S0-ASB-790

JW MARRIOTT.
CANCUN RESORT & SPA

Mexico

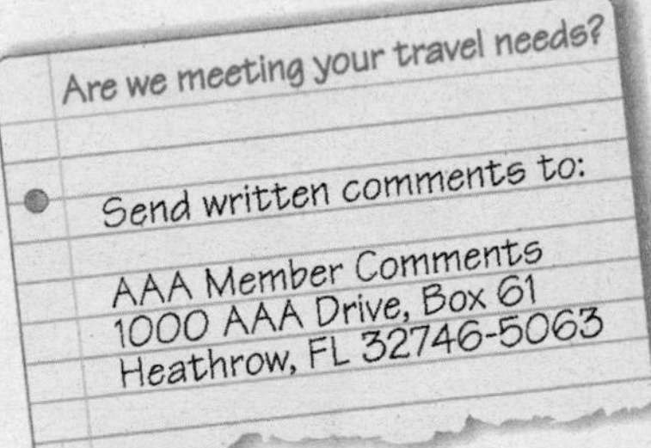

Published by AAA Publishing
1000 AAA Drive
Heathrow, FL 32746-5063

Advertising Rate and Circulation Information: (407) 444-8280

Printed in the USA by Quebecor World, Buffalo, NY

Photo Credit: (Cover & Title Page)
Temple of the Warriors,
Chichén Itzá, Yucatán Peninsula
© SIME s.a.s / eStock Photo

Printed on recyclable paper.
Please recycle whenever possible.

Stock #5022

Mexico

The Pacific Coast

Mexico City & Vicinity

Central Mexico

Southern Mexico

Featured Information

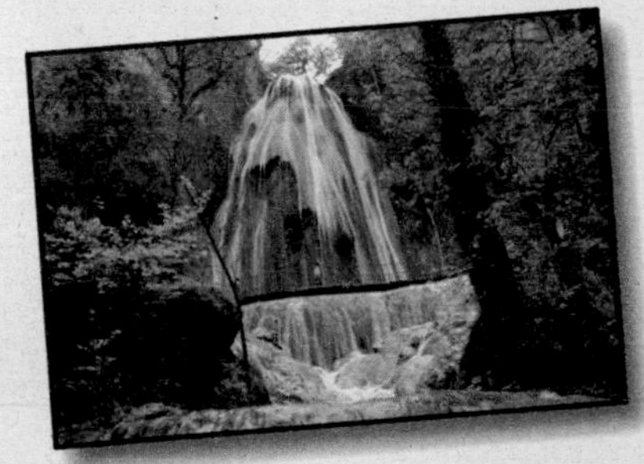

Acquainting yourself with the warmth of the sun.
It's our pleasure.

Tips for AAA.com's

Quick tips for using TripTik® Travel Planner's enhanced features.

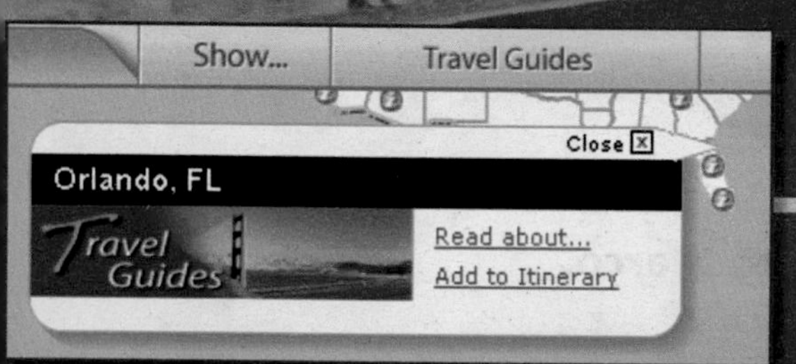

TRAVEL GUIDE
Select the 'Travel Guides' button to get AAA's exclusive travel information.

HOTEL BOOKING AT LOW RATES
Click to book partner hotels at low online rates.

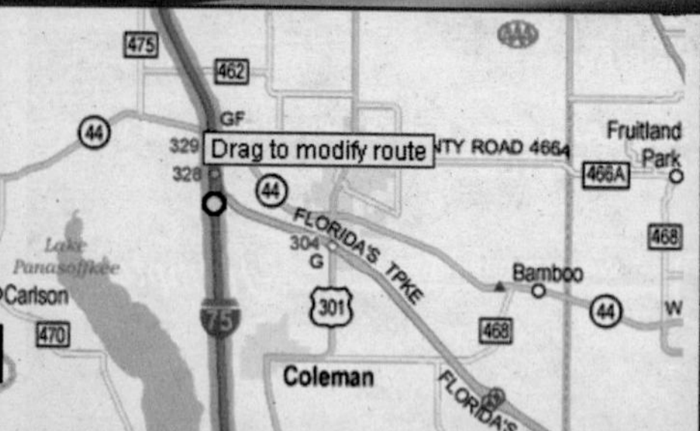

CLICK AND DRAG ROUTE MODIFICATION
Click and drag the route to the roads you prefer to travel.

TripTik® Travel Planner

CUSTOM MAPS

Click to add points of interest to MyPlaces then 'Print' full color maps showing just the places you chose.

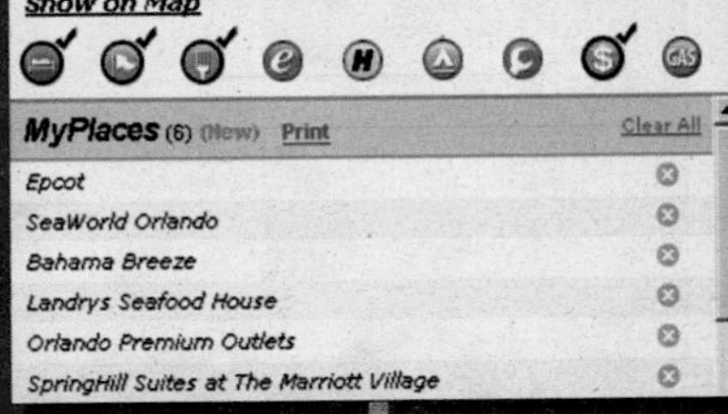

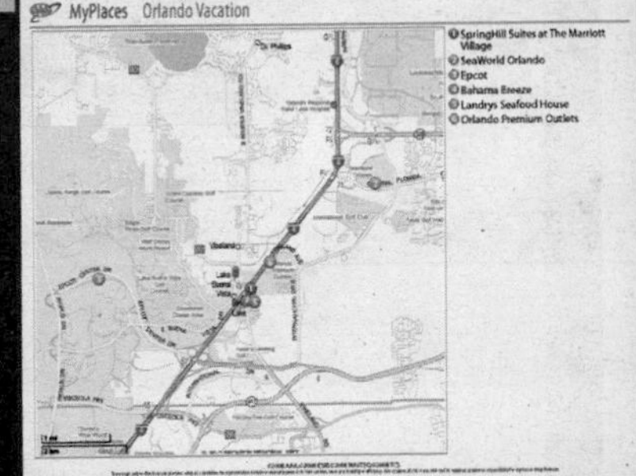

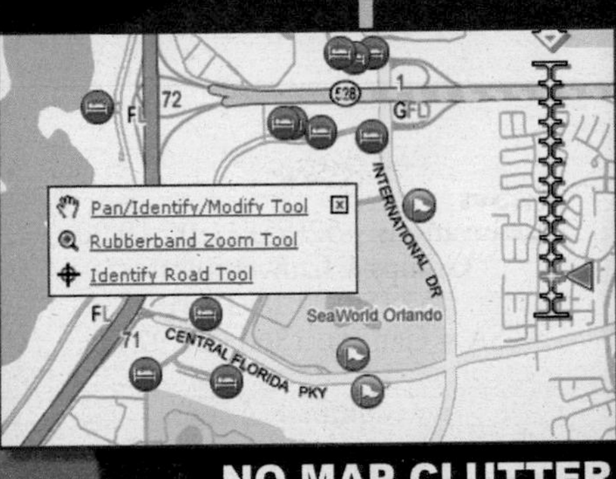

NO MAP CLUTTER

Right click for more navigation tools.

TripTik Travel Planner
AAA.com's all-in-one maps, directions and travel information resource.

Attractions, lodgings and restaurants are listed on the basis of merit alone after careful evaluation and approval by one of AAA/CAA's full-time, professionally trained inspectors. Evaluations are unannounced to ensure that we see an establishment just as you would see it.

An establishment's decision to advertise in the TourBook guide has no bearing on its evaluation or rating. Advertising for services or products does not imply AAA endorsement.

Information in this guide was believed accurate at the time of publication. However, since changes inevitably occur between annual editions, we suggest you work with your AAA travel professional or check on AAA.com to confirm prices and schedules.

How the TourBook Guide is Organized

The TourBook guide is organized into three distinct sections.

The **Points of Interest** section helps you plan daily activities and sightseeing excursions and provides details about the city or attraction you are visiting.

The **Lodgings and Restaurants** section helps you select AAA Approved accommodations and dining facilities meeting your specific needs and expectations.

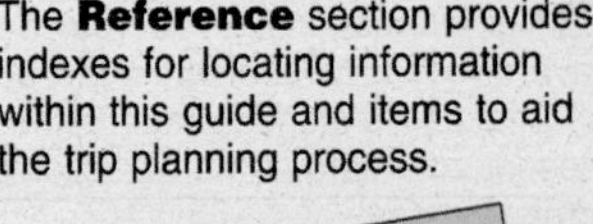

The **Reference** section provides indexes for locating information within this guide and items to aid the trip planning process.

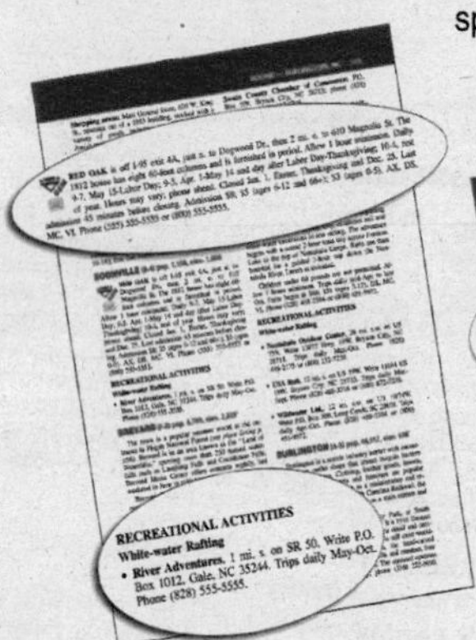

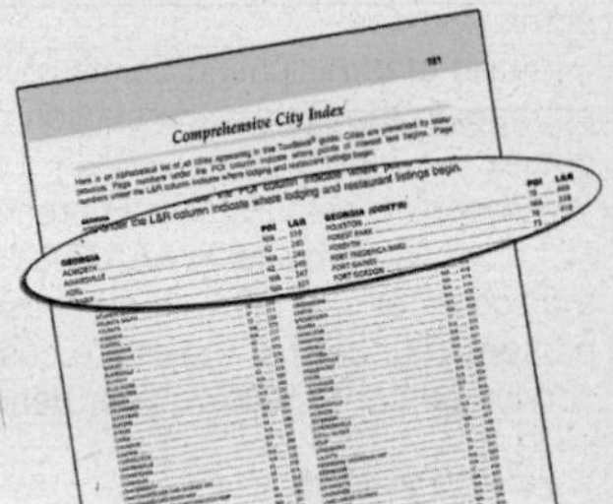

Locating the Attractions, Lodgings and Restaurants

Attractions, lodgings and restaurants are listed under the city in which they physically are located - or in some cases under the nearest recognized city. Most listings are alphabetically organized by state, province, region or island, then by city and establishment name.

A color is assigned to each state or province so that you can match the color bars at the top of the page to switch from the **Points of Interest** section to the **Lodgings and Restaurants** section.

Spotting maps help you physically locate points of interest, lodgings and restaurants in the major destinations.

The Comprehensive City Index located in the **Reference** section contains an A-to-Z list of cities.

Destination Cities and Destination Areas

Destination cities, established based on government models and local expertise, include metropolitan areas plus nearby vicinity cities. **Destination areas** are regions with broad tourist appeal; several cities will comprise the area.

If a city falls within a destination's vicinity, the city name will appear at its alphabetical location in the book, and a cross reference will give you the exact page on which listings for that city begin.

An orientation map appears at the beginning of each destination section to familiarize you with that destination.

Understanding the Points of Interest Listing

GEM Designation

A [GEM] indicates the attraction has been rated a AAA GEM, a "must see" point of interest that offers a *Great Experience for Members®*. These attractions have been judged to be of exceptional interest and quality by AAA Inspectors.

A GEM listing page with a brief description of individual GEM attractions follows the Orientation map near the beginning of each state or province Points of Interest section. Cross-references guide the reader to the attraction's listing page.

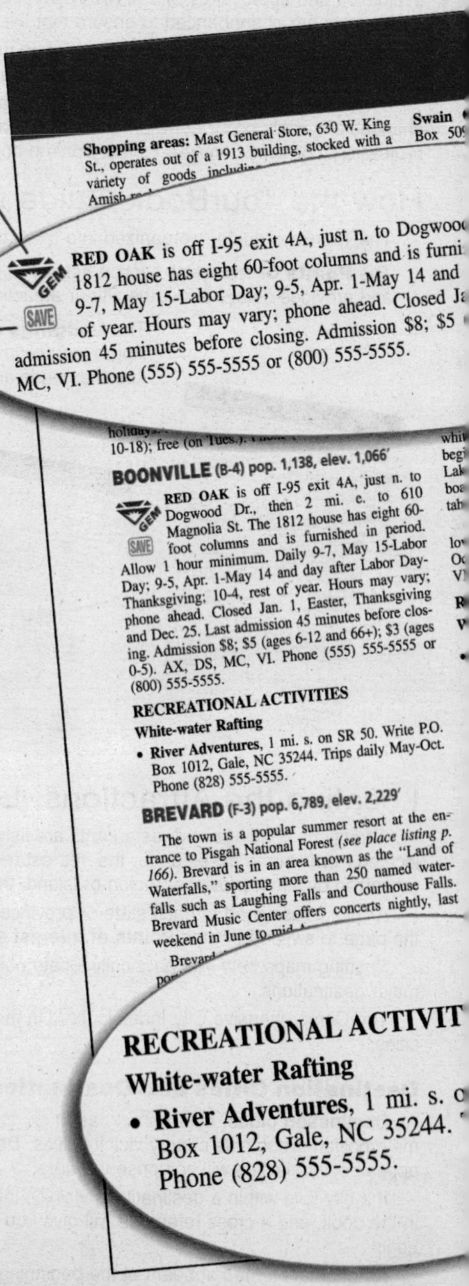

Discount Savings

The [SAVE] icon denotes those attractions offering AAA/CAA, AAA MasterCard, AAA VISA or international Show Your Card & Save discount cardholders a discount off the attraction's standard admission. Present your card at the attraction's admission desk.

A list of participating points of interest appears in the Reference section of this guide.

Shopping establishments preceded by a [SAVE] icon also provide to AAA/CAA members a discount and/or gift with purchase; present your card at the mall's customer service center to receive your benefit.

Exceptions

- Members should inquire in advance concerning the validity of the discount for special rates.
- The [SAVE] discount may not be used in conjunction with other discounts.
- Attractions that already provide a reduced senior or child rate may not honor the [SAVE] discount for those age groups.
- All offers are subject to change and may not apply during special events, particular days or seasons or for the entire validity period of the TourBook guide.

Adventure Travel

There are inherent risks with adventure travel activities like air tours, hiking, skiing and white-water rafting. For your own safety, please read and adhere to all safety instructions. Mentions of these activities are for information only and do **not** imply endorsement by AAA.

BOONVILLE (B-4) pop. 1,138, elev. 1,066'

[GEM] [SAVE] **RED OAK** is off I-95 exit 4A, just n. to 610 Dogwood Dr., then 2 mi. e. to Magnolia St. The 1812 house has eight 60-foot columns and is furnished in period. Allow 1 hour minimum. Daily 9-7, May 15-Labor Day; 9-5, Apr. 1-May 14 and day after Labor Day-Thanksgiving; 10-4, rest of year. Hours may vary; phone ahead. Closed Jan. 1, Easter, Thanksgiving and Dec. 25. Last admission 45 minutes before closing. Admission $8; $5 (ages 6-12 and 66+); $3 (ages 0-5). AX, DS, MC, VI. Phone (555) 555-5555 or (800) 555-5555.

RECREATIONAL ACTIVITIES

White-water Rafting

- **River Adventures**, 1 mi. s. on SR 50. Write P.O. Box 1012, Gale, NC 35244. Trips daily May-Oct. Phone (828) 555-5555.

BREVARD (F-3) pop. 6,789, elev. 2,229'

The town is a popular summer resort at the entrance to Pisgah National Forest (*see place listing p. 166*). Brevard is in an area known as the "Land of Waterfalls," sporting more than 250 named waterfalls such as Laughing Falls and Courthouse Falls. Brevard Music Center offers concerts nightly, last weekend in June to mid-

ONE — BURLINGTON, NC 125

y Chamber of Commerce: P.O.
yson City, NC 28713; phone (828)

., then 2 mi. e. to 610 Magnolia St. The
in period. Allow 1 hour minimum. Daily
after Labor Day-Thanksgiving; 10-4, rest
., Easter, Thanksgiving and Dec. 25. Last
s 6-12 and 66+); $3 (ages 0-5). AX, DS,

Bryson City, combines rail and
ter excursions in one outing. The adventure
ith a scenic 2-hour train trip across Fontana
the top of Nantahala Gorge. Rafts are then
for a guided 3-hour trip down the Nan-
iver. Lunch is included.

ren under 60 pounds are not permitted. Al-
ours minimum. Trips daily mid-Apr. to late
res begin at $66; $51 (ages 3-12). DS, MC,
one (828) 488-2384 or (800) 451-9972.

REATIONAL ACTIVITIES

-water Rafting

ntahala Outdoor Center, 26 mi. s.w. on US
V. Write 13077 Hwy. 19W, Bryson City, NC
713. Trips daily Mar.-Oct. Phone (828)
8-2175 or (800) 232-7238.

SA Raft, 12 mi. s. on US 19W. Write 11044 US
)W, Bryson City, NC 28713. Trips daily Mar.-
ept. Phone (828) 488-3316 or (800) 872-7238.

Vildwater Ltd., 12 mi. s.w. on US 19/74W.
Vrite P.O. Box 309, Long Creek, SC 29658. Trips
daily Apr.-Oct. Phone (828) 488-2384 or (800)
451-9972.

URLINGTON (A-5) pop. 44,917, elev. 656'

Burlington is a textile industry center with numer-
outlet shops that attract bargain hunters
Clothing, leather goods, towels,
and furniture are popular
as a maintenance and re-
Carolina Railroad; the
as a train station and

SR 50. Write P.O.
ps daily May-Oct.

ity Park, at South
is a 1910 Dentzel
eir detail and intri-
ls still exist world-
s, the hand-carved
ffe and reindeer, four
s. The carousel operates
, phone (336) 222-5030.

Directions

Unless otherwise specified, directions are given from the center of town, using the following highway designations:

I=interstate highway
SR=state route
FM=farm to market
Mex.=Mexican highway
US=federal highway
CR=county road
FR=forest road
Hwy.=Canadian or Caribbean highway

Prices and Dates of Operations

Admission prices are quoted without sales tax. Children under the lowest age specified are admitted free when accompanied by an adult. Days, months and age groups written with a hyphen are inclusive.

Prices pertaining to points of interest in the United States are quoted in U.S. dollars; points of interest in Canada are quoted in Canadian dollars; prices for points of interest in Mexico and the Caribbean are quoted as an approximate U.S. dollar equivalent.

Schedules and admission rates may change throughout the validity period of this guide. Check AAA.com for the most current information.

Credit Cards Accepted

AX=American Express
CB=Carte Blanche
DC=Diners Club
DS=Discover
JC=Japan Credit Bureau
MC=MasterCard
VI=VISA

Bulleted Listings

Gambling establishments within hotels are presented for member information regardless of whether the lodging is AAA Approved.

Recreational activities of a participatory nature (requiring physical exertion or special skills) are not inspected.

Wineries are inspected by AAA Inspectors to ensure they meet listing requirements and offer tours.

All are presented in an abbreviated bulleted format for informational purposes.

Understanding the Lodging Listing

Local Member Value

AAA or CAA and SAVE identify hotels that offer members a rate guarantee and up to two free special amenities as part of their Official Appointment partnership with AAA. Rate guarantee: Discounted standard room rate (usually based on last standard room availability) or the lowest public rate available at time of booking for dates of stay. Free special amenity options are included in the listing and could be either: breakfast, local telephone calls, newspaper, room upgrade, preferred room, or high-speed Internet.

Diamond Rating

The number of Diamonds informs you of the overall complexity of a lodging's amenities and service. Red indicates an Official Appointment lodging. An fyi in place of Diamonds indicates the property has not been rated but is included as an "information only" service. A detailed description of each rating level appears on page 20.

Classification

All Diamond Rated lodgings are classified using three key elements: style of operation, overall concept and service level. See pages 22-23 for details on our classifications.

Rates

The property's standard 2-person rates and effective dates are shown.

Rates are provided to AAA by each lodging and represent the publicly available rate or ranges for a standard room. Rates are rounded to the nearest dollar and do not include taxes. U.S., Mexican and Caribbean rates are in U.S. dollars; rates for Canadian lodgings are in Canadian dollars.

Information about cancellation and minimum stay policies is provided in the **Terms** section of the property's listing.

Online Reservations

This notation indicates AAA/CAA members can conveniently check room availability, validate room rates and make reservations for this property in a secure online environment at AAA.com.

Service Availability

Unit types, amenities and room features preceded by the word "Some" indicate the item is available on a limited basis, potentially within only one unit. The term "Fee" appearing to the left of an amenity icon indicates an extra charge applies.

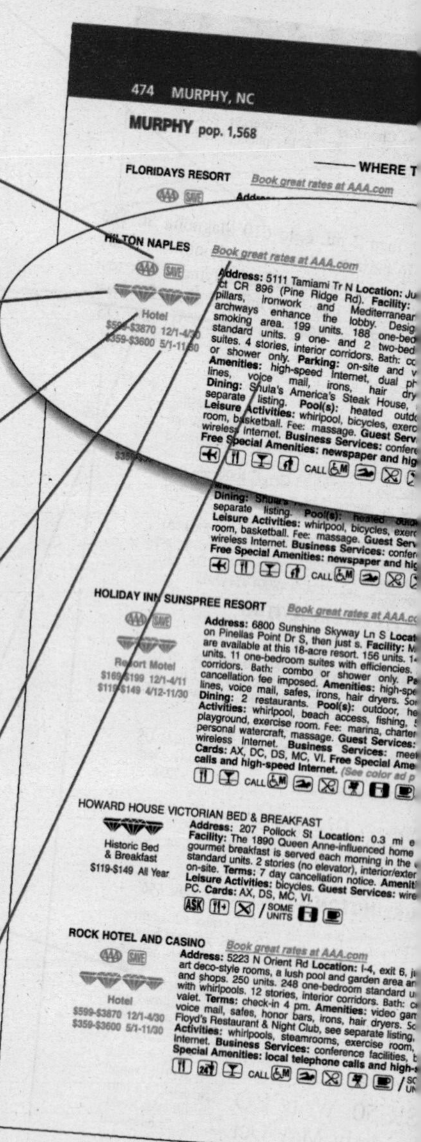
474 MURPHY, NC

MURPHY pop. 1,568

WHERE T

FLORIDAYS RESORT — Book great rates at AAA.com

HILTON NAPLES — Book great rates at AAA.com

Hotel
$599-$3870 12/1-4/30
$359-$3600 5/1-11/30

Address: 5111 Tamiami Tr N **Location:** Ju... ct CR 896 (Pine Ridge Rd). **Facility:** ... pillars, ironwork and Mediterranean ... archways enhance the lobby. Desig... smoking area. 199 units. 188 one-bed... standard units. 9 one- and 2 two-bed... suites. 4 stories, interior corridors. Bath: co... or shower only. **Parking:** on-site and v... **Amenities:** high-speed Internet, dual ph... lines, voice mail, irons, hair dry... **Dining:** Shula's America's Steak House, ... separate listing. **Pool(s):** heated outd... **Leisure Activities:** whirlpool, bicycles, exerc... room, basketball. Fee: massage. **Guest Serv...** wireless Internet. **Business Services:** confer... **Free Special Amenities: newspaper and hig...**

HOLIDAY INN SUNSPREE RESORT — Book great rates at AAA.co...

Resort Motel
$169-$199 12/1-4/11
$119-$149 4/12-11/30

Address: 6800 Sunshine Skyway Ln S **Locat...** on Pinellas Point Dr S, then just s. **Facility:** M... are available at this 18-acre resort. 156 units. 1... units. 11 one-bedroom suites with efficiencies. ... corridors. Bath: combo or shower only. **Pa...** cancellation fee imposed. **Amenities:** high-spe... lines, voice mail, safes, irons, hair dryers. So... **Dining:** 2 restaurants. **Pool(s):** outdoor, he... **Activities:** whirlpool, beach access, fishing, ... playground, exercise room. Fee: marina, charter... personal watercraft, massage. **Guest Services:** ... wireless Internet. **Business Services:** meet... **Cards:** AX, DC, DS, MC, VI. **Free Special Ame... calls and high-speed Internet.** (See color ad p...

HOWARD HOUSE VICTORIAN BED & BREAKFAST

Historic Bed & Breakfast
$119-$149 All Year

Address: 207 Pollock St **Location:** 0.3 mi e... **Facility:** The 1890 Queen Anne-influenced home... gourmet breakfast is served each morning in the ... standard units. 2 stories (no elevator), interior/exter... on-site. **Terms:** 7 day cancellation notice. **Amenit...** **Leisure Activities:** bicycles. **Guest Services:** wire... PC. **Cards:** AX, DS, MC, VI.

ROCK HOTEL AND CASINO — Book great rates at AAA.com

Hotel
$599-$3870 12/1-4/30
$359-$3600 5/1-11/30

Address: 5223 N Orient Rd **Location:** I-4, exit 6, ... art deco-style rooms, a lush pool and garden area a... and shops. 250 units. 248 one-bedroom standard u... with whirlpools. 12 stories, interior corridors. Bath: c... valet. **Terms:** check-in 4 pm. **Amenities:** video gam... voice mail, safes, honor bars, irons, hair dryers. So... Floyd's Restaurant & Night Club, see separate listing, ... **Activities:** whirlpools, steamrooms, exercise room, ... Internet. **Business Services:** conference facilities, ... **Special Amenities: local telephone calls and high-...**

Nationwide Member Value

The blue box in the listing identifies hotel brands that offer an everyday member benefit at all AAA Approved locations. (See page 19 for additional program benefits.)

Spotting Symbol

Black ovals with white numbers are used to locate, or "spot," lodgings on maps we provide for larger cities.

Credit Cards Accepted

AX=American Express
CB=Carte Blanche
DC=Diners Club
DS=Discover
JC=Japan Credit Bureau
MC=MasterCard
VI=VISA

Some properties accept cash but require a credit card at registration. If you plan to pay in cash, call in advance for restrictions.

Icons

Lodging icons represent some of the member values, services and facilities offered.

Discounts

- ASK May offer discount

Member Services

- Airport transportation
- Pets allowed (call property for restrictions and fees)
- Restaurant on premises
- Restaurant off premises (walking distance)
- 24-hour room service
- Full bar
- Child care
- Accessible features (call property for available services and amenities)

Leisure Activities

- Full-service casino
- Pool
- Health club on premises
- Health club off premises
- Recreational activities

In-Room Amenities

- Designated non-smoking rooms
- VCR
- Movies
- Refrigerator
- Microwave
- Coffee maker
- No air conditioning
- No TV
- No cable TV
- No telephones

Safety Features

(see page 24)
(Mexico and Caribbean only)

- S Sprinklers
- D Smoke detectors

Understanding the Restaurant Listing

Official Appointment

(AAA) or (CAA) indicates Official Appointment (OA) restaurants. The OA program permits restaurants to display and advertise the AAA or CAA emblem. These establishments are highlighted in red to help you quickly identify them. The AAA or CAA Approved sign helps traveling members find restaurants that want member business.

Local Member Value

SAVE identifies restaurants that offer a Show Your Card & Save® discount to AAA/CAA members.

Diamond Rating

The number of Diamonds informs you of the overall complexity of food, presentation, service and ambience. Red indicates an Official Appointment restaurant. A detailed description of each Diamond level appears on page 21.

Cuisine Type

The cuisine type helps you select a dining facility that caters to your individual taste. AAA currently recognizes more than 120 different cuisine types.

Prices

Rates shown represent the minimum and maximum entree cost per person. Exceptions may include one-of-a-kind or special market priced items. Rates are rounded to the nearest dollar and do not include taxes. U.S., Mexican and Caribbean rates are in U.S. dollars; rates for Canadian restaurants are in Canadian dollars.

Icons

Icons provide additional information about services and facilities.

- No air-conditioning
- Accessible features offered (call property for available services and amenities)
- Designated smoking section available

Menus

This notation indicates AAA/CAA members can conveniently view the restaurant's menu in a secure online environment at AAA.com.

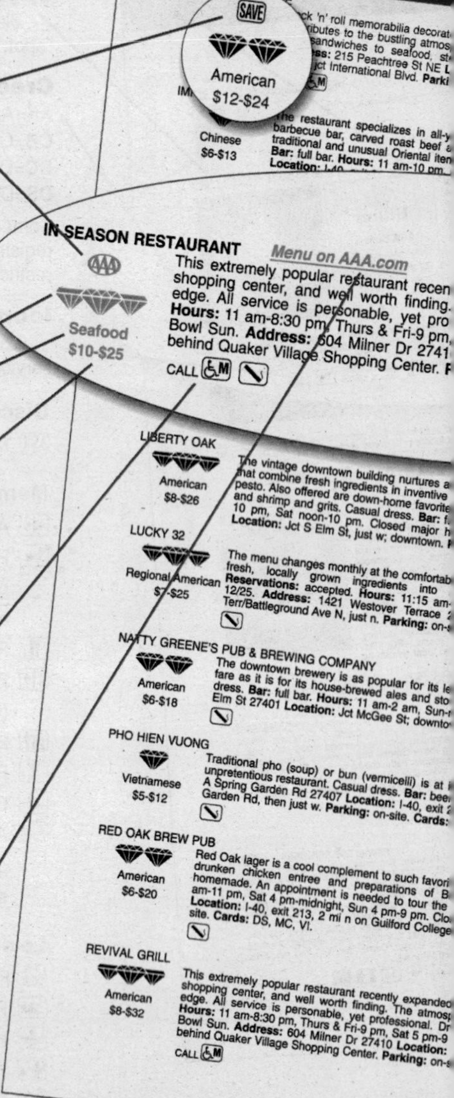

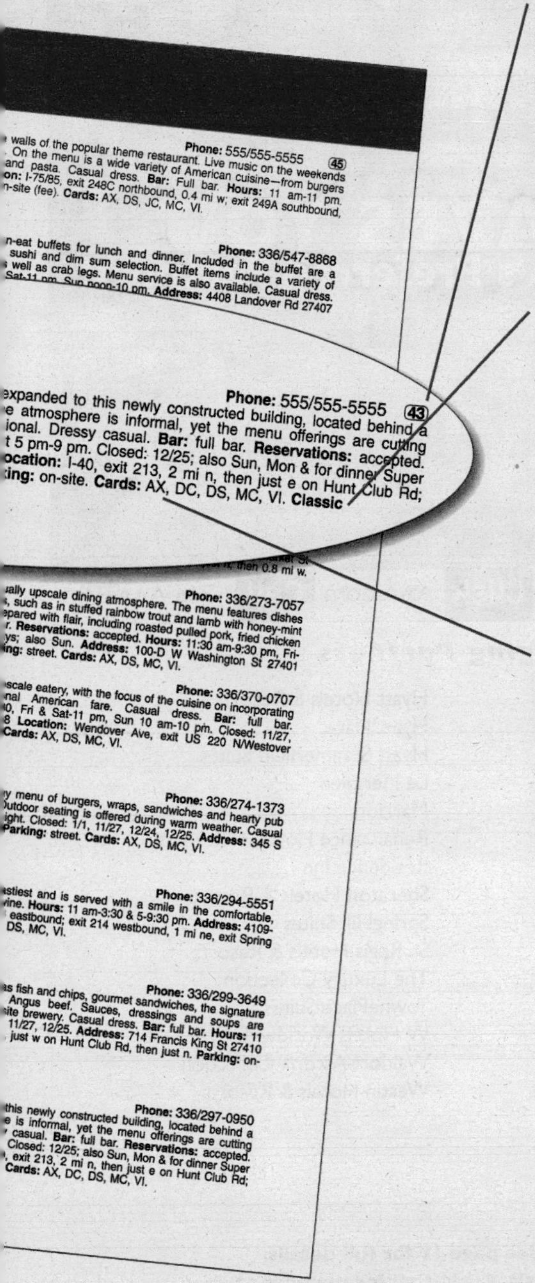

Spotting Symbol

White ovals with black numbers serve as restaurant locators and are used to locate, or "spot," restaurants on maps for larger cities.

Classifications

If applicable, a restaurant may be defined as:

Classic - renowned and/or landmark restaurant in business longer than 25 years, known for unique style and ambience.

Historic - establishments must meet one of the following criteria:

- Listed on the National Register of Historic Places
- Designated a National Historic Landmark
- Located in a National Register Historic District

Separate criteria designate historic properties in Canada, Mexico and the Caribbean.

Credit Cards Accepted

AX = American Express
CB = Carte Blanche
DC = Diners Club
DS = Discover
JC = Japan Credit Bureau
MC = MasterCard
VI = VISA

RELAX

AAA SAVES YOU
5-15% with AAA's Preferred Partners!

Visit Over 1,100 AAA Offices **Click** AAA.com **Call** 1-866-AAA-SAVE

AAA Preferred Lodging Partners

- aloft
- Andaz
- Best Western International
- Conrad Hotels & Resorts
- Courtyard by Marriott
- Doubletree
- element
- Embassy Suites
- Fairfield Inn
- Four Points by Sheraton
- Hampton Inn & Suites
- Hilton
- Hilton Garden Inn
- Hilton Grand Vacations
- Homewood Suites
- Hyatt Hotels & Resorts
- Hyatt Place
- Hyatt Summerfield Suites
- Le Meridien
- Marriott
- Renaissance Hotels & Resorts
- Residence Inn
- Sheraton Hotels & Resorts
- SpringHill Suites
- St. Regis Hotels & Resorts
- The Luxury Collection
- TownePlace Suites
- W Hotels Worldwide
- Waldorf-Astoria Collection
- Westin Hotels & Resorts

– see page 19 for full details.

Visit, Click, Call for member savings.

AAA/CAA members can generally expect to pay no more than the maximum regular rate printed in the TourBook guide in each rate range for a standard room. On rare occasions AAA receives or inadvertently publishes incorrect rates.

Obtain current AAA/CAA member rates and make reservations at AAA.com. Rates may vary within the range, depending on season and room type. Listed rates are usually based on last standard room availability.

Discounts

Member discounts, when offered, will apply to rates quoted within the rate range and are applicable at the time of booking. Special rates used in advertising, as well as special short-term promotional rates lower than the lowest listed rate in the range, are not subject to additional member discounts.

Exceptions

Rates for properties operating as concessionaires for the U.S. National Park Service are not guaranteed due to governing regulations. Rates in the Mexico TourBook are not guaranteed and may fluctuate based on the exchange rate of the peso.

Lodgings may temporarily increase room rates, not recognize discounts or modify pricing policies during special events. Examples of special events range from Mardi Gras and the Kentucky Derby (including pre-Derby events) to college football games, holidays, holiday periods and state fairs. Although some special events are listed in AAA/CAA TourBook guides and on AAA.com, it is always wise to check in advance with AAA travel professionals for specific dates.

Get the Room You Reserved

When making your reservation, identify yourself as a AAA or CAA member and request written confirmation to guarantee: type of room, rate, dates of stay, and cancellation and refund policies. At registration, show your membership card.

When you find your room is not as specified, and you have written confirmation of reservations for a certain type of accommodation, you should be given the option of choosing a different room or finding one elsewhere. Should you choose to go elsewhere and a refund is refused or resisted, submit the matter to AAA/CAA within 30 days, along with complete documentation, including your reasons for refusing the room and copies of your written confirmation and any receipts or canceled checks associated with this problem.

If you are charged more than the maximum rate listed in the TourBook guide for a standard room, question the additional charge. If management refuses to adhere to the published rate, pay for the room and submit your receipt and membership number to AAA/CAA within 30 days. Include all pertinent information: dates of stay, rate paid, itemized paid receipts, number of persons in your party and the room number you occupied, and list any extra room equipment used. A refund of the amount paid in excess of the stated maximum will be made if our investigation indicates that unjustified charging occurred.

Deposit, Refund and Cancellation Policies

Most establishments give full deposit refunds if they have been notified at least 48 hours before the normal check-in time. Listing prose will note if more than 48 hours' notice is required for cancellation. Some properties may charge a cancellation or handling fee. When this applies, "cancellation fee imposed" will appear in the listing. If you cancel too late, you have little recourse if a refund is denied.

When an establishment requires full or partial payment in advance and your trip is cut short, a refund may not be given.

When canceling a reservation, phone the lodging immediately. Make a note of the date and time you called, the cancellation number if there is one, and the name of the person who handled the cancellation. If your AAA/CAA club made your reservation, allow them to make the cancellation for you as well, so you will have proof of cancellation.

Check-in and Check-out Times

Check-in and check-out times are shown in the lodging listings, under Terms, only if they are before 3 p.m. or after 10 a.m. respectively.

Members Save With Our Partners

These National Show Your Card & Save® partners provide the listed member benefits. Visit AAA.com/Save to discover all the great Show Your Card & Save® discounts in your area. Admission tickets that offer greater discounts may be available for purchase at the local AAA/CAA club. A maximum of six attraction tickets is available at the discount price at the gate; six discounted tickets is also the maximum for Amtrak and Gray Line.

SeaWorld, Busch Gardens, Sesame Place
AAA.com/SeaWorld, AAA.com/BuschGardens, AAA.com/SesamePlace

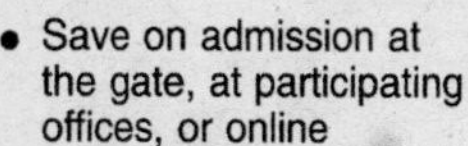

- Save on admission at the gate, at participating offices, or online

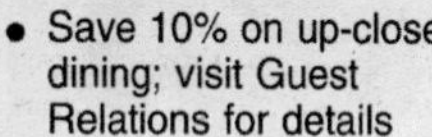

- Save 10% on up-close dining; visit Guest Relations for details

Six Flags AAA.com/SixFlags

- Save on admission at the gate, at participating offices, or online
- Save 10% on merchandise purchases of $15 or more at in-park stores

Universal Orlando Resort and Universal Studios Hollywood
AAA.com/Universal

- Save on admission at the gate, at participating offices, or online
- Save 10% at select food and merchandise venues in-park and at Universal CityWalk®

Restaurant Partner
Savings applies to AAA/CAA members and up to five guests.

Joe's Crab Shack

- Save 10% on food, non-alcoholic beverages and merchandise

Landry's Seafood House, The Crab House, Chart House, Muer Seafood Restaurants, and Aquarium and Downtown Aquarium Restaurants

- Save 10% on food and non-alcoholic beverages at all of the above restaurants
- Save 10% on merchandise at Aquarium and Downtown Aquarium restaurants

Hard Rock Cafe

- Save 10% on food, non-alcoholic beverages and merchandise at all U.S. and select Canadian and international locations

Tanger Outlet Centers www.tangeroutlet.com

- Save up to 20% on total purchase at select merchants with AAA/CAA coupon booklet
- Member BONUS: FREE $5 gift card for each additional Tanger Outlet Center visited after first within same calendar year
- Show membership card and register at the AAA customer service desk when you visit

Amtrak

- 10% discount on rail fare when booked at least 3 days in advance of travel date

Grand Canyon Railway

- Save up to 20% on rail fare, hotel accommodations, restaurant and gift shop purchases sold outside of Grand Canyon National Park

Gray Line
AAA.com/GrayLine

- Save 10% on sightseeing tours of 1 day or less worldwide

AAA Preferred Lodging Partners

EXPECT SAVINGS, SELECTION, AND SATISFACTION

- **Best AAA/CAA member rates for your dates of stay.** Provide valid membership number when placing reservation and show your card at hotel check-in.
- **Satisfaction guarantee.** Notify the property if you are dissatisfied with any part of your stay. If the matter cannot be resolved, you may be entitled to compensation (see page 17).
- **Seasonal promotions and special member offers.** Visit AAA.com to view current offers.
- **Everyday member benefit.*** Look for the blue boxes in the TourBook listings for everyday values offered at all AAA Approved locations.

**Offer good at time of publication: Chains and offers may change without notice. Preferred Hotel Partner discounts may vary in Mexico and the Caribbean.*

10% Off Best Available Rates
Best Western International

5% or more Off Best Available Rates
Conrad, Doubletree, Embassy Suites, Hampton, Hilton, Hilton Garden Inn, Hilton Grand Vacations, Homewood Suites, and Waldorf=Astoria Collection

10% Off Best Available Rates
Andaz, Grand Hyatt, Hyatt Place, Hyatt Regency, Hyatt Summerfield Suites, and Park Hyatt

5% or more Off Best Available Rates
Courtyard, Fairfield Inn, JW Marriott, Marriott, Renaissance Hotels & Resorts, Residence Inn, SpringHill Suites, and TownePlace Suites

5-15% Off Best Available Rates.
aloft, element, Four Points, Le Meridien, Sheraton, St. Regis, The Luxury Collection, Westin, and W Hotels

Understanding the Diamond Ratings

AAA/CAA inspectors have evaluated and rated each of the 58,000 lodging and restaurant establishments in the TourBook series to ensure quality travel information for our members. All properties must meet AAA's minimum requirements (for lodgings) concerning cleanliness, comfort and security - or - AAA's minimum requirements (for restaurants) pertaining to cleanliness, food preparation and service.

Eligible applicants receive an unannounced evaluation by a AAA/CAA inspector that includes two distinct components:

- **AAA Approval:** The inspector first must determine whether the property meets the criteria required to be AAA Approved. Every establishment that meets these strict guidelines offers AAA members the assurance that, regardless of the Diamond Rating, it provides acceptable quality, cleanliness, service and value.
- **AAA Diamond Rating:** Once an establishment becomes AAA Approved, it is then assigned a rating of one to five Diamonds, indicating the extensiveness of its facilities, amenities and services, from basic to moderate to luxury. These Diamond Ratings guide members in selecting establishments appropriately matched to their needs and expectations.

LODGINGS

1 Diamond

One Diamond lodgings typically appeal to the budget-minded traveler. They provide essential, no-frills accommodations and basic comfort and hospitality.

2 Diamond

Two Diamond lodgings appeal to family travelers seeking affordable yet more than the basic accommodations. Facilities, decor and amenities are modestly enhanced.

3 Diamond

Three Diamond lodgings offer a distinguished style. Properties are multi-faceted, with marked upgrades in physical attributes, amenities and guest comforts.

4 Diamond

Four Diamond lodgings are refined and stylish. Physical attributes are upscale. The fundamental hallmarks at this level include an extensive array of amenities combined with a high degree of hospitality, service and attention to detail.

5 Diamond

Five Diamond lodgings provide the ultimate in luxury and sophistication. Physical attributes are extraordinary in every manner. Service is meticulous, exceeding guest expectations and maintaining impeccable standards of excellence. Extensive personalized services and amenities provide first-class comfort.

fyi The lodging listings with **fyi** in place of Diamonds are included as an *information only* service for members. The icon indicates that a property has not been rated for one or more of the following reasons: too new to rate, under construction, under major renovation, not evaluated, may not meet all AAA requirements.

A property not meeting all AAA requirements is included for either its member value or because it may be the only accommodation available in the area. Listing prose will give insight as to why the **fyi** designation was assigned.

RESTAURANTS

1 Diamond 

One Diamond restaurants provide simple, familiar specialty food (such as burgers, chicken, pizza or tacos) at an economical price. Often self-service, basic surroundings complement a no-nonsense approach.

2 Diamond 

Two Diamond restaurants offer a familiar, family-oriented experience. Menu selection includes home-style foods and family favorites, often cooked to order, modestly enhanced and reasonably priced. Service is accommodating yet relaxed, a perfect complement to casual surroundings.

3 Diamond 

Three Diamond restaurants convey an entry into fine dining and are often positioned as adult-oriented experiences. The atypical menu may feature the latest cooking trends and/or traditional cuisine. Expanded beverage offerings complement the menu. The ambience is well coordinated, comfortable and enhanced by a professional service staff.

4 Diamond

Four Diamond restaurants provide a distinctive fine-dining experience that is typically expensive. Surroundings are highly refined with upscale enhancements throughout. Highly creative chefs use imaginative presentations to augment fresh, top-quality ingredients. A proficient service staff meets or exceeds guest expectations. A wine steward may offer menu-specific knowledge to guide selection.

5 Diamond

Five Diamond restaurants are luxurious and renowned for consistently providing a world-class experience. Highly acclaimed chefs offer artistic menu selections that are imaginative and unique, using only the finest ingredients available. A maitre d' leads an expert service staff in exceeding guest expectations, attending to every detail in an effortless and unobtrusive manner.

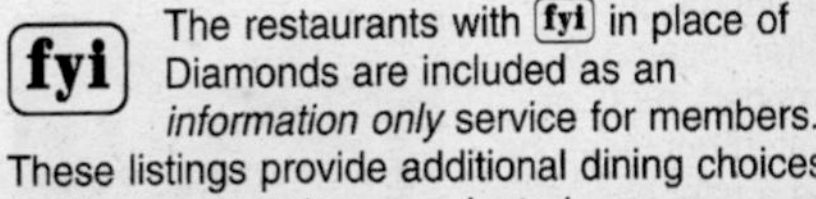

fyi The restaurants with **fyi** in place of Diamonds are included as an *information only* service for members. These listings provide additional dining choices but have not yet been evaluated.

Understanding the Lodging Classifications

To ensure that your lodging needs and preferences are met, we recommend that you consider an establishment's classification when making your travel choices. While the quality and comfort at properties with the same Diamond Rating should be consistent (regardless of the classification), there are differences in typical decor/theme elements, range of facilities and service levels.

Lodging Classifications

Bed & Breakfast

Typically smaller scale properties emphasizing a high degree of personal touches that provide guests an "at home" feeling. Guest units tend to be individually decorated. Rooms may not include some modern amenities such as televisions and telephones, and may have a shared bathroom. Usually owner-operated with a common room or parlor separate from the innkeeper's living quarters, where guests and operators can interact during evening and breakfast hours. Evening office closures are normal. A continental or full, hot breakfast is served and is included in the room rate.

1884 Paxton House Inn
Thomasville, GA

Cabin

Vacation-oriented, typically smaller scale, freestanding units of simple construction—roughly finished logs or stone—and basic design or décor. Often located in wooded, rural, or waterfront locations. As a rule, basic cleaning supplies, kitchen utensils, and complete bed and bath linens are supplied. The guest registration area may be located off site.

Greenbrier Valley Resorts
Gatlinburg, TN

Condominium

Vacation-oriented—commonly for extended-stay purposes—apartment-style accommodations of varying design or décor. Routinely available for rent through a management company, units often contain one or more bedrooms, a living room, full kitchen, and an eating area. Studio-type models combine the sleeping and living areas into one room. As a rule, basic cleaning supplies, kitchen utensils, and complete bed and bath linens are supplied. The guest registration area may be located off site.

Sands of Kahana
Kahana, Maui, HI

Cottage

Vacation-oriented, typically smaller scale, freestanding units with home style enhancements in architectural design and interior décor. Often located in wooded, rural, or waterfront locations. Units may vary in design and décor. As a rule, basic cleaning supplies, kitchen utensils, and complete bed and bath linens are supplied. The guest registration area may be located off site.

Paradise Villas, Little Cayman Island

Country Inn

Although similar in definition to a bed and breakfast, country inns are usually larger in scale with spacious public areas and offer a dining facility that serves—at a minimum—breakfast and dinner.

Greenville Inn, Greenville, ME

Hotel

Commonly, a multistory establishment with interior room entrances offering a variety of guest unit styles. The magnitude of the public areas is determined by the overall theme, location and service level, but may include a variety of facilities such as a restaurant, shops, fitness center, spa, business center, and/or meeting rooms.

The Grand America Hotel
Salt Lake City, UT

Motel

Commonly, a one- or two-story establishment with exterior room entrances and drive up parking. Typically, guest units have one bedroom with a bathroom of similar décor and design. Public areas and facilities are often limited in size and/or availability.

Best Western Deltona Inn, Deltona, FL

Ranch

Typically a working ranch with an obvious rustic, Western theme featuring equestrian-related activities and a variety of guest unit styles.

Lost Valley Ranch, Deckers, CO

Vacation Rental House

Vacation-oriented—commonly for extended-stay purposes—typically larger scale, freestanding, and of varying design or décor. Routinely available for rent through a management company, houses often contain two or more bedrooms, a living room, full kitchen, dining room, and multiple bathrooms. As a rule, basic cleaning supplies, kitchen utensils, and complete bed and bath linens are supplied. The guest registration area may be located off site.

ResortQuest, Hilton Head Island, SC

Lodging Sub-classifications

The following are sub-classifications that may appear along with the classifications listed previously to provide a more specific description of the lodging.

Boutique

Often thematic and typically an informal, yet highly personalized experience; may have a luxurious or quirky style which is fashionable or unique.

Casino

Extensive gambling facilities are available, such as: blackjack, craps, keno, and slot machines. **Note:** This sub-classification will not appear beneath its Diamond Rating in the listing. It will be indicated by a 🎲 icon and will be included in the row of icons immediately below the lodging listing.

Classic

Renowned and landmark properties, older than 50 years, well-known for their unique style and ambience.

Contemporary

Overall design and theme reflects characteristics of the present era's mainstream tastes and style.

Extended Stay

Offers a predominance of long-term accommodations with a designated full-service kitchen area within each unit.

Historic

These properties are typically over 75 years of age and exhibit many features of a historic nature with respect to architecture, design, furnishings, public record, or acclaim. Properties must meet one of the following criteria:

- Maintained the integrity of the historical nature
- Listed on the National Register of Historic Places
- National Historic Landmark or located in a National Register Historic District

Separate criteria designate historic properties in Canada, Mexico and the Caribbean.

Resort

Recreation-oriented, geared to vacation travelers seeking a specific destination experience. Travel packages, meal plans, themed entertainment, and social and recreational programs are typically available. Recreational facilities are extensive and may include spa treatments, golf, tennis, skiing, fishing, or water sports. Larger resorts may offer a variety of guest accommodations.

Retro

Overall design and theme reflect a contemporary design reinterpreting styles from a bygone era.

Vacation Rental

Typically houses, condos, cottages or cabins; these properties are a "home away from home" offering more room and greater value for the money. In general, they provide the conveniences of home, such as full kitchens and washers/dryers. Located in resort or popular destination areas within close proximity to major points of interest, attractions, or recreation areas, these properties may require a pre-arranged reservation and check-in at an off-site location. Housekeeping services may be limited or not included.

Vintage

Offers a window to the past and provides an experience reflecting a predominance of traits associated with the era of their origin.

Guest Safety

Room Security

In order to be approved for listing in AAA/CAA TourBook guides for the United States and Canada, accommodations must have dead bolt locks on all guest room entry doors and connecting room doors.

If the area outside the guest room door is not visible from inside the room through a window or door panel, viewports must be installed on all guest room entry doors. Bed and breakfast properties and country inns are not required to have viewports. Ground floor and easily accessible sliding doors must be equipped with some type of secondary security locks.

Even with those approval requirements, AAA cannot guarantee guest safety. AAA Inspectors view a percentage of rooms at each property since it is not feasible to evaluate every room in every lodging establishment. Therefore, AAA cannot guarantee that there are working locks on all doors and windows in all guest rooms.

Fire Safety

Because of the highly specialized skills needed to conduct professional fire safety inspections, AAA/CAA Inspectors cannot assess fire safety.

Properties must meet all federal, state/province and local fire codes. Each guest unit in all U.S. and Canadian lodging properties must be equipped with an operational, single-station smoke detector. A AAA/CAA Inspector has evaluated a sampling of the rooms to verify this equipment is in place.

Mexico and the Caribbean

Requirements for some features, such as door locks and smoke detectors/sprinkler systems, differ in Mexico and the Caribbean. If a property met AAA's security requirements at the time of the evaluation, the phrase "Meets AAA guest room security requirements" appears in the listing.

Service Animals

The Americans with Disabilities Act (ADA) prohibits U.S. businesses that serve the public from discriminating against persons with disabilities. Some businesses have mistakenly denied access to persons who use service animals. Businesses must permit entry to guests and their service animals, as well as allow service animals to accompany guests to all public areas of a property.

A property is permitted to ask whether the animal is a service animal or a pet, and whether the guest has a disability. The property may not, however, ask questions about the nature of the disability, the service provided by the animal, or require proof of a disability or certification that the animal is a service animal. These regulations may not apply in Canada, Mexico or the Caribbean.

No fees or deposits, even those normally charged for pets, may be charged for service animals. Service animals fulfill a critical need for their owners—they are not pets.

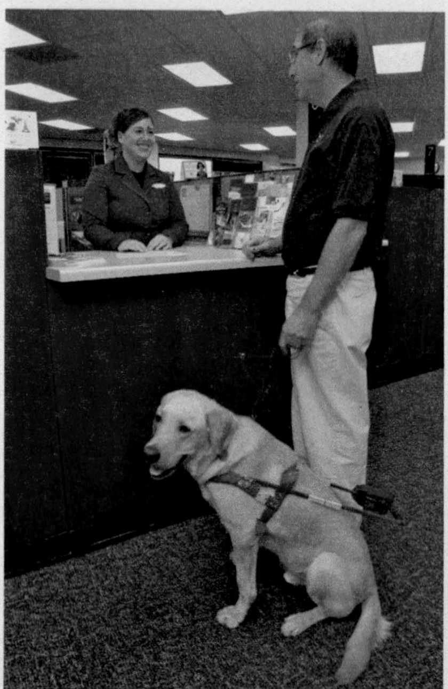

Frank Frand with his seeing eye dog, Cardinal.

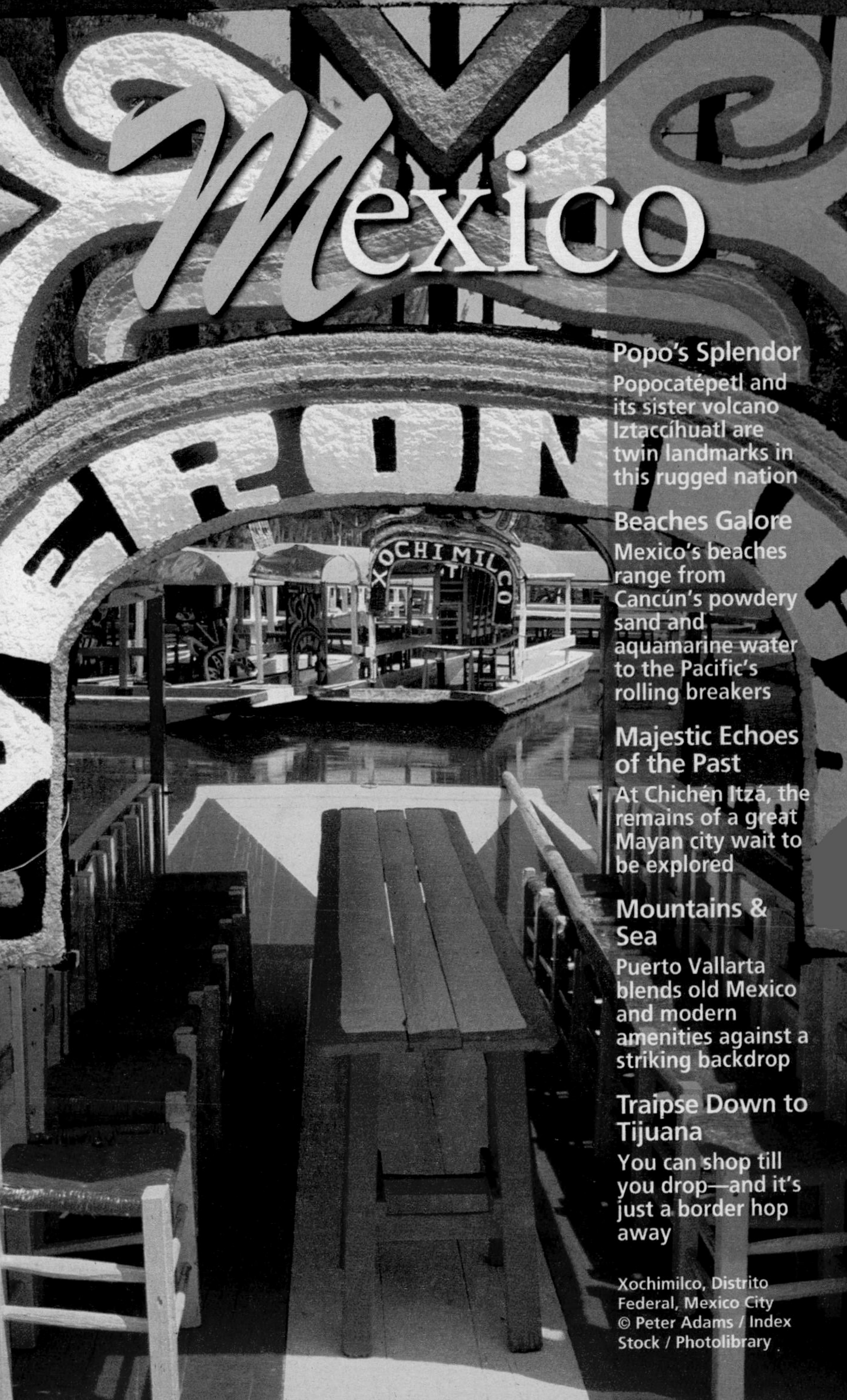
Mexico
Popo's Splendor
Popocatépetl and its sister volcano Iztaccíhuatl are twin landmarks in this rugged nation
Beaches Galore
Mexico's beaches range from Cancún's powdery sand and aquamarine water to the Pacific's rolling breakers
Majestic Echoes of the Past
At Chichén Itzá, the remains of a great Mayan city wait to be explored
Mountains & Sea
Puerto Vallarta blends old Mexico and modern amenities against a striking backdrop
Traipse Down to Tijuana
You can shop till you drop—and it's just a border hop away
XOCHIMILCO

Xochimilco, Distrito Federal, Mexico City © Peter Adams / Index Stock / Photolibrary

Near Lover's Beach, Cabo San Lucas, Baja California / © Prisma / SuperStock

Mexico in the 21st century stands at a crossroads of sorts. Perhaps nowhere else on Earth is there such a difference between old and new, between the traditional past and the unpredictable future.

Timeless "Mexican" images still exist, of course. Donkeys amble down dusty paths, and ancient ruins stand silhouetted against the sky. But for every small village where a herd of goats comprises the local traffic, there is a vehicle-choked freeway. And for every local market displaying live chickens, handwoven baskets and piles of dried chilies, there is a glitzy mall offering the latest in upscale merchandise.

The extremes of wealth and poverty here can be shocking. Half an hour away from Cancún's glittering resorts are windowless, thatch-roofed huts with dirt floors. In bursting-at-the-seams Mexico City, high fashion and haute cuisine coexist with sprawling shantytowns lacking running water.

But while a Third World way of life is still unfortunately the norm for many Mexicans, visitors benefit from a strong and growing first world of hotels, restaurants and related amenities, as well as a cultural heritage richly expressed through fiestas and national celebrations. This makes Mexico a fascinating country that can be explored rather easily. What are you waiting for?

Historical Overview

Mexican history has been particularly tumultuous, encompassing cultural peaks as well as the suffering borne out of conquest, war and subjugation. No one knows for sure where the native peoples of Mexico originally came from. Somewhere around 5000 B.C., in the valley of Tehuacán southeast of present-day Mexico City, a straggling community of seed gatherers discovered how to domesticate maize, becoming farmers in the process and beginning the establishment of permanent villages.

Eventually the stage was set for the building of cities. At a time when much of Europe was decidedly primitive, civilizations in the New World were carving out sophisticated architectural, scientific and artistic achievements. Scattered throughout central and southern Mexico, the ruins of pyramids, palaces and temples all bear witness to the highly developed skills of the Olmec, Maya, Toltec and Aztec cultures that flourished, in some instances, more than a thousand years before the arrival of Spain. Some waged war; all trafficked and explored, leaving behind a fascinating legacy.

Many historians consider the Maya to be the crown jewel of pre-Columbian cultures. They developed the mathematical concept of zero and produced a calendar that enabled their priests to predict eclipses and plot the movements of the solar system. In contrast to these refined achievements, the Maya also participated enthusiastically in brutal games, human sacrifice and ritual bloodletting, which they believed helped them communicate with the gods. From about 200 B.C. through the eighth century, the vast Mayan empire spread north from Guatemala to the Yucatán Peninsula.

In the early 1300s the fierce, nomadic Mexica, now known as the Aztecs, moved from place to place in search of a prophetic vision foretold by the Toltec people: an eagle perched on a cactus pad, clutching a serpent in its beak. According to legend, that vision was seen on an island in the middle of Lake Texcoco, within the Valley of Mexico—the site of present-day Mexico City. Aztec civilization was well advanced by the beginning of the 16th century, but ironically it was their ruthless dominance that led to their undoing at the hands of the Spanish *conquistadores*.

The equally ruthless conquest of the Aztecs gave Spain the infamous distinction of wiping out hundreds of years of Indian achievements

Mexico Historical Timeline

200 B.C.-A.D. 900
Mexico's first great urban civilizations are built, including Chichén Itzá, Palenque, Teotihuacán and Uxmal.

1325
The Aztecs establish the city of Tenochtitlan, later to become Mexico City.

Library of Congress

1521
Tenochtitlan falls to conquistador Hernando Cortés, inaugurating 3 centuries of Spanish rule.

1810
Father Miguel Hidalgo issues the *Grito de Dolores*, a call for freedom that sparks the War of Independence.

Library of Congress

1823
A new constitution is drafted proclaiming Mexico a federal republic.

1848
The Treaty of Guadalupe Hidalgo forces Mexico to cede its territories north of the Rio Grande River to the United States.

in Mesoamerica. Spanish reign was insignificant politically but momentous socially. Mexico's colonial cities, its grand cathedrals and most of its historic buildings were constructed during 3 centuries of Spanish rule. Spain justified its continued presence in Mexico on the basis of converting the natives—considered barbarians—to Christianity. The church thus played a singular role in the colony of New Spain, which consisted of all Spanish possessions in North and Central America. Augustinian, Dominican and Franciscan friars (and later the Jesuits) all journeyed to New Spain to minister and teach, founding missions in the depths of the wilderness.

Mexico's push for independence came out of the divisiveness resulting from rigid societal classes that emerged over the course of colonial rule, and from continuing exploitation of the vast outpost off which the Spanish colonists profited. It was finally achieved in 1821, but political turmoil was the rule rather than the exception throughout the remainder of the 19th century and into the 20th.

Social change, rapid industrial growth and economic improvement came in the mid-20th century. The new Mexican prosperity was put on world view during the 1968 Summer Olympics, held in Mexico City. By the dawn of the 1990s the leap from developing nation to recognized world player seemed likely. Then a guerrilla uprising, a political assassination and a devastating currency devaluation (all in 1994) threatened hard-won stability. The United States bailed the country out of a monetary crisis with a $20 billion international financial aid package, but by 1997 Mexico had fully repaid its debt. The peso never recovered to pre-devaluation levels, however, so visitors with dollars to convert will find a country eager to accept them.

Natural Features

Mexico, while part of North America, also marks the transition from that vast continent's topographic and climatic extremes to the more uniformly tropical features of Central America and the Caribbean basin. Although its sun-scorched deserts and jagged mountain ranges look harsh, they also possesses an austere beauty. And not all is geographically forbidding—there are verdant valleys, cool highlands and mile after mile of sandy, palm-fringed beaches.

Roughly triangular in shape, Mexico narrows from an expanse of 1,300 miles across its northern frontier to a mere 140 miles at the

1862
French emperor Napoleon III is defeated at the Battle of Puebla.

1910
Growing opposition to the dictatorship of Porfirio Díaz sets off the bloody, protracted Revolution of 1910.

Library of Congress

1929
Mexico's dominant political party, the Partido Revolucionario Institucional (PRI), is founded.

1968
Summer Olympics are held in Mexico City.

1994
Indian guerrillas calling themselves the Zapatista National Liberation Party lead a rebellion for land and self-rule in the state of Chiapas.

2000
Vicente Fox of the National Action Party defeats the PRI candidate in the presidential election, dethroning the country's ruling political dynasty.

©Keith Dannemiller Digital Railroad

Isthmus of Tehuantepec. Two peninsulas—Baja (Lower) California and the Yucatán Peninsula—are appendages to the mainland.

Most of the country consists of hills or mountain ranges broken by level plateaus; the plateaus in turn are carved into many canyons and valleys. Central Mexico is a vast elevated landscape dominated by high mountains to the east and west, many of which are of volcanic origin. The east coast is low and flat, but in the state of Veracruz the lofty mountains advance almost to the coast. The northwestern coastal plain is another relatively flat area, broken in parts by low hills and mountains.

The Sierra Madre comprises three great mountain ranges. The Sierra Madre Oriental and the Sierra Madre Occidental form the eastern and western boundaries of the central plateau region. The Sierra Madre del Sur frames the Pacific coast through the states of Guerrero and Oaxaca.

The height of the mountains is accentuated by deep valleys and canyons, which can plunge more than 1,500 feet below the general level of the plateau. At the bottom of some of these canyons the climate and vegetation are subtropical and distinctly different from conditions at the canyon rim. This is particularly true of the Copper Canyon area in the state of Chihuahua. Shadowed by the lofty Sierra Madre Occidental, it derives its name from the rust coloring of many of the canyon walls.

There are hundreds of volcanic peaks in Mexico; in the state of Michoacán alone there are more than 80. Volcanoes active in the last half century or so include Volcán de Fuego de Colima, near the city of the same name; Paricutín, near Uruapan but now dormant; and El Chichonal. Born in the fall of 1943 when a cornfield suddenly erupted, Paricutín grew more than 1,700 feet in 10 months. In 1982 the long-dormant volcano El Chichonal spewed a billion tons of ash and rock across a wide area near the small town of Teapa in southeastern Mexico.

A recent increase in seismic activity has been noted within Popocatépetl, at 17,883 feet Mexico's second highest peak. Although snow perpetually covers its upper flanks, Popocatépetl has historically spewed ash over extensive areas. Tests conducted in 1994 measuring sulfur dioxide emissions showed the volcano to be among the world's five or six most active, although scientists cannot predict whether this is a significant indication of any future activity. Over time, dozens of villages have sprouted up on Popocatépetl's lower slopes, but as with earthquakes, most Mexicans treat the possibility of an erupting volcano as simply a fact of life.

The backbone of Baja California consists of several westward-sloping mountain ranges. The Yucatán Peninsula, on the other hand, is primarily flat or rolling; its highest point is barely 1,000 feet above sea level. Much of the subsurface rock is limestone, and subterranean erosion has produced many sinkholes (cenotes), some of which are used as natural swimming pools.

The Coasts

Mexico has four distinct coastal regions. The Baja California Peninsula, bathed by both the Pacific Ocean and the Sea of Cortez (Gulf of California), is marked by numerous bays and coves, as is the northwestern mainland coast. Farther south, Pacific breakers crash against the feet of the Sierra Madre Occidental and the Sierra Madre del Sur. The Pacific Coast cities of Manzanillo and Acapulco boast fine natural harbors.

The eastern coastal plain along the Gulf of Mexico is essentially featureless. The flat terrain is characterized by broad beaches, swamps and palm-lined lagoons. Sandbars and lagoons also are features of the western and northern coasts of the Yucatán Peninsula. The peninsula's eastern coast borders the Caribbean Sea and is marked by extensive coral reefs. The islands of Cozumel and Mujeres are off its northeast corner. Powdery sands and clear, aquamarine waters are the Yucatán's greatest natural resource.

For average monthly high and low temperatures and precipitation amounts for representative cities, *see page 50.*

People

The Mexican people are a vibrant and complex group, despite being the product of a historical legacy that is in many ways tragic and divisive. And just as the country is a land of extremes—from baked desert to dripping jungle, from craggy mountain to swampy coast—there are differences among the people as well. You'll likely encounter both ostentatious wealth and startling poverty, impeccable politeness and stony indifference, gracious manners and leering *machismo.*

The Indígenas

When Hernando Cortés arrived in 1519, the land now comprising Mexico was inhabited by some 15 to 20 million people, a number of whom were under the savage domination of the Aztecs. Many lived in the elevated plateau region of central Mexico, where the weather and soil were most favorable for agriculture. By 1521, a handful of

Spanish *conquistadores* had toppled the vast Aztec civilization and went on to subjugate an entire country.

Spaniards subsequently came to New Spain, amassed riches and returned to the mother country. The Indians, meanwhile, were put to work in the silver mines, toiled in fields or performed backbreaking manual labor constructing lavish cathedrals and public buildings, laboring side by side with Africans brought into the country for the same purpose. Although the Spanish contributed only minimally to growth—during 300 years of rule only about 300,000 settled in Mexico—a combination of introduced diseases, cultural upheaval and strict suppression decimated the natives.

The Indians, or *indígenas,* living in Mexico today—an estimated 15 percent of the total population—are direct descendants of the Aztec, Maya and other ancient civilizations. These natives speak a primary language other than Spanish, and many might express surprise if referred to as "Mexican." Some are small groups living in self-sufficient isolation; others occupy large territories. While it is convenient for the sake of categorization to lump all Indians together, Mexico's native peoples are characterized by linguistic and cultural differences that can be as distinct as those defining Norwegians and Italians.

Approximately 50 of the numerous ethnic groups populating Mexico at the time of the Spanish arrival remain in existence. They include the Tarahumara, who dwell in the Copper Canyon region of northwest Mexico; the Yaqui, in the state of Sonora; the Huichol and the Tarasco, near and along the central Pacific coast; the Nahua and the Otomí, in the central plateau region; the Zapotec and the Mixtec, in the state of Oaxaca; the Chamula, Tzeltal and Tzotzil, in the state of Chiapas; the Huastec, along the eastern Gulf of Mexico coast; and the Maya, throughout the Yucatán Peninsula.

The status of *indígenas* in today's Mexico, unfortunately, is not a whole lot better than it was during the colonial era. Poverty is a chronic, debilitating fact of life for more than three-quarters of the country's Indian communities, including many in the economically challenged southern states of Chiapas, Guerrero and Oaxaca. Indian rights—particularly the demand for self-rule—has been a thorny issue for the Mexican government since the January 1994 uprising led by the Zapatistas. Life is still hard for "Mexico's most forgotten people," as many *indígenas* refer to themselves, but their plight has garnered international attention and forced ongoing government negotiations.

The gulf between Mexico's industrialized north and the poor south was underscored by the 2006 presidential election, the closest and most bitterly contested in the country's history. Ruling National Action Party (PAN) candidate Felipe Calderón won a razor-thin margin of victory over leftist Democratic Revolutionary Party (PRD) candidate and former Mexico City mayor Andrés Manuel López Obrador. Obrador, whose impassioned supporters were largely from Mexico City and the southern states, mounted a legal challenge disputing the vote count amid allegations of fraud, although in the end Mexico's Federal Election Tribunal court ruled that the results were valid.

Mestizos and the "Thousand Families"

The great majority of Mexicans—75 percent—are *mestizos,* of mixed European and Native American descent. They have perhaps the strongest sense of national identity, although occupying various levels of prosperity and social standing. The small percentage of citizens of purely European ancestry—some 10 percent of the population and often referred to as the "Thousand Families"—control the country's political power and economic wealth, just as the Spanish did more than 3 centuries earlier.

There are signs of change, however. The PRI's 1997 political defeats came largely at the hands of the youth vote. An estimated 65 percent of the population is under age 30, and this new generation of Mexicans may prove to be as influential on the nation's economics and culture as the baby boomers have been in the United States.

Mexico is the second most populous country in Latin America after Brazil. Within its 31 states and the Federal District live some 109 million citizens—up from just 30 million in 1950. But over the last several decades the fertility rate has fallen dramatically, and this generational shift has resulted in a trend toward smaller families that will have far-reaching social and economic effects.

The Mexican Character

Many Mexicans have a strong streak of fatalism. The country has weathered hurricanes, erupting volcanoes and severe earthquakes, particularly the one that leveled parts of Mexico City in 1985. More telling is the violence associated with history. Aztec ceremonies revolved around blood-spattered human sacrifice, with hearts literally torn from victims' chests. The Spanish conquest wiped out entire cities. Post-independence Mexico endured war, revolution, assassination and civil strife. Death is thus both honored and mocked in such celebrations as the Day of the Dead, when decorated sugar skulls are sold, costumed children bear mock coffins in street parades and families pay tribute to deceased members in front of lavish home altars.

This is a country that knows how to have fun, and priority is given to family and holidays. On weekends, city dwellers exit the concrete jungle en masse for beaches, parks and lakeside resorts. A minor saint's day is reason enough to hold a fiesta, and the birthday of a national hero or the date commemorating an important historical or religious event merits a major celebration.

Many Mexicans are rather formal in their dealings with strangers, and very polite as well; try to respond in kind. Older citizens can be very conservative, and provocative or skimpy dress—on men or women—is frowned upon if worn in churches or other inappropriate places. When sightseeing, dress with both comfort and common sense in mind. Mexican men also love to charm, and female travelers may receive openly admiring looks or remarks. If such behavior is bothersome, it's best to simply ignore it rather than to get angry, and to minimize or eliminate overtures by dressing conservatively.

Architecture

Mexico is particularly rich with reminders of its earliest architects' work. Innumerable archeological sites—some little more than a few earthen mounds or a crumbling platform, others the spectacular remains of cities—have left behind intriguing clues related to the puzzle of their abandoned cultures.

Early Builders

The first great architects were the Maya. They constructed numerous ceremonial centers connected by straight, wide roadways of crushed limestone called *sacbe* (sack-BEH). These ancient roads were marvels of engineering, since the flat land denied builders an elevated vantage point while planning construction through the dense, scrubby jungle.

Mayan buildings took three main forms: the pyramid, often with a temple capping the summit; the palace, consisting of a central court surrounded by chambers; and the ball court, a wide, flat area used for playing a mysterious but presumably sacred ball game.

Another early site is the ceremonial center of Teotihuacán, northeast of present-day Mexico City. Pyramids with sloping sides created an impression of great mass. They were adorned with stucco reliefs, murals and the carved heads of gods that frequently resembled animals. The Zapotecs, who dominated the Valley of Oaxaca in southern Mexico, created Monte Albán. Its ball court, raised platforms and temples bear the influence of Teotihuacán, Mayan architects and the Pre-Classic Olmec people, who inhabited the coastal regions of the present-day states of Tabasco and Veracruz.

Mexican pyramids did not necessarily resemble the familiar form of the Egyptian variety—a square base with four sloping, triangular sides meeting at the top. Created essentially as religious monuments, they frequently had steps built into the sides. Exterior carvings not only served as decoration but also depicted historical and mythological events. The ceremonial centers from which these pyramids rose were dedicated to fanciful gods and paid tribute to the priest rulers who presided over rigidly hierarchical societies.

The medium of choice was stone, a common building material in Mexico and one suitable for long-lasting creations. Frequently employed was a porous, volcanic rock known as *tezontle,* also used by the Aztecs. Although the sheer scope of the structures is awe-inspiring, other archeological remnants—for example, the free-standing arch at Labná, on the Yucatán Peninsula—hint at the direction in which the Maya and other early architects might have headed.

Subsequent tribes such as the Toltecs, Mixtecs and Aztecs expanded on the architectural themes developed by the great Classic civilizations. Pyramids and palaces continued in importance, serving the needs of highly complex religious ceremonies. It was a period of military maneuvers and violent conquest, and the murals, carvings and bas-reliefs applied as decoration depicted scenes of war and human sacrifice.

European Influence

The arrival of Spain in the early 16th century brought an abrupt end to Indian achievements, as most of the existing civilizations were destroyed. The conquerors frequently chose such razed ground as the place to begin their own construction. The Spanish conquest ushered in a 300-year period during which ecclesiastical architecture predominated, often imitating prevailing European trends.

Augustinian, Dominican, Franciscan and Jesuit friars built churches throughout Mexico as part of a large-scale attempt to convert the natives to Christianity. These structures, distinguished by thick walls and simple interiors with vaulted ceilings, were impressively fortified to serve as protection against Indian attack. A monastery built around an enclosed patio was usually connected to the church. Decoration also served an educational purpose, as frescoes and stone carvings vividly depicted the symbolic themes of the new religion.

Several decorative motifs were developed to enhance the aesthetics of the buildings themselves. A combination dome and tower often was used; the dome, constructed of arched masonry, frequently was covered with colorful tiles arranged in geometric designs. Plateresque decoration foreshadowed the more extravagant flourishes of the 17th and 18th centuries. The word comes from the Spanish *platero,* or silversmith, and the delicate ornamentation that often was placed around doorways or entrances resembled silverwork designs. The Convent of San Agustín Acolman (Convento de San Agustín Acolman) in the town of Acolman, México, and the doorway of the Montejo House (Casa de Montejo) in Mérida, Yucatán, are two good examples of the Plateresque style.

The wealth amassed from Mexico's silver and gold mines and from the huge sugar-producing *haciendas* (plantations) led to a spate of ostentatious construction in the 17th and 18th centuries. The baroque style, characterized by lavish ornamentation, came into popularity, and baroque cathedrals began springing up in the central plazas of cities throughout the country. Notable examples are the Metropolitan Cathedral (Catedral Metropolitana) and the Church of Santo Domingo (Iglesia de Santo Domingo) in Mexico City and the Cathedral of the Immaculate Conception in Puebla.

The ultimate baroque expression was a Mexican development known as Churrigueresque, or ultra-baroque. It was named after Spanish artisan José de Churriguera, whose own work, curiously, was much more restrained. Buildings exploded with carved geometric forms, leafy vines, frolicking cherubs, scrolls and other imaginative accents, often to the point that formal structure seemed an afterthought.

The style extended inside as well, and Churrigueresque interiors were a cornucopia of extravagant embellishment, often executed in gold. The overall intent was literally to knock one's eyes out. Stunning examples of this ornate style are the Church of San Francisco Xavier (Iglesia de San Francisco Xavier) in Tepotzotlán, México; the Church of Santa Clara (Iglesia de Santa Clara) and the Church of Santa Rosa de Viterbo (Iglesia de Santa Rosa de Viterbo), both in the city of Querétaro; the Cathedral in the city of Zacatecas; and the interior of the Church of Santo Domingo (Iglesia de Santo Domingo) in the city of Oaxaca.

Another form used in Mexico during this period was *mudéjar,* derived from the Spanish Moors. The *mudéjar* style also favored lavish decoration; interiors and exteriors were plastered with colored tiles. Puebla is particularly noted for churches with intricate tiled designs; a secular example is the House of Tiles (Casa de Los Azulejos) in Mexico City, a former mansion occupied since 1919 by a Sanborn's restaurant.

After the excesses of the Churrigueresque, something had to give. The end of the colonial era saw a return to the more restrained neoclassic style. Buildings often incorporated several styles of architecture, however. Sometimes more than a century passed before work was finished; as a result, influences overlapped, particularly on the larger cathedrals. Mexico City's massive Metropolitan Cathedral took 240 years of off-and-on construction to complete; its facade is primarily baroque but also exhibits neoclassic elements, while the ornamentation of the altars is Churrigueresque.

During much of the 19th century Mexican life was disrupted by war and political turbulence, and architectural development was given short shrift. When relative prosperity returned under dictator Porfirio Díaz, a new round of public buildings appeared, mostly massive structures in a variety of styles that again imitated what was happening in Europe. Mexico City's Palace of Fine Arts (Palacio de Bellas Artes) was designed and executed by Italian architects following classic blueprints. Mérida's ornate mansions took on a Parisian influence, as wealthy hemp exporters strove to emulate the refined atmosphere of that French city.

The Modern Era

The early 20th century found Mexican architects struggling for a style to call their own. Attempts at monumentality produced such misguided curiosities as the gigantic statue of José María Morelos, a hero of the Mexican War of Independence. Built on an island in Lake Pátzcuaro, it depicts an ungainly-looking figure reaching toward the sky. Skyscrapers began to sprout in industrial centers like Mexico City and Monterrey, but their functional steel and concrete construction tended to resemble the tall buildings found in any big city.

In the last half of the century, innovative architecture resulted from the combination of old and new design elements, such as the buildings at the National University of Mexico (UNAM) in San Angel, the National Museum of Anthropology in Mexico City and large-scale resort properties in places like Cancún and Acapulco. One of the most recent examples is the National Center of the Arts, inaugurated in 1994. The complex, south of downtown Mexico City, incorporates futuristic forms—a vivid orange tower studded with exaggerated window frames—as well as a lecture hall resembling mission churches built during the colonial era.

Music and Dance

To a Mexican, a love of music is as fundamental a pleasure as the loving bonds of family. The country's musical traditions are exceedingly rich and abundantly varied. As with architecture and art, styles have tended to originate elsewhere before being assimilated and frequently adapted to suit the national preferences: passion, romance and insistent rhythms. Popular folk and dance music in particular vividly evokes the sights, sounds and moods of the country.

A broad distinction can be made between the music of Mexico's *indígena* and *mestizo* groups. Indian musical expression is ceremonial in nature, linked to religious rituals or village fiestas. Within the dominant, mixed *mestizo* population, on the other hand, music has a genuinely mass appeal that is strengthened by a healthy recording industry, ceaseless radio play and impromptu performances that enliven the central plazas of practically every town in the country.

From Marimba to Mariachi

Little is known about what sort of sounds were created by pre-Hispanic civilizations. Music, singing and dancing did, however, play a large role in daily ceremonial life. The mesmerizing beat of the drum was foremost among ancient instruments. Drums were fashioned out of clay, wood, bones and turtle shells. Rattles complemented the beat, and simple reed or clay flutes added a melodic counterpoint. It may well have sounded similar to what can be heard in some Indian villages today.

Spanish *conquistadores* and the missionaries who followed them imported European culture, which began to have an influence on native song and dance. Folk orchestras began to accommodate new instruments, chief among them various types of guitars. The *son* (also called *huapango*), a driving dance rhythm with plenty of instrumental flourishes, is the basic form of *mestizo* music. Regional styles have different names, such as *son huasteco* (northeastern Mexico), *son jarana* (the Yucatán Peninsula), *son jarocho* (around Veracruz) or *son mariachi* (the state of Jalisco). Whatever the region, the guitar is the lead instrument, replaced by violin in the *huasteco* style and harp in the *jarocho* style.

Another of Mexico's traditional sounds is that of the marimba, a percussion instrument similar to a xylophone. When struck with small rubber mallets, the marimba's hardwood bars produce clear, breezy-sounding tones. Marimba music is most commonly heard in southern Mexico and Guatemala, where on fiesta days town plazas resonate with lively rhythms, sputtering firecrackers and all manner of merriment.

Popular Mexican songs have long evoked the trials and tribulations of daily life. The *corrido*, a folk narrative descended from Spanish balladry, emerged during the turbulent period of the 1910 Revolution and served as a news service of sorts in the days before radio. In exchange for a meal, wandering minstrels would travel from one rural town to another, singing songs about historical events, heroes, villains and the travails of unrequited love.

The *canción* (literally, song or lyric) was usually a slow, unabashedly sentimental ballad appealing to the passionate aspect of Mexican character. No less dramatic were the *rancheras,* nostalgic paeans to home and country originally sung by Mexican cattlemen, thus giving them a sort of country-and-western flavor.

The music most emblematic of Mexico is the sound of the mariachis. The custom of hiring a group of professional musicians to play at weddings, birthdays and other special occasions began in the state of Jalisco; "mariachi" is said to be an adaptation of the French word *mariage.* Mariachi bands deck themselves out in the costumes of the *charro,* or Mexican cowboy: tight-fitting pants, wide-brimmed sombreros and lots of silver spangles. Today they can be found all over Mexico—regaling foreign tourists in flashy Cancún, playing to homesick laborers in border towns, or serenading the object of a young suitor's desire—all for a fee, of course.

Mariachi bands started out playing guitars, violins and harp, with the harp later replaced largely by the brassy sound of trumpets. The style reached its peak in the 1950s, when Mexican matinee idols in Hollywood films sang their love songs to the strains of mariachis. The two best places for visitors to see them in action today are Plaza Garibaldi in Mexico City and Plaza de Los Mariachis in Guadalajara. A mariachi band worth its salt will be able to reel off an astonishing variety of songs, from long-established classics to customer requests in styles from achingly sad to irresistibly upbeat—and all delivered with undeniable heart and soul.

With the shrinking of the global village over the last couple of decades, Mexico—like many countries throughout the world—has been exposed to a tidal wave of Americanized pop culture. In the cities, radios, bars and dance clubs *(discotecas)* blare the latest pop, rock and hip-hop. Jay-Z, the Jonas Brothers, Rihanna and other international acts are as popular here as anywhere. But despite the invasion, music with a Mexican feeling continues to thrive.

Norteña, appropriately, originated in the working-class *cantinas* and speak-easies of the northern border area. Springing from the *corrida* tradition of lyric-driven balladry, *norteña* songs often spin tales involving small-time thieves, drug runners, illegal immigrants and other antiheroes who buck a system they consider crooked. Musically, *norteña* is like a Mexican polka, with the accordion typically the lead instrument.

Cumbia, a seductive, danceable import from the Caribbean, was the most popular music in Mexico in the 1980s; the songs are distinguished by their flirtatious lyrics, often spiced with double entendres. Equally danceable salsa, which originated in Cuba and Puerto Rico and is influenced by jazz and rock, is popular as well. *Banda* musicians play various popular styles, all arranged with an emphasis on brass and percussion. And concerts given by brass bands fill parks and town halls throughout the country.

All of these influences—spliced together with bits of American rock 'n' roll, pop, country, jazz and rap—combine to produce *tejano,* a cross-cultural musical blend embraced by Americans of Mexican descent. The center of *tejano* music is Texas (specifically, the gulf coast city of Corpus Christi), although its popularity extends south of the border as well. *Tejano's* rising star was a young woman named Selena, sometimes referred to as the "Mexican Madonna," who was murdered in 1995 by her fan-club president as she was about to break into the English-language market.

Pole Flyers, Hats and Little Old Men

Rich in history and spectacle, native folk dances are one of Mexico's most enjoyable traditions for visitors. They include those that predate the Spanish arrival, as well as European dances adapted to suit the Mexican character. Although the *conquistadores* initially tried to eradicate what they viewed as simply pagan rites, Franciscan and Dominican missionaries encouraged the continuation of Indian dances and wove these age-old rituals into their ongoing efforts to convert the natives to the Catholic church. The symbolism may have been changed—substituting Moors and Christians in place of warring tribes, for instance—but the costumes and movements remained essentially the same.

Like musical styles, folk dances vary by region. Around Papantla in the state of Veracruz, Totonac Indians still perform the flying pole dance, originally a ceremony meant to appease the rain gods. In the states of Sonora and Chihuahua, Yaqui and Tarahumara Indians perform the deer dance, a ceremony once meant to impart good luck on the hunt. A dancer in this vivid re-enactment may even wear the stuffed head of a deer. *Los Viejitos,* the "Dance of the Little Old Men," originated in the state of Michoacán. It is danced by young boys wearing masks carved to resemble the visages of elderly men. The dancers begin by moving arthritically in a parody of old age; by the end, however, their pace has enlivened considerably.

Popular traditional dances are based, not surprisingly, on Spanish steps. Perhaps the one most widely known and closely associated with the country is the *jarabe tapatío,* or Mexican hat dance. The costumes for this passionate interlude are flamboyant: for men, the silver-embroidered shirt and trousers and wide-brimmed sombrero of the horseman *(charro);* for women, the national costume, a *china poblana* dress. The dance ends with the man's sombrero placed on the floor and the couple parading around it.

Food and Drink

Authentic Mexican dishes have many influences, among them Maya, Aztec, Spanish, French, Moorish and even Chinese. There is much more to the cuisine, however, than the commonly mistaken notion that it is always hot. Many items that are in use throughout the world originated in Mexico. Corn is the country's greatest contribution to global cookery, but the list also includes tomatoes, chocolate, avocados, squashes, beans, pumpkins, chilies and turkeys (the only bird bred in pre-Hispanic Mexico).

Corn, the centerpiece of the Indian diet, took on an almost magical significance in many cultures, being used in religious rituals and ceremonies. Called *teoxintle* until the Spaniards renamed it *maíz*, the different corn varieties enabled native cooks to put this versatile vegetable to assorted uses—grinding kernels to make tortillas, thickening soups, creating beverages.

Squash and beans were other basic foodstuffs, providing practical as well as nourishing applications. Gourds, for example, were fashioned into handy household items. The cacao bean, from which chocolate is made, was so valued that the Indians used it for money, and hot chocolate whipped to a fragrant froth was at one time a drink quaffed only by the upper classes. Another native plant highly prized in pre-Hispanic kitchens was the nopal (prickly pear) cactus. Its juicy fruit was cooked and added to soups and stews, or stuffed with meat. Nopal cactus pads are a common sight in Mexican markets today.

It was with chilies, however, that early cooks could fully utilize their creative talents. Using the entire chile ensured maximum firepower, while removing the veins or seeds lessened the fiery impact. Although eaten alone as a garnish, chilies most often contributed to sauces—either salsa, made from a combination of ingredients, or mole (MOH-leh), a blend of chilies.

All of this native bounty must have mesmerized the Spanish *conquistadores* who arrived in Mexico. Bernal Díaz, a historian who marched with Hernando Cortés, described the *tianguis* (the Aztec word for marketplace) at Tlatelolco, an important trading center located just north of present-day Mexico City. Wild game included pigeon, duck, rabbit, deer, boar and iguana. From fresh water came frog legs and the larvae of water gnats. Many of the exotic fruits, vegetables and herbs—among them chilies, avocado, cilantro, cumin, papaya, mango, guava and jicama—the Spaniards had never before seen.

The Spanish themselves influenced the native cuisine, introducing cattle, sheep, goats, pigs, chickens, sugar, olive oil, rice, citrus fruits, lettuce, pepper, cinnamon and other products. Many of Mexico's most enduring dishes were developed in the Spanish convents by nuns, who had the time and patience to painstakingly combine spices, herbs and chilies into complex sauces. Eggs, lard, sugar and milk formed the basis for pastries and candies, as well as new, improved versions of the traditional tortilla. The invading French also added to the culinary mix. Wine, butter and cream added a refined touch to sauces, and such herbs as dill and mustard lent flavor to French soufflés, omelettes and pâtes.

Staples and Street Food

The tortilla, also common in Central America, is as ubiquitous in Mexico as a hamburger in the United States. This thin wrapper made of coarse cornmeal appears in many guises, and a basket of warm flour or corn tortillas frequently replaces bread or rolls on a Mexican table.

A tortilla wrapped around a filling is a taco, one of the earliest Mexican foods as well as the one most commonly embraced north of the border and around the world. Although the term is Spanish for "light snack," the taco had its origins in pre-Hispanic times, when the Aztecs used tortillas to scoop up other food. Later, the wives of agricultural workers *(campesinos)* wrapped the mid-day meal, or *comida*, in tortillas so that it could be eaten in the field. As Mexico underwent urbanization and people migrated from the country to the city, modest businesses began popping up to provide this simple, tasty regional fare.

In general, flour tortillas are used for northern Mexican grilled meat tacos, replaced by smaller yellow or white corn tortillas in central and southern Mexico. These small, soft tortillas are often doubled to hold a filling and sold in orders of two or three. Tortillas also are rolled around fillings and then fried until the tortilla is crispy, a nod to the hard taco shells popular north of the border.

Chopped onion and cilantro are the classic toppings, augmented by salsas, chopped radishes and cucumbers, grilled green onions *(cebollitas)* and the juice of lime wedges *(limones)*. Salsas are varied. Fresh chopped salsa with tomatoes, onions and cilantro is called *salsa casera*. Cooked red salsas utilize dried chilies, while *salsa verde*, made with tomatillos—the small, tart-tasting tomato native to Mexico—is green. Another garnish is guacamole, usually a thinner version than the chunky variety used as a dip.

A street taco is a two- or three-bite bit of satisfaction usually eaten on the go, and there is an art to consuming one. The tortilla and its contents are folded over to form a tube shape, then grasped between thumb and fingers so that the end closest to the mouth can be bitten off. Eating tacos in a sit-down restaurant does, however, make it easier to sop up all the salsa and meat juices.

There are numerous versions of the standard street taco, and different regional favorites throughout the country. Taco vendors tend to operate in the morning and the evening. *Tacos de canasta* are often wrapped in layers of paper or cloth, piled into a basket and sold on the street or delivered to businesses for a quick breakfast. Small corn tortillas are stuffed with such fillings as potatoes and *chorizo* (pork sausage), *frijoles* (beans) or *chicharron* (pork rinds).

Also popular in the morning are *tacos de barbacoa,* which have a filling of beef, lamb or goat. The meat for these tacos is traditionally cooked in an underground pit, but a simpler method is to steam the taco. The outer layer from a *maguey* (century plant) leaf—similar to parchment paper in thickness and consistency—also is a traditional wrapping, but nowadays a plastic baggie wrapped in foil is a common substitute. *Tacos de barbacoa* often are served with *salsa borracha* (drunken sauce), made with tomatillos, *pasilla* chilies, garlic and beer.

A traditional breakfast in northern and central Mexico is *tacos de cabeza,* literally "head tacos." The long-steamed meat is shredded and simmered in its broth. Customers can choose from a variety of cuts, including tongue *(lengua),* ear *(oreja)* and brains *(sesos).* The squeamish can opt for *maciza,* boneless shredded beef. These tacos are topped with cilantro, chopped onions and red or green salsa.

Around dusk the storefront *taquerías* open, street carts begin setting up and the air is filled with the tantalizing aroma of grilling meat. In the evening tacos can be the basis for a light supper *(cena)* and also are a preferred late-night snack. *Tacos al pastor* and *tacos de carnitas* are twin favorites. A Mexican adaptation of Middle Eastern spit-grilled meat, *tacos al pastor* are made with marinated pork stacked on a vertical spit above a gas flame. As it roasts the meat is shaved off, heaped on a tortilla and topped with grilled onions, cilantro and often pieces of fresh pineapple. In Puebla a variation of *tacos al pastor* called *tacos arabes* is wrapped in a thicker tortilla similar to pita bread and served with a spicy, deep-red salsa flavored with *chipotle,* dried *jalapeño* chilies.

Tacos de carnitas also are made from pork; the cuts are displayed in a glass case kept warm with a heat lamp. Customers choose the part of the pig they want, from a boneless cut of meat, ribs *(costilla)* or cracklings (skin) to the more exotic heart, liver or pork cheeks. The chunks of meat are then cooked in lard, which gives them a golden-brown color. *Tacos al carbón,* also known as *tacos de carne asada,* utilize thin slices of quickly grilled beef stuffed into tortillas and garnished with green onions, sliced radishes and cucumbers, salsa and lime.

Tacos de fritangas are tacos made with meat—chicken breast, pork or blood sausage, even lamb testicles—that is fried in a metal pan. *Guisados* (stews) of beef, chicken, turkey, pork, lamb or goat are simmered in a clay pot with chilies and such vegetables as mushrooms, squash blossoms and cactus pads *(nopales),* and these mixtures also are used as taco fillings. *Tacos dorados,* also called *taquitos* or *flautas,* are tortillas rolled around a filling, usually cooked chicken or beef, then fried and topped with shredded lettuce, cream *(crema)* and grated Mexican cheese. The fish tacos of Baja California and the Pacific coast are tasty morsels of batter-dipped and fried filets with accompaniments of shredded cabbage, guacamole, salsas and onions marinated in vinegar.

As long as visitors follow a couple of basic common-sense rules, indulging in street tacos—some of the tastiest food in Mexico—should not result in digestive problems. Trust the judgment of locals and look for a taco stand that has lots of customers, a sure sign the food is good. Pick one that specializes in a certain type of taco rather than offering a wide variety; fewer ingredients mean that they are likely to be fresher. You also will be able to watch your order being prepared, and part of the fun of eating on the street is observing the cooks and vendors as they deftly go about the business of assembling their specialties.

There are taco variations as well. When served with tomato sauce and sprinkled with cheese, soft rolled tacos are called enchiladas. Crisp fried tortillas spread with minced chicken, meat or salad are called *tostadas.* Tortilla dough turnovers filled with cheese are *quesadillas;* when filled with potato, pork sausage or refried beans and then fried in fat, they are *empanadas.*

Tamales, like tacos, also are made from a corn-based dough to which lard is added, creating a mealier texture. A *tamale* is filled with bits of chicken, pork or such sweets as chocolate, wrapped in corn husks or banana leaves and then steamed. *Sopes* are flat, thick disks of dough made from ground corn treated with lime juice *(masa)* that are baked on a griddle. Topped with various combinations of meat and vegetables and garnished with cheese, salsa and cilantro, *sopes* are best eaten right after they're made.

Tortas, the Mexican counterpart of sandwiches, are prepared with a small loaf of bread called *telera* or *bolillo* and then filled with different meats, lettuce, onion, tomato, cheese and avocado. The *cemita,* which originated in the city of Puebla, is a sandwich on a soft, sesame-seed egg roll. The meat is usually pork or beef pounded thin and then deep-fried; fillings include onions, sliced avocado and mild white cheese.

Like the taco, two Mexican side dishes are known around the world. *Frijoles* (beans) are cooked in various ways and served either whole or mashed, or combined with rice, vegetables, chicken livers, plantains or eggs. Guacamole, mashed avocado seasoned with onion, hot peppers and tomato, makes a tasty chip dip and also is used as a salad garnish.

Other street food comes in an almost overwhelming variety of forms. Sometimes it's simple: pieces of freshly peeled fruit sold in a plastic cup or threaded on a skewer. A popsicle vendor can be found on almost every city street corner. *Churros,* sold from carts, are ridged, tube-shaped pieces of fried dough, doughnut-like in texture, that are dusted with sugar or filled with fruit or chocolate. Corn on the cob *(elote)* is roasted in the husk, then speared on a stick and spread with condiments like butter or sour cream and sprinkled with cheese or red chili powder. The kernels also are cut off the cob and served in a styrofoam cup to which the condiments can be added.

Festive and Regional Fare

The nation's favorite special preparation is *mole de guajolote,* turkey served with a rich, thick sauce made from various chilies, peanuts, spices, sesame seed and unsweetened chocolate. As many as 30 different ingredients, all of which must be ground or pureed, may go into the sauce's preparation.

Another distinctly Mexican concoction is *chilies rellenos,* or stuffed chilies. A dark green chili pepper—not the sweet bell variety popular in the United States—is stuffed with cheese or ground meat, fried in a coating of egg batter and then simmered in tomato sauce. A variation of this dish is called *chile en nogada.* Instead of tomato sauce, the chili (stuffed with beef, pork and fruits) is covered with ground fresh walnuts and a pureed white cheese similar to cream cheese. When sprinkled with red pomegranate seeds and garnished with parsley, the dish represents the red, white and green colors of the Mexican flag. It is frequently served in conjunction with independence celebrations during the month of September.

If you're fond of gastronomic adventure, Mexico has some exotic choices. At the time of the Spanish arrival, the staple diet of the Indians included such items as grasshoppers, ant eggs, rats, armadillos, monkeys, parrots and rattlesnakes. Fine restaurants in Mexico City and Oaxaca still offer insect dishes, including crunchy fried grasshoppers *(chapulines)* dashed with chili powder and lime juice, ant eggs *(escamoles)* and worms *(gusanos de maguey)*—also crisply fried—that live on the maguey plant, from which tequila is made. *Huitlacoche* is a black, truffle-like fungus that grows on ears of corn; it is often served with crepes. In the northern part of the country, broiled goat *(cabrito)* is popular.

Different areas of Mexico are known for their style of cooking or for specific dishes. In and around Veracruz the specialty is *huachinango a la Veracruzana,* red snapper broiled in tomato sauce and served with onions, olives and capers. Acapulco and other Mexican seaside towns are famous for their ceviche (say-VEE-cheh). Pieces of raw fish or shellfish are marinated in lime juice for at least eight hours, "cooking" the fish. Chopped tomatoes and onions, chilies and such herbs as cilantro are then added to this dish, which is served chilled and often as an appetizer. In Baja California and the northwestern coastal cities, lobster and shrimp are scrambled into eggs, or replace chicken and pork as taco fillings.

Historical and geographical isolation have had perhaps their greatest impact on regional cuisine in the Yucatán Peninsula. Here the food has Cuban, Caribbean, European and Asian influences. The fiery habanero chile common in Yucatecan cookery grows nowhere else in Mexico. Achiote, the tiny red seed of the annatto tree, is the primary ingredient of a pungent paste with a distinctive orange-red color that seasons pork, chicken or fish cooked *pibil* style—sort of a distant relative of American barbecue.

Yucatecan menus offer such authentic dishes as *cochinita pibil,* pork rubbed with achiote, wrapped in banana leaves and baked in an underground oven; *frijol con puerco,* a pork and black bean stew garnished with cilantro, radishes and onions and served with rice; and *huevos motuleños,* a filling breakfast dish featuring a tortilla covered with refried black beans, topped with a fried egg and smothered with tomato sauce or chile-spiked salsa, peas, diced ham and crumbled white cheese, usually served with slices of fried banana or plantain.

Soups and Desserts

Soups are tasty and varied. Mexican chicken soup is laden with chunks of chicken, rice, vegetables and often sliced avocado. Rich cream soups are made from such unlikely vegetable by-products as squash blossoms.

Pozole, a hearty soup native to the state of Jalisco but popular in many parts of Mexico, incorporates hominy and pork or chicken in a flavorful broth. Shredded lettuce, chopped onions, strips of fried tortilla and splashes of lime juice are frequently tossed in. This stew-like concoction also takes on red or green hues from the addition of ancho chilies or green tomatoes mixed with various greens, respectively. **Note:** Most Mexican chilies are hot, and some are incendiary. If in doubt about their firepower, ask, *"Es muy picante?"* ("Is it very hot?").

Desserts are not the focal point of a good Mexican meal. Many are overwhelmingly sweet. Flan (browned custard), which is widely served, is a Spanish creation. Although there is a large variety of egg-based, pudding-like sweets, a better choice would be one of the country's tropical fruits, such as papaya, passion fruit, pineapple or mango. Remember to avoid those that are unpeeled.

Mexican confections, or *dulces,* are most often fruit-flavored hard candies, sugar-glazed fruits in their natural form or little cakes made of honey, grated coconut, almonds and other ingredients. Some restaurants feature good ice cream *(helado).*

Beverages

A good way to begin the day in Mexico is to have a steaming cup of coffee. *Cafe de olla* is flavored with cinnamon and sugar, although you'll have to ask for cream (which usually turns out to be evaporated milk). Espresso and cappuccino are widely available—and undistinguished instant is frequently served in restaurants—but Mexicans favor *cafe con leche,* a combination of strong black coffee and hot milk that is often poured into a tall glass. Another favorite is Mexican hot chocolate, which is not as sweet as the American version.

Freshly squeezed fruit juices are inexpensive and refreshing. Ask for a *licuado* (fruit shake) made with bananas or papayas. Also inexpensive are soft drinks, the ubiquitous Coca-Cola as well as local brands *(refrescos).* They are not only safe to drink out of the can but one of the few luxuries that the country's poorer citizens can afford. Tehuacán, in the state of Puebla, is famous for bottled mineral waters made with and without natural fruit flavors. Local bottling plants draw from the mineral springs around the city.

Cerveza (beer) is as ubiquitous as Coke *(Coca).* Two Mexican varieties—Corona and Tecate—are sold everywhere (the latter is the country's No. 1 cheap alcoholic beverage). Quality brews like Dos Equis and Bohemia are appreciated throughout the world.

Mexico's viticultural history was relatively late in developing. Although pre-Hispanic peoples enjoyed fermented beverages, those derived from the grape were not among them. Spanish colonists introduced the first vine cuttings, and Mexican wines soon began competing with those of the homeland. A marauding insect almost destroyed the grape crop in the late 19th century, but plague-resistant cuttings from California were grafted onto the diseased ones, saving the wine industry. Today almost 80 percent of all domestic vintages are produced in the state of Baja California. Other major wine-producing areas are in the states of Aguascalientes, Querétaro and Zacatecas.

From the several varieties of the maguey (mah-GAY) plant, a cactuslike jack-of-all-trades, come highly intoxicating liquors that are uniquely Mexican. Tequila is the quintessential one, traditionally downed from a salt-rimmed glass and immediately followed by a bite into a lime wedge. Bottles of mezcal from the vicinity of Oaxaca sometimes include a worm that lives on the plant. Other alcoholic beverages produced from the maguey are *comiteco* (Chiapas), *charanda* (Michoacán), *sotol* (Chihuahua) and *bacanora* (Sonora).

Pulque, manufactured in central Mexico from the maguey's unfermented juice, has less of a kick and is considered to have both nutritious and medicinal properties. *Colonche* is prepared in the states of Aguascalientes, Guanajuato, Jalisco and San Luis Potosí with fermented fruit from the prickly pear cactus. *Rompope* originated in the state of Puebla as a family beverage for festive occasions. Similar to eggnog, its ingredients include milk, egg yolks, sugar, vanilla, cinnamon and a dash of rum.

Dining Tips

In large cities, restaurants serving top-quality French, Italian or Continental cuisine are easy to find. But it's worth the effort to seek out places that focus on traditional Mexican cooking, which is not necessarily the tacos and enchiladas so common north of the border.

Native foods can be found in smaller restaurants called *cenadurías, taquerías* or *merenderos,* which cater more to Mexican customers than to foreign tourists. In such establishments diners can order *carne en su jugo* (meat in its juice), tamales and a great variety of *antojitos* (snacks). The sign "Antojitos Mexicanos" indicates that these and other specialties are on the menu. An added bonus at these country-style restaurants are the shows, accompanied by mariachi music, often put on for diners.

Another way to sample local fare is to buy it off the street. Even the smallest town square will have vendors selling roasted meat, cut-up fruit, soft drinks, sweets or other edibles. Levels of sanitation, however, vary greatly, and the advice of most veteran travelers who stay healthy is to avoid street vendor offerings.

For those accustomed to an early breakfast, Mexican restaurants are not particularly accommodating; many don't open until around 9 a.m. Markets, however, normally open early and are good places to pick up something for a morning meal. Another tip: Buy croissants or sweet rolls at a bakery the night before and have your own breakfast before starting the day.

Because many Mexicans make something of a ceremony out of meals, restaurant service tends to be slower than in the United States. If you follow the Mexican schedule for dining, you will have lunch no earlier than 2 p.m., cocktails at 7 p.m. and dinner at 9 or 10 p.m.

Lunch, or *la comida,* is the main meal of the day (*el almuerzo* also means lunch but tends to be a late morning snack eaten on the run). Many restaurants still offer a *comida corrida,* or lunch special, which usually includes soup, a main course, a dessert and coffee. For those on a budget, making lunch the big meal of the day is the most economical way to dine.

Gracious service is the rule rather than the exception. When you're ready for the check, simply say *"la cuenta, por favor"* ("the check, please"). Making scribbling motions on your hand to imply writing is commonly recognized international sign language.

Regardless of the establishment, always ask about policies and double check the total amount of the bill. You might assume, for example, that there are free refills for coffee when in actuality you'll be charged for each cup you drink (a free second cup is more common at breakfast).

Some restaurants may compute the tab by adding up the number of glasses and plates on the table. The 15 percent IVA service tax (10 percent in the state of Quintana Roo and the Baja California Peninsula) may be added (sometimes the charge is 17 percent, which includes local tax); again, double check the individual amounts. This does not take the place of a tip, so leave what you think is appropriate, usually 10 to 20 percent of the bill.

Celebrations

Perhaps the clearest view into the heart of a nation is through its celebrations. This is especially true in Mexico, with its distinctive yet endlessly varied blending of Indian and Hispanic cultures. Each town has its own traditions, stemming from centuries of ancestral practices and beliefs combined with the Christian influences introduced by the Spaniards.

Fiestas

The country's most dynamic—and ubiquitous—special event is the fiesta. A fiesta takes place somewhere in Mexico every day of the year, in the tiniest villages and the biggest cities. There's much to celebrate; in addition to observing national holidays and such country-wide fiestas as Carnaval and the Day of the Dead, every town salutes its patron saint's day.

Fiestas take on myriad forms, but almost every one includes a parade. The procession is usually in association with a revered religious image but also can be secular in nature, often capped off by fireworks. Music, dancing and an array of local edibles are essential elements. Costumed dancers may portray historical, mythological or imagined happenings to the accompaniment of indigenous instruments.

Sometimes there are regional or folkloric dances representative of the area or state; mariachi or harp ensembles are the usual accompaniment. The Yucatán, for example, has its evocative *jaranas,* danced by couples in white costumes to the lilting sound of a band. Yucatecan fiestas, called *vaquerías,* brim with joy and merrymaking.

On a more official note is the observance of Independence Day on Sept. 16, commemorating the 1810 proclamation of the *Grito de Dolores,* a rallying cry for freedom from Spain, by Father Miguel Hidalgo y Costilla. The town of Dolores Hidalgo, where Father Hidalgo read the *grito* from his parish church, still figures prominently in Independence Day festivities. The biggest celebration by far, however, is in Mexico City, where the huge *Zócalo* swarms with crowds and fireworks fill the air.

Religious Observances

Some of Mexico's loveliest traditions center on Christmas, despite the American influence of Santa Claus and Christmas trees. Foremost are the *posadas,* which take place for 9 days beginning Dec. 16 and represent the search for an inn *(posada)* in preparation for the holy birth. Bearing candles and figures of Mary and Joseph, guests circle a house begging for a place to stay, but are refused until the Pilgrims are identified. After that the party begins, with hot punch, sweets and the breaking open of *piñatas.* More and more, gift giving is on Dec. 25, although in smaller towns presents are still exchanged on the traditional Twelfth Night, or Epiphany (Jan. 6).

Another Christmas season tradition is the presentation of *pastorelas* in public plazas, schools and theaters. Based on the events immediately before Jesus' birth, they often have a comic touch. Over time *pastorelas* have come to include in their cast of characters such historical figures as Aztec emperor Cuauhtémoc and revolutionary Emiliano Zapata, who take part as if they had lived during that first Nativity.

Mexico precedes the Lenten season with an uproarious celebration of Carnaval. Festivities usually begin on the Saturday before Ash Wednesday and end on Shrove Tuesday night, often with the burning of a papier-mâché figure of Juan Carnaval to signal the beginning of Lent. Carnaval is particularly exuberant in Mazatlán and Veracruz.

The Lenten season culminates in Holy Week *(Semana Santa)* from Palm Sunday to Easter Sunday, which is marked by solemn *pastorelas* or a re-enactment of the Passion from Judgment to Resurrection. The young man chosen to portray Jesus undergoes rigorous preparation for his role, which in some places includes being whipped and then tied to a cross. Again, the observance often ends with the burning of a papier-mâché figure, this time Judas. Many Holy Week celebrations also venerate the Virgin Mary, with processions bearing some form of her image.

Laughing at Death

Mexico's best-known celebration, one in which both Indian and Catholic traditions blend into a unique expression of love for the deceased, is *Los Dias de Muertos,* or Days of the Dead, which are celebrated on Nov. 1 and 2. A straightforward approach to the uncomfortable subject of mortality, the holiday—celebrated in Mexico for centuries—mixes mourning with macabre humor and pagan rites with the Catholic observances of All Souls' and All Saints' days.

Day of the Dead celebrations are similar to, although more serious than, the celebration of Halloween north of the border. But as with Christmas, the American influence has become pervasive, and some Mexican traditionalists worry that the proliferation of Halloween parties in Mexico City and elsewhere, as well as the sale of "spooky" items like vampire masks and plastic jack-o-lanterns, threatens to overshadow the meaning of their own holiday.

Families may honor departed loved ones by telling stories, eating candy skulls or even camping all night in the local cemetery, decorating gravesites, praying and sharing memories. The holiday tends to be downplayed by the wealthier and more educated segments of Mexican society as superstitious ritual or quaint religious holdover, although much of the country continues to explode each November with food, drink, flowers and skeletal figures (which are known as *calaveras;* literally, "skull"). The most traditional Day of the Dead celebration takes place on the island of Janitzio, in Lake Pátzcuaro, although local and regional variations abound.

The popular belief that the dead are permitted to visit their living kin provides the latter a chance to prepare sometimes ostentatious culinary offerings, which usually include sweet loaves of *pan de muerto* (bread of the dead). A lavish *ofrenda,* or altar, could include candles, mementos, pictures of the departed, a bottle of favorite liquor, dancing skeletons, a portrait of the Virgin of Guadalupe and a display of marigolds *(zempoalxóchitl),* known as the "flower of the dead." Everyone sings, dances and prays, simultaneously sending up and accepting the inevitability of death.

Note: Many Mexicans travel during Holy Week and the Christmas holidays, and visitors should make hotel reservations in advance if planning to be in the country during those times. Local transportation systems also tend to be jammed during Holy Week. For a listing of representative fiestas, fairs and celebrations in Mexico, *see Fiestas and Holidays, pages 675.*

Recreation

Spectator Sports

The earliest known sport played in Mexico was a form of ball game; the ruins of courts on which it was played exist at various archeological sites. While the rules are unknown, it is believed that the final outcome for some of the players was death. Fortunately, today's organized recreational activities are decidedly safer. The national sport is **soccer. Baseball** and **football** also are popular.

Bullfighting was introduced by the Spaniards. More spectacle than sport, the bullfight, or *corrida de toros,* is an elaborate ceremony that begins with a parade and ends with the flamboyantly attired matador taking a tour of the ring to the accolades of spectators while a team of mules drags away the dead bull. In between is a series of encounters between man and beast, kept thrilling by the matador's dramatic skill and by the continual goading of the animal with viciously barbed lances.

While bullfighting is very much a part of Mexican lore, those with an aversion to such brutality would be better off not attending. Bullfights can be seen throughout the country but are regularly scheduled in Mexico City, Guadalajara and Tijuana.

Equally spectacular but more humanitarian are the Mexican **rodeos** called *charreadas.* The *charro,* a gentleman cowboy, competes in various displays of skill. These events, usually held on Sunday mornings, feature colorful costumes, music and a general air of showmanship; charro associations from all over Mexico compete. Guadalajara has some of the best exhibitions.

Jai alai, an exciting game similar to squash that often is accompanied by spirited betting, is played countrywide but particularly in Mexico City. **Competitive cycling, horse racing** and **cockfights** (the last supposedly illegal) all take place in various locations; check at your hotel desk or consult the local tourist office for details.

Golf, Tennis and Riding

In Mexico you can play **golf** at a variety of world-class courses located in all of the major metropolitan areas and at the beach and vacation resorts. Los Cabos, at the southern tip of the Baja peninsula, is famed for its immaculately groomed and devilishly challenging courses, including three designed by old pro Jack Nicklaus. Many courses boast stunning backdrops, from Baja's deserts to Cancún's beaches to the colonial charm of San Miguel de Allende.

Among the outstanding courses are those located at the Moon Palace Golf Resort south of Cancún; the Ocean and Desert courses at the Cabo del Sol resort in Los Cabos; the Club de Golf México in Mexico City; the Tres Vida Golf Club in Acapulco; the Grand Bay Hotel at Isla Navidad, north of Manzanillo; and the Vista Vallarta Golf Club in Puerto Vallarta.

Almost all golf courses in Mexico are private and can be played by visitors only if they are accompanied by a member. Hotel-owned courses give preference to guests, although the hotel might be able to arrange access to a nearby facility. Fees at the better course are comparable to those in the United States. Bring your own clubs if possible; purchasing equipment is even more expensive than playing.

The Mexican Ministry of Tourism (SECTUR) publishes an Official Golf Course Tourist Guide that provides general information about a number of courses throughout the country. Information also can be accessed through the Mexico Tourism Board's Web site, www.visitmexico.com.

Tennis courts are plentiful in resort areas. Equipment can be rented but varies in quality; again, serious players should bring their own.

The horse was considered a strange, frightening beast to superstitious Aztecs who first laid eyes on the steeds brought over by Hernando Cortés. These fears were overcome, and today Mexicans are enthusiastic riders. **Horseback riding** is an invigorating way to explore the arid, beautifully scenic stretches of northern Mexico, and this part of the country has a number of stables and ranches that rent horses and arrange riding expeditions. Another popular activity is horseback riding along the beach, available at Acapulco, Mazatlán, Puerto Vallarta and along both coasts of Baja California.

The Lure of the Water

Mexico has some wonderful beaches along its Pacific and Caribbean coasts. The major resorts all offer the usual water sports, from **water skiing** and **windsurfing** to **sailing** and **parasailing,** and any necessary equipment is easily rented. Pay close attention to local warnings regarding surf conditions; many Pacific beaches have dangerous undertows and strong currents. In addition, some ocean waters can be polluted.

Snorkeling is best around Cancún and the islands of Cozumel and Isla Mujeres. The clear, shallow waters here brim with brilliantly hued fish and intricate coral formations. The Baja California and Pacific coasts are more suitable for **scuba diving,** although Baja's Pacific waters are quite cold and the diving spots tend to be hard to reach. La Paz, in southern Baja on the Gulf of California, and Guaymas, on the northwestern mainland coast, have inviting waters, equipment rentals and resort facilities.

Other good bases for snorkeling and scuba explorations are Puerto Vallarta, situated amid the coves, rock formations and underwater ledges of the Bay of Banderas; Ixtapa/Zihuatanejo, where offshore rock formations create a variety of underwater sites; and Bahías de Huatulco, with nine lovely bays to explore.

Note: If you're taking scuba lessons or have a referral letter from your home training center, check to make sure that the instructor or dive center you choose in Mexico holds

U.S.-recognized certification, such as NAUI, PADI, SSI or YMCA.

While **surfing** has little appeal to most Mexicans, American surfers claim that the country's Pacific breakers are some of the best. Accessible spots include the beaches in the vicinity of Cabo San Lucas at the southern end of Baja California; around Mazatlán and south toward San Blas; and at Puerto Escondido, west of Bahías de Huatulco. Those pursuing surfing opportunities in Mexico should keep in mind that very few boards are available for rent.

Getting Back to Nature

The most popular areas for **camping** are in Baja California and along the Pacific Coast beaches of the mainland. The desolate beauty of Baja is often accessible only via four-wheel-drive vehicle; campers straying off the beaten path should be experienced and properly equipped.

Some of Mexico's national parks permit camping as well. Many offer a backdrop of cool pine forests or sparkling lakes, as well as good **hiking** trails and scenic spots for **picnicking.** For listings of AAA-RATED campgrounds and trailer parks, *see How to Read a Campground Listing, beginning on page 678.* **Note:** Avoid camping at deserted beaches or in other isolated areas, where banditry tends to occur.

For the prodigiously fit, Mexico has several challenging peaks for **mountain climbing.** Organized expeditions are available to the dormant volcano Iztaccíhuatl, near Mexico City, and to Citlaltépetl (Pico de Orizaba), in the state of Veracruz. Needless to say, experience is essential.

Major equipment is available in Mexico, but plan on bringing personal items (backpack, footwear, sleeping bag). Do not attempt to climb during the rainy season, June through September. For further information, contact the Exploration Club of Mexico (Club de Exploraciones de México, or CEMAC), Calle Juan A. Mateos #146, Col. Obrera, 06800 México, D.F.; phone (55) 5740-8032.

Fishing

Mexico offers some of the best deep-sea **fishing** in the world, particularly around the southern tip of Baja California, in the Gulf of California, along the Pacific coast and off the eastern coast of the Yucatán Peninsula; its excellence is attested to by the numerous tournaments held each year. As with hunting, Mexican authorities are taking greater steps to preserve the country's natural resources, and a catch-and-release policy is advocated for sports anglers.

Locations noted for their deep-sea fishing opportunities include Acapulco for pompano, barracuda and shark; Cabo San Lucas for blue and striped marlin, sailfish and swordfish; Cancún and Cozumel for sailfish, swordfish, marlin, dolphin and barracuda; Ensenada for yellowtail; Guaymas for marlin, sailfish, dolphin and yellowtail; La Paz and Loreto for marlin and sailfish; Los Mochis and Topolobampo for marlin, sailfish, pompano and roosterfish; Manzanillo for sailfish; Mazatlán for sailfish and marlin; Mulegé for snook; and Puerto Vallarta for sailfish, marlin, bonito, red snapper and shark.

Rivers and lakes contain many varieties of freshwater fish. A man-made lake near Valle de Bravo, in the state of México, is known for black bass and trout. Bass also is the lure at Vicente Guerrero, another man-made lake in the state of Tamaulipas. El Novillo Dam, east of Hermosillo in the state of Sonora, has good bass fishing. Whitefish, esteemed as a national delicacy, can be caught in Lake Catemaco, in the state of Veracruz; Lake Chapala, in the state of Jalisco; and Lake Pátzcuaro, in the state of Michoacán.

Fishing regulations, which apply to both freshwater and saltwater species, are not complicated—the only requirement is a license. A Mexican sport-fishing license covers all types of fishing and is valid anywhere in Mexico.

If you intend to fish in Baja California or Pacific waters, contact the California office of the Secretaría de Pesca (Mexican Department of Fisheries) in San Diego for an application; phone (619) 233-6956. You also can obtain the necessary license at fishing and tackle supply stores in San Diego.

License fees vary depending on boat size and time spent fishing (1 day to 1 year). They range from about $15 to $40 but are subject to change; contact the Department of Fisheries for updates. The cost is the same whether the angler is alone or part of a tour group. Everyone aboard private boats in Mexican waters must have a fishing license regardless of age and whether or not they are fishing. Licenses are not transferable. Skin divers and scuba divers who fish need a license as well.

Spear fishing is legal only with hand-held or spring-powered spears. The taking of mollusks, crustaceans, sea turtles, totoaba (totuava, or sea trout) and marine mammals is prohibited. It is illegal to sell, trade or exchange any fish caught.

The maximum catch per day varies by species. Generally authorized maximums are 10 fish caught per day, but not more than five of the same species. Catches of marlin, sailfish, swordfish and shark are limited to one per day per species; catches of tarpon, roosterfish, dorado and shad are limited to two per day per species. The limit on inland bodies of water is five fish per day, regardless of species. To preserve game species, many of Mexico's top sport-fishing destinations emphasize a catch-and-release policy.

Major hotels and independent companies at the resorts and in port cities can arrange fishing expeditions or provide boats and gear for hire. All nonresident private boats entering Mexican waters must obtain certification and a temporary boat permit from the Mexican Department of Fisheries in San Diego, a Mexican consulate office or a customs broker.

The Mexican Ministry of Tourism (SECTUR) publishes an Official Sports and Recreation Fishing Guide that includes general information about the best salt and freshwater fishing opportunities in various parts of the country. The information also can be accessed through the Mexico Tourism Board's Web site.

Spas

For some, the focus of recreation is on relaxation and restoration rather than physical activity. Visitors to a Mexican spa can benefit from the same therapeutic resources used for centuries by indigenous peoples—the country's immense variety of native plants.

Mexico's botanical wonders are many. The nopal, a tropical prickly pear cactus, is a source of vitamin C and amino acids; helps the body pull fluids from tissues back into the bloodstream, thus diminishing cellulite and water retention; and is effective in regulating blood sugar for those who are diabetic. The so-called "magic bark" of the tepezcohuite tree, indigenous to the state of Chiapas, has skin-healing and regenerative properties used to treat sunburn, blisters and blemishes. Mexicans also have long extolled the use of mineral-rich volcanic mud to stimulate circulation and relieve muscular and arthritic pain.

The precursors to today's world-class spa facilities are the hot springs and mineral water bathing resorts that still can be found in central Mexico towns like Cuautla, Ixtapan de La Sal and Tepoztlán. But contemporary beauty and health services are increasingly adopting such pre-Hispanic spa techniques as the *temazcal,* a type of sweat house using hot stones and herbs to purify the body.

Mexico's spa offerings include resort facilities set against breathtaking natural backdrops, often incorporating golf, swimming or eco and adventure tourism activities to enhance the experience. The spa at the Las Ventanas al Paraiso resort along the Los Cabos Corridor offers everything from an aromatic exfoliation and soak to nontraditional plant medicine therapies and sacred healing rituals. And Cabañas Copal, a secluded seaside resort an hour and a half south of Cancún, offers a spa where you can cleanse body and mind through holistic principles performed by local shamans.

Fast Facts

POPULATION: 100,124,800 (2002 estimate).

AREA: 1,972,554 sq km (761,603 sq. mi.).

CAPITAL: Mexico City, D.F.

HIGHEST POINT: 5,657 (meters 18,555 feet). Pico de Orizaba, Ver.

LOWEST POINT: 13 meters (43 feet) below sea level. South of Mexicali, B.C.

LANGUAGE: Spanish; some 50 Indian languages and many more dialects are spoken outside of major cities and towns. English is widely spoken, particularly in larger cities and at resorts.

UNIT OF CURRENCY: The monetary unit is the peso. The exchange rate in July 2008 was about 10.3 pesos=$1 U.S., although the rate is subject to small daily fluctuations.

BANK HOURS: Most banks are open Mon.-Fri. 9-1:30; in some larger cities, they may reopen 4-6 and are open Sat. 10-1:30. Large hotels usually exchange money, although at varying rates. Banks are closed on all national holidays, and also may close to celebrate local holidays.

BUSINESS HOURS: In most cities, businesses operate Mon.-Sat. 9-7; many are closed from 2-4 for the traditional long lunch break. In resort areas stores and shops are often open into the evening and on Sunday. Shop hours may not always correspond to what is advertised. Shopping malls are generally open daily; they are closed Jan. 1, Good Friday, May 1 (Labor Day) and Dec. 25.

TAXES: Mexico levies a 15 percent value-added (Impuesto de Valor Agregado, or IVA) tax on all goods and services, even telephone and Internet services (10 percent in the state of Quintana Roo and the Baja California Peninsula). An additional tax on hotel and beverage services means that some items can carry a 17 percent IVA tax. The tax is supposed to be included in the posted price or rate but is not always itemized separately on your bill; inquire if you feel you are being doubly charged.

HOLIDAYS: New Year's Day; Constitution Day, Feb. 5; Birthday of Benito Juárez, Mar. 21; Holy Week (Semana Santa); Good Friday through Easter Sunday; Labor Day, May 1; Battle of Puebla (Cinco de Mayo), May 5; Independence Day, Sept. 16; Day of the Race (Columbus Day), Oct. 12; Christmas, Dec. 25. Banks, government offices and most stores are closed.

MEDIA: Mexico has no national English-language newspapers. *USA Today* is usually available in big cities or resorts. The Sanborn's chain, with outlets in the larger cities, carries English-language magazines. Hotels usually provide free magazines that list what is happening around town; most hotels also offer U.S. TV channels.

ATTRACTION SCHEDULES: Before setting out for a day of sightseeing, check with the front desk at your hotel regarding schedules for local museums, archeological sites or historic buildings. Many museums in Mexico are open 9-5 and are closed on Monday. Admission fees are inexpensive, usually less than $5 (U.S.). While free admission days or reduced fees for different age groups technically apply only to Mexican citizens, policies will vary depending on the attraction. The listings in this TourBook provide hours and admissions where known.

PUBLIC RESTROOMS: Take advantage of those in hotels, restaurants, airports or bus stations wherever possible, as public restrooms otherwise are difficult to find. Those in out-of-the-way places, particularly at gas stations, often have primitive plumbing and are definitely not up to the standards of public restrooms in the United States. Always carry a roll of toilet paper and a small bar of soap; both of these necessities can be in short supply away from your hotel.

POLICE: Few tourists ever run into trouble with the law, but you may need to ask police for directions or seek assistance for other reasons. While officers normally are helpful, other encounters—mainly those involving alleged traffic violations—can be exasperating or even intimidating, especially if you don't speak fluent Spanish. Always cooperate if stopped, but try to resolve the situation right away.

RESOURCES: Bilingual telephone operators with the Mexico Ministry of Tourism (Secretaría de Turismo, or SECTUR) provide 24-hour information about tourist destinations and services. In Mexico City, phone (55) 5250-0123 or (55) 5250-0151; elsewhere within Mexico, phone 01 (800) 903-9200 (toll-free long distance).

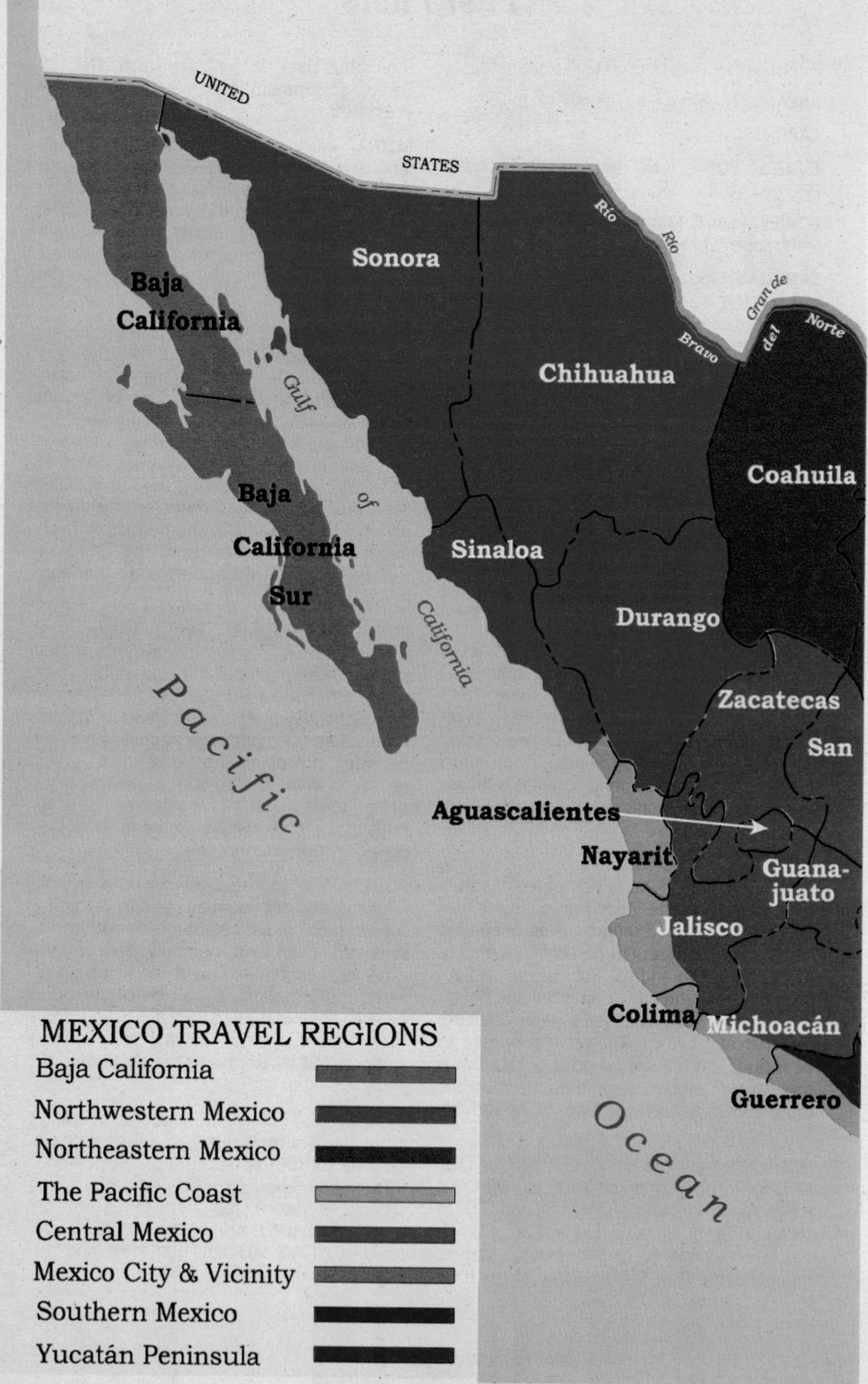
UNITED
STATES
Sonora
Baja
California
Gulf
of
California
Baja
California
Sur
Chihuahua
Río
Río
Bravo
Grande
del
Norte
Coahuila
Sinaloa
Durango
Zacatecas
San
Aguascalientes
Nayarit
Guana-
juato
Jalisco
Colima
Michoacán
Guerrero
Pacific
Ocean
MEXICO TRAVEL REGIONS
Baja California
Northwestern Mexico
Northeastern Mexico
The Pacific Coast
Central Mexico
Mexico City & Vicinity
Southern Mexico
Yucatán Peninsula

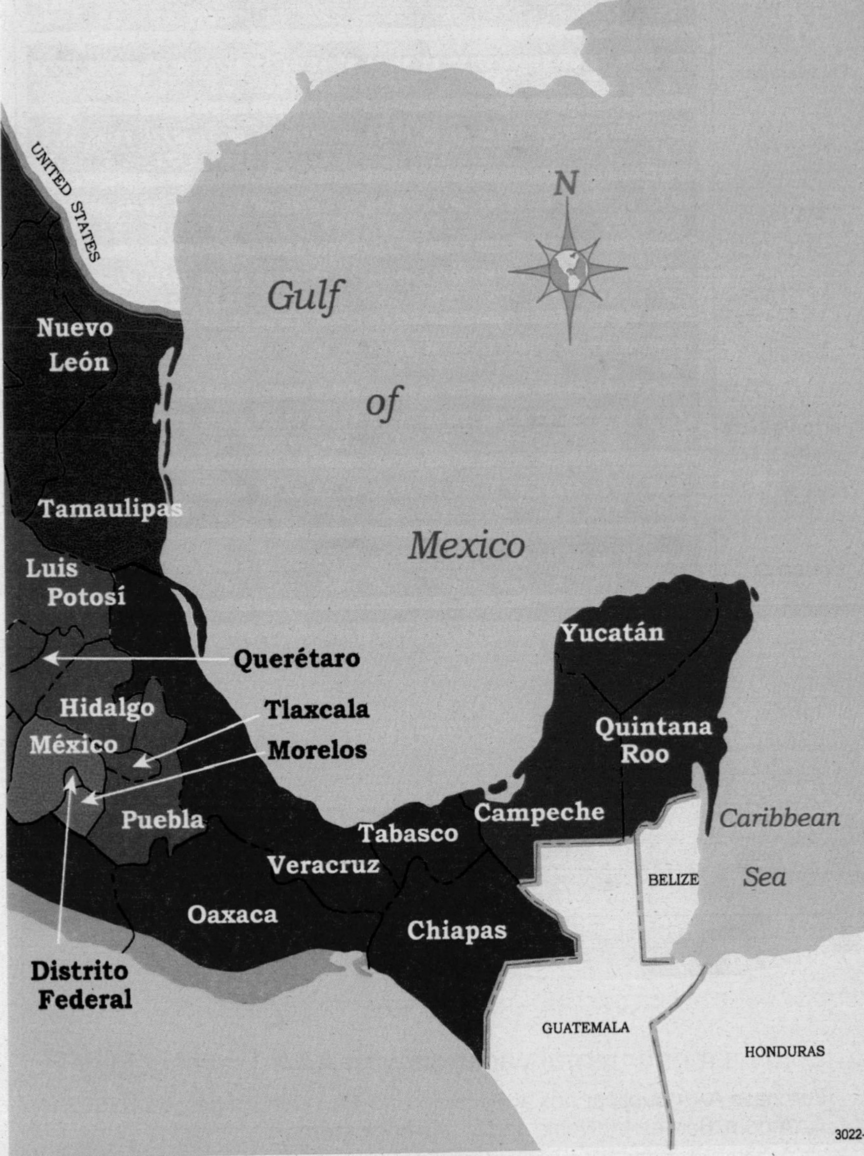
© AAA
MEXICO
Orientation
0 Miles 291
0 Kilometers 469
UNITED STATES
N
Gulf
of
Mexico
Nuevo
León
Tamaulipas
Luis
Potosí
Querétaro
Hidalgo
Tlaxcala
México
Morelos
Puebla
Distrito
Federal
Veracruz
Oaxaca
Tabasco
Chiapas
Campeche
Yucatán
Quintana
Roo
Caribbean
Sea
BELIZE
GUATEMALA
HONDURAS
3022-C

Mexico Temperature and Rainfall Averages

From the records of Comisión Nacional del Agua (Servicio Meteorológico Nacional)

	JAN	FEB	MAR	APR	MAY	JUNE	JULY	AUG	SEPT	OCT	NOV	DEC
Acapulco	87/74 .5	87/74 .1	87/75 0	87/75 .2	89/77 .9	89/77 10.3	90/77 9.6	90/77 11.0	89/77 11.8	89/77 5.0	89/77 .7	88/75 .5
Cancún	82/69 5.4	84/69 1.8	86/71 2.1	89/74 1.5	91/76 3.5	91/77 5.4	92/77 2.2	93/77 4.3	91/77 8.8	88/75 8.7	85/73 5.2	83/70 3.8
Guadalajara	77/50 .8	80/52 .2	85/55 .2	88/59 .3	90/63 .7	87/64 7.3	81/62 10.8	81/62 8.6	81/62 6.5	81/60 .2	80/55 .6	77/52 .3
Mazatlán	75/60 .7	75/59 .2	76/60 .1	78/64 .1	82/69 0	86/76 1.2	88/77 7.4	88/77 7.6	88/77 8.9	87/75 3.2	82/68 .5	77/63 .7
Mérida	88/63 1.5	89/63 1.2	93/65 1.0	96/67 1.0	97/70 2.8	95/70 5.6	95/70 6.7	95/69 5.5	93/70 6.8	91/69 4.8	89/67 2.4	88/63 1.9
Mexico City	70/42 .4	73/45 .2	78/49 .4	80/51 1.0	80/53 2.2	76/54 5.3	73/53 6.9	74/53 6.7	72/53 5.7	72/50 2.6	71/46 .5	69/44 .2
Morelia	77/42 .6	80/43 .2	84/47 .4	87/51 .4	89/54 1.7	85/55 5.4	81/54 7.3	80/55 6.4	80/54 5.2	80/51 2.1	79/46 .4	78/43 .2
Puerto Vallarta	84/62 1.3	84/61 .2	85/62 .1	86/63 .1	88/68 .6	90/73 7.4	92/73 12.9	93/73 12.3	93/73 14.6	93/72 3.7	90/68 .8	86/64 .9
Tijuana	69/45 1.7	70/47 1.7	69/49 2.4	71/51 .8	75/56 .1	78/60 0	83/63 0	82/64 0	82/63 .2	78/56 .4	74/50 1.3	69/44 1.4
Veracruz	76/65 .9	77/66 .6	80/69 .6	84/73 .7	86/76 1.9	87/76 11.7	87/75 16.5	88/75 12.7	87/75 14.1	85/73 6.0	81/70 2.3	78/66 1.0

Mexican State Chart

State	Abbreviation	Area (sq. miles)	Population	Capital
AGUASCALIENTES	Ags.	2,112	1,065,416	Aguascalientes
BAJA CALIFORNIA	B.C.	26,996	2,844,469	Mexicali
BAJA CALIFORNIA SUR	B.C.S.	28,369	512,070	La Paz
CAMPECHE	Camp.	19,619	754,730	Campeche
CHIAPAS	Chis.	28,653	4,293,459	Tuxtla Gutiérrez
CHIHUAHUA	Chih.	94,571	3,241,444	Chihuahua
COAHUILA	Coah.	57,908	2,495,200	Saltillo
COLIMA	Col.	2,004	567,996	Colima
DISTRITO FEDERAL	D.F.	571	8,720,916	Mexico City
DURANGO	Dgo.	47,560	1,509,117	Durango
GUANAJUATO	Gto.	11,946	4,893,812	Guanajuato
GUERRERO	Gro.	24,819	3,115,202	Chilpancingo
HIDALGO	Hgo.	8,038	2,345,514	Pachuca
JALISCO	Jal.	31,211	6,752,113	Guadalajara
MEXICO	Mex.	8,245	14,007,495	Toluca
MICHOACAN	Mich.	23,138	3,548,200	Morelia
MORELOS	Mor.	1,911	3,966,073	Cuernavaca
NAYARIT	Nay.	10,417	949,684	Tepic
NUEVO LEON	N.L.	25,067	4,199,292	Monterrey
OAXACA	Oax.	36,275	3,506,821	Oaxaca
PUEBLA	Pue.	13,090	5,383,133	Puebla
QUERETARO	Qro.	4,420	1,598,139	Querétaro
QUINTANA ROO	Q.R.	19,387	1,135,309	Chetumal
SAN LUIS POTOSI	S.L.P.	24,351	2,410,414	San Luis Potosí
SINALOA	Sin.	22,520	2,608,442	Culiacán
SONORA	Son.	70,290	2,394,861	Hermosillo
TABASCO	Tab.	9,756	1,989,969	Villahermosa
TAMAULIPAS	Tamps.	30,650	3,024,238	Ciudad Victoria
TLAXCALA	Tlax.	1,551	1,068,207	Tlaxcala
VERACRUZ	Ver.	27,683	7,110,214	Jalapa
YUCATAN	Yuc.	14,827	1,818,948	Mérida
ZACATECAS	Zac.	28,283	1,367,692	Zacatecas

Source: 2005 Mexican Census

GEM Points of Interest Offering A *Great Experience for Members®*

Yucatán Peninsula

CHANKANAAB LAGOON PARK—Saltwater Chankanaab Lagoon is part of a national park that provides sanctuary for multicolored tropical fish and fun for swimmers and snorkelers. See Cozumel p. 122.

CHICHEN ITZA—The Yucatán Peninsula's best known and most visited ruin is one of the archeological wonders of the world. See p. 107.

TULUM RUINS—The remains of this Mayan fortress-city overlooking the turquoise Caribbean are a popular day trip for visitors based in Cancún. See Tulum p. 147.

UXMAL—The majestic Pyramid of the Magician is a highlight of the Uxmal ruins, built by the Maya more than 1,000 years ago. See p. 150.

XCARET—Xcaret is a big seaside theme park of an attraction and a fun all-day destination. The ecological slant won't stop kids from loving it. See Playa del Carmen p. 143.

XÉL-HA—Xel-Ha, a series of freshwater lagoons fed by underground springs, is a pretty place to swim and go snorkeling or scuba diving. See Tulum p. 149.

Northwestern Mexico

COPPER CANYON—A rail excursion through Copper Canyon country offers a chance to see some of Mexico's most spectacular mountain scenery. See p. 195.

Mexico City and Vicinity

BASILICA OF OUR LADY OF GUADALUPE—Two basilicas in the northern Mexico City suburb of Villa de Guadalupe honor the Guadalupe Virg2in, the nation's patron saint and most revered iconic religious figure. See Mexico City p. 302.

DOLORES OLMEDO PATINO MUSEUM—Beautiful grounds and a notable collection of art make this tranquil retreat a must-see escape from Mexico City's hubbub. See Xochimilco p. 320.

METROPOLITAN CATHEDRAL—This towering church is a magnificent example of baroque architecture and also contains beautiful chapels and prized works of art. See Mexico City p. 291.

MUSEUM OF MODERN ART—The country's best modern art museum has works by Diego Rivera, Rufino Tamayo and other Mexican masters. See Mexico City p. 301.

NATIONAL MUSEUM OF ANTHROPOLOGY—One of the world's foremost museums, the National Museum of Anthropology exhibits an outstanding collection of treasures covering all of Mexico's early civilizations. See Mexico City p. 301.

NATIONAL PALACE—The chief attraction at the National Palace is a mesmerizing series of historical murals created by famed Mexican artist Diego Rivera. See Mexico City p. 293.

PALACE OF FINE ARTS—The Palacio de Bellas Artes is the capital's cultural center and a showcase for the music and dance performances of the Ballet Folklórico. See Mexico City p. 299.

TEOTIHUACAN—Teotihuacán is one of Mexico's most impressive and easily accessible archeological zones, and also one of its most mysterious. See p. 313.

Central Mexico

AMPARO MUSEUM—This collection of pre-Hispanic and colonial art is one of the best in the country, impressively displayed in a building that was formerly a college. See Puebla p. 355.

CABANAS CULTURAL INSTITUTE—Designated a World Heritage Site by UNESCO in 1997, Guadalajara's cultural and performing arts center is graced with powerful murals by Mexican artist José Clemente Orozco. See Guadalajara p. 333.

CHURCH OF LA VALENCIANA—Officially the Iglesia de San Cayetano (Church of San Cayetano), La Valenciana is a visual feast of wood carvings, gold leaf and lovely religious paintings. See Guanajuato p. 345.

DIEGO RIVERA MUSEUM—The birthplace of Mexico's celebrated muralist houses works tracing the development of his art, including sketches for his controversial mural commissioned by New York City's Rockefeller Center in the early 1930s. See Guanajuato p. 345.

DON QUIXOTE ICONOGRAPHIC MUSEUM—The hero of Miguel de Cervantes' novel is artistically celebrated in the form of paintings, sculpture and even clocks at this thoroughly enjoyable museum. See Guanajuato p. 346.

PARISH CHURCH—San Miguel's historic center is dominated by this beautiful church, which stands over the main plaza. See San Miguel de Allende p. 367.

RAFAEL CORONEL MUSEUM—The Rafael Coronel Museum features an incredible array of creative, colorful masks *(máscaras)* displayed in a gracious 18th-century building that was formerly a convent. See Zacatecas p. 374.

STATE HISTORICAL MUSEUM—The Alhóndiga de Granaditas, a former granary, played an important role in the fight for Mexican independence, and this excellent museum provides a historical perspective. See Guanajuato p. 347.

TULA RUINS—The Chac Mool figure, an international artistic symbol of Mesoamerican culture, was first discovered at this archeological site. See Tula p. 372.

Southern Mexico

CHURCH OF SANTA PRISCA—Built in the mid-18th century, Taxco's Santa Prisca Church is one of Mexico's finest examples of baroque architecture. See Taxco p. 397.

CHURCH OF SANTO DOMINGO—Mexico has no shortage of lovely churches, but Oaxaca's Iglesia de Santo Domingo boasts an especially breathtaking interior of lavish gold leaf ornamentation. See Oaxaca p. 387.

MONTE ALBAN RUINS—The religious center of the Zapotec people, Monte Albán boasts a dramatic setting overlooking the Valley of Oaxaca. See Oaxaca p. 387.

MUSEUM OF ANTHROPOLOGY—Jalapa's Museo de Antropología houses a superb collection of artifacts focusing on the Indian groups that inhabited Mexico's gulf coast region. See Jalapa p. 381.

PALENQUE RUINS—What these Mayan ruins lack in sheer scope is made up for by a primeval air that makes them worth visiting, despite the remote location. See p. 389.

SANTO DOMINGO CULTURAL CENTER—Priceless jewelry, precious stones and other treasures excavated from the Monte Albán site are the standout exhibits at the Santo Domingo Cultural Center. See Oaxaca p. 388.

Planning Your Trip

Planning for a Mexican vacation first depends on whether you'll be driving your own vehicle around the country, flying to one destination only, or flying to one destination and then driving a rental car to another. If you drive your own vehicle, specific regulations govern its temporary importation across the border. There's also your day-to-day, on-the-road itinerary to consider. Flying eliminates many of these additional details, particularly if a travel agency or tour operator is handling the logistics.

Trip cost will largely be determined by your agenda. If you want frills or as many of the comforts of home as possible, travel exclusively by air or take a guided package tour; stay at internationally recognized hotels or all-inclusive resorts; and eat and don't shop at establishments that cater primarily to tourists. Your vacation will be essentially hassle-free, but it also could be very expensive. But if you are willing to put up with the occasional lumpy bed or misguided detour and don't mind a few unexpected departures from an otherwise orderly schedule, you will not only reduce expenses but experience Mexico on a much more intimate level.

Cathedral, Guadalajara, Central Mexico / © age fotostock / SuperStock

Practical Advice and Tips

While not essential, a knowledge of Spanish is helpful. English is spoken widely, especially in large cities and at the popular beach resorts. Elsewhere, Mexicans who work in hotels, restaurants or other aspects of the tourism industry usually speak and understand basic English. Shop owners and market sellers likely will be familiar with numbers, which is helpful when bargaining.

Out-of-the-way places, particularly Indian villages and rural areas in the Yucatán Peninsula and southern Mexico, are another story. But if you know some words or phrases in the native tongue, Mexicans tend to overlook a visitor's halting pronunciation and mixed tenses. Speak slowly, distinctly and be patient if you have trouble making yourself understood. Where some knowledge of the language is necessary, the "Speaking of Spanish" section in this TourBook provides words and phrases that identify common needs.

Keep in mind that the high-school Spanish many Americans learned—and promptly forgot—is based on the Castilian form of the language. Expressions that are innocuous in one Spanish-speaking country can take on an offensive tone in another. Practice is the only way to pick up such nuances.

Mexico Travel Regions

Tourism is big business in Mexico; the country welcomes more than 20 million visitors annually, and those with U.S. dollars can find some very good travel bargains. But no visitor takes on all of Mexico in one vacation. And with its sheer size and enormous variety, who would want to?

This book divides the country into eight travel regions, with geography the primary determining factor: Baja California, Northwestern Mexico, Northeastern Mexico, The Pacific Coast, Central Mexico, Mexico City and Vicinity, Southern Mexico and the Yucatán Peninsula. Each of these regions is color-coded on the Mexico Orientation map. Mexico provides varying levels of visitor amenities and many different things to see and do, so a knowledge of what each region offers can aid in trip planning.

Where To Go

Generally speaking, Mexico's priciest destinations are its big beach resorts. For the first-time visitor, they offer the exotic lure of a foreign country without too much cultural displacement. One will find American fast-food joints as well as thatch-roofed seafood shacks—and a large proportion of locals who speak English. Cancún, Los Cabos, Puerto Vallarta, Acapulco, Ixtapa, Mazatlán, Manzanillo and Bahías de Huatulco all fall into this category.

Travel Advisories

The U.S. Department of State issues Consular Information Sheets and Travel Warnings concerning serious health or security conditions that might affect U.S. citizens. They can be obtained at U.S. embassies and consulates abroad, regional passport agencies in the United States and from the Office of Overseas Citizens Services, 2201 C St. NW, Room 4811, Department of State, Washington, D.C. 20520; phone (202) 647-5225, fax (202) 647-3000. For the latest information about travel advisories or warnings, consult the Bureau of Consular Affairs home page; the Web site address is www.travel.state.gov. Updated information on Mexico travel and security issues can be obtained by calling (888) 407-4747 (from the United States).

Consular Information Sheets provide information about entry requirements, currency regulations, health conditions, security, political disturbances, areas of instability and drug penalties. A Travel Warning is issued when the situation in a country is dangerous enough for the Department of State to recommend that Americans not travel there.

Also pricey is Mexico City, which is not a place for those seeking laid-back relaxation. Museum lovers, however, will find some truly outstanding ones that exhibit the artistic and historical treasures associated with Mexico's long history.

Much of Mexico away from the resorts and the big cities provides a maximum of scenic splendor and local flavor and a minimum of pampering. Those with a taste for adventure and no need for luxury will relish the opportunity to camp along a deserted stretch of beach or explore little-visited archeological ruins.

Ecotourism is booming in Mexico among travelers and tour operators alike. Getting close to nature at relatively remote and unspoiled areas is a trend that goes hand in hand with the recognition that preserving the environment also benefits tourism. A bewildering number of tour companies offer specialized excursions based around biking, diving, hiking, kayaking and numerous other outdoor activities; consult a travel agency for details.

The Mexican government promotes ecological awareness in various ways. Biosphere reserves, such as Sian Ka'an in the state of Quintana Roo, protect the country's rich variety of indigenous flora and fauna. The El Rosario Monarch Butterfly Sanctuary, in the wooded mountains west of Mexico City, is a refuge for the insects, which annually migrate by the millions to the central Mexican highlands. In the Gulf of California commercial fishing is strictly regulated in order to protect the sport-fishing industry, and a catch-and-release policy is advocated. California gray whales, which migrate to Baja's Pacific coast each winter, also are protected.

For travelers accustomed to a high level of comfort, an ecotour may not be a wise choice. But for those who prefer unspoiled environments and scientific authenticity over fine dining and five-diamond accommodations, Mexico offers a multitude of choices, from backpacking through the Baja desert to bird-watching along the northern Yucatán coast to mountain biking through the highlands of Oaxaca state.

Perhaps the best bet for combining affordable and acceptable comfort with the pleasure of experiencing new cultural perspectives is a visit to one of the interior cities. Such colonial cities as Guanajuato, Querétaro, San Miguel de Allende, Taxco and Zacatecas, built by the Spanish, have fascinating historical and architectural legacies.

Often overlooked on tourist itineraries is Morelia, the capital of Michoacán and perhaps the city in Mexico most reminiscent of Spain. Residents of Oaxaca, San Cristóbal de Las Casas and Mérida produce some of the best native handicrafts in Mexico. Guadalajara offers big-city amenities, Mexican atmosphere and Western familiarity, the last resulting in part from a large resident population of American retirees.

When To Go

When to go is as important a consideration as where to go. From a weather standpoint, the dry season—October through May—is the best time to visit most of the country. Rainfall patterns, however, vary greatly. In the highland region of central Mexico afternoon showers are likely at any time from June through September, but over a large portion of northern—and especially northwestern—Mexico, rain is infrequent throughout the year. In Chiapas and the normally wet coastal areas, heavy rains can wash out roads or cause mudslides.

Much of northwestern Mexico and Baja California is uncomfortably hot in the summer; in the coastal regions summer heat is exacerbated by high humidity. Conversely, fall and winter evenings in high-altitude locations can get quite nippy.

December through February or March is the high season at Mexico's beach resorts, and accommodation rates at the major tourist destinations, such as Cancún and Puerto Vallarta, are at their peak. April through November is the off season, when rates come down and crowds let up. Each resort has its own timetable; Cancún, for example, is crowded with U.S. spring breakers during March and April.

Easter week is perhaps the most popular time of the year for Mexican families to vacation. Many Mexicans also travel over the Christmas holiday period and during such major national celebrations as the Fiesta of the Virgin of Guadalupe on Dec. 12. For good weather, lower cost and crowd avoidance, a general rule of thumb is to go in the spring or fall.

It's a good idea to obtain advance confirmed reservations for accommodations at beach resorts and in most other Mexican cities during the peak travel seasons—roughly speaking, December through June at the resorts and June through August at the inland cities. Reservations are imperative for the week preceding and following Easter.

You may want to time your arrival to coincide with a significant annual event, such as Oaxaca's Guelaguetza celebration in July or Guanajuato's International Cervantes Festival (Festival Cervantino) in October. The whole country celebrates occasions like Independence Day (Sept. 15 and 16) and the Days of the Dead (Nov. 1 and 2). And almost every day of the year some village or town honors its patron saint or commemorates a historical occasion.

All things considered, one of the nicest times to visit is in November: Temperatures are moderate, summer rains have turned much of the normally brown landscape a lusher green, and the peak holiday season is still a month away.

Calling Mexico

Trip planning may necessitate making phone calls to Mexico for the purpose of setting up hotel reservations, obtaining information about special events, etc. When calling Mexico from the United States and Canada, first dial 011 (the international access code), then 52 (the country code), then the area code and local phone number. For credit card and operator-assisted calls, dial 0152, then the area code and local phone number. While major hotels in tourist areas normally employ English-speaking staffs, a basic knowledge of Spanish will come in handy should you encounter an exception.

What May Be Taken Into Mexico

If you're driving across the border, your baggage will be examined at the Mexican customs checkpoint. Although there's always the possibility that this procedure can turn into an ordeal of exasperating interactions with customs officials—or time-consuming additional inspections at customs or immigration substations—it has been streamlined for the most part.

Each vehicle must pass through an automated "traffic light" signal system. After submitting a customs declaration form or oral declarations, the driver presses a button that activates a randomly flashing signal. If the light flashes green no further action is taken; if it flashes red your luggage will be inspected, regardless of previous declarations made to customs officials. By law, if the signal is not operating properly no inspections are allowed unless the previous declaration involves goods on which fees are required.

The best time to cross the border is early in the morning on weekdays. Weekends—and especially holiday weekends—are the worst time, and there may be a long wait depending on what time you arrive at the border.

Airline passengers receive a customs declaration form (printed in English) on the flight listing all items that can be brought into Mexico duty-free and without prior authorization. The form should be filled out and is then submitted to customs officials upon arrival at the entry point. At most airports (for example, Mexico City's), after retrieving your luggage you'll proceed to a similar automated mechanism and press a button that activates a randomly flashing signal. If the light flashes green simply hand in your declaration; if it flashes red your luggage will be inspected.

Note: Complaints regarding treatment by Mexican customs officials may be registered by contacting the Department of the Comptroller (SECODAM) in Mexico City; phone 01 (800) 001-4800 (toll-free long distance within Mexico), or (888) 594-3372 (from the United States). English is not likely to be spoken.

Money: Up to $10,000 in U.S. currency and traveler's checks (or the equivalent in other currencies) may be taken into Mexico; any greater amount must be declared. It is advisable to have the bulk of funds in traveler's checks. U.S. traveler's checks, particularly those issued by the most recognized institutions, are

Mexico Tourism Board Offices

CHICAGO

225 N. Michigan Ave., Suite 1850, 60601; (312) 228-0517

MIAMI

5975 Sunset Dr., Suite 305, 33143; (786) 621-2909

NEW YORK

375 Park Ave., Suite 1905, 10152; (212) 308-2110

MONTREAL, QUEBEC

1 Place Ville Marie, Suite 1931, H3B 2C3; (514) 871-1103

TORONTO, ONTARIO

2 Bloor St. West, Suite 1502, M4W 3E2; (416) 925-0704

VANCOUVER, BRITISH COLUMBIA

999 W. Hastings St., Suite 1110, V6C 2W2; (604) 669-2845

Weather Notes

Mexico encompasses some 760,000 square miles and varies in elevation from sea level to more than 18,000 feet above. This wide range of terrain guarantees a correspondingly wide range of climatic conditions. The weather can be oppressively sultry or refreshingly cool, extremely dry or persistently rainy. Because much of the country lies within the tropics, altitude rather than latitude tends to determine the temperature. Two characteristics more or less stand out: a large number of hours of annual sunshine, and distinct wet and dry seasons.

Many of Mexico's major inland cities, including Mexico City, Guadalajara, Puebla, Guanajuato, Morelia and Querétaro, are at altitudes that give them springlike weather year-round. Northwestern cities such as Chihuahua and Hermosillo experience greater seasonal extremes. Here summers are sizzling, while temperatures during winter can drop below freezing and occasional light snow falls. Cancún, Acapulco, Puerto Vallarta and other coastal resorts, on the other hand, show little temperature variation from month to month. The nicest weather in these cities is from November through March, when humidities are fairly low and little rain falls.

Severe weather and natural disasters in Mexico are sporadic in nature. Localized heavy rains—particularly in low-lying, tropical coastal areas—can cause flooding, bridge washouts and mud or rock slides that adversely affect transportation. Occasional hurricanes affect the eastern Yucatán Peninsula, the lower Gulf of Mexico coast, and the Pacific coast from the southern part of the normally arid Baja California Peninsula south to Acapulco. Earthquakes, however, cause the most catastrophic damage. While they are an ever-present possibility, the great majority of visitors will hopefully never experience these tremors.

normally easy to cash. It may be more difficult to cash Canadian currency and traveler's checks, so many Canadian travelers convert their money into U.S. currency beforehand.

Small-denomination traveler's checks and also a fair amount of cash come in handy when traveling in Baja California and the more remote areas of mainland Mexico. When presented with sufficient identification, major credit cards are accepted in the larger cities provided that the credit card company normally operates in Mexico.

You can make your dollars go further by exchanging them only as you need them. Exchange rates are posted at hotel front desks, currency exchange offices and banks. Banamex and Bancomer are two of the largest Mexican banks; most cities and towns have branches of one or the other.

If you transport or cause to be transported (including by mail or other means) more than $10,000 in currency or negotiable instruments such as traveler's checks into or out of the United States, you must file a copy of Customs Form 4790 with U.S. Customs and Border Protection, 1300 Pennsylvania Ave. N.W., Washington, D.C. 20229.

Personal items: You may take with you into Mexico duty free clothing, footwear and other personal items. The allowance includes jewelry, perfume, toiletries, books and magazines (in a quantity that does not indicate them to be the object of commercialization), and medicines for personal consumption (accompanied by prescriptions as appropriate and in accordance with quantities prescribed).

Unless acceptable proof of prior ownership is presented upon return to the United States, duty may be required on personal articles that are foreign-made. This proof can be a bill of sale, insurance policy, jeweler's appraisal or original receipt of purchase. Items with serial numbers or other permanently affixed identification can be registered with the nearest Bureau of Customs and Border Protection office before departure. The certificate of registration will facilitate re-entry into the United States should any question of prior possession arise.

Photographic equipment: One camera with up to 12 rolls of unused film, as well as one video camera and 12 blank cassettes, are admissible; this includes the camera's power source. Foreign-made cameras can be registered at the point of departure to prove that they were not purchased in Mexico. Airline passengers should have all photographic film hand-inspected at boarding points to ensure against damage from baggage inspection equipment at check-in locations.

Note: Photography must not be for commercial purposes. Tripods and flash equipment require special permits for use at archeological sites, museums and monuments.

Weapons: Strict regulations govern the temporary importation of firearms and ammunition into Mexico. Tourists are not permitted to import pistols, revolvers, automatic firearms or weapons of any type. Technically this includes all knives (pocket and Swiss Army knives, as well as switchblades and other knives that could be classified as weapons). Although tourists are not likely to be fined or incarcerated for bringing in knives normally used for camping purposes, it may be safer to purchase such a knife while in Mexico.

U.S. citizens are most often arrested for firearms possession in border areas, but arrests have been made in every part of the country—including on private boats in Mexican territorial waters. Ignorance of the law in no way guarantees leniency or prevents prosecution. The only way to legally import firearms and ammunition into Mexico is to secure a permit in advance from the nearest Mexican consulate office.

Drugs: The possession, use or sale of illegal drugs in Mexico is extremely risky. Mexican law, to which tourists in Mexico are subject, deems that trafficking in and/or possession of illegal drugs is a federal offense. All such cases are prosecuted rigorously by the Mexican government regardless of the nature of the drug. During the extensive trial process, which could possibly last more than a year, offenders are not eligible for bail; if found guilty, they are ineligible for parole.

If you require medicines containing habit-forming drugs or narcotics, take precautions to avoid any misunderstanding. Properly identify all drugs, carry only the necessary quantity and have with you a prescription or written statement from a physician. These safeguards will also help to avoid potential customs problems upon return to the United States.

Other duty-free items: Also allowed are one tent and camping equipment, one surfboard, two tennis rackets, a pair of skis, one pair of binoculars, one new or used laptop or other portable computer, one cellular phone, one pager, one portable radio/cassette player, one CD player, one portable television set, one VCR, up to 20 CDs or audiocassettes, up to five laser discs or DVDs, a musical instrument that can normally be carried by one person, one portable typewriter, up to five used toys (if the tourist is a minor), and personal items that compensate for or aid individuals with a disability.

The duty-free limit for the above items is usually per person or per each family member. Also admissible are gifts or items up to a total value of $300 (provided none are restricted) if arriving by air or sea, $50 if arriving by land. These duty-free limits apply per each crossing or arrival. There are no restrictions on the containers in which items are imported.

Each tourist, provided that he or she is not a minor, may bring in 3 liters of wine or another alcoholic beverage and two cartons of cigarettes, 25 cigars or 200 grams of loose tobacco. Recreational vehicle owners can bring in kitchen, dwelling and/or bedroom furniture or utensils, a videocassette player and a bicycle (with or without motor).

Cuauhtémoc Monument, Mexico City / © age fotostock / SuperStock

Tourists are *not* permitted to bring any type of live animal, fresh food products of animal or vegetable origin, or plants, flowers or fruits into Mexico. The following foodstuffs are allowed: dehydrated foods or canned fruit or vegetables, packaged roasted coffee, dried spices, dry herbal medicines, canned or bottled jellies or fruit preserves, canned or bottled nuts and sauces, and U.S.- or Canadian-processed cheeses.

Packing Hints

Heed the old adage to "pack light." The weather in most areas ranges from mild to warm, and consequently you will not need a great deal of clothing. Bring items that are comfortable and easy to care for. In Mexico City and other high-altitude areas, a light coat is a good idea during the winter months, a sweater or jacket for other times. Sweaters also can ward off the chill of air conditioning, which can be icy in those establishments that have it. Lightweight summer clothing is necessary in tropical areas, which include practically all of the coastal lowlands.

Although Mexico is not a particularly formal country, neither is it lacking in modesty. Some of the native peoples are very conservative, and revealing clothing on either sex is frowned upon, regardless of the heat. Away from the main tourist areas women will attract much unwanted attention by going braless or wearing very short skirts or otherwise provocative attire.

Slacks or jeans are fine for sightseeing and shopping. Shorts and/or bathing suits are more appropriate at the beach and in cosmopolitan cities than they are in small towns or outlying areas, although personal comfort should be the deciding factor. If you plan to dine in an upscale restaurant, it's a good idea to keep casual evening clothes (a sports jacket and tie for men, a dress or suit for women) on hand. Bring a raincoat or umbrella for the rainy-season months of June through September.

A pair of sturdy, comfortable walking shoes is essential for exploring ruins, hiking through forests or climbing up hills, and even for walking the frequently cobblestoned streets of cities and towns. A luggage cart can be useful if you'll be traveling by bus, as stations in smaller towns rarely have porters, and it can save money at airports. For those who plan to be on the go much of the time, a shoulder bag may be more appropriate than a suitcase; make sure it fastens securely.

Take an extra pair of sunglasses, a good sunscreen, insect repellent (absolutely necessary in lowland and coastal areas and not always available in Mexico), a vacuum or plastic bottle for drinking water, eyedrops to ease discomfort from wind or glare, and a combination pocketknife with bottle opener and corkscrew attachments.

Mexican pharmacies carry aspirin and other standard toiletry items, but you should bring your own prescription drugs. Toilet paper is often missing in out-of-the-way restrooms; bring several rolls, and always try to carry at least one. Purchase film and batteries before you leave, as they are more expensive in Mexico. Another useful item is a bathtub plug; in many hotel rooms they are missing or don't fit properly.

Electrical current in Mexico is 110-volt, 60-cycle AC—the same as in the United States and Canada—which permits the use of such small standard appliances as shavers, travel irons or hair curlers. In smaller towns, electricity may be weak or even unavailable, so bring a small flashlight and disposable razor.

Crossing the Border

All U.S. and Canadian citizens entering Mexico by land must stop at the international border to show proof of citizenship and pay a fee to have their tourist permit validated. If you are planning on driving beyond the 20-kilometer (12-mile) mainland border zone you also must provide the necessary forms for temporarily bringing a vehicle into the country, which necessitates a stop at a Mexican customs and immigration office. Hours of operation for these offices at major border crossing points are as follows:

CALIFORNIA/MEXICO

Calexico/Mexicali—Daily 24 hours

San Diego/Tijuana—Daily 24 hours

ARIZONA/MEXICO

Douglas/Agua Prieta—Daily 24 hours

Lukeville/Sonoyta—Daily 6 a.m.-midnight

Nogales/Nogales—Daily 24 hours

TEXAS/MEXICO

Brownsville/Matamoros—Daily 24 hours

Del Rio/Ciudad Acuña—Daily 24 hours

Eagle Pass/Piedras Negras—Mon.-Fri. 8-8, Sat. 10-2

El Paso/Ciudad Juárez—Daily 24 hours

Laredo/Nuevo Laredo—Daily 24 hours

McAllen/Reynosa—Daily 24 hours

U.S. and Canadian citizens traveling to Mexico must carry proof of citizenship. A valid (unexpired) passport book is the most convenient, since it ensures problem-free re-entry into the United States, serves as a photo ID and facilitates many transactions, such as cashing traveler's checks.

You can request a passport application form by contacting the National Passport Information Center; phone (877) 487-2778, or TTY (888) 874-7793. Comprehensive passport information and application forms also are available on the U.S. Department of State Department Web site; the address is travel.state.gov (link to "passports").

It's a good idea to keep a record of your passport number. Make two photocopies of your passport identification page and other personal documents before leaving home. Leave one set at home, and carry the other set with you in a separate place from your actual documents.

U.S. citizens who travel across the Mexican border regularly for business reasons can apply for a passport card, a wallet-sized document that will facilitate entry and expedite document processing at official land and sea points of entry. The passport card has the same validity period as the standard passport book: 10 years for adults, 5 years for children

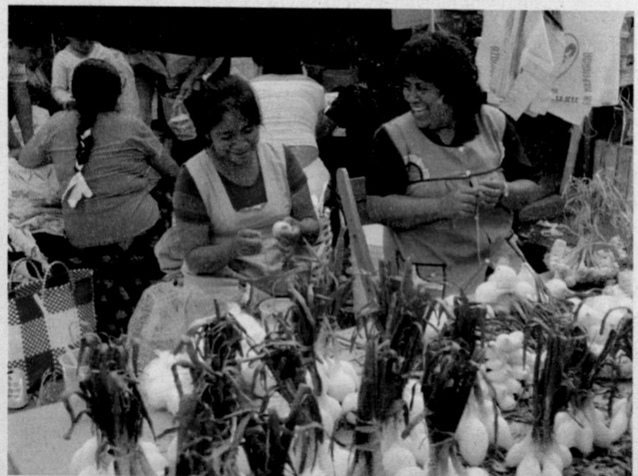

Zaachila, Oaxaca / © R.H. Productions / Robert Harding / Digital Railroad

under 16. Passport cards cannot be used for air travel.

Note: All U.S. and Canadian citizens traveling *by air* between the United States and Mexico are required to show a passport or other accepted secure document. The passport requirement will be extended to land and sea border crossings on June 1, 2009. Up until this date the U.S., Canadian and Mexican governments also will accept a birth certificate, which must be a certified copy with a raised seal from the government agency that issued it and be accompanied by government-issued photo identification (such as a driver's license).

Tourist Permits

A government-issued tourist permit (commonly referred to as a tourist card, but actually a form) must be obtained in order to travel within Mexico. For general information about tourist permits *see the Border Information section in the back of this book.*

If you're entering Mexico by land it is advisable to obtain your tourist permit prior to leaving the United States. A permit can be obtained upon presentation of proof of citizenship from Mexican consulates in the United States and Canada *(see page 65)* or immigration offices at official points of entry.

When applying for a tourist permit, minors (under age 18) traveling without their parents—i.e., alone or with friends or relatives—must present proof of citizenship (a valid passport or birth certificate) and a notarized, signed letter of consent from both parents granting permission for the minor to travel in Mexico. If the minor's parents are divorced or separated, the letter must be accompanied by divorce or separation papers, or proof of sole custody. Even if one parent goes along, a minor must submit from the absent parent a notarized, signed letter of consent, or when applicable, divorce, death certificate or guardianship papers.

Canadian citizens, including parents, traveling abroad with a minor should be prepared to document their legal custody of that child. If a minor is traveling with a friend or relative, the individual with the minor must have a notarized letter of consent from both parents (including a telephone number) or a custody document. In all cases it is important for the minor to have a valid Canadian passport. Mexican citizens living in the United States must go to the Mexican consulate nearest their place of residence and sign the legal documents granting permission for the minor to travel in Mexico.

Cancún, Yucatán Peninsula

When departing Mexico your tourist permit must be returned to Mexican immigration. All visitors departing through land points of entry also should request that their passport be stamped with an "exit" designation. You can be fined by Mexican immigration officials on your next trip into the country via a land point of entry if your passport does not show the "exit" designation from a prior visit.

Arriving by Air

There are international airports in all major Mexican cities and resort areas that receive regular flights from the United States and Canada, either directly or through Mexico City. Some airports receive charter flights as well. Major Mexican cities that receive direct U.S. flights are so identified in their descriptive listing. **Note:** Unlike nonstop service, a direct flight stops at least once and may involve changing planes.

The following airlines provide service from selected cities in the United States and Canada to Mexican destinations:

Aero California, (800) 237-6225 from the United States

Aeroméxico, (800) 237-6639 from the United States; www.aeromexico.com

Alaska Airlines, (800) 252-7522 from the United States; www.alaskaair.com

American Airlines, (800) 433-7300 from the United States; www.americanair.com

Continental Airlines, (800) 523-3273 from the United States; www.continental.com

Delta Airlines, (800) 241-4141 from the United States; www.delta.com

Mexicana Airlines, (800) 531-7921 from the United States; www.mexicana.com

Northwest Airlines, (800) 225-2525 from the United States; www.nwa.com

United, (800) 538-2929 from the United States; www.ual.com

US Airways, (800) 428-4322 from the United States; www.usair.com

The two major domestic airlines are Mexicana and Aeroméxico, with flights linking the resorts and larger cities to Mexico City. Smaller regional airlines operate in different parts of the country. Aeromar serves central Mexico; Aviacsa the Yucatán Peninsula and southern Mexico. Other regional airlines are Aerocaribe and Aerolitoral. Traveling between destinations within the country often involves changing planes in Mexico City. Schedules, fares and routes all are subject to change. Smoking is generally prohibited on all international flights; check with the appropriate Mexican carrier regarding its smoking policy.

All arriving passengers must present valid proof of citizenship along with a filled-out tourist permit. Tourist permit and customs declaration forms are distributed on the flight (the tourist permit per individual, the customs declaration per individual or family). At the Immigration counter your tourist permit will be stamped with a "fee paid" designation before you proceed to the baggage claim area to retrieve your belongings. The last stop is Mexican customs; make sure your declaration form is properly filled out. Mexico uses a random "Red Light-Green Light" system. If you are just bringing personal items and have nothing to declare, you will be asked or directed to push a button. If the light is green you may proceed without inspection. If the light flashes red your luggage will be routinely searched. If you do *not* declare items over and above the $300 allowance and pay all applicable duties and are caught by a red light, you will be fined.

Airports almost always offer fixed-rate transportation via bus, minivan or taxi to downtown or hotel zone areas. Usually there is a booth at the airport where you can purchase a ticket or voucher. You also may have the option of riding in a private taxi (which costs more) or sharing the ride (and paying less). For safety reasons, never hail an unmarked cab outside the terminal.

There are frequent flights to Mexico from such "gateway" cities as Dallas/Fort Worth, Houston, Los Angeles and Miami. A bewildering array of fares, vacation packages and promotions also are available, and it often pays to search for a bargain. AAA/CAA members can obtain fare and schedule information and make reservations through AAA Travel Agencies. When making reservations, be sure you confirm all flights at least 72 hours prior to departure—particularly the return leg of a round trip.

Charter flights, while offering low fares, also are subject to the greatest number of restrictions. The charter operation can cancel a flight up to 10 days before it is scheduled to depart; if *you* cancel, you may not be able to recoup your money. When considering a charter flight, review the refund policy and contract stipulations carefully. **Note:** Mexico charges an airport tax on all departing flights. At press time the charge was about $25 (U.S.) for international flights and $16 for domestic flights; this fee normally is included in the cost of your airline ticket, but double check to make sure.

Car Rentals

U.S. rental cars generally cannot be driven across the border into Mexico. One exception is Hertz, which permits designated vehicles rented at airport facilities in San Diego, Tucson and Yuma to be taken across the border; special paperwork is required.

If you're flying into Mexico but plan on taking a side trip from your main destination, renting a car is an easy way to sidestep dealing with unfamiliar local transportation. AAA/CAA members can reserve a rental car through their local club; it is highly recommended that you make all necessary arrangements prior to your departure.

The major U.S. franchises are located in the larger cities. There are numerous Mexican companies as well, but although their rates may be less the vehicles also may be less reliable, and available insurance protection should be carefully reviewed. Overall, the cost of renting a car in Mexico is at least, if not more, expensive than in the United States.

U.S. car rental companies require a credit card. Few if any will accept a cash deposit, and if allowed it will be substantial. A U.S. or Canadian driver's license is acceptable. The usual minimum age limit is 25. With Hertz, renters ages 21-24 will incur an age differential charge, and certain restrictions may apply. Special restrictions also may be placed on drivers above a certain age. Extras such as air conditioning or automatic transmission may incur additional costs.

Also take your itinerary into account when deciding how long to rent. While most companies will allow you to rent in one location and drop off at another, the drop-off charge can be quite steep. Request that a copy of the reservation confirmation be mailed to you; this should reduce the chance of overcharging, since the rate will be printed on the confirmation slip.

Booking a vehicle in advance simplifies matters, but it may not guarantee the make and model of your choice when you arrive. Many Mexican rental vehicles are Volkswagen Beetles, and if one is unavailable a company may try to send you elsewhere or charge for an upgrade. Inspect the car carefully before you drive off the lot. Check the windshield for cracks; the windshield wipers; the body and fenders for dents, rust, etc.; the head and taillights; the tires for wear and pressure; and note any missing items, such as the gas cap or floor mats. Seat belts and a fire extinguisher are required by law. A thorough inspection is well worth the time, as you will be charged for anything that is perceived damaged or missing.

Mexican automobile insurance is required; it is provided by the rental company and figured into the total cost of the contract. Standard contracts normally offer both liability coverage and collision coverage after payment of a deductible. Accepting an optional Collision Damage Waiver (CDW) will be an additional charge but means that you won't have to pay the deductible (which can be as much as $5,000) in the event of an accident. Also, if you decline the CDW, some companies will apply an amount equal to 10 percent of the commercial value of the vehicle to your credit card.

Note: It is strongly recommended that if renting a car you check with your personal automobile insurer to confirm that coverage is provided for a rental in Mexico; if not, definitely accept the Loss Damage Waiver option. Driving conditions in some areas of Mexico make it advisable to have the additional protection provided by the Loss Damage Waiver.

While the extras add up, they're worth it for peace of mind. In any event, the more coverage you have the better; speed bumps on many Mexican free roads, for example, can cause damage even if negotiated at slow speeds. Look into what your own automobile insurance covers—it might, for example, take care of damages to a rental car.

Keep the rental company's toll-free emergency number handy in case you run into trouble on the road. And when you return the vehicle, remember to fill the gas tank; the refueling charge will be much more expensive than any pump.

Copper Canyon, Chihuahua, Northwestern Mexico
© Luc Novovitch / Offiwent / Digital Railroad

Arriving By Personal Vehicle

If you're driving into Mexico, a little advance preparation can prevent crossing the border from becoming a lengthy process. Both a temporary vehicle importation permit and a promise to return vehicle form are required for travel beyond 20 to 30 kilometers (12 to 19 miles) of the mainland border (depending on the Mexican state). For general information about regulations involving the temporary importation of a motor vehicle *see the Border Information section in the back of this book.*

Note: To be on the safe side, bring the original as well as two copies of your current vehicle license/registration receipt to present at the point of entry, as border officials may insist on seeing the original. Keep the original in a safe place while you are in Mexico and keep the copies with the temporary vehicle importation permit and the promise to return vehicle form.

For leased or company-owned vehicles, a notarized letter of authorization (printed on stationery showing the company's or leasing agency's letterhead) that permits the driver to take the vehicle out of the United States or Canada and into Mexico is required, and an employee ID card must be presented. If the vehicle is not fully paid for, a notarized letter from the lienholder authorizing use of the vehicle in Mexico for a specified period must be presented.

Rented vehicles require a rental agreement and a notarized affidavit from the rental car company stating the company's permission to bring the car into Mexico. The same name must appear on the rental agreement and on the temporary vehicle importation permit.

If the owner does not have or does not wish to use a major credit card, a bond—based on the value of the vehicle—must be posted with a Mexican bonding firm (Afianzadora) at the point of entry. However, this is a costly procedure that involves much paperwork; fees range from $200-$400, depending on the vehicle's make and model year.

For the temporary importation of two vehicles at least two persons must travel as tourists, and separate permits must be obtained for each vehicle. For example, one individual will not be allowed with both a car and a motorcycle, even if he or she owns both vehicles. One of the vehicles must be registered to another qualified driver in the same party, or a second person can obtain a permit for the additional vehicle by presenting a notarized affidavit of permission from the owner.

It is not mandatory for a group of people arriving in Mexico in the same vehicle to leave in the same vehicle; however, the individual who obtained and filled out the temporary vehicle importation permit must leave the country in the same vehicle in which he or she arrived. The vehicle may be driven by the importer's spouse or adult children, as long as they have the same immigration status; other persons may drive the vehicle as long as the owner is in it. Drivers crossing and recrossing the border need not obtain a new temporary vehicle importation permit with each crossing, provided that the initial permit is still valid.

The temporary importation regulations for automobiles also apply to recreational vehicles. Equipment and luggage should be packed to permit easy customs inspection. Vehicles exceeding 3.5 metric tons in weight require a special permit, as do buses. If in doubt as to how your vehicle will be classified, consult the nearest Mexican consulate office before starting your trip.

Trailers and motor homes can only stay in Mexico 6 months unless they are left in bond at an authorized trailer park. Such trailer parks have placed a bond with the nearest Mexican customs office, making them responsible for the storage of the recreational vehicle.

When you pay the administrative fee and enter Mexico with your own vehicle, a guarantee must be signed on your credit card, giving the Mexican government authority to track down the owner or driver if the vehicle is left behind. If a fine is incurred, it may be charged against the credit card. Should your vehicle become incapacitated, arrangements to leave without it can be made through the U.S. Embassy or one of its consulates, or through a Mexican customs (Aduana) office.

The Mexican government does not provide facilities for storing an automobile if you must suddenly leave the country due to emergency. It can, however, be left for up to 10 days after the temporary importation permit expiration date, provided that you apply for a *Retorno Seguro* permit at the nearest Mexican customs office.

Hacienda (the Mexican Treasury Department) has the authority to confiscate any vehicle that has been illegally imported into the country. Hacienda also has the authority to confiscate a vehicle whose owner (or driver) cannot produce the proper temporary vehicle importation documentation. **Note:** It is illegal for a foreigner to sell a motor vehicle in Mexico.

Automobile Insurance

U.S. automobile insurance is *not* valid in Mexico. It must be replaced by insurance from a Mexican company. While some American companies may extend their coverage a certain number of miles from the border or number of days in Mexico, *only* a Mexican automobile liability policy is acceptable as evidence of financial responsibility if you have an accident in that country. Arrange for a policy with full coverage issued through a reliable Mexican insurance company with complete adjusting facilities in cities throughout the country.

All AAA offices in Southern California, New Mexico and Texas sell a Mexican automobile insurance policy issued by Grupo Nacional Provincial (GNP). Members also can purchase the policy online through www.AAA.com, following the appropriate link to the local Web sites for the Automobile Club of Southern California, AAA New Mexico or AAA Texas.

AAA Arizona offices sell Mexican insurance as well. Members who also are Arizona residents can purchase a policy for an automobile, RV, trailer or towed boat online at the club's Web site: www.AAA.com.

Most California State Automobile Association offices also sell Mexican automobile insurance. AAA and CAA members can purchase a policy online by accessing the club's Web site: www.csaa.com. Look for the Mexico auto insurance link under the Travel section.

To obtain Mexican insurance, you will need to provide the following: current vehicle title or registration, a valid U.S. or Canadian driver's license, and proof that you currently have U.S. or Canadian automobile insurance (the policy's declaration sheet lists all coverages). Call ahead to determine what additional specific information (vehicle identification number, included accessories, etc.) is needed so that the policy can be accurately written.

The Mexican government has no minimum requirement for insurance; the agent will help you obtain the coverage best suiting your needs. If you obtain Mexican insurance through a AAA club office the policy will be written by the day, with a discount for more than 30 days' coverage, and will be issued immediately upon application. Towed vehicles *must* be identified in the policy; if not, the policy can be declared void.

To obtain a policy for a vehicle rented through Hertz, a letter of authorization must be presented along with the rental contract, stating that the renter has obtained permission to take the vehicle into Mexico. Without these documents a policy cannot be written.

If the vehicle is leased or not owned by you, a notarized letter from the leasing company or the registered owner giving you permission to take the vehicle into Mexico must be provided, and must include the vehicle identification number and the dates of your entry into and departure from Mexico.

Unlike the prevailing tenet of U.S. and Canadian law, Mexican law is based on the Napoleonic Code, *which presumes guilt until innocence is proven.* As a result, *all* parties (operators of vehicles, but in some cases even passengers) involved in an accident in Mexico are detained for assessing responsibility. If the accident involves no personal injury, the drivers may be asked to go with the attending officer to the police station to complete the necessary accident report, and the vehicles will usually be impounded for investigation. Once blame is established, the negligent driver's vehicle will remain impounded until he or she pays the damages.

If the accident causes injury or death, the operators will be jailed until the authorities determine who was at fault. Then only the responsible driver will remain incarcerated until he or she guarantees restitution to the victims and payment of the fine imposed for causing the accident (under Mexican law an automobile accident is a criminal offense).

A Mexican insurance policy is recognized by the authorities as a guarantee of proper payment for damages according to the terms of the policy. When presented, it can significantly reduce red tape and help to bring about an early release. However, a Mexican insurance policy may not prevent a motorist from actually being detained *if* he or she is involved in an accident that results in injury or death.

Note: Automobile Club of Southern California border offices in California and Texas offer optional coverage with their policy that provides professional legal services necessary to deal with Mexican authorities. Under

Mexican Consulates in North America

ARIZONA

NOGALES—Consul de Mexico, 571 N. Grand Ave., 85621; (520) 287-2521

PHOENIX—Consul General de Mexico, 1990 West Camelback Rd., Suite 110, 85015; (602) 242-7398

TUCSON—Consul de Mexico, 553 S. Stone Ave., 85701; (520) 882-5595

CALIFORNIA

LOS ANGELES—Consul General de Mexico, 2401 W. Sixth St., 90057; (213) 351-6800

SACRAMENTO—Consul General de Mexico, 1010 8th St., 95814; (916) 441-3287

SAN DIEGO—Consul General de Mexico, 1549 India St., 92101; (619) 231-8414

SAN FRANCISCO—Consul General de Mexico, 532 Folsom St., 94105; (415) 354-1700

COLORADO

DENVER—Consul de Mexico, 5350 Leetsdale Dr., Suite 100, 80246; (303) 331-1110

DISTRICT OF COLUMBIA

WASHINGTON, D.C.—Consul de Mexico, 2827 16th Street N.W., 20009-4260; (202) 736-1000

FLORIDA

MIAMI—Consul General de Mexico, 5975 S.W. 72nd St., Suite 101, 33143; (786) 268-4900

ORLANDO—Consul de Mexico, 100 W. Washington St., 32801; (407) 422-0514

GEORGIA

ATLANTA—Consul General de Mexico, 2600 Apple Valley Rd., 30319; (404) 266-2233

ILLINOIS

CHICAGO—Consul General de Mexico, 204 S. Ashland Ave., 60607; (312) 855-1380

MASSACHUSETTS

BOSTON—Consul de Mexico, 20 Park Plaza, Suite 506, 02116; (617) 426-4181

MICHIGAN

DETROIT—Consul de Mexico, 645 Griswold Ave., Suite 1700, 48226; (313) 964-4515

MISSOURI

KANSAS CITY—Consul de Mexico, 1600 Baltimore Ave., Suite 100, 64108; (816) 556-0800

NEBRASKA

OMAHA—Consul de Mexico, 3552 Dodge St., 68131; (402) 595-1841

NEW MEXICO

ALBUQUERQUE—Consul de Mexico, 1610 4th St. N.W., 87102; (505) 247-4177

NEW YORK

NEW YORK—Consul General de Mexico, 27 E. 39th St., 10016; (212) 217-6400

NORTH CAROLINA

RALEIGH—Consul de Mexico, 336 E. Six Forks Rd., 27609; (919) 754-0046

OREGON

PORTLAND—Consul de Mexico, 1234 S.W. Morrison, 97205; (503) 274-1450

PENNSYLVANIA

PHILADELPHIA—Consul de Mexico, 111 S. Independence Mall East, Suite 310, 19106; (215) 922-3834

TEXAS

AUSTIN—Consul General de Mexico, 800 Brazos St., Suite 330, 78701; (512) 478-2866

BROWNSVILLE—Consul de Mexico, 301 Mexico Blvd., Suite F2, 78520; (956) 542-4431

DALLAS—Consul General de Mexico, 8855 N. Stemmons Frwy., 75247-3855; (214) 252-9250

EL PASO—Consul General de Mexico, 910 E. San Antonio Ave., 79901; (915) 533-8555

HOUSTON—Consul General de Mexico, 4506 Caroline St., 77004; (713) 271-6800

LAREDO—Consul de Mexico, 1612 Farragut St., 78040; (956) 723-6369

SAN ANTONIO—Consul General de Mexico, 127 Navarro St., 78205; (210) 271-9728

UTAH

SALT LAKE CITY—Consul de Mexico, 155 S. 300 St. W., 3rd floor, 84101; (801) 521-8502

WASHINGTON

SEATTLE—Consul de Mexico, 2132 Third Ave., 98121; (206) 448-3526

CANADA

MONTREAL—Consul General de Mexico, 2055 Peel St., Suite 1000, Quebec H3A 1V4; (514) 288-2502

TORONTO—Consul General de Mexico, 199 Bay St., Suite 4440, Commerce Court West Building, Ontario M5L 1E9; (416) 368-1847

VANCOUVER—Consul General de Mexico, 1177 W. Hastings St., Suite 710, British Columbia V6E 2K3; (604) 684-1859

this coverage, a bond will be submitted in order to obtain the release of the automobile and bail for the insured party who is involved in legal proceedings.

If an accident in which a driver is at fault results in damage to government property, such as road signs, safety fences, light or telephone poles, toll stations, street pavement or sidewalks, he or she must pay for the repairs needed even if no other vehicle was involved or no injury or death occurred.

All accidents or claims *must* be reported before leaving Mexico. If you need assistance with a claim, you should obtain it *only* from an authorized agent or adjuster of the insurance company that issued the policy. Official release papers should be kept as evidence that the case is closed, especially if the car shows obvious damage from the accident.

Rates are based on the current value of the vehicle; towed vehicles are covered separately. Policies are written in both English and Spanish. In the event of a disagreement, the Spanish text will prevail. Read your policy carefully before entering Mexico to discern what is and isn't covered. Most companies, for example, do not include lawyer's fees or bail to defend the policyholder against criminal charges, although adjusters in the larger cities may keep lawyers on a retainer who will act on behalf of the insured free of charge.

A separate policy may be required to pay for translating and notarizing a driver's license or other documents. Personal accident insurance, baggage insurance and medical coverage are all wise investments when considering the amount of coverage you think you'll need.

For Assistance

Special needs frequently require a special kind of help, particularly when you are visiting a foreign country. The following sources of aid are suggested for travelers to Mexico.

Medical Assistance

Ask at your hotel desk or consular office for the name and address of the nearest hospital and English-speaking doctor. Several Mexican and U.S. companies offer medical evacuation service by air; the U.S. Embassy in Mexico City provides a list of these firms. Tourist publications often print names and addresses of local hospitals. Most Mexican cities and towns also have a Red Cross (Cruz Roja) facility.

The U.S. Department of State has a Web site link with general medical information for U.S. citizens traveling abroad: travel.state.gov/travel/abroad_health.html. *Also see The Informed Traveler page under the listings for Acapulco, page 222, Cancún, page 90, Guadalajara, page 330, Mexico City, page 280, and Puerto Vallarta, page 256.*

Legal Difficulties

Assistance often is provided by Tourist Assistance *(Protección al Turista).* Offices are in Ensenada, Mexicali, Rosarito, San Felipe, Tecate and Tijuana on the Baja California Peninsula and in the capital of each state on the mainland, normally in the same building that houses the State Tourism Office. The U.S. Embassy and Mexican consulate offices in the United States and Canada can provide lists of attorneys who speak English. Federal Consumer Protection Agency *(Procuraduría Federal del Consumidor)* offices are in all state capitals and other major cities.

If you run into problems with the police in Mexico, Tourist Assistance recommends that the following steps be taken:

Observe or ask for the officer's name (most police wear nameplates), badge number, department (federal, state or municipal), and vehicle number.

Go to the nearest police station to pay any traffic-related fine and ask for a receipt.

Write out the nature of the complaint and mail it to the Tourist Assistance Director.

Although the vast majority of tourists return home without encountering any legal difficulties, you could be arrested for breaking laws you didn't know about or for what would be considered a minor offense in Canada or the United States. For example, if you are involved in a traffic accident that causes injury you will automatically be taken into police custody, regardless of who is at fault. If detained or arrested, you should contact one of the following organizations:

Your embassy or consulate. By international law, you have the right to call a consular officer *(see Embassies, Consulates and Consular Agencies, page 67).* **Note:** The long distance access code for the United States and Canada from within Mexico is 95 (station to station). For Mexico from within the country the code is 91. To make a direct international call to the United States or Canada from within Mexico, dial 001 before the area code and phone number; to call long distance from one Mexican destination to another, dial 01 before the area code and phone number.

Embassies and consulates advise and assist their nationals in case of accident, arrest, serious illness or death. Consular agents can help in such matters as lost passports. Important travel information, compiled by the U.S. Embassy in Mexico City, is contained in the brochure "Tips for Travelers to Mexico." Obtain a copy before your trip by enclosing $1 and writing the Superintendent of Documents, U.S. Government Printing Office, Washington, D.C. 20402, or the Consumer Information Center, Pueblo, CO 81009.

The International Legal Defense Counsel. This association allows access to a worldwide network of reputable attorneys. Their address is 1429 Walnut St., 8th Floor, Philadelphia, PA 19102; phone (215) 977-9982, fax (215) 564-2859.

The United States Embassy. The U.S. Embassy cannot represent U.S. citizens in court or provide legal counsel, but does maintain a list of local attorneys who speak English and who can provide advice on options and

Embassies and Consulates

Note: If calling or faxing from outside Mexico, dial 01152 before the area code and phone number. The U.S. Embassy's fax number is (55) 5525-5040; the Web site address is www.usembassy-mexico.gov. Office hours vary but are indicated where known. Offices are closed on U.S. and Mexican holidays.

U. S. EMBASSY:

Mexico City, Distrito Federal, Paseo de la Reforma #305, Colonia Cuauhtémoc, (55) 5080-2000; Mon.-Fri. 9-2 and 3-5

CANADIAN EMBASSY:

Mexico City, Distrito Federal, Calle Schiller #529, Colonia Polanco, (55) 5724-7900; Mon.-Fri. 8:45-5:15

U. S. CONSULATES:

Ciudad Juárez, Chihuahua, Avenida López Mateos #924-N, (656) 613-1655; Mon.-Fri. 8-4:45

Guadalajara, Jalisco, Progreso #175 at Avenida López Cotilla, (33) 3268-2100; Mon.-Fri. 8:30-noon and 2-3

Hermosillo, Sonora, Calle Monterrey #141 (between calles Rosales and Galeana), (662) 289-3500; Mon.-Fri. 8-4:30

Matamoros, Tamaulipas, Calle Primera #2002, Colonia Jardín, (868) 812-4402; Mon.-Fri. 9-noon and 1:30-3:30

Mérida, Yucatán, Paseo Montejo #453 at Avenida Colón, (999) 925-5011; Mon.-Fri. 7:30-4

Monterrey, Nuevo León, Avenida Constitución #411 Pte., (81) 8345-2120; Mon.-Fri. 8-5

Nogales, Sonora, Calle San José, about 3 miles south of the border and a block west of Avenida Obregón, (631) 311-8150; Mon.-Fri. 8-5

Nuevo Laredo, Tamaulipas, Calle Allende #3330, Colonia Jardín, (867) 714-3954; Mon.-Fri. 8:30-11:30

Tijuana, Baja California, Avenida Tapachula #96, Colonia Hipódromo, (664) 622-7400; Mon.-Fri. 8-4:45

U. S. CONSULAR AGENCIES:

Acapulco, Guerrero, Costera Miguel Alemán #121 (in the Hotel Acapulco Continental Emporio), (744) 469-0556; Mon.-Fri. 10-2

Cabo San Lucas, Baja California Sur, Boulevard Marina #C-4, Plaza Nautica, Colonia Centro, (624) 143-3566; Mon.-Fri. 9-2

Cancún, Quintana Roo, Plaza Caracol II, 3rd level (Boulevard Kukulcán, Km 8.5), (998) 883-0272; Mon.-Fri. 9-2

Cozumel, Quintana Roo, Villa Mar Mall, 2nd floor (avenidas Melgar and 5 Norte on the main plaza), (987) 872-4574; Mon.-Fri. noon-2

Ixtapa, Guerrero, Hotel Fontan, (755) 553-2100; Mon.-Fri. 1-5

Mazatlán, Sinaloa, Avenida Playa Gaviotas #202, Golden Zone (in the Hotel Playa Mazatlán), (669) 916-5889; Mon.-Fri. 10-2

Oaxaca, Oaxaca, Calle M. Alcalá #407, Office 20, (951) 514-3054; Mon.-Fri. 10-3

Puerto Vallarta, Jalisco, Paseo de los Cocoteros #1 in Paradise Plaza, Nuevo Vallarta, (322) 222-0069; Mon.-Fri. 8:30-12:30 (closed third Wed. of the month)

San Luis Potosí, San Luis Potosí, Avenida Venustiano Carranza #2076-41 (Las Terrazas Building), (444) 811-7802; Mon.-Fri. 8:30-12:30

San Miguel de Allende, Guanajuato, Dr. Hernández Macías #72, (415) 152-2357; Mon. Fri. 9-1

CANADIAN CONSULATES:

Acapulco, Guerrero, Costera Miguel Alemán and Prolongación Farallón, Centro Comercial Marbella, (744) 484-1305; Mon.-Fri. 9-5

Cancún, Quintana Roo, Plaza Caracol II, 3rd floor (Boulevard Kukulcán, Km 8.5), (998) 883-3360; Mon.-Fri. 9-5

Guadalajara, Jalisco, Aurelio Aceves #225 on Minerva Circle (in the Hotel Fiesta Americana Guadalajara), (33) 3615-6215; Mon.-Fri. 8:30-2 and 3-5

Mazatlán, Sinaloa, Rodolfo Loaiza #202 (in the Hotel Playa Mazatlán), (669) 913-7320; Mon.-Fri. 9-1

Monterrey, Nuevo León, Constitución and Zaragoza #1300 Sur (Kalos Building), (81) 8344-2753; Mon.-Fri. 9-1:30 and 2:30-5:30

Oaxaca, Oaxaca, Pino Suárez #700, (951) 513-3777; Mon.-Fri. 11-2

Puerto Vallarta, Jalisco, Calle Zaragoza #160, (322) 222-5398; Mon.-Fri. 9-4

San José del Cabo, Baja California Sur, Boulevard Mijares at Plaza José Green, (624) 142-4333; Mon.-Fri. 9-1

Tijuana, Baja California, Avenida Germán Gedovius, Zona Río, (664) 684-0461; Mon.-Fri. 9-1

remedies within the Mexican legal system. For information phone (55) 5080-2000, ext. 4780.

Government Officials

Visitors who encounter trouble or require emergency services while in Mexico should contact the appropriate office of the State Tourism Department or, if there is no office nearby, notify local police. Outside major cities, Mexican government authority rests with the *delegado*, an elected official who presides over emergencies and civil or legal disputes. This individual can be found at the *delegación municipal* or *subdelegación*. Offices are often at the *palacio municipal* (City Hall); ask at your hotel desk for directions. In isolated rural areas, authority is usually vested in an appointed citizen who reports to the nearest *delegado*. Since tourist crime rarely occurs in out-of-the-way places, it shouldn't be necessary to resort to the last measure.

If you have problems bringing a vehicle into Mexico, or want to report improper treatment, SECODAM, or the Department of the Comptroller, can help with complaints. SECODAM offices are located at all border crossings. Phone 01 (800) 001-4800 (toll-free long distance within Mexico) or (888) 594-3372 (from the United States).

State Department Services

The U.S. State Department's Office of Overseas Citizens Services office deals with such situations as notifying home if you are caught in a natural disaster or political disturbance, locating someone in the event of an emergency, delivering emergency messages, making emergency money transfers and providing emergency loans. In these and other instances, have friends or family phone (202) 647-5225 (24 hours). Information also is provided for nonemergency questions. For emergency situations dealing with minors, contact the Office of Children's Issues; phone (202) 736-7000.

Note: Should you lose your money or other financial resources while in Mexico, the U.S. Embassy can help you contact your family, bank or employer to arrange for the transfer of funds. To transfer funds commercially to Mexico, contacts in the United States should go to the nearest Western Union office and have money sent to an "Elektra" store in Mexico. The funds should be sent in care of your name, either *Dinero en Minutos* (Money in Minutes) or *Va a Llamar* (Will Call).

The Elektra store closest to the embassy is the Insurgentes Elektra Store, Tonalá #15, Colonia Juárez, 06600 Mexico, D.F.; phone (55) 5525-1608. The sender(s) must provide a 10-digit confirmation number along with their name and phone number, and the name, address and phone number of the Western Union office from which the money was sent. Photo identification is needed when the money is picked up.

Mexico's Highways

Mexico forever seems to be in the midst of a massive road-building program. Many old roads follow ancient Indian causeways or the cobblestone *caminos carreteros* (carriage-ways) of colonial days. But new construction is ongoing, and bypasses and loop roads are standard features around cities and towns that have a central core with narrow streets and heavy traffic.

Roads in Mexico are generally not marked as clearly as those in the United States. Signs for turns and route directions will sometimes consist of city or town names only. Ideally, route numbers are posted every 5 kilometers (3 miles) on small roadside markers, but these also can be few and far between.

Each Mexican state is responsible for the maintenance of its roads, and some are better kept than others. Weather conditions, especially heavy rains, and such natural occurrences as mud or rockslides can keep roadways in disrepair. Lanes on nontoll roads tend to be narrow, and shoulders are either narrow or nonexistent.

If you plan to drive little-used or unpaved roads, inquire locally about conditions before heading out. Even a good map may not be accurate regarding the conditions of unpaved or ungraded routes; deep sand "roads" can stall even a four-wheel-drive vehicle, and seasonal downpours can render unpaved roads impassable. Put a protective covering over your luggage to keep out dust, and store camera equipment in plastic bags.

Toll Roads

A network of toll highways *(autopistas)* covers large sections of the country. Most of the newer tollways are divided four-lane highways with road shoulders and are comparable in quality to U.S. highways. Many are patrolled by the Green Angels as well. For the most part, toll roads are safe, speedy and scenic, and some are all but deserted because Mexican motorists can't afford to use them.

Most toll roads have a free alternative route. Toll roads are designated on signs by the word *cuota* (and also by the letter "D" following the route number), nontoll roads by *via libre* (free road). *Libramiento* indicates a route that circumvents big city centers or bypasses smaller towns entirely. These bypasses, which sometimes are part of the toll route, can save time by avoiding congested areas.

Following are some major Mexican toll road routes. Fees at individual tollbooths are usually less than $3 (U.S.) and can be paid in dollars or pesos; to be on the safe side, however, have peso denominations handy. At each booth you will receive a receipt in return for payment, which also acts as an insurance certificate to avoid paying road repair charges if you are involved in an accident.

Mex. 1-D (Tijuana to Ensenada): Runs about 114 kilometers (71 miles) south from the U.S. border to Ensenada in the state of Baja California.

Mex. 2-D (Tijuana to Mexicali): Runs east-west along the U.S. border in the state of Baja California.

Mex. 15-D (Nogales to Mazatlán): Runs about 1,212 kilometers (727 miles) from the U.S. border south to Mazatlán through the states of Sonora and Sinaloa.

Mex. 15-D (Tepic to Guadalajara): Runs about 228 kilometers (137 miles) southeast through the states of Nayarit and Jalisco.

Mex. 15-D (Guadalajara to Mexico City): Runs about 668 kilometers (401 miles) southeast through the states of Jalisco, Michoacán and México.

Mex. 57-D (Mexico City to Querétaro): Runs about 210 kilometers (126 miles) northwest from Mexico City through the states of México and Querétaro.

Mex. 85-D (Nuevo Laredo to Monterrey): Runs about 235 kilometers (141 miles) south from the U.S. border through the state of Nuevo León.

Mex. 55-D/95-D (Mexico City to Acapulco): Runs about 415 kilometers (249 miles) south from Mexico City via Cuernavaca to Acapulco (states of Morelos and Guerrero).

Mex. 180-D (Mérida to Cancún): Runs about 242 kilometers (145 miles) from the junction with Mex. 180 east to the junction with Mex. 307 through the states of Yucatán and Quintana Roo.

Chiapas, Southern Mexico / Nadine Markova / Mexico Tourism Board

Driving Precautions

Do not expect most free roads in Mexico to compare to the interstate highway system in the United States. Following the dictates of mountainous terrain, these roadways are mostly rolling or winding, although there are many straight and/or level stretches in northern Mexico and the Yucatán Peninsula. Some of them have a sandpaper texture that affords better traction on curves but is wearing on tires.

Above all, motorists in Mexico should heed this advice: **Do not drive after dark if at all possible.** Few roads aside from the toll highways are equipped with street lights or shoulders, and night visibility is poor. Vehicles, which are sometimes driven with no headlights, might suddenly swerve to your side of the road to avoid potholes (which become invisible after dark). Bicycles without lights or reflectors are ridden, and pedestrians commonly use the roads at night. In addition, the Green Angels *(see "The Green Angels" subheading)* stop patrolling at 8 p.m. If you intend to cover a certain distance during any one day, get an early start and estimate your total driving time on the side of caution. *Never* pull off the road to sleep.

The possibility of robbery is another reason to curtail driving after dark. Bandits are likely to target foreign vehicles and have been known to pose as stranded motorists or police officers, so it's never a good idea to stop and offer assistance if you're unsure of the situation. You must stop, however, at designated police checkpoints *(see the "Law Enforcement" subheading)*.

Livestock—principally cattle, goats and donkeys—may unexpectedly appear on rural roadways at night (and even during the day). A fence is no guarantee that an animal won't suddenly appear in the road. Slow down and give them a wide berth. Furthermore, animals will be almost invisible on unlighted roads at night—and can cause tremendous damage to your vehicle if they are struck.

Another requirement is to drive defensively. Always be alert to road conditions and other motorists. Bus, truck and other drivers who are familiar with local routes will drive faster and negotiate maneuvers more boldly than tourists, who will likely find the highways more narrow, winding and weathered than those in the United States. **Note:** Using a cellular phone while driving is a traffic violation in the state of Baja California.

On some main corridors truck traffic is moderate to heavy, and truckers may drive aggressively or inconsiderately. If a truck begins to pass on a two-lane road, be prepared to pull off onto the gravel or graded dirt flanking the road surface if necessary to give the truck adequate room. Exercise caution; along the sides of roadways without shoulders there often is a full or partial covering of brush or undergrowth. Be particularly careful if you are attempting to pass a slow-moving truck—the driver isn't likely to pull over to give you more maneuvering room. Also be on the lookout for vehicles that are temporarily stopped in the roadway, particularly in rural areas.

Signaling one's intentions can have a different meaning than it does in the United States or Canada. For instance, a left turn signal in Mexico also means an invitation to pass on the left. Buses and trucks may flash their left blinker to guide you around them, but attempt to pass only when it can be done safely.

At intersections with a left-turn lane, there usually is a separate left-turn arrow; to turn left legally you must wait for the arrow. If making a left turn off a two-lane roadway where there is no separate left-turn lane, you are expected to pull over to the right as far as possible and wait for traffic to clear before making the turn. A right turn on red is generally not permitted unless there is a sign giving permission to do so; use your best judgment in situations when it is unclear whether you can legally turn right on red.

Heed the signals given by other drivers as well. When an oncoming truck flashes its headlights a couple of times, the driver is warning you to slow down or pull over. Since this signal is usually made when both you and the truck are approaching a one-lane bridge or narrow section of the road, you had better comply—the truck driver generally will not.

Speed bumps *(topes)* and potholes *(baches)* constitute perhaps the greatest danger to motorists on Mexican highways. Speed bumps are at the entrance to almost every town, no matter how small, and also can be encountered within towns. Warning signs will say *Topes, Vibradores* or *Reductor de Velocidad* (speed reducer) and give the distance in meters. Instead of words, some signs show a picture symbol and the distance in meters. In small towns these signs can appear suddenly, and not just at the entrance to town. Some speed bumps may not be preceded by a warning sign, however.

Topes are raised cobblestone bumps that can damage the underside of a vehicle unless negotiated at a very slow speed (in other words, you basically must come to a stop). *Vibradores* are corrugated, both lower and wider than *topes*. Speed bumps are prohibited on open sections of road and on toll roads, except at the entrance to toll stations.

Potholes are a particular problem along older free (nontoll) roadways and are exacerbated in areas that have a summer rainy season. Short-term maintenance may be nothing more than filling the pothole with sand or dirt. As some can be large enough to swallow a tire, caution is advised wherever potholes occur.

In the downtown sections of larger cities there are likely to be a number of one-way streets. Instead of signs, small arrows on the side of buildings or on lampposts often will indicate traffic direction. Follow the flow; if in doubt as to whether you are driving in the right direction, note which way parked vehicles are facing.

Recreational Vehicle Travel

Travel in recreational vehicles—campers, motor homes, trailers and similar vehicles—should be confined to the main highways. Do not park in isolated areas or camp along the highway or on beaches. Vehicles left unattended should be securely locked, with the shades or curtains drawn and all equipment (bicycles, chairs, etc.) removed from the outside. Never sleep in any vehicle parked along the roadside.

Propane gas is obtainable by vacationers traveling in recreational vehicles more than 50 kilometers (30 miles) below the U.S. border. This policy ensures that tourists who use propane for their engines, stoves and heaters will have an adequate supply.

Gasoline, Oil and Repairs

All gas stations in Mexico are concessions granted by the federally run oil company, Pemex. Fuel prices are fixed by the government. To avoid being overcharged by service station operators (a practice that targets foreign motorists in particular), be certain you are charged the correct amount; make sure the pump is turned back to zero before your tank is filled; know exactly how many gallons/liters your tank holds; and keep smaller denominations of pesos in case attendants run out of change. Stations on major routes are spaced at adequate intervals but occasionally run out of supplies; it's a good idea to always keep your gas tank at least half full.

Most Pemex stations sell two grades of unleaded *(sin plomo)* gas: "Magna," dispensed from green pump handles, is the cheaper of the two; the "Premium" grade is dispensed from red pump handles. Pemex stations no longer offer Nova (leaded) gas, although diesel fuel is available.

Fuel quality is comparable to U.S. unleaded grades. In July 2008, a gallon of regular Magna was equivalent to about $2.65 (U.S.); a gallon of premium, about $3.35. Diesel fuel is less expensive. Gas prices in the northern border region are a bit higher than in central and southern Mexico, but as is the case north of the border there are regional fluctuations. Stations are full service; let the attendant fill the tank, but make sure he zeroes out the pump. Tipping is customary; a few pesos is fine.

Since unleaded pump nozzles in Mexico are sometimes larger than those in the United States, it's a good idea to keep a funnel in the car. Remember that pumps in Mexico register liters, not gallons; 10 liters is equal to about 2.5 gallons. For conversion information, *see the metric equivalents chart in the Featured Information section at the back of this book.*

Stations with a "GasoPLUS" sign accept credit cards of the same name for gasoline purchases, but otherwise you'll have to pay cash, so keep peso amounts handy. Payments must be made in pesos, although some

Pemex stations now accept credit cards. Along the border and in areas frequented by tourists (for example, in Cancún and Playa del Carmen) dollars also are accepted.

Service stations and private garages carry oils made in Mexico by foreign companies and by Pemex. Its brand, Brio, comes in several grades which are indicated by the color of the can; gold, black and blue are the best.

If your own vehicle or a rental car requires routine maintenance or major repairs while on the road, there are plenty of automotive repair shops (indicated by signs that say *taller mecánico*) in most parts of the country. Make sure you have a complete understanding about any work to be done as well as its cost. If a part must be ordered there could be additional expense and long delays, as permission from Mexican customs is needed to import parts.

A knowledge of Spanish is usually necessary when negotiating with car repair shops, and it could be difficult finding a mechanic familiar with the make and model of your vehicle. Also keep in mind that businesses in Mexico may close from around 2-4 p.m. for *siesta.*

National University of Mexico, south of San Angel, Distrito Federal / © Christian Heeb Photo

The Green Angels

The idea of having a vehicle breakdown in Mexico can be unnerving, but motorists unfortunate enough to find themselves stranded do have a resource: the Green Angels. Since the early 1960s, these crews have patrolled roadways throughout the country. "Angeles Verdes" are identified by their distinctive green uniforms and green-and-white pickup trucks.

The Green Angels patrol more than 260 routes—both toll highways and "free" roads—that collectively cover every Mexico state capital and all major tourist destinations. Most Green Angel patrols are linked to 32 base stations, one in each of the 31 Mexican states plus the Federal District (Mexico City); routes are patrolled daily 8-8, year-round.

Green Angels personnel are carefully selected and should be familiar with the facilities along their routes. Services offered include vehicle mechanical aid, towing, adjustment or changing of tires, road condition information, medical first aid and protection. Motorists pay for the cost of automobile parts, gasoline and oil, but service is rendered free of charge. A tip is customary, although not required. Although all crew members are supposed to be bilingual, a knowledge of Spanish will still come in handy.

The program is in the midst of an expansion phase that will not only increase the capacity of Green Angels teams to respond to motorists in need of mechanical assistance, but also will provide advanced first aid and protection in conjunction with ambulance and emergency vehicle services. A prevention program focusing on the precautions visiting motorists need to take before and during their travels on Mexican roadways is being developed as well.

To enlist the assistance of a crew, pull completely off the highway and lift the hood of your vehicle. Contact the Mexico Ministry of Tourism (SECTUR) to obtain help or to have a crew dispatched; phone their national hotline, 01 (800) 903-9200 (toll-free long distance).

If you break down in a remote area and don't have a cell phone, it may be necessary to hail a passing motorist, or preferably a bus or truck driver, and ask that he or she stop at the nearest available location to place the call. You also may be able to use one of the emergency telephones found along most of the newer toll highways and also along some older roads. Since Green Angel crews constantly cover their assigned sector, however, the chances are good that a patrol will soon locate you. Repairs, unfortunately, are another matter *(see the "Gasoline, Oil and Repairs" subheading).*

Road Signs

Road signs are a mix of international picture symbols and signs in Spanish. A sign saying *Via Corta* indicates a short or alternate route. Right turns on red are prohibited unless a sign is marked *Continua.* A sign with the word *Retorno* means a U-turn is permitted. Signs often posted just before entering small towns are *Poblado Proximo* (upcoming town), *Disminuya su Velocidad* (reduce your speed) or those that show the maximum speed limit allowed.

Common signs along highways include *Arbochate el Cinturon* (Buckle Your Seat Belt) and *No Deje Piedras Sobre el Pavimento* (Don't Leave Stones on the Pavement); the latter refers to the common practice of placing rocks in the road to denote a hazard or disabled vehicle. Some intersections without traffic signals have signs that say *Ceda el Paso a un Vehiculo* (Cede the Right of Way to One Vehicle); they are posted on each intersecting road and indicate that one vehicle at a time may proceed.

Be careful when approaching bridges. Those marked *Un Solo Carril* or *Puente Angosto* are narrow, one-way bridges. When two cars approach such a bridge from opposite directions, the first driver to flick his or her headlights has the right-of-way. The other should pull to the side of the road, allowing the first driver to cross. Although not a regulation, it is a general practice.

Many traffic signals are positioned horizontally rather than vertically. Also, on some signals the green light flashes three times before the yellow light appears. Motorists stopped at red lights in cities will often be approached by people attempting to earn money by washing windshields. If you're not interested, mouth the words *"no tengo dinero"* or shake your head "no" and rub your thumb and index finger together—the international symbol for "I have no money."

Parking

If possible, schedule daily activities so that your car does not have to remain unattended for any length of time. Heed "no parking" signs, which depict a red circle with a diagonal line superimposed over a capital "E." Illegally parked cars will be towed, or their license plates will be removed. Recovering either item can result in a nightmare of time, expense and frustration. If in doubt, park in a guarded lot rather than on the street. Never leave valuables in plain sight in a parked vehicle.

On a one-way street, make certain your vehicle is parked on the left side, not the right. Parking on the street also likely means being approached by a youngster who will offer to watch your vehicle while you're gone. This often is a good idea, since the couple of pesos you hand over are a small price to pay for peace of mind. If a group of boys appears on your return, however, pay only one.

Law Enforcement

On main highways the speed limit is generally about 100 km/h (60 mph) or as posted. In many cities the limit is about 40 km/h (25 mph); in some small towns it may be as low as 30 km/h (18-20 mph). Always obey the speed limit; while local police are generally lenient toward tourists who commit minor traffic violations, they make an exception in the case of speeding.

In Mexico City and those parts of the state of Mexico falling within the greater metropolitan area (particularly north and east of the Federal District), motorists with foreign license plates may be stopped by police for alleged driving infractions. If you commit an infraction and recognize it, accept the *boleta de infracción* (ticket) without arguing.

If you are stopped and did not do anything wrong, however, do not give in to a demand for graft. Take the officer's number and ask to speak with his *jefe* (HEH-feh), or boss, or to be taken to the nearest *delegación de policía* (police station) to explain your situation. In Mexico City, the Secretaría de Turismo (the Ministry of Tourism, or SECTUR) may be able to provide assistance if you feel you have been unfairly accused of a traffic violation; phone (55) 5250-0123 or (55) 5250-0151. Elsewhere within Mexico, phone 01 (800) 903-9200 (toll-free long distance), or contact the nearest State Tourism Office.

Note: Motorists in northwestern Mexico—primarily those heading north toward the border—may occasionally be stopped by narcotics police, members of the military or inspection station personnel who are searching for arms or, more likely, drugs. These individuals may also speak only Spanish, which can make the situation stressful for those not fluent in the language.

While you should cooperate fully—even if it means explaining in English that you do not speak Spanish—by all means report any unfair treatment to the U.S. Embassy in Mexico City or to the nearest Mexican consulate office upon your return home. Such checkpoints are most likely to occur from Sinaloa north through Sonora, although they are a possibility practically anywhere in the country.

Bus Service

Mexico has a well-developed bus system, and this is an economical way to travel around the country. More than a dozen Mexican bus lines maintain frequent express service from U.S. border points to most cities, and also between major Mexican cities. Although service is less extensive in Baja California, buses travel practically everywhere. Among the major lines are Autobuses de Oriente (ADO), Enlases Terrestres Nacionales (ETN), Transportes del Norte (TN) and Elite.

Most of these companies offer first-class service that is comparable in quality to first-class U.S. bus service. Referred to as *ejecutivo, lujo, primera plus,* "deluxe," "super first class" and similar terms, these buses often include such amenities and extras as air conditioning, reclining seats, footrests, restrooms, movies, free snacks and beverages, as well as controlled 95 km/h (60 mph) speed. First-class buses also make few—sometimes no—stops and carry fewer passengers.

For long trips, bring your own food—in case you don't want to eat in the restaurant where the bus stops—drinking water and a roll of toilet paper. Seats on first-class buses are normally reserved in advance. Smoking is usually not permitted on these buses.

Note: Travel only during the day; avoid overnight trips. First-class and luxury buses use toll highways and are less likely to encounter incidents of robbery or assault.

Second- and third-class buses should by no means be compared to U.S. lines. You can hail one of these buses just about anytime and anywhere simply by standing at the side of the road and waving, and they're certainly a great way to experience local life. However, they make interminable stops, the vehicles themselves are frequently antiquated and can be unpleasantly hot, and you may have to share your seat with a pig or chicken. Furthermore, they cost only slightly less than first-class or luxury buses, and without the convenience of making advance reservations.

Many Mexican cities have one central bus station *(Central Camionera* or *Central de Autobuses)*, which may or may not be near the main plaza or center of town. The various bus lines maintain offices at the central station. In some cities there may be several stations in different locations that serve specific companies or destinations. If you're unsure where to go, ask for the *estación del autobús* and give your destination. For trips between major cities, purchase a reserved-seat ticket from the station in advance; this is imperative for long weekends, and around school holidays, holiday seasons and important fiestas.

Note: Round-trip fares are not sold. Although buses frequently run behind schedule, be punctual—yours might depart the second it's supposed to.

Routes, fares and departure times are always subject to change, and the only way to obtain this information is directly from the station. English is not likely to be spoken, so write your destination down and make certain you're getting on the right bus. Mexican bus schedules usually indicate whether the bus is *local* or *de paso* (which means it is en route from another location). *Directo* or *expresso* indicate a nonstop route. *Salida* means departure; *llegada,* arrival.

Do not use local buses for in-town transportation; a taxi, although more expensive, is safer. Exceptions are buses that travel specifically to tourist attractions; while these may be slow, they allow you to relax and enjoy the scenery.

The American bus line Greyhound Lines Inc. provides limited schedule and fare information for major Mexican bus lines and can ticket passengers to most U.S. border cities, in addition to Tijuana. Once across the border, passengers make arrangements with a Mexican bus line. Often there are buses that shuttle between the U.S. and Mexican stations. From Mexico City, bus trips to points of interest throughout the country are easily arranged; the major bus lines operate out of four huge terminals located in the northern, southern, eastern and western sections of the city.

One option to using buses as your main means of on-the-road transportation is to take a guided motor coach tour. Prior to 1991, U.S. and Canadian visitors were required by law to use Mexican buses and take Mexican tours once they crossed the border, but American buses now are able to make the entire journey. Such U.S. companies as Gray Line Tours offer trans-border bus excursions from several hours to

Floating Gardens, Xochimilco, Distrito Federal / © Angel Cavalli / SuperStock

several days' duration that visit various parts of Mexico. Contact a travel agency for details.

Rail Service

Passenger rail service in Mexico is a thing of the past, eclipsed by first-class bus service that reaches just about every part of the country. If you want to see Mexico while someone else does the driving, bus travel is recommended. The one popular tourist train trip is the Chihuahua al Pacífico railway that runs through the rugged Sierra Madre Mountains and the spectacularly scenic Copper Canyon region *(see Copper Canyon listing under Northwestern Mexico).*

© David Sanger Photography / Alamy

Ferry Service

Passenger and vehicle ferry service is provided between the Mexican mainland and Baja California, connecting the ports of Santa Rosalía-Guaymas, La Paz-Topolobampo (Los Mochis) and La Paz-Mazatlán.

Normally, ferries run four times a week between Santa Rosalía and Guaymas (sailing time about 8 hours) and daily between La Paz and Topolobampo (sailing time about 6 hours). They depart from La Paz for Mazatlán on Monday, Wednesday and Friday, and from Mazatlán to La Paz on Tuesday, Thursday and Saturday (sailing time about 18 hours).

Advance reservations are required and can be made by phone as well as in person at one of the ferry offices. As a knowledge of fluent Spanish is necessary, it's easier to make reservations through a local travel agency at the port of departure. The Web sites www.bajaferries.com (in Spanish only) and www.ferrysantarosalia.com provide fare, schedule and contact information.

Fares are one way and per person, sharing the accommodation. *Salon* seats, the least expensive, are airplane-type seats. *Cabina,* cabin lodging with restroom facilities, also is available but is more expensive. Children ages 1-11 are charged half the adult fare. If you're prone to seasickness, bring the appropriate medications. Pregnant women are not allowed onboard. If transporting a vehicle, take everything you'll need out of it before the journey begins.

Note: If you plan on transporting a vehicle from Baja California to the Mexican mainland, it is necessary to obtain a temporary vehicle importation permit. To avoid frustration and disrupted travel plans, obtain the permit and have all related temporary vehicle importation documents filled out at the border before entering Mexico. When applying for a vehicle permit, acceptable proof of citizenship, a copy of the current registration and a notarized letter of permission from the lienholder (if a vehicle is not fully paid for) all must be presented for each vehicle being transported (including motorcycles).

Your vehicle must be weighed before you purchase your ticket. Arrive at the ticket office as soon as possible (check in advance; opening times vary from location to location), and inquire where to park your vehicle for weighing *(la balanza).* Passenger and vehicle tickets are usually sold in separate lines. Also keep in mind that if you have entered Mexico via Baja California and then cross over to the mainland, you will have to go through customs before boarding the ferry and pay whatever duty fees are assessed.

In La Paz, the Sematur ticket office (for ferries to Mazatlán) is at Guillermo Prieto and Calle 5 de Mayo, 2 blocks southeast of Plaza Constitución. The Baja Ferries ticket office (for ferries to Topolobampo) is at the corner of Calle Isabel La Católica and Navarro. Both ferry terminals are at Pichilingue, the deep-water port for La Paz, about 16 kilometers (10 miles) north of the city via Mex. 11.

In Santa Rosalía, the ferry office is in the terminal building on Mex. 1, just south of the main entrance into town. In Topolobampo, Guaymas and Mazatlán, offices are at the ferry terminal. *Also see the separate listings for La Paz and Santa Rosalía under Baja California, the listings for Guaymas and Los Mochis under Northwestern Mexico and the listing for Mazatlán under The Pacific Coast.*

In the state of Quintana Roo, a daily ferry carries passengers and vehicles from Puerto Morelos to Cozumel; however, variable schedules can cause long waiting periods. Passenger boats also make regular daily trips between Playa del Carmen and Cozumel, and from Puerto Juárez, just north of Cancún, to Isla Mujeres. *See Cancún listing, page 94,* *and the separate listings for Playa del Carmen and Puerto Morelos under Yucatán Peninsula.*

Health and Safety

Sanitation and hygiene in Mexico have improved considerably in the last several decades.

Several endemic infectious diseases have been eradicated, and today life expectancy at birth is 70 years for men, 78 years for women. Reasonable precautions will eliminate serious health risks for almost all foreign visitors.

Visiting High-Altitude Areas

If you live in or are used to a lower altitude, you may need a short adjustment period when visiting areas above 1,525 meters (5,000 feet). Don't push yourself too hard; a light diet and reduced intake of alcoholic beverages are recommended. Move about in a leisurely fashion for the first few days. If you're affected by the altitude (headache or nausea), rest quietly until you feel comfortable; it may take from 12 to 36 hours before you feel better. Another health consideration at high altitudes is overexposure to the sun; use a suntan lotion that has an effective sunscreen agent.

Persons with weak hearts or of very advanced age should consult their physician before undertaking prolonged visits to cities at high elevations. Travelers with specific health concerns should inquire about recommended immunizations or medications to carry with them.

Acute Mountain Sickness (AMS), which can strike at altitudes of 2,450 meters (8,000 feet) or more, is the body's way of coping with reduced oxygen and humidity. Also known as altitude sickness, its symptoms include headaches, double vision, shortness of breath, loss of appetite, insomnia and lethargy. Some people complain of temporary weight gain or swelling in the face, hands and feet. Even those used to high altitudes may feel the effects of AMS. If symptoms strike, stop ascending. A quick descent will alleviate the discomfort.

The negative reaction of your body to changes in altitude is lessened if you're in good physical shape and don't smoke. Ascend gradually, eat light but nutritious meals and drink plenty of bottled water. Alcohol consumption may aggravate AMS symptoms if they occur.

Note: The elevation for city and place descriptions is given when it is over 762 meters (2,500 feet).

Air Quality

As is common when traveling anywhere in the world, a change in weather or lifestyle can particularly affect the health of elderly visitors, young children or those who suffer from cardiac or respiratory conditions. Mexico City's dense traffic and air pollution, conditions present in any large metropolis, are factors that nevertheless should be taken into consideration. Air pollution also is a factor in Guadalajara and Monterrey.

Mexico City's location is partly responsible for its pollution problem: More than 7,000 feet above sea level, it is situated at the bottom of a valley ringed with mountains. Despite the unfavorable geography, a thin atmosphere and an estimated 3.5 million vehicles on the streets, federal and city authorities continue to take steps toward a cleaner environment.

Eating and Drinking

Follow the cardinal rule for fruits, vegetables and seafood: Do not eat anything that has not been peeled by you, or that cannot be cooked or boiled. Avoid unpasteurized dairy products as well. Otherwise, take every opportunity to enjoy the country's many distinctive regional dishes. Avoid food sold by street vendors, but at the better restaurants in Cancún, Mexico City, Puerto Vallarta and other cities where tourism is big business, virtually anything on the menu can be enjoyed without fear.

Mexican restaurants traditionally do not have a separate nonsmoking area. One exception is Vips, a restaurant chain that is casual, clean, efficient and springing up everywhere.

Bottled water in liter or smaller sizes is sold throughout Mexico at gas station convenience stores, grocery stores and shops catering to tourists. Chemical disinfecting tablets also are available from pharmacies and supermarkets.

If the hotel has its own purification system, tap water can be used for brushing your teeth or rinsing contact lenses; ask to make sure, and also ask about the ice dispensed by ice machines. Most hotels routinely provide bottled water for drinking (some may charge for it when you check out). If in doubt about the water in smaller towns, ask for bottled water. Remember that this includes ice cubes. If you find yourself in an area where bottled

San Miguel de Allende, Guanajuato / DreamPictures / Getty Images

water is not available, boil water vigorously for one full minute to kill disease-causing organisms.

These precautions should serve to ward off the most common visitor ailment, diarrhea (which Mexicans call *turista*). Bed rest and a liquid diet (unsweetened tea is best) will cure most cases. If these preventive measures fail, see a doctor. There are physicians, surgeons, specialists, good hospitals and Mexican Red Cross clinics in all the major cities and larger towns. In many villages, visitors can receive medical assistance from clinics or hospitals run by the Instituto Mexicano del Seguro Social (IMSS), the Instituto de Seguridad y Servicios Sociales de los Trabajadores del Estado (ISSSTE) or the Secretaría de Salud.

Most of the better hotels have house doctors; if not, your hotel manager or the local police will help you find medical assistance. It's not a good idea to buy over-the-counter antibiotics.

Diseases

The risk of contracting typhoid or cholera is minimal, despite sporadic cholera outbreaks. Vaccinations will offer protection in areas off the tourist itinerary, where running water and drainage systems frequently are inadequate, but vaccinations should not be considered a substitute for caution in selecting food and drink. In the case of cholera or other intestinal ailments, this means avoiding raw or undercooked seafood and cold seafood dishes.

The presence of mosquitoes that transmit malaria is dependent on such local conditions as weather, altitude, mosquito control efforts and the prevalence of disease. Mosquitoes also can spread dengue fever. In coastal areas, the risks of being bitten are greater. Use mosquito repellent if you plan on spending time outdoors. Brands containing DEET are the most effective; be sure to read and follow the directions and precautions on the label. Try to avoid being outside between dusk and dawn, when mosquitoes are most likely to bite.

According to the Centers for Disease Control and Prevention (CDC), the following states have a risk of malaria in rural areas: Campeche, Chiapas, Guerrero, Michoacán, Nayarit, Oaxaca, Quintana Roo, Sinaloa and Tabasco. If you plan to explore remote areas of any of these states, consult your physician or local health department before leaving for the advisability of taking a preventive drug.

Tourists arriving in Mexico from yellow fever-infected areas must have a yellow fever vaccination certificate; tourists arriving directly from the United States or Canada are not required to have the certificate.

The CDC operates a hotline with international health requirements and health recommendations for foreign travelers. Topics include general vaccinations, food and water guidelines and current disease-outbreak reports. Phone (877) 394-8747; for the immunization hotline, phone (800) 232-4636. The Web site address is www.cdc.gov.

Personal Safety

Crimes against tourists in Mexico are unlikely. But the possibility does exist, due in part to several factors: a criminal justice system that investigates few of these crimes and punishes even fewer perpetrators; law enforcement officers who may be in tacit partnership with organized criminal activity (and out-of-work former soldiers and police who turn to such activity); unemployment fueled by economic hardship; and the ever-growing gap between rich and poor that makes crime an increasingly lucrative career option.

The Mexico City metropolitan area, where an estimated 21 million people are crammed together, has been hit especially hard. Tijuana and Ciudad Juárez—both centers of the flourishing border drug trade—have seen violent crime escalate as well.

Although not directed at foreigners, politically motivated violence occurs from time to time in the states of Guerrero, Oaxaca and particularly Chiapas. And like resorts in many other countries, even the tourist haven of Cancún is not immune from hotel room thefts, purse snatchings and pickpocketing incidents.

But regardless of your itinerary, employing the same common sense you would at home to maintain personal safety will reduce the chance of becoming a crime victim. For example, it is very important to look and act confident rather than bewildered when out in public. Don't, however, flaunt expensive watches, jewelry or clothing; you're more likely to be targeted for robbery or assault if you are easily identifiable as a well-off or wealthy tourist.

Avoid putting your wallet in a back pocket or wearing a purse with a shoulder strap that can be grabbed by a passerby. Petty thieves and pickpockets use a razor to slash pockets or bags, so keep your belongings close to you at all times. Put cameras in briefcases or bags with a chain-reinforced strap.

Stash traveler's checks and cash in different places; for example, in money belts and extra pockets sewn inside clothing. Keep photocopies of passports, credit cards and other documents in a separate place from the originals. Be very cautious around ATM machines. If possible, use one during the day inside a large commercial facility; avoid nighttime transactions at glass-enclosed street machines.

When planning a day of sightseeing, try to keep informed regarding any political developments where you are staying. Tense local politics can sometimes result in rowdy demonstrations. Hotel staff, taxi drivers and tour guides are good sources of information in such instances and can offer practical advice should it be necessary to temporarily steer clear of certain parts of town for any reason.

If you're driving, do not leave valuables in plain view in your car; stow possessions out of sight. Use parking lots or garages whenever possible. Parking areas are designated by a sign with the word *"Estacionamiento"* and the international symbol of a red circle with a capital "E" inside.

Always lock your car, roll up the windows and park in a well-lighted area. If traveling by bus or train, be especially careful at the station; never leave your luggage unattended, and lock all items together with a chain or cable if possible.

As crime is an unfortunate byproduct of widespread poverty, highway robberies do occur, particularly outside of tourist areas and in the southern part of the country. To avoid becoming a target, stick to toll highways wherever possible, and above all do not pull off the road to sleep. **Never drive after dark.** Camp in designated national parks or at RV sites rather than along lonely beaches or other unsupervised wilderness areas.

Puerto Peñasco, Sonora, Northwestern Mexico
© Gibson Stock Photography

Motorists driving on free roads may be stopped at military checkpoints and approached by official-looking men in green uniforms who request identification and ask where you are going. This normally happens in less-traveled areas of Mexico—particularly near the northern and southern international borders in Sonora and Quintana Roo, respectively; in parts of the Baja California Peninsula; and in the states of Chiapas, Guerrero and Oaxaca. Most often these checkpoints are conducting random searches for firearms or drugs.

Be sure to slow down and stop if motioned to do so. Remain calm and polite, comply with instructions and speak as little Spanish as possible. If asked to hand over your wallet, give them *only* the proper identification; if necessary, remove all your money first. Get badge numbers and names, and report any irregularities to the appropriate embassy, consumer protection agency or consular office.

Poorly paid police may intimidate foreign motorists into paying "fines" for minor or alleged infractions. This is particularly true in and around Mexico City, where visitors with non-Mexican license plates may find themselves victims of harassment. You could also encounter a situation in which you are charged with an infraction that you are certain you did not commit.

Such an incident can be both frightening and infuriating, but if it happens, try to remain calm. Ask to be shown documentation of the rule you violated. Request to speak with someone of higher authority if necessary, and beware of "plainclothes policemen"; insist on seeing identification.

Very obviously writing down all the details of the incident—name, badge number, the nature of the alleged violation, the exact location where it occurred—may help defuse the situation. Avoid handing over an original driver's license, car rental contract, vehicle registration or any other document; always carry photocopies.

If resistance provokes further trouble, ask for the ticket, pay it at a bank and claim a receipt. To register a complaint, contact the Secretaría de Turismo (the Ministry of Tourism, or SECTUR) in Mexico City; phone (55) 5250-0123 or (55) 5250-0151, or 01 (800) 903-9200 (toll-free long distance) elsewhere within Mexico.

Women, either traveling alone or with others, normally do not need to take special precautions, but there are a few things that should be kept in mind. While ethnic or sexual stereotyping is unfortunate, it can occur. Female travelers who look obviously foreign, or those with fair skin and hair, may attract unsolicited attention. If this happens, the best response is no response. In many *cantinas,* bars with a macho, often hard-drinking male clientele, female customers are unwelcome.

Sexual assault is not out of the question, particularly in Mexico City. In bars and nightspots (even those in areas frequented by tourists) avoid accepting a drink from a stranger; it may be drugged.

Currency

The monetary unit is the peso (its symbol is the dollar sign, or $). One peso equals 100 centavos. There are 5-centavo, 10-centavo, 20-centavo and 50-centavo coins; peso coins are in denominations of $1, $2, $5, $10 and $100. Banknotes are in denominations of 20, 50, 100, 200, 500 and 1,000 pesos. Banco de México issues the frequently used 20-peso banknote in both paper and synthetic polymer versions; the latter has a longer life and added safety features such as a transparent window.

The 5-, 10- and 20-centavo coins are not often used, but they come in handy as spare change to give to the needy, if you're so inclined. The 50-centavo coin can help facilitate small transactions like bus fares and souvenir purchases at markets. Hang on to smaller denomination banknotes and coins as you accumulate them, or exchange a dollar amount that will yield smaller denominations.

Cash payments for amounts that include centavos are rounded off to the nearest 10 centavos. An item costing 11.52 pesos, therefore, would be rounded off to a cash payment of 11.50 pesos; an item costing 11.56 pesos would be rounded off to a cash payment of 11.60 pesos. Check and credit card payments will show the exact amount and must be paid in that amount. Credit card charges are converted into dollars by the bank issuing the card, usually at a favorable bank rate.

National Museum of Anthropology, Mexico City
© Christian Heeb Photo

In border cities and some tourist resorts, prices in Mexican currency may carry the abbreviation "m.n." (moneda nacional); prices in American currency, "dlls." (dollars). As a general rule, Mexican establishments rendering services to tourists quote and charge in pesos. In many of Mexico's resort areas, however, U.S. dollars are as readily accepted as pesos. Information sheets showing pictures of Mexican coins and bills are normally available at airports and border crossings, or appear in tourist publications.

Note: As a convenient reference, any prices or rates appearing in this book are quoted in the approximate U.S. dollar value, unless stated otherwise. In July 2008 the exchange rate was approximately 10.3 pesos to the dollar. However, the peso is a floating currency subject to small daily fluctuations.

Credit cards should cover almost all hotel, restaurant and store charges, as well as airline tickets for flights within Mexico. (**Note:** Gasoline purchases normally cannot be charged unless you have a GasoPLUS credit card—issued only in Mexico—which can be used at Pemex gas stations. Some Pemex stations will accept U.S. credit cards, but have cash on hand just in case.)

Many Mexican banks exchange dollars for pesos or cash traveler's checks only during morning business hours. Also, some banks may require you to open an account before any business can be conducted, so it pays to inquire about this in advance.

If you're using traveler's checks, exchange only what you think you'll need for the next day or two. Keep in mind that all Mexican banks charge a service fee or commission to exchange dollars for pesos; beware of banks that charge a flat fee per traveler's check cashed. Traveler's checks denominated in pesos can be purchased at banks and currency exchange offices in the United States and will be easier to cash in small towns and areas away from tourist centers, where banks may be less likely to cash a traveler's check.

Casas de cambio (currency exchange offices) usually offer a better rate of exchange than banks. They often are located next to big hotels in cities, or in malls in resort areas. A driver's license is needed to cash U.S. traveler's checks. Some exchange offices may cash checks issued by all three major U.S. credit card companies (American Express, MasterCard and Visa), while others may not. Some also charge a commission for transactions, so it pays to find one that does not.

Automated teller *(caja permanente)* machines are available in major cities and resort areas; most ATMs accept the widely honored Cirrus and PLUS cards. Expect peso denominations in return, and to be charged a service fee by your bank for each transaction.

There is always the possibility that foreign travelers will be forced to withdraw money from an ATM. Make all transactions during daylight hours, preferably at machines inside commercial establishments.

Currency exchange also is a standard service at hotel front desks, and this is the most convenient alternative if you don't feel like hunting down a bank or a currency exchange office. Call the hotel or hotels at which you'll be staying just prior to your trip to see what exchange rate is being offered. Trying to find the best rate usually boils down to a matter of convenience, since differences are normally minimal and rates can change daily. If you're shopping around for the best rate or trying to save pennies a pocket calculator will come in handy.

Unfortunately, the threat of purse or wallet snatching is ever present in crowded areas or a busy marketplace. Keep your money and important documents separate. Consider depositing surplus currency and jewelry in hotel vaults. When out in public, ignore remarks from strangers such as "What's that on your shoulder?" or someone yelling "Thief!" in a crowded area—both may be setups used by pickpockets or scam artists to distract your attention or trick you into revealing where you carry your money.

Tipping

While tipping is virtually universal, the matter of whom, when and how much to tip varies. In Mexico, waiters, maids, porters and other workers whose wages are low must rely to a great extent on tips for their living. Let your conscience be your guide, and don't hesitate to reward outstanding service or penalize poor service.

Percentages for hotel and restaurant staff are similar to those in the United States and Canada. In restaurants, make sure that a service charge has not already been added onto the bill. Taxi drivers are not usually tipped unless they've performed some special service, such as waiting while a bit of shopping is done. Gas station attendants, however, expect a tip.

Sightseeing tour guides should be tipped. There also are individuals whom you would not normally tip at home but should in Mexico; for example, theater ushers, washroom attendants and parking attendants.

Economic reality makes it necessary for some Mexicans to resort to begging as a means of survival. Women or children will ask for coins on the street or outside the town cathedral. Another frequently employed location, particularly in larger cities, is a busy intersection. Here an entire family may gather—washing windshields or even putting on an impromptu performance in costume—in return for small change from motorists stopped at the red light. Whether to give under such circumstances is up to the individual, of course, but considering the very real poverty with which many people must cope, any gift will be much appreciated.

Street vendors can be ubiquitous, particularly in the main plazas of towns, at archeological sites and other places where tourists are likely to be, and at beaches where vending is not prohibited. If you do decide to purchase something from a roving vendor, be very discreet; otherwise you will be inundated by insistent hawkers pushing everything from fruit to straw baskets. If you don't intend to buy, firmly communicate your lack of interest.

Young children frequently will offer special services to visitors. Even if it is performed in an unsolicited manner—for example, cleaning your windshield while you're stopped at a red light—compensation is expected. Again, if you are not interested in what a child is offering, whether it be carrying your bags at the airport or promising to guard your car while you shop or see the sights, be very firm about declining.

Youngsters also will charm coins or other gifts out of visitors, and it may be hard to resist these overtures. If you do succumb, hand something directly to a child. Children have been killed running across busy streets to pick up "gifts" tossed from car windows. Better yet, buy some pieces of fruit or other inexpensive foods at the local market. A few clothing items, pencils, pens or simple toys can be packed along with your own personal belongings if you enjoy contributing such gifts to the needy.

Mail Service

All letter mail to Mexico travels by air. First class mail service from Mexico to other countries is by air; parcel post and second class mail is by land. If you want to send mail from Mexico, use post mail only in those cities with airline service. **Note:** Mail service is notoriously slow, and mail can take up to a month to reach destinations in the United States, even that marked "via air mail." Do not expect postcards, letters or packages to arrive back home before you do.

Postal codes in Mexican addresses should be placed before the name of the destination town or city, as in the following example: Hotel Imperial, Avenida Guadalupe #210, 45040 Guadalajara, Jal., Mexico.

Addresses

If you've ever had difficulty hunting down an address in almost any large city in the United States, prepare for the same possibility in Mexico. Street names tend to change mysteriously on either side of a town's main square, or capriciously after traversing several blocks. Street signs may be outdated or even nonexistent. Addresses frequently do not include numbers. All of this can be frustrating if trying to locate an out-of-the-way shop or restaurant; however, there are some general guidelines that can be relied on to aid in the search.

Although used where known in this book for purposes of clarification, designations such as *avenida* and *calle* usually are not posted, and streets are referred to by name only. That name may include a compass direction—*Nte.* or *Norte*, *Sur*, *Pte.* or *Poniente* and *Ote.* or *Oriente* for north, south, east and west, respectively.

When an address includes *s/n* it means there is no number. In numbered addresses, the number follows rather than precedes the name. Addresses on main routes outside of cities or towns will often be stated in terms of the number of kilometers from town; for example, *Km. 18 a Mérida.*

Sprawling urban areas (Guadalajara and Monterrey, for example) have their own inscrutable logic regarding street names and configurations, and trying to find something outside of well-known tourist areas can turn into an adventure. In a class of its own is Mexico City, where hundreds of new thoroughfares are added to the metropolitan area each year and existing streets are often renamed.

Streets in smaller cities are usually laid out in a simple grid pattern radiating from the central plaza (technically, only the square in Mexico City is referred to as the *zócalo*). Specific locations within the core downtown area can thus be pinpointed relatively easily in terms of the number of blocks north, south, east or west of the plaza.

If you become lost in an unfamiliar city or town, asking a local taxi driver for directions or having him lead you where you want to go can save a lot of headaches. A knowledge of Spanish is helpful in these situations, and agree on a price first if he transports you anywhere.

If you need to ask directions from someone on the street, you may be steered off course; Mexicans tend to improvise rather than admit they don't know. But again, there are certain strategies that can increase your chances of success. Keep questions brief and to the point, and ask them with a smile; most people will be happy to try and help. Women who were brought up not to talk to strangers may ignore you, and don't bother asking a child, particularly if your Spanish is rusty. Maps are not likely to be understood; pointing is more direct. If you ask how long it will take to reach a specific destination, or what the exact distance is, remember that the answer is likely to be subjective.

Church of Santo Domingo, Oaxaca, Southern Mexico
© Carlos S. Pereyra / age fotostock

Phone Service

When making telephone calls within Mexico, remember one thing: They are frequently more expensive than back home. Also keep in mind that if you do not speak fluent Spanish, local calls to businesses, police stations or public service agencies can easily grind to a halt.

There are very few coin-operated public pay phones in Mexico, and they tend to be out of order. Most public phones are labeled Telmex, the name of the national telephone company, and are part of a system called Ladatel—literally, long distance *(lada)* telephone. Ladatel phones allow direct dialing without operator assistance and are less expensive than making phone calls from a hotel room. Local calls also can be made from Ladatel phones.

Most Ladatel pay phones have a slot in which to insert a disposable Ladatel phone card. Some have two slots—one for the Ladatel card and one for Mexican bank credit cards (Banamex, Bancomer or Carnet). They also may accept MasterCard or Visa, but not U.S. telephone calling cards. Ladatel phone cards can be purchased in various peso denominations (typically 30, 50 or 100 pesos) at most pharmacies and gas station mini-markets, as well as from machines at airports and bus stations.

To make a call with a Ladatel card, insert the card into the appropriate slot, with the computer chip facing up and toward the phone. Dial the access code (if necessary) plus the number you're trying to reach. The card is left in the slot while the call takes place. If the call does not go through, the card is returned. If the call is for less time than the value of the card, it is returned with a credit amount shown (the card does not expire). If the call is still in progress when the card's value has been used up, the phone will beep and another card must be inserted to continue the call. Some phones have a digital display window that monitors the cost of the call.

When calling long distance from one Mexican location to another, dial 01 (the access code), then the three-digit area code (two-digit area code in metropolitan Guadalajara, Mexico City and Monterrey), then the seven-digit local phone number (eight-digit local number in metropolitan Guadalajara, Mexico City and Monterrey). Mexican phone numbers shown in this book include only the 10-digit format (area code plus the local number), not the access code that also must be dialed if making a long-distance call. Local calls in Mexico do not require dialing the access or area codes.

Free tourist publications usually include phone numbers for hotels, restaurants, attractions, travel agencies, airlines and so forth, as well as emergency and general information numbers. For additional assistance, consult a Telmex directory.

All Mexican toll-free numbers have an 800 area code. You must first dial the 01 access code, then the 800 prefix and the seven-digit number. **Note:** Mexican numbers with an 800 prefix will work *only* in Mexico; the call will not go through if dialed from outside the country.

If your cellular phone is activated for international roaming and has worldwide capability it can be used in Mexico; otherwise you will need to have it programmed for a Mexican number. You also can rent one and prepay for the minute allotment you'll need. Calls to Mexican cell phone numbers—either locally or long distance within the country—must be prefaced by dialing 044, which replaces the access code 01. The 044 prefix does not need to be dialed if calling a Mexican cell phone number from outside the country, although you will still need to dial the international access number and the appropriate area code.

If you want to connect directly to an international destination without speaking to an operator, use your calling card and dial 01 (for AT&T) or 001 (for MCI or Sprint) plus the 800 access number for your long-distance carrier. AT&T's USA DIRECT number is (800) 288-2872; MCI WorldPhone, (800) 674-7000; and Sprint, (800) 877-8000. To avoid having expensive hotel surcharges tacked on to your bill, don't call from your room.

Some hotels may block one or more access code numbers if you try to call from the room; if that is the case, make the call from a public pay phone with a U.S. calling card. Some also add a charge for local calls made from the room in addition to the hefty surcharge placed on all international calls. Inquire when you check in whether local calls are extra. Avoid public phones claiming to offer low long-distance rates for calls to the United States and Canada; the cost per minute will be exorbitant.

If you have a problem trying to make a specific local or long-distance call, enlist the aid of an operator; there are few recordings advising callers of phone number or area code changes. To reach a long-distance operator within Mexico, dial 020; for directory assistance, dial 040; for emergency assistance, dial 060 or 066; for an international operator, dial 090. Keep in mind that English may not be spoken.

To make an international call to the United States or Canada on a private phone line in Mexico, dial 001, then the area code and phone number. If calling collect, dial 91, then the area code and phone number. If you call collect from your hotel room and the call is not accepted, however, you may still be charged.

Time Zones

Most of Mexico's states are on Central Standard Time. Exceptions are the states of Chihuahua, Nayarit, Sonora, Sinaloa and Baja California Sur, which are on Mountain Standard Time, and Baja California, which is on Pacific Standard Time.

Note: Mexico began observing daylight saving time (DST, referred to as *horario de verano,* or "summer time") in 1996 in accordance with the United States and Canada—from the first weekend in April through the last weekend in October. This schedule will continue in 2009, although U.S. daylight saving time observation begins 3 weeks earlier and ends 1 week later. The state of Sonora does not observe daylight saving time.

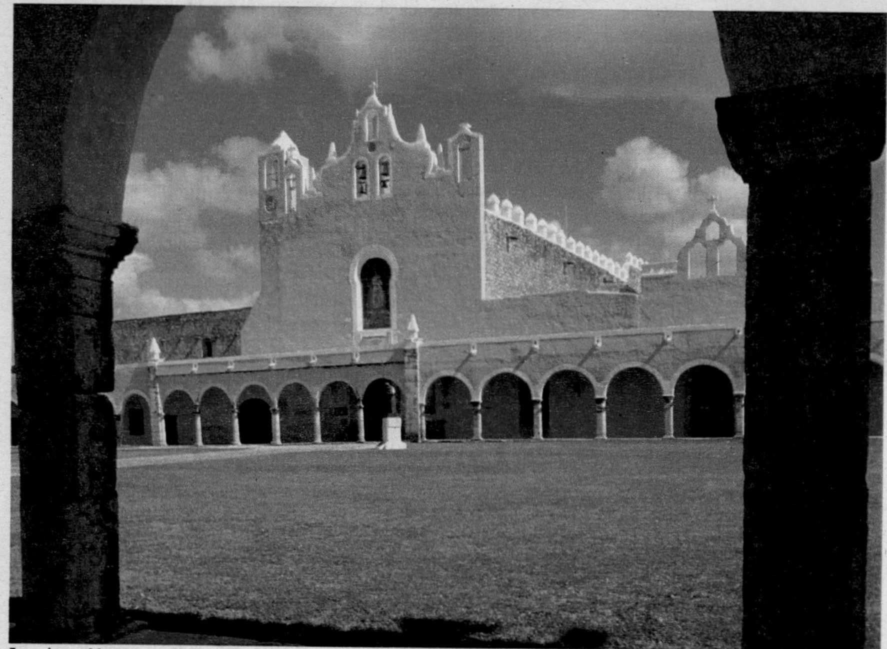

Franciscan Monastery, Izamal / © age fotostock

Yucatán Peninsula

Consisting of three states—Campeche, Quintana Roo and Yucatán—the Yucatán (yoo-cah-TAHN) Peninsula is an intriguing juxtaposition of old and new, natural and man-made, primitive and master-planned. Geographic, ethnographic and historical factors combine to separate the Yucatán somewhat from the rest of Mexico, a feeling shared by the people who live here—most think of themselves as *yucatecos* first, Mexicans second.

The first Spaniards who arrived at the Yucatán's eastern shore in the early 16th century believed it to be a huge island in between the Caribbean Sea and the Gulf of Mexico. Certainly the region's physical characteristics, which are more similar to the state of Florida than to the Mexican mainland, could qualify it as a separate country. The peninsula's most exploitable natural resource is its Caribbean coastline, bathed by aquamarine water and lined with gorgeous white-sand beaches, and the wealth of fishing, diving, snorkeling, swimming and boating opportunities draws multitudes of tourists to the Yucatán's shores.

It wasn't always so. As early as 400 B.C., the ancient Mayan civilization was beginning to evolve in the Mexican state of Chiapas and the countries of Belize, Guatemala and Honduras. Its origins remain one of history's puzzles, although it is believed that the Maya were descended from the Olmec, whose own civilization flourished along Mexico's lower gulf coast in what is now the state of Tabasco. Over a period of time roughly parallel to the rise of the Roman Empire the Maya developed their own sophisticated civilization, as well as a reputation for bizarre, blood-spattered rites.

The Maya migrated northward from Central America to the present-day states of Campeche and Yucatán. Between 1000 and 1500, such major cities as Chichén Itzá, Cobá,

Dzibilchaltún, Edzná, Ek Balam, Mayapán, Tulum and Uxmal were built. Over time the focus of Mayan civilization moved from the observance of elaborate religious rituals toward commercial, governmental and militaristic concerns. Some cities functioned as trade centers between the Caribbean and gulf coasts and Mexico's interior as the peninsula was infiltrated by various tribes. It was the squabbling among these different factions that set the stage for Spanish conquest of the Yucatán, which was absolute by the end of the 16th century.

The Yucatecan people—direct descendants of the Maya—are one of Mexico's largest *indígena* groups. They live throughout the peninsula, particularly in the state of Yucatán, and their short stature, dark-skinned complexions and sculpted cheekbones bear unmistakable witness to their forebears. Mayan dialects are as readily spoken as Spanish, although residents employed in the tourist industry usually speak English as well. Yucatecans are friendly; don't be afraid to ask for the time or for directions, but return the kindness with a smile and a thank-you. You could also try thanking in Mayan, which (spelled phonetically) is "dios boteek." Always ask first if you wish to photograph someone; this can be requested as simply as holding up your camera and saying *"por favor"?*

Adventurous travelers might want to head for Campeche, the least-explored state, where ancient ruins poke up out of thick jungle. Hardwoods traditionally furnished much of Campeche's wealth, although oil is the leading industry today. The capital of Campeche, walled in the 17th century as a defense against pirates, has the easygoing charm of a tropical port, and ongoing efforts are under way to renovate the city's numerous colonial-style buildings.

Rising from the flat scrubland of Yucatán state are the archeological sites of Chichén Itzá, Ek Balam and Uxmal. These former ceremonial centers contain monumentally scaled buildings created without benefit of such basics as the wheel, metal tools or proven beasts of burden. And among the small villages dotting the Yucatán's rolling hills, one bona fide city stands out: Mérida, one of the first cities to be built by the Spanish. Ornate mansions, fine old buildings and lively plazas combine to give this vibrant capital a distinctly European feel—despite the exotic flowers and sultry heat.

Quintana Roo, which occupies the eastern part of the peninsula, was almost wholly isolated from the rest of the country until the completion of two roads (Mex. 180 and Mex. 186). Today, however, the great majority of Quintana Roo's visitors fly in, and their destination of choice is Cancún, which as recently as the late 1960s was a sleepy, unknown fishing village. No more—hordes of spring breakers, winter-weary gringos and beach lovers have made this sun-splashed resort one of the world's top tourist destinations.

In stark contrast to Cancun's manufactured paradise is the primeval wilderness of the Sian Ka'an Biosphere Reserve, established as a protected area by the Mexican government in 1986 and designated a World Heritage Site by the United Nations Educational, Scientific and Cultural Organization (UNESCO) in 1987. This 1.3 million-acre ecological preserve, located on the Yucatán Peninsula's eastern coast, boasts a rich spectrum of habitats: tropical forests, lagoons, mangrove marshes and an offshore barrier reef, all protected from encroachment or commercial development.

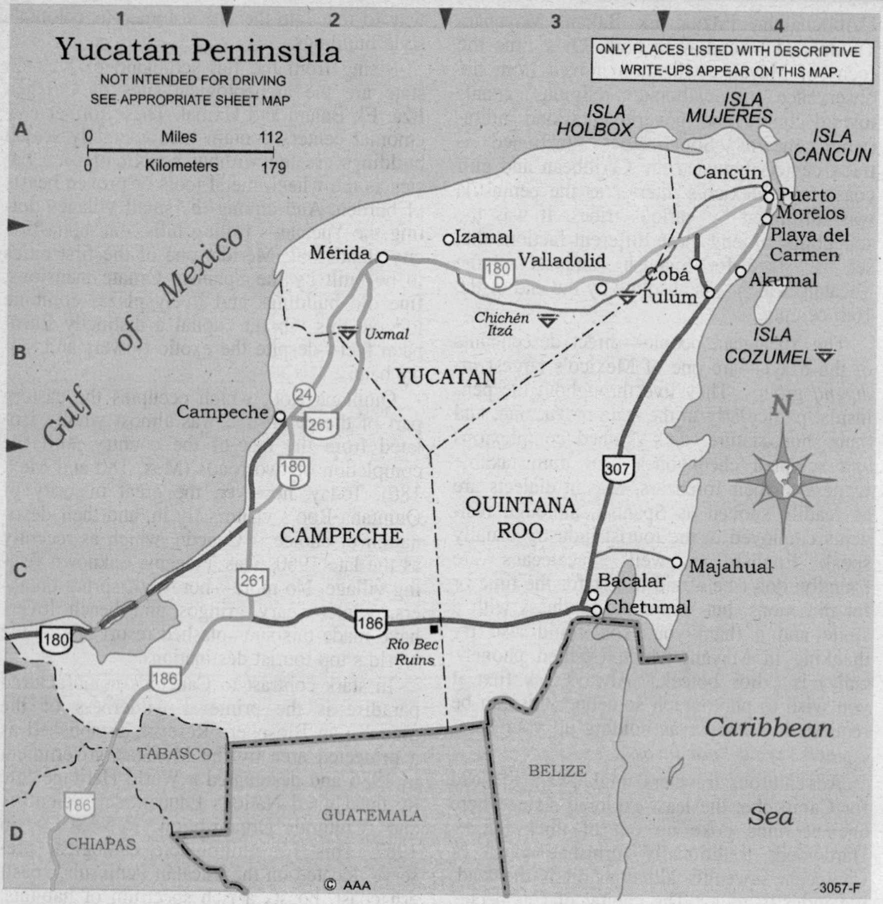

Yucatán Peninsula

NOT INTENDED FOR DRIVING
SEE APPROPRIATE SHEET MAP

ONLY PLACES LISTED WITH DESCRIPTIVE WRITE-UPS APPEAR ON THIS MAP.

0 Miles 112
0 Kilometers 179

Gulf of Mexico
ISLA HOLBOX
ISLA MUJERES
ISLA CANCUN
Cancún
Puerto Morelos
Playa del Carmen
Akumal
Izamal
Mérida
Valladolid
Cobá
Tulúm
Chichén Itzá
Uxmal
ISLA COZUMEL
YUCATAN
Campeche
CAMPECHE
QUINTANA ROO
Majahual
Bacalar
Chetumal
Río Bec Ruins
Caribbean Sea
TABASCO
BELIZE
GUATEMALA
CHIAPAS
180 D
24
261
307
186
180

© AAA
3057-F

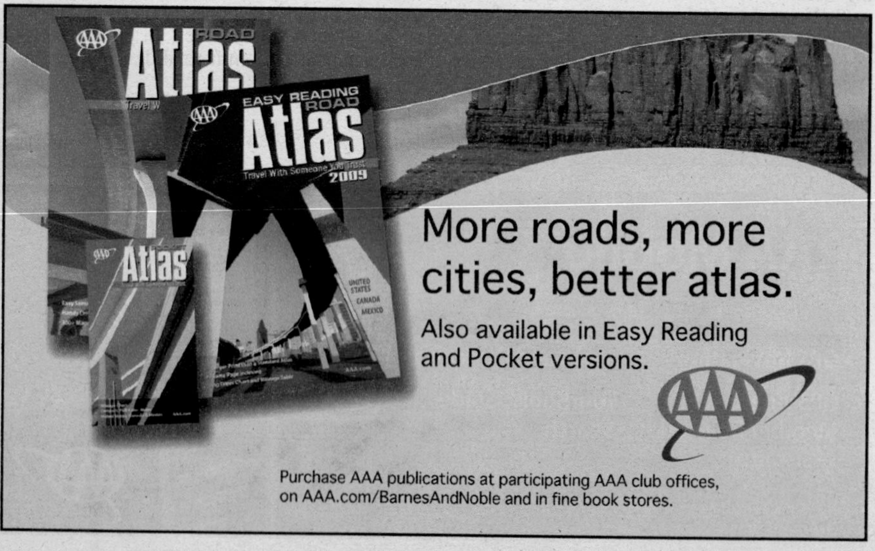

Points of Interest

AKUMAL, QUINTANA ROO (B-4)

A once-humble fishing village turned diving and snorkeling center, Akumal ("place of the turtles" in the Mayan language) is off Mex. 307 about 26 kilometers (16 miles) north of Tulum. Although centered around several resort complexes, you don't need to be a guest at any of them in order to enjoy the long, curving beaches or swim in the warm Caribbean surf. Akumal is laid-back and friendly, a great place to drop your anchor and get into the relaxed rhythms of the Riviera Maya coast.

Getting here is a bit tricky. If heading southbound on Mex. 307, you'll encounter a concrete center median at the Akumal turn-off that prevents vehicles from making a left turn onto the access road. Continue a hundred yards or so beyond the turn-off to the signed turnaround *(retorno)*; make a U-turn here, head back north and turn right at the access road junction.

Less than half a mile down the road you'll drive under a white arch. Stay to the left to get to the Akumal beach parking lot (there are spaces on either side of the road); an attendant will usually wave you in and collect a small parking fee. Past the parking lot, a dirt road continues on to Half Moon Bay. A short distance beyond Half Moon is Yal-ku Lagoon *(see attraction listing)*.

The town of Akumal spreads out along the shore of exceptionally pretty Akumal Bay, the largest of three bodies of water comprising this stretch of coast. It has a beautiful white-sand beach and two full-service dive shops that provide scuba instruction as well as reef diving, sport fishing and snorkeling excursions. From shore it's an easy swim to Akumal's offshore reef, where the chances of spotting a sea turtle are high. As you snorkel, be mindful of boat traffic in the bay.

Grocery stores, restaurants, beach bars and other tourist amenities are plentiful in town. The beachfront bar at Restaurante Lol Ha is popular with Akumal regulars and has great views of Akumal Bay. To the north, Half Moon Bay is lined with a fine-sand beach backed by villas and condos. There's good snorkeling here as well. You can rent kayaks and other water sports equipment at both bays.

Akumal Dive Adventures, a PADI-certified dive center located on Half Moon Bay, offers a variety of scuba and snorkeling trips that emphasize a low-impact approach to the fragile offshore reef environment, as well as deep-sea fishing excursions for mahi mahi, marlin, sailfish and wahoo. Accompanied by a cave-certified instructor, divers can explore the wonderland of Dos Ojos (Two Eyes), a cenote (freshwater sinkhole) that leads to a vast subterranean cavern filled with intricate limestone formations in crystal-clear water. Phone (984) 875-9157.

AKTUN CHEN is about 4 km (2.5 mi.) s. of Akumal (watch for the signed turn-off on the right side of Mex. 307 going southbound), then another 4 km (2.5 mi.) down a narrow dirt road to the entrance. This nature park offers a guided half-mile walking tour through a dry cave festooned with stalactites, stalagmites and other natural limestone formations, all enhanced by indirect artificial lighting as well as natural light coming through openings in the cave ceiling.

The tour ends at a freshwater underground cenote with clear, green-hued water that reaches a depth of 36 feet. Animal exhibits include deer, spider monkeys, toucans, parrots and snakes, and such local wildlife as wild turkeys and iguanas also can be seen.

Guided tours in English are available. A small restaurant is on the premises. On-site parking is available. Restrooms are provided. Insect repellent is recommended. Allow 3 hours minimum. Daily 9-7 (last tour begins at 6 p.m.), June-Aug.; 9-5 (last tour begins at 4:30), rest of year. Admission about $24 (U.S.); $13 (ages 3-10). MC, VI. Phone (984) 109-2061.

YAL-KU LAGOON is about 2 km (1 mi.) n. of town past Half-Moon Bay; take the marked Akumal exit off Mex. 307 and stay to the left past the center of town. The entrance to the lagoon is down a short, winding walking path. A brackish mix of fresh and salt water, Yal-ku offers the opportunity to snorkel in a sheltered environment (currents are stronger near the open sea). Sets of stairs lead down to a sandy bottom. Entry is easy and the water is calm, but due to poor water flow clarity is on the murky side. You will, however, see rock formations and the

---

DID YOU KNOW

Hurricane Wilma, which hit Cancún, Cozumel, Isla Mujeres and the Quintana Roo coast in October 2005, caused nearly $3 billion in damage.

---

usual small reef fish. It's a good choice for beginning snorkelers and families with kids. There also are sculptures and gardens on the grounds.

On-site parking is available. Restrooms are provided. Daily 8-5:30. Admission about $7 (U.S.); there are extra fees for snorkel equipment rental and life jackets.

BACALAR, QUINTANA ROO (C-3)

Bacalar (ba-cah-LAHR) barely registers a blip on the mass tourism radar, which means adventurous travelers who journey to this spot in southern Quintana Roo are rewarded with a gorgeous turquoise lagoon and an authentic town unspoiled by Cancún-like commercialism. Located on the lagoon's western shore, Bacalar has a handful of small hotels (some with lagoon views) that mainly cater to vacationing Mexican families, while a couple of rustic eco lodges with cabana-type accommodations appeal to international visitors.

Founded in 1528, Bacalar was the first Spanish colonial settlement in the region that became Quintana Roo. Although the colonists lived in relative peace for more than 100 years, Spanish-Mayan hostility simmered under the surface, exploding when four local farmers were savagely murdered. The Mayan community in Chetumal retaliated with equal savagery; the site was finally destroyed by pirates in 1652.

In 1726, Bacalar was resettled by Spanish expatriates from the Canary Islands. They built Fort San Felipe (Fuerte de San Felipe), a massive fortification completed in 1733 that was encircled by a most effective deterrent: a crocodile-filled moat. At the outbreak of the Castes War in 1848 the Maya, after brutal fighting, again reclaimed the settlement and the fort. Bacalar remained in Mayan hands until 1901, when the Mexican government reclaimed it peacefully.

Fort San Felipe, now surrounded by landscaped gardens rather than hungry reptiles, has a watchtower that overlooks the fishing and boating activities on Bacalar Lagoon. It houses the Museum of the Piracy (Museo de la Piratería), which focuses on the area's pirate past and contains displays of weapons and artifacts. Information panels are in Spanish and English. The museum is closed Monday.

Next to the fort is the main plaza. There's an ATM on the west side of the square. On the surrounding streets you may see a curious sight: horse-drawn buggies driven by Mennonites, a religious Christian group similar to the Amish. Seeking religious freedom, Mennonites began establishing communities in rural areas of northern Mexico, and also around Bacalar. Their small farming settlement is located west of Mex. 307.

Bacalar Lagoon (Laguna de Bacalar) is east of town; follow the signs from Mex. 307. This 31-mile-long body of water is a spectacular natural wonder in the midst of the otherwise unremarkable jungle scrub of southern Quintana Roo. Salt and fresh water mix in the lagoon, accentuating beautiful hues from deep turquoise to almost black (it is also known as "Lake of the Seven Colors"). The lagoon's clear water is ideal for swimming, boating, kayaking, snorkeling and scuba diving.

Along the western shore, a good swimming spot is the Balneario Magico beach club. Located a few minutes' drive north of the town plaza (take the waterfront road), the club has a simple restaurant, a pier and picnic tables with a view of the lagoon. Parking is about $1 (U.S.), and admission to the facility is about 50c per person. At the southern end of town, there's more good swimming in front of the bluff-top Hotel Laguna. Keep in mind that you will be expected to order something from the hotel's bar or restaurant to use the waterfront facilities.

About 5 kilometers (3 miles) south of town, almost at the edge of the lagoon, is Cenote Azul (Blue Cenote). This freshwater sinkhole is the largest in the Yucatán and reputedly the largest in the world. Some 600 feet across and estimated at more than 250 feet deep, it is filled with blue water that is unusually clear. Surrounded by green vegetation, Cenote Azul is popular with swimmers, snorkelers and divers. Camping facilities are available nearby.

CAMPECHE, CAMPECHE (B-1)

pop. 195,700

Capital of the state of the same name, Campeche (kahm-PEH-cheh) is the largest city between Villahermosa and Mérida. Its waterfront, dotted by offshore oil rigs, is the base of Mexico's largest gulf coast shrimp fleet.

Hernández de Córdova and his *conquistadores* stopped in this area in 1517 to obtain fresh water. Founded in 1540 by Don Francisco de Montejo, the city flourished from the export of hardwoods and dyewoods to Europe. One of the foremost cities of New Spain in the mid-16th century, Campeche preserves buildings that date from this period in its old San Francisco section. One such structure was the house where Montejo planned his conquest of the Yucatán.

Campeche's most remarkable attraction is a massive 1.5-mile hexagonal wall with eight fortresses that was erected for protection against repeated sackings by European pirates in the 16th and 17th centuries. Begun in 1686, the fortification took 18 years to build. The historic fortified section of the city was designated a World Heritage Site by UNESCO in 1999.

Fort Soledad (Fuerte de la Soledad), 3 blocks north of the ancient Puerta del Mar entranceway, has been converted into a museum displaying Mayan artifacts, an arms collection and exhibits on colonial history. On the outskirts of the city is one of the most impressive of all the fortresses, Fort San Miguel (Fuerte de San Miguel). Its moat supposedly contained crocodiles.

Fort San Carlos (Fuerte de San Carlos), a government-sponsored handicrafts market today, has intriguing secret underground passageways. Linked to many houses in the city, the tunnels provided a hiding place for women and children when pirate ships came to plunder. Most passageways are sealed off with bricks, but guides offer tours into the fort's basement for a small fee. The fort's roof, still equipped with ancient cannon, offers a spectacular view of the gulf.

Among the words coined in Campeche is *campechano,* used to describe a pleasant, easygoing person. Local tradition has it that the word "cocktail" originated here centuries ago because English pirates were served drinks adorned by palm fronds resembling cocks' tails. Happily, the root of Campeche's name, taken from the Mayan words *kim* and *pech,* meaning "serpent" and "tick," has no modern application.

Although the city is studded with ancient walls and fortresses, it also contains such buildings as the Government Palace and the Legislative Palace, respectively referred to as "the jukebox" and "the flying saucer" for their modern architecture, which blends surprisingly well with the native buildings. Local markets sell such handicrafts as Panama hats and articles made of alligator skin. The regional cuisine includes such exotic dishes as shark stew.

Other points of interest include the 1540 Franciscan Cathedral, the oldest convent church in the Yucatán Peninsula; the 1546 Convent of San Francisco, the site of one of the first masses in Campeche; the Temple of San Francisquito, which now houses the Campeche Cultural Institute (Instituto Cultural Campechano); and the House of the King's Lieutenant (Casa del Teniente del Rey), which contains colonial furnishings. Alameda Park's Bridge of Dogs (El Puente de Los Perros), a colonial bridge guarded by carved stone dogs, honors the Dominican missionaries called the "Dogs of God" for their zealous hounding of converts.

Campeche State Tourism Office: downtown at Plaza Moch-Couoh, on Avenida Ruiz Cortines; phone (981) 816-6829.

EDZNA RUINS are about 53 km (33 mi.) s.e. of Campeche; take Av. Central out of the city, following signs for the airport and Edzná. This Mayan city was first inhabited about 600 B.C. and abandoned by the 15th century; as is true of other archeological sites in Mexico, the reasons for its decline remain a mystery.

The closest major ruins to Campeche may not be worth the trip if you've seen Chichén Itzá or Uxmal, but there is one standout building: the 98-foot-tall Temple of Five Stories (Templo de Cinco Cuerpos), a five-level structure with a central staircase and an impressive roofcomb. South of this temple is the Temple of Masks, with carvings of heads that have jaguar-like faces.

Site open daily 8-5. Admission 39 pesos (about $3.80 U.S.). The fee to use a video camera is $4.

Cancún

City Population: 436,000 (estimated)
Elevation: 7 meters (23 feet)

Editor's Picks:

Interactive Aquarium Cancún ..... *(see p. 97)*
Tulum Ruins .... *(see p. 147)*
Xcaret................................ *(see p. 143)*

It began in the southwestern Caribbean Sea as a tropical depression on Oct. 15, 2005—a year that was to go down in the meteorological record books as the most prolific and destructive year in history in terms of Atlantic basin hurricanes. Within days a storm by the name of Wilma had morphed into a terrifying category 5 hurricane with sustained winds of 185 mph. Although that fearsome intensity fortunately was not sustained, Wilma was still a destructive category 4 cyclone as it bore down on Cancún, the most popular resort destination in Mexico.

Although deaths were few, Wilma's aftermath plunged this tourism-dependent region into near chaos. Thousands of tourists were stranded, basic communications were disrupted and luxury hotels had blown-out windows and flooded lobbies. But with remarkable resourcefulness, Cancún got back on its feet as local citizens—many with jobs directly linked to the tourism industry—pitched in to help clean up, remodel and renovate. Within weeks most of the city had reopened for business, and things were back to normal in a matter of months.

Cancún's post-Wilma rebirth was just the latest chapter in a city with a brief but remarkable history. At the beginning of the 1970s this world-famous playground didn't even show up on maps. There were no throngs of vacationers; Cancún was home to a handful of fishermen eking out a living along a stretch of gorgeous coast once home to the ancient Maya and later a refuge for pirates. The area appealed to serious scuba divers and committed beach bums, but a lack of all but the most basic amenities was an impediment to widespread leisure travel. Those in search of inviting Mexican beaches that actually had hotels at which to stay headed for Acapulco or Puerto Vallarta.

Stunning natural attributes, however, meant that a sandbar lying just offshore the northeastern Yucatán Peninsula was paradise waiting to blossom. The Mexican government, in the midst of ambitious plans to maximize the country's tourism potential, selected the little spit of land as a prime location for a new resort, and it was promptly handed over to eager developers.

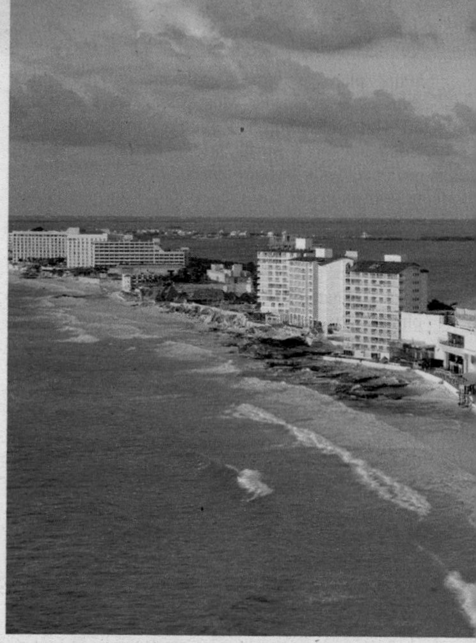

The blueprint called for a tourist zone, a residential area and an airport to serve visitors. Bridges were built to connect Cancún Island to the mainland, and a makeshift city (which grew into downtown Ciudad Cancún) was erected to house workers who literally built a vacation playground from scratch. Cancún opened for business in 1974, the same year that the territory of Quintana Roo became a Mexican state.

A building boom took off in the mid-1980s, and the city has never looked back. Today some 3 million vacationers come each year for beaches of fine-grained sand and beautiful turquoise-hued water; for accommodations from budget-priced to downright luxurious; for rowdy, high-energy nightlife that doesn't quit; for a dining scene that encompasses both elegant hotel restaurants and local joints specializing in Yucatecan cuisine; for shopping at an assortment of bright, shiny malls; for sightseeing boat cruises and all sorts of water recreation; and last but not least, to relax, kick back and soak up the sun.

Getting There — *starting on p. 91*
Getting Around — *starting on p. 93*
What To See — *starting on p. 95*
What To Do — *starting on p. 97*
Where To Stay — *starting on p. 415*
Where To Dine — *starting on p. 427*

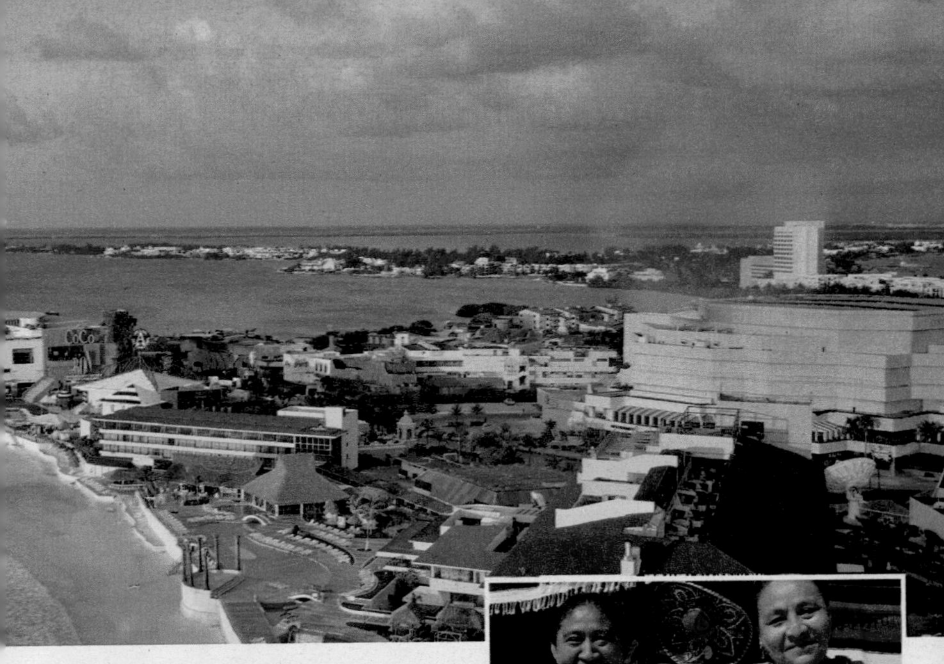

Cancún also is a spring break hotspot, a major convention city and a popular getaway for honeymooners.

Ciudad Cancún, known locally as "El Centro," is on the mainland, a commercial and business center that is very much like any other Mexican town. Cancún Island (Isla Cancún), known as the Hotel Zone (Zona Hotelera), is where all the resorts are concentrated. This elbow-shaped sandbar is nearly 15 miles long but just a quarter-mile wide, separated from the mainland by narrow causeways at either end.

In between are the calm waters of Nichupté Lagoon (Laguna Nichupté). The island's seaward side fronts Mujeres Bay from Ciudad Cancún east to Cancún Point (Punta Cancún). The point is the crook of the elbow; south of it the shoreline faces the open Caribbean.

While the Hotel Zone has its scruffy aspects—dust, cement, broken sidewalks—it also is crowded, busy and booming. It's a mix of upscale luxury hotels and youth-oriented nightspots, trendy designer shopping and souvenir markets, buzzing energy and tropical languor (the sound of coconut palm fronds rustling in the breeze is a constant backdrop). The hotels in particular are Cancún's real "attractions"—architecturally distinctive, lushly landscaped and opulently appointed, they have a backdrop of intensely aquamarine Caribbean surf and are etched under sunlight bright enough to make sunglasses a full-time accessory.

Many hotels took advantage of the damage caused by Wilma not only to repair but to upgrade. While Cancún lodgings come in all price ranges, the latest trend is toward upscale properties catering to a sophisticated, well-heeled clientele. One of the Hotel Zone's hippest places to stay is the ME by Meliá. The look is sleek, minimalist and contemporary, with dramatic lighting and funky art. At night the entire hotel seems to throb to the beat of moody techno music as guests hit the pool-side bars or dine at one of two side-by-side restaurants. At the Fiesta Americana Aqua Cancún, the enticements include celebrity chefs, aromatherapy sessions and a choice of eight different pillows to ensure a good night's sleep.

© Jon Arnold Images / Danita Delimont Stock Photography

As befits a tropical resort, the weather here is balmy year-round. Although constant sea breezes temper the summer heat, humidity is high; the winter months are the most pleasant. The water is warm enough for swimming all year. Most visitors wear shorts and T-shirts; casual but stylish resort wear is appropriate at the nicer restaurants or for an evening out. Bring sunblock, and pack a sweater for the occasional cool, blustery winter day or icily air-conditioned summer interior.

The greatest chance for tropical disturbances is from August through October, and Cancún, by virtue of its location, is vulnerable. The city received yet

The Informed Traveler

WHOM TO CALL

Police (emergency): Dial 060 and ask to be connected to an English-speaking operator.

Consumer Protection Agency (Procuraduría Federal del Consumidor): Av. Cobá #9 (2nd floor) in downtown Ciudad Cancún; phone (998) 884-2369. The office is open Mon.-Fri. 9-3.

Immigration Office: avenidas J.C. Nader and Uxmal in Ciudad Cancún; phone (998) 884-1404. The office is open Mon.-Fri. 9-noon and can provide assistance if you lose your tourist permit.

Hospitals: Most of the major hotels have their own in-house or on-call doctor. If in doubt, obtain a list of physicians from the U.S. Consular Agency, located at Plaza Caracol Two (third level, #320-323), Boulevard Kukulcán Km 8.5; phone (998) 883-0272. Local clinics do not accept U.S. health insurance, often charge fees well above U.S. rates and have been known to charge for services not rendered.

In case of emergency, the Red Cross (Cruz Roja) is in Ciudad Cancún on Avenida Yaxchilán, between avenidas Xcaret and Labná. It is open 24 hours; phone (998) 884-1616.

WHERE TO LOOK

Newspapers

The *Miami Herald* and *USA Today* are available in the bigger hotels.

Television

Most hotels have a cable TV system that offers the ABC, CBS, NBC and Fox networks via a U.S. affiliate, such staples as CNN and ESPN, and HBO or another movie channel, in addition to Spanish-language channels.

Publications

Cancún Tips is a quarterly magazine with easy-to-read maps and information about restaurants, shopping, entertainment, sightseeing and local services. The pocket-size version also has numerous restaurant discount coupons. The *Mapa Pocket Guide,* published twice yearly, contains maps and useful phone numbers. Pick up these and other free tourist-oriented brochures at shopping centers and sidewalk booths. The open-air building on Boulevard Kukulcán just west of the Fiesta Americana Grand Coral Beach hotel has information about local attractions and guided tours down the coast.

Visitor Information

Quintana Roo State Tourism Office (Secretaría de Turismo de Quintana Roo, or SEDETUR): Boulevard Kukulcán Km marker 9 (Hotel Zone), on the first floor of the Cancún Center. Open Mon.-Fri. 9-5; phone (998) 881-9000.

WHAT TO KNOW

Currency Exchange

Casas de cambio (currency exchange offices) and banks are along Avenida Tulum in downtown Ciudad Cancún. Most banks are open Mon.-Fri. 9-5; currency exchange normally is confined to the morning hours. Exchange offices also are located in the Hotel Zone shopping areas around Cancún Point. You also can exchange currency at your hotel's front desk.

ATM withdrawals are in pesos, although some machines dispense dollars as well. Since the rates offered by exchange offices, banks and hotels differ only slightly and fluctuate daily, exchanging dollars boils down to a matter of convenience. You'll want to keep some pesos on hand, since not everything (bus and taxi fares, the ferry fare to Isla Mujeres) can be paid for by credit card. Keep a supply of change and smaller denomination bills on hand.

Staying Safe

Crime directed at tourists is not prevalent, but do use common sense. Always put jewelry and other valuables in the hotel safe, or don't bring them at all. Be on guard for potential pickpocket or purse-snatching incidents in crowded public places or when using public transportation. Car break-ins can occur in the Hotel Zone's shopping areas; don't invite one by leaving valuables in plain view. Always take a taxi after dark, whether in Ciudad Cancún or the Hotel Zone.

another scare in August 2007, when Hurricane Dean was forecast at one point to deliver a direct hit. But the storm's course shifted south and it eventually came ashore as a powerful category 5 hurricane near Chetumal, more than 150 miles to the south.

Often linked with Cancún in the minds of travelers, Cozumel *(see separate listing within this region)* is a major destination all its own, since it is a major cruise ship stop. Mexico's largest populated island, it lies about 12 miles offshore and has a deserved reputation among divers for water of unsurpassed clarity, inhabited by an amazing variety of marine life.

Isla Mujeres *(see separate listing within this region)*, an island 4 miles off the coast, is just north of Cancún opposite mainland Puerto Juárez. Much smaller than Cozumel, it's a delightful and very popular day trip from Cancún via small passenger ferries or larger sightseeing cruise vessels.

The mainland town of Playa del Carmen *(see separate listing within this region)*, about 45 minutes south of Cancún, is experiencing its own boom. The beaches here are just as pretty, nightlife is almost (but not quite) as frenetic, and a steadily growing number of big resort properties rival Cancún's in terms of luxury. Playa also has its workaday side, a typical Mexican town that is far removed in character (if not physical distance) from the touristy Hotel Zone.

Cancún makes a convenient base for exploring other parts of the Yucatán, particularly its archeological riches. The ruins of Chichén Itzá *(see separate listing within this region)*, the remains of a once-great Mayan city and one of the world's best-known archeological sites, are about 2 hours away by car or tour bus. About 90 minutes south of Cancún are the Tulum Ruins *(see attraction listing under Tulum)*, dramatically situated on a cliff overlooking the Caribbean.

The 60-mile stretch of Quintana Roo coastline from Puerto Morelos south to the town of Tulum is known as the Riviera Maya. It is a rapidly growing region of nature-oriented attractions where visitors can snorkel and dive in cenotes (freshwater sinkholes), view a rich diversity of wildlife and explore stunningly beautiful beaches. The sport fishing is rewarding, and an offshore coral reef guarantees superb diving and snorkeling. Accommodations along the Riviera Maya range from rustic lodges to pricey all-inclusive resorts.

South of Tulum the coast is less developed. For a real adventure, journey from Tulum south to Punta Allen. The coastal road is narrow and bumpy, with sandy, rutted and potholed intervals. But the scenery is wildly lovely—miles of deserted beaches with powdery white sand, serene mangrove-lined estuaries and the odd Mayan ruin poking up through scrubby jungle. Punta Allen is the end of the line, a slip of a lobster fishing village catering to sport-fishing enthusiasts that lazes in an idyllic setting of coconut palms and thatched *palapas*. Nature is protected in wilderness sanctuaries like the 1.5-million acre Sian Ka'an Biosphere Reserve *(see attraction listing under Tulum)*.

Even farther south, the stretch of coast from Punta Herrero south to Xcalak (shka-LAK) at the Belize border—known as the Costa Maya—is steadily being developed for eco tourism. Small resorts and campsites cater to visitors who come for the excellent sport fishing, snorkeling, diving and bird-watching opportunities. This also has become a big international cruise ship destination, and there is a major cruise ship pier at Majahual *(see separate listing within this region)*. The Costa Maya bore the brunt of Hurricane Dean's fury, and the pier and port facilities were heavily damaged. Rebuilding soon got under way, though, and at press time the pier was expected to reopen sometime in fall 2008.

Cancún is not colonial Mexico, steeped in time and tradition. It has a pervading sense of newness that is especially evident post-Wilma. From Subway to Starbucks, you'll see—at least in the Hotel Zone—fast food outlets and stateside franchises. Themed shopping complexes rule here, not historical and cultural shadings. But there also is a comforting familiarity. English is commonplace—although Spanish might be spoken first. Dollars are routinely accepted. The widespread Americanization makes Cancún a good choice for travelers hesitant about vacationing in a foreign country, or for those who desire a higher level of amenities and fewer hassles than are routinely encountered in Mexico's less-developed areas.

Despite the ongoing challenge of balancing growth and preserving the natural environment, Cancún and the Caribbean coast do boast an unbeatable trio—sun, sea and sand. And there are plenty of options for visitors to enjoy these natural attributes, from economical trip packages to the pampering that is to be expected at an exclusive luxury resort. Locals take great pride in their city and welcome tourists—and judging from the planeloads of satisfied vacationers, Cancún must be doing something right.

Getting There

By Air

Cancún International Airport is on the mainland off Mex. 307, about 16 kilometers (10 miles) southwest of downtown Ciudad Cancún and about 10 kilometers (6 miles) from the southern end of Cancún Island. It receives regular flights from major cities in the United States and Mexico; many are daily.

Aeroméxico, 01 (800) 021-4010 (toll-free long distance within Mexico), and Mexicana, 01 (800) 509-8960 (toll-free long distance within Mexico), offer direct flights from some U.S. cities. Other airlines serving the airport include American, 01 (800) 904-6000 (toll-free long distance within Mexico); Continental, 01 (800) 900-5000 (toll-free long distance within Mexico); and Northwest, 01 (800) 907-4700 (toll-free long distance within Mexico). A number of charter companies fly to Cancún as well.

Note: There are no direct flights from Canada to Cancún; most major U.S. airlines meet connecting flights from Canada in Dallas, Houston or New York. To confirm schedules, contact the appropriate airline or a travel agency. For additional information about airlines *see Arriving by Air, page 61*.

Click Mexicana, Mexicana's low-cost carrier, flies to nearby Yucatán destinations, including Chichén Itzá, Mérida and Playa del Carmen, as well as to Oaxaca. For information phone (800) 112-5425 (toll-free long distance within Mexico).

Cancún's airport is modern and clearly marked with bilingual signs for arrivals, departures, gates, immigration and restrooms. After arriving you must first proceed to Immigration and have your tourist permit validated before heading to the baggage claim area. The last stop is Mexican customs, where you will hand over your completed declaration form, put your luggage on a conveyor belt and push a button that activates the random green light/red light system; if the red light flashes your bags will be briefly searched.

The airport's Terminal 3 opened in May 2007, easing some of the congestion that travelers had experienced previously. The new terminal has plenty of restaurants, gift shops and duty-free stores on the upper departure level. The rental car counters are now in a consolidated location as you exit the baggage claim/customs area. (Unfortunately, getting through the lines at Immigration takes as long as ever.) Terminal 3 handles most, but not all, international arrivals/departures, while Terminal 2 handles most, but not all, domestic flights. Free shuttle service runs between the two terminals.

Don't immediately exchange dollars for pesos, as your hotel may well offer a better rate. Hotels will not change Mexican currency back into dollars, however, so do this at the airport exchange office when you depart (although you will be shortchanged by the rate).

A noisy crowd of sign-bearing taxi drivers and shuttle bus operators congregate outside the airport. Shuttle service via passenger van *(colectivo)* is available to Ciudad Cancún and the Hotel Zone for a fixed rate of about $10 (U.S.). These vehicles usually take a maximum of 10 passengers. They are less costly than van pickup associated with your hotel or a private taxi, either of which will cost about $35-$40 (U.S.) to the Hotel Zone, plus tip.

You can purchase a ticket for a *colectivo* or a chartered airport taxi at the taxi counter in the terminal. *Colectivos* do not provide service back to the airport, making a private taxi or hotel-associated fleet ride necessary upon departure. Cabs affiliated with the bigger hotels often charge a fixed rate for service back to the airport, which should be less than the trip from the airport.

Confirm your reservation and departure time with your airline at least 24 hours prior to departing Cancún. For international flights, arrive at least 2 hours before scheduled departure time; lines can be long, and all carry-on luggage is inspected by hand at the gate even after you've cleared security. There are numerous snack carts, fast-food restaurants and places to pick up a sandwich and beverage. The airport also has a number of shops for last-minute souvenir purchases; prices are a bit steep, but U.S.

dollars are accepted. Prices for duty-free merchandise—mostly liquor, cigars and perfume—may not be as much of a bargain as advertised, so shop carefully.

By Car

Mexico's easternmost city is located at the Yucatán Peninsula's northeastern tip. From the west, the main route is Mex. 180 via Veracruz, Villahermosa, Campeche and Mérida; it ends at Punta Sam, north of Cancún. From Villahermosa, an alternate route is Mex. 186 east to Escárcega, Camp., and then north on Mex. 281 to Champotón. It carries heavy truck traffic and has very few gas stations or mechanical services. This route should only be driven during daylight hours.

Mex. 180 is two lanes between Mérida and the small town of Hoctún. Four-lane toll *(cuota)* highway Mex. 180-D begins about 60 kilometers (37 miles) east of Mérida and roughly parallels Mex. 180 for a distance of about 240 kilometers (144 miles). All of Mex. 180-D is in very good condition, lightly traveled and quicker than Mex. 180, which passes through small towns with lots of speed bumps *(topes)*. It is, however, isolated if you happen to break down.

Kilometer markers are along the right side of the highway, and there are regular intervals, indicated by signs, to make a U-turn *(retorno)*. Signage is good (both speed limit and mileage signs and the international blue highway signs). Toll plazas are located at the Chichén Itzá exit (Pisté) and at the Yucatán/Quintana Roo state line (Xcan), which also is a customs checkpoint. For cars, motorcycles, vans and pickup campers, toll charges for the entire stretch of Mex. 180-D total about $30 U.S. There are only a few gas stations along the length of the route, so make sure your tank is always at least half full.

Mex. 180-D ends about 16 kilometers (10 miles) west of the airport; follow the sign that says "Cancún/Puerto Juárez" to stay on the mainland, or the sign "Tulum/Aeropuerto" to get to the Hotel Zone.

An access route to Cancún from the south is Mex. 307, which begins about 19 kilometers (12 miles) west of Chetumal off Mex. 186 in southern Quintana Roo and proceeds north through Bacalar and Tulum. The section of Mex. 307 from Tulum north to Cancún offers easy access to attractions and beach resorts along the Riviera Maya coast.

A highway branching northwest at Tulum offers access to the Cobá archeological zone and joins Mex. 180 at the town of Xcan—a distance of about 85 kilometers (53 miles). It saves time and mileage if you want a more direct route from Tulum to Mérida.

By Bus

The bus terminal is in downtown Ciudad Cancún at the intersection of avenidas Tulum and Uxmal, in front of the Plaza Caribe Hotel. The ADO line offers first-class service to and from various points on the Yucatán Peninsula, including Chetumal, Chichén Itzá, Mérida, Playa del Carmen, Tulum and Valladolid. Frequent first-class service is available from Mérida, with stops en route at Chichén Itzá and Valladolid. For additional information about buses *see Bus Service, page 72.*

By Cruise Ship

Cancún has no docking facilities for cruise ships. Only an occasional ship stops offshore from Playa Tortugas, at Km marker 7 on Boulevard Kukulcán; passengers are ferried to land. If you're on a ship that docks at Cozumel and want to spend some time in Cancún, you'll be tendered from Cozumel to Playa del Carmen, about a 45-minute drive south of Cancún (or check with your ship's shore excursion desk to see if they offer a Cancún package). Depending on the length of shore leave, you could squeeze in a shopping trip or a visit to one of the beaches.

Note: If a shore excursion is arranged through the cruise line the ship will wait if you aren't back at the scheduled departure time. This is not the case, however, if you arrange the excursion yourself, so keep timing in mind.

Getting Around

City Layout

The main streets in downtown Ciudad Cancún (often called "El Centro") are east-west Avenida López Portillo, the in-town section of Mex. 180, which extends from the western city limits northeast to Puerto Juárez and Punta Sam; and north-south Avenida Tulum, the in-town section of Mex. 307, which runs south toward the airport and on down the coast. Many souvenir shops and restaurants are along or near avenidas Tulum and Cobá; the latter street becomes Boulevard Kukulcán as it heads east and enters the Hotel Zone.

Ciudad Cancún is divided into districts called *super manzanas* (shortened to SM), each containing several blocks surrounding a central square or park. Driving can be daunting even if you know where you're going, however. There are numerous one-way streets and traffic circles *(glorietas)*, as well as crowds of pedestrians and unfamiliar traffic signals. For an excursion into El Centro for dinner or shopping, take a bus or taxi.

If you'd like to experience Cancún away from the touristy Hotel Zone, spend some time in Parque las Palapas. It's centrally located in downtown Ciudad Cancún—a block west of Avenida Tulum, bordered by calles Tulipanes, Gladiolas, Margaritas and Alcatraces. This is a family-oriented park where craft sellers set up their wares and food vendors offer popcorn, fried bananas and *churros* (doughnut-like snacks). There are usually outdoor art exhibits and festivals on the weekend. Live music on Friday evenings ranges from jazz to salsa, and on Sunday afternoons the Cancún Municipal Orchestra gives a free performance. Casual restaurants line Calle Tulipanes, a pedestrian alleyway, and some of the city's popular local eateries, including La Habichuela and Restaurante Labná, are within walking distance of the park.

Boulevard Kukulcán (also referred to as Paseo Kukulcán but usually just called "Kukulcán") is a four-lane divided thoroughfare running the length of narrow Cancún Island and is the Hotel Zone's only main traffic artery. It actually begins at the junction with Avenida Bonampak, on the eastern edge of Ciudad Cancún. Past Punta Nizuc (Nizuc Point), the island's southern tip, Kukulcán runs into southbound Mex. 307 at the overpass leading to the airport.

Kukulcán's four lanes divide briefly to encompass Cancún Point, the elbow of the island's "seven" configuration. Where U-turns are permitted, signs in the median say *retorno.* **Note:** The speed limit along most of Kukulcán is 40 km/h (25 mph); the limit increases to 60 km/h (37 mph) at the southern end of the island.

Numbered addresses are rarely given for places in the Hotel Zone. Kilometer markers installed in the median (from Km 1, just past the mainland, east and south to Km 25 beyond Nizuc Point) are used to designate locations. Directions also are given in reference to well-known landmarks or hotels. Because there is only one road, it's almost impossible to get lost.

Rental Cars

It's not really necessary to rent a car if you're limiting your vacation to Cancún and vicinity; bus and taxi service is frequent. But you'll need one if you plan a day or overnight trip down the coast toward Tulum or inland to the ruins of Chichén Itzá or Cobá and don't want to be part of an organized tour. The quality of most regional roads is good. Do not underestimate the amount of time it will take to arrive at your destination, however, and in general avoid driving after dark.

Rates are expensive if you rent on the spot; make reservations in advance through a U.S. 800 number to get the best deal. Arranging for pickup and drop-off at the airport will eliminate taxi fares. Make certain you fully understand the terms of any rental contract. If the car only has half a tank of gas when you pick it up, you can return it with half a tank; double check before you drive off.

Inspect the vehicle carefully inside and out, and check for the required in-car fire extinguisher. Inventory thoroughly for nicks and dents as well. Keep in mind that license plates on rental vehicles say *renta,* marking you as a visitor. It is becoming more common for major rental car agencies to provide (for an added charge) a driver; consider this option if you don't feel entirely comfortable driving in unfamiliar surroundings. **Note:** In the event of damages caused by a hurricane, all insurance claims are void.

Hertz is one of several rental car agencies available, with offices at the airport, in downtown Ciudad Cancún and on Boulevard Kukulcán in the vicinity of Cancún Point. AAA/CAA members receive discounts through Hertz for vehicles booked in the United States or Canada; phone (800) 654-3080.

Buses

Ruta 1 and *Ruta 2* buses (marked R-1, *Hoteles* or *Zona Hotelera* on the windshield) run regularly from the mainland along Boulevard Kukulcán to the southern end of the Hotel Zone (around the Km 20 marker) and back daily 24 hours (buses are more frequent from 6 a.m.-10 p.m.). The fare is inexpensive—6.5 pesos (about 65c U.S.). The *Ruta 8* bus goes to Puerto Juárez and Punta Sam for the ferries to Isla Mujeres.

You'll need Mexican currency; drivers will return change up to a 20-peso bill. There are frequent designated stops along the length of Boulevard Kukulcán (or you can tell the driver where you want to get off), and buses can be flagged from hotel driveway entrances. Using the bus is much cheaper than taking a cab, especially if you're staying at the southern end of the Hotel Zone.

Buses are likely to be crowded mornings and evenings, when mainland locals use them to get to and from work. They jolt along and can stop suddenly, so watch your footing. There also can be impromptu entertainment in the form of a guitar player who will board the bus, sing a song or two and then pass the hat for spare change.

Taxis

Taxis within the Hotel Zone are very expensive, costing $5 (U.S.) per ride, even if it's just from one hotel to the next. They also are not metered; fares are based on a zone system. Arranging for a cab directly at your hotel is convenient, but these cabs also tend to have the highest rates. Some hotels list fares to various destinations at the front entrance; if not, ask the doorman. Always confirm the rate with the driver before setting out. Better hotels will arrange "payouts," putting cab fares on the bill so they show up on your credit card receipt as a recorded expense.

Green city taxis can be hailed on the street in Ciudad Cancún. The driver should be able to provide a rate list if you ask, although it is likely to be in Spanish. If you're going from the Hotel Zone to Ciudad Cancún, Puerto Juárez or Punta Sam, take the Kukulcán bus to the mainland, then a taxi to your destination, since the city taxis have a cheaper rate structure (also based on a zone system) than the Hotel Zone taxis. A taxi also can be hired to Chichén Itzá or for a drive south along the Riviera Maya, although you'll pay a steep hourly rate for this convenience.

Ferries

Enclosed, air-conditioned passenger ferries run between Puerto Juárez, about 3 kilometers (2 miles) north of Cancún via Avenida López Portillo (Mex. 180), and Isla Mujeres. To get to the municipal dock, take the R-1 bus from the Hotel Zone into

Ciudad Cancún, then take a taxi or the R-15 bus to Puerto Juárez. The taxi fare shouldn't be more than about 20 pesos, but be prepared to haggle that rate on the return trip.

The ferry departs every half-hour daily from 6:30 a.m. to 9 p.m., then departs hourly until midnight. The final departure from Isla Mujeres back to Puerto Juárez is at 11:30 p.m. The trip takes about 30 minutes; one-way fare is 35 pesos (about $3.40 U.S.). Double-check the final departure time when you arrive at Isla Mujeres. Since this is the least expensive alternative to Isla the boat can be crowded, but passengers are counted to make sure everyone gets a seat.

A newer ferry service, UltraMar, provides the same trip from the Gran Puerto dock, a short distance away on Avenida López Portillo. These ferries also depart every half-hour daily; the trip takes about 15-20 minutes. Always double check the final departure time back to Cancún when you arrive. Round-trip fare (including tax) is about $6.50 (U.S.). **Note:** The ride on the smaller ferries can be choppy even in good weather, so it's a good idea to take the proper precautions if you're prone to seasickness.

There are three Hotel Zone departure points that are closer but more expensive than the Puerto Juárez ferries. The *Mexicano,* an open-air boat, departs from the El Embarcadero dock, Km marker 4 on Boulevard Kukulcán, daily at 9:30 and 11:30, returning from the main pier at Isla Mujeres at 3:30 and 5:30; the trip takes about 45 minutes. Additional departures vary seasonally.

Boats also depart from the dock at Playa Tortugas, Km marker 6 on Boulevard Kukulcán (next to Fat Tuesday's restaurant), and from the Club Nautico dock, at Km 8.5 across from the Plaza Caracol mall. The boat departs from Playa Tortugas daily every 60 to 90 minutes from 8:30 to 4:15; it returns from Isla Mujeres approximately every 90 minutes 10:15-6:15. Boats depart from the Club Nautico dock daily at 9, 11 and 1, returning from Isla at noon and 5. The round-trip fare for each is about $15 (U.S.).

The car ferry from Punta Sam, abut 5 kilometers (3 miles) north of Puerto Juárez, departs for Isla Mujeres five times daily. The first departure is at 8 a.m.; the last departure is at 8:15 p.m. The first departure from Isla Mujeres back to Punta Sam is at 6:30 a.m.; the last departure is at 7:15 p.m. The trip takes about an hour. Double check the schedule at the dock ticket booth, as bad weather can affect departure times.

The fare for a car is 185 pesos (about $18 U.S.) and includes the driver; each additional passenger pays 14 pesos. Plan on arriving at least 1 hour before departure, and purchase your ticket before boarding. Isla Mujeres is so small, however, that there's no reason to bring a car for a day visit. For additional information about ferry schedules, *see "Sightseeing," page 99.*

Parking

There are very few municipal parking lots in Ciudad Cancún or the Hotel Zone. Park on city streets at your own discretion. If you've rented a car or are driving your own vehicle, keep it in the hotel lot—most of them are guarded—and use buses or cabs for local excursions.

Guides/Tours

The most popular day excursions from Cancún are to Xcaret, Xel-Ha and Tulum, all south along the Caribbean coast. Guided tours to Chichén Itzá, Cobá and Uxmal also are available. The Xcaret building next to the Fiesta Americana Grand Coral Beach in the Hotel Zone is a convenient place to arrange a trip and purchase tickets. There also are numerous in-town tour operators, and many hotels have a travel agency on site or a concierge who can help with tour arrangements.

Gray Line Cancún, Km 3.5 on Boulevard Kukulcán (in Plaza Nautilus), offers motorcoach tours to various regional points of interest; including Chichén Itzá, Cozumel, Isla Mujeres, Playa del Carmen, Xcaret and Xel-Ha; phone (998) 849-4545 or 01 (800) 800-0952 (toll-free long distance within Mexico).

What To See

AQUA WORLD is at Km 15.2 on the lagoon side of Blvd. Kukulcán. In addition to organizing deep-sea fishing trips and diving and snorkeling excursions, Aqua World rents equipment for windsurfing, jet skiing and wave running. The *Sub See Explorer,* an air-conditioned, glass-bottomed boat, cruises from Nichupté Lagoon past Caribbean coral reefs to man-made Paradise Island for lunch and snorkeling. The Skyrider offers both ocean and lagoon-side parasail "flights" high above Cancún Island.

Scuba diving instruction is available. Arrange cruise excursions or fishing trips in advance. Aqua World sales kiosks are located at most major hotels. Daily 6:30 a.m.-9:30 p.m. Fees for activities, cruises and equipment rentals vary. AX, MC, VI. Phone (998) 848-8327.

CANCUN ARCHEOLOGICAL MUSEUM (Museo Arqueológico de Cancún) is to the right of the main entrance in the Cancún Center, Km marker 9 on Blvd. Kukulcán. It exhibits a collection of pre-Hispanic artifacts gathered from various Quintana Roo archeological sites. Guided tours are available. Tues.-Sun. 9-7. Admission about $3.50 (U.S.); free to all Sun. and holidays. Phone (998) 883-0305.

EL EMBARCADERO is at Blvd. Kukulcán Km marker 4. This municipal dock is a base for several tourist-oriented activities. It's a convenient departure point for the boat trip to Isla Mujeres, especially if you're staying in the Hotel Zone and don't want to take the bus into Ciudad Cancún, then a taxi to get to the ferry dock at Puerto Juárez.

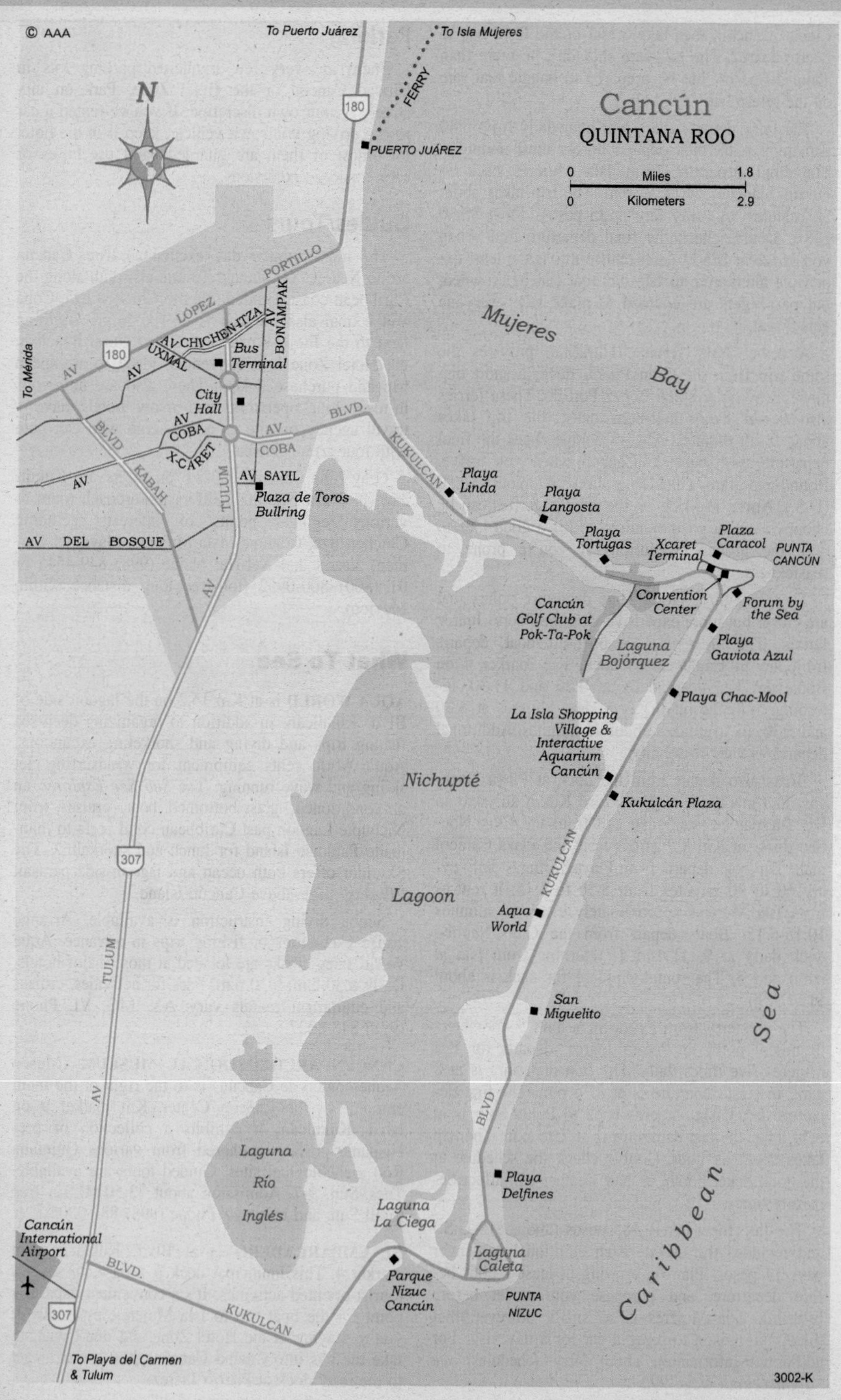
© AAA
To Puerto Juárez
To Isla Mujeres
FERRY
180
PUERTO JUÁREZ
N
Cancún
QUINTANA ROO
0 Miles 1.8
0 Kilometers 2.9
PORTILLO
LÓPEZ
AV BONAMPAK
AV CHICHEN-ITZA
UXMAL
Bus Terminal
To Mérida
180
AV
AV
City Hall
BLVD
AV COBA
AV COBA
X-CARET
KABAH
AV
TULUM
AV SAYIL
Plaza de Toros Bullring
AV DEL BOSQUE
AV
BLVD
KUKULCAN
Mujeres
Bay
Playa Linda
Playa Langosta
Playa Tortugas
Xcaret Terminal
Plaza Caracol
PUNTA CANCÚN
Convention Center
Forum by the Sea
Cancún Golf Club at Pok-Ta-Pok
Laguna Bojórquez
Playa Gaviota Azul
Playa Chac-Mool
La Isla Shopping Village & Interactive Aquarium Cancún
Nichupté
Kukulcán Plaza
KUKULCAN
307
Lagoon
Aqua World
TULUM
San Miguelito
Sea
AV
BLVD
Laguna Río Inglés
Playa Delfines
Caribbean
Laguna La Ciega
Cancún International Airport
Laguna Caleta
BLVD.
Parque Nizuc Cancún
PUNTA NIZUC
307
KUKULCAN
To Playa del Carmen & Tulum
3002-K

The Captain Hook dinner cruise includes a lobster or steak dinner aboard twin galleons that are "attacked" by pirates. The boats light up after the sun sets, with music and dancing under the stars. The Breathing Observation Bubble (BOB) is a submersible, scooter-like ride tethered to a boat and lowered 25 feet into the water, with a plastic bubble around the rider's head supplying oxygen. Excursions are subject to weather conditions; participants must be at least 12 years of age.

Food is available. Isla Mujeres boat rides depart daily at 9:30 and 11:30, returning from the main pier at Isla Mujeres at 3:30 and 5:30; the trip takes about 45 minutes. Additional departures vary seasonally. Captain Hook dinner cruise departs daily (except Jan. 1 and Dec. 25) at 7 p.m. and returns at 10:30 p.m.; hotel pickup and drop-off is not included. Breathing Observation Bubble rides daily at 9, 11:30 and 2 (also 4:30 in summer). Round-trip boat fare 170 pesos (about $16.50 U.S.); credit cards are not accepted. Captain Hook dinner cruise about $78 (U.S.) per person. Breathing Observation Bubble rides $75. MC, VI. Phone (998) 849-4451 for dinner cruise reservations or (998) 849-4440 for Breathing Observation Bubble reservations.

EL REY RUINS (Ruinas El Rey) are on the lagoon side of Blvd. Kukulcán at Km marker 17, a short distance past the Hilton Cancún Golf & Spa Resort (watch for the sign); take the stairway down to the entrance. The site, which is reached via a short trail, consists of a few temple platforms that once supported roofs. Although much smaller than the Yucatán's well-known archeological sites, El Rey is a nice, quiet change of pace from Cancún's malls and rowdy nightspots. The chief attraction here is not the ruins but the many iguanas that sun themselves on the rocks. Fed by park guards, they're used to people and will come running for bread, crackers or tortillas.

Restrooms are on site. Wear a hat and sunscreen and bring water. Open daily 8-5. Admission 35 pesos (about $3.40 U.S.).

INTERACTIVE AQUARIUM CANCUN is on the lagoon side of Blvd. Kukulcán at Km 12.5, in La Isla Shopping Village. Here you can swim with dolphins or feed sharks in a special underwater cage. Touch exhibits allow visitors to observe rays, starfish and other marine animals up close, and all guests can feed stingrays and young nurse sharks or have their picture taken with a macaw. Trained dolphins perform daily at 5 p.m.

Food is available. Daily 10-9. Admission $13 (U.S.); $9 (ages 3-10). Dolphin swim $125 per person, shark tank feeding $65 per person (includes aquarium admission). Advance reservations are recommended. Parking fee $2. AX, CB, DC, DS, MC, VI. Phone (998) 883-0411 or 01 (800) 012-0856 (toll-free long distance within Mexico).

NICHUPTE LAGOON lies between the Hotel Zone and the mainland. It contains a combination of fresh and salt water. A few small islands are within the lagoon, and peninsulas punctuate the shoreline. Two smaller lagoons are connected to Nichupté by narrow waterways: Laguna Bojórquez, at the northeastern end, and Laguna Río Inglés, at the southwestern end. Nichupté is home to many different bird species. Swaths of dead mangroves are about the only remaining visual evidence in Cancún of Hurricane Wilma's wrath.

PLAZA DE TOROS BULLRING is at the intersection of avs. Bonampak and Sayil in Ciudad Cancún; buses from the Hotel Zone drop visitors off about 3 blks. away at Blvd. Kukulcán and Av. Bonampak, but pick them up in front of the bullring when returning to the Hotel Zone. Unlike most Mexican bullrings, which have shaded and unshaded sections, this one is entirely covered.

Prior to the main event, volunteers from the crowd take part in mock match-ups with smaller but still dangerous bulls (a doctor and ambulance are present just in case). After these participant games professional matadors take over. **Note:** The bull is traditionally killed during these performances, and anyone upset by blood or the inherent cruelty of the spectacle should not attend.

Vendors at the bullring hawk beverages and snacks. Allow 3 hours minimum. Bullfights take place Wed. afternoon at 3:30. Tickets can be obtained at the bullring or from local travel agencies and cost about $35 (U.S.).

SIAN KA'AN BIOSPHERE RESERVE—*see Tulum p. 148.*

TULUM RUINS—*see Tulum p. 147.*

XCARET—*see Playa del Carmen p. 143.*

XEL-HA—*see Tulum p. 149.*

WET 'N WILD (Parque Nizuc Waterpark) is at the southern end of Blvd. Kukulcán and the Hotel Zone at Km marker 25. Owned by Palace Resorts, it has thrill waterslides like Kamikaze, Twister and the Double Space Bowl, a lifeguard-supervised children's play area and the Lazy River for inner tube floating. You also can interact with dolphins and sea lions as part of a program run by the animal research center Atlantida.

Food is available. Daily 10-5:30. Admission $49 (U.S.); $24.50 (ages 5-11). Reduced rates apply to guests staying at Palace Resorts properties. Dolphin swim $125 (includes park admission). Lockers, towels and inner tubes can be rented. AX, MC, VI. Phone (998) 881-3030.

What To Do

Dining

Hotel restaurants offer the gamut of casual and fine dining choices, with uniformly reliable quality and predictable expense. Most hotels go to great lengths to keep their guests on the premises, and some may charge for meals whether they are eaten or not. Dress is usually casual but not unkempt (no shorts or T-shirts). Don't expect much in the way of regional cookery in the Hotel Zone; U.S. fast-food and chain restaurant franchises, as well as Mexican chains like Sr. Frog's, are the norm.

Ciudad Cancún is a different story. Avenida Tulum is lined with restaurants, and most have outdoor tables. Look for places where locals congregate if you want authentically prepared Yucatecan dishes like *sopa de lima*—soup with a chicken broth base, vegetables and a tangy dose of fresh lime juice—or *poc-chuc,* spicy marinated pork grilled with onions.

One local favorite—and a place where you can sample home-style cooking for a fraction of the cost of the Hotel Zone restaurants—is Checándole, Av. Xpuhil #6 (SM 18). It serves tacos, steak *tampiqueña* and other Mexican standards, along with fresh fruit juices. A three-course lunch is about $3 (U.S.). The easiest way to get there from the Hotel Zone is to take a bus downtown, then a taxi to the restaurant. There also are branches on Mex. 307 at Km 13.5, just before the airport exit, and in the Plaza Flamingo food court.

For a reasonably priced Mexican-style breakfast try one of Cancún's coffee shops. At Vips, a popular chain with branches all over the country, you can order standards like *huevos motuleños*—two fried eggs, peas and diced ham atop a crispy tortilla covered in tomato sauce, with pureed black beans and slices of fried banana on the side. This, plus toast, orange juice and good *cafe americano,* will fill you up for about $10. The Hotel Zone Vips is next to the Cancún Center.

Restaurants in the large hotels use purified water for cooking and for washing produce; inquire about this health procedure specifically at places on the mainland. In general, avoid ice cubes in drinks unless you know purified water has been used. *For a list of AAA-RATED dining establishments in Cancún, see the Lodgings & Restaurants section.*

Shopping

Shopping in Cancún's Hotel Zone usually focuses on two things: pricey specialty items, or T-shirts and beach supplies. Window-shopping is a popular pastime, but don't expect a lot of bargains. For garden-variety souvenirs it pays to look around, as merchants compete vigorously for tourist dollars and prices can be on the steep side. Inspect carefully before buying; quality can vary greatly.

As a duty-free zone Cancún does offer potential bargains on international merchandise. High-quality tequila and cigars are two of the most popular purchases. Ultra Femme, downtown on Avenida Tulum, has good buys on cosmetics, jewelry and imported perfume; there also are branches in several of the Hotel Zone malls and at the airport.

In Ciudad Cancún, a variety of shops and open-air craft markets line Avenida Tulum. Ki-Huic, near the intersection with Avenida Cobá, is a flea market a block long with more than 100 vendors offering handicrafts, knickknacks, marble chess sets, men's *guayabera* shirts, *huipil* (ee-PEEL) dresses and Panama hats. Another downtown crafts market is Mercado Plaza, at the corner of avenidas Tulum and Uxmal. Bargaining is expected at the markets; never offer to pay the initial asking price.

If you feel the need to shop for basics, branches of three familiar stateside retailers also are in Ciudad Cancún: Costco (Price Club), at the corner of avenidas Kabah and Yaxchilán; Sam's Club, at the corner of avenidas Xcaret and Yaxchilán; and Wal-Mart, at the corner of avenidas Kukulcán and Mayapán. Pick up convenience items at an Oxxo store (similar to 7-11); there are several branches in the Hotel Zone.

The Hotel Zone has both enclosed, air-conditioned malls and open-air complexes. Elegant Plaza Caracol is at Km 8.5 next to the Cancún Center. Cool marble walls and floors are the setting for some 200 shops and boutiques offering jewelry, designer clothing, resort wear, silver and decorative art. You'll also find pharmacies, art galleries, cafes and restaurants here.

Forum-by-the-Sea, Km 9.5 near the Cancún Center, is a three-level entertainment complex. There are specialty boutiques like Swatch and Tommy Hilfiger, but the emphasis is on restaurants, bars and nightspots, which include the Cancún branch of the Hard Rock Café. Flamingo Plaza, Km 11.5 on Kukulcán (lagoon side), is a smaller shopping center with several duty-free stores and boutiques, as well as a currency exchange office and restaurants like Jimmy Buffett's Margaritaville. It also has a branch of the Mexican chain Sanborn's that is open 24 hours and has a pharmacy and newsstand.

Cancún's hottest mall is La Isla Shopping Village, Km 12.5 on Kukulcán (lagoon side). La Isla is as bright and shiny as anything you'll find in the states. The stores and shops are linked by crisscrossing bridges and walkways running over small canals. Johnny Rockets and Chili's are two of the several familiar stateside eateries here. There also is a 10-screen multiplex, the Interactive Aquarium Cancún *(see attraction listing)* and other family-friendly features. It's upscale and expensive but a fun place to spend a few hours, especially on a rainy day.

At Km marker 13 is one of the largest malls, Kukulcán Plaza, which also caters to tourists with stores and boutiques offering gifts, handicrafts, perfume, leather goods, jewelry and silver. It also contains a parking garage, bank, currency exchange offices, drugstores, a kiosk providing Internet access and a food court with a number of U.S. fast-food franchises. The mall's "Luxury Avenue" features such high-end retailers as Baccarat, Cartier, Louis Vuitton and Tiffany & Co.

If you enjoy the bargaining experience, browse the many craft stalls at the Mercado de Artesanías Coral Negro (Flea Market), a peach-colored building just south of the Cancún Center (at the point where

Blvd. Kukulcán splits). The selection of items is large, and it's open daily.

Most of the mall stores are open daily 10-8 or 10 p.m. Outside the Hotel Zone some stores observe the traditional *siesta* and close for a few hours in the afternoon. The sales tax is 10 percent, which may be waived at some shops if you pay in cash. Paying with cash instead of a credit card may also lower the price when bargaining with vendors. Almost all stores will accept U.S. dollars, and at some establishments prices are quoted in dollars rather than pesos.

Beaches

Hurricane Wilma decimated Cancún's spectacular beaches, but by mid-2006 they had been restored. The beaches along the Caribbean were literally replaced; sand was dredged from the bottom 20 miles offshore and dumped on top of areas where the storm's fury had completely washed it away. The new beaches are thus artificial, but that makes little difference to visitors. The white sand is soft and fine grained, and the water—which is warm enough for swimming all year—provides a gorgeous counterpoint, its ever-shifting hues ranging from opalescent green to vivid turquoise. The beaches at the northern end of the Hotel Zone, which front Mujeres Bay (Bahía Mujeres), are narrow and have calm, shallow water. The beaches along the Caribbean are wider and more dramatic, with occasional crashing breakers and dangerous undertows.

The best beaches are in front of the big hotels. All beaches in Mexico, however, are federally owned and therefore public, even stretches that may seem like they are on hotel property. Keep in mind that you cannot use hotel facilities unless you are a guest, although changing areas and outdoor showers are available. Note the flags posted to indicate surf conditions. White or green flags indicate safe conditions for swimming; yellow indicates caution; and red or black, dangerous conditions.

The "inner" coast of Cancún Island borders saltwater Nichupté Lagoon. Much of the lagoon is lined with stands of mangrove. Wilma killed many of the trees, but they are starting to grow back, with patches of green showing up amid the dead wood. Nichupté doesn't have the Caribbean's beauty, but the calm water is ideal for boating and water skiing, and the restaurants along the shore are popular places for sunset watching.

The following designated public beaches are described in the order they appear along Cancún Island, beginning at the top of the island's "seven" configuration after leaving the mainland. *See map page 96.*

PLAYA LINDA is just before the bridge over Canal Nichupté, at Km marker 4. Boat tours to Isla Mujeres embark from the Playa Linda pier, and there are snack and dive equipment shops in the vicinity.

PLAYA LANGOSTA is next to the Casa Maya Hotel at Km marker 5. The beach is close to several yacht clubs, water sports facilities and restaurants. Tour boats leave from the dock here.

PLAYA TORTUGAS is near the Intercontinental Presidente Cancún at Km marker 6. Frequented by locals, the beach faces the calm waters of Mujeres Bay.

PLAYA CARACOL is close to the Fiesta Americana Grand Coral Beach. Farther east is Cancún Point, the crook of the Cancún elbow. The very tip of the point, behind the Camino Real hotel, is where Mujeres Bay meets the open Caribbean. Isla Mujeres is visible in the distance. Waves crash against the rocks and send up plumes of spray on the Caribbean side, while just around the point the water is calm, shallow and translucent.

PLAYA CHAC-MOOL is at Km 9.5. This popular stretch is conveniently located and washed by the Caribbean surf, but also is subject to large waves and strong undertows.

PLAYA DELFINES is at Km marker 18 toward the southern end of the Hotel Zone. It offers some nice views, although swimming can be hazardous due to the rough surf conditions.

Sightseeing

People come to Cancún not to sightsee but to sun, swim, eat, party and relax. One fun—and free—diversion is to go hotel hopping. The Hotel Zone is chock-full full of architecturally striking resorts, and even if you're staying at one it's worth checking out some of the others (consider it research for your next vacation). The public "Hoteles" buses that travel the length of Boulevard Kukulcán *(see "Buses" under Getting Around)* are the best way to get from one property to another, as they stop frequently and will let you off right at the hotel entrance (keep in mind, however, that you must pay bus fare each time you reboard).

Cancún's resorts are state-of-the-art examples of imaginative design, with lavish public areas and swimming pool complexes looking out onto the Caribbean's aquamarine waters. It doesn't cost anything to tour a property, and you can take your pick of restaurants and lounges to indulge in a leisurely lunch or a relaxing pit stop. **Note:** While you can enter most of the hotels if you're not a paying guest, many of the all-inclusive resorts, such as the Cancún Palace and the Hotel RIU Cancún, do not allow non-guests to walk around their public areas.

Which ones should you see? The Fiesta Americana Grand Coral Beach has a spacious, high-ceilinged lobby that radiates understated luxury—marble floors, giant flower arrangements and fine art displayed in recessed wall nooks, with cozy sitting areas scattered about. The ME by Meliá is hip and contemporary; its public areas have funky artwork, sleek furniture and fountains with sheets of water flowing over cool black marble slabs. The postmodern vibe extends to the pool complex, where there is an infinity pool—so named for the visual effect of water appearing to extend to the horizon and merge seamlessly with the sea.

The Gran Meliá Cancún Beach & Spa Resort is one of the largest properties in the Hotel Zone, with the guest rooms housed in five soaring, pyramid-shaped buildings. The public areas here are towering and jungle-like, festooned with hanging plants, dripping with water and incorporating decorative elements—including oversized statues, frescos and calendars—that reflect Mayan motifs and culture. The very large lobby at the Fiesta Americana Condesa Cancún is shaded by a colossal *palapa.* Soaring five stories, the thatched roof provides a rustic contrast to the lobby's extravagant decoration. "Expansive" best describes the Hilton Cancún Golf & Spa Resort, a dramatic pyramidal building with an enormous lobby and a series of interconnected pools that end up looking out on a spectacular stretch of beach.

Cancún is not a cruise ship stop, but that doesn't mean you can't take a cruise. Boats ply Nichupté Lagoon and the waters around Cancún Island, Cozumel and Isla Mujeres. Prices range from about $50-$70 (U.S.) per person, including beverages and entertainment. Boat operators and itineraries change, so check with your hotel or a local travel agency to see what's available.

Aqua World's paddlewheeler the *Cancún Queen* cruises along the shores of Nichupté Lagoon. The excursion includes a gourmet dinner followed by dancing to live band music on the top deck. The boat departs Wednesdays and Fridays at 6 p.m. from the Aqua World marina at Km 15.2 on Boulevard Kukulcán. For reservation information phone (998) 848-8327.

The 300-person capacity *Dolphin Express* cruiser travels to Isla Mujeres; activities include shopping, snorkeling and dolphin observation. Cruises depart daily at 10 a.m. from the Playa Langosta Dock, next to the Casa Maya Hotel at Km marker 5 on Boulevard Kukulcán, and return at 4:30.

If you would rather explore Isla Mujeres on your own take the Magaña Express, a commercial passenger ferry that leaves from the public dock at Puerto Juárez, about 3 kilometers (2 miles) north of downtown Ciudad Cancún via Avenida López Portillo (Mex. 180). There are daily half-hourly departures in each direction. The enclosed, air-conditioned boat has bench seats, holds about 30 passengers and docks at the main pier at the northern end of the island; the trip takes about 30 minutes. The final departure from Isla back to Puerto Juárez is normally 11:30 p.m., but double-check at the dock to make sure. One-way fare is 35 pesos (about $3.40 U.S.) and is collected after you board.

UltraMar passenger ferry service departs from the nearby Gran Puerto dock. Round-trip fare (including tax) is about $6.50 (U.S.); purchase your ticket at the dock booth before boarding. The trip takes about 15-20 minutes. These ferries have individual seats instead of benches. There are daily half-hour departures in each direction; double-check the final departure back to Gran Puerto if you intend to make an evening of it. Facilities at this dock include clean restrooms, a coffee shop, a convenience store and a couple of fast-food outlets. Waiting in line is a possibility during the high tourist season, so checking on crowds at both docks could save you time.

Besides the various package excursions that include snorkeling, lunch, shopping trips and visits to such attractions as Garrafón, there are three Hotel Zone departure points for boats to Isla: the El Embarcadero dock at Km 4.5 on Boulevard Kukulcán; the dock at Playa Tortugas, Km marker 6 on Kukulcán; and the Club Nautico dock, Km 8.5 on Kukulcán (across from Plaza Caracol). Departures are daily; always double-check the final departure from the Isla Mujeres pier if you don't intend to spend the night. Round-trip fares average about $15 (U.S.).

Note: Although Isla Mujeres is just 4 miles off the mainland and the boat ride is a lovely trip in stunningly turquoise water, the small boats can encounter choppy water conditions even on fair weather days. Those prone to seasickness may want to take something to calm their stomach before the trip.

A few miles north of Puerto Juárez is Punta Sam, from which a car/passenger ferry departs for Isla Mujeres several times daily (weather permitting). Because Isla Mujeres is so small, however, a car isn't necessary for routine day trips or an afternoon at the beach. Passengers not transporting a vehicle can use the Punta Sam ferry as well.

There are significantly more sightseeing options if you consider broadening your base outside Cancún. Extending south from Cancún is the Riviera Maya, a stretch of Caribbean coastline sprinkled with scenic beaches and protected by a series of offshore coral reefs. Mex. 307 traverses the length of this corridor, offering easy access to a mushrooming number of all-inclusive vacation resorts and nature-oriented attractions. While organized tours target such established tourist draws as Xcaret, Xel-Ha and the Tulum ruins, driving offers greater flexibility and the opportunity to see secluded spots the tour buses don't visit.

Note: Mex. 307 as far south as Playa del Carmen is a four-lane divided highway in good condition. Speed bumps appear frequently in Mexico, and on this highway they are installed before traffic lights at intersections; road signs denote their presence. Speed limits are enforced and vary from 70 km/h (about 45 mph) to 100 km/h (about 65 mph), but along most stretches the limit is 80 km/h (about 50 mph), dropping to 40 km/h (about 25 mph) per hour when approaching Puerto Morelos, Playa del Carmen and Tulum.

International green road signs with picture symbols denote towns, points of interest, gas stations, resort hotels, etc. Pemex gas stations are along the highway at the Puerto Morelos and Playa del Carmen turn-offs; gas can be paid for with pesos or dollars. Most points of interest are just a kilometer or so east or west of Mex. 307 via paved, dirt or rutted roads; they are denoted by crude signs as well as prominent billboards. Mileage signs are posted in kilometers, and kilometer markers are installed along the right-hand side of the highway. Drive defensively, as many motorists, especially locals, tend to drive too fast for conditions. Avoid driving after dark.

From Cancún it takes about an hour and a half to reach Tulum. From Ciudad Cancún, take Avenida Tulum (which becomes Mex. 307) south. From the Hotel Zone, take Boulevard Kukulcán south toward the airport. After rounding Nizuc Point (Punta Nizuc), the southern tip of the island, Kukulcán curves west toward Mex. 307. Continue to the highway interchange and follow the signs for Playa del Carmen and Tulum.

The thick jungle that once blanketed this coastal region is largely gone; the flat terrain and open scrubland isn't unlike rural southern Florida in appearance. Although the highway offers no glimpses of the Caribbean, the coastline is only a mile or two to your left. Roadside establishments along Mex. 307 offer hammocks, blankets and crafts for sale.

The main turn-off for Puerto Morelos (an intersection with a traffic signal) is about 36 kilometers (22 miles) south of Cancún's Hotel Zone. This laidback village *(see separate listing within this region)* has a delightful setting—beaches backed by coconut palms, fishing boats, a municipal dock and the turquoise hues of the Caribbean. The snorkeling and diving is excellent due to a protected coral reef less than 2,000 feet offshore. For a perfect afternoon, stroll along the sandy beach in the center of town and then grab a bite to eat at one of the casual restaurants on the main square *(zócalo).*

The turn-off for Punta Beté, about 58 kilometers (36 miles) south of Cancún, is signed "Punta Beté/ Xcalacoco"; the bumpy dirt road leads to a rocky beach where inexpensive cabana-type lodgings and residential dwellings are sprouting up. Despite development, the atmosphere here remains serene.

There are two main roads into Playa del Carmen *(see separate listing within this region),* about 68 kilometers (42 miles) south of Cancún. Either the first or second turn-offs (Avenida Constituyentes and Avenida Juárez, respectively) will take you to downtown Playa; Avenida Juárez goes straight to the main plaza. Both intersections have a traffic signal; stay in the inside lanes to turn left or you'll have to proceed south to the turnaround and double back.

This is the Riviera Maya's largest city, with a full quotient of glitzy resorts and a hopping nightlife. But in spite of Playa's rapid growth it remains a small town at heart. In contrast to downtown's bustle the pace along pedestrian-only 5th Avenue (Quinta Avenida), which runs a block off the beach, is leisurely. You can lunch al fresco, browse block after block of craft stalls or just relax on a bench at the palm-shaded plaza *(zócalo),* with its lovely view of the Caribbean.

South of Playa del Carmen Mex. 307 continues as a four-lane divided highway for another dozen or so miles before alternating between two- and three-lane stretches (with the third lane used as a passing lane by both southbound and northbound vehicles). Be careful when passing, as drivers in the oncoming lane may cross over the center line unexpectedly. Also use caution when making left turns; turn lanes are marked by reflectors on the road.

The turn-off for Xcaret *(see attraction listing under Playa del Carmen)* is about 72 kilometers (45 miles) south of Cancún. Once nothing but a peaceful cove, Xcaret has grown over the years to become a big aquatic theme park, albeit one that puts an emphasis on the preservation of Mayan heritage and the Yucatán Peninsula's natural resources. One of the highlights here is an underground river that flows through a series of caves to the beach; swimmers float along with the current.

The most popular day trip in the Mexican Caribbean is an organized bus excursion to Xcaret, which departs from a number of hotels in Cancún, Playa del Carmen and elsewhere along the Riviera Maya coast. This is the most convenient way to visit the park if you don't have a rental car.

Tour packages include round-trip transportation and park admission. Pickups are daily between 8 and 10 a.m.; check with your hotel regarding schedule and ticket purchase. From Cancún hotels the cost is $116 (U.S.); $58 (children 40 to 55 inches tall). From Playa del Carmen and Riviera Maya hotels the cost is $99; $49.50 (children 40 to 55 inches tall). For reservation information phone 01 (800) 292-2738 (toll-free long distance within Mexico). For additional information contact the Xcaret information center in Cancún, phone (998) 883-0470; in Playa del Carmen, phone (984) 803-1298.

Ten kilometers (6 miles) beyond Xcaret, just north of Puerto Aventuras, is the signed turn-off for Paamul (paul-MOOL), a sheltered cove with a rocky beach. This beach is popular with RV owners. You can swim here when seas are calm, and the snorkeling is good due to the nearby presence of the offshore coral reef. The beach is sandier and less rocky at the south end.

The turn-off for Puerto Aventuras *(see attraction listing under Playa del Carmen)* is about 85 kilometers (53 miles) south of Cancún. This planned resort community also is a sport fishing center and has the only marina along the Riviera Maya coast. The marina is surrounded by shops and casual open-air restaurants. Much of the beachfront here is occupied by resort properties; the main beach area is along Fatima Bay between the Chac Hal condominium development and the Grand Peninsula hotel.

A few kilometers south of Puerto Aventuras are several turn-offs for Xpu-Ha (take the one signed "La Playa" for public access to the beach). This stretch of powdery white sand reflects the ongoing balancing act between preserving and developing the Quintana Roo coast's abundant natural beauty.

Xpu-Ha was once nothing but deserted shoreline edging a lagoon. The Palace chain of all-inclusive resorts bought the land and created an eco park that was soon dismantled in favor of three resort properties. The beach remains lovely, however—it is cleaned and raked of seaweed—and, like all beaches in Mexico, is open to the public (although beach chairs, *palapas* and other amenities are reserved for hotel guests). The beach is nicest toward the north end (in front of the Xpu-Ha Palace and Copacabana hotels), and there are several casual restaurants and bars.

South of Xpu-Ha and about 105 kilometers (65 miles) south of Cancún is the turn-off for Akumal *(see separate listing within this region)*. To the right is the tiny Mayan *pueblo* (community) of Akumal, which consists of one main thoroughfare with a couple of small businesses and a few side streets.

Getting to the Akumal Bay resort area is a bit tricky. If heading southbound on Mex. 307, you'll encounter a concrete center median barrier at the Akumal turn-off that prevents vehicles from making a left turn onto the access road. Continue a hundred yards or so beyond the turn-off to the signed turn-around *(retorno)*; make a U-turn here, head back north and turn right at the access road junction. Less than half a mile down the road you'll drive under a white arch. Stay to the left to get to the Akumal beach parking lot. Past the parking lot, continue on a dirt road to reach Half Moon Bay. A short distance beyond Half Moon is Yal-ku Lagoon *(see attraction listing under Akumal)*; calm water makes this protected inlet a good snorkeling spot.

South of Akumal Mex. 307 reverts back to a two-lane road, although this will likely change in the future as the highway continues to be widened all the way down to Tulum and beyond. Unless traffic is light, the safest thing to do when making a left turn is to pull off the road to your right, put on your left blinker or emergency flashers and wait until it is clear in both directions; do not stop in the middle of the road.

A few kilometers south of Akumal is the signed turn-off for Xcacel *(see attraction listing under Tulum)*, a lovely white-sand beach on a crescent-shaped bay with calm, clear water. The area is an important nesting site for Atlantic green and loggerhead turtles, both on the endangered species list, and efforts are ongoing to ensure their preservation. At the south end of the beach is a path that leads through the jungle to a small cenote. The area is a nature preserve, and boating, sport fishing and overnight camping are prohibited.

About 122 kilometers (76 miles) south of Cancún is the well-marked turn-off to Xel-Ha *(see attraction listing under Tulum)*, an ecologically oriented park centered around a large lagoon. Xel-Ha (shell-HAH) is a breeding ground for parrotfish and other tropical fish species. It's an ideal spot for kids and novice snorkelers. Tour buses regularly pack the parking lot, so try to get there early. On the west side of the highway and close to the park entrance is a group of restored Mayan ruins.

A few kilometers beyond Xel-Ha is the signed turn-off for Soliman. The unpaved road heads toward the beach and arrives at a "T" intersection. To the left is the northern half of Soliman Bay; to the right, the southern half. The halves are separated by a headland. The white-sand, palm-backed beach along the northern section of Soliman, unlike some areas of the Riviera Maya, has remained primarily undeveloped. However, ground was recently broken for condo and home development, and beach access is problematic.

Note: While all Mexico beaches are indeed public, you may not use private property to access them. As the Riviera Maya coast continues to build up, more and more beaches that were once wide open are now becoming part of planned developments.

The southern section of Soliman has long been lined with private beachfront homes and small bed-and-breakfast inns. The latter are a nice lodging alternative for travelers leery of massive all-inclusive resorts. Protected by the outer reef break, the water at Soliman is tranquil—perfect for snorkeling and kayaking. The beach is narrow but lovely, and swimming is good when the sea is calm. Keep in mind that Soliman and other natural beaches along the Quintana Roo coast can have rocky, silt-laden or grassy bottoms; foot protection is recommended when going in the water.

Just south of Soliman is the turn-off for Tankah. The unpaved access road is marked by a highway sign that reads "Casa Cenote-Tankah Tres." There's more good snorkeling and kayaking in this bay due to the sheltering effect of the offshore coral reef. The bay is lined with private homes and small inns. Beach width varies from wide to narrow, but the white sand is fine-grained. Manatee Cenote, behind the Casa Cenote restaurant on the beach, is a good snorkeling spot. Actual manatees used to be seen swimming in the cenote, but there hasn't been a sighting in years.

One look at the ruins of Tulum *(see attraction listing under Tulum),* about 131 kilometers (81 miles) south of Cancún (the turn-off to the ruins is prominently signed), and it's easy to see why the Maya chose this site: This is the only place on the low-lying Yucatán Peninsula where limestone deposits built up to form coastal cliffs. The most distinctive feature of these fortresslike ruins is their location overlooking the turquoise Caribbean. Visitors to the site can hike to the beach below and enjoy a swim in the sea. Tulum is a popular day trip from Cancún, often combined with a stop at Xel-Ha.

The town of Tulum is a growing *pueblo* where many of the residents work at nearby resort properties. Mex. 307 is the main thoroughfare, lined with souvenir shops, open-air restaurants, fruit markets and local businesses (everything from muffler repair shops to Internet cafes). A gazebo stands in the middle of Tulum's small, palm-shaded plaza, just east of Mex. 307 behind the City Hall (Ayuntamiento) building/police headquarters. Kids play basketball during the day and families gather at the park in the cool of the evening, when vendors sell snacks from pushcarts.

Past the town of Tulum Mex. 307 angles southwest into the scrubby flatlands of interior Quintana Roo. Hugging the coast directly to the south is the 1.3-million-acre Sian Ka'an Biosphere Reserve *(see attraction listing under Tulum).* This vast tract of jungle, honeycombed with cenotes (freshwater sinkholes), is a haven for numerous kinds of wildlife, including some endangered species.

At the northern end of town Mex. 307 intersects with a paved road that runs northwest to the ruins of Cobá. Take this road east (the sign at the intersection says "Playas/Punta Allen") if you want to visit the beaches and Tulum's hotel zone. The road passes through open scrubland for about 5 kilometers (3 miles) before reaching the Hotel Posada del Sol, where there also are several restaurants, a currency exchange office, a grocery store and a couple of mini-markets.

This is the beginning of the hotel zone, which extends south for several miles along a narrow paved drive shaded by palms and other tropical vegetation; watch for occasional *topes* (speed bumps). Cabanas, thatched *palapa* huts, small hotels and other accommodations line the road. Many advertise yoga and holistic massages, underscoring the relaxed, get-away-from-it-all feeling. The beachside properties are steps away from the surf, although you can't see the beach from the road. Several beachfront restaurants and a few nightspots also are mixed in.

After winding through the hotel zone the road continues south down the length of the Boca Paila Peninsula. This narrow isthmus of land constitutes Sian Ka'an's buffer zone, the only portion of this protected wilderness reserve that is open to visitors. You must stop and pay a registration fee of 21 pesos per person at the reserve's official point of entry (marked by a guardhouse) if you intend to drive down to Punta Allen.

At the guardhouse, set your car's trip meter to zero. Ten kilometers (6.2 miles) down the road is a small visitor center with a handful of displays focusing on Sian Ka'an's flora, fauna and history. Information panels are in Spanish and English. A short trail leads inland to a wooden dock fronting an expansive lagoon. Here you can arrange kayak rentals (about $20 U.S. per hour) and 90-minute boat tours of the lagoon ($40 U.S. per person). Reservations are not necessary.

Beyond the visitor center the setting is dense scrub jungle, with empty, palm-studded beaches and mangrove-lined estuaries along the Caribbean coast and a network of lagoons and waterways between the peninsula and the mainland. At one point along the road, your peripheral vision will encompass sea, land and lagoon. Several rustic eco lodges cater to dedicated birders (species common to this region include frigate birds, brown pelicans, woodpeckers, parrots and the Yucatán jay) and anglers who come for the superb sport fishing.

Some 17 kilometers (10.6 miles) past the guardhouse there is easy beach access and good swimming at a gorgeous semi-sheltered cove. Park anywhere along the side of the road. If hunger and thirst strike before you reach Punta Allen, stop at Xamach Dos (24 kilometers south of the guardhouse), a sleepy beachfront hotel with a few rental cabanas and a small *palapa* restaurant. There are picnic tables and beach chairs at the water's edge. If you've always fantasized about having a Caribbean beach all to yourself, continue toward Punta Allen and pull off at any of the small, unmarked turn-outs along the beach side of the road. Cancún this is not.

The journey ends at the tiny lobster-fishing village of Punta Allen. Truly the end of the line, Punta Allen consists of several restaurants (Casa Cuzan is a solid choice), a handful of convenience stores and a few fishing and eco tour guide services, albeit in an idyllic setting of coconut palms, thatched *palapas* and beautiful Caribbean views.

The road ends at a lighthouse with a *mirador* (viewing platform) that looks out over expansive Ascension Bay (Bahía de la Ascensión). The bay's vast saltwater flats are some of the best fly-fishing spots in the world for tarpon, bonefish and the elusive permit, a saucer-shaped game fish with a deeply forked tail that is related to the pompano.

Note: It is approximately 45 kilometers (28 miles) from the Sian Ka'an guardhouse to Punta Allen. Much of the route—which is gradually being paved and improved—is a narrow one-lane trail of packed dirt and sand over limestone. It winds through dense scrub jungle, passing deserted beaches, mangrove flats and even an occasional Mayan ruin. Iguanas scurry across the road. Ruts and potholes are more evident after crossing the Boca Paila bridge, about 24 kilometers (15 miles) south of the Sian Ka'an guardhouse.

The drive can be made in a car, but a jeep or four-wheel-drive vehicle is recommended. Make sure you have a full tank of gas and bring drinking water, food and insect repellent. Plan on at least 2 hours (not including stops) to reach Punta Allen from Tulum, although once you're familiar with the road it's safe to shave a good 20 minutes off your estimated return drive time. If you're not spending the night in Punta Allen allow enough time to get back to Mex. 307 before dusk.

Recreation

Water sports, not surprisingly, top Cancún's list of leisure activities. **Fishing** is excellent; the open Caribbean, Mujeres Bay, the channel between Cozumel and the mainland, and the waters of Nichupté Lagoon together are home to some 500 species, including all types of game fish. Bonito, dorado and sailfish run from March into July; bluefin tuna from April through June. Barracuda, grouper, mackerel and red snapper can be hooked all year.

Hotel Zone marinas offer a range of vessels and top-of-the-line equipment. Larger boats are 35-40 feet long; single-engine diesel boats average 26-28 feet. Four- and 8-hour charter excursions normally include a captain, first mate, gear, bait and soft drinks. Cost varies and the marinas compete for business, so it pays to shop around; ask at your hotel for recommendations. Bluewater Adventures, Km 6.5 on Kukulcán, charters fishing trips and also offers snorkeling and sightseeing boat tours; phone (998) 849-4444.

In addition to the islands, fishing opportunities are plentiful all along the Caribbean coastline and farther south at La Ascención and Espíritu Santo, two large bays along the shore of the Sian Ka'an Biosphere Reserve. Shark fishing is good in Yalahau Lagoon, the body of water between the mainland and Cape Catoche at the northeastern tip of the Yucatán Peninsula. Boats can be hired in the port town of Chiquilá, reached via a paved road branching north off Mex. 180 at the town of El Ideal, and on Isla Holbox *(see separate listing within this region).*

Scuba diving and **snorkeling** also are rewarding, particularly at the southern end of Cancún Island around Nizuc Point, off Cozumel and Isla Mujeres, and in Nichupté Lagoon. Dive shops along Kukulcán rent equipment, give lessons and schedule trips; some hotels also can arrange dive excursions. Check credentials, boats and equipment, and if possible get the inside scoop from a diver familiar with the area. Conditions are best from May or June through August.

Scuba Cancún, on the lagoon side of Kukulcán at Km marker 5 (across from Playa Langosta), offers a 5-hour "resort course" that includes pool practice and a one-tank dive at a shallow reef with a certified PADI instructor. They also organize all-day snorkeling and cavern diving excursions (on Tuesday, Thursday and Saturday) to freshwater cenotes in the jungles just north of the Tulum ruins. Transportation, wet suits and gear are included; open water certification is required to participate in the cavern dive. Phone (998) 849-7508.

Other activities include **water skiing, windsurfing, parasailing, swimming** and **boating.** The best place to water ski is Nichupté Lagoon; ski clubs along Kukulcán on the lagoon side rent boats and equipment. Windsurfing propels its participants across the water at exhilarating speeds; the sailboard used by windsurfers is comprised of a masted sail attached to a surfboard. The pools at the big resort hotels are masterfully designed, with the added bonus of the Caribbean as a backdrop.

For landlubbers there's **golf** at the Cancún Golf Club at Pok-Ta-Pok, a championship 18-hole course designed by Robert Trent Jones Jr. Located on an island between Laguna de Bojórquez and Laguna Nichupté (access is off Kukulcán at Km 7.5), it offers fine views of both lagoons and the Caribbean. Shoes, carts and clubs are available for rent, and there is a pro shop. Reservations are advised; phone (998) 883-1230 or (998) 883-1277.

Another championship 18-hole course is at the Hilton Cancún Golf & Spa Resort, off Kukulcán at Km 17; phone (998) 881-8000 for reservations information. Greens fees vary depending on the season and are less for hotel guests.

Horseback riding trips take in locations from jungle to seashore. Rancho Loma Bonita, off Mex. 307 just south of Puerto Morelos (Km 49), provides transportation to and from the ranch, in addition to a guide and lunch. Phone (998) 887-5465, or make arrangements through your hotel or a local travel agency.

Tennis is offered at the big resort hotels; there are courts at the Crown Paradise Club Cancún, Fiesta Americana Condesa, Fiesta Americana Grand Coral Beach and Le Meridien Cancún Resort & Spa, among others. A **jogging** and **bicycling** path—also used for roller blading—parallels the sidewalk along the northern (bay) side of Kukulcán, extending as far as Cancún Point; a path also parallels the sidewalk along most of the southern half of the Hotel Zone. Runners should make the circuit in the early morning before it gets too hot.

If you just want to relax—and are willing to pay the price—the spa at the J.W. Marriott Cancún Resort & Spa, Km 14.5 on Kukulcán, offers hydrotherapy, massage and facial and body treatments, plus a state-of-the-art gym, an indoor pool, steam and sauna rooms and a natural juice bar. An appointment is required; for information phone (998) 848-9600.

Nightlife

Cancún provides something for everyone after dark, from rowdy spring break hangouts to Mexican and Caribbean-themed dinner shows. The clubs, needless to say, offer plenty of high-decibel action. Hotels also get in the act with lobby bars, happy-hour specials and varied entertainment.

Most clubs open around 10 or 10:30 p.m. and stay open until as late as 6 a.m. Cover charges begin at about $12 (U.S.), go up to $25 or $30 with an open bar, and may be waived on certain nights; at some places women are routinely admitted free of charge. Inquire about the dress code; some don't allow jeans or shorts.

La Boom, at Km 3.5 on Kukulcán, is divided into two sections: a video bar and a two-level dance floor with a laser light show and blasting music. Almost nightly themed events and special deals bring in a young, partying crowd. The Bulldog Cafe, at Km marker 8, also features a laser light show along with video screens and music that ranges from hip-hop to rock.

Coco Bongo, at Km 9.5 on Kukulcán in the Forum-by-the-Sea shopping complex, draws young scenesters with a mix of recorded techno, hip-hop, house, salsa and '70s and '80s hits, as well as live bands. There's no actual dance floor, you gyrate wherever there's a spot. This cavernous space regularly packs in as many as 3,000 people.

The City, also at Km 9.5 in front of Coco Bongo, attracts visiting international DJs who spin pulsating dance music accompanied by dizzying light shows. With nine bars and lounges and a beach club that has a wave pool, cabanas and food and drink service, this is basically a 24-hour hangout.

Dady'O, at Km 9.5 on Kukulcán (near the Cancún Center), is a granddaddy as far as longevity goes but is still very popular; like the other clubs it's loud and wild, and the sound and lighting are first-rate. Dady Rock Bar & Grill, next door to Dady'O, has both live bands and DJ-spun music, karaoke contests, T-shirt giveaways, an open bar and a restaurant.

A somewhat less frantic atmosphere prevails at Glazz, in the La Isla Shopping Village complex. This lounge and nightclub targets the over-30 crowd with DJ dance music, a huge selection of martinis and varied live entertainment. The La Madonna restaurant, also at La Isla Shopping Village, has a European-style ambiance and a well-stocked martini bar. If you prefer a quieter evening, most of the resort hotels have a nightclub or lobby bar with jazz or other live music; the lobby lounge at The Ritz-Carlton Cancún is particularly elegant.

For those who love to party there are plenty of places that combine food, music and a frathouse sense of fun. Two Mexican chains—Carlos 'n Charlie's, at Km 5.5 on the lagoon side of Kukulcán (across from the Casa Maya Hotel), and Señor Frog's, at Km 9.5 on Kukulcán—are noisy and popular, with waiters who get as crazy as the patrons. Cancún's Hard Rock Cafe, in the Forum-by-the-Sea complex, has live rock bands every night except Wednesday, a menu of Mexican and American favorites and a view of the Caribbean.

Note: Cancún's spring break begins in mid-February and lasts for about 2 months. Excessive alcohol consumption associated with partying is common; the legal drinking age in Mexico is 18 but is not uniformly enforced. Much of the rowdy behavior takes place at nightspots that target a younger crowd.

Planet Hollywood, in La Isla Shopping Village, sticks to the movie memorabilia formula that has sustained the chain's worldwide popularity. Mango Tango, at Km 14.2 on the lagoon side of Kukulcán (opposite The Ritz-Carlton), accompanies dinner with a lively floor show staged outdoors nightly at 8:30, with live music (usually salsa or reggae) following at 9:30.

For those who don't want to stand in line, the Bar Leaping Tour does the work for you. Departing at 7:30 p.m. from La Isla Shopping Village, it includes stops at four nightspots, with transportation en route aboard the air-conditioned Froguibus—an easy way to spend a night on the town. The cost is about $50 (U.S.) per person. For information phone (998) 883-5402.

Mexican-style entertainment in Cancún is still available amid the lasers and fog machines. The Ballet Folklórico de Cancún performs Tues.-Sat. at the Cancún Center. The ticket booth is just inside the center; tickets can be purchased for a Mexican buffet dinner and the show, or for the show only. Dinner begins at 7 p.m.; the show begins at 8. Tickets are about $50 (U.S.) for dinner and the show (ages 6-12, $25), about $30 for the show only (ages 6-12, $15). For more information check with your hotel or a local travel agency.

The El Mexicano Restaurant, in the Costa Blanca shopping center at Km 8.5 on Kukulcán, also offers a folkloric ballet show beginning nightly at 8 p.m. Dinner at this beautifully decorated restaurant, which re-creates the look of a 19th-century Mexican hacienda, comes complete with strolling mariachis.

Romantics will enjoy a moonlit cruise. The Lobster Dinner Cruise sets sail for Nichupté Lagoon from the Aquatours Marina pier at Km 6.5 on Kukulcán (across from Playa Tortugas). A lobster or surf-and-turf dinner is served aboard the 60-foot galleon *Columbus,* along with dancing to live jazz music. Departures are Mon.-Fri. at 5 and 8 (arriving 30 minutes before scheduled departure is recommended). Under 12 are not permitted. Transportation to the pier is not included. Reservations are required; for information phone (998) 193-3360 or (866) 393-5158 (toll-free from the United States).

Special Events

The Day of the Kings (Feast of the Epiphany, or El Día de Los Reyes) on Jan. 6 is a day of gift-giving. Local restaurants serve a King's Cake (Rosca de Reyes) that contains a small plastic Jesus doll (El Niño) inside. The person receiving the piece with the doll acts as a host on Candlemas (La Candeleria), the season's final Chrismas celebration held the first week in February, when a meal of *tamales* and hot chocolate is served in homes and restaurants.

Carnaval, a fiesta in the spirit of Mardi Gras, is held the week preceding Ash Wednesday. Residents dress up in elaborate costumes, floats parade down the streets of Ciudad Cancún, and there are street parties featuring dancing, fireworks and regional foods and beverages.

On Mar. 21 the Vernal Equinox (Inicio Primavera) is observed at Chichén Itzá. When the late afternoon sun shines on El Castillo, a shadow remarkably reminiscent of a slithering serpent appears on the side of the pyramid. Thousands of people attend this event. The Cancún Jazz Festival over Memorial Day weekend has drawn such celebrated musicians as Carlos Santana, Ray Charles and Diana Krall. Concerts take place in and around the Hotel Zone and at a park in downtown Ciudad Cancún.

As in all of Mexico, Independence Day (Patria de la Independencia) festivities take place Sept. 15-16 and include fireworks, a parade (on the 16th) and traditional food. Father Miguel Hidalgo's famous speech *Grito de Dolores* is re-enacted as people gather at midnight to shout out *Viva México!*"

The Eve of All Souls' Day, Oct. 31, is observed throughout the Yucatán by adorning headstones with wreaths of marigolds and placing candles and offerings of food and tequila at gravesites. Day of the Dead graveside and church ceremonies take place amid a party-like atmosphere Nov. 1 and 2, with bakeries doing big business turning out various skull-shaped pastries.

The ITU World Cup Triathlon, held in early November, attracts triathletes from around the world who compete in swimming, running and bicycling. Events are held at Playa Langosta. Also in November is the International Caribbean Cultural Festival, held in downtown Ciudad Cancún. It brings artists, dancers, musicians and in particular salsa groups from all over the Caribbean.

Christmas celebrations begin 9 days prior to Dec. 25 and feature *posadas* (processions) of families and friends who take part in *pastorelas* (plays) portraying Jesus' birth, along with street fairs, *piñata* smashing and other festivities. One highlight of the season is the display of nativity scenes.

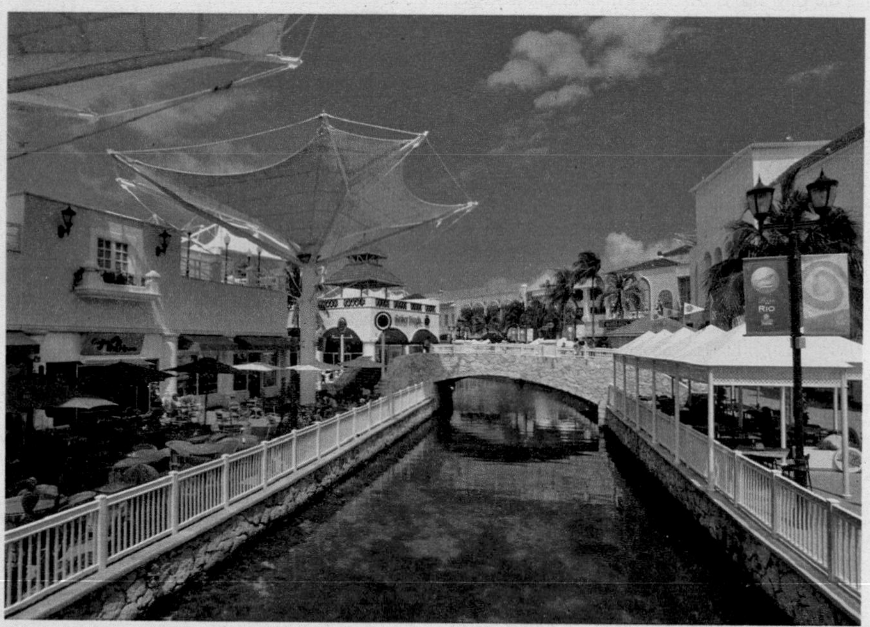

This ends listings for Cancún.
The following page resumes the alphabetical listings of cities in Yucatán Peninsula.

CHETUMAL, QUINTANA ROO (C-3)

pop. 126,700

One of the oldest cities on the Yucatán Peninsula, Chetumal (cheh-too-MAHL) was a former Mayan stronghold. Three centuries of back-and-forth battles—some viciously barbaric—were waged as the Spanish attempted to wrest control of the region from the Maya. The city was renamed Payo Obispo in 1898 and recast as a border town dealing in jungle hardwoods, arms and smuggled goods. These profitable dealings came to an abrupt end in 1955, when a hurricane all but flattened the city.

The capital of Quintana Roo reflects the stages of its checkered history. It is at once a thriving port and a steamy backwater. The older part of town, with its rickety clapboard buildings huddled under trees ablaze with tropical blooms, has a marked Central American atmosphere (the nation of Belize, with which Chetumal shares tourist and commercial traffic, is just across the river). Boulevard Bahía, bordered by small plazas, follows the bay for several kilometers. The large, modern bus terminal is north of downtown near the intersection of avenidas Héroes and Insurgentes. First-class bus service to Cancún and Mérida is offered by ADO.

Quintana Roo State Tourism Office (Secretaría de Turismo): Av. Del Centenario #622; phone (983) 835-0860, ext. 1809 or 1810. The Chetumal Tourism Office, downtown at Avenida 5 de Mayo and Calle Carmen O. de Merino, has free maps, tourist publications and brochures and is more conveniently located for visitors. It's open Mon.-Fri. 9-5.

Shopping areas: Many of Chetumal's stores line Avenida Héroes, which begins at the bay and runs west through the market area. An incongruous touch in this downtown shopping district are the numerous shops selling Dutch cheeses, Japanese stereo equipment, French perfume and other international products, all at duty-free prices. The chance to purchase such items draws crowds of Mexican and Belizean tourists. While it is possible to find good buys on Yucatecan hammocks, U.S. and Canadian visitors should save their pesos and purchase Mexican crafts elsewhere. Like most Mexican markets, Chetumal's enormous and lively central market, across the street from the Museum of Mayan Culture, is fun to wander through.

Downtown, you'll find excellent food in a tourist-friendly atmosphere at Restaurant El Fenicio, at the corner of avenidas Héroes and Zaragoza. The tortilla and cheese soup is delicious, and the *Haga su taco* (make your own taco) plate for two people is a good way to sample El Fenicio's various taco fillings.

MUSEUM OF MAYAN CULTURE (Museo de la Cultura Maya) is downtown on Calle Niños Héroes, 5 blks. e. of Av. Alvaro Obregón (across from the Holiday Inn). Occupying an entire city block, it presents an excellent historical account of all things Mayan from around 1,000 B.C. to the conquest of the Yucatán in 1590. Touch screens, interactive exhibits and displays of paintings, sculpture and stela provide a detailed understanding of Mayan astronomy, architecture, mathematics, art, music, politics and religion. The central courtyard features a recreation of a typical Mayan village complete with thatch-roofed huts, mini altars and work areas.

Most (not all) of the stela and artifacts are reproductions. There is a small museum bookstore near the ticket window that has books about the Maya in English. Exhibit information is in English and Spanish. The museum also is air conditioned, a rarity in this Third World border city. Allow 2 hours minimum. Tues.-Sun. 9-7 (also Fri.-Sat. 7-8 p.m.). Admission 50 pesos (about $4.85 U.S.). Phone (983) 832-6838.

GEM CHICHEN ITZA, YUCATAN (B-3)

The pyramids, temples and shrines at Chichén Itzá (chee-CHEHN eet-SAH)—the magnificent remains of a once-great Mayan city—were designated a World Heritage Site by UNESCO in 1988. It is believed that Chichén Itzá was founded sometime around A.D. 435; the first large-scale excavations of the site began around the turn of the 20th century. Of the several hundred buildings believed to have once stood, only about 30 are fully restored. A few more remain as they were found, and the rest are hidden under rough, underbrush-covered mounds in the thick jungle scrub of the north-central Yucatán Peninsula.

Northern Zone

Chichén Itzá is remarkable for both monumental scope and architectural variety. The ruins consist of two complexes connected by a dirt path. Generally speaking, the older southern section contains mostly Mayan ruins and the structures in the northern section combine Mayan and Toltec influences, although the blending of pre-Hispanic cultures is apparent throughout. The militaristic Toltec influence is evident in the images—jaguars, sharp-taloned eagles, phalanxes of marching warriors, feathered serpents—employed to decorate the exteriors of pyramids and temples.

El Castillo *(see attraction listing)* dominates the other Northern Zone ruins sprinkled over a level, grassy area. That this pyramid's builders were mathematically precise in their construction is borne out by a natural phenomenon that occurs at the spring and fall equinoxes (on or around Mar. 21 and Sept. 21). As the sun begins its descent, the shadows cast by the terraces on the north staircase form the body of a serpent, whose actual sculpted head rests at the base of the stairs. In the spring, the serpent appears to be slithering down the stairs; in the fall, the illusion is reversed. **Note:** Visitors from around the world attend this semiannual event, and although it is well worth seeing, expect large and boisterous crowds.

El Castillo also is deceptively steep; the large stone steps ascend to the top at a 45-degree angle.

Visitors have traditionally been able to climb the 100-foot-tall pyramid using the staircases on three of its sides, with most people climbing the steps on the western side (the side you see as you first enter the site). But because of erosion to the steps and a fatality that occurred in 2006, the base is roped off and climbing is not permitted.

Temples are at both ends of the ball court *(see attraction listing)* near El Castillo. The temple at the northern end has a short stairway ascending to two columns supporting a roof. It retains only a few remnants of its former murals and sculptures. The Temple of the Jaguars, at the southeastern corner of the ball court, has columns carved in the shape of serpents and panels depicting jaguars and Mayan warriors.

Just east of the ball court is the Temple of the Skulls (Tzompantli), decorated in macabre fashion with rows of human skulls. This artistic rendering reflects the gruesome act of human sacrifice that was integral to Mayan religious rites, as the heads of victims were often stuck on the ends of poles. The adjacent Platform of the Eagles and Jaguars has carvings showing these creatures grasping human hearts. A short distance east of this structure and north of El Castillo is the Platform of Venus, which has depictions of a feathered serpent (a reference to the god Quetzalcóatl) holding a human head in its mouth. Serpent carvings ascend the stairways.

Just south of the Temple of the Warriors *(see attraction listing)* are the partially restored remains of what archeologists believe were steam baths and a market complex. Further to the southeast are unrestored mounds of rubble beneath the trees.

Note: All of the major structures at Chichén Itzá, including El Castillo, are roped off and can no longer be climbed.

Central Zone

The southern complex of ruins (often mistakenly referred to as Old Chichén), accessible from the northern complex via a short dirt pathway, consists of mostly Mayan ruins. The first structure you come to is the Ossuary (High Priest's Grave), thought to be a burial ground. This partially reconstructed pyramid is topped with the remains of a temple and has distinctive serpent head carvings at the base. Its interior (not open to the public) leads to an underground cave in which human skeletons and offerings have been found.

Across the path and south of this pyramid is El Caracol *(see attraction listing)*, an astronomical observatory dating from the 10th century that may have been one of the last Mayan buildings erected at this site. The short stairway leading to the dome can be climbed, and there are fine views from the top of the wall, particularly of the nearby Nunnery.

East of El Caracol a winding path leads north through dense underbrush to the Cenote Xtoloc. Unlike the Sacred Cenote *(see attraction listing)*, this well was not used for human sacrifice; it provided

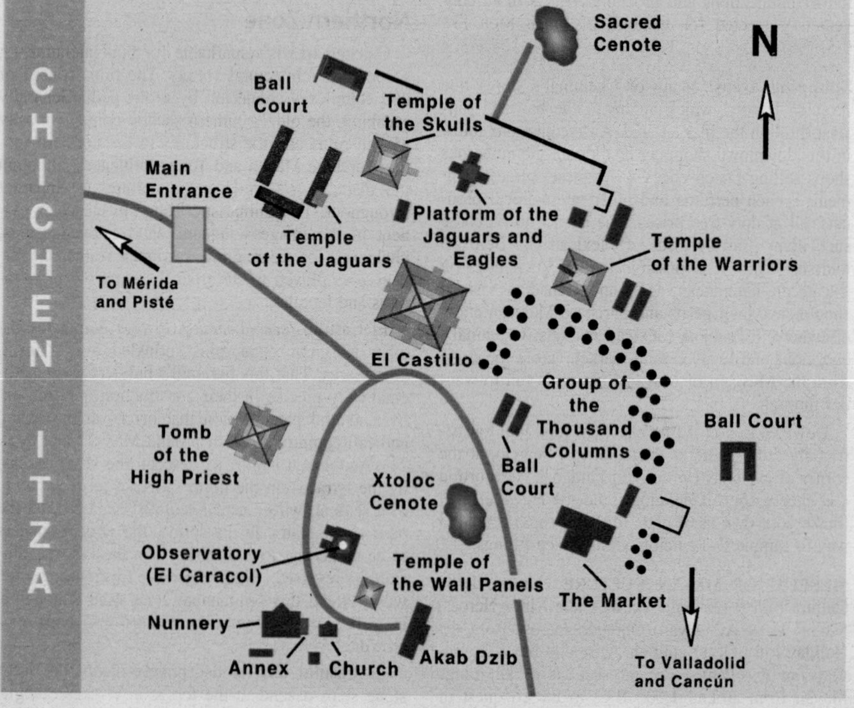

Chichén with its drinking water. South of El Caracol is the Nunnery (Casa de Las Monjas), so named by the Spaniards because it reminded them of a European convent. This large complex has exquisitely carved facades of animals, flowers and designs that are reminiscent of latticework. Next to the Nunnery is The Church (La Iglesia), also named by the Spanish. While it in no way resembles a church, this small building is lavishly decorated, primarily with beak-nosed carvings of Chac.

The exterior carvings on the Temple of the Carved Panels (Templo de Los Tableros Esculpidos), east of the Nunnery, are more difficult to discern, but may refer to Toltec warrior symbology. A rough path, also beginning east of the Nunnery, runs through the scrub for several hundred feet to the Akab-Dzib, a classically designed Mayan temple believed to be one of Chichén Itzá's oldest structures. Traces of red handprints are faintly visible in some of the interior rooms, and above one doorway are carved Mayan hieroglyphics that have yet to be deciphered.

General Information and Activities

Arrangements to join a group tour aboard a first-class bus can be made in Mérida, about 120 kilometers (75 miles) west, and Cancún, about 200 kilometers (125 miles) east. A group tour eliminates the hassle of driving but can make for a long, hectic day and requires sticking to a rigid schedule. Cancún-based Mayaland Tours offers a day trip package that includes round-trip transportation from Mérida, guide service, park admission, a buffet lunch and a 30-minute swim at one of the nearby hotels—a nice refresher after touring the hot, humid site. For reservations information phone (998) 887-2450 (in Mexico) or (800) 235-4079 (from the United States).

If you're driving, the ruins are a few miles south of the Chichén Itzá exit off Mex. 180-D; Yuc. 79 is the local road. One of the highway's two toll plazas is at this exit; at press time the toll was 85 pesos (about $8.25 U.S.). You'll first pass through the small town of Pisté, on Mex. 180 about 2 kilometers (1.2 miles) west of the Chichén Itzá entrance. Here there are budget accommodations, restaurants and basic travel services for those who prefer to stay overnight. Taxi service also is available from Pisté to the site entrance. Several more upscale hotels are grouped east of (and within walking distance) of the southern complex of ruins.

Chichén Itzá can be explored on your own or as part of a group led by a staff guide. A guide isn't necessary to appreciate the grandeur of the major landmarks, however, and information plaques in Spanish and English give a general architectural and historical background.

If you're visiting on your own, begin early in the morning if possible, before it gets too hot and the tour buses begin arriving. A hat or other headgear is advised since there is little shade. Sturdy walking shoes with nonslip soles come in handy for clambering over rocks and especially for climbing El Castillo. Bring bottled water and/or snacks as well as insect repellent for any extended walking excursions. Three hours or so is enough to see everything, although archeology buffs could easily spend the entire day.

A sound-and-light show is presented nightly. The ruins are bathed in colored lights, and Spanish narration recounts the history of and legends associated with the site. Headsets in several languages can be rented. Confirm the start time at the visitor center ticket window.

The visitor center at the main entrance has an information desk (where admission tickets are purchased); a small museum; an air-conditioned auditorium, Chilam Balam, where an audiovisual presentation is shown; and a bookstore, restaurant and restrooms. There also are restrooms off the path between the northern and central zone complexes.

Food is available. Site open daily 8-5. Sound-and-light show begins at 7 or 8 p.m. (depending on season) and lasts about 45 minutes. Admission (includes museum) 100 pesos (about $9.70 U.S.). Sound-and-light show admission 50 pesos (about $4.85 U.S.). Parking fee 10 pesos. Video camera fee about $6 (U.S.).

Points of Interest

BALANCANCHE CAVES (Grutas de Balancanché) are about 5 km (3 mi.) e. of Chichén Itzá off Mex. 180 via a very short gravel road; follow signs. This series of illuminated underground passages, discovered in the mid-1960s, extends for about half a mile past large stalactite formations. Three of the seven chambers are open to the public. In various niches along the way are offertory urns, incense burners and other artifacts. Outside is a small botanical garden.

Note: The walk through the passages can be slippery. Some crawling is required; wear sturdy shoes. The caves are not recommended for those who are claustrophobic.

Guided tours in English are given daily at 11, 1 and 3 for groups of between six and 30 persons (double-check tour times at the Chichén Itzá visitor center); self-guiding tours are not permitted. A sound-and-light show accompanies the tour and recounts the cave's history. Admission 35 pesos (about $3.40 U.S.).

BALL COURT is a short distance west of El Castillo. Two walls run parallel to the playing field. The object of this ancient game was for two teams of players to maneuver a heavy rubber ball—without using their hands—through one of two stone rings placed high on each wall. Some participants (opinion is divided on whether they were winners or losers) apparently suffered death by decapitation. Stone carvings depict this act as well as players sporting protective padding and feathered headdresses. The acoustics are startling: Two people standing on opposite sides of the field and speaking in normal voices can easily hear each other.

The Maya World

The Maya evolved into one of Mexico's most intriguing ancient civilizations. At the same time Europe was suffering through the Dark Ages, the Maya people were enjoying a creative flowering without precedent in the known world. They built temples and ceremonial centers that evoke wonder to this day; developed an astronomical calendar and predicted both solar and lunar eclipses; pioneered the mathematical concept of zero; and produced a highly refined hieroglyphic writing system. As if that weren't enough, these multi-taskers also were accomplished artists, historians and road builders.

Maya civilization spread as far south as northern Central America and as far north as the northern Yucatán Peninsula, an area that includes all of Belize, most of Guatemala, portions of Honduras and El Salvador, and all or part of the Mexican states of Campeche, Chiapas, Quintana Roo, Tabasco and Yucatán. Its history can be divided into Preclassic, Classic and Postclassic eras. The earliest Maya settlements date from around 1800 B.C.; one important Preclassic site was Dzibilchaltún, north of Mérida.

The Classic period, from approximately A.D. 300 to 900, represented the peak of development in terms of large-scale construction of independent Maya city-states. Well-known sites include Copan and Tikal in Guatemala, and Palenque in the state of Chiapas. For reasons that are still unknown—theories range from tribal invasion to peasant revolt against the elite to crop failure caused by climate change to an epidemic of disease—major ceremonial centers such as Palenque and Tikal declined by the early 10th century, as Mayan civilization shifted northward to the Yucatán Peninsula and such cities as Chichén Itzá and Uxmal.

THE CASTLE (El Castillo) is a short walk from the visitor center at the main entrance. Also called Kukulcán, the Mayan name for the Toltec king Quetzalcóatl, this 100-foot-tall pyramid has a perfectly symmetrical design. Each of the four sides is scaled by 91 steps; the total of 364 steps plus the top platform equaled the number of days in the Mayan year. El Castillo also is deceptively steep; the large stone steps ascend to the top at a 45-degree angle. Visitors have traditionally been able to climb the 100-foot-tall pyramid using the staircases on three of its sides, with most people climbing the steps on the western side (the side you see as you first enter the site)

An additional step underneath the pyramid, the 365th, signified a trip to the underworld. Each side also has 18 terraced sections—nine on either side of a central staircase, equaling the 18 months of the Mayan year—and 52 panels, corresponding to the number of years in the Mayan calendrical cycle.

Inside El Castillo is an older temple accessed via a stairway at the foot of the north staircase (on the western end). A very narrow set of steps ascends to two humid, claustrophobic inner chambers. One contains a reclining Chac Mool figure, the other a reddish throne in the shape of a jaguar with green jade eyes. **Note:** Visitors are not currently permitted to enter this temple.

OLD CHICHEN (Chichén Viejo) is about a 15-minute walk down a dirt path that begins southwest of the Nunnery. A sincere interest in archeology and a local guide are both recommended for a trek to this area of little-restored buildings, which is mosquito-infested (wear plenty of insect repellent) and overgrown with jungle scrub. Avoid exploring during the June-through-September rainy season, when the narrow pathways can become difficult to navigate.

The barely uncovered buildings feature masks of Chac and gargoyle-like creatures carved along cornices. The Date Group of ruins includes the House of the Phalli, so named for some sculptures carved into the walls of one room. The earliest date discovered in Chichén Itzá—the equivalent of A.D. 879—is carved into a lintel supported by columns; the rest of what was once a pyramid no longer remains.

SACRED CENOTE is about a 5-minute walk due n. of the Platform of Venus along a dirt path. This path was once a Mayan *sacbe,* or paved causeway. Two cenotes, or limestone sinkholes, served Chichén Itzá. The Sacred Cenote is a 190-foot-wide pit that was used for human sacrifice to appease the rain god Chac. The skeletons of men, women and children have been excavated, which suggests that in addition to young maidens—the preferred sacrificial victim—the diseased and mentally ill also may have been drowned in the well.

Excavations of the cenote have unearthed bones, idols, jewelry, jade objects and other artifacts from different parts of Mexico, leading archeologists to believe that pilgrimages to Chichén Itzá continued long after its abandonment.

THE SNAIL (El Caracol) is in the southern group of ruins. Also called "The Winding Stair," its name is a reference to the interior winding staircase (not open to the public) that leads to the dome (which can be entered). This ruin's round construction is quite possibly unique in Mayan architecture. Stones could be removed from slits within the dome—nine in all—enabling Mayan astronomers to study different parts of the heavens. Some interesting carvings decorate the dome's exterior.

TEMPLE OF THE WARRIORS is a short distance e. of El Castillo. This Toltec-influenced temple has impressive rows of carved warriors and a roof boasting fine sculptural details of the rain god Chac, feathered serpents and mythical animals; it is guarded by a reclining Chac Mool figure. Next to the temple is the Group of the Thousand Columns, thought to have housed the residences of Chichén's ruling elite. The rows of Toltec-style pillars (in actuality, far fewer than 1,000) are covered with bas-relief. **Note:** At press time, the Temple of the Warriors was roped off to visitors.

COBA, QUINTANA ROO (B-3)

Cobá (coh-BAH) translates roughly as "waters stirred by wind." This small village is about 66 kilometers (40 miles) northwest of Mex. 307; the Tulum/Cobá road branches off Mex. 307 just north of the town of Tulum. From Cancún, take Mex. 180 west to Xcan, then the paved road south about 43 kilometers (26 miles). The village is about a mile west of the road via a turn-off.

COBA RUINS spread e. from the shore of Lake Cobá just outside of town. This city/ceremonial center dates from between A.D. 600 to 900—older than both Chichén Itzá and Tulum—and at its height may have supported as many as 50,000 inhabitants. Archeologists theorize that Cobá was an important trade link between Mayan outposts on the coast and cities in the interior.

The ruins were first discovered in the early 1890s, but excavations did not begin in earnest until 1973. It is believed that as many as 6,500 structures exist. Those temples, pyramids and elaborately carved stela (vertical stone tablets) that have been excavated are surrounded by palm tree thickets, tropical hardwoods, roping vines and other vegetation.

Nohoch Mul ("large hill"), a 138-foot-high pyramid towering above the flat landscape (about a half-hour walk from the site entrance), is the tallest structure of its kind in the northern Yucatán—rising even higher than the Pyramid of the Magician at Uxmal. Climbing is permitted. The Cobá Group, a cluster of ruins on the right after you enter the site, contains another massive pyramid, the Temple of the Churches (Templo de las Iglesias), which cannot be climbed.

The Maya World (continued)

The Postclassic period from the 10th to early 16th centuries saw the rise of such sites as Cobá, Edzná, Mayapán and Tulum. These city-states competed for power until the arrival of Spanish *conquistadores* in the early 16th century. The first Spanish stronghold in the Yucatán Peninsula was established in 1542 at Mérida. Thus began a protracted attempt to subjugate the Maya and exert control over their lands. But unlike the Aztecs, where power was consolidated at a single political center (the city of Tenochtitlan), the individual Maya city-states each put up determined resistance. It was not until 1697 that the last one—Tayasal, in Guatemala—surrendered.

After being conquered by the Spanish the surviving Maya peoples retreated to the jungles of Quintana Roo, where fierce revolts continued until Mexico finally won its freedom in 1821. Even afterward the fighting continued, and the Yucatán twice declared its own independence in the 19th century.

As impressive as those created by the ancient Greeks and Romans, Maya buildings are all the more notable when one considers the primitive way in which they were constructed—without benefit of draft animals, wheeled conveyances, metal tools or pulleys. Structures were built primarily from limestone that most likely was quarried locally.

Maya architecture took several characteristic forms. Platforms, constructed in the manner of a typical foundation and often embellished with carved figures, were the site of public ceremonies and religious rites. Observatories aided Maya astronomers in mapping out the heavens. Ritualistic ball games were played on an "I"-shaped court enclosed on two sides and decorated with militaristic themes or images of eagles or jaguars that suited the savage nature of the competition.

The Maya World (continued)

Palaces, which presumably housed members of royalty, were large, highly decorated edifices divided up into a warren of small chambers or rooms. Maya pyramids made the grandest statement of all. Often a temple was built atop a pyramid. Extensively decorated and capped by a distinctive-looking but nonfunctional wall known as a roof comb, these temples conveyed a not-so-subtle message that the city in question was important.

The Maya left behind examples of architecture both monumental and exquisite. The El Castillo pyramid at Chichén Itzá, among the world's best-known archeological sites, was designated one of the "new seven wonders of the world" in 2007. The buildings at Uxmal have an intricately detailed beauty, and the Palace of the Masks at Kabah, a small site nearby, is one of the most amazingly decorated structures in all of Mexico. While the ruins of Tulum pale in comparison, their location—on a cliff-top overlooking the turquoise waters of the Caribbean—is stunning. These and other archeological sites are among the Yucatán's most outstanding attractions.

Chichén Itzá
Nadine Markova
Mexico Tourism Board

Guides can be hired at the entrance, and mountain bike rentals are available. Try to visit early in the morning; the heat, humidity and mosquitoes can be formidable. Sturdy walking shoes, insect repellent and drinking water are necessary for those planning to spend any time exploring the site. Daily 7-6. Admission 48 pesos (about $4.65 U.S.). Parking $1.25.

COZUMEL, QUINTANA ROO (B-4)

pop. 64,100

Surrounded by the intensely turquoise Caribbean Sea, Cozumel (koh-soo-MEHL) is not only Mexico's largest inhabited island; many feel it's the country's most beautiful as well. Famed underwater explorer Jacques Cousteau would likely agree. His early 1960s documentary on Cozumel's spectacular coral reefs caught the attention of scuba fanatics, and today this tropical isle 12 miles off the Yucatán coast is one of the top diving destinations on the planet.

But if you step ashore at San Miguel de Cozumel, the island's only town, during the tourist high season (December through April), don't expect to see marine biologist types gearing up for a dive. Instead, you'll be surrounded by a human flood of cruise ship day-trippers shuffling past the wall-to-wall shops and restaurants lining the waterfront. And if this is all you see of Cozumel, you'll leave with the wrong impression.

Cozumel has two faces. There's the commercial aspect, which puts its best foot forward in San Miguel. And then there's Cozumel's wild side, a land of sugar-white beaches, ancient Mayan ruins and mind-blowing subaquatic scenery. For many, the highlight of an island visit is a drive (preferably in a jeep) along Cozumel's unspoiled windward coast. Dotted with rustic seafood restaurants and lashed by turquoise-blue breakers, the rugged eastern shore is worlds removed from the bustle of downtown San Miguel.

For the ancient Maya, Cozumel was an important ceremonial and trading center. The present name is a derivation of the word Cuzamil, or "the island of swallows." In the 1500s, Spanish explorers used the island as a base from which to launch attacks against mainland Indians. A port was established, but by the end of the 16th century European-introduced diseases had wiped out most of the local population. From the early 1600s through the mid-19th century, Cozumel was a favorite hideout for fiendish pirates.

Around this time Indian survivors of the War of the Castes fled mainland Yucatán and began to resettle the island. The shipping of henequen (a natural fiber derived from a type of agave plant), coconuts and chicle (used to make chewing gum) triggered an economic boom, which went bust when moving shipments by road instead of by water essentially put Cozumel out of business. The island fell off the radar until the U.S. Air Force was stationed here during WWII to scout for Nazi submarines in the Caribbean.

U.S. servicemen, and later Cousteau, spread the word abut Cozumel's amazing reefs, and tourism took off. Hotel construction followed, but it is not on the massive scale found in Cancún. Despite the arrival of up to eight cruise ships a day, the island takes it all in stride and sways to its own lazy tropical rhythm.

Island Layout

Cozumel is located off the coast opposite Playa del Carmen; a 3,000-foot-deep channel separates it from the mainland. Mexico's largest populated island, it has a total area of 189 square miles (about one-sixth the size of Rhode Island), is approximately 29 miles long and averages 9 miles wide.

Most of the interior comprises patches of insect-ridden jungle, expanses of thorny, uninviting scrub and scattered Mayan ruins, none of them well preserved. The terrain is uniformly flat—the highest point is less than 50 feet above sea level—and inaccessible. It's a desolate landscape, which makes the beaches all the more inviting. Those on the western (leeward) side of the island are protected from the open Caribbean; they have calm waters and sandy shores. The eastern (windward) coast is rockier and faces the open sea. Pounding surf and powerful undertows create dangerous swimming conditions, but these beaches also have a wild beauty.

On the western coast is Cozumel's only town, San Miguel de Cozumel, usually referred to as San Miguel. The island's hub, it is a conglomeration of budget hotels, businesses, shops, restaurants and nightspots. Many of them line San Miguel's main street, Avenida Rafael Melgar, which runs north-south along the waterfront. A cement walkway, locally referred to as the *malecón,* divides the avenue from the shore. Avenidas run north-south, calles run east-west, forming an easy-to-negotiate grid pattern. (An exception is Avenida Benito Juárez, which begins at the passenger ferry pier and runs due east.)

A short block inland from the *malecón* is Plaza Principal, the central plaza, bounded on the north by Avenida Benito Juárez and on the south by Calle 1 Sur. A bright, mustard-yellow clock tower rises behind the plaza, and a red tile-roofed gazebo sits at its center. Tourists stroll the square's perimeter while local vendors relax and gossip on wooden benches. Studded with rustling palms and graced with a statue of Mexican president and hero Benito Juárez, the plaza is especially pretty in spring when royal poinciana trees are covered with orange blooms. The streets a block north, east and south of the plaza are pedestrian only. **Note:** Other downtown streets also are closed to vehicular traffic, and street parking is scarce.

Hotel zones comprising Cozumel's more exclusive accommodations are to the north and to the south of San Miguel. One paved road, the Carretera Transversal (the eastward extension of Avenida Benito Juárez), crosses the island west-east. At Cozumel's eastern (windward) shore, this paved road heads south along the coast, rounds the southern tip of the island and becomes the Carretera Costera Sur. Continuing north along the island's western (leeward) shore, the road offers access to Cozumel's best beaches before it becomes Avenida Rafael Melgar as it enters the town of San Miguel. There are no paved roads in the northern half of Cozumel, and very little development.

Practicalities

Cozumel International Airport is about 3 kilometers (2 miles) north of San Miguel via Boulevard Aeropuerto Internacional, which runs off Avenida Rafael Melgar. American Airlines offers direct flights from Dallas and Miami. Atlantic Southeast Airlines and Continental offer nonstop service from Atlanta and Houston, respectively. Several charter airlines offer direct flights as well. Make airline and hotel reservations well in advance if you'll be visiting during the peak tourist season, mid-December through mid-April. Mexicana airline's low-cost carrier, Click Mexicana, offers regular flights to Mexico City and other mainland destinations; for schedule information phone (800) 112-5425 (toll-free long distance within Mexico).

Ground transportation from the airport to your hotel is available via private taxi vans or shared passenger vans *(colectivos).* Fares for private van service are expensive and range from 100 pesos (about $9.70 U.S.) per person to downtown hotels to 350 pesos per person to the far southern hotel zone. Shared passenger vans wait until the vehicle is full; cost ranges from 50 pesos per person to downtown hotels to 80 pesos per person to the far southern hotel zone. Tickets can be purchased at the airport exit or from the drivers themselves. Take an inexpensive city taxi back to the airport upon departure.

Travel agencies, tour operators, hotels and airlines offer a variety of air/hotel package deals. For additional information about airlines *see Arriving by Air, page 61.*

Two different ferry companies carry passengers between Cozumel and Playa del Carmen *(see separate listing within this region).* The passenger ferry pier is off Avenida Rafael Melgar across from San Miguel's main plaza. Between the two companies a ferry departs for Playa del Carmen every hour on the hour beginning at 5 a.m.; the last scheduled departure is around 10 p.m. The last scheduled departure from Playa del Carmen back to Cozumel is around 11 p.m. Tickets for both ferries can be purchased from booths at the pier. Signs posted outside the ticket booths indicate each ferry's next departure time. If you're carrying luggage, you can check your suitcase with ferry baggage handlers free of charge. Double-check the schedule, and in particular confirm the time of the last departure from Playa if you're planning a day trip to the mainland.

Both ferry companies operate modern, air-conditioned vessels. UltraMar has a fleet of blue and gold boats, while Mexico Waterjets sport an orange, white and blue color scheme. The trip takes about 35 to 45 minutes and both companies charge roughly the same price. One-way fare (including

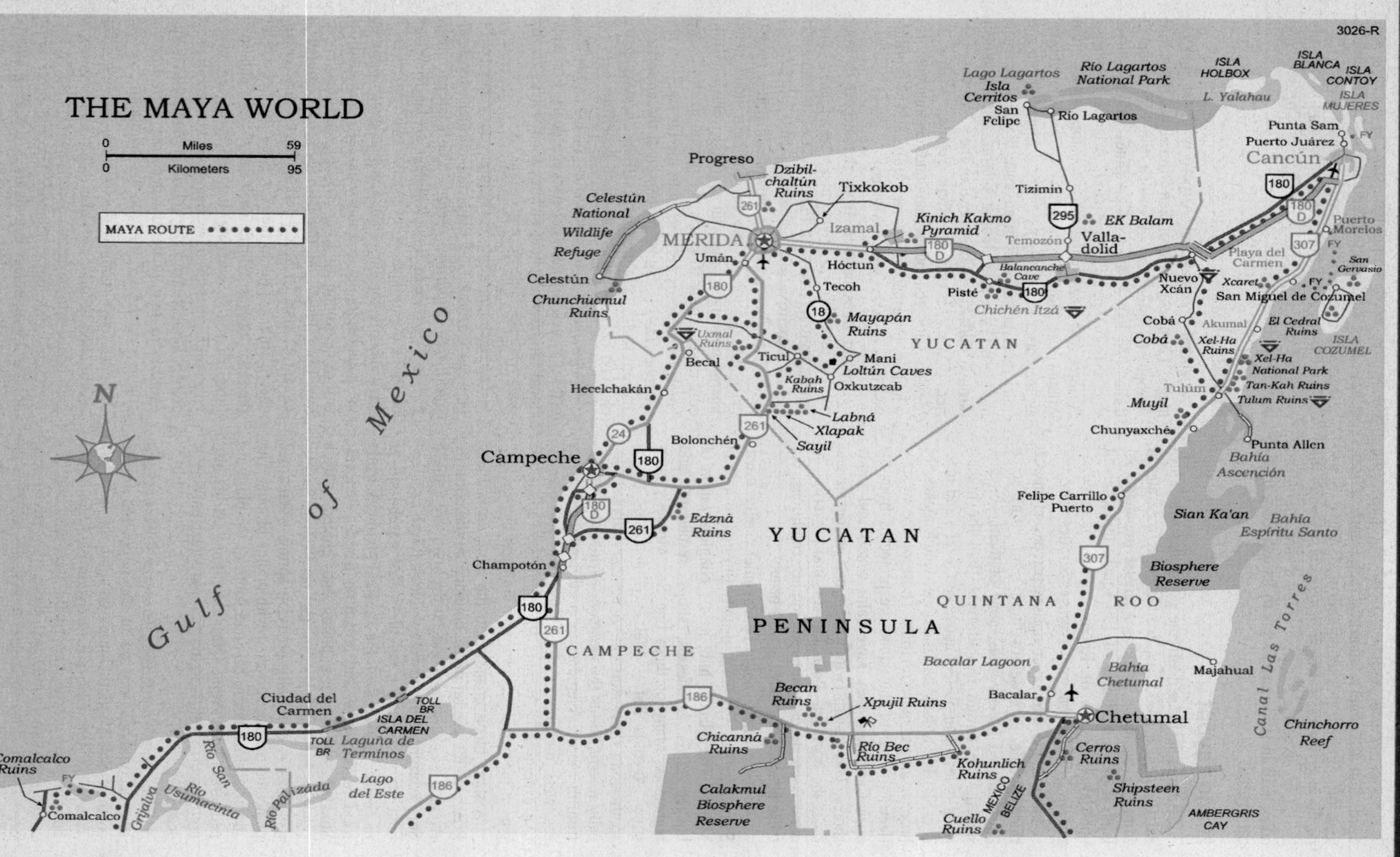
THE MAYA WORLD
0 Miles 59
0 Kilometers 95
MAYA ROUTE
3026-R
N
Gulf of Mexico
Progreso
Dzibilchaltún Ruins
Tixkokob
Celestún National Wildlife Refuge
Celestún
Chunchucmul Ruins
MERIDA
Umán
Izamal
Kinich Kakmo Pyramid
Hóctun
Tecoh
Mayapán Ruins
Temozón
Valladolid
EK Balam
Tizimín
Lago Lagartos
Isla Cerritos
San Felipe
Río Lagartos
Río Lagartos National Park
ISLA HOLBOX
L. Yalahau
ISLA BLANCA
ISLA CONTOY
ISLA MUJERES
Punta Sam
Puerto Juárez
Cancún
Puerto Morelos
Playa del Carmen
San Gervasio
Balancanche Cave
Pisté
Chichén Itzá
Nuevo Xcán
Xcaret
San Miguel de Cozumel
Cobá
Akumal
El Cedral Ruins
Xel-Ha Ruins
Xel-Ha National Park
ISLA COZUMEL
Tulum
Tan-Kah Ruins
Tulum Ruins
Muyil
Chunyaxché
Punta Allen
Bahía Ascención
Uxmal Ruins
Becal
Ticul
Mani
Loltún Caves
Kabah Ruins
Oxkutzcab
YUCATAN
Hecelchakán
Labná
Xlapak
Sayil
Bolonchén
Campeche
Edzná Ruins
Champotón
YUCATAN
PENINSULA
CAMPECHE
QUINTANA ROO
Felipe Carrillo Puerto
Sian Ka'an
Bahía Espíritu Santo
Biosphere Reserve
Canal Las Torres
Bacalar Lagoon
Bahía Chetumal
Majahual
Bacalar
Chetumal
Chinchorro Reef
Becan Ruins
Xpujil Ruins
Chicanná Ruins
Río Bec Ruins
Kohunlich Ruins
Cerros Ruins
Shipsteen Ruins
Calakmul Biosphere Reserve
MEXICO
BELIZE
Cuello Ruins
AMBERGRIS CAY
Ciudad del Carmen
TOLL BR
ISLA DEL CARMEN
Laguna de Términos
Lago del Este
Comalcalco Ruins
Comalcalco
Grijalva
Río Usumacinta
Río San
Río Palizada
FY
180
180 D
295
307
261
18
24
186

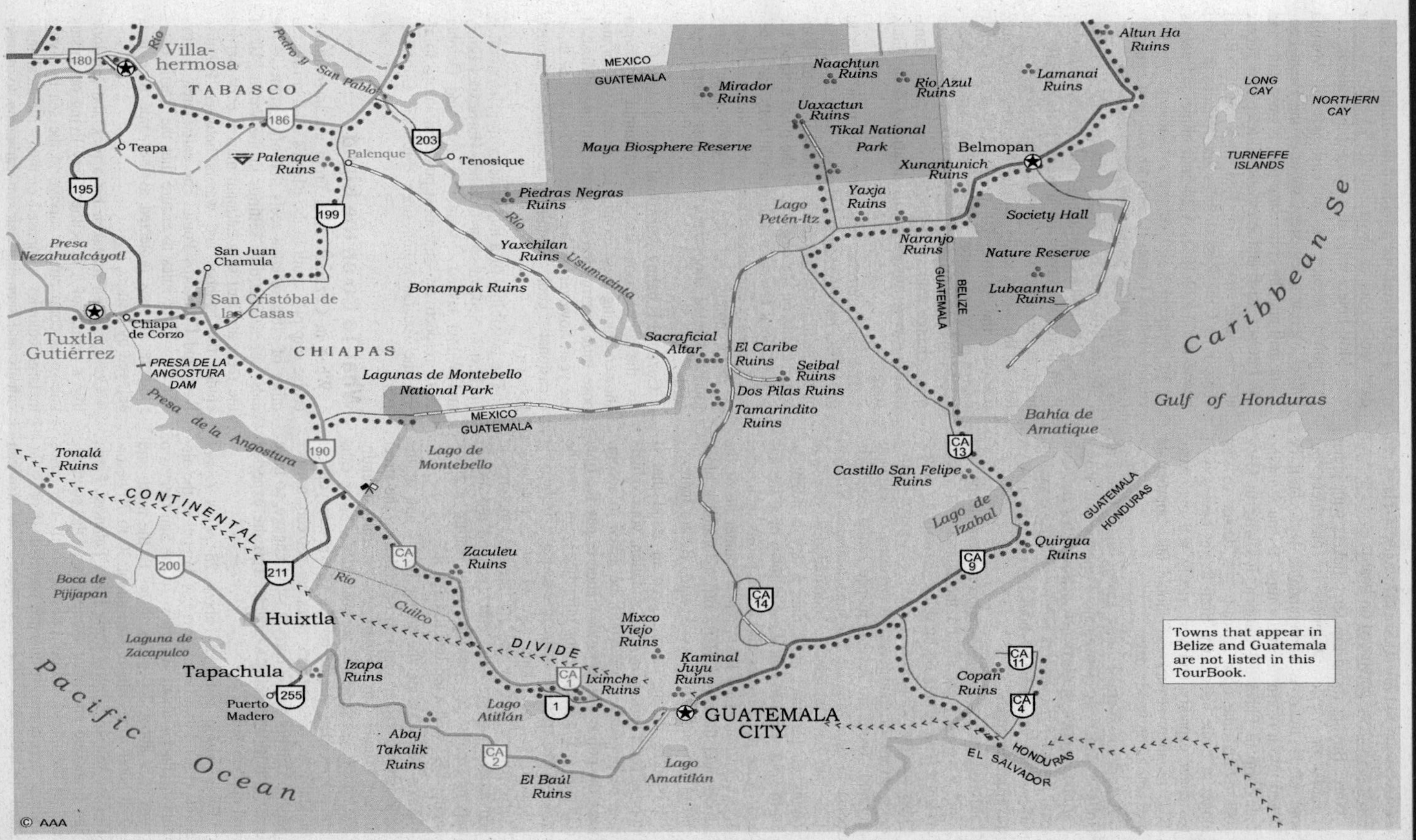
Villa-hermosa
Río
Pedro y San Pablo
TABASCO
Teapa
Palenque Ruins
Palenque
Tenosique
MEXICO
GUATEMALA
Mirador Ruins
Naachtun Ruins
Río Azul Ruins
Lamanai Ruins
Altun Ha Ruins
LONG CAY
NORTHERN CAY
TURNEFFE ISLANDS
Uaxactun Ruins
Tikal National Park
Maya Biosphere Reserve
Belmopan
Xunantunich Ruins
Piedras Negras Ruins
Yaxja Ruins
Society Hall
Lago Petén-Itz
Naranjo Ruins
Nature Reserve
Lubaantun Ruins
BELIZE
GUATEMALA
Presa Nezahualcáyotl
San Juan Chamula
Yaxchilan Ruins
Río Usumacinta
Bonampak Ruins
San Cristóbal de las Casas
Tuxtla Gutiérrez
Chiapa de Corzo
CHIAPAS
Caribbean Se
Sacraficial Altar
El Caribe Ruins
Seibal Ruins
Dos Pilas Ruins
Tamarindito Ruins
PRESA DE LA ANGOSTURA DAM
Lagunas de Montebello National Park
Presa de la Angostura
MEXICO
GUATEMALA
Gulf of Honduras
Bahía de Amatique
Lago de Montebello
Tonalá Ruins
Castillo San Felipe Ruins
CONTINENTAL
Lago de Izabal
GUATEMALA
HONDURAS
Zaculeu Ruins
Quirgua Ruins
Boca de Pijijapan
Río Cuilco
Huixtla
Mixco Viejo Ruins
Laguna de Zacapulco
DIVIDE
Kaminal Juyu Ruins
Towns that appear in Belize and Guatemala are not listed in this TourBook.
Tapachula
Izapa Ruins
Iximche Ruins
Copan Ruins
Puerto Madero
Lago Atitlán
GUATEMALA CITY
Pacific Ocean
Abaj Takalik Ruins
El Baúl Ruins
Lago Amatitlán
HONDURAS
EL SALVADOR
© AAA

tax) is about $11.50 (U.S.); $7 (ages 4-11). Cold beverages can be purchased on board.

Note: Buying round-trip ferry tickets with either UltraMar or Mexico Waterjets is convenient, but your return ticket is nonrefundable and you'll be locked into a return departure time. If you're taking a day trip to Playa del Carmen, it's wise to leave your return time open in case you decide to stay longer or come back early. Both ferries have a high passenger capacity and very rarely sell out. Also, those prone to seasickness should take appropriate precautions on windy days.

A number of cruise lines, among them Carnival, Holland America, Norwegian, Princess and Royal Caribbean, dock at Cozumel and/or Playa del Carmen. AAA/CAA members receive exclusive savings on cruising vacations by booking through a AAA travel professional.

Mopeds, motorcycles and open-air jeeps are popular ways to get around the island, but streets crowded with people on bicycles, jaywalking pedestrians and the ubiquitous scooters can make them a risky means of transportation. Wearing a helmet is required. There are several moped rental establishments in San Miguel. The rate averages $25-$30 (U.S.) per day; insurance is not included. If you're staying on Cozumel more than a day it might be worth your while to rent a car in town or at the airport, since the beaches and other points of interest are spread out. Hertz has a rental counter inside the airport, and there is a Hertz office located a block east of the central plaza on Avenida Benito Juárez.

If you're renting a car, keep in mind that if stopped for a serious moving violation, your vehicle may be impounded and you'll be asked to accompany the police officer to the station to pay the fine. (Of course fines for minor infractions can often be paid on the spot, in cash; in Mexico a bribe is a common way of taking care of such situations.) Curbs painted yellow are for bicycle, motorcycle and moped parking only; curbs painted red are no parking zones. No parking signs feature a black capital "E" with a red line through it.

Taxis wait outside the major hotels and at the passenger ferry pier, and can be hailed on the street in San Miguel. Taxi drivers are generally friendly and courteous, and fares are reasonable. Since cabs are not metered, decide on the fare before you get in. Cabs are not metered; fares are per cab, not per person. Drivers do not carry a lot of change, so have smaller bills and coins available. Tips are expected and appreciated.

Fares within town run about 25 pesos (about $2.40 U.S.). From downtown San Miguel to the airport the fare is about 40 pesos. To the San Gervasio ruins it is about 200 pesos. Fares to the north and south hotel zones range from about 30 to 70 pesos. To Chankanaab Lagoon Park, Playa Palancar, Playa San Francisco and other attractions at the southern end of the island, expect fares of about 100 pesos and up, depending on distance traveled. If possible, share the cost with other passengers. You also can hire a taxi driver for a tour of the island; the standard fee begins at about $80 (U.S.) for a 4-hour tour. Most hotels will call a taxi for their guests.

VigoNet, located on the east side of Avenida Rafael Melgar a few steps south of the Punta Langosta mall and the cruise ship pier, is open daily and has Internet, wi-fi and international telephone access at reasonable rates. The Red Cross (Cruz Roja) clinic is at Calle Rosada Salas and Avenida 20 Sur; phone (987) 872-1058. A 24-hour clinic and access to air ambulance service are available at the Cozumel Medical Center (Centro Médico de Cozumel), Calle 1 Sur #101; phone (987) 872-9400.

Since Cozumel is a major port of call for cruise ships, U.S. dollars are almost universally accepted. Even if you're staying for a week, there's really no need to exchange U.S. currency for pesos. Regardless of the small, daily official exchange rate fluctuations, the simple 10 pesos-to-$1 U.S. dollar exchange is common among many smaller businesses and taxi drivers, and you'll find some even make change with a mix of dollars and pesos. Canadian currency, however, will invariably draw blank stares.

There's a currency exchange office attached to the HSBC bank/ATM located at the southeast corner of the main plaza. There also is an ATM at the Bancomer bank, on the east side of the plaza behind the yellow clock tower; withdrawals at both are in pesos. Currency exchange offices are at the airport and at major hotels, but rates are often poor. Many tourist-oriented shops and restaurants accept credit cards.

Cozumel is balmy year-round. June through October, the rainy season, also is more humid. Afternoon showers during these months are generally brief and pose little interruption to leisure activities. Most of the year, however, is dry, warm and sunny, with an occasional cool evening December through February.

The possibility of a hurricane or tropical storm is likeliest in September or October. Hurricanes Emily and Wilma lashed Cozumel in July and October 2005, respectively—the most powerful storms to affect the Yucatán region since Hurricane Gilbert in 1988.

What To Do on the Island

When in Cozumel, dive. From the international cruise ship pier south to the island's southern tip are miles of offshore coral reefs that offer some of the most spectacular dive settings in the world. All of the reefs are part of a national marine park that includes the beaches and waters between Paradise Reef and Chiqueros Point. The entire area is governed by strict rules to ensure that the fragile environment remains protected at the same time it is enjoyed by visitors.

Coral is often mistaken for a rock and can look like a plant, but it is neither. Tiny living organisms known as coral polyps survive in the sea by living in large colonies composed of many identical individuals and secreting calcium carbonate to protect them by means of a hard outer skeleton. A coral formation constitutes not one organism but thousands of genetically identical organisms that reproduce asexually. As old generations of coral polyps die, new generations grow on top of their skeletons, and over time coral reefs are formed.

Corals obtain most of their nutrients from algae, which is why many species grow in clear, shallow water penetrated by sunlight. Although comprising less than 1 percent of its surface, coral reefs provide a refuge for more than 25 percent of the world's marine life despite being one of the most fragile and endangered of all ecosystems.

Life among the reefs is diverse and amazing. Sedentary animals such as sponges provide shelter for small crustaceans, shrimps and fishes. Another mostly sedentary animal is the sea anemone, a close relative of the corals and jellyfish. Although anemones resemble beautiful flowers (and are named after a terrestrial flower that is a member of the buttercup family), they are actually aggressive predators that sting their prey with poisonous tentacles.

Echinoderms include sea stars, sea urchins and sea cucumbers. Crustaceans like crabs and lobsters hide from predators in reef crevices. Such mollusks as snails, clams, scallops, octopus and squid are reef dwellers, along with the most colorful residents—the fishes. Tropical reef fish are legion: angelfish, butterfly fish, damsel fish, parrotfish, triggerfish, puffer fish, barracuda, grouper, eels, wrasses. Other marine species that frequent the reefs are sharks, rays, sea snakes and sea turtles.

Cozumel has many rewarding dive sites that are classified primarily by skill level and the depth of the dive. The reefs are all off the western (leeward) coast. Paradise Reef, a series of three separate reefs lying about 200 yards offshore, is the only reef accessible from the beach. The marine life here is abundant, and the shallow depth (40 to 50 feet) is suitable for novice divers. Another good location for beginning divers is Yucab Reef, where the swift currents attract barracuda.

Tormentos Reef is suitable for intermediate divers. Colorful coral heads, valleys of sand and marine life that includes moray eels, angelfish, grouper and snapper can be found at depths of 50 to 70 feet. San Francisco Reef is the shallowest of Cozumel's wall dives—half a mile of reef broken into three sections that is teeming with sea life. The Santa Rosa Wall is a very popular deep dive; the wall begins at a depth of 50 feet and drops straight down, with sponge-covered coral overhangs and a myriad little caves and tunnels to explore.

Palancar Reef is one of the island's best known, and with good reason; the marine environment is full of caverns, tunnels and huge, tightly packed coral heads. Colombia Reef matches it in underwater grandeur; the towering pinnacles of coral are pocked with caverns and tunnels. Divers are joined by large turtles, rays and barracuda.

Punta Sur and Maracaibo Reef are Cozumel's most demanding dives. Punta Sur is known for the "Devil's Throat," a dark, narrow tunnel at a depth of 90 feet that opens to a sunlit section of reef wall 130 feet below the surface. A large cave opening is called the "cathedral" for the cross shape on the cavern ceiling created by growths of sponges. Diving conditions at Maracaibo, the southernmost of the island's reefs, are greatly affected by surf and currents, but at around 150 feet the reef wall is incredible. This is decompression diving and thus should be attempted only by the most expert divers. This reef is not on the regular dive boat itinerary and requires advance reservations.

The peak diving season is June through August, when the Caribbean waters are calm and warm and hotel rates tend to be lower. A wetsuit top is recommended for winter diving, when water temperatures are slightly lower. Night dives, underwater photography or making a customized video are among the available options. A scale map of all of Cozumel's reefs, complete with water depths and other information, can be obtained from most of the local dive shops.

A variety of packaged excursions, which usually include airfare, accommodations and diving costs, can be booked in the United States. In addition, the island's dive outfits compete vigorously for both seasoned divers and beginners, offering equipment rentals, instruction, guides and organized expeditions that range from an afternoon to several days.

Many hotels organize their own dive trips as well, and their facilities, while likely to be more expensive, also are more convenient. If you're not on a packaged trip or making your own arrangements, take the time to investigate credentials, boats and equipment; if possible, get the inside scoop from a diver familiar with the area. It's customary to tip the dive crew, as they are responsible for your safety.

One in-town dive shop is Aqua Safari, in the Safari Inn at Av. Rafael Melgar #429 (at Avenida 5 Sur), phone (987) 872-0101. The Scuba Shack, affiliated with Blue Bubble Divers, is at Carretera Costera Sur Km 3.5, between the Casa del Mar and Park Royal hotels; phone (987) 872-4240. **Note:** Make certain the instructor you choose has PADI certification and is affiliated with the island's Buceo Médico Mexicano recompression chamber, located on Calle 5 Sur just off Avenida Rafael Melgar; phone (987) 872-1430 or (987) 872-2387.

Snorkeling is excellent in Chankanaab Bay, at Playa San Francisco and around the offshore reefs near Colombia Lagoon, at the island's southern tip. Morning feedings from the piers of the Stouffer Presidente and La Ceiba Beach hotels attract schools of hungry fish, some of which are bold enough to break the surface of the water and take food from outstretched hands (but beware of sharp teeth). An upside-down plane, deliberately sunk for a movie production, sits on the sandy bottom a short distance from the La Ceiba pier. Those who want to view the colorful marine life but don't want to get wet can take a glass-bottom boat trip.

Snorkeling gear can be cheaply rented at Playa San Francisco, Chankanaab Lagoon Park *(see attraction listing)* or from the larger hotels. In addition, the dive shops and travel agencies provide organized snorkeling excursions to the various reefs. A representative agency is Turismo Aviomar, which has a central office at Avenida 5 Norte between Calles 2 and 4 Norte; phone (987) 872-0477. Other Turismo Aviomar offices are in the lobbies of the major hotels, including the Presidente Intercontinental. The Fiesta Cozumel Holidays agency also has offices in the major hotels.

Sport fishing is superb, and Cozumel was an angler's paradise long before it gained renown as a dive destination. Catches differ according to the season. From April through June blue and white marlin, dorado, tuna and sailfish are hooked; fishing for amberjack, barracuda, bonito, mackerel, shark, snapper and wahoo can be done all year. Lagoon fishing yields bonefish, snook and tarpon.

Charters range from about $400 to $700 (U.S.) according to the length of the trip (half day or full day), size of the vessel, the number of people and the season. To get an idea of what's available and how much it costs visit the Club Abrigo Náutico de Cozumel marina, a mile north of downtown near the airport, in the late afternoon when the boats are returning and talk to a couple of the captains.

Nauti Girl Charters offers guided sport-fishing trips in the waters off Cozumel, Playa del Carmen and Akumal aboard the *Nauti Girl,* a 41-foot vessel powered by twin diesel engines. Half- or full-day charters include crew, fishing gear, safety equipment and boat amenities. The office is at Avenida 25 Sur #480 (at Calle 19 Sur); for information phone (987) 872-3270. Snail mail in Mexico can be exceedingly slow, so to arrange a fishing trip in advance e-mail Nauti Girl Charters at eddscozumelprodigy.net.mx.

You also can hire a boat and a guide through the Cozumel Angler's Fleet at Club Naútico de Cozumel, at the Puerto de Abrigo Marina on Avenida Rafael Melgar, just north of downtown; phone (987) 872-1113, or write Club Naútico at P.O. Box 341, Cozumel, Quintana Roo 77600.

Sightseeing excursions to Cancún, Playa del Carmen, Xel-Ha, Tulum and other nearby points of interest can be easily arranged; information is available at most hotels. Travel agencies also offer Cozumel tours that include such activities as sunbathing at the beach, snorkeling at Chankanaab Lagoon Park, a visit to the San Gervasio ruins or a day trip to the Xcaret ecological theme park on the mainland *(see Playa del Carmen),* which includes ferry transportation.

The Cozumel Country Club is on the north side of the island, near the airport. The island's first golf course has 18 holes, a pro shop, a driving range, and club and shoe rental. Carts are required. Guest privileges are available for those staying at the Playa Azul and Presidente Inter Continental hotels. For greens fees and additional information phone (987) 872-9570.

Rancho Buenavista offers a 4-hour guided horseback riding trek into the interior jungle scrub, with stops at several Mayan ruins. The tours depart from the Acuario Restaurant on Avenida Rafael Melgar and include round-trip transportation to the ranch; phone (987) 872-1537.

Carnaval, the island's version of Mardi Gras, is held in February on the 3 days preceding Ash Wednesday. Colorful float parades along the *malecón,* masquerade balls, street dances and the "burning" of Juan Carnaval (a Carnaval king) take place during this exuberant fiesta. The Billfish Release Tournament and the Marlin Tournament are both held in early May. Cozumel also celebrates the patron saint of San Miguel with a fiesta on Sept. 29.

Beaches and Ruins

As in the rest of Mexico, all of Cozumel's beaches are public, even those that appear to be the property of hotels. North of San Miguel are several of the more luxurious accommodations and some condominium developments. Playa San Juan extends to Punta Norte, where the highway ends. This beach is good for swimming and water recreation. Beyond Punta Norte is miniscule Isla de la Pasión, in the middle of calm Abrigo Bay. Local boat owners can take you to this secluded spot, where there are deserted beaches and opportunities for fishing, but no facilities.

South of San Miguel, Avenida Rafael Melgar becomes the coastal highway (Costera Sur) and passes several beach and snorkeling spots. Heading south, the first beach club worth a stop is The Money Bar, next to the Fiesta Americana Cozumel Dive Resort (watch for the signed hotel turn-off on the main road). This large *palapa* restaurant has beach chairs, umbrellas and a booth that rents snorkel equipment. The snorkeling is decent just offshore along the Dzul-Ha Reef.

The beach at Chankanaab Lagoon Park *(see attraction listing)* is studded with *palapas* that provide welcome shade, the sand is soft and powdery, and there are opportunities for snorkeling, diving and interactive dolphin swims. South of the park off the Costera Sur (coastal highway), beautiful Playa San Francisco is hugely popular with cruise ship passengers. Here you'll find public showers and changing rooms, as well as the Carlos 'n Charlies and Playa San Francisco beach clubs. Drinks, food, beach chairs, shade and snorkel gear can all be had for moderate prices.

For a mellower beach scene, continue south to the Playa Palancar beach club (watch for signs). You'll find the usual *palapa* seafood restaurant and beach chairs, minus the cruise ship crowds. For snorkelers, the main draw is an opportunity to see a relatively shallow section of the famous Palancar Reef. Boats leave from shore and charge about $35 (U.S.) per person for a guided 90-minute snorkel tour.

The eastern (windward) coast is far less developed and thus more dramatic. The beaches, interspersed among rocky coves, are frequently empty. The open Caribbean is intensely turquoise, but the surf and undertows are often strong; swim at your own risk.

Near the entrance to Punta Sur Park *(see attraction listing),* hand-painted signs featuring the visage of Bob Marley direct day-trippers to Freedom in Paradise (also called "Rasta Bar"), Cozumel's very own mini Jamaica. The rustic two-story *palapa* restaurant has a relaxed tropical feel and sports the requisite red, green and yellow rasta colors, while the reggae icon's greatest hits seemingly play on a constant loop. The beach is gorgeous, but mostly rocky and not good for swimming.

From the southern end of the island at Punta Celarain, a paved road follows the coast north toward Punta Morena. Dotting the coastline are several beach clubs where you can grab a bite, sip a margarita, clock some serious hammock time and watch the surf roll in.

For sunbathing or a lazy beach stroll, try the long powder-white stretch of sand at the appropriately named Playa Bonita. For swimming, the calmest windward shore waters are usually found at Chen Río Beach, a protected cove farther up the road. There are *palapa* bars at both beaches, but there are better views and better food at Coconuts, a few minutes' drive north. Perched on a high bluff overlooking the Caribbean, Coconuts is a must for east shore first-timers. Ask for an outdoor table to fully absorb the unbeatable ocean panorama.

Located roughly halfway between Coconuts and the Carretera Transversal (cross-island road) turnoff, the Punta Morena beach club dishes up impressive lunches on a beachfront, white canvas-shaded patio. The fresh lobster tacos and chicken club sandwich are both delicious, and the new age background music encourages chilling out.

Near Punta Morena the road runs into the end of the east-west Carretera Transversal (cross-island road), about 15 kilometers (9 miles) from San Miguel. Playa Oriente, the rocky beach, is scenic but not safe for swimming. There also are two beach clubs here, and employees try hard to wave you in.

North of the Carretera Transversal junction the coastal route becomes a dirt road, passing waterfowl-filled lagoons and a smattering of ruins, among them Castillo Real—a former Mayan fortification where the few remains include a lookout tower. The snorkeling is outstanding in this little-visited area, but a jeep or four-wheel-drive vehicle is necessary to reach it. At the northern tip of Cozumel is the Punta Molas Lighthouse, where bird-watching is rewarding and it is possible to camp (again, no facilities).

Note: The road was severely damaged by Hurricane Wilma, and travel north of the turn-off is not recommended. A few organized four-wheel-drive tours still visit this remote area; inquire locally about conditions.

The San Gervasio Ruins *(see attraction listing)* are also north of and accessible from the cross-island road. At Km 17.5 on the Costera Sur, a turn-off leads about 3 kilometers (2 miles) east to the ruins of El Cedral. One small structure is all that remains at this site, believed to be the oldest on the island and the one first discovered by the Spanish. A tree grows from the roof, its roots snaking around the crumbled stones. Faint traces of paint and stucco are still visible. A small farming settlement named Cedral—the island's agricultural center—has grown up here, dominated by a rural church painted bright green.

Dining

Cozumel's restaurant scene, like shopping, centers on San Miguel. Island eateries range from drop-in casual to suitable for a special occasion. There are a variety of cuisines (French, Italian, Japanese) in addition to Mexican, and also a number of local places dishing up terrific Yucatecan food that are off the beaten tourist path but definitely worth searching out.

Guido's, on the waterfront between calles 6 and 8 Norte, specializes in wood-fired pizzas but also offers fish and shellfish dishes. Another house specialty is *pan de ajo,* bread infused with olive oil, garlic and rosemary. The bougainvillea-draped outdoor dining area is a lovely spot for dinner. For a relaxing break from shopping, Pancho's Backyard, inside the Los Cinco Soles craft store, serves standard Mexican dishes in a courtyard garden setting complete with live marimba music—although you may have to share this place with the cruise ship crowd. Menu prices are listed in both dollars and pesos.

La Veranda, on Calle 4 Norte between avenidas 5 and 10 Norte, also has a lovely setting—a Caribbean-style wooden house and romantic backyard garden with a fountain and gazebo that are illuminated in the evening. Caesar salad for two is prepared tableside, and the seafood dishes, in keeping with the ambience, have a Caribbean flavor. La Cocay ("the firefly"), Calle 8 Norte between avenidas 10 and 15 Norte, is a sophisticated spot where you can order a range of appetizers to nibble on, or entrees like sauteed sea scallops, lobster tail or a rib-eye steak.

Lobster aficionados will certainly want to try the Lobster House (La Cabaña del Pescador), in the hotel zone at the northern end of the island (on the east side of the road across from the Playa Azul Hotel). The atmosphere is romantic and candlelit, with starfish-studded fishing nets hanging from the ceiling. The crustacean is the only thing on the menu—simply boiled and served with melted butter, steamed vegetables and bread. At market price, a jumbo lobster tail sure to satisfy two people will cost about $60 (U.S., cash only). After dinner, ask the waiter to take you for a walk through the gardens out front and shine a flashlight on the massive iguanas sleeping in the trees. (**Note:** The restaurant has no air conditioning, and cash only is accepted.)

La Lobsteria, a block off the waterfront at the corner of Avenida 5 Sur and Calle 7 Sur (4 blocks south of Plaza del Sol), also specializes in lobster—lobster tails served with drawn butter, rice and vegetables. Other choices include coconut shrimp and seafood soup *(sopa de mariscos).* The restaurant is in a building reminiscent of a typical Mayan house with a thatched *palapa* roof.

Johnny Bravo's, on Avenida 15 Sur between calles Rosado Salas and Calle 3 Sur, dishes up *arrancheros* (are-raun-CHAIR-ohs). Tough cuts of beef are pounded thin to tenderize them, then grilled over hot charcoal. The meat is sliced with a sharp knife, piled on freshly made tortillas and topped with grilled onions, sliced radishes, cilantro and hot sauce.

Casa Denis has traditional Yucatecan dishes like *cochinita pibil, poc chuc, sopa de lima* and phenomenal *papadzules* (warm tortillas stuffed with chopped hard-boiled egg and soaked with a tasty pumpkin seed sauce). Family owned and operated, this longtime local favorite opened in 1945 and is on the pedestrian-only section of Calle 1 Sur, half a block east of the main plaza. Seating is available inside the historic *casa* or at the sidewalk tables out front. Service is fast and friendly.

Some of Cozumel's best eating is at the unassuming places that locals frequent. On the east side of the main plaza, below the yellow clock tower, La Parroquia is a simple taco stand with a few tables off to the side. Local vendors and tourists alike line up for cheap *cerveza* and beef, chicken or fish taco plates that cost between 50 and 85 pesos. Kick back here and do some people watching.

Taco lovers also should seek out El Foco (The Light Bulb), on Avenida 5 Sur a short distance south of the main plaza. Grilled meats topped with grilled onions and peppers and melted cheese are served with flour tortillas. There are various combination plates, all for 70 pesos (about $6.50 U.S.).

Las Seras, on the corner of Avenida 30 Sur and Calle Morelos (between calles 2 and 4 Sur) has *tacos al pastor*—slivers of barbecued pork, minced onion, cilantro and pieces of fresh pineapple on a corn tortilla—for about six pesos apiece, plus tasty bean soup garnished with cheese and onions. The restaurant is open only in the evening. Los Tres Gatitos (The Three Kittens), in a quiet residential neighborhood on Calle 7 Sur between avenidas 10 and 15 Sur, is another evening-only place that serves various soups as well as *antojitos* (snacks) like *panuchos*, chewy fried corn tortillas topped with black bean paste, shredded chicken, cheese, chopped lettuce, tomatoes and pickled onions.

Restaurante Manati occupies a tin-roofed, bright yellow clapboard building at the corner of Avenida 10 Norte and Calle 8 Norte. The decor is shabby-chic, and the *comida corrida* (fast food) menu is outstanding. For about $6 (U.S.) you can choose from fresh grouper, breaded steak in wine sauce, homemade pasta or orange chicken. Meals come with your choice of salad or soup of the day. Wash it all down with one of Manati's potent mango margaritas. A tiny stage hosts a local salsa band on Thursday nights and a classic rock outfit on Saturdays.

For a morning pick-me-up, head to one of the island bakeries *(panaderías)*. They offer fresh-baked French rolls *(bolillos)*, sweet breakfast breads *(pan dulce)* and pastries; try *orejas*, crunchy morsels shaped like an ear and drenched with honey, or nut cookies topped with freshly grated coconut. Customers take a round metal tray and a pair of tongs, select the items they want from the bakery shelves and then take them to the counter to be bagged and paid for.

Zermatt, at the corner of Calle 4 Norte and Avenida 5 Norte (a block east of the waterfront) has fresh bread, yummy desserts and pizza by the slice in the afternoon. The St. Martin Bakery, on Avenida 30 Sur between calles 5 and 7 Sur, has excellent flan and homemade *tamales* in banana-leaf wrappers (available in the afternoon). Café Caribe on Avenida 10 Sur offers ice cream, carrot cake and other sweets along with fresh-roasted coffee.

Ice cream parlors *(neverias)* serve ice cream *(helado)* made with milk or bottled water in flavors both standard (chocolate) and exotic (corn). A *paletería* is a shop that sells both ice cream and iced juice drinks *(agua frescas)*. The *agua fresca de sandía*—watermelon juice mixed with sugar and water—is utterly refreshing on a hot day. Another refreshing treat is mango; when the fruit is in season (spring and summer), street vendors sell them on a stick, peeled and carved into different shapes.

Dress is casual at all island restaurants, and reservations are advised only at the most expensive places. Service is invariably relaxed and friendly. There's no need to worry about health concerns at restaurants that cater to tourists. At local joints, follow the standard rule—if it's cooked it should be safe to eat. English isn't spoken at the small family-run places, but it doesn't really matter; most have a wall menu, so just point to what you want to order and remember to add *"por favor."* Some restaurants close on Sunday. *For a list of AAA-RATED dining establishments on Cozumel, see the Lodgings & Restaurants section.*

Shopping

For shoppers, Avenida Rafael Melgar is the place to go. Shops and boutiques offer duty-free imported goods, chic sportswear and high-quality folk art reproductions, as well as T-shirts and cheap souvenirs. The shops cluster around the main plaza and extend for about five blocks north and eight blocks south along the waterfront. Keep in mind, however, that prices will be more expensive here than in the shops on the side streets just a couple of blocks off Melgar. Also, prices at many shops magically drop on days when cruise ships are few and business is slow.

Five blocks north of the plaza is the Forum Shops, an air-conditioned, marble-floored mini mall on Avenida Rafael Melgar at Calle 8 Norte. Inside you'll find a Diamonds International outlet, plus shops selling quality beachwear, leather, silver, glass, tequila and cigars. Ride the escalator to the second floor for clean restrooms, a pharmacy, a restaurant/bar and a jewelry factory where you can peer through glass windows and watch jewelers at work.

Next door is Los Cinco Soles, a big, rambling store that sells a huge selection of crafts, art and clothing imported from all over Mexico. From furniture, ceramics, wood carvings and masks to textiles, hand-blown glass and obsidian figurines, prices on craft items are relatively reasonable. Clothing and jewelry prices, on the other hand, are high. For the budget-minded there's also an endless selection of affordable knickknacks.

Souvenir T-shirt shoppers flock to the Cozumel outpost of Florida's Ron Jon Surf Shop (at the corner of Avenida Rafael Melgar and Calle 4 Norte), where high-quality logo T-shirts, caps, souvenirs and beachwear fly off the shelves. For T-shirts of comparable quality at better prices, try Piraña Joe, on Avenida Rafael Melgar between Calle 2 Norte and Calle 4 Norte.

While doing the shopping shuffle along the waterfront, you'll notice there's no shortage of jewelry merchants in San Miguel. The salespeople posted in front of these stores can be annoyingly aggressive in their attempts to get you inside, often luring unsuspecting shoppers with promises of a "free gift." If your idea of a gift is a high-pressure sales pitch, by all means have at it. If not, it's best to ignore them and keep walking.

The plaza's northern side (the pedestrian-only section of Benito Juárez) is chock-a-block with souvenir shops and stalls, most selling identical merchandise (think blankets, sombreros, T-shirts and jewelry). While good quality is hard to come by, a little bargaining should yield low prices. On the east side of the plaza, the white-trimmed, bright yellow Plaza del Sol building is undergoing renovations, and new shops are scheduled to open sometime in the fall of 2008.

Other shops are on downtown's more relaxed side streets. Muebles de la Santa Cruz, on Avenida 15 Norte between Avenida Benito Juárez and Calle 2 Norte, has wrought-iron and hand-carved wood furniture, talavera tile, picture frames and lamps. Unahi Pax, at the corner of Benito Juárez and Avenida 15, carries musical instruments from all over the country.

Galería Azul, on Avenida 10 Sur between Calle 1 Sur and Calle Rosado Salas (a block and a half southeast of the main plaza), is owned by Greg, an exceptional Washington state artist who specializes in unique blown-glass pieces incorporating intricate undersea-themed designs. The gallery is open daily 5:30-9:30 p.m., but he will gladly open the shop for you during non-business hours; phone (987) 872-4493. Colorful hand-painted pottery spills out of the Talavera Store, on Calle 1 Sur between avenidas 20 and 25 (3 blocks east of the plaza).

Inspiración Galería de Arte, on Avenida 5 Sur near the corner of Calle 3 Sur (not far from the main plaza), deals in contemporary paintings and sculpture, plus Jicara gourd bowls. A few doors down, Puro Mar, at the corner of Avenida 5 Sur and Calle 3 Sur, sells top-quality swim trunks, bikinis, flip-flops, backpacks and other beach gear at tourist-inflated prices. Near the plaza, Miguelon y Hijos, on Calle 5 Sur between avenidas 10 and 15 Sur (watch for the doorway on the left side of the street), features the work of a local Cozumeleño artist who specializes in painstakingly carved shell cameos.

At the Punta Langosta Pier (Avenida Rafael Melgar, just south of Calle 7 Sur), cruise ship passengers disembark and walk directly into the Punta Langosta mall, a modern open-air building with shops, jewelry stores, clothing boutiques and eateries on two levels. Los Cinco Soles has a small satellite location here, as does the Hard Rock Cafe. Starbucks addicts can get their fix at the thatch-roofed franchise fronting the mall.

The Chedraui grocery store, on Avenida Rafael Melgar just south of downtown San Miguel, is a big, modern supermarket that stocks a variety of fresh produce, meats, seafood, cheeses and other staples. Also in the Chedraui shopping center is a movie theater that screens first-run Hollywood fare and Spanish language features.

El Mercado, at the corner of Avenida 25 Sur and Calle Rosado Salas, is the biggest of the traditional Mexican markets on the island. All kinds of fruits and vegetables are for sale here, along with cilantro, fresh and dried chilies, freshly squeezed fruit and carrot juices, honey and *jamaica* (dried hibiscus blossoms), sold by the kilo. When boiled in water and allowed to steep for at least several hours, strained into a pitcher along with sugar and lime juice and then served over ice, the blossoms make a refreshing tea. *Pescaderías* (fish markets) sell freshly caught fish like grouper *(mero)* and snapper *(huachinango)* as well as shrimp, octopus and conch.

Nightlife

After a strenuous day of diving, swimming or exploring, most visitors are content to turn in early. For after-dinner relaxation, the outdoor cafes on the south side of the main plaza are pleasant places to enjoy the evening breeze. On Sunday evenings the plaza comes alive when families gather to hear Latin bands or be serenaded by mariachis. This is a good opportunity to dance and mingle with the locals, who take tourism in stride and are friendly toward visitors.

For those with energy to burn, the ever-reliable Carlos 'n Charlie's, in the Punta Langosta mall, is a raucous spot with beer-drinking contests and high-decibel music. Patrons also know what to expect at the Cozumel branch of the Hard Rock Cafe, Av. Rafael Melgar #2A (second floor), just north of the main plaza.

Fans of Polynesian-style tiki bars should drop by Tiki-Tok, a friendly second-floor *palapa* bar on Avenida Rafael Melgar between Calle 2 Sur and Calle 4 Sur. In addition to the usual lineup of tropical cocktails (mai tais, daiquiris and piña coladas), house specialties include original concoctions named after major Atlantic hurricanes (beware: Wilma packs a wallop). Tables along the front railing are situated in a sandbox and overlook the waterfront action below; there's live music on Thursday, Friday and Saturday nights.

Parrotheads belly up to the bar at Margaritaville (corner of Avenida Rafael Melgar and Calle 11 Sur), the Cozumel branch of Jimmy Buffett's wildly successful theme restaurant chain. This place draws big crowds during the day when cruise ships are in port. Revelers pack the outdoor waterfront terrace; DJs spin Buffett tunes and classic rock. A cheeseburger (in paradise?) and fries will set you back about $12 (U.S.).

Next door to Margaritaville is the 1.5 Tequila Lounge, a late night hipster hangout. A chic club overlooking the Caribbean, the lounge pours high-end tequila shots and designer martinis. DJs specialize in electronica, jazz fusion, trance and the like. With the exception of theme party nights, there's usually no cover charge; drinks are pricey, however.

Tourist information office: second floor of the Plaza del Sol building behind the main plaza, corner of Benito Juárez and Avenida 5 Norte. Open Mon.-Fri. 9-3; phone (987) 869-0211. The magazine *Cozumel Today,* available around town, is published by the tourism office and is a source for local visitor information.

What To See

***ATLANTIS* SUBMARINE** departs from the Atlantis office, Km marker 4 on Carretera Chankanaab (Chankanaab Highway), across the street from the Casa del Mar Hotel; passengers are taken from the pier to the submarine via a 12-minute ferry ride. The submarine accommodates 48 passengers for a 40-minute undersea tour of Chankanaab Reef at depths of up to 100 feet. Large portholes running the length of the sub offer views of coral formations and marine life in crystal-clear water.

Note: Entering the sub involves climbing backwards down seven steep stairs (handrails are available). Children under age 4 or under 36 inches tall are not permitted, and the trip is not advised for those prone to claustrophobia or confined to a wheelchair. Sub departs daily (weather permitting) at 9, 11 and noon. Fee $81 U.S. (includes $2 entrance fee for visiting the reef area); $47 (children 36 inches tall through age 12). AX, MC, VI. Phone (866) 546-7820 (from the United States), (987) 872-5671 or 01 (800) 715-0804 (toll-free long distance within Mexico) for reservation information.

GEM **CHANKANAAB LAGOON PARK** (Parque Laguna de Chankanaab) is on the leeward side of the island, about 9 km (5.5 mi.) s. of town off the Costera Sur (Coastal Highway), the southward extension of Avenida Rafael Melgar. This large beach park took the opportunity to install new *palapas* and other facilities following Hurricane Wilma. Chankanaab, which means "small sea," refers to the natural saltwater lagoon inside the park, which provides sanctuary for such marine life as corals, sponges, crustaceans, turtles, moray eels and tropical fish.

Snorkeling is not permitted in the lagoon, nor is feeding the fish; observation areas are provided. Surrounding the lagoon is a shady botanical garden with tropical and subtropical plant species, many native to Cozumel; for a tip, local youths will give impromptu tours and point out the different flora and fauna

The beach fronting the bay is wide and pretty. In addition to swimming and snorkeling (submerged religious statues and encrusted anchors and cannons are popular dive sites), beach activities include snuba (a combination of snorkeling and scuba diving) and Seatrek, an underwater breathing helmet. A small museum has exhibits about local plant, animal and marine life. There also are hammocks for "frond snoozing" and a children's play area. Several dive shops on site, as well as restrooms, changing areas and showers.

Food is available. Picnicking is permitted. Allow 3 hours minimum. Daily 7-5. Admission (includes access to the beach and use of park facilities) $16 (U.S.); $8 (ages 3-11). There are extra fees for snuba, Seatrek, a sea lion show and dolphin swim programs. Snorkel and scuba equipment can be rented; you also can bring your own. Phone (987) 872-0914.

MUSEUM OF THE ISLAND OF COZUMEL (Museo de la Isla de Cozumel) is on Avenida Rafael Melgar just n. of the main ferry landing, between calles 4 and 6 Norte. This museum's four exhibit halls chronicle the island's human history, from its reputation as a revered Mayan religious destination through pre-Hispanic trade and navigation to its settlement by Mayan refugees from the 19th-century War of the Castes. An overview of natural history (with information in Spanish and English) focuses on endangered species and local plant and animal life.

A restaurant on the second floor has expansive waterfront views. There also is a bookstore and library with a few selections in English. Guided tours in English are available. Restrooms are provided. Allow 2 hours minimum. Daily 9-5 (may vary seasonally). Admission $3 (U.S.), free (0-7). Phone (987) 872-1434.

PUNTA SUR PARK (Parque Punta Sur) is at Km 28 at the southern end of the Costera Sur (coastal highway), about 28 km (17 mi.) s. of the main ferry landing; take the Punta Sur turn-off and proceed about 100 yards down a dirt road to the entrance ticket booth. This national ecological reserve focuses on the conservation of local wildlife, including crocodiles, iguanas, egrets and herons, and therefore has few tourist-oriented facilities.

The Celarain Lighthouse, built in 1934, stands guard at the island's southern point. The steep circular staircase can be climbed, and there are outstanding views of turquoise waters and sandy beaches from the top. Next to the lighthouse is a squat white building, formerly the lighthouse keeper's home and now the Navigation Museum, which has displays of ship models, nautical artifacts, maps and exhibits relating to the history of the lighthouse. Next to the museum are a few thatched-roofed souvenir stalls. Beyond the vendor stalls several well-marked, sandy paths lead to the edge of a low bluff offering more coastal views.

Flatbed trucks with bench seating shuttle visitors to La Playa mas Hermosa ("The Most Beautiful Beach") for snorkeling. You can swim out to the reef from shore; two floating platforms anchored offshore provide a place to rest en route. It took quite a beating from Hurricane Wilma, but the farther west you swim along the reef the better the underwater scenery gets (swaying purple sea fans and large schools of tropical fish).

A portion of the beach is a sea turtle nesting area that is blocked off to visitors; other beaches within the park are accessible. Forty-minute catamaran rides explore the mangroves and bird life of Colombia Lagoon. A wooden lookout tower on the shore can be climbed for views out over the lagoon. **Note:** Cars are permitted only as far as the lighthouse parking lot.

A map of the park is handed out at the entrance booth. A snack bar at the snorkeling beach sells soda, cold beer and chips. Restrooms are on site. Snorkeling gear can be rented. Allow 2 hours minimum. Park open daily 9-4:30. Shuttle trucks run continuously between the lighthouse and the snorkeling beach, but there is no set schedule. Admission 110 pesos or $10 (U.S.); free (ages 0-9). Catamaran rides $3. Round-trip taxi service from San Miguel runs $40-$50. Phone (987) 872-0914.

SAN GERVASIO is e. on the Carretera Transversal (Avenida Benito Juárez) to the well-marked San Gervasio turn-off, then n. 6.3 km (about 4 mi.) on a paved two-lane access road to the entrance gate. Not nearly as impressive architecturally as other archeological sites on the Yucatán Peninsula—Chichén Itzá this isn't—San Gervasio (san her-BAH-see-oh) was nevertheless inhabited for more than 1,000 years. Cozumel's largest remaining Mayan ruin, it was once a sanctuary to the goddess Ixchel and an important pilgrimage site.

There are no grandly restored pyramids here. Bear left after walking through the site entrance and you'll come to Plaza Central. Nine spread-out structures sit low to the ground and are in various states of disrepair. However, there are more interesting ruins beyond this plaza. From the back side of the plaza, take the well-marked, jungle-lined walking path that leads to Ka'Na Nah, a Post-Classic (1200-1650) temple reputedly built in dedication to Ixchel. It features some interesting, although decayed, carvings around the base.

Another path leads east from Ka'Na Nah to Murcielagos, a building set deep in the jungle that is not roped off like the other structures. Numerous iguanas sunning themselves on rocks offer good photo opportunities. A separate trail branching off to the left leads back to Plaza Central by way of Nohoch Nah. This boxy temple, set atop a stepped pyramid-like platform, is classic Mayan architecture—with the out-of-character addition of a screen door that has been installed across the front entrance. On the way back to the plaza is El Arco, an intact arch that presents another good photo opportunity. The site's other significant structure is Manitas, a small temple that retains faint traces of red-colored hand prints.

The site's thatch-roofed entrance pavilion has restrooms, vendor stalls and a snack bar that sells bottled water and sodas. Information plaques in Spanish and English provide historical background. The structures are roped off and cannot be climbed. Daily 7-5. Admission (paid at the entrance pavilion) 33 pesos (about $3.20 U.S.). A second fee of 39 pesos (about $3.80 U.S.) per person must be paid at the official entrance to the ruins; this fee is charged by INAH (National Institute of Anthropology and History), the organization that manages almost every archeological site in the country. Parking is free, but expect to give someone a few pesos to "watch your car" (standard procedure at attraction parking lots all over Mexico). San Miguel taxi drivers will take you to the site entrance and wait while you view the ruins; the fare is negotiable, but expect to pay about $30 U.S.

ISLA HOLBOX, QUINTANA ROO (A-3)

The very definition of "laid back," Isla Holbox (EES-lah hole-BOSH) lies in the Gulf of Mexico 7 miles off the northern tip of the Yucatán Peninsula, or about 40 miles northwest of Cancún as the crow flies. It was once visited by pirates who subsequently intermarried with Mayans living on the island, and descendants of the original families still live here. The first Europeans arrived in 1856 to harvest tropical hardwoods and founded a small village.

Although off the beaten path and yet to be discovered by mass tourism, Holbox—some 7 miles long and about a mile wide—is growing, and not just in popularity: Land is being bought for multistory resort hotels, and efforts have begun to control both their construction and the island's ambience. For now, though, this is as good a spot as any to get away from it all.

And getting away from it all is the whole point. On Holbox the key word is relaxation. The exceptionally wide, sandy beaches are ideal for ambling. Shell collectors will delight in the variety of intact, unbroken seashells deposited on the beach by gulf currents. The water is warm, shallow, relatively clear and emerald green, without the dangerous undertows and large waves that can affect Quintana Roo's Caribbean coast beaches. The only thing the gulf lacks is the dazzling turquoise hues of the Caribbean.

Other pleasures are of the laid-back variety as well—paddle boating and kayaking, strolling around the village or just lazing the afternoon away in a hammock. A daily ritual is sunset watching from the beach or the main pier in town, a view that takes in fishing boats silhouetted against the sky. A more adrenaline-fueled activity is the relatively new sport of kite surfing, which utilizes a surfboard with foot straps and a large kite that together propel a user both through the air and on the water.

Holbox Village has a prototypical tropical seaside look. The streets are sand; golf carts, bikes and walking are the preferred modes of transportation. Dogs nap in the shade. Dust devils swirl down the sandy streets. Local kids shoot hoops on the main plaza's basketball court. Tourists snooze on the beach. The wood and cinder block buildings are painted bright colors and roofed with either corrugated tin or traditional thatched *palapas*. Fancy? No—but a bit of paradise nevertheless.

Practicalities

There's a reason that Isla Holbox is known for its tranquility—getting there involves a bit of effort. The island is about a 3-hour drive from Cancún via free Mex. 180 (not toll highway Mex. 180-D) west to the Nuevo X-Can exit (signed "Nuevo X-Can/Kantunil"). The highway runs north to the land's end village of Chiquilá and south to the ruins of Cobá. Toward Chiquilá the road becomes very narrow, and sections of it are rough.

Vehicles can be left at a guarded parking lot in Chiquilá for a daily fee of about $4 (U.S.), cash only. Estacionamiento Cirilo has covered spaces and is located on the east (right) side of Avenida Delfines (Chiquilá's main drag) as you drive into the heart of town. The lot is next door to the Hotel La Puerta del Sol. If the lot is full, there are other lots along the waterfront, closer to the ferry pier. No matter where you park, do not leave valuables in your vehicle. There also is a twice-daily car ferry, but you won't need a car on the island.

Second-class buses travel to Chiquilá from the central bus station in downtown Ciudad Cancún (at the intersection of avenidas Tulum and Uxmal in front of the Plaza Caribe Hotel). There are normally three departures a day for Holbox; the earliest bus leaves around 8 a.m. A private taxi from downtown Cancún to Chiquilá costs about $70 (U.S.) one way; fare from the Cancún Hotel Zone is about $80.

From Chiquilá, water taxis and a ferry service take passengers on the 30-minute ride across Yalahau Lagoon to the island. The fare for a water taxi is 50 pesos (about $4.85 U.S.). The ferry is less expensive—45 pesos (about $4.40 U.S.) one way (25 pesos for children). The "9 Hermanos" ferry ticket booth is located on the pier. Departures are approximately every 2 hours; the last crossing departs at 7 p.m. If you miss the last boat, it's possible to hire a private water taxi; expect to pay $25 to $30 (U.S.) for a ride to the island.

Golf cart taxi fares are inexpensive, and a ride from the ferry dock to your hotel (including properties outside of downtown) should cost no more than 30 pesos. While most everything of visitor interest on Holbox is within a 10- or 20-minute walk, renting a golf cart might be a good idea if the weather is too hot for foot travel or you're staying at a hotel on the beach east of town.

There are several rental agencies *(rentadoras)* that all charge basically the same rates. Rentadora Moguel, across from the plaza at the corner of Calle Igualdad and Tiburon Ballena, rents carts for 100 pesos (about $9.70 U.S.) per hour, 350 pesos for 5 hours and 600 pesos for 24 hours.

There are no banks or ATMs on the island. Most local businesses prefer cash (pesos or U.S. dollars). Exchanging money also can be a hassle, so don't count on using traveler's checks. You can check your e-mail and the weather in air-conditioned comfort at Internet Cyber Shark, on Calle Igualdad just east of Avenida Carite.

Aerosaab, a regional airline, can arrange private flights from Cancún, Cozumel and Playa del Carmen to the small airstrip on Isla Holbox. The short flights (20 minutes to 1 hour) are aboard a four-seat Cessna aircraft. Aerosaab also offers all-day whale shark tours that depart from Cancún, Cozumel and Playa del Carmen.

During the whale shark off-season, consider the daylong tour that flies out of Playa del Carmen only and visits Bird Island, Yalahau spring and the Holbox Village. Flights leave Playa on Tuesday, Thursday and Saturday at 9 a.m., returning at 5 p.m., and take a minimum of four passengers; smaller groups should contact the airline and ask to be put on a waiting list. For additional information phone (984) 873-0804.

Recreation

Many of Holbox's approximately 1,500 permanent residents are fishermen. They set out each morning before sunrise, pulling in catches of grouper, barracuda, red snapper, yellowtail and shark. Most families on the island make their living from commercial fishing or diving for conch, lobster and octopus. Local skippers also serve as guides for sport-fishing excursions; the waters around Cape Catoche (Cabo Catoche), where the Gulf of Mexico and the Caribbean merge, are fertile fishing grounds. Boat trips for deep sea or fly fishing can be arranged at the main pier.

Yalahau is the name of the lagoon between Isla Holbox and the mainland as well as a natural spring-fed pond on the island that once was a source of drinking water for Mayan fishermen. According to folklore the pond was the private swimming pool of a Mayan king and later the refuge of a pirate, "Yellow Beard." Local legend also maintains that Yalahau is a fountain of youth. It can be reached by boat, and while swimmers may not feel any younger, the clear, cool water is decidedly refreshing on a hot day.

Isla Pájaros, or Bird Island, is a small islet only 200 feet wide that lies in a shallow portion of Yalahau Lagoon. This protected wildlife sanctuary is accessible only by boat. Covered by thick stands of mangrove, cacti and underbrush, it is a feeding and nesting haven for more than 150 different species. Flamingos visit from April to October; other frequently seen birds include frigates, white ibises, snowy egrets, spoonbills, pelicans and ducks. The island also is home to iguanas, horseshoe crabs and such plants as bromeliads and wild orchids.

Tours to Isla Pájaros depart from the main pier on Holbox Island. In order to protect the fragile ecosystem, visitors are not allowed to walk on the island; birds can be observed in their natural surroundings from elevated walkways and observation lookout points.

The most notable attraction Holbox offers is the opportunity to get up close and personal with whale sharks (*tiburon ballena* in Spanish). The world's largest living fish species, it attains a length of up to 45 feet. Also called domino shark for the distinctive pattern of pale yellow spots marking its body, the whale shark—unlike many of its more fearsome brethren—is harmless to humans. This shark is a filter feeder: It pumps sea water through five large pairs of gills that act as sieves, trapping plankton, algae, krill, small vertebrates and other food that are then swallowed.

The manta ray, another giant marine creature, is much less frequently spotted. A relative of the shark, it is the largest ray in the world—up to 25 feet wide when measured across the pectoral fins, and weighing more than 1.5 tons. The manta, unlike other species of ray, does not have a stinging spine. And like the whale shark, it too is a filter feeder, feasting on plankton, small fish and crustaceans that are swept into its wide mouth with the aid of two fleshy lobes that resemble horns (hence the nickname "devil ray"). These solitary creatures are harmless to swimmers and divers and thus a highly prized sighting.

Whale sharks and manta rays visit the waters around Holbox from mid-June to early September. Boat trips to the whale shark feeding waters (about 1 hour away from the Holbox pier) allow visitors the opportunity to swim and snorkel alongside the surprisingly docile giants without touching them (scuba diving is not permitted). Only two snorkelers and a guide are allowed in the water at a time, and the first thing you'll notice is how fast these jumbo fish move. If you're not a strong swimmer, keeping up with them is out of the question. Regardless, simply being in the open water next to a whale shark is an incredible once-in-a-lifetime experience for most visitors.

Note: Although it is not guaranteed that you'll see a shark, the probability in the heart of the season (July and August) is high. If you're visiting at this time, make lodging and tour reservations far in advance.

There are about ten whale shark tour operators in town. Holbox regulars have their favorites, and two of them always rank at or near the top. Operadora Turística Monkey's (aka Monkey Tours) is the largest outfitter in town, and their red-and-white boats are manned by some of the best whale shark spotters on the island.

Excursions depart early in the morning and last 5 to 6 hours. Each boat takes a maximum of 10 people; snorkel equipment and lunch are included. The tour is not recommended for children under 8. Space is limited (especially in season), and advance reservations are necessary. Expect to pay about $80 (U.S.) per person. For more information and to make reservations, visit their office on the west side of Calle Tiburon Ballena, just north of Aguilar, or phone (984) 875-2029. Tours offered by Hotel Mawimbi also are well regarded; for information phone (984) 875-2003.

Holbox Tours & Travel on Calle Bravo offers all-inclusive trip packages that include ground transportation to and from Cancún International Airport and hotel accommodations in addition to a guided all-day whale shark excursion. Trips are offered June through August. For additional information or to book reservations phone (984) 875-2173 or (305) 396-6987 (from the United States).

Shopping, Dining and Nightlife

Several interesting shops are on Calle Igualdad, east of the plaza. Artesanía Las Chicas is an offbeat little boutique specializing in handmade *henequen* clothing with a bohemian bent. Las Chicas also has a nice selection of purses, jewelry and aromatic incense. Next door, Caracol is the place to go for colorful nylon and cotton hammocks handmade by local women.

Also on Calle Igualdad is PLATA Mexicana 925, Agua y Tierra. The name refers to silver that's 92.5 percent pure. Obviously, this tiny shop is packed with jewelry, though not all of it is sterling. You'll also find rings, necklaces and bracelets made from seashells and other humble materials. Artesinas Puesta del Sol sells beachwear, flip-flops, tote bags and jewelry, plus an array of good-quality Mexico keepsakes, including hand-painted margarita glasses.

West of the plaza, seashell collectors head for Lalo, on Avenida Canané just south of Avenida Coldwell. The shop is on the second floor of a thatch-roofed house. You can't miss the sign out front. Inside, polished seashells of all shapes and sizes command high prices. Bargains come in the way of souvenir knickknacks and cool items like handbags made from seashells. Another trove of Mexican handicrafts is nearby at La Bambina, at the corner of Avenida Coldwell and Esmedregal.

Restaurants are simple and casual. Restaurante Zarabanda, a block south of the main plaza (look for the thatched roof and red-and-white trim) is a rustic, family-owned place that serves fresh seafood like grilled fish filets and conch or shrimp ceviche. You also can get breakfast here. Viva Zapata, just west of the main plaza, is a popular Mexican restaurant with sombrero-shaped lamps dangling over the tables and pictures of Pancho Villa covering the walls. Ask for a table on the breezy second-floor balcony and try the surf-and-turf platter for two. The food is very good, but service can be slow.

Always busy at dinner time, Restaurante y Pizzeria Edelyn bakes tasty thin crust pies in a log cabin-like building opposite the southeast corner of the plaza. While most first-timers order the house specialty, lobster pizza (covered with garlicky chunks of crustacean), don't overlook the linguine or the #10 pizza, loaded with the works. Seating is inside (hot in summer), on the front porch or at plastic tables set out in the street.

At funky La Isla del Colibre, opposite the southwest corner of the plaza, you can ponder the Frida Kahlo paintings on the walls (seven and counting) while you wait for your meal to arrive. Housed in a colorful clapboard building decorated with surrealist art, the restaurant specializes in seafood and also serves excellent breakfasts. This is a favorite haunt of street performers and musicians; bring change for *propinas* (tips).

Antojitos El Chivo, on the west side of Calle Tiburon Ballena half a block north of the plaza, dishes up cheap and delicious Mexican food in a simple setting (think plastic tables and zero romantic ambience). It's only open for dinner, but if you forgo the fancier places in town and give El Chivo a shot, you won't be disappointed.

In town, beachfront dining is limited to three restaurants: Cariocas (favored by locals), Buena Vista Grill (romantic but expensive) and the casual Villa Mar. Tables at the latter are shaded by mini *palapa* umbrellas and offer views of the beach and pier. Breakfasts are hearty, tasty and (late risers take note) served until 1 p.m. Mexican standards and drink specials draw a steady stream of tourists the rest of the day.

It won't take you long to figure out that there's no wacky Cancún-type nightlife on Holbox, but there *are* a handful of mellow bars on the west side of the plaza. On Saturday nights the plaza fills up with locals and tourists alike who come to watch live music and traditional Mayan dances performed under a white concrete bandshell. Think of it as the island's very own Hollywood Bowl.

ISLA MUJERES, QUINTANA ROO (A-4)

pop. 10,800

Laid-back Mexican beach vacations don't get much better than Isla Mujeres (EES-lah moo-HEH-rehs). While single male travelers might be disappointed to find that the male-female ratio on the "Island of Women" is actually rather balanced, no one can deny Isla's considerable charms.

This little slip of an island in Mujeres Bay is within sight of Cancún's Hotel Zone, and getting there on a ferry boat is part of the fun. As soon as you leave the Cancún dock you're surrounded by intensely hued water that ranges from sea foam green to pastel aquamarine to deep, deep turquoise, the colors constantly shifting with the interplay of sun and clouds. The little boat bobs up and down on the waves, sending salt spray flying. (A word of advice: Even on tranquil days the ride tends to be choppy, so if you're prone to seasickness take the appropriate precautions.)

The island, first appearing as an indistinct blur on the horizon, begins to take shape as the boat draws closer. Details emerge—palm trees, clapboard buildings, fishing boats. And before you know it you've reached another dock and disembark to a scene that is a bit different than the one you left.

Gold-seeking Spanish explorers led by Francisco Hernández de Córdoba accidentally discovered Isla Mujeres in 1517 after a storm blew their expedition off course. The origin of the name is based on two legends. One maintains that seafaring buccaneers used the island as a hideaway for stowing their female captives; slave trader Fermín Mundaca built a beautiful hacienda here in an effort to woo an island girl. But a more likely explanation is that it refers to the carved stone images of Ixchel, the Mayan goddess of love and fertility, discovered by the Spaniards.

After the era of pirates and smugglers passed, Isla Mujeres was quite content to be just another idyllic Caribbean island where people fished for a living. It was discovered again during the 1960s, this time by hippies and beach bums who dug the laid-back atmosphere. And since Cancún's ascendance to world-famous tourist destination Isla has gotten more and more spillover from its big, flashy mainland neighbor. But it's also a place where people live; while you're on vacation, for residents it's just another day. And the chance to be part of daily Mexican life—if only for a few hours—is what makes this island special.

You'll get into the spirit as soon as you start strolling along Avenida Rueda Medina, the *malecón,* which runs along the waterfront. The sidewalk is a jumble of sunburned gringos, locals and occasional dogs that might suddenly plop down under the shade of a coconut palm (the sound of palm fronds rustling in the ever-present breeze is a constant backdrop). Vendors sit next to their displays—bead necklaces, seashells, starfish, sandals, sombreros. The street is clogged with taxis, mopeds, golf carts and scooters, but no one is really in a hurry. Stop and breathe in the aroma of fresh fish grilling at a *loncheria* (casual open-air restaurant).

Then explore a few of the downtown side streets. Narrow Avenida Hidalgo, 2 blocks inland from the waterfront, is for pedestrians only, and thus invites browsers to linger at the many shops and vendor stalls. Turn a corner and you might see a group of school kids in immaculate uniforms skipping along the sidewalk. Many of the buildings have festive crayon colors—pink, peach, lime green, bright blue. Stop at a cafe for a cup of coffee or a freshly blended fruit smoothie. Above all, relax.

Many people spend their entire vacation on Isla Mujeres, since accommodations run the gamut from no-frills in-town motels to exclusive beachside retreats. But one of the island's calling cards is that it's just a half-hour boat ride away. You can leave Cancún in the morning, go shopping, have lunch and take an afternoon ferry back. You can leave around noon, go snorkeling or while away an afternoon sunning on the beach, and be back in time for dinner. Or you can leave in the late afternoon, enjoy dinner and a fun evening on Isla, and catch the last ferry back to the mainland. It's the perfect day trip.

Practicalities

Isla Mujeres, located about 5 miles off the easternmost tip of the Yucatán Peninsula, is accessible by ferry or boat from mainland Puerto Juárez (passengers only) or Punta Sam (passengers and/or vehicles). There also are three Cancún Hotel Zone departure points for passenger ferries to the island: the El Embarcadero dock at Km marker 4 on Boulevard Kukulcán; the dock at Playa Tortugas, Km marker 6 on Boulevard Kukulcán (next to Fat Tuesday's restaurant); and from the Club Nautico dock, at Km marker 8.5 on Boulevard Kukulcán (across from the Plaza Caracol mall).

The Puerto Juárez public ferry departs every half-hour daily from 6:30 a.m. to 9 p.m., then departs hourly until midnight. The final departure from Isla Mujeres back to Puerto Juárez is at 11:30 p.m. The trip aboard the enclosed, air-conditioned vessel, which holds about 30 passengers, takes about 30 minutes; one-way fare is 35 pesos (about $3.40 U.S.). Schedules are normally posted at the docks but are subject to change; always double-check the final departure time if you are going to Isla on a day trip from Cancún, or vice versa. Since the public ferries are the least expensive alternative to Isla the boat can be crowded, but passengers are counted to make sure everyone gets a seat.

A newer ferry service, UltraMar, provides the same trip from the Gran Puerto dock, a short distance away on Avenida López Portillo. These ferries also depart every half-hour daily; the trip takes about 15-20 minutes. Always double-check the final departure time back to Cancún when you arrive. Round-trip fare (including tax) is about $6.50 (U.S.). **Note:** The ride on the smaller ferries can be choppy even in good weather, so it's a good idea to take the proper precautions if you're prone to seasickness.

The car ferry from Punta Sam departs for Isla Mujeres five times daily. The first departure is at 8 a.m.; the last departure is at 8:15 p.m. The first departure from Isla Mujeres back to Punta Sam is at 6:30 a.m.; the last departure is at 7:15 p.m. Double check the schedule, as bad weather can affect departure times. Isla Mujeres is so small, however, that there's no reason to bring a car for a day visit. For additional information about ferry service, *see Sightseeing under the Cancún listing, page 99.*

If you're basing a vacation in Isla Mujeres and have several pieces of luggage, taxis line up by the two town docks for the short ride to the hotels concentrated in town and scattered along the beaches. The fare shouldn't be more than a dollar or two. Taxis also can be hired (at an hourly rate) for a tour of the island or to reach beaches at the southern end. A municipal bus travels from the Posada del Mar Hotel on Avenida Rueda Medina south to Playa Lancheros; the fare is inexpensive. The tourist information office *(see below)* can provide bus schedules.

Renting a "moto," the local term for mopeds, or an electric golf cart is an easy way to get around, and there are several places in town that rent both (many of the hotels also rent golf carts). Keep in mind, however, that the rental fee does not include insurance. Some hotels also rent bicycles, which cost considerably less.

The "downtown" section of Isla Mujeres occupies the island's northern end. The main street, referred to locally as the *malecón,* is Avenida Rueda Medina, which runs the length of the island. The main streets are north-south avenidas Guerrero and Hidalgo, and east-west avenidas Madero and Morelos. These are all narrow, one-way, pedestrian-friendly streets where traffic (mostly taxis and mopeds) moves slowly. Everything—the ferry docks, in-town hotels, restaurants, shops, travel agencies, City Hall, the police station, the post office, a couple of *farmacias* (pharmacies), the island's one bank, *casas de cambio* (currency exchange offices) and several Internet cafes—are all within a compact area of about 4 by 6 blocks.

Islander, a monthly magazine available at hotels, provides tourist information. A Red Cross (Cruz Roja) clinic is about 5 kilometers (3 miles) south of town, near Playa Lancheros; phone (998) 877-0280.

What To Do on the Island

The most popular beach is Playa Norte, located at the northern edge of town. It's a lovely white-sand beach sprinkled with coconut palms and thatch-roofed *palapas.* The water is clear, calm and shallow, perfect for swimming or wading. Umbrellas, chairs, jet-skis, three-wheeled water "trikes" and other equipment can be rented. **Note:** You may encounter discreet topless sunbathers at this beach.

Other options are Playa Lancheros and Playa Garrafón, both toward the opposite end of the island on the western (leeward) side. Playa Lancheros is the southernmost beach on the local bus route. The surf is rougher along Isla's eastern coastline, which faces the open Caribbean.

At the very southern tip of the island, on a bluff overlooking the sea, once stood the reconstructed remains of a Mayan temple believed to have been built in honor of the fertility goddess Ixchel. Archeologists believe that the Maya, en route to Cozumel on pilgrimages to worship Ixchel, stopped over at Isla Mujeres. Gilbert reduced it to a pile of stones, but there are fine views of the sea. A 30-foot-tall lighthouse nearby was left standing. A taxi ride from downtown costs about $4 (U.S.).

Branching east off Rueda Medina, a paved road follows the eastern edge of the island back toward town. One justification for bringing a car to Isla Mujeres is to drive this route, stopping at one of the pull-offs for a view of the open sea.

Offshore coral reefs and the Cave of the Sleeping Sharks (Cueva de Los Tiburones Durmientes) attract scuba divers. The underwater cave, off the northern tip of Contoy Island National Park *(see attraction listing),* was discovered in the late 1960s. The reason for the sharks' seemingly narcotized state has been attributed to everything from varying salinity levels to lack of carbon dioxide in the underwater caverns to constant currents that supply the oxygen allowing the creatures to remain stationary. Whatever the cause, this is a challenging dive to depths of 150 feet or more, with no guarantee that the sharks will be around.

Another site for advanced divers is the Ultrafreeze (El Frio) wreck, a cargo ship that caught fire in 1979 and was towed to the open sea to be sunk. Many forms of marine life, including small and large fish, stingrays and turtles, can be seen.

Manchones Reef, just off the island's southern tip, is more than 2,500 feet long. Blue tangs, wrasses, parrot fish, angelfish and red snapper are among the tropical species that swarm over the reef, which exhibits a variety of coral formations. The water depth is 30 to 40 feet. Manchones also is the site of the underwater statue Cross of the Bay (Cruz de la Bahía).

The summer months of June, July and August, when the water is calm, are best for diving. The Bahía Dive Shop, on Avenida Rueda Medina across from the ferry dock, offers certification classes. Their knowledgeable instructors can arrange fishing excursions as well as trips to local dive sites; phone (998) 877-0340. Coral Scuba Dive Center, Av. Matamoros #13-A at Avenida Rueda Medina (3 blocks north of the passenger ferry dock), also offers certified instruction and organizes snorkeling and fishing trips; phone (998) 877-0763.

The Boatmen's Cooperative (Cooperativa Isla Mujeres), on Avenida Rueda Medina at the foot of Avenida Madero (near the ferry dock), handles snorkeling and sport-fishing excursions as well as day trips to Isla Contoy. Some outings require a minimum number of passengers. Billfish (swordfish and marlin) are a good possibility in April and May; during the rest of the year catches include bonito, grouper and red snapper.

Shopping, Dining and Nightlife

Although craft shop prices are lower than in Cancún, bargaining is still the best way to come out ahead. Wood carvings, ceramic and clay figurines, pottery, handmade clothing, T-shirts, and decorative objects made of sea and snail shells are among the possible purchases. Sidewalk vendors set up small displays along Avenida Rueda Medina in the vicinity of the passenger ferry dock, selling shells, jewelry, trinkets and souvenirs. The other side of the street is lined with gift shops.

Avenida Hidalgo, 2 blocks in from the waterfront, is a pedestrian-only thoroughfare with more shops and vendor stands, along with several restaurants that have outdoor tables. It's a pleasant little street to wander along. Fire Opal (Opalo de Fuego), Av. Juárez #7 (at Avenida Nicolas Bravo) specializes in hand-crafted jewelry made from opals, amethysts and other gemstones. Also downtown is Galería de Arte Mexico; the handicrafts for sale include ceramics, silver jewelry, talavera tile and hand-painted Oaxacan rugs.

One of the nicest restaurants on the island is Zazil-Ha, in the Hotel Na Balam on Calle Zazil (at Playa Norte). The seafood dishes are well-prepared, and diners have a choice of eating indoors or in an open-air garden setting. Pizza Rolandi, on Avenida Hidalgo between avenidas Madero and Abasolo, is a reliable chain that features pizza, calzones and pasta dishes along with fish; it's a good spot to take a break in the shade and people watch.

Roticerias are tiny joints that sell whole roasted chickens, which come with rice, beans, marinated onions and tortillas. It's a good takeout meal for a beach picnic. There are two locations: on Avenida Hidalgo at Plaza Isla Mujeres, and at Av. Guerrero #4. The beachside restaurant at Playa Lancheros offers fresh ceviche and the Yucatecan style of fish preparation known as *tikin xic*. Look for the thatched *palapa* roof. If you want to sample local cookery, check out the food vendors at the Municipal Market (Mercado Municipal), on Avenida Guerrero next to the post office.

Isla Mujeres is not known for frenetic nightlife, which suits most visitors just fine. The *palapas* along Playa Norte are a great place for sunset-watching. Most of the restaurant bars have a late afternoon happy hour, and a few offer live music and dancing.

Tourist information office: Av. Rueda Medina #130, between Madero and Morelos (just north of the ferry dock). Open Mon.-Fri. 8-8, Sat.-Sun. 8-2; phone (998) 877-0767.

What To See

CONTOY ISLAND NATIONAL PARK (Parque Nacional Isla Contoy) is about 32 km (20 mi.) n. of Isla Mujeres. The uninhabited island is the site of a wildlife reserve and bird sanctuary. Four miles long and half a mile wide, Contoy has nature trails winding through tropical vegetation. Pelicans, egrets, cormorants and flamingos are among the species that nest here. In addition to park rangers, iguanas, turtles and hermit crabs live on the island, and marine life—which includes seasonal armies of migrating lobsters—is plentiful. There also is a fine outdoor nature museum.

Contoy is protected and can only be visited on a guided tour. Tours depart from Isla Mujeres, Cancún and Puerto Juárez. The Isla Mujeres tours are run by people familiar with the island and dedicated to preserving its natural environment, and the boats are smaller. But regardless of the operator, the itinerary is the same: snorkeling en route to the island, time to relax or explore, and a grilled fish lunch prepared Mayan style *(tikin-xic)*, plus an open bar. Activities include visiting an aviary, hiking along protected dunes, snorkeling or simply resting on the beach prior to the return voyage.

Life jackets and snorkeling gear are provided. Insect repellent is advised. The nature museum has restroom facilities. The boat trip is normally about 45 minutes one way but can take up to 2 hours if seas are rough. Kolumbus Tours offers an all-day trip that departs Tues., Thurs. and Sun. from the Hacienda del Mar marina in Puerto Juárez, north of Cancún. Departures from Isla Mujeres are every 2 hours beginning at 9 a.m. and can be arranged through Delfin Discovery or Guadalupana Tours. Tours from Isla Mujeres average about $58 (U.S.)

per person. The Kolumbus Tours excursion is $80; ages 6-12, $42.50. MC, VI. Phone (998) 877-0305 for Delfin Diving, (998) 877-0229 for Guadalupana Tours, or (998) 884-5333 or 01 (800) 715-3375 (toll-free long distance within Mexico) for Kolumbus Tours.

DOLPHIN DISCOVERY is at Villa Discovery on Discovery Island, reached via a bridge across Makax Lagoon (Laguna Makax). At this facility visitors can enjoy interactive encounters with dolphins. There are three different 1-hour programs that range from non-swimming sessions (includes touching the animals and watching them perform) to full-fledged water encounters. The program also features an educational video (watching it is required before you can enter the water). For trips from Cancún transportation is aboard the 110-foot cruiser *Discovery.*

Food is available. Allow 2 hours minimum. Advance reservations are necessary. Children under 8 must be accompanied by an adult. Boat transportation from Cancún departs daily at 9, 11 and 1 from the Playa Langosta dock, Km 5 on Boulevard Kukulcán (next to the Casa Maya Hotel); check-in at the Dolphin Discovery office (just before the entrance to The Cove restaurant) is required 30 minutes prior to departure. Departures from Isla Mujeres back to Cancún are at noon, 4:15 and 6 p.m. Dolphin programs take place daily beginning at 10:30, noon, 2 and 3:30. Dolphin encounter $79 (U.S.); $69 (under 12). Dolphin swims $99 and $139 (children must be at least 8 years of age and/or 48 inches tall). Round-trip boat fare is $5 for dolphin program participants, $10 for nonparticipants. Phone (998) 193-3360, (866) 393-5158 (from the United States), (866) 793-1905 (from Canada) or 01 (800) 727-5391 (toll-free long distance within Mexico).

GARRAFON PARK is at the southern tip of the island off Carretera Garrafón, Km marker 6. This "natural park" has seen its share of environmental damage. Sections of the offshore coral reef have been killed by the dropped anchors of too many tour boats (a practice now outlawed) and were further damaged by Hurricane Gilbert in 1988. In 2005 Hurricane Wilma devastated this area, but Garrafón bounced back and reopened the next year.

Multicolored tropical fish can be seen in calm, clear water that has an average depth of 13 feet. A zipline allows thrill seekers to skim above the island's coastal cliffs. Garrafón's swimming pool has a waterfall and a view of the Caribbean. Two ocean platforms anchored to a sandy bottom near the reef, one for sunbathers and one with a diving board, are connected by ropes that can be crossed "monkey" style, walking on one while hanging on to the other.

If all this sounds too strenuous, relax in the shady Garden of Hammocks and listen to the breeze rustling the palm fronds. In order to protect the environment, use of biodegradable sunscreen (available at the park's gift shops) is advised.

Food is available. Picnicking is permitted. Locker rooms and showers are provided. Allow 4 hours minimum. Daily 10-5. Garrafón Discovery package admission (includes snorkeling and use of pool and bicycles) $65 (U.S.); $49 (ages 0-12). Other combination packages that include dolphin encounters are available. There are separate fees for round-trip transportation from the Cancún pier, snorkel gear (a $20 refundable deposit also is required), access to the beach, use of hammocks and the zipline, a lunch buffet and playing with dolphins. AX, MC, VI. Phone (998) 849-4748 or (800) 417-1736 (from the United States) for reservation information.

IZAMAL, YUCATAN (B-3) pop. 14,300

A significant pre-Columbian political and religious center, Izamal (ee-sah-MAHL) developed around a Franciscan monastery. Diego de Landa, the Spanish bishop responsible for the annihilation of most of the Mayan civilization's *codices* (picture books) and documents, deliberately chose Izamal as the seat of his diocese because it was a religious center of the Maya-speaking tribe known as the Itzae.

Izamal was a center of commerce and trade during the Spanish colonial period. When Mérida took over as the Yucatán's chief city, it slipped into obscurity. One recent momentous event in this slow-paced town was a 1993 visit by Pope John Paul II. The mustard-colored government buildings surrounding the central plaza give it the nickname "Ciudad Amarilla" (Yellow City). A relaxing way to view the colonial-era architecture is by horse-drawn carriage; rides can be arranged at the plaza, where the guides congregate.

Dilapidated houses and commercial buildings attest to the poverty that most Yucatecans endure. Downtown clusters around the small central plaza, shaded by trees and furnished with wrought-iron benches.

About 74 kilometers (46 miles) east of Mérida via two-lane Mex. 180, Izamal makes for an interesting day trip. From Mérida, watch for the signed turn-off that says "Yuc. 53"; if approaching from Cancún, the signed turn-off from toll highway Mex. 180-D says "Izamal" and also merges into Yuc. 53. The narrow, two-lane road, which has no shoulders and occasional potholes, passes through thick green scrubland interspersed with fields of spiky, blue-green agave plants.

Between the 180-D turn-off and Izamal—a distance of about 18 kilometers (11 miles)—are three small villages: Xanaba, Sudzal and Cuauhtémoc. Cobbled *topes* (speed bumps) force vehicles to slow to a crawl when entering each one, as do the wandering dogs, chickens, turkeys and children. Xanaba has a large yellow church with white trim opposite its small central plaza. In Sudzal and Cuauhtémoc you'll see typical Mayan houses—thatch-roofed huts with open doorways, dirt floors and walls constructed of upright wooden stakes—surrounded by banana trees and other tropical vegetation. This is rural life at its most basic, a world away from Cancún's glitter and Mérida's big-city bustle.

From Izamal, there are two ways to return to Mex. 180: Backtrack on Yuc. 53, or take another local road to the small town of Hoctún (which is on Mex. 180). The latter route passes through Citilcum and Kimbila en route; all three villages are representative of the rural Yucatán countryside. Make certain you're back on Mex. 180 before dark.

Because of the slow-paced driving conditions and the fact that it's easy to lose your orientation in Izamal—small as it is—this trip is most conveniently taken with a hired taxi driver or guide from Mérida. Check with one of the city's tour operators or arrange for a driver through your hotel.

FRANCISCAN MONASTERY dominates the main plaza. It was originally dedicated to St. Anthony of Padua and was later known as the Church of Our Lady of Izamal. It was completed in 1561 atop a Mayan pyramid. In 1618, monks added the monastery and an arcade. The atrium of this enormous church is reputed to be second in size to that of St. Peter's Basilica in Rome. The church's simple, mustard-colored exterior contrasts with the rough-hewn, fortresslike monastery compound; the original access ramps and stairways built by the Maya remain.

KINICH KAKMO PYRAMID (Pirámide Kinich Kakmo) is about 4 blocks n. of the plaza. In the Mayan language, its name means "Solar-Faced Macaw of Fire." Kinich Kakmo is one of Mexico's largest pyramids—some 115 feet high and almost 660 feet wide. It sits in the middle of town; there are houses just across the street. One of the four sides remains unexcavated and is covered with a thick green matting of tangled underbrush. Admission is charged.

MAJAHUAL, QUINTANA ROO (C-4)

Majahual (mah-ha-WAL) sits at about the midpoint of an extensive, largely unspoiled stretch of shoreline lacking anything that remotely resembles an all-inclusive mega resort. Known as the Costa Maya, this coastal region encompasses Quintana Roo's southern Caribbean coast, from Punta Herrero (which is within the Sian Ka'an Biosphere Reserve) south to the village of Xcalak near the Mexico-Belize border. The Costa Maya has a recurring motif of tangled mangroves, placid lagoons and swaying palms backing white-sand beaches. Just offshore, sea life thrives along one of the most pristine sections of the great Mesoamerican barrier reef.

In other words, this is the serene and sparsely developed late 1970s version of the Riviera Maya—the strip of coast from Puerto Morelos south to Tulum—with one notable exception: the Puerto Costa Maya cruise ship dock that sits next to this once-sleepy fishing village. Opened in 2001, the port and cruise ship facilities were the first major step in a tourism development plan cooked up by FONATUR, Mexico's tourism promoter. And according to FONATUR's ambitious plans, "When the project is developed to its maximum potential, it will complement the level of services offered by Cancún and the Mayan Riviera."

Hurricane Dean, however, had other ideas. When the storm roared over the Costa Maya as a Category 5 hurricane on Aug. 21, 2007, it came ashore just north of the cruise ship port. The pier and facilities sustained heavy damage. The town of Majahual itself was devastated, most of its wooden buildings destroyed by the massive storm surge and sustained 170 mph winds.

But rebuilding has been swift. At press time, cruise ships (including the Holland America line) were scheduled to return sometime in the fall of 2008. And in an effort to make Majahual's once-sandy main street more tourist-friendly, FONATUR has paved paradise and put up a $4 million (U.S.) concrete *malecón* (seaside promenade).

Despite Dean's depredations and in spite of temporarily sidetracked plans for mass tourism, the Costa Maya retains a feeling of idyllic isolation and has much to offer cruise ship passengers weary of overcrowded Caribbean ports 'o call. Adventurous travelers who make the 4-hour drive south from Cancún will find small, independently run hotels in Majahual proper, as well as in more remote locales along the coast. Located just a few kilometers south of Majahual, the Balamku Inn and Hotel Maya Luna are two good choices; the latter's restaurant is excellent.

Practicalities

Driving from the Cancún airport, it's a good 3.5-hour trip down Mex. 307 to the Majahual turn-off, on the east side of the road just beyond the tiny village of Limones. The paved, two-lane access road is not numbered, but is well signed. From the turn-off, the highway heads east toward the coast. It's about 57 kilometers (35 miles)—a 40-minute drive—to Majahual. **Note:** There is only one Pemex gas station along the entire stretch of the Costa Maya; it's located on the south side of the Majahual road about 4 kilometers (2.5 miles) before you reach town.

If you're driving from the Riviera Maya south to Majahual, there is a Pemex station with restrooms in the mainland town of Felipe Carrillo Puerto at the corner of Calle 70 (Mex. 307) and Calle 69. Next to the gas station is a bank with an ATM. From Felipe Carrillo the drive time to Majahual is about 1 hour and 30 minutes. When driving through rural areas in Mexico, always fill your tank whenever you have the chance.

From Bacalar, near Chetumal at the southern end of Quintana Roo, the distance to Majahual is about 137 kilometers (85 miles); drive time is about an hour and a half. There are two Pemex stations in Bacalar, both on Mex. 307. The station at the north end of town (on the east side of the highway) has a mini mart with an ATM.

Majahual (the official name, although the spelling shown on road signs and around town is "Mahahual") exhibits a dual personality. On cruise ship days, tourists shop and eat their way down the *malecón,* ATVs carrying sightseers buzz along the region's dirt roads, snorkeling boats bob near the reef and tour buses head inland to visit the Mayan ruins of Chacchobén *(see attraction listing).* When there's no ship in port, Majahual becomes a ghost town. Many restaurants and shops are closed and you'll likely be the only gringo on the beach.

If arriving by cruise ship, you'll step ashore at the port facility, a modern complex with gift shops, restaurants and the only ATM on the entire coast. **Note:** The cash machine, located inside the port facility, can only be accessed by cruise ship passengers. But since Majahual is a cruise ship port of call, U.S. dollars are widely accepted. Some businesses accept credit cards, but most don't. To be on the safe side, bring more cash than you think you'll need.

From the port it's a 5-minute taxi ride to Majahual, where a tall white lighthouse that miraculously survived Dean's fury marks the north end of town. From here, the *malecón* winds its way south. Fringed with newly planted palms and offering views of the crystal clear Caribbean, the promenade is lined with *palapa* restaurants serving fresh seafood and small shops hawking the usual beachwear, jewelry and trinkets.

Dining and Recreation

The restaurants themselves are located on the inland side of the *malecón* and are backed by a dirt road (in the process of being paved) that runs the length of town and continues south. If you want to sip a *cerveza* and wiggle your toes in the sand, most dining establishments also set up chairs, tables and umbrellas directly on the beach.

Near the lighthouse, the Tequila Beach Club occupies a huge, two-story *palapa* overlooking the *malecón* and a small wooden pier, the departure point for many snorkeling and fishing trips. About halfway down the *malecón,* El Sabor de Mi Tierra sets up a half-dozen tables at the shoreline and operates out of a proper restaurant located a block behind the promenade. A fresh lobster tail swimming in a rich chipotle cream sauce costs about $30 (U.S.).

Farther south, La Posada de Los 40 Cañones is a hotel and restaurant that also operates the Pez Quadro Beach Club, which offers a few dozen umbrella-shaded lounge chairs. Mexican, Italian and seafood dishes dominate the menu; a lobster taco platter will set you back $10 (U.S.). Classic rock and Top 40 pap boom from the sound system.

If you're itching to snorkel the nearby reef and don't want to spend a half-hour swimming to it from shore, Dreamtime Diving offers 90-minute trips that usually visit two sites, where you'll see healthy coral and the usual posse of reef fish. Keep an eye peeled for rays. Dreamtime's boats are well maintained, guides are bilingual and most of the trip is spent in the water. Cost is $35 (U.S.) per person; snorkel gear, bottled water and snacks are included. Phone (983) 834-5823 for more details.

Of course the subaquatic marquee attraction in these waters is Banco Chinchorro, the largest coral atoll in the Northern Hemisphere. Located some 31 kilometers (19 miles) from Majahual, Chinchorro's abundant marine life and eye-popping coral (including huge barrel sponges and compact car-sized brain coral) attracts scuba divers and marine biologists from around the world. Chinchorro's distance from shore (between 1.5 and 2 hours) means the ocean must be calm for boats to go out, and because it's a protected federal marine reserve, dive operators need special permits.

In Majahual, Bucanero del Caribe offers all-day, two-tank Chinchorro trips for $150 (U.S.) per person. Snorkelers can tag along for $100. You'll find Bucanero's reservation booth in front of the La Posada de Los 40 Cañones hotel; phone (983) 120-5306. The most highly regarded Chinchorro operator is XTC Dive Center, based in the tiny fishing village of Xcalak, about a 45-minute drive south of Majahual. XTC's all-day, three-tank Chinchorro excursions cost $165 per person. Snorkelers are welcome to ride along for $105. The fabled shipwrecks littering Chinchorro's shallow reefs are best explored sans oxygen tank. The dive center has no phone; for information e-mail infoxtcdivecenter.com.

The small coastal town of Xcalak (shka-LAK) is about 55 kilometers (34 miles) south of Majahual and can be reached by two roads. The bumpy dirt-and-sand beach track that heads due south from Majahual will take you hours. Alternately, a narrow, two-lane paved road splits south off the access road to Majahual about 53 kilometers (33 miles) east of the Mex. 307 junction; taking this detour cuts the drive down to 45 minutes.

Xcalak was founded in 1900 as an outpost for the Mexican navy. Fishing and coconut plantations supported a healthy population until 1955, when Hurricane Janet wiped out this town at Quintana Roo's southernmost point, just a stone's throw from Belize. Today, Xcalak has a ramshackle, end-of-the-road ambiance that has attracted a number of American and European expatriates. Longing for a simpler life, they've built small boutique hotels and bed-and-breakfast properties that cater to the adventurous traveler.

Xcalak's beaches are not of the deep, powdered sugar variety. But the laid-back vibe, excellent fishing and superb diving and snorkeling more than make up for the hard-packed sand. Colorful clapboard homes and hurricane-proof cinder block houses line the town's dirt roads. The restaurant at the Costa de Cocos Resort dishes up delicious seafood in a rustic setting.

North of Majahual, a paved inland road and a potholed beach road lead to the loose-knit coastal communities of Rio Indo, El Placer and El Uvero, the areas hardest hit by Hurricane Dean. Scores of beachfront homes, most built by expats, were completely leveled. While the vegetation will take years to recover, rebuilding is well underway.

Farther north, within the Sian Ka'an Biosphere Reserve *(see attraction listing under Tulum)*, you'll need a sturdy high-clearance vehicle to tackle the sandy beach road leading to some of the most beautiful, unspoiled Caribbean beaches on the entire Yucatán Peninsula. If you make it to gorgeous Punta Herrero, a tiny fishing village at the mouth of Bahía del Espíritu Santo, congratulations are in order. You've reached the real Mexican Caribbean.

CHACCHOBEN RUINS are about 73 km (45 mi.) w. of Majahual. The signed turn-off is on Mex. 307 just s. of the Mex. 307/Majahual access road junction; from this point, the site is 9 km (5.5 mi.) w. of the highway. Chacchobén is an old site, believed to have been settled around 200 B.C., although most of the nicely restored structures here date to around A.D. 200-700. The most impressive pyramid (Templo 1) is in Group A, just beyond the Gran Plaza. The parklike setting, shaded by palms and banyan trees, is usually peaceful; however, the site does see large tour groups when cruise ships are in port at Majahual. If you're on a cruise ship that stops at Majahual, these are the Mayan ruins you'll most likely be visiting on a shore excursion.

Daily 8-5. Admission 39 pesos (about $3.80 U.S.).

MERIDA, YUCATAN (B-2)

pop. 680,300, metro area 875,200

Capital of the state of Yucatán and metropolis of the Yucatán Peninsula, Mérida (MEH-ree-dah) fits the description of a "colonial city" but somehow seems different from other places in Mexico. It is a peculiar mixture of the modern and the timeless, presenting the visitor with images both comfortingly familiar and exotically foreign.

Mérida was founded in 1542 by Francisco de Montejo (the son of Montejo the Elder) at the site of T'ho, an ancient Mayan city. The crumbling temples and palaces at the site were razed to make way for cathedrals, ornate mansions and parks, many of which survive to this day. Over time Mérida became the commercial, governmental and religious center of the Yucatán, with the Spaniards living in luxury made possible by Indian toil.

Mérida became even wealthier in the last half of the 19th century because of a tough, thorny plant. Henequén, a member of the agave family, thrived in the rocky soil and seasonally dry conditions prevalent in the northern Yucatán. The fibrous leaves were made into a variety of products, including twine, burlap sacks, furniture stuffing and hammocks. Although sophisticated machinery now processes, weaves and dyes henequén fibers, in the heyday of the large haciendas (plantations) Indian field workers manipulated this intractable plant by hand.

By World War I the city claimed more millionaires per capita than any other in the world as a result of the monopoly on sisal fiber, the valuable henequén extract. The product was named after the port town of Sisal, 50 kilometers (31 miles) northwest of Mérida, from where it was once shipped.

Although plantation barons were swimming in the revenue generated by this profitable export, they were an island unto themselves. The Yucatán Peninsula was still considered Mexico's mosquito-ridden backwater, and a lack of road and rail access isolated it as well. As a result, privileged Meridanos looked to Europe as their model for cultural sophistication. Fueled by henequén's "green gold," they built imposing, Moorish- and rococo-style mansions with arched doorways and marbled tile interiors. These buildings line Paseo Montejo, Mérida's wide showcase boulevard, and give the city its air of graceful elegance.

The henequén haciendas are long abandoned now, although some have been turned into luxury hotels and spas. As in other large Mexican cities, tourism is becoming a leading industry. Mérida's tropical ambience and variety of cultural offerings make it an established destination among European travelers. It also is the most convenient base from which to explore nearby archeological ruins or the Yucatán's northern and western coasts.

Planning Your Stay

Many Yucatán travelers bypass Mérida in favor of Cancún and the Mexican Caribbean coast, but the city is a fascinating travel destination in its own right. There's plenty to do: visiting the museums and public buildings that cluster around the main square, Plaza de la Independencia (also called Plaza Grande); wandering through the bustling market district; taking a horse-drawn carriage ride down Paseo Montejo; or sampling authentic Yucatecan cuisine at local restaurants

Perhaps no other city in Mexico offers as many outdoor performances as Mérida, where there is something going on every day of the week. Better yet, most of the evening concerts or folkloric shows held at the downtown plazas are free.

For *Mérida en Domingo* (Mérida on Sunday), the streets surrounding Plaza de la Independencia are closed to traffic. Mexican families dressed in their Sunday best make for a great people-watching promenade as they stroll among the pushcart vendors selling *tortas* (sandwiches), fruit drinks, corn on the cob, fried cornmeal balls and little cups of sliced mango dusted with chile powder. Handicraft sellers and food stalls set up shop around the plaza and also in Hidalgo Park and Santa Lucía Park.

Sunday also is one of the high points of Mérida's excellent public events program. In the late morning the city police orchestra performs typical Yucatecan music in Santa Lucía Park, on Calle 60 about 3 blocks north of Plaza de la Independencia. Groups of musicians in front of the Government Palace (Palacio del Gobierno), on Plaza de la Independencia, play everything from classical to jazz. A folkloric ballet interpretation of a Yucatecan wedding celebration is enacted at City Hall (Palacio Municipal), on the west side of Plaza de la Independencia, while marimba music percolates at Hidalgo Park (also called Cepeda Peraza Park), a block northeast of the main plaza at calles 59 and 60.

Saturday evenings also are active; the downtown area is closed to traffic, and restaurants move tables outside so diners can listen to the bands scattered around the plazas. The music starts at 8:30 and continues until around 2 a.m.

Guided tour operators abound in Mérida, and many of them offer the same destinations with differing forms of conveyance (from economical buses to luxurious private vehicles). City tours last a couple of hours and take in the public buildings around the main plaza, Paseo Montejo, and the Museum of Anthropology and History. Popular day trips travel to Chichén Itzá or Uxmal, with admission to the ruins, lunch, a guide and often a swim at a hotel pool included in the price.

Mérida puts up with sultry heat most of the year. April through September are quite hot and humid, and in May temperatures can soar above 100 degrees. If you're visiting during one of these months, sightsee in the morning, take it easy in the afternoon and venture out again in the evening, when it cools down somewhat. December through February have the most pleasant temperatures and lower humidity. The rainy season is June through September, but precipitation isn't usually heavy or persistent enough to affect travel plans. The greatest chance for hurricanes or other stormy weather is in September and October.

The city is very crowded in July and August, when many Mexican families go on vacation; if that's when you'll be there as well, make hotel reservations in advance.

Practicalities

Manuel Crecencio Rejon International Airport is off Avenida Benito Juárez, also called Avenida Itzaes (Mex. 180), about 7 kilometers (4 miles) southwest of the city center. Aeroméxico, phone 01 (800) 021-4010 (toll-free long distance within Mexico), offers direct flights from Miami. Continental offers direct flights from Houston. Mexicana and the Mexicana subsidiary Aerocaribe offer connecting flights from various destinations in the Yucatán, including Cancún, Cozumel and Chetumal, as well as from Mexico City. For additional information about airlines *see Arriving by Air, page 61*.

City bus #79 (designated "Aviación") takes airport passengers to the downtown area but is unreliable and slow; if you're carrying any amount of luggage it's more convenient to take a taxi. *Colectivo* (group) minivans transport passengers from the airport to downtown hotels for about $8 (U.S.) per person; taxi fare runs about $18 between the airport and downtown hotels.

The first-class bus station, Terminal CAME (CAH-me), is on Calle 70 between calles 69 and 71, about 7 blocks southwest of Plaza de la Independencia. Buses travel frequently to and from Chichén Itzá, Uxmal, Cancún, Campeche, Playa del Carmen, Tulum and Palenque. "Deluxe" service to many of these destinations is offered by ADO's GL and UNO lines. For additional information about buses *see Bus Service, page 72*.

Sitios (taxi stands) are located in the vicinity of Plaza de la Independencia, or use a cab affiliated with your hotel. Rates to in-town destinations are fixed and can be expensive; ask what the fare is before getting in the cab. *Colectivo* taxis (usually white Volkswagen minivans) also take passengers to various city destinations on a first-come, first-serve basis; look for these around Plaza de la Independencia.

Mérida has a tourist police force who patrol on foot and on motorcycle in the downtown core and also in the hotel zone, the area along Avenida Colón between Paseo Montejo and Calle 60. Officers wear white-and-brown or blue uniforms and a sleeve patch that says "Policia Turística." To contact police in case of an emergency, phone (999) 925-2555.

To register a complaint with the Consumer Protection Agency (Procuraduría del Consumidor), phone (999) 923-4927. If you lose your tourist permit, contact the Mexican Immigration Office; phone (999) 928-5823. In case of medical emergency, contact the Red Cross (Cruz Roja); phone (999) 924-9813.

Currency exchange is most conveniently expedited at your hotel front desk, as the rates offered by hotels, banks and *casas de cambio* (currency exchange offices) do not differ greatly. There's an exchange office next to the Hotel Fiesta Americana Mérida.

The Mérida English Library, Calle 53 #524 (between calles 66 and 68), functions as a meeting place for the English-speaking community throughout the city. The library offers English-language books and Internet access as well as community information, and also sponsors seasonal guided house and garden tours. It is open Mon.-Fri. 9-1 (also Tues. and Thurs. 4-7), Sat. 10-1; phone (999) 924-8401.

Getting There

By car, the main approach from the east is Mex. 180, which becomes east-west Calle 65 within the city limits. To get to the downtown hotel zone (where such major hotels as the Hyatt and the Fiesta Americana are located), take Calle 65 west to north-south Calle 60 and turn right.

Mex. 180 also approaches Mérida from the southwest via Campeche. Mex. 261 approaches from the south, joining Mex. 180 at the town of Umán, just south of the city limits. North of downtown, the northern extension of Calle 60 continues north as Mex. 261 to Progreso on the gulf coast.

A loop road, the Anillo Periférico, encircles Mérida, offering access to regional destinations without having to negotiate the downtown area. It can be confusing, however, unless you're familiar with the exits. If you're driving, the most direct way out of the city from the Paseo Montejo/hotel zone area is to take east-west Avenida Colón west to Avenida Itzaes, a major north-south thoroughfare on the west side of town. Turn left (south); you'll pass Centenario Park and the turn-off to the airport before reaching the Anillo Periférico—a distance of about 12 kilometers (7 miles).

Note: Avenida Itzaes changes names twice without warning—to Avenida Internacional and then to Avenida Benito Juárez—as it proceeds south. Don't get sidetracked by the name changes; stay on the avenue.

At the periférico junction there are signs for Cancún (Mex. 180 east), Progreso (Mex. 261 north) and Campeche (Mex. 180 southwest). To head south toward Uxmal and nearby archeological sites, continue south a mile or two on Avenida Itzaes/Internacional/Juárez to Umán. Watch for signs saying "To Campeche via Uxmal on Mex. 261," "Zona Arqueologica Uxmal" and "Ruta Puuc." Follow these signs to access Mex. 261 south.

To head east toward Cancún, turn left onto the periférico at the sign that says "Cancún/Motul." Take this four-lane divided highway about 15 kilometers (9 miles) to the Mex. 180/Cancún exit. From this point, two-lane Mex. 180 runs about 48 kilometers (30 miles) east to the town of Hoctún. At Km marker 66, Mex. 180 divides. The two-lane "libre" (free) road continues east toward the town of Kantunil, and the four-lane divided Mérida-Cancún "cuota" (toll) highway begins.

City Layout

Mérida has long been known as the "White City." Visual evidence does not automatically bear the name out (it could be the impression created by strong sunlight reflecting off the marble and stone surfaces of white buildings), but one thing is certain: The downtown core (often called *El Centro*) is compact, dense and an assault on the senses.

Downtown streets are laid out in a standard grid pattern radiating from the central plaza. They are numbered rather than named; even-numbered streets (calles) run north-south, odd-numbered streets run east-west. They are lined with many beautiful old buildings, and many more shabby ones. Most of these streets are narrow and one way. Vespa motor scooters and beat-up bikes abound, and traffic is heavy and slow. Elsewhere in the city thoroughfares are not well signed and change names without warning. They also can twist and turn confusingly, so know where you're going.

Note: In the *centro,* where buildings sit close together and sidewalks are very narrow, exhaust spewed by green city buses is a near-constant irritant. This central area is roughly bounded by Calle 49 on the north, Calle 67 on the south, Calle 52 on the east and Calle 66 on the west.

Fortunately Mérida also is a city of plazas, bursting with royal poinciana trees and other tropical greenery, that are oases of relative tranquility amid the street noise and traffic jams. Plaza de la Independencia is bounded east and west by calles 60 and 62 and north and south by calles 61 and 63. Here and at other city plazas you'll see *confidenciales,* S-shaped white stone benches that allow two people to face each other while talking. The cathedral and the aristocratic facades of government buildings border the plaza.

A good way to experience the local atmosphere is to stroll up and down Calle 60, a busy street filled with restaurants, handicraft shops selling clothing, jewelry and trinkets, and several fine examples of colonial architecture. From the northeast corner of Plaza de la Independencia, walk north. In the next block is cozy little Hidalgo Park, where there are several outdoor restaurants. At the corner of calles

60 and 57 is the imposing, Italianate Peón Contreras Theater (Teatro Peón Contreras); climb the marble steps and wander around inside.

Mérida's "show street" is four-lane Paseo Montejo, which begins at Calle 47, about 7 blocks northeast of the main plaza. Broad and tree-lined, it also has much wider sidewalks than you'll encounter in other parts of the city, a relief from the cramped spaces of the *centro*. Montejo runs north for 10 blocks past hotels, shops, sidewalk cafés and several large, ornate 19th-century mansions. It culminates at the Monument to Patriotism (Monumento a la Patria), a grouping of sculptures within a traffic circle that depict various stages of Mexican history.

Along Paseo Montejo is the Mérida Sculpture Walk, a collection of changing outdoor art. It begins with the large sculpture in the traffic circle at Montejo and Calle 47; from there walk south along Montejo to the corner of Avenida Colón, near the U.S. Embassy. The final sculpture is the beautifully carved trunk of a tree that was killed by Hurricane Isidore in 2002.

For a peek inside one of the street's impressive residences, take a guided tour of La Quinta Montes Molina, Paseo de Montejo #469 (at Calle 56). Still owned by the same family, the mansion now functions as a location for wedding receptions and "sweet 16" parties. The lavish rooms are filled with European furniture, alabaster and porcelain sculptures, sumptuous crystal chandeliers and Art Deco decorative accents. One-hour tours are given Mon.-Fri. at 8:30 and 2; the fee is 50 pesos (about $4.85 U.S.). Other times are available by appointment; phone (999) 925-5999.

Mérida's streets were originally meant to accommodate *calesas* (horse-drawn carriages). Sunday is the best day to take a tour. Most of the carriages can be found in the vicinity of Plaza de la Independencia or along Calle 60, and they have designated routes. A 45-minute ride should cost from $15 to $20 (U.S.); determine the fare before you set out.

Shopping

Shopping is serious business in Mérida, where a multitude of goods are offered for sale. The city is particularly known for hammocks *(hamacas)*, clothing (especially the men's shirt called a *guayabera)*, Panama hats *(jipis)* and henequén handicrafts.

The market district spreads across several blocks and encompasses hundreds of shops and open-air stalls. Roughly, the area extends from calles 63 to 69 north-south and from calles 54 to 62 east-west (the area just southeast of Plaza de la Independencia). The Municipal Market (Mercado Municipal), centered at calles 65 and 56, is a dizzying hodgepodge of fruit, vegetables, live chickens, tortilla stands, spices and candy, all presided over by *huipil*-clad *señoras* who have brought their wares from the small Mayan villages around Mérida. Among the items for sale are baskets, pottery, gold earrings, gold and silver filigree jewelry, and pieces of amber-colored incense.

Native handicrafts from all over Mexico, but particularly the Yucatán region, are in a separate building at calles 56 and 67. Look for table mats, purses, leather goods, hammocks, piñatas, clothing, ceramics and *huaraches* (sandals with leather straps and soles made from old tires). Fixed prices prevail at many shops, but you can bargain at some of the market stalls and with street vendors.

Note: Haggling in this crowded, noisy atmosphere is not for everyone. Although many vendors speak English, a knowledge of Spanish would be very handy for asking specific questions about merchandise. If you're uncomfortable around high-pressure sales tactics, stick to the fixed-price shops.

Hammocks—often used in the rural Yucatán in place of beds—are fashioned from various materials and come in several sizes. To judge the proper size, hold one end of the hammock even with the top of your head. Let the other end drop—if it reaches the floor and then some, it's probably big enough. Those made from cotton tend to be the most durable. Ask for a demonstration; loosely woven hammocks are an indication of poor quality.

Street vendors will assail prospective hammock purchasers, but their low prices may also indicate low quality. Shops specializing in hammocks offer a greater selection. Wherever you buy a hammock, check the workmanship carefully, since a poorly made one will wear out quickly.

The *guayabera*, a loosely worn, lightweight cotton shirt, is about as formal as men's clothing gets in sweltering Mérida. Upper-class Yucatecans in the late 19th century bought them during trips to Cuba. The garment is worn by businessmen and local politicians instead of a shirt and tie. Traditionally it is white, with a bit of colored embroidery around the front buttons, and has four pockets—two at the chest and two at the waist. Guayaberas Jack, on Calle 59, is one of the few city factories that still produces custom-made shirts.

Just as traditional as the *guayabera* is the *huipil*, a white cotton dress with a squared neck that often is edged with embroidered flowers. A similar but longer and more elaborate garment is the *terno*. Many women who live in rural areas still wear these garments. Handmade dresses have largely been supplanted by machine-made ones, although the latter are usually of good quality.

A jauntily positioned *jipi* (HEE-pee) provides an effective screen against the hot Yucatán sun. The hats are made in several small towns in neighboring Campeche; residents store palm fronds in damp basements until they become soft and pliable, then weave them. Panama hats cost anywhere from about $6 to more than $60 (U.S.); the price is determined by the closeness of the weave and the quality of the fibers (coarse to fine). A good-quality, closely woven hat should bounce back into shape even after being folded into a suitcase or rolled up and stuck in a pocket.

Mexican markets are known for their exotica, and Mérida is no exception; here you can buy live "jeweled" beetle pins called *maquech* (ma-KETCH). The insects are displayed in glass bowls along with a few pieces of wood (their food). Bits of multicolored glass are glued to their backs, and the beetle is attached to a gold chain which hooks to a safety pin. If you do choose to indulge in a live lapel ornament, find another buyer before you leave the country; U.S. Customs and Border Protection officials won't allow it across the border.

Dining and Nightlife

Be sure to sample some of the culinary specialties associated with the Yucatán. *Papadzules* are tortillas stuffed with chopped hard-boiled eggs and topped with pumpkinseed or tomato sauce. *Poc-chuc* is slices of pork marinated in sour orange juice and served with pickled onions; *pollo pibil* is herb-infused chicken wrapped in banana leaves and baked.

Sopa de lima is a soup containing shredded chicken and strips of fried tortilla and flavored with lime juice. *Salbutes* are puffy fried tortillas topped with shredded turkey, lettuce and pickled onions. The incendiary habanero chile is provided on the side rather than in the dish at most establishments (ask to make doubly sure).

Beverages are intriguing as well. While *licuados*—liquified fruit drinks—are sold in many parts of Mexico, they are especially refreshing in Mérida, where the vendors can draw from a variety of melons, pineapple and other tropical flavors. *Licuado* stands are marked by rows of colorful fruit.

More unusual are drinks quaffed for centuries by the Maya and their descendants. One example is *horchata,* a blend of ground rice and almonds, water and ice, sweetened with raw sugar, cinnamon, vanilla or honey.

Café Montejo, in the lobby of the Hotel Fiesta Americana Mérida, is a pleasant spot for lunch or dinner. *For a list of AAA-RATED dining establishments in Mérida, see the Lodgings & Restaurants section.*

Mérida is a friendly city, and one that's fairly safe to walk around in after dark. At dusk, Plaza de la Independencia and adjoining Hidalgo Park are alive with crowds watching street performers, listening to musicians, grabbing a bite to eat or just relaxing on benches. Sidewalk vendors set up along nearby streets, and a head-spinning array of stores and walk-in eateries sell everything from *tortas* to heavy metal CDs. To fully experience this vibrancy, hit the streets on your own two feet.

There is free evening entertainment at downtown parks and plazas several nights a week, courtesy of an active cultural arts scene. On Monday beginning at 9 p.m. a folkloric dance troupe performs *vaquerías* (traditional Yucatecan dances) in front of City Hall (Palacio Municipal), on Calle 62 across from Plaza de la Independencia. For event schedule information, check with the information center in the Peón Contreras Theater or one of the city tourist offices.

Yucatán State Tourism Office: in the Peón Contreras Theater, on Calle 60 between calles 57 and 59. The office is open daily 8-8; phone (999) 924-9290 (English spoken). There also is a branch of the State Tourism Office inside the Government Palace (Palacio de Gobierno) on the main plaza. Another office is on the second level of the Century XXI Yucatán Convention Center, north of downtown on Calle 60 (the road to Progreso). It is open daily 9-7; phone (999) 930-3760.

The publication *Yucatán Today,* available at the airport and most hotels, has detailed information about city and state attractions and includes maps.

What To See

Downtown

CATHEDRAL (Catedral) is on the e. side of Plaza de la Independencia, opposite the Government Palace. Much of the stone used in its construction came from the ruined buildings of T'hó, the ancient Mayan city upon which Mérida was built. The interior is stark, in marked contrast to the lavish decoration of other Mexican colonial churches. One painting, hanging over a side door to the right of the main altar, depicts a meeting between the Spanish and the Xiu Indians.

To the left is a chapel containing a replica of the Christ of the Blisters (Cristo de las Ampollas), an image of Christ carved from a tree that was said to be struck by lightning but did not burn; it survived a fire in another church and was brought to the cathedral in 1645. Daily 6 a.m.-noon and 4-7. Free.

CITY HALL (Palacio Municipal) is on Calle 62 on the w. side of Plaza de la Independencia. More commonly known as the Ayuntamiento, it was built atop a Mayan pyramid. The exterior, yellow with white trim, shows a Moorish influence, and the clock tower is typical of Mexican government buildings. Adjoining it is the Olimpo, a cultural center with space for concerts and art exhibitions; schedules for upcoming performances are posted on the bulletin board in the pretty courtyard.

CITY MUSEUM (Museo de la Ciudad) is at calles 61 and 58 across the street from Plaza de la Independencia. It has paintings, photographs and drawings illustrating Mérida's history, with exhibit information in English. Tues.-Fri. 10-2 and 4-8). Free.

GOVERNMENT PALACE (Palacio de Gobierno) is on the n. side of Plaza de la Independencia. It dates from 1892. Take the wide stairway to the second floor, where the walls of one room are adorned with murals by Meridano artist Fernando Castro Pacheco depicting traditional Mayan symbology as well as the violent appropriation of their culture by the Spanish. A hall of history, also on the second floor, chronicles the destruction by Spanish bishop Diego de Landa of the Mayan *codices,* pictorial history books. Mon.-Sat. 8-8, Sun. 9-5. Free.

MACAY MUSEUM (Museo de Arte Contemporáneo Ateneo de Yucatán) is on Calle 60 next to the cathedral. It exhibits the work of Yucatecan artists in two floors of rooms built around an interior patio. There are paintings by Fernando Castro Pacheco, who created the murals in the Government Palace. The museum also presents temporary exhibits of art from other parts of Mexico. The Revolution Passage (Pasaje de la Revolución), a pedestrian walkway connecting the museum and the cathedral, is an outdoor exhibit space for various sculptures.

Wed.-Mon. 10-6 (also Fri.-Sat. 6-8 p.m.). Free. Phone (999) 928-3236.

MONTEJO HOUSE (Casa de Montejo) is on Calle 63 (s. side of Plaza de la Independencia). It was built in 1549 by the son of Francisco de Montejo, the Yucatán conqueror. Montejo the Younger employed Indian labor to create the richly ornamented facade and doors, fine examples of Plateresque decoration. A reminder of Spanish cruelty are the carvings of *conquistadores* with feet firmly planted on top of wailing Mayan heads. This restored family home now houses a Banamex Bank branch with a huge, lushly landscaped patio. Business hours Mon.-Fri. 9-5, Sat. 9-2.

NATIONAL MUSEUM OF POPULAR ART (Museo Nacional de Arte Popular) is 6 blks. e. of the plaza on Calle 59, between calles 48 and 50. It is housed in one of Mérida's venerable mansions. The collection of Yucatecan handicrafts here includes regional costumes, pottery, masks, woven baskets, musical instruments and beautifully carved conch shells. Tues.-Sat. 9-6. Admission about $2 (U.S.).

PEON CONTRERAS THEATER (Teatro Peón Contreras) is on Calle 60 between calles 57 and 59, just n. of Cepeda Peraza Park (Hidalgo Park). It was built in the early 20th century in the grand Italianate style of European opera houses. The main entrance features a staircase of Carrara marble, and the interior is typically and richly ornate. Changing exhibitions feature the work of contemporary painters, sculptors and photographers from all over Mexico. This venue for the performing arts also houses a tourist information center that is a good place to find out what's going on around town.

In and Around the City

ANTHROPOLOGY MUSEUM (Museo Regional de Antropología) is on Paseo Montejo at Calle 43. It is housed in the Palacio Cantón, the former home of Mérida's prominent Cantón family. The museum has an extensive collection of stone carvings, figurines and relics, including jade and gold objects retrieved from the Sacred Cenote at Chichén Itzá. Particularly interesting are the sections devoted to daily Mayan life, showing how babies' heads were elongated and how teeth were filed to achieve their rather bizarre standards of beauty.

Exhibit information is mostly in Spanish. Tues.-Sat. 9-8, Sun. 8-2. Admission 33 pesos (about $3.20 U.S.).

CENTENARIO PARK AND ZOO is about 12 blks. w. of Plaza de la Independencia, running along Av. Itzaes between calles 59 and 65. Handsome, colonial-style yellow stone archways flank the park entrance. It is large, shady and particularly fun for children. The zoo displays a variety of animals and birds, from peacocks and flamingos to alligators, lions and jaguars, as well as species native to the Yucatán Peninsula. A miniature train offers rides through the park. Park open Tues.-Sun. 6-6, zoo Tues.-Sun. 8-5. Free.

DZIBILCHALTUN RUINS (zeeb-eel-chal-TOON) are about 15 km (9 mi.) n. of Mérida; take Calle 60 n. out of the city, following signs for Progreso and Mex. 261. The paved turn-off is marked by a sign that says "Dzibilchaltún/Universidad del Mayab." The site entrance is another 5 km (3 mi.) e. Although this is one of Mexico's largest archeological discoveries, not much remains of its former glory. More than 8,000 ruins, mostly mounds of rubble or the remains of low platforms, have been uncovered so far. The cluster of excavated altars and other structures are aligned along a walkway.

The reconstructed House of the Seven Dolls (Templo de las Siete Muñecas), a raised temple, was named for the seven primitive figures discovered buried under the structure's floor. Exhibiting such deformities as a hunchback and a swollen belly, they may have served as spiritual "messengers" during ceremonies to cure illness. There is a good site museum that exhibits carved stone tablets and stela, panels and finely detailed limestone carvings (including a life-size gorilla carrying a human); paintings and Yucatán artifacts from the Spanish colonial period; weapons associated with the 19th-century War of the Castes; and machines used to harvest henequén.

Guided tours and food are available. Allow 2 hours minimum. Ruins daily 8-5; museum Tues.-Sun. 8-4. Admission (includes museum) 46 pesos (about $4.50 U.S.). Parking fee $1.

HERMITAGE OF SANTA ISABEL (La Hermita de Santa Isabel) is s. of Plaza de la Independencia at calles 66 and 77. It was built in 1748. In colonial days it became known as the Convent of Safe Travel, since travelers on their way to the busy port of Campeche would stop to pray for a safe journey. The restored hermitage is surrounded by a serene, pretty garden accented with Mayan and Toltec statues and a waterfall.

MAYAPAN RUINS are about 64 km (40 mi.) s.e. of Mérida. To get there from downtown, take Calle 59 e. to the Anillo Periférico (the loop road around the city). Take the Anillo Periférico s. to the exit for Mex. 18. Continue s. on Mex. 18, a two-lane blacktop, past the villages of Kanasin, Acanceh, Tecoh and Telchaquillo; a short distance past Telchaquillo watch for the sign (on the right) directing you to the ruins entrance. From Cancún or Chichén Itzá, take Mex. 180-D w. to the Ticopo exit and follow signs

The Art of the Retablo

Churches and cathedrals in Mexico are renowned for their beauty both inside and out. Many of them positively brim with stone carvings, statues and extravagant ornamentation. And a particularly lovely feature in some churches is the display of *retablos,* or devotional paintings. Combining centuries-old Catholic iconography, traditional religious beliefs and indigenous artistry, the *retablo* is a distinctly Mexican example of popular folk art.

Vibrantly colorful and rife with symbolic overtones, these small oil paintings of Catholic saints were created on zinc, wood, copper and tin. *Retablos* were employed by Spanish priests as part of an effort to convert the Indians to Christianity after Spain's conquest of Mexico in the early 16th century. Tall, multi-paneled structures displaying an array of saints and other religious figures were typically erected behind a church's main altar; the word *retablo* means "behind the altar."

Small factories sprang up to mass produce *retablos* (also called *laminas* in Mexico). *Retableros,* artists who were both skilled and unskilled, made their living reproducing the images of many different saints, from venerated individuals like St. Francis of Assisi, founder of the Franciscan order, and biblical translator St. Jerome (San Jerónimo) to San Ysidro Labrador, the patron saint of farmers. Over a lifetime a *retablero* might end up creating the same image literally thousands of times. At the height of their popularity in the late 19th century *retablos*—in addition to being placed in churches and at shrines—were sold to devout believers who graced home altars with the likeness of their patron saint.

to Mex. 18; continue s. on Mex. 18 past Acanceh, Tecoh and Telchaquillo to the Mayapán entrance.

This walled city flourished after the heyday of Chichén Itzá and Uxmal; it was reduced to rubble in the 16th century by Spanish conqueror Francisco de Montejo's forces. The site is impressively large, with eight buildings more than 30 feet tall and another two dozen smaller ruins and platforms. The structural similarities with Chichén Itzá are evident: high, sloping walls with steep steps built into the sides.

Most of the pyramidal structures can be climbed, although the very narrow steps make it difficult to do so. The remote location and slow pace of ongoing restoration work means there are few visitors, and those fascinated by ruins will have these crumbling temple platforms and weathered sculptures basically to themselves.

Note: There are no restrooms or other amenities at the site. Allow 2 hours minimum. Daily 8-5. Admission 29 pesos (about $2.80 U.S.). Parking fee 10 pesos. The fee to use a video camera is $5. Phone (999) 942-1900.

Nearby Destinations

Mérida makes a good base for day trip excursions to the small towns and villages in the state of Yucatán. Most of them have interesting churches and bustling markets, and it's a nice opportunity to get out of the city, see the countryside and mingle with the locals.

If you want to visit a typical Yucatecan *pueblo* located just outside the Mérida city limits, take Avenida Itzes (Mex. 180) southbound past the airport to the Anillo Periférico loop road, then follow the directional signs for Umán. In the vicinity of the town's main plaza, which is dominated by a large church, are small shops and sidewalk vendors selling food and trinkets. *Triciclo* drivers line up waiting to transport locals. A *triciclo* is the reverse of a tricycle—two wheels in front supporting a cargo/carrier area, and one in the back below the driver's seat. Everything from people to live chickens to crates of produce are transported by means of this cheap transportation.

Hacienda Yaxcopoil is about 32 kilometers (20 miles) south of Mérida. From downtown take Avenida Itzaes southbound to the Anillo Periférico. Access Mex. 180 (the road is signed "Libramiento Umán" but bypasses the town of Umán), continue south and exit at Mex. 261. Stay on Mex. 261, following the signs for Uxmal. The small village of Yaxcopoil (yawsh-koe-poe-EEL) is about 11 kilometers (7 miles) south of the exit; watch for the marked turn-off to the hacienda ("Antigua Hacienda y Museo Yaxcopoil"), distinguished by a Moorish double arch, on the right at Km marker 186.

Operating first as a cattle ranch and later as a henequén plantation, this was once one of the most important haciendas in the Yucatán. Although now showing great age and some ruin, the Moorish-style architecture of Casa Principal, the main building, and its drawing rooms, high-ceilinged corridors and lush garden areas hint at the gracious lifestyle enjoyed by wealthy late 19th-century plantation owners. The Maya Room in the main building has displays of pottery and artifacts excavated from nearby Mayan ruins. The property is safe to visit and interesting to explore. Hacienda tours are given Mon.-Sat. 8-6, Sun. 9-1. Admission 50 pesos (about $4.85 U.S.). Phone (999) 900-1193.

The Convent Route

The Convent Route (Ruta de Los Conventos) south from Mérida via Mex. 18 passes through a string of rural towns and villages. From the downtown historic center, take Calle 59 east to the Anillo Periférico loop road, then take the Anillo Periférico south to the exit for Mex. 18 (signed "Kanasin"). Two-lane Mex. 18 heads south, passing through small Yucatecan communities distinguished by their impressively large churches.

About 22 kilometers (14 miles) south of Kanasin is the town of Acanceh (ah-con-KAY). A Mayan pyramid undergoing restoration, a colonial-era church and a present-day church all stand on the town plaza. About 8 kilometers (5 miles) beyond Acanceh is Tecoh (tay-KO), where the town market is dwarfed by a large church and convent dedicated to the Virgin of the Assumption. Built atop the raised platform that was once the foundation for a Mayan pyramid, the church is reached by a broad stone stairway.

This 16th-century building has a rough stone exterior capped by twin towers similar in appearance to the cathedral in Mérida *(see attraction listing)*. Inside is a soaring, beautifully ornamented *retablo* that was restored in the late 1990s. It features four large paintings that are the work of Mexico's famed baroque artist Miguel Cabrera. In addition to the main altarpiece, the church also is graced with two smaller *retablos* dedicated to the Virgin Mary, both resplendent with gold decoration in the extravagant Mexican Churrigueresque style.

Several miles south of Tecoh is the small village of Telchaquillo (tel-chah-KEY-yoh). On the plaza stands a small, plain-looking chapel, and nearby is a cenote (limestone sinkhole) with stone stairs leading down into the water. A short distance south of Telchaquillo is the turn-off (on the right) for the Mayapán Ruins *(see attraction listing)*.

About 18 kilometers (11 miles) south of Telchaquillo is a larger village, Tekit (teh-KIT). Tekit's parish church of San Antonio de Padua has a simple altar and elaborately decorated statues of saints. About 7 kilometers (4 miles) south of Tekit is Mamá, another small village dominated by a large church and convent built in the 17th century. The exterior is crowned by lovely decorative stonework; inside are wall frescoes, baroque *retablos,* recessed wall niches holding statues of saints and a spectacularly ornate altar.

About 13 kilometers (8 miles) south of Mamá is Teabo (tay-AH-bow), which like other towns in this region is known for the manufacture of the *huipil* dress, the traditional white cotton shift with colorful

The Art of the Retablo (continued)

A similar expression of devotion is the *ex-voto,* a painting on canvas or a sheet of tin that was accompanied by a written testimonial. The assistance of a particular saint might be requested to help cure a health problem, or an expression of thanks was offered in return for a perceived benevolent act or answered prayer. In addition to featuring the saint's image, an *ex-voto* also told a story through pictures, depicting such scenes as a person rising miraculously from a sickbed or a farmer praying for rain for his crops.

Churches with fascinating collections of *retablos* include the Basilica of Our Lady of Guadalupe in Mexico City; the Parish of the Immaculate Conception in Real de Catorce, a former mining town in the state of San Luis Potosí; and the Temple and Ex-Convent of Santo Domingo in San Cristóbal de Las Casas. The Church of La Valenciana, just outside of Guanajuato, features three soaring *retablos*—one behind the main altar and two in the transepts to either side—adorned with life-size statues of saints and biblical figures and a profusion of ornate gold-leaf decoration.

And in Tecoh (tay-KO), a little Yucatán village southeast of Mérida, stands a huge fortress-church and convent that was built in the 17th century atop a Mayan pyramid. Inside the imposing structure stands a tall, four-tiered *retablo* highlighted by four large paintings depicting St. John the Baptist and three archangels. Painstakingly restored, this visual feast of elaborate red-and-gold ornamentation is a stunning reminder of Mexico's rich legacy of colonial art.

embroidery around the neckline worn by Yucatecan women. Teabo's 17th-century Temple of St. Peter the Apostle is part of a complex of colonial buildings. There are beautiful frescoes in the sacristy.

From Teabo, it's another several miles to Maní. It was here in 1562 that Diego de Landa, a Spanish bishop, ordered the destruction by fire of the Mayan *codices,* or hieroglyphic picture books, believing them profane. The historical loss resulting from this act was incalculable, leaving Landa's own treatise on Mayan history, *"Relación de las Cosas de Yucatán"* ("Yucatán Before and After the Conquest"), the only known account.

Maní is a quiet, peaceful town that sees little tourist traffic. Visit the town church, which has artwork displaying both Mayan and Spanish influences. The carefully preserved *retablos,* each replete with red and gold ornamentation, are noteworthy. Be sure to look up at the vaulted ceiling above the gilded gold *retablo* behind the altar; it is covered with exquisite frescoes. The church's adjacent open-air Indian chapel dates from the late 16th century. The park on the main plaza, complete with the bust of an unidentified Mexican statesman atop a green stone pedestal, is a shady spot to relax.

From Maní continue south to Oxkutzcab (osh-koots-KAHB), located in a fertile farming region that produces sugar cane, tobacco, corn, bananas and citrus fruits. It's a bustling place, with fleets of foot-pedaled *triciclos* (and more recently, motorized three-wheeled taxis) waiting to pick up passengers.

Oxkutzcab's market, near the main plaza, has stacks of plump green watermelons, wooden crates filled with fruits and vegetables, and vendor stalls in an open-air building with a long, colorful mural extending across the front. Go in the morning, before it gets too hot or crowded, for a Yucatecan breakfast of *salbutes*—handmade corn tortillas fried and topped with lettuce, chopped tomatoes and shredded chicken. Also on the plaza is the Church and Convent of San Francisco de Asis, which has a tan exterior. Inside this meticulously renovated church are several beautiful *retablos,* the statues of saints surrounded by gold-leaf ornamentation.

From Oxkutzcab, take the Mérida-Chetumal Highway (Mex. 184) north about 19 kilometers (12 miles) to Ticul. This busy regional center specializes in the manufacture of pottery and women's shoes. It's also larger than most of the other towns; the streets are filled with *triciclos* (and dogs).

A domed 18th-century church stands next to Ticul's central plaza. An interesting exterior decoration is the facial features—two half-moon eyes and a nose—carved below the roof. Many of the shops lining the downtown streets sell nothing but shoes. Craft shops offer ceramic bowls, and street vendors hawk embroidered *huipiles* and Panama hats made from woven palm fronds.

From Ticul continue north on Mex. 184 to Muna, then take Mex. 261 from Muna north to Mérida. From Ticul you also can get to the ruins at Uxmal *(see separate listing within this region).*

Celestún

A day trip also is possible is to the fishing village of Celestún, on the western Yucatán coast. To get there, take Mex. 281 (Calle 59A within the city) about 97 kilometers (60 miles) west. En route are the towns of Hunucma and Kinchil, as well as fields of henequén and old haciendas that drove this once-thriving industry.

The village sits at the tip of a strip of land separating the Celestún Estuary (*ría* in Spanish) from the Gulf of Mexico. The atmosphere is decidedly laid-back; there are no resort amenities here. A stretch of white-sand swimming beach is at the north edge of town, although constant winds make the water choppy and silt-laden. The harbor is picturesque in a scruffy sort of way, filled with small boats and fishing nets drying in the sun.

The main reason to visit Celestún is the surrounding wildlife refuge, home to a large colony of flamingos. While these spindly-legged, coral-plumaged birds are the area's most spectacular residents, numerous species of waterfowl also live here. In addition, Celestún is on the flyway of many species migrating from northern climates to South America.

Tours of the estuary can be arranged just past the bridge leading into town, where there is a parking lot, ticket window, restrooms and a snack bar. The fare for a 75-minute tour is about $45 (U.S.) per boat (cash only), in canopied boats that accommodate up to six passengers. Bring sunscreen and water. The tour includes bird-watching (in addition to flamingos, you're likely to see pelicans, herons, egrets, spoonbills and ducks) as well as an excursion through dense mangroves to a freshwater spring welling up within the saltwater estuary. The number of flamingos seen depends on the season, tide and time of day, but in any event refrain from encouraging your boat captain to get too close, which causes the birds undue stress.

PLAYA DEL CARMEN, QUINTANA ROO (A-4) pop. 47,200

Playa del Carmen once was the mainland departure point for Mayan pilgrims visiting the sanctuaries and temples on Cozumel. That connection is maintained today, but ferry boats have supplanted canoes and bear tourists, not worshippers. And "Playa," as it is usually referred to, has long surpassed its function as simply a ferry departure point. Growth in the last decade or so has been explosive, and while it might not rival Cancún in size or popularity, the town has become a destination in its own right.

Playa sits in the approximate middle of a stretch of Quintana Roo coastline known as the Riviera Maya. It begins at Puerto Morelos and extends south to the fishing village of Punta Allen, at the tip of the Boca Paila Peninsula. A rapidly developing vacation area, the coast is an alternative to the more established destinations of Cancún and Cozumel.

The Riviera Maya seems simultaneously trendy and timeless. Ecological awareness is a major theme at the nature park attractions opening along the coast. Environmentalism is actively promoted, and visitors are encouraged to participate in such programs as preserving nesting sites of the threatened sea turtle population. Some accommodations also promote a "back to nature" slant—rustic, thatch-roofed seaside "eco-hotels" nestled under palm trees, where the standard guest activities include yoga classes, meditation in a flotation tank or a full-body exfoliation treatment. Many hotels and restaurants here have European owners, giving Playa a strong international influence.

And a number of tour companies are popping up to take advantage of the surge in eco tourism along Mexico's Caribbean coast. Playa del Carmen-based Alltournative specializes in outings like a visit to the Tulum Ruins *(see attraction listing under Tulum)* combined with snorkeling in a cenote and a zipline thrill ride above the jungle, or exploring underwater caverns and then piloting a sea kayak to an offshore coral reef. These guided day trips also involve the community, putting the focus not only on adventure but on education and giving back to local families. For more details phone (984) 803-9999 or (800) 507-1092 (from the United States or Canada).

Practicalities

Most visitors fly into Cancún and then drive to Playa del Carmen, about 68 kilometers (42 miles) south via Mex. 307, the highway that connects the coastal communities. There are three turn-offs that run east into town. The first, Avenida 34, accesses the northern end of Playa. The main turn-offs (Avenida Constituyentes and Avenida Juárez) will take you downtown; Avenida Juárez goes straight to the main plaza and the ferry pier to Cozumel. (Both of these intersections have a traffic signal; stay in the inside lanes to turn left or you'll have to proceed south on Mex. 307 to the turnaround and double back.) The Pemex gas stations, new car dealerships and branches of Sam's Club and Office Depot along the highway are evidence that this is the biggest town along the Riviera Maya coast.

Taxis from Cancún are expensive, averaging about $70 (U.S.) one way. A far less expensive option is taking the bus. Autobuses Riviera provides frequent daily service between Cancún International Airport and Playa del Carmen. One-way fare is about $8 (U.S.). Bus tickets can be purchased at Terminals 2 or 3. Look for a bus ticket counter inside the terminal entrance doors, or purchase a ticket from the driver; the red buses, which have "Riviera" and "ADO" written on the side and the destination on the front, pick up passengers outside the terminals.

Playa has two bus stations. Buses from Cancún and other points north and from Tulum and other points south arrive at the Riviera bus station, at the corner of Avenida Juárez and 5th Avenue (Avenida 5), just up the street from the main plaza. Buses from Mérida and other interior points arrive at the newer ADO bus station, northwest of downtown on Avenida 20 between calles 12 and 14. *Colectivos* are an equally inexpensive alternative to the bus. These air-conditioned, government-regulated vans run the length of Mex. 307, providing transportation from Playa to various destinations between Cancún and Tulum.

Drivers on large yellow tricycles *(triciclos),* the Mexican version of a rickshaw, congregate in front of the downtown station; it's an inexpensive way to get to nearby hotels or take a spin around town. Playa is small enough, however, that practically everything of interest to casual visitors is within walking distance. There are several bike rental shops at the northern end of 5th Avenue, and bicycling is a pleasant way to get around.

Taxi fares within the downtown area shouldn't be more than 20 pesos (about $1.95 U.S.). Make sure you confirm the rate with the driver before getting in the cab. Many drivers don't speak English, so it helps to have directions to your destination written down. You also can hire a taxi for the day, which is convenient if you don't have a rental car; the driver will take you to the places you want to visit and wait while you sightsee. Rates are negotiable, but expect to pay a minimum of about $70 (U.S.).

Two different ferry companies carry passengers between Playa del Carmen and Cozumel *(see separate listing within this region).* The centrally located ferry pier is off Avenida 5, a block south of the main plaza. Cars are not transported; there is a guarded parking lot across the street from the pier. Departures to Cozumel are approximately every hour and begin around 5 a.m.; the last scheduled departure is around 11 p.m. The last scheduled departure from Cozumel back to Playa del Carmen is around 10 p.m. Cold beverages can be purchased on board.

Tickets can be purchased at booths along 5th Avenue and close to the pier. If you're going on a day trip to Cozumel, simply arrive at the pier early and buy a ticket for the next available trip. Early morning rides may sell out due to workers commuting to the island, but in general seats are always available. Double-check the schedule at the pier, and in particular confirm the time of the last departure from Cozumel if you're planning a day trip to the island. On Cozumel tickets can be purchased at the dock where you board the ferry.

Modern, air-conditioned vessels operated by UltraMar depart regularly for Cozumel daily 8 a.m.-9 p.m. The trip takes about 45 minutes. Round-trip fare (including tax) is about $20 (U.S.); ages 4-11, $11.

Note: Ferry schedules are subject to change due to weather conditions, as seas can sometimes be quite rough; make sure you carry appropriate medication if you're prone to seasickness.

About four kilometers (2.5 miles) south of the turn-off for Xcaret *(see attraction listing)* is the Puerto Calica cruise ship pier. Passengers on ships docking here avoid the tender ride to the mainland from Cozumel. Fewer ships dock on the weekend, which is a better time to visit such tourist attractions as Xcaret, Xel-Ha and the Tulum ruins if you want to avoid cruise ship crowds.

Several banks are located on Avenida Juárez. Most have ATMs; withdrawals are in pesos. A Banamex bank branch with an ATM is at the corner of Avenida 10 and Calle 12. There also are several *casas de cambio* (currency exchange offices) in town. Many shops and restaurants accept U.S. and Canadian dollars, however.

City Layout

Playa is somewhat of a hybrid—explosive growth has resulted in luxury resorts and a hopping nightlife, but it still has the workaday feel of typical Mexican town. The small, compact downtown area bustles with traffic and pedestrians. Merchandise is displayed outside shop doors. There are grocery, hardware and convenience stores, dive shops, hair salons, laundromats, tattoo parlors. Shoeshine men and vendors selling hot dogs and hamburgers from wheeled carts set up on the sidewalk. The nicest part of Playa is right along the beach; west of Avenida 10, two blocks inland, the streets start to have a scruffier look common to many Mexican towns.

Downtown is laid out in a simple grid pattern and is easy to negotiate. Avenidas run north-south; calles run east-west. Traffic congestion is common, however, due partly to a number of newer unpaved, sandy streets and their water-filled potholes that require careful maneuvering. The busiest part of town is where Avenida Juárez ends at 5th Avenue (also called Avenida 5 or Quinta Avenida), in the vicinity of the Riviera bus station and the ferry pier to Cozumel. The public pay parking lot near the bus station, just north of Juárez and just west of 5th Avenue, is a convenient place to leave your car if you feel like getting out and exploring.

The tourist action centers on 5th Avenue, just inland from the beach. The 15-block stretch from Avenida Juárez north to Calle 26 has the greatest concentration of restaurants, hotels, shops and nightspots. Playa's small *zócalo* (main plaza), a block east of 5th Avenue and a block south of Avenida Juárez, is just off the beach. Shaded by coconut palms and a lush green canopy of almond trees, this little brick-paved plaza has benches, a gazebo with black wrought-iron trim and a view of the Caribbean; it's a lovely spot to relax. Next to the plaza vendors set up tables shaded by brightly colored umbrellas; in fact, almost everywhere you turn there are umbrella-shaded stands selling just about everything.

The Playacar hotel zone is south of the ferry pier. Residential homes, condos, hotels and all-inclusive resorts are within this designated area; the cobblestoned main thoroughfare is called Paseo Xaman-Ha (sha-MAN hah). A genuine lodging bargain might be found here during the off season (after Easter through November). Cruise ship passengers and day visitors from Cancún take advantage of Playacar Club de Golf, a public, 18-hole golf course designed by Robert Von Hagge that includes an outstanding clubhouse and pro shop. Greens fees drop significantly if you're a guest at a hotel affiliated with the club.

Playa's beaches have the powdery white sand and beautiful turquoise water characteristic of the entire Mexican Caribbean coast, and offshore reefs guarantee good snorkeling and diving. The main public beach, between the ferry pier and Calle 10, is the most crowded. It's wide and sandy near the pier, narrowing somewhat as it runs north past restaurants, beach bars, dive shops and varied water sports operators. If you prefer fewer crowds and more seclusion, keep walking north past the jetty at the Porto Real Hotel. The wide sand beach here is quieter as long as you avoid the activities around the Playa Tukan and Mamitas beach clubs. You can, however, rent an umbrella and a lounge chair from these places if you intend to stay the day; just get there early.

Note: Playa's air of funky informality attracts a young, open-minded crowd of international vacationers, and topless sunbathing is nonchalantly accepted at a few spots (although against the law in Mexico).

Shopping and Nightlife

Avenida 5 is a pedestrian-only thoroughfare between calles 1 and 6. The numerous shops and souvenir stands here and on little side streets sell T-shirts, jewelry, knickknacks, handmade pottery, New Age paraphernalia and a wide variety of crafts from all over Mexico. While it's fun to browse the avenue checking out everything that's on display, some merchants can be quite persistent in their attempts to entice potential customers; be prepared to keep walking if you're not really interested in buying.

Strolling, shopping and the heat combine for a laid-back scene during the day. Avenida 5 really comes alive in the evening, when people stroll around the plaza, flock to restaurants and congregate at sidewalk cafes. Reggae music fills the air, and a carnival-like atmosphere prevails. A number of dance clubs and beach bars offer a partying atmosphere and live music.

The Blue Parrot, on the beach between calles 10 and 14 (next to the Hotel Costa del Mar), is a popular bar that attracts a rowdy crowd. This longtime favorite has an outdoor beachside dance floor that throbs with techno music until the wee hours. For those over 30 it's a nice spot for lunch or a late afternoon drink on the beach. La Santanera, on Calle 12 between 5th and 10th avenues, has an open-air upper level where you can lounge on couches under a *palapa* roof and a downstairs disco where DJs spin house and other dance music.

Dining

For its size, Playa has an impressive number of restaurants offering a smorgasbord of variety. Mexican, American, Italian, German, seafood, steak, pizza and taco vendors, ice cream and popsicle stands—it's all here. If you want something healthy to nibble on while walking around town, stop at a fruit stand. For about 10 pesos, women wearing traditional Mayan blouses (white with colorful embroidery) will give you a large cup filled with chunks of fresh pineapple, mango, coconut and watermelon. *Churros,* sold from street carts, are sticks of dough pressed through a tube shaped like a star, then fried in oil and rolled in cinnamon sugar or filled with fruit jam or melted chocolate. Another tasty snack is *tacos al pastor,* shredded, marinated pork cooked on a rotisserie, heaped on a small corn tortilla and garnished with chopped onions, cilantro and a slice of pineapple.

Restaurants can be found up and down the length of 5th Avenue. La Parilla (at Calle 8) is one of the most popular, a fun place that serves Mexican standards like tortilla soup, enchiladas and quesadillas. Mariachis serenade evening diners. For more sophisticated dining try Byblos Restaurant, on Calle 14 just off 5th Avenue. Candlelit tables draped with white linens create a romantic mood, and the menu choices—from escargot to duck foie gras sauteed with vegetables and cider, all matched with selections from the wine list—is classic French. At the north end of 5th Avenue (at Avenida Constituyentes) is Ah Cacao Chocolate Café. Pull up a chair at one of the little sidewalk tables, linger over an espresso, latte or iced coffee and sample one of the cafe's signature chocolate brownies.

And don't limit your restaurant sampling to 5th Avenue alone. Babe's Noodles and Bar, on Calle 10 between 5th and 10th avenues, is representative of Playa's international flavor. At this Swedish-owned restaurant—decorated with Barbie dolls and lava lamps—a Mexican server will bring you Thai-style noodles in green or coconut curry, or perhaps a shrimp salad with vegetables, rice noodles and a Vietnamese dressing. Eat in the Buddha Garden, an open-air terrace surrounded by tropical trees and hung with Asian lanterns. More off the beaten path is La Pesca, on 30th Avenue between calles 14 and 16 (across from the Mega supermarket). Some locals say it serves the best seafood in town. Try the ceviche, octopus *(pulpo)* in a spicy sauce or *cazuela de camarones* (shrimp casserole).

Playa is very casual, and casual dress is appropriate even at the more expensive places. There's no need to watch what you order at restaurants targeting the tourist trade. Use your own judgment regarding local hangouts or street food, but as a general rule if it's cooked it should be safe to eat. *For a list of AAA-RATED dining establishments in Playa del Carmen, see the Lodgings & Restaurants section.*

Riviera Maya Tourism Board: north of downtown in the Professional Building (Edificio Profesional), corner of Mex. 307 (Carretera Federal) and Calle #28; phone (984) 206-3150 or (877) 746-6292 (from the United States). The organization provides general visitor information about the Quintana Roo coast from Cancún south to Tulum.

Nearby Destinations

ECOPARK KANTUN-CHI is on the inland side of Mex. 307, 22 km (14 mi.) s. of Playa del Carmen, 2 km (1.2 mi.) s. of Puerto Aventuras and just n. of Xpu-Ha Beach. The park entrance road is prominently signed with a roadside billboard; a faux Mayan pyramid sits at the front entrance.

The 1-hour guided tour of Kantun-Chi's underground cavern system begins when you descend (via wooden ladder) a deep hole that resembles a well. Several pools feature ceilings dripping with stalactites and have cold water that is inhabited by tiny cave fish. The dry sections of the cavern are festooned with more stalactite and stalagmite formations illuminated by colored lights. You can swim and snorkel in the pools. In addition to the underground caverns, visitors can explore four aboveground cenotes—pools sheltered under limestone overhangs—that are linked by jungle-lined pathways.

Snorkel masks, life jackets and lockers are included. Waterproof sport sandals are highly recommended, but you can get by with flip-flops. Walking through the dry sections of the underground cavern involves negotiating some tight passageways and low overhangs. Restrooms are on site. Children under age 7 are not permitted on the cave tour. Open daily 9-5 (also 5-6 during the summer months). Admission (cash only, pesos or U.S. dollars) for the guided cavern tour plus access to the above-ground cenotes $38 (U.S.); $30 (ages 8-12). Access to cenotes only $23; $13 (ages 0-12). Phone (984) 873-0021.

PUERTO AVENTURAS is 20 km (12 mi.) s. of Playa del Carmen off Mex. 307. This planned resort community of hotels, condominiums and residential areas has its own golf course, marina, dive centers, shops and restaurants. The landscaped grounds are adorned with imported palms and orchids. Tennis, swimming, scuba diving, deep-sea fishing and swimming with dolphins are among the recreational activities offered.

CEDAM Museum is 2 blks. s. of the Omni Puerto Aventuras Resort. Known locally as the Shipwreck Museum, this small space exhibits artifacts and wreckage obtained from shipwrecks that have occurred off the Quintana Roo coast. Cannons, dinnerware, gold coins and an elephant tusk are some of the objects on display from wrecks that include the *Matanceros* (which means "the killers"), a Spanish merchant ship that ran into the coral reefs just offshore in 1741. Food is available. Allow 1 hour minimum. Daily 10-1 and 2-6, although hours may vary. Donations.

GEM **XCARET** is about 6 km (4 mi.) s. of Playa del Carmen at Mex. 307 Km marker 282 (follow the marked turn-off). At one time Xcaret (ISH-kah-ret) was a tranquil series of interlocking lagoons in the midst of pristine jungle. No more—this is a full-scale tourist attraction with a multitude of things to see and do. Preserving the natural environment, however, is given as much emphasis as showcasing it, and equally important is the park's dedication to educating visitors regarding Mayan history, culture and traditions.

One of the most popular activities for swimmers, snorkelers and divers is paddling through interconnected cenotes (freshwater sinkholes) and two natural underground rivers. There also are beaches and inlets for swimming and snorkeling, along with educational programs that include interaction and swimming with dolphins. **Note:** Using suntan lotion is not permitted in the lagoons and other waterways because of its effect on the marine habitat.

In addition to water-based recreation, Xcaret offers a living coral reef aquarium; jaguar, deer and monkey island habitats; an aviary; a bee farm; regional wildlife exhibits, including tapirs, flamingos, manatees and sea turtles; a nature trail through tropical jungle; a bromeliad and orchid greenhouse; and several small archeological sites on the grounds. Regional species flit through a botanical garden at the Butterfly Pavilion.

Xcaret's replica of a Mayan Village (Pueblo Maya) depicts how life is still lived in many rural Yucatán towns. The re-created village cemetery, with colorful grave displays and catacombs running underneath, has a hilltop setting. Entertainment features performances of the ceremonial flying pole dance by the Papantla Flyers and the rousing evening show "Xcaret Mexico Espectacular," with traditional music and dance performances and an overview of Mexican history as seen through the eyes of a young girl.

Visitors are not permitted to bring food, beverages, audio devices or sunblock lotions into the park. Food is available. Allow a full day. Daily 8:30 a.m.-9 p.m. (also 9-10 p.m. in summer). Admission $69 (U.S.); $34.50 (children 40 to 55 inches tall). The basic admission includes use of showers, changing rooms, beach chairs and hammocks, as well as all water, wildlife and botanical areas, the Butterfly Pavilion, archeological sites and entertainment. There are separate rental fees for snorkeling equipment, lockers, towels, wheelchairs and baby strollers. Depending upon crowds, however, the park may run out of supplies; bring your own towels and snorkeling gear if possible. There also are separate fees for scuba diving instruction, guided diving and snorkeling excursions and the dolphin swim programs (which should be reserved in advance). AX, MC, VI. Phone (998) 883-0470 in Cancún, (984) 803-1298 in Playa del Carmen or 01 (800) 292-2738 (toll-free long distance within Mexico).

PUERTO MORELOS, QUINTANA ROO (A-4)

The turn-off for Puerto Morelos (PWEHR-toh moh-REH-los) is about 36 kilometers (22 miles) south of Cancún off Mex. 307 (watch for the traffic light and prominent signage). From the highway it is a short 2-kilometer (1.2-mile) jaunt to this peaceful, unhurried fishing village with palm-shaded beaches and restaurants serving fresh seafood. The town's pride and joy is a large offshore coral reef, recently designated a national park; in addition to offering excellent snorkeling and diving it helps break up the waves reaching the shore, making the beaches good for wading and swimming.

In 2005 Hurricane Wilma took dead aim on this tourist town, which experienced more damage from the ocean than the unrelenting winds. Waves removed tons of sand and redistributed it along the coast, although the beaches are now longer and wider than they were before the storm hit. Sea grass—the by-product of a healthy reef environment—grows on the bottom and washes up on the beaches, which are cleared daily.

There is frequent first-class bus service from Puerto Morelos to both Cancún and Playa del Carmen. Two stations, one for northbound buses and one for southbound buses, are on Mex. 307. The fare to either city is 16 pesos (about $1.55 U.S.). *Colectivos* (white minivans) also provide transportation both in town and between towns; the in-town fare is an inexpensive 4 pesos (about 40 cents U.S.). Taxi rates are set, not metered; agree on a price before you get in. **Note:** Traffic around the town square is one-way clockwise.

While away the afternoon at the square, where there is a large bookstore, Alma Libre Books, that has thousands of new and used titles in English. It's open Tues.-Sat. 10-3 and 6-9 p.m., Sun. 4-9, Oct.-Apr. Also on the square is the Casa Martín grocery market. A produce market sets up Wednesday mornings next to the church.

The town's lighthouse, damaged by a hurricane, now leans precariously; a newer one stands behind it. For a good photo opportunity, walk to the end of the town dock and then turn around to face the shore. Another favored activity in laid-back Puerto Morelos is taking a beachside snooze in a hammock.

Dive shops in town provide guided deep-sea fishing trips on local *pangas* or a larger vessel with a cabin; catches include barracuda, billfish and grouper. They also offer scuba and snorkeling excursions to the reef, which teems with brilliantly colored tropical fish, all sorts of crustaceans, rays, eels, nurse sharks and sea turtles, plus a wrecked military vessel that divers can explore.

Dive Puerto Morelos, Av. Rojo Gómez #14 (several doors north of the town square), has knowledgeable, PADI-certified guides. Prices range from $25 (U.S.) for a reef snorkeling trip (plus a 20-peso park fee) to $65 for a half-day jungle tour that includes a stop at a freshwater cenote. For reservation information phone (998) 830-7244 (cellular number).

A passenger car/ferry leaves from the Puerto Morelos dock for Cozumel, where it docks at the International Pier just south of the La Ceiba Hotel. The ferry takes about 3 hours to reach Cozumel, but the wait can be tedious and trucks carrying fuel and other cargo take precedence over automobiles. A much quicker alternative for visitors not taking a vehicle to the island (which is not recommended due to limited parking) is to board one of the passenger ferries departing from Playa del Carmen.

There are normally daily departures at 9 a.m. and 1 p.m. It is necessary to arrive at least several hours prior to scheduled departure time in order to purchase a ticket and secure a place in line. This ferry also can be docked for as long as a week during prolonged periods of bad weather.

CROCO CUN is just n. of the Puerto Morelos turn-off on Mex. 307, at Km marker 31. This small zoo, which also functions as a crocodile-raising farm, emphasizes environmental education. On display are crocodile specimens of all ages and sizes, along with rattlesnakes, boa constrictors, iguanas, macaws, tapirs, spider monkeys, menacing-looking tarantulas and other regional species. Visitors can hold young crocodiles and feed baby deer. Guided tours in English are available. Food is available. Insect repellent is strongly advised. Daily 8:30-5:30. Admission $17 (U.S.); $11 (ages 6-12). Phone (998) 850-3719.

DR. ALFREDO BARRERA BOTANICAL GARDEN (Jardín Botánico Dr. Alfredo Barrera) is just s. of the Puerto Morelos turn-off; the entrance is right off Mex. 307. This protected area features a nature trail that winds through a variety of native and regional plants, including a grove of sapodilla trees (from which the sticky substance used to make chewing gum is extracted), a mangrove swamp, an orchid garden, a section where epiphytes (air plants) grow and an area containing a reproduction of a Mayan dwelling. It will be of most interest to visitors familiar with the flora, although bird-watching is rewarding and there are occasional monkey sightings.

Signs give plant names in Spanish and English. Wear plenty of insect repellent. Mon.-Sat. 9-5. Admission about $7 (U.S.).

RIO BEC, CAMPECHE (C-2)

Discovered at the turn of the 20th century, Río Bec (REE-oh bek) is the collective designation for an archeological zone comprising several Mayan sites. All but two are in the state of Campeche. They generally flourished between about A.D. 400 and 1000 and are believed to have served as trade routes between Mayan outposts established along the Caribbean and Gulf of Mexico coasts. The most interesting of these—Kohunlich, Dzibanché, Xpujil, Becan, Chicanná and Calakmul—are all accessible from east-west Mex. 186.

Architecturally the sites exhibit what is referred to as the "Río Bec" style. Features include tower-like structures more visually pleasing than functional and temple entrances carved to look like the open jaws of a snake, dragon or other monstrous creature. These ruins are largely unexplored and little visited, although more and more restoration efforts are being made. What remains intact is the mystery and sense of wonder surrounding these ancient cities.

One or more of the Río Bec sites can easily be visited in the course of a day. As far as staying overnight (highly recommended if you plan on visiting the far-flung Calakmul ruins), there are tourist-class accommodations and a restaurant at the Chicanná Ecovillage Resort, located across the highway from the Chicanná ruins *(see attraction listing)*. The rooms lack air conditioning, but the resort is surprisingly luxurious considering its remote location. Non-guests are welcome to eat at the restaurant; simply tell the guard at the front gate that's what you want to do.

Each archeological site has a parking/entry area and restrooms. Water and food are not available; bring your own. Insect repellent and sturdy shoes are essential for those who plan to do any amount of walking or ruin climbing, which is allowed at all the sites.

Note: Mex. 186 is a long, hot route with few services of any kind. ADO operates first-class bus service from Chetumal west to Escárcega and Villahermosa; while the buses may stop at ruins along the way, it is much more convenient to drive your own vehicle. Make sure the car is in good condition and the tank is full (there is a gas station shortly before reaching Xpujil, near the Quintana Roo-Campeche state line). It is strongly recommended that Mex. 186 only be traveled during daylight hours. The sites below are listed based on their distance from Chetumal. One-way drive time (with no stops) from Chetumal to Xpujil is about 90 minutes.

DZIBANCHE ruins are about 64 km (40 mi.) w. of Chetumal on Mex. 186 to the well-signed turn-off, then about 19 km (12 mi.) n. of the highway via a paved road. Only open to the public since the mid-1990s, Dzibanché dates to between A.D. 300 and 1200. It receives few visitors despite containing a small but impressive collection of structures. Temples 1 and 6 soar above the wooded site (the ceiba trees that grow here were sacred to the ancient Maya). Just beyond Dzibanché is the smaller Kinichná archeological zone.

Daily 8-5. Admission (good for both sites) 39 pesos (about $3.80 U.S.).

KOHUNLICH ruins are about 66 km (41 mi.) w. of Chetumal to the signed turn-off (just before the village of Francisco Villa), then about 8 km (5 mi.) s. of the highway via a paved road. Parklike and shady, Kohunlich (koh-hoon-LEECH) may once have been an oasis. The most notable structure among the rubble-strewn mounds is the pyramid-like Temple of the Masks (Templo de Los Mascarones), which has a central stairway flanked with carved faces, strongly Olmec-influenced, that resemble masks. Hints of red are still visible on these figures, which are protected by thatched coverings. Daily 8-5. Admission 46 pesos (about $4.50 U.S.).

XPUJIL ruins are about 72 km (45 mi.) w. of Kohunlich, on the n. side of the highway just past the village of Xpujil. Xpujil (sh-pooh-HEEL), which means "place of the cattails" in the Mayan language, flourished between A.D. 400 and 900. The largest building at the site consists of three towers that once had steep ornamental stairways extravagantly decorated with jaguar masks; traces of its former grandeur remain. Daily 8-5. Admission 35 pesos (about $3.40 U.S.).

BECAN ruins are about 7 km (4 mi.) w. of Xpujil on the n. side of the highway and can be reached via a short road (watch for the turn-off sign). Surrounded by a dry moat that probably was used as a fortification (the name means "ravine formed by water"), the site once was accessed by seven causeway bridges. This is the most developed of the Río Bec sites and has some of the largest structures, including a twin-towered temple (Structure IX), plazas surrounded by low-rise buildings and a ball court. There also is a nicely preserved stucco mask on display (behind glass) at Structure X.

Daily 8-5. Admission 39 pesos (about $3.80 U.S.).

CHICANNA ruins are about 2 km (1.2 mi.) w. of Becán on the s. side of the highway; a short road leads to the site. They stand within an enticing grove of tropical trees and other vegetation. The buildings are a mix of Río Bec and Chenes architectural styles. Most notable is Structure II, which stands in the main plaza. It features elaborate carvings and a huge doorway fashioned after the jaws of a monster's open mouth, complete with stone teeth. Other buildings include a twin-towered temple and Structure XX, which also has a monster mouth doorway. Daily 8-5. Admission 35 pesos (about $3.40 U.S.).

CALAKMUL ruins are a good 2-hour drive w. of Chicanná; from the Mex. 186 turn-off (watch for signs), a winding road heads s. about 60 km (37 mi.) into the Calakmul Biosphere Reserve. This huge archeological zone—a UNESCO World Heritage Site—sits in the state of Campeche near the Guatemala border. A Classic-era superpower that often battled nearby Tikal, Calakmul is one of the largest Mayan cities ever discovered and boasts the tallest Mayan pyramid (180 feet) in Mexico. Allow a full day to explore the ruins. Daily 8-5. Admission 39 pesos (about $3.80 U.S.). The toll charge for the biosphere reserve road is about $4 (U.S.) per person.

TULUM, QUINTANA ROO (B-3)

Four separate Mayan cities—Solimán, Tankah, Xel-Ha and Tulum—once flourished close to where Tulum (too-LOOM) now stands. This small but growing town is benefiting not only from the upsurge in tourism along the Mexican Caribbean coast but from its proximity to the Tulum Ruins *(see attraction listing)* and several other nearby attractions.

Tulum is small enough that it's easy to walk around and soak up the local atmosphere. Mex. 307 is the main thoroughfare, and for about a mile it is lined with restaurants, souvenir shops and small businesses. Internet cafes sit next to laundromats, *loncherías* (open-air lunch counters), tortilla stands, ice cream parlors, *zapaterías* (shoe stores) and auto repair shops. Produce markets are filled with clusters of bananas on stalks, green coconuts, tropical fruits and sacks of beans. Craft shops offer the usual array of hammocks, textiles, rugs, jewelry, masks and ceramics, while other stores sell housewares and other everyday items.

Explore the side streets, which extend a couple of blocks on both sides of the highway. Tulum's town plaza is just east of Mex. 307 behind the Ayuntamiento (City Hall) building. Shaded by coconut palms, it has a gazebo and is a community gathering place where kids play basketball and vendors set up shop on the sidewalk. Many locals work in nearby resorts or in construction. The local neighborhoods are a mix of cement block houses, traditional Mayan huts and dwellings with thatched roofs and walls made of sticks. **Note:** Lateral streets with diagonal parking spaces run along either side of Mex. 307; use caution when entering the highway from one of these streets.

Evening is a pleasant time to stroll around town. The restaurants along Mex. 307 are casual, and several of them have open-air seating in a garden setting. Some feature live music and dancing on certain nights. Sidewalk taco vendors fill the air with the tantalizing aroma of grilling chicken and pork, and reggae music wafts out of doorways and courtyards. Tulum is a bit of an international melting pot; you'll see American tourists, young European backpackers and elderly local matriarchs likely garbed in a *huipil,* the embroidered white cotton blouse that has long been worn by Yucatecan women.

To reach Tulum's beaches, take the Cobá/Boca Paila road east (the intersection with a traffic signal at the northern end of town; make a left turn if traveling southbound or a right turn if traveling northbound). The paved road has no highway number; the sign at the intersection says "Playas/Punta Allen." It runs east through open scrub for about 3 kilometers (2 miles) before forking north (toward the Tulum Ruins, with access to beaches along the way) and south to the hotel zone.

Take the right fork (south), a narrow, winding paved road that follows the coast. Campgrounds, cabanas and small spa hotels line this lovely drive, bordered by lush growths of palms and other tropical vegetation. Some properties are nothing more than a grouping of *palapa* huts just steps away from the beach. Several of these laid-back accommodations have signs designating them as "eco chic" resorts—which means that they might rely on a generator for electricity and dispense with such amenities as TVs and phones.

Even if you're not staying in the Tulum hotel zone, it's well worth stopping at one of the casual hotel restaurants for lunch and picture-postcard Caribbean views. Head south along the coast road to Zamas; it draws a loyal following to a breezy dining deck overlooking an unspoiled stretch of beach. Farther down the road, Ana y José Beach Club serves great seafood and cocktails. You can eat inside the big *palapa* restaurant, or if you prefer, in a king-size beach bed. Bring lots of cash. Near the southern end of the hotel zone, rustic-chic La Zebra attracts lots of European backpacker hipsters, but the excellent food and drink will satisfy anyone. And La Zebra's beach is gorgeous.

Some of the beaches along this stretch of coast, in addition to boasting powdery white sand and luminous turquoise water, are all but deserted. South of the entrance to the buffer zone of the Sian Ka'an Biosphere Reserve *(see attraction listing)* are miles of uninhabited beaches that edge the Boca Paila Peninsula.

Note: These are natural beaches, unlike the "groomed" stretches that front resort hotels; foot protection is recommended since the bottom can be rocky. Swim or snorkel only when seas are calm, beware of strong currents and stay close to shore; there are no lifeguards. Do not park along the coast road, and do not leave valuables in your car. There are no facilities at these beaches; bring your own water and food.

Numerous cenotes dot the jungles outside Tulum. Technically a cenote (pronounced say-NOH-tay) is a sinkhole that forms when the ceiling of an underlying cave collapses. The Yucatán Peninsula, honeycombed with an underground network of porous limestone rock, also has many cavern systems through which subterranean rivers often flow. The pile of rubble left by a collapsed cave ceiling typically contains very few nutrients, so trees and plants that do manage to sprout send their roots through the rocks to tap the water below; this is why you'll often see tree roots descending into an underground cave from above.

From above ground many cenotes look just like normal ponds, and locals use them as swimming holes. Small tropical fish—such species as tetras and mollies that are commonly seen in home aquariums—live in these freshwater sinkholes, making them great places to snorkel. Most also have remarkably clear water, although the tannin from fallen dead leaves can stain the water in some cenotes, giving it the appearance of freshly brewed tea, and in the heat of summer warm water temperatures promote algae bloom that can turn it a cloudy green.

Cenote Cristal and Cenote Escondido are about 4 kilometers (2.5 miles) south of Tulum on opposite sides of Mex. 307 and can be reached via short gravel walking paths. These are typical cenotes of the "pond" variety, and the cool, clear water is good for a refreshing dip. Snorkelers will see turtles and small tropical fish. Watch for the parking area on the right side of the highway, where you pay the 40-peso entrance fee; lock your car and do not leave valuables inside. Cenote Cristal has a sloping path to the water's edge; at Cenote Escondido a ladder descends from a stone platform to the water. There are no facilities, so bring your own drinking water and snacks. Open daily 8-5.

GRAN CENOTE is about 3.6 km (2.1 mi.) w. of Tulum via the road to the Cobá ruins (the jct. with Mex. 307 is at the n. end of town); watch for the signed turn-off on the right side of the road. This freshwater limestone sinkhole—shaped like a half moon—leads to a huge underground cave system. It offers good swimming and snorkeling in cool, clear blue water. Beneath the surface are caverns and passageways, limestone stalactites and stalagmites, and schools of tropical fish. From the entrance/parking area, access to the cenote is down a short path. Divers suit up on the wooden decks overlooking the cenote, and ladder steps lead down to the water. Wear nonslip shoes while swimming or snorkeling.

About 3 kilometers (2 miles) farther down the road (watch for the turn-off on the left) is Car Wash Cenote, so named because locals once washed their vehicles here and you can drive right up to the water's edge. A diving platform has been installed for swimmers. This freshwater pond is home to lots of small tropical fish. Algae growth is heavy in the summer; the water is clearer during the winter months.

Bring your own mask and snorkel or scuba gear. Parking and very basic restrooms are on site. Food is available. Allow 2 hours minimum. Gran Cenote open daily 8-5; Car Wash Cenote open daily 9-5. Gran Cenote admission 100 pesos (about $9.70 U.S.); 50 pesos (children under 48 inches tall). Snorkel gear rental fee 60 pesos, life jacket rental 30 pesos. Car Wash Cenote admission 50 pesos (about $4.85 U.S.). Phone (984) 146-2323.

GEM **TULUM RUINS** are about a mile n. of the town of Tulum. The well-marked turn-off is on the e. side of Mex. 307; a large parking lot is less than 100 yds. e. of the highway. While not nearly as impressive or varied architecturally as Chichén Itzá or Uxmal, Tulum is notable for its dramatic setting overlooking the turquoise Caribbean.

One of the later Mayan outposts, this small but powerful city-state rose to prominence sometime during the 12th century. It was fortified on three sides by a wall—rather uncommon among Mayan cities—due to the coastal location, which was both strategic and vulnerable. A center for maritime commerce, Tulum was never conquered by the Spaniards, although it was abandoned some 75 years after the Spanish conquest of Mexico in 1521.

Some 60 structures are spread over a level, grassy area. The most imposing is The Castle (El Castillo), a pyramidal structure capped by a small temple that stands at the edge of a cliff above the sea. Also worth seeing is the Temple of the Frescoes (Templo de los Frescos) near the site entrance. It features interior murals that display typical Mayan motifs and exterior statues bearing still-discernible traces of paint. Just north of El Castillo is the Temple of the Descending God; the winged stucco figure over the doorway suggests a plummeting diver.

Note: The structures cannot be climbed, and most have roped-off areas that visitors must stand behind, obscuring the view of some interior details. Wear nonslip walking shoes; the sandy, rocky terrain can be unexpectedly slippery. The porous limestone has created a few blowholes through which geysers of sea water can unexpectedly erupt. Weather permitting, bring a swimsuit—the lovely beach below can be reached by walking down a long staircase. Licensed, English-speaking guides are available, although the information you receive may or may not be historically accurate. The ruins are a popular day trip from Cancún and can be crowded depending on the time of year.

There are restrooms, a bookstore, a restaurant and a few souvenir stands in the visitor center at the far end of the parking lot; the entrance to the site is about a 10-minute walk from the parking lot. Open daily 8-5. Admission 48 pesos (about $4.65 U.S.). Parking 40 pesos (about $3.90). Shuttle ride from the visitor center to the site $1.50. The fee for using a video camera is $4. Guided tour fee about $20.

Nearby Destinations

CUZAN BONEFISH FLATS is within the lobster-fishing village of Punta Allen at the tip of the Boca Paila Peninsula. From the jct. of Mex. 307 and the Boca Paila access road at the northern end of the town of Tulum (signed "Playas/Punta Allen") the distance to Punta Allen is about 56 km (35 mi.). Cuzan is known for its wade fishing in Ascención Bay, a stretch of uniformly shallow water covering flats of sand and turtle grass. Bonefish, tarpon and ladyfish are among the game species anglers will encounter. Saltwater reef fishing opportunities include barracuda, grouper, king mackerel and jack crevalle.

Guided eco tours during the winter months include half-day excursions to two rookery islands, one for observation of migratory species like herons, spoonbills and egrets and another to view the frigate bird. This prehistoric-looking relative of the pelican has the largest wingspan-to-bodyweight ratio of any bird and is almost completely aerial, alighting only to roost or breed. Males display a large red throat pouch during mating season.

Accommodations at the Cuzan guest house are thatched cabanas or breezy open-air *palapas*. Waterproof sunscreen, polarized sunglasses and insect repellent all are essential for a stay at Cuzan. There is no public transportation to Punta Allen; the easiest way to schedule a stay is to make reservations directly through Cuzan or AGI Tours in Cancún, which includes transportation from the Cancún airport or your hotel. If driving a rental car, follow the access road through the Tulum hotel zone that heads south to Punta Allen. The road is paved most of the way, becoming a well-maintained dirt road as it nears Punta Allen.

Rates for trip packages ranging from 3 days to a week include accommodations, fishing excursions with a local guide and meals; ground transportation to and from Punta Allen is not included. Credit cards are not accepted. Phone (983) 834-0358, or (998) 887-6967 or (877) 244-6090 (toll-free from the United States or Canada) for AGI Tours.

HIDDEN WORLDS CENOTES PARK is off Mex. 307 about 10 km (6 mi.) n. of the Tulum Ruins (the signed turn-off is on the right if going southbound); watch for the large billboard just before the park entrance. The park offers guided snorkeling and diving excursions to cenotes (freshwater sinkholes) that are part of an extensive subterranean river system. Snorkelers can explore Hilario's Well, a labyrinthine waterway packed with elaborate stalactite and stalagmite formations; a cavern dive in the Dreamgate Cenote reveals an otherworldly environment of elaborately decorated underwater chambers.

Other activities include a 600-foot zipline, which enables thrill seekers to "fly" above the jungle canopy while wearing a safety harness before being dumped into a cenote. The Skycycle also skims above the trees via a kilometer-long, cable-supported bicycle; at the halfway point riders can stop at a cenote to swim or snorkel before continuing to peddle through above-ground caverns.

Transportation from the park entrance to snorkel and dive sites is provided. Insect repellent is recommended. Food is available. Picnicking is permitted. Allow 2-3 hours minimum depending on the activity. Open daily 9-5. Snorkel tours depart at 9, 11, 1, 2 and 3; cavern diving tours depart at 9, 11 and 1. Last admission is at 3. Snorkel tour $28 (U.S.); ages 8-12, $22. Cavern diving tour $50 (one tank), $100 (two tanks). Guides are included; equipment and tanks are not (rentals are available). MC, VI. Phone (984) 115-4514.

MUYIL is about 22 km (13 mi.) s. of Tulum on the east side of Mex. 307. This archeological site—also known as Chunyaxché (choon-yahsh-CHEH)—is on the banks of Muyil Lagoon (there also is a pueblo called Muyil on the west side of Mex. 307). The main structure is the Castle (El Castillo), a well-restored pyramid about 70 feet tall. Lesser structures in varying degrees of repair surround it. From the site a path leads to the lagoon (technically a bay since it opens to the sea).

Note: This is a tropical scrub jungle environment, and visitors may encounter large horseflies or the occasional poisonous snake. About 300 feet south on Mex. 307 is a turn-off; turn left (east) on this narrow *sacbe* (white road), which also leads down to the bay. On weekends and holidays locals gather at the impressively large two-story building here (constructed entirely from large bamboo sticks) and will take visitors for a cruise on the bay.

Parking and restrooms are on site. There are no other facilities; bring your own water and food. Allow 1 hour minimum. Site open daily 8-5. Admission 29 pesos (about $2.80 U.S.); free (ages 0-11). There is an additional 40-peso fee to access the walkway down to the lagoon. The fee for a 1-hour boat cruise is negotiable and runs $8-$20.

SIAN KA'AN BIOSPHERE RESERVE (Reserva de la Biosfera Sian Ka'an) encompasses the Boca Paila Peninsula and mainland Quintana Roo s. of Tulum and e. of Mex. 307. Designated as a protected area by the Mexican government in 1986, Sian Ka'an (the name means "place where the sky is born") includes a variety of habitats: tropical jungle, drier areas of tree-speckled savanna, coastal mangrove flats and some 70 miles of offshore coral reefs.

This vast region is a haven for flora and fauna. Among the resident animals are deer, jaguars, ocelots, tapirs, peccaries (a form of wild pig), howler monkeys, crocodiles, manatees and sea turtles. Bird life is diverse; the 339 known species range from egrets, herons and roseate spoonbills to toucans, parrots and the frigate bird. About 1,200 different kinds of plants can be found here. There also are some 30 Mayan archeological sites within Sian Ka'an's borders.

Most of the reserve is off limits to tourists, but the beaches and jungles on the Boca Paila Peninsula can be explored by visitors. To get a taste of this wild and beautiful place, take the Boca Paila/Punta Allen road off Mex. 307 (turn left if traveling southbound, right if traveling northbound; the intersection has a traffic signal and is signed "Playas/Punta Allen"). The road runs east for a few miles and then continues south through Tulum's hotel zone. About 15 kilometers (9 miles) from the Mex. 307 junction is the entrance to the reserve, marked by a guardhouse building (Caseta de Control). Day visitors must register at the guardhouse; the registration fee is 21 pesos (about $2 U.S.). From this point there is access to secluded beaches, and kayaks and bikes can be rented.

Centro Ecológico Sian Ka'an (CESIAK), an organization that promotes environmental awareness of this wilderness sanctuary, offers guided tours that include lagoon kayaking around mangrove islands, an all-day canal boat trip through mangrove swamps and savanna grasslands to palm-lined beaches, and a sunset bird-watching excursion. Tours are offered on a seasonal basis. Tour fees range from $45-$70 (U.S.). Phone (984) 871-2499 for information and reservations.

TANKAH is about 3.5 km (2 mi.) n. of the Tulum Ruins and e. of Mex. 307. It was one of the satellite cities of Tulum; the others were Solimán and Xel-Ha. The few ruins that remain are hidden in the underbrush and have not been fully explored.

XCACEL (ISH-ca-sell) is about a quarter mile e. of Mex. 307 between Playa Chemuyil and Xel-Ha, about 19 km (12 mi.) n. of the town of Tulum (watch for the signed turn-off); access to the beach is via a dirt road to a gate with a welcome sign in Spanish. Bypassed by most tourists, this wide, sandy beach is one of the prettiest along the Riviera Maya. There is good snorkeling at the north end, but be mindful of the currents and stay close to shore. Toward the south end of the beach is a path into the jungle; a 5-minute walk leads to a cenote (freshwater sinkhole) where you can swim and snorkel. There is normally a security guard on duty.

Xcacel is a protected refuge and a nesting site for endangered loggerhead and green turtles. From May through October, female turtles laboriously leave the sea at night to build nests on the beach and lay their eggs in the sand. Many turtle nesting sites are being destroyed by the tourism-related development occurring along much of this coast.

Note: Be careful when turning off the highway; there is a fairly steep dropoff onto the access path. Park within sight of the security guard and do not leave valuables in your car. Open daily 6 a.m.-10 p.m., Nov.-Apr.; 9-6, rest of year (during turtle nesting season). Day use fee 20 pesos (about $1.95 U.S.).

XEL-HA is about 16 km (10 mi.) n. of the town of Tulum via a well-marked turn-off on the e. side of Mex. 307 (Km marker 240). The centerpiece of this water park (pronounced shell-HAH) is a beautiful lagoon surrounded by jungle. A natural aquarium, it allows visitors to observe a variety of marine inhabitants in a mix of salt and fresh water; schools of brightly colored tropical fish gather around the underwater rock formations. Snorkeling can be enjoyed without the undertows or strong currents that can make the beaches dangerous, and the clarity of the water is excellent. Snuba gear enables snorkelers to stay under water longer by breathing air through tubes that run to air tanks floating on the surface. Platforms built over the lagoon offer easy underwater viewing for landlubbers.

Another favorite activity at Xel-Ha is river floating. Visitors are taken to a drop-off point by a shuttle train and then float slowly along with the current toward the sea. Mo's Flight, a rope swing, and the Cliff of Courage both offer an exhilarating plunge into the lagoon waters. Xel-Ha also has an interactive dolphin swim program. Other activities include visiting a nursery/apiary where honey is harvested from stingless bees, hiking the Path of Conscience bordering the lagoon, crossing the lagoon via a floating bridge, exploring freshwater sinkholes or relaxing in the shade on appropriately named Hammock Island.

Xel-ha is a popular day trip from Cancún and is often combined with a stop at the Tulum ruins; contact a local travel agency for information. Dress casually and bring comfortable shoes. Life jackets are provided, and there is a first-aid station on site. An ATM accepts international credit cards.

Food is available (all food services close at 5 p.m.). Park open daily 8:30-7, in summer; 8:30-6, rest of year. To fully enjoy Xel-ha get there early; when the tour buses arrive it can become very crowded. Admission (includes entry fee, use of showers, changing rooms and hammocks, life jacket, river float, river shuttle and a bag for transporting personal belongings, plus food and beverages) 806 pesos (about $78 U.S.); 530 pesos/$51 U.S. (children 36-54 inches tall). Package tours from Cancún and Playa del Carmen (includes all-inclusive admission and round-trip transportation) are available. Snorkeling gear and locker rentals are available; photo identification and a $20 (U.S.) deposit (refundable on return of gear) are required. There are separate fees for Snuba snorkeling and other underwater activities as well as for the dolphin swim (make reservations in advance). AX, MC, VI. Phone (998) 884-7165 Mon.-Fri. 8-2 and 4-7, Sat. 9-noon for customer service information. *See color ad on insert.*

GEM UXMAL, YUCATAN (B-2)

If Chichén Itzá is considered the Yucatán Peninsula's most impressive archeological site, Uxmal (oosh-MAHL) is the most beautiful. Unlike the structures at Chichén Itzá, with their Toltec-influenced images of violent conquest, Uxmal's architecture is more purely Mayan, with richly ornamented stone facades and a majestic pyramid. The ruins were designated a World Heritage Site by UNESCO in 1996; don't miss them.

Uxmal rose to prominence concurrently with the great civilizations at Palenque *(see separate listing under Southern Mexico)* and Tikal in Guatemala, flourishing between A.D. 600 and 1000. Little is known about its history. The name means "thrice built" in Maya, although it was actually reconstructed five times, suggesting that drought forced abandonment followed by resettlement. The subsequent importance of Chichén Itzá and the increased intermingling of Mayan cultures with those from the central Mexican highlands were likely contributors to the city's decline, which appeared to be complete by the 14th century.

The first excavations were begun in 1929 by Danish archeologist and explorer Frans Blom, who also conducted research at other Mayan archeological sites. The Mexican government has since worked with a number of archeologists to reconstruct the site, and the main buildings have all been restored.

Uxmal is the defining example of the Puuc architectural style (the name refers to the region's hilly terrain), which emphasized elegant, horizontal proportions and intricately detailed building exteriors of cut stones assembled in geometric patterns. Cornices and entryways often feature beak-nosed representations of the rain god Chac. The detail of the stonework is even more amazing when one considers that the Maya created their buildings without benefit of metal tools.

This part of the peninsula has a hot climate with seasonal precipitation and is subject to prolonged dry spells. Unlike other Mayan cities, Uxmal did not have ready availability to a source of water. Instead, they depended upon the *chultun* (a man-made cistern) to collect precious rain.

Visitors enter the site via a short path that begins at the visitor center. The first building is immediately evident: The Pyramid of the Magician *(see attraction listing)*. This structure probably functioned as a ceremonial building where Uxmal's rulers were crowned.

The Nunnery *(see attraction listing)*, named by the Spaniards, was probably used by Uxmal's elite ruling class. Just south of the Nunnery is a ball court, smaller and simpler than the one at Chichén Itzá. South of the ball court is the small, classically designed House of the Turtles (Casa de las Tortugas), named for the border of turtles carved along its upper molding. Stand on the south side of this temple and look through the central doorway (of three) for a nicely framed view of the Nunnery.

The Governor's Palace *(see attraction listing)* was most likely Uxmal's administrative center and may also have served an astrological purpose; it faces east while the other buildings face west, perhaps to better sight the planet Venus, which the Maya associated with war. From this elevated vantage point there is an expansive view of the Nunnery and the Pyramid of the Magician.

The Great Pyramid, partially restored, is just southwest of the Governor's Palace. Originally terraced with nine levels, it is topped by a palace decorated with Chac masks and bird carvings that probably represent parrots. The climb to the palace level is steep but doable (be particularly careful descending if you're prone to vertigo), with sweeping views of the surrounding jungle scrub.

Just west of the Great Pyramid are the remains of a building called the Dovecote because its lattice design somewhat resembles a bird nesting house. The view of this ruin is particularly fine from the summit of the Great Pyramid.

Other buildings at the site are only partially reconstructed, or unexcavated mounds hidden in the brush. The House of the Old Woman (Casa de la Vieja), an old, ruined pyramidal structure southeast of the Great Pyramid, is reached by an overgrown path. Further southeast is the Temple of the Phalli, another ruined structure with phallic-shaped sculptures along the cornices, presumably to divert and collect rainwater from the roof.

General Information and Activities

Mérida is the most convenient base from which to explore the Puuc region. Cancún-based Mayaland Tours offers two packages: a day tour of Uxmal and the nearby Kabah archeological site that departs at 9 a.m., and an afternoon tour of Uxmal that departs at 1:30 p.m. and includes the evening sound-and-light show. Both tours include round-trip transportation, guide service and lunch or dinner. For reservation information phone (998) 887-2450 (in Mexico) or (800) 235-4079 (from the United States). Tour groups usually have access to a swimming pool; bring a suit and towel, as they aren't provided.

Uxmal is about 80 kilometers (50 miles) south of Mérida via Mex. 261. If driving, take Avenida Itzaes (Mex. 180) south from downtown Mérida past the airport to the Anillo Periférico (loop road) and the junction with Mex. 261.

Note: Highway construction now gives motorists the option of bypassing the quaint villages of Umán, Yaxcopoil and Muna en route to Uxmal. This cuts some time off the trip, which takes about an hour from Mérida. If you want to experience rural Yucatán take the old road, which runs through largely undeveloped scrub country. Muna is a typical Yucatecan small town of thatch-roofed stone dwellings that has a large Franciscan church.

For those who want to spend the night near the ruins, there are AAA Approved lodgings along Mex. 261 near the site entrance. More budget-minded travelers might consider an overnight stay in the nearby town of Ticul, about a 15-minute drive from Uxmal, which offers very basic services.

Guide fees are posted on a board next to the ticket window. Although you don't need a guide to appreciate the architecture, and the information may be embellished with fanciful details, a guide's general knowledge will be helpful to those unfamiliar with Mayan history. The main buildings have informational plaques in English, Spanish and Maya. Plan on spending half a day at the ruins if not part of an organized tour group, or devote a full day to see Uxmal and the other sites along the "Puuc Trail" *(see below)*.

A 45-minute sound-and-light show is presented nightly from a vantage point overlooking the Nunnery quadrangle. Colored lights, recorded symphonic music under the stars and melodramatic narration provide an appropriate backdrop for Mayan legends. Although the "history" can be taken with a grain of salt, the artificial lighting illuminates architectural details that are missed under sharp sunlight. The narration is in Spanish, but headsets offering the show in several languages (including English) can be rented.

Most of the site is unshaded; bring a hat or other headgear for protection from the strong sun. An early start will allow you to beat not only the heat but the tour bus crowds that begin arriving before noon. Comfortable, nonslip walking shoes are a must if you plan to do any climbing. It's also a good idea to bring bottled water and insect repellent (particularly if you're attending the sound-and-light show).

The visitor center at the entrance has very clean restrooms, a bookstore, first-aid station, gift shop, coffee shop, casual restaurant and convenience store (where film and disposable cameras can be purchased). A few souvenir and T-shirt stands set up next to the visitor center parking lot. Uxmal is open daily 8-5. The sound-and-light show begins at 7 or 8 p.m., depending on the season. Admission (includes sound-and-light show) about $9 (U.S.). Parking fee about $1. Video camera fee 50 pesos (about $4.85 U.S.).

Points of Interest

GOVERNOR'S PALACE is s. of the Nunnery and just s.e. of the House of the Turtles. This building is widely considered to be among the finest Mayan architectural achievements. The low, narrow structure, more than 300 feet long, is built on three levels. Its upper facade is covered with intricately carved stone figures and geometric designs. Serpents, masks and mosaic patterns all blend into a beautifully harmonious whole. Stand back from the palace's eastern side to discern the 103 stone carvings of Chac that together form the image of an undulating serpent (dramatically illuminated during Uxmal's sound-and-light show).

NUNNERY (Casa de las Monjas) faces the western stairway of the Pyramid of the Magician. More than 70 rooms are in the long, low buildings that surround a large quadrangle. Stand in the center of the courtyard to appreciate the overall harmony that prevails, even though the buildings are terraced and on different levels. The exteriors of each wing have beautiful decorative details, including stone masks of Chac (recognized by their elongated noses), entwined serpents, mosaic patterns and latticework designs. The southern wing has an arched entryway, once the complex's main entrance.

PYRAMID OF THE MAGICIAN is near the site entrance. Also called The Sorcerer (El Adivino), this impressive structure is both taller (some 125 feet) and steeper than El Castillo, the pyramid at Chichén Itzá. It actually contains five superimposed layers that correspond to Uxmal's five separate periods of construction. The walls are rounded rather than sharply angular, an unusual feature. Stairways ascend the eastern and western sides. The western stairway is very steep (a 60-degree angle); the eastern stairway is not quite as steep. **Note:** Visitors are not permitted to climb this pyramid.

Nearby Puuc Ruins

For true aficionados of Mayan history and culture, a full day can be spent exploring the ruins along the Puuc Trail south and east of Uxmal, all within easy driving distance. Some tour buses visit these small archeological sites, but driving allows you to see them at your own pace. Roadside services are minimal, so make sure your gas tank is full and bring food, water, insect repellent and comfortable, nonslip walking shoes. The following sites are listed in order of location from Uxmal.

KABAH is about 19 km (12 mi.) s. on Mex. 261; park in the small dirt lot on the e. (left) side of the road. Although small—there are only two main buildings—it is well worth visiting to see the lavishly decorated Palace of the Masks, or Codz-Pop (in Maya, "rolled mat"). Its entire west exterior is emblazoned with elaborately carved stone masks of the rain god Chac. The busy architectural style reflects the ornate Chenes influence, which is not often seen in this region.

As amazing as the front is, make sure you walk around to the back (east) side. There are no Chac masks here, but jutting off the upper facade are the sculptures of two warriors who seem to be guarding the palace. Below them on one of the side panels (at ground level) are bas-reliefs depicting one warrior subjugating another in classic Mayan fashion.

The other major building on this side of the road is the well-restored Palace (El Palacio), built on two levels, which features a Puuc-style colonnaded facade. Across Mex. 261 is the Great Temple, a large conical mound rising above the thick scrub. It is only partially restored. Beyond the Great Temple is a freestanding arch marking the spot where a Mayan *sacbe* (limestone causeway) road once entered Kabah from Uxmal; compare it to the one at Labná *(see below)*.

Daily 8-5. Admission 35 pesos (about $3.40 U.S.). The fee to use a video camera is 50 pesos.

SAYIL is about 5 km (3 mi.) from Kabah; take Mex. 261 to the junction with Mex. 184 (the road to Oxkutzcab), then e. about 4 km (2.5 mi.) to the ruins. The aptly named site, which means "place of ants," contains several hundred known structures, almost all on the south side of the road. There is one standout: the Palace (El Palacio), a grand three-level building more than 200 feet long. The second level features rows of Grecian-style columns as well as a profusion of stone carvings. Most are of the rain god Chac, but there are additional depictions of an upside-down "diving god."

Most of the other buildings are in ruins or obscured by jungle. South of the Palace is El Mirador, a small temple, and beyond it a primitive stele (carved stone). Also at this site are a number of man-made cisterns that were built to catch seasonal rainfall. Daily 8-5. Admission 35 pesos (about $3.40 U.S.). The fee to use a video camera is 50 pesos.

XLAPAK is about 6 km (3.5 mi.) e. of Sayil. Xlapak (shla-PAHK) means "old walls" in Maya. The notable structure at this small site on the south side of the road is the partially restored Palace of Xlapak, which is decorated with Chac masks, some flaunting curled noses. The restored portions are lighter in tone than the weathered, unrestored sections. Daily 8-5. Admission 35 pesos (about $3.40 U.S.). The fee to use a video camera is 50 pesos.

LABNA is about 3 km (2 mi.) e. of Xlapak. Here the best-known ruin is a restored, freestanding stone arch larger and more ornately decorated than the one at Kabah. It features ornate decoration on the west side and a more geometric pattern on the east side. Pass through the arch to El Mirador, a pyramidal structure resting on a pile of rubble. Labná, like Sayil, contains the remains of many *chultunes* (cisterns) that collected rainwater.

Labná's impressive Palace building is similar to the one at Sayil, although not in as good condition. See it for the ornamentation, which is—as on so many Mayan buildings—bizarrely imaginative. Daily 8-5. Admission 35 pesos (about $3.40 U.S.). The fee to use a video camera is 50 pesos.

LOLTUN CAVES (Grutas de Loltún) are about 6 km (10 mi.) s.w. of Oxkutzcab via the Sayil-Labná road. The entrance to the caves is reached from a gravel path that branches off the n. side of the road; the turn-off is not signed. Hieroglyphic inscriptions and carvings of flowers on the cave walls are estimated to be some 1,000 years old; the name, loosely translated, means "one flower in the stone." Throughout the caves are *chultunes* (cisterns), stone troughs which were placed to collect water dripping from the roof. Natural formations include giant stalactites and stalagmites that emit an echoing hum when struck.

The caverns can be seen by guided tour only. Tours are given daily at 9:30, 11, 12:30, 2, 3 and 4; double-check this schedule at the Uxmal visitor center. Some passages are dark and the paths may be slippery or steep; wear comfortable, nonslip walking shoes. Most tours are given in Spanish; ask at the front ticket office regarding the availability of an English-speaking guide. Daily 8-5. Admission 35 pesos (about $3.40 U.S.).

VALLADOLID, YUCATAN (B-3)

pop. 38,000

Valladolid (vah-yah-doh-LEED) was founded in 1543 by Francisco de Montejo, who established Spanish rule over much of the Yucatán Peninsula. The Spaniards constructed their churches over the site of a former Mayan town, Zací. Many revolts occurred in this region during the mid-19th-century War of the Castes, when rebellious and oppressed descendants of the Maya clashed with privileged landowners. Here too was one of the first uprisings against dictator Porfirio Díaz, which foreshadowed the Mexican Revolution of 1910.

The commercial center for an agricultural district, Valladolid is on Mex. 180 and is one of the three exits off toll highway Mex. 180-D. A colonial atmosphere, now somewhat gone to seed, pervades this unpretentious market town. Old buildings still bear weathered Spanish coats of arms above their doorways. The main plaza is bounded by calles 39, 40, 41 and 42; here visitors can browse among shops selling leather goods or sit on one of the curved stone benches and observe the local scene.

Several kilometers north of Valladolid on Mex. 295, on the way to the Ek Balam ruins *(see attraction listing)* is the little village of Temozón. It's worth stopping here to take a look at the beautifully weathered church that dates from the early 18th century. There's a small plaza in front of the church that makes for a good photo opportunity.

The ruins themselves are the most noteworthy attraction in the Valladolid vicinity. Ongoing restoration work at this archeological site deep in the jungle began in 1997. Still primitive, Ek Balam receives relatively few visitors and thus retains more of a sense of mystery than other Yucatán ruins.

Dining options in the immediate vicinity are few—with one rather surprising exception. The Dolce Mente, a New Age hotel/retreat that opened in late 2007, has an Italian restaurant with very good food and friendly service. It's in the pueblo of Ek Balam; to get there from the ruins, watch for the signed turn-off to the pueblo branching off the Ek Balam entrance road (the road that connects the ruins to Mex. 295). From the turn-off it's about a 5-minute drive to the pueblo; then follow the signs to Dolce Mente.

CENOTE DZITNUP is about 4 km (2.5 mi.) s.w. of town on the south side of Mex. 180 (there is a signed turn-off). This is a better alternative than Cenote Zací if you want to try swimming. The natural pool of clear, blue water is inside a cavern where artificial lighting illuminates the stalactites hanging from the roof. The short flight of stone steps leading down into the cavern can be slippery. Daily 7-6. Admission about $3 (U.S.).

CENOTE ZACI is on Calle 36 2 blks. e. of the main plaza, between calles 37 and 39. This huge underground sinkhole is reached by worn stone stairs that descend into a dark cavern, the upper reaches of which are populated by bats. The murky water is flecked with green scum that the locals call "lake lettuce." Zací (sah-KEE) is spookily atmospheric but unsuitable for swimming. It is located in a park that has a restaurant as well as examples of traditional thatch-roofed Mayan houses. Daily 8-5. Admission about $3 (U.S.).

CHURCH AND CONVENT OF SAN BERNARDINO DE SIENA is about 6 blks. s.w. of the main plaza. The fortifications of this massive complex, founded in 1552 by the Franciscan Order, were built to ward off the warring Mayas, who sacked it repeatedly. Looting during the War of the Castes has robbed the church of much of its interior ornamentation; there is, however, a likeness of the Virgin of Guadalupe on the altar.

EK BALAM is about 15 km (9 mi.) n. of the Mex. 180-D Valladolid exit via Mex. 295, following signs. To get there from Valladolid, take Calle 40 out of town to Mex. 295 and proceed n. about 18 km (11 mi.) to the Ek Balam turn-off (watch for the sign marking the turn-off). Archeologists believe the site achieved its greatest prominence between A.D. 400 and 600; the name Ek Balam means "black jaguar."

Stony, muddy walkways connect ruins unusual in the fact that the buildings have round corners where there are normally sharp right angles. Structure 1 (known as the Acropolis) dominates the main plaza. About 100 feet tall, it has very narrow, steep stairs that can be climbed for fantastic views of the surrounding area. Thatched roofs protect statues and carvings on the different levels. About two-thirds of the way up is the recently uncovered tomb of Ukit Kan Lek Tok, one of Ek Balam's rulers. Decorative features include a wall covered with intricate carvings and, most interestingly, statues of winged warriors reminiscent of angels.

Smaller edifices surround the base of the main pyramid. Large thatched roofs protecting new excavation sites provide welcome shade. At the entrance is a restored Puuc-style gateway arch that once was connected to an ancient Mayan road, or *sacbe*.

There are restrooms in the ticket building. Wear comfortable walking shoes and bring drinking water. Allow 2 hours minimum. Daily 8-4:30. Admission 29 pesos (about $2.80 U.S.); free (ages 0-12). The fee to use a video camera is 35 pesos.

RIO LAGARTOS NATIONAL PARK is about 100 km (62 mi.) almost due n. of Valladolid at the end of Mex. 295. **Note:** The *topes* (speed bumps) along Mex. 295 can significantly damage the underside of a vehicle if negotiated at too fast a speed. Mexico's largest flamingo sanctuary comprises some 120,000 acres of protected mangrove swamps, sand dunes, mud flats and shallow estuaries along the Yucatán Peninsula's northern coast. In addition to flamingos, the park is home to herons, egrets, cormorants, ducks, pelicans and many other bird species.

Boat tours can be arranged with local guides at the dock area in the fishing village of Río Lagartos. Bring a hat or other protection from the sun, your own water and a snack. The winter months are a better—and cooler—time to observe young flamingos and other bird species. Don't allow the boatman to scare flamingos into flight for a photo opportunity, as this will eventually drive them from their habitat. Rates vary according to boat, destination and tour size, but an excursion for five people should be about $45 (U.S.).

Puerto Paraiso Entertainment Plaza, Cabo San Lucas / © Kim Karpeles / age fotostock

Baja California

In 1535, a shipwreck survivor regaled Hernando Cortés with reports of an island populated by Amazonian women and brimming with gold and pearls. The *conquistador,* believing it to be the fabled land of California, set sail for the elongated peninsula known as Baja (Lower) California with three galleons and 600 prospective settlers. He landed near the present site of La Paz, toward the peninsula's southern end. Finding neither pearls, gold nor Amazons—but encountering impoverished land and fierce Indians—Cortés abandoned the area. The Spanish, busy plundering other parts of Mexico, all but forgot Baja.

It was not until 1697 that a permanent settlement was established, a Jesuit mission and presidio at Loreto. Throughout the 18th century, the Indians in this barren land were ministered to by the Jesuits, who founded the first missions and also taught the Indians how to farm.

When the Jesuits were banished from Mexico in the 1760s, the Franciscans and the Dominicans followed. But along with churches, the missionaries brought disease. Smallpox had almost wiped out the indigenous population by the middle of the 19th century. Meanwhile, primitive settlements accessible only by boat or on foot slowly developed.

Except for quintessential border town Tijuana and seaside Ensenada, Baja for the most part remained a lonely outpost for hardy fishermen through the first half of the 20th century. Much of the peninsula remains isolated, although the opening in 1974 of Mex. 1, the Transpeninsular Highway, opened the more far-flung parts to visitors and ushered in economic development.

Nearly 800 miles in length and varying from about 30 to 110 miles in width, the Baja

Peninsula extends south from the U.S. border like a giant appendage paralleling the northwestern Mexican mainland. It broke off millions of years ago, in the process creating the Gulf of California (also known as the Sea of Cortez).

Baja's backbone is made up of two westward-sloping mountain ranges. Sierra de San Pedro Mártir dominates the north; Sierra de la Giganta, the south. In the former, Picacho del Diablo attains an elevation of 10,073 feet, the highest point on the peninsula.

Both the gulf and Pacific coastlines are indented by an endless string of bays and coves, with many islands scattered offshore. Both bodies of water are home to an amazing variety of fish, making the peninsula a sportfishing paradise.

The state of Baja California, comprising all territory north of the 28th parallel, consists mostly of rugged mountains or harsh desert, although irrigation of the hot, arid valleys around the border city of Mexicali has turned them into a productive agricultural region. Easily accessible Tijuana—big, bustling, equal parts flashy tourist trap and working-class city—draws hordes of stay-for-a-day visitors, the partying college crowd and dedicated souvenir shoppers. The port of Ensenada is a popular weekend destination offering beaches, dining and nightlife. Between the two is Rosarito Beach, a casual, rapidly growing resort area.

The state of Baja California Sur, occupying the southern portion of the peninsula, is even more barren. Occasional oases such as the village of San Ignacio, a mirage of date palms and pastel-colored buildings, pop up in the middle of the desert. Toward the peninsula's end is La Paz, the capital, a laid-back, quintessentially Mexican city.

At Baja's dramatically beautiful southern tip is its most popular vacation spot, and one of Mexico's most popular destinations. Los Cabos (the Capes) refers to the twin resort towns of Cabo San Lucas and San José del Cabo, where outstanding sport fishing and an unbeatable lineup of championship golf courses are complemented by pricey all-inclusive resorts.

Vagabundos Del Mar Travel and Boat Club provides assistance to RV travelers in Baja. Services include roadside aid, RV park information, insurance needs, and medical air services and evacuation. For information phone (800) 474-2252 (from the United States).

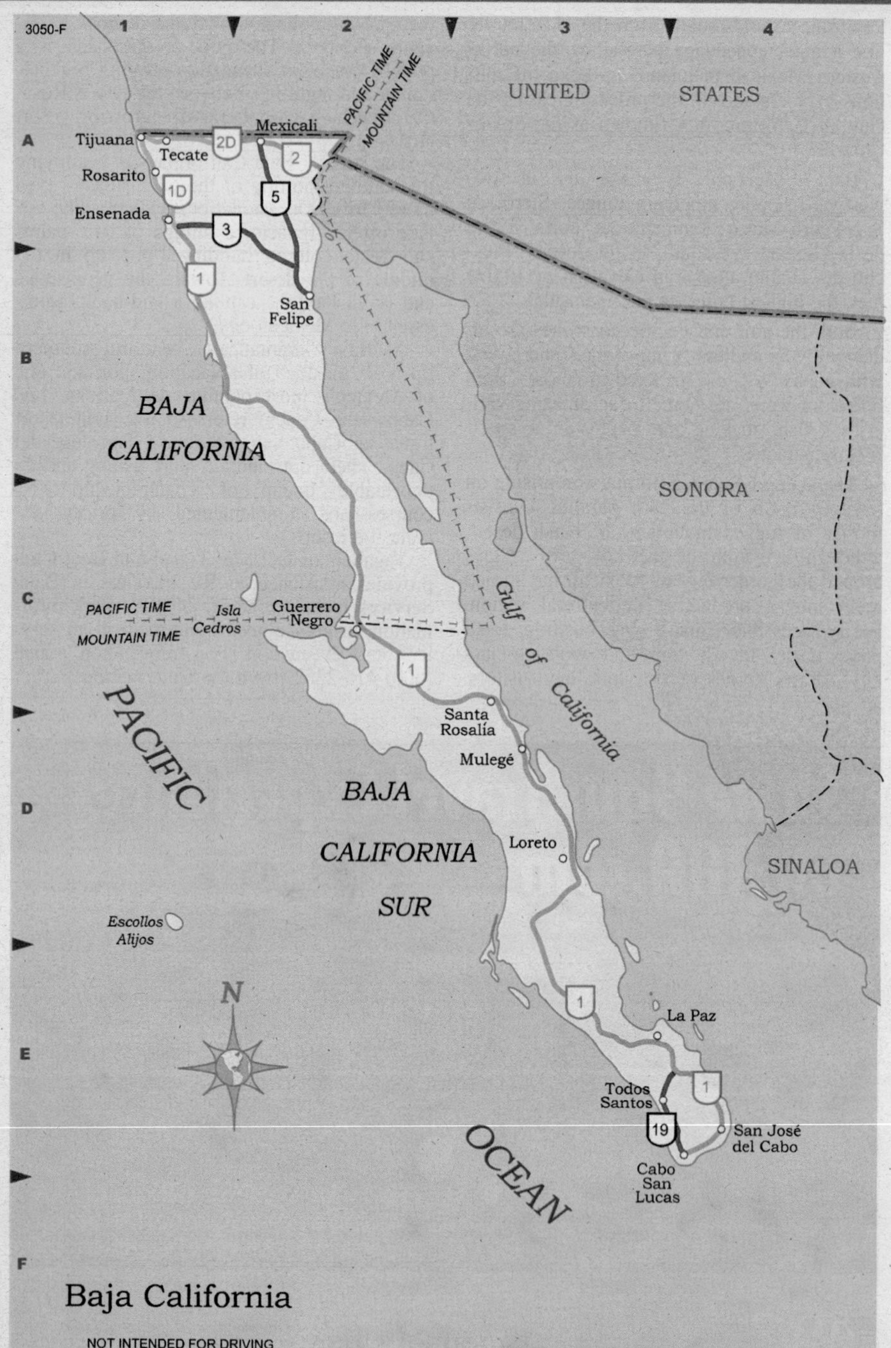

3050-F
1
2
3
4
A
B
C
D
E
F
UNITED STATES
PACIFIC TIME
MOUNTAIN TIME
Mexicali
Tijuana
Tecate
Rosarito
Ensenada
2D
2
1D
5
3
1
San Felipe
BAJA CALIFORNIA
SONORA
Gulf of California
PACIFIC TIME
MOUNTAIN TIME
Isla Cedros
Guerrero Negro
Santa Rosalía
Mulegé
PACIFIC
BAJA CALIFORNIA SUR
Loreto
SINALOA
Escollos Alijos
N
La Paz
Todos Santos
19
San José del Cabo
Cabo San Lucas
OCEAN
Baja California
NOT INTENDED FOR DRIVING
SEE APPROPRIATE SHEET MAP
0 Miles 133
0 Kilometers 213
ONLY PLACES LISTED WITH DESCRIPTIVE WRITE-UPS APPEAR ON THIS MAP.
© AAA

Points of Interest

CABO SAN LUCAS, BAJA CALIFORNIA SUR (E-3) pop. 40,300

See map page158.

Cabo San Lucas (KAH-boh sahn LOO-kahs) perches at the southern tip of Baja California, where the waters of the Gulf of California (Sea of Cortez) and the Pacific Ocean converge. Although offering some of Mexico's nicest luxury resorts and a full slate of outdoor-oriented recreational activities, it is still very much a laid-back place where local fishermen go about their daily business. The stark, stunning scenery—rocks, water and big blue sky—is, of course, the stuff of tourist brochure dreams. And Cabo has a well-deserved reputation for attracting those who like to party, if only for a getaway weekend.

Not so very long ago Cabo San Lucas was the quintessential dusty village. Due in large part to its remoteness, it wasn't until after World War II that well-heeled Southern Californians and rich American sportsmen took notice of the world-class deep-sea fishing in both the ocean and the gulf. There were no roads yet: Visitors arrived via pleasure yacht or private aircraft.

Early hotels like the La Palmilla, which opened in 1956 (now the One & Only Palmilla), the Solmar (now the Solmar Suites Resort) and the Hotel Cabo San Lucas catered to such Hollywood notables as Bing Crosby and John Wayne. Cabo remained a well-kept secret until 1974, when the Mex. 1 transpeninsular highway made automobile travel viable. But it was the expansion of the airport in 1986 that was the springboard to explosive growth. Condominiums and luxury hotels sprouted from the barren land, international sport-fishing tournaments proliferated and golf became very big business.

Cabo San Lucas and neighboring San José del Cabo *(see separate listing within this region)*—plus the 20-mile stretch of highway between them—are collectively known as Los Cabos. This is one of Mexico's leading resort areas, rivaling such hotspots as Cancún and Puerto Vallarta, and its popularity shows no sign of slowing down.

Each Cabo has a distinctly different personality. Cabo San Lucas draws golfers and sport-fishing fans as well as Generations X and Y, who come for the surfing, beaches and rowdy nightlife. San José del Cabo is a much more traditional Mexican small town, complete with a central plaza and cathedral. It's quieter and more family-oriented than Cabo San Lucas, but also offers a growing number of sophisticated shops, galleries and restaurants.

Between the two Cabos runs divided four-lane Mex. 1. "The Corridor" has developed into its own destination. The wild, rocky landscapes along the highway once hid only secluded fishing lodges and a few hotels. Now the views of rugged cliffs and the glimpses of steely blue gulf water and white-sand beaches are punctuated by a string of lushly groomed and lavishly appointed resorts. The Corridor also is where you'll find Cabo's championship golf courses. The resort communities of Cabo Real and Cabo del Sol are centers of tourist-oriented development.

Due to geographic isolation from the Mexican mainland and a tourism infrastructure with close ties to California and other Western states, there is a more pronounced "north of the border" sensibility here than at other Mexican resorts. American cars, products and dollars are all highly visible. But Los Cabos also has a by-the-seaside feel that is distinctly Mexican, aided immeasurably by the unspoiled grandeur of its desert setting.

It's a setting that comes at a price, however. If you're in search of a bargain Mexican vacation, you won't find it in Los Cabos. Hotels, restaurants, taxis, shops and tour operators charge some of the steepest prices in Mexico, if not *the* highest in the entire country. Locals jokingly refer to Cabo San Lucas as "*Caro* San Lucas" (*caro* means "expensive"). That said, prices for goods and services do drop the farther you stray from the main tourist areas.

Practicalities

San José del Cabo International Airport is about 13 kilometers (8 miles) north of San José del Cabo and 48 kilometers (30 miles) northeast of Cabo San Lucas. Alaska, American and Mexicana airlines offer direct flights from Los Angeles; Aeroméxico flies direct from San Diego. Alaska Airlines has flights from several California cities as well as Phoenix, Portland and Seattle. America West flies from Phoenix. American, Continental and Delta offer service from U.S. East Coast cities, with most connecting flights via Atlanta, Dallas or Houston. For additional information about airlines *see Arriving by Air, page 61.*

Note: Avoid the time share sellers who bombard arriving visitors, unless you're really interested in spending 4 hours enduring an aggressive sales pitch for a new condominium development. The lure of free lunches and drinks or so-called discounted activities is definitely not worth it.

Private taxis from the airport to your hotel are very expensive; a ride to San José del Cabo can cost up to $60 (U.S.), while fares to Cabo San Lucas reach into the $90 stratosphere and beyond. Returning to the airport via private taxi is slightly cheaper. Rates from San José are in the $30 to $35 (U.S.) range; from Cabo San Lucas prepare to shell out $50 to $60.

Los Cabos Express provides air-conditioned shuttle van and bus transportation from the airport

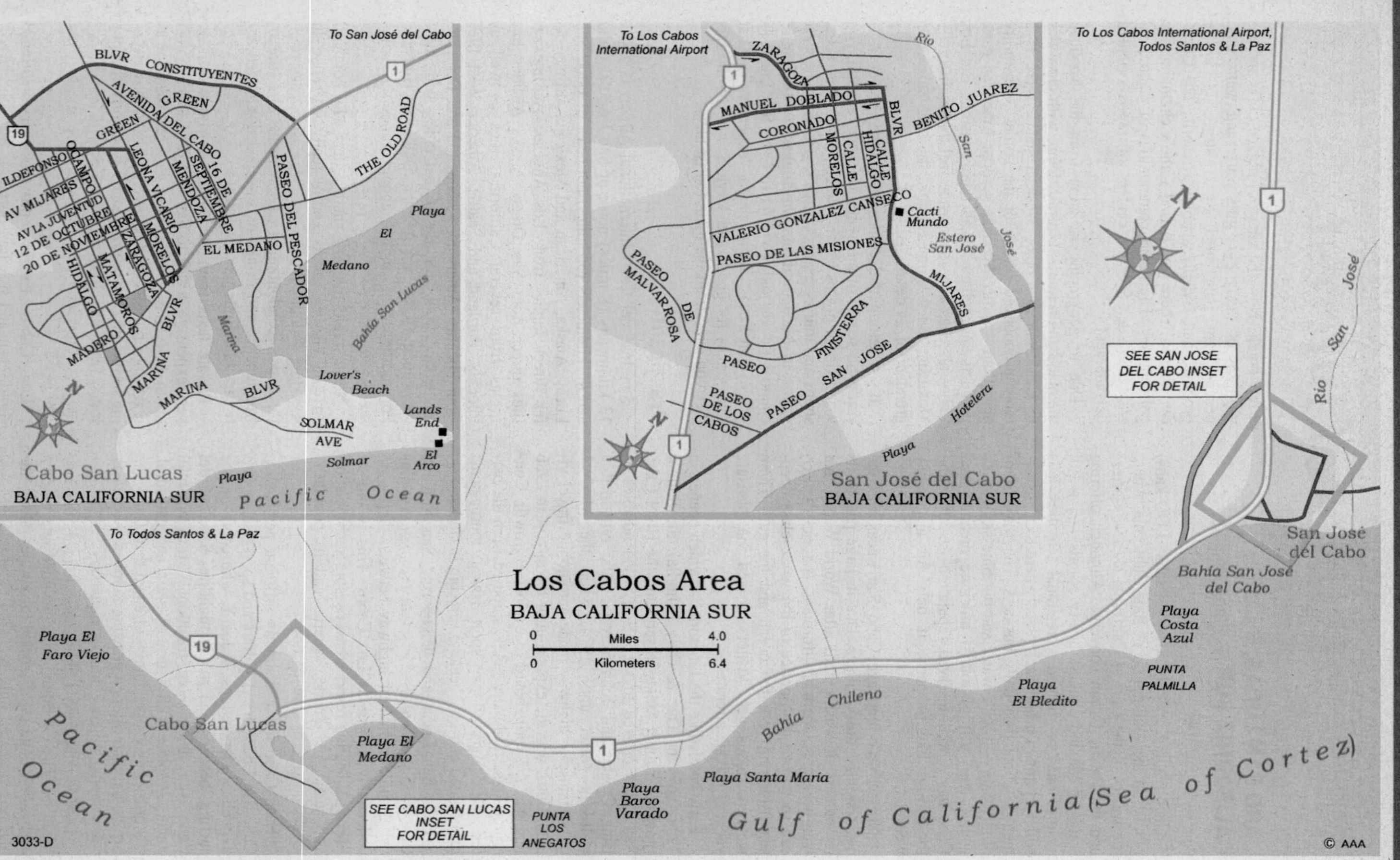

Cabo San Lucas
BAJA CALIFORNIA SUR
To San José del Cabo
BLVR CONSTITUYENTES
AVENIDA DEL CABO
GREEN
GREEN
THE OLD ROAD
PASEO DEL PESCADOR
16 DE SEPTIEMBRE
MENDOZA
LEONA VICARIO
MORELOS
ZARAGOZA
MATAMOROS
HIDALGO
MADERO
OCAMPO
ILDEFONSO
AV MIJARES
AV LA JUVENTUD
12 DE OCTUBRE
20 DE NOVIEMBRE
EL MEDANO
BLVR MARINA
MARINA BLVR
Marina
Playa El Medano
Bahía San Lucas
Lover's Beach
Lands End
El Arco
SOLMAR AVE
Solmar
Playa
Pacific Ocean
San José del Cabo
BAJA CALIFORNIA SUR
To Los Cabos International Airport
ZARAGOZA
MANUEL DOBLADO
CORONADO
MORELOS
CALLE HIDALGO
CALLE
BLVR BENITO JUAREZ
VALERIO GONZALEZ CANSECO
PASEO DE LAS MISIONES
Cacti Mundo
Estero San José
Río San José
MIJARES
FINISTERRA
PASEO SAN JOSE
PASEO
PASEO DE MALVARROSA
PASEO DE LOS CABOS
Playa Hotelera
To Los Cabos International Airport, Todos Santos & La Paz
SEE SAN JOSE DEL CABO INSET FOR DETAIL
Río San José
San José del Cabo
Bahía San José del Cabo
Los Cabos Area
BAJA CALIFORNIA SUR
Miles
Kilometers
4.0
6.4
To Todos Santos & La Paz
Playa El Faro Viejo
Cabo San Lucas
Playa El Medano
Pacific Ocean
SEE CABO SAN LUCAS INSET FOR DETAIL
PUNTA LOS ANEGATOS
Playa Barco Varado
Playa Santa Maria
Bahía Chileno
Playa El Bledito
Playa Costa Azul
PUNTA PALMILLA
Gulf of California (Sea of Cortez)
3033-D
© AAA

to hotels based on a zone system. One-way rates average $12-$15 per person; for information phone (624) 115-4972. If you arrive at the airport without a reservation, look for the green-and-white Los Cabos Express bus, which is usually parked outside the terminal; buy your ticket from the driver. Another less expensive option than a cab is an airport transfer, which some hotels offer for a fee; inquire about this service when you make your reservations.

Because the Los Cabos area is spread out and expensive, taxi fares will quickly add up. Renting a car is a viable option if you're staying more than a few days or want to explore the surrounding area. If you only want a car for a day or two, consider renting one in town at the end of your trip and dropping it at the airport on your departure day. The car rental company's one-way drop-off fee will usually be cheaper than a taxi ride back to the airport.

If you've rented a car at the airport and want to bypass the stoplights and frequently heavy traffic on Mex. 1, take the Los Cabos Airport-San José del Cabo toll road. This modern, four-lane highway departs the airport (watch for signs) and travels about 20 kilometers (12 miles) to San José, where it terminates at Mex. 1, just west of the waterfront hotel zone. The toll booth is at the southern end of the road; the toll is about 30 pesos ($2.90 U.S.). To reach Cabo San Lucas, just continue southwest on Mex. 1. **Note:** There are no gas stations along the toll road.

Note: AAA/CAA members enjoy discounts through Hertz for vehicles booked in the United States. Consult your local AAA/CAA club or phone Hertz, (800) 654-3080. There's a Hertz office in Cabo San Lucas at Blvd. Lázaro Cárdenas #6, the city's main thoroughfare. For additional information about renting a car *see Car Rentals, page 62.*

It's a long drive to Los Cabos from the border at Tijuana—some 1,050 miles via Mex. 1 (also called the Carretera Transpeninsular). From La Paz, the quicker and less winding route to Cabo San Lucas is Mex. 1 south to the junction with Mex. 19, then Mex. 19 south through Todos Santos to Cabo San Lucas.

Except for the four-lane Corridor and four-lane Mex. 1-D from Tijuana to Ensenada, Mex. 1 is a two-lane road that runs through frequent desolate stretches. Gas stations and traveler facilities can be few and far between. A temporary vehicle importation permit is not required anywhere on the peninsula, unless the vehicle is put on a ferry bound for the mainland.

Mex. 1 is narrow compared to highways in the United States and Canada, and road shoulders are nonexistent along many stretches. The quality of the road is generally good, but there are potholes in the vicinity of Cataviña in the state of Baja California. Avoid driving at an excessive speed (above 50 mph), and above all **do not drive at night.** This and other roads are not lit at night, and cows congregating on the road surface pose an ever-present danger.

Note: While it seldom rains much of the year in southern Baja, streams (called *arroyos*) are subject to flash floods during infrequent storms. Flooding, although rare, can make vehicle travel impossible when it occurs. Elevated bridges have solved this problem along the Corridor (the stretch of Mex. 1 between San José del Cabo and Cabo San Lucas).

Baja's main overland bus line, Autotransportes de Baja California (ABC), travels from Tijuana to La Paz several times a day; the trip (including stops en route) takes about 22 hours. From La Paz, the Aguila bus line provides frequent service to both San José del Cabo and Cabo San Lucas for about $11-$15 (U.S.); this trip takes another 2 to 3 hours. A valid tourist permit is required. Greyhound buses take passengers from the Greyhound terminal at 120 W. Broadway in downtown San Diego to Tijuana's Central Bus Terminal (Centro de Autobuses) in La Mesa; for fare and schedule information phone (800) 231-2222 (from the United States). For additional information about buses *see Bus Service, page 72.*

Taxis from Cabo San Lucas to San José del Cabo or the Corridor hotels are convenient but expensive, averaging $25-$30 or more, depending on destination. The local Suburcabos buses are a much cheaper alternative, running regularly between the two Cabos; the fare for the 45-minute trip is $2.50. The Aguila bus line provides service from Cabo San Lucas to San José del Cabo and also to Todos Santos. The central bus station is at the junction of Mex. 19 and Mex. 1.

Currency can be exchanged at banks during their normal Mon.-Fri. business hours; however, make sure this service is offered before getting in line. *Casas de cambio* (currency exchange offices) are another option; their exchange rates may not be as favorable, but they're more convenient. ATMs are plentiful, and some dispense dollars in addition to pesos. Avoid using an ATM after dark.

As in other parts of Mexico, making phone calls from your hotel room, calling collect or using a credit card can all end up being prohibitively expensive. Instead, buy a prepaid Ladatel/Telmex calling card, available in various denominations at mini markets, pharmacies and other local businesses. The cards offer relatively low per-minute rates and can be used at any public phone marked "Telmex" or "Ladatel." Avoid using phones that say "To call long distance to the USA and Canada, simply dial 0"; they are installed by a private company, and the charge will be exorbitant.

The English-language *Gringo Gazette* is published every other week. There are two separate editions covering southern and northern Baja. The newspaper is a good source for local tourist-related news, plus restaurant and entertainment listings. The Cabo Coffee Co., at the corner of Avenida Madero and Calle Hidalgo (across the street from the main square) has high-speed Internet connections and serves java made from organically grown Mexican coffee. Cabo Clipper, at the Puerto Paraiso mall (third level) on Boulevard Lázaro Cárdenas, also offers computers with fast connections.

In case of emergency dial 066 to reach local police, the fire department or the Red Cross. The AmeriMed Cabo San Lucas Hospital, on Avenida Lázaro Cárdenas near the Bancomer bank branch and a McDonald's outlet, offers a wide range of routine and emergency services and has a 24-hour pharmacy. Insurance is required for medical emergencies; phone (624) 105-8500.

To contact the municipal police, phone (624) 143-3977. The Red Cross (Cruz Roja) is at Mex. 19 Km marker 221 (on the way to Todos Santos); phone (624) 143-3300. As is the case with most local offices in Mexico, the ability to speak fluent Spanish will come in handy.

Cabo San Lucas is warm all year. Daytime highs are around 80 degrees in winter but can soar to over 100 during the summer months; bring plenty of sunscreen. The Gulf of California waters warm well into the 80s in summer and are close to 80 degrees the rest of the year, making conditions for diving and snorkeling ideal. The Pacific is about 10 degrees cooler. The high tourist season is primarily November through April; bring a sweater for occasional cool evenings if visiting in January or February. September and October are the rainiest months, but in general the climate is arid.

City Layout

Despite its popularity as an exclusive resort area, Cabo San Lucas is still a small town at heart. It spreads north and west from Cabo San Lucas Bay (Bahía de Cabo San Lucas). The main street is Avenida Lázaro Cárdenas, the westward extension of Mex. 1. Boulevard Marina branches off it, curves around the harbor and leads to a few beachfront hotels located beyond downtown. Almost everything of visitor interest clusters around the harbor; the streets in the vicinity of Plaza Amelia Wilkes, the central town square; and along the Mex. 1 Corridor.

Downtown Cabo lends itself to strolling. The shopping centers, restaurants and nightspots along Boulevard Marina and on the surrounding streets can all be easily reached on foot. In addition, a pedestrian walkway *(malecón)* wraps around the large Cabo San Lucas Marina, a modern harbor packed with everything from humble *pangas* to huge luxury yachts. The harbor *malecón* can be traversed in about an hour and the people-watching is always interesting.

Stop by the sport-fishing docks at the harbor's southern end in late afternoon, when local boats return from a day's fishing, for a firsthand look at the many game varieties found in the surrounding waters. If you're driving in from one of the Corridor hotels, there is a large free parking lot off Boulevard Marina, next to the Plaza Nautica shopping center.

Beaches

The beaches of southern Baja are renowned for their beauty as well as their tranquility. The scenery is magnificent: intensely blue water, a backdrop of mountains and rugged cliffs, stands of huge cacti. It's still not all that difficult for solitude seekers to find a secluded beach and spend the day picnicking, surfing or snorkeling sans crowds.

You will, however, need a car for beach exploring. With the exception of Medano Beach, private taxi rides to and from the Corridor beaches are expensive. Public bus transportation is an option and drivers will generally let you disembark at beach turn-offs. However, walking from the highway to the beaches themselves often involves a long trek without any shade (i.e., miserably hot).

Cabo's most popular sunbathing spot is Medano Beach (Playa El Medano), which curves gracefully along the shore of Cabo San Lucas Bay just north of town and encompasses the beachfront hotel zone. The water here is usually safe for swimming, the sand is soft, and people-watching from the outdoor bars and restaurants lining the beach is always entertaining.

Cruise ships anchor just off shore. Parasailers soar overhead. Beach vendors trudge through the sand. Catamarans, sea kayaks and *pangas* ply the bay. Rowdy co-eds rent wave runners and other water toys. To reach the beach from Avenida Lázaro Cárdenas, head south on Paseo de Pescador. **Note:** During college spring break weeks Medano's raucous beachfront bars are party central.

Land's End *(see attraction listing)*, or "Finisterra," is literally that—the tip of the Baja California Peninsula. Both the approach to Cabo San Lucas via Mex. 1 and elevated spots in town offer panoramic views of Baja's final frontier. Some of the beaches in this area, however, are accessible only by boat.

Located just west of Land's End, Lover's Beach (Playa del Amor) may well be the most idyllic, although it's almost always crowded unless you arrive early in the day. A water taxi can be hired either at Medano Beach or the Cabo San Lucas marina to take you to the beach, drop you off and then return at a predetermined time; bring along drinking water and a lunch. Swimming and snorkeling are usually safe along the cove that faces the Gulf of California side, although the water can occasionally get a bit rough.

At Lover's Beach it's also possible to walk coast to coast—literally and in a matter of minutes. From the gulf shore, the sand extends across the cape to another beach facing the Pacific Ocean. Known as Divorce Beach, this stretch's white sand is great for strolling or beachcombing, but crashing waves and strong rip currents make swimming dangerous.

Solmar Beach (Playa Solmar) is a wide stretch of sand running west from the rocks at Land's End. Several large hotels, including the Solmar Suites Resort, the Hotel Finisterra, the Terra Sol Beach Resort and the Playa Grande Resort, front this beach. The powerful Pacific undertow and currents make swimming here dangerous as well, but the views are spectacular.

Land's End is noted for two dramatic rock formations sculpted by the elements. El Arco *(see subattraction listing)*, Cabo's signature landmark, is the famous natural rock arch featured on everything from tourist brochures to souvenir shot glasses. The other photogenic formations here are the pinnacles of The Friars (Los Frailes)—chiseled granite formations shaped like hooded monks. Intense blue water surrounds them at Land's End, a point where the Gulf of California mingles with the mighty Pacific.

For close-up views of El Arco you'll need to hit the water. Everything from water taxis and kayak tours to booze cruises and glass-bottom boats make the short trip from either Medano Beach or the Cabo San Lucas marina. Glass-bottom boat tours last an hour, cost about 120 pesos ($11.65 U.S.) per person and depart from the docks at the far southern end of the marina. You'll find ticket booths along the *malecón.*

At Cabo Falso, a lighthouse once guided ships between the U.S. West Coast and Panama. Old Lighthouse Beach (Playa El Faro Viejo) offers sweeping views of towering sand dunes *(las dunas).* The lighthouse still stands and is undergoing renovations. However, the trip (accessible by rental car) to a hilltop overlook to view the dunes is now in limbo, as there are plans to develop a luxury mega resort at this site.

If you have a car, the Gulf of California coast between Cabo San Lucas and San José del Cabo, also known as "the Corridor," is sprinkled with surfing areas, hidden beaches and secluded little coves that can be explored. Turn-offs branching off Mex. 1, some no more than dirt paths, lead to these spots. Generally these beaches are not considered safe for swimming (there are no lifeguards, for one thing), but they offer excellent snorkeling and diving opportunities. Heading northeast on Mex. 1 from Cabo San Lucas toward San José del Cabo, here are a few worth visiting.

Shipwreck Beach (Playa Barco Varado) is at Km 11, about 7 miles north of downtown Cabo (access to the beach is via the entrance to the Cabo del Sol resort development). The beach is named for a Japanese freighter that ran aground in the 1960s; the rusted hulk still remains on the rocks. The wreck provides golfers a spectacular backdrop on the last few holes of the Ocean Course at Cabo del Sol.

Widow's Beach (Playa las Viudas) also is known as Twin Dolphin Beach because of its location near the Hotel Twin Dolphin. Swimming is usually good at this series of scalloped, coarse sand beaches separated by rocky outcroppings. When the surf's up, however, the pounding shore break will surely finish you off. But the wild beauty and splendid isolation of Viudas make it a worthwhile stop at any time, regardless of ocean conditions. The turn-off for the unpaved beach access road (signed "Acceso a la Playa") is just past the Km 12 marker; watch for the "Twin Dolphin" radio tower and bunker on the north side of Mex. 1.

Snorkelers are drawn to Playa Santa Maria, a picturesque horseshoe-shaped bay endowed with colorful underwater scenery. Around mid-day an armada of tour boats arrive at the cove, blasting high-decibel party music and dispensing pods of snorkelers. In other words, it's best to visit in the morning or late afternoon. There are no snack bars, so pack a cooler. Shade is nonexistent, but roving umbrella rental boys will set you up for a few pesos. The signed beach turn-off is on Mex. 1 just past Playa la Viudas. Parking is available in a "guarded" lot near the highway, or farther down the dirt road at the beach itself.

Chileno Bay, about 14 kilometers (9 miles) northeast, is one of the most beautiful areas along the Los Cabos coast, and a prime swimming, snorkeling and scuba destination. A gorgeous bay backed by rocky bluffs and a shady palm grove, Playa Chileno caters to civilized beachgoers with bathrooms, showers and a booth renting snorkel equipment. The Mex. 1 Chileno turn-off is clearly signed "Chileno Bay Playa Público"; a paved road leads down to a free parking lot.

Playa Palmilla, about 27 kilometers (17 miles) northeast, is near the luxurious, long-established One & Only Palmilla resort hotel. A long crescent of sand, Palmilla's dependably calm surf makes it one of the best swimming beaches along the Corridor. If you've brought your mask and fins, there's decent snorkeling along the rocks toward the point. Thatched *palapa* umbrellas provide welcome shade, and if you're in the mood to fish, the Fisherman's Cooperative in the beach parking lot will gladly arrange a trip. The well-signed turn-off (look for the Palmilla resort signs) is near the Km 27 marker. The paved access road winds through Palmilla's golf course before reaching the beach.

Note: Most of the beaches facing the Gulf of California are safe for swimming; those facing the open Pacific should be appreciated only for the view. Pay attention to any warning signs: Some beaches are prone to riptides and dangerous breakers, or have deep drop-offs close to shore. All beaches in Mexico are the property of the government and consequently are accessible to the public. Parking at or camping on deserted beaches is perfectly legal; it is not legal, however, to leave behind garbage of any kind. Driving on beaches in Mexico also is illegal.

Outdoor Recreation

Two pursuits define the outdoor life at Los Cabos: sport fishing and golf. The waters of the Gulf of California and the Pacific Ocean are home to some 850 species of fish. The gulf in particular has a rich and varied marine population, including whale sharks, manta rays, schooling hammerhead sharks, stingrays, moray eels and sea turtles.

Of the two dozen or so game species widely caught in Baja waters, striped marlin run year-round. The season for the majestic blue marlin is June through mid-November. Others commonly hooked include amberjack, black marlin, bonito, black sea bass, corbina, dorado (mahi mahi), roosterfish, sailfish, snapper, wahoo, yellowfin tuna and yellowtail.

During the season it is advisable to book fishing trips well in advance; some participants reserve boats as much as a year in advance for the Bisbee's Black and Blue Marlin Jackpot Tournament and the Los Cabos Offshore Tournament, both held the second half of October. These are among the world's richest marlin fishing tournaments, with base entry fees of several thousand dollars.

A catch-and-release policy is strongly emphasized; anglers experience the thrill of battle, but after their catch is reeled in it is tagged and set free, helping to preserve billfish species and ensure the continuation of the sport.

Most of the larger resort hotels have their own sport-fishing fleets, making it easy to plan an excursion if you're a guest. The Fiesta Americana Grand Los Cabos, the Solmar Suites Resort and the One & Only Palmilla have fleets with boats anchored at the Cabo San Lucas marina.

If you prefer to make your own arrangements, several fleet operators operate from the marina's docks on the south side of the harbor. *Pangas* (small, outboard motor-powered skiffs) holding two or three people can be rented by the hour, including equipment and a fishing license (required). ABY Charters is at the marina's main dock, next to the Flea Market (Mercado de Artesanías); phone (624) 143-0831 or (866) 751-3505 (from the United States).

More expensive sport-fishing cruisers normally rent for parties of four to six people so expenses can be shared; the cost usually includes tackle, bait, licenses, lunch and a captain and mate, but not taxes or tips. Rates range from $700 to more than $1,000 per day, depending on the size of the boat. Trips depart around 7 a.m. and return by 2 or 3 in the afternoon. Most boats either head east to the fertile fishing grounds of the Gordo Banks or around Los Arcos toward the open Pacific.

Several water sports centers provide a full range of rental equipment as well as organized snorkeling and scuba trips. Cabo Acuadeportes specializes in scuba and snorkeling excursions to Chileno Bay. They also conduct single-tank boat dives with an English-speaking guide to nearby sites daily at 9, 11 and 2:30. Bringing your own dive gear is recommended, although rental equipment is available. The center is located at the Hacienda Beach Hotel, on Cabo San Lucas Bay at the southern end of Medano Beach; phone (624) 143-0117.

Amigos del Mar, on Boulevard Marina across from the sport-fishing docks, offers guided natural history, scuba and snorkeling tours. These excursions venture to such prime spots as the Socorro Islands, about 200 miles southwest of Cabo San Lucas, inhabited by 400-pound tuna and exotic species of reef fish; Land's End, home to octopus, tropicals and sea lions; and Cabo Pulmo National Marine Park, site of a living coral reef that offers experienced divers some of the clearest water and richest marine life in the world.

Most trips are aboard a 22-foot canopied skiff that accommodates four people plus a divemaster. For additional information and reservations phone (624) 143-0505, or (513) 898-0547 (from the United States).

Gray whales complete their long-distance migration from the Bering Sea to the warm Pacific waters of the mid- and lower Baja coastline each year from January through March. They can sometimes be spotted from the beaches and rocky overlooks along the Mex. 1 Corridor and the rocks around Land's End.

The adventure tour company Aereo Calafia offers flights to Magdalena Bay, the southernmost gray whale calving area, which is about 200 miles up the Pacific coast. *Panga* boats take passengers into the coastal lagoons for an up-close look at these fascinating creatures. There is an Aereo Calafia office downtown inside the Hotel Tesoro; phone (624) 143-4302, or (818) 206-3255 (from the United States).

As popular as sport fishing—if not more so—is golf. Not so long ago, golf meant one nine-hole course, the Mayan Palace Golf Course (formerly Campo de Golf) in San José del Cabo. A process that allows reclaimed water to be used for irrigation purposes makes it possible to maintain manicured greens and fairways in the midst of arid conditions.

Today world-class courses are scattered along the Corridor between the two Cabos—with more on the drawing board—all laid out against the stunning natural backdrop of desert terrain. Some—like Querencia, an exclusive residential community with an 18-hole course designed by Tom Fazio—are open to members only. Golfing in Los Cabos also is a very expensive pastime; greens fees for 18 holes average more than $200 (somewhat less in the low season), cart and bottled water included.

The signature hole at the Nicklaus-designed Palmilla Golf Club, at the One & Only Palmilla resort, is the par-4 fifth. The tee shot must carry over a cactus-filled canyon, which also wraps around in front of the green. The desert vegetation, Gulf of California vistas and view from the mountaintop clubhouse are all breathtaking, and the play is a strategic challenge. This is a semiprivate club, and eventually will be open to guests only. For information phone the resort at (624) 144-5250.

The Golden Bear also designed the highly regarded and recently renovated Ocean Course at the Cabo del Sol resort development. The final three holes offer dramatic waterfront scenery as well as an assortment of hazards in the form of cactus, rock cliffs and treacherous bunkers. Instead of negotiating long fairways, players tee off over deep ravines to landing pads and then chip to the green. Even the short par 3 holes are formidable.

The Tom Weiskopf-designed Desert Course features an inland layout that nevertheless provides a view of the gulf from every hole. For information about either course phone the resort at (624) 145-8200, or (213) 891-6385 or (877) 703-4394 (from the United States).

The Cabo Real Golf Course, at Corridor Km marker 19.5, was designed by Robert Trent Jones. It winds its way among beautiful homes and the exclusive Las Ventanas al Paraiso resort. Average players can handle the layout, which doesn't mean play is easy. The palm-flanked 14th-hole fairway sweeps down to the beach, while the 15th tee, right at the surf, offers the most spectacular view of the course. Reservations can be made by phoning (800) 543-2044 (toll-free long distance within Mexico) or (877) 795-8727 (from the United States).

The Nicklaus-designed course at the Eldorado Golf Club, next to the Westin Regina Golf & Beach Resort at the northeast end of the Cabo Real development, has six holes right along the beach. The layout winds from seaside to rocky canyons and back, with the green at the par-5 16th hole framed by the gulf's cobalt-blue waters. For reservations, phone (624) 144-5450 or (877) 795-2727 (from the United States).

The Cabo San Lucas Country Club is just a short distance east of Cabo San Lucas. This is the only course in Los Cabos with a view of the Land's End rocks, which look particularly impressive from the 18th hole. The gently sloping fairways look out on a desert landscape that features giant cardon cacti. The seventh hole, a par 5 double dogleg that wraps around a lake, is a whopping 620 yards. Greens fees are not quite as expensive as they are at the other championship courses. For information phone (624) 143-4653 or (877) 461-3667 (from the United States).

Dining

Hotel restaurants in Los Cabos are expensive and, on the whole, predictably good. For more local fare, hit the streets. Cabo is famed for fish tacos, but you'll also find shrimp, pork, chicken and beef varieties. For the most part, the food at the bars and restaurants lining Medano Beach and the marina *malecón* is very good, but also overpriced. For better *comida* at more digestible prices, try the open-air restaurants in the downtown area, many run by families. These are good places for late night tacos or a hearty morning meal of *huevos rancheros,* eggs and black beans drenched in tomato salsa, sprinkled with cheese and served with tortillas.

El Pollo de Oro ("The Golden Chicken"), at the corner of Morelos and 20 de Noviembre, specializes in juicy, fall-off-the-bone Sinaloa-style barbecued chicken. Seating is in a large patio courtyard perpetually packed with locals and a sprinkling of tourists. In addition to the must-order *pollo,* the menu is loaded with tempting Mexican dishes—all authentic and affordable.

Torta (sandwich) stands also pop up on downtown street corners after dark. Ham and cheese is a common and tasty variety. Many stands grill hot dogs and whip up tacos as well. Use the same common sense at these places that applies whenever sampling street food in Mexico—if there's a crowd hovering around a cart and the food looks hot and fresh, it should be fine. Squeezing lots of lime juice over the meat helps kill any lingering bacteria. *For a list of AAA-RATED dining establishments in Cabo San Lucas, see the Lodgings & Restaurants section.*

Shopping

A one-stop destination for shopping and entertainment in downtown Cabo is the Puerto Paraiso mall, off Avenida Lázaro Cárdenas between Plaza Bonita Mall and the Marina Fiesta resort. On a par with American malls, Paraiso is a modern, three-level collection of clothing chains (Kenneth Cole, Nautica, Tommy Bahama), boutique-type shops, gift stores, high-end jewelry merchants and restaurants. The center is designed for open-air strolling along attractively landscaped terraces, as well as window shopping in air-conditioned comfort.

On the lower level, American restaurant chains like Johnny Rockets, Harley-Davidson Restaurant & Bar and Ruth's Chris Steakhouse front the marina. For kids there is a bowling alley and video arcade, a 10-screen movie theater complex and a fast-food court. Puerto Paraiso is open daily 7 a.m.-10 p.m.

Plaza Bonita, an open-air shopping center next door to Puerto Paraiso, has a few interesting shops, includding the Sergio Bustamente Gallery (near the Hard Rock Cafe). The famed Guadalajaran artist is known for his whimsical ceramic, wood, bronze and papier-mâché sculptures, which elicit opinions as wildly mixed as his art. Check out the two-level gallery and decide for yourself.

The Souvenir Outlet, across the street from Puerto Paraiso at the corner of Avenida Lázaro Cárdenas and Vicario, occupies a faux lighthouse packed with all manner of souvenir cheese. We're talking fridge magnets, twisted Corona beer bottles, El Arco paperweights, snow globes and other assorted dust collectors. If this is what you're after, the prices here are noticeably lower than at other gift shops around town. You'll also find a well-stocked pharmacy *(farmacia)* inside.

More traditional craft shops are located on or near Lázaro Cárdenas and Boulevard Marina. They offer the usual T-shirts and other touristy trinkets in addition to blankets, folk art, woven goods and black coral jewelry. Open-air flea markets in the downtown area sell ceramics, pottery, silver jewelry, leather goods and hand-carved wooden animal figures. One of the largest flea markets is on the ground level of Plaza del Sol, on Boulevard Marina. Bargaining is expected.

No shopping tour of Cabo is complete without wandering the streets in the vicinity of Plaza Amelia Wilkes, a traditional Mexican square with a gazebo at its center. On the plaza's northwest corner is the Cabo Museum, which has natural history exhibits and is a cool place (both figuratively and literally) to wander around for a few minutes. It's open Tues.-Sun. 10-3 and 6-8 p.m., and admission is free.

Among the countless souvenir shops, clothing boutiques and jewelry stores you'll find a couple of unusual galleries. Worth a visit is the Golden Cactus Gallery/Studio, at the corner of Guerrero and Madero just east of the plaza. This second-floor gallery exhibits works by regional artists and also sells fine art prints and inexpensive posters. Magic of the Moon, in the vicinity of the plaza on Hidalgo (near the corner of Zapata) sells designer women's fashions—casual, colorful outfits with tropical motifs that fit right in at a beachside resort. The vivacious owner, Pepita, will gladly show you around.

Zen Mar, near the corner of Avenida Lázaro Cárdenas and Calle Matamoros, is a combination art gallery and museum with an outstanding variety of ethnic masks from all over Mexico, including Day of the Dead designs. *Ex-votos* have facial writings describing why the mask was made for a particular religious ceremony; *retablos* (small devotional paintings) depict emotions without the use of words. Most of the works are for sale.

Costco, the American warehouse-like discount chain, is on the inland side of the Transpeninsular Highway (the Corridor) at Km 4.5. If you're staying in a condo with a kitchen, it's a good place to load up on staples; don't forget to bring your Costco card from home. In addition, there are well-stocked Mexican grocery stores in town.

Nightlife

Given the surfers and other youthful revelers who flock to Cabo, bars and rock 'n' roll pretty much sum up the casual, lively nightlife. The Cabo Wabo Cantina, on Calle Vicente Guerrero just south of Avenida Lázaro Cárdenas, is owned by rocker Sammy Hagar. Young crowds pack the place for regular live shows by a rock cover band and occasional visits from big-name acts, including Hagar himself; hard rock and dance pop blasts from the sound system on other nights. It's open daily until 4 a.m.

The Giggling Marlin, on Boulevard Marina at Calle Matamoros, blasts classic rock and dance hits, has frequent live music and puts on a saucy audience-participation show. The attraction here is a pulley device that dangles patrons upside down—rather like a captured fish—to the great amusement of the masses. There's also a restaurant on the premises that serves good Mexican and seafood dishes. To find it, look for the beer bottle-toting marlin atop the entrance.

Also high on the see-and-be-seen circuit is El Squid Roe, on Avenida Lázaro Cárdenas at Boulevard Marina (across from Plaza Bonita Mall). This three-level nightclub is loud, raucous and invariably packed. Be forewarned: It's the kind of place where waiters brandishing spray tanks of tequila move through crowds of people dancing on top of tables. An open-air dance floor is on the main level.

The trendiest dance club on the Cabo party scene is Zoo, on Boulevard Marina opposite Plaza Bonita. The decor (African safari chic) and the music (hip-hop, house and electronica) draw a young dressed-to-impress crowd that downs 2-for-1 drink specials and gyrates til dawn.

For a decidedly mellower evening, the Whale Watcher's Bar in the Hotel Finisterra, off Boulevard Marina heading out toward Land's End, is an ideal place to watch the sun slowly drop into the Pacific. Mariachis play on Friday evenings. You can watch the big game and wager on the outcome at the Caliente Sports Book on Boulevard Marina (in Plaza Nautica). Clean, well-lit, air conditioned and loaded with TVs, Caliente also offers off-track betting in case you've got a hot tip on a horse. There's a full bar.

Los Cabos Tourism Office (Secretaría Municipal de Turismo): on Mex. 1 in San José del Cabo, just north of Valerio Gonzalez Canseco at Plaza San José. Open Mon.-Fri. 10-3; phone (624) 146-9628. The office is way off the beaten tourist track; brochures and visitor information also are available in the courtyard at City Hall (Palacio Municipal), on the main plaza in downtown San José.

LAND'S END (Finisterra) is at the confluence of the Pacific Ocean and the Gulf of California (Sea of Cortez). This southernmost tip of the Baja California peninsula generally refers not just to one specific outcropping, but rather the slender chain of rocks protruding from the waters south of Cabo San Lucas. The most well-known of this group is El Arco (The Arch).

Although visible from shore, the best way to see the eroded formations that constitute Land's End is from the water. Fleets of water taxis (many of the "glass-bottom" variety) line up at the marina to take passengers on a roughly 45-minute trip for up-close looks at these unusual rocky outcroppings. Among the formations along the way are Pelican City, a group of rocks where members of that large-billed species congregate; another clump of rocks where a colony of seals likes to hang out; a cave said to have been a favorite of pirates; Lover's and Divorce beaches; and, of course, El Arco.

Since these water taxi excursions are extremely popular, in order to provide good views the guide may have to maneuver his craft past numerous other water taxis; boats carrying snorkelers and scuba divers to nearby offshore locations; fishing boats; and other watercraft towing parasailers. Before returning to shore, the boat swings by a small rock jutting up from the water, the actual "land's end."

El Arco (The Arch) is part of the Land's End formation stretching offshore near the point where the Gulf of California and the Pacific Ocean meet. The iconic image of Cabo San Lucas, El Arco is a natural granite arch that has been carved by wind and water.

While the arch is readily visible from shore, its size and beauty are best appreciated close up. Water taxis, available at the marina, take passengers past the arch and will drop guests off on request at nearby Lover's Beach (Playa del Amor), which faces the swimmable Gulf of California. The opposite side of the beach, which faces the rough waters of the Pacific Ocean, is not safe for swimming. **Note:** If you opt for some time at Lover's Beach, remember to set a time for the water taxi to pick you up for the trip back to Cabo San Lucas.

ENSENADA, BAJA CALIFORNIA (A-1)

pop. 280,000

One of Baja California's foremost summer resorts, Ensenada (ehn-seh-NAH-dah) spreads over scrub-covered hills that slope down to the shores of large, lovely Bahía de Todos Santos (Todos Santos Bay). The city (its name, not surprisingly, means "bay") boasts a scenic setting, pleasant weather, duty-free shopping, fine sport fishing and close proximity to the United States; for many weekend visitors, Ensenada is the farthest they ever get into Mexico.

This area was still relatively isolated before the completion of Mex. 1 from Tijuana and the development of port facilities in the mid-1930s. But more than 300 years earlier, Spanish explorer Sebastián Vizcaíno had sailed into the bay and, entranced by its beauty, named it Ensenada de Todos Santos—"All Saints' Bay." A lack of fresh water prevented any permanent settlement from taking hold, although the bay often sheltered whaling ships, treasure-laden galleons and the privateers who preyed upon them.

The first real roots were put down by ranchers, who began settling the area in the early 19th century. Ensenada temporarily boomed in 1870 with the discovery of gold at nearby Real del Castillo. The town became a supply depot for miners and was designated the capital of the Baja California Territory in 1882. By the early 20th century, however, the mines had given out, the capital was relocated to Mexicali and Ensenada lapsed back into obscurity.

After U.S. Prohibition went into effect in the late 1920s, Ensenada—along with Tijuana—became a favored drinking and gambling destination for Hollywood stars and other well-heeled types. Real revitalization came with agricultural reform and development in the Mexicali Valley. A nearby port was needed to handle the export of farm produce to the United States and mainland Mexico, and Ensenada's harbor facilities made it an obvious choice for development. Tuna fishing provided further economic incentive. But it was the completion of paved highway Mex. 1 from Tijuana that opened the city up to American vacationers and sport-fishing enthusiasts.

Connected to Tijuana by the Mex. 1-D toll highway, Ensenada is the governmental seat of the *municipio* of Ensenada, which extends south to the Baja California Sur state line and includes shoreline on both the east and west coasts of the peninsula. The local economy has long relied on the cultivation of olives and grapes, the harvesting of halibut and yellowtail and commercial shipping, but tourism is becoming more important than ever before.

While Ensenada is a little far for a day trip from the United States, it makes a great weekend getaway and a good choice for dining, strolling, shopping, perhaps some fishing or a drive to a winery, or attending one of the city's many annual events. Summer is the high season; to avoid crowds, visit April-May or October-November.

Practicalities

Ensenada is about 109 kilometers (68 miles) south of Tijuana. The city's small airport, south of town off Mex. 1, currently accommodates only private planes. A tourist permit is not required for stays of less than 72 hours or if you do not travel any farther south than the town of Maneadero, south of Ensenada. For additional information about border crossing regulations *see the Border Information section in the back of this book.*

Four-lane toll highway Mex. 1-D is a quick, convenient route south from Tijuana. From the border, follow the prominent "Ensenada Toll Road" *(Ensenada Cuota)* signs along westbound Calle Internacional, which parallels the border fence to the junction with Mex. 1-D. Make sure you choose the proper exit lane, or you could be routed back to downtown Tijuana. The first of three toll booths between the two cities is at Playas de Tijuana. The second is on the southern edge of Rosarito Beach; the third is at the village of San Miguel, about 13 kilometers (8 miles) north of Ensenada. At press time, combined tolls were about $7.25 (U.S.). The final stretch from San Miguel to Ensenada is via four-lane, non-toll Mex. 1.

Although towing and Green Angels assistance are free, motorists who run out of gas on this stretch are required to pay for it. Call boxes appear at intervals for travelers to use in case of emergency. Off-ramps provide access to points of interest along this fast-growing corridor, and there are frequent panoramic views of the scenic Baja coastline. Some of the highway's curves can be daunting to drivers not used to them. About 28 kilometers (17 miles) north of Ensenada is El Mirador, a rest stop with an overlook high above the water.

Alternative free Mex. 1 (look for signs that say *Libre*) parallels Mex. 1-D most of the way, although it turns inland south of the village of La Misión, about 44 kilometers (27 miles) north of Ensenada. The driving time is longer, and the road has some rough spots. Avoid night driving along this and other two-lane secondary roads in northern Baja, as both cattle and pedestrians frequently cross them.

The main bus station is in the northern part of town on Avenida Riveroll, between calles 10 and 11. Bus service is inexpensive; local routes are designated by street name, usually painted on the windshield. The Autotransportes de Baja California bus line provides regular service to cities up and down the peninsula. For additional information about buses *see Bus Service, page 72.*

Taxis, many of them minivans, congregate near the hotels along Avenida López Mateos. Although their ubiquitous solicitations can be annoying, drivers are normally courteous and knowledgeable. Make sure, however, that the fare is decided before you set off. Taxis can be hired for trips to such outlying destinations as La Bufadora *(see attraction listing)* and the Guadalupe Valley wineries. Round-trip rates run $40-$50 (U.S.), depending on the number of passengers.

In the event of emergency, dial 066 (English may not be spoken). For nonemergency tourist assistance or help with legal problems, dial 078, which should connect to the nearest State Tourism Office during normal working hours. A calling card is not needed to dial either of these three-digit numbers from a public phone. For medical emergencies, Clinica Hospital Cardiomed is located downtown at Av. Obregón #1018. Phone (646) 178-0351 (English spoken).

The English-language *Gringo Gazette* publishes two editions, one for northern and one for southern Baja, containing travel-related information and lots of local advertising. *Casas de cambio* (exchange booths) offer the best foreign exchange rates. ATM machines dispense pesos and also may charge a withdrawal fee.

One of Ensenada's best features is its mild climate, similar to coastal Southern California and with fewer extremes of heat than almost any other Baja city. Winter evenings can be chilly, but the temperature seldom drops below 40 F. Summers are warm and dry, with occasional hot spells caused by Santa Ana winds blowing in from the desert. Almost all of the annual precipitation falls between December and March. Fierce Pacific storms sometimes bring torrential winter rains, and early summer can be quite foggy.

Personal safety is a matter of common sense. Although it has experienced tremendous growth, Ensenada still has a relaxed, laid-back atmosphere. Tourists are invariably welcomed, as their dollars sustain many local businesses. If traveling by car, the best advice is to drive safely and defensively; traffic accidents are one of the biggest sources of vacation headaches in Mexico. One way to minimize risk is to stop at every intersection, even those that don't have stop signs.

City Layout

The preferred route into downtown Ensenada (signed "Centro") branches off Mex. 1 about 2.5 miles north of the city and follows the coastline. It becomes Boulevard Lázaro Cárdenas (more commonly known as Boulevard Costero), one of two main thoroughfares traversing the waterfront tourist zone. Boulevard Costero runs along the harbor; Avenida López Mateos is a block inland. These two streets are lined with hotels, restaurants, bars, shops, nightspots and other businesses catering to visitors.

Heading south, Boulevard Costero ends at Calle Agustín Sangines (also called Calle Delante), which proceeds east to Mex. 1. Mex. 1, the Transpeninsular Highway, then continues south to Maneadero and on down the peninsula.

The *malecón,* a bayside walkway running for half a mile between Boulevard Azueta and Avenida Castillo, has been widened and refurbished. Here are the sport-fishing piers, a towering flagpole and huge Mexican flag, Plaza Civica *(see attraction listing)* and the cruise ship terminal. It's the best place in town for a breezy stroll, and there are benches for relaxing.

Away from the waterfront, Ensenada is easy to negotiate. The terrain is flat, and the layout is a basic grid. Avenues (avenidas) are named and run north-south; streets (calles) are numbered and run east-west. Streets and avenues are often unmarked, however. To orient yourself, count off city blocks inland from Avenida López Mateos, which is also known as Calle 1; successive streets are Calle 2, Calle 3, etc. The commercial business district centers around avenidas Ruíz and Juárez (the in-town extensions of Mex. 1) at the western end of downtown.

Driving tips to keep in mind: As in other Baja cities, traffic lights are small and often hard to spot from a distance. Stop *(alto)* signs placed at intersections can be obscure, so always proceed slowly and with caution. Some downtown streets are one way. The pay lot at the Plaza Marina shopping center, on Boulevard Costero just north of the sport-fishing piers, is convenient for nearby waterfront wandering.

The city's low skyline is distinguished by the twin spires of Our Lady of Guadalupe (Nuestra Señora de Guadalupe), at the corner of Calle 6 and Avenida Floresta. The cathedral, built in typical Spanish colonial style, is one of Ensenada's most prominent structures and can be used as a downtown orientation landmark. Named for the Virgin of Guadalupe, Mexico's patron saint, it is the focus for celebrations on Dec. 12 *(see Special Events)*.

Northwest of the downtown area, Avenida Alemán (accessible via Avenida Reyerson) encircles Chapultepec Hills (Lomas de Chapultepec), an attractive residential area. Several parking pull-offs offer different city perspectives, from the port and downtown waterfront south to the Punta Banda Peninsula and Todos Santos Bay.

Shopping

Some people prefer Ensenada's low-pressure shopping environment to Tijuana's more raucous atmosphere. Like that city, Ensenada is a duty-free zone, and savvy shoppers can purchase imported items at significant savings over U.S. prices.

The main tourist shopping area is along Avenida López Mateos. Gift shops lining the blocks between avenidas Castillo and Ruíz feature such imported items as silver and gold jewelry, onyx chess sets, leather boots and fine liquor. Some of the shops have fixed prices; English is usually spoken and credit cards are welcomed. Los Castillo, Avenida López Mateos #1076, carries Taxco silver jewelry guaranteed to be at least 92.5 percent pure (designated by the numerals ".925").

This upscale merchandise is augmented by curio shops that stock traditional Mexican craft and clothing items like baskets, ceramics, guitars, jewelry, wrought-iron furniture and leather jackets, purses and sandals. On Boulevard Costero at Avenida Castillo is the Handicrafts Center (Centro Artesenal), a cluster of craft stalls. In particular, take time to wander through Galería de Pérez Meillon, which sells Casas Grandes pottery, Kumeyaay baskets and other handmade items fashioned by northern Mexican artisans using age-old techniques.

Ensenada's outdoor flea markets offer a chance to find the odd treasure amid piles of utilitarian wares. Los Globos, bordered by Calle 9, Calle Coral, Avenida Morelos and Avenida Juárez (3 blocks east of Avenida Reforma and about a mile from the waterfront), is especially busy on weekends. In one area there are foodstuffs—fruit, vegetables, nuts, grains, freshly made tacos and *churros,* a sweet tube-shaped fritter similar to a doughnut. Although you won't find many souvenirs, this full-blown Mexican marketplace is a change of pace from the tourist district.

For local shopping, the supermarket chains Calimax and Gigante are convenient for picking up grocery staples as well as Mexican liquors and wines. Libros Books, on Avenida López Mateos between avenidas Miramar and Macheros, has newspapers and magazines in English. And although such items as name-brand clothing and electronic equipment often cost more in Mexico than the United States, prescription drugs and pharmaceuticals tend to be considerably less expensive. There are several *farmacias* (drugstores) in the downtown area.

Outdoor Recreation

Fishing is Ensenada's most popular recreational activity. Todos Santos Bay and the Pacific yield such cool-water species as albacore, barracuda, bonito, rockfish and yellowtail. Summer is the best time for sport fishing, although such bottom dwellers as sea bass, ling cod, rock cod, halibut and whitefish can be caught all year.

Charter arrangements can be made at the piers off the *malecón.* Rates for private groups range from about $200 (U.S.) to upward of $550 per day, depending on the size of the craft (an outboard-powered *panga* or a larger cruiser) and the number of passengers. Party boats for bigger groups cost about $40 per person for an 8-hour day of fishing, plus an extra $10 or so for a required Mexican fishing license. Bait and tackle are usually included, as is pick-up and drop-off from your hotel.

In addition to fishing trips, Gordo's Sport Fishing Fleet offers 30- to 40-minute sightseeing tours of the bay; phone (646) 178-3515. Sergio's Sportfishing runs daily trips all year to Punta Banda, San Miguel Reef and the Todos Santos Islands, plus longer trips to the Outer Banks (about 35 miles offshore), usually from late May through September; phone (646) 178-2185, or (800) 336-5454 from the United States (Mon.-Fri.).

Northern Baja diving conditions are similar to those off the coast of Southern California. Within easy reach of Ensenada are thick kelp forests sheltering a wide range of marine life. The tip of the Punta Banda Peninsula is a favored dive site; underwater mountains (sea mounts) are blanketed with colonies of anemones and sponges, and a variety of fish swim through growths of brilliant blue algae. Water temperatures are bracing—around 55 to 64 degrees F. Dale's La Bufadora Dive, near the end of the road to La Bufadora *(see attraction listing),* offers half-day diving and fishing trips. Equipment, wet suit and kayak rentals also are available; phone (646) 154-2092.

Punta Banda also has an abundance of hot springs; at spots along the beaches here, it is possible to dig into the sand and create your own hole from which soothing hot waters bubble. There are a couple of RV parks and camping areas along BC 23, the paved road that traverses the peninsula. Several unmarked hiking trails also lead off this road.

Ensenada is on the last leg of a gray whale migration journey that begins in the Bering Sea and ends at coastal bays and lagoons along the southern half of the Baja Peninsula. From late December through March the whales pass between the shoreline and the Todos Santos Islands, a little more than a mile offshore. Some of them come close enough to scratch their backs along the bay floor, removing barnacles and parasites. The rugged coastline north and south of town, and especially the end of the Punta Banda Peninsula, provides some excellent lookout points. Gordo's Sport Fishing Fleet, Sergio's Sportfishing and Dale's La Bufadora Dive all offer whale-watching trips in tour boats during the peak viewing months.

There are no beaches within the city proper. Most visitors head for Estero Beach, about 12 kilometers (7 miles) south of downtown Ensenada via Mex. 1; the turn-off, about 7.5 kilometers (4.5 miles) south, is well marked. Along the shore of Estero Inlet there are gentle waves and a long stretch of sand.

Southern California surfers gravitate to several spots in the vicinity of Ensenada, including Punta San Miguel, a point next to the village of the same name; Punta Salsipuedes, north of Punta San Miguel; and Estero Beach. But the ultimate surf location in northern Baja is off the Todos Santos Islands (Islas Todos Santos), located at the mouth of Todos Santos Bay. These twin islands catch the full brunt of winter swells from the north Pacific, and waves can reach 30 feet. The San Miguel Surf Shop, on Avenida López Mateos between avenidas Miramar and Gastélum, is the local surfer hangout.

Dining and Nightlife

Fishy delights await at Ensenada's traditional open-air Seafood Market, at the north end of Boulevard Costero at Avenida Miramar, just north of the sport-fishing piers. Known to locals as the Mercado de Mariscos, the covered sheds displaying freshly caught fish and shellfish have a suitably salty ambience. Handcart vendors hawk fresh clams, oysters shucked on the spot and seafood cocktails.

Fish tacos are an Ensenada staple. Stands opposite the Seafood Market offer strips of savory fried fish wrapped in a folded tortilla along with sour cream, guacamole, salsa (both *verde* and *roja*, green and red), cabbage, onions and cilantro. Avoid the mayonnaise that is left out on the tables, though. You also can get fish tacos, soups *(caldos)* and other reasonably priced seafood at the nearby outdoor food court Plaza del Marisco.

Stumbling into a small, out-of-the-way seafood restaurant hidden on a side street is one of the joys of exploring the city. Check the customers; if a place is full of locals, it's likely to be good. Mariscos Bahía Ensenada, at the corner of avenidas López Mateos and Riveroll, is a downtown fixture with an extensive menu and a lively atmosphere complete with roving string trios. *For a list of AAA-RATED dining establishments in Ensenada, see the Lodgings & Restaurants section.*

Although Ensenada is quiet during the week, particularly in winter, it becomes a party town on summer weekends and U.S. holidays. But unlike Tijuana or Rosarito, where the crowds are largely young and rowdy, Ensenada tends to attract an older and more diverse group of revelers.

Most of the bars and clubs catering to tourists are downtown in the vicinity of Avenida López Mateos and Boulevard Costero. Hussong's Cantina, on Avenida Ruíz just east of Mateos, treats the designated driver in a group to free soft drinks while his or her companions indulge in margaritas and *cerveza*. Sawdust covers the hardwood floor and mariachi bands provide the music at a watering hole that has atmosphere to spare. Across from Hussong's is Papas & Beer, three floors of fun with free-flowing margaritas, blasting rock and high energy dance music, occasional live bands and numerous theme events.

An alternative to all this raucousness can be found at Bar Andaluz, in the Riviera del Pacífico *(see attraction listing)*. This low-key lounge is a relaxed place to have an early evening drink. La Capilla, in the Best Western El Cid on Avenida López Mateos (between avenidas Alvarado and Blancarte), has a clubby feel and features live Cuban jazz on weekend evenings.

Mexican dance, ballet and theatrical productions, plus performances by such visiting artists as the San Diego Symphony, take place at the City Theater (Teatro de la Ciudad), on Calle Diamante between avenidas Pedro Loyola and Reforma. For event information phone (646) 177-0392.

Special Events

Something always seems to be going on in Ensenada. Carnaval (Mardi Gras) is usually celebrated in mid-February on the 6 days prior to Ash Wednesday. A downtown street fair takes place each night, with midway rides, live entertainment, food vendors, parades of flower-covered floats and other merriment. The festivities climax with a masquerade ball; prizes are awarded for the best costume.

The LEXUS Newport to Ensenada Race from Newport Beach, Calif., to Ensenada is held the last weekend in April. Hundreds of yachts depart from Newport Beach at noon, ending up in Ensenada about 11 hours later. Most remain in the city for a day or two, and a huge party with food, music and dancing follows. For information contact the Newport Ocean Sailing Association; phone (949) 644-1023 (from the United States).

Thousands of cyclists make the 50-mile trek from Rosarito to Ensenada along Mex. 1 (the free road) during the Rosarito-Ensenada Bike Ride, which is held twice a year, in late April and late September. Following the event, participants and supporters party at the Finish Line Fiesta, held at the Ensenada city fairgrounds off Boulevard Costero near the cruise ship terminal.

The Estero Beach Volleyball Tournament takes place in late June on the sands in front of the Estero Beach Hotel, south of Ensenada. The tournament attracts some of the best volleyball players in North America. Food, beverages and live entertainment are on hand for spectators.

Franciscan and Dominican missionaries first introduced wine culture to Baja California in the 16th century as a way to celebrate holy Mass, and today a thriving wine industry is centered in the Guadalupe Valley. With an ideal climate for grape production and rich volcanic soil, vineyards in northeastern Baja California state produce some 90 percent of Mexican wines.

For 2 weeks in the first half of August the Grape Harvest Festival (Fiesta de la Vendimia) celebrates this bounty. Area wineries, many with vineyards in the nearby Guadalupe and El Escondido valleys, also offer tours *(see Wineries)*. For more information contact the Association of Wine Growers of Baja California (Asociación de Viticultores), downtown at Av. de la Marina #10, third floor; phone (646) 178-3038.

Restaurants from all over northern Baja and Southern California enter dishes to be judged at the Ensenada International Seafood Fair, which normally takes place in late September. Also in September is the J.D. Hussong Baja International Chili Cookoff, which brings together chili cooks and connoisseurs from both sides of the border for a day-long event at the Quintas Papagayo Resort. Mexican beers, local wines and margaritas help the fiery concoctions go down more smoothly. Live entertainment, a salsa-making competition and a chili-eating contest also take place. Admission is charged and includes chili and salsa samplings, raffle tickets and food coupons.

Ensenada, like most of Mexico, honors the deceased during Day of the Dead celebrations Nov. 1-2. Beginning in mid-November is the Tecate SCORE Baja 1000 (commonly known as the Baja Mil), one of the world's most prestigious off-road races. There are separate categories for cars, trucks, motorcycles and ATVs. The course alternates between an 800-mile loop beginning and ending in Ensenada and a longer run from Ensenada to La Paz that takes place every third year. For information contact SCORE International in the United States; phone (818) 225-8402.

Another major festival is the Feast Day of Our Lady of Guadalupe (Día de Nuestra Señora de Guadalupe), celebrated Dec. 12. It honors the nation's patron saint, the Guadalupe Virgin. All manner of amusement rides are set up in front of Our Lady of Guadalupe Church, and another attraction is the array of culinary specialties from all over Mexico.

Baja California State Tourism Office: across from the Corona Hotel in a one-story white building on Boulevard Lázaro Cárdenas (Boulevard Costero) at Calle Las Rocas. Open Mon.-Fri. 8-8, Sat.-Sun. 9-1; phone (646) 172-3022 (English spoken). This office also can provide legal assistance to tourists.

The Tourism and Convention Bureau (Comité de Turismo y Convenciónes) operates a booth on Boulevard Lázaro Cárdenas near the western entrance to the city. Open Mon.-Fri. 9-7, Sat. 10-4, Sun. 10-3 (but may vary by season); phone (646) 178-2411 (English spoken).

What To See in and Around Town

CIVIC PLAZA (Plaza Cívica) is off Blvd. Lázaro Cárdenas (Costero) at the foot of Av. Riveroll. Also known as Three Heads Park, it has a small landscaped court with 12-foot-high bronze busts of Mexican freedom fighter Father Miguel Hidalgo and former presidents Benito Juárez and Venustiano Carranza. Horse-drawn sightseeing carriages, or *calandrias,* depart from the plaza. There also are public restrooms.

CONSTITUTION OF 1857 NATIONAL PARK (Parque Nacional Constitución de 1857) is n.e. of the city. To get there, take Mex. 3 from Ensenada e. about 40 km (25 mi.) to the small farming community of Ojos Negros; continue e. on Mex. 3 approximately 16 km (9.6 mi.) to a dirt turn-off (watch for the "Parque Nacional" sign). Proceed n.e. on a series of dirt roads, following park directional signs, to the village of Aserradero; the park entrance is a short distance past the village. The total distance from the Mex. 3 turn-off is approximately 32 km (20 mi.).

In the high plateau country of the Sierra de Juárez range, this small park offers a distinct contrast to Ensenada's seaside air. The rugged terrain, highlighted by unusual rock formations, is blanketed with thick forests of cedar and ponderosa pine. In the middle of the park is small Lake Hanson (Laguna Hanson), surrounded by primitive but adequate campsites. Fishing is permitted (bass and catfish inhabit the lake when rainfall is adequate); hunting is prohibited. Solitude is the main reason to make the trip, since the park receives only a handful of visitors most of the year.

Note: The ungraded route from the Mex. 3 turn-off to the park entrance is normally negotiable in a passenger vehicle, although a fair-sized stream that crosses it about 5 kilometers (3 miles) from the turn-off may be too deep to ford during winter and spring, depending on weather conditions. Avoid visiting Lake Hanson during Easter week (Semana Santa), the busiest week of the year. A $3 (U.S.) per person entrance fee is periodically charged.

LA BUFADORA (The Buffalo Snort) is about 32 km (20 mi.) s.w. of downtown Ensenada. Take Mex. 1 s. to the jct. with BC 23, which branches w. just n. of Maneadero. The two-lane road, offering spectacular views of Bahía Todos Santos and the Pacific, winds past olive orchards, cultivated fields, trailer parks and the private Baja Beach and Tennis Club before ending at a paved parking lot near the western tip of the Punta Banda Peninsula.

From the parking lot it's a short walk to a viewing area where you can observe a hollow rock formation that acts as a natural sea spout. During incoming tides, water rushes into an underground cavern, sending spray shooting into the air like a geyser. Snack vendors congregate along the path to the blowhole, and there are curio shops where you can browse for souvenirs, but the main attraction is the dramatic mountain scenery en route. Public restrooms are on site. A $1 (U.S.) parking fee is charged.

REGIONAL HISTORICAL MUSEUM (Museo Histórico Regional) is on Av. Gastélum, just w. of Av. López Mateos. The oldest public building in the state of Baja California, it was built in 1886 and served as an army barracks during its early years. It also was a prison, and the cellblocks and guard towers remain. Exhibits focus on city history. Tues.-Sun. 10-5. Admission about $2.50 (U.S.). Phone (646) 178-3692.

RIVIERA DEL PACIFICO is off Blvd. Lázaro Cárdenas (Costero) near Av. Club Rotario. Also referred to as the Civic, Social and Cultural Center (Centro Cívico, Social y Cultural), this elegant Mediterranean-style mansion was formerly a gambling casino and hotel as well as a favored gathering place for wealthy Americans and Mexicans during the Prohibition era. Visitors can view the lavish murals and ornate wood paneling in the entry hall, explore the restored salon and gambling rooms or wander through the gardens, beautifully landscaped with subtropical foliage.

The building also houses the Museum of History (Museo de Historia), which has artifacts and dioramas recalling Baja's early days. Grounds open daily 8 a.m.-9 p.m., in summer; 8-7 rest of year. Museum daily 9-2 and 3-5. Grounds free. Museum admission $1 (U.S.); 50c (ages 7-12 and students). Phone (646) 177-0594 for the museum.

WINERIES

- **Bodegas de Santa Tomás** is downtown on Av. Miramar #666 (at Calle 7). Baja's oldest and largest winery began selling wine by the barrel in 1888, and today the firm's huge Ensenada aging and storage facility produces a variety of wines and liquors. One-hour guided tours in English begin daily at 11, 1 and 3. Fee $5-$10 (U.S.). Phone (646) 174-0836, ext. 22.

- **Casa Pedro Domecq** is on Mex. 3 (Carretera Tecate-El Sauzal), Km marker 73, a few miles n. of the town of Guadalupe; from Ensenada, take Mex. 1-D n. about 10 km (6 mi.) to the junction with Mex. 3, then proceed n.e. toward Tecate. Tours and tastings Mon.-Fri. 10-4, Sat.-Sun. 10-1:30. Phone (646) 155-2249.

- **Château Camou** is off Mex. 3 in the Guadalupe Valley. One tour includes lunch. Tours and tastings Mon.-Sat. 8-3, Sun. 9-2. Fee $5-$40 (U.S.). Phone (646) 177-3303or (646) 177-2221.

- **L. A. Cetto Winery** is on Mex. 3 at Km 73.5. Tastings and tours of the facility daily 10-4. Phone (646) 177-2352.

- **Monte Xanic Winery** is off Mex. 3 near the village of Francisco Zarco. Tours and tastings Mon.-Fri. 9:30-4. Phone (646) 174-6155.

GUERRERO NEGRO, BAJA CALIFORNIA SUR (C-2) pop. 10,900

Guerrero Negro (geh-REH-roh NEH-groh) is located within the barren Vizcaíno Desert (Desierto Vizcaíno), just south of the Baja California Sur state border. The name, which means "black warrior" in Spanish, was the moniker of an American whaling ship wrecked at the entrance to nearby Scammon's Lagoon (Laguna Ojo de Liebre). Summer temperatures here are much cooler than in the interior of the peninsula due to the cold California Current, which extends north off the Pacific coast.

The area around Guerrero Negro is part of the El Vizcaíno Biosphere Reserve, designated a World Heritage Site by UNESCO in 1993. Encompassing bays, lagoons, vast expanses of the Sonoran Desert and the rugged Sierra mountains, El Vizcaíno is an important breeding and wintering site for the California gray whale and also is home to four species of endangered sea turtle.

Approximately 1,500 whales migrate south some 6,000 miles each year from the Bering Sea off Alaska to several lagoons along the central Baja coast: Scammon's Lagoon (Laguna Ojo de Liebre), Magdalena Bay (Bahía Magdalena) and San Ignacio Lagoon (Laguna de San Ignacio). The whales venture from their Arctic feeding grounds to mate and calve in these comparatively warm waters.

Most tours to view the whales depart from Magdalena Bay or San Ignacio Lagoon, about 100 miles to the south, although arranging for a boat to nearby Scammon's Lagoon is most conveniently arranged in Guerrero Negro.

To reach Scammon's Lagoon by car, take Mex. 1 south about 9 kilometers (5.5 miles) to the graded dirt turn-off (sandy but passable) that branches southwest; signs at this junction read "Laguna Ojo de Liebre" and "Parque Natural de la Ballena Gris/Gray Whale Natural Park." There is a salt company checkpoint about 6 kilometers (4 miles) west of the turn-off. About 16 kilometers (10 miles) farther is a shack where admission to the natural park is charged. Just beyond the shack is a fork; the road to the left leads to the beach offering the best views. Since the whales are usually some distance offshore, bring a pair of binoculars.

From late December through March, group tours in outboard motor-powered boats *(pangas)* are offered by local fishermen, who charge $30-$40 (U.S.) per person. Private boats are not permitted anywhere in the lagoon during the season; local operators receive special permits. Morning is the best time to spot whales, as afternoon fog frequently obscures visibility.

The easiest way to experience the whales up close is to take part in an organized trip from Guerrero Negro. Malarrimo Eco-Tours offers 4-hour excursions with English-speaking guides aboard a 23-foot outboard boat with a maximum of 10 passengers. In addition to the whales, marine birds, sea lions and dolphins can be seen. Van transportation to and from Scammon's Lagoon is included.

Warm clothing, a waterproof jacket or windbreaker, sunblock and rubber-soled shoes are recommended. Trips depart daily Dec. 15-Apr. 15 from the Malarrimo Restaurant and campground complex on Boulevard Zapata. The cost per person (includes park fee) is $48 (U.S.); under 11, $38. Reservations should be made several months in advance; for information phone (615) 157-0100.

Significantly more expensive, but worth it if you want convenience and a complete experience, is an all-inclusive package excursion under the guidance of an experienced naturalist. Most of these trips depart from San Diego and include transportation and accommodations. A representative package tour company is the environmentally oriented, San Diego-based Baja Expeditions, Inc.; phone (800) 843-6967 (from the United States).

LA PAZ, BAJA CALIFORNIA SUR (E-3) pop. 168,600

La Paz (lah PAHS) is the commercial and governmental capital of the state of Baja California Sur. Its name means "peace," and the Dove of Peace Monument, a large contemporary sculpture of a dove in flight just off Mex. 1 at the northern entrance to town, serves as a gateway to the city. A plaque greets visitors with the following inscription: "And if you want peace, I offer it to you in the sunny peace of my bay."

Ironically, La Paz's history is one of the most turbulent of any community on the entire Baja California Peninsula. Two years after the bay was discovered by a Spanish expedition in 1535, supply problems doomed a colonization attempt by Hernando Cortés. Nearly 300 years of isolation and hardship prevented a permanent settlement from taking hold. The most persistent inhabitants were the privateers who sought haven in the bay. The name of one—Cromwell—lives on (Hispanicized) in the *coromueles,* or offshore breezes, and in such local place names as Playa Coromuel.

Rich oyster beds below the surface of the Gulf of California attracted a handful of fortune seekers throughout the 17th century. The Jesuits founded a mission at La Paz in 1720 and kept it going despite a series of Indian uprisings. It was abandoned nearly 30 years later after disease had virtually wiped out the area's indigenous population; the city's cathedral stands on the site today.

A group of determined Spaniards finally established a settlement in 1811. Continued pearl diving and some mining provided impetus for growth, and when Loreto *(see separate listing within this region)* was destroyed by a hurricane in 1829, La Paz was named the territorial capital. But conflict broke out again, this time in the form of the Mexican-American War. Battles were fought in the city's streets, but American soldiers departed after the Treaty of Guadalupe Hidalgo was signed in 1848.

Southern Baja's remoteness continued to hinder any large-scale development. After the pearl and mining industries gave out toward the end of the 1930s, La Paz languished. But as was the case with Ensenada and Cabo San Lucas, sportsmen and tourists slowly rediscovered the area's balmy winter climate and fine fishing. After years of existence as a neglected territory, Baja California Sur—along with Quintana Roo, one of Mexico's two newest states—suddenly exploded with economic and population growth, and La Paz evolved from a sleepy port into a modern state capital.

This jolt into the Mexican mainstream came with a few rude awakenings—the traffic congestion on downtown's cramped, narrow streets being but one example. But the shady plazas and renovated, palm-fringed *malecón,* the waterfront promenade along the bay, still retain some of the colonial grace of old. And for every contemporary structure there is a quaintly arched doorway or an old cobblestone sidewalk.

Despite its commercial bustle, La Paz is a laid-back city. Residents carry themselves with pride and respect, and drivers actually stop for pedestrians crossing the street. While tourism is accommodated willingly, a thoroughly Mexican atmosphere prevails. This old-fashioned charm is most evident on Sunday evenings, when throngs of couples and families stroll along the *malecón,* often against the backdrop of a spectacular sunset.

Practicalities

Marquéz de León International Airport is about 13 kilometers (8 miles) southwest of downtown off Mex. 1 (north toward the town of Ciudad Constitución). Aero California and Aeroméxico both fly from Los Angeles, and also offer service from other Mexican cities, including Mexico City and Tijuana. For additional information about airlines *see Arriving by Air, page 61.*

Colectivos (shared shuttle vans) transport passengers from the airport into the city for about $12 (U.S.), but not the other way around; you'll need to take a taxi when departing. Taxi rides to the airport average $15-$20.

The central bus station (Central Camionera) is southwest of downtown at Calle Jalisco and Héroes de la Independencia. Another station is on Paseo Alvaro Obregón, just south of Avenida 5 de Mayo. Autotransportes de Baja California buses provide regular service between La Paz and Tijuana—a 22-hour trip that includes stops at towns along the route. *Aguila* buses travel to San José del Cabo and Cabo San Lucas, about 209 kilometers (130 miles) to the south. In-town fares are inexpensive, but a knowledge of both Spanish and the city's layout is helpful.

Taxis are plentiful, especially along Paseo Alvaro Obregón. Rides within the downtown area average less than $5 (U.S.), to the port of Pichilingue about $10. A car will come in handy for exploring outlying beaches, but keep in mind that rental cars tend to be more expensive in Mexico than in the United States. Major car rental agencies have offices on Paseo Alvaro Obregón; unless otherwise specified, the vehicles tend to be Volkswagen Beetles.

Ferry service links La Paz with the mainland ports of Mazatlán and Topolobampo, near Los Mochis. Reservations to Mazatlán can be made in person at the Sematur ticket office, which is downtown on Guillermo Prieto at Avenida 5 de Mayo, 2 blocks southeast of Plaza Constitución. The office is open Mon.-Sat. 8-3; phone 01 (800) 718-9531 (toll-free long distance within Mexico).

Reservations to Topolobampo can be made in person at the Baja Ferries ticket office, on the corner of Calle Isabel La Católica and Navarro. The office is open Mon.-Sat. 8-6; phone (612) 125-7443 or 01 (800) 122-1414 (toll-free long distance within Mexico).

Both ferry terminals are in Pichilingue, about 16 kilometers (10 miles) north of La Paz via Mex. 11, and are located on opposite sides of the harbor. A knowledge of Spanish is helpful when making reservations, which should be booked at least a couple of days in advance.

Separate fares are charged for passengers and for vehicles; the rate for vehicles is determined by the length of the vehicle in meters. The maximum vehicle width is 2.6 meters (about 8.6 feet); vehicles that exceed this width are charged double the rate, as they will take up two spaces. Fares are subject to frequent change, and discounts for students and children are regularly offered.

If you plan to transport a vehicle on the ferry, contact a Mexican consulate office prior to your trip for the latest updates regarding laws and regulations. Random but thorough searches may occur before vehicles are boarded. Owners are not permitted to retrieve articles from their vehicles after they have been boarded. For additional information, *see Ferry Service, page 74.*

The southern Baja edition of the English-language *Gringo Gazette* has tourist-related articles and advertisements pertaining to La Paz and other cities in the state of Baja California Sur. Libros Books, on Avenida Constitución a block northeast of Plaza Constitución, has a good selection of English-language publications. The satellite dish antennas at the large hotels bring in TV stations from Mexico City as well as the United States.

Banks with ATM machines are concentrated a block or two inland from Paseo Alvaro Obregón. Baja Net, Av. Madero #430, offers Internet access for an hourly fee. For medical emergencies, the Hospital Especialidades Médicas is in the Fidepaz Building at the north end of town, on Mex. 1 at Km marker 5.5; phone (612) 124-0400.

November through April or May is the best time to visit La Paz, when days are warm and nights can be comparatively cool. Summer's sticky heat and humidity is uncomfortable, to say the least, despite afternoon breezes coming off the bay. Rainfall in this desert region is scant and varies from year to year, although violent tropical storms called *chubascos* bring occasional downpours in late summer or fall.

City Layout

La Paz appears as somewhat of a mirage in the midst of the barren, cactus-covered foothills of southern Baja. The city spreads out from the curving shoreline of beautiful Bahía de la Paz, the largest bay along the Baja Peninsula's eastern coast. Situated at the bay's southern end, La Paz faces northwest rather than east. While this location is ideal for viewing the frequently impressive sunsets, it can be somewhat confusing when it comes to getting your bearings.

Fortunately, city streets are laid out in a simple grid pattern, oriented northwest-southeast and southwest-northeast. Hotels and tourist-oriented facilities are concentrated along Paseo Alvaro Obregón and the bayside *malecón* promenade, roughly between northwest-southeast avenidas Sinaloa and Colegio Militar. Adjoining the bayfront is downtown, a congested section of irregular streets that is more easily navigated on foot than by car.

The *malecón,* a traditional feature of every Mexican port town, is the city's gathering place. Hugging the shore of Bahía de la Paz, this boardwalk runs parallel to Paseo Alvaro Obregón in the heart of the tourist and shopping district. Here are a pair of wharves, one serving tour boats and one for commercial vessels. Benches and statuary along the length of the *malecón* make it the most scenic spot in La Paz, just the place for an early morning or evening walk.

Many streets are one way, although clearly marked. Besides Paseo Alvaro Obregón, the major thoroughfares are Avenida 5 de Mayo, Avenida 16 de Septiembre and Avenida Bravo. Most visitor points of interest are a few blocks inland from the waterfront, but you'll need a car for trips to the outlying beaches and the port of Pichilingue.

Recreation and Beaches

La Paz, like Los Cabos and Ensenada, is famed for its sport fishing. Blue marlin weighing up to 1,000 pounds are found in offshore waters from mid-March through October; sailfish can be hooked from the end of May through October. Bonito, roosterfish and yellowtail are available all year. Other fish anglers may encounter include black marlin, cabrilla, dorado, grouper, red snapper, wahoo and yellowtail. Although the northern end of the bay still offers good fishing, the open gulf is where the real action is, especially in the waters off Isla Cerralvo southeast of the city.

Boats for a day of deep-sea fishing—either an outboard motor-powered *panga* or a more expensive cruiser for four or more people—usually include tackle, bait and a fishing license, but double check when you make arrangements. A *panga* for two or three anglers averages about $250 (U.S.) for a day; a 30-foot cruiser accommodating four will cost about $350-$450. Many boats depart from beaches north and southeast of the city.

Baja Diving & Service, which operates from the Club Cantamar Resort & Sports Center, offers a variety of sport-fishing excursions. Their downtown office is at Paseo Alvaro Obregón #1665-2 at Plaza Cerralvo; phone (612) 122-1826. Fishermen's Fleet operates out of the Hotel Los Arcos on Paseo Alvaro Obregón. Their guided charters to Isla Cerralvo, Muertos Bay and Bahía de la Paz aboard a 22-foot *panga* include bait, tackle, breakfast and lunch; phone (612) 122-1313.

Diving is rewarding in the La Paz area, which has perhaps a dozen spots where coral reefs and sunken shipwrecks can be explored and sea lions, sharks and numerous tropical fish can be viewed. Among the most popular locations are Isla Espíritu Santo north of the Pichilingue Peninsula; Los Islotes, a group of islets off that island's north coast; El Bajo, a grouping of underwater rock pinnacles east of Isla Espíritu Santo; and around the northern and southern tips of Isla Cerralvo.

Local snorkeling trips cost less than diving excursions. Scuba gear can be rented from area outfitters, and basic instruction courses are available. Baja Quest, Calle Rangel #10 between avenidas Sonora and Sinaloa, offers single- and multiday diving excursions. From June to October experienced divers with valid certification can enter a shark cage for an underwater encounter with the torpedo-shaped, jumbo-sized Humboldt squid. Phone (612) 123-5320.

Sea kayaking is another popular activity. Due to its scenic qualities, numerous sheltered coves, prime diving conditions and easy shore access, Isla Espíritu Santo is one of the best kayaking destinations in Baja California. Isla la Partida, a smaller island just north, is home to a large colony of friendly sea lions. El Mogote, a spit of sand across the bay from downtown La Paz, and Playa Balandra, a few miles north of La Paz, are good nearby destinations. Both single-seat and tandem models can be rented. The outfitters referenced above also organize kayak trips. A few hotels offer kayaks to their guests for local use; check when you make reservations.

Although gray, sperm, humpback and enormous blue whales are sometimes spotted off local waters, La Paz is not considered a primary whale-watching destination. Bahía Magdalena, a shallow, protected bay on the Pacific coast about 160 miles north, offers a much better opportunity for whale observation. Here gray whales mate and give birth from January through March. Baja Diving & Service and Baja Quest offer full-day trips including transportation, meals and viewing time aboard a local licensed *panga*.

San Diego-based Baja Expeditions offers a number of different excursions with a focus on environment, education and adventure. Most trips include accommodations, equipment, meals and a knowledgeable trip leader. Operations are based in La Paz; many trip organizers live in the city and are well acquainted with the area. For additional information, write Baja Expeditions at 2625 Garnet Ave., San Diego, Calif. 92109, or phone (800) 843-6967.

The nicest beaches are north of the city via Mex. 11 (known locally as the Pichilingue Highway) as it heads to the northern end of the Pichilingue Peninsula. The highway is not marked, although signs indicate that you are heading in the direction of Pichilingue and the ferry docks. Mex. 11 continues north all the way to Playa Tecolote.

A short distance north of the tourist wharf in town is Playa El Coromuel, a sandy stretch convenient for wading and sunbathing. There is an open-air seafood restaurant here as well. About 13 kilometers (8 miles) north of town via Mex. 11 is Playa El Tesoro, a crescent-shaped beach with some *palapas* for shade.

Pichilingue itself was once a haven for pirates plundering the bounty of black pearls harvested from oysters residing in the bay. By about 1940, however, the mollusks had mysteriously disappeared, presumably wiped out by disease. Today the town functions as the deep-water port for La Paz and a recreational getaway where sport-fishing boats bring in the day's catch.

About 5 kilometers (3 miles) north of Pichilingue is Playa Pichilingue. Stop here for a dip in the clear blue water followed by a cold beer and some freshly grilled fish at one of the beachside *palapa* eateries. Next is Playa Balandra, which fronts a narrow inlet. In addition to a small coral reef that is one of the few good spots for snorkeling close to La Paz, this beach is known for a distinctive mushroom-shaped rock formation that balances on an almost absurdly tiny base.

At the peninsula's northern tip is Playa El Tecolote, where conditions for swimming and diving are just about ideal. The gently sloping beach is equipped with *palapas*, there are casual open-air restaurants, and the water is beautifully blue and crystal clear. The water sports center here rents ski boats, kayaks and other craft and also can arrange trips to Isla Espíritu Santo.

Shopping, Dining and Nightlife

La Paz offers the savvy shopper good buys on such handicrafts as coral jewelry, seashell knickknacks, leather goods and woven baskets. Tourist-oriented shops cluster along the stretch of Paseo Alvaro Obregón between avenidas Bravo and 5 de Mayo. Antigua California, Paseo Alvaro Obregón #220 (at Avenida Arreola), carries a good selection of folk art from different parts of the country.

Ibarra's Pottery, about 6 blocks inland from the waterfront at Calle Guillermo Prieto #625, is a workshop where the Ibarra family fires pottery the old-fashioned way. Artisans carefully hand-paint exquisite floral designs on plates, mugs, tiles and vases. At Artesanía Cuauhtémoc (The Weaver), southwest of downtown on Avenida Abasolo (Mex. 1) between calles Jalisco and Nayarit, Fortunato Silva creates and sells handwoven cotton and woolen articles—rugs, tablecloths, placemats, blankets, *sarapes* and the like.

Dorian's, at Avenida 16 de Septiembre and Calle 21 de Agosto, stocks typical department store items. Due to La Paz's status as a duty-free port, it also has excellent prices on cosmetics, perfume, clothing and other merchandise.

Local restaurants are big on steak, seafood and traditional Mexican favorites. You'll find Burger King and other fast-food franchises as well. The open-air restaurants at the beaches have a decidedly casual ambience and are good places to go for fresh grilled fish and other simply prepared seafood.

Non-carnivores will appreciate El Quinto Sol, downtown at the corner of Avenida Independencia and Belisario Domínguez (a block northwest of Plaza Constitución). Proudly vegetarian, if offers meatless versions of such standbys as tacos, burritos and *tortas*, along with refreshing *licuados* (fresh fruit shakes). *For a list of AAA-RATED dining establishments in La Paz, see the Lodgings & Restaurants section.*

Nightlife here doesn't compare to Cabo San Lucas, but there are still options. Local and visiting performing arts groups take to the stage at the 1,500-seat City Theater (Teatro de la Ciudad), at Miguel Legaspy and Héroes de la Independencia.

Las Varitas, on Avenida Independencia at Belisario Domínguez, is a dance club that plays everything from salsa to Mexican rock. There is a cover charge to get in. La Paz Lapa (Carlos 'n Charlie's), the local branch of the popular Mexican chain, is a typically rowdy restaurant/bar/dance club with live music on weekends. The nightclub La Cabaña, which also has a cover charge, is on the lobby floor of the Hotel Perla, on Paseo Alvaro Obregón between Avenida Arreola and Callejón La Paz. The music is a mix of salsa, disco and oldies.

The most enjoyable activity, though, might be to simply take a seat at an outdoor café along the *malecón* at sunset as the waters of the bay turn to spectacular hues of red and gold. La Terraza, at the

Hotel Perla, is a good spot to watch the passing parade. Another hangout and gringo favorite is Pelícanos, in the Hotel Los Arcos, Paseo Alvaro Obregón at Calle Rosales. In addition to a nice view of the bay, this low-key bar has a vintage collection of black and white photos.

Baja California Sur State Tourism Office (Coordinadora de Promoción al Turismo): on Mex. 1 at Km marker 5.5, at the north end of town in the Fidepaz Building (near the marina). Open Mon.-Fri. 8-8; phone (612) 124-0100. The staff is helpful and bilingual.

Another office is on Paseo Alvaro Obregón at Calle Mutualismo, in front of the Cabañas de Los Arcos hotel near Cuauhtémoc Park. It has information about various city tour packages and is open Mon.-Fri. 8 a.m.-10 p.m., Sat.-Sun. noon-10; phone (612) 122-5939.

ANTHROPOLOGICAL AND HISTORICAL MUSEUM OF BAJA CALIFORNIA SUR (Museo de Antropología y Historia de Baja California Sur) is at Ignacio Altamirano and Av. 5 de Mayo. It features exhibits on the geology, geography, flora and fauna of the state. Evocative murals and dioramas depict the region's Indian cultures and La Paz's early days. Spanish mission settlement, Mexican ranch life and three major conflicts—the War of Independence, the Mexican-American War and the Mexican Revolution—are among the historical subjects covered. Most exhibit information is in Spanish.

Mon.-Fri. 9-6, Sat.-Sun. 9-3. Donations. Phone (612) 125-6424.

OUR LADY OF LA PAZ (Nuestra Señora de la Paz) is on the s.e. side of Plaza Constitución. The church, originally a Jesuit mission, has lovely stained glass. The present building dates from 1861; a second tower was added in the early 20th century. Large bilingual plaques relate the church's history as well as La Paz's beginnings.

Plaza Constitución is a traditional main square, with tiled, tree-shaded paths and a gazebo. It's a peaceful spot to relax while city life goes by, or to gather with the locals and listen to a band concert. On the plaza's northwest side is the old state capitol building, which houses the Historical Library of the Californias (Biblioteca de Historia de las Californias). In addition to historical documents, the library has some striking paintings depicting Baja California Sur's early days.

LORETO, BAJA CALIFORNIA SUR
(D-3) pop. 10,600

Loreto (loh-REH-toh) dates from 1697, when a mission was founded by Jesuit padre Juan María Salvatierra. It became the first capital of both Alta (the present state of California) and Baja California. Loreto also was the departure point from which Junípero Serra launched his northward quest in 1769 to establish a chain of missions in Alta California.

After Mexico won its independence from Spain in 1821, the missions began to decline. When a devastating hurricane struck in 1829, the capital was moved south to La Paz. Loreto fell into near oblivion until its impressive natural attributes began attracting U.S. sportsmen, who discovered that the fishing was outstanding.

Loreto is easily reached from points north via the transpeninsular highway (Mex. 1). The airport is about 7 kilometers (4 miles) southwest of town. Direct flights are offered from Los Angeles by Aero California, and also Thursdays and Sundays by Alaska Airlines. Continental flies from Houston to Loreto on Thursdays and Sundays during peak travel season (winter, spring and summer) and once a week on Saturdays during fall.

The *malecón* (boardwalk) has benches for taking in the view, but beach lovers should skip the rocky public stretches in town and head for the indented shores of Bahía Concepción, about an hour's drive north up the Gulf of California coast toward Mulegé.

At Nopolo Bay, about 8 kilometers (5 miles) south of Loreto, there is a championship 18-hole golf course (located just south of the Camino Real Hotel). The challenging course features numerous sand traps and is laid out along the Gulf of California coastline, blending into the surrounding desert and the Sierra de la Giganta mountains. For information on tee times and facilities, phone (613) 133-0554.

There are several fishing outfits based in town. Alfredo's Fleet, on Boulevard Benito Juárez across from the marina, has knowledgeable guides; phone (613) 135-0165. Arturo's Sport Fishing, on Calle Hidalgo between the main plaza and the marina, is a family-owned business that offers diving, snorkeling, kayaking and whale-watching excursions in addition to fishing trips; phone (613) 135-0766.

A boat excursion can be taken to Coronado Island, about a mile and a half offshore, part of Bay of Loreto National Marine Park. The clear, tranquil water harbors a great variety of tropical fish. The best months for snorkeling and scuba diving are June through October, when the water is warmest. Whale sightings are possible in winter. Trip arrangements can be made through local hotels or Arturo's Sport Fishing.

Note: Few merchants in town take credit cards or traveler's checks for payment, although both pesos and U.S. dollars are readily accepted. Currency can be exchanged at the Bancomer bank, on the main plaza, Mon.-Fri. during the morning.

Adventurous travelers can make the trip to the San Javier Mission (Misión San Javier), which is west of town; from a signed junction about 2 kilometers (1.1 miles) south of the Loreto turn-off on Mex. 1, a rough access road (recommended only for high-clearance vehicles) proceeds southwest through stunning canyon and mountain scenery for about 37 kilometers (23 miles). The beautifully restored structure of dark volcanic rock in the *mudéjar* (Moorish) style sits at the bottom of a deep valley.

The second oldest of the Jesuit missions established on the peninsula, it was founded in 1699 but not completed until 1758. The towering walls feature exemplary stonework, and the gilded altar was brought from Mexico City. It's possible to climb the winding stairs to the roof and bell tower, which offers a panoramic view of the valley below. A guided tour can be arranged through Loreto hotels or Desert and Sea Expeditions; phone (613) 135-1979.

Tourist information office: in the Palacio de Gobierno building across from the main plaza. Hours vary; phone (613) 135-0411.

MISSION MUSEUM (Museo de Las Misiones) is next to the Mission of Our Lady of Loreto. Artifacts and manuscripts on display relate to Baja California's historic missions. Other exhibits include religious art and saddles used in colonial times. Tues.-Sun. 9-6. Admission about $3 (U.S.). Phone (613) 135-1831.

MISSION OF OUR LADY OF LORETO (Misión de Nuestra Señora de Loreto) is a block w. of the main plaza. Severely damaged by earthquakes, the 1752 mission—including the tower with its modern clock—has been almost completely rebuilt and still functions as an active church. It features baroque stone ornamentation, a bell tower and a collection of gilded altar paintings.

MEXICALI, BAJA CALIFORNIA (A-2)

pop. 575,300, metro area 830,600

A remote and blazingly hot desert seems an unlikely location for a big city, but Baja California's second largest city has grown up in just such an environment. Mexicali (meh-hee-CAH-lih) is an unlikely metropolis developed as a market center for surrounding farms in the early 20th century. It became the capital of the territory of Baja California Norte in 1915. Visitors from across the border were attracted by legalized alcohol and gambling as well as by land speculation. *Maquiladoras*, foreign-owned businesses established in Mexican border areas because of low production costs, have further bolstered the economy.

Capital of the state of Baja California, Mexicali is a border city and duty-free port opposite Calexico, Calif. Mexican and U.S. Customs and Border Protection offices are open 24 hours daily.

A number of shops and restaurants are near the international border in an irregular rectangle bounded by avenidas Cristóbal Colón and Alvaro Obregón, the Río Nuevo and Calle C. Mexico's largest Chinatown (La Chinesca) also is near the border, concentrated south of Calzada López Mateos around avenidas Juárez and Altamirano. In the former state governor's residence at Avenida Alvaro Obregón #1209, between calles D and E, is The City Gallery (Galería de la Ciudad), an art gallery displaying works by Mexican artists.

Secture (Secretaría de Turismo del Estado): calzadas Montejano and Benito Juárez in the Hotel Zone (Zona Hotelera), south of Plaza Azteca. Open Mon.-Fri. 8-5, Sat. 10-3; phone (686) 566-1116 (English spoken). The office provides visitor information as well as tourist assistance.

REGIONAL MUSEUM, UNIVERSITY OF BAJA CALIFORNIA (Museo Regional, Universidad de Baja California) is at Av. Reforma and Calle L. It has exhibits focusing on paleontology, archeology, ethnography, landscape photography and the missions of Baja California. Mon.-Fri. 9-6, Sat.-Sun. 10-4. Admission about $1 (U.S.).

MULEGE, BAJA CALIFORNIA SUR (D-3)

Mulegé (moo-leh-HEH) is an old, traditional Mexican town and an oasis in the middle of the inhospitable Baja California desert. Perched on a terrace above the Río Mulegé—one of the peninsula's few rivers—it has dirt streets and a laid-back air. Mulegé also offers easy accessibility to the stunning beaches and tucked-away coves of Bahía Concepción, which begins 19 kilometers (12 miles) south of town.

Mulegé's history dates back to 1705 with the founding of the Mission of Santa Rosalía Mulegé *(see attraction listing)*. Mulegé, which means "large creek," thrived as a producer of subtropical fruits and as a regional market center long before the completion of Mex. 1 brought tourists from the United States.

About 3 kilometers (2 miles) northeast of town is the public beach, at the end of a dirt road where the Río Mulegé empties into the Sea of Cortez. The beach has dark sand, a few waves and, in summer, jellyfish. Nearby El Sombrerito, at the mouth of the river, is a hat-shaped monolith with stone steps leading to a lighthouse at the summit.

Mulegé offers outstanding fishing and boating opportunities. Fishing arrangements can be made through most hotels or at one of the many RV parks along the river south of town. The area also attracts scuba divers and snorkelers; the underwater life in Bahía Concepción includes impressively large sea turtles. Cortez Explorers, Calle Moctezuma #75A (near the telegraph office), can arrange scuba and snorkeling expeditions and rents equipment; phone (615) 153-0500.

The shell-studded beaches of coarse white sand south off Mex. 1 along the shores of the bay are known for warm, clear and gloriously blue water. For a backdrop, there are mountains tinted shades of rose by the sun. All are accessible from Mex. 1, with signs posted at each turn-off; however, the access roads are likely to be sandy, rutted or both. If you wish to hike from the highway (wear sturdy shoes), bus drivers will make drop-offs at the access roads; double-check the time the last northbound bus heads back to town. Expect to share these beaches with an army of RVers and campers.

The first beach south of Mulegé is Playa Punta Arena, about 16 kilometers (9 miles) south. Palm-thatched *palapas* line the sand, and hillside caves south of the beach are littered with shells discarded by ancient inhabitants. Playa Santispac, crowded with campers, is the most active; craft from sailboats to yachts cruise on the bay.

Playa El Coyote fronts a cove and has several trees, rare on Baja's desert beaches. Playa El Requesón, a narrow point of land connected to an offshore island that can be reached by vehicle at low tide, is a prime windsurfing location. Don't expect much in the way of tourist facilities at any of these beaches, aside from some *palapa* shelters and a few toilets.

MISSION OF SANTA ROSALIA MULEGE (Misión Santa Rosalía de Mulegé) is just upstream from the Mex. 1 Bridge over the Mulegé River. It can be reached by a pathway shaded by broad-leafed banana plants. Sunday services are still held in the solid stone structure, which was abandoned as a mission in 1828. The hilltop view takes in date palm groves spreading toward the mountains.

ROSARITO, BAJA CALIFORNIA (A-1)

pop. 53,700

One of northern Baja's most popular destinations, this resort town, easily reached from the United States, is about 29 kilometers (18 miles) south of Tijuana. Also known as Rosarito (roh-sah-REE-toh) Beach and Playas de Rosarito, it is located at the junction of free Mex. 1 and toll Mex. 1-D, both four lanes from Tijuana.

The opening of the Rosarito Beach Hotel in 1925 launched the town's vacation reputation, and it soon became a favorite fly-in spot for Hollywood stars. Still a small town in 1960, Rosarito has since expanded in each succeeding decade—particularly the 1980s—mirroring the growth of tourism in general in Baja California. Rosarito and Tijuana, in fact, are merging together into one coastal/border urban and resort area.

A major boost came in the 1990s, when Fox Studios built a huge movie production facility a short distance south of town. A 90-percent scale model of the ship that appeared in the blockbuster 1997 film "Titanic" was constructed, and Rosarito became the beneficiary of a tremendous amount of "Titanic"-related publicity. Movies continue to be made at the production lot, local shops still sell "Titanic" memorabilia, and the Xploration movie theme park *(see attraction listing)* helped bring in a new wave of tourists.

Numerous hotels line Mex. 1 (the Old Ensenada Highway), which is called Boulevard Juárez in town. Juárez also swarms with restaurants, bars and tourist-related businesses. Weekends and the spring break months of March and April bring bumper-to-bumper traffic as visitors converge on the beaches. The main tourist strip is little more than a mile long, from La Quinta Plaza south to the Rosarito Beach Hotel, but the *municipio* of Rosarito stretches more than 25 miles south to the village of La Misión, with the beachfront in between rapidly filling up with hotels, condo developments and gated residential communities.

Driving can be a hassle here, although the main tourist stretch is spread out and impractical to walk. For those who prefer not to drive, taxis make regular trips to Rosarito from Tijuana and also travel the stretch of Mex. 1 south of town to popular destinations like Puerto Nuevo *(see attraction listing)*. Taxis also cruise up and down Boulevard Juárez, although the main pick-up and drop-off point is across from the Rosarito Beach Hotel. Rates are typically negotiated per carload of passengers, since most of the cabs are full-size station wagons.

Mexicoach is the primary bus service for tourists. Round-trip shuttle service from the Border Station parking lot (next to the San Diego Factory Outlet Center) or the trolley station in San Ysidro, Calif., is offered to Rosarito and Xploration. The bright-red buses depart Tijuana every 20 minutes daily 8 a.m.-9 p.m. Round-trip shuttle service to Rosarito is $12. Phone (619) 428-9517 (from the United States), or (664) 685-1470 in Tijuana.

A huge assortment of gift shops, curio stands and open-air markets earns Rosarito its stripes as a tourist town. Souvenir shops line Boulevard Juárez along with *farmacias* and liquor stores, the latter two aimed at border-crossing day visitors picking up prescription drugs and alcoholic beverages, respectively, at bargain prices. Souvenir hunters will want to check out the Handicrafts Market (Mercado de Artesanías), on the west side of Boulevard Juárez south of Calle Acacias. Some 200 shops sell merchandise running the gamut from tacky to exquisite and everything in between.

The bigger hotels have shopping arcades where you can poke around for craft and household items. There also are numerous pottery outlets along Mex. 1 south of town. Pots, fountains, busts, birdbaths and many other wares line the road for several miles. Rosarito also is a good place to shop for carved wood furniture, paintings, tile and wrought iron.

The Rosarito Beach Hotel, on Boulevard Benito Juárez at the south end of town, is worth a visit even if you don't spend the night. The ornate main lobby has 20-foot ceilings, elaborate woodwork and nostalgic murals depicting missions, volcanoes and tropical scenes. The stained-glass *señorita* above the arched entryway is a local icon.

The Calafia Historical and Cultural Center, about 8 kilometers (5 miles) south of town on free Mex. 1, is a picturesque seaside retreat with a hodgepodge of attractions, from Japanese-style gardens and replicas of Spanish missions to a large model of Christopher Columbus' vessel the *Santa María* overlooking the ocean. It's a favored location for weddings and also has a popular seaside restaurant.

At the corner of Boulevard Juárez and Calle del Nogal, just north of the Rosarito Beach Hotel, is Festival Plaza, an eight-story hotel and nightlife complex that is a phantasmagoria of watermelon sculptures, metallic streamers, tiled waterfalls and a giant concrete sombrero. A mix of restaurants, clubs and bars make this a popular evening hangout for a young and rambunctious crowd. Live music concerts take place most weekends, especially during spring break.

Papas & Beer, an offshoot of the Ensenada original, is on the beach off Boulevard Juárez, near the Rosarito Beach Hotel. It claims to be the biggest bar in Baja and is a local favorite for volleyball, dancing, music and knocking back an ice-cold beer. The setting is faux tropical, with a waterfall, wooden decks and palm trees. There's also occasional live music. Rene's Sports Bar, on free Mex. 1 at the south edge of town, draws a somewhat older crowd of gringos for dancing to rock and salsa, singing along to mariachi bands or shooting a friendly game of pool.

Several annual events take place in and around Rosarito. Thousands of cyclists make the 50-mile trek to Ensenada along Mex. 1 (the free road) during the Rosarito-Ensenada Bike Ride, which is held twice a year, in late April and late September. Participants and supporters party after the ride at the Finish Line Fiesta, held at the Ensenada city fairgrounds.

As its name implies, the Mexican Food Festival, in May, focuses on tried-and-true favorites. Festivities include the creation of what is claimed to be the world's biggest enchilada. More traditional eats, along with carnival rides and music concerts, add up to a month of fun during the Rosarito Fair in July. Also in July, the Rosarito International Seafood Festival puts the spotlight on local restaurants. Along with sampling their culinary specialties, there's music, dancing and other entertainment.

Puerto Nuevo is all about lobster, and the village basically salutes itself during the Puerto Nuevo Lobster Festival in early October. Local restaurants feature the crustacean in all sorts of dishes, while mariachi bands provide musical accompaniment.

Rosarito Tourist Office: at the south end of town on Mex. 1 (the Rosarito-Ensenada free road) at Km marker 28. The office is open Mon.-Fri. 8-8, Sat.-Sun. 9-1; phone (661) 612-0200. The Tourism and Convention Bureau (Comité de Turismo y Convenciónes) is in Oceana Plaza, on Boulevard Juárez in the south part of town. The office is open Mon.-Fri. 9-5, Sat.-Sun. 10-2; phone (800) 962-2252 (from the United States).

PUERTO NUEVO is about 18 km (11 mi.) south of Rosarito via free Mex. 1. This tiny, unremarkable fishing village is known for one thing: some 30 restaurants specializing in Pacific lobster *(langosta)*. Some have an ocean view and a touch of elegance; others are down-home places operated by local families. The menu at each is similar—a clawless lobster (ordered by size) sliced lengthwise and pan fried in lard, along with rice, refried beans and flour tortillas, plus melted butter and chili sauce on the side. Beverages are equally standardized, running to soft drinks, wine or beer.

Hucksters shout the merits of their particular establishment to potential customers, but the final decision boils down to ambience—or a line indicating popularity. Expect to pay about $15 (U.S.) per person for dinner. Dollars are accepted, but few restaurants take credit cards. Summer weekends are the peak dining time.

XPLORATION is 5 km (3 mi.) s. of Rosarito and about 34 km (21 mi.) south of the San Ysidro, Calif., border crossing into Tijuana; take the last of four Rosarito exits off Mex. 1-D (signed "La Paloma-Popotla-Calafia"), then proceed s. on Mex. 1 to Km 32.5. This movie theme park features exhibits and memorabilia from films made entirely or in part at neighboring Baja Studios. Attractions include original sets, props and wardrobe items from "X-Men: The Last Stand" and the first two "X-Men" movies; Cinemagic, an interactive examination of the filmmaking process; and the Titanic Museum, a guided tour of sets, costumes and props from the blockbuster 1997 film.

Local musicians give weekend performances at the seaside Los Olas Amphitheater. Dolly Plaza, complete with the grand fountain that made an appearance in 1969's "Hello, Dolly!", also has an ocean view. Food is available. Mexicoach shuttle buses provide round-trip transportation from the Border Station parking lot in San Ysidro. Wed.-Fri. 9-4:30, Sat.-Sun. 10-5:30. Admission $12 (U.S.); $9 (ages 3-11 and 62+). MC, VI. Phone (866) 369-2252 (toll-free from the United States), or (661) 612-4294 in Mexico.

SAN FELIPE, BAJA CALIFORNIA (B-2)

pop. 14,000

Although nomadic fishermen first gravitated to the area around San Felipe (sahn feh-LEE-peh) in the mid-19th century, the town was not permanently settled until the 1920s. The completion of Mex. 5 from Mexicali in 1951 brought a steady stream of American sportsmen who have helped transform San Felipe into a major winter vacation destination. Rapid expansion that began in the 1980s has produced a slew of waterfront trailer parks, condominiums and hotels. Even so, do not expect a luxury-style resort: San Felipe's style is distinctly no-frills.

About 193 kilometers (120 miles) south of Mexicali, the town's location combines the inviting—the Gulf of California's shimmering blue waters—with the forbidding—an extremely arid desert environment. Mex. 5 south from Mexicali is in excellent condition, including an initial stretch of four-lane divided highway. **Note:** There are only two gas stations between the village of La Puerta and San Felipe—a distance of some 100 miles—and only one selling unleaded fuel. Make sure your tank is full before starting out.

After traversing open desert, an archway heralds the arrival into town. The steep eastern flank of the Sierra San Pedro Mártir range—which includes Baja California's tallest mountain, Picacho del Diablo—is clearly visible to the west. The town spreads out under 940-foot-tall Punta San Felipe, a promontory that forms the northern end of Bahía San Felipe. Yellow-sand beaches line the coast southeastward from the crescent-shaped bayfront to Punta Estrella, about 19 kilometers (12 miles) distant. A splendid view of the town and coastline is available from the Virgin of Guadalupe Shrine, atop a hill just north of San Felipe.

The bay, along with the entire northern Gulf of California, has an extreme tidal range that often reaches more than 20 feet, requiring an experienced boater to successfully navigate the waters. At high tide waves break against the shore; at low tide it is possible to wade far out over sand and mud flats.

South of town, an unnumbered, very rough road passes the airport and continues 85 kilometers (53 miles) to Puertecitos. Along the way are turn-offs leading to vacation home communities and trailer camps, but very few motorist facilities.

About 21 kilometers (13 miles) south of San Felipe via the Gulf of California coast road is the Valley of the Giants (El Valle de Los Gigantes). Watch for the sign for Colonia Gutierrez Polanco, then take the sandy road going in the opposite direction—southwest—about 5 kilometers (3 miles). The cluster of very large, very old cardón cactuses and other desert vegetation makes for an intriguing sight. It is recommended that this excursion be made only in a sturdy, high-clearance vehicle.

San Felipe attracts campers, anglers, road racers and beachcombers. Dwellings are modest, vegetation scarce, and litter sometimes an eyesore. The town attracts a rowdy crowd of motorcyclists and dune buggy fanciers on holiday weekends and the 2 weeks around Easter. At these times noise and congestion reign. Also avoid the blistering summer months, when temperatures can soar to 120 degrees under cloudless skies. The weather November through April is much more pleasant, although still crowded on such holiday weekends as Washington's Birthday and Thanksgiving.

At this major fishing center shrimp are caught commercially, and surf fishing and package or chartered fishing trips are available. Cabrilla, white sea bass, yellowtail, dorado and other game species are found in the gulf waters. Boat rentals range from oar-propelled *pangas* to large craft that can accommodate a party for several days. Local boating outfits are concentrated along Mar de Cortés, as are San Felipe's restaurants, bars and nightspots.

Tourist information office: on the south side of town at Manzanillo and Mar de Cortés, the *malecón* (waterfront drive); phone (686) 577-1155.

SAN JOSE DEL CABO, BAJA CALIFORNIA SUR (E-4) pop. 33,000

Fronting the steely blue Gulf of California at the eastern end of the Los Cabos resort area, sedate San José del Cabo (sahn hoh-SEH dehl KAH-boh) is the anti-Cabo San Lucas. While young couples and rowdy college kids dance and drink themselves into a Mexi-coma near Land's End, San José attracts a slightly older tourist crowd that bypasses hyper-Americanized Cabo in favor of a more relaxed resort. That's not to say that San José is a sleepy Baja backwater: It's plenty modernized, but the town's colonial roots and pockets of late 19th-century architecture remind visitors they are indeed vacationing in Mexico.

Those roots date back to the late 17th and early 18th centuries, when Spanish galleons dropped anchor here to obtain fresh water for the last leg of their lengthy voyage from the Philippines to Acapulco. The nearby bays provided good hiding places for British pirates, who plundered the ships for their riches. As these raids increased, it became necessary for Spain to establish a permanent settlement at the end of the Baja Peninsula.

In 1730 Jesuit padre Nicolás Tamaral founded Mission San José del Cabo on a mesa overlooking the Río San José, but due to a plague of mosquitoes it was soon moved to the mouth of the inlet. Inhospitable Pericu Indians, rebelling against Tamaral's indictment of their predilection toward polygamy, killed the padre and burned the mission down 4 years later.

The Spanish promptly built a military outpost *(presidio)* that both protected the settlement from Indian attack and guarded the inlet against pirate raids. After that Baja's tip lapsed back into obscurity, although San José del Cabo continued to serve as a trade center for passing ships.

Following the end of the 1846-48 Mexican-American War, Baja (Lower) California remained a part of Mexico, while Alta (Upper) California became part of the United States. In 1853 a Tennessee-born lawyer, journalist and soldier of fortune, William Walker, set out to conquer the Mexican territories of Baja California and Sonora, proclaiming them the Republic of Lower California. Walker actually captured the city of La Paz before his ragtag campaign was quelled by the Mexican government. He later was tried in California for conducting an illegal war, although the jury—presumably influenced by the then-popular doctrine of Manifest Destiny—acquitted him almost instantly.

After this failed attempt at colonization, regional mining operations quietly came and went in the late 19th and early 20th centuries. A few farmers began trickling into the area in the 1930s, but San José basically snoozed in the sun until neighboring Cabo San Lucas started luring sport fishermen and vacationers in the 1960s. When San José International Airport opened, this quiet riverside village suddenly found itself the gateway to Los Cabos.

San José is one of the three main ingredients that make up Los Cabos—the other two being Cabo San Lucas *(see separate listing within this region)* and the Mex. 1 Corridor between the two towns. In contrast to its party animal sibling, the "other" Cabo manages to retain some small-town charm, even if its sleepy days are pretty much a thing of the past. While San José has certainly benefited from the tourist surge in recent decades, and residents take pride in preserving its small-town character—evident in the vicinity of Plaza Mijares, the large main square—growth *does* bring change.

And change is exemplified by Puerto Los Cabos, which continues to take shape along 3 miles of beachfront just east of town. This 2,000-acre, master-planned resort community is anchored by a recently opened, 535-slip marina sandwiched between the untamed San José Estuary (Estero San José) and the small fishing village of Pueblo La Playa. Naturally, a breakwater had to be built at the mouth of the marina, which has resulted in dependably calm surf at the adjacent La Playita *(see Beaches and Recreation)*. As for Pueblo La Playa, local residents banned together and rejected lucrative offers to sell their land.

The pueblo is surrounded by newly constructed homes and condos that stretch back into the hills and spread eastward along the coast. The master plan also includes an elevated access road from San José (construction is well under way), shopping plazas and two championship golf courses. A Jack Nicklaus-designed course is already open for business, while the inaugural tee-off at a Greg Norman signature course is expected by the end of 2008.

The serene flip side to all this unabated growth is Cabo Pulmo National Marine Park *(see Beaches and Recreation)*, a colorful coral realm teeming with sea life that lies beneath the Sea of Cortez. Driving to Cabo Pulmo from San José entails a long, bumpy journey along the unpaved East Cape Road, but it's doable in one very full day. Those who make the trip will be rewarded with some of the finest diving and snorkeling in Baja—in an unspoiled environment blissfully free of T-shirt shops, raucous watering holes and gaggles of sunburned, camera-toting tourists.

Practicalities

San José del Cabo International Airport is about 13 kilometers (8 miles) north of San José del Cabo and 48 kilometers (30 miles) northeast of Cabo San Lucas. Aeroméxico, Alaska Airlines, America West, American, Continental, Delta and Mexicana airlines all offer either direct or connecting flights from various U.S. cities. For additional information about the airport *see the Cabo San Lucas listing;* for additional information about airlines *see Arriving by Air, page 61.*

Because the Los Cabos area is spread out and expensive taxi fares will quickly add up, renting a car is a viable option if you're staying more than a few days or want to explore the surrounding area. **Note:** AAA/CAA members enjoy discounts through Hertz for vehicles booked in the United States. Consult your local AAA/CAA club or phone Hertz, (800) 654-3080. For additional information about renting a car *see Car Rentals, page 62.*

Taxis from San José del Cabo to Cabo San Lucas or the Corridor hotels are convenient but expensive, averaging $15-$30 depending on destination. The local Suburcabos buses are a much cheaper alternative, running regularly between the two Cabos; the fare for the 45-minute trip is $2.50. The Aguila bus line also provides service between the two towns.

Walking from the far eastern end of the beachfront hotel zone to downtown San José will take about 20 minutes. If you're staying at a hotel located west of town, you'll save time, energy and a $6 (U.S.) taxi fare by taking the bus. San José employs a fleet of converted yellow school buses, which you'll see running during daylight hours along Paseo San José, the wide boulevard behind the hotel zone. Flag down any eastbound bus and simply tell the driver, *"La Plaza, por favor."* The fare is six pesos per person. **Note:** Unless you're familiar with the city, taking the bus beyond Plaza Mijares is not recommended.

Currency can be exchanged at banks during their normal Mon.-Fri. business hours, but make sure this service is offered before getting in line. Banks also may be open Saturday morning. You'll find branches of Mexican banks (with attached ATMs) all over downtown and along Mex. 1 west of town. If you're staying in the beachfront hotel zone, head for the modern, two-level Mega Comercial shopping center at the junction of Mex. 1 and Paseo de Los Cabos. There's an ATM inside the Mega grocery store, plus two banks/ATMs in a strip mall next door. Some ATMs dispense dollars in addition to pesos, but beware of stiff transaction fees.

In case of emergency dial 066, which can be used to reach local police, the fire department or the Green Angels. There is a 24-hour medical clinic and pharmacy (Médica Los Cabos) on Calle Zaragoza near the corner of Avenida I. Green, about 3 blocks west of the main plaza. English is spoken; phone (624) 142-2770. The Red Cross (Cruz Roja) is on Boulevard Mijares next to the post office; phone (624) 142-0316. To contact the local police at City Hall, phone (624) 142-0361.

City Layout

This is—for now—the quiet alternative to the fiesta-like atmosphere of Cabo San Lucas 20 miles down the road. Downtown San José is about a mile from the Gulf of California (Sea of Cortez), separated from the beachfront hotel zone by a series of low hills and the condos and private homes surrounding the Mayan Palace Golf Course. Some of downtown's narrow streets are lined with historic Spanish-colonial style buildings that have been converted into stylish shops and restaurants. Flowering trees, including the purple-blossomed jacaranda, arch overhead. The orderly grid of streets is small and compact, and conducive to walking.

Mex. 1 runs along the western edge of town before turning west toward Cabo San Lucas to form the Corridor. Another main thoroughfare is north-south Boulevard Mijares. It begins at Avenida Zaragoza and heads south to Paseo San José, which follows the waterfront. San José's hotel zone is along this wide boulevard.

Avenida Zaragoza borders the south side of Plaza Mijares. The name commemorates Mexican naval officer José Antonio Mijares, who prevailed in a bloody skirmish against U.S. forces deployed from the frigate *Portsmouth* during the Mexican-American War. Tourists tote shopping bags through the cobbled square, pausing to snap pictures or rest on the wrought-iron park benches.

On the south side of the plaza a yellow clock tower rises above the traditional Palacio Municipal (City Hall), built in 1927. Inside, city offices surround a shady courtyard where you'll find an ATM and racks full of tourist brochures. The east side of the square is graced with a large fountain backed by the Jardín del Los Cabaños, a half-dozen bronze busts of historical big shots. A giant Mexican flag waves overhead. There is a small but ornate wrought-iron bandstand near the plaza's east side.

Across Avenida Miguel Hidalgo from the plaza stands the twin-steepled San José Church; it was rebuilt in 1940 on the spot where the town's original mission stood. Above the entrance is a tiled mural depicting the unwelcome fate of San José mission founder Nicolás Tamaral—being dragged to his death toward fire by Indians. The church is usually open if you want to peek inside.

The Arroyo San José, more a stream than a river, flows along the eastern side of town and empties into San José Inlet (Estero San José). The estuary, east of the Presidente Intercontinental Los Cabos Resort, was long ago a pirate hideout and more recently a waterfowl sanctuary. The new Puerto Los Cabos Marina has displaced some of the wetlands on the estuary's eastern side, but the grassy marshes near town remain unspoiled.

Beaches and Recreation

The stretch of beach along the San José del Cabo waterfront is impressive to look at, but pounding shore breakers make it generally unsafe for swimming. Guided horseback rides along the shoreline are popular and can be booked on the beach or through your hotel.

La Playita is a calm, pretty curve of sand at Pueblo la Playa, a small fishing village about 4 kilometers (2.5 miles) east of San José. Adjacent to the Puerto Los Cabos Marina, La Playita was recently endowed with new public facilities. A cobbled walkway runs behind the beach, while an oceanfront playground for kids sits directly on the sand. *Palapa*-shaded picnic tables, showers and bathrooms are set back near the marina.

To reach La Playita, take paved Avenida Juárez out of town for 2.4 kilometers (1.5 miles) to the beach turn-off, simply signed "La Playa." From here, drive 1.6 kilometers (1 mi.) down the unpaved beach access road. Tommy's Barefoot Cantina, on the east side of the road just before the beach, has excellent seafood, ice-cold beer and live music most nights.

The most popular surfing beach is Playa Costa Azul, a short distance south of San José at Mex. 1 Km marker 29. The Costa Azul Surf Shop at Km marker 28 rents boards by the day, and also offers lessons. Since surfing is a tricky art, most visitors will be content to watch the experts take on the waves from a lookout point at the top of a hill just south of the beach.

The diving and snorkeling are superb at Cabo Pulmo National Marine Park, which protects the only coral reef in the Sea of Cortez. There are several reef fingers in Pulmo Bay (Bahía Pulmo), most of which are best left to divers. However, the inner reef can be easily accessed by snorkelers. A handful of dive shops offer tours that depart from the tiny town of Cabo Pulmo itself. Boats stop for exceptional snorkeling off rocky Mermaid Beach (Playa La Sirenita) and then visit a sea lion colony where you'll actually swim alongside the barking beasts. The Cabo Pulmo Dive Center is a long-established local dive shop; phone (624) 141-0885.

It's also possible to reach beautiful Mermaid Beach by car and a short hike. Just five minutes south of Cabo Pulmo village, look for the well-signed turn-off to Playa Arbolitos. A short dirt road leads to the beach, where *palapa* umbrellas and good snorkeling await. To find Mermaid Beach, face the ocean and look to your right. There's a narrow unmarked trail that climbs a hill and heads south along the bluffs. The hike takes about 15 minutes **Note:** Sections of the trail are narrow, with steep drop-offs; use caution. This trail is only recommended for people in fairly good physical condition.

To reach Cabo Pulmo by car, you can take one of two routes. The paved option involves driving north out of San José on Mex. 1 toward La Paz. At the town of Las Cuevas, head east toward the coast on a paved road that eventually veers south and approaches Cabo Pulmo from the north. Only the last 10.5 kilometers (6.5 mi.) are unpaved, but can still be negotiated by a regular passenger car.

The scenic route follows the unpaved East Cape Road (usually passable in a regular car), which heads east out of San José (follow Avenida Juárez out of town), veers north, skirts the coast and affords gorgeous views of stark, cactus-studded desert hills tumbling into the deep blue Sea of Cortez. One-way drive time is between 2.5 and 3 hours. You'll see an ever-growing number of luxury beachfront homes along the coastal road, but visitor services and gas stations are nonexistent.

Baja Wild offers full-day Cabo Pulmo kayak and snorkel trips that depart from the San José area and include round-trip, air-conditioned van transportation to the marine park. The company also organizes ATV, jeep and whale-watching tours. Phone (624) 172-6300 for tour fees and additional information.

Note: All beaches in Mexico are the property of the government and consequently are accessible to the public. Driving on beaches in Mexico is illegal. For information about other beaches in Los Cabos, *see the Cabo San Lucas listing*.

Due to a combination of game fish migrations, bait supply, water temperature and ocean currents, the Gordo Banks, about 10 miles east of San José del Cabo, are considered to be among the richest fishing grounds in the Gulf of California. Gordo Banks Pangas, headquartered in the village of

Pueblo la Playa, offers chartered 6-hour sportfishing trips in outboard motor-powered *pangas* that are launched from the new Puerto Los Cabos marina.

Rates for a standard 22-foot *panga* holding up to three passengers begin at about $210 (U.S.). Tackle and equipment are included; lunch, live bait and transportation to and from the launch area are not. Reservations should be made several months in advance for the October-November peak season; phone (624) 142-1147 or (800) 408-1199 (from the United States).

The nine-hole Mayan Palace Golf Course is the granddaddy of Los Cabos links. Although not the caliber of the world-class courses down the road, this public course suits duffers as well as intermediate golfers—and it's much cheaper to play. Tee times are on a first-come, first-served basis; phone (624) 142-0905.

The newly opened course at Puerto Los Cabos is another Jack Nicklaus signature layout. (Play at a second course designed by Greg Norman is restricted to residents and members.) For rates and reservations, phone (624) 144-1200. For information about other courses *see the Cabo San Lucas listing.*

Shopping

Shops of varying quality can be found along Calle Zaragoza near Plaza Mijares, and also up and down Boulevard Mijares. ADD Curios Gallery (Arte, Diseño y Decoración), or Art, Design and Decoration, sells a range of hand-crafted home accessories, from ceramics to furniture. The shop is at the corner of Calle Zaragoza and Avenida Hidalgo. Copal, on Plaza Mijares, will entice browsers with its selection of handicrafts and jewelry from all over Mexico.

Also on Plaza Mijares is Necri Boutique. It specializes in hand-painted Talavera tile, Majolica ceramics, dinnerware sets and pewter creations—all made in Mexico. Prices are a bit steep, but the craftsmanship is superior. If you want a good deal rather than pricey quality try Curious Carmela, at the corner of Boulevard Mijares and Coronado. It's a huge store packed to the rafters with ceramic plates, glassware, blankets, toys, clothing, decorative items and cheap Mexico mementos.

At last count, some 16 art galleries dot Avenida Obregón and the narrow streets behind the San José Church. Easily explored on foot, the area is known as the San José del Cabo Art District, and behind its pastel storefronts you'll find some of the most interesting shopping in all of Los Cabos. A free guide map is available at the galleries.

At the corner of Avenida Obregón and Morelos, a colorful mural featuring Frida Kahlo serves as a backdrop for the gourmet coffee patio at El Armario, the self-proclaimed "cutest shop in town." Housed in an old gas station building, the gallery sells handmade folk art, unusual gift items and jewelry, plus eye-pleasing abstract paintings by up-and-coming local artists.

Old Town Gallery, Avenida Obregón #20, features paintings by local artists and a nice selection of original crystal sculptures. The tiny Doña Pitaya Gallery, Avenida Obregón #8, is devoted to the colorful, psychedelic bead art created by Huichol Indians. Across the street, the Arenas Mata Ortiz Art Gallery sells much sought-after Mata Ortiz pottery, as well as paintings and exquisite jewelry.

Corsica Galería de Arte deals in contemporary works by internationally known Mexican artists like Leonardo Nierman and Manuel Felguerez. Unless you've got a few thousand extra U.S. dollars burning a hole in your pocket, you'll have to be content with simply admiring Corsica's museum-quality paintings, large-scale sculptures and various *objets d'art.*

For a more down-to-earth shopping experience, walk through the Municipal Market (Mercado Municipal), off Calle Manuel Doblado. Locals gather here to buy fish, produce and flowers. Next door, a large yellow building houses a half-dozen *lonchería* stands where you can get a fairly inexpensive lunch. Lonchería Ely dishes up outstanding *pozole* (hominy stew), while Lonchería Sonia makes a mean fish taco. Seating is at communal tables, packed with locals at lunchtime.

Dining and Nightlife

Many downtown restaurants are either on or a block or so away from Plaza Mijares. Open-air courtyards, garden patios, sidewalk tables and distant Gulf of California views all make dining out a delightfully relaxed affair. *For a list of AAA-RATED dining establishments in San José del Cabo, see the Lodgings & Restaurants section.*

Even more casual is Zippers, just south of town on the road to Cabo San Lucas (Mex. 1 Km marker 28.5). This surfer and gringo hangout at Playa Costa Azul serves up burgers, fries, ribs, steaks, seafood and Mexican standards, usually with a helping of TV sports events, and you can chow down in your bathing suit if you wish.

Compared to Cabo San Lucas, nightlife in San José is downright sedate. Cactus Jack's, on Boulevard Mijares just north of Juárez, is a big, friendly party bar with dancing and karaoke on most nights. The TVs at Shooters Sports Bar, at the corner of Boulevard Mijares and Doblado, are tuned to NFL, NHL, NBA and MLB action. The Tropicana Bar & Grill at the Tropicana Inn, Blvd. Mijares #30, is a longtime local gathering place that sometimes has live music.

Baja Brewing Co., on Morelos just north of Avenida Obregón (in the Art District), is owned by a couple of beer aficionados from Colorado. The on-site brewery produces impressive ales and lagers, and the kitchen (open late) turns out tasty pub grub and thin-crust pizzas. There's sports on TV as well as live salsa and reggae music on most nights.

Live bands also occasionally play beachside at Zippers. For most visitors, however, a stroll around Plaza Mijares caps off a pleasant evening—it's safe, the trees are wrapped in twinkling lights, and the square is filled with vendors and families.

Los Cabos Tourism Office (Secretaría Municipal de Turismo): on Mex. 1, just north of Valerio Gonzalez Canseco at Plaza San José. Open Mon.-Fri. 10-3; phone (624) 146-9628. The office is way off the beaten tourist track; brochures and visitor information also are available in the courtyard at City Hall (Palacio Municipal), on the main plaza in downtown San José.

CACTI MUNDO is on the w. side of Blvd. Antonio Mijares, about halfway between Plaza Mijares and the eastern end of San José's beachfront hotel zone. While the orderly collection can't compare with seeing wild cactus in Baja's starkly beautiful desert landscapes, this small, contemporary-style outdoor garden does feature artfully arranged plantings of cactuses and succulents. Paved walkways are lined with some 850 species from around the world, many rare or endangered. You also can purchase a hunk of cactus candy, which comes in a shrink-wrapped Styrofoam tray.

Allow 30 minutes minimum. Daily 8-6. Admission 30 pesos (about $2.90 U.S.); $1 (ages 0-12). Phone (624) 146-9191.

SANTA ROSALIA, BAJA CALIFORNIA SUR (C-3) pop. 11,300

A mining town that has been designated a national historic monument, Santa Rosalía (SAHN-tah roh-sah-LEE-ah) was established by the French-owned El Boleo Copper Co. during the 1880s. Prosperity reigned until the mines gave out in 1953. Mining operations were later reactivated with the discovery of new copper and manganese deposits, but these too failed. Commercial fishing and boat building contribute to today's economy.

The French left their mark on Santa Rosalía's narrow, bustling streets. Instead of Mexican-style stucco walls and tiled roofs, many houses are built of wood painted in pastel shades, and gardens are enclosed by picket fences. One of these residential neighborhoods sits on a plateau north of town and offers a panoramic view of the old copper smelter. Another European touch shows up on some of downtown's 19th-century buildings, which are topped with square clock towers.

Santa Rosalía also is known—somewhat incongruously—for bread. The El Boleo Bakery (Panadería El Boleo), Avenida Obregón and Calle 4, has earned a regional reputation for its fresh-baked specialties, particularly baguettes (arrive early if you want to stock up; they tend to sell out quickly).

The small harbor serves as the terminal for Santa Rosalía ferry service to Guaymas *(see separate listing under Northwestern Mexico)* on the Mexican mainland. Reservations are recommended; double-check rates and schedules prior to departure. The ferry office is in the terminal building just south of town on Mex. 1; phone (615) 152-1246. For reservations information phone 01 (800) 505-5018 (toll-free long distance within Mexico). For additional information *see Ferry Service, page 74.*

A pleasant side trip is the farming community of San José de Magdalena, reached via a well-marked turn-off that branches west off Mex. 1, about 27 kilometers (17 miles) south of Santa Rosalía. The road is graded dirt and can be negotiated by a high-clearance vehicle, but it becomes rough past the village. An oasis sheltered by palm groves, the village dates from Baja California's Spanish colonial period, when it served as a visiting station of the Mission Santa Rosalía Mulegé *(see Mulegé listing).* In the vicinity are the ruins of a chapel built by the Dominicans in 1774.

SANTA BARBARA CHURCH (Iglesia Santa Barbara) is in the center of town at Av. Obregón and Calle 1. Santa Rosalía's most interesting architectural feature is this prefabricated, galvanized-iron church designed by Gustave Eiffel for the 1898 Paris World's Fair. It was shipped in pieces from France and reassembled here. Note the stained-glass windows.

TECATE, BAJA CALIFORNIA (A-1) pop. 55,200

Tecate (teh-KAH-teh) is Baja's oldest border town, first settled in 1831. The region's dry, mild climate, suited to growing grapes, olives and wheat, led to the development of farming as an important industry. The town grew following the completion in 1915 of a rail line between Tijuana and Mexicali, facilitating the export of agricultural products to the United States. Tecate also was a whiskey smuggling point during U.S. Prohibition in the 1920s. Beer replaced whiskey in the local economy when the Cuauhtémoc Brewery *(see attraction listing)* opened in 1944.

Tecate is accessible from the Otay Mesa border crossing into Tijuana *(see Border Tips under Tijuana).* From the border, proceed south about a mile on Boulevard de los Aztecas to Boulevard Industrial and turn left (east). Toll Mex. 2-D begins after about 2 miles. The toll for cars and light trucks is about $6.25 (U.S.), but this is a faster, non-congested alternative to free Mex. 2. Once you leave the industrial zone behind the route enters open countryside, first tracing a narrow canyon (watch for falling rocks along the roadside) and then continuing past rolling hills dotted with farms and ranches. The total distance is about 34 kilometers (21 miles).

The Tecate border crossing is at the junction of Calle Cárdenas and SR 94 in California. From the border, Calle Cárdenas runs south 4 blocks before ending at the junction with Mex. 2. A block east is the northern terminus of Mex. 3, which runs southwest through the Guadalupe Valley and connects with Mex. 1 just north of Ensenada.

A new crossing facility for vehicles returning to the United States opened just east of the former location in early 2005. There can be a wait to cross the border back into the United States on busy summer weekends. Mexican customs offices are open daily 8-4; U.S. Customs and Border Protection offices are open daily 5 a.m.-11 p.m.

Tecate is the largest town on Mex. 2 between Tijuana and Mexicali. It lies in a bowl-shaped valley below 3,900-foot Tecate Peak. The mountain's rocky, brush-covered slopes, inhabited by many kinds of wildlife and the site of sacred Kumeyaay Indian grounds, are protected by both the U.S. and Mexican governments. The land is so rugged in parts that no border fence marks the boundary between the two nations.

Unlike much of the rest of the Baja border region, and despite steady growth, Tecate has managed to maintain much of its Mexican small-town atmosphere and remains relatively un-Americanized. Daily life centers on Hidalgo Park (Parque Hidalgo), the tranquil, tree-shaded main plaza, which has fountains, tile walkways and a Spanish-style gazebo. A statue of Benito Juárez stands at the plaza's northeast corner. Lingering here, it's hard to believe that California is a mere 4 blocks north.

Another authentic Mexican experience can be had at the El Mejor Pan de Tecate bakery, on Avenida Juárez between calles Rodríguez and Portes Gil (about 2 blocks east of Hidalgo Park). It offers cakes, *bolillos* (rolls), *pan dulce* (lightly sweetened breakfast breads) and other treats in traditional serve-yourself style. Downtown's walk-up *taquerías* and taco stands are inexpensive places to fuel up on burritos, *tortas* and other Mexican standbys.

Although it remains a commercial center for the surrounding grape-, olive- and grain-growing area, Tecate also attracts artists. As a result, shops and handicraft centers often sell locally made pottery, tile and glassworks instead of the more typical curios and souvenirs. About 4 miles west of town is Rancho La Puerta, a well-known health resort and spa that has offered guests facilities for physical, mental and spiritual rejuvenation since 1940. Its location was no doubt influenced by the weather, perhaps the best in northern Baja: pleasantly mild in winter, cooler in summer than desert areas to the east and south, and almost entirely free of the fog that affects the Pacific coast in late spring and early summer.

The Tecate Beer Festival, held in July, pays tribute to the popular libations produced at the Cuauhtémoc Brewery. Food, music and of course ice-cold *cerveza* are part of the celebration, which takes place in the brewery's beer garden. In October the Tecate Founders Fiesta at Hidalgo Park commemorates the city's founding. For information about both events contact the State Tourism Office.

Baja California State Tourism Office: Callejón Libertad #1305 on the south side of the main plaza. Open Mon.-Fri. 8-8, Sat.-Sun. 9-1; phone (665) 654-1095.

CUAUHTEMOC BREWERY is 6 blks. s. of the border at Av. Hidalgo and Calle Carranza. This is where Baja's famed Tecate and Carta Blanca beers, among other brands, are brewed. The Tecate logo—a red and gold symbol with a stylized eagle—is a familiar sight throughout Baja California. The beer garden offers one free beer per person. Beer garden open Mon.-Fri. noon-4, Sat. 10-2. Free guided tours are given Mon.-Fri. at noon and 3; Sat. tours are by appointment. Phone (665) 654-9478.

TIJUANA, BAJA CALIFORNIA (A-1)

pop. 1,228,700, metro area 1,700,000

Tijuana (tee-HWAH-nah), some 29 kilometers (18 miles) south of San Diego, is a major U.S. point of entry to Baja California. While tourism has resulted in a proliferation of shops, restaurants and bars aimed squarely at the hordes of incoming visitors, it is industry that has really transformed this former tawdry border town. Hundreds of international companies have set up shop here, making Tijuana one of Mexico's largest manufacturing centers.

"The World's Most Visited Border City" (as its boosters proclaim) extends for more than a dozen miles along the international border; its downtown core is less than a mile from the United States and about 6 miles inland from the Pacific Coast. Tijuana is a window to Mexico, although it's not necessarily typical of how the rest of the country lives. San Diego is linked to the city via two border crossings. The bustling port city of Ensenada lies an hour south. To the east via Mex. 2 is the Baja California state capital, Mexicali.

Tijuana, often referred to as "TJ," is the farthest point in the country from Mexico City and does indeed seem apart. The area was settled relatively recently in comparison to other areas of Mexico—the 1860s—although the region has been inhabited by indigenous peoples for centuries. The city's name is derived from "Tia Juana," a former 10,000-hectare working ranch. When Mexico lost Upper California to the United States as a result of the Mexican-American War in 1848, the area around the ranch became the new border between the two countries.

The city's urban beginnings date from 1889, when the streets of the central downtown area were laid out. Californians first filtered across the border to watch horse races and boxing matches, shop around for souvenirs and enjoy hot springs bathing. Northwestern Baja has welcomed Golden State residents seeking an easily accessible weekend retreat ever since.

The 1920s brought important changes. Prohibition fueled tremendous growth as well as Tijuana's sinful reputation for drinking, gambling and worse. Upon Prohibition's repeal and the Great Depression's onset, the resort folded, the jetsetters moved on and Tijuana slumped. President Lázaro Cárdenas' administration closed down the casinos in the 1930s, furthering the city's decline. The government did, however, designate all of Baja California a duty-free port, and shoppers came calling in search of bargains.

U.S. servicemen kept alive the city's reputation as a bawdy center for illicit fun. Reform laws instituted in the 1930s began curbing some of the more undesirable aspects, but it was not until the 1960s that city leaders took steps to create a more family-friendly image for Tijuana.

This is one of Mexico's largest urban areas. Millions of people pour back and forth across the San Ysidro border crossing—said to be the world's busiest—each year, and the combination of tourism, manufacturing and commerce places Tijuana among the country's top destinations.

In the decades since 1970 the city really began reaping the rewards of a vast, money-spending gringo population just across the border. College students and weekend tourists flock to Tijuana to shop, play golf, have dinner, bet on sports and party the night away, although not all at once. But while the city receives 10 times as many annual visitors as Cancún, its challenge is to keep them for more than a day.

Tijuana is a hybrid—it's an Americanized place where English is widely spoken, yet has the curiosity appeal of a foreign country. It also is a city of contrasts. Viewed from the United States side, Tijuana looks decidedly ramshackle. But in the fashionable Zona Río district, Paseo de Los Héroes (Avenue of the Heroes) is lined with substantial hotels and office buildings. The avenue's name refers to the statues of historical figures, such as Aztec ruler Cuauhtémoc and U.S. President Abraham Lincoln, that stand in the center of several traffic circles.

The passage of the North American Free Trade Agreement (NAFTA) furthered the proliferation of foreign-owned businesses, the majority of them attracted by Tijuana's low production costs, an educated and relatively cheap labor force and a prime location. The factories, or *maquiladoras,* in sprawling areas like the Otay Mesa Industrial District churn out millions of manufactured goods every year.

Over the years Tijuana has shed some of its less savory aspects in the quest to lure visitors. Avenida Revolución, the main street and traditional tourist zone, once was lined with rowdy bars and sleazy strip joints in addition to the omnipresent cheap souvenir stands. But while many endearingly kitschy curio shops remain, and the nightspots are still loud, much of the street has been extensively cleaned up.

Practicalities

Tijuana International Airport is on the eastern edge of the city near the Otay Mesa border crossing. Aeroméxico, Mexicana and Aero California are among the airlines serving the airport, flying to cities on the Baja Peninsula and mainland Mexico. *Colectivos* (shared shuttle vans) and taxis provide transportation to downtown hotels. *Colectivo* fares are about $5 (U.S.). Taxis are more expensive; fares are posted at the counters where you purchase tickets. For additional information about airlines *see Arriving by Air, page 61*.

Greyhound buses travel frequently between Tijuana and San Diego; for fare and schedule information phone (800) 231-2222 (from the United States). Tijuana's Central Bus Terminal (Centro de Autobuses) is on Calzada Lázaro Cárdenas at Río Alamar in La Mesa, en route from downtown to the airport. Regular passenger service is offered to the nearby cities of Ensenada, Mexicali and Tecate. The Autotransportes de Baja California line offers first-class service; phone (664) 621-2424, ext. 121. For additional information about buses *see Bus Service, page 72*.

Five Star Tours provides charter service from San Diego to locations in northern Baja. Buses depart from San Diego's Amtrak depot, Broadway at Kettner Boulevard, to Avenida Revolución in downtown Tijuana, Tijuana International Airport, Rosarito, the Puerto Nuevo lobster village and the cruise terminal in Ensenada. For schedule and fare information phone (619) 232-5040 or (800) 553-8687 (from the United States).

Mexicoach offers round-trip shuttle service from the Border Station parking lot (next to the San Diego Factory Outlet Center) or the trolley station in San Ysidro, Calif., to Rosarito, the Xploration movie theme park and Bullring-by-the-Sea. The bright-red buses depart every 20 minutes daily 8 a.m.-9 p.m. A round-trip ticket is $5, round-trip shuttle service to Bullring-by-the-Sea $8 and round-trip shuttle service to Rosarito $12. Phone (619) 428-9517 (from the United States), or (664) 685-1470 in Tijuana.

Most shopping centers have free parking lots. There are pay lots along Avenida Revolución downtown, and these are preferable to parking on the street. For day visitors who want to avoid traffic congestion and the hassle of finding a parking space, it's much more convenient to just park north of the border and enter the city on foot via an elevated pedestrian crossing.

Taxis are not metered, so always ask how much the fare is *("Cuanto?")* and state your destination before getting in, as drivers may try to get more money out of tourists or take you somewhere other than where you want to go. Cab drivers congregate around the stand just south of the border. Fares from the border to Avenida Revolución run about $6 (U.S.); within the downtown area $4 to $5; from downtown to the racetrack and El Toreo bullring about $10; and to the airport or Bullring-by-the-Sea about $12.

The nearest RV park is the El Oasis Resort & Trailer Park, off Mex. 1-D about 5 kilometers (3 miles) north of Rosarito (southbound, Oasis exit; northbound, San Antonio exit). Another facility between Tijuana and Rosarito is KOA Rosarito, about 11 kilometers (7 miles) north of Rosarito via Mex. 1-D (San Antonio exit); phone (661) 613-3305.

Note: Keep in mind that facilities, maintenance and services at trailer parks in Baja California may not be up to U.S. standards. Tap water is not fit for drinking, and bathroom facilities can be rustic. Campgrounds in the southern part of the peninsula may not have English-speaking employees; a knowledge of basic Spanish comes in handy. For listings of AAA-RATED campgrounds and trailer parks, *see How to Read a Campground Listing, beginning on page 678.*

Hospital General is located at Av. Centenario #10851 in the Zona Río neighborhood; phone (664) 684-0922. The U.S. consulate office is on Calle Tapachula near the Caliente Racetrack (Hipódromo). Assistance is offered to U.S. citizens who receive inappropriate treatment by Mexican police while traveling in northern Baja California. The office will furnish a questionnaire pertaining to incidents of mistreatment, or write to the American Consulate General, P.O. Box 439039, San Diego, CA 92143-9039. In case of an after-hours emergency, phone (619) 692-2154.

The weather in Tijuana is similar to that in southern California—mild, overcast and rather wet in winter, warm and dry in summer. Daily maximums are usually in the 60s during the winter months, rising to the low 80s in summer. While there are occasional hot spells, the moderating influence of the Pacific Ocean largely spares the city from the blazing temperatures common in many other parts of Baja. Precipitation averages only about 10 inches a year, with almost all of it falling during the winter; the months of May through September are essentially rainless.

Like many big cities, Tijuana has a rough side. Stick to the established tourist zone—roughly Avenida Revolución east to Paseo de los Héroes, the area just south of the San Ysidro border crossing, and along Boulevard Agua Caliente as it extends southeast off Avenida Revolución. At night, avoid side streets and unlighted areas.

Despite an emphasis on family entertainment, Tijuana still attracts a large contingent of partying revelers. Those who end an evening overindulging on margaritas or Tecate beer should take the appropriate measures to get back to their hotel room (or car) safely. Don't even consider purchasing drugs; penalties are swift and severe, with little possibility of intervention from U.S. sources.

Border Tips

There are two border crossings—at Tijuana-San Ysidro and at Otay Mesa, just east of Tijuana International Airport and south of SR 117 (Otay Mesa Road). U.S. Customs and Border Protection offices are open 24 hours daily. Mexican customs offices are open Mon.-Fri. 8 a.m.-9 p.m., Sat. 8-5. Both crossings are open to travelers daily 24 hours. For additional information *see the Border Information section in the back of this book.*

Crossing the border south into Tijuana can usually be accomplished without delay. However, travelers are likely to encounter backups during the late afternoon or early evening on weekdays, as thousands of commuters return from their jobs on the U.S. side of the border. Friday afternoon backups are especially common at both the San Ysidro and Otay Mesa crossings.

The best times to cross the border north into the United States are before 10 a.m. and after 10 p.m. spring through fall, and before 2 p.m. and after 8 p.m. during the winter (except holidays). Occasional cloudy summer days—locally referred to as "June gloom"—often prompt weekend visitors to leave earlier on Sunday afternoons.

Crossing on or around major holidays—Memorial Day, July 4, Labor Day, Thanksgiving and Christmas—can entail waits of up to 3 hours. The 2-week college spring break and the first 2 weeks of December, when citizens of both countries are traveling back and forth doing their Christmas shopping, are other times when significant delays can be expected, as are Mexican holidays.

Note: All U.S. and Canadian citizens traveling *by air* between the United States and Mexico are required to show a passport or other accepted secure document. The passport requirement will be extended to land and sea border crossings on June 1, 2009. Up until this date the U.S., Canadian and Mexican governments also will accept a birth certificate, which must be a certified copy with a raised seal from the government agency that issued it and be accompanied by government-issued photo identification (such as a driver's license).

For those who choose to leave their vehicle on the U.S. side and walk across the border, Border Station Parking, next to the San Diego Factory Outlet Center at the San Ysidro crossing, is open and attended 24 hours daily. It is fenced, lighted and equipped with surveillance equipment. Both short- and long-term pay parking is available. Mexicoach buses depart from the lot for Tijuana and Rosarito Beach. Phone (619) 428-1422.

San Diego Trolley provides transportation to its San Ysidro station (East Beyer Boulevard and East San Ysidro Boulevard) from various downtown San Diego stations, including America Plaza (West C Street and Kettner Boulevard), Civic Center (C Street and 3rd Avenue), 5th Avenue (5th Avenue and C Street) and Gaslamp (5th Avenue and Harbor Drive).

There are public parking lots at each station; daily rates range from $5 to $7. One-way fare from downtown San Diego $3; over 59, $1. For information and schedules phone (619) 233-3004 or (800) 266-6883 (from the United States), (619) 685-4900 (recorded information) or (619) 234-5005 (TTY/TDD); closed Thanksgiving and Dec. 25.

City Layout

The intermittently flowing Tijuana River passes through the heart of Tijuana on its way northwest across the U.S. frontier, where it empties into the Pacific Ocean. The old downtown (referred to as El Centro) is just south of the river and less than a mile south of the San Ysidro border crossing. Busy Avenida Revolución, the heart of the tourist zone, is lined with restaurants, nightclubs and souvenir shops. About a mile to the southeast rise Tijuana's newer, modern office buildings and shopping centers.

Crossing the border on foot is by far the most convenient way to visit Tijuana. If you do choose to drive, follow the signs that say "Downtown Centro"; they will lead you to Calle 3, which runs west to Avenida Revolución. City driving is a daunting task; north-south avenidas Revolución and Constitución and east-west calles 2 and 3, which traverse the downtown core, are very congested. The old-fashioned traffic signals are not readily visible; watch carefully for them.

Traffic circles, or *glorietas,* along northwest-southeast Paseo de los Héroes and Paseo de Tijuana can be confusing; always bear right when entering a traffic circle, following the flow of traffic counterclockwise. There are many one-way street signs. Side streets away from the main business districts are often unpaved, rutted or potholed. Fortunately, several wide through streets facilitate traffic flow through central Tijuana.

Mex 1-D, a divided, fully access-controlled toll highway, provides a quick and safe route south to Ensenada and is preferable to old, free Mex. 1. From the international border, it proceeds west, paralleling the border fence and bypassing much of Tijuana's congestion (follow the "Ensenada Cuota" signs along Calle Internacional). You may, however, encounter detours that route traffic along downtown streets.

Mex. 1-D continues west to Playas de Tijuana, then turns south, with the ocean in view along most of the scenic route. There are three toll plazas between the two cities; the total charge is about $7.25 (U.S.). Toll highway Mex. 2-D runs parallel to the border from Tijuana east to Mexicali; expect to pay about $20 in tolls.

Shopping

Shopping is the No. 1 tourist activity in a city where the options range from French perfume to false teeth. Although the cheap souvenirs manufactured locally for the tourist trade are inescapable (yet somehow irresistible), there is much more to tempt the eyes and wallets of shoppers. Good buys can be found on many Mexican-made articles, including blankets, blown glass, ceramics, guitars, jewelry, leather goods, piñatas, pottery, silver and tin objects, stoneware, straw baskets, sweaters, wrought-iron furniture, hand-tooled saddles and decorative objects.

Because of its status as a duty-free port of entry, Tijuana also offers Rolex watches, Russian caviar, Italian shoes, French cosmetics, European designer fashions, Scottish cashmere sweaters, Oriental rugs, fine crystal, gold jewelry and other international goods, as well as fine-quality Mexican crafts. But although there are certainly bargains to be had, don't assume that prices will automatically be lower than back home; compare before you buy.

Some 10 blocks of Avenida Revolución downtown are lined with souvenir stalls and maze-like arcades filled with curio shops. Shopkeepers call out from doorways, entreating you to stop and look. Haggling is expected if you're buying from street vendors or open-air stalls; in more established shops, ask if bargaining is accepted. The only ground rule is to maintain a serious yet light-hearted approach, for a merchant's initial offering price will usually be about twice what the item is worth.

In this swirl of buying and selling, keep expectations in mind. For example, if you're looking for quality and authenticity in silver jewelry instead of a simple trinket, avoid the street vendors whose arms are garlanded with necklaces. Tijuana is considered the leather capital of Baja, and boots, shoes, sandals, luggage, purses, wallets, briefcases, belts and coats can all be bargained for—but again, check for quality before committing your dollars.

Tijuana has great bargains on such Mexican liquors as Kahlua, tequila, rum, brandy and local Baja wines. The best buys are found not in the smaller liquor stores but in the Mexican grocery stores called *supermercados.* Nondrinkers can stock up on gourmet coffees. Calimax is one of several chains in the city.

For those who would rather browse in a more concentrated area, Tijuana also has standard shopping malls. Plaza Río Tijuana, along Paseo de los Héroes next to the Tijuana Cultural Center, has more than a hundred shops and restaurants, including several department stores, as well as a movie theater multiplex. Pueblo Amigo, a 5-minute walk from the border, has shops, restaurants, nightspots and a Caliente Sportsbook betting facility.

The Hidalgo Market (Mercado M. Hidalgo), a block south of the cultural center, is a typically lively public market filled with fresh produce stalls, art and craft shops, a mind-boggling array of spices, chilies and candy, and a great selection of piñatas.

The Mexican peso and the American dollar are practically interchangeable in Tijuana. This is the one Mexican city where visitors rarely have to worry about currency exchange. Prices are fixed in department stores and the finer shops selling imported items; elsewhere, bargaining is expected. Some stores accept U.S. credit cards.

Sports and Recreation

Recreational diversions in Tijuana have changed little over the years. Some of the world's top matadors perform at two bullrings in town. Bullfights are held on selected Sunday afternoons at 4:30 from May through September; July and August are the busiest months.

During the season sites alternate between Tijuana Bullring (El Toreo de Tijuana), about 3 kilometers (2 miles) east of downtown on Boulevard Agua Caliente, and the larger Bullring-by-the-Sea (Plaza de Toros Monumental), 10 kilometers (6 miles) west of downtown via Mex. 1-D. Reserved and general admission seating is available. Ticket prices range from $15-$50 (U.S.); seats on the shady side of each arena are more expensive. Tickets can be purchased at each bullring; phone (664) 686-1219 for the Bullring-by-the-Sea, (664) 686-1510 for the Tijuana Bullring.

The fast and furious action of jai alai once took place at the Jai Alai Palace (Frontón Palacio), at the corner of Calle 7 and Avenida Revolución. Matches (and the attendant betting) have been discontinued, but the building itself remains a Tijuana landmark, a Moorish-inspired structure with tile mosaics adorning its front.

Next to the Jai Alai Palace is a Caliente Sportsbook betting facility. There are 12 locations scattered throughout Tijuana, including three within walking distance of the border. Here wagers can be placed for most major U.S. and Latin American sporting events; multiple giant-screen TVs broadcast the action.

The Caliente Racetrack (Hipódromo de Caliente), about 5 kilometers (3 miles) east of downtown off Boulevard Agua Caliente, presents greyhound racing nightly at 7:45, plus matinees at 1 Mon.-Tues. and 2 Sat.-Sun. General admission is free. For additional information phone (664) 681-7300.

The Tijuana Country Club (Club Campestre Tijuana), also east of downtown via Boulevard Agua Caliente, boasts an 18-hole golf course designed by Alister MacKenzie, the man responsible for the Pebble Beach and Augusta National courses in the United States. Some tee times are reserved for members. For reservations information, phone (888) 217-1165 (from the United States).

Dining and Nightlife

Gastronomic lore names Tijuana as the birthplace of the Caesar salad, originally intended to serve a crowd of late diners from a restaurant's depleted food supply. Victor's, on Boulevard Sanchez Taboada at Calle Juaquin Clausell in the Zona Río neighborhood, is said to have the best *carne asada* and Caesar salad in the city.

More meat, in the form of huge steaks and lamb chops, can be found at Restaurante Argentino de Tony, in the Pueblo Amigo Center in the Zona Río. For a gourmet Mexican dining experience, try Cien Años, Calle José María Velazco #1407 (just off Paseo de los Héroes) in the Zona Río. The specialties here range from daring (ant eggs) to soothing (squash blossom soup), and the food is stylishly presented. Reservations are recommended.

Hacienda de la Tia Juana, on Calle 1 next to the Tijuana Wax Museum, has a lovely courtyard that is one of the few places in the city where you can have a quiet lunch. The menu includes Caesar salads, Mexican combination plates and beef *tampiqueña*.

For those in search of quick, inexpensive street food, there is a large taco stand at the corner of Calle 3 and Avenida Revolución. These snacks are filling but can play bacterial havoc with stomachs not made of steel. If you indulge, look for food that is hot, freshly prepared and cooked using purified water. For the gastronomically unadventurous, Tijuana has a full complement of familiar franchises such as Dennys, Jack in the Box and McDonalds.

Do not include the 10 percent IVA tax that is automatically added to the check in restaurants when deciding what to tip. A 20 percent tip is not expected in Mexico; 10 percent is acceptable, unless you feel the service has been truly outstanding. *For a list of AAA-RATED dining establishments in Tijuana, see the Lodgings & Restaurants section.*

Loud music—both recorded and live—pours out of the clubs along Avenida Revolución, and shills are stationed at every door luring potential customers with free drink cards. If you do go in, don't look for bargains, as cover charges and drink prices are frequently equal to if not more than similar prices in the states. Most clubs are open Thursday through Sunday evenings.

The Tijuana branch of the Hard Rock Café, Av. Revolución #520 (between calles 1 and 2), is a popular hangout that draws a young, noisy clientele, as does Señor Frog's, part of a Mexican chain, in the Pueblo Amigo shopping center on Paseo Tijuana. Local institution Tijuana Tilly's, next to the Jai Alai Palace on Avenida Revolución at Calle 7, attracts the sports crowd.

Rodeo Santa Fe, also in the Pueblo Amigo center, sports glowing purple and gold icicles on its roof and three levels of music and dancing more or less modeled on the "wild, wild West." There's even a live rodeo at midnight. This club is open late and packed on Friday and Saturday nights.

More sedate are the lobby bars and lounges in such hotels as the Lucerna, in the Zona Río neighborhood along Paseo de los Héroes. Bacarat, in the Grand Hotel Tijuana on Boulevard Agua Caliente, offers a quiet and upscale evening of dinner and dancing. The Zona Río also has a popular dance club, Baby Rock, at Calle Diego Rivera #1482. Expect a dress code; those in jeans and T-shirts won't get in.

Note: While Tijuana promotes fun, remember that you are in a foreign country where a different set of rules and laws are in effect. The police invariably arrest those who are inebriated and causing a disturbance in public, and nothing will ruin a vacation like a night in a Mexican jail and the ensuing bureaucratic hassle to get out.

Baja California State Tourism Secretariat (Secretaría de Turismo): Paseo de los Héroes #10289 at Avenida José Velasco, on the fourth floor of the Nacional Financiera (NAFIN) building; phone (664) 634-6330.

The Tijuana Convention & Visitors Bureau operates three visitor centers with English-speaking staff where you can pick up brochures and obtain information about local attractions and tours. The center located just south of the San Ysidro border crossing is open Mon.-Thurs. 8-5, Fri.-Sat. 8-7, Sun. 8-3; phone (664) 683-1405.

The center across from the elevated pedestrian border crossing is open Mon.-Thurs. 9-5, Fri.-Sat. 8-5, Sun. 8-3; phone (664) 683-4987. The center on Avenida Revolución (between Calles 3 and 4) is open Mon.-Thurs. 10-4, Fri.-Sun. 10-7; phone (664) 685-2210.

There also is a tourist information booth at the Border Station Parking facility just north of the San Ysidro border crossing. It is open daily 9-5; phone (619) 428-6200.

What To See

TIJUANA CULTURAL CENTER (Centro Cultural Tijuana, or CECUT) is on Paseo de los Héroes between calles Javier Mina and Centenario, just n. of the Plaza Río shopping center in the Zona Río section of downtown. Shaped like a giant golf ball, the complex includes a museum, exhibit halls, the Cine IMAX theater (with daily showings in English), a 1,000-seat performing arts theater (Sala de Espectáculos), art gallery, bookstore, shopping arcade and an outdoor sculpture garden (Jardín Caracol). The Museum of the Californias (Museo de las Californias) has historical and geological exhibits about the Baja Peninsula.

Sunday jazz, pop and rock concerts take place on the paved concourse in front of the complex. "Baja P" buses drop passengers off here from the border.

Food is available. Complex open daily 9-7; hours for specific facilities vary. Museum of the Californias Tues.-Sun. 10-6:30. Outdoor sculpture garden Tues.-Sun. 10-7. IMAX film showings Mon.-Fri. on the hour 4-9, Sat.-Sun. on the hour 11-9. Complex free. Museum admission 20 pesos (about $1.95 U.S.), 12 pesos (children); 10 pesos for all Tues.-Wed. Sculpture garden admission 10 pesos, 5 pesos (children); 5 pesos for all Tues.-Wed. IMAX films 45 pesos (about $4.40 U.S.); 25 pesos (ages 3-11). Parking 10 pesos for 3 hours. Phone (664) 687-9650.

TIJUANA WAX MUSEUM is downtown at the corner of Calle 1 and Av. Madero. Figures depict both the famous and infamous from Mexico, the United States and around the world. While some of them bear little resemblance to the actual personage—John F. Kennedy, for example—Michael Jackson is suitably lifelike, and Christopher Columbus, Marilyn Monroe and Jack the Ripper are here as well. Another feature is the convincingly gory Aztec sacrifice diorama.

Mon.-Fri. 10-7, Sat.-Sun. 10-8. Admission $2 (U.S.), free (ages 0-5). Phone (664) 688-2478.

WINERIES

- **L. A. Cetto Winery** is downtown at the corner of Callejón Johnson and Av. Constitución Sur. This large brown building is the aging and tasting complex for the L.A. Cetto Vineyards in the Guadalupe Valley. Tastings and tours of the facility are available. Open Mon.-Fri. 10-6:30, Sat. 10-5. Last tour begins 30 minutes before closing. Tastings $2 (U.S.). Phone (664) 685-3031.

TODOS SANTOS, BAJA CALIFORNIA SUR (E-3)

An old farming and fishing community about 80 kilometers (50 miles) north of Cabo San Lucas, Todos Santos (TOH-dos SAHN-tos) was long isolated from visitors. That changed in 1986 with the completion of Mex. 19 from La Paz south to Cabo San Lucas. Even though large-scale resort development has begun to take shape south of town, Todos Santos ("All Saints") retains a relaxed air and the charms of a traditional Mexican town.

Located just south of the Tropic of Cancer, Todos Santos is tropical but not quite as torrid as the towns lying next to the warm Gulf of California waters. Underground water from the Sierra de la Laguna range, which rises to the east, provides irrigation for groves of mangoes, papayas and avocados. The town's 19th-century status as a sugar cane producer is evidenced by the ruins of a few sugar mills.

The peak tourist season is from October through February; many businesses are closed or open irregular hours from July through September, when the weather is hotter and more humid and the beaches are plagued by mosquitoes. From Oct. 10-14 Todos Santos puts on the Founder's Festival (Festival Fundador), which celebrates the town's founding in 1723.

A persistent urban legend claims that the Hotel California, on Calle Juárez, is the lodging with "plenty of room" referred to in the well-known song by the Eagles and shown on the cover of their same-named 1976 album. The myth (there's no connection) helped bring tourists to town in the 1980s, when the reggae-influenced tune regularly wafted out of the hotel bar. The Hotel California first opened in 1950, closed in the late 1990s for an extensive renovation and reopened in 2004. Standing under the building's arches makes for a popular souvenir photo opportunity. The Hotel's La Coronela Restaurant has live music on Saturday evenings.

Café Todos Santos, on Calle Centenario at Calle Topete (across from the Todos Santos Inn), is where many visitors head for breakfast. The cafe latte comes in a cup the size of the bowl; pair it with a cinnamon bun, sit in the charming garden and while away the morning.

Todos Santos has become an established bohemian enclave. Local galleries include Galería de Todos Santos, Legaspi #33, where works by Mexican and American artists are on display, and Galería Santa Fe, Centenario #4 next to Café Santa Fe, where there is a delightful collection of Mexican folk art.

About 3 kilometers (2 miles) west of town on a dirt road is Playa Punta Lobos. Here local fishermen embark in their *pangas* for the day's catch; visitors can enjoy the dramatic Pacific surf. South of town via Mex. 19, dirt-road turn-offs offer access to unspoiled, unpopulated beaches—good for surfing—along the rocky coastline. Just 23 kilometers (14 miles) east the Sierra de la Laguna Mountains rise to 6,000 feet; pack trips to explore the area can be arranged in town.

Urique River, Copper Canyon, Chihuahua / © A. Littlejohn / Robertstock

Northwestern Mexico

Northwestern Mexico encompasses three of the country's four largest states—Chihuahua, Durango and Sonora—and vast expanses of insurmountable territory. Desolate plateaus stretch for miles, and the sun sets over panoramic mountain and desert vistas. This part of Mexico also is economically rich. Irrigated river valleys produce flourishing crops of cotton, peanuts, sugar cane, tobacco, fruits and vegetables. Extensive ranchlands in Sonora yield what is considered to be the country's best beef cattle. And mining remains important; looming over the city of Durango is one of the world's largest single iron deposits, Mercado Hill (Cerro de Mercado).

One of the most rewarding ways to view northwestern Mexico's rugged scenery is from the window of a passenger train traversing the Copper Canyon region, a complex of interconnected canyons almost four times larger and some 280 feet deeper than the Grand Canyon. Traveling across the rugged Sierra Madre Mountains between the cities of Los Mochis and Chihuahua, the Chihuahua al Pacífico railway traverses the rugged scenery of this spectacular natural area.

The rail line was begun in the late 19th century, envisioned as the shortest trade route linking Kansas City with Mexico's Pacific coast. Finally finished in 1961, it made engineering history after intermittent work was delayed by lack of funds, the 1910 Revolution and what seemed like insurmountable terrain and engineering problems associated with crossing the Sierra Madre. Years of construction, 39 bridges and 87 tunnels were required to move a train from sea level to a maximum altitude of 8,056 feet.

Travel to this remote region, which has increased markedly in recent years, is seen as one way of stemming the uncontrolled logging that continues to take place. Copper Canyon travel packages—many emphasizing an eco-tourism angle—feature coach tours, and some also include guided hiking or horseback riding expeditions or overnight camping trips to canyon-bottom locations.

The region's ruggedness also attracts devotees of extreme sports, and athletes from around the world make their way here to participate in mountain and desert biking competitions, triathlons and one ultra marathon covering 60 miles. For those who aren't prodigiously fit but still desire an active vacation experience, tour companies offer more moderate biking and hiking excursions to such natural wonders as Basaseáchic Falls.

The Copper Canyon is the domain of the Tarahumara Indians, Mexico's largest surviving tribe. Of all of this vast country's native peoples, they have perhaps been the most successful in preserving their centuries-old culture; many still dwell in the shadow of vast mountains and in the isolation of caves set in deep canyons.

The Tarahumara refer to themselves as *rarámuri,* or "foot runners," and it is said that they can run wild turkeys or deer to exhaustion. Both men and women compete in races called *rarajípari,* marathons of stamina that can last several days and cover hundreds of miles.

A harsh climate and landscape long impeded large-scale settlement of this part of Mexico, and there are few ancient ruins or cultural reminders of past greatness. One exception is the Paquimé archeological zone, near the town of Nuevo Casas Grandes in the state of Chihuahua. Designated a World Heritage Site by UNESCO in 1999, this former city was once an important trade and cultural link between the Pueblo culture of the southwestern United States and the more advanced civilizations of Mesoamerica. Paquimé was mysteriously abandoned around the time of the Spanish conquest, and the extensive ruins left behind have only been partially excavated.

The industrialized big cities are not as immediately appealing as, say, Mexico's beach resorts. Hermosillo was named after Jaliscan general José María González Hermosillo, a patriot in the Mexican War of Independence from Spain. A huge Ford assembly plant is representative of the region's industrial expansion. Appropriately, the city's most distinctive landmark is a rocky outcrop right in the center of town that is covered with a web of radio antennas.

Chihuahua, founded in 1709, is one of northwestern Mexico's major cities. *Perritos chihuahueños,* the very small dog breed that shares the city's name, is not originally from Mexico; it is thought that Jesuit priests brought the first chihuahuas to the country from the Philippines in the 18th century.

A day-trip destination and the gateway to north-central Mexico is the major border city of Ciudad Juárez, opposite El Paso. Home to nearly 1.5 million people, it is an interesting hybrid of both countries, much like Tijuana. The traditional tourist shopping area is within walking distance of the border, along Avenida Juárez. English is as widely spoken here as Spanish.

Durango, officially known as Victoria de Durango, is a major crossroads, sitting at the junction of Mex. 40, which connects Monterrey and Mazatlán, and Mex. 45, which leads to Mexico City. The city rises from the level Guadiana Valley, which is bordered by the foothills of the Sierra Madre Occidental. Visitors passing through on the main roadways linking Mex. 40 and 45 will see few of the city's attractions; much of Durango's charm lies in a 17th- and 18th-century architectural legacy, for which it has been designated a national historic monument. Fortunately, the mild climate (due to elevation) makes the city pleasant to explore on foot.

Two small but growing gulf of California resorts are in the state of Sonora. San Carlos, just outside the port city of Guaymas, is in an area known for deep-sea fishing, while Puerto Peñasco is especially popular with residents of nearby California and Arizona due to its easy accessibility.

For a taste of authentic Mexico, head to Alamos, situated in the foothills of the Sierra Madre Occidental in Sonora's southeastern corner. This designated national historic monument is the site of an established expatriate community. Some 52 kilometers (32 miles) east of Navojoa via Mex. 10, it's about a 5-hour drive from the U.S. border at Nogales. The presence of cottonwood trees, blooming flowers and elegantly restored colonial-era mansions make Alamos an oasis of sorts in the otherwise barren landscape of coastal Sonora.

Perhaps the spookiest place in all Mexico is the Zone of Silence (Zona del Silencio), at the point where the state borders of Chihuahua, Coahuila and Durango meet. For unexplained reasons it attracts meteor showers and also is said to prevent radio wave activity, hence the name. The mysteries associated with this remote area—about 130 kilometers (81 miles) north of the city of Torreón to the village of Ceballos, then about 40 kilometers (25 miles) east via a rough road—intrigue stargazers as well as proponents of UFOs.

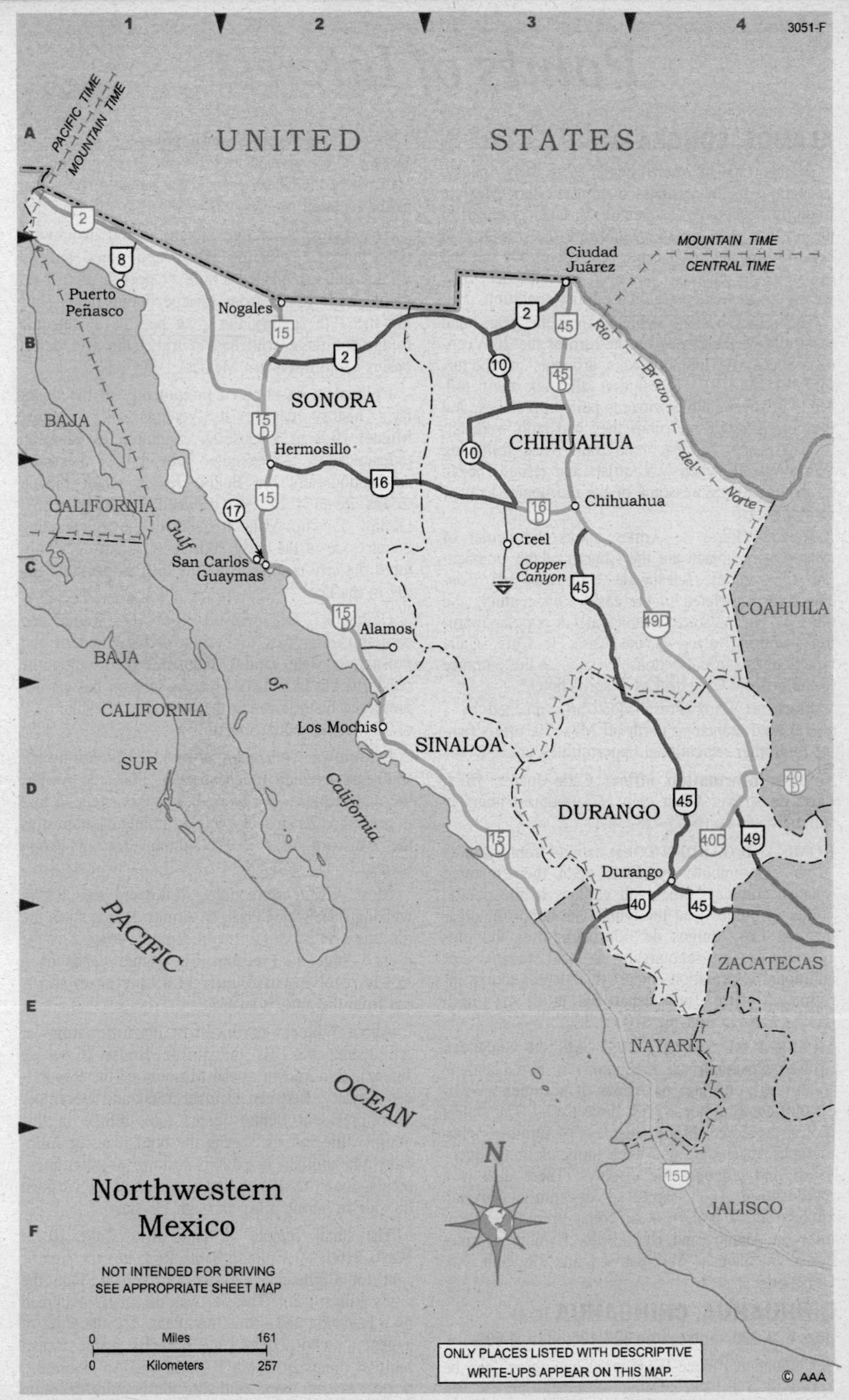

1
2
3
4
3051-F
A
B
C
D
E
F
PACIFIC TIME
MOUNTAIN TIME
UNITED
STATES
MOUNTAIN TIME
CENTRAL TIME
Ciudad Juárez
Puerto Peñasco
Nogales
SONORA
CHIHUAHUA
BAJA
CALIFORNIA
Hermosillo
Chihuahua
Río Bravo del Norte
Creel
Copper Canyon
San Carlos
Guaymas
Gulf of California
COAHUILA
Alamos
BAJA
CALIFORNIA
SUR
Los Mochis
SINALOA
DURANGO
Durango
PACIFIC
ZACATECAS
NAYARIT
OCEAN
N
JALISCO
Northwestern Mexico
NOT INTENDED FOR DRIVING
SEE APPROPRIATE SHEET MAP
0 Miles 161
0 Kilometers 257
ONLY PLACES LISTED WITH DESCRIPTIVE WRITE-UPS APPEAR ON THIS MAP.
© AAA

Points of Interest

ALAMOS, SONORA (C-2)

Alamos (AH-lah-mohs) began as an early Spanish stronghold in the vastness of northwestern Mexico. Explorer Francisco Vásquez de Coronado camped in the area as early as 1540, unaware that the ground beneath him held rich deposits of silver. By the end of the 17th century, however, a settlement had sprung up to service regional mining operations.

The mines became depleted over the years, and were all but abandoned by the turn of the 20th century. Successive Indian attacks, droughts and the turmoil of the 1910 Revolution all took their toll. Many of the wealthier citizens pulled up stakes, and the colonial-style mansions they had built were left to deteriorate. A turnaround took place following World War II, when U.S. artists and retirees began to arrive and restore some of the old homes to their former glory.

Arcaded Plaza de Armas marks the center of town. On the plaza are the Church of the Immaculate Conception (Iglesia de la Inmaculada Concepción), completed in the early 19th century, and the City Hall (Palacio Municipal). A popular morning gathering place is the Casa de Café, Calle Obregón #10, a coffeehouse located at the entrance to the historic Casa de Los Tesoros hotel.

Mocuzari Dam (Presa Mocuzari), reached by a gravel road branching north off Mex. 10, offers fishing and other recreational opportunities.

Tourist information office: Calle Juárez #6 at Plaza de Armas. Open daily 9-7 (reduced hours in summer); phone (647) 428-0450.

HOME AND GARDEN TOUR departs from Plaza de Armas. Community residents open their restored Spanish colonial homes and gardens to the public; volunteer guides lead the tours. The nonprofit organization Los Amigos de Educación uses the proceeds to provide scholarships to local students. For additional information contact the Alamos tourist information office. Tours depart Sat. at 10 a.m., mid-Oct. to May 1. Tour fee $10 (U.S.).

MUSEUM OF SOCIAL CUSTOMS OF SONORA (Museo Costumbrista de Sonora) is at Guadalupe Victoria #1 on Plaza de Armas. It occupies a 19th-century colonial house with three patios. The state's past is preserved through displays of furniture, photographs, machinery and work tools, clothing, documents and ethnographic displays. There also is a reproduction of a typical 19th-century Mexican kitchen and a collection of coins from the former mints in Alamos and Hermosillo. Exhibit information is in Spanish. Wed.-Sat. 9-1 and 3-6, Sun. 9-6. Donations.

CHIHUAHUA, CHIHUAHUA (C-3)

pop. 678,000, metro area 822,100, elev. 4,690′

Chihuahua's (chee-WAH-wah) beginnings can be traced to a frontier mining settlement in the late 17th century. When Spanish governor Antonio de Deza y Ulloa arrived in 1709, he decided upon the spot where the Chuvíscar and Sacramento rivers met as the location for a new townsite.

The Spaniards drafted Indians to toil in labyrinthine mines, extracting silver and other mineral wealth, and established a military post to protect regional trade routes from Apache Indian raids. During the 19th century the town became a welcome refuge for those who had to travel the arid desert basins of northwestern Mexico.

Chihuahua has figured prominently in the country's history despite its geographical isolation. Miguel Hidalgo y Costilla, champion of Mexican independence, was executed here in 1811. It served as headquarters for Benito Juárez when French troops invaded Mexico between 1862 and 1867. Outlaw Pancho Villa frequented the surrounding countryside in the early 20th century and once captured the city by disguising his men as peasants going to market.

Chihuahua has evolved from its mining and cattle-breeding past to become a big, modern and prosperous state capital. Industrial plants clog the outskirts, but like many Mexican cities it has a well-preserved historic center that manages to evoke a bit of 19th-century atmosphere.

Downtown Chihuahua is divided by northwest/southeast Avenida Independencia; Plaza de Armas, the main square, is a block below this street. A taxi is needed to reach such outlying points of interest as the Museum of the Revolution *(see attraction listing)*.

Most visitor attractions, however, are within walking distance of Plaza de Armas. Rising from the plaza is a 115-foot-tall marble column topped by the bronze Angel of Freedom. The statue stands on a slowly revolving base; at night a laser beam shoots out from the angel's sword.

About 3 blocks northwest of Plaza de Armas at Av. Juárez #321 is the Juárez House (Casa de Juárez), also known as the Museum of the Republican Loyalty. Between October 1864 and December 1866 president Benito Juárez took refuge in this house while in exile during the brief reign of Archduke Maximilian. It exhibits historic objects, documents signed by Juárez and a replica of the carriage he rode in during a trip through the state.

The small Temple of Santa Rita, Calle 10 de Mayo #1601-A, Colonia Santa Rita, is very significant for Chihuahuans, who consider St. Rita the city's patron saint. The site was originally occupied by a hacienda and a smelting plant. The daughter of a general who acquired the property had a chapel built in honor of Santa Rita. In 1837 it became a hospice for the poor, initiating the popular devotion for Santa Rita. The chapel was restored in 1949 and retains its original beams.

The city's ancient aqueduct was begun in 1706, prior to its founding, in order for canoes to carry water from the Chuvíscar River to a smelting hacienda. The ditches dug for the canoes provided the foundation for a stone aqueduct completed in 1854; some of the semicircular arches can still be seen.

Lerdo Park, on Paseo Bolívar southeast of Plaza de Armas, is the scene of Sunday concerts. Seasonal Sunday afternoon bullfights take place at the 7,500-seat Plaza La Esperanza. For a good selection of Tarahumara and other regional crafts, visit the House of Crafts of the State of Chihuahua (Casa de las Artesanías del Estado de Chihuahua), at Av. Juárez #705 (across from the Federal Palace).

The El Tarahumara Trolley is a convenient way to sightsee in downtown Chihuahua. Service begins in front of the city's cathedral, facing the main plaza; the 19-passenger trolley completes the tour loop in 1 hour and runs daily 9-6. One ticket allows passengers to get on and off at different stops up to four times in the same day.

The 2-week Santa Rita Fair, which takes place in mid-May, is a major local event dating back to colonial-era celebrations of Chihuahua's patron saint. This family-oriented fair offers rides, arts and crafts, traditional food and cultural events.

Interesting day trips can be made to Aquiles Serdán (also known as Santa Eulalia), east of the city via Mex. 45, and to Aldama, north via Mex. 16. Reputedly the oldest mining town in northern Mexico, Santa Eulalia has been restored and has a cathedral, the Templo de Santa Eulalia de Mérida, that contains impressive religious artwork. Near Aldama, in the center of an important fruit-producing area, are the ruins of the Santa Ana de Chinarras Mission, founded by Jesuits in 1717.

Note: Many roads out of the city are four-lane and divided for a considerable distance, traversing open, desertlike areas; driving at night is not recommended.

Chihuahua State Tourism Office (Información Turística del Estado): Av. Libertad and Calle 13, 2nd floor; phone (614) 429-3596 or 01 (800) 508-0111 (toll-free long distance within Mexico). A branch office is at the main entrance to the Government Palace; phone (614) 429-3300, ext. 4515.

CASA REDONDA MUSEUM (Museo Casa Redonda) is n.w. of Plaza de Armas via Av. Independencia to Av. Escudero; the museum is at Av. Escudero and Av. Tecnológico/Colón. The name (Round House) is a reference to the building's circular shape and original purpose: It was once a maintenance and repair shop for steam locomotives. In addition to a permanent exhibit documenting the history of railroads in the region, there are rotating displays of contemporary art.

Allow 1 hour minimum. Tues.-Sun. 10-8, Feb.-Nov.; 10-6, rest of year. Admission 5 pesos. Phone (614) 414-9061.

CATHEDRAL faces Plaza de Armas. This ornate, twin-towered church of pink-hued stone is perhaps northern Mexico's finest example of baroque architecture. Although it was begun in 1725, Indian wars delayed completion until 1826. The Museum of Sacred Art (Museo de Arte Sacro) in the cathedral basement has a collection of 18th-century religious-themed paintings by Miguel Cabrera, José de Alcíbar and Antonio de Torres.

To the left of the main entrance is the beautiful Christ of Mapimí Chapel, where a cross-shaped niche holds a venerated image of Christ. Museum open Mon.-Fri. 10-2. Cathedral free, museum admission about $1.50 (U.S.).

CHURCH OF SAN FRANCISCO (Iglesia de San Francisco) is n.e. of Plaza de Armas on Calle Libertad (at Calle 15). Begun by Franciscan missionaries and dedicated to St. Joseph, it was consecrated in 1721. Architecturally similar to Franciscan missions in northern Mexico, the church's exterior is relatively plain. The interior has a roomy cross-shaped nave, beamed roofing, 18th-century altarpieces and a majestic cupola. Bricklayer Nicolás Muñoz built the bell tower in 1740. Open daily. Free.

FEDERAL PALACE (Palacio Federal) is several blks. e. of Plaza de Armas via pedestrian-only Calle Libertad, at Av. Juárez and Vicente Guerrero. It dates from 1910 and houses the main post office. Within the building is Hidalgo's Dungeon, which preserves the cell in which Father Miguel Hidalgo was held prisoner by the Spanish while awaiting execution. It exhibits the freedom fighter's crucifix, pistol and other personal belongings, as well as a plaque inscribed with a message Hidalgo dedicated to his captors for their humane treatment.

Museum open Tues.-Sun. 9-6. Admission about 50c (U.S.).

GOVERNMENT PALACE (Palacio de Gobierno) is a block s. of the Federal Palace, on the n. side of Plaza Hidalgo at Calle Aldama and Calle Venustiano Carranza. The Chihuahua state capitol was built 1881-92; a third floor was added during reconstruction after a 1941 fire destroyed a large part of the building. Inside are enormous archways, a large central patio and first-floor walls covered with noteworthy murals depicting the state's history. A beautiful stained-glass window above the main staircase illustrates themes of law and justice.

It was here that Father Miguel Hidalgo was executed by firing squad in 1811 during the War of Independence. The Nation's Altar (Altar de la Patria) on the ground floor marks the exact spot where he died. The Hidalgo Museum has a re-creation of the church facade in Dolores Hidalgo from which the priest turned freedom fighter issued his call for independence, while the Gallery of Arms displays an impressive array of weapons. Both museums incorporate state-of-the-art interactive media displays.

Allow 1 hour minimum. Daily 8-8. Free.

MUSEUM OF THE REVOLUTION (Museo de la Revolución) is about 1 km (.6 mi.) s. of the historic city center at Calle 10 Norte #3014. It was the home of Pancho Villa, a revolutionary leader who sympathized with the hardships endured by the Mexican peasant majority. It also is known as Quinta Luz in honor of Villa's wife Dona Luz, who lived here until her death in the early 1980s.

The 50-room mansion, a museum dedicated to the Mexican Revolution of 1910, displays military uniforms, period firearms (including some machine guns), and a collection of photographs of Villa and his cohorts. The bullet-riddled Dodge in which he was ambushed and killed is parked in a courtyard.

An equestrian statue of the *generalísimo* by Chihuahuan sculptor Ignacio Asúnsulo stands at avenidas Universidad and División del Norte. Exhibit information is in Spanish. Allow 1 hour minimum. Tues.-Sat. 9-1 and 3-7, Sun. 10-4; closed May 1 and Dec. 25. Admission 10 pesos. Phone (614) 416-2958.

NOMBRE DE DIOS CAVERNS (Grutas de Nombre de Dios) are in the northeastern part of the city, about a 20-minute drive from downtown Chihuahua via Calz. H. Colegio Militar, then along dirt roads following the blue-and-white signs. Stalactite and stalagmite formations in these small caves are said to resemble Don Quixote, a dinosaur head and the Leaning Tower of Pisa, among other things. Tours with English-speaking guides are available.

The path through the caverns is fairly dark and has some tight passages and a couple of steep inclines; the tour is not recommended for those prone to claustrophobia. Food is available. Allow 1 hour, 30 minutes minimum. Tues.-Fri. 9-4, Sat.-Sun. and Mexican holidays 10-4:30. Admission 40 pesos (about $3.90 U.S.); 20 pesos (ages 5-10).

QUINTA GAMEROS is at Paseo Bolívar #401, about 8 blks. n.w. of the main plaza. The cultural center for the University of Chihuahua occupies a restored turn-of-the-20th-century mansion—named for Manuel Gameros, the wealthy mining engineer who commissioned its construction—and furnished in Art Nouveau style. The main reason to visit is not the university's collection of art on the second floor but the building's stained-glass windows, intricately carved wooden staircases and lavish interior decoration and furniture.

Tues.-Sun. 11-2 and 4-7. Admission about $3 (U.S.). Phone (614) 416-6684.

CIUDAD JUAREZ, CHIHUAHUA (B-3)

pop. 1,257,200, elev. 5,000′

On the Rio Grande opposite El Paso, Tex., the sprawling border city of Ciudad Juárez (HWAH-res) is an overall economic success story: More than 400 manufacturing plants in 17 industrial parks employ some 250,000 people. Northern Mexico's principal highways and railroads converge here, making Ciudad Juárez a transportation center as well.

In 1581 Don Juan de Onate crossed the Rio Grande River in the vicinity of present-day Juárez, the first Spanish explorer to do so. It wasn't until 1668, however, that Franciscan friar Father Garcia de San Francisco founded the Mission of Our Lady of Guadalupe (Misión de Nuestra Señora de Guadalupe), which still stands on the west side of Plaza de Armas in downtown Ciudad Juárez. While it has a very plain exterior, the interior beamed roofing is profusely decorated with geometric designs.

Next to the mission is the much newer Cathedral, built in 1935 but restored and enlarged in 1976. It boasts lovely stained-glass windows.

Much of the fighting during the 1910 Mexican Revolution took place around Ciudad Juárez and Chihuahua. The treaty ending the conflict and resulting in the resignation of president and dictator Porfirio Díaz was signed in the old Customs House, now the History Museum (Museo Histórico), on the east side of Plaza de Armas. This distinctive-looking building, which dates from 1889, features finely carved wood and beautiful ironwork.

Just across the Bridge of the Americas off Avenida Lincoln is El Chamizal Park. Mexico claimed El Chamizal after the Mexican-American War established the Río Grande as the international border in 1848. However, the land fell into U.S. possession when the river changed its course 16 years later. It wasn't until 1967 that President Lyndon Johnson returned approximately 640 acres to Mexico, a goodwill gesture initiated by John F. Kennedy; the land was turned into a park.

Within the park is the Archaeology Museum. It contains mostly replicas of representative pre-Hispanic artifacts—such as a Chac Mool sculpture, an Olmec head and decorative motifs associated with the ruins of Uxmal and Teotihuacán—displayed in an outdoor garden.

Bullfights take place at the Plaza de Toros Monumental, on the east side of town just south of Avenida 16 de Septiembre (Mex. 45) and east of the junction with Avenida López Mateos. Famous bullfighters come here during the season, which runs from April to September.

Expo-Juárez is held each year in June and July. This major fair offers more than 200 booths displaying everything from locally made crafts and candy to furniture and jewelry, along with rides, theatrical performances, regional cuisine and performances by the Papantla Flyers. An arena, or *palenque*, is the setting for cockfights, bingo games and concerts by international singers.

Border Tips

The border crossing at Santa Teresa, New Mexico, just west of El Paso, is recommended only for travelers who plan to bypass Ciudad Juárez and continue into Chihuahua; the crossing is in a rural area, off the beaten track for tourists. Banjercito offices here and at the 30-kilometer (19-mile) mark on Mex. 45 (Juárez-Chihuahua Highway) are the only local agencies that will process the paperwork necessary for vehicle travel into the interior.

Several bridges facilitate travel into Ciudad Juárez. The Ysleta-Zaragoza Bridge (toll) on Zaragoza Avenue enters Mexico east of Ciudad Juárez. From US 54 south of I-10, the Cordova Bridge (Bridge of the Americas, or the "free bridge") enters Juárez via Avenida Lincoln.

The Santa Fe Street Bridge is the most convenient bridge to use if you are walking across the border for a day visit; there is plenty of parking on the U.S. side. Once across the border, Santa Fe Street becomes Avenida Juárez. The bridge is one way northbound for vehicles.

The Stanton Street Bridge (toll fee $1.25 per vehicle, free for pedestrians) is one way southbound, entering Juárez from Stanton Street in El Paso; once across the border the street becomes Avenida Lerdo.

Motorists returning to the United States from downtown Juárez must use the northbound-only Paseo del Norte Bridge (toll fee $2 per vehicle, $1.50 for pedestrians) via Avenida Juárez to Santa Fe Street, or the nontoll Bridge of the Americas via Avenida Lincoln. Lines are often long, especially at the free bridge. **Note:** Dollars or pesos are accepted when entering or departing Mexico or the United States. Baggage may be inspected at the customs offices.

Both Mexican and U.S. Customs and Border Protection offices are open 24 hours daily. AAA/CAA members can obtain Mexican auto insurance and make arrangements for bus tours of the city through the El Paso office of AAA Texas; phone (915) 778-9521 (from the United States).

Note: All U.S. and Canadian citizens traveling *by air* between the United States and Mexico are required to show a passport or other accepted secure document. The passport requirement will be extended to land and sea border crossings on June 1, 2009. Up until this date the U.S., Canadian and Mexican governments also will accept a birth certificate, which must be a certified copy with a raised seal from the government agency that issued it and be accompanied by government-issued photo identification (such as a driver's license).

Note: Mexico's border region continues to experience drug-related violence. Visitors should stick to established tourist areas during daylight hours only. Avoid the area west of Avenida Juárez as it extends south toward Avenida 16 de Septiembre in general, and especially after dark. If driving in the city, do not park in any area that appears to be restricted, as your license plates may be confiscated.

Tourist information center: in El Chamizal Park, just across the border via the Bridge of the Americas (Cordova Bridge). Open daily 9-9; phone (888) 654-0394 (from the United States), or 01 (800) 201-5589 (toll-free long distance within Mexico). The center offers travel guides and bilingual assistance to those visiting the state of Chihuahua, as well as general information about Mexico.

Shopping areas: Shoppers will want to visit the orange-and-blue Juárez Market (Mercado Juárez), on Avenida 16 de Septiembre a couple of blocks east of Plaza de Armas. It offers a variety of low-priced handicrafts from all over Mexico, including blankets, silver and turquoise jewelry, leather goods, pottery and curios. There also are a couple of open-air cafes in front of the market.

The Arts and Crafts Center (Centro Artesanal), at avenidas Lincoln and Ignacio Mejía across from the Museum of Art and History, also has a wide selection of high-quality crafts.

MUSEUM OF ART is e. of downtown and s. of Chamizal Park at avs. Lincoln and Coyoacán, in Plaza de las Americas (the Zona Pronaf area). Built in 1964 and designed by architect Pedro Ramírez Vázquez, the museum displays works by both local and international artists. Tues.-Sun. 11-7; closed Mexican holidays. Admission $1 (U.S.).

GEM COPPER CANYON, CHIHUAHUA (C-3)

The Copper Canyon (Barranca del Cobre) area of northwestern Mexico was created by more than 60 million years of geological upheaval. Over time the ash deposited by volcanic eruptions built up to form massive plateaus; further volcanic activity created gaping cracks that were subsequently eroded by rain and subterranean water to carve twisting canyons. Within this extensive canyon system are rivers that are rendered all but unnavigable due to boulder fields and lofty waterfalls.

The name "Copper Canyon" is something of a misnomer; although one canyon along a section of the Urique River is named Barranca del Cobre, the Copper Canyon as a whole actually comprises more than 20 canyons covering some 25,000 square miles. There are six main canyon systems: the Urique, Copper, Cusarare and Tararecua canyons; Batopilas Canyon; Candamena Canyon; Huapoca Canyon; the Oteros, Chínipas and Septentrion canyons; and Sinforosa Canyon. Mountain elevations within the entire region range from 7,500 to 9,500 feet, with a few peaks reaching 12,000 feet.

This rugged and forbidding region has long been inhabited by the Rarámuri Indians. Also known as the Tarahumara, these mountain dwellers have managed to preserve their ancient way of life more successfully than other Native American groups. Although sharing a common ancestry with the warrior-like Aztecs, the peaceful Tarahumara could not have been more different. Settling the plains of central Chihuahua, they grew corn, beans and squash, constructing irrigation canals to make the arid land productive. The Tarahumara took advantage of more than 250 varieties of edible and medicinal plants, and also were renowned for their stamina, chasing down game through sheer dogged determination until the animals collapsed from exhaustion.

By the end of the 16th century Spanish explorers, searching for silver and other precious metals, had penetrated Mexico's northern territories and the region occupied by the Tarahumara. Commissioned to

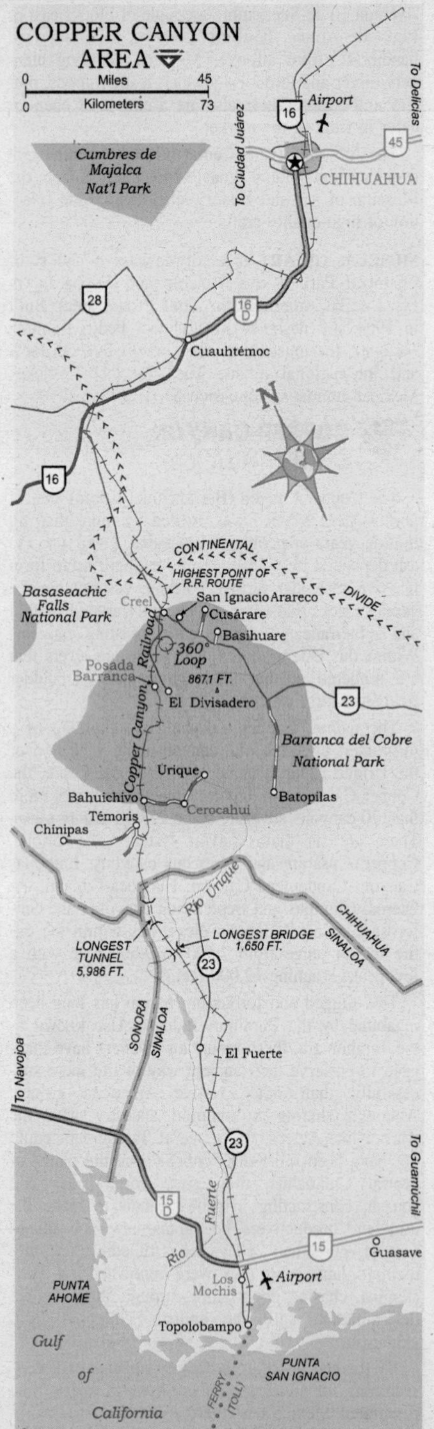

secure new lands for the Spanish crown and lured by tales of unimaginable wealth, these men were recruited with the promise of an *encomienda*—a grant to employ the native people, who were in turn supposed to be paid for their services. The expedition parties were accompanied by missionary priests, who established churches and schools meant to "civilize" and convert the Indians to Christianity.

During the 17th century Spanish settlers enslaved many Tarahumara, forcing them to toil in mines and carry goods across terrain that was too rough for even horses to negotiate. To escape servitude many of them retreated deep into the remote Copper Canyon sierra country. Their descendants continue to live here today, working small ranches or farms and living in simple huts. Some of the more reclusive Tarahumara still dwell in remote mountain caves in the summer, migrating to the warmer *barrancas* (canyon bottoms) in winter.

It was not until the beginning of the 20th century that this vast and inhospitable region was penetrated by a railroad. Construction of the Chihuahua-Pacific Railway (Chihuahua al Pacífico) began in 1898 but was not completed until 1961. One of Mexico's noteworthy engineering feats, the 941-kilometer (588-mile) rail line begins at Ojinaga, just across the border from Presidio, Tex., and ends at the Pacific coast port of Topolobampo. It boasts 99 tunnels and 39 bridges. Within a distance of less than 125 miles, numerous switchbacks drop from an elevation of more than 7,000 feet in the mountains to near sea level on the coastal plain.

One of the railway's most dramatic stretches is the approach to the station at Témoris, where three different levels of track hug one mountainside. Another breathtaking view unfolds at the small mountain village of Divisadero, at an elevation of about 7,400 feet. Here the Urique, Copper and Tararecua canyons are all visible, a vast overlapping series of rust-colored walls punctuated by the green of pine-clad ridges.

A fascinating aspect of the Copper Canyon region is the dramatic difference between environments. On canyon rims and atop high plateaus—where the altitude exceeds 8,000 feet—winters are cold and summers mild, with abundant rain. Fragrant forests of pine and Douglas fir cloak these highlands, and the verdant mesa tops are bright with wildflowers from the end of September into October.

At lower levels grow pines, junipers and oaks, with shade-tolerant, red-barked madrona trees flourishing in their understory. Alders and poplars add blazing color in the fall. In contrast, canyon bottoms—often a mile below the rim—are subtropical. Palms and towering fig and ceiba trees—the latter characterized by buttressed roots and a huge, spreading canopy of leaves—grow where water is available. Wildlife is plentiful, ranging from badgers, otters and skunks to little-seen ocelots to such endangered bird species as the military macaw and the thick-billed parrot.

Creel *(see separate listing within this region)* is a major stop on the rail line and functions as a base for trips to explore towns and villages in the Copper Canyon. Hotels in Creel can arrange guided day or overnight trips to towns on the canyon floor. Rough paved or dirt-gravel roads descend to the towns of Cusárare, Basíhuare and Batopilas; from Bahuichivo to Cerocahui; and from Témoris to Chínipas. Some lodgings in the Copper Canyon, while comfortable, lack electricity and telephones; the key word is rustic.

The usual mode of transportation for a trip to canyon-bottom towns is a school bus, and the ride can be dusty and bone-jarring. Sturdy walking shoes are absolutely essential for exploring; even guided hikes may involve anything from fording a brook to clambering over fallen logs. If you hire a guide make certain that he is familiar with your destination, for much of this region is still authentic wilderness.

From the train station at Bahuichivo, a trip can be arranged to the mountain village of Cerocahui, where a Jesuit mission was established in the late 17th century. Local hotels can arrange round-trip excursions from Bahuichivo to the canyon-bottom village of Urique. Cusárare, about 19 kilometers (12 miles) from Creel, also has a Jesuit mission that was built in order to minister to the Tarahumara. In the vicinity is Lake Arareco *(see Creel)* and an area of volcanic rock formations that resemble mushrooms.

A trip to the town of Batopilas, about 129 kilometers (80 miles) southwest of Creel, is an 8-hour adventure if taken by local bus. The narrow, dusty dirt road to the canyon bottom passes Cerro El Pastel (Cake Mountain), named for its alternating layers of pink and white volcanic rock. The Urique and Basíhuare rivers trace tight, meandering paths before their headwaters lose themselves in unnamed chasms. As the route descends temperatures rise, and forest of pine are replaced by stands of cactus.

Batopilas itself is a former silver-mining town. It began to boom in the 1740s, although mining operations had been in existence for more than 100 years before that. According to local legend, the town's cobblestone streets were once paved with silver. Distinctly different from the canyon-top villages, Batopilas has whitewashed houses, swaying palm trees and gardens of subtropical flowers—temperatures here are some 30 degrees warmer than at the top of the canyon. Local ranchers ride into town on horseback, and the occasional goat or pig can be seen wandering the streets. Accommodations for overnight stays are modest.

Practicalities

Allow plenty of time to take this rail journey. First-class trains depart from both Chihuahua and Los Mochis in the early morning (around 6 a.m.) and take anywhere from 14 to 17 hours (depending on whether there are weather-related delays) to cover the 654-kilometer (406-mile) distance between the two cities. Because of the length of the journey it's necessary to spend at least one night en route to better experience what the region has to offer. Creel has the most lodging options, but hotels in the vicinity of the train stations also can be quite expensive. More rustic cabin accommodations are a short taxi ride from the stations, but amenities are likely to be quite basic.

During the winter months, leaving from Los Mochis or El Fuerte guarantees seeing the most spectacular scenery in full daylight; coming from Chihuahua, towering canyon walls can block the last rays of the sun and magnify the gathering gloom of evening. Summer's extended daylight hours, however, make this decision less crucial. Also keep in mind that you will not really experience the true magnificence of the Copper Canyon from either a train car or a station platform; take a bus or horseback tour to one of the various canyon rim viewing points in order to fully appreciate the views.

Temperatures can be quite cold December through February at the higher elevations, and the canyon bottoms are uncomfortably hot in May and June. The best times of the year to take this trip are March and April or late September through October, when both the sierra wildflowers and fall foliage are at their colorful peak. There may be fewer travelers from August into September, and the landscape will be green from summer rains. Avoid May and June, the driest time of the year; browned-out vegetation and hazy skies are not the best showcase for the Copper Canyon's natural beauty.

Noteworthy fiestas focusing on Indian rituals are held during Holy Week (Palm Sunday to Easter Sunday) and during the Christmas holiday season in Cusárare, Chínipas, San Ignacio Arareco and other Tarahumara towns.

The easiest way to arrange a tour of the Copper Canyon is through a travel agency or rail tour company that offers an all-inclusive trip package. These packages normally include applicable ground transportation (but not airfare to and from the point of departure), lodgings, meals and sightseeing excursions. Mexico-based Camp David provides organized train tours (*See color ad p. 197*) on the Chihuahua-Pacific rail line that depart from Los Mochis and also feature sightseeing in Cerocahui, Creel and at the Gulf of California coast; phone (866) 247-3464 (from the United States or Canada).

Sharing the rails with the Chihuahua-Pacific Railway are deluxe classic cars like those operated by the Arizona-based Sierra Madre Express tour company. Their standard Copper Canyon itinerary departs from Nogales, Son., and includes stays at Divisadero and Cerocahui plus sightseeing trips to the villages of Cusárare and Bahuichivo. For further information write Sierra Madre Express, P.O. Box 2475, Cortaro, AZ 85652-2475; from the United States or Canada phone (520) 747-0346 or (800) 666-0346.

Note: Tour companies outside of Mexico do not sell individual train tickets, only tickets that are part of a tour package that includes lodgings and transportation. They cannot provide information regarding point-to-point travel along the Chihuahua-Pacific Railway route.

If you would rather schedule your own itinerary, travel agencies in Chihuahua and Los Mochis sell individual train tickets that can be ordered by phone. In Chihuahua, Turismo al Mar, Calle Berna #2202, sells train tickets in addition to organized Copper Canyon tour packages ranging from 4 to 8 days; phone (614) 410-9232 or (877) 228-1288 (from the United States).

In Los Mochis, the Viajes Flamingo travel agency in the Hotel Santa Anita, downtown at avenidas Gabriel Leyva and Hidalgo, sells advance first-class train tickets from Los Mochis to Chihuahua (a service fee is charged) and can make arrangements for an overnight stay at the hotel and early morning shuttle transportation to the train station. The agency also sells organized Copper Canyon tour packages that include train tickets, transfers and hotel accommodations; phone (668) 818-7046 or (800) 896-8196 (from the United States).

Since the train passes through flat, visually uninteresting grasslands for the first hour or so out of Los Mochis, an alternative is to begin the trip in El Fuerte, a small, bustling town on the banks of the El Fuerte River that dates back to 1564. The original Spanish fort here has been preserved as a historical museum, and there are fine views of the river and the town from the parapets. El Fuerte has a number of reasonably priced lodging choices as well as a more leisurely departure time for the train (around 8:30 a.m.). The railway station is about 6 kilometers (4 miles) east of town, so allow enough time to get there.

Although tickets can be purchased on the train, if you're planning your own trip it's advisable to purchase them in advance to ensure reserved seating; also inquire about which side of the train offers the best views. The Chihuahua-Pacific Railway was privatized in 1998; the passenger train popular with tourists ("El Chepe") was refurbished, and security measures were tightened. First-class service features air-conditioned cars, reclining seats and picture windows.

Although most first-class trains have dining car service, and vendors at stops hawk homemade burritos and other items, you may want to pack your own food. It's also a good idea to bring water and toilet paper, just in case. Second-class passenger trains, used as transportation by locals, are not recommended for touring unless you want an authentic Mexican experience (complete with livestock).

URIQUE CANYON LOOKOUT TOUR departs from the village of Cerocahui, which is accessible only by train. If you've only seen the Copper Canyon from a train window, this guided tour organized by the Hotel Misión is well worth it for breathtaking, up-close vistas of the region's deepest canyon. The tour includes a visit to a Tarahumara cave home/shop selling handmade baskets. The drive from Cerocahui to the lookout point takes about 2 hours one way.

Daily tours depart in the morning and afternoon. Fee $22 (U.S.). Phone (668) 818-7046.

CREEL, CHIHUAHUA (C-3) elev. 7,650′

The logging village of Creel (creh-EHL) was once the western terminus of the Chihuahua al Pacífico Railway; it is now the approximate midway point. Although the quantity of pine shipped from the vicinity has diminished over the years, active lumber camps still operate. A concrete statue of Christ gazes down from the cliffs north of town, testimony to the Jesuit priests who have ministered to the Tarahumara since the early 17th century.

Creel retains much of its raw charm despite an ever-developing tourist industry. Almost every lodging, restaurant and service is on or within walking distance of the main street, López Mateos. Men ride by on horseback, and resplendently dressed Tarahumara women sell pottery and baskets from the curbsides. Several shops also sell Tarahumara arts and crafts, which include rugs, wood carvings, necklaces, dolls and violins. The Tarahumara Mission Store also has crafts, and the Indians benefit from all sales.

This is the largest settlement in the Copper Canyon area and makes a good base for exploration of the region. Dirt-gravel roads lead to Tarahumara villages at the edges of scenic canyons. **Note:** If you're planning to drive to the Copper Canyon area, fill the gas tank in Chihuahua or the town of La Junta, on Mex. 16. Driving time from Chihuahua to Creel is about 3.5 hours; a sturdy vehicle is recommended.

Basaseáchic Falls National Park is about 5 hours away via a paved road running from Creel north to the Mex. 16 junction, then west on Mex. 16 to the park. The falls plunge some 800 feet into an open cylinder formed by huge rock columns. The spray nourishes pine trees growing at the base of the falls, and a marked footpath allows hikers access to the bottom of the canyon. At the top there are basic camping facilities.

LAKE ARARECO is 7 km (4 mi.) s. on a paved road. This horseshoe-shaped, man-made lake is surrounded by diversified forest and oddly-shaped rock formations. Lodging, horseback riding, boat rental and food service facilities are available. Fishing and camping are permitted.

DURANGO, DURANGO (D-3)

pop. 435,400, elev. 6,196′

Not many travelers make it to Durango (doo-RAHN-goh), situated in the high desert country of north-central Mexico. Comparative isolation is one of the main reasons: Mazatlán, the nearest city of any size, is nearly 200 miles away, and the Sierra Madre Occidental mountains form an inhospitable barrier to the west. So despite being an important commercial crossroads due to the fact that it sits at the junction of two major highways (Mex. 40 and Mex. 45), Durango's tucked-away location makes it a bit of a diamond in the rough for visitors.

The city was founded in 1563 by Spanish *conquistador* Francisco de Ibarra, who also established the city of Fresnillo in the neighboring state of Zacatecas. Ibarra explored large sections of northwestern Mexico while exploiting the land's rich deposits of silver and other minerals. He named Durango for his home town in the Spanish province of Vizcaya. It was an early outpost in a vast region Ibarra named Nueva Vizcaya, covering an area equal to the present-day states of Chihuahua, Durango, Sinaloa and Sonora.

Hostilities with indigenous groups impeded early development, but by the mid-18th century construction of the colonial buildings that make up today's historic center was well under way. Durango received a further boost when the lumber and mining camp of El Salto was founded by English timber interests around the turn of the 20th century. After a railway was constructed between El Salto and Mexico City, Durango became an important shipping point for lumber and minerals taken from the surrounding mountains.

Local legend maintains that it was in a cave in one of the buttes punctuating the countryside north of Durango that revolutionary Pancho Villa traded his soul to the Devil in return for mastery over other men. Villa was born Doroteo Arango in 1877 on a hacienda near the village of San Juan del Río, 110 kilometers (68 miles) north of Durango on Mex. 45. He grew up an uneducated peasant, working as a sharecropper. After killing a man who had seduced and then abandoned his younger sister, Villa began a life on the run from the law.

After becoming involved in the fight to overthrow the iron rule of dictator Porfirio Díaz Villa went on to become one of the Mexican Revolution's foremost figures, envisioning himself as a Mexican Robin Hood who took from the rich hacienda owners and gave back to poor farmers and sharecroppers. Commanding a fiercely loyal band of supporters collectively known as the Division of the North (División del Norte), Villa was an able military leader as well as a flamboyant personality who today is one of Mexico's most admired folk heros.

City Layout

Durango—officially Victoria de Durango—sits in a valley strewn with craggy buttes that are an otherworldly shade of orange. It's a beautiful natural setting that initially seems compromised by modern industry; like other Mexican cities founded during the colonial era, the outskirts of town look grimy and industrial. To experience the best of what the city has to offer head straight for the historic downtown core, where the 17th- and 18th-century colonial architecture has for the most part been handsomely preserved.

Plaza de Armas, the main plaza, is between avenidas 20 de Noviembre and 5 de Febrero and calles Constitución and Juárez. It has pretty gardens and a circular bandstand, and is the scene of Sunday band concerts. The major visitor points of interest are all within several blocks of the plaza, making Durango easy to explore on foot.

A block southwest of Plaza de Armas, facing the north side of Plaza Centenario, is the Government Palace (Palacio de Gobierno), an 18th-century baroque building distinguished by its arcades. Inside are murals illustrating Durango state history.

A block north of the Government Palace on Avenida 20 de Noviembre, between calles Zaragoza and Bruno Martinez, is the Ricardo Castro Theater (Teatro Ricardo Castro), originally called the Teatro Principal but renamed for a Durangueño pianist and composer when it was renovated in 1990. Used for performances by visiting music, theater and dance troupes, it has beautiful marble and tile flooring.

Shoppers can browse through the Municipal Market (Mercado Gómez Palacio), 3 blocks east of Plaza de Armas (entrances on Calle Pasteur and Calle Patoni). In addition to the standard displays of produce and foodstuffs the market has stalls selling *charro* (Mexican-style rodeo) clothing, leather goods, wool *sarapes,* locally made handicrafts and souvenirs with scorpion motifs; the stinging arachnids are a common sight in this desert country.

The Durango area has long been used by filmmakers for location shooting, particularly Hollywood westerns *(see Movie Sets attraction listing).* Golden age icons Lillian Gish, John Wayne and Clark Gable as well as more recent stars like Jack Nicholson, John Belushi and John Travolta have all been in movies filmed around Durango. The Museum of the Cinema (Museo Temático de Cine), Calle Florida #1006, has a collection of old movie posters, photographs and vintage film equipment. Open Tues.-Sun. 10-6.

A downtown restaurant popular with Durangueños is Los Farolitos, on Calle Martinez near the intersection with Avenida 20 de Noviembre. Huge, freshly made flour tortillas are wrapped around a variety of tasty fillings, from *carne asada* (grilled steak) to cheese spiked with bits of green chilies *(queso con rajas).* A branch of the Mexican chain Sanborn's on Avenida 20 de Noviembre offers a reliably standard menu and good coffee.

The central bus station is east of downtown near the junction of avenidas Felipe Pescador and Colegio Militar (Mex. 40). Transportes del Norte offers first-class bus service from Chihuahua, Mazatlán, Mexico City, Zacatecas and other Mexican cities. The *Ruta 2* line running west from the station along Avenida 20 de Noviembre (the city's main east-west thoroughfare) to Plaza de Armas stops within easy walking distance of downtown points of interest. The fare is inexpensive (about 40c U.S.).

Nearby Destinations

The 312-kilometer (195-mile) journey west from Durango to Mazatlán via two-lane Mex. 40 passes through some of Mexico's most spectacular scenery. The views of the Sierra Madre Occidental range are truly spectacular. The roadway also is in good condition, although locals—quite appropriately—call it the Road of 3,000 Curves (Camino de Tres Mil Curvas).

Make certain that your vehicle is in tip-top shape; outside of a few tire shops *(llanteras),* repair facilities between the two cities are nonexistent. Also plan on taking between 6 and 7 hours to complete this drive; the narrow stretch of highway is used by trucks and buses that must negotiate the frequent hairpin curves, and opportunities for passing are infrequent.

From Durango, the road ascends through stands of pine to the straggling logging town of El Salto, about 100 kilometers (62 miles) west. Two public parks in the vicinity—El Tecuán and Puerto de Los Angeles—offer picnic areas and rustic cabin rentals in a region of waterfalls, thick forests and interesting geological formations, all at elevations of up to 8,500 feet.

Continuing west, La Ciudad is another mountain town with very basic services, including a couple of bare-bones diners *(comedores)* with wood-burning stoves and cement floors. Beginning a short distance west of La Ciudad is the most spectacular—and unnerving—part of the route. The Devil's Backbone (El Espinazo del Diablo) is a narrow, 5-mile-long mountain ridge with precipitous dropoffs falling away from both sides of the road. Mazatlán and the Pacific, more than 90 kilometers (55 miles) southwest, can be seen on clear days from this dizzying height; the road is a triumph of man's ingenuity over a challenging environment.

Durango State Tourism Office (Dirección General de Turismo y Cinematografía): downtown at Calle Florida #1106, on the second floor of the Barrio del Calvario. Open Mon.-Fri. 8-8; phone (618) 811-1107.

What to See

CATHEDRAL (Catedral Basílica Menor) is on Av. 20 de Noviembre facing the n. side of Plaza de Armas. Construction was begun in 1695 and completed in 1750. The massive structure is surmounted by two square towers. The exterior is a mixture of styles, with baroque predominating. The entrance is richly decorated. Inside are choir stalls adorned with finely carved wooden figures of saints and apostles. Bell ringers in the towers are visible from the plaza.

The ghost of an 18th-century nun *(monja)* is said to inhabit the church. According to local legend she fell in love with a French soldier who had deserted the Napoleonic army. He was killed by his countrymen before returning to France and seeking a pardon for deserting; unaware of his fate, the nun climbed one of the cathedral's towers each night to await his return, finally dying of a broken heart. Her silhouette is supposedly visible on nights when there is a full moon.

GANOT-PESCHARD MUSEUM OF ARCHEOLOGY (Museo de Arqueología Ganot-Peschard) is 2 blks. w. of Plaza de Armas at Calle Zaragoza #315 Sur, between avs. 20 de Noviembre and 5 de

Febrero. It chronicles the indigenous cultures of this part of Mexico from prehistoric times through the Spanish conquest. Highlights are an underground re-creation of tombs and their contents and an exhibit detailing the methodology of archeological research. Background information is in Spanish. Tues.-Fri. 10-6, Sat.-Sun. 11-7. Admission about 50c (U.S.).

HOUSE OF THE COUNT OF SUCHIL (Casa del Conde del Valle de Súchil) is 2 blks. e. of Plaza de Armas at Av. 5 de Febrero and Calle Francisco I. Madero. This is a fine example of mid-18th-century Spanish colonial architecture. Built for a wealthy landowner, the restored mansion's former grandeur is evident in such exterior features as the roof-line sculptures and elaborate molding around the main doorway. The building is occupied by a Banamex bank branch, but visitors can wander around the interior courtyard.

MERCADO HILL (El Cerro de Mercado) is just n. of the city. A mound of high-content iron ore said to be one of the largest single iron deposits in existence, it rises some 700 feet above the surrounding plain and is still producing. The hill was named for the man who discovered it in 1552, Ginés Vázquez del Mercado.

MOVIE SETS (Escenarios) in the city vicinity are permanent fixtures. Durango's heyday as a movie-making center began in the 1950s and continued through the '70s, as actors like John Wayne, Burt Lancaster and Robert Ryan came here to film Hollywood westerns. Among the classics shot in the vicinity were Raoul Walsh's "The Tall Men" and Sam Peckinpah's "The Wild Bunch" and "Pat Garrett and Billy the Kid."

For information contact the State Cinematography Office (Dirección Estatal de Cinematografía), located in the same building as the State Tourism Office.

Chupaderos is about 14 km (9 mi.) n. of Durango off Mex. 45. An actual Mexican village, it has been used for filming more than any other area location. The town's original structures have been augmented over the years by Old West-style buildings fabricated for the movies, which ironically are occupied by local families. Among the Westerns filmed here was the 1970 oater "Chisum," starring John Wayne.

A few kilometers to the south on Mex. 45 is Villa del Oeste, a village that first came into being as a constructed "Western" town. It's now a tourist attraction offering shops, restaurants and re-enactments of Old West-style shootouts and barroom brawls on weekends.

Los Alamos is about 29 km (18 mi.) s. of Durango on the paved road to the village of La Flor; take Blvd. Domingo Arrieta (about 7 blks. e. of the main plaza) s. out of town. This set was built to re-create the town of Los Alamos, New Mexico, for the 1989 film "Fat Man and Little Boy," about the development of the atomic bomb. The rugged canyon scenery en route is quite impressive.

GUAYMAS, SONORA (C-1) pop. 99,800

Backed by bare mountains that advance almost to the coast, Guaymas (GWAY-mahs) is one of Mexico's principal seaports. The surrounding area was originally occupied by Indians known as Guaymenas, thought to be an offshoot of the Seri tribe. Spanish explorers discovered the region in the 1530s, but it wasn't until 1701 that a nearby mission was established jointly by Fathers Eusebio Francisco Kino and Juan María Salvatierra. The settlement of Guaymas was founded in 1769.

The old city sits along the shore of a fine natural harbor crowded with freighters, tankers and shrimp boats. This part of Guaymas is divided by a mountainous peninsula from the newer resort area, which spreads out to the northwest along Bacochibampo and San Carlos bays. The mountain backdrop, brilliant blue sky and equally blue gulf waters are best appreciated by strolling along the waterfront section of Avenida Serdán, the main east-west thoroughfare.

Two blocks to the north is the 19th-century Church of San Fernando (Iglesia de San Fernando). In front of the church is a small park complete with white wrought-iron bandstand and benches set under trees that provide welcome shade. Nearby, at Avenida Serdán and Calle 23, is the Plaza of the Three Presidents (Plaza de Los Tres Presidentes). In front of City Hall (Palacio Municipal) on the plaza are statues honoring Plutarco Elías Calles, Adolfo de la Huerta and Abelardo Rodríguez, all former Mexican presidents born in Sonora.

Native heritage is evident in the celebrations and ritual dances of the Yaqui Indians, who still inhabit the villages in the Yaqui River valley southeast of Guaymas. One of Mexico's most fiercely independent ethnic peoples, the Yaqui staged frequent rebellions against ruling governments during the 18th and 19th centuries.

Politically assimilated into contemporary Mexico, the Yaqui have nevertheless maintained certain aspects of their culture, most notably the Deer Dance *(Danza del Venado)*, which is performed both locally and at folkloric festivals throughout the country. The main participant wears a deer's head to enact the dance's symbolic representation of the battle between good and evil.

The Guaymas area is well known to deep-sea fishing enthusiasts. Prized catches include marlin, sailfish, yellowtail, corbina, sea bass and red snapper. Even the local oysters are celebrated for their flavor. Fishing excursions and sunset cruises can be arranged in nearby San Carlos *(see separate listing within this region)*.

Practicalities

Aeroméxico offers direct flights to Guaymas from Tucson; for additional information about airlines *see Arriving by Air, page 61.* Taxis provide service to and from the airport, which is located west of town. First-class bus service to border cities and other Mexican destinations is provided by several bus companies, including Elite, TAP, Transportes del

Pacífico and Tufesa. Schedule and fare information can be obtained at one of the city's three downtown bus stations, all located in the vicinity of Calle 14 and Avenida 12. In addition, local buses to Playa Miramar and San Carlos make stops at various points along Avenida Serdán.

Despite breezes coming off the water, Guaymas is uncomfortably hot (and often humid) during the summer months. The winter season, roughly November through March, is much more pleasant—warm days, rather cool nights and mostly sunny skies.

The Santa Rosalía ferry provides automobile-passenger service linking Guaymas and Santa Rosalía *(see separate listing under Baja California)* on the Bajá California Peninsula. The ferry terminal is just east of downtown on Avenida Serdán. There are normally four departures a week; sailing time is 8 hours. Schedules and rates are subject to change and should be double-checked in advance. Phone (622) 222-0204, or 01 (800) 505-5018 (toll-free long distance within Mexico) for reservations information. For additional information about ferries *see Ferry Service, page 74.*

Tourist information office: downtown at Calle 19 and Avenida 6. For information about the San Carlos area, contact the Sonora State Tourism branch office in San Carlos, located at Hacienda Plaza #264 Int. 6, Sector Crestón; phone (622) 226-0202.

HERMOSILLO, SONORA (B-2)

pop. 559,600, metro area 657,200

Capital of the state of Sonora, Hermosillo (ehr-moh-SEE-yo) rises abruptly from the sparsely settled terrain of northwestern Mexico. Big and spread out, the city is not conducive to sightseeing but is a popular stop for motorists proceeding south to Pacific coast resorts. Aeroméxico flies direct from Tucson and from Los Angeles via Tijuana, and has direct flights to Hermosillo from Mexico City, Guadalajara and other Mexican cities. Aero California flies direct from Los Angeles and Tucson. First-class bus service from Nogales is provided by several companies, including Elite, Norte de Sonora, TAP and Tufesa.

Aside from the colonial-era architecture of the 18th-century Cathedral of the Assumption (Catedral de la Asunción), the Government Palace (Palacio Gobierno) and the pink-hued City Hall (Palacio Municipal), most of Hermosillo looks blandly modern. Plaza Zaragoza, the central plaza, provides welcome shade trees and an oasis from the crowded and frequently dusty downtown streets. Also check out the colorful murals depicting Sonoran history in the Government Palace courtyard.

Mex. 15, also called the Pacific Coast Highway, extends from the U.S. border at Nogales south and east to Mexico City. It is mostly a divided four-lane highway except where it passes through some small towns and villages. Watch for occasional potholes and rocks, especially in the vicinity of hills or low mountains. Highway repair work is frequent, and traffic may be diverted to the two-lane stretch that is open. Periodic agricultural checkpoints and gun/drug checks may be encountered in each direction. These stops involve no monetary transactions and are normally routine; English is spoken, although being able to speak Spanish is helpful.

There are presently 11 tollbooths along Mex. 15/15-D between Nogales and Mazatlán. Combined toll charges for automobiles are a little over 500 pesos (about $48.50 U.S.). **Note:** Toll charges can go up without warning, and rates for different types of vehicles aren't always posted. Avoid SIN-1 (Sinaloa Highway 1), a toll road between Guamúchil and Culiacán that has been known to be targeted by robbers.

Mex. 16 connects Hermosillo with Chihuahua and cuts through the Sierra Madre range. Before it opened, the only paved road running east-west through the Sierra Madres was Mex. 2, roughly paralleling the U.S. border between Agua Prieta and Janos in the state of Chihuahua. Mex. 16 is a narrow, two-lane blacktop without shoulders. There are many turns and steep grades, and horses, burros or grazing cattle may be encountered at almost any point. For the adventurous traveler with a reliable vehicle, the route offers breathtaking mountain scenery of canyons, cliffs, rivers and masses of vegetation.

Mex. 16 also can be used to access the Copper Canyon area *(see Copper Canyon listing)*. Those who do decide to travel on Mex. 16 should keep in mind that viewing scenic areas or dealing with a flat tire will require stopping on the roadway. There are no guardrails, and rock falls from the cliffs above may require sudden stops or veering into the opposite lane. Due to a lack of service stations, make sure your gas tank is full before starting out.

Saltwater fishing is the main attraction at the Gulf of California resort town of Kino Bay (Bahía Kino), some 105 kilometers (65 miles) southwest of Hermosillo via Mex. 16. Named for Jesuit missionary Francisco Eusebio Kino, this was long a hideaway known only to a few intrepid RV owners. Lately condominiums and secluded vacation homes have been springing up, although the mountain-backed beaches of golden sand for the most part remain unspoiled.

Tourist facilities are concentrated in Kino Nuevo (New Kino), separated by some 4 kilometers (2.5 miles) of open beach from Kino Viejo, the Mexican village. The beaches are practically deserted during the summer months, but they also are uncomfortably hot.

Across a narrow channel is Shark Island (Isla Tiburón), which is being developed into a game and wildlife refuge. A special permit is necessary to visit the island; check with one of the hotels or RV parks in town regarding guide service. About 24 kilometers (15 miles) north of Bahía Kino via a winding gravel road is the fishing village of Punta Chueca, where Seri Indians offer wood carvings and shell necklaces for sale.

Sonora State Tourism Office (Subsecretaría de Fomento al Turismo): on the third floor of the State Government Building, North Wing, located at Comonfort and Paseo Río Sonora Sur (about 7 blocks south of Plaza Zaragoza and 4 blocks east of Mex. 15); phone (662) 217-0076 or (662) 217-0060, ext. 125.

To receive visitor information from the Sonora Department of Tourism, phone (800) 476-6672 (from the United States) or 01 (800) 716-2555 (toll-free long distance within Mexico).

What To See

REGIONAL MUSEUM OF SONORA (Museo Regional de Sonora) sits on the eastern slope of Cerro de la Campana (Hill of the Bells), which overlooks the city. It is housed in a former penitentiary dating from the beginning of the 20th century. Some of the underground dungeons and wards have been preserved. The museum's archeological, ethnological and historical exhibits emphasize northwestern Mexico. Open Wed.-Sun. Admission is charged.

REGIONAL MUSEUM OF THE UNIVERSITY OF SONORA (Museo Regional de la Universidad de Sonora) is at calles Luis Encinas and Rosales. It has exhibits relating to the Yaqui, Mayo, Pima, Pápago and Seri Indian groups. Also on view are photographs of Mexican Revolution activities in Sonora, exhibits pertaining to the local history of the area and the university, and numismatic collections. Open Wed.-Sun. Admission is charged.

SONORA ECOLOGICAL CENTER (Centro Ecológico de Sonora) is about 3 km (2 mi.) s. of the city on Mex. 15. A zoological park, it exhibits flora and fauna native to the region's varied ecosystems, from arid desert to the rich marine environment of the Gulf of California. Snakes, tortoises, sea lions and the Mexican gray wolf can all be seen. Notable are the more than 300 species of cacti, many of them labeled. The zoo covers a large area and thus is more pleasant to walk during the cooler winter months. Bottled water is available. Open Wed.-Sun. Admission is charged.

LOS MOCHIS, SINALOA (D-2)

pop. 204,900

Los Mochis (los MO-chees) was founded in 1893 by Benjamin Johnston, who arrived from Pennsylvania to grow sugar cane. Johnston also founded the Ingenio Azucarero, an enormous sugar refinery around which the city developed; visitors can tour the building.

Los Mochis is the major coastal terminus of the Chihuahua al Pacífico Railway, which travels across the rugged Sierra Madre Occidental to Chihuahua via the spectacular Barranca del Cobre (Copper Canyon) region *(see Copper Canyon listing)*.

Technically the end of the rail line is 24 kilometers (15 miles) south at Topolobampo. This deep sea port, known for its shrimp fleet and fishing, is connected by ferry to La Paz, B.C.S.

Topolobampo is the site of a colony developed in the late 19th century by a group of Americans headed by Alfred K. Owens, who originally conceived the Chihuahua-Pacífico Railway as part of a trade route linking Kansas City with Mexico's Pacific coast. Owens was an idealistic socialist intent on establishing a utopian community that would rival San Francisco in importance. Disillusioned followers and the ravages of typhoid eventually caused the colony to fail, and construction of the rail line faced a formidable obstacle burrowing through the Sierra Madre. Nevertheless, Owens' dream of success was realized in part; the completion of the line in 1961 brought new opportunities to the area.

Los Mochis is an agricultural boomtown and the export center of the state of Sinaloa. A dam on the Río Fuerte, part of a tri-river federal irrigation program in northern Sinaloa and southern Sonora, has increased the productivity of this semiarid region.

Aeroméxico offers flights to Los Mochis from some U.S. cities. Aero California has daily flights to Los Mochis from Los Angeles. Baja Ferries service links Topolobampo with La Paz; the trip takes about 6 hours. Schedules and rates are subject to change and should be double-checked in advance with the Topolobampo ferry office; phone (668) 862-1003 or 01 (800) 718-2796 (toll-free long distance within Mexico). For additional information *see Ferry Service, page 74*.

The Hotel Santa Anita, downtown on Avenida Gabriel Leyva, is a good city orientation landmark. The Viajes Flamingo travel agency, on the hotel's first floor, has Copper Canyon train information and sells advance tickets for the train trip as well as tour packages that include tickets, transfers and hotel accommodations. This travel agency also may be able to provide information about ferry service; phone (668) 818-7046. Elite offers first-class bus service; the bus station is nearby on Avenida Degollado.

Tourist information office: in the back of the State Government (Gobierno del Estado) building on Calle Allende.

NOGALES, SONORA (B-2)

pop. 164,700, elev. 3,674'

The border city of Nogales (noh-GAH-lehs) is sometimes referred to as Ambos Nogales ("both Nogales") in recognition of the sister city of Nogales, Ariz. on the other side of the international boundary fence. Settlement of the area began shortly after present-day Arizona, New Mexico and California were ceded to the United States according to the terms of the Treaty of Guadalupe Hidalgo, which ended the Mexican-American War. It was not until 1882, however, that the town was officially established. It not only became—and continues to be—larger than its U.S. counterpart, but also has managed to retain a strong sense of Mexican identity.

Nogales is the gateway into northwestern mainland Mexico and points south, although many visitors just come for the day. Things heat up on weekends, when the underage Arizona crowd makes the hour pilgrimage south from Tucson to patronize the local bars and nightspots.

Mexican and U.S. Customs and Border Protection offices are open 24 hours daily. A tourist permit is not needed for in-town stays of less than 72 hours, but proof of citizenship is required. For motorists traveling into the interior, the official checkpoint—where your temporary vehicle importation permit must be presented, the $25 (plus IVA tax) administrative fee paid and a windshield sticker obtained—is 21 kilometers (13 miles) south of Nogales on Mex. 15.

Note: All U.S. and Canadian citizens traveling *by air* between the United States and Mexico are required to show a passport or other accepted secure document. The passport requirement will be extended to land and sea border crossings on June 1, 2009. Up until this date the U.S., Canadian and Mexican governments also will accept a birth certificate, which must be a certified copy with a raised seal from the government agency that issued it and be accompanied by government-issued photo identification (such as a driver's license).

From Tucson, I-19 south ends at Nogales, Ariz.; signs point the way to the border crossing. Mex. 15 begins at the border but passes through the most congested part of the city. Motorists intending to bypass Nogales for points south can save time by using the international truck crossing, which connects with Mex. 15 south of Nogales at the 21-kilometer (13-mile) immigration checkpoint. At press time, the toll was about $2 (U.S.).

If you're driving through downtown Nogales back to the United States, watch for the sign that says "Linea International"; follow the directions for the road that leads to the border crossing.

Since almost all of the tourist-oriented shopping is within easy walking distance of the border, it is recommended that day visitors park on the Arizona side and head into Mexico on foot. From the Nogales-Santa Cruz, Ariz., Chamber of Commerce, 123 W. Kino Pkwy. (just off the intersection of Grand Avenue and US 82), it's about a 1.5-mile drive south to a series of guarded lots; all-day parking fees average about $8. The turnstiles to Mexico are at the foot of the Port of Entry.

The shops and vendor stalls catering to tourists are concentrated within easy walking distance of the border along north-south Avenida Obregón. They sell pottery, baskets, fabrics, ceramics, leather goods, glassware, carved pine furniture, rugs, jewelry and more. Most business is conducted in English, bargaining is acceptable and even expected, and American currency is preferred. More exclusive establishments have fixed prices and carry crafts and gift items from all over Mexico. When buying at stalls or from street vendors, always check for quality.

Along with shopping, Nogales offers such "touristy" experiences as having your picture taken astride a donkey and listening to mariachi bands. Like other Mexican border cities, it also is a place to get prescriptions filled at a cost that is often far less than stateside. There are good restaurants that specialize in traditional Mexican dishes, have English-speaking servers and offer menus with prices quoted in dollars. Two reliable longtime establishments are El Cid and the Elvira Restaurant, both close to the border on Avenida Obregón.

PUERTO PEÑASCO, SONORA (B-1)

pop. 31,600

Puerto Peñasco (PWEHR-toh peh-NYAHS-coh) is an oasis of sorts situated in the midst of some of Mexico's most inhospitable territory: blazingly hot, extremely arid and impressively desolate. As a result this small but growing resort area—about 100 kilometers (68 miles) south of the U.S. border, 4 hours from Tucson and 4 to 5 hours from Phoenix—attracts legions of campers, RVers and tourists.

Puerto Peñasco might today be an Arizona seaport were it not for the Mexican government's negotiating skills. Following the end of the Mexican-American War in 1848, border disputes between the two countries continued. Under the terms of the Treaty of Guadalupe Hidalgo, Mexico ceded territories that comprise present-day California, Nevada and Utah, most of Arizona and New Mexico and part of Colorado. But the United States also was interested in the region now occupied by much of the Mexican states of Sonora and Chihuahua in order to have a southern transcontinental railroad route to the Pacific Ocean.

American diplomat James Gadsden went to Mexico to bargain for the acquisition, but Gen. Antonio López de Santa Anna—a charismatic but ideologically unfocused military leader who was president of Mexico no less than 11 different times between 1833 and 1854—did not want to give up the land bridge connecting mainland Mexico and the Baja California Peninsula. The Gadsden Purchase of 1853 gave the United States territory that finalized the boundaries of Arizona and New Mexico, but Mexico retained access to the Gulf of California.

In the 1920s Mexican fishermen discovered huge schools of shrimp in the waters off Cerro de Peñasco (Rocky Point), and the town of Puerto Peñasco was established. A pier was built for the local fishing fleet in 1936, and during World War II a paved road (Mex. 8) was constructed from the Arizona border by the U.S. Army Corps of Engineers—with the cooperation of the Mexican government—to provide shipping access to the Gulf of California in the event of Japanese attacks on American West Coast ports.

By the early 1980s commercial fishing and shrimping accounted for more than 80 percent of the local economy. Fishing was prohibited north of Puerto Peñasco a decade later, when Mexico designated the northern gulf coast and desert region a protected area, and today these activities have largely been supplanted by tourism. The character of the coast also is changing as more and more high-rise condominium and resort complexes, vacation homes, marinas and golf courses are being planned and built.

The beaches around Puerto Peñasco are generally wide and flat, with both sandy and rocky areas. While the coarse, tan-colored grains are no match for the powdery sand at some of Mexico's other beach resorts, the blue-green water is calm and shallow, waves are gentle and there are no riptides—ideal conditions for wading and swimming. Beachcombers take note: The northern Gulf of California coast experiences an extreme tidal range of more than 20 feet, which exposes a treasure trove of shells and marine life at low tide.

Playa Hermosa, just west of Puerto Peñasco, is the locals' beach and the one closest to town. It has restrooms, showers and snack stands. To the east at Playa Las Conchas are tide pools teeming with crabs, mussels, sponges and other creatures. Farther east, the Morua Estuary (Estero Morua) and the La Pinta Estuary (Estero La Pinta) provide habitats for shore and wading birds, fish and invertebrates. In between the two estuaries are three beaches—Playa Encanto, Playa Dorada and Playa Miramar—lined with condos, resort complexes and rental homes. Keep in mind that all beaches in Mexico are public, even stretches that may seem like they are on hotel property.

The Intercultural Center for the Study of Oceans and Deserts (CEDO) is on the eastern edge of town at Playa Las Conchas; from Boulevard Benito Juárez take Boulevard Fremont and then an access road east, following signs. This biological field station is devoted to researching and conserving the surrounding marine and desert environments. Free public tours of the facility are offered Tuesdays and Saturdays. The center also organizes occasional tide pool explorations, bird-watching excursions, coastal desert walks and other guided activities; for information phone (638) 382-0113 or (520) 320-5473 (from the United States).

Also on the access road to Playa Las Conchas a short distance west of the center is the Cet-Mar Aquarium (Acuario Cet-Mar). It has tanks displaying invertebrates and fish that inhabit the coastal intertidal zone, as well as a couple of turtles and sea lions. Other things to do in Puerto Peñasco include shore fishing, chartered sport-fishing excursions, sailing, snorkeling, scuba diving, kayaking, whale watching (during the winter months) or just kicking back and enjoying the sunset.

The Sonoran Desert, which covers some 120,000 square miles in northern Baja as well as neighboring Arizona and California, may look forbidding, but it is actually a region of biological diversity. Wet pockets in the overall arid landscape—such as oases and riverbanks—can support a variety of plant and animal life, although all desert species are specifically adapted to coping with life in a harsh environment. The Sonoran, in fact, is considered to be a lush desert, although that designation is highly dependent on one key ingredient: scarce seasonal rainfall.

One of the Baja desert's distinctive plants is the organ pipe cactus, which often grows on south-facing hillsides where it can absorb a maximum amount of sunlight as well as gain protection from winter frosts (the coldest air usually sinks to the flat desert floor). Its name refers to the several vertical stems that extend upward from a short trunk. Like many other cactuses, the organ pipe produces large, eye-catching flowers in the spring. Most of the desert's animal inhabitants, such as jackrabbits, snakes and kangaroo rats, are nocturnal. This austerely beautiful wilderness can be explored at Pinacate Biosphere Reserve *(see attraction listing)*.

The Old Port section of town, perched at the tip of a rocky cape overlooking the gulf, is the site of the original fishing settlement. Browse the craft shops along waterfront Malecón Kino, where vendors sell—in addition to the ubiquitous T-shirts, ceramics and seashell necklaces—carvings fashioned from ironwood, a desert tree known for its extremely hard and dense wood. Another interesting place to wander through is the open-air seafood market and its displays of freshly caught fish.

Taquerias set up along the *malecón* and around the harbor area. These stands dish up handmade corn tortillas filled with strips of meat or fish cooked on a charcoal griddle and garnished with such toppings as grilled onions and peppers, beans, chopped cabbage, radishes, cilantro and salsa. The tacos are an inexpensive and tasty on-the-spot snack. They also should be safe to eat as long as you avoid adding the lettuce, tomatoes or carrots that are often provided (and may not be rinsed with purified water). Another good rule of thumb is to patronize a stand that is popular with Rocoportenses (locals).

Practicalities

Easy access is perhaps Puerto Peñasco's biggest lure. Sonoyta, the small town just across the border from Lukeville, Ariz., has the usual assortment of tourist-oriented shops but lacks the excitement of bigger and more bustling border cities like Nogales, Mexicali and Tijuana. Unless you're intent on scoring a souvenir, stay on Boulevard de las Américas, following the signs for Puerto Peñasco.

Note: A temporary vehicle importation permit is not needed if traveling to Puerto Peñasco from the United States. Motorists must, however, carry Mexican automobile insurance. If you plan on bringing a boat, ATV or other type of recreational vehicle, take along a copy of the ownership documents. For additional information about bringing personal items into the country *see What May Be Taken Into Mexico, page 57*.

Mex. 8, the direct route to the Gulf of California, is a two-lane road that has a couple of sharp turns. The approximately 105-kilometer (65-mile) drive through open range country takes over an hour; note the lower speed limit of 65-75 kilometers per hour (about 45 mph). Because of the lack of roadside facilities, the trip from the border should be made only during the daytime.

Puerto Peñasco is most crowded from November through May, when the weather is cooler. Most weekends the rest of the year also see an influx of visitors, despite the extreme summer heat. The busiest months are March and April, when Holy Week (Easter) coincides with an invasion of U.S. college students on spring break.

The Serfin Bank at Boulevard Benito Juárez and Calle 13 has an ATM machine; withdrawals are in pesos. Many local businesses, however, accept or even prefer U.S. dollars. In case of medical emergency, contact the Red Cross (Cruz Roja); phone (638) 383-2266. To reach the local police department, phone (638) 383-2626.

Rocky Point Convention & Visitors Bureau: Boulevard Benito Juárez and Calle 11; phone (638) 388-0444 or (877) 843-3717 (toll-free from the United States).

The local tourist office is on Boulevard Benito Juárez at the northern entrance to town; phone (638) 383-6122.

PINACATE BIOSPHERE RESERVE is part of northwestern Mexico's Gran Desierto; the information center is about 52 km (32 mi.) s. of Lukeville, Ariz., just off Mex. 8 at Km marker 52. This trackless, otherworldly region was created over time by subterranean pools of molten rock that exploded up through the desert floor and then cooled, leaving behind a wasteland of towering sand dunes, lava tubes, cinder cones and dormant volcanic craters.

The area was designated as a biosphere reserve in 1993 to preserve both its volcanic rock formations and such endemic species as the desert octopus (which lives in the Sonoyta River), the flat-tail chameleon and the Gila monster. From the top of El Pinacate, a hill about 3,960 feet above sea level, there are panoramic views of the Baja California Peninsula.

Visitors must register at the information center before hiking or driving in the reserve. A high-clearance vehicle is recommended. There are no facilities; bring plenty of water, a hat and sun protection and wear comfortable hiking shoes. Camping is permitted at two designated locations (a permit is required). The best time to visit is January through April. Daily 9-5. Donations accepted.

SAN CARLOS, SONORA (C-1)

San Carlos, "just over the mountain" from the port city of Guaymas *(see separate listing within this region)*, is actually about 8 kilometers (5 miles) north of Guaymas via Mex. 15, then 24 kilometers (15 miles) west on a four-lane highway. Guaymenas Indians occupied this area for a few thousand years before the Spanish arrival in the mid-16th century; Jesuit priests built a mission in 1710. San Carlos flourished as a major supply center during the Mexican-American and U.S. Civil wars, but following the Mexican Revolution of 1910 sport fishing took precedence over port activities.

Quiet San Carlos "went Hollywood" in the late 1960s when the movie "Catch 22" was filmed at nearby Playa Algodones. A Club Med followed, and today's resort was born. Natural beauty remains in the tranquil white-sand beaches and the clear, blue-green waters of the Sea of Cortez—which are inhabited by more than 650 species of game fish—and red-tiled roofs retain a Spanish flavor. Well-to-do Mexicans and foreign tourists will find upscale condominiums and the most luxurious accommodations in Sonora here, but there also are inexpensive motels and RV parks that cater to budget travelers.

Marina San Carlos, one of Mexico's largest yacht marinas, has extensive docking facilities as well as moorings on outer San Carlos Bay. The San Carlos Country Club, Avenida Cristobal #1390, has an 18-hole golf course; most hotels in the area can arrange a temporary membership. Gary's Dive Shop, on Avenida Bay, and the El Mar Diving Center, Avenida Creston #263, offer fishing and scuba excursions.

Sonora State Tourism Office: A branch office is located at Hacienda Plaza #264, Int. 6, Sector Crestón; phone (622) 226-0202.

Horsetail Falls, El Cercado, Nuevo León / © Peter Langer / Danita Delimont Stock Photography

Northeastern Mexico

Northeastern Mexico is not the Mexican vacation paradise touted in glossy travel brochures. Take the gulf beaches along the low-lying, marshy, lagoon-fringed coastal strip in the state of Tamaulipas, for example; they're muddy and rife with mosquitoes. The sprawling state of Coahuila is arid, largely undeveloped and sparsely populated, with tourist facilities few and far between. The clang of machinery is the pulsebeat of Nuevo León, where heavy industry—ironworks, steelworks, smelting plants—takes precedence over touristic charm.

Matamoros and Reynosa, just across the southeastern Texas border, are easy day-trip destinations for shopping expeditions and a Mexican dinner. Matamoros, settled around 1700, was burned twice and pillaged several times, in the process earning the title "Thrice Heroic" city.

A major gas-processing and oil-refining center, Reynosa is decidedly short on charm but does have a small tourist district, the Zona Rosa, where there are a few shops and restaurants. More shopping can be found in the vicinity of Plaza Principal, the main plaza (some 20 blocks in from the toll bridge), a typical Mexican square with a colonial-style cathedral upon which has been grafted an ultramodern addition.

Saltillo, in a broad valley surrounded by the imposing peaks of the Sierra Madre Oriental, was founded as a Spanish outpost in 1577 by Alberto del Canto. In 1591, Francisco de Urdiñola established a mining settlement populated by relocated Tlaxcaltec Indians. By the early 17th century, the town was a strategic center for Spanish expeditions embarking on explorations to the north. From 1835 to 1847 Saltillo was capital of a territory that included Texas and extended as far northward as present-day Colorado.

Capital of the state of Nuevo León, industrial powerhouse Monterrey is Mexico's third largest city. Numerous factories produce transportation equipment, electrical appliances, cement, steel, chemicals, clothing, beer, cut glass and many other products. Industrialization also has made the city a major Mexican rail center and an important point of commerce with the United States. Monterrey's business muscle is exemplified by the Centro Internacional de Negocios (CINTERMEX), said to be the largest trade and convention center in Latin America.

Passage of the North American Free Trade Agreement (NAFTA) in the early 1990s added further economic impetus to an already-healthy industrial environment. Multinational corporations drawn by the availability of cheap Mexican labor meant jobs for Mexican workers, and *maquiladoras*—assembly plants—sprang up here and in northeastern Mexico's border cities. Real prosperity, however, is a fact of life for only a small—although growing—percentage of the population.

Known locally as the "Sultana del Norte," or Sultan of the North, Monterrey is a favored weekend getaway for nearby Texans (just a 3-hour drive from the border). Sheer size can make it a daunting choice for the casual tourist. But Monterrey's old center—with its flower-filled plazas, narrow thoroughfares, centuries-old buildings and colorful patios—retains the flavor of Spanish colonial days, and a handful of pedestrian-only streets provide welcome relief from big-city congestion.

A world away from Monterrey's urban sprawl is the El Cielo Biosphere Reserve, south of the Tamaulipas state capital of Ciudad Victoria. This 357,000-acre refuge stretches from the eastern to western slopes of the Sierra Madre Oriental, encompassing a transition zone of tropical, semidesert and temperate ecosystems.

Within the reserve is a cloud forest that is home to numerous species of orchids and birds. Several hiking trails begin in the little village of Gomez Farías, about 100 kilometers (62 miles) south of Ciudad Victoria and 40 kilometers (25 miles) north of Ciudad Mante on a side road branching west off Mex. 85. Guides are available in the village for this truly off-the-beaten-path ecotour adventure.

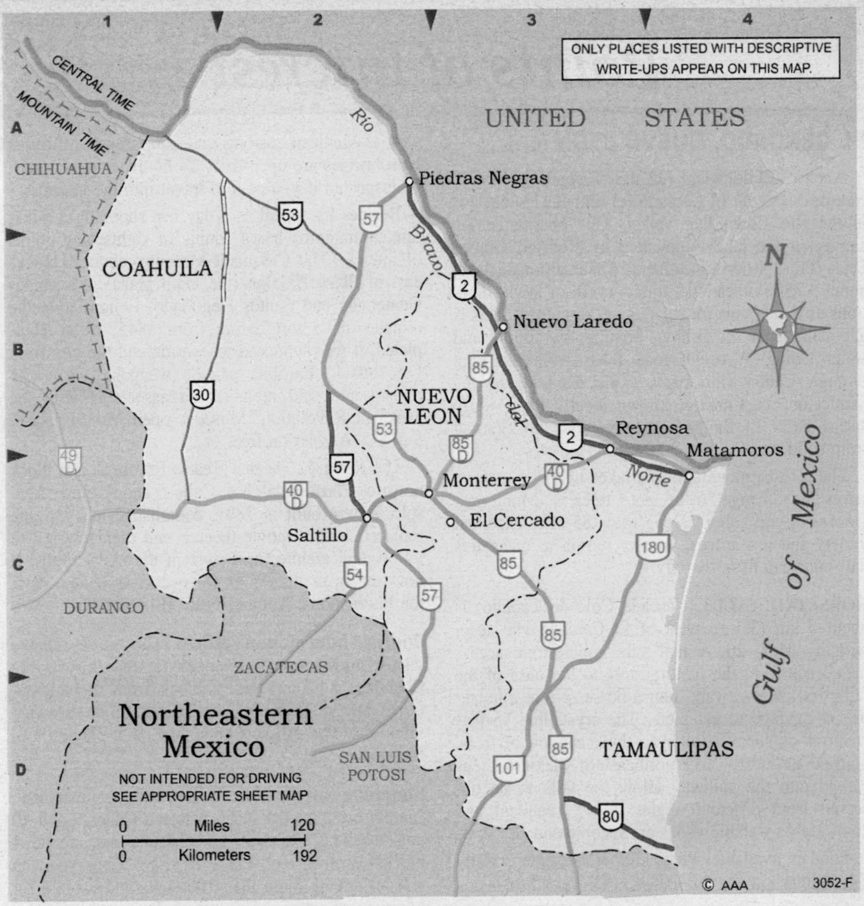

Northeastern Mexico

NOT INTENDED FOR DRIVING
SEE APPROPRIATE SHEET MAP

ONLY PLACES LISTED WITH DESCRIPTIVE WRITE-UPS APPEAR ON THIS MAP.

UNITED STATES
CENTRAL TIME
MOUNTAIN TIME
CHIHUAHUA
COAHUILA
NUEVO LEON
TAMAULIPAS
DURANGO
ZACATECAS
SAN LUIS POTOSI
Gulf of Mexico
Rio Bravo del Norte
Piedras Negras
Nuevo Laredo
Reynosa
Matamoros
Monterrey
El Cercado
Saltillo
2, 30, 40 D, 49 D, 53, 54, 57, 80, 85, 85 D, 101, 180
N

0 Miles 120
0 Kilometers 192

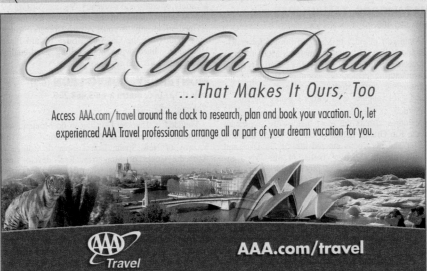

© AAA 3052-F

Points of Interest

EL CERCADO, NUEVO LEON (C-3)

About 36 kilometers (22 miles) south of Monterrey on Mex. 85, El Cercado (el sehr-KAH-doh) sits in the Río Escamillas Valley. This boat-launching site is on the lake impounded by Rodrigo Gómez Dam (Presa Rodrigo Gómez). The man-made lake, about 3.25 kilometers (2 miles) north of town, functions as a reservoir for the city of Monterrey. This is a popular spot for fishing, boating, swimming and water skiing. A rough road leads from the dam through Cañón Garrapatas (Tick Canyon) to the hamlet of Los Canelos, known locally for a warm spring and "El Bañito," a huge "bathtub" carved from solid rock.

The forests, mountains and lakes in this area are a refreshing change from hot, treeless Monterrey. Dozens of curio shops along Mex. 85 offer excellent variety and low prices, another reason to make this half-hour trip from the city.

HORSETAIL FALLS (Cascada Cola de Caballo) is about 5 km (3 mi.) west of El Cercado via steep, winding Mex. 20. A half-mile cobblestone access path leads from the parking area to the base of the falls; visitors can walk, rent a horse or hire a horse-drawn carriage to get there. The crystalline 75-foot waterfall is surrounded by a thick canopy of trees, unusual in mostly arid northeastern Mexico. Steps carved into the pathway allow the falls to be observed from different angles. Insect repellent and comfortable walking shoes are recommended.

Food is available. Picnicking is permitted. Daily 8-6. Admission about $4 (U.S.); $3 (ages 5-16).

MATAMOROS, TAMAULIPAS (C-4)
pop. 395,400

Main port of entry to Mexico from the lower Rio Grande Valley, Matamoros (mah-tah-MOH-rohs) is connected with Brownsville, Tex. The city is a manufacturing center, the commercial hub of the surrounding cotton-producing and cattle-raising region, and is popular with border-hopping tourists.

Settled at the beginning of the 18th century, Matamoros also is the most historically significant of the Rio Grande border towns. U.S. Gen. Zachary Taylor and his troops entered the city in 1846 and waged the first major battle of the Mexican-American War. Matamoros profited during the U.S. Civil War, when Confederates smuggled contraband cotton across the border for shipment to European markets.

Three bridges span the Rio Grande. The two most helpful to visitors are the B & M Bridge, which enters Matamoros via Mexico Street in Brownsville, and the Gateway Bridge, also called the International Bridge, which enters via International Boulevard. U.S. Customs and Border Protection offices as well as Mexican customs and immigration offices at both bridges are open daily 24 hours. Baggage must be inspected if you plan to travel into the interior.

Besides its appeal as a day trip shopping destination, Matamoros has a couple of sightseeing points of interest. The Casamata Museum, about 6 blocks east of Plaza Hidalgo (the main plaza) at avenidas Guatemala and Santos Degollado, is housed in the remains of a fort dating from 1845; never completed, it was supposed to help defend the city from U.S. attack. Exhibits include weapons, early city photographs and memorabilia associated with the Mexican Revolution. Museum open Mon.-Fri. 8-4, Sat. 8-2. Admission free.

The Reforma Theater (Teatro Reforma) is a block north of Plaza Hidalgo at Calle 6 and Avenida Abasolo. It was built in 1861, demolished in 1956 and replaced with a movie theater, and then restored to its original architectural style in the early 1990s. It now serves as the venue for events associated with the International Autumn Festival in October.

Tourist information office: The most reliable visitor information is available at the Brownsville Chamber of Commerce, a block from the international bridge at 1600 E. Elizabeth St. in Brownsville, Tex. The office is open daily 9-5; phone (956) 542-4341.

Shopping areas: The Juárez Market (Mercado Juárez) occupies the block between Calles 9 and 10 and avenidas Abasolo and Matamoros, about 4 blocks northwest of Plaza Hidalgo. Here you can wander among more than 100 stalls and bargain for a variety of crafts and souvenirs. Sections of Calle 9 and Avenida Abasolo in the vicinity of the market are pedestrian only. Avenida Alvaro Obregón, which runs south from the Gateway Bridge toward Plaza Hidalgo, is lined with shops selling good-quality handicrafts, gifts and silver jewelry.

MONTERREY, NUEVO LEON (C-2)
pop. 1,127,000, metro area 3,468,200

See map page 211.

Founded in 1596 by Don Diego de Montemayor, Monterrey (mohn-teh-REY) was named for the Viceroy of New Spain, Don Gaspar de Zúñiga y Acevedo, Count of Monterrey. Real development began in the 18th century, when El Obispado, or the Bishop's Palace *(see attraction listing)*—initially built as a place of retirement for Catholic bishops—became the seat of the religious diocese.

The city lies in a valley ringed with craggy mountains, including 5,700-foot Hill of the Saddle (Cerro de la Silla) and 7,800-foot Hill of the Miter (Cerro de la Mitra). The former is saddle-shaped; the latter resembles a bishop's headdress. The mountains trap smog created by the dense concentration

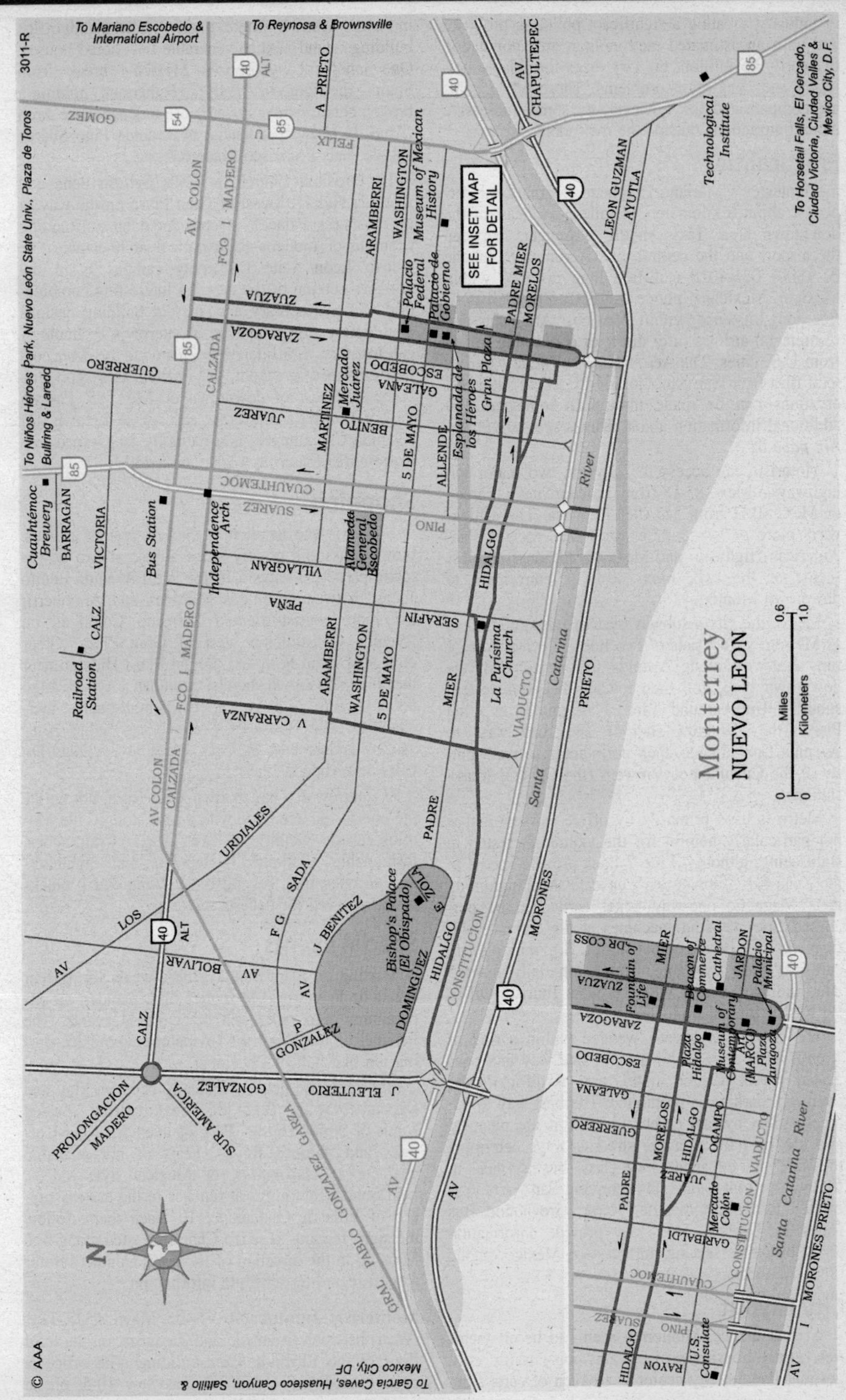
Monterrey
NUEVO LEON
SEE INSET MAP FOR DETAIL
To Mariano Escobedo & International Airport
To Reynosa & Brownsville
To Niños Héroes Park, Nuevo León State Univ., Plaza de Toros
To Horsetail Falls, El Cercado, Ciudad Victoria, Ciudad Valles & Mexico City, D.F.
To Garcia Caves, Huasteco Canyon, Saltillo & Mexico City, DF
Cuauhtémoc Brewery
Bullring & Laredo
Bus Station
Independence Arch
Railroad Station
Alameda General Escobedo
Mercado Juárez
Palacio Federal
Palacio de Gobierno
Museum of Mexican History
Esplanada de los Héroes
Gran Plaza
La Purísima Church
Bishop's Palace (El Obispado)
Technological Institute
Santa Catarina River
Fountain of Life
Beacon of Commerce
Cathedral
Palacio Municipal
Plaza Hidalgo
Museum of Contemporary Art (MARCO)
Plaza Zaragoza
Mercado Colón
U.S. Consulate
Miles 0 0.6
Kilometers 0 1.0
3011-R
© AAA

of industry, creating a significant pollution problem, and with an estimated metropolitan area population of nearly 3.5 million, the city faces formidable pollution and congestion problems. These urban pains are compensated for, however, by some impressive natural attractions outside the metropolitan area.

Practicalities

Monterrey's Mariano Escobedo International Airport is about 6 kilometers (4 miles) northeast of the downtown area. Taxis shuttle passengers between the airport and the central city. Aeroméxico, phone 01 (800) 021-4010 (toll-free long distance within Mexico), Mexicana, phone 01 (800) 509-8960 (toll-free long distance within Mexico), American and Continental airlines offer direct or connecting flights from U.S. cities. The Aeroméxico subsidiary Aerolitoral flies from San Antonio and McAllen, Tex.; reservations can be made through Aeroméxico. For additional information about airlines *see Arriving by Air, page 61*.

Motorists can access the city via two major toll highways—Mex. 85-D from Laredo/Nuevo Laredo or Mex. 40-D from McAllen/Reynosa. These highways more or less parallel free Mex. 85 (the Pan-American Highway) and Mex. 40. Although the less scenic of the two, Mex. 40-D is convenient to downtown Monterrey.

Metro, the city's subway system (also referred to as Metrorrey), consists of two lines. Elevated Line 1 runs east-west along Avenida Colón, north of the downtown core, and then toward the northwestern suburbs. Underground Line 2 originates at Gran Plaza (the Zaragoza station) and runs west to Avenida Cuauhtémoc, then north-south to the vicinity of the Cuauhtémoc Brewery (the General Anaya station).

Metro is used primarily by office workers and is not particularly helpful for the visitor interested in sightseeing, although Line 2 does provide access to the Zona Rosa, downtown's upscale shopping/dining area. Magnetic one-way ticket cards can be purchased from vending machines at the entrance stations for 4.5 pesos (about 40c U.S.); multiple-trip cards also are available. Trains run daily from 5 a.m.-midnight. Check with the State Tourism Office for further information.

The downtown streets, wedged within a ring of expressways, tend to be narrow, one way and congested. Street parking in this area is difficult, and overnight parking is prohibited. The best way to see the sights is by taxi or bus tour. Taxis are plentiful and can be hailed on the street; always determine the fare in advance. First-class bus service to Monterrey from Dallas, Houston and San Antonio is offered by Transportes del Norte. Greyhound Bus Lines in Laredo, Tex., can provide information about bus lines serving northeastern Mexico; phone (956) 723-4324.

City Layout

At first glance, Monterrey seems to be all factories, grimy housing projects and noisy traffic congestion. But the city center is a haven of sorts from industrial sprawl, where modern hotels and office buildings stand next to venerable flat-roofed houses. One landmark symbolizes Mexico's break from Spain—the figure of "Patria" (Fatherland) holding a broken chain, which sits atop the Independence Arch (Arco de la Independencia) at Avenida Pino Suárez and Calzada Francisco Madero.

La Purísima Church, at Calle Serafín Peña and Avenida Hidalgo (west of Gran Plaza on the way to the Bishop's Palace), is considered an outstanding example of modern ecclesiastical architecture. The Nuevo León State University campus is in the northern section of the city. An interesting combination of contemporary and age-old building designs distinguishes the campus of Monterrey's Technological Institute. Considered by many to be Mexico's best engineering school, the institute is a short distance southeast of downtown on Mex. 85. Pastora Park (Parque la Pastora), east of downtown off Avenida Chapultepec, is a naturally landscaped recreation area featuring a lake and a zoo.

Shopping

Folk arts and handicrafts such as leather articles, blown glass and pottery are available at two downtown markets. Mercado Juárez is off Avenida Benito Juárez between avenidas Martínez and Aramberri; the more tourist-oriented Mercado Colón is on Avenida Constitución west of Gran Plaza. Other craft shops can be found around Plaza Hidalgo near the big downtown hotels; Carapan, Av. Hidalgo #305 Oriente, offers a variety of high-quality merchandise. The House of Crafts (Casa de las Artesanías) is just east of Gran Plaza at avenidas Dr. Coss and Allende.

Monterrey also has its own Zona Rosa, not unlike the one in Mexico City, which runs along Calle Morelos in the vicinity of Gran Plaza. Craft shops, fashionable boutiques, restaurants and nightclubs line an open mall several blocks long and 2 blocks wide, reserved for pedestrians only.

Special Events

Starting on Palm Sunday, the 2-week Spring Fair (Feria de Primavera) festivities offer parades, art expositions, auto races and other sports events. The Festival of the Virgin of Guadalupe take place during the first half of December.

Bullfights are held periodically between May and December at the Plaza de Toros bullring, located south of Niños Heroes Park at avenidas Ruíz Cortines and Alfonso Reyes. Feats of horsemanship characterize *charreadas*, or Mexican-style rodeos, held Sunday mornings at ranches in the eastern suburb of Villa de Guadalupe. To reach them, follow the signs reading "Lienzo Charro" posted along free Mex. 40 in the direction of Reynosa. Contact Infotur Centro regarding schedule information.

Monterrey Infotur: Av. 5 de Mayo #525 Ote. (West) between Escobedo and Zaragoza, on the third floor of the Elizondo Páez building. The office is open Mon.-Fri. 9-1 and 3-7, Sat.-Sun. 10-5; phone

01 (800) 832-2200 (toll-free long distance within Mexico) or (800) 235-2438 (from the United States or Canada).

What to See

ALFA CULTURAL CENTER (Centro Cultural Alfa) is s.w. of downtown on Av. Manuel Gómez Morín (at Roberto Sada). Housed in a building that looks like a leaning cylinder, it has one of Mexico's best planetariums, an IMAX theater and numerous hands-on exhibits. Free buses run hourly to the center from the Alameda, a downtown park just west of Avenida Pino Suárez between avenidas Aramberri and Washington. Tues.-Sun. 3-9 (also Sat.-Sun. noon-3). Admission is charged.

BISHOP'S PALACE (El Obispado) is in the western part of the city at the w. end of Av. Padre Mier. It was built by Fray José Rafael Verger in 1787, a year of famine, to employ Indian victims of a severe drought. During the Mexican-American War, it resisted an onslaught by the invading U.S. Army for 2 days after the city had fallen. The building also served as a stronghold against the French in 1864, as a hospital during a 1903 yellow fever epidemic, and as temporary quarters for Pancho Villa during the 1910 Revolution. On smog-free days, it offers a wonderful view of the city.

Regional Museum of Nuevo León (Museo Regional de Nuevo León) is inside the palace. It has displays tracing the industrial, cultural and artistic development of the Monterrey area. Of note are the guns that were used to execute emperor Archduke Maximilian. Tues.-Sun. 10-5. Admission is charged.

CUAUHTEMOC BREWERY (Cervecería Cuauhtémoc) is n. of downtown at Av. Universidad #2002 Norte, following signs; there is no street parking, but limited free parking is available within the entrance gate. Bohemia, Tecate and Carta Blanca beers are produced at the rate of more than a million bottles a day; samples are served in the large beer garden. A Baseball Hall of Fame (Salón de la Fama) displays memorabilia associated with Mexican professional baseball players, including historic announcements, uniforms, bats and silver glove awards. There also is an interactive batting and catching area.

Food is available. Visitors taking the tour must wear an orange vest and be able to climb steep, narrow metal stairs. Allow 2 hours minimum. Guided brewery tours given on the hour daily 11-4. Beer garden open daily 10:30-6. Hall of fame open Mon.-Fri. 9:30-6, Sat.-Sun. 10:30-6. Tour and hall of fame free. Phone (81) 8328-6060.

Monterrey Museum (Museo de Monterrey) is in the old brewery warehouses. The museum displays original copper brewing vats and other artifacts, regional costumes, and works by Latin American artists.

GRAN PLAZA is bounded by Av. 5 de Mayo on the north and Av. Constitución on the south. Monterrey's immense central plaza is one of the world's largest city squares. Also known as the Macro Plaza, its construction during the 1980s helped revitalize the downtown area. Graced by fountains, statuary, gardens and boldly modern buildings, the 100-acre expanse stretches from City Hall (Palacio Municipal) north to the Government Palace (Palacio de Gobierno). Several streets pass beneath the raised plaza, helping to alleviate traffic congestion and giving it a surprisingly relaxed feel.

Beacon of Commerce (Faro del Comercio) stands in the center of Plaza Zaragoza. This 230-foot-tall, bright-orange laser beam tower dominates the plaza and bathes it with green light in the evenings.

Cathedral is on Calle Zuazua at the southern end of Gran Plaza. Built over a period of more than 2 centuries, it reflects several architectural styles. The pale yellow facade is baroque, while Plateresque decoration adorns the entrance door.

Esplanade of the Heroes (Explanada de Los Héroes) is just s. of the Government Palace. This is the most formal looking part of Gran Plaza in terms of its resemblance to a traditional Mexican plaza. It contains monuments to Mexican historical figures Father Miguel Hidalgo, Benito Juárez and José María Morelos. Just south is the Hidden Garden (Bosque Hundido), a relaxing green space with trees, burbling fountains and sculptures.

Fountain of Life (Fuente de la Vida) is in the center of Gran Plaza between avenidas Matamoros and Padre Mier. This impressive fountain boasts a bronze statue of Neptune surrounded by cavorting steeds and nymphs.

Government Palace (Palacio Gobierno) anchors the n. end of Gran Plaza, just south of Av. 5 de Mayo. The Nuevo León state capitol, this Spanish colonial-style building was built in 1908 of pink stone quarried from around San Luis Potosí; it has a typically Spanish patio.

Plaza Hidalgo is across Gran Plaza from the cathedral. Another traditional Mexican square, Hidalgo is framed with colonial-style buildings and dotted with shops and little outdoor cafes.

HEROIC CHILDREN'S PARK (Parque Niños Héroes) is on Av. Alfonso Reyes, just s. of Nuevo León State University. It was named in honor of the young cadets who defended Mexico City's Chapultepec Castle from U.S. forces during the Mexican-American War. Within the park is the Museum of Fauna and Natural Sciences (Museo de la Fauna y Ciencias Naturales); the Nuevo León Art Gallery (Pinacoteca de Nuevo León), which surveys the state's artistic heritage; a baseball stadium; gardens; and a man-made lake. Tues.-Sun. 10-7. Admission is charged. Phone (81) 8331-3890.

MUSEUM OF CONTEMPORARY ART (Museo de Arte Contemporaneo) is at calles Zuazua and Ocampo at the southern end of Gran Plaza, next to the cathedral. MARCO, as this museum is popularly known, is a spacious, ultramodern building designed by noted Mexican architect Ricardo Legorreta. Exhibits in the 14 galleries emphasize Mexican and Latin American artists. Works by 20th-century masters like Diego Rivera and David Alfaro Siqueiros share space with cutting-edge artists like Juan Soriano, who created the gigantic bronze sculpture of a dove, "La Paloma," that stands at the front entrance.

Food is available. Allow 2 hours minimum. Tues.-Sun. 10-6 (also Wed. 6-8 p.m.). Admission about $3.80 (U.S.); about $2 (ages 1-6). Free to all Wed. Phone (81) 8342-4820.

MUSEUM OF MEXICAN HISTORY (Museo de Historia Mexicana) is on Plaza 400 Años, a few blks. e. of the Government Palace It focuses on the Revolution of 1910. Multimedia exhibits, including a railroad car that transported rebels under leader Pancho Villa, chronicle the political turmoil of that era. Also on display is a collection of Huastec Indian artifacts. Guided tours in English are available. Daily 11-6:30 (also Fri.-Sun. 6:30-7:30 p.m.). Donations.

Nearby Destinations

GARCIA CAVES (Grutas de García) are n.w. of downtown Monterrey via Mex. 40. A paved road runs to the caves, which are about 8 km (5 mi.) east of the village of Villa de García. Discovered about 1843 by parish priest Juan Antonio Sobrevilla, these caves are among the largest and most beautiful in Mexico. Their estimated age is 50 to 60 million years; it is presumed the caves were once submerged due to the shellfish fossils scattered over the walls and ceilings. Ten "rooms" contain stalagmite and stalactite formations.

A swimming pool, restaurants, and picnic and recreational areas cluster at the foot of the mountain where the caves are located. From the parking area, a cable car transports visitors past rugged scenery to the cavern entrance, tucked high on a cliffside. The cement passageways connecting the caves are well lighted. Open daily. Admission includes the cable car ride and a guided tour.

HUASTECA CANYON is about 32 km (20 mi.) w. of Monterrey on Mex. 40 to the village of Santa Catarina, then 3 km (2 mi.) s. The magnificent rock gorge of Huasteca (wahs-TEH-kah) is located in Monterrey Heights National Park (Parque Nacional Cumbres de Monterrey). The sheer walls reach heights of 750 to 1,000 feet. In places the softer rock has been eroded into curious formations. Restrooms, a snack bar and picnic areas are on site.

NUEVO LAREDO, TAMAULIPAS (B-3)

pop. 322,100, metro area 533,900

Nuevo Laredo (noo-EH-voh lah-REH-doh) is a major point of entry to the Mexican mainland from the United States. It is connected to Laredo, Tex., by four international toll bridges across the Río Grande. International Bridge 1 (Gateway to the Americas) is open to vehicular and pedestrian traffic; International Bridge 2 (Juárez Lincoln) is open to vehicular traffic only. Either one can be used if you plan on driving beyond the border zone. Bridge 3 (Columbia Solidarity) primarily serves commercial vehicles, and Bridge 4 (World Trade Bridge) is reserved for commercial vehicles only. Tolls for International Bridge 1 and 2 are $3 (U.S.) southbound, $2.25 northbound; 50c southbound, 25c northbound for pedestrians (International Bridge 1).

For shopping day trips, it is recommended that you leave your car in Laredo and walk across the border, which eliminates time-consuming crossing procedures. The Mexican customs and immigration office at Bridge 1 is open 24 hours daily. U.S. Customs and Border Protection offices at Bridge 1 and Bridge 2 are open 24 hours daily.

Note: Nuevo Laredo continues to experience a high level of violence due to the warring between Mexican drug cartels. Although tourists are not targeted, visits to the city should be confined to established tourist areas during daylight hours only.

PIEDRAS NEGRAS, COAHUILA (A-2)

pop. 130,700

Piedras Negras (pee-EH-drahs NEH-grahs) faces Eagle Pass, Tex., across the Rio Grande. Two bridges extend across the border. International Bridge One is a two-lane bridge with pedestrian walkways that connects the towns' shopping areas;

it is open daily 7 a.m.-11 p.m. International Bridge Two carries vehicle traffic into Mexico; it is open daily 24 hours. Tolls are 25 cents for pedestrians, $2.50 (U.S.) for automobiles and pickups. If you're traveling into the interior the Mexican customs office is open Mon.-Fri. 8-8, Sat. 10-2. For those returning from Mexico the U.S. Customs and Border Protection office is open 24 hours daily.

This typical border city is notable chiefly as the beginning of Mex. 57—the Carretera de la Constitución (Constitution Highway), which runs south to Mexico City—and as the setting for the popular novel "Like Water for Chocolate."

REYNOSA, TAMAULIPAS (B-3)

pop. 431,900

On the Rio Grande just south of McAllen, Tex., Reynosa (reh-NOH-sah) is reached via the McAllen International Toll Bridge. The toll to enter Mexico is $2 (U.S.) per vehicle; to return to the United States the toll is $2.05 per vehicle. Both Mexican and U.S. Customs and Border Protection and immigration offices are open 24 hours daily. The city provides access to fishing camps around El Azucar (Sugar) Dam, some 81 kilometers (50 miles) to the west, which teems with bass and other freshwater game species.

Note: The border region continues to experience periodic drug-related violence. Although tourists are not a target, visits to Reynosa should be confined to established tourist areas during daylight hours.

SALTILLO, COAHUILA (C-2)

pop. 581,400, metro area 657,800, elev. 5,245′

About 85 kilometers (53 miles) southwest of Monterrey on Mex. 40, Saltillo (sahl-TEE-yoh) is the capital of and leading industrial city in the state of Coahuila. Its outskirts are a sprawl of manufacturing plants producing automobiles, engine parts and textiles. Saltillo's wool, silk and cotton mills are the source of brightly colored *sarapes,* the familiar woolen blanket worn as an outer garment. Although artificial fibers and chemical dyes are steadily replacing the old methods, *sarapes* and small throw rugs are still made by hand in shops clustered along Calle Victoria downtown; visitors are welcome to watch the weaving process. Unglazed terra-cotta tiles are another local product.

Because of its altitude and dry, mild climate, Saltillo is a popular summer resort. Golf, tennis, polo and swimming are popular recreational pursuits. The city's annual *feria* (fair) takes place the first half of August.

There are two downtown plazas. Dignified monuments and well-preserved colonial buildings line the streets around Plaza de Armas. The feeling of formality is reinforced by its paved surface, a central fountain overlooked by four female statues, and the lack of trees and benches. The plaza is flanked by the city's grand 18th-century cathedral and the Government Palace (Palacio de Gobierno), which contains murals illustrating regional history.

Much livelier is Plaza Acuña, 2 blocks northwest. Here there are an abundance of shops, and the square is ringed with little cafes and bars. Occupying one corner is Mercado Juárez, which is a good place to browse for handicrafts, *sarapes,* rugs, pottery, silverwork and bizarre-looking tin masks. Families and wandering musicians make this a fun spot to soak up the local atmosphere.

A monument to Emilio Carranza, who made the first nonstop flight from Mexico City to New York, stands along Calle Victoria. The street begins at the Alameda, a shady park just west of Plaza de Armas that is frequented by students and joggers. Here stands an equestrian statue of General Ignacio Zaragoza, hero of the 1862 Battle of Puebla. Zaragoza was born in 1829 in Bahía del Espíritu Santo, near what is now Goliad, Tex. The central bus station is southwest of downtown on Boulevard Luis Echeverría.

Coahuila State Tourism Office (Instituto Estatal de Turismo): Blvd. Venustiano Carranza #3206 in the Latinoamericana district of the city; phone 01 (800) 718-4220 (toll-free long distance within Mexico).

What to See

FUENTE ATHENEUM (Fuente Ateneo) is on Boulevard Venustiano Carranza on the University of Coahuila campus. This Art Deco-style building contains an art gallery with works by well-known European and Mexican painters.

HERRERA MUSEUM is at Bravo Norte #342. It occupies the former home and studio of early 20th-century Mexican painter Rubén Herrera. The 18th-century residence contains more than 400 of his paintings, mostly Italian landscapes and pastoral scenes representing the artist's apprenticeship in Rome.

LA ANGOSTURA BATTLEGROUND is about a half-hour drive south of the city off Mex. 54. A monument on the east side of Mex. 54 marks the site of a bloody Mexican-American War battle on Feb. 22-23, 1847.

SANTIAGO CATHEDRAL is at calles Hidalgo and Juárez facing Plaza de Armas. Built 1746-1801, it exhibits a mix of architectural styles, most notably the Mexican Churrigueresque. Decorative baroque carvings representing plants and shells adorn its facade and doors. The interior features a gilded altarpiece and a pulpit covered in gold leaf. The 1762 chapel contains a Spanish image of Christ associated with numerous legends. A 200-foot tower dominates the church and offers a panoramic view of the city.

Malecón, Puerto Vallarta / © Irene Chan / Digital Railroad

The Pacific Coast

Also known as the Mexican Riviera, Mexico's Pacific Coast boasts hundreds of miles of surf-pounded shoreline and a string of destinations stretching from Mazatlán south to Bahías de Huatulco. They range from funky beach communities—traditional getaways for budget-conscious backpackers and Mexican families of modest means—to luxurious oceanfront retreats catering to the well-heeled international set.

The Mexican Riviera unofficially begins at Mazatlán, "the Pearl of the Pacific," a shrimping center, commercial port and beach resort that has long attracted sport-fishing enthusiasts. The name is derived from the Náhuatl Indian word *mazatl,* meaning "place of deer"—a reference to former inhabitants, as these fleet creatures are nowhere to be seen in the midst of today's oceanfront bustle.

Now a year-round resort, Mazatlán blends colonial charm with the modern allure of high-rise hotels. Strung along miles of scenic Pacific shoreline and with some 10,000 hotel rooms and condominium units covering all categories and rates, the city is northwest Mexico's major beach destination. The seaside boulevard, or *malecón,* stretches for more than 10 miles past golden sands and crashing waves. The combination of sun, sea and sand draws more than half a million visitors each year.

Balancing the tourist atmosphere are the activities of a busy commercial port. Minerals and agricultural products—tomatoes, cantaloupes, cotton—from throughout the fertile state of Sinaloa are brought to the city's harbor for export. Mazatlán maintains the largest fleet of shrimp boats in Mexico, and thousands of tons of the frozen crustaceans find their way to the United States and Japan, the two main foreign markets.

Those who opt for a more laid-back time head for Manzanillo, where sun, sea and sand mix with the matter-of-fact grime of a real working city. Manzanillo doesn't go out of its way to lay out the welcome mat for visitors, which gives it an unpretentious air. Again, sport fishing is one of the big draws. And Manzanillo all but shuts down on Sunday, when practically everyone heads for—where else—the beach.

Puerto Vallarta was a tiny fishing village blessed with a stunning natural backdrop until the early 1960s. The event that put it on the tourist map was the 1964 filming of "Night of the Iguana." John Huston's movie showcased the tropical beauty of Mismaloya Beach, and the torrid romance between star Richard Burton and tagalong Elizabeth Taylor—both of whom were married to others—titillated millions and generated an avalanche of publicity. Visitors came pouring in, hoping to glimpse a movie star, and an international destination was born.

Puerto Vallarta is basically a one-stop vacation destination, where an idyllic locale is complemented by a full spectrum of luxury amenities. It combines a leisurely, slow-paced ambience with such expected big-resort features as fine dining and flashy nightlife. Accommodations range from small and unpretentious to decidedly upscale. Most of the city's older section is postcard pretty and pleasant to stroll.

The surrounding region is rich in natural beauty as well, and eco-tourism is in full swing here. Many day trips revolve around the inviting beaches lining Banderas Bay. Mismaloya, Quimixto and Yelapa, all south of Puerto Vallarta, are secluded spots (the latter two accessible only by boat) made to order for a relaxed outing away from the tourist hustle. More strenuous but equally rewarding options include taking in the jungle scenery by bike or on foot, or perhaps exploring coastal lagoons by kayak.

Ixtapa and Zihuatanejo are twin resorts, only 4 miles apart but decidedly different in atmosphere. Ixtapa, created in the early 1970s, has a glittery but planned look; Zihuatanejo, founded by Spanish conquistadores in the early 16th century, is much more down-home.

Perennially popular Acapulco now plays second fiddle to Cancún as Mexico's beach of choice, but its excess and boisterous nightlife remain in a class of their own. This Pacific playground instantly conjures images of idle days spent soaking up the sun and evenings of dining, dancing and revelry. Certainly Acapulco fulfills the scenic requirements for a tropical resort. Lofty mountains and green foothills extend to the sparkling blue of bay and ocean waters. Tall palm trees stand silhouetted against picturesque sunsets. And the view of Acapulco Bay at night, set off by thousands of city lights, is breathtaking.

Rounding out the Riviera is Bahías de Huatulco, built along a series of bays that scallop the Pacific coast like a necklace of aquamarine jewels. At some point in the future this fledgling resort might rival such hotspots as Acapulco, Cancún and Puerto Vallarta as one of Mexico's most desirable beach getaways. Located on the rugged Pacific Coast in Oaxaca, one of Mexico's poorest states, it has yet to graduate to major-league resort status, to date attracting mainly Mexican families, European tourists and diving enthusiasts.

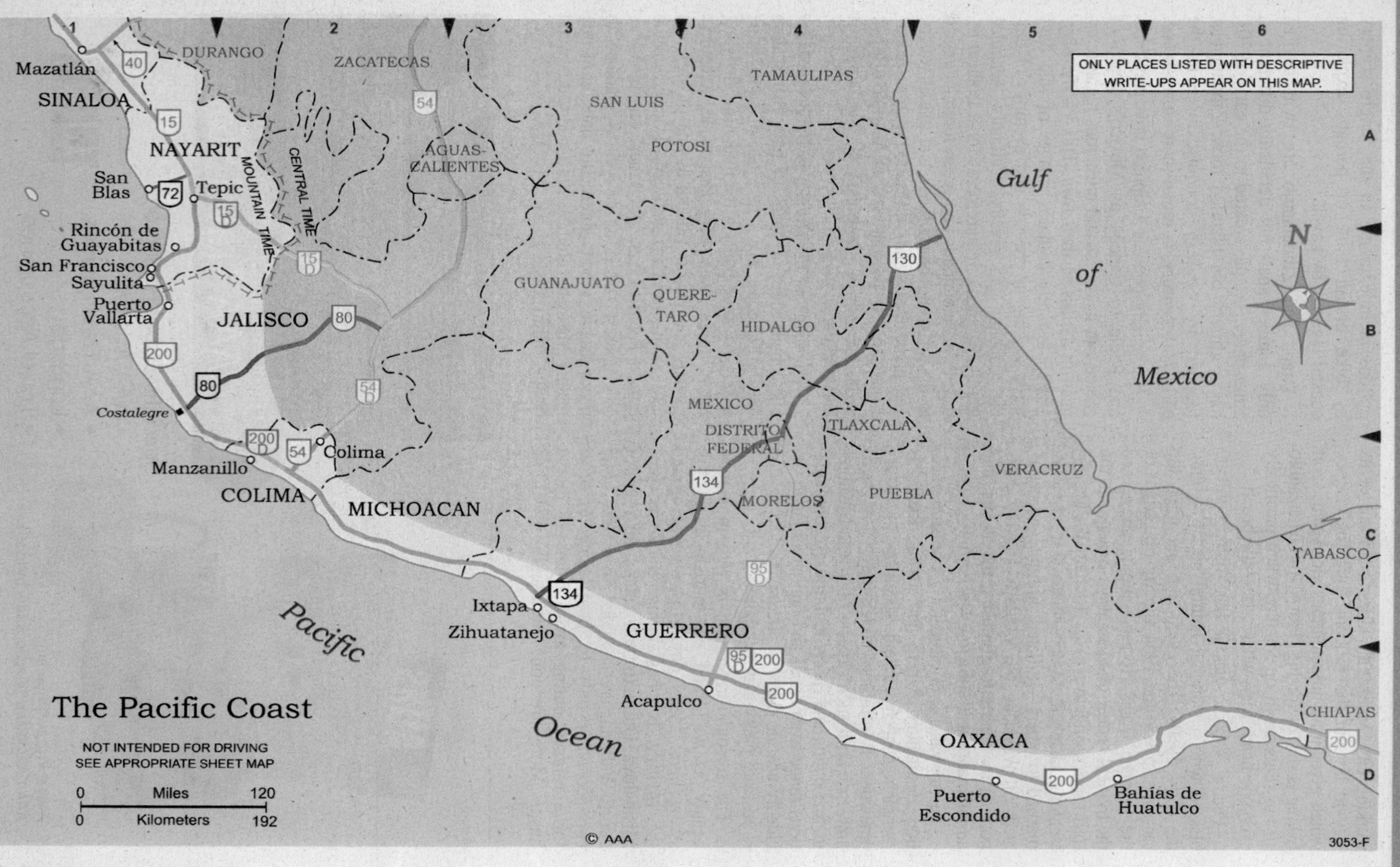
ONLY PLACES LISTED WITH DESCRIPTIVE
WRITE-UPS APPEAR ON THIS MAP.
1
2
3
4
5
6
A
B
C
D
N
Gulf of Mexico
Pacific Ocean
SINALOA
DURANGO
ZACATECAS
NAYARIT
AGUAS-CALIENTES
SAN LUIS POTOSI
TAMAULIPAS
MOUNTAIN TIME
CENTRAL TIME
JALISCO
GUANAJUATO
QUERE-TARO
HIDALGO
MEXICO
DISTRITO FEDERAL
TLAXCALA
VERACRUZ
PUEBLA
MORELOS
COLIMA
MICHOACAN
GUERRERO
OAXACA
TABASCO
CHIAPAS
Mazatlán
San Blas
Tepic
Rincón de Guayabitas
San Francisco
Sayulita
Puerto Vallarta
Costalegre
Manzanillo
Colima
Ixtapa
Zihuatanejo
Acapulco
Puerto Escondido
Bahías de Huatulco
40
15
15 D
72
54
54 D
80
130
134
95 D
200
200 D
The Pacific Coast
NOT INTENDED FOR DRIVING
SEE APPROPRIATE SHEET MAP
0 Miles 120
0 Kilometers 192
© AAA
3053-F

Acapulco

City Population: 632,300,
metro area 877,000 (estimated)
Elevation: 13 meters (43 feet)

Editor's Picks:

Acapulco Bay / © Carlos S. Pereyra / age fotostock

As early as the 1530s, ships for exploration purposes were built at a Spanish settlement occupying Acapulco's present site. Due to its excellent natural harbor, Acapulco (the name is an Indian word meaning "place where the reeds were destroyed") became the main Mexican west coast seaport for galleons bound from Manila. It was designated a city in 1599 and established as the only authorized trading port between the Americas and Asia.

From Acapulco silks, spices and other exotic goods were carried overland on mules to Mexico City and then Veracruz for shipment to Spain, while galleons moored in Acapulco Bay refilled their holds with silver and other Mexican products. That mercantile tradition continues, as the city remains a major export point for coffee, sugar and other products.

The rich Asian trade brought Mexico City merchants to Acapulco for annual unloading fairs. It also attracted Dutch and English pirates. Sir Francis Drake supposedly lay in wait for laden galleons near Puerto Marqués, just east of the present city, and pounced upon them as they left the sheltered harbor. To protect the ships from such raiders, the Spanish built Fort San Diego in 1616.

Commerce between Acapulco and Manila lasted some 250 years but came to a close in 1815 with the Mexican War of Independence. This conflict and the continued discovery and settlement of North and South America contributed to the rerouting of the China trade. As a result, Acapulco lapsed into the lethargy of an almost forgotten fishing village, punctuated by the excitement that accompanied a brief boom period during the California gold rush.

Not until 1927 was a road cut through the mountains to form an overland connection with the progressive cities to the north, particularly Mexico City. Acapulco's beaches are the country's closest to Mexico City by road, and although the trip took more than a week, the sleepy port was roused into a fever of development. When a new highway from Mexico City was completed in 1955, Acapulco was on its way to becoming Mexico's most notorious party spot.

Direct international air service began in 1964, ushering in the city's '60s and '70s heyday of glorious excess as it became a haven for the international and Hollywood jet sets, as well as one of the world's top resort destinations. Movie stars like John Wayne, Johnny Weismuller, Elvis Presley, Elizabeth Taylor and Rita Hayworth lounged at luxurious hotels. The shore along Acapulco Bay was transformed into a 9-mile swath of glitter and indulgence patronized by *la gente bonita* (the beautiful people).

Although Cancún is now Mexico's beach of choice for many foreign visitors, Acapulco retains its popularity, especially among Mexicans. A new condominium development or resort hotel project is always on the drawing board. Boat sweepers clean the bay daily (the beaches are swept daily as well), although pollution is evident in some locations, notably the area around La Quebrada, where Acapulco's famous cliff divers plunge into the surf.

Getting There — *starting on p. 221*
Getting Around — *starting on p. 224*
What To See — *starting on p. 224*
What To Do — *starting on p. 226*
Where To Stay — *starting on p. 513*
Where To Dine — *starting on p. 517*

The weather is always balmy: highs average in the upper 80s or low 90s, lows in the 70s. The ocean and bay are warm enough for swimming year-round. June through October is humid as well as hot, and these months also produce brief but torrential rains. Occasional hurricanes affect Mexico's Pacific coast. November is one of the nicest months, as high-season prices haven't yet kicked in. Formality can be left at home with your coat; standard attire consists of shorts, T-shirts and scandalous bathing suits.

Acapulco contains neither sober historical monuments nor venerable colonial architecture. Although it is a real city and important commercial center, the economy depends most heavily on the tourist trade. Visitors come not so much to sightsee but to relax. In addition to letting life's cares melt away at the beach, water recreation—from motorboat tours and fishing excursions to water skiing and parasailing—shopping and nightlife are favorite diversions.

For those with money to burn, the fun and flash are indeed heady. Big hotels pamper guests with private villas and every convenience; their swimming pool complexes in particular are some of the most elaborate in Mexico. Dining here is an event, where al fresco tables at intimate restaurants overlook the bay. And night owls flock to the city's flamboyant discos, which don't get started until midnight and wind down when the sun comes up. But Acapulco also has budget-friendly alternatives—low-key motels, simple fish shacks and a fun-filled atmosphere suitable for families.

Getting There

By Air

Acapulco International Airport is about 23 kilometers (14 miles) southeast of the city and the hotel zone, near Puerto Marqués. Major carriers frequently fly into Mexico City, where connections can be made to Acapulco.

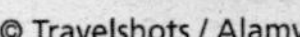

American, Continental, Delta and Mexicana airlines offer direct flights from U.S. cities. Aeroméxico, phone 01 (800) 021-4010 (toll-free long distance within Mexico), and Taesa airlines offer direct flights from Mexico City and other major Mexican cities; Aeroméxico also offers nonstop service from Los Angeles. For additional information about airlines *see Arriving by Air, page 61.*

Transportes Terrestres is an airport taxi service that transports visitors from the airport to the city's hotel zone along Costera Miguel Alemán. The 30-minute ride in a shared minivan *(colectivo)* costs about $10 (U.S.) per person; a non-shared cab starts at about $30, depending on the destination. Phone (744) 462-1095.

By Car

From Mexico City, toll highway Mex. 95-D, the Autopista del Sol (Sun Highway), is by far the

The Informed Traveler

WHOM TO CALL

Police (emergency): Dial 060 and ask to be connected to an English-speaking operator.

Police Assistance: (744) 485-0650. English-speaking tourist police on the streets wear white uniforms and safari hats and are very helpful to tourists.

Highway Patrol (Policía Federal de Caminos): (744) 486-0647 or (744) 485-0439

LOCATEL (provides assistance in locating vehicles or missing persons, or to those in need of public services): (744) 481-1111

Hospitals: Hospital Privado Magallanes, Calle Wilfrido Massieu #2, (744) 485-6544; IMSS (Mexican Social Security Hospital), downtown at Av. Cuauhtémoc #95, (744) 483-5550; Red Cross (Cruz Roja), Av. Ruíz Cortines #126, (744) 485-4100. Most hotels have an in-house doctor or a doctor on 24-hour call.

Local Phone Calls: Local calls in Acapulco cost about 15c (U.S.) for 3 minutes. Many public phones take Ladatel credit cards only; these can be purchased in stores and other locations that display the Ladatel logo.

WHERE TO LOOK

Newspapers

The bigger hotels offer *USA Today,* the *New York Times* and the *Los Angeles Times.*

Publications

Sanborn's, a Mexican restaurant chain, has English-language books and periodicals. There are branches on Costera Miguel Alemán near Playa Condesa and in the old downtown area. *Adventure in Acapulco* is a monthly publication in English that offers information on what's happening around town.

Visitor Information

Guerrero State Tourism Office (Secretaría de Fomento Turístico): Costera Miguel Alemán #4455 in the Acapulco International Center (Centro Internacional de Acapulco); phone (744) 484-2423 (English spoken). The center also contains the local Green Angels office. It is open Mon.-Fri. 8-8, Sat.-Sun. 10-6.

State Attorney General's Tourist Office (Procuraduría del Turista): Costera Miguel Alemán (in front of the Acapulco International Center); phone (744) 484-4416. The office is open daily 9 a.m.-10 p.m. and provides maps as well as tourist assistance.

WHAT TO KNOW

Currency Exchange

Most banks along the Costera, both in the downtown area and the hotel zone, are open Mon.-Fri. 9-5 (some also Sat. 10-2) and may have better currency exchange rates than the hotels. *Casas de cambio* (currency exchange offices) line the Costera in the vicinity of the big hotels; these are open daily and often until 8 p.m. ATM machines are plentiful and accept international credit cards; withdrawals are in pesos.

Staying Safe

Areas frequented by tourists are generally safe, even after dark. However, tourists often are targeted for petty theft; stay alert in crowded public places like markets or on buses. Don't take large sums of money or other valuables to the beach, and always keep your hotel key with you.

quickest and best option. Between Mexico City and Cuernavaca the funnel highway is toll Mex. 55-D. Mex. 95-D splits off from old Mex. 95 near Puente de Ixtla, proceeds south to Chilpancingo and Tierra Colorada, and then on to the international airport. Total driving time is about 3.5 hours.

The four-lane, largely traffic-free highway twists and turns through beautiful valleys and around mountainous curves. Signs denote scenic stops. About halfway to Acapulco a suspension bridge 600 feet above a river affords a spectacular view; acrophobes will probably want to keep their eyes shut.

The one drawback to traveling this well-maintained, 415-kilometer (249-mile) route is the cost: tolls are expensive. Tolls must be paid for and gas must be purchased in pesos. The highway is economically out of the question for the average Mexican driver; most of the traffic is luxury buses, long-distance trucks and tourists willing to pay for convenience.

Mex. 95, an older, free highway, begins at Mexico City and proceeds south through Cuernavaca, Taxco, Iguala and Chilpancingo to Acapulco, roughly paralleling toll Mex. 95-D. It's scenic, but also very winding. Coastal Mex. 200 links Acapulco with Bahías de Huatulco to the southeast and with Ixtapa/Zihuatanejo to the northwest.

Acapulco is a long way from the United States; from McAllen, Tex., one of the closest U.S. border points, the distance is nearly 900 miles. From points north or south along the Pacific coast, Mex. 200 is the only route. Portions of this roadway within the state of Guerrero, however, can be potholed or marked with detours that slow driving time. As a result, most visitors fly directly to the city or drive from Mexico City.

By Bus

First-class *(ejecutivo)* buses operated by Tres Estrellas de Oro make daily runs on the Autopista del Sol between Mexico City's southern bus terminal and Acapulco; the trip takes 5 to 6 hours and costs about $30 (U.S.) one way. This bus line also has service to Taxco, Ixtapa and Zihuatanejo. Buses coming from Mexico City on Friday and departing Acapulco on Monday are often very crowded. **Note:** This highway is very steep and winding in places. *For additional information about buses see Bus Service, page 72.*

By Cruise Ship

Acapulco is a major port of call for cruise ships, most of which originate from Los Angeles. Ships dock at Puerto Acapulco, near the old downtown area. Lines that visit the city include Cunard, Holland America, Norwegian, Princess Cruises and Royal Caribbean. The ship's excursion manager plans tours of the city; onshore visits include Fort San Diego (across the street from where the cruise ships are moored); La Quebrada, where the cliff divers perform; the city market; and the Mercado de Artesanías (flea market). The fine harbor and 4-mile-long bay also teem with smaller pleasure and commercial vessels.

Nadine Markova / Mexico Tourism Board

Getting Around

City Layout

The oldest part of Acapulco fills a peninsula that forms the western side of the bay. This is where residents attend to such daily errands as grocery shopping and stopping at the post office. Plaza de Toros, where occasional bullfights are held, is south of the central downtown area. On the western side of the peninsula is La Quebrada.

Besides the Mercado Municipal (city market), Old Acapulco features a Moorish-looking cathedral—complete with onion-shaped blue bulb and yellow spires—that dominates Plaza Alvarez, the city's main square. The cathedral's appearance can be misleading: It was actually constructed from parts of an uncompleted movie theater. The main square, shaded by large trees, is a meeting place at which to stop and socialize, or peruse the newspaper over a cup of coffee. Band concerts are held here on Sunday evenings.

The waterfront contains the docks and fishermen's wharves, reminders of Acapulco's continuing importance as a commercial port. This is where both cruise ships and smaller fishing boats dock. Historic Fort San Diego is in this section.

Along the bay runs Costera Miguel Alemán, the scenic boulevard named for the former Mexican president who was responsible for much of Acapulco's resort development. Most of the luxury hotels, along with many restaurants and shops and the major beaches, are in the central bay area lining the "Costera," as the thoroughfare is commonly known. Beyond the junction with Mex. 95, the coastal drive follows Acapulco Bay toward Puerto Marqués and the airport, where another group of newer luxury hotels are clustered. Inland, the major route is Avenida Cuauhtémoc, which roughly parallels the Costera.

As in many other parts of Mexico, streets are bewilderingly named and frequently change names as well. Street signs are difficult to locate. Orient yourself by using the Costera as a reference point—the great majority of Acapulco's accommodations, restaurants, nightspots and attractions are on or a short distance off it.

Rental Cars

Hertz is one of several rental car agencies with offices in Acapulco. Be sure you fully understand the terms of any rental contract. Some luxury hotels provide jeeps for their guests.

Note: AAA/CAA members enjoy discounts through Hertz for vehicles booked in the United States. Consult your local AAA/CAA club or phone Hertz, (800) 654-3080.

Buses

Local buses connect the city with the beaches and various points of interest; fares are inexpensive, and the newer tourist buses are air-conditioned. If you are taking a bus to one of the outlying areas, such as Pie de la Cuesta or Puerto Marqués, find out when and where to board the last bus going back into town. Buses run regularly all along the Costera, and maps at covered bus stops illustrate routes to major hotels and tourist attractions. Stay alert while on the bus and beware of pickpockets, who sometimes target foreign tourists.

Taxis

Hotel taxis are the most expensive, but they also are the most comfortable. A list showing the rates to which drivers must adhere is posted in most hotel lobbies. Rates usually go up at night. Taxis not affiliated with the hotels are usually white or blue-and-white Volkswagen Beetles. They usually charge by zone, destination or the distance traveled. Make certain that you come to an agreement on a rate before getting in the cab.

Parking

Old Acapulco has narrow streets and is better suited to walking than driving. It is illegal to park anywhere along Miguel Costera Alemán. An easier alternative is to use city buses or take a taxi where you want to go.

Guides/Tours

With the focus on sunning, shopping and eating out, a guide is not really necessary in Acapulco. If you do hire one, make certain he or she is a reputable, bonded guide licensed by the State Department of Tourism. Guides can usually be found in the lobbies or at the entrances of the more expensive hotels.

Better yet, take an organized excursion. A standard city tour, a day trip to Taxco or an evening tour of the city's nightclubs are all easily arranged. Local tour operators often have desks at the large hotels. Acuario Tours is a representative company. Their office is at Costera Miguel Alemán #186-3; phone (744) 485-6100.

What To See

CHILDREN'S INTERNATIONAL CENTER (Centro Internacional de Convivencia Infantil, or CICI) is on Costera Miguel Alemán at Calle Cristóbal Colón. It contains a wave pool, waterslides, swimming pools with water pistols and boats, and a small aquarium. There also are shows featuring performing dolphins and seals. The most popular activity is swimming with dolphins, which includes a half-hour orientation and another half-hour of swimming time. Food is available. Daily 10-6. Admission is charged to the water park. Dolphin swim about $95 (U.S.); reservations are required. Phone (744) 484-8210.

FORT SAN DIEGO (El Fuerte de San Diego) stands on a hill e. of the main square in Old Acapulco, overlooking the harbor and the oldest section of the city's port. Originally built in 1616 as a series of ramparts to ward off Sir Francis Drake and other

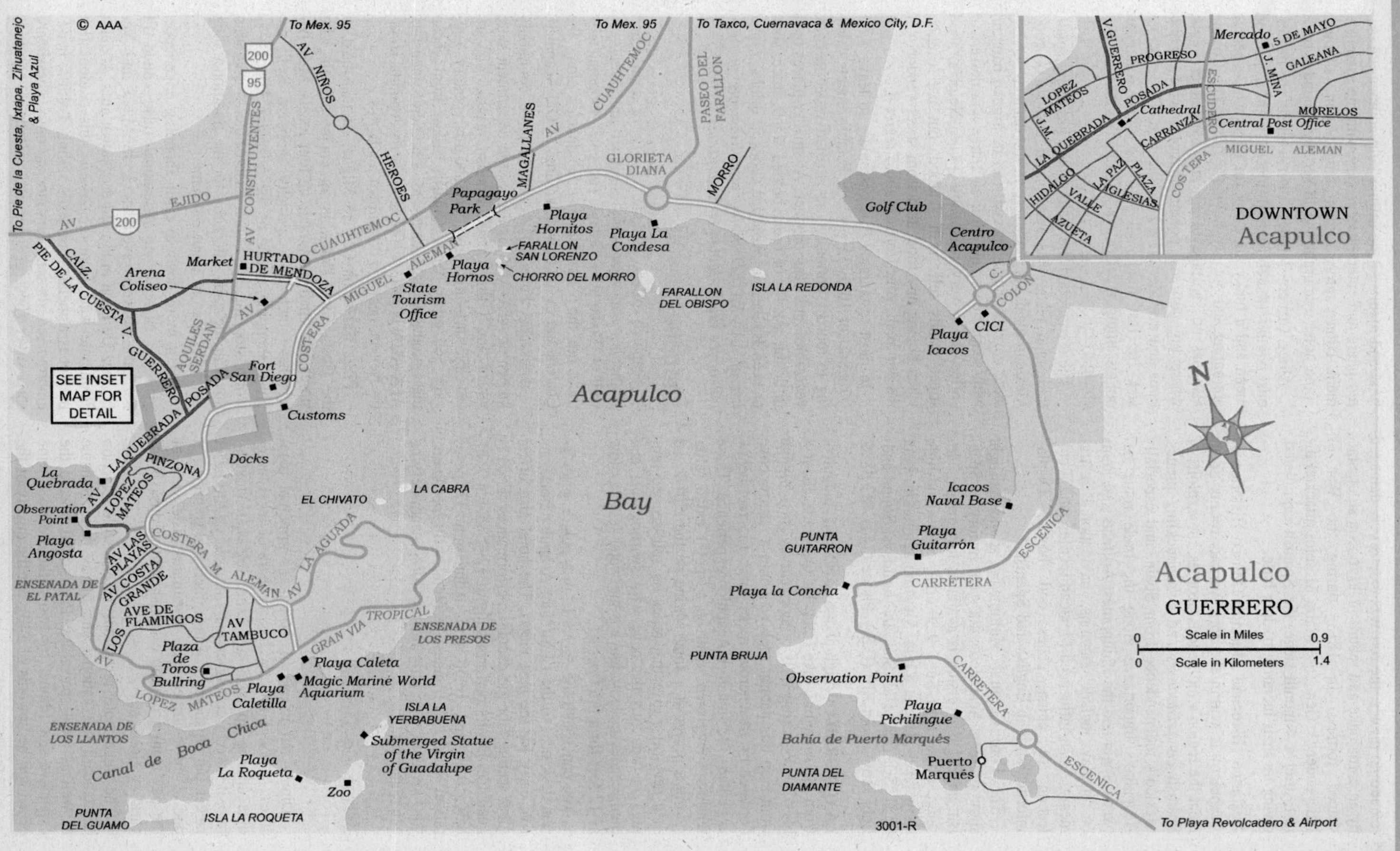

© AAA
To Pie de la Cuesta, Ixtapa, Zihuatanejo & Playa Azul
To Mex. 95
To Mex. 95
To Taxco, Cuernavaca & Mexico City, D.F.
200
95
AV NIÑOS
HEROES
CUAUHTEMOC
AV
MAGALLANES
PASEO DEL FARALLON
GLORIETA DIANA
MORRO
AV EJIDO
200
AV CONSTITUYENTES
CUAUHTEMOC
Papagayo Park
Playa Hornitos
Playa La Condesa
Golf Club
Centro Acapulco
CALZ. PIE DE LA CUESTA
Arena Coliseo
Market
HURTADO DE MENDOZA
FARALLON SAN LORENZO
Playa Hornos
CHORRO DEL MORRO
FARALLON DEL OBISPO
ISLA LA REDONDA
C.
COLON
CICI
Playa Icacos
COSTERA MIGUEL ALEMAN
State Tourism Office
AQUILES SERDAN
AV
V. GUERRERO
SEE INSET MAP FOR DETAIL
POSADA
Fort San Diego
Customs
Acapulco
LA QUEBRADA
PINZONA
Docks
La Quebrada
AV LOPEZ MATEOS
Observation Point
Playa Angosta
EL CHIVATO
LA CABRA
Bay
Icacos Naval Base
AV LAS PLAYAS
AV COSTA GRANDE
COSTERA M ALEMAN
AV LA AGUADA
ENSENADA DE EL PATAL
AVE DE FLAMINGOS
LOS
AV TAMBUCO
GRAN VIA TROPICAL
ENSENADA DE LOS PRESOS
Plaza de Toros Bullring
Playa Caleta
Magic Marine World Aquarium
Playa Caletilla
AV LOPEZ MATEOS
ISLA LA YERBABUENA
Submerged Statue of the Virgin of Guadalupe
ENSENADA DE LOS LLANTOS
Canal de Boca Chica
Playa La Roqueta
Zoo
PUNTA DEL GUAMO
ISLA LA ROQUETA
PUNTA GUITARRON
Playa Guitarrón
ESCENICA
Playa la Concha
CARRETERA
PUNTA BRUJA
Observation Point
CARRETERA
Playa Pichilingue
Bahía de Puerto Marqués
PUNTA DEL DIAMANTE
Puerto Marqués
ESCENICA
3001-R
To Playa Revolcadero & Airport
N
Acapulco
GUERRERO
Scale in Miles
0
0.9
0
1.4
Scale in Kilometers
V. GUERRERO
PROGRESO
Mercado
5 DE MAYO
J. MINA
GALEANA
LOPEZ MATEOS
POSADA
ESCUDERO
MORELOS
J.M.
LA QUEBRADA
Cathedral
CARRANZA
Central Post Office
COSTERA
MIGUEL ALEMAN
HIDALGO
LA PAZ
PLAZA
IGLESIAS
VALLE
AZUETA
DOWNTOWN
Acapulco

marauding pirates, the fort was extensively damaged by an earthquake and rebuilt in 1776 as a stout, star-shaped fortress. In 1813, during the War of Independence, Gen. José María Morelos attacked the fort; after a 4-month siege, the Spanish capitulated, giving up their lucrative trading base.

Acapulco Historical Museum (Museo Histórico de Acapulco) is within the fort. Various rooms document the region's indigenous peoples, the exploits of Spanish *conquistadores* and swashbuckling pirates, Mexico's independence from Spain, and especially Acapulco's importance along the trade route between Spain and the Philippines. Artifacts and items on display include cannons, navigational instruments, Asian-influenced Mexican textiles, and a collection of china plates and bowls. Display information is in English and Spanish.

The Foro Cultural Multimedia sound-and-light show presents Acapulco's 400-year history in Spanish; an English version is available for groups. Museum open Tues.-Sun. 9:30-6:30; sound-and-light show takes place at 8 p.m. Museum admission about $3 (U.S.); free to all Sun. and holidays. Sound-and-light show about $10 (U.S.). Phone (744) 482-3828.

LA QUEBRADA is high above downtown Acapulco; from the cathedral, take Calle La Quebrada about 4 blks. w. Watching cliff divers *(clavadistas)* plunge from atop this natural rock wall into a narrow cove bordered by treacherous rocks some 135 feet below is perhaps the signature Acapulco experience. These fearless young men stand on a spotlit ledge (after saying a prayer at a small shrine on the cliffs) and then perform a dive that relies on split-second timing; the tide fills the cove with swirling surf and then recedes quickly, leaving the water level as low as 12 feet for a brief period.

You can watch the divers from a public observation deck next to the El Mirador Acapulco hotel; arrive early for the best views. The hotel also offers meal seatings for the evening performances. Food is available. Divers perform daily at 12:45 and at 7:30, 8:30, 9:30 and 10:30 p.m. Admission 37 pesos (about $3.60 U.S.); many people also tip the divers, who are paid very little for providing death-defying entertainment.

What To Do

Dining

Dining out is one of Acapulco's principal pleasures. Although the city has its share of local hangouts dishing up tacos and other regional Mexican fare, it's worth getting casually dressed up (no tie or jacket, but no shorts or jeans either) and splurging at one of the gourmet hotel restaurants. The view of the bay from a rooftop establishment at dusk is invariably glorious.

The bigger hotel restaurants offer a wide selection of standard international and trendy fusion cuisine as well as local specialties. Prices tend toward the expensive side (dinner for two without drinks, wine or tip will be upwards of $40), but the quality of the food and luxury of the setting help compensate. Atmosphere and entertainment vary with the establishment. Dinner rarely begins before 9 p.m., although some hotel restaurants begin serving around 6 or 7.

Along Costera Miguel Alemán there are numerous *palapa* (thatch-roofed) places with a seafood menu and a funky air. Look for those where people are eating and not just having a drink. The Costera also has no shortage of rib and hamburger joints, where big portions, potent libations, wild decorations and a wilder crowd are the rule. Those homesick for fast food will find the usual American outlets lining the Costera, although prices are not cheap.

The area around the main square has many small, traditional restaurants where you can get a good Mexican meal. As elsewhere in the country, the *comida corrida* (lunch special) can be a good bargain, with soup, rice or noodles, an entree and dessert or coffee for a very reasonable price. Neighborhood street stands sell fresh seafood, but use caution when buying any food item from street vendors—if it's *not* fresh, your stomach could regret it.

In most restaurants it is customary to leave a tip (*propina*) of 10 to 15 percent. Establishments catering to tourists normally use purified water to cook vegetables and wash produce. At smaller places or if in doubt, ask for or order bottled water, juice, soda or beer. It's best to avoid ice cubes in drinks. *For a list of AAA-RATED dining establishments in Acapulco, see the Lodgings & Restaurants section.*

Shopping

Acapulco offers a wide variety of men's and women's resort wear—both designer and casual—as well as Taxco silver items. The chief shopping districts are the air-conditioned complexes along the Costera and in the downtown area of Old Acapulco.

Artesanías Finas de Acapulco, more commonly known as AFA-ACA, is a one-stop department store where you'll find carved wooden masks, folk art, jewelry, furniture, onyx chessboards, pottery, luggage and other items. Quality varies, from cheap mass-produced souvenirs to fine craftsmanship. AFA-ACA is just off the Costera on Avenida Horatio Nelson, near the downtown Sanborn's.

Plaza Bahía, on Costera Miguel Alemán next to the Costa Club Hotel, is an enclosed mall with stores and small restaurants on four levels. Most hotels have their own specialty shops as well; the plush shopping arcade at the Acapulco Princess is worth stopping by. Some establishments still shut down in the early afternoon for the traditional long lunch break from about 2-4 p.m.

For a more down-to-earth shopping experience, visit the Mercado de Artesanías (also called El Parazal), between avenidas 5 de Mayo and Velazquez De León in the old downtown area. About a 20-minute walk from the *Zócalo,* this outdoor flea market is a melange of stalls selling T-shirts, hand-embroidered dresses, hammocks, onyx chessboard sets, silver (both genuine and imitation), ceramics and assorted curios. Here the time-honored custom of bargaining prevails. The selling price is apt to be outrageous. If you don't have the time or patience to stand and haggle, pretending to walk away often brings the price down quickly. Go early in the morning, before it gets too hot or crowded.

The Municipal Market (Mercado Central), a few blocks off the Costera at avenidas Cuesta Hurtado de Mendoza and Constituyentes, offers a distinct change from the upscale stores of the tourist strip. This is where the locals do their shopping, and the tarp-covered stalls display everything from fresh produce to good luck charms. Souvenirs abound, and fans of kitsch will appreciate the gaudy ashtrays and shell ornaments.

Beaches

Noisy band concerts and frivolous teeny-bikini contests notwithstanding, Acapulco's shoreline does have its business side. The bay is anchored by a commercial port at one end and a naval base at the other. Still, there is plenty of room in between for a swath of sand that is broken only by a few rock outcroppings, and more secluded beaches stretch northwest of the bay along the Pacific coastline. Keep in mind that all beaches in Mexico are federally owned property and therefore public, even stretches that may seem private because they are in front of one of the big hotels.

For safety's sake, avoid completely isolated beaches. Chairs, umbrellas, showers, hammocks and refreshments are available at most locations. Due to unpredictable or rough surf conditions, the beaches facing the open Pacific—northwest of more protected Acapulco Bay—are better suited for watching the sky turn a pretty pink at sunset or taking a romantic stroll along the shore than for swimming. The following beaches are listed alphabetically.

PIE DE LA CUESTA is about 16 km (10 mi.) n.w. of Acapulco. "Foot of the Hill" is an uncrowded, golden-sand beach that makes a good day trip by car or taxi. Thatched *palapa* restaurants shaded by coconut palms are a perfect place to savor the local fish, caught fresh in the morning and broiled over charcoal fires. Crashing breakers and treacherous currents make swimming or bodysurfing at this beach very risky; there are no lifeguards.

Watching the sun go down over the water is a daily ritual. Families line up rows of chairs pointed toward the descending sun. Vendors mill around selling snacks and trinkets. All heads turn at sunset. If there are clouds in the sky, the patterns of color will be magnificent; even if the weather is perfect, the Pacific turns into pale gold as the sun drops.

PLAYA CALETA is along the peninsula where Old Acapulco is located. Caleta Beach and its twin, Playa Caletilla, used to be known as the "morning beaches." Once attracting the city's chic elite, the beaches today cater more to families. The ocean water is very calm here. Inner tubes and other water sports equipment can be rented.

Across from Caleta Beach is the secluded island of La Roqueta, reached by a 15-minute trip aboard a motorboat or glass-bottom boat. A lighthouse stands on the island. It's a peaceful place to sunbathe, snorkel or windsurf; boards, beach chairs, inner tubes and canoes all can be rented at Caletilla Beach.

Standing submerged in the harbor near the island is a bronze statue of the Virgin of Guadalupe. It is best seen on a glass-bottom boat ride, as the shrine is not easily visible from the surface.

PLAYA HORNOS is just off Costera Miguel Alemán. Twin beaches Hornos and Hornitos once were fashionable spots for afternoon bathers; both are now packed with Mexican tourists. Here the water of Acapulco Bay is calm, although not particularly clean. But palm trees shade the sand, and there are numerous casual, thatched-roof restaurants lining the beach.

PLAYA LA CONDESA faces the middle of Acapulco Bay. La Condesa Beach is crowded with singles—the place to see and be seen, view Acapulco's most daring swimwear (on both sexes) and watch the parasailers. Vendors hawking trinkets also roam this beach. There are many lunch spots along Costera Miguel Alemán.

PLAYA PUERTO MARQUES stretches along a narrow neck of little Puerto Marqués Bay e. of Acapulco. The water is calm and suitable for swimming or water skiing, and the beach is lined with seafood restaurants that are literally at the water's edge. Puerto Marqués is popular with Mexican tourists and is crowded on weekends. The real attraction is the 18-kilometer (11-mile) drive via the Carretera Escénica (Scenic Highway), the eastward extension of Costera Miguel Alemán that winds past Icacos Naval Base, which offers magnificent views of the city and Acapulco Bay.

DID YOU KNOW

The Mexican coastline is nearly four times longer than the combined coasts of California and Florida.

PLAYA REVOLCADERO is approximately three-quarters of a kilometer (half a mile) beyond Playa Puerto Marqués. On the open ocean, Revolcadero Beach is popular for swimming and surfing, although the waves can be rough and there is a powerful undertow; stay close to shore. The wide strip of sand is ideal for a beachside horseback ride.

Sightseeing

The sights here are seenic, not historic. Brightly decorated *calandrias* (horse-drawn carriages) regularly parade along Costera Miguel Alemán, a leisurely way to tour the city. They also can be hired as taxis. In Fraccionamiento Las Brisas, an upscale subdivision of homes, is La Capilla de la Paz, a simple, modern chapel. From this mountainside location a large white cross overlooks the east side of the bay. The attractive grounds offer a peaceful retreat from Acapulco's hectic pace.

Rental cars and jeeps are available for drives along the outlying coastal roads. An interesting side trip is through the Costa Chica (Little Coast), a 240-kilometer (150-mile) stretch of coastline that stretches southeast of Acapulco to the Guerrero-Oaxaca border. Mex. 200, in poor paved condition in some areas of this coastal route, runs past the town of San Marcos through a deserted terrain of lagoons and rocky cliffs in the shadow of the Sierra Madre mountains.

Costa Chica is inhabited by descendants of two boatloads of slaves who managed to evade their intended Acapulco destination. Many African customs have been preserved among the Costa Chicans, who are descendants of the Bantu tribe. This cultural enclave is most evident in and around the small mining village of Ometepec.

Driving northwest from Acapulco on Mex. 200 (the Costa Grande, or Big Coast) is another scenic excursion encompassing palm-lined lagoons and secluded beaches. Jungle-covered hills and high rock promontories finally yield to the high-rise hotels of Ixtapa.

Yachts that depart daily from the *malecón* offer morning, afternoon and moonlight cruises around Acapulco Bay. Tickets can be purchased at the boat or from any hotel travel agent. Lunch or dinner, music and dancing are frequently part of the package. The water also is a prime vantage point from which to view Acapulco's sunsets or the La Quebrada cliff divers. Glass-bottom boat tours of the bay are available at Caleta Beach and several other waterfront locations.

Outdoor Recreation

All forms of water recreation are natural choices for leisure activity. Big-game **fishing** for marlin, sailfish, dolphin, barracuda, yellowtail, shark, red snapper and pompano is excellent all year. An international sailfish tournament is held in late November or early December. Besides deep-sea fishing, there's freshwater fishing in Tres Palos Lagoon and Coyuca Lagoon, near Pie de la Cuesta. Small boats can be rented, with catfish the frequent catch. Favored spots for inland river fishing are along the Río Papagayo, east of Acapulco just beyond Tres Palos Lagoon, and the Río Coyuca, just beyond Coyuca Lagoon and west of Pie de la Cuesta.

Guides are available for hire, and fishing trips also can be arranged through your hotel or the Pesca Deportiva, near the dock across from the main square. Rates at the dock are negotiable; select a reliable outfit whose equipment is in good, safe condition. Deep-sea boats with experienced crews can be rented by the day; these excursions usually leave in the early morning and return in the early afternoon. Make arrangements ahead of time. A fishing license is required, but local companies frequently will take care of this for you.

Almost every type of **boating** can be enjoyed. Sailboats, speedboats, catamarans and other pleasure craft prevail on the bay. Yachts and deep-sea fishing vessels are available as well; some host sunset and moonlight cruises complete with champagne. Arrange boat rentals through hotels or travel agents. For larger vessels with fully-equipped crews, make reservations in advance. An information booth at Caletilla Beach rents canoes, paddleboats and other small craft and can arrange water skiing and scuba diving excursions.

Swimming in certain areas of Acapulco Bay is not recommended, despite the enticing hue of its waters. Although cleanup efforts are ongoing, pollution is still evident. The beaches tend to have rough surf and strong undertows; pay particular heed to any warning flags posted. There also are periodic shark sightings. Fortunately, almost every hotel has a pool, if not several. Some of them are huge, set against a backdrop of rustling palms and tropical plantings, and have swim-up bars for the truly indolent. Luxury hotels feature private or semiprivate pools.

All of the major hotels offer **scuba diving** lessons and equipment. The waters off Roqueta Island are especially suited to diving. Divers de México provides dive packages with English-speaking instructors, plus lessons beginning in a swimming pool; phone (744) 482-1398. Boats for **water skiing** can be booked at hotels as well. The gentler waters at Puerto Marqués and Caleta Beach are good for beginners. Exhibitions of barefoot skiing can be viewed at Coyuca Lagoon. **Surfing** is not permitted in Acapulco Bay; the best place to surf is Revolcadero Beach, near Puerto Marqués.

Another popular sport is **parasailing,** although it is not without risks. From a standing position, a speedboat hauls a "sailor" to an altitude of more than 325 feet. This thrill can be had at almost any beach, although many parachute operators set up at La Condesa. **Windsurfing** is good at Puerto Marqués and also can be arranged at Caleta Beach. **Horseback riding** is best at Playa Revolcadero and Pie de la Cuesta.

Bullfights are held on Sundays and some holidays January through April at the Plaza de Toros bullring, off Avenida López Mateos in Old Acapulco (up the hill from Caletilla Beach). Tickets are available through travel agencies or hotels; tickets purchased through agencies normally include transportation to and from the hotel. The *corrida* begins promptly at 5:30, so arrive early, particularly if you plan to buy a ticket at the ring.

General admission ticket are about $5 (U.S.); reserved seats average about $20 but vary with the location of the seat. *Sombra* (in the shade) seats are more expensive but more desirable than *sol* (in the sun). If it's your first bullfight, try to obtain seats near the top of the arena, which provide a sweeping view of the spectacle. **Note:** The bull is traditionally killed during these performances, so if the inherent cruelty is upsetting do not attend.

Fans of **jai alai** can watch this fast-paced sport at the Jai-Alai Stadium, also in Old Acapulco near the bullring. This state-of-the-art complex contains restaurants, specialty shops and an art gallery, in addition to a Racing & Sports Book betting facility where wagers can be placed.

Most accommodations provide **tennis** courts for their guests; nonguests can use the facilities but will pay more per hour for court fees. There are both indoor and outdoor courts; some are lighted for night play. Lessons with English-speaking instructors are available. A tennis center at the Vidafel Mayan Palace hotel, in the Punta Diamante area at the eastern end of Acapulco Bay, has 12 clay and synthetic-floor courts surrounded by nylon netting that screens the sun but allows cooling breezes in.

Championship **golf** courses include the 18-hole course at the Acapulco Princess Hotel and the 18-hole course at the Pierre Marqués Hotel, both along Revolcadero Beach, and the Tres Vidas Golf & Country Club at Punta Diamante, designed by renowned golf course architect Robert von Hagge. There also is a nine-hole public course off Costera Miguel Alemán, next to the Acapulco International Center. All four charge greens fees, although reduced fees are offered to Acapulco Princess and Pierre Marqués hotel guests. Advance reservations are suggested during the winter season. Try to schedule a weekday round, when courses are generally less crowded.

Opportunities for **jogging** are not plentiful. A morning run is possible along the sidewalk on the beach side of Costera Miguel Alemán; do it before traffic gets too heavy. The truly dedicated can run on the shifting sands of the beaches. For those unwilling to sacrifice regular workouts just because they're on vacation, the Villa Vera Hotel & Racquet Club has a **fitness center** with step aerobic machines and free weights. The center is open to nonguests.

Nightlife

Acapulco's reputation for wild nightlife is renowned: The fun usually begins after a long dinner and can last until dawn. Much of the activity centers on nightclubs and hotel bars; for a full night on the town, try several establishments for dinner, dancing and drinks. Other options, such as flamenco dancers, drag shows, stand-up comedy or live salsa music, are plentiful.

The city's glitzy dance clubs feature elaborate light shows, mirrored walls, fireworks and dance beats pounding from state-of-the-art sound systems. The music ranges from techno to hip-hop to alternative rock to Top 40. Some places have breathtaking views of Acapulco Bay. They start hopping after 10:30 p.m. and stay open until the wee hours. While always crowded, most are conveniently located along Costera Miguel Alemán and are grouped in clusters; if there's a line at one place, try another.

A dress code is standard (jeans and T-shirts are usually frowned on). Cover charges are steep ($30 or more during the winter high season, less at other times), although they are sometimes waived to draw customers. Women normally pay a reduced charge. In addition to the cover, you also can run up a hefty drink tab if you're not careful.

Present hot spots include El Alebrije, Costera Miguel Alemán #3308 (across from the Hyatt Regency Acapulco); Baby'O, Costera Miguel Alemán #22; Mandara, on Carretera Escénica (the Costera) near the La Vista Shopping Center; and the Palladium, on Carretera Escénica (the Costera) at Las Brisas. Zucca, in the La Vista Shopping Center on Carretera Escénica (the Costera), attracts an older crowd (which in Acapulco means over 25).

Just as much fun but more casual (especially in regard to dress code) is Disco Beach, Costera Miguel Alemán #111 (at Playa Condesa). This open-air club is right on the sand. It opens earlier, and the cover charge is lower. Rock bands frequently play on the street-level stage; the DJ area opens onto the beach. Foam parties rule on Friday nights. Another popular watering hole is the Acapulco branch of the Hard Rock Café, at Costera Miguel Alemán #37.

The city's most celebrated nighttime attraction, however, is the diving from La Quebrada cliff *(see attraction listing)*. Young men belonging to the Association of Professional Cliff Divers (Clavadistas Profesionales de la Quebrada) perform these spectacular dives, which date back to 1934, when La Quebrada first became a popular spot for local divers to display their talent.

A successful dive depends as much on timing as on skill, since a diver enters a channel less than 25 feet wide and must wait for an opportunity when the water is deep enough to permit a safe entry at a speed of about 55 miles an hour. Getting to the top of the cliff is risky as well—barefoot divers scale the steep, vertical cliffside by grasping at rocky outcrops that occasionally snap off.

The last two evening dives incorporate blazing torches for a truly theatrical effect. The traditional place to view the cliff divers is from the bar or terraces of the La Perla restaurant at the El Mirador Acapulco hotel, but you'll be required to pay a cover charge (which includes two drinks) or have dinner. Reservations are advised during the winter high season; phone (744) 483-1155.

In keeping with the local love for feats of daring, the celebrated Papantla Flyers (Voladores de Papantla) perform a flying pole act Wednesday and Friday evenings in Aztec Plaza at the Acapulco International Center, Costera Miguel Alemán #4455, as part of Fiesta Mexicana nights. With poles far higher than those traditionally used, the Indians' act is very hazardous and dramatic. The show begins at 8 p.m. Those who prefer less life-threatening drama can take in native dance performances of the Acapulco Ballet Folklórico. General admission or dinner show tickets can be purchased; phone (744) 484-7050 for reservations, or consult your hotel tour desk or a local travel agency.

The high-rise hotels frequently offer nightly entertainment, such as Mexican-style fiestas or theme parties. Live music accompanies the happy hour at these establishments, which also have the usual poolside cocktail bars and evening floor shows. The Acapulco International Center, in addition to hosting the flying pole dancers, has several entertainment facilities, including mariachi and piano bars and outdoor performance areas.

Special Events

The year's greatest influx of visitors is during Holy Week and the week after, marked by several religious observances. Many local businesses close, and the city becomes so crowded that some people sleep on the beach. Those wishing to visit during this time should make reservations far in advance.

For music lovers the Acapulco International Music Festival, which takes place in May, draws participants from many countries. The offerings encompass everything from top-of-the-charts pop to traditional boleros, and are performed by orchestras, bands, trios and individual artists. Concerts are given at the Acapulco International Center, the Plaza de Toros bullring and at beaches, hotels and other open-air spots around the city.

The Virgin of Guadalupe is the focus of a nationwide pilgrimage on Dec. 12 to the Basilica of Our Lady of Guadalupe, in a northern suburb of Mexico City *(see the Mexico City attraction listing, page 302)*. The event, celebrated with dancing and other forms of merriment, is observed with special exuberance in Acapulco. Also in December are the Cliff Diving Championships. Acapulco closes out the year with a huge party on New Year's Eve.

This ends listings for Acapulco.
The following page resumes the alphabetical listings
of cities in The Pacific Coast.

BAHIAS DE HUATULCO, OAXACA

(D-5)

FONATUR, Mexico's government-funded tourist development agency, officially inaugurated Bahías de Huatulco (wah-TOOL-co) in 1988, selecting a 22-mile stretch of bays, coves and inlets as the site for a master-planned vacation getaway. But while its resort aspects are a recent development, the settlement of Huatulco has been around for quite awhile.

Zapotec, Mixtec and Aztec merchants established a trade route through this region during pre-Hispanic times, and the coastal settlement of Santa Cruz Huatulco became a thriving port and shipyard. By the late 16th century, however, Acapulco had absorbed the galleon trade, and pirate attacks brought about a further decline. Until recently, Huatulco and other small villages along this stretch of coast remained forgotten outposts.

Jagged boulders and small islands characterize this section of Mexico's Pacific coastline, much of which is backed by dense tropical forest. The resort area comprises nine bays in all. Thanks to their natural layout, large-scale development will be broken into a series of resort areas targeting budget, mid-range and upper-end travelers. Ecotourism is promoted heavily, and there are increasing opportunities for jungle hikes, river rafting, rappelling and other vigorous activities.

Planners also have vowed to set aside the majority of the resort's approximately 52,000 acres as ecological preserves in order to protect the area's natural environment. If projected development comes to pass, by the year 2018 Bahías de Huatulco is expected to have some 30,000 hotel rooms (compared to about 2,300 now), bring in 2 million visitors annually, and generate nearly 25 percent of the state of Oaxaca's total revenue.

Practicalities

Huatulco International Airport is off Mex. 200, about 19 kilometers (12 miles) northwest of the Tangolunda resort area. To those travelers arriving by air, Huatulco from above resembles more than anything a vast green carpet of jungle descending from the foothills of the Sierra Madre del Sur to the ocean shore.

The tropical feeling is reinforced by the airport's appearance. The two terminals—one for international flights, one for domestic flights—are large, *palapa*-style hardwood structures with high ceilings and thatched roofs. Unfortunately, arriving visitors may encounter roaming time share representatives; avoid their high-pressure sales tactics.

Mexicana, phone 01 (800) 509-8960 (toll-free long distance within Mexico), flies from Chicago, Los Angeles, San Francisco, Toronto and other international cities to Huatulco via Mexico City. Mexicana and its subsidiary, Aerocaribe, also offer domestic flights to Huatulco from Mexico City, Oaxaca and other Mexican cities. For additional information about airlines *see Arriving by Air, page 61*.

Transportes Terrestres, phone (958) 581-9014 or (958) 581-9024, operates shared minivan *(colectivo)* service that shuttles passengers from the airport to the resort hotels; expect to pay about $9-$10 (U.S.) per person. A private taxi (often a Chevrolet Suburban) is much more expensive—about $40 and up, depending on the amount of luggage you have—and drivers can be aggressive about soliciting fares.

Taxi service also links the three separate areas of Tangolunda, Santa Cruz and La Crucecita. Cabs wait in front of the big hotels and also congregate around the plazas in Santa Cruz and La Crucecita. Fares average about $5 (U.S.) from La Crucecita to Tangolunda and $3 from Santa Cruz to Tangolunda or Santa Cruz to La Crucecita. Rates are posted at the travel booth on the main plaza in La Crucecita.

Since Huatulco is spread out and also has a good road network, a rental car can come in handy for exploring as well as for trips to nearby destinations. AAA/CAA members can reserve a rental car through their local club; it is recommended that you make all necessary arrangements prior to your departure. It also helps to know the peso equivalent of the dollar rate you are charged, since the charge in Mexico will be in pesos.

The climate is tropical, with an average annual temperature of 82 degrees. Temperatures in May, the hottest month, can reach 100. January through May is practically rainless; heavy rains fall July through September. As in Mexico's other Pacific coast resorts, the "winter" months, December through March, are the sunniest, driest and least oppressive. **Note:** Mosquitoes can be fierce all along the coast. Pack an effective insect repellent or pick up Autan Classic, a widely available Mexican brand.

The Bays

From east to west, the nine bays of Huatulco are Conejos, Tangolunda, Chahué, Santa Cruz, El Organo, El Maguey, Cacaluta, Chachacual and San Agustín. Conejos, Tangolunda, Chahue, Santa Cruz, El Maguey and El Organo are accessible by car; others can be reached only by boat. Bahía Conejos has minimal tourist facilities but offers excellent snorkeling, diving and fishing at its four beaches.

Luxury hotel development in Huatulco is focused along Bahía Tangolunda, which means "place where the gods live" in the Zapotec dialect. High-rise buildings are absent—no structure here is more than six stories tall. As a result, the Mediterranean-, Moorish- and Mexican-style resorts that hug the bay offer unobstructed views from many different vantage points. Careful attention has been given to paving and landscaping, with sculptured rocks separating the roads running to and from the resort properties.

Several beaches line this bay, including Playa La Hierbabuena, Playa del Amor (Love Beach), Punta Paraiso and Playa La Entrega, where a coral reef lies just a few feet offshore. Most of the resorts are all-inclusive, with shuttle service to the beach and such diversions as themed evening shows and Mexican Fiesta nights.

Bahía Chahué (Chah-WAY) is the largest of the nine, with three separate stretches of sandy beach. A marina for private yachts is in operation. Many hotel employees live in La Crucecita, a planned town and residential area a mile or so inland off Mex. 200. Its main square, while not particularly authentic, is attractive, graced with a central bandstand, brick walkways, green lawns, shade trees and white stone benches.

Surrounding this plaza are modest hotels, restaurants, shops specializing in Oaxacan handicrafts and an Internet café, an establishment fast becoming ubiquitous in Mexico. Horse-drawn carriages depart from the plaza for leisurely tours. The central part of town is very lively in the evening, when locals and visitors mingle at the restaurants and in the square.

Bahía Santa Cruz is the site of the original fishing settlement of Huatulco. Day cruises to the other eight bays depart from the marina here; arrangements can be made at your hotel or through local travel agents. An international cruise ship dock was completed and opened in 2003 at the entrance to the Santa Cruz Marina.

The village of Santa Cruz, which developed in the wake of Huatulco's resort unveiling, has a shady main square surrounded by shops, restaurants, bars and a few Mexican-style, middle-class hotels. Playa Santa Cruz, the main beach, is a short distance from the marina. It has clear, calm water and refreshment facilities, making it a pleasant spot to snorkel or simply lay around after lunch. Nearby Playa Yerbabuena and Playa La Entrega are accessible by boat, either an outboard motor-propelled *panga* (skiff) or a deluxe cruise vessel.

Bahía El Organo has gentle surf, nearby parking facilities and a few open-air *palapa* restaurants. The four westernmost bays—El Maguey, Cacaluta, Chachacual and San Agustín—were designated a national park in 1998, protecting them from commercial development, although they can still be visited. Cacaluta and Chachacual have long, deserted stretches of beach; San Agustín is excellent for diving. All of the bays, in fact, boast lovely golden-sand beaches and pristine waters, the result of a sewage system that permits nothing to be dumped into the ocean.

What To Do

Huatulco's cove-pocked coastline is its major attraction, and the best way to experience it is to take a cruise. Boat tours visit the more pristine of the nine bays, such as El Maguey or Chachacual, with time out for swimming or snorkeling in the crystal-clear water and lunch on the beach. Guided kayaking trips also are available up the Copalita River, which winds into the nearby mountains.

Isla La Blanquita, off Bahía Santa Cruz, looks white from a distance, crowded as it is with seagulls, ducks, pelicans and albatrosses. Bahía El Organo's U-shaped Playa Violín has very fine sand and gentle waves that form a sort of natural swimming pool. Here also are two natural phenomena: El Bufadero, a blowhole in a shoreline cliff from which spouts of water occasionally erupt, and the "Stone Face," a rock formation just above the water that resembles the visage of an old man.

The bays are ideal for swimming, sailing and snorkeling, but surf conditions can fluctuate greatly at Tangolunda Bay; heed the colored flags posted along the beach that advertise swimming conditions. Tangolunda and Santa Cruz bays have the most extensive equipment rental facilities. Among the prettiest beaches are Bahía Chahué's Playa Esperanza and Playa Tejón, and Bahía Chachacual's Playa la India. Swimming is best at Conejos, Tangolunda, Santa Cruz, El Organo and El Maguey bays.

In the mountains above Huatulco are coffee plantations begun by German immigrants. The tropical highlands in the vicinity offer ideal conditions for growing coffee, an evergreen shrub native to East Africa. Methods of harvesting and processing the plant's seeds, or beans, have changed little over time.

The trek up into this mountainous area is not for the faint of heart. Roads leading to the plantations must be traversed by four-wheel-drive vehicle. As the route ascends the vegetation changes, becoming more lush. Particularly beautiful are the intertwined limbs of saba trees, which are considered sacred. Scattered waterfalls and numerous streams in the vicinity feed into the Copalita River. Some of the plantations are only accessible via horseback.

For those who don't mind a rough journey, this is an opportunity to explore southern Mexico's rugged back country. Café Huatulco *(see Dining and Nightlife)*, a venture organized by the local coffee producers' association, can provide information about guided coffee plantation tours; phone (958) 587-0339.

Rancho Caballo del Mar, at Bahía Conejos, offers horseback rides along the beach, including hotel pickup. Reservations are required; phone (958) 587-0530.

The easiest way to arrange most activities is through a travel agency. Bahías Plus has offices in the major hotels and offers a variety of different tours, such as snorkeling and diving trips to the bays; sunset cruises; bird-watching excursions; ATV jungle trips; sport-fishing trips; eco-tours to view turtles, crocodiles and native wildlife; and day trips to Puerto Angel and Zipolite Beach. The all-purpose "Huatulco Discovery" sightseeing tour includes a swim at El Maguey Bay, a stop in downtown La Crucecita and time out for shopping.

If necessary, bring comfortable shoes, sunblock, insect repellent and/or a bathing suit or change of clothes. Expect to get dusty on the ATV jungle trip. Some excursions (for example, the ATV trips) are advised only for those in good physical condition. Bahía Plus agency's main office is at Av. Carrizal #704 in La Crucecita.

Dining and Nightlife

Dining choices in Huatulco are not necessarily limited to the expensive hotel restaurants. Restaurant

Ve El Mar, on the water's edge at Playa Santa Cruz, is a casual, friendly place serving lobster, ceviche, shrimp and other seafood dishes.

El Sabor de Oaxaca, Avenida Guamúchil #206 in La Crucecita (just east of the plaza, in the Hotel Las Palmas), is airy and colorful and features such regional fare as chicken in *mole* sauce, *tlayudas* (big corn tortillas with cheese and other fillings), *chilies rellenos* (stuffed chilies) and tamales. For an inexpensive, tasty meal try Pollo Imperial, on Avenida Carrizal between Guamúchil and Boulevard Chahué. The healthy portions of rotisserie chicken come with charro beans and a macaroni and ham salad.

Café Huatulco has two branches, one on the plaza in Santa Cruz (near the marina) and one in the Plaza Esmeralda shopping center at Tangolunda. It serves a variety of caffeinated concoctions utilizing good locally grown coffee, and also sells whole beans.

Nightlife has a long way to go before catching up with Acapulco or Cancún. Most of the hotels have their own bars, and the bigger ones stage Mexican Fiesta nights. **Note:** Finding a cab late at night can be difficult. Make any necessary arrangements for transportation back to your hotel before stepping out for the evening.

Nightspots tend to open and close with regularity, but one local hangout that has been around awhile is the La Crema Bar, on the main plaza in La Crucecita (above the Tropicana Restaurant and across from the Hotel La Flamboyant). You can't miss the guitar-playing dude hanging from the outside of the building. Loud rock and a couple of PCs for Web surfing attract a young crowd. The wood-fired oven turns out a surprisingly good pizza.

Nearby Destinations

Northwest of the airport off Mex. 200, sitting at the foot of the jungle-carpeted Sierra Madre del Sur, is Santa María Huatulco, which functioned as a trade center for the coastal region during pre-Hispanic times. Today the town serves as the governmental center for the different districts that make up Huatulco. It is about 10 kilometers (6 miles) from the airport and west of the developed bays; watch for the marked turn-off on Mex. 200.

Unlike the resort area, Santa María Huatulco has the look of a typical Mexican small town. Activity centers on the main square, where there is a museum housing an interesting collection of masks. Also on the square is the 18th-century, red-and-white cathedral; inside is a fragment of wood that is said to be part of Jesus' cross.

A day trip can be made to the coastal town of Puerto Angel, about 49 kilometers (30 miles) west of Huatulco via Mex. 200 to the town of Pochutla, then about 12 kilometers (7 miles) south on the Puerto Angel-San Antonio highway. Buses travel from Huatulco to Pochutla, from which a taxi can be taken to Puerto Angel. This small fishing village was severely damaged by Hurricane Pauline in 1997 but has been rebuilt. The beaches are rocky but pretty, and the bay is dotted with *pangas*—small, motor-propelled skiffs.

Morning activity centers around Playa Principal and the town pier, where fishing boats arrive with the day's catch. The most popular in-town swimming and sunning beach is Playa Panteón, where there are sandy-floored *palapa* eateries and an oceanfront graveyard filled with colorful tombstones.

Playa Zipolite, about 5 kilometers (3 miles) west of Puerto Angel toward Mazunte, is one of the few beaches in Mexico where nudity is tolerated. In addition to *au naturel* sunbathers (who congregate at one end of the beach), Zipolite attracts a young crowd of surfers and backpackers. Strung along the sand are huts where one can eat, drink or just lounge in a hammock. Camping is permitted at the beach's trailer park. If you do venture here, don't bring anything valuable, as petty theft is common.

Note: Zipolite faces the open ocean, and the undertow is treacherous; swimming is not advised. Also avoid walking on the beach after dark, as armed robberies have occurred.

Oaxaca State Tourism Office (Sedetur): on Boulevard Benito Juárez in Tangolunda; phone (958) 581-0176. Travel agents in the bigger hotels are probably the best sources for tourist information, however.

The Huatulco Hotel and Motel Association office (Asociación de Hoteles y Moteles de Huatulco) is at Blvd. Benito Juárez #8 (in the Crown Pacific Huatulco hotel). The staff can provide information about a variety of local excursions, including day trips to Puerto Escondido and Puerto Angel. The office is open Mon.-Fri. 9-6, Sat. 9-1; phone (958) 581-0486, or (866) 416-0555 (from the United States).

NATIONAL MEXICAN TURTLE CENTER (Centro Mexicano de la Tortuga) is about 12 km (7 mi.) west of Puerto Angel on the Puerto Angel-San Antonio highway, in the small seaside village of Mazunte. It is dedicated to the ongoing preservation of endangered sea turtle species inhabiting Mexican coastal waters. Prior to 1990, when the government imposed a ban on turtle hunting, the local economy depended upon the slaughter of turtles for their meat and leathery hides; the center's opening refocused efforts toward conservation. Sea turtles are on view in large tanks.

Guided tours in English are available. Tues.-Sat. 10-4:30, Sun. 10-2:30. Tour fee about $5 (U.S.).

COLIMA, COLIMA (C-2) pop. 123,500

Although the city of Colima (koh-LEE-mah) is little visited, it makes it a very pleasant day trip from Manzanillo and a nice break from the beach. The 70-minute drive—via the Manzanillo-Colima toll highway to the town of Tecomán, then north on Mex. 110—passes beautiful tropical and mountain scenery. If you don't have a car, trips to Colima can be arranged through travel agencies at Manzanillo resorts *(see What To Do under the Manzanillo listing).* **Note:** The toll charge is about $6.75 (U.S.) each way.

Colima itself lies in a fertile valley. Although tropical in appearance, it is cooler than the lowlands along the coast. The Río Colima divides the city in two, running through tropical fruit orchards and clusters of coconut palms (the region is an important producer of coconuts, bananas and lemons). Entering the city via Mex. 110 from Manzanillo, the first landmark visitors see is the King Colima Monument, a sculpture erected in 1955.

What makes Colima especially enticing—besides the remarkable cleanliness of its streets and parks—is the carefully preserved colonial atmosphere of the town center. Many of the downtown buildings were constructed in the neoclassic style during the later years of dictator Porfirio Díaz's regime. Earthquakes in 1932 and 1944 leveled some of the structures, which were later rebuilt.

Plaza Principal, the main square, is located between avenidas Madero, Hidalgo, Degollado and Reforma. The plaza is surrounded by the Liberty Garden (Jardín Líbertad), where there are white benches and huge, sculpted iron fountains shooting streams of water 20 feet into the air. Arcades on the north and south sides of the plaza shelter shops and commercial businesses.

On the plaza's east side are the Government Palace *(see attraction listing)* and the cathedral (Santa Iglesia), erected by the Spanish in 1527 but rebuilt several times since then. The Hidalgo Theater (Teatro Hidalgo), a block southwest of Plaza Principal at the corner of Degollado and Independencia, was originally completed in 1883 and reconstructed after earthquakes in 1932 and 1941. Its interior has a 19th-century elegance. Check with the State Tourism Office for information about scheduled performances.

Four blocks east of Plaza Principal is Jardín Nuñez, a park with lush greenery that makes it a good spot for relaxing. Just south of the House of Culture complex *(see attraction listing)* and east of Calzada Galván is Piedra Lisa Park (Parque Piedra Lisa). The name means "sliding stone," and those who do slide on the namesake rock will supposedly return to Colima one day.

For lunch, try Samadhi, about 3 blocks north of Jardín Nuñez on Avenida Filomena Medina (where it branches off Avenida Juárez). This vegetarian restaurant has a shady courtyard and serves a tasty, inexpensive *comida corrida.* Have a *licuado* (fruit shake) or juice rather than taking a chance on the water.

The Main Bus Terminal (Central Camionera Foránea), also called Terminal Nuevo, is a little over a mile east of the city center via Avenida Guerrero to Avenida Niños Heroes.

About 7 kilometers (4 miles) north of Colima (via Avenida Herrera out of town) is the village of Comala ("the place of the griddles"). It's a quick trip by car or bus; "suburban" buses leave from the Central Camionera Suburbana station at Plaza Colimán, on the western outskirts of town via Carretera a Coquimatlán. Comala was once known as El Pueblo Blanco ("The White Town") for its all-white buildings with red-tiled roofs.

Passing time in the central plaza, with its shade trees and white benches, makes for a pleasant afternoon outing. A group of small restaurants on the plaza's south side (including local favorite Comala Bucaramanga) serve a variety of *botanas,* or appetizers, for the price of potent Mexican libations. As the afternoon wears on, the square fills with the sound of music as mariachi bands try to outdo each other for customers' business.

The Sociedad Artesanías Cooperativa Pueblo Blanco, a short walk south from the town center, is a factory and crafts school. Local artisans create colonial-style wood furniture and ironwork using traditional methods. Good buys are possible.

Twin volcanoes just 3 miles apart are the focus of Volcán Nevado de Colima National Park, about 40 kilometers (25 miles) north of the city via Highway 16 (the road to the villages of Comala, Suchitlán and San Francisco). Dormant Volcán Nevado de Colima, 14,365 feet tall, has flanks cloaked with forests of green conifers. Its neighbor, 12,989-foot Volcán de Fuego, has acted up numerous times since a disastrous eruption in 1941. The most recent outburst occurred in May 1999, spewing rocks and lava, necessitating the evacuation of nearby villages and creating spectacular night scenes for intrepid photographers.

From May through July, orchids line the paved, winding road to tiny San Antonio, just outside the national park. The clear, dry winter months, when the volcanoes are snowcapped, is the best time for viewing them. Experienced mountaineers often hike or climb to the summit of Nevado de Colima.

Colima State Tourism Office (Secretaría de Turismo): on the west side of Plaza Principal, across from the Government Palace at Calle Hidalgo #96. Open Mon.-Fri. 8:30-8, Sat. 10-2; phone (312) 312-4360 (English spoken).

What To See

COLIMA REGIONAL HISTORY MUSEUM (Museo Regional de Historia de Colima) is on Calle 16 de Septiembre at Av. Reforma, on the s. side of Plaza Principal. It exhibits archeological and craft displays and a group of pre-Hispanic ceramics (primarily dogs and human figures), smaller than the collection at the Museum of the Western Cultures but just as fascinating. Tues.-Sat. 9-6. Admission about $3 (U.S.). Phone (312) 312-9228.

GOVERNMENT PALACE (Palacio de Gobierno) is on the e. side of Plaza Principal. Built between 1884 and 1904, it has a cool inner courtyard. Covering four walls around an interior staircase is a mural by Jorge Chavez Carrillo illustrating scenes from Mexican history, beginning with the Spanish conquest and ending with the 1910 Revolution.

HOUSE OF CULTURE (Casa de la Cultura) is on Calz. Galván at Ejército Nacional, about half a mile e. of Plaza Principal; it is most easily reached by bus. This is the University of Colima's arts center. The modern buildings of this extensive complex include a theater and an art gallery displaying a permanent collection of paintings by Colima artist Alfonso Michel, all set among landscaped grounds. Temporary art exhibits and traditional music and dance performances are regularly scheduled; contact the State Tourism Office for information.

Museum of the Western Cultures (Museo de las Culturas de Occidente) is part of the Casa de la Cultura complex. It has a superb collection of pre-Columbian pottery and artifacts. Male and female statues depict many aspects of daily life in pre-Hispanic western Mexico. Noteworthy are the Izcuintli, or "Colima dog" figurines, playful representations of dancing canines. Deposited in the tombs of the departed, they were said to guide the dead in the journey toward *tlalocan* (paradise). Exhibit information is in Spanish.

The museum's café has a smoky ambience accentuated by Salvador Dalí posters hanging on the walls. Tues.-Sun. 9-7. Admission about $2 (U.S.). Phone (312) 313-0608.

LA COMPANA RUINS are on the city's n.w. side in the village of Villa de Alvarez, next to the Technological Center on Av. Tecnológico, following signs. The earliest remains of this important pre-Hispanic settlement are believed to date from around 1500 B.C. Seven pyramid-like buildings and a tomb have been excavated; structures No. 5 and 6 are the largest, and Structure No. 7 has a tunnel tomb beneath it. Buses run from the city center to the site.

Background information is present in Spanish and English. Allow 30 minutes minimum. Tues.-Sun. 9-6. Admission 35 pesos (about $3.40 U.S.).

UNIVERSITY MUSEUM OF POPULAR ARTS (Museo Universitario de Artes Populares) is about 8 blks. n. of Plaza Principal at calles 27 de Septiembre and Manuel Gallardo. Here the emphasis is on traditional masks; there also are displays of musical instruments, textiles and furniture. Exhibit information is in Spanish. Tues.-Sat. 10-2 and 5-8, Sun. 10-1. Admission about $1 (U.S.); free to all Sun.

COSTALEGRE, JALISCO (B-1)

Travelers who want to experience a bit of seaside old Mexico should explore the Costalegre (Happy Coast)—also known as the Costa Careyes, or Turtle Coast—which extends from Chamela south to Barra de Navidad. A few expensive, exclusive, secluded resorts catering to celebrities and the wealthy are tucked among a string of modest beach towns that are popular weekend getaways for Guadalajarans.

To reach the area by car, simply take Mex. 200 south from Puerto Vallarta. (Buses traveling between Puerto Vallarta and Manzanillo also make stops along the coast.) At Boca de Tomatlán, south of Puerto Vallarta, the road swings inland, bypassing Cabo Corrientes (the southern tip of Banderas Bay) before nearing the Pacific again in the vicinity of Chamela. Although not strictly a coastal route, the highway does offer occasional views of the ocean.

The scenery is varied—hills spiked with cactus give way to palm groves as the route winds south, and views shift from craggy mountains to waterfowl-filled lagoons. Many of the villages, beaches and private resorts along the Costa Alegre are accessed from dirt roads branching off Mex. 200.

Just north of Chamela is the resort property of Las Alamandas, hidden off Mex. 200. A dirt road that passes through the village of Quémaro leads to the entrance of this small (six guest villas) but extravagantly appointed resort hideaway developed by the granddaughter of Bolivian tin baron Antenor Patiño.

The village of Chamela sits on bluffs overlooking Bahía Chamela. First settled in 1525, it served as a fortified anchoring ground for Spanish galleons returning from the Orient. Sea turtles and good-sized oysters inhabit the local beaches. During February and March, huge flocks of migrating sea birds settle on the small islands in the bay. A few rustic bungalows, restaurants and campsites accommodate travelers.

The next major development is Costa Careyes, where two luxury, all-inclusive resort developments—one of them a Club Med—are situated along a series of rocky, jungle-edged coves protected from the open ocean. Further south is the tranquil, mile-long beach at Tenacatita, which is reached by a 8-kilometer (5-mile) dirt road turn-off. There are a number of restaurants at the western end of the beach.

The most popular stretch of the Costalegre is anchored by the towns of Barra de Navidad and San Patricio Melaque (meh-LAH-keh), just north of the Colima state border. They lie about 2 miles apart along the shore of crescent-shaped Bahía de Navidad, which is edged by a long, curving beach. Small, inexpensive hotels and thatch-roofed restaurants line the beach, known for its blazing sunsets. This area is much less crowded during the week than it is on weekends (and particularly during the Easter and Christmas holidays).

Barra de Navidad, on a sandbar lying between the bay and a lagoon, is the more picturesque of the two towns and the one most dependent on tourism. While not luxurious, it has more upscale accommodations than San Patricio Melaque. Hotels line Avenida Lopez de Legazpi, the beachfront street (although it is actually a short walk to the beach from most of them). Simple, casual eateries serve standard Mexican dishes; Restaurante Pati, on Calle Jalisco, dishes up *carne asada* and barbecued chicken.

The redbrick-tiled *Zócalo*, on Calle Jalisco, is part of a pedestrian mall closed to traffic. This plaza is the place to relax, browse the many small shops *(tiendas)*, have a cup of coffee or a cold beer *(cerveza)*, or perhaps have your hair braided by one of the local women. On Thursdays, a street market sets up along Calle Guanajuato between avenidas Veracruz and Tampico.

There are views of the bay and beaches along the length of the *malecón* (sea wall), where *pangas* (small open-air ferries) and yachts can be seen entering and leaving the harbor. On the ocean side of the *malecón* stands the Nereida Triton, which commemorates the 400th anniversary of the discovery of the Philippine islands by a Spanish expedition that departed here in 1554.

An established group of American expatriates lives in Barra de Navidad; one of them runs Beer Bob's, a local gathering place and paperback book exchange located at Av. Tampico #8 (the first canal-side street). It's usually open Mon.-Fri. 1-3.

The *panga* docks are at the south end of Avenida Veracruz, on the lagoon side of the sandbar. The local *cooperativa*—an association of individual boat operators—is further up the street. They can arrange fishing excursions, a tour of the lagoon or a quick trip across it to one of the half-dozen seafood restaurants in the little village of Colimilla. Lagoon tours are 150 pesos (about $14.50 U.S.).

Local buses connect Barra de Navidad with San Patricio Melaque, toward the northern end of Bahía de Navidad. Melaque is more like a typical Mexican town with its main plaza, church, municipal market and bus station. It has a greater number of hotels in the budget range. For RV owners, a designated camping area is located along the rather unattractive stretch of beach just west of town, as well as the Playa Trailer Park, closer to the main beach area.

IXTAPA/ZIHUATANEJO, GUERRERO

(C-3) pop. 75,900

Ixtapa (eeks-TAH-pa) and Zihuatanejo (see-wah-tah-NEH-ho) are geographically close resorts on Guerrero's Pacific coast, but they are altogether different in character. Ixtapa materialized in the 1970s, largely through the efforts of FONATUR, the Mexican government's tourism development agency. Zihuatanejo, in contrast, was a quaint little fishing town long before its northern neighbor's first lofty hotel rose from the sand. While Ixtapa indulges visitors with luxurious amenities at world-class hotels, Zihuatanejo beguiles them with centuries-old traditions and—despite its own increased growth—a relaxed village feel.

Artifacts, stone carvings and stela found in the vicinity of Zihuatanejo offer evidence that the region has been inhabited as far back as 3,000 B.C. Spanish *conquistadores* first sailed from Bahía de Zihuatanejo in the 16th century, their galleons returned laden not only with silks and spices but with coconut palms brought from the Philippines (the graceful fronds of this palm are now a common sight at seaside resorts up and down the Mexican Pacific coast). However, Acapulco quickly took over the Orient trade.

During an early Spanish exploration of the area, an officer under Hernando Cortés is said to have asked his guide the name of the place. In the Náhuatl language, the guide replied "Cihuatlán," meaning "place of women"—a reference to the existing matriarchal society, in which weaving was the chief occupation. Along the way, Cihuatlán was mispronounced and the somewhat dismissive Spanish suffix "nejo" was tacked on at the end, resulting in the present name.

Ixtapa, on the other hand, blossomed almost overnight after FONATUR determined the stretch of sand a few miles northwest of Zihuatanejo Bay to be ripe for resort development. The construction of hotels, restaurants, shopping plazas and a marina created employment opportunities in a largely impoverished state. As Ixtapa grew, Zihuatanejo followed suit, albeit at a slower pace. For starters, many of the dirt streets were paved. Although restaurants and boutiques give the *malecón* (waterfront promenade) a touristy look, Zihuatanejo to a large degree has managed to hold on to its charm.

Those who decry Cancún level the same criticisms at Ixtapa—too big, too expensive, soulless, manufactured. But like Cancún, Ixtapa appeals to the traveler who craves a getaway from any and all daily concerns. Beauty and pampering come with a price, of course, but for those willing to pay it, the big-league resort trappings of Ixtapa definitely satisfy. Here, however, vacationers can have the best of both worlds—sampling Ixtapa's air-conditioned luxury as well as Zihuatanejo's down-to-earth informality.

Practicalities

Zihuatanejo International Airport is off Mex. 200 (referred to as the Carretera Costera, or Coastal Highway), about 10 kilometers (6 miles) east of Zihuatanejo and 17 kilometers (10.5 miles) southeast of Ixtapa. Continental, phone 01 (800) 900-5000 (toll-free long distance within Mexico) flies direct from Houston, with connecting flights linking other U.S. cities. For information about Continental vacation packages to Ixtapa/Zihuatanejo, phone (800) 301-3800 (from the United States).

Aeroméxico, phone 01 (800) 021-4010 (toll-free long distance within Mexico), offers flights to Mexico City, where connections can be made to Zihuatanejo. Aerolitoral, an Aeroméxico subsidiary, has daily nonstop flights from Guadalajara. Mexicana, phone 01 (800) 509-8960 (toll-free long distance within Mexico), offers flights from U.S. cities to Guadalajara and Mexico City, where connections can be made to Zihuatanejo. For additional information about airlines *see Arriving by Air, page 61*.

Fixed-price *colectivos* (minivans) shuttle groups of passengers from the airport to hotels in either Ixtapa or Zihuatanejo. Tickets are purchased at the transportation desk in the arrival area. It will cost slightly more for a ride to Ixtapa. Private taxis from the airport are more than twice as expensive. Arrange transportation back to the airport through your hotel.

Getting to Ixtapa and Zihuatanejo by motor vehicle is much more of a challenge. The main—really the only—route is Mex. 200, which winds along the coast. Acapulco is about 256 kilometers (160 miles) to the southeast; Manzanillo is 560 kilometers (356 miles) to the northwest. While the condition of the roadway is generally good, heavy summer rainstorms can create potholes or trigger mudslides.

It is the mountainous terrain, however, that makes driving such an adventure. South of Manzanillo between the small towns of Placita and Caleta de Campos Mex. 200 is a series of very sharp bends, with steep grades both ascending and descending. Drivers pulling an RV trailer will average only about 50 km/h (about 31 mph) on this part of the journey, which takes more than 2 hours to drive approximately 40 miles. In addition, there are only a couple of gas stations along the highway between Tecomán and Playa Azul. If driving north from Acapulco, numerous speed bumps *(topes)* are scattered along Mex. 200 all the way to Zihuatanejo.

From Mexico City, Ixtapa and Zihuatanejo are about 575 kilometers (360 miles) to the southwest via Mex. 134, the most direct route. Do not attempt to negotiate this road unless you have a four-wheel-drive vehicle. From the vicinity of Ciudad Altamirano all the way to the junction with Mex. 200, Mex. 134 is filled with potholes, and portions of the roadway can be washed out or blocked by rock slides. One more word of caution: Regardless of the route, **do not drive after dark.**

Taxis are a convenient way to shuttle between Zihuatanejo and Ixtapa's Hotel Zone (about a 10-minute ride), but they're expensive. It costs at least $5 (U.S.) to travel between the two, and a minimum of $2.25 within each town. Fares go up after midnight. Current rates are posted in hotel lobbies. Fortunately, both the Hotel Zone and downtown Zihuatanejo are easily negotiated on foot. Regardless of where you're going, agree to a fare before getting in the cab.

City buses run frequently between Ixtapa and Zihuatanejo. The fare is inexpensive, about 50c (U.S.) one way. Buses make numerous stops along Boulevard Ixtapa; in Zihuatanejo, they stop near the intersection of avenidas Morelos and Benito Juárez, some 3 blocks north of the city market. If you're driving from one town to the other, use caution; the road narrows and widens unexpectedly, and there are several speed bumps.

Moto Rent, located in the Los Patios shopping center on Boulevard Ixtapa, rents mopeds, mountain bikes and rollerblades; phone (755) 553-1630. **Note:** While a moped is a convenient way to get around, keep in mind that the rental fee may not include insurance.

Currency can be exchanged at hotels, banks and *casas de cambio* (exchange offices). Banks usually

---

DID YOU KNOW

There are four mountain peaks within Mexico greater than 15,000 feet in elevation. The tallest, the 18,850-foot extinct volcano Citlaltépetl, is the third-highest point in North America.

---

have the best rates and are open Mon.-Fri. 9-1. A Banamex branch is at the corner of Ejido and Vicente Guerrero in downtown Zihuatanejo. In Ixtapa, there are 24-hour Banamex automatic teller machines (designated *Caja Permanente*) on Boulevard Ixtapa next to the Hotel Fontan and at other locations. In Zihuatanejo, there are ATMs at Ejido and Vicente Guerrero and on Benito Juárez in the Comercial Mexicana, as well as several other locations. The machines accept MasterCard or Visa and dispense pesos.

For assistance or in case of an emergency, contact the Ixtapa tourist police; phone (755) 554-5360. The Red Cross (Cruz Roja), in Zihuatanejo, provides 24-hour ambulance service; phone (755) 554-2009. Major hotels should be able to provide the names and phone numbers of English-speaking doctors.

The average annual temperature at this tropical location is a balmy 79 degrees. Summers are hot, with temperatures ranging from the upper 70s to the low 90s. The winter months—high tourist season—are slightly cooler, with lows in the low 70s, highs in the upper 80s. The rainy season, from June through October, turns the normally brown countryside a brilliant green. The rain frequently falls at night, guaranteeing sunny days almost all year. Pacific hurricanes occasionally strike this section of the coast.

Layout

The coastal strips of both Guerrero and Michoacán states are essentially undeveloped and remote, giving Ixtapa/Zihuatanejo somewhat the feel of an oasis. This twin resort area encompasses some 16 miles of sandy beaches, tiny offshore islets, scalloped coves and placid lagoons, all backed by the Sierra Madre del Sur.

An impressive string of high-rise hotels, surrounded by clusters of palms, make up the 2-mile stretch of Ixtapa's Hotel Zone, which fronts broad Palmar Bay. Boulevard Ixtapa is the main street and runs behind the hotels. On the other side of this thoroughfare are a number of small shopping malls. At the Hotel Zone's eastern end is the Ixtapa Golf Club. Almost anything of interest to visitors will be on either side of Boulevard Ixtapa.

About a mile before the end of the Hotel Zone (if you're heading north), a road branching to the right off Boulevard Ixtapa leads to Mex. 200, and also is the way to get to Playa Quieta, Playa Linda and other beaches north of Ixtapa proper (watch for signs indicating the destination). Boulevard Ixtapa itself ends in a traffic circle at the 450-acre Marina Ixtapa complex, where luxury villas and condominiums share space with a 622-slip yacht marina, the Marina Golf Course and a dockside promenade lined with restaurants. Overlooking the marina is El Faro, an 85-foot-tall tower that offers a 360-degree view of the surrounding area.

Ixtapa is connected with Zihuatanejo, about 7 kilometers (4 miles) to the southeast, by Mex. 200 (which is referred to as the *carretera*) between the two towns). Zihuatanejo (affectionately referred to by locals as "Zihua") spreads along the shores of oyster-shaped Bahía de Zihuatanejo, a naturally protected harbor. Less than 2 miles wide, this is one of the more picturesque bays along Mexico's Pacific coast.

Zihuatanejo's small downtown lies north of the bay; to the east are unobstructed beaches and the foothills of the Sierra Madre del Sur. Locals and tourists alike congregate along the *malecón* (waterfront promenade), officially called Paseo del Pescador. In Zihuatanejo, the basketball court fronting the beach right in the center of town takes the place of the traditional Mexican main square.

East-west Avenida Juan Alvarez, a block north of and paralleling the *malecón,* is one of the main traffic arteries; it takes traffic out of the commercial area while Avenida Ejido, a block farther inland, takes traffic in. The main north-south thoroughfares are 5 de Mayo, Cuauhtémoc (which is pedestrian-only for a couple of blocks), Vicente Guerrero and Benito Juárez.

Hotels perch atop the cliffs surrounding the bay. A clifftop *mirador* (lookout point) along Camino a Playa la Ropa, the road that connects Zihuatanejo and La Ropa Beach, offers a spectacular view of the town and the bay. A bronze plaque (in Spanish) commemorates the first commercial maritime expedition that departed from the port, bound for the Philippines.

The Beaches

The coastline between Ixtapa/Zihuatanejo and Acapulco is known as "La Costa Grande" because of its broad, open beaches. The swath fronting the Ixtapa Hotel Zone is called Playa del Palmar. The dramatic arc of white sand forms a wide curve, with clusters of rock formations rising out of the offshore waters. This beach faces the ocean, and the surf is rough at times. At the eastern end of the Hotel Zone, near the Ixtapa Golf Club, is Playa Vista Hermosa. Between Ixtapa and Zihuatanejo is Playa Majahua, a secluded, little-visited beach slated for resort development.

At the northwest end of Palmar Bay is Ixtapa Point (Punta Ixtapa). A residential and recreational complex is being constructed on this peninsula. Just off the tip of the point is Isla de a Pie ("island on foot"), so named because it can be reached at low tide by traversing the rocks. Marine birds, especially pelicans and seagulls, congregate on the islet. Along the west side of the peninsula is Playa Quieta (Quiet Beach), which is now largely devoted to the water sports facilities of Club Med and is closed to the public.

Playa Linda, about a mile up the coast from Playa Quieta, has a jungly backdrop of coconut plantations. Open-air restaurants along the beach serve fresh seafood. Outboard motor-powered skiffs *(pangas)* depart from the small jetty for the 10-minute boat ride to Isla Ixtapa, a short distance offshore. The wooded island is a pleasant place to spend a day sunning, snorkeling or diving. Playa Cuachalalate, the main beach, is lined with *palapa* restaurants. On the other side of the island, behind the El Marlin Restaurant, is tiny Playa Coral, with calm, crystal-clear water ideal for snorkeling. Basic gear is available for rent on the island.

Round-trip tickets for the boat ride to Isla Ixtapa can be purchased at the Playa Linda pier landing for about $2.25 (U.S.). The last boats leave for the mainland around 5 p.m.; keep your ticket stub for the return trip. **Note:** Only take a boat displaying the local *Cooperativa* emblem.

Zihuatanejo's main beach is Playa Principal, a sandy stretch in front of the *malecón* (Paseo del Pescador). At the *malecón's* western end is the town pier *(muelle)*. Local fishermen store their boats and gear on the sand after returning with the morning's catch. At the western end of the *malecón*, a concrete bridge crosses a narrow canal; to the south is the Puerto Mío resort and marina.

Just east of Playa Principal and the main part of town is Playa la Madera (Wood Beach). The name comes from colonial days, when pine, oak, cedar and mahogany cut from the mountain forests were shipped back to Spain. Small hotels, private bungalows and restaurants crowd Cerro la Madera (Madera Hill), which rises behind the narrow beach. A bayside footpath (known as "Continuación del Paseo del Pescador") cuts through the rocks that once separated the two beaches. It's a pleasant walk if not attempted at high tide, when you're bound to get wet. Also avoid the footpath after dark.

Particularly pretty is Playa la Ropa (Clothes Beach), on the protected eastern side of the bay and a 5-minute taxi ride from downtown Zihuatanejo. The name refers to the cargo of silks that were strewn all over the beach when a Spanish galleon shipwrecked here. Palm trees fringe the mile of soft white sand, and several sand-floored, open-air *palapa* eateries offer both seafood and Mexican cooking. Playa la Ropa is good for swimming, water skiing, jet skiing, parasailing and windsurfing. A steep rock bluff separates this beach from Playa la Madera.

Divers and snorkelers head for the crystalline waters of Playa las Gatas, which is reached by boat. Harmless nurse sharks once populated the shallow, rocky bay bottom, hence the name. Legend has it that the long row of rocks that functions as a breakwater were deposited by a pre-Hispanic ruler as a shelter for his daughter's private beach, although it is possible they could also be ballast dumped from Spanish galleons. There are a number of *palapa* restaurants here.

Small, canopied *pangas* depart from the Zihuatanejo town pier for a scenic 10-minute ride across the bay to the small dock at Las Gatas. Round-trip tickets cost about $2.50 (U.S.) and can be purchased at the *Cooperativa* office at the head of the pier. The boats, often called "water taxis," run frequently; keep your ticket stub for the return trip.

Playa Blanca is about 10 kilometers (6 miles) east of Zihuatanejo; it is accessible via a dirt road that branches off Mex. 200. The scenic stretch of sand curves southeast to Barra de Potosí, off the tip of this hook-shaped peninsula is a group of rock islets, called *morros*, that are characteristic of this section of coastline. One of them, "The Iceberg," gets its name from the shower of white guano left behind by innumerable marine birds.

Outdoor Recreation

Although Mazatlán and Baja California are better-known Pacific coast sport-fishing destinations, anglers are discovering the offshore waters here. Sailfish is the pre-eminent big-game catch, along with blue and black marlin, dorado (mahi-mahi) and yellowfin tuna; smaller species like barracuda, grouper, roosterfish, Spanish mackerel and wahoo also put up a spirited fight. An environmentally friendly tag-and-release policy is promoted.

The Boat Cooperative (Cooperativa de Lanchas de Recreo) at the Zihuatanejo town pier can arrange an excursion; phone (755) 554-2056. Prices vary based on the size of the boat and the number of people and can be negotiated with the boat owners. Most of the boats depart the bay by 7 a.m. and return around 3. Your hotel may be able to arrange a fishing trip, although it will cost more.

The Zihuatanejo Scuba Center arranges scuba and snorkeling trips and also organizes night dives and excursions for underwater still and video photography. Visibility is best from May through December, although diving is possible year-round. Juan Bernard, a marine biologist and the center's dive instructor, is very knowledgeable about the area's scuba sites, which range from shallow reefs to submerged shipwrecks to canyons 100 feet below the surface. One of the most recent discoveries was made by divers exploring the rock islets off Barra de Potosí; they found a series of caverns leading to a large dome rising above the water's surface.

Snorkelers favor Playa Manzanillo, just south of Zihuatanejo Bay and accessible only by boat. Here, offshore in 15 to 20 feet of water, dwell an impressive variety of coral reef fish.

The scuba center operates two full-service dive shops. One is in downtown Zihuatanejo at Calle Cuauhtémoc #3 (across from the Banamex bank). The other is at the main dive facility within the private marina at the Puerto Mío resort, just inside the mouth of Zihuatanejo Bay. Full-day packages include separate morning and afternoon dives, all equipment, instructors and soft drinks on board. Morning, afternoon and night dives also are available. For information and reservations phone (755) 554-2147.

Yates del Sol's trimaran *Tristar* departs from the marina at the Puerto Mío resort for "sunshine" cruises to Ixtapa Island and a stop for lunch, snorkeling and swimming. A snorkeling cruise casts off for Playa Manzanillo, and a "magical sunset" cruise sails from the bay into the open Pacific for sunset watching and a view of Ixtapa's Hotel Zone. Reservations are required. Cruises can be arranged through a local travel agency, or phone Yates del Sol at (755) 554-2694 or (755) 554-8270.

The usual water sports—water and jet skiing, windsurfing, parasailing—can be enjoyed at both Ixtapa and Zihuatanejo. Facilities and equipment rentals are usually available at Playa del Palmar, Playa la Ropa and Playa las Gatas. Surfers favor Playa Troncones, which faces the open ocean northwest of Ixtapa. **Note:** Make certain that parasailing is arranged only through a reputable outfit. Not all boat operators have the required level of experience, and accidents have occurred.

There are two 18-hole golf courses in the area. The Ixtapa Golf Club, a Robert Trent Jones, Jr.-designed course at the eastern end of the Hotel Zone, extends to the ocean's edge. The grounds, considered a wildlife preserve, are lush with tropical vegetation and home to numerous exotic birds. Crocodiles inhabit some of the water hazards, discouraging any attempts to search for balls lost in the drink; zoologists from Mexico City visit once a year and retrieve the largest specimens for relocation to Mexican zoos. Clubhouse facilities include a pro shop, restaurant and pool with a lounge deck. For reservations information phone (755) 553-1062.

The Marina Golf Course, within the Marina Ixtapa complex just past the western end of the Hotel Zone, was designed by Robert von Hagge. Recreational boaters take advantage of the course's criss-crossing canals, and water hazards come into play on 14 holes. The challenging 600-yard, par-5 18th is known locally as "el hoyo del diablo" (the devil's hole). Golfers have the use of a clubhouse, restaurant, pro shop, pool and tennis courts, and the marina's dockside promenade is close by. For reservations information phone (755) 553-1410.

Tennis courts are located at the Ixtapa Golf Club, the clubhouse at Marina Ixtapa, at the major Ixtapa hotels, and at the Hotel Villa del Sol at Playa la Ropa in Zihuatanejo. Most courts are illuminated for night play; nonguests can usually play at the hotel courts for a fee.

At Playa Linda and Playa Larga, both northwest of Ixtapa's Hotel Zone, horses can be rented by the hour for rides along the beach or through one of the nearby coconut plantations. Sunset rides are especially nice (wear insect repellent). Local travel agencies can arrange a trip, or make reservations through Rancho Playa Linda; phone (755) 554-3085.

Shopping

There are no malls in the traditionally sprawling sense in either Ixtapa or Zihuatanejo. Instead, small complexes with (usually) air-conditioned shops line Boulevard Ixtapa, across the street from the big hotels. Fashionable resort wear, sportswear, jewelry, art and handicrafts fill the boutiques at Ixpamar, La Puerta, Las Fuentes and Los Patios, among other shopping plazas.

Laddi Guichi, in the Los Patios shopping center, specializes in woven goods made in the state of Oaxaca. La Fuente, also in the Los Patios center, has a fine selection of talavera pottery, hand-blown glass, ceramics and papier-mâché figures. Mic-Mac, in the La Puerta center, offers native handicrafts, embroidered clothing and wall hangings. All of the shopping centers contain restaurants and snack shops for those in need of refueling. Most of the stores are open daily; many of them close from 2-4.

Downtown Zihuatanejo has its share of souvenir stands and T-shirt emporiums, but it's also a good place to search out Mexican crafts. Shops and stalls line Paseo del Pescador and the adjacent streets. Mario's Leather Shop, Calle Vicente Guerrero #12, features custom-made saddles, hats, vests, purses and belts. Galería Maya, Av. Nicolas Bravo #31, and Arte Mexicano Nopal, Av. Juan Alvarez #13B (at Calle Agustín Ramirez), display such items as pewter frames, straw baskets, wooden sculptures and handmade leather bags. Coco Cabaña, at Avenida Juan Alvarez and Calle Vicente Guerrero, also has a high-quality collection of handicrafts.

Casa Marina, Paseo del Pescador #9 (near Calle 5 de Mayo), consists of five family-owned folk art and handicraft shops under one roof. There are displays of pottery, rugs, pillows, regional costumes, silver jewelry, hammocks, hand-painted lacquer boxes and masks created by Guerrero artisans. Visitors can observe weaving demonstrations at La Zapoteca, one of the stores. Within the complex is Café la Marina, where you can have a pizza and a beer and then browse through the large collection of used books for sale and trade.

Vendors, formerly a persistent presence at the beaches, now hawk their wares at specially designated handicrafts markets. At the Mercado de Artesanía Turístico, on Boulevard Ixtapa across from the Ixtapa Sheraton, there are numerous souvenir and handicraft stands.

In Zihuatanejo, a similar tourist-oriented market is located along Calle 5 de Mayo across from the church. Families operate many of the stalls at these markets, producing hand-painted ceramics, seashell knickknacks and embroidered goods. Zihuatanejo's Central Market (Mercado Central) spreads along Avenida Benito Juárez several blocks inland from the waterfront. Here the emphasis is on foodstuffs—tropical fruits, vegetables, seafood and medicinal herbs. Good buys at the market include Guerrero coffee and leather *huaraches* (sandals).

Dining and Nightlife

For an expensive but reliably good dining experience, the Ixtapa Hotel Zone is an obvious choice. Zihuatanejo has a lower price range and a greater variety of eateries; imported fast-food chains are conspicuously absent. Fresh seafood—lobster, clams, squid, *huachinango* (red snapper) and a local specialty, *camarones al ajo* (shrimp encrusted with garlic)—are on many Zihuatanejo menus.

Sample the local bounty at Chez Arnoldo, the only tile-roofed structure among the thatched, open-air restaurants dotting Playa las Gatas. Here you can feast on expertly prepared seafood dishes in your bathing suit.

La Sirena Gorda (The Fat Mermaid), on the *malecón* next to the town pier, is known for its fresh seafood tacos—fish, shrimp, octopus and conch—and also is a pleasant spot for breakfast. Coconuts is a local gathering place on Calle Agustín Ramirez; Igorian Hacienda, the original building occupying the location, served as a weigh-in station for the coconut plantations that once surrounded Zihuatanejo.

Nueva Zelanda, Calle Cuauhtémoc #23 (at Avenida Ejido), is casual and family-oriented, specializing in *tortas* (Mexican sandwiches), enchiladas and *licuados* (fruit shakes). There is a branch in Ixtapa as well.

Pozole is a hearty, hominy-thickened soup with a chicken or pork stock base. Toppings include avocado slices, chopped onion, white cheese, lettuce and cabbage; herbs and spices vary depending on who is making the *pozole*. Less adventurous diners will appreciate the fact that pickled pig knuckles are normally served on the side. The addition of chilies gives *pozole* three different colors—red, green or white. Thursday is the traditional day to eat this thoroughly Mexican dish, and most lunch spots in Zihuatanejo include it on their Thursday *comida corrida* menu.

Mexican "Fiesta Nights" are popular evening entertainment in Ixtapa during peak tourist season (November to April). They start around 7 p.m. with a lavish buffet spread, after which live music and folkloric dance performances are presented. The cost, about $30-$40 (U.S.) per person, normally includes dinner, drinks and the show. The Westin Brisas Ixtapa offers its Fiesta Night on Sunday; the Hotel Krystal in Ixtapa on Monday; the Hotel Villa del Sol in Zihuatanejo on Friday. The Sheraton Ixtapa presents a Wednesday Fiesta Night all year. Reservations or advance tickets are necessary; call the hotel or make arrangements through a local travel agency.

Casual is the standard attire in both Ixtapa and Zihuatanejo, although shorts and sandals are frowned on for an evening out at an expensive restaurant or fashionable nightspot. Most restaurants use purified water to make the ice in drinks (check to see if the cubes have holes). If in doubt, order bottled mineral water (the brands Agua de Taxco or Tehuacán are good), beer or a soft drink; the *limón* flavor of Yoli, a soft-drink brand sold only in the state of Guerrero, is similar to 7-Up. *For a list of AAA-RATED dining establishments in Ixtapa and Zihuatanejo, see the Lodgings & Restaurants section.*

Nightlife is concentrated in Ixtapa. Christine, in the Hotel Krystal, has a laser light show set to music beginning at midnight; after that dancing takes over. Tiers of tables overlook the dance floor. The doors open nightly around 10:30 p.m. (the off-season schedule varies); there is a cover charge. Shorts, jeans and tennis shoes are not allowed.

Other clubs are Euforia, on Boulevard Ixtapa in front of the Best Western Posada Real, and Visage. Also on Boulevard Ixtapa (near the Best Western) is an outpost of Carlos 'n Charlie's, which offers food, drinks and dancing to rowdy rock on an elevated platform by the beach. Señor Frog's, in the La Puerta shopping center, also serves food to the accompaniment of loud rock 'n' roll. There is a cover charge here for dancing.

Special Events

Two major tournaments draw serious sportfishing enthusiasts to Ixtapa/Zihuatanejo: the Billfish Classic in January and the International Sailfish Tournament in May. Other sporting events include a Pro-Am tournament held at the Ixtapa Golf Club in June or July, a national triathlon in Ixtapa during September, and a high-powered boat race in Zihuatanejo in November. Amateur golf and tennis tournaments and a marathon are organized annually in Ixtapa as well; check with the tourism office for dates, which tend to be erratic.

Cultural Sunday takes place every Sunday at the basketball court in downtown Zihuatanejo. Young children are in the spotlight at this delightful event, performing regional dances from all over Mexico in full, colorful costume. The festivities begin around 6 p.m.

Guerrero State Tourism Office: in the La Puerta shopping center on Boulevard Ixtapa (across the street from the Presidente Forum Resort). Open Mon.-Fri. 9-2 and 4-7; phone (755) 553-1968.

The Ixtapa/Zihuatanejo Hotel Association also can provide general information about the area; phone (755) 553-1566. Avoid booths with "Tourist Information" signs (found mostly at the airport), which are essentially pushing time-shared properties.

ARCHEOLOGICAL MUSEUM OF THE COSTA GRANDE (Museo Arqueológico de la Costa Grande) is on the Zihuatanejo waterfront at the eastern end of Paseo del Pescador (near Calle Vicente Guerrero). This small but nicely displayed museum contains artifacts, pottery and paintings relating to the Costa Grande, the section of coastline between Zihuatanejo and Acapulco. Exhibit information is in Spanish.

Allow 30 minutes minimum. Tues.-Sun. 10-6; closed Dec. 25. Admission 10 pesos.

MANZANILLO, COLIMA (C-1) pop. 100,200

Manzanillo (mahn-sah-NEE-yoh) may have participated in trade with the Orient before the arrival of the Spanish. Settled by Europeans shortly after the Spanish conquest, it became an important departure point for Spanish expeditions, not only to other parts of Mexico but to such far-flung locations as the Philippines and Alta California (the present state of California). Hernando Cortés established what is believed to be Latin America's first shipyard at Manzanillo in 1531. This maritime legacy thrives today, and tourism—although well developed—takes a back seat to commerce.

Manzanillo began attracting foreigners in the 1970s, along with new seaside playgrounds like Cancún and Ixtapa. As with Puerto Vallarta, its neighbor some 259 kilometers (160 miles) to the north, Manzanillo was blessed with natural attributes. Twin bays, golden-sand beaches and a lush tropical backdrop of jungle and banana plantations drew U.S. and Canadian vacationers searching for something a little off the beaten track.

What put the city on the tourist map for good was the 1974 opening of Las Hadas, a luxurious beach retreat conceived by Bolivian tin magnate Antenor Patiño. The opulent hotel began attracting an international set of moneyed pleasure seekers. Manzanillo gained further exposure when the hotel was chosen as the setting for the 1979 film "10," although for many the movie's most striking image was a cornrowed Bo Derek jogging down the beach.

Practicalities

Playa de Oro International Airport is located about 47 kilometers (29 miles) northwest of Manzanillo, on the way to Barra de Navidad. Inside the small terminal building are rental car counters, several shops, a restaurant and a lovely mural. International flights are limited. Aeroméxico, Alaska Airlines and Mexicana offer flights from Los Angeles, with connections en route. America West flies from Phoenix; Aero California, from Los Angeles. Most flights to Manzanillo arrive via Mexico City.

The commuter airlines Aeromar, phone 01 (800) 237-6627 (toll-free long distance within Mexico), and Aerolitoral, phone 01 (800) 800-2376 (toll-free long distance within Mexico), offer flights to Manzanillo from Mexico City as well as from other Mexican destinations. Charter packages to Manzanillo from various U.S. cities are available during the winter months; consult a travel agency for details. For additional information about airlines *see Arriving by Air, page 61.*

Transportes Turísticos Benito Juárez provides shuttle service from the airport. The fare averages about $20-$25 (U.S.) per passenger. Make advance arrangements for a ride back to the airport upon your departure; a taxi ride between the airport and most hotels averages about $25 (U.S.).

First-class bus service from Manzanillo to Puerto Vallarta and Guadalajara is provided by ETN. The terminal is in the Santiago area, on Mex. 200 at Km marker 13.5. For additional information about buses *see Bus Service, page 72.*

From Guadalajara, Manzanillo can be reached by car via two-lane Mex. 80, which runs into coastal Mex. 200 at Barra de Navidad, or by the toll highway Mex. 54-D, which passes through Colima. Driving Mex. 200 southeast from Puerto Vallarta or northwest from Ixtapa/Zihuatanejo can be an adventure, particularly during the July-through-September rainy season, when downpours can create hazardous potholes and unexpected detours.

City Layout

Manzanillo is first and foremost a commercial port. With a fine natural harbor and rail connections to the interior, it handles an enormous amount of Mexican industrial and agricultural output. The downtown district occupies a narrow isthmus at the southern end of Manzanillo Bay. It's a noisy, bustling jumble of shipyard activity and railroad tracks. Few tourist amenities will be found among the businesses, cheap hotels and no-frills restaurants, although an ongoing port beautification project—undertaken to help establish Manzanillo as a port of call for cruise ships—has resulted in a landscaped promenade.

Jardín de Obregón, the main plaza, is at the north end of downtown overlooking the harbor, which is studded with Mexican military vessels. This small square has an elaborate bandstand and a gazebo. Near the plaza are courts where pickup basketball and *fútbol* games attract lively crowds of spectators. Avenida México, the city's main commercial thoroughfare, runs south from the plaza.

The resort area spreads out north and then west of town along the shores of twin bays, Bahía de Manzanillo and Bahía de Santiago. Manzanillo Bay encompasses the harbor and some of the more reasonably priced hotels. The Santiago Peninsula, on which Las Hadas and the Hotel Sierra Plaza are located, separates the bays. This tourist-oriented area includes the Santiago and Salahua developments, where there are homes, restaurants and shopping centers. On the other side of the peninsula is Santiago Bay, where luxury homes and condominiums have begun springing up.

Note: In the Manzanillo area, Mex. 200 is referred to variously as the Santiago-Manzanillo Highway or the Costera Highway; the official name is Boulevard Miguel de la Madrid. Between the Santiago area and downtown, there are three major junctions along this highway: with the road to the Santiago Peninsula and Las Hadas; with the road to the Las Brisas Peninsula, the resort area closest to town (known as the *crucero,* or crossroads); and with the highway leading into downtown Manzanillo. At the last junction, Mex. 200 continues southeast down the coast toward Colima and Ixtapa/Zihuatanejo, while the Santiago-Manzanillo Highway bears south toward downtown, running into Calzada Niños Heroes.

Roads, many of them dirt, branch off Mex. 200, leading to resort and condominium developments. While Mex. 200 and other major roadways are in good condition, streets within the city can be potholed. City buses (the newer ones are blue and white) make a circuit from downtown north along Mex. 200 and the shores of the two bays. Destinations are marked on the left side of the windshield; for example, "Centro" (downtown), "Las Brisas," "Las Hadas" or "Santiago." The fare is inexpensive—just 25c (U.S.) from the main resort areas to downtown—and is an easy way to get a look at the coastline and some of the hotels without driving.

The Beaches

There are several beaches to choose from along the wide curve of Manzanillo's two bays. Playa las Brisas is the closest to town, although to reach it by road requires detouring around Laguna de San

Pedrito to the narrow strip of land fronting Manzanillo Bay. Older hotels and restaurants line both sides of the bayfront drive, a popular destination for weekenders from Guadalajara.

Beyond Playa las Brisas is the long curve of golden-brown sand called Playa Azul. The water gets rougher heading north toward the Santiago Peninsula, and the bottom drops off sharply along much of this stretch, making it problematic for wading or swimming.

The water in Santiago Bay, which is not used for shipping, tends to be cleaner than at the beaches fronting Manzanillo Bay closer to town. One of the area's best swimming beaches is Playa la Audiencia, which occupies a pretty, sheltered cove below jungle-covered hills on the north side of the Santiago Peninsula. The rocky outcroppings here are one of Manzanillo's few good snorkeling spots.

Farther around Santiago Bay is Playa Miramar, another nice beach popular with windsurfers and boogie boarders. Beyond Playa Miramar, the shoreline curves to form the Juluapan Peninsula. Here the water becomes tranquil and the beach is dotted with thatch-roofed souvenir shops. Locals crowd this area on Sundays.

Swimmers should exercise care due to occasional rough surf; flags are posted at most beaches to indicate conditions. Red flags mean potentially dangerous conditions; white flags mean safe conditions.

About 49 kilometers (30 miles) southeast of Manzanillo and accessible by bus is Playa Cuyutlán, a beach known for the *Ola Verde,* or "Green Wave." This mountainous wave—with crests that are said to reach 30 feet or more from March through May—seems to be more talked about than actually seen. The greenish hue is due to the glow of phosphorescent marine organisms.

Despite their color, the waves pounding this beach are impressive at any time. The black sand is the result of crushed volcanic rock. The long, open beach, backed by coconut palms, is all but deserted during the summer; lifeguards are normally present during the high season (December to May). Swimmers should beware of rough seas and strong undertows.

The tiny village of Cuyutlán, which consists of a few budget hotels and small seafood restaurants, drowses away most days, although *Semana Santa* (Holy Week) brings an influx of Mexican families. Facilities are spartan, but it's an appealing day trip for those seeking solitude. To get there, take a local bus to the town of Armería, south of Manzanillo on Mex. 200; buses leave frequently from Armería for Cuyutlán. If you're driving, there is a signed turnoff for Cuyutlán on Mex. 200 about 5 kilometers (3 miles) before Armería, or take the Manzanillo-Colima toll highway that parallels the railroad line.

What To Do

Several of the major resort properties in Manzanillo are all-inclusive, providing guests with an array of entertainment and recreational options in addition to lodging and meals. It therefore tends to be easier to arrange such activities as tennis, horseback riding, scuba trips, sunset cruises, or fishing and golf packages if you are staying at a hotel that provides them. If you're not, try one of the local travel agencies, which have offices along Boulevard Miguel de la Madrid. These agencies can arrange tours of the city and trips to such nearby destinations as Colima, the state capital, and Barra de Navidad.

Like other resorts along Mexico's Pacific coast, Manzanillo claims to be the sport-fishing capital of the world, particularly with regard to sailfish. Marlin, dorado, tuna and wahoo are also hooked. The peak season is November through March. There are two annual fishing tournaments, one in early November and one in early February. Reservations for fishing excursions can be arranged through any of the resorts; booking as part of a group will lower costs.

Ocean Pacific Adventures offers deep-sea fishing excursions departing from La Perlita Plaza in downtown Manzanillo; phone (314) 335-0605. They'll also cook your catch for free at the Colima Bay Café. Again, going with a group will lower the cost. Less expensive are the *pangas* (outboard motor-powered launches) operated by individual owners; determined haggling can lower the fee.

Honeycombed with lagoons, the coastal region offers good bird-watching. Laguna de Cuyutlán, just south of Manzanillo, is populated by different species depending on the season. Herons, pelicans and flamingos can be seen at Laguna de las Garzas (Lagoon of the Herons), the waterway separating the Las Brisas Peninsula from the mainland. The views here are especially nice at sunset.

There are three area golf courses. The Club Santiago Resort has a nine-hole course. The 18-hole La Mantarraya, at the Las Hadas resort, offers plenty of water hazards, notably the water-encircled tee-off at the finishing hole. The course is open to the public, although hotel guests receive preferred tee times. To make reservations phone (314) 334-0000.

The 27-hole course at the Grand Bay Hotel on Isla Navidad, about 30 kilometers (19 miles) north of the airport and a 45-minute trip from Manzanillo, was designed by Robert von Hagge. Laid out along the ocean, with breathtaking views at the 13th and 14th holes, the course is lushly landscaped and immaculately maintained.

Tennis courts, all lighted for night play, are located at the following resorts: Club Maeva, on Boulevard Miguel de la Madrid at Playa Miramar; Las Hadas Resort, on the Santiago Peninsula off Boulevard Miguel de la Madrid; and the Hotel Sierra Manzanillo, on the Santiago Peninsula at Av. de la Audiencia #1.

Although Manzanillo is geared more toward relaxing at the beach than to sightseeing, its premier resort, Las Hadas, is an attraction in itself. Set against the eastern side of the Santiago Peninsula, this blindingly white hotel is a dazzling spectacle.

With its minarets, cupolas and turrets, Las Hadas resembles a Moorish village. If you're not a guest, you can still stop in and stroll the luxuriously landscaped grounds (although restaurant reservations are needed to enter the property through the guarded gate). The marina here accommodates up to 45 vessels; a fee is charged. Adjacent to the marina is a calm bay where boats can be moored without a fee.

The University Museum of Archeology is on Avenida Niños Héroes a few minutes north of the downtown area, on the San Pedrito campus of the University of Colima. Displays include numerous metal and shell artifacts from western Mexico as well as fabrics, looms and fabric-making implements. Hours vary, so call ahead to make sure the museum is open; phone (314) 332-2256.

Shopping, Dining and Nightlife

Manzanillo is not a shopper's paradise. A couple of shops on and around the main downtown plaza offer shell jewelry and a few handicrafts, but they're not worth a special trip. Pricey boutiques appear here and there along Boulevard Miguel de la Madrid and at the shopping arcade at the Las Hadas resort. Galería de Arte, in the Sierra Hotel, displays a selection of works by Sergio Bustamante. Plaza Manzanillo, on Boulevard Miguel de la Madrid in the Salahua neighborhood, is an air-conditioned mall with a Comercial Mexicana department store, specialty boutiques and a food court.

Fresh seafood is the specialty at Bigotes 1, Boulevard Miguel de la Madrid # 3157 (Mex. 200) at Playa Las Brisas. One of the house specialties is *pescado zarandeado*, a whole fish marinated in lime juice and soy sauce, grilled and served with a tomato sauce. American-owned Juanito's, on Boulevard Miguel de la Madrid at Km 14, Playa Olas Altas, is a relaxed hangout popular for breakfast as well as burgers, fries, crispy chicken tacos, ribs, milkshakes and fresh fruit smoothies. You also can check your e-mail and access the Internet here.

Casual dress is appropriate at all Manzanillo restaurants (resort wear at the more expensive places). Keep in mind that a service charge may automatically be added to the bill (in addition to the 15 percent IVA tax). While purified water is used at the well-known restaurants, for gastrointestinal reasons it's best to steer clear of the *enramadas* (beach shack restaurants) and outdoor taco stands. *For a list of AAA-RATED dining establishments in Manzanillo, see the Lodgings & Restaurants section.*

Nightlife centers around the resorts. A Mexican "Fiesta Night" is offered at the Club Maeva resort during the high tourist season. Clubs include Boom Boom, also at Club Maeva, and Disco Vog, in the vicinity of Playa Azul. There is a cover charge at both, and shorts and sandals are not permitted (this dress code is more likely to apply to men than to women). Hours at all of the clubs may vary outside of the high season.

Colima State Tourism Office: Blvd. Miguel de la Madrid #1033 (Mex. 200), in the vicinity of Playa Azul. Open Mon.-Fri. 9-3 and 5-7, Sat. 10-2; phone (314) 333-2277 (English spoken).

The Manzanillo Foreign Community Association is a nonprofit organization that assists foreign visitors with information about the Manzanillo/Santiago area in particular and Mexico in general, and also provides translation services, documentation assistance and help with emergency illness, legal or immigration matters. Phone (314) 334-0977 (English spoken).

MAZATLAN, SINALOA (A-1) pop. 335,900

Mazatlán (mah-saht-LAHN) is the stress-free Mexican beach resort that typifies the good old days, when all you needed was a clean hotel room, reliable sunshine and cheap tacos. But since the late 1980s, this port city on the shimmering blue Pacific has been overshadowed by the likes of Cancún and Cabo San Lucas, gringo-friendly destinations that have gone increasingly upscale with a glut of all-inclusive luxury resorts and over-the-top nightlife.

Meanwhile, the "Pearl of the Pacific" is stealthily staging a comeback—and not in the way you might suspect. Yes, new resorts and condos are springing up along the city's far northern shoreline. But it's Old Mazatlán, the city's historic core, that's enjoying a renaissance well worth your precious time.

Founded in 1531 by a group of Spanish *conquistadores* led by Nuño de Guzmán, Mazatlán (which means "land of the deer" in the Nahuatl language) enjoyed nearly 3 centuries of peace and undeveloped quiet. The first real settlement took root in the 1820s. By the late 19th century, German immigrants had helped transform Mazatlán into an international shipping port.

Today the German influence is still evident in Old Mazatlán, where the European architecture and wrought-iron balconies have something of a French Quarter feel. The miraculous refurbishment of the once-crumbling Angela Peralta Theater *(see attraction listing)* and the ongoing restoration of countless other historic structures have spurred a blossoming cultural scene. A number of art galleries and specialty shops ensure that you'll bring home something more unique than a Pacífico beer T-shirt, while beautiful Plazuela Machado, ringed with breezy sidewalk cafes, is the Mexico you won't find in Cancún.

Mazatlán's first international tourists began to arrive in the 1950s, bedding down in newly built hotels along Playa Olas Altas. By the '70s, major resort development had spread north along the coast and formed the Zona Dorada (Golden Zone), where you'll likely be staying during your visit. While the hotel district lacks the charm of Old Mazatlán, it does boast the city's best beaches—golden stretches of wave-lapped sand that offer dreamy views (especially at sunset) of three not-too-distant islands.

Practicalities

Besides affordability, one of Mazatlán's attractions is its relative proximity to the U.S. border. As

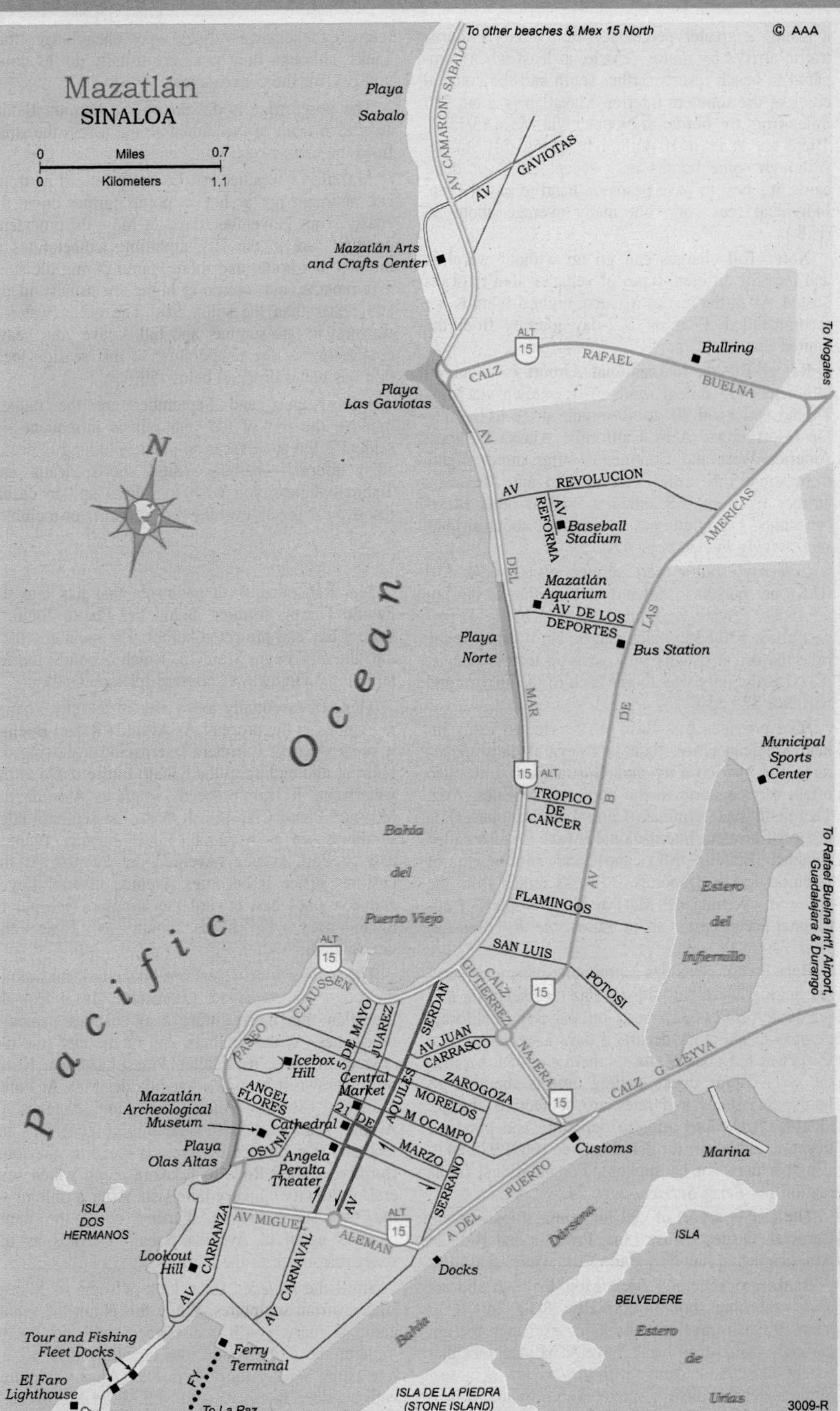
Mazatlán
SINALOA
0 Miles 0.7
0 Kilometers 1.1
© AAA
To other beaches & Mex 15 North
Playa Sabalo
AV CAMARON SABALO
AV GAVIOTAS
Mazatlán Arts and Crafts Center
ALT 15
CALZ RAFAEL BUELNA
Bullring
To Nogales
Playa Las Gaviotas
N
AV DEL MAR
AV REVOLUCION
AV REFORMA
Baseball Stadium
AV DE LAS AMERICAS
Mazatlán Aquarium
AV DE LOS DEPORTES
Bus Station
Playa Norte
Pacific Ocean
AV B DE LAS
Municipal Sports Center
15 ALT
TROPICO DE CANCER
Bahía del Puerto Viejo
Estero del Infiernillo
To Rafael Buelna Int'l. Airport, Guadalajara & Durango
FLAMINGOS
SAN LUIS POTOSI
CALZ GUTIERREZ NAJERA
ALT 15
PASEO CLAUSSEN
5 DE MAYO
JUAREZ
SERDAN
AV JUAN CARRASCO
Icebox Hill
Central Market
AQUILES
ZAROGOZA
MORELOS
M OCAMPO
21 DE MARZO
ANGEL FLORES
Mazatlán Archeological Museum
Cathedral
OSUNA
Angela Peralta Theater
Playa Olas Altas
SERRANO
CALZ G LEYVA
Customs
Marina
AV DEL PUERTO
Dársena
ISLA DOS HERMANOS
AV CARRANZA
AV MIGUEL ALEMAN
ALT 15
AV CARNAVAL
Lookout Hill
Docks
ISLA BELVEDERE
Estero de Urías
Bahía
Tour and Fishing Fleet Docks
Ferry Terminal
FY
El Faro Lighthouse
To La Paz
ISLA DE LA PIEDRA (STONE ISLAND)
3009-R

a result, a greater percentage of the city's tourist traffic arrives by motor vehicle, at least when compared to beach resorts farther south and the colonial cities of the southern interior. Mazatlán is about 750 miles from the border at Nogales via Mex. 15/15-D. There are at least 10 tollbooths along this stretch. Although some booths may accept credit or debit cards, it's best to have pesos on hand to pay the fee. Individual fees vary, but many average about $7 (U.S.).

Note: Toll charges can go up without warning, and fees for different types of vehicles aren't always posted. As in the rest of Mexico, night driving is not recommended. Plan on a 2-day journey from the United States.

Rafael Buelna International Airport is about 40 kilometers (25 miles) south of downtown via Mex. 15 and is a good 30- to 40-minute drive to the major resort areas. Aero California, Alaska Airlines, America West and Continental offer direct flights from some U.S. cities. Aeroméxico and Mexicana airlines fly from U.S. cities as well as other Mexican cities. For additional information about airlines *see Arriving by Air, page 61.*

Colectivo shuttle van service costs about $10 (U.S.) per person to downtown Mazatlán or the hotel zones. Private taxis hired in front of the airport cost about $30-$35, which can be cut by sharing the ride; the driver usually will carry up to four people. A taxi is the only way to get back to the airport, and will cost $25-$30.

Elite provides first-class bus service to many inland Mexican cities, including several daily departures for Mexico City and Guadalajara. Elite also offers service north to the border at Nogales, Ariz. The main bus terminal (Central de Autobuses) is just off Carretera Internacional (Mex. 15, also called Avenida Ejército Méxicano) and just south of Avenida de Los Deportes, 3 blocks inland from the *malecón* (Avenida del Mar) at Playa Norte. For additional information about buses *see Bus Service, page 72.*

Baja Ferries provides automobile-passenger service linking Mazatlán with La Paz *(see separate listing under Baja California)* on the Baja California Peninsula. The ferry departs 3 days a week from the Playa Sur terminal, at the southern end of town near the sport-fishing docks; sailing time is about 15-18 hours. Schedules and rates are subject to change. Double-check both prior to departure and purchase tickets in advance; for details phone (669) 985-0470 (English may not be spoken). For additional information *see Ferry Service, page 74.*

The city is a port of call for cruise ships as well. Carnival, Disney Cruise Line, Princess and Holland America arrive regularly during the winter season.

Banks are generally open Mon.-Fri. 9-6 and set aside morning hours—normally 8:30 to 11:30 a.m.—to cash traveler's checks or exchange foreign currency. Almost all banks have ATM machines that accept most bank cards; withdrawals are in pesos. Some machines also dispense U.S. dollars, which are widely accepted in Mazatlán. *Casas de cambio* (currency exchange offices) stay open longer than banks, although their rates are usually not as good; you pay for the convenience.

The post office is downtown on Avenida Benito Juárez, in front of the cathedral and across the street from the main plaza.

Mazatlán's weather can be characterized as tropical, although not as hot as points farther down the coast. From November through May, daytime temperatures are in the 70s, nighttime temperatures in the 60s. It's hotter and more humid during the summer months, but afternoon highs are usually in the 80s rather than the sultry 90s. The ocean water is warmest in late summer and fall. Leave your heavy coat at home; the temperature at this seaside location has never dropped below 50 F.

July, August and September are the rainiest months; the rest of the year rain is infrequent and seldom a threat to vacation plans. Clothing is decidedly informal—bathing suits, shorts, jeans and T-shirts—unless you wish to "dress up" in casual resort wear for an evening out to dinner or a club.

City Layout

Mazatlán occupies a peninsula that juts into the Pacific Ocean, forming Bahía del Puerto Viejo, a natural bay and protected harbor. The main approach into the city is via Mex. 15, which becomes the International Highway (Carretera Internacional).

Mex. 15 essentially loops around the city, changing names in the process. As Avenida Rafael Buelna, it veers west off Carretera Internacional, passing the bullring and ending at the Sábalo traffic circle at the waterfront. It then proceeds south as Avenida del Mar and Paseo Claussen. It skirts the southern edge of downtown as Avenida Miguel Alemán, running east to Port Avenue (Avenida del Puerto). At the customs office it becomes Avenida Gabriel Leyva and continues east toward the airport. Once out of town, Mex. 15 heads south to Tepic and Guadalajara.

The *malecón,* or waterfront boulevard, runs along the coast for some 17 kilometers (11 miles). In Mazatlán this thoroughfare also changes names—four times. At the southern end of the city (the old downtown area), it is called Paseo Claussen. North of downtown it becomes Avenida del Mar. At Punta Camarón (Shrimp Point), the name changes to Avenida Camarón Sábalo. At this point it runs inland and is paralleled by Avenida Playa las Gaviotas (formerly called Rodolfo Loaiza), along which several of the city's luxury hotels sit. After a mile or so the two streets rejoin. Farther north the name changes again to Avenida Sábalo Cerritos as the street runs north to the marinas.

Stroll the *malecón* for a look at some of Mazatlán's seafront sculptures. While this is not the avant-garde statuary you'll see farther south in Puerto Vallarta, these often-audacious creations make for an interesting walk. Along Playa Olas Altas, sculptures depict a deer, mermaids and "La Mujer Mazatleca," a woman dramatically embracing the heavens. "La

Continuidad de la Vida" (The Continuity of Life) features a nude man and woman perched atop a huge seashell, the man gesturing to a pod of leaping dolphins.

The Fisherman's Monument (Monumento al Pescador), on Avenida del Mar north of Playa Olas Altas, is a local landmark. This sculpture of a woman and a fisherman dragging his net—both of them again sans clothing—is a curious sight. Farther north, along Avenida del Mar across from Avenida Lola Beltran, suds lovers will find a tribute to Mazatlán's very own Pacífico Brewery in the form of a huge copper beer vat.

The section of town north of the *malecón* along Avenida Camarón Sábalo is known as the Golden Zone (Zona Dorada). Welcome to *turista* central. Here, a chain of high-rise hotels and mega resorts front some of Mazatlán's finest beaches. Running behind the hotels is a garish commercial drag jam-packed with fast food joints, bars, restaurants, mini markets, souvenir shops, car rental offices and banks. While the comforts of home are certainly convenient, the area isn't exactly picture postcard material.

Near the Golden Zone's southern end, where Avenida Playa las Gaviotas splits off from the main thoroughfare and runs behind the hotels fronting Playa Gaviotas, are more restaurants and several nice shops. But no matter where you go in the Golden Zone, be aware that you're also in the "Time Share Zone"—and the sharks here are particularly aggressive. If you're not interested in a "free tour" (read: time share presentation), it's advisable to give them the cold shoulder.

Icebox Hill (Cerro de la Nevería), in the Olas Altas area, is residential. A gradually ascending road reaches its summit, from which are views of a great part of the city, the immense blue bay and awe-inspiring sunsets that tint the sea and clouds a brilliant orange-red. Nearby El Mirador, off Paseo Claussen, is where daring locals plunge from a platform 45 feet above turbulent water surrounded by dangerous rocks. The feat requires expert timing; without the cushioning effect of a wave, a diver meets just 6 feet of water. In the evening these young daredevils carry flaming torches for a theatrical effect. Tips are expected.

Old Mazatlán, just inland from Playa Olas Altas, is the oldest part of the city. Here ongoing renovation is preserving a number of historical structures. Blocks of buildings and private residences—including rows of town houses with wrought-iron and stone trim—line the narrow streets, especially along avenidas Heriberto Frias, Venus and Niños Héroes.

Although it remains unseen by many tourists staying in the Zona Dorada to the north, a day in Old Mazatlán (the Centro Histórico) is a must. This is where the city's daily business is conducted amid the rushing of people and vehicles. Plaza Principal, the main plaza (also called Plaza Revolución), sits in the heart of the historic center across the street from Mazatlán's 19th-century cathedral, the Basilica of the Immaculate Conception.

With its wrought-iron benches, shoeshine stands and vendor carts shaded by bushy trees and palms, the plaza is the city's communal hub. Old-timers read newspapers and smoke cigars. Downtown workers eat lunch and chat on cell phones. Schoolchildren run and play after being cooped up in a classroom all day. Tourists wander through, trying to find the "other plaza," Plazuela Machado. To reach it, walk to the south end of Plaza Principal (away from the cathedral) and head west 2 blocks on Calle Angel Flores. Make a left on Avenida Carnaval and follow it for 2 blocks to Plazuela Machado.

Here, on the plaza's east side, Old Mazatlán's revival essentially began with the early 1990s restoration and reopening of the Angela Peralta Theater, now the city's cultural showplace. This beautiful little plaza is a shady oasis surrounded by colorful colonial buildings that have been converted into cafes and restaurants. Teenagers smooch on the wooden benches. In the late afternoon, local expatriates walk their dogs. Outdoor art shows are held regularly, and occasional music concerts take place under the green wrought-iron gazebo. After dark the atmosphere *es muy romántico.*

The Mazatlán Art Museum (Museo de Arte de Mazatlán), Calle Sixto Osuna and Avenida Venustiano Carranza, displays works by Mazatleco artists as well as such nationally known figures as José Luis Cuevas. Film screenings, concerts and other cultural events also take place.

At the southern end of town are the ferry terminal, tour boat operators, sport-fishing fleets and commercial port activities. Standing guard over the harbor's entrance is El Faro, said to be the tallest lighthouse in the Western Hemisphere and second only to Gibraltar in the world, with a range of some 35 nautical miles. Those undertaking the strenuous half-hour hike up the rocky pinnacle will be rewarded with an expansive view of the harbor and ocean.

Another vista of the city and its watery surroundings—particularly lovely in the evening—can be seen from the top of Lookout Hill (Cerro de Vigía), a short distance north of El Faro. This climb, also steep, is better made via taxi.

Back in the Zona Dorada, more great city views abound at the historic Hotel Posada Freeman, now run by the Best Western chain. An elevator whisks you to the 12th-floor "Sky Room," a casual bar with big picture windows offering panoramas of city and sea. The rooftop has a swimming pool and lounge chairs; the latter are available to non-hotel guests who order drinks. Nicknamed "Mazatlán's Skyscraper," the Freeman welcomed its first guests in 1944.

Because of Mazatlán's waterfront sprawl, walking is an ill-advised choice for exploration. Fortunately, there are several public transportation options. *Pulmonías,* the city's signature taxis, are essentially souped-up golf carts powered by Volkswagen Bug engines. They make the Zona Dorada circuit, travel up and down the *malecón* and seat three passengers comfortably (four is a squeeze).

The vehicles were nicknamed *pulmonía* by rival cabbies, who told potential fares that riding in a chilly open-air car would result in the flu (it apparently didn't, judging from their ubiquity, and the name stuck). Always negotiate the fare in advance, as *pulmonías* tend to be more expensive than a taxi. A word of caution: *Pulmonías* do not have seat belts and they emit strong exhaust fumes; if either is a concern, opt for a regular taxi instead.

For 5 pesos one can get to just about any place in the city via local bus lines. The "Sábalo-Centro" route is the most useful for tourists. These buses run along the waterfront between the Zona Dorada hotels and downtown. Buses marked "Sábalo-Cocos-Centro" or simply "Centro" also travel between the two areas, but unless you're interested in a lengthy detour through the city's working class neighborhoods, avoid them.

"Cerritos Juárez" buses follow a route from Mazatlán's coffee factory to the Zona Dorada and then north to the marinas, ending at Playa Los Cerritos. The fare for the comfier, air-conditioned green buses, which are only available on the "Sábalo-Centro" and "Sábalo-Cocos-Centro" routes, is 8 pesos. A knowledge of Spanish is helpful if you intend to get around by bus. During rush hour, about 5 to 7 p.m., buses that are full may pass waiting passengers. During off hours it's often possible to hail a bus as you would a taxi.

Mazatlán is a favorite destination for RV travelers due to its access from the United States via Mex. 15. Most of the RV parks are at the north end of the city, along avenidas Camarón Sábalo/Cerritos. Mar Rosa, in the Zona Dorada at Av. Camarón Sábalo #702, has about 80 sites, some of them beachfront; phone (669) 913-6187.

Beaches

Mazatlán's beaches offer something for everyone and accordingly attract different groups of sunseekers. Some are visited mainly by Mazatlecos; others draw tourists. The following beaches are described as they are located from south to north along the coast.

Stone Island (Isla de la Piedra), at the southern end of the city, is actually a peninsula offering miles of mostly undeveloped oceanside beaches that can be explored on horseback. Small motorboats carry passengers to and from the island (about a 5-minute ride), departing from a launch along the harbor channel north of the ferry terminal. On weekends—and particularly Sunday—entire families spread out along the sand or under the coconut palm groves. Open-air restaurants offer smoked fish, shrimp and beer along with music and dancing.

Playa Olas Altas was the city's first tourist beach and is where the *malecón* begins. The name means "high waves," and surfers congregate here during the summer. This is not the best beach for swimming; instead, enjoy the tremendous views of the surf from one of the many outdoor cafés that line the seaside walkway.

Playa Los Piños, located between the Marine House and the Fisherman's Monument, is where local fishermen sell their catch. If you're interested in purchasing fresh fish without angling for it, arrive early; the catch disappears quickly. Just north of Playa Los Piños is Playa Norte, which stretches between the Fisherman's Monument and Punta Camarón. This beach is popular with locals who play impromptu baseball and soccer games in the sand or take to the water on a three-wheeled floating trike.

Playa Martín fronts the seaside promenade along Avenida del Mar. A tunnel connects the beach with the Hotel Hacienda Mazatlán. Big Pacific rollers crash against the rocks at Punta Camarón. On the north side of this outcrop jutting into the water is Playa las Gaviotas, popular with tourists who want to soak up some sun or play a game of beach volleyball.

Farther up is Playa Sábalo, where the wide, white sand beach attracts droves of tourists and what seems like an equal number of Mexican vendors. Parasailers and windsurfers utilize this stretch fronting the Golden Zone. It is protected from the open surf by Bird, Deer and Goat islands, which rise out of the water a short distance offshore.

Beyond Playa Sábalo, at the north end of Mazatlán, are Playa Brujas (Witches' Beach) and Playa Los Cerritos, which stretch north to Cerritos Point (Punta Cerritos). To reach these beaches, either hire a taxi (about $8-$10 U.S. one way from the Golden Zone) or hop on the "Cerritos-Juárez" bus heading north. The line ends near Playa Los Cerritos. To get to the shore, walk straight ahead past a long, squat building packed with souvenir stalls. Rustic *palapa* restaurants sit on a low bluff overlooking the beach, which is crowded with Mexican families on weekends. During the week, swimming is good at this mostly unspoiled stretch of sand protected by rocky outcroppings.

Playa Brujas also is within walking distance of the bus stop. Head west up the only narrow paved road in sight and follow it to Restaurant Playa Bruja, a nice *palapa* bar overlooking the sand. Playa Brujas was once an isolated surfing outpost, but condo and hotel development continues to creep ever closer.

Sports and Recreation

Fishing in Mazatlán ranks among the best anywhere. Striped marlin are hooked between November and April; sailfish and black marlin are caught between May and October. Other game species taken from the Pacific waters include blue marlin, bonito, dolphin and yellowfin tuna. Well-equipped fleets are headquartered at the docks at the southern end of town, where the ferry and charter tour boats are moored, and at Marina El Cid in the Golden Zone.

Charter fishing boat rates start at about $270 (U.S.) a day for a small boat (up to four people) and include bait and tackle, but not fishing licenses or refreshments. Tipping the captain and first mate is customary, particularly if the day's catch has been bountiful. A catch-and-release policy is emphasized. Make fishing arrangements in advance of your arrival with either the fleet itself or through your hotel. Hotels will usually try to arrange group excursions, thereby sharing the cost of boats.

The El Cid Resort offers a variety of fishing packages utilizing its own Aries fleet of boats. For information and reservations phone (669) 916-3468, or contact a travel agency. Local charter companies include Star Fleet, phone (669) 982-2665, and Flota Bibi Fleet, phone (669) 981-3640. Sport-fishing guides depart from dock 10 at Marina Mazatlán in the Golden Zone; for reservation information phone (669) 916-7799.

Baseball in Mazatlán is considered something of a tradition. Loyal fans fervently support the local Pacific League team, the Mazatlán Venados, which has produced players who have gone on to the American majors. Games are played at Teodoro Mariscal Stadium, off Avenida del Mar and convenient to the tourist zone. Check with the Sinaloa State Tourism Office for game schedules; the season runs October through January.

Bullfights take place on Sundays and holidays at 4 p.m. from December to early April at the Plaza de Toros Monumental bullring on Avenida Rafael Buelna. Tickets can be purchased at the bullring, at most hotels or through a travel agency. Prices depend on where you sit; seats in the shade *(sombra)* are more expensive and run $20-$30 (U.S.).

A popular activity is parasailing, which provides 15 minutes of sheer thrills for those not prone to vertigo. Arrangements can be made in front of the Playa Mazatlán and Las Flores hotels in the Golden Zone.

The Aqua Sports Center at the El Cid Resort rents a variety of water sports equipment, from jet skis and Hobie Cats to kayaks and snorkeling gear. The resort also has a challenging 27-hole golf course—18 holes designed by Robert Trent Jones Jr. and nine by Lee Trevino. It is open to the public on a limited basis, although preferred tee times are given to hotel guests. Phone (669) 913-3333 for equipment rental or golf reservation information.

Another Jones-designed championship course is at the Estrella del Mar resort community on Isla de la Piedra, just south of Old Mazatlán. Six of the 18 holes border the ocean, offering spectacular views. Amenities include a pro shop and clubhouse. For information, phone 01 (800) 776-4653 (toll-free long distance within Mexico) or (800) 967-1889 (from the United States).

Good for a casual round is the nine-hole course at the Mazatlán Country Club (Club Campestre Mazatlán), and the $25 (U.S.) greens fee is significantly less expensive. The club is on Mex. 15 at the south end of town but is hard to find; take a taxi. To schedule a tee time, phone (669) 980-1570.

Shopping

Shopping in Mazatlán is centered primarily along avenidas Playa las Gaviotas and Camarón Sábalo in the Golden Zone. The shops and galleries here feature the usual assortment of T-shirts, sportswear, resort wear, jewelry, handicrafts and leather goods. Most are open Monday through Saturday; some do not accept credit cards.

Be sure to stop by Sea Shell City, a combination museum and shop on Av. Playa las Gaviotas #407. A kaleidoscopic variety of shells from around the world are on display, and there are many shell craft items as well as Mexican handicrafts for sale. Upstairs is an amazing fountain covered in shells that holds colorful koi.

Across the street, the open-air Las Cabañas Shopping Center is a narrow corridor lined with small gift shops, some of them interesting, others stocked with the usual trinkets. At the far end of this mini shopping arcade you'll find Pancho's Restaurant and steps leading down to Playa las Gaviotas, where roving beach vendors are waiting to pounce.

The nearby Mazatlán Arts and Crafts Center, on Avenida Playa las Gaviotas, stocks everything from tablecloths and rugs to pottery, *guayabera* shirts, embroidered dresses and footwear. Artisans can sometimes be seen creating both artwork and jewelry designs. Purchases here are cash only.

If you're looking for jewelry of a better pedigree than what the beach vendors are peddling, Cielito Lindo, Av. Playa las Gaviotas #501, has a huge selection at surprisingly reasonable prices. For artistic (i.e., expensive) jewelry, check out Isabella Matiella Jewelry inside the Royal Villas Resort on Avenida Camarón Sábalo. Matiella incorporates ancient petroglyphs into some of her designs.

For a more authentic Mexican shopping experience, head downtown. In the Central Market *(mercado)*, at avenidas Ocampo and Juárez in Old Mazatlán, you'll find aisle after aisle crammed with vendor stalls selling everything from fresh meat, seafood and produce to *piñatas*, shoes and Che Guevara T-shirts. More stalls line the outside walls of the market building. As far as non-food items go, good quality can be hard to find, but for dedicated bargain hunters the opportunity to haggle with local merchants is the real fun.

The rebirth of Old Mazatlán has seen a number of art galleries crop up in recent years, most located on the streets west of Plazuela Machado. Art Walk Mazatlán publishes a free map available at many of the galleries.

Nidart (Nido de Artesanos) occupies a bright purple and red-trimmed building next to the Angela Peralta Theater in Old Mazatlán. This gallery and studio complex (the name means "nest of artisans") features leather masks, sculptures, burlap dolls, decorated coconut shells, jewelry, clay figurines and other crafts expertly fashioned by local artisans. It is open Mon.-Sat. 10-3 during the high tourist season.

Casa Etnika, Calle Sixto Osuna #50, is a contemporary Mexican art gallery that occupies a large 19th-century house. The ground-floor rooms are filled with fine furniture, sculpture, paintings, wildlife photography prints, baskets, jewelry and more.

You'll also find gifts for children (Mazatlán coloring books) and high-quality T-shirts (a rarity in Mexico). There's a small gourmet coffee bar next to the gallery entrance.

South of Avenida Rafael Buelna on Avenida de los Deportes, about 3 blocks inland from the *malecón* (Avenida del Mar), is La Gran Plaza, a mall offering American-style shopping. The supermarket and department stores make this a convenient place to stock up on basics. It is easily reached by taxi or the Sábalo Cocos bus.

Dining and Nightlife

Everything from American fast food to spicy Creole fare is available in Mazatlán. But for a city that touts itself as "the shrimp capital of Mexico," seafood understandably is the star on many local menus. Shrimp dishes are prepared in every way imaginable, and almost nowhere else is the crustacean fresher or more tempting.

In addition to the big hotel restaurants and fine dining spots, there are numerous establishments along the *malecón* serving fish filets, various shrimp concoctions or such Pacific coast specialties as *pescado zarandeado,* filleted and grilled snapper coated with a chile/achiote marinade.

In and around Old Mazatlán's Central Market, you'll find several food stands selling tasty tacos, *tortas* and the like. Better yet, head a few blocks southwest to Plazuela Machado and dine al fresco at one of the sidewalk cafes. If you don't care to eat another shrimp as long as you live, try Beach Burger, at Constitución #513. Their signature Kahuna burger is thick, juicy and delicious, and the margaritas pack a wallop.

Café Pacífico, in Old Mazatlán at the corner of calles Constitución and Heriberto Frias (also on Plazuela Machado), has a pool table, walls hung with old photographs and a laid-back air. The cafe's outdoor tables are a nice spot for a leisurely lunch.

The Hotel Playa Mazatlán, on Avenida Playa las Gaviotas in the Golden Zone, presents "Fiesta Mexicana" on Tuesday, Thursday and Saturday evenings from November through May (less frequently the rest of the year) beginning at 6 p.m. An all-you-can-eat buffet of charbroiled steaks and chicken, tacos, burritos, guacamole, salsa and fresh fruit is followed by folkloric dance and music performances from various regions of Mexico. The entertainment includes an amazing display of rope twirling by a *charro,* or Mexican cowboy, and a flamboyantly costumed troupe who re-enact a bit of Carnaval.

Admittance to the shows is first-come-first served. Dress is casual, but shorts are not permitted. For information and tickets phone (669) 989-0555, or contact the tour desk inside the hotel lobby.

Most of the restaurants and hotels in Mazatlán offer purified water and ice. There should be no cause for concern about drinking the water in these establishments, but double check if in doubt. Purified water can be bought in any of the mini markets around town. *For a list of AAA-RATED dining establishments in Mazatlán, see the Lodgings & Restaurants section.*

Note: Some restaurants add a standard 10 to 15 percent gratuity to the bill. Be sure to differentiate between this charge and the 15 percent IVA tax that is added to every check, and tip accordingly.

Many of the big hotels in the Golden Zone have bars or lounges, with plenty of evening happy hours featuring two-for-one drink prices. The Fiesta Land complex, perched atop Punta Camarón, the rocky outcrop near the Sábalo traffic circle, has several clubs. The techno, hip-hop and Latin music at Valentino's attracts a glamorous crowd for dancing and scene-making. Cover charge is $8 (U.S.), $22 if you choose the open bar option. Bora Bora has a great view of the surf below to complement the music menu of '70s and '80s pop and rock, hip-hop and techno. Cover charge is $6 (U.S.). Canta Bar is a karaoke club. All three venues stay open into the early morning hours.

Another loud, rollicking spot is Joe's Oyster Bar. There's a well-signed entrance on Avenida Playa las Gaviotas, or you can enter this thatch-roofed *cantina* from the Golden Zone beachfront. The music is mostly hip-hop, with a few Latin jams mixed in for the local clientele. Late afternoon happy hour sees college kids dancing on tables, older tourists eating jumbo oysters and two-man volleyball teams engaged in heated matches on the sand volleyball court. The scene gets much wilder after the sun sets.

In the mood to hear a classic rock cover band play Toto's "Africa" or Santana's "Black Magic Woman"? Then head to Gus Gus, in the Golden Zone at Av. Camarón Sábalo #1730 (across the street from the Costa de Oro Hotel). A party atmosphere prevails at this casual bar and grill, with the menu offering above-average Mexican staples.

Events

The year's biggest party is the pre-Lenten Carnaval, or Mardi Gras, held in late February or early March. All Mazatlán—not to mention revelers from around the world—gathers for 5 days and nights of fireworks, parades with elaborate floats, the coronation of a festival queen *(La Reina de Carnaval)* and of course, plenty of music and dancing. If you'll be visiting around this time, make hotel reservations several months in advance and inquire regarding exactly when Carnaval begins. Expect prices to climb as well.

Historical records of the event date to 1827, when military men demanding salaries staged a protest by masquerading. Over the years the tradition grew, with mask wearing becoming part of the festivities at both public assemblies and private parties. By the end of the 19th century, French, German and Italian immigrants were adding facets of their own culture to Carnaval, and today the city claims that its celebration is the world's third largest after those in Rio de Janeiro and New Orleans. The revelry culminates on Shrove Tuesday, when the *malecón* is packed with merrymakers.

Mazatlán recognizes Day of the Dead celebrations Nov. 1 and 2 with a combination of feasting and somber remembrances. Several sport-fishing tournaments also occur in November.

Guided Tours

A guided tour is a good way to see both the city and several interesting towns in the surrounding area. Information about city and vicinity tours can be obtained through all of the major hotels or at any local travel agency.

Olé Tours, Av. Camarón Sábalo #7000 in the Golden Zone, offers a 3-hour city historical tour that includes the cathedral, central market, Old Mazatlán, the Angela Peralta Theater, Icebox Hill, Plaza Machado and residential areas. It departs Mon.-Sat. at 9 a.m.; the fee is $23 (U.S.). There also are tours to Rosario and Concordia/Copala; hotel pickup is included. Phone (669) 916-6288.

Marlin Tours, Av. Camarón Sábalo #1504, organizes city excursions as well as day trips to Concordia/Copala, Rosario and Teacapán; phone (669) 913-5301. **Note:** Beware the numerous sidewalk entrepreneurs who offer free tours; their real goal is to pitch the sale of time share units.

Day excursions also can be arranged to the islands off the Golden Zone section of the coast: Goat Island (Isla de Chivas), Bird Island (Isla de Pájaros) and Deer Island (Isla de Venados), a nature preserve where seashell collectors can search along the shore and snorkelers will find decent submarine scenery when waters are calm.

The El Cid Resort offers a trip to Deer Island aboard an amphibious vehicle for $10 (U.S.) per person; snorkeling gear is available for rent. Daily departures are at 10, noon and 2. There are no services or restaurants on the island, so pack a cooler with drinks and snacks. If you forget, the men who rent out beach umbrellas also sell beer and soda on the sly. For information contact the resort's Aqua Sports Center; phone (669) 913-3333.

Perhaps the most popular guided day trip from Mazatlán takes in the former mining outposts of Concordia and Copala, both on Mex. 40 as it heads east toward Durango *(see place listing under Northwestern Mexico)*. These two colonial-era towns offer a charming, laid-back contrast to Mazatlán's seaside partying atmosphere.

Concordia, in the foothills of the Sierra Madre Occidental, is surrounded by mango and banana plantations. Founded in 1565 by Spanish *conquistador* Francisco de Ibarra, it is still a furniture, brick and pottery making center; roadside stands sell furniture, pottery and fresh mangos. The main plaza contains a gazebo and an enormous wooden chair that provides an amusing photo opportunity. Across from the plaza is the baroque Church of St. Sebastian, a lovely old building that has an ornate stone facade.

Copala, about 24 kilometers (15 miles) east of Concordia, is smaller and not as bustling but just as picturesque. A walk down this village's cobblestoned main street past red tile-roofed, whitewashed buildings is like a journey back in time. Little has changed in the town's more than 400 years of existence. Cars are few and far between. Dogs, chickens, pigs and donkeys wander the streets, and dawn is greeted by the sound of crowing roosters. Adding to the scene is the brilliantly colored bougainvillea that spills over roofs and cascades down walls.

Up until the late 19th century Copala was a center for silver mining operations in the surrounding mountains, and old homes still cling precariously to the hillsides. The tree-shaded town plaza has wrought-iron lampposts and an ornate bandstand and is bordered by small gift shops selling silver jewelry and regional handicrafts. At one end of the plaza stands the baroque Church of San José, which was completed in 1775; it has a vaulted interior with gold leaf decoration and colorful polychrome statues of saints.

Also on the plaza is the Copala Butter Company. Charles Butter, an American entrepreneur, played a role in much of the mining effort in this region, and a restaurant and small inn are named after him. The restaurant is known for its homemade tacos and enchiladas as well as banana cream pie. Banana cream pies are, in fact, a local specialty; tiny Chalva's Pie Shop bakes them to go, and Daniel's restaurant, which caters to tour bus groups, offers a version that also includes coconut.

South of Mazatlán via Mex. 15 is Rosario, another old mining community. At the end of the 18th century it had a population of 7,000 and was one of the richest towns in northwest Mexico. Mining activities ceased in the 1940s. Of particular interest is Our Lady of the Rosary, the town's beautiful colonial church; its marvelous altarpiece is completely covered with intricate gold-leaf designs. Some 70 kilometers (43 miles) of underground tunnels, dug over a 300-year period to aid in extracting gold and silver, remain behind; locals attest that they outnumber the surface streets.

Sinaloa State Tourism Office (Coordinación General de Turismo de Sinaloa): downtown at Av. Carnaval #1317 (at Avenida Mariano Escobedo). The staff is friendly and speaks English. Open Mon.-Fri. 9-5; phone (669) 981-8883.

What To See in Town

ANGELA PERALTA THEATER (Teatro Angela Peralta) is 3 blks. s. of Plaza Principal at Av. Carnaval #47 (at Calle Libertad). It opened in 1874 as the Teatro Rubio. Renowned opera singer Angela Peralta, dubbed "the Mexican Nightingale," arrived for an engagement in 1883 but contracted cholera and tragically died (along with most of her company) before uttering a single note.

After stints as a Mardi Gras ballroom, movie palace, boxing arena and parking garage, the theater was abandoned and in ruins before restoration efforts began in 1987. It reopened in 1992 and today is the pride of Mazatlecos. The most important cultural center in town, it houses a performing arts school and presents a varied schedule of performances, including ballet, folkloric dance, concerts, operas and plays. The opulent interior can be toured; photo displays on the second-floor mezzanine chronicle the theater's history and restoration.

Allow 30 minutes minimum. Daily 9-6. Tour fee $1 (U.S.). Phone (669) 982-4446.

BASILICA OF THE IMMACULATE CONCEPTION (Basilica de la Inmaculada Concepción) is downtown on the n. side of Plaza Principal, at avs. Juárez and 21 de Marzo. The city's cathedral is easily recognized by its gold-colored twin spires. The late 19th-century exterior is rather plain, but the beautifully preserved interior is very ornate, with numerous gold accents. Open daily. Free.

MAZATLAN AQUARIUM (Acuario Mazatlán) is half a blk. e. of Av. del Mar at Av. de los Deportes #111. It displays 250 species of fresh and saltwater marine life, from colorful reef fish to moray eels to sea turtles, in some 50 tanks. A sea lion show is presented several times daily in an open-air amphitheater. There also is an exotic bird show utilizing birds confiscated from vendors who captured them illegally. Daily 9:30-5:30. Admission about $5.50 (U.S.); $3 (children). Phone (669) 981-7815.

MAZATLAN ARCHEOLOGICAL MUSEUM (Museo Arqueológico de Mazatlán) is at Calle Sixto Osuna #76, just e. of Paseo Claussen. The small collection focuses on paintings, clay figurines and regional artifacts. There also is an exhibit that covers the Mexican Revolution and Mazatlán's early history. Most background information is in Spanish. Guided tours are available. Mon.-Sat. 10-5, Sun. 10-3. Admission about $1.50 (U.S.).

MAZATLAN JUNGLE TOUR is not really a jungle excursion but a sightseeing trip along the waterfront. The tour boat passes shrimp fleets and the navy base, proceeds through inlets and waterways lined with mangroves, and ends up at Stone Island (Isla de la Piedra). A bus takes visitors to the island's beach. A charcoal-grilled fish lunch, prepared beachside, is included; horseback rides along the beach are extra.

The boat departs at 9 a.m. and returns at 3; the schedule varies according to season but tours are normally Tues.-Thurs. and Sat. Reservations are required. All-inclusive fare (includes round-trip transportation and hotel pickup) about $45 (U.S.). Phone (669) 914-1444 for reservations information through King David Tours.

PUERTO ESCONDIDO, OAXACA (D-5)

pop. 19,000

Puerto Escondido (PWEHR-to ehs-cohn-DEE-doh) means "hidden port," and until fairly recently the translation was quite appropriate. The town was named for Punta Escondida, the rocky outcrop that protects a half-moon bay. A port was established here in 1928 as a shipping point for coffee grown on the forested seaward slopes of the Sierra Madre del Sur. Coastal Mex. 200 came through in the 1960s, opening up the area to tourism.

Among the first visitors were surfers, who were drawn by the big waves and dirt-cheap lodgings. Today they're still here, but Puerto Escondido is no longer a hideaway and not quite as cheap. Instead, it's an established destination, frequented by an international group of travelers preferring a more laid-back alternative to the shiny expense of Bahías de Huatulco and other carefully planned seaside resorts.

Practicalities

Puerto Escondido is about 113 kilometers (70 miles) west of Huatulco via Mex. 200. This highway, often referred to as the Carretera Costera (Coastal Highway), divides the town roughly in half. The older, upper section, above the highway, is where most residents live and conduct their daily business.

Below the highway is the newer, tourist-geared waterfront, where hotels, restaurants and shops spread for about a mile along the main thoroughfare, Avenida Peréz Gasga. At noon each day, chains are raised at the eastern and western ends of the beachfront strip, closing the street to vehicular traffic. At the western end of this pedestrian zone, Gasga begins winding uphill and crosses Mex. 200, where its name changes to Avenida Oaxaca (Mex. 131). The junction, marked by a traffic signal, is known as El Crucero.

The local bus stations are all within a block or so of the El Crucero intersection. Estrella Blanca provides first-class service along Mex. 200 between Acapulco and Bahías de Huatulco (be sure to specify the La Crucecita terminal as your destination if you're taking a bus to Huatulco from Puerto Escondido). The station is on Avenida Oaxaca, just north of the El Crucero junction.

By car, Puerto Escondido can be reached from Oaxaca by taking Mex. 175—a winding 6- to 8-hour drive over mountainous terrain—to the junction with coastal Mex. 200 (just south of Pochutla), then west about 81 kilometers (50 miles). Avoid Mex. 131, a direct route between Oaxaca and Puerto Escondido but one that has long unpaved stretches.

Coastal Mex. 200 southeast from Acapulco or west from Bahías de Huatulco is generally negotiable, although the route winds between Acapulco and Puerto Escondido and is likely to be potholed in spots during the summer rainy season (roughly July through September). A word of caution: **Do not drive after dark.**

The international airport is about 3 kilometers (2 miles) west of town off Mex. 200, near the newer hotel and resort development around Playa Bacocho. It receives flights from Mexico City (via Mexicana/Aerocaribe) and Oaxaca (via Aerotucan). Taxis and less expensive *colectivos* (minibuses) operated by Transportes Terrestres shuttle airport passengers to and from hotels. For additional information about airlines *see Arriving by Air, page 61*.

There is a *casa de cambio* (currency exchange) office on each side of Peréz Gasga near the Rincón

Pacífico Hotel. Graficom, Av. Peréz Gasga #302, has telephone, fax and Internet services.

The Beaches

A lighthouse atop Punta Escondida at the western end of the bayfront affords a panoramic view of town. Running east from the rocky cove beneath the lighthouse is Playa Principal, the in-town beach. Here the stretch of sand is narrow, the water calm and the beach backed by rustling palms. It can be crowded: Mexican families flock here on Sundays and holidays to wade and paddle in the shallows, and local fishermen cast their nets at the sheltered west side of the bay or launch small, colorfully painted boats. **Note:** Avoid walking along any of Puerto Escondido's beaches at night, as robberies and muggings have occurred.

To the east of Playa Principal is Playa Marineros, which begins at the jutting rocks below the Hotel Santa Fe. Here the shoreline begins curving toward the south and increasingly faces the open ocean. The surf gets rougher, and swimmers should exercise caution.

Farther to the southeast is Playa Zicatela, considered to be one of the world's best surfing beaches. The wide expanse of golden-colored sand stretches for miles, and the thundering Pacific breakers crashing onto it are impressive indeed. The biggest waves occur between August and November. Surfers from all over the world congregate at Zicatela, especially for the international tournament held annually in November. Spectators line the beach to watch these daredevils finesse the "pipeline," a long tubular swell of water. Needless to say, swim here at your own risk.

West of town are the coves of Puerto Angelito and Carrizalillo. With small beaches, submerged rock formations and close-in shelves of coral, these sheltered spots are ideal for snorkeling and scuba diving (bring your own gear, as facilities are limited at best). Both coves can be reached either by taxi, a boat launched from Playa Principal or a circuitous concrete footpath (wear a hat and bring water if you decide to walk). Farther west is Playa Bacocho, another open strip of sand; the waves and undertow make it better for sunning and hiking than swimming. Most of the more expensive hotels cluster around this beach.

What To Do

The main reason to visit Puerto Escondido is to relax at the beach; shopping and entertainment are not high on its list of diversions. The local *mercado* (municipal market) is in the upper section of town on Avenida 10 Norte, several blocks west of Avenida Oaxaca. It sells mostly produce, but one group of stalls offers a selection of regional handicrafts. Along the tourist strip, there are a few clothing shops and the usual hodgepodge of T-shirts, postcards and souvenirs.

Several restaurants line beachside Avenida Peréz Gasga, with fish and seafood—from sushi to octopus—the main menu items. Most places provide a view of the beach and the activity along it. The restaurant in the Hotel Santa Fe, on Avenida del Morro at the eastern end of the bay (about half a mile southeast of the town center), has good food and a breezy atmosphere, with tables overlooking the Playa Zicatela surf.

Art and Harry's Surf Inn, as the name suggests, attracts the local surfer contingent. The fresh fish, salads and unobstructed sunset views are a good way to cap off a day at the beach. The restaurant is on Avenida del Morro, at the southern end of Zicatela.

The best places to watch the sun sink into the Pacific are along Playa Zicatela, where there is an unobscured view of the western horizon. The cliff-top lawn on the grounds of the Posada Real Hotel, west of town overlooking Playa Bacocho, is an ideal perch for sunset watching. A taxi can get you there. There are a couple of noisy bars and dance clubs in the tourist zone along Avenida Peréz Gasga and in the hotels around Playa Bacocho.

The surrounding coastal region is a natural paradise, and because most locations are inaccessible except by boat, eco-tourism is actively promoted. Hidden Voyages Ecotours offers seasonal guided bird-watching and nature trips to some of the lagoons that indent the Oaxacan coast. Early morning trips visit Manialtepec Lagoon, about 15 kilometers (9 miles) west of Puerto Escondido, which is encircled by mangroves and home to a rich variety of wetland bird species and tropical vegetation.

An all-day excursion to Lagunas de Chacahua National Park, a larger series of lagoons west of Manialtepec, includes a midday swim and a visit to a crocodile hatchery. Sunset cruises also are available.

Round-trip transportation is provided from Puerto Escondido hotels. Food is not included; the Chacahua tour stops at a restaurant for lunch. The restaurant at the departure dock sells beverages to go. Bring a hat, sunblock and a dollar or two to tip the boatman. Binoculars are provided. There is a four-person minimum for tours. Fees range from $30 to $40 (U.S.) per person.

Reservations must be made through the Turismo Rodimar Travel Agency, Av. Peréz Gasga #905 on the beachfront. It is usually open daily 7:30 a.m.-10 p.m.; phone (954) 582-0734. This agency also can arrange three- or four-person fishing trips to the waters off Puerto Escondido for mackerel, sea bass, snook or tuna. Boats depart from Playa Principal.

Tourist information office: near the airport, at the intersection of Mex. 200 (Carretera Costera) and Avenida Benito Juárez. Open Mon.-Fri. 9-2 and 5-8, Sat. 9-1; phone (954) 582-0175 (English not likely to be spoken). An information booth operated by the Oaxaca Tourist Bureau, located near the western end of beachside Avenida Peréz Gasga, is normally open the same hours.

Puerto Vallarta

City Population: 350,000 (estimated)
Elevation: 6 meters (20 feet)

Editor's Picks:

Church of Our Lady of Guadalupe.................... *(see p. 260)*
El Centro............................ *(see p. 260)*
Playa Mismaloya.................... *(see p. 264)*

On the shores of sparkling blue Bahía de Banderas (Bay of Flags), jungle-cloaked mountains plunge into the Pacific. Here lies the treasure at the foot of the Sierra Madre: Puerto Vallarta. Luxury resorts fronted by warm water and golden-sand beaches are the main draw for some 2 million annual visitors, many of them content to simply unwind, soak up the sun and watch azure waves wash ashore—and we can't say we blame them. But Puerto Vallarta offers more. Dig a little deeper and it won't take long for the city's alluring combination of modern sophistication and vintage character to get under your skin.

Vallarta (as the locals call it) knows what tourists crave, and along the city's cobbled streets you'll find the usual line-up of gringo-friendly businesses, from casual Mexican restaurants and hip clothing boutiques to American chain stores and party-til-dawn nightclubs. But the town also is known for its artistic bent. Surrealistic sculptures dot the bustling beachfront *malecón* (boardwalk), where locals and visitors alike enjoy sunset strolls. One-of-a-kind art galleries and shops pepper the compact downtown area. Souvenir vendor stalls line shady Isla Río Cuale, a long, slender islet in the middle of the Río Cuale, which bisects the downtown area on its journey from mountains to sea.

Unlike some pre-fab Mexican beach resorts (Cancún springs to mind), Vallarta does have a pre-tourism, human history. In the 1500s, Spanish explorers on a quest to conquer Mexico for the mother country discovered the bay and took advantage of the refuge it offered their galleons from marauding pirates. Indigenous peoples had inhabited the area

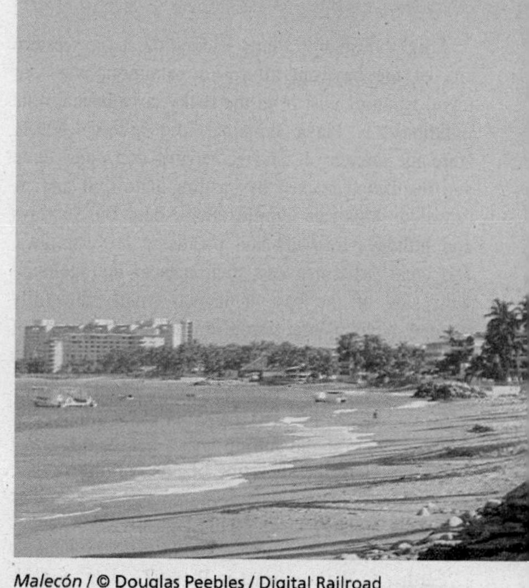

Malecón / © Douglas Peebles / Digital Railroad

for centuries, but it wasn't until the 19th century that anything resembling a permanent *pueblo* took shape.

In 1851, on the site of present-day Puerto Vallarta, settlers involved in the refinement of silver mined in the surrounding mountains (and later, farmers and fishermen) established the town of Las Peñas. Economic booms and busts followed. On solid footing by 1918, the town's name was changed to Puerto Vallarta in honor of former Jalisco state governor Ignacio Luis Vallarta.

Adventurous travelers began to trickle in during the 1940s and '50s. But it would take a Hollywood director and a scandalous romance to put Vallarta on the mass tourism radar. Long before paparazzi chased celebutants and washed-up pop stars around the globe, they pursued real movie stars. Elizabeth Taylor came to Puerto Vallarta in 1963 to be near Richard Burton, who was on location filming John Huston's "The Night of the Iguana." At the time, Taylor and Burton were having a highly publicized extramarital affair. Photographers followed their every move, and Vallarta instantly became world famous.

Heavily promoted flights from U.S. cities (especially Los Angeles) led to serious investments in

Getting There — *starting on p. 255*
Getting Around — *starting on p. 258*
What To See — *starting on p. 260*
What To Do — *starting on p. 260*
Where To Stay — *starting on p. 554*
Where To Dine — *starting on p. 564*

tourism infrastructure, and by the 1970s and '80s resort and condominium development had spread far north and south of the original village. The Marina Vallarta complex, completed in the mid-'90s to accommodate high-end resorts and cruise ships, sits just north of the Hotel Zone. Here, American discount chains Costco and WalMart have set up shop to serve the ever-growing population of Mexican transplants and expatriates from *el norte*. Yet somehow name-brand consumerism never seems to overshadow the prevailing sense of Old Mexico charm that makes Puerto Vallarta so appealing.

The weather is balmy year-round. Daily highs range from the 80s to the low 90s, nightly lows from the low 60s to low 70s. The temperature rarely drops below 60 degrees, making heavy jackets unnecessary. The nicest weather is during the high tourist season, from mid-December through mid-April. This is also the time preferred by vacationing humpback whales that swim down from the Arctic to laze in the relatively warm Pacific waters.

Vallarta is very casual; most visitors wear shorts and T-shirts. Slacks or nice jeans for men and summer-type dresses for women are appropriate for more upscale restaurants and some nightclubs. A sweater comes in handy for winter evenings; an effective sunblock is a must all year. Pack a hat and bring along an effective insect repellent, as mosquitoes can be a nuisance at any time of year. A formula containing at least 40 percent DEET will usually do the trick. If you arrive without bug dope, Autan Classic is a widely available Mexican brand.

If you plan on visiting during the high season, reservations will need to be booked several months in advance. With all the activities at hand—sun, sand, strolling, shopping, swimming, fishing, boat trips or just kicking back and doing nothing—it's easy to spend a week or two.

© Chad Ehlers / Stock Connection / Digital Railroad

Getting There

By Air

Gustavo Díaz Ordaz International Airport is on the main highway about 7 kilometers (4 miles) north of downtown. Aeroméxico, Alaska Airlines, American, America West, Continental, Delta and Mexicana all provide service to Puerto Vallarta from U.S. cities. Connections for flights from the United States are normally via Mexico City. Charter flights from Canada are available through Toronto and Vancouver. Aeroméxico and Mexicana also provide service from other cities within the country, including Guadalajara, León, Mexico City and Tijuana.

For flight information contact the individual airline; within Mexico, phone 01 (800) 021-4010 (toll-free long distance) for Aeroméxico, 01 (800) 904-6000 (toll-free long distance) for American, 01 (800) 900-5000 (toll-free long distance) for Continental, 01 (800) 123-4710 (toll-free long distance)

The Informed Traveler

WHOM TO CALL

Police (emergency): Dial 060 and ask to be connected to an English-speaking operator. For non-emergencies, phone (322) 290-0507.

Consumer Protection Agency (PROFECO): Calle Morelos #883; phone (322) 225-0000 (English may not be spoken fluently). The office is open Mon.-Fri. 9-3 and can assist with time share, taxi, store and other consumer-related issues.

Hospitals: Ameri-Med Hospital, in Plaza Neptuno at the entrance to Marina Vallarta (Boulevard Francisco Medina), (322) 226-2080; CMQ Hospital, Basilio Badillo #365 at Insurgentes, (322) 223-1919 or (322) 222-3572; Red Cross (Cruz Roja), (322) 222-1533. All of these facilities are open 24 hours.

Local phone calls: Use public Telmex phones marked "Ladatel" rather than calling from your hotel room, which almost always incurs a hefty charge (as much as $7 U.S. per minute). These phones require a Ladatel phone card, available in various denominations from most local stores. Avoid phones showing pictures of credit cards or plastered-on decals saying *"3 minutos gratis"* that advertise long distance calling to the United States and Canada. You'll pay dearly for the convenience.

WHERE TO LOOK

Newspapers

Vallarta Today is an English-language daily newspaper geared toward tourists; it has information on everything from restaurants to currency exchange rates. The English-language *Vallarta Tribune* is a free weekly containing local news as well as restaurant and entertainment listings.

Visitor Information

Municipal Tourist Office: in the City Hall (Presidencia Municipal) building at avenidas Juárez and Independencia. The office is open daily 8 a.m.-9 p.m.; phone (322) 223-2500. It's a good source for general city information and has current events listings. This also is the office of the tourist police.

The Web site www.virtualvallarta.com provides local news and comprehensive information about everything from airlines to restaurants to city services. In addition, Puerto Vallarta has numerous Internet cafes where you can check e-mail and surf the Web for about $4 (U.S.) per hour. Aquarius Internet, Av. Juárez #523 (on the west side of the street between avenidas Corona and Galeana) is open daily; phone (322) 223-5700.

WHAT TO KNOW

Currency Exchange

Banks and currency exchange offices *(casas de cambio)* are located throughout the city and at the airport. Banks are usually open Mon.-Fri. 9-5, although hours for exchanging foreign currency may be restricted. Currency exchange offices are open longer hours. Hotels traditionally offer the worst exchange rates, although convenience may render the difference a moot point. Stores, restaurants, taxi drivers and even street vendors will often take U.S. dollars, and credit cards are widely accepted. ATMs are plentiful; withdrawals are in pesos. Some machines dispense U.S. dollars as well, but this option usually requires a Mexican bank-issued ATM/credit card.

Staying Safe

Tourist crime is uncommon, and it's safe to walk the downtown streets. However, visitors would do well not to carry large amounts of cash in public. Avoid walking back streets after dark. If your hotel provides safety deposit boxes, they are a good place to keep money, passports, airline tickets, tourist permits and so forth. Bilingual "tourist police" wearing white safari outfits and baseball caps patrol the downtown area and are generally friendly and helpful.

for Delta and 01 (800) 509-8960 (toll-free long distance) for Mexicana. For additional information about airlines *see Arriving by Air, page 61.*

The ticketing and arrival area is on the main level; customs is located in the baggage claim area. Beyond customs is the main lobby, where you'll be approached by overly friendly men offering to arrange discounted ("almost free") ground transportation. These are time share salesmen. Unless you're willing to endure a high-pressure time share sales pitch, ignore them. Just beyond the hustler gauntlet you can pick up tourist brochures, make arrangements for no-strings-attached ground transportation and exchange currency. The upper level is the departure area, which requires a boarding pass to enter. Phone (322) 221-1537 for airport information.

Colectivos (minivans) operated by Transportes Terrestres provide shared transportation for a per-person fare from the airport to area hotels. Tickets can be purchased at booths just outside the terminal. Specially licensed airport taxis also take passengers to hotels. In both cases, fares are based on a zone system. Zones are posted at the minivan and taxi ticket booths; ask if you don't know the zone in which your hotel is located.

Airport taxis are notoriously expensive; don't be surprised to fork over as much as $18 (U.S.) for a ride to the main Hotel Zone north of town. For budget-friendly taxi transportation to your hotel, exit the far end of the airport lobby and walk over the pedestrian bridge to the other side of the main highway. Here you can hire a regular city taxi for about $6 to $10 (U.S.) depending on your destination.

By Car

Reaching Puerto Vallarta by car involves a lengthy journey; the city lies some 1,200 miles south of the border at Nogales, Ariz., via Mex. 15/15-D and Mex. 200. Traffic on the Mex. 15 free road (*libre* in Spanish) slows considerably in the city of Mazatlán and beyond. Alternately, the Mex. 15 toll road *(cuota)* is usually wide open. However, be prepared to pay several pricey tolls ranging from $7 to $16 (U.S.). Carry plenty of cash. State and federal police conduct frequent inspections, particularly at state lines. Trucks can slow traffic down around Tepic, the Nayarit state capital. From Tepic, Mex. 200 proceeds south to Puerto Vallarta.

Mex. 161 connects San Blas, on the Nayarit coast, with Puerto Vallarta, bypassing Mex. 15's uphill slog through Tepic. While it's not any faster than 15, the Mex. 161 route is incredibly scenic. The generally well-maintained two-lane road snakes through jungle-cloaked hills, skirts the coast and passes through arid farmland. If heading south from San Blas (which is accessible from Mex. 15 via Mex. 54), take the marked Puerto Vallarta turn-off just before the entrance to town and head south. Mex. 161 connects with Mex. 200 at the town of Las Varas; from there, proceed south. Plan on a 3-hour drive from San Blas to Puerto Vallarta.

To reach Puerto Vallarta from Guadalajara, take toll highway Mex. 15 west toward Tepic. At Chapalilla, take the Mex. 200-D turn-off (toward Compostela); at Compostela, proceed south on Mex. 200 for about 130 kilometers (80 miles) to Puerto Vallarta.

Note: Mex. 200 is a precipitously winding two-lane road that passes through extremely mountainous terrain (the mountains here reach all the way to the coast). In addition to the numerous twists and turns, road shoulders are narrow and have steep drop-offs. Only experienced motorists familiar with mountain driving should attempt to navigate this route, and **never drive it at night.** Plan on taking up to 6 hours to get to Puerto Vallarta from Guadalajara. A less sinuous toll highway linking Puerto Vallarta and Guadalajara is supposed to be in the works.

By Bus

Puerto Vallarta's modern central bus station, Central Camionera de Puerto Vallarta, is located just off the Tepic Highway about a kilometer north of the airport. It has a ticket office, baggage storage, restaurants, long distance phone and fax services and guarded overnight parking. The major first-class lines operate out of this station.

Vallarta Plus is a popular line offering daily first-class bus service to and from Guadalajara (about 5 hours). Elite travels the route as well, and also offers service north to Tepic, Mazatlán, Mexicali and Tijuana and south to Manzanillo, Zihuatanejo, Acapulco and Puerto Escondido. Some buses require transfers or stop along the way, while others do not; the ticketing agent will be able to clarify routes and answer questions.

ETN (Enlaces Terrestres Nacionales) specializes in "executive-class" service to Mexico City, Guadalajara and Manzanillo. Travel agencies around town can sometimes provide bus routes and schedules. For additional information about buses *see Bus Service, page 72.*

By Cruise Ship

Puerto Vallarta is a major port of call for cruise ships, most arriving from Los Angeles during the peak tourist season. Cruise lines dock at the Terminal Marítima (Maritime Terminal), north of downtown at the Marina Vallarta complex, and include Carnival, Disney Cruise Line, Holland-America, Norwegian, Princess and Royal Caribbean. From the dock, a road lined with gift shops and guided tour kiosks leads to the main highway. Taxis are readily available n the terminal area; a ride downtown will cost about $6 to $7 (U.S.).

Getting Around

City Layout

North of the Río Cuale, the different parts of the city are connected by one primary thoroughfare. Officially called Avenida Francisco Medina Ascencio, it changes names several times. The stretch of busy four-lane highway heading south from the airport and running behind the beachfront Hotel zone is also known as the Carretera Aeropuerto (Airport Highway). South of the Hotel Zone, the road narrows and becomes Avenida México and then Paseo Díaz Ordáz as it runs along the waterfront.

El Centro *(see attraction listing),* the central downtown area, is small and compact, hemmed in as it is between the mountains and the bay. The Río Cuale divides it into two sections. North of the river is the *malecón,* a mile-long oceanfront boardwalk that runs along Paseo Díaz Ordáz. Throngs of vacationers and locals alike come to enjoy the cool sea breeze, people watch and ponder the *malecón's* beautiful—and often times bizarre—collection of bronze sculptures. Master sand castle artists create additional eye candy on the narrow shore below the seawall. On the opposite side of the street you can browse boutiques and souvenir shops, scout the nightclubs or sip a margarita on one of several restaurant balconies and watch the sun set over the bay.

The heart of Vallarta, tree-shaded Plaza de Armas (also called Plaza Principal), sits just off the *malecón* between avenidas Morelos and Juárez. A central gazebo and a statue of Don Ignacio L. Vallarta, for whom the city was named, adorn this traditional town square where schoolchildren chase pigeons and overheated street vendors nap on wrought-iron benches. Tourists stroll by on their way to the Church of Our Lady of Guadalupe *(see attraction listing),* its crown-topped spire soaring over the city.

On Avenida Juárez, facing the north side of the plaza, is City Hall (Presidencia Municipal). The mural of Puerto Vallarta hanging above the stairwell was painted by local artist Manuel Lepe in 1981. On the west side of the plaza between Avenida Morelos and the southern end of the *malecón* is an outdoor amphitheater, the site of evening concerts. The white arches (Los Arcos) backing the amphitheater were rebuilt after being destroyed by Hurricane Kenna in 2002.

Casa Kimberley, Elizabeth Taylor's former residence, is in an area known as Gringo Gulch. Named for the intellectual and artsy Americans who settled in Puerto Vallarta during the 1950s and '60s, this steep ravine overlooking the Río Cuale is lined with beautiful red tile-roofed, colonial-style villas, many of them tucked away off cobbled alleyways festooned with pink bougainvillea.

To reach the gulch, walk up Calle Zaragoza toward the hillside above town. The street appears to dead-end, but look closely and you'll see a steep stone staircase. Climb it to continue on Zaragoza. Richard Burton bought the home at #445 for Taylor during their whirlwind romance while he was on location filming "The Night of the Iguana." An arched pink "love bridge" connects it to a home across the street that the actor also owned. **Note:** Formerly a bed & breakfast inn and museum, Casa Kimberly is undergoing renovation and is closed to the public.

Río Cuale Island (Isla Río Cuale), a long, narrow island-oasis in the middle of the Río Cuale, can be accessed from the northern and southern sections of El Centro by two road bridges, a pair of wood-plank suspension foot bridges and a concrete pedestrian bridge that spans the mouth of the river. The island's main attraction is its meandering fig and rubber tree-shaded walkway, lined with colorful souvenir stalls and a handful of riverside eateries. Just east of the Avenida Insurgentes road bridge, a shady plaza is home to a statue of Hollywood legend John Huston, who directed "The Night of the Iguana." At the island's western end, where the river meets the sea, local kids play and swim in water that appears less than pristine.

The area south of the Río Cuale is known as the "Zona Romantica." This is one of Vallarta's oldest neighborhoods, and though the whitewashed building facades don't look radically different from what you'll see north of the river, the narrow cobbled streets exude more of a ragged "Old Vallarta" feel. An eclectic mix of shops, restaurants and bars can be found along Basilio Badillo, 5 blocks south of the river and the main east-west thoroughfare.

The Zona Romantica's main beach is Playa los Muertos, a popular stretch of sand lined with casual *palapa* (thatched-roof) restaurants and mid-range hotels. North of El Centro, luxury properties fronting pretty Playa de Oro (Golden Beach) form the upscale Hotel Zone. High-rise resort towers boast sweeping views of palm-fringed Banderas Bay. Running behind the Hotel Zone is busy, four-lane Avenida Francisco Medina Ascencio. While it's not exactly ideal for a romantic stroll, the boulevard does offer a convenient assemblage of shopping centers packed with a predictable lineup of minimarkets, banks, gift shops, restaurants and American fast-food joints. Plaza Caracol, near the Fiesta Americana Hotel, is anchored by a Gigante supermarket.

Feeling more like a yachtsman's enclave in the United States rather than part of Mexico, Marina Vallarta aims to be a resort destination unto itself and wholly succeeds. This modern development near the airport encompasses major chain hotels, upscale condos, an enormous marina and yacht club and the 18-hole Marina Vallarta Club de Golf. Deluxe mega-resorts occupy beachfront real estate, while the pleasant marina boardwalk is lined with tourist-geared shops, galleries, cafes and restaurants. Hotel shuttles, city buses and taxis provide service to downtown. The marina is a good choice if you're a first-timer or part of a package tour, although it lacks the charm of Puerto Vallarta proper.

Nuevo Vallarta, about 19 kilometers (12 miles) north of the airport, is just over the Nayarit state line at the mouth of the Río Ameca. This planned resort area is a mix of condominiums, time share units, private bayfront homes and fancy all-inclusive accommodations.

A bit farther north is the village of Bucerías ("place of the divers"), an enclave of cobblestone streets, walled villas and tidy little hotels. Some travelers prefer this lower-cost alternative to Puerto Vallarta for its many shops, town square market and casual open-air restaurants. The 5-mile stretch of white sand is the longest along the Banderas Bay coastline. The shallow shoreline is perfect for wading, body surfing and shell collecting, and the beach draws throngs of local families on Sundays. Bucerías is most easily reached by bus; minivans also shuttle passengers from the airport to the village and back.

Rental Cars

If you've driven your own vehicle or rented one for exploring areas to the north or south, avoid driving after dark; cows wandering onto the roadway can be a very real hazard. Keep in mind that rental cars are expensive, and downtown parking is difficult. For sightseeing in and around the city, take advantage of the green-and-white or blue-and-white city buses that cover the area from Marina Vallarta south to Mismaloya Beach.

Note: AAA/CAA members enjoy discounts through Hertz for vehicles booked in the United States. Consult your local AAA/CAA club or phone Hertz, (800) 654-3080. The local Hertz office is on the east side of Avenida Francisco Medina Ascencio, just south of the airport.

Buses

City buses are inexpensive and take passengers to almost all points along Banderas Bay, from the airport south through the Hotel Zone, into downtown via the Ignacio Vallarta Bridge, and to points as far south as Mismaloya Beach. The fixed fare is 5 pesos. The exact amount is appreciated, but drivers will make change for a $20 peso note. Change for a $50 peso bill comes with a heavy sigh and a side of grumbling. In addition to the newer minibuses (*combis* or *colectivos*) that are equipped with emission controls, there are still old public buses on the streets spewing clouds of exhaust.

Stops are designated by a white bus outlined on a dark blue sign. If traffic is light, it's often possible to flag down a bus anywhere along the street. Destinations and routes (for example, *"Olas Altas," "Ixtapa," "Zona Hoteles"* or *"Aeropuerto"*) are posted on the front of the bus or painted on the windshield. As you climb aboard and pay your fare, tell the driver where you want to be let off. Most drivers don't speak English but they do understand, for example, "El Sheraton Hotel, por favor." Local routes are normally covered from 6 a.m. to 11 p.m.

The local bus station is on Avenida Olas Altas at Plaza Lázaro Cárdenas, south of the Río Cuale and just inland from the beach. City buses also depart from Plaza de Armas, the main square.

Taxis

Taxis are plentiful and cover the same routes as buses, but are more expensive. Fares are based on set rates and defined zones. The average fare within town is about $4 to $5 (U.S.); trips from downtown north to the Hotel Zone or Marina Vallarta will run up to about $7, depending on the destination. A ride across town from Marina Vallarta south to Playa los Muertos is about $10 to $12. Fares *should* be posted in each taxi and are printed in the *Vallarta Today* newspaper. Many hotels post a list of rates to specific destinations, which can come in handy if you're unfamiliar with the city. Taxis also can be hired by the hour or by the day for out-of-town trips.

Always ask how much the fare is *("Cuanto?")* and come to a decision before you get in the cab, which might save a few pesos. Resist efforts by any driver to steer you to a particular restaurant; some restaurateurs pay commissions to drivers for bringing them customers. It also is customary not to tip drivers.

Parking

Parking in the compact downtown area is scarce, and driving around the city in general presents a challenge. During the winter tourist season from December through April the narrow streets are jammed; from July through October heavy rains can make them flooded and muddy. Many roads leading in to Puerto Vallarta are just two lanes and descend from the mountains; drive with caution.

Guides/Tours

The standard city tour provides an all-purpose Puerto Vallarta orientation. A short version of the tour covers the local sights by air-conditioned minibus, including the main plaza, cathedral and the exclusive neighborhoods of Conchas Chinas and Gringo Gulch. A shopping trip is usually made to either Isla Río Cuale or the Municipal Market.

The jungle tour is a longer version that throws in trips to a tequila tasting room and Mismaloya Beach, plus lunch in a tropical setting at Chico's Paradise. Hotel pickup and drop-off is included in the fee; lunch is not. Several companies offer daily city and jungle tours lasting 4 and 6 hours, respectively. Make arrangements through your hotel or at one of the guided tour reservation booths you'll see all over town.

Canopy tours, a fancy name for zipline tours that skim through jungle treetops, have become popular in recent years. Canopy Tours de los Veranos offers daily 4-hour excursions to their zipline course near Mismaloya Beach. Transportation from the tour office on Mex. 200 (just south of downtown) is included. Reservations are required; phone (322) 223-0504.

What To See

CHURCH OF OUR LADY OF GUADALUPE (La Iglesia de Nuestra Señora de Guadalupe) is on Calle Hidalgo, a block e. of Plaza Principal. It took 33 years to build. The church is noted for the large crown atop the steeple, modeled after one worn by Carlota, wife of Archduke Maximilian, Mexico's ruler for 3 years in the 1860s. Made of fiberglass, it replaced the original crown, which collapsed during an earthquake in 1995. Angels clasping hands decorate the exterior. Do not wear shorts or T-shirts if you wish to enter the church. Open daily. Free.

CUALE MUSEUM (Museo del Cuale) is on Isla Río Cuale at the island's far western end, near Oscar's restaurant. Focusing on the indigenous peoples of western Mexico, this tiny archeology museum displays ancient pottery, figurines, jewelry and other objects. Information panels are in Spanish and English. Tues.-Sat. 10-3 and 4-7. Free.

EL CENTRO encompasses the area inland from the *malecón* and n. of the Río Cuale. Puerto Vallarta's old downtown core is a delightful contrast to the newer resort development that has spread both north and south along the beaches. An irregular grid of narrow streets, lined with whitewashed stucco buildings with red-tiled roofs, extends some 6 blocks up into the hills above the bay. The cobblestone streets, full of little shops and offering vistas of lush green hills tumbling down to the bay, are a pleasure to stroll (wear comfortable shoes). Street names are denoted on Mexican tiles on the sides of buildings.

El Centro exudes charm despite sputtering taxicabs, aggressive bus drivers and occasional construction; such sights as the odd donkey clopping along the cobblestones are a flashback to a more prosaic Mexico.

***MALECON* SCULPTURES** dot the *malecón* boardwalk along Paseo Díaz Ordáz. Walking from south to north, you'll see a beautiful collection of bronze public sculptures that includes the "Fountain of Friendship" (Fuente de la Amistad), a dome-shaped fountain crowned with three leaping dolphins. The romantic "Triton & Nereida" depicts the son of Neptune reaching for his mermaid lover, perched atop a curling wave just beyond his grasp.

A Vallarta icon, "El Caballito del Mar" is the famous statue of a young boy riding a seahorse. Farther along the sculptures take a surrealistic turn. "In Search of Reason," by Guadalajara artist Sergio Bustamente, features a ladder to nowhere being climbed by two pillow-headed children. Perhaps the *malecón's* strangest installation is Alejandro Colunga's "Rotunda of the Sea" (La Rotunda del Mar); ringed by alien creatures with twisted shapes that form high-backed chairs, this is by far Vallarta's most bizarre photo-op. Nearby is an 8-foot-high, Dali-esque statue of a man filling his black obsidian pot belly with rocks; Jonás Gutierrez's 2006 installation is called "Eating Stones" (Come Piedras).

At the *malecón's* northern end is Mathis Lidice's "Millennium"; a wave twists and arcs toward the sky, topped by a female figure releasing a dove to the heavens. The sculpture represents "the feminine energy that will lead us into a new age."

What To Do

Dining

Vallarta offers many options for dining well, if not particularly cheaply. A plus for foreign visitors is the purified water—including ice—that is universally used by licensed food and beverage establishments. (If in doubt, ask for bottled water, juice, beer or a soft drink.) While food quality is dependable, it is the striking ocean views that distinguish many

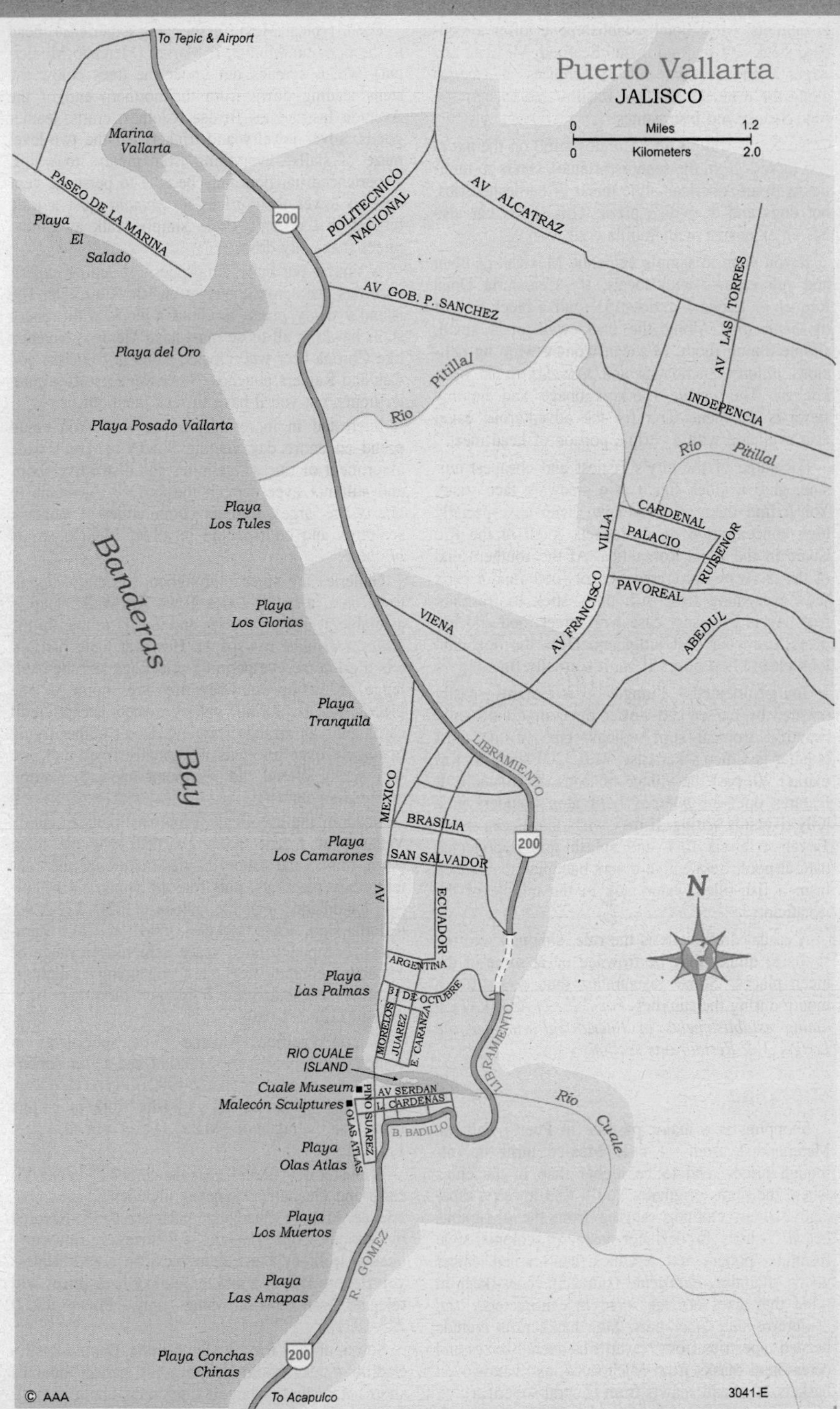
Puerto Vallarta
JALISCO
0 Miles 1.2
0 Kilometers 2.0
To Tepic & Airport
Marina Vallarta
PASEO DE LA MARINA
Playa El Salado
200
POLITECNICO NACIONAL
AV ALCATRAZ
AV GOB. P. SANCHEZ
AV LAS TORRES
Playa del Oro
Río Pitillal
INDEPENCIA
Playa Posado Vallarta
Río Pitillal
CARDENAL
PALACIO
RUISENOR
VILLA
Playa Los Tules
Banderas
PAVOREAL
AV FRANCISCO
Playa Los Glorias
VIENA
ABEDUL
Playa Tranquila
Bay
LIBRAMIENTO
AV MEXICO
BRASILIA
Playa Los Camarones
SAN SALVADOR
200
N
ECUADOR
ARGENTINA
Playa Las Palmas
31 DE OCTUBRE
MORELOS
JUAREZ
E. CARANZA
LIBRAMIENTO
RIO CUALE ISLAND
Cuale Museum
Malecón Sculptures
AV SERDAN
L. CARDENAS
PINO SUAREZ
OLAS ATLAS
B. BADILLO
Río Cuale
Playa Olas Atlas
Playa Los Muertos
R. GOMEZ
Playa Las Amapas
Playa Conchas Chinas
200
© AAA
To Acapulco
3041-E

restaurants. Most hotel establishments offer a standard steak and seafood menu. Seafood, Mexican and Argentinian are some of the choices at eateries along the 3 blocks of Calle Basilio Badillo between Pino Suárez and Insurgentes.

No Name Cafe, Calle Morelos #460 on the *malecón* (across from the seahorse statue), caters to families with an American-style menu of barbecued ribs, hot dogs and deep-dish pizza. This sports bar also has an extensive memorabilia collection.

If you want to sample authentic Mexican cooking and rub elbows with locals, try Cenaduria Doña Raquel, at Leona Vicario #131 (half a block east of the *malecón*). Along the back wall of a small, simple dining room, Mexican women whip up delicious *flautas*, enchiladas and *tostadas* in an open kitchen. The *pozole* (pork, cabbage and hominy stew) is excellent—and for the adventurous eater, also available with a "triple portion of head meat."

For some of the city's tastiest and cheapest cuisine, grab a quick lunch at a sidewalk taco stand. You'll find them all over town, with an especially high concentration on the streets south of the Río Cuale in the Zona Romantica. At the southern end of the *malecón* a congregation of food vendor carts sells everything from fish on a stick to fresh-cut fruit. As is the usual case with street food and hygiene, use your best judgment. Does the operation look clean? Is it busy? If so, it's usually fine.

Tourist-oriented "jungle" restaurants—easily reached by car or taxi—offer open-air dining amid beautiful tropical surroundings. One of the most popular is Chico's Paradise, Mex. 200 south to Km marker 20, past the village of Boca de Tomatlán. It features open-air *palapas* built atop boulders in a hilly riverside setting. If they wish, guests can swing Tarzan-style via rope and splash into a protected natural pool. Less active diners handpick their lunch from a fish-filled water tank in the middle of the restaurant.

A casual dress code is the rule, although wearing shorts to dinner may be frowned on at some of the nicer places. Some restaurants shut down for a month during the summer. *For a list of AAA-RATED dining establishments in Puerto Vallarta, see the Lodgings & Restaurants section.*

Shopping

Shopping is a major pastime in Puerto Vallarta. Merchandise from all over Mexico turns up, although prices tend to be higher than in the cities where the items originate. You'll find jewelry, especially silver; clothing ranging from the ubiquitous beach T-shirts to designer fashions; colonial-style furniture; pottery and ceramics; hand-tooled leather goods, including *huaraches* (sandals); shoes (keep in mind that sizes are measured in centimeters); and sombreros and other hats. Fine handicrafts include beaded tapestries from Nayarit, lacquered boxes and ceremonial masks from Michoacán, and handwoven baskets, rugs and shawls from Central America.

For a typical Mexican shopping experience, head to the open-air Municipal Market (Mercado Municipal), which spreads out under the trees below the steps leading down from the northern end of the Avenida Insurgentes Bridge. Clothes, crafts, leather goods, silver jewelry and trinkets fill the two-level maze of stalls—everything from piñatas to whips. Experienced hagglers may be able to persuade vendors to lower their prices *un poquito* (just a little bit). If that doesn't work, simply walk away and prices magically drop.

A similar but more atmospheric shopping experience lies just across the river on Isla Río Cuale. The island's shady *paseo* is chock-a-block with vendor stalls hawking all those must-have Mexico souvenirs like Corona beer wall clocks, *lucha libre* masks and Oakland Raiders ponchos. Some vendors offer quality items, but you'll have to seek them out.

Interested in more than a souvenir? You could spend an entire day visiting Puerto Vallarta's wide assortment of fine art galleries and distinctive shops and still not even scratch the surface. As home to one of the largest resident communities of painters, sculptors and craftspeople in all of Mexico, art is *big* here.

Galleries are spread throughout the entire downtown area; a handy "Old Town Art Walk" map is available at many galleries and also is printed in the *Vallarta Tribune* newspaper. However, with fine objets d'art come eye-popping price tags and the challenge of getting your new treasures home in one piece. Most (if not all) gallery owners accept credit cards and can arrange shipping. Don't bother trying to haggle over price, as it's usually fixed and you will surely offend the proprietor—not to mention embarrass yourself.

North of the Río Cuale, standouts include Galería Vallarta, at Juárez #265. Located near the main plaza, this casual gallery carries traditional and contemporary paintings, plus fine art prints and beautiful handmade jewelry; phone (322) 222-0290. Galería Uno, Calle Morelos #561 (at Calle Zaragoza), occupies a huge space exhibiting a range of Mexican contemporary art, including paintings, graphics and sculptures. It is open Mon.-Sat. 10-8; phone (322) 222-0908.

Galería Pacífico, Aldama #174, specializes in contemporary works by Mexican and Latin American artists; phone (322) 222-1982. Galería de Ollas, Corona #176, carries the exquisite work of potters from the village of Mata Ortiz; phone (322) 177-2213.

A cluster of galleries near the corner of Leona Vicario and Guadalupe Sánchez includes Corsica Galería de Arte, at Guadalupe Sánchez #735. Favored by serious collectors, it specializes in museum-quality work by big-league Mexican artists. Unless you flew to PV on a private jet, sky-high prices will relegate you to browsing only. Phone (322) 223-1821.

South of the Río Cuale, Galería Dante, Basilio Badillo #269, should be on every gallery hound's short list. Vallarta's largest (and many claim its best) gallery, Dante features a sculpture garden filled with contemporary pieces by international artists, plus high-quality re-creations of classical statues. The painters represented are primarily Mexican; phone (322) 222-2477.

A few storefronts north of Basilio Badillo, the Zona Romantica's main drag, is quirky Puerco Azul (The Blue Pig) at Constitución #325. This funky little folk art gallery/shop is packed with kitschy curios and whimsical paintings, many of them by owner Lee Chapman. Movie fans can flip through boxes of vintage Mexican "lobby cards" once used to promote American films; phone (322) 222-8647. Back on Basilio Badillo, more galleries, boutiques and jewelry shops line the street all the way down to the beach.

Downtown shops carry an excellent selection of home decor. Prices tend to be high, but so does quality. The warehouse-like Mundo de Cristal, south of the river at Insurgentes #333 (at the corner of Basilio Badillo) is the place to go for all things glass—from plates, stemware and vases to art glass handblown on site. Mundo de Azulejos (World of Tiles), Venustiano Carranza #374 (also south of the river), has a huge selection of handpainted Talavera tiles, as well as plates and murals. On display at Alfarería Tlaquepaque, Av. México #1100 (just off the *malecón*), are baskets, woodcarvings, glassware and ceramics from various Mexican states.

Huichol (pronounced we-CHOL) bead and yarn art is hand-crafted by Huichol Indians, who live in the Sierra Madre Mountains not far from Puerto Vallarta. Shamanistic traditions and peyote-fueled visions inspire the Huichol to create colorful yarn "paintings." Threads of yarn are pressed into a wax-coated wood tablet to create mythological imagery. The same general process is employed when using tiny, colored beads to decorate wooden animal figures with psychedelic patterns.

A good place to learn more about the animistic Huichol and the symbolism reflected in their art is the Huichol Collection Gallery, Paseo Díaz Ordaz #732 (across the street from the *malecón*). Deer, snake, wolf, jaguar and iguana figures fill the shelves. Prices for larger items reach into the hundreds of dollars, but smaller pieces can be had for about $15 (U.S.). Huichol artisans demonstrate their craft at a worktable in the center of the gallery.

Puerto Vallarta's shopping centers feature boutiques offering sportswear and casual yet fashionable evening wear. They are located primarily along the *malecón* and north into the Hotel Zone. Most stores are open until at least 8 p.m., and some may close from 2-4 for *siesta.* Many stores are closed on Sunday.

Among the arcades with browsing potential are Plaza Malecón, on the oceanfront at Paseo Díaz Ordaz and Calle Allende; Plaza Marina, within the Marina Vallarta complex; and Villa Vallarta, on Avenida Francisco Medina Ascencio in the Hotel Zone. Just north of the cruise ship terminal and WalMart, the sleek new Galerías Vallarta mall is anchored by Mexican department store Liverpool (think Nordstrom).

Worlds removed from the hustle and bustle of downtown, the relaxed Marina Vallarta boardwalk caters to tourists staying in the Marina Vallarta resort area. Yachts glisten in the sun, couples stroll hand in hand along the water's edge and families dine al fresco at gringo-friendly eateries. Roving souvenir vendors are nonexistent. Restaurants outnumber retail establishments, but there are a handful of shops, clothing boutiques and galleries worth investigating. **Note:** Finding the boardwalk can be tricky as it's hidden behind a string of condominium developments. From the marina's main thoroughfare, Paseo de la Marina, access is via calles Timón, Ancla or Vera.

Galería EM deals in gorgeous high-end art glass. Prepare to dole out some serious *dinero* for one of EM's elaborate stained-glass windows, fused-glass creations or eye-catching "floating crystal" sculptures. Next door, Art by Design carries a nice selection of contemporary paintings and sculpture. Kupuri Arte Huichol sells cool-looking yarn and bead art made by Huichol Indians. You can check e-mail, sip *cafe* and pick up a Danielle Steel paperback at Once Upon a Bean, a combination Internet cafe, coffee shop and used bookstore (closed Sundays).

A small flea market offering the usual T-shirts and souvenirs sets up at the Maritime Terminal docks where the cruise ships anchor. And finally, swarms of vendors peddle their wares at all Vallarta beaches, but they're practically a plague at Playa de los Muertos, and their persistence can be annoying. If you're not interested in purchasing anything, shaking your head "no" or simply saying *"Gracias, no"* will usually do the trick. If that doesn't work, it's best to ignore them completely. Also be aware that if you eat at one of the *palapa* restaurants fronting the beach boardwalk, vendors will approach you constantly. If this bugs you (and who *wouldn't* it bother?), ask for a table located well inside, away from the front row action.

Beaches

Beaches are divided into three zones: north of town, in town and south of town. In summer there are efforts at all of the beaches to protect the eggs of endangered sea turtles, evidence of an increased ecological awareness throughout the country. Puerto Vallarta's sea turtle release programs involve regular patrols of turtle nesting grounds. Eggs are taken to protected nurseries, and hatchlings are released in the open water.

PLAYA DE ORO is on the n. side of town and is backed by the Hotel Zone. Although it may seem like the stretches of golden-brown sand in front of the big hotels are private, they are not; all beaches in Mexico are federal property and thus open to the public. The wide, flat expanse of sand, divided into sections by rocky jetties, faces the open bay; waves can be surprisingly rough.

PLAYA DE LOS MUERTOS (Beach of the Dead) is s. of the Río Cuale and can be accessed from Calle Olas Altas. City officials have long tried to rename this popular beach Playa del Sol. Better for sunning than for swimming (the water is somewhat polluted), Playa de los Muertos attracts locals, European tourists and budget travelers. Sunbathers crowd the sand (particularly on Sundays and holidays), parasailers soar above it and roaming vendors hawk barbecued fish on a stick—the PV equivalent of a Coney Island hot dog. At the southern end of the beach is El Púlpito, a rock formation shaped like a pulpit.

PLAYA MISMALOYA (Mismaloya Beach) is about 10 km (6 mi.) s. of town off Mex. 200 (the southward extension of Av. Insurgentes). Protected by a pretty cove, it is where "The Night of the Iguana" was filmed. An easy walking path along the cove's southern end leads to the ruins of the movie set, most of it surrounded by chain-link fencing hung with signs warning visitors to stay out.

Although the spot's tranquil beauty has been compromised by hillside home development and the sprawling La Jolla de Mismaloya hotel complex, the water is clear, the sand white and the beach backed by jungle-cloaked hills. A string of shoreline *palapa* restaurants sell beer and seafood, and also rent out tables and beach chairs. At the far southern end of the beach, Teos Restaurant & Bar serves delicious jumbo shrimp wrapped in greasy bacon and drizzled with pineapple juice. In the rugged country above Mismaloya another movie was made—Arnold Schwarzenegger's 1987 action opus "Predator."

Sightseeing

Nearby beaches and islands make easy day trip destinations from Puerto Vallarta. More and more eco-tourism activities allow participants to explore or learn about the local environment without disturbing it. Vallarta Adventures organizes a variety of sightseeing and eco tours; phone (322) 297-1212, or (888) 303-2653 (from the United States).

Several companies organize guided trips into the surrounding region. Open Air Expeditions, downtown at Guerrero #339, specializes in adventure travel, taking small groups on hiking, kayaking, bird-watching and whale-watching excursions; phone (322) 222-3310.

Terra Noble is an arts center and spa situated on a high plateau at the north end of town, surrounded by mountains and jungle. Visitors can attend hands-on clay or painting workshops utilizing pre-Hispanic techniques, or relax with a massage and an invigorating sea salt exfoliation. Reservations can be made through local travel agencies, or phone (322) 223-0308.

About 16 kilometers (10 miles) south of the city, just before Mex. 200 veers inland, is the village of Boca de Tomatlán, at the mouth of the Río

Tomatlán. It is easily reached by taxi or bus (buses post their destination in the window or above the windshield). Lush hillsides, freshwater pools and water burbling past huge rocks all evoke a relaxed tropical atmosphere.

The small but enticing beach at Boca de Tomatlán is sheltered by a narrow cove. Here you can hire a *panga* (skiff) for trips to the remote beaches of Playa de las Animas, Playa Quimixto (key-MISH-toh) and Playa Yelapa, all located southwest of town and only accessible by boat. Prices range from about $10 to $20 (U.S.).

All three beaches also can be reached by slightly larger and more expensive water taxis that depart from the pier at Playa de los Muertos. Tour booths at the foot of the pier can offer more details; look for booths advertising "Tour information only. No time share." Separate catamaran and boat cruises set sail daily for the coastal villages of Animas, Quimixto and Yelapa from both Playa de los Muertos and Marina Vallarta's Maritime Terminal. Cruises typically depart between 9 and 10:30 a.m. and return around 4 or 5; they usually include lunch and use of snorkeling equipment.

The coastline here is a series of small coves set against a jungle backdrop. Cruceros Santamaría, phone (322) 221-2511, offers a daily yacht cruise that visits Animas and Quimixto beaches. You'll also drop anchor for a half hour of snorkeling at Los Arcos, an underwater eco-preserve surrounding the huge offshore rocks that lie just north of Mismaloya Cove. Playa de las Animas is a striking stretch of sand backed by a string of *palapa* restaurants and a small fishing village. Water activities abound; swimming, jet skiing (rentals are available) and snorkeling are popular. Quimixto's main draw, besides its beach, is a pretty waterfall reached by an easy half-hour hike or horseback ride (about an extra $20 U.S. per person).

Yelapa, the farthest afield of the three main beaches, sees the fewest day trippers. That doesn't mean you'll have the beach to yourself; not by a long shot. But its distance from Vallarta means that all-day Yelapa cruises typically *only* visit Yelapa, and those that do number far fewer than the Animas/Quimixto/Los Arcos boats—something to consider if you desire fewer crowds.

The *Princess Yelapa* departs the Maritime Terminal daily at 9:30 a.m., cruises the coast, stops for snorkeling off Playa Majahuitas and spends between 2 and 3 hours (although often longer) at Yelapa. Jungle-cloaked hills surround the small bay, and a half-dozen *palapa* restaurants line the coarse-sand beach. Chico's Restaurant accepts credit cards (there are no ATMs here). Rogelio's serves fresh ceviche and fish tacos. For dessert, Yelapa's roaming "pie ladies" sell slices from lemon meringue and pecan pies that they balance on their heads.

Yelapa itself is reached by a short water taxi ride from the main beach. The steep, sandy streets of the tiny pueblo are blissfully free of cars. A 10-minute walk along the Yelapa River leads to a 150-foot-high waterfall. Tempted to stay the night? Yelapa offers a handful of rustic accommodations, and you can always catch a water taxi back to Vallarta in the morning. Reservations for the *Princess Yelapa* can be made at most of the tour booths around town. Kon Tiki Tours offers an all-day trimaran cruise that visits the beaches at Majahuitas and Colomitos; phone (322) 145-6429.

Recreation

Water sports are a given in an environment where there is access to modern marine facilities within a protected bay. The Bay of Banderas extends north to Punta de Mita (Mita Point) and south to Cabo Corrientes (Corrientes Cape), where the foothills of the Sierra de Cuale range begin. Water depths of up to 1,500 feet give the bay characteristics normally associated with oceans, but it also is protected due to its shape and the surrounding geography. The result is generally calm water and clear visibility, which makes it ideal for **boating.**

For snorkelers, the bay teems with tropical fish. Dolphins, sea turtles, giant manta rays and migrating humpback whales also can be seen. A favorite **snorkeling** destination is the underwater park at Los Arcos (also called Las Peñas), a short distance offshore from Mismaloya Beach. The oddly eroded formations jutting out of the bay served as an early landmark for ships. Colorful marine life is particularly evident around these rocks.

A favored destination for kayakers and experienced divers is the Marietas Islands (Islas Marietas), off Punta de Mita at the bay's northern end. Comprising the tips of an undersea mountain range, these islets were once used as a hiding place by pirates who plundered galleons loaded with silver from Sierra Madre mines. Tropical fish thrive here, dolphins are frequently sighted, and the islands also are a protected bird sanctuary. Chico's Dive Shop, Paseo Díaz Ordaz #772 at the northern end of the *malecón,* rents equipment and organizes dive trips to the Marietas; phone (322) 222-1895.

Boats for **sport fishing** can be hired through the Fishing Cooperative (Cooperativo de Pescadores), at the northern end of the *malecón*. There are reservation booths out front; phone (322) 222-1202. Fishing charters can also be booked through your hotel or travel agent. Rates for fishing vessels depend on the size of the boat, where you fish, and whether bait and tackle are supplied. Bring your own refreshments, since most trips don't include them.

Sailfish and blue marlin are hooked November through February; smaller game species such as dorado, roosterfish and tuna can be caught seasonally most of the year. A catch-and-release policy is stressed if the fish is not going to be eaten.

Marina Vallarta has more than 500 slips and offers boaters fresh water, as well as cable TV and telephone hookups. Hardware and boating supply outlets are located along the boardwalk of this sprawling complex, which also has an 18-hole golf course, luxury hotels and condominiums. Tour boats and fishing excursions depart from the marina's Maritime Terminal. Boaters can explore a variety of tiny coves and hidden beaches along the shore of Banderas Bay, or drop anchor for awhile at Bahía de Banderas in Nuevo Vallarta.

Swimming, water skiing, parasailing and other watery pursuits can be enjoyed at many spots along the bay. Surfers head for the open waters and bigger waves around Punta de Mita. For those who would rather view the bay than venture into it, saddle horses for shoreline rides can be rented through a travel agency or the beachfront hotels.

Rancho El Charro and Rancho Ojo de Agua organize guided 2- to 3-hour **horseback riding** excursions into the foothills of the Sierra Madre, past jungle plantations and rural villages. Transportation is included and reservations are necessary; phone (322) 224-0114 for Rancho El Charro, (322) 224-0607 for Rancho Ojo de Agua.

There are several 18-hole **golf** courses in the area. Water comes into play on 11 holes at the Marina Vallarta Club de Golf course. A cart or caddy is mandatory, and member privileges are extended to guests staying at certain hotels. Greens fees range from $100-$130 (U.S.). Golfers wishing to play outside peak tourist season should check with the club; phone (322) 221-0073.

The Flamingos Golf Club is about 13 kilometers (8 miles) north of the airport off Mex. 200, in the state of Nayarit. Greens fees at this older, par-71 course range from $80-$120 (U.S.); caddies and motorized carts are available. (**Note:** Nayarit observes Mountain Standard Time, which is an hour earlier than Puerto Vallarta and the rest of Jalisco.) Reservations and transportation can be arranged through your hotel, or phone (329) 296-5006.

The Vista Vallarta Club de Golf, 653 Circuito Universidad, Colonia San Nicolas, is about 3 miles inland from Marina Vallarta. There are two courses, one designed by Jack Nicklaus and one by Tom Weiskopf. Greens fees range from $130-$185 (U.S.). For tee times and hotel package information phone (322) 290-0030.

Most of the resorts provide clay **tennis** courts for their guests. PV also has two tennis centers: the Canto del Sol Tennis Club, at the Canto del Sol Plaza Vallarta resort in the Hotel Zone; and the Los Tules Tennis Center, near the Fiesta Americana Hotel. For **bullfighting** fans, the La Paloma Bullring is across Avenida Francisco Medina Ascencio from Marina Vallarta. Bullfights begin Wednesday afternoons at 5, November through April; tickets can be obtained through travel agencies.

Nightlife

The cheapest after-dark option is strolling along the *malecón* (Paseo Díaz Ordaz). Sunday evenings in particular bring out local families, mariachi bands, street performers and the ubiquitous vendors.

The loud, flashy nightclubs along the *malecón* tend to attract younger crowds. Hip-hop booms at Mandala, a sleek, partially open-air dance club where flat-screen TVs play the latest rap videos and a giant Medusa statue towers over the bar. Next door, techno pulses in the cave-like Zoo, a safari-themed club complete with a bouncer in a gorilla suit and an elevated "dance cage." A few blocks south is Hilo, a smaller club with a dance floor that boogies way past the witching hour.

These and other clubs usually stay open into the wee hours, and often until dawn during spring break weeks. Dress codes aren't strict, but don't show up in your soggy swim trunks and flip-flops. There's usually no cover charge; however, drink prices are steep.

Vallarta's party bars cater to a diverse demographic—from frat boys to boomers in tacky Hawaiian shirts—with rock, reggae and pop hits. Gringo-friendly grub, drinking contests, conga lines and over-the-top party boy waiters are all part of the fun. Carlos O'Brien's is along the *malecón* at the corner of Paseo Díaz Ordaz and Pipila. Señor Frog's is at Galeana #518, across the street from the seahorse statue. The PV branch of the Hard Rock Café draws a mellower clientele who come to chow down on reliable burgers and check out the rock memorabilia; there's live music most nights.

Puerto Vallarta also has a number of American-style sports bars where you can grab a bite to eat, play a board game, watch sports on TV or just sit and chat. El Torito, on Ignacio L. Vallarta (#290), features satellite broadcasts of sports events and a casual menu with the likes of nachos, ribs and beer-battered shrimp. Steve's Sports Bar, at Basilio Badillo #286 across the street from Memo's Pancake House, is a casual sports pub frequented by local expats and NASCAR, NHL and NFL enthusiasts.

The Kit Kat Club, at Playa de los Muertos, is a hip, snazzy New York-style lounge with cool music, martinis and some outstanding desserts. For a more romantic evening, catch a live jazz combo at Le Bistro, a stylish supper club at the eastern end of Isla Río Cuale.

Christine, in the Hotel Zone next to the Krystal Vallarta Hotel, is a mega disco with a laser light show and performing acrobats suspended from the ceiling. The club opens around 10 p.m. but usually doesn't heat up until after midnight. The cover charge varies but is normally $15-$20 (U.S.). It doubles if you indulge in the "open bar" option.

Mexican-style fiestas are another popular diversion and include dinner buffets, folk dancing, live music and even fireworks. One of the oldest is La Iguana, south of the river at Calle Lázaro Cárdenas #311 (at Constitución). A Mexican buffet dinner is accompanied by live music, mariachis, rope twirling, colorfully costumed folk dancers and breaking open a piñata. Shows begin Thurs. and Sun. at 7 p.m.; phone (322) 222-0105.

Other fiestas take place at big hotels like the Krystal Vallarta and the Sheraton Buganvillias. For schedule and reservation information, check with the hotels or a local travel agency.

Pirates of the Bay sets sail nightly on a 4-hour, adults only dinner cruise and pirate show. Passage on the replica pirate ship includes live entertainment, a buffet meal, open bar, dancing and a fireworks display launched from the boat. Cruises depart the Maritime Terminal at 6 p.m.; a family-friendly version of the cruise is available every morning at 9 a.m. Make reservations through your hotel or phone (322) 223-0309.

Special Events

Luckily for visitors, Puerto Vallarta's biggest events occur during the peak tourist season. The Festival of the Sea (Fiesta del Mar) is celebrated during November. Golf tournaments, art exhibits, an international boat show and a gourmet dining festival all take place, as well as a couple of fishing tournaments—the International Sailfish & Marlin Tournament and the World Billfish Series Puerto Vallarta Classic—that attract anglers from all over Mexico and the United States. For dates and details on specific events, contact the Puerto Vallarta Tourist Office.

The yachting season kicks off in late fall with the San Diego to Puerto Vallarta Annual Regatta, which heralds the arrival of some impressive craft. The patron saint of mariachis is honored Nov. 23 during the Festival of Santa Cecilia, when a lineup of mariachi bands plays at the cathedral.

Perhaps the year's biggest celebration is the Fiesta de Guadalupe, honoring the Virgin of Guadalupe, Mexico's patron saint. Daily evening processions, called *peregrinaciones,* make their way to the Church of Our Lady of Guadalupe from various *colonias* (neighborhoods) and local businesses the week prior to Dec. 12. Young and old alike participate in the celebration, many carrying candles or offerings of food and flowers to be exchanged for a blessing by the priest. Mass is held in front of the cathedral, accompanied by dancing and singing. The festivities culminate on Dec. 12 with a grand fireworks display.

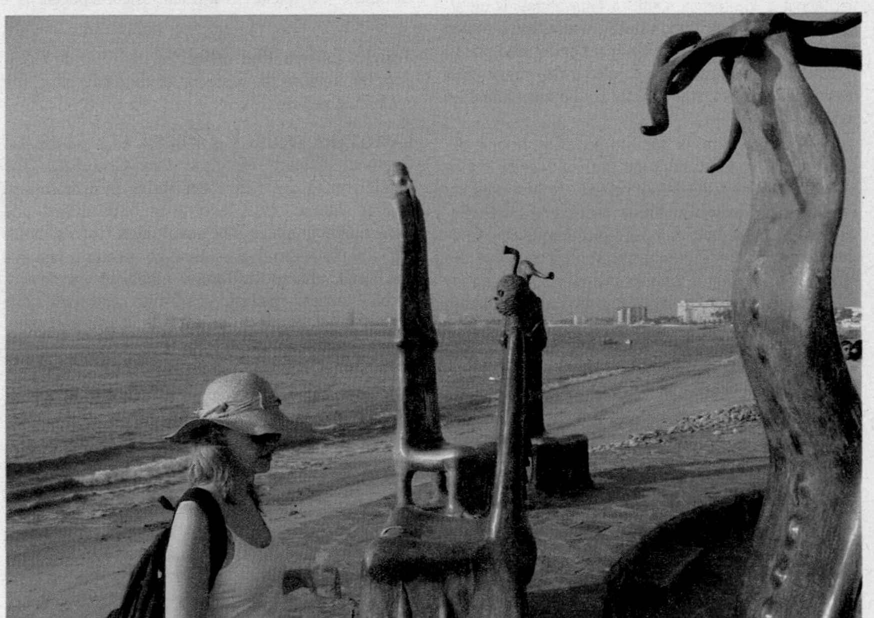

Malecón / © Ryan J. Hollander

This ends listings for Puerto Vallarta.
The following page resumes the alphabetical listings of cities in The Pacific Coast.

RINCON DE GUAYABITOS, NAYARIT

(B-1) pop. 1,800

While the "Riviera Nayarit" towns of Sayulita and San Francisco court tourists with gringo-friendly amenities (read: cute shops), Guayabitos sits on pretty Jaltemba Bay and mainly draws vacationing Mexican families in search of budget beachfront accommodations and mild surf. Guayabitos is also popular with Canadian snowbirds, who are attracted by the town's affordability.

Guayabitos is about 61 kilometers (39 miles) north of the Puerto Vallarta airport via Mex. 200—just over an hour's drive. You'll find the usual *palapa* bars serving seafood and cold *cerveza,* although not on the wide, flat beach itself; local law doesn't allow alcohol sales on the sand. Instead, vendor carts hawking fish-on-a-stick, fresh fruit and inflatable beach toys are the norm.

There's decent snorkeling around Isla Islote, which is a few kilometers offshore and accessible by *pangas* that depart from Guayabitos beach. You should be able to hire a boat for about $30 (U.S.) round-trip. Los Ayala, about 2 kilometers south of Guayabitos, is an attractive curve of sand lined with thatch-roofed restaurants serving fresh seafood at non-inflated prices. Local kids play beach soccer. Fishermen repair their nets. On weekdays, you'll likely be the only *gabachos* there.

For those who really want to get away from it all, gorgeous Playa Chacala is the stuff of Mexico coffee table books. Tall palms sway behind a golden crescent of sand. The deep blue Pacific is framed by jungle-covered points at both ends of a picturesque bay. Children play in the shore breakers. Pelicans dive for lunch. A smattering of tourists and RVers sip *cervezas* at a string of rustic *palapa* restaurants. And there isn't a time share hustler in sight.

Playa Chacala is slightly less than a 2-hour drive north of Puerto Vallarta. From the airport, take Mex. 200 about 103 kilometers (64 miles) to the Chacala turn-off. (**Note:** The turn-off sign is badly faded. When you reach a large collection of roadside produce markets, watch for a paved road heading west.) A 9-kilometer (5.5 mile) stretch of blacktop leads to the little town of Chacala; the main thoroughfare is a dirt loop road running behind the beach. Rough, cobbled side streets lead up into the residential areas.

Among the *palapa* bars, Las Brisas caters to gringos with comfy lounge chairs, good seafood and clean bathrooms. But don't overlook the excellent grilled lobster at Chico's. On the beach, you can rent kayaks or arrange snorkeling excursions with local fishermen. Shopping is limited to a few stalls selling the usual souvenir T-shirts and trinkets. Lodging options range from a beachfront campground to a pair of "eco-resorts" in the hills just south of town. **Note:** There are no ATMs in Chacala. The nearest machines are in the town of Las Varas, on Mex. 200 about 5 minutes north of the Chacala turn-off.

SAN BLAS, NAYARIT (A-1)

The fishing village of San Blas (sahn BLAHS) was a major port from the late 16th into the 19th centuries. Galleons involved in the Manila trade routinely stopped here. During the mid-18th century San Blas also became a shipbuilding center and was a garrison for the Spanish armada, which fought French, Dutch and British pirates; the ruins of a Spanish fortress occupy a hill looming above the town.

Adventurous travelers who want to avoid the hub-bub of Mazatlán to the north or Puerto Vallarta to the south might consider San Blas, which is accessible via Mex. 11 branching off Mex. 15-D. (**Note:** Mex. 11 is isolated and jungle-lined; make sure the gas tank is full and your vehicle is in tip-top shape.)

The main draw for tourists are the tan-colored beaches, which encircle nearby Matanchen Bay. Playa Borrego is the most convenient to town. This typical Mexican beach has few amenities other than the open-air shacks serving cold beer and whole smoked fish. Playa Los Cocos, reachable by taxi, has a backdrop of palm trees. The rainy summer season is plagued by mosquitoes; *jejenes* (hey-HAY-nays), or "no-see-ums," are bothersome biting gnats that materialize at dawn and dusk year-round. As a result, insect repellent is a necessity.

Tourist information office: in the Casa de Gobierno building on the east side of the main plaza (on Avenida Canalizo).

LA TOVARA SPRINGS is n. of San Blas via the San Cristóbal Estuary (Estuario San Cristóbal). The jungle trip to this freshwater spring in a motorized dugout *(lancha)* is a favorite of birdwatchers and nature photographers. The small boats (usually holding six passengers) pass through swampy lagoons and dense mangrove forests inhabited by herons, egrets, turtles, iguanas, crocodiles and fish. The spring itself forms a cool, clear freshwater pool where swimming is possible. For the best wildlife views, go early in the morning.

It is possible to arrange an excursion with a local guide that departs from the boat launch at the bridge leading into town; check with the tourist information office for details. Banderas Bay Tours & Travel in Puerto Vallarta offers a guided day trip to La Tovara that includes a visit to the springs, a crocodile reserve where the reptiles are bred for repopulation, a stop in downtown San Blas and lunch on the beach at Matachen.

Trips from the San Blas dock last 3 to 4 hours. Guided tours from Puerto Vallarta depart Tues. and Thurs. at 8 a.m.; allow a full day for the excursion. The fee for boat trips from San Blas is negotiable and starts at about $10 (U.S.) per person; lunch at the restaurant at the springs is not included. Per-person trip cost from Puerto Vallarta (transportation, lunch and entry fees included) $110 (U.S.); $55 (children). Phone (322) 145-6429 or 01 (800) 502-0622 (toll-free long distance within Mexico) for Banderas Bay Tours & Travel.

SAN FRANCISCO, NAYARIT (B-1)

The secret is out on the string of beach villages along the southern coast of Nayarit state, christened the "Riviera Nayarit" by Mexico's tourism developer, FONATUR. Largely spared from the condo construction around Punta Mita and Sayulita, low-key Playa San Francisco (nicknamed "San Pancho") isn't quite what Puerto Vallarta was like 40 years ago, but it comes close. From the signed turnoff on Mex. 200, 38 kilometers (23 miles) north of the Puerto Vallarta airport (about a 45-minute drive), the town's cobbled main street leads to a wave-pounded, deep sand beach beloved by surfers. Bookended by jungly headlands, the long, palm-backed strand is refreshingly crowd free. A pair of *palapa* restaurants provide fine spots for sunset watching.

You'll find more dining along the drowsy main drag, curiously named Avenida Tercer Mundo (translation: Third World Avenue). Expatriates get their American-style breakfast fix at Maria's, a homey diner that whips up outstanding chorizo-and-potato omelets and pours an eye-opening Bloody Mary (closed Wednesday). The wood-fired oven at La Casa del Gallo bakes the town's best pizza, a crispy thin crust pie available with a variety of fresh toppings; try the spicy "Mexicana" combo (closed Tuesday).

San Francisco has a sprinkling of small shops and galleries. And if you're inclined to spend a night or two, a couple of hotels and bed & breakfasts are just north and south of town. The Costa Azul Adventure Resort and Bungalows Lydia are solid choices. **Note:** Some establishments accept credit cards, but San Francisco has no ATMs; the nearest machine is at the Pemex gas station about 11 kilometers (7 miles) north of town on Mex. 200.

SAYULITA, NAYARIT (B-1)

Sayulita was a little-known fishing village until surfers "discovered" its extra-long waves in the early 1970s. Good paved roads connect the town to Puerto Vallarta, 33 kilometers (20 miles) northwest of the airport via Mex. 200 (about a 40-minute drive) and to the nearby Four Seasons Punta Mita resort, a favorite of celebrities hiding from paparazzi.

Back in the '70s, surf pilgrims made do with a case of beer and a beach tent, grooving on the beautiful views of Banderas Bay and the rich tropical forest environment that characterizes the base of the coastal Sierra Madre mountains. Nowadays, Sayulita's scruffy beach town charm attracts hippie dropouts, families, bohemian hipsters and rich retirees from los Estados Unidos who demand certain creature comforts. Recently, upscale bed and breakfasts, cafes and boutiques (think deep tissue massages, chai lattes and designer handbags) have sprung up around town. But it's Sayulita's bay that remains the star attraction. A string of *palapa* restaurants and a handful of surf schools line the gray-sand shoreline. When waves are small, boogie boarders and beginning surfers head for the water en masse.

Painted in red, green and yellow pastels, Plaza Pública sits in the center of town. Local families spill out of the church next door and lounge on the plaza's palm-shaded benches. Huichol Indian artisans on cell phones hurry past, carting their wares to the small vendor market at the plaza's northeast corner. The narrow streets leading down to the beach are peppered with real estate offices (lots here are being gobbled up at a phenomenal rate), clothing boutiques and shops.

The funky Gypsy Galería (Calle Marlin #10) is packed with hand-painted plates, masks, tiles and figurines from all over Mexico, plus Guatemalan handbags, Chiapan shawls and a slew of Dia de Los Muertos (Day of the Dead) crafts from Michoacán. The pricier El Ojo de Venado (Calle Marlin #6) has suede and leather purses, pottery and eye-catching fused glass jewelry. Overlooking the beach, two-story Don Pedro's Restaurant & Bar (Calle Marlin #2) dishes up Mexican and seafood classics; there's live salsa music on Monday nights.

TEPIC, NAYARIT (A-1) pop. 305,200

Tepic (teh-PEEK), the state capital, lies at the foot of the extinct Sangangüey (sahn-gahn-GWAY) volcano. The city dates from the 16th century, but grew slowly at first because of its isolated location. Today Tepic (a Náhuatl Indian word meaning "hard stone") functions mainly as a stopover for travelers en route to Guadalajara or Puerto Vallarta.

The cathedral bordering Plaza Principal has twin towers and a yellow exterior. At the summit of a hill south of the town center is the 18th-century Convent of the Holy Cross (Convento de la Santa Cruz). The restored former convent was built around a growth of grass in the shape of a cross, said to be a miraculous site.

The surrounding countryside is mountainous and isolated, although it has a wild beauty. Here live the Huichol and Cora Indians, among the least affected of Mexico's indigenous peoples by the intrusions of modern life. Appropriately, religion and ritual are an integral part of daily life. Huichol art, particularly the brightly colored wall hangings, incorporates symbols relating to fertility, nature and the heavens. Shops bordering Plaza Principal sometimes offer beads and other handicrafts made by local Huichol and Cora artisans.

The Regional Museum of Anthropology (Museo Regional de Antropología), south of Plaza Principal at Av. México #91 Norte (at Avenida Zapata), is housed in an 18th-century mansion, the former House of the Counts of Miravalle. On view are a collection of Huichol artifacts, including animal-shaped pottery, and an exhibit pertaining to the archeological site surrounding the town of Ixtlan del Río, which is distinguished by a circular pyramid. Open Tues.-Sun.

Nayarit State Tourism Office (Subsecretaría de Turismo): downtown at Avenida México and Calzada del Ejército, in the Ex-Convent of La Cruz (Ex-Convento de La Cruz); phone (311) 214-8071 or 01 (800) 523-0160 (toll-free long distance within Mexico).

ZIHUATANEJO—

see Ixtapa/Zihuatanejo p. 236.

National University of Mexico, south of San Angel, Distrito Federal / © Steve Vidler / SuperStock

Mexico City and Vicinity

Floating on a lake bed a mile and a half high, Mexico City is, in a word, unique. This ancient land of the Aztecs is a thoroughly modern world capital, yet a city with roots deeply entrenched in its indigenous and colonial Spanish cultures. It is the oldest (more than 675 years) and second highest (7,350 feet) capital in North America, and one of the most populous cities in the world.

Distinguished colonial buildings fill Mexico City's historic center. More than 2,000 years of history unfurl at the city's wealth of museums and their collections of priceless artifacts. The world-famous Ballet Folklórico celebrates the history of Mexican folk music and dance. If you are a gourmand on a culinary quest, the capital offers memorable gastronomic experiences. And ardent shoppers will find a treasure trove of brightly colored bargains.

Mexico City's neighborhoods are as varied as the city itself. Polanco is a small residential area filled with art galleries, hotels, restaurants and foreign embassies. The shopping malls and exclusive international boutiques along Presidente Masaryk, the main street, are Mexico City at its most chic. Condesa is a middle-class neighborhood filled with parks and lovely turn-of-the-20th-century homes. San Angel and Coyoacán, two distinctive neighborhoods in the southern part of the city, reflect the Spanish colonial era in the form of venerable plazas, colorful markets and a vibrant sense of artistic expression. This is "old Mexico" at its most beguiling.

Sunday is the best time to visit Coyoacán, when it is the site of a lively street bazaar. City residents converge at Plaza Hidalgo against a heady backdrop of sights, colors and aromas. Vendors display their wares—clothing, jewelry, balloons, trinkets, plants, paintings, puppies, paper flowers, incense, carved figurines, housewares and myriad other

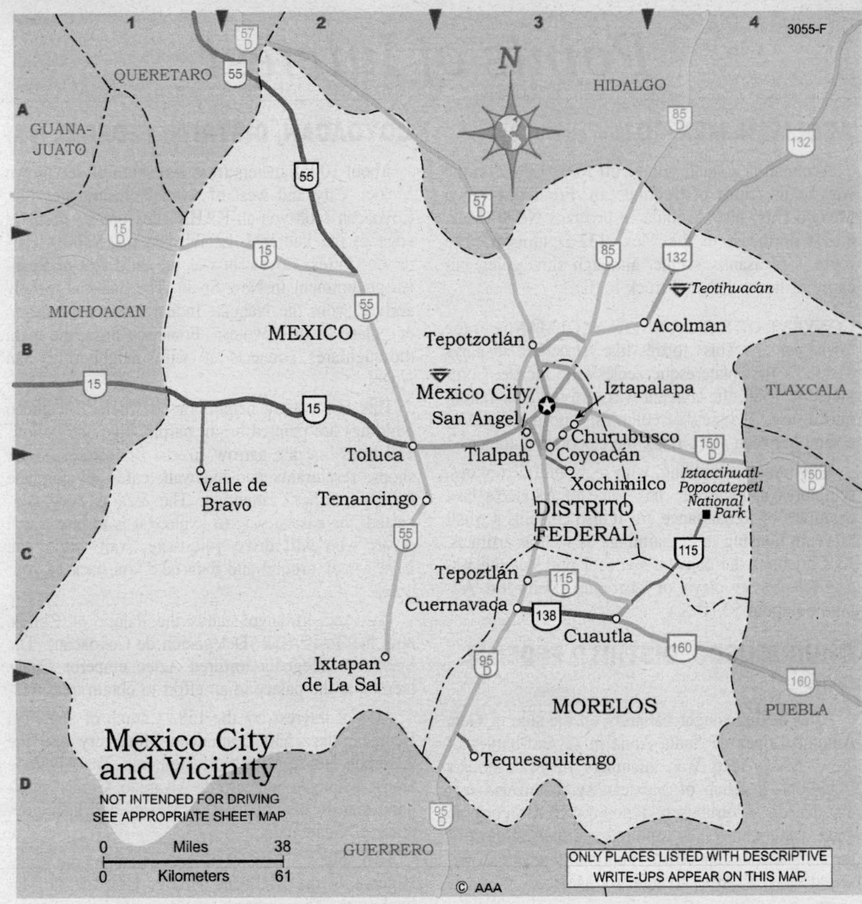

items—in stalls or spread on the ground on blankets.

Side trips are a relatively short hop away. Perhaps the most impressive is Teotihuacán, easily reached from Mexico City. While it lacks the lush jungle backdrop of Palenque, in southern Mexico, Teotihuacán is the most monumentally scaled of all the country's archeological zones. The temple remains and two majestic pyramids rise from a flat, open plain, with little surrounding vegetation to obscure the view. The wide open spaces and awe-inspiring ruins are the perfect antidote to the city's sometimes claustrophobic congestion.

DID YOU KNOW

One-fifth of Mexico's total population lives in or around Mexico City.

Points of Interest

ACOLMAN, MEXICO (B-4) elev. 7,511′

Acolman is a small village off Mex. 132-D on the way to the ruins of Teotihuacán. From downtown Mexico City, take Avenida Insurgentes Norte (Mex. 85-D) northeast to the Mex. 132-D turn-off. The route is pleasantly scenic, although slow going because of heavy bus and truck traffic.

CONVENT OF SAN AGUSTIN ACOLMAN is in the town center. This fortresslike structure displays Mexico's first plateresque ecclesiastic facade. Completed in 1560, the convent was restored after falling into disuse. Two sets of columns, with the statue of a saint between each, flank the elaborate entrance.

The immense building, with its beautiful frescoes, sculptures and cloister, has some of Mexico's best examples of Renaissance art. It also contains a small museum housing more paintings as well as artifacts. At Christmas the convent's chapel provides the setting for nativity plays, or *pastorelas*. Daily 9-6. Admission about $3 (U.S.).

CHURUBUSCO, DISTRITO FEDERAL (B-3)

After having fought valiantly on the side of Gen. Antonio López de Santa Anna in several battles of the U.S.-Mexican War, members of St. Patrick's Battalion—a group of Mexican sympathizers—met disaster in Churubusco (choo-roo-BOOS-coh) in 1847. American forces captured and hanged most of the battalion of 260 Irish immigrants who had deserted the U.S. Army to fight for Mexico.

Thankfully, Churubusco is much more tranquil today. Mexico's major film studios also are concentrated in this suburb just east of Coyoacán.

EX-CONVENT OF CHURUBUSCO is between Calz. de Tlalpan and Av. División del Norte (M: General Anaya, line 2). It was built in 1678 over the ruins of an ancient Aztec temple. This former Franciscan convent, which includes the Church of St. Matthew, served as a fortress against invading U.S. forces in August 1847. There are lovely gardens on the grounds of the restored structure.

National Museum of Interventions (Museo Nacional de las Intervenciones) is within the convent complex. It chronicles the exploits of those adventurers, pirates and foreign armies—the United States and France chief among them—who have invaded Mexico over the past 4 centuries. Weapons, flags, medals and other war memorabilia make up the displays. Exhibit information is in Spanish.

Guide service in English is available. Tues.-Sun. 9-6. Admission about $3.25 (U.S.); free to all Sun. Phone (55) 5604-0699.

COYOACAN, DISTRITO FEDERAL (B-3)

About 10 kilometers (6 miles) south of downtown Mexico City and west of Avenida Insurgentes Sur, Coyoacán (coh-yoh-ah-KAHN) lies on the northern edge of the Pedregal. Established in 1521 by Hernando Cortés, Coyoacán was the third seat of Spanish government in New Spain. The name is loosely derived from the Náhuatl Indian term *coyohuacan*, or "place of the coyotes." Francisco Sosa, the main thoroughfare, connects it with neighboring San Angel.

This is an artsy neighborhood where the stucco buildings are painted bright purple, blue and yellow. Tall trees line the narrow streets. Bookstores, sweet shops, restaurants and sidewalk cafés all compete for the stroller's attention. The area is very congested; the easiest way to explore it is to hire a taxi driver who will drive you there, wait while you have a look around and then take you back to your hotel.

On Plaza Hidalgo stands the Palace of Cortés, now the Town Hall (Delegación de Coyoacán). The Spaniards allegedly tortured Aztec emperor Cuauhtémoc at the palace in an effort to obtain treasure.

Also of interest are the 1583 Church of San Juan Bautista, the 1530 Dominican Monastery and the Alvarado House, now a private home. The Alvarado House belonged to Pedro de Alvarado, Cortés' right-hand man in his conquest of Mexico and later governor of Guatemala.

Two blocks east of Plaza Hidalgo on Calle Higuera is the Malinche House (Casa de la Malinche), the former home of Cortés' Indian mistress, interpreter and chief aide on his march through Mexico. Malinche, a major and much-maligned figure in Mexican legend, was supposedly condemned to 300 years of martyrdom for her act of betrayal. The solemn-looking dwelling sits across from Plaza de la Conchita, a peaceful little park.

DIEGO RIVERA MUSEUM (Museo Anahuacalli) is on the s. side of the city, off Av. División del Norte at Calle del Museo #150 (M: Coyoacán, line 3). It was designed by Rivera and constructed from black volcanic stone. This stark, pyramidal building contains the muralist's vast personal collection of pre-Hispanic art. The Aztec and Toltec civilizations and the ancient city of Teotihuacán are well represented, and there is an outstanding collection of objects from the states of Colima, Jalisco and Nayarit.

Rivera also set up a studio on the upper floor of the building; mementos and works in progress now occupy the restored space. There are spectacular views from the building's hilltop location, particularly of twin volcanoes Popocatépetl and Iztaccíhuatl. Tues.-Sun. 10-6 (closed 2-3 p.m.).

Admission about $2.25 (U.S.). Phone (55) 5617-3797.

FRIDA KAHLO MUSEUM (Museo Frida Kahlo) is at Calle Londres #247 (at the corner of Allende), 5 blks. n. of Plaza Hidalgo (M: Coyoacán, line 3). This adobe house was the celebrated Latin American painter's lifelong residence; from 1929 until her death in 1954 she shared it with her husband Diego Rivera, Mexico's equally celebrated muralist. Through their tempestuous relationship Rivera and Kahlo forged the nucleus of contemporary Mexican art.

"Casa Azul" is an explosion of color, not the least of which is the cobalt-blue, red-trimmed exterior. Personal possessions include the four-poster bed in which Kahlo was born and died. *Calaveras* (papier-mâché skeletons) and carved death masks are reminders of the physical suffering that plagued Kahlo's everyday life and provided the fuel for her creativity. Works on display by this self-taught artist include some surrealistic self-portraits.

A spacious studio contains the artist's wheelchair, paintbrushes and an easel on which rests an unfinished portrait of Joseph Stalin. Wooden spoons and ceramic jugs and bowls fill the kitchen. Be sure to stroll through the garden, full of luxuriant vegetation, sculptures, pre-Hispanic pottery and descendants of Kahlo's beloved cats. There is a cafe on the museum's first floor. The surrounding neighborhood, with its bookstores and coffee shops, has a bohemian air well suited to this iconoclastic figure. Tues.-Sun. 10-6. Admission 35 pesos (about $3.40 U.S.); 20 pesos (ages 6-12). Phone (55) 5554-5999.

LEON TROTSKY MUSEUM (Museo Casa de Leon Trotsky) is n. of Plaza Hidalgo at Av. Río Churubusco #410 (M: Coyoacán, line 3). The Russian revolutionary took up residence here after being exiled from the Soviet Union in 1929. He was murdered at home on Aug. 20, 1940. An axe-wielding assassin (a Spanish communist) accomplished the deed, which had been attempted months earlier when Stalinist sympathizers showered the house with a hail of bullets.

The fortresslike dwelling is capped with turrets once occupied by armed guards. Inside are Trotsky's modest belongings, preserved largely as he left them, and newspaper clippings recounting the event. Tues.-Sun. 10-5. Admission about $2.25 (U.S.), $1 (students); free to all Sun. Phone (55) 5554-0687 or (55) 5658-8732.

CUAUTLA, MORELOS (C-3)

pop. 140,400, elev. 4,198′

Cuautla (coo-WOW-tlah), popular with the Aztecs for its mineral springs, became a fashionable Spanish spa early in the 17th century. The city witnessed one of the most dramatic battles of Mexico's War of Independence when patriot José María Morelos and 3,000 rebels managed to withstand a 58-day siege by Royalist troops.

Some 31 kilometers (19 miles) south of Cuautla is Chinameca, the hacienda where Emiliano Zapata was assassinated; the site has been designated a national historic monument. Another historical site is Ayala, about 6 kilometers (4 miles) south of Cuautla. In 1910, Zapata issued a declaration of land reform here; later the townsite was a battlefield during the Revolution of 1910.

AGUA HEDIONDAS are about 3 km (1.9 mi.) e. of town. The "stinking waters" are a series of connected thermal pools. Aztec emperor Moctezuma is said to have spent time improving his health in the spa's sulphurous waters. Facilities include swimming pools, bathhouses, dressing rooms, a pavilion and gardens.

LAS ESTACAS is s.w. off Mex. 115. This popular swimming resort is built over several deep and powerful springs. Blue Wells Spring is a skin diving and snorkeling spot. The resort also contains three swimming pools, a wading pool, a restaurant, sports facilities and camping and picnicking areas. **Note:** Pools are normally drained on Monday for weekly cleanings.

At the entrance road to Las Estacas is the town of Tlaltizapán, which was the site of Emiliano Zapata's headquarters during the Revolution of 1910. The town's Zapata Headquarters Museum (Museum Cuartel General de Zapata) displays photographs, weapons and clothing, including the clothes Zapata had on when he was assassinated.

CUERNAVACA, MORELOS (C-2)

pop. 334,400, metro area 737,000, elev. 5,058′

See map page 275.

Capital of the state of Morelos, Cuernavaca (kwehr-nah-VAH-cah) is one of the most attractive spots in Mexico. Pink, blue and yellow houses with red-tiled roofs, luxuriant vegetation and brilliant flowers add to its charm. Many affluent Mexico City residents have second homes here, with swimming pools and extravagant gardens hidden behind high walls. Some of the homes are opened to the public on Thursdays during the first 3 months of the year.

At Mex. 95 and Avenida Fundadores a grand equestrian statue pays tribute to Emiliano Zapata, the leader of the Revolution of 1910. Zapata's battle cry of "Land and liberty, and death to the hacendados" struck at the great hacienda owners throughout the state. His Plan de Ayala, the beginning of a program toward agrarian reform, was signed near Cuautla on Nov. 28, 1911. In 1914 Zapata briefly joined Pancho Villa in occupying Mexico City before returning to Cuernavaca to prevent its seizure by federal troops.

Those maintaining summer homes in Cuernavaca over the centuries have included Aztec emperors, Hernando Cortés, Archduke Maximilian and his wife Carlota, various Mexican rulers and José de la Borda, the "silver king" *(see Taxco listing under Southern Mexico)*. On the outskirts of town in the suburb of Acapantzingo is the Olvido House, Maximilian and Carlota's summer home. The restored structure is now known as the Municipal Herb Museum (El Museo de Herbolaria).

Quaint furniture, fine silver and leather articles, colorfully woven *huaraches* and straw hats can all be purchased in Cuernavaca; on market day wares are sold in the streets and plazas as well as at the market. The main plaza teems with vendors and also has restaurants and cozy cafés. Distinctive silver religious items are hand wrought by monks at the Emaus Monastery, Calle Laurel off Boulevard Zapata, and sold there on Sundays or in the atrium of the cathedral daily.

A colorful local fiesta is the Flower Fair, held the first week in April. It features exhibits and competitions in floriculture and gardening as well as a sound-and-light show and performances by popular entertainers.

Morelos State Tourism Office (Subsecretaría de Turismo): Av. Morelos Sur #187 in the Palmas neighborhood (south of the cathedral). Open Mon.-Fri. 8-5; phone (777) 314-3872 (English spoken). There also is a visitor kiosk on the cathedral grounds that is open daily.

What To See In and Around Town

ASUNCION CATHEDRAL (Catedral de la Asunción de María) is at avs. Hidalgo and Morelos, a block or so from the Borda Gardens. It was founded by Hernando Cortés in 1529 and is one of the oldest churches in Mexico. The cathedral was the focal point of activities by Franciscan missionaries in Far Eastern countries during the colonial era.

The interior was renovated in the 1960s in a spare, modern style, but remains of early frescoes can still be seen. At the back of the cathedral is the Chapel of the Third Order (Capilla de la Tercer Orden). Sculptures by Indian artists flank the atrium. Daily 8-2 and 4-10 p.m. Free.

BORDA GARDENS (Jardín Borda) are across Calle Morelos from the cathedral. They are part of the mansion, landscaped grounds and botanical gardens built by José de la Borda, a Frenchman who came to Mexico in 1716 and made a fortune in mining. Archduke Maximilian turned the palatial estate into his summer retreat in 1864. Borda is buried in the Church of Guadalupe (Parroquía de Guadalupe), next to the main house.

The gardens are formally laid out in a succession of terraces. The front buildings contain an art gallery; on the south side of the inner court is a cafe serving light snacks. Rowboats are available for rent. Tues.-Sun. 10-5:30. Admission about $1.25 (U.S.); free to all Sun.

CUAUHNAHUAC MUSEUM (Museo de Cuauhnáhuac) flanks the e. side of the main plaza. This museum is housed in the Cortés Palace (Palacio Cortés), the former home of the Spanish conqueror. Begun in 1530, the medieval-style stone fortress has been considerably altered since that time.

The museum contains many interesting paintings and sculptures, as well as exhibits chronicling Mexico's evolution from the age of the dinosaur to contemporary Indians. Diego Rivera murals donated by former U.S. Ambassador Dwight Morrow depict the conquest of Mexico, the War of Independence and the Mexican Revolution of 1910. Tues.-Sun. 9-6. Admission about $2.50 (U.S.); free to all Sun.

LAKES OF ZEMPOALA NATIONAL PARK (Parque Nacional Lagunas de Zempoala) is 22 km (14 mi.) n. on old Mex. 95 to the town of Tres Marías, then some 15 km (9 mi.) w. on a narrow, winding road that passes the village of Huitzilac. The seven lakes *(lagos)* comprising this national park—Zempoala, Compela, Tonatihagua, Quila, Hueyapan, La Seca and Ocoyotongo—lie about 9,500 feet above sea level.

The bracing scenery—lofty mountain peaks and thick stands of tall green pine trees—looks more like Oregon or Canada than it does Mexico. Some of the lakes are stocked with bass and trout, and simple roadside restaurants hawk the latter (called *trucha*) grilled, fried and smoked. The park offers plenty of opportunities for boating, hiking, bicycling, camping and jet-skiing.

Note: Do not drive after dark, as the access road is extremely winding and can be dangerous. A toll is charged at a forest ranger station.

ROBERT BRADY MUSEUM (Museo Robert Brady) is next to the cathedral at Calle Netzahualcóyotl #4. The museum occupies Casa de la Torre, the former home of American artist Robert Brady, a native Iowan who settled in Cuernavaca in 1960. Brady restored the 16th-century stone and adobe mansion, formerly a Franciscan convent.

Brady collected as well as created art, and the museum displays more than 1,300 pieces—everything from Balinese masks to Mexican colonial carvings. They adorn the shelves, walls and tables of 14 rooms, essentially as Brady left them. The bright yellow and deep red walls and exuberantly colorful artwork combine for a surreal effect. Also noteworthy are the hand-painted tiles covering the kitchen and bathrooms. Artists represented include Diego Rivera, Rufino Tamayo, Frida Kahlo, Milton Avery and Marsden Hartley.

Guided tours in several languages are available by appointment. Food is available. Allow 2 hours minimum. Tues.-Sun. 10-6. Admission 30 pesos (about $2.90 U.S.). Phone (777) 318-8554.

SAN ANTON FALLS (Salto de San Antón) are less than a mile w. of the Borda Gardens. A walkway, where there are a few picnic tables, is cut into the rock behind the cascade. Clinging to a ledge above the falls is the tiny village of San Antón, where celebrated Cuernavaca pottery is produced. Tues.-Sun. 10-6. Free.

TEOPANZOLCO PYRAMID (Pirámide de Teopanzolco) is e. of downtown near the railroad station, off Calle Río Balsas. Built by the Aztecs but never completed, it was discovered in 1910 during the Mexican Revolution, when a large hill on the outskirts of Cuernavaca was used as a platform for attacks on the city. Tremors resulting from gunfire

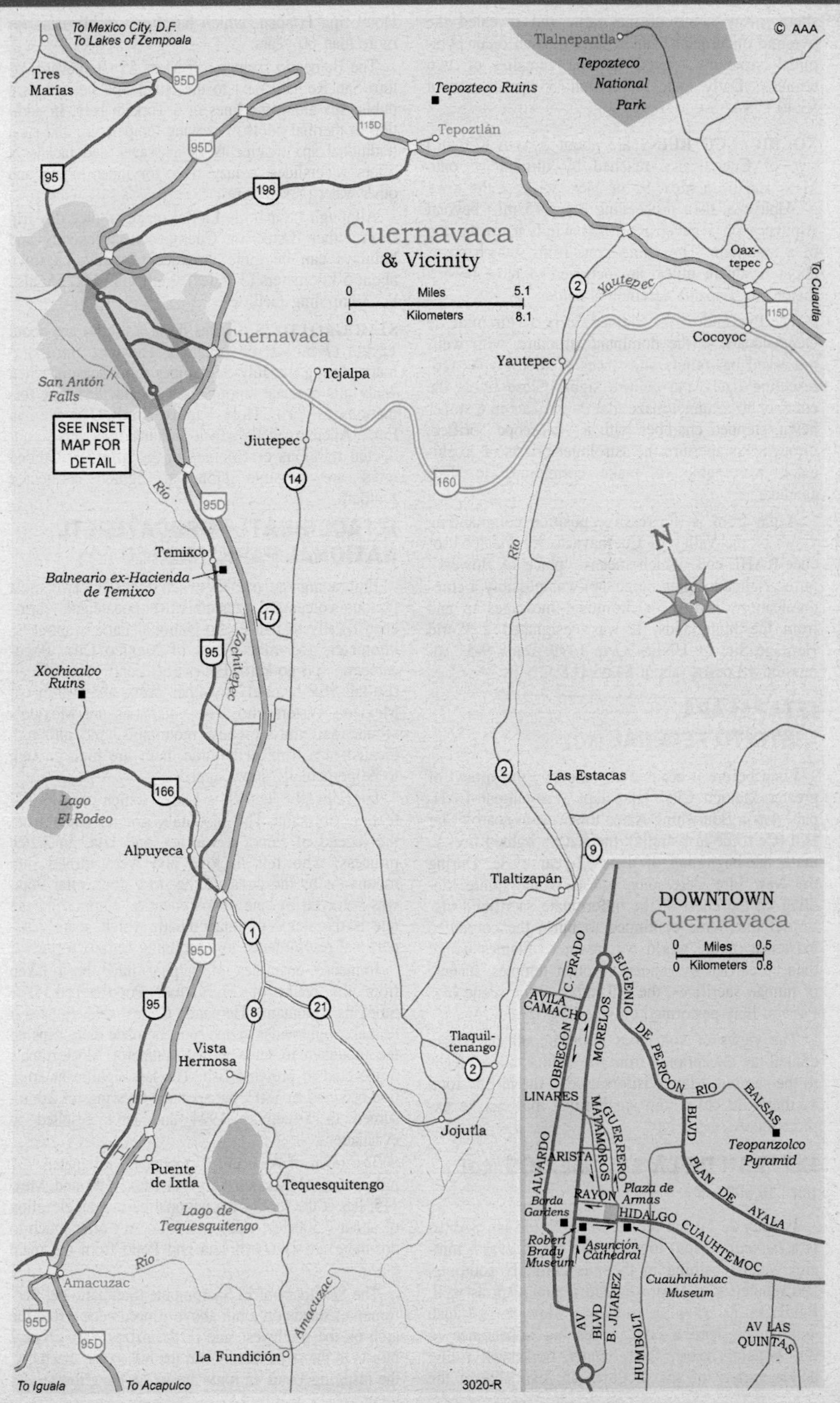
© AAA
Cuernavaca
& Vicinity
0 Miles 5.1
0 Kilometers 8.1
To Mexico City, D.F.
To Lakes of Zempoala
Tres Marías
Tlalnepantla
Tepozteco National Park
Tepozteco Ruins
Tepoztlán
Oax-tepec
To Cuautla
Yautepec
Cocoyoc
Cuernavaca
San Antón Falls
SEE INSET MAP FOR DETAIL
Tejalpa
Jiutepec
Río
Temixco
Balneario ex-Hacienda de Temixco
Zochitepec
Xochicalco Ruins
Lago El Rodeo
Alpuyeca
Las Estacas
Tlaltizapán
Vista Hermosa
Tlaquil-tenango
Jojutla
Puente de Ixtla
Tequesquitengo
Lago de Tequesquitengo
Amacuzac
La Fundición
To Iguala
To Acapulco
3020-R
DOWNTOWN
Cuernavaca
0 Miles 0.5
0 Kilometers 0.8
C. PRADO
AVILA CAMACHO
OBREGON
MORELOS
EUGENIO DE PERICON
RIO BALSAS
LINARES
MATAMOROS
GUERRERO
BLVD PLAN DE AYALA
Teopanzolco Pyramid
ALVARDO
ARISTA
RAYON
Plaza de Armas
Borda Gardens
HIDALGO
CUAUHTEMOC
Robert Brady Museum
Asunción Cathedral
Cuauhnáhuac Museum
AV
BLVD
B. JUAREZ
HUMBOLT
AV LAS QUINTAS
95D
95
115D
198
160
2
14
17
166
1
8
21
9

shook away some of the earth and revealed the pyramid underneath, which surrounds an older pyramidal structure topped by the remains of two temples. Daily 9-5. Admission 35 pesos (about $3.40 U.S.).

XOCHICALCO RUINS are about 37 km (23 mi.) s.w. of Cuernavaca, reached by turning w. onto Mex. 166 from Mex. 95 or Mex. 95-D at the town of Alpuyeca, then proceeding 8 km (5 mi.) beyond Alpuyeca on a paved road that winds n. to the top of a mountain. The white-stone ruins, which cover about 6 square miles, are believed to have been a major pre-Hispanic ceremonial center.

The Pyramid of the Plumed Serpent (Pirámide de Quetzalcóatl) is the dominant structure, with well-preserved bas-reliefs and traces of hieroglyphs representing dates and eclipse signs. Close by is the entrance to a tunnel/maze that culminates in a stone-hewn, stepped chamber with a "telescope" orifice; through this aperture the astrologer-priests of Xochicalco were able to make corrections to their calendar.

Aside from its fortresslike position commanding views of the Valley of Cuernavaca, Xochicalco (so-chee-KAHL-coh, which means "place of flowers" in the Náhuatl Indian language) was possibly a communications center for drummed messages to and from the hinterlands. It was designated a World Heritage Site by UNESCO in 1999. Daily 9-5. Admission 48 pesos (about $4.65 U.S.).

IZTAPALAPA, DISTRITO FEDERAL (B-3)

Long before it became absorbed by the sprawl of greater Mexico City, Iztapalapa (ees-tah-pah-LAH-pah) was a flourishing Aztec town. Atop nearby Star Hill (Cerro de la Estrella), the Aztecs lighted fires to mark the beginning of their 52-year cycle. During the New Fire Ceremony, priests would ignite kindling on the chest of the unfortunate sacrificial victim. If the flame continued to burn, the continued existence of the world was assured. Flames would then be carried by runners to other temples. Instead of human sacrifices, the hill today is the scene of a Passion Play performed on Good Friday.

The views of volcanoes Popocatépetl and Iztaccíhuatl are exceptional from the hilltop; a road leads to the summit. Many visitors ascend the hill by foot, as there are caves and small ruins that can be explored along the way.

IXTAPAN DE LA SAL, MEXICO (C-2)

pop. 16,600, elev. 6,311′

Ixtapán de La Sal (ees-tah-PAHN deh lah SAHL) is a *balneario* (spa) town known for its warm mineral waters; bathing in them is certainly soothing, and reputed to aid arthritis and rheumatism as well. Public pools, flowing fountains, flowers and lush landscaping lend a cool, refreshing appearance to this popular resort. Golf, tennis, horseback riding and a variety of spa facilities are available at the Hotel Spa Ixtapan, which has been in business for more than 60 years.

The Balneario Ixtapan, off Mex. 55 (Boulevard Arturo San Román) next to the Hotel Spa Ixtapan, is a public spa along the lines of a Turkish bath. In addition to thermal pools of varying temperature and such traditional spa treatments as massages and facials, it offers waterslides, a lazy river for inner tubing and other water park features.

Although Ixtapán de La Sal makes a nice day trip from either Taxco or Cuernavaca, weekends and holidays can be quite crowded. Tonatico, a town about 5 kilometers (3 miles) south via Mex. 55, also has swimming facilities.

STAR GROTTOES (Grutas de la Estrella) are about 12 km (7 mi.) s. of Tonatico. They are most dramatic during the July-September rainy season, when waterfalls cascade among such spectacular rock formations as "The Holy Family" and "The Human Ear." Ancient Matlaltzinca Indians may have conducted religious ceremonies in the grottoes. Guided tours are possible along a lighted, protected footpath.

IZTACCIHUATL-POPOCATEPETL NATIONAL PARK, MEXICO (C-4)

Embracing the pass between Mexico's two most famous volcanoes, Iztaccíhuatl-Popocatépetl (shortened locally to Izta-Popo) National Park is about 83 kilometers (52 miles) east of Mexico City. Popocatépetl (po-po-kah-TEH-pet-el) and Iztaccíhuatl (iss-tah-SEE-hwat-el) together form the Valley of Mexico's eastern rim. The volcanoes are Mexico's second and third highest mountains, and although located in a tropical latitude, both are high enough to be perpetually snowcapped.

Iztaccíhuatl (The White Lady), which rises 17,343 feet, is dormant. The mountain got its name from the legend of Popo, a warrior, and Izta, an Aztec princess, who fell in love and were turned into mountains by the gods, so the story goes, after Popo was betrayed by one of his enemies. Supporting the tale is the shape of Iztaccíhuatl, which bears a superficial resemblance to a reclining female form.

Immense quantities of sulphur have been taken from the crater of 17,887-foot Popocatépetl (The Smoking Mountain); Hernando Cortés' soldiers used it to make gunpowder. Aztec runners made daily trips up the mountain to fetch ice for Emperor Moctezuma's drinks and to preserve fish. The last significant eruption occurred in 1802, but sporadic spewings of ash resumed in December 1994 and have resulted in evacuations.

The town of Amecameca, about 60 kilometers (37 miles) east of Mexico City via Mex. 190 and Mex. 115, lies at the foot of the national park at an elevation of about 7,500 feet. Although it doesn't offer much to do, there are views of Izta and Popo from the main plaza.

The Sanctuary of El Sacromonte (Santuario del Sacromonte) stands on a hill above Amecameca. From the arch on the southwest side of the plaza, walk about 2 blocks to the steps that ascend the hill to the sanctuary; the inspiring vistas en route are worth the effort.

To get to the park from downtown Amecameca, take Mex. 115 south to the Pemex gas station at the city's southern edge, then take the paved road east toward Tlamacas (watch for the highway sign). The narrow, two-lane blacktop passes through the town of San Pedro Nexapa; watch for the highway signs that say "Ruta de Acesso" (route access). The road ascends to the town of Paso de Cortés, where the main park office is located; this is where visitors check in. The office has wall-mounted maps of the park.

Dirt and cobblestone hiking and bicycling trails branch out into various sections of the park, offering beautiful views of rugged mountains and thick pine forests. Interestingly, the terrace farms and fruit orchards in this region are more reminiscent of Europe than Mexico. Burnt-out land and lava flows are evidence of Popo's recent activity, and the mountain remains off limits to the public.

Note: Military checkpoints may be encountered. Watch for electric cattle fences that are scattered throughout the park. Picnicking is permitted. Allow 2 hours minimum. Izta-Popo National Park is open daily 8 a.m.-9 p.m. Admission is about $2 (U.S.). For information phone (597) 978-3829 (English may not be spoken).

Mexico City

City Population: 9,000,000, metropolitan area 20,965,400 (2002 estimate)
Elevation: 2,240 meters (7,347 feet)

Editor's Picks:

Plaza de la Constitución

Mexico City lies in the Valley of Mexico, or Anáhuac, a great basin about 60 miles long and 30 miles wide, bounded by mountains on all sides except the north. From the air, the vastness of the city sprawl is startling—a solid sea of buildings stretching across the valley floor to the distant horizon. The most conspicuous landmarks, however, are the snowcapped peaks of Popocatépetl and Iztaccíhuatl and to the southeast. The looming mountains hemming Mexico City in are chiefly responsible for creating the smog problem that threatens the environment. And at elevations ranging from about 7,200 to 8,000 feet, this is one of the world's loftiest cities.

Much of the valley, including the area occupied by Mexico City, is an old lake bed with no underlying bedrock. The combination of unstable subsoil and the volcanic nature of the region makes sinking and earthquakes the two greatest threats to the city's buildings. The metropolis, in fact, is settling under its own weight even as it continues to rise story upon steel, glass and stone story—although it only yields about an inch each year. But despite the preponderance of stone and concrete, Mexico City is surprisingly green (when it rains). Tamarind, cypress and rubber trees lines the streets, date palms adorn parks, clipped shrubs border sidewalks.

Earthquakes—the result of unfortunate geography—are in the back of every resident's mind. Mexico City's greatest natural catastrophe in modern times was the massive earthquake and aftershocks on Sept. 19 and 20, 1985. Some 10,000 people died, and scores of buildings were destroyed or later razed. There are still abandoned, decrepit structures here and there that were ruined but never torn down.

Mexico City normally experiences no severe temperature extremes aside from a very occasional heat wave in May or early June. Days are generally sunny and pleasant and nights comfortably cool throughout the year. The arrival of spring somewhat diminishes the severe smog and pollution problem, which peaks from mid-November through January and is exacerbated by the tremendous amount of automobile traffic. Afternoon showers are most likely from June through September.

Dress in the capital ranges from casual to elegantly formal, depending on your agenda. The most expensive restaurants may require a jacket and tie for men. A sweater, jacket or light topcoat is advisable for evenings or for trips to nearby mountain resorts.

The entire city is designated a national historic monument, and the enormous *Zócalo,* or main square, is its centerpiece. (Although most Mexican cities and towns have a central plaza that may be locally referred to as the *zócalo,* it is only Mexico City's that receives the official designation.) It is the world's second largest public gathering place after Moscow's Red Square. Once a verdant green common strolled by privileged aristocrats, the *Zócalo* is now a vast expanse of concrete (the plaza was paved over during the Revolution of 1910) that, appropriately, is best known as a very public stage for political rallies.

Visitors will see sharp contrasts. As an important business center, Mexico City has a distinctly international air. In blatant contrast, however, are ragged children and the destitute elderly begging for a few coins, sad reminders of the rampant poverty suffered by millions trying to eke out a life. The green expanses of Chapultepec Park and the charm of colonial plazas are counterbalanced by the ceaseless noise and congestion of the city's traffic, some of the worst anywhere.

Although Mexico City's sheer size can seem overwhelming to the first-time visitor, there are pleasant retreats amid the hubbub. One such area is Condesa, a *colonia* (neighborhood) centered along Avenida Michoacán off Calzada J. Vasconcelos, southeast of Chapultepec Park's eastern end.

This part of the city was the early 20th-century home of well-to-do residents who later abandoned the area, leaving behind dilapidated mansions. As recently as the 1985 earthquake this was a largely run-down area. But Condesa (which means countess) has been revitalized by an influx of young artists and expatriates and now offers tree-lined boulevards, good restaurants, plenty of sidewalk bistros and the Federal District's largest concentration of Art Deco buildings.

Noted for its strolling pedestrian traffic, Condesa is one of the best places to mingle with Mexico City's middle class. Leafy Parque México, on Avenida Michoacán near Avenida Insurgentes Sur, is delightfully well-kept and has plenty of benches. Families gather at the park on Sundays, when there are all sorts of arts and crafts activities for kids. But Condesa also is a magnet for sleek, well-dressed 20-somethings who congregate for a night out hopping among the fashionable *cantinas* and bars, many of which are open until the wee hours.

Zócalo / Carlos Sanchez / Mexico Tourism Board

So despite the inevitable big-city headaches, it is neighborhoods like Condesa—not to mention the obvious draws of history, culture and world-class museums—that make Mexico City such an enthralling experience overall. Residents are fond of saying, with an innate sense of pride, *"Como México no hay dos,"* or "There is no place like Mexico."

Historical Overview

The Aztec people, like the Toltecs before them, were originally from the Big Horn Basin region in the present-day state of Wyoming. The Aztecs then migrated south over many centuries before ending up in the Valley of Mexico in 1168 to fulfill a priestly prophecy: They were destined to settle where an eagle, carrying a serpent in its beak, was perched on a cactus (an image that appears on the Mexican flag). According to legend that spot was on an island in the middle of Lake Texcoco. It was there that the great capital of Tenochtitlan was founded.

The Aztecs soon controlled the riches of the Valley of Mexico, an important trade center, and by the

The Informed Traveler

WHOM TO CALL

Tourist Protection (Protección Legal al Turista): Secretaría de Turismo (SECTUR) headquarters, Presidente Masaryk #172; phone (55) 5761-4371 (English spoken). Persons needing legal assistance should contact this department at the Ministry of Tourism. SECTUR's 24-hour hotline also can help tourists in difficulty or coordinate aid in an emergency; phone (55) 5250-0123 or (55) 5250-0151.

Police (emergency): Dial 060 and ask to be connected to an English-speaking operator if you need immediate assistance.

Police (non-emergency): In general, the police in Mexico City should be contacted only as a last resort. If your car is stolen, however, you must report it to the police, as you will be liable for any subsequent crimes committed in or with the vehicle. To reach the highway police phone (55) 5684-2142; to report a robbery, assault or mugging, phone (55) 5625-8008 or (55) 5625-8646.

U.S. Embassy: Paseo de la Reforma #305 (M: Sevilla or Insurgentes, line 1); phone (55) 5080-2000. The embassy is open for general business Mon.-Fri. 9-2 and 3-5. There is a protection officer on 24-hour duty to advise you in case of such serious trouble as robbery, assault, major loss, accident, illness or death. In any event, Mexican law takes precedence and must be observed. A list of attorneys and translators also is available.

Canadian Embassy: Calle Schiller #529, just north of the National Museum of Anthropology (M: Auditorio, line 7); phone (55) 5724-7900. The office is open Mon.-Fri. 8:45-5:15. Both embassies are closed on U.S., Canadian and Mexican holidays.

LOCATEL: phone (55) 5658-1111 (English not likely to be spoken). This government-operated agency can help coordinate a search for missing persons or lost, stolen or towed vehicles and is available 24 hours.

Consumer Protection Office (Procuraduría del Consumidor): Phone (55) 5568-8722 if you feel that you've been cheated or ripped off regarding a service or purchase.

Hospitals: American British Cowdray (ABC) Hospital, in the southern part of the city at Calle Sur #136 and Avenida Observatorio (M: Observatorio, line 1, west bus terminal); phone (55) 5230-8000. All major credit cards are accepted. The Mexican Red Cross (Cruz Roja), Ejército Nacional #1032 in the Polanco neighborhood, is open 24 hours; phone (55) 5395-1111.

A list of doctors and hospitals in Mexico City is available from the U.S. Embassy, phone (55) 5080-2000, ext. 4780 (during working hours); the Canadian Embassy (see phone number above); the British Embassy, Av. Río Usumacinta #26 (2 blocks north of Paseo de la Reforma near the Sheraton María Isabel Hotel), phone (55) 5242-8500 (Mon.-Thurs. 8:30-1, Fri. 8:30-11:30); or your hotel front desk.

Local Phone Calls: Card-operated Ladatel phones have replaced most coin-operated phones. Ladatel phone cards in 20-, 50- and 100- peso denominations can be purchased at pharmacies or newsstands. To reach information, dial 040.

WHERE TO LOOK

Newspapers

Tiempo Libre, published every Thursday, has information about restaurants, museums, galleries and cultural events. Major U.S. newspapers are available at many newsstands the day after they are printed.

The Informed Traveler

Publications

The American Bookstore, Av. Bolívar #23 near Avenida Francisco Madero (M: Allende, line 2), has U.S. newspapers and magazines, books and an extensive selection of travel guides. The Sanborn's chain of restaurants also carries newspapers, magazines and books. Mexico City has numerous branches; one is in the House of Tiles *(see attraction listing)*, Av. Madero #4 (M: Bellas Artes, lines 2 and 8). Gandhi Bookstore, Av. Juárez #4 at Avenida Lázaro Cárdenas (across from the Palace of Fine Arts), has books about Mexico as well as an international selection of CDs and DVDs.

Visitor Information

Mexico Ministry of Tourism (Secretaría de Turismo, or SECTUR): Av. Presidente Masaryk #172 (ground floor), near the northeastern edge of Chapultepec Park in the Chapultepec Morales neighborhood (M: Polanco, line 7). Printed information can be obtained during office hours (Mon.-Fri. 8-6, Sat. 10-3), or phone (55) 3002-6300, ext. 1133.

Contact SECTUR for answers in English to questions about tourist attractions, destinations and services. In Mexico City, phone (55) 5250-0123; elsewhere within Mexico, phone 01 (800) 903-9200 (toll-free long distance). These hotline phones are staffed 24 hours a day.

Most of the big hotels offer Internet access in their business centers. Java Chat, an Internet cafe at Calle Génova #44 in the Zona Rosa (near Calle Hamburgo), is open daily until 11 p.m.; an hour of surfing costs about $3 (U.S.).

WHAT TO KNOW

Currency Exchange

While the rates charged by banks and *casas de cambio* (currency exchange offices) differ, they are invariably better than the rates offered by hotels. Most banks exchange currency Mon.-Fri. 9-noon, but you may have to wait in line; exchange offices often are open weekdays until 5 and may be open Saturdays as well. Your hotel front desk is likely to be the most convenient option. Exchange offices and ATMs are concentrated along Paseo de Reforma, in downtown's Historic Center and in the Zona Rosa. The Sanborn's chain of restaurants also provide ATMs.

Almost all ATMs take Visa and MasterCard; withdrawals are in pesos. Only use ATMs inside commercial establishments and be alert for suspicious behavior around the machine—criminals may target tourists withdrawing cash. Above all, do not make street transactions at night. Also be careful when leaving banks or exchange offices, which can be targeted by petty thieves.

Staying Safe

Street crime—from relatively benign offenses like pickpocketing and purse snatching to dangerous armed robbery—is an ever-present risk. No part of the city is immune, even the upscale Polanco neighborhood and other areas frequented by tourists. If going out for the evening, arrange designated hotel taxi transportation to and from your destination, particularly if you're unfamiliar with your surroundings. One way to avoid being mugged or robbed is not to wear expensive jewelry or watches.

Taxi robberies are among the most frequently reported crimes. The Zona Rosa and the area behind the U.S. Embassy are particularly vulnerable to street crime against foreigners; also avoid taxis parked in front of the Palace of Fine Arts. For safety's sake, it is advisable to arrange any excursion—even if only several blocks away—with a driver affiliated with your hotel.

Avoid participating in any demonstrations, strikes or other disputes that might be deemed political by Mexican authorities. Avoid the *Zócalo* and surrounding streets if protest activity is taking place. The Mexican Constitution prohibits foreigners from engaging in political activities; those who do may be detained and/or deported.

3005-R
To Querétaro & Monterrey
© AAA
To Pachuca
57D
Tepotzotlán
57
Tecámac
Coacalco
85
85D
Cuautitlán
VIA LOPEZ PORTILLO
Lechería
Mexico City
& Vicinity
132D
Venta de Carpio
San Cristóbal Ecatepec
132
N
0 Miles 3.7
0 Kilometers 6.0
Tepexpan
To San Martín de las Pirámides
85
QUEBRADA
Atizapán de Zaragoza
Ecatepec de Morelos
Tequesquinahua
146
LA
To Veracruz via Tlaxcala & Jalapa
Santa Cecilia
JOSE M MORALES
Tulpetlac
San Andrés Atenco
Tlalnepantla
85D
136
To Mex. 136
CHAMAPA
Tenayuca Pyramid
Santa Clara
Tepetlacalco
ANILLO
VIA
Texcoco
AV
CALZ
Fondo del Lago de Texcoco
Xocoyahualco
Ciudad Satélite
PERIFERICO
AUTOPISTA MEXICO-TEXCOCO
Huexotla Ruins
57
AQUILES SERDAN
Basilica Our Lady of Guadalupe
Naucalpán
Chapingo
CALZ CAMARONES
VALLEJO
NORTE
CALZ MISTERIOS
SAN JUAN DE ARAGON
Coatlinchán
Los Remedios

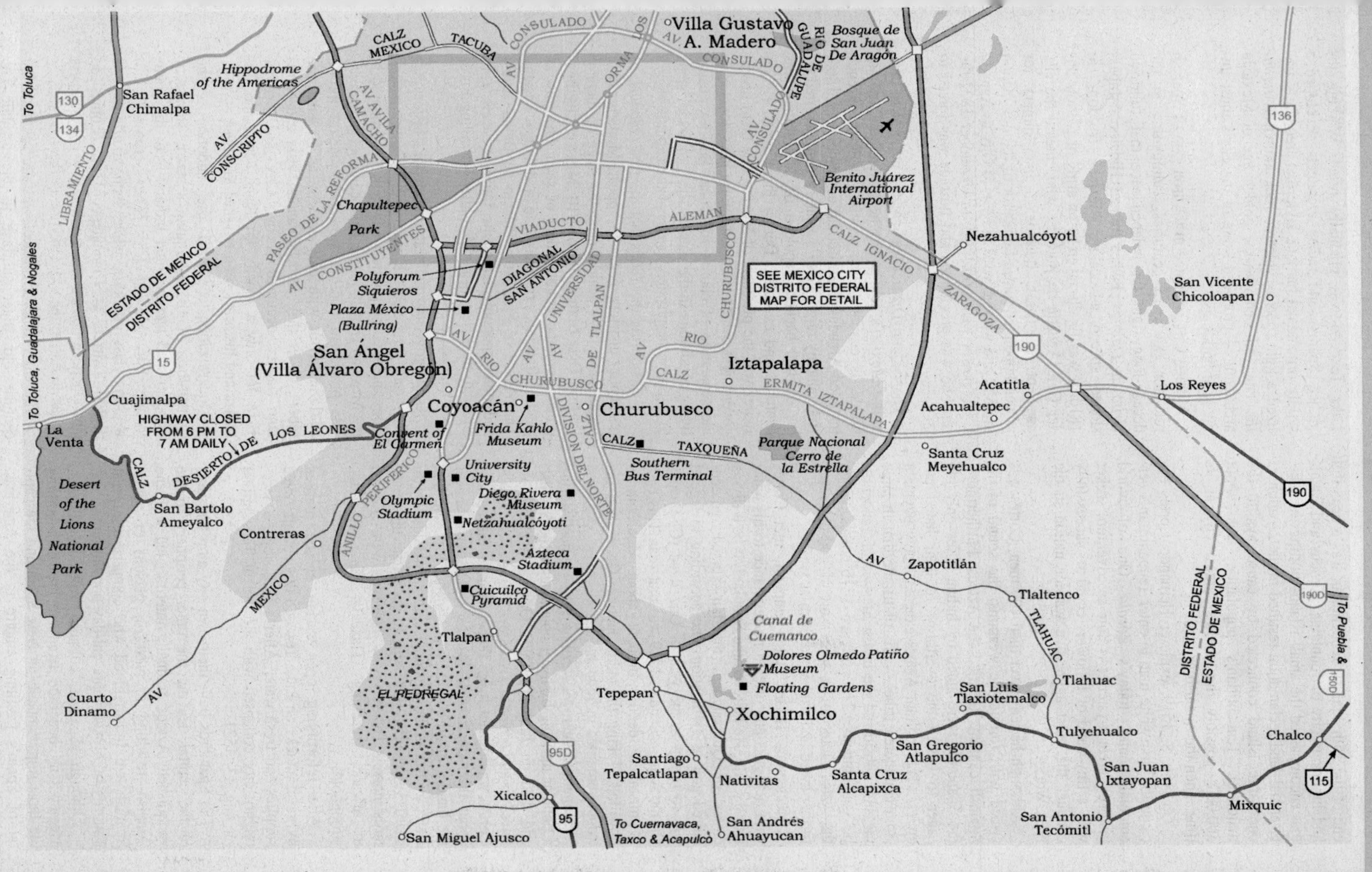
Villa Gustavo A. Madero
Bosque de San Juan De Aragón
Hippodrome of the Americas
San Rafael Chimalpa
To Toluca
Benito Juárez International Airport
Chapultepec Park
Polyforum Siqueiros
Plaza México (Bullring)
Nezahualcóyotl
SEE MEXICO CITY DISTRITO FEDERAL MAP FOR DETAIL
San Vicente Chicoloapan
ESTADO DE MEXICO
DISTRITO FEDERAL
San Ángel (Villa Álvaro Obregón)
Iztapalapa
Acatitla
Los Reyes
Cuajimalpa
To Toluca, Guadalajara & Nogales
Coyoacán
Churubusco
Acahualtepec
La Venta
HIGHWAY CLOSED FROM 6 PM TO 7 AM DAILY
Convent of El Carmen
Frida Kahlo Museum
Southern Bus Terminal
Parque Nacional Cerro de la Estrella
Santa Cruz Meyehualco
Desert of the Lions National Park
University City
Olympic Stadium
Diego Rivera Museum
Netzahualcóyotl
San Bartolo Ameyalco
Contreras
Azteca Stadium
Zapotitlán
Cuicuilco Pyramid
Tlaltenco
Tlalpan
Canal de Cuemanco
Dolores Olmedo Patiño Museum
Floating Gardens
To Puebla &
Tlahuac
Cuarto Dinamo
EL PEDREGAL
Tepepan
Xochimilco
San Luis Tlaxiotemalco
Tulyehualco
San Gregorio Atlapulco
Chalco
Santiago Tepalcatlapan
Nativitas
Santa Cruz Alcapixca
San Juan Ixtayopan
Xicalco
Mixquic
To Cuernavaca, Taxco & Acapulco
San Andrés Ahuayucan
San Antonio Tecómitl
San Miguel Ajusco

end of the 15th century Tenochtitlan was a beautiful and luxurious city of fountains, gardens and canals that encompassed the small islands dotting the lake. Eventual land reclamation resulted in the creation of one large island connected by causeways to the mainland. Tenochtitlan's population was about 300,000—possibly the world's largest city at its time. Then the Spanish arrived.

On Nov. 8, 1519, explorer Hernando Cortés became the first white man to enter Tenochtitlan's ceremonial center, today's *Zócalo.* One of world history's great mysteries is how an adventure seeker with a tiny band of followers could so successfully conquer the most aggressive warrior nation in the New World.

Although he led fewer than 400 men, Cortés was armed with formidable weapons; the sound of the Spanish cannons terrified the Aztecs. Furthermore, the Spaniards were aided by Indian allies only too eager to hasten the overthrow of their hated enemies. (The militant Aztecs exacted heavy payment from conquered tribes—gifts of tribute that in large measure subsidized the lavish lifestyle of Tenochtitlan's inhabitants.) The presence of 16 horses, which the Aztecs took to be some sort of god-monsters, further awed and frightened them as well.

Moctezuma II, the Aztec emperor, met Cortés with rich gifts and offered no resistance to his entry into the city. He believed the Spaniard to be a divine envoy of Quetzalcóatl, the fair-skinned, golden-haired god of civilization who according to legend was to return in the year of One Reed (Ce Acatl). On the Aztec calendar, 1519 was that year. This case of mistaken identity brought about Moctezuma's downfall. Taking the ruler captive, Cortés and his troops remained in Tenochtitlan.

Sometime later, Moctezuma was wounded during a popular uprising by his people against the Spanish and died on June 30, 1520. On that evening, referred to as *La Noche Triste,* or "Night of Sadness," Cortés was driven from Tenochtitlan at the cost of about three-quarters of his force. The savagery of the hand-to-hand combat was horrific. It is said that Aztec warriors brandishing clubs embedded with shards of obsidian were able to decapitate the Spaniards' horses. The survivors, however, were allowed to escape, reaching Tlaxcala, an anti-Aztec stronghold.

After refortifying, open warfare ensued, marked by naval attacks on Lake Texcoco that cut off Aztec supplies and fresh water. After a long siege, a once-mighty city collapsed with the fall of Tenochtitlan on Aug. 13, 1521.

The Spaniards built their own city atop the ruins of the capital, leaving the outer periphery to the vanquished. Aztecs gradually intermingled with the Spanish, resulting in *mestizos,* persons of mixed Spanish and Indian blood who comprise the great majority of Mexico's present-day population.

Although Spanish colonial rule was harsh, Mexico City benefited from the crown, becoming the most important city in New Spain and the capital of Spain's far-flung empire in the Americas. Lake Texcoco was gradually filled. Working together, Spanish and Indian architects developed a wildly ornamental baroque style that frequently utilized a light, porous volcanic rock known as *tezontle.* The 18th century—the golden age of Mexican architecture—produced some of the city's most impressive buildings.

Mexico City remained in the iron grip of Spanish rule for exactly 3 centuries, culminating in the decade-long fight for independence that followed *Grito de Dolores,* Father Miguel Hidalgo's impassioned speech advocating Mexican freedom, in 1810. It was finally taken by an army of patriots under Gen. Agustín de Iturbide, who entered the city on Sept. 27, 1821. Iturbide, a man hungry for power, appointed himself emperor of the new nation in 1822 and was crowned in Mexico City as Agustín I. His power was short lived; in December 1822 the republic was proclaimed and Iturbide was forced to abdicate.

The Federal District was created in 1824 to centralize Mexico's new government. Mexico City continued as capital of the republic until the French installed Archduke Maximilian as emperor in 1864. His unhappy reign lasted 3 years, when, deserted by his original backer, Napoleon III, Maximilian was captured and executed. During these years, Benito Juárez was the president of Mexico's de facto liberal government, which instituted reform laws devoted to the separation of church and state. Besides raising living conditions in the country, he took major steps to improve the physical layout of the capital.

It was during the 1860s that the first *colonias,* or residential districts, began to appear. Modernization began on a large scale during the reign of dictator Porfirio Díaz from 1876 to 1910. Mexico City benefited from the establishment of such amenities as electric lighting, streetcars and a drainage system. The Palace of Fine Arts (Palacio de Bellas Artes) and other monumental public buildings were constructed, their design modeled after prevailing European neoclassic styles.

As the governmental seat, the capital's history has obviously paralleled the history of the entire nation. Consequently, the political unrest that culminated in the Mexican Revolution of 1910 centered in the city. The protracted conflict turned the capital into a battlefield. But with only anarchy as a cause, the rebels, under their leaders Pancho Villa and Emiliano Zapata, occupied Mexico City in December 1914 for only a month; President Venustiano Carranza and his army soon returned to power.

Modernization continued after adoption of the Constitution of 1917, bringing a steady stream of impoverished *mestizos* and Indians from the countryside into Mexico City. They crowded into working-class *colonias,* while such luxurious residential districts as Chapultepec Hills (Lomas de Chapultepec) housed the wealthy few. Skyscrapers began to define the city's skyline in the 1930s.

One early renewal project was the relief of the centuries-old water shortage in the capital. The springs of Laguna del Río Lerma, beyond the mountains west of the city in the Valley of Toluca, now bring water by aqueduct to reservoirs in Chapultepec Park. The first sections of a modern subway system were completed in 1971; today the Metro's nine lines provide efficient and inexpensive city transportation. Construction of the system also brought to light some ancient archeological treasures, notably the Templo Mayor, or Great Temple of the Aztecs.

Since German traveler Baron Alexander von Humboldt described 18th-century Mexico City as a city of palaces centered on the *Zócalo,* the capital has expanded to become a metropolis. In addition to its business and commercial districts, Mexico City is honeycombed with hundreds of separate residential neighborhoods. In the last half of the 20th century the metropolitan area exploded in all directions, incorporating such former towns as Churubusco, Coyoacán, Iztapalapa, San Angel, Tlalpan, Villa de Guadalupe and Xochimilco.

Getting There

By Air

Benito Juárez International Airport is about 13 kilometers (8 miles) east of the *Zócalo.* Some 35 airlines, both international and domestic, maintain regular flights to and from Benito Juárez.

Aeroméxico, (55) 5133-4010 or 01 (800) 021-4010 (toll-free long distance within Mexico), and Mexicana, (55) 5448-1050 or 01 (800) 509-8960 (toll-free long distance within Mexico), offer service from U.S. cities. Alaska Airlines, American, America West, Continental, Delta, Northwest, United and US Airways offer direct flights to Mexico City from Houston.

Numerous facilities cater to foreign travelers, including Banamex and Bancomer bank branches, cellular phone rental, Internet access, ATMs and *casas de cambio* (currency exchange offices), a food court, short-term parking garage, and a variety of gift and duty-free shops. Rental car agencies include Hertz.

Representatives of the Mexican Ministry of Tourism (SECTUR) and the Hotel Association in the arrivals area can assist in booking a room according to location and price specifications. Authorized baggage handlers are identified by the "Union" ID placard attached to their hand carts. Phone (55) 5571-3600 for airport information.

Contact the airline directly when making reservations for flights to other cities within Mexico, or if you need price or schedule information. This can be frustrating if you reach someone who doesn't speak good English; airline numbers also change frequently. If possible, make all flight arrangements prior to your departure; then the only reason you may need to call is to confirm times.

When departing Mexico City, make sure to allow for sufficient travel time to the airport—a minimum of 45 minutes if you're based in the downtown area. Arrive at least an hour before departure for domestic flights, 90 minutes before departure for international flights. If you have an early morning flight, staying at the Marriott Aeropuerto is convenient; an elevated skywalk connects the hotel and Terminal B. For additional information about airlines *see Arriving by Air, page 61.*

Authorized airport taxis are the safest way to reach the downtown area. The yellow-and-white vehicles, sedans or minivans, have a black aircraft symbol on the door and are labeled *"Transportación Terrestre"* (Ground Transportation). Taxis require prepayment at the official airport taxi counter; look for the *Taxi Autorizada* booth in the baggage claim area.

Rates are based on a zone system and vary according to distance; consult the map at the taxi counter to verify your destination. The fare to downtown Mexico City averages about $14-$16 (U.S.). Yellow-outfitted escorts show you to an available taxi; vouchers are given to the driver. Do not negotiate with anyone who approaches you with the offer of a ride into town. There are no buses that travel directly to the city center. The ride to the city center takes 25 minutes to an hour, depending on the time of day. Tipping is customary if the driver helps with your luggage.

If you're traveling light, you might consider using Metro, Mexico City's rapid transit system. Large pieces of luggage aren't allowed on board, however, and riding a crowded subway car weighed down with anything more than an overnight bag is not only cumbersome but unsafe. The airport station is Terminal Aérea (Air Terminal Building, line 5) on Boulevard Puerto Aéreo. The main terminal is within walking distance; follow the signs. To reach the downtown area from the airport, take the subway to the Pantitlán station and switch to line 1.

By Car

Mex. 15-D, 57/57-D and 85-D are the major highways approaching Mexico City from the west and north. From the south and east come Mex. 95-D and Mex. 150-D. Other routes are likely to be slow, winding or of substandard quality, and one—Mex. 134, which travels northeast to Mexico City from Mex. 200 along the Pacific Coast—should be avoided entirely.

Leaving the city, the main thoroughfares are Avenida Insurgentes Sur, which becomes Mex. 95-D as it heads south to Cuernavaca, Taxco and Acapulco; running north, Avenida Insurgentes Norte becomes Mex. 85-D/85 heading toward Pachuca. The Periférico, which loops around the city's western and southern sides, is called Avenida Avila Camacho within the city and becomes Mex. 57-D heading northwest toward Querétaro. Avenida Constituyentes runs west past Chapultepec Park and becomes Mex. 15 as it heads toward Toluca; Calzada Ignacio Zaragoza leads east out of the city, becoming Mex. 190-D as it heads toward Puebla.

Try to time both arrival and departure times into and out of Mexico City as early in the morning as possible to avoid the near-constant traffic.

Note: Seat belt use by the driver and all passengers is required within the Federal District.

By Bus

With interconnections between Mexican and U.S. bus lines, it is possible to travel economically by bus from several U.S. border cities to Mexico City. Transportes del Norte, Tres Estrellas de Oro, Transportes Chihuahuenses and Omnibus de México are linked with Greyhound Lines Inc. From Tijuana it takes about 40 hours to reach Mexico City; from Ciudad Juárez, across the border from El Paso, Tex., about 24 hours; from Matamoros, across the border from Brownsville, Tex., about 14 hours.

Bus travel is available from Mexico City to nearly every town in the republic, but reservations must be made. Most major Mexican lines offer first-class *(lujo)* bus service; these companies include Autobuses Cristóbal Colón, Autobuses del Oriente (ADO), ETN, Omnibus de México, Primera Plus and Tres Estrellas de Oro. **Note:** Arrivals and departures at bus stations in Mexico are usually announced in Spanish only. For additional information about buses *see Bus Service, page 72.*

Mexico City has four main bus terminals that correspond to the four compass points. Each terminal has luggage storage facilities, a post office, ATMs, a cafeteria and long-distance (Ladatel) telephones.

By far the largest of the four is the Terminal Central de Autobuses del Norte, Av. Cien Metros #4907 (M: Autobuses del Norte, line 5). Most of the buses traveling from the northern border arrive at this terminal, also known as "Terminal Norte" or "Camiones Norte." From here, buses travel to almost every destination north of the capital, including the Pacific Coast resorts from Manzanillo northward; inland cities such as Aguascalientes, Guadalajara, Guanajuato, Monterrey, Morelia, Querétaro and San Miguel de Allende; and the nearby archeological sites of Teotihuacán and Tula.

The terminal offers currency exchange services (during normal banking hours) and has a hotel reservations booth. Taxis charge standard fares based on a zone system; tickets are purchased at booths inside the station. Count your change carefully, as overcharging is common.

Terminal de Autobuses de Pasajeros de Oriente (TAPO) is at Calzada Ignacio Zaragoza #200, near the airport (M: San Lázaro, line 1). The most modern of the four stations, it handles buses to and from such eastern destinations as Jalapa, Puebla, Veracruz, Villahermosa and cities on the Yucatán Peninsula, as well as Oaxaca, San Cristóbal de Las Casas, Tuxtla Gutiérrez, Guatemala and other places to the south. Taxi ticket booths and currency exchange services are available.

Terminal Central de Autobuses del Sur is at Av. Taxqueña #1320 (M: Taxqueña, line 2). At the end of Metro's line 2, this also is a major terminus for local city buses from downtown and other points north. From here buses arrive and depart for Acapulco, Cuernavaca, Ixtapa/Zihuatanejo, Taxco and other points south of Mexico City. For day trips to

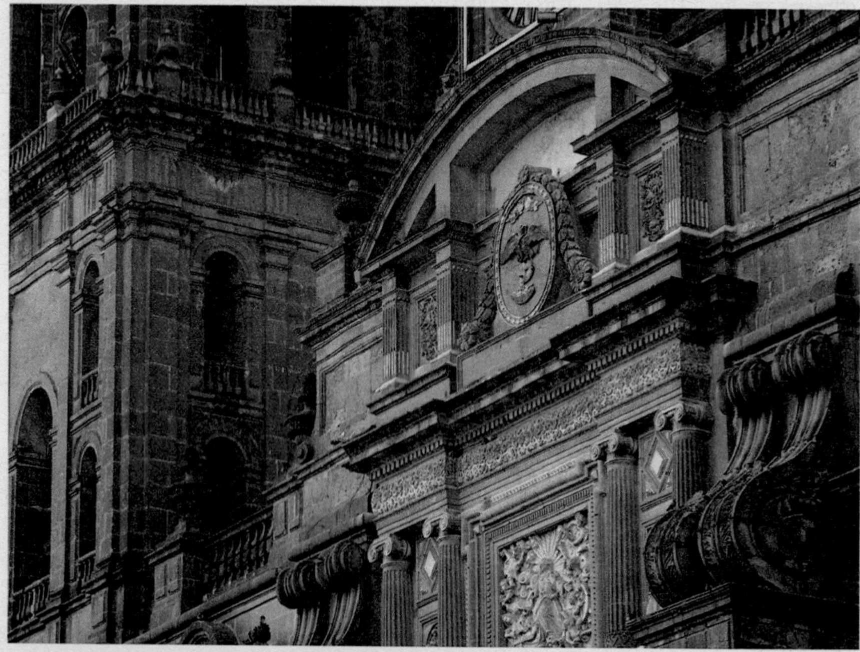

Metropolitan Cathedral / © David Mendelsohn / Masterfile

the tourist destinations of Cuernavaca and nearby Cuautla and Tepoztlán, take one of the Pullman de Morelos buses, which depart frequently for Cuernavaca. Estrella de Oro has first-class service to Acapulco and Zihuatanejo. The terminal also has a travel agency.

The smallest of the four is the western station, Terminal de Autobuses del Poniente, Av. Sur #122 at Tacubaya (M: Observatorio, line 1). This is the easiest way to take a day trip to Toluca by bus. Service also is available to Morelia and Guadalajara; the going is slow but the scenery is pleasant.

Getting Around

City Layout

Mexico City's *colonias,* or neighborhoods—more than 300 of them—are served by a maze of *calles, avenidas* and *calzadas*. Some narrow alleyways, or *callejones,* are cobblestoned relics from earlier days. Major thoroughfares, on the other hand, can have eight lanes.

Most of the signs tend to be more confusing than enlightening. There is no real logic to the city's streets, which are named after rivers, mountains, foreign cities and countries, musicians, writers, doctors, composers, the states of Mexico and just about everything else. They also change names frequently.

A system of connected highways combine to form the Circuito Interior, which roughly encircles the central city. Beginning at the airport, on the east side of town, Avenida Río Consulado runs north and then west, becoming Calzada Melchor Ocampo. Ocampo swings south, passing east of Chapultepec Park and intersecting Paseo de la Reforma, at which point it continues as Calzada Vasconcelos. Angling off Vasconcelos is Avenida de la Revolución, which runs south to Avenida Río Churubusco. Churubusco then proceeds east before turning north to connect with Río Consulado, southwest of the airport, and completing the circuit.

Theoretically, this loop provides a less congested alternative to the jam-packed streets within it. However, these roads themselves are usually crowded, particularly during the morning and evening rush hours.

Also within the Circuito Interior are axis roads *(ejes),* a series of numbered boulevards running one way only, with special lanes reserved for trolleys and buses circulating in the opposite direction. East-west Eje 1 Norte and Eje 2 Norte are north of the *Zócalo,* Eje 2 Sur through Eje 8 Sur run progressively south of the *Zócalo.* North-south Eje 1 through 3 Oriente are east of Eje Central Lázaro Cárdenas, which divides the central city in half; Eje 1 through 3 Poniente are to the west.

The most magnificent of the broad principal arteries that intersect the central city is the Paseo de la Reforma. A legacy of French emperor Maximilian, it runs southwest to northeast for more than 7 miles. From the eastern end of Chapultepec Park to past Alameda Park, Reforma is exceptionally wide and beaded with monument-adorned *glorietas* (circles).

One good point of reference is the Independence Monument at the intersection of Reforma, Florencia and Tiber. The 150-foot-tall spire, topped by a gold angel, is easy to spot. Another is the major intersection at Paseo de la Reforma and Avenida Insurgentes, marked by the Cuauhtémoc Monument.

Insurgentes, the capital's longest thoroughfare, runs north/south, bisecting western and eastern sections of the city. East-west Viaducto Miguel Alemán runs south of downtown, connecting Calzada Ignacio Zaragoza at the eastern end of the city with the Anillo Periférico at the western end. The Periférico (Mex. 57) traverses the city's western and southern sections.

Driving just about anywhere within Mexico City is a daunting prospect and not recommended. The sheer number of vehicles makes for an extremely slow pace. Add to that aggressive tactics (the locals often disregard traffic signals), frequent construction, detours and a plethora of one-way streets, and visitors are far better off relying on taxi transportation provided by their hotel. Above all, never drive alone after dark due to the risk of car hijacking, robbery or assault.

If circumstances dictate that you must drive, carry a good city map and always park the vehicle in a guarded lot. Street parking is not only rare but chancy, as vandalism often occurs. Any vehicle parked illegally is likely to have its license plate removed by police; expect to pay a fee to get it back. Never leave valuables in your car, even if hidden.

Note: Motorists in Mexico City who are stopped for a red light at many downtown intersections are besieged by everyone from beggars to performing children (whose parents are often sitting on a nearby corner) to vendors selling newspapers, flowers, candy and trinkets. The best defense if you're part of this captive audience is to keep your door locked, your window rolled up and look straight ahead, avoiding eye contact.

Speed limits are shown in kilometers. If a road, avenue or street is unmarked, follow these general guidelines: school zones, 20 km/h (10-12 mph); residential streets, 30 km/h (20 mph); main streets, 50 km/h (30 mph); avenues, bypasses, loop roads and overpasses within the city, 60 km/h (35 mph); main roads, 100 km/h (60 mph); selected main roads and toll roads, 110-120 km/h (65-75 mph).

Taxis

The most important safety advice for visitors is to never hail a cab on the street. Avoid the constantly cruising green and white Volkswagen Beetle taxis (often referred to as *ecologicos* or *magna sins*), or cabs with license plates containing the letter "L" (*libre* cabs). While residents must use them to get around an overcrowded city, drivers often are involved in robberies against passengers. The drivers themselves also are frequent victims of assault, making this a dangerous profession.

Major hotels maintain fleets of *turismo* taxis associated specifically with the hotel. These can be used for short hops to a nearby restaurant and back, or for longer excursions to shop or sightsee. For an hourly rate (and normally a 2-hour time minimum), you can arrange to have the driver wait at a specific location in addition to providing transportation. Rates for individual trips are negotiated with the driver; establish the fee for any excursion in advance. Although *turismo* taxis are expensive (a ride just a few blocks in length can cost several dollars), the peace of mind is well worth the cost.

J.R. Taxi is a reliable service; the driver speaks English, is familiar with all of the city's major tourist attractions, can pick up passengers at the airport or at designated bus stations, and offers favorable rates to AAA members. Phone (044) 55-5100-7542 (cellular number) in Mexico City, (044) 5100-7542 elsewhere within Mexico, or (55) 5100-7542 outside of Mexico. A similar service is Laupac Taxi; phone (044) 55-2523-1499 (cellular number) in Mexico City, (044) 2523-1499 elsewhere within Mexico, or (55) 2523-1499 outside of Mexico.

If your hotel doesn't provide transportation or you otherwise need a cab, the U.S. Embassy strongly urges that you ride only in a taxi summoned by phone from a designated *sitio* (SEE-tee-oh) stand. They are considered safer than taxis that circulate because the driver can be easily traced back to the stand. Many of the stands list telephone numbers where the taxi can be called. Arrangements also can be made to have these cabs pick you up at a predetermined time and place.

Ask for the license plate number and the cab driver's name, and only use cabs with plates beginning with the letter "S," which are assigned to a particular site—such as a hotel—and registered. The number on the license plate should match the number painted on the side of the cab. It's much easier to negotiate for a *sitio* taxi if you speak fluent Spanish.

Authorized taxis at the airport and at bus stations charge fees based on a zone system; tickets to pay the fee are purchased at booths inside the terminal. *Also see Getting There—By Air, page 285.*

Rental Cars

There are many car rental agencies in Mexico City. The larger companies also have branches in major cities where you can leave your car at trip's end. Be sure you fully understand the terms of any rental contract, especially in regard to insurance coverage. It's much less expensive to reserve before you leave home; make reservations at least 1 week in advance. AAA/CAA members enjoy discounts through Hertz for vehicles booked in the United States. Consult your local AAA/CAA club or phone Hertz, (800) 654-3080.

Note: Although having a vehicle at your disposal can be convenient for sightseeing trips outside the metropolitan area, keep in mind that a rental car driven by a foreigner may unfortunately become a target for police who will try to extract a bribe.

Vehicles in the Mexico City metropolitan area, including the Distrito Federal (Federal District) and parts of the state of Mexico, may *not* be driven on certain days based on the last digit of the license plate. Make certain your rental car can be driven when you wish to use it. A rental agency may inadvertently provide a vehicle with a license plate with a last digit that corresponds to the day on which it cannot be driven. For additional information, *see the Day Without Car Program box on page 292.*

Buses

City buses go just about everywhere and are inexpensive, but the system is not user-friendly for visitors. Routes and bus numbers change frequently, and route maps are practically nonexistent. Some signs at the downtown bus stops bear route descriptions. Buses run daily 5 a.m.-midnight, but show up much less frequently after 10 p.m.

Two major bus routes put visitors within walking distance of many of the city's attractions. The east-west route links the *Zócalo* with the National Auditorium in Chapultepec Park and continues to the Observatorio Metro station (line 1), traveling along avenidas Francisco I. Madero and Juárez and Paseo de la Reforma. These buses are usually marked *"Zócalo."*

Buses running north-south along Avenida Insurgentes connect the huge Terminal Norte station with the southern suburbs of San Angel and University City via the Zona Rosa. These buses are usually marked *"Indios Verdes-Tlalpan."* Routes are marked on the windshield.

Never carry valuables onto a city bus, and know exactly where you're going before you board. But unless you simply want to have the experience, it's safer and much more convenient to use a taxi associated with your hotel for getting around.

Peseros

These vehicles resemble a minibus or van. *Peseros,* also called *colectivos, combis* or *rutas,* travel along established routes and charged flat rates (according to distance) that are a bit more than the bus but less than taxi fares. Route destinations (often a Metro station) are marked on the windshield or shown on a sign. Flag down a *pesero* as you would a bus, and tell the driver your destination when you board.

Major routes include the principal east-west and north-south tourist corridors (the *Zócalo* to Chapultepec Park and Avenida Insurgentes Sur, respectively). This is an alternative to the crowded and often chaotic city buses, although using a designated taxi is still the safest way to travel. Try to have the exact change in pesos, and never pull out a wallet, which will attract the attention of pickpockets.

Metro

Metro—one of the world's busiest subway systems—is faced with the formidable task of moving some 6 million riders daily over both surface and subterranean track. Metro lines cover most of the city. In addition, a *tren ligero* (light rail) line provides service to the popular tourist attraction of Xochimilco. The two lines most helpful to visitors are Lines 1 and 2, as they cover major sightseeing points of interest.

Line 1 runs roughly west-east from the Observatory, near Chapultepec Park, to Pantitlán in the eastern suburbs, passing south of the Zona Rosa and the *Zócalo*. Subway riders bound for the airport switch to line 5 at the Pantitlán station. Line 2 begins in the northwest part of the city at the Cuatro Caminos station, proceeds east, burrows under the *Zócalo* and then runs above ground due south to the Taxqueña station.

Line 3 runs from the Indios Verdes station, north of the Basilica of Guadalupe, south past Alameda Park to University City (National University of Mexico campus). Line 4 runs north-south east of downtown, from the Martín Carrera to the Santa Anita stations. Line 5 runs from the Politécnico station south to the La Raza station, then east and south to Pantitlán, with a stop (Terminal Aérea) at the airport. **Note:** To switch from line 3 to line 5—or vice versa—at the La Raza station requires a 10- to 15-minute walk through a long tunnel.

Line 6 runs north of downtown, proceeding east from the El Rosario station to the Martín Carrera station via the Instituto del Petróleo and Deportivo 18 de Marzo stations. Line 7 runs north-south along the city's western edge from the El Rosario station to the Barranca del Muerto station. Line 8 runs from the Garibaldi station (one stop north of the Bellas Artes station on line 2) south and east to the Constitución de 1917 station, in the southeast section of the city. Line 9 parallels line 1 and runs south of it, from the Tacubaya station in the west to the Pantitlán station in the east.

Two additional lines provide light rail service. Line A runs from the Pantitlán station (the eastern terminus of lines 1, 5 and 9) south to the La Paz station; Line B serves the Buenavista Railroad Station and runs east to the Garibaldi station (the northern terminus of line 8), then north to the Ciudad Azteca station. The *tren ligero* line runs south from the Taxqueña station south to Xochimilco.

The flat fare, which includes transfers, is 2 pesos. Tickets, which are valid indefinitely, are purchased at booths at the stations; the magnetically encoded stub allows passage through the turnstiles. If you plan on using the system, purchase several tickets at one time to avoid spending time standing in lines.

You also can purchase an *abono* ticket, which allows use of the entire system for a multiple-day period. (With this type of ticket, enter Metro stations only through the blue turnstiles; otherwise the ticket will be taken and not returned.)

At the stations, on signs and in guidebooks and brochures, Metro lines are designated by the following colors: lines 1 and A, bright pink; line 2, blue; line 3, olive green; line 4, light blue; line 5, yellow; line 6, red; line 7, orange; line 8, dark green; and line 9, brown. You can consult a color-coded subway guide at Metro information booths, or try obtaining a map of the system from the ticket booths at the larger stations.

The rubber-wheeled trains are fast and frequent, and the stations are modern. But keep in mind that Metro is used daily by millions for commuter travel, so sardine-can conditions usually prevail. During weekday rush hours (both morning and evening) the trains are crammed and guards are employed to control the crowds; avoid using the system during these times.

Single women, unfortunately, may have to fend off unwelcome advances or inappropriate male conduct. Foreign visitors are prime targets for pickpockets and purse snatchers, especially at stations near major tourist sights. There are separate cars for women and children during rush hours, but regulations are not strictly enforced.

Although it can be convenient to use the subway for sightseeing, especially to get to Xochimilco or the southern neighborhoods of Coyoacán and San Angel, for safety's sake it's best to hire a taxi affiliated with your hotel if you intend to visit these areas. If you do need to take Metro for any reason, make certain you know which direction the train is heading. Check the signs on the loading platforms *(andenes);* they denote the last station on the line in each direction. For example, *Dirección Pantitlán* and *Dirección Observatorio* indicate the last stations for line 1. Transfer gates, where more than one line shares a subway station, are marked *Correspondencia;* exits, *Salida.*

Metro is least crowded on weekends and holidays. In general trains begin running at 5 a.m. Mon.-Fri., 6 a.m. Sat., 7 a.m. Sun., and operate until 12:30 a.m. Luggage and backpacks are technically not permitted on any of the subway cars, nor is the taking of photographs allowed.

Note: Points of interest and other locations described in the text for Churubusco, Coyoacán, Mexico City and San Angel include, where applicable, the name of the individual Metro station (M) and the subway line (1 through 9). Attraction listings without this designation are located away from Metro routes.

Guides/Tours

The services of a good guide can be expensive but invaluable, particularly for the first few days in this huge city. If you go with this option, obtain the services of a bonded guide licensed by the Secretaría de Turismo (the Mexican Ministry of Tourism, or SECTUR). Ask to see his or her official guide card marked with "Departamento de Turismo" and take special note of the expiration date to the right of the photograph. Additional fees are charged for guided trips outside Mexico City.

Taxi drivers also can function as a driver/bodyguard/guide, even if it means waiting by the car for an hour while you stroll one of the city's tourist-friendly neighborhoods. Rates are negotiable, but

METRO LINES

N
El Rosario
Tezozomoc
Aquiles Serdán
Azcapotzalco
Ferreria
Norte 45
Vallejo
Politécnico
Instituto del Petróleo
Lindavista
Indios Verdes
Basílica
La Villa
Martín Carrera
Ciudad Azteca
Plaza Aragón
Olimpica
Tecnológico
Muzquiz
Rio de los Remedios
Impulsora
Continentes
Villa de Aragón
Bosque de Aragón
Deportivo Oceanía
Camarones
Autobuses del Norte
Potrero
Talisman
Bondojito
Refineria
Consulado
La Raza
Misterios
Valle Gómez
Eduardo Molina
Aragón
Cuatro Caminos
Tlatelolco
Garibaldi
Lagunilla
Tepito
Panteones
Tacuba
Cuitlahuac
Popotla
Buenavista
Guerrero
Bellas Artes
Canal del Norte
Oceanía
San Joaquín
Colegio Militar
Normal
San Cosme
Revolución
Hidalgo
Allende
Morelos
Romero Rubio
Terminal Aérea (Benito Juárez International Airport)
Polanco
San Juan de Letrán
Zócalo
Gran Canal
Juárez
Hangares
Auditorio
Salto del Agua
Pino Suárez
Merced
Moctezuma
Balbuena
Balderas
Cuauhtémoc
Insurgentes
Constituyentes
Sevilla
Niños Héroes
Doctores
Isabel la Católica
Candelaria
San Lázaro
Aeropuerto
Pantitlán
San Antonio Abad
Fray Servando
Gómez Farías
Zaragoza
Chapultepec
Obrera
Chabacano
Juanacatlán
Hospital General
Tacubaya
Observatorio
Patriotismo
Chilpancingo
Centro Médico
Lázaro Cárdenas
Jamaica
Mixihuca
Velódromo
Ciudad Deportiva
Puebla
San Pedro de los Piños
Etiopía
Viaducto
La Viga
Santa Anita
San Antonio
Eugenia
Xola
Coyuya
Tezontle
Villa de Cortés
Apatlaco
Mixcoac
División del Norte
Nativitas
Aculco
Escuadrón 201
Zapata
Portales
Atlalico
Tren Ligero
Barranca del Muerto
Coyoacán
Ermita
Iztapalapa
General Anaya
Cerro de la Estrella
Viveros
La Purísima
Constitución de 1917
Miguel A. de Quevedo
Taxqueña
La Paz
Copilco
Universidad

expect a minimum of 230 pesos (about $22 U.S.) an hour. Most visitors will find the peace of mind that comes from not having to negotiate city traffic or use public transportation well worth the expense.

What To See

Note: To make it easier to plan a sightseeing itinerary in this sprawling city, the following attraction listings are grouped under nine separate, geographically based subheadings and spotted on three different maps. For the Mexico City & Vicinity map, see pages 282-283; for the Mexico City Distrito Federal map, see pages 296-297; for the Downtown Mexico City map , see page 303.

Around the Zócalo

CALLE MONEDA begins just e. of the *Zócalo* at Av. Seminario (M: Zócalo, line 2). It takes its name from the country's first mint, which now houses the National Museum of the Cultures *(see attraction listing)*.

Many of the colonial-era buildings lining this thoroughfare, one of the city's oldest, are constructed of *tezontle,* the reddish volcanic rock used by the Aztecs to build their pyramids and temples. Near the *Zócalo* they are carefully refurbished but become more dilapidated as the street heads east. Vendors add to the bustle of this downtown corridor, which is closed to traffic and therefore pleasant to stroll (during daylight hours only).

GRAN HOTEL is just w. of the *Zócalo* at Av. 16 de Septiembre #82 (M: Zócalo, line 2); the parking entrance is located between avenidas 5 de Febrero and Palma. Built in 1895, this five-story marble structure—a grand example of turn-of-the-20th-century architecture—reopened a couple of years ago following an extensive remodeling. The spacious atrium lobby is worth a peek; it boasts a spectacular Tiffany stained-glass ceiling and gilded, open-cage elevators. The hotel also has a rooftop terrace restaurant overlooking the *Zócalo.* Parking is available for an hourly fee.

GREAT TEMPLE (Templo Mayor) encompasses a city block just n. of the *Zócalo;* the site entrance is on Av. Seminario (M: Zócalo, line 2). The only available parking is a commercial underground garage near the Palace of Fine Arts. The Great Temple, or Teocalli, of the Aztecs was a monumental pyramid that served as a religious, political and sacrificial center. The ruins, located in the heart of today's metropolis, are striking evidence of a separate civilization that flourished hundreds of years earlier.

Demolished and buried by the conquering Spaniards, the structure—originally thought to be beneath the nearby Metropolitan Cathedral—was rediscovered in 1978 by a subway construction worker. The excavated ruins reveal successive layers of older temples, each built atop the other, and include other structures as well as a stone replica of a *tzompantli,* or wall of skulls. Plaques in Spanish explain the origin of the different temples. **Note:** Visitors must proceed through the complex in one direction and are not permitted to turn around and go back once inside the site.

Allow 1 hour, 30 minutes minimum. Site open Tues.-Sun. 9-4:30. Admission (includes site and Great Temple Museum) 45 pesos (about $4.40 U.S.), free (ages 0-12); free to all Sun. The fee to use a video camera is $3.50. Phone (55) 5542-4943.

Great Temple Museum (Museo Templo Mayor) is at avs. Guatemala and Seminario within the site. The museum provides a valuable historical perspective, especially for those unfamiliar with Aztec lore. On display are more than 7,000 items recovered from the site and locations as far away as the present-day states of Veracruz and Guerrero. There are eight exhibit rooms (*salas*) on three levels, organized around a central open space dominated by the original discovery, the enormous stone depicting a beheaded and limbless Coyolxauhqui.

Among the more impressive artifacts are life-size, terra-cotta eagle warrior statues and stone masks that were offered as tributes by subjugated tribes. Open same hours as the site.

GEM **METROPOLITAN CATHEDRAL** (Catedral Metropolitana) is on the n. side of the *Zócalo* (M: Zócalo, line 2). This enormous church seems even bigger rising up from the vast expanse of the *Zócalo.* A church built in 1525 was demolished in 1573 to make way for the present structure, which was not completed until some 215 years later. The exterior is a mingling of architectural styles, from baroque ornamentation to a neoclassic clock tower.

Along the interior side aisles are five naves and 14 chapels variously adorned with statuary, ornate altars, paintings, gilded surfaces, priceless tapestries and various representations of Christ, including a black Christ figure. The Chapel of the Kings, at the end of the nave behind the main altar, is graced by gilded wood carvings and an extravagantly Churrigueresque altarpiece. **Note:** Visitors to the cathedral (or any church in Mexico) should respect those who are there to worship.

All manner of crystals, herbs, gemstones and religious paraphernalia are sold in front of the cathedral. On the west side more vendors set up shop, selling everything from crafts to Mexican jumping beans, and laborers sit on the curb next to small signs advertising their trade.

A sound-and-light presentation, "Voices of the Cathedral," features choral music and actors in period costume. Performances are Wed. at 8:30 p.m. Tickets are available through Ticketmaster. Cathedral daily 7-7. Free. "Voices of the Cathedral" tickets about $25 (U.S.). Phone (55) 5325-9000 for tickets.

Sacristy (El Sagrario) adjoins the cathedral. This church, built in the mid-18th century to house vestments and sacred relics, has an elaborate baroque facade. Both the Sacristy and the cathedral were damaged in the 1985 earthquake, and each has tilted

"Day Without Car" Program

In a continuing effort to reduce air pollution, city government officials in 1989 established driving restrictions on all vehicular traffic, including vehicles carrying non-Mexican registration and regardless of license plate origin. The restriction is based on the last digit of a vehicle's license plate and pertains to the days of the week. It is in effect throughout the Mexico City metropolitan area, which includes the Distrito Federal (Federal District) and parts of the state of México.

Vehicles may not be driven on certain days according to the following schedule: MONDAY—license plates that end with 5 or 6; TUESDAY—license plates that end with 7 or 8; WEDNESDAY—license plates that end with 3 or 4; THURSDAY—license plates that end with 1 or 2; FRIDAY—license plates that end with 9 or 0. All vehicles may be driven SATURDAY and SUNDAY. The restrictions **do not** apply from 11 p.m. to 5 a.m. Failure to comply with "Day Without Car" (Hoy No Circula) regulations will result in vehicle impoundment and a hefty fine.

These restrictions are ongoing and apply to both permanent and temporary plates. **There is no specific provision regarding plates with letters only.** If you are visiting Mexico City and plan to rent a car and drive anywhere in the greater metropolitan area, contact the rental car agency in advance and make certain the vehicle can be driven when you wish to use it.

noticeably over decades as they ever so slowly sink into the underlying lake bed. Ongoing work to repair the effects of uneven settling has been successful, however, and some of the ever-present scaffolding that seemed to have become a permanent part of the cathedral has been removed.

MEXICO CITY HISTORIC CENTER (Centro Historico de México) is the area that radiates out from the *Zócalo*. It has been the city's hub since its founding by the Aztecs in 1168. Cortés and his followers decimated the Indian structures, building their own monuments atop the rubble. Today the district—designated a World Heritage Site by UNESCO in 1987—encompasses more than 1,500 historic structures, including the Templo Mayor, or Great Temple of the Aztecs, the National Palace and the Metropolitan Cathedral *(see separate attraction listings)*.

A multitude of businesses, including the National Pawn Shop, operate amid restaurants, museums, theaters, churches and the ubiquitous street vendors, who peddle everything from lottery tickets to holy water. Some of the streets around the *Zócalo*, where restoration efforts are ongoing, are closed to vehicular traffic. Visitors, at any rate, will definitely want to explore on foot.

MUNICIPAL PALACE (Palacio del Ayuntamiento) faces the *Zócalo's* s. side (M: Zócalo, line 2). It serves as City Hall. The original building at the square's southwest corner dates from 1724. On the front arcade are coat-of-arms mosaics depicting Mexican cities, states and regions, including Coyoacán, site of the first city hall in the Valley of Mexico; the 1168 founding of Aztec capital Tenochtitlan; and the Villa Rica de la Vera Cruz, said to be the first city hall in the continental Americas.

In order to see the Hall of Rulers (Salón Virreyes) and the Legislative Assembly Hall (Sala de Cabildos) visitors must present identification and sign in at the visitor desk on the first floor. The exhibit halls are located on the second floor. The Hall of Rulers is a collection of paintings—including one of Hernando Cortés—displayed in two rooms. Adjacent to these rooms is the room where the Mexican legislative assembly met until 1928; it contains original furniture. Spanish-only guided tours are available. Allow 30 minutes minimum. Tues.-Sun. 10-5; closed major holidays. Free.

NATIONAL MUSEUM OF CULTURES (Museo Nacional de Las Culturas) is at Calle Moneda #13, near the cathedral and just e. of the *Zócalo* (M: Zócalo, line 2). This museum once displayed the Mexican archeological treasures now housed at the National Museum of Anthropology in Chapultepec Park *(see attraction listing on page 301)*. Now it provides a general overview of anthropology by means of various artifacts and replicas, with three floors of exhibit halls grouped around a lovely central patio. The African and South Seas displays are particularly noteworthy. A striking Rufino Tamayo mural in the lobby depicts the 1910 Revolution. Exhibit information is in Spanish.

Allow 2 hours minimum. Tues.-Sun. 9:30-5:45; closed major holidays. Free. Phone (55) 5542-0165.

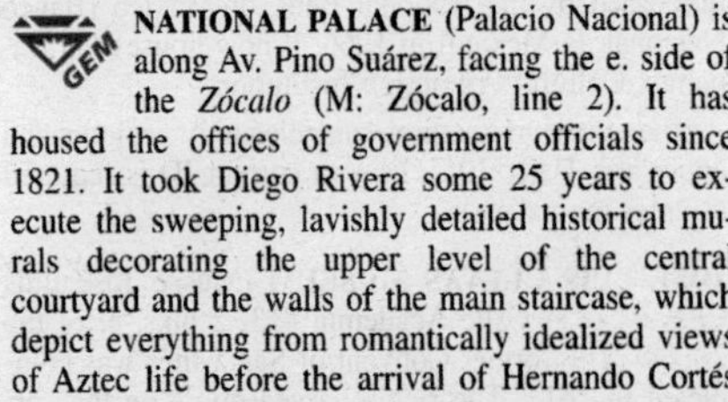

NATIONAL PALACE (Palacio Nacional) is along Av. Pino Suárez, facing the e. side of the *Zócalo* (M: Zócalo, line 2). It has housed the offices of government officials since 1821. It took Diego Rivera some 25 years to execute the sweeping, lavishly detailed historical murals decorating the upper level of the central courtyard and the walls of the main staircase, which depict everything from romantically idealized views of Aztec life before the arrival of Hernando Cortés to the bloody 1910 Revolution.

Hanging over the central doorway is the Independence Bell, tolled by Father Miguel Hidalgo in 1810 to proclaim Mexican independence from Spain; on Sept. 15 Mexico's president rings the bell in an annual ceremonial re-enactment of Hidalgo's plea for freedom.

There also are two museums inside the palace. The Benito Juárez Museum consists of several large rooms displaying furnishings, manuscripts, artwork and other artifacts associated with the former Mexican president; the Parliamentary Museum has elegant fabric-covered walls, gold chandeliers, flags and the formal "well" used for parliamentary sessions. At the palace's far end is a relaxing garden with benches and stone fountains.

Allow 1 hour, 30 minutes minimum. Tues.-Sun. 9-4:30. Free (personal identification is required).

NATIONAL PAWN SHOP (Nacional Monte de Piedad) is near the n.w. corner of the *Zócalo* at Monte de Piedad #7 and Av. 5 de Mayo (M: Allende or Zócalo, line 2). This four-story structure stands on the site of an Aztec palace occupied by the emperor Moctezuma and later entirely rebuilt in colonial style by Hernando Cortés. The pawn shop was established in 1775 to provide poor citizens with loans on personal property at low interest rates. Run by the government, it houses a vast quantity of items—everything from jewelry and antique clocks to huge crystal chandeliers and framed art. While this is strictly a commercial operation, the exhibit salons are fascinating to wander through.

Public parking is not available. Allow 1 hour minimum. Mon.-Fri. 9-6, Sat. 9-3; closed Mexican holidays. Free. Phone (55) 5278-1800.

ZOCALO is bounded by avs. Corregidora, Seminario (Pino Suárez), Madero and Monte de Piedad (M: Zócalo, line 2). The *Zócalo* (SOH-cah-loh), officially Plaza de la Constitución, is a vast, open expanse of concrete covering nearly 10 acres; only Moscow's Red Square is larger. Emperor Moctezuma's palace and the Templo Mayor stood on the site when the Spanish made their way into the city of Tenochtitlan and proceeded to tear it to the ground.

The *Zócalo* (the word means "base of a pedestal") follows the Spanish blueprint for colonial

Day Without Car (continued)

Physically disabled drivers are not exempted from the regulation. If you're driving your own vehicle, keep in mind that police officers in jurisdictions within the greater metropolitan area may stop drivers with foreign plates for "violating" driving restrictions in an attempt to extract a bribe. Signs explaining the program are posted along major highways entering the metropolitan area. Many of the signs, however, are in Spanish. There is a Web site that provides air quality reports and related information; the address is www.sima.org.mx.

Note: When pollution is extremely heavy (particularly during the winter months), emergency driving restrictions may be mandated. "Double Day Without Car" (Doble Hoy No Circula) means that driving is prohibited a second day during the week, based on whether the last digit of the license plate is odd (1, 3, 5, 7 or 9) or even (2, 4, 6, 8 or 0). Before any such decision is made, announcements are broadcast on radio and TV specifying the contingency days added to the normal restriction, and those vehicles affected.

settlements staked out in the Americas: a central plaza surrounded by a cathedral and government buildings. A Mexican flag stands in the center of the square; residents come here to protest as well as to celebrate and stroll.

Special events are held regularly. An elaborate flag-lowering ceremony performed daily at 6 p.m. is filled with the flourishes of formal pomp and circumstance. Hundreds of thousands of people flock to the square for the Sept. 15 and 16 Independence Day celebrations. (For a panoramic view of either proceeding, sit outside on the seventh-floor dining terrace at the Majestic Hotel, Avenida Madero on the west side of the *Zócalo.*)

Note: This is a very crowded, congested part of the city. Do not even attempt to negotiate the traffic or find a place to park on your own. If you want to walk around and explore for an hour or so, hire a licensed guide, a private driver or a hotel taxi to drop you off, wait and then take you back to where you're staying. Avoid the *Zócalo* and surrounding streets after dark.

Within the Historic Center

CHURCH AND HOSPITAL OF JESUS THE NAZARENE (Iglesia y Hospital de Jesús Nazareno) are 3 blks. s. of the *Zócalo* on Avenida República del Salvador, between avenidas 20 de Noviembre and Pino Suárez (M: Pino Suárez, lines 1 and 2). The first hospital in Mexico is said to stand on the site where Hernando Cortés and Aztec emperor Moctezuma had their first meeting in 1519; a large stone tablet on Pino Suárez next to the church commemorates the occasion. The chapel has an entrance on Salvador at Pino Suárez; inside are Cortés' remains. A plaque marking the tomb of the *conquistador* can be seen on the left wall of the main altar.

The dramatic José Clemente Orozco mural "Apocalypse" covers the ceiling and upper walls of the church's choir mezzanine. Allow 30 minutes minimum. Sat. 1-8, Sun. 7 a.m.-8 p.m.; hours vary Mon.-Fri. Rectory open Tues.-Fri. 11-noon and 1:15-2. Free.

EX-CONVENT AND TEMPLE OF REGINA COELI (Ex-Convento y Templo de Regina Coeli) is about 5 blks. s.w. of the *Zócalo* at calles Regina and Bolívar (M: Isabel la Católica, line 1); street parking is very limited. Construction began in 1655, although it was not consecrated until 1731. Once the Convent of the Nuns of the Conception in Mexico, it received its present name in 1756.

The sumptuous Medina-Picasso Chapel, built in 1733, encompasses an entire block and is considered a masterpiece of Churrigueresque architecture. It contains three altarpieces with works by Villalpando Rodríguez Juárez and other 18th-century painters. A striking niche in the main altar is adorned with tortoiseshell and mother-of-pearl. Allow 30 minutes minimum. Daily 8-1 and 4-8. Donations.

ITURBIDE PALACE (Palacio de Iturbide) is w. of the *Zócalo* at Av. Madero #17 near Bolívar (M: Bellas Artes, lines 2 and 8). Commissioned by the Count of San Mateo de Valparaíso as a dowry for his daughter, this building exhibits the characteristic 18th-century baroque architectural style, with some Italian influence. It became a hotel in 1850 and was purchased by the National Bank of Mexico (Banco Nacional de México) in 1966. It now houses the Banamex Cultural Promotion Institution.

The interior features an elegantly colonnaded courtyard. Daily 10-7. Free (a current ID is required to enter the palace).

JOSE LUIS CUEVAS MUSEUM (Museo José Luis Cuevas) is at Calle Academia #13, 2 blks. e. of the *Zócalo*. The former Convent of Santa Inés was completed in 1612. The richly carved doors on the corner of Called Moneda depict the saint's life and death and portraits of the convent's founders. Cuevas, a highly regarded contemporary artist, created the monumental sculpture "The Giantess" that stands in the center of the courtyard. Of the museum's approximately 3,000 works, about a third are by Cuevas. Tues.-Sun. 10-6. Admission about $1 (U.S.).

MINISTRY OF PUBLIC EDUCATION (Secretaria de Educación Pública) is n. of the Great Temple at República de Argentina #28 (M: Zócalo, line 2). The walls of this building were perhaps Diego Rivera's greatest canvas; almost every space on the three floors is covered with murals symbolizing Mexican life, history and culture.

The first floor contains images of daily rural life, depictions of industry and the celebration of such truly Mexican festivities as the Day of the Dead. Notably missing from these scenes is Rivera's customary political satire; instead, he emphasized national pride. Panels on the second and third floors focus on Mexican workers, the nation's heroic leaders, the 1910 Revolution and such familiar Rivera targets as capitalist greed. Mon.-Fri. 9-6. Free.

MUSEUM OF MEXICO CITY (Museo de la Ciudad de México) is 3 blks. s. of the *Zócalo* at Pino Suárez #30, near República del Salvador (M: Pino Suárez, line 2). The building housing this museum was originally given by Hernán Cortés to a member of his crew; in the late 19th century it was converted into a two-story palace with stone archways and several interior courtyard gardens.

The vast collection surveys the history, culture and people of both the ancient and modern city. Large exhibits that can be observed from overhead catwalks depict daily life in the early 1500s in the Aztec city of Tenochtitlan, where canoes were the primary means of conveyance for people and goods. Other displays show how neighborhoods that exist today, like Tacuba and Coyoacán, looked back then. Artwork on view includes Aztec sculptures, feather-adorned pieces, gold bracelets, murals and paintings by Frida Kahlo and Diego Rivera.

Another permanent display features black-and-white images of gridlocked cars, turbulent political scenes, earthquake damage and a sea of humanity in the *Zócalo,* all dramatically evoking the day-to-day challenges of living in this enormous metropolis. Temporary rotating exhibits are presented regularly.

Allow 2 hours minimum. Tues.-Sun. 10-6. Admission about $3.50 (U.S.); free (ages 0-2). Phone (55) 5522-9936.

OLD COLLEGE OF SAN ILDEFONSO (Antiguo Colegio de San Ildefonso) is just n. of the Great Temple (Templo Mayor) and 2 blks. n. and just e. of the *Zócalo* at Avenida Justo Sierra #16, between avenidas República de Argentina and del Carmen (M: Zócalo, line 2). This outstanding colonial edifice was built in 1749 as the Jesuit School of San Ildefonso. Converted to a museum, the renovated structure has three floors exhibiting colonial works of art, paintings by Fernando Leal and traveling exhibitions.

José Clemente Orozco murals depicting post-Revolutionary Mexico surround the main patio. The Patio of the Undergraduates (Patio de Los Pasantes), with just three corridors, has a small courtyard featuring Orozco and Diego Rivera murals painted in the 1920s. Guided tours are available. Allow 2 hours minimum. Tues.-Sun. 10-5:30; closed major Mexican holidays. Admission about $4.50 (U.S.), free (ages 0-12). Admission for murals only $2. Free to all Tues. Rental fee for audio guide $5.

SANTO DOMINGO CHURCH (Iglesia de Santo Domingo) is on República de Venezuela (M: Allende, line 2), facing the n. side of Santo Domingo Plaza. The original church, destroyed by a flood, was the first founded in Mexico by the Dominicans. The present building, dating from 1736, has a beautiful baroque exterior highlighted by ornately carved Corinthian columns. Inside is a chapel containing *milagros,* offerings given by the devout in thanks for a miraculous cure from infirmity or disease.

SANTO DOMINGO PLAZA is 3 blks. n.w. of the *Zócalo,* bounded by República de Venezuela, República de Peru, República de Chile and República de Brasil (M: Zócalo, line 2). It is one of the best preserved colonial squares in the city. Dating from about 1550, the plaza is surrounded by charming old buildings. It also is the home of *los evangelistas.* These professional typists, writers and editors ply their trades from under arcades on the west side of the plaza, a service begun by public scribes in the 1850s for citizens unable to write.

Museum of Mexican Medicine (Museo de Medicina Mexicana) is at the opposite end of the plaza at República de Brasil and República de Venezuela. Formerly a college of medicine, it has rooms dedicated to medical equipment—some of it archaic—and a re-creation of an old pharmacy. Some of the exhibits, such as one detailing aborted fetuses at different stages, are quite graphic. **Note:** Although a few exhibit areas are open, the majority of the museum is closed for ongoing renovations. Daily 10-6. Free.

SUPREME COURT OF JUSTICE (Suprema Corte de Justicia) is just s. of the National Palace at Pino Suárez and Corregidora. Built between 1935 and 1941 at the site of ancient Plaza del Volador, this building has a sober exterior, but the interior features an interesting set of staircases leading to the Hall of Lost Steps (Salón de los Pasos Perdidos), which contains two José Clemente Orozco murals depicting workers' rights, nationalism and concepts of justice.

Calle Corregidora runs between the court building and the National Palace. Prior to the Spanish conquest a canal traversed this area, part of a system that connected Tenochtitlan to other Aztec centers around Lake Texcoco. Today evidence of the ancient waterway can still be seen, although Corregidora is now a pedestrian-only thoroughfare filled with vendor stalls. Court open Mon.-Fri. 9-5:30. Free.

Alameda Park and Vicinity

ALAMEDA PARK lies just w. of the Palace of Fine Arts between avs. Juárez and Hidalgo. Two Metro stations are close by: Hidalgo (lines 2 and 3) is at the intersection of Hidalgo and Paseo de la Reforma, a block off the park's northwest corner; Bellas Artes (lines 2 and 8) is at the park's northeast corner. A green retreat in the middle of Mexico City's concrete jungle, this rectangular, centrally located park—formerly an Aztec market—is surrounded by museums, theaters, hotels and restaurants.

Landscaped with poplars, ash and willow trees, the Alameda contains fountains, 19th-century French sculptures and a Moorish kiosk. Sundays bring out the crowds, with families, cotton candy and ice cream vendors, and lovers of all ages sharing the park. Organ grinders delight children, and there are free music concerts.

Juárez Monument (Juárez Hemiciclo) faces Av. Juárez along the park's southern boundary. "Hemiciclo" refers to the monument's semicircular design. It honors the liberal president of Mexico (1858-72); his marble statue sits on a pedestal surrounded by columns. Benito Juárez's Mar. 21 birthday is celebrated at the park.

CHURCH OF THE CONVENT OF CORPUS CHRISTI is at Av. Juárez #44, opposite the s. side of Alameda Park (M: Bellas Artes, lines 2 and 8). Part of the first convent to accept noble indigenous women and the daughters of Indian chieftains, this sober baroque building was later a training college for teachers and until 1985 housed the National Museum of Popular Art and Industries. The central portal has arched doors flanked by pilasters supporting a cornice and a small pediment.

DIEGO RIVERA MURAL MUSEUM (Museo Mural Diego Rivera) is at calles Balderas and Colón, just w. of Alameda Park (M: Hidalgo, lines 2 and 3). It was built specifically to house the epic mural "Dream of a Sunday Afternoon in the Alameda Central," which had originally been painted on a wall of the Hotel del Prado across the street. Although the hotel was torn down following damage

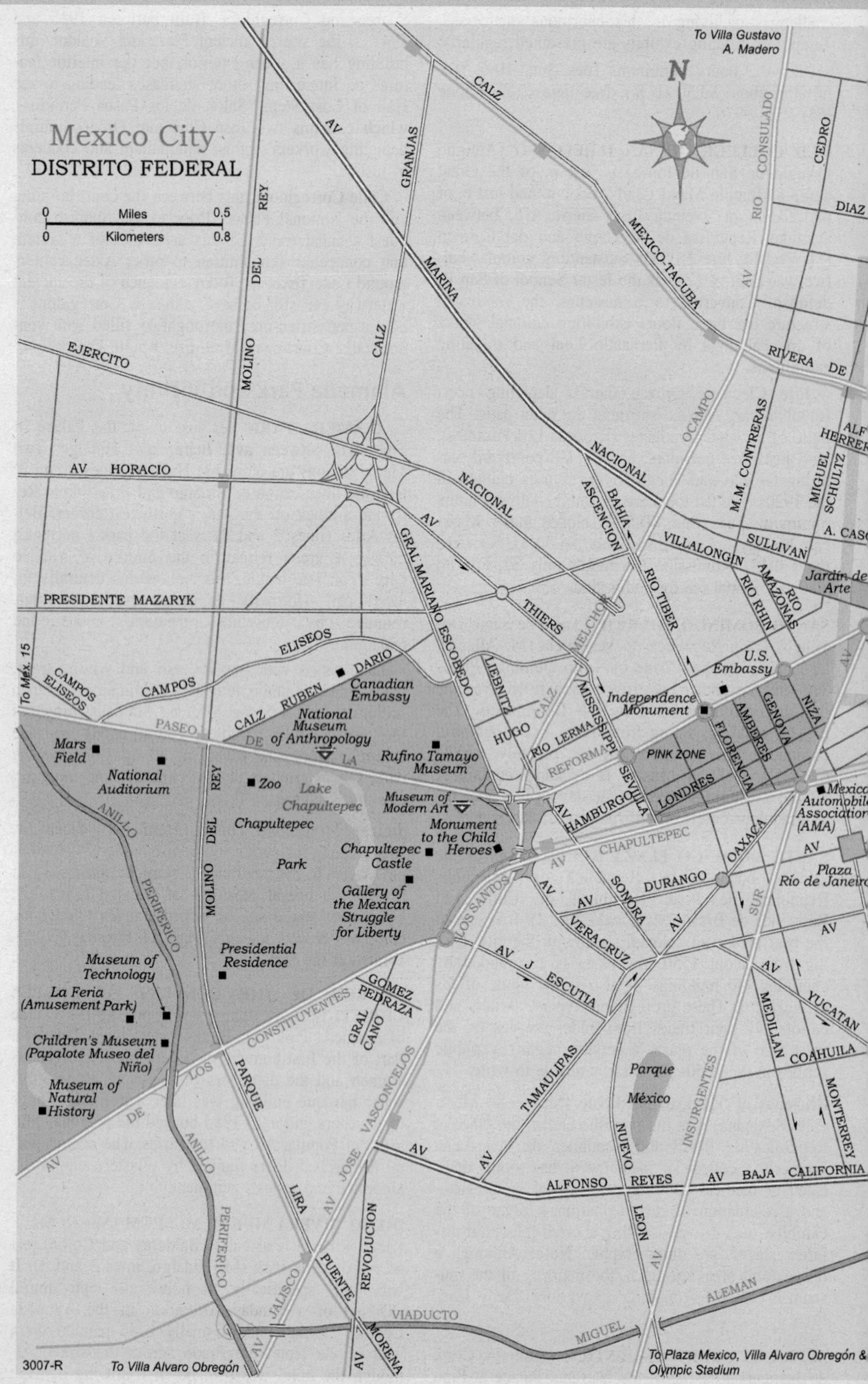

Mexico City
DISTRITO FEDERAL
0 Miles 0.5
0 Kilometers 0.8
N
To Villa Gustavo A. Madero
Mars Field
National Auditorium
Zoo
Lake Chapultepec
Chapultepec Park
National Museum of Anthropology
Canadian Embassy
Rufino Tamayo Museum
Museum of Modern Art
Monument to the Child Heroes
Chapultepec Castle
Gallery of the Mexican Struggle for Liberty
Presidential Residence
Museum of Technology
La Feria (Amusement Park)
Children's Museum (Papalote Museo del Niño)
Museum of Natural History
Independence Monument
U.S. Embassy
PINK ZONE
Jardín de Arte
Mexico Automobile Association (AMA)
Plaza Río de Janeiro
Parque México
To Méx. 15
To Villa Alvaro Obregón
To Plaza Mexico, Villa Alvaro Obregón & Olympic Stadium
3007-R

© AAA
To Villa Gustavo A. Madero & Basilica of Our Lady of Guadalupe
To Basilica of Our Lady of Guadalupe
FOR MORE DETAIL SEE DOWNTOWN AREA MAP
Plaza of the Three Cultures
Mercado Lagunilla
MEXICO CITY HISTORIC CENTER
Monument to the Revolution
Plaza de la República
Alameda
Zócalo
Legislative Palace
Parque de las Americas
To Benito Juárez International Airport
To Coyoacán
To Tlalpan & Xochimilco
RAPID TRANSIT
STATION
MANUEL GONZALEZ
CANAL DEL NORTE
RICARDO FLORES MAGON
MIRON
MOSQUETA
VIOLETA
RAYON
HEROS DE GRANADITAS
ECUADOR
COSTA RICA
RIVERO
PASEO DE LA REFORMA
HEROES FERROCARRILES
DE LA REVOLUCION
SAN COSME
AV PUENTE DE ALVARADO
AV HIDALGO
CALZ. TACUBA
REP DE VENEZUELA
GUATEMALA
MONEDA
EMILIANO ZAPATA
CORREGIDORA
5 DE MAYO
AV MADERO
AV JUAREZ
16 DE SEPTIEMBRE
V CARRANZA
ARTICULO 123
COLON
D GUERRA
ATENAS
GEN PRIM
TOLSA
ARCOS DE BELEN
JM IZAZAGA
DR. RIO DE LA LOZA
FRAY SERVANDO DE TERESA MIER
CARRETONES
AV DEL TRABAJO
GUERRERO
LAZARO CARDENAS
CHILE
AV PERALVILLO
JESUS CARRANZA
ORTEGA
ALLENDE
REP DE BRASIL
AV REP DE ARGENTINA
AZTECAS
VIDAL ALCOCER
CARMEN
CALLE ACADEMIA
CORREO MAYOR
JESUS MARIA
ANILLO DE CIRCUNVALACION
MORAZAN
AV BUCARELI
BALDERAS
LUIS MOYA
BOLIVAR
ISABEL LA CATOLICA
5 DE FEBREDO
AV 20 DE NOVIEMBRE
CALZ PINO SUAREZ
ARRIAGA
RAMIREZ
PARIS
VERSALLES
ROMA
LIVERPOOL
MARSELLA
INSURGENTES
DURANGO
OBREGON
DR. CLAUDIO BERNARD
LICEAGA
ALEMAN
PASTEUR
JOSE T CUELLAR
DR VERTIZ
CUAUHTEMOC
CALZ. SAN ANTONIO ABAD
CALZ DE LA VIGA
FRANCISCO
AV DEL TALLER
DR MARQUEZ
JUAN A MATEOS
ORIZABA
AV MORELOS
CALZADA DEL CHABACANO
AV CENTRAL
PEON CONTRERAS
VIADUCTO MIGUEL ALEMAN
COYUYO
DIAGONAL SAN ANTONIO
AVENIDA

caused by the 1985 earthquake, the mural weathered the disaster and was carefully moved to this museum. The central figures—among a gallery of Mexican historical characters—enjoying a Sunday promenade in the park are the artist (portrayed as a child); his wife, fellow painter Frida Kahlo; and Catrina, a clothed skeleton *(calavera)* representing the works of satirist José Guadalupe Posada.

Publications and lithographs on the walls provide information about the historical characters depicted in the mural. The second floor has information about Rivera's life and work and also is used for temporary art exhibits. Allow 30 minutes minimum. Tues.-Sun. 10-6; closed major Mexican holidays. Admission about $1.50 (U.S.); free to all Sun. Phone (55) 5510-2329.

FRANZ MAYER MUSEUM (Museo Franz Mayer) is at Av. Hidalgo #45 (Plaza de la Santa Veracruz), opposite the n. side of Alameda Park (M: Bellas Artes, lines 2 and 8). A former convent dating from the second half of the 16th century, it was a hospital for much of its existence until closing in 1966; in 1989 it was restored to house an enormous and valuable collection of viceregal, European and Asiatic paintings and sculptures.

Among the objects on view are ceramics, silver, textiles, maps and navigation instruments. The museum also organizes temporary exhibits. Food is available. Tues.-Sun. 10-5. Admission about $1.50 (U.S.); free to all Tues. Phone (55) 5518-2265.

HOUSE OF TILES (Casa de Los Azulejos) is at Av. Francisco I. Madero #4, about 2 blks. e. of the Alameda (M: Bellas Artes, lines 2 and 8). This is one of the city's finest colonial mansions. It was built in 1596 to be the residence of the Counts of Orizaba. The entire exterior is covered with decorative blue and white tiles from Puebla; the bronze balustrade was brought from China.

The flagship of the Sanborn's restaurant chain has occupied the building since 1919. Stop in for a look at the murals in the main dining room and the José Clemente Orozco mural that adorns the wall of the huge staircase. Daily 7 a.m.-1 a.m.

LATIN-AMERICAN TOWER (Torre Latino) is at avs. Madero and Lázaro Cárdenas (M: Bellas Artes, lines 2 and 8); entrances are on both streets. At 595 feet, this slender, 44-story glass skyscraper was once the city's tallest but now ranks fourth. The tower rests on floating piers sunk deep into the underlying clay; as the city's first building to have an adequate foundation, it has survived every earth tremor that has occurred since its 1956 construction. An elevator takes visitors to the 37th floor, where there is a cafe; a small museum is on the 38th floor.

The open-air observation deck on the 44th floor offers magnificent views of the city and the surrounding mountains on rare smog-free days; the 42nd and 43rd floors are enclosed for rainy day viewing. Allow 1 hour minimum. Daily 9 a.m.-10 p.m. Observation deck admission about $5 (U.S.), $4 (children and senior citizens); tickets can be purchased at a booth near the elevators. Phone (55) 5518-7423.

MAIN POST OFFICE (Correo Mayor) is on the corner of avs. Tacuba and Eje Central Lázaro Cárdenas across from the Palace of Fine Arts (M: Bellas Artes, lines 2 and 8). Designed by Italian architect Adam Boari—who also was responsible for the Palace of Fine Arts—and in operation as a post office since 1907, this building incorporates Gothic, Moorish, Renaissance, Spanish and Venetian elements. The facade is covered with yellow-rose quarry stone from the state of Hidalgo. Most of the interior ironwork, banisters and furnishings were imported.

Within the building, the Philatelic Museum (Museo Filatélico) displays stamp collections and antique Mexican postal equipment. The post office also is the point of reference for the city's street numbering system. Museum open Mon.-Fri. 9-6, Sat. 10-2.

NATIONAL ART MUSEUM (Museo Nacional de Arte) is at Calzada Tacuba #8, directly e. of the Palace of Fine Arts (M: Bellas Artes, lines 2 and 8). Formerly the Hospital of San Andrés and later the Palace of Communications, this building's gray stone facade is enhanced by wrought iron and wooden doors and window frames. The museum provides an overview of Mexican art, its 24 halls exhibiting works ranging from 17th- and 18th-century paintings of New Spain through 19th-century landscapes and portraits to 20th-century modernism.

Particularly noteworthy are the rooms devoted to José Guadalupe Posada and María Asúnsolo. Two elegant curved staircases at the back of the museum lead to the upper levels; at the bottom are two lions supporting a buttress with five lamps. The underside of one stairwell is decorated with the painting "Peace Defeating War." Tues.-Sun. 10-5:30. Admission about $3.25 (U.S.) but can vary by exhibition; free to all Sun. Phone (55) 5130-3400.

El Caballito stands in the center of the square fronting the museum. "The Little Horse" is the work of Manuel Tolsá. The 30-ton sculpture, showing King Charles IV of Spain astride his horse, is considered one of the world's finest equestrian statues. It was cast in 1803 from a single piece of bronze.

Palace of Mining (Palacio de Minería) is across from the museum at Tacuba #5. This impressive neoclassic building, also designed by Tolsá, has several patios and exhibits finely crafted stonework. Mon.-Fri. 9-8. Free.

NATIONAL MUSEUM OF ENGRAVING (Museo Nacional de la Estampa) is at Hidalgo #39 next to the Franz Mayer Museum (M: Bellas Artes, lines 2 and 8). Housed in a handsomely restored 16th-century building, it focuses on the graphic arts. The second floor has permanent exhibits, notably the pointed political cartoons and cavorting skeleton figures of 19th-century Mexican artist José Guadalupe

Posada. Temporary exhibits of contemporary art are on the first floor. Tues.-Sun. 10-6. Admission 10 pesos.

GEM **PALACE OF FINE ARTS** (Palacio de Bellas Artes) is on Calle Lopez Peralta at the e. end of Alameda Park (M: Bellas Artes, lines 2 and 8). It was begun in 1904 by Italian architect Adamo Boari, interrupted by the Revolution of 1910 and finally dedicated in 1934, a legacy of Porfirio Díaz's economically progressive but politically oppressive regime. Because of enormous weight and a swampy subsoil, the building has settled considerably since its construction.

The decorative sculptures on the facade are the building's highlight. They include garlands, flowers, masks and a sculptural group called "Harmony." A sculpture of Pegasus stands in the outdoor esplanade. Inside the look is pure 1930s Art Deco, augmented by second- and third-floor murals by Diego Rivera, José Clemente Orozco and David Alfaro Siqueiros. Note in particular "Man in Control of His Universe," Rivera's caustic rendering of capitalism, originally commissioned for New York City's Rockefeller Center in 1933.

The city's premier cultural center is the home of the National Opera Company, the National Ballet of Mexico, the National Dance Company and the National Symphony Orchestra. The building also houses the National Museum of Architecture, which contains models, sketches, photographs and draft plans. Temporary exhibitions of art, sculpture and photography are regularly mounted.

Open daily 9-9. Admission to museum and to view the murals 25 pesos (about $2.40 U.S.), free (ages 0-11 and students with ID). Phone (55) 5512-2593, ext. 152.

Ballet Folklórico de México is presented in the palace theater. This theatrically colorful spectacle showcases many forms of Mexican folk music and dance. The theater is famed for its 22-ton crystal curtain; actually a double-walled steel curtain, the side facing the audience was crafted from 1 million pieces of opalescent glass that resemble a large window and depict snowcapped peaks Popocatépetl and Iztaccíhuatl. The half-hour curtain show is given only before the Sunday morning performance. *Also see Concerts, page 310.*

Performances are given Sun. at 9:30 and 8:30 p.m., Wed. at 8:30 p.m. Tickets $25-$40 (U.S.). Phone (55) 5325-9000 for Ticketmaster.

SAN FERNANDO CHURCH AND CEMETERY is n.w. of Alameda Park at Vicente Guerrero #39 (M: Hidalgo, lines 2 and 3). At one end of the plaza is the church, a former monastery built in the mid-18th century. The Churrigueresque facade survived the monastery's dismantlement after the monks were expelled in 1860. The adjacent cemetery holds the remains of several prominent Mexican families; the last person buried here was former president Benito Juárez. Daily 8-3. Free.

SAN FRANCISCO CHURCH is on Av. Madero, 2 blks. e. of Alameda Park and almost directly across from Sanborn's (M: Bellas Artes, lines 2 and 8). Begun in 1524 with money granted by Hernando Cortés, it was long the center of Catholicism in America and headquarters of the Franciscan Order. The original complex, fragments of which are still visible, also comprised a monastery and training school for Franciscan missionaries. The present church dates from the 18th century and has an elaborately Churrigueresque facade.

Chapultepec Park and Vicinity

CHAPULTEPEC CASTLE (Castillo de Chapultepec) is within Chapultepec Park (M: Chapultepec, line 1). It stands atop a 200-foot-high hill overlooking the central part of the city; the stony outcrop was once used by Aztec emperors as a summer retreat. Construction of the castle began in 1783. Completed in 1840, it was fortified and became a military college. When it was attacked and taken in 1847 by U.S. forces during the Mexican-American War, the castle was defended solely by its young cadets. After passing through a succession of leaders it was finally bequeathed to the nation in 1939 by President Lázaro Cárdenas.

The climb to the castle along a paved walkway winding up Chapultepec Hill is fairly steep and takes about 20 minutes. En route there are frequent views of the downtown skyline. A train that is boarded inside the park entrance also carries passengers up the hill. Admission $4.50 U.S. (includes admission to the National Museum of History), free (ages 0-12 and 60+). Free to all Sun. Parking fee for Chapultepec Park $3 per day. Train fare about $2.

Caracol Museum/Gallery of History (Museo de Caracol/Galería de Historia) is within Chapultepec Park, about halfway up the hill to Chapultepec Castle. The name "caracol" refers to the building's spiral shape, which resembles a snail's shell.

Twelve descending *salas* (exhibit halls) offer detailed, colorful dioramas that depict memorable past events in Mexican history, including Father Miguel Hidalgo's military campaign to secure independence from Spain, the Mexican-American War, French intervention in the 1860s and the Mexican Revolution of 1910. The chamber of red *tezontle* (volcanic) stone at the end of this walk through the past is covered with an impressive dome and is dominated by three objects: the national flag, a carved-stone eagle and a facsimile of the 1917 Constitution. Explanations are in Spanish.

Allow 1 hour minimum. Tues.-Sun. 9-4; guided tours are given Tues.-Fri. at 10 and 2. Admission $3.70 (U.S.), free (ages 0-13 and 60+). Free to all Sun. Parking fee for Chapultepec Park $3 per day.

National Museum of History (Museo Nacional de Historia) is the first building before Chapultepec Castle and adjacent to it; there is no sign. A guided tour proceeds through 12 *salas* (exhibit halls) tracing Mexican history from the Spanish conquest to the Revolution of 1910 and the adoption of the 1917 constitution. Weapons, paintings, clothing, furniture and maps are displayed. The *Salón de Virreyes* contains portraits of historical figures and rulers from Hernando Cortés to 20th-century Mexican presidents, while the *Salón de Malaquitas* has doors and other objects fashioned out of malachite.

Murals depict important events in the nation's history, and there also is a striking mural painting of Mexican artists such as Jorge Gonzalez Camarena and José Clemente Orozco. Exhibit information is in Spanish.

Flash photography is not permitted. Allow 2 hours minimum. Tues.-Sun. 9-5.

CHAPULTEPEC PARK (Bosque de Chapultepec) sprawls on either side of Paseo de la Reforma beginning about 4 blks. w. of the Zona Rosa (M: Chapultepec, line 1; Auditorio and Constituyentes, line 7). It is the oldest natural park in North America and one of the largest and most varied in the world. After the establishment of Tenochtitlán, Aztec emperors used Chapultepec Hill, within today's park, for summer relaxation.

Despite the wear and tear it's fascinating to stroll along the cobbled walkways, as much for the people-watching as anything else. You won't see many foreign tourists here; the park is very much a gathering place for city residents. Sunday is the best day to visit, as families converge to enjoy their day off at this enormous green space.

Chapultepec is divided into three sections. Some of the city's most notable museums are grouped in the oldest (eastern) section ("1a Sección"), including the National Museum of Anthropology, the Museum of Modern Art and the National Museum of History in Chapultepec Castle. The section of the park west of Calzada Molino del Rey ("2a Sección") is newer and contains many of the kid-oriented attractions. The Pines (Los Piños), the Mexican president's residence, is just east of Molino del Rey; it is heavily guarded and cannot be visited.

If you plan to spend most of the day and would rather not sample the offerings of food vendors, bring a lunch. Eastern section open daily 5-5; some attractions are closed Mon. Free; separate admissions charged for attractions. Most are free on Sun.

Chapultepec Park Zoo (Parque Zoológico de Chapultepec) is in the eastern section, s. of Paseo de la Reforma off Calz. Chivatito (near the National Museum of Anthropology). It displays giant pandas—this is one of the few zoos to have successfully bred them in captivity—a white tiger and other animals in natural habitats. There's also an aviary, a venomous snake exhibit and a miniature train ride. Tues.-Sun. 9-4:30. Free; admission to snake exhibit about $2.25 (U.S.).

Children's Museum (Papalote Museo del Niño) is at Av. Constituyentes #268 in the park's second (western) section (near the Anillo Periférico). Themed areas explore the human body, science, computers and artistic expression, among other subjects. Kids will love the contraption that makes giant soap bubbles. In addition to the many interactive, hands-on activities, the museum also has an IMAX theater alternating two different films several times daily.

Food is available. Mon.-Fri. 9-6 (also Thurs. 6-11 p.m.), Sat.-Sun. 10-7. Admission 70 pesos (about $6.80 U.S.); 65 pesos (ages 2-11). Phone (55) 5237-1773.

Don Quixote Fountain (Fuente de Don Quijote) stands in Quixote Square, just off Gran Avenida, w. of Lake Chapultepec and s. of the Botanic Garden. The fountain is within a pavilion designed in the shape of a simple cube. A mural by Diego Rivera covering its bottom depicts the evolution of life by water. The hydraulic works in the vicinity receive water from the Río Lerma. Also on the square is a metallic structure housing two small sculptures of Quixote and sidekick Sancho Panza in the midst of an argument.

La Feria is in the park's second (western) section off the Circuito Bosque de Chapultepec, w. of the Anillo Periférico. This amusement park is dominated by a giant roller coaster, the Russian Mountain (Montaña Rusa), and has a number of other rides, as well as bumper cars and go-carts. Tues.-Sun. 10-6 (also Sat.-Sun. 6-9 p.m.). Admission about $6.50 (U.S.), $1 (children).

Lake House (Case del Lago) is in the heart of the park's old section, on the western shore of Lake Chapultepec (Lago de Chapultepec). It functions as a cultural center and as a setting for public events. Rowboats can be rented. A short distance west of the lake is the park's Botanical Garden (Jardín Botánico).

Monument to the Child Heroes (Monumento de Los Niños Héroes) is near the park's main entrance. The group of columns memorializes six cadets who were among those defending Chapultepec Castle, then a military college, against American troops at the height of the Mexican-American War in 1847. They reputedly leaped to their deaths wrapped in the Mexican flag rather than be captured.

Museum of Natural History (Museo de Historia Natural) is in the park's second (western) section off the Circuito Bosque de Chapultepec. It consists of 10 interconnecting domes that house nature dioramas and biological, geological and astronomical exhibits. The museum's insect collection is a highlight. Tues.-Sun. 10-5. Admission about $1.75 (U.S.); free to all Tues.

Museum of Technology (Museo Tecnológico) is in the park's second (western) section off the Circuito Bosque de Chapultepec, s. of the amusement park. Housed in a pyramidal structure, the museum has a planetarium and exhibits on aviation, energy, science and industry. The grounds feature installations of railroad cars and other industrial equipment. Tues.-Sun. 10-5. Free.

Rotunda of Illustrious Men (Rotonda de Los Hombres Ilustres) is in the western section of the park at avs. Constituyentes and Civil Dolores (M: Constituyentes, line 7). Dolores Cemetery, Mexico's national cemetery, is where many of the country's military leaders, political figures and important citizens have been laid to rest. The markers are arranged in circular fashion around an eternal flame. Artists Diego Rivera, David Alfaro Siqueiros and José Clemente Orozco are just a few of the notables interred. A map is available at the entrance building. Daily 6-6. Free.

INDEPENDENCE MONUMENT (Monumento a la Independencia) is in the circle at Paseo de la Reforma and Tiber (M: Insurgentes, line 1). A 150-foot-high column dating between 1901 and 1910, it is topped by a winged statue of Victory. The central figure at the base is Father Miguel Hidalgo; he is flanked by other leaders in the war for independence, including José María Morelos and Nicolás Bravo. The female statues represent Law, Justice, War and Peace.

This is one of several commanding landmarks that stand in the middle of *glorietas* (traffic circles) at principal intersections along Reforma; locals and visitors alike use them as geographical reference points.

GEM **MUSEUM OF MODERN ART** (Museo de Arte Moderno) occupies a circular building on the s. side of Paseo de la Reforma (at Calle Gandhi), near the entrance to Chapultepec Park (M: Chapultepec, line 1). It celebrates the diversity of 20th-century Mexican modern art and also presents temporary exhibitions by important international artists.

The permanent collection is housed in Xavier Villaurrutia and Carlos Pellicer halls. Among its many highlights are works by Mexico's three leading muralists—Diego Rivera, David Alfaro Siqueiros and José Clemente Orozco. Paintings by another major Mexican modern artist, Rufino Tamayo, include "The Sleeping Musicians" and "The Man Radiant in Happiness." This museum also contains Frida Kahlo's "The Two Fridas," one of the surrealist's most striking works.

José Guadalupe Posada, José Luis Cuevas and Juan Soriano are other well-known artists represented, along with contemporary figures like Oliverio Hinojosa and Irma Palacios. There is a sculpture garden surrounding the museum. Exhibit information is in Spanish. Food is available. Tues.-Sun. 10-5:30; closed official holidays. Admission 20 pesos (about $1.95 U.S.). Phone (55) 5553-6233.

GEM **NATIONAL MUSEUM OF ANTHROPOLOGY** (Museo Nacional de Antropología) is in Chapultepec Park off Calz. Mahatma Gandhi, facing the n. side of Paseo de la Reforma (M: Chapultepec, line 1 or Auditorio, line 7). A must-see stop for any Mexico City visitor, this is one of the world's finest museums.

The halls (*salas*) devoted to Mexico's early civilizations exhibit every conceivable type of artifact, including temple reconstructions, stone carvings, sculptures, ceramics, antique furniture, jewelry, masks, decorative objects, and arts and crafts. Dramatic lighting accentuates the remarkable artistry of the larger sculptures. Upstairs exhibit areas focus on the country's Indian cultures, showcasing musical instruments, traditional costumes and giant papier-mâché dolls.

Guided tour tickets can be purchased in the main entrance hall, which also has a bookstore selling English-language museum guides and an orientation theater where a 20-minute orientation film is shown. Most exhibit labeling is in Spanish; newer exhibits also include an English translation.

Guided tours in English are available. Food is available. Wheelchairs are available. Restrooms are provided. Tues.-Sun. 9-7. Admission 9-5 45 pesos (about $4.40 U.S.); admission 5-7 150 pesos (about $14.50). Free to all Sun. Guided tour fee 60 pesos (about $5.80). The fee to use a personal video camera is 30 pesos. Phone (55) 5553-6381, or (55) 5553-6386 for guided tour information.

Aztec Hall (Sala Mexica), on the ground floor, has as its focal point the 24-ton Aztec calendar stone, the Stone of the Sun (Piedra del Sol), with the face of the sun god carved in its center. The vivid statue of the goddess Coatlicue is rendered beheaded and wearing a skirt of snakes, and a scale model of the center of pre-Hispanic Tenochtitlan includes hundreds of detailed miniatures and an accompanying mural depicting the lake that once covered the area.

Maya Hall (Sala Maya), on the ground floor, spotlights a culture that was arguably the most advanced in all Mesoamerica. While the artifacts displayed here may not equal the grandeur of their lavishly decorated temples—the singular Mayan architectural achievement—they affirm the beauty of Mayan art. Many of the ceramic figurines, pieces of jewelry and death masks were retrieved from burial sites.

Teotihuacán Hall (Sala Teotihuacána), on the ground floor, is devoted to the first of Mexico's great pre-Hispanic cities. Here visitors can see a reproduction of the site's Temple of Quetzalcóatl, a huge statue of Chalchiuhtlicue, the Teotihuacán goddess of the "running waters," and displays from Cholula *(see separate listing under Central Mexico)*.

RUFINO TAMAYO MUSEUM (Museo Rufino Tamayo) is in Chapultepec Park, on the n. side of Paseo de la Reforma and west of Calzada Gandhi (M: Chapultepec, line 1). It displays the personal modern art collection of the Oaxacan painter and muralist, who died in 1991. Although Tamayo's work was initially criticized for its lack of political content, his reputation as a key figure of 20th-century Mexican art has grown over the years. In addition to Tamayo's own paintings, there are works by Pablo Picasso, Francis Bacon, Salvador Dali and Joan Miró. There also are changing international exhibitions.

Tues.-Sun. 10-6; closed Jan. 1, May 1 and Dec. 25. Admission 15 pesos (about $1.45 U.S.); free to all Sun. Phone (55) 5286-6519.

UNITED STATES EMBASSY is at Paseo de la Reforma and Río Danubio, just n. of the Zona Rosa (M: Insurgentes, line 1). Like many city buildings, it was built to withstand the impact of a powerful earthquake. Phone (55) 5080-2000 for Citizens Consular Services.

ZONA ROSA (Pink Zone) is about halfway between Alameda Central and Chapultepec Park (M: Insurgentes or Sevilla, line 1), roughly bordered by Paseo de la Reforma on the n., Av. Chapultepec on the s., Insurgentes on the e. and Sevilla on the w. This was long Mexico City's trendsetting neighborhood and favored tourist hotspot. However, its popularity has been eclipsed by the Polanco area, north of Chapultepec Park, which has many of the city's best hotels, restaurants and retailers.

Although still filled with shops, eateries and flashy nightspots, the Zona Rosa has become worn around the edges and also attracts groups of youth gangs who prey on anyone perceived to have money. Be careful if coming here for a night out, and arrange designated hotel taxi transportation both to and from your destination.

North of Downtown

BASILICA OF OUR LADY OF GUADALUPE (Basilica de Nuestra Señora de Guadalupe) is at Plaza de las Américas #1, about 10 km (6 mi.) n. of the Historic Center (M: La Villa, line 6). The site is located on a rocky hill (Cerro del Tepeyac) in the neighborhood (*colonia*) of Villa de Guadalupe. From the La Villa Metro station, walk n. 2 blks. on Calz. de Guadalupe, or take a taxi. The basilica, one of Roman Catholicism's holiest shrines, honors the Guadalupe Virgin, Mexico's patron saint.

Mexican Catholics believe that at this site in December 1531 the Virgin appeared to Juan Diego, a peasant Indian, and asked him that a church be built. After hearing this story, the local bishop requested proof. Diego returned on Dec. 12, his cape filled with roses that the Virgin had directed him to pick (a rather miraculous occurrence itself, considering the time of year). When the cape was opened, the roses had disappeared and a vivid image of the dark-skinned Virgin appeared on the folds of cloth.

A plaza with a visitor information center and a museum anchors the sprawling complex. A large underground parking lot is filled with a bazaar-like assemblage of religious-themed shops and street vendors selling handicrafts. Visitors enter the plaza through steel gates manned by armed guards. At the far end of the plaza is the ornate Old Basilica (Basilica Antigua), built about 1709 to house the sacred image.

Near the main entrance soars the New Basilica (Basilica Nueva), which can accommodate more than 10,000 people. Daringly modern in contrast, it was built in 1976. The cloth, in a gold frame and protected by bulletproof glass, hangs above the main altar; visitors pass beneath it via two moving walkways going in opposite directions. To the rear of the Old Basilica is a museum that displays religious artworks, including a collection of *retablos* (small devotional paintings). Other churches within the complex are the Church of the Indians (Parroquía de Indios) and the Chapel of the Well (El Pocito).

Allow 1 hour minimum. Tues.-Sun. 10-6. Churches free, museum admission about 55c (U.S.). Parking fee about $3, free with $10 worth of merchandise purchased from adjacent shops. Phone (55) 5577-6022.

CONVENT OF SAN AGUSTIN ACOLMAN—
see Acolman listing p. 272.

PLAZA OF THE THREE CULTURES (Plaza de Las Tres Culturas) is n. of the Historic Center and w. of Paseo de la Reforma Norte, at Av. Lázaro Cárdenas and Ricardo Flores Magón (M: Tlatelolco, line 3). The name comes from three vastly different influences—pre-Hispanic Aztec, colonial Spanish and contemporary Mexican—that have left their individual imprints on this plaza.

The ceremonial and trading center of Tlatelolco (tlah-tay-LOHL-koh) considerably predated the Aztec capital of Tenochtitlan. Even after it was absorbed by the Aztec city in 1473, Tlatelolco continued to function as an important market. It was from Tlatelolco that the Aztecs made their final stand against Spanish forces on Aug. 13, 1521.

Nearly 450 years later, the plaza was the scene of another massacre. On the eve of the 1968 Summer Olympic Games—with Mexico City in the world spotlight—a massive student protest over prevailing economic and social policies turned deadly when government troops were ordered to open fire.

The site ruins can be seen from raised walkways and give an indication of its former size. The Church of Santiago Tlatelolco, dating from 1609, has a restored interior that contains several frescoes and a strikingly simple stone altar. Next to the church are the remains of a monastery and former college where Franciscan friars taught the sons of Aztec nobility.

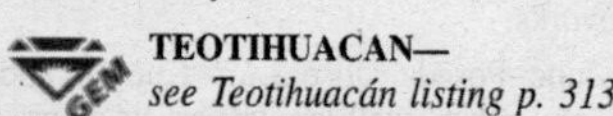

TEOTIHUACAN—
see Teotihuacán listing p. 313.

West of Downtown

REVOLUTION MONUMENT (Monumento a la Revolución) stands in the Plaza de la República, n. of Paseo de la Reforma and w. of the Alameda (M: Revolución, line 2). Topped by an imposing copper dome that surmounts four arches, it rises 250 feet. Buried under the four columns are four former presidents—Venustiano Carranza, Plutarco Calles, Lázaro Cárdenas and Francisco I. Madero—as well as revolutionary Pancho Villa. Porfirio Díaz, the dictator deposed by the Revolution of 1910, intended the building to house the government's legislative offices, but the uprising halted construction; it was dedicated as a monument in the 1930s.

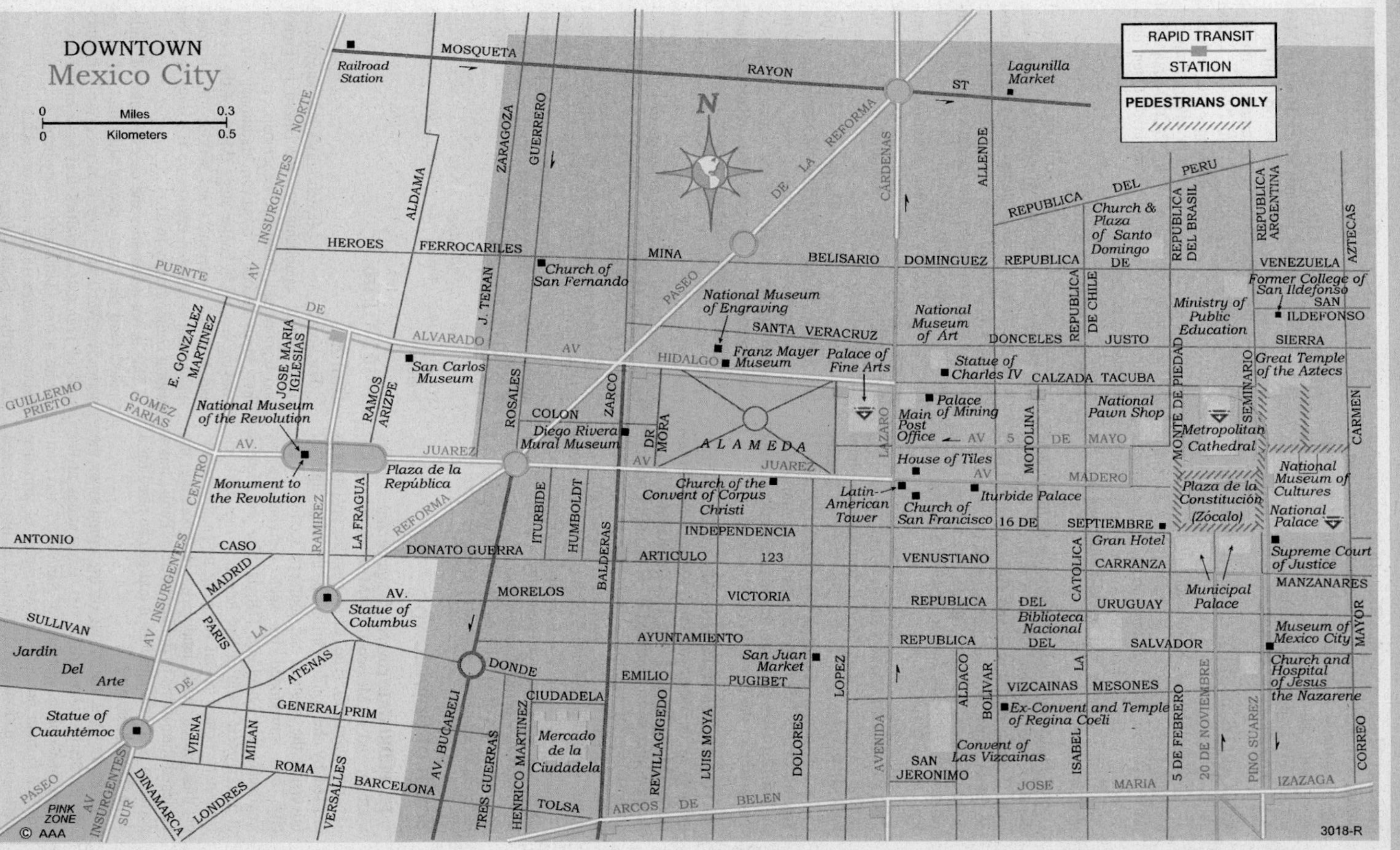
DOWNTOWN
Mexico City
Miles 0 0.3
Kilometers 0 0.5
RAPID TRANSIT STATION
PEDESTRIANS ONLY
Railroad Station
Lagunilla Market
Church & Plaza of Santo Domingo
Former College of San Ildefonso
Ministry of Public Education
Great Temple of the Aztecs
Metropolitan Cathedral
National Museum of Cultures
National Palace
Plaza de la Constitución (Zócalo)
Supreme Court of Justice
Municipal Palace
Museum of Mexico City
Church and Hospital of Jesus the Nazarene
Gran Hotel
National Pawn Shop
National Museum of Art
Statue of Charles IV
Palace of Mining
Main Post Office
House of Tiles
Iturbide Palace
Church of San Francisco
Latin-American Tower
Palace of Fine Arts
Biblioteca Nacional
Ex-Convent and Temple of Regina Coeli
Convent of Las Vizcainas
San Juan Market
National Museum of Engraving
Franz Mayer Museum
ALAMEDA
Church of the Convent of Corpus Christi
Church of San Fernando
Diego Rivera Mural Museum
Mercado de la Ciudadela
San Carlos Museum
Plaza de la República
Statue of Columbus
National Museum of the Revolution
Monument to the Revolution
Statue of Cuauhtémoc
Jardín Del Arte
PINK ZONE
© AAA
3018-R

National Museum of the Revolution (Museo Nacional de la Revolución) is inside the lower part of the monument. It houses a collection of weapons, along with paintings and sculptures depicting the revolution's leading figures. Tues.-Sat. 9-5, Sun. 9-3. Admission about 65c (U.S.).

SAN CARLOS MUSEUM (Museo de San Carlos) is about 3 blks. n. of Plaza de la República at Puente de Alvarado #50 (M: Revolución, line 2). It houses an impressive collection of paintings by European artists spanning the 15th through the 19th centuries, including works by Francisco José de Goya, Tintoretto, Titian, Anthony Van Dyck, Rembrandt and Peter Paul Rubens.

The lovely neoclassic building was the private home of such notable Mexican military figures as Gen. Agustín de Iturbide and Gen. Antonio López de Santa Anna. A small public park off Puente de Alvarado faces the rear facade. Wed.-Mon. 10-6. Admission 25 pesos (about $2.40 U.S.); free to all Sun. Phone (55) 5566-8522.

STATUE OF COLUMBUS stands within the *glorieta* (traffic circle) on Paseo de la Reforma at Av. Morelos (M: Revolución, line 2). The work of Charles Cordier, it depicts the explorer (Cristóbal Colón in Spanish) and is one of several statues commissioned by Porfirio Díaz to grace major intersections along this stretch of the city's widest boulevard.

STATUE OF CUAUHTEMOC (Monumento a Cuauhtémoc) is on Paseo de la Reforma at Av. Insurgentes (M: Insurgentes, line 1). Cuauhtémoc, the last Aztec emperor, was tortured by Hernando Cortés in an unsuccessful attempt to force him to reveal the hiding place of the vast treasure of Moctezuma. The statue, created by Miguel Moreña, shows the proud ruler garbed in a plumed robe and standing imperiously with his spear, surrounded by warriors. Pedestal engravings depict Cuauhtémoc's torture and the burning of his feet. The circle at Insurgentes and Reforma is a major crossroads for city traffic.

South of Downtown

EL PEDREGAL covers 15 square miles at the southern end of Mexico City (M: Universidad, line 3, south terminal). The great basaltic lava bed is crossed by the Anillo Periférico, the loop highway traversing the western and southern sections of the city, and surrounded by such communities as Coyoacán, San Angel and Tlalpan. The lava flow is at its craggiest south of San Angel. In the 1950s ultramodern homes began cropping up in the middle of this barren rock landscape, incorporating the hardened formations to dramatic effect. Public transportation is scarce, although a taxi can be hired for a drive through the area.

El Pedregal is the result of the eruption of the volcano Xitle around A.D. 400. Excavations at the quarry of Copilco, just east of San Angel, have uncovered human remains and examples of primitive craftsmanship from a civilization that likely existed sometime during the Middle Preclassic period (1200-400 B.C.).

POLYFORUM SIQUEIROS is at Av. Insurgentes Sur and Filadelfia, on the grounds of the Hotel de México. An eight-sided, four-story exposition hall for the arts, it is the work of and a monument to muralist David Alfaro Siqueiros (1896-1974). Garish Siqueiros murals cover the building's exterior walls, and inside on the upper level a revolving floor permits an unimpeded view of his 26,150-square-foot ceiling mural "March of Humanity." Open daily. Admission is charged.

The Southern Suburbs

Churubusco, Coyoacán, Iztapalapa, San Angel and Tlalpan, all within the Mexico City limits, were once individual *pueblos* (towns) that for the most part have maintained their distinct identities despite being swallowed up by the capital's rampant 20th-century growth. The Federal District, the 571-square-mile seat of national government, encompasses Mexico City and several separate municipalities, including Xochimilco, site of the popular floating gardens.

North-south Avenida Insurgentes Sur—a major thoroughfare lined with office buildings and commercial sprawl—is the easiest way to reach the southern suburbs, especially the tourist hotspots of San Angel and Coyoacán, both relatively quiet, well-to-do enclaves somehow removed from the rest of the city's clamor. Colonial charm, good restaurants, several museums, weekend arts and crafts shopping, and the cultural offerings of the National University of Mexico make this area a popular destination for visitors.

The safest and easiest way to reach the southern suburbs is to take a taxi; taxis also come in handy for making short trips from one point of interest to another. For an hourly fee you can hire a taxi driver to get you there and also wait while you shop or sightsee.

For more information about these destinations see their individual alphabetical listings under this region.

What To Do

Dining

For years, most of Mexico City's best known and most elegant establishments specialized in French and Continental, those two benchmarks of fine dining. More recently, however, traditional Mexican cooking has taken center stage. Many of the newest and trendiest restaurants are serving time-honored dishes that originated during pre-Hispanic days, but with a contemporary twist.

This is not necessarily the cheese-slathered, chile-spiked food that many people still think of as generically "Mexican," nor is it necessarily reminiscent of regional specialties that have ended up on menus across the country. Ingredients are frequently exotic—*nopales,* fleshy pads of cactus; *huitlacoche,* the earthy black fungus that is Mexico's version of the truffle; or *cajeta,* a sweet caramel flavoring made from goat's milk. Menu choices can be exotic, too: squash flowers, *chapulines* (fried grasshoppers) or *gusanos de maguey* (worms) fried and served with guacamole.

Diners still crave robustly traditional fare, of course—*sopa de tortilla* (tortilla soup); *chilies rellenos* (stuffed chilies); *huachinango a la Veracruzana* (a whole fish, usually sea bass or red snapper, awash in a sauce of tomatoes, onions, olives and capers); and *cochinita pibil* (pork wrapped in banana leaves and baked). La Fonda del Recuerdo is a boisterous, fun family restaurant featuring platters of delicious Mexican seafood accompanied by roving *jarocho* musicians. It's located at Bahía de las Palmas #37 in Colonia Veronica Anzures; take a taxi.

For those who demand world-class haute cuisine (with prices to match), Mexico City has some dependable choices. Such restaurants are usually located in the big, expensive hotels. Fouquet's de Paris, in the Camino Real Hotel at Mariano Escobedo #700—a branch of the Parisian outpost—offers as refined and elegant a setting as you'll find in the capital for food that is a combination of international and Mexican flavors. At this and other high-end restaurants, reservations are required or advised, and a jacket and tie are required for men.

Mesón El Cid, Humboldt #61 in the Historic Center, dishes up Spanish classics like paella and roast Cornish hen during the week and offers a medieval banquet on Saturday evening, complete with costumed waiters and singers. If you're in a hurry or just want a casual meal, eat at Vips or Sanborn's, both Mexican chains with numerous Mexico City locations. The food is dependably prepared and reasonably priced; they're good choices for breakfast.

Another casual alternative is one of the sandwich stands that occupy almost every street corner. Try *tacos al pastor*—shreds of roast pork with grilled onions and cilantro heaped on a small tortilla, the whole thing rolled up burrito-style and popped in the mouth. At 5 pesos apiece, they're a popular late-night snack.

The El Globo bakery chain, with locations throughout the Federal District, offers good-quality breads and pastries at low prices. For the homesick and/or unadventurous, there are plenty of American fast-food outlets, including Burger King, McDonald's, Pizza Hut and Subway.

Many restaurants are concentrated in the Polanco and Zona Rosa areas; reservations are recommended or necessary. Another cluster of good restaurants and cozy sidewalk cafes are in the southern suburbs of San Angel and Coyoacán. Casual neighborhood eateries and family-style places are the rule in the downtown area and around the *Zócalo.* Many restaurants close on Sunday. Pay with a major credit card if possible, as the rate of exchange is better than that offered by banks or currency exchange offices.

Approach cocktails and liquors with caution if you are unaccustomed to the altitude. Also be aware that imported wines and spirits are heavily taxed; Mexican beers and wines are much less expensive. Although the better restaurants customarily use purified water, avoid green salads, unpeeled raw vegetables and unpeeled fruit if you have a sensitive stomach. To be completely safe, order drinks without ice cubes, or drink bottled water.

In general, restaurants cater to the local custom of eating the main meal of the day in the early afternoon, then a lighter supper around 9 p.m. or later. Most begin to serve breakfast around 7:30 a.m., *comida* (lunch) about 1 p.m. and dinner after 7:30 p.m. From 2 to 4, restaurants can be crowded with lingering diners; if you eat dinner before 9, on the other hand, you might have the place to yourself.

Even in the finer establishments, don't expect every server to have a fluent command of English. A knowledge of basic Spanish or a handy phrase book not only helps in communication but also in deciphering menus. *For a list of AAA-RATED dining establishments in Mexico City, see the Lodgings & Restaurants section.*

Shopping

Whether it's a cheap souvenir or an expensive, finely crafted work of art, chances are you'll find it here. In particular, look for intricate silverwork, hand-carved masks, jewelry, tinted onyx and obsidian, carved wooden chests, boxes of inlaid wood, furniture, paintings, picture frames, fine glassware and pottery, lacquerware, hand-tooled leather and textiles—especially *sarapes, rebozos* (shawl-like garments), embroidery and fine table linens. Merchandise is sold either in fixed-price shops where you pay the posted sale price or in markets where bargaining determines the cost.

One of Mexico City's major shopping areas is the Zona Rosa, off Paseo de la Reforma and encompassing calles Amberes, Génova, Hamburgo, Niza and Londres (M: Sevilla or Insurgentes, line 1). Galleries and boutiques abound, and outdoor cafes provide a relaxing break. For music purchases, there is a Tower Records at Niza #19-A.

A more exclusive shopping area is the Polanco neighborhood (M: Polanco, line 7). Armani, Cartier, Perry Ellis, Hermes and other chic fashion boutiques line a section of Avenida Presidente Masaryk that is Mexico City's version of L.A.'s Rodeo Drive.

Condesa (M: Juanacatlan, line 1), which spreads east from the eastern end of Chapultepec Park, is another neighborhood that is both pedestrian and shopper friendly. The trendiest shops are concentrated near the intersection of avenidas Michoacán and Atlixco and along Avenida Tamaulipas. Avenida Michoacán also has retail outlets selling clothes, CDs and other merchandise.

Hundreds of shops and vendor stalls line avenidas Juárez and Francisco I. Madero in the vicinity of the *Zócalo.* This old downtown section of Mexico City is packed with stores and shops. From the *Zócalo* west to Avenida Lázaro Cárdenas, every other side street is closed to traffic and paved with brick tiles.

The government-run FONART stores offer a variety of arts and crafts—rugs, glassware, folk art, pottery—from all parts of the country at reasonable prices. A centrally located outlet, also known as Exposición Nacional de Arte Popular, is at Av. Juárez #89, just west of Alameda Park (M: Hidalgo, line 2).

The major department stores are Liverpool and Palacio de Hierro; each has several city branches. The Mexican restaurant chain Sanborn's has numerous locations throughout Mexico City, including the original outpost in the House of Tiles *(see attraction listing)* and several along Paseo de la Reforma and in the Zona Rosa. Almost all Sanborn's have an attached store that is a convenient place to pick up toiletries and English-language publications, as well as quality craft items and ceramics. Many also have a pharmacy and an ATM machine.

Among the suburban shopping malls, the largest is Centro Santa Fe, in the western part of the city. Although inconvenient for tourists because there is no Metro station nearby, it does have nearly 300 stores, as well as movie theaters, restaurants and play areas for kids. To get there, take the Anillo Periférico expressway (Avenida Avila Camacho) south to the exit marked *Centro Santa Fe.* Another big, pricey mall is Perisur, located on the southern outskirts close to where the Periférico expressway connects with Avenida Insurgentes Sur.

Mexico City's *mercados* were once areas of stalls open to the weather, roving dogs, and plagues of insects and bacteria. Long on merchandise, they were short on sanitation. City officials stepped in, and the markets are now housed in clean, properly ventilated buildings. Here you can haggle to your heart's content—and should, for a vendor normally asks at least 25 percent more than he or she expects to receive.

A suitable arena in which to practice the art of bargaining is the San Juan Market (Mercado de Curiosidades San Juan). The principal section is in a modern three-story building at Ayuntamiento and Dolores, 4 blocks south of Alameda Park (M: Salto del Agua, line 1). It offers an assortment of such wares as baskets, leather goods, jewelry, linens and shawls and is open Mon.-Sat. 9-7, Sun. 9-4.

The huge Buenavista Artisan Center (Centro Artesanal Buenavista), Aldama #187 near the Buenavista train station northwest of the Historic Center, markets handicrafts from throughout Mexico. Specialties include leather goods, pottery, stained-glass lamps and clothing. Prices are fixed. Open daily 9-6.

The city's biggest food market is La Merced, several blocks east of the *Zócalo* along Circunvalación (M: Merced, line 1). The huge buildings are crammed with a multitude of vendors selling produce, housewares and other everyday items. The selection of fruits, vegetables and spices in particular is staggering. While you're not likely to find many souvenirs, the sheer scope of the commerce makes it a fascinating place to wander through.

The Mercado Insurgentes, also called the Mercado Zona Rosa, fills an entire block along Calle Londres between Florencia and Amberes in the Zona Rosa (M: Insurgentes, line 1). A typical neighborhood crafts market, it has a maze of stalls selling everything from baskets to ponchos. Bargaining is expected, and good buys are possible. Open Mon.-Sat. 9:30-7:30, Sun. 10-4.

The Lagunilla Market is east of the intersection of Lázaro Cárdenas and Paseo de la Reforma, between República de Chile and Calle Allende (M: Allende, line 2). A modern triple-roofed building of enormous proportions, Lagunilla is especially busy on Sunday, when vendors from all over the city set up tables or booths to sell used clothing, silver of varying quality and other goods. Antiques, coins, blankets and rare books are good buys here. Watch out for pickpockets. Within walking distance, north of Paseo de la Reforma, is the Plaza of the Three Cultures *(see attraction listing)*.

Serious silver fanciers should head for Tane, Amberes #70 in the Zona Rosa and several other city locations, where the jewelry, candelabra and museum-quality reproductions are expensive but exquisitely crafted. The striking work of contemporary Mexican artist and sculptor Sergio Bustamente is available at his gallery on Amberes #13 in the Zona Rosa; another outlet is in the Hotel Nikko México, at Campo Elíseos #204 in the Polanco neighborhood.

Handcrafted items from all over the country are sold at the Mercado de la Ciudadela, about 6 blocks southwest of Alameda Park on Plaza de la Ciudadela at Avenida Balderas (M: Balderas, line 1). More than 300 covered booths display everything from leather moccasins to custom guitars. Some of the most interesting items at La Ciudadela are the handcarved wooden masks, with colorful and creatively rendered visages ranging from whimsical to demonic. Expect to bargain here.

Scores of Mexican artists exhibit and sell paintings and sculpture in the city's many art galleries. Of special interest is the Saturday Bazaar (Bazar Sábado), at Plaza San Jacinto #11 (M: Miguel A. de Quevedo, line 3) in San Angel. Set up in a beautifully renovated 18th-century mansion—but usually spilling out of it as well—the bazaar is held only on Saturdays from 10-7.

The emphasis here is on art and features works by a tightly knit group of contemporary artisans, some of them U.S. expatriates. Paintings, sculpture, ceramics, textiles and garments, rugs and high-quality jewelry are sold; prices are high, but so is quality. Search out the *animalitos,* bizarrely carved and painted wooden creatures for which Oaxaca is famous, and the "Tree of Life" candelabras exploding with flowers, animals and other figures.

Gilded statues of the Virgin Mary, Our Lady of Guadalupe and other Mexican patron saints are exquisite examples of handiwork and command high prices. More affordable merchandise—and a greater chance to bargain—can be found outside the bazaar, where merchants offer wooden toys, decorative gourds and beaded bracelets. Local artists exhibit their work, and the lively scene frequently includes dancers and other entertainment.

Sightseeing

Mexico City's enormous size makes it difficult to plan a sightseeing itinerary. Although many museums and other points of interest are concentrated in certain areas—the Historic Center, Chapultepec Park, the southern suburbs of San Angel and Coyoacán—getting to them can take effort, given the formidable traffic congestion. If the prospect of hitting the streets on your own seems too stressful, consider taking a guided tour.

The easiest way to obtain guided tour information is to check with the staff at your hotel; the hotel may either have its own travel agency or be able to recommend a reliable one. An alternative is to visit one of the city's tourist information modules (Módulo de Información y Orientación Turística) operated by the Tourism Secretariat of Mexico City. A number of these modules are located in the Historic Center, in the vicinity of Alameda and Chapultepec parks, in the Pink Zone (Zona Rosa) and along Paseo de Reforma.

Guided tours of the Historic Center (via Tren Turístico) and Coyoacán (via Paseo por Coyoacán) depart daily aboard trolley buses built to resemble the trams that crisscrossed Mexico City streets in the early 20th century. The narrated tours are in

Spanish; the fare is about $3.50 (U.S.). For schedules and other information, check at any tourist information module.

Turibuses travel a route that takes in the Historic Center, Paseo de la Reforma, Chapultepec Park and the Condesa and Roma neighborhoods—an area filled with museums, monuments, art galleries, parks and restaurants. Each red, double-decker Turibus can hold up to 70 passengers, and the tour includes a simultaneous translation in several languages. One ticket allows you to use the service all day, disembarking and reboarding at 25 stops.

Buses run daily 9-9 and pass each stop approximately every half hour. Tickets Mon.-Fri. cost 100 pesos (about $9.70 U.S.); ages 4-12, 50 pesos (about $4.85). Tickets Sat.-Sun. cost 115 pesos (about $11); ages 4-12, 55 pesos (about $5.30). Two- and 3-day tickets also are available. For more information check with your hotel or at a tourist information module.

Another easy way to see the sights is to have your hotel arrange for a private car and a guide, either by the hour or by the day. Although you'll pay for the convenience, this option allows greater flexibility and more personal service. The larger hotels should be able to arrange such an excursion; check with the concierge. Guests at the Four Seasons Hotel, for example, can take advantage of guided weekend cultural tours.

The best day to sightsee in Mexico City is Sunday, when many attractions are free.

Sports and Recreation

For the spectator, opportunities in Mexico City are legion. Besides the major sports mentioned below, there are basketball games, boxing and wrestling matches and a growing collegiate schedule of American-style football. Refer to the sports pages of the newspapers for current activities and schedules. Your hotel can help you get tickets.

The best **bullfighting** in the republic can be found at Plaza México (M: San Antonio, line 7). Accommodating about 50,000 spectators—one of the world's largest bullrings—it is located on Calle Augusto Rodín a few blocks west of Avenida Insurgentes, about 6 kilometers (4 miles) south of the traffic circle at Paseo de la Reforma (the Cuauhtémoc Monument).

The season for top matadors runs from early November through March. During other months novice bullfighters *(novilleros)* take the ring. Bullfights start promptly at 4 p.m. on Sunday; buses marked "Plaza México" travel along Insurgentes Sur throughout the afternoon. Plan on arriving early to get a good seat, and hang on to your ticket stub so you can reclaim your seat if you need to leave it.

To avoid long lines at the bullring's ticket windows *(taquillas)*, buy tickets in advance or book a tour that includes a bullfight through your hotel or a travel agency. Ticket prices range from about $4 to $45 (U.S.); they vary according to proximity to the ring and the side on which you sit. Sun *(sol)* is cheap, shade *(sombra)* is expensive. Seats in the sun tend to attract the more unruly fans. For more information phone (55) 5563-3959. **Note:** The bull is traditionally killed during these performances; plan not to attend if you find the spectacle's inherent cruelty upsetting.

The country's most popular game is **soccer** *(fútbol)*. It is played almost every weekend by the big leagues at Azteca Stadium, in the southern part of the city on Calzada de Tlalpan, north of the Periférico Sur. Shuttles are available from the Taxqueña Metro station (line 2). There are winter (August to December) and summer (January to May) seasons. The city's most popular team, América—nicknamed Las Aguilas (the Eagles)—draws huge crowds, especially when they play arch-rival Guadalajara in a match called El Clásico.

The university-sponsored Pumas play soccer at Olympic Stadium (Estadio Olímpica) on the National University of Mexico campus. Reconstructed and enlarged for the 1968 Summer Olympics, it can accommodate some 72,500 people. The oval design somewhat resembles the crater of a volcano. A Diego Rivera mosaic of colored rocks, illustrating human endeavor in sports, covers the stadium's sloping walls. Tickets for all games are normally available right up to game time and range from about $2 to $11 (U.S.).

NBA **basketball** exhibition games are played at the Sports Palace (Palacio de Deportes), Avenida Río Churubusco and Calle Añil (M: Velódromo or Ciudad Deportiva, line 9). Designed by Félix Candela for the 1968 Olympic Games, it seats 25,000.

Professional **baseball** is popular in Mexico City, where teams in the Mexican League play from the beginning of April through mid-September. Games are announced in Spanish, but little is lost in the translation as the rules are the same. Some key terms: *el lanzador* is the pitcher, *la entrada* is the inning, *pegar* means hit, *un sencillo* is a single.

Many games are played at the Parque Foro Sol, a very modern facility on Avenida Río Churubusco in front of the Sports Palace. It is shared by two teams, the Diablos Rojos and the Tigres; the season is from March through August. General admission seats are inexpensive, less than $5 (U.S.). Tickets can be purchased through Ticketmaster; phone (55) 5325-9000.

Horse races are held at the lovely Hippodrome of the Americas (Hipódromo de las Américas). The track is in the northwestern part of the city between avenidas del Conscripto and Industria Militar, west of the Anillo Periférico. Buses and *peseros* (minivans) marked "Hipódromo" travel west along Paseo de la Reforma to the track. Races are held Friday through Sunday throughout the year beginning at 3 p.m.

General section admission is 15 pesos; box seats are more expensive. Tickets are available through Ticketmaster. There are fast-food outlets, the fashionable restaurant La Terraza and a sports book facility on the premises. For further information phone (55) 5387-0600.

Tennis and **golf** clubs are private; if you want to play tennis, make arrangements to stay at a hotel that offers courts. The Bella Vista Golf Club, an 18-hole course northwest of the city off Mex. 57-D (the Querétaro Highway), offers playing privileges to guests staying at the Camino Real and Sheraton María Isabel hotels. Greens fees are expensive, especially on weekends. Phone (55) 5360-3501.

Nightlife

More often than not, nightlife in Mexico City means nightclubs—both independent establishments and the lobby bars in the big hotels. Nightclub tours are an easy way to visit some of the city's hot spots, since transportation and reservations are arranged for you. These tours usually last several hours and include dinner at a nice restaurant and perhaps a floor show or a stop at Plaza Garibaldi *(see below)*. For more information check with your hotel desk or a travel agency. The weekly publication *Tiempo Libre*, published on Thursday and available at newsstands, provides entertainment and performing arts listings in Spanish.

Just as they do in Acapulco and Cancún, people in Mexico City tend to keep the evening going practically all night. Dinner might begin at 9 or 10 p.m., and most of the clubs don't kick into high gear until midnight. Many nightspots are closed on Sunday. Keep in mind that altitude can greatly magnify the effects of alcohol.

Note: Always be careful when venturing out after dark anywhere in Mexico City, even in tourist-frequented areas like the Zona Rosa and Polanco. Metro is not recommended as a way of getting around at night, and never hail a taxi on the street. The safest way to travel is to make drop-off and pickup arrangements with your hotel taxi service. Thieves also frequent the popular nightlife districts, so carry a minimum of cash and guard your personal belongings carefully.

Hotel lobby bars offer an elegant atmosphere, a sophisticated clientele and music for dancing. Good bets include the bars in the Intercontinental Presidente Mexico City, Campos Elíseos #218, Colonia Polanco; the Camino Real Mexico, Mariano Escobedo #700 (near the main entrance to Chapultepec Park); the Sheraton María Isabel Hotel and Towers, Paseo de la Reforma #325 (opposite the Independence Monument); and the Westin Galería Plaza, Hamburgo #195 in the Zona Rosa.

Avoid *cantinas*, small, dimly lit places that tend to attract hard-drinking patrons. An exception is the La Opera Bar, Av. 5 de Mayo #10 at Filomeno Mata, 3 blocks east of Alameda Park (M: Bellas Artes, lines 2 and 8). By day this is a crowded lunch spot, with jacketed waiters and formal service. In the evening dinner is served, but the gilded ceiling, mirrored walls, dark paneled booths and clubby feel also make La Opera an intimate place for an early evening cocktail. Your waiter is likely to show you the bullet hole Pancho Villa supposedly fired into the ceiling.

Dance to live salsa and merengue at Bar León, República de Brasil #5 in the Historic Center (behind the Metropolitan Cathedral). The cover charge begins at about $5.50 (U.S.). The club is open Thurs.-Sat. evenings; phone (55) 5510-3093.

The Art Deco Bar Mata, Filomena Mata #11 at Avenida 5 de Mayo in the Historic Center (near the La Opera Bar), occupies two floors in a colonial building near the Palace of Fine Arts. Dancing is to jazz, blues and rock. The rooftop bar offers fresh air and great views of the illuminated city. El Hijo del Cuervo, Jardín Centenario #17 in Coyoacán, attracts hip students and a mix of locals and foreigners. The music is hip as well; there is a cover charge for occasional live shows.

Floor shows are another option. International headliners appear at El Patio, an old-fashioned nightclub at Atenas #9 (east of the Zona Rosa and a block south of Paseo de la Reforma). Bar Jorongo, in the Sheraton María Isabel Hotel and Towers at Paseo de la Reforma #325, is a popular nightspot where well-known mariachi trios play in upscale surroundings. There is a cover charge. The rooftop bar at the Hotel Majestic, Av. Francisco I. Madero #73 (M: Zócalo, line 2), often has live entertainment in a setting overlooking the *Zócalo*.

For those seeking an indubitably Mexican nightlife experience, Plaza Garibaldi offers it. Bounded by calles República de Peru and República de Honduras, about 5 blocks north of the Palace of Fine Arts (M: Garibaldi, line 8), this square is ruled by the city's mariachi bands, who serenade paying customers every night of the week. The typical outfit includes violin, trumpet, guitar and a heart-tugging vocalist, and the songs almost always address the travails of love (usually at the hands of an unfaithful woman—a nod to Mexican *machismo*).

Decked out in tight, silver-spangled costumes and wide-brimmed sombreros, the musicians unabashedly solicit business from the throngs of people crowding the plaza (about $5 U.S. for a song). Sunday night is the best time to hear music in the square itself. Mariachis also perform in the surrounding *cantinas* and clubs, which stay open into the wee hours.

Plaza Santa Cecelia nightclub, across Calle Amargura from the plaza, puts on first-rate mariachi shows. At the establishments El Tenampa and Tlaquepaque you can sit and listen to the mariachis while nibbling *botanas* (snacks).

Note: Plaza Garibaldi is at its most exuberant late at night and is a traditional last stop for an evening on the town, but the surrounding neighborhood is unsavory, filled with cheap hotels and gaudy burlesque theaters. Unfortunately, street crime has become all too common here, even during daylight hours. If you do go, exercise caution. Guard closely against pickpockets, and arrange in advance for safe transportation to the plaza and back to your hotel. Some places have been known to gouge money from tourists by raising quoted prices for food and/or drinks, so stick to the larger, well-known establishments.

Concerts

Your hotel or a travel agency may be able to obtain tickets for popular performances, such as those by the Ballet Folklórico de México, which should be obtained in advance. Tickets for many events also can be purchased through Ticketmaster. Phone (55) 5325-9000; www.ticketmaster.com.mx. There is a Ticketmaster outlet in the National Auditorium, Paseo de la Reforma #50 in Chapultepec Park (M: Auditorio, line 7).

The Palace of Fine Arts (M: Bellas Artes; lines 2 and 8) is the home of the National Symphony Orchestra. The National Opera Company also stages productions here, usually January through March and August through October. The Mexico City Philharmonic Orchestra (Filarmonica de la Ciudad de México) gives concerts at Silvestre Revueltas Hall (Sala Silvestre Revueltas). It is located at Anillo Periférico Sur #5141, just east of Avenida Insurgentes at the southern end of the city (near San Angel).

International symphony, ballet and opera companies also perform at the National Auditorium. Tickets can be purchased at the auditorium box office Mon.-Sat. 10-7, Sun. 11-6; for information phone (55) 5280-9250.

The acclaimed National University Symphony mounts its concert program at Justo Sierra Auditorium (M: Universidad, line 3, south terminal), on the National University of Mexico campus. The hall is famed for its acoustics. Nezahualcoyotl Hall regularly presents performing artists and groups, including the University of Mexico Philharmonic Orchestra. It is located within the University Cultural Center, which is off Avenida Insurgentes south of the main campus buildings.

Music al fresco is particularly popular and can be heard on the street or at parks throughout the capital. Better yet, many of these performances—which range from mariachi music to heavy metal—are free. Sunday concerts often take place in Alameda Park, usually around noon, and near the Lake House (Casa del Lago) in Chapultepec Park.

The central plazas in the southern suburbs of Coyoacán and San Angel often are the scene of weekend musical offerings. Big-name pop, rock and hip-hop concerts by international acts take place at the National Auditorium; the Sports Palace (Palacio de Los Deportes), Avenida Río Churubusco and Calle Añil; and Parque Foro Sol stadium, in front of the Sports Palace.

The Ballet Folklórico de México *(see Palace of Fine Arts attraction listing)* is one of the city's standout offerings. Although tickets are sold in advance at the Palace of Fine Arts box office (on the ground floor at the main entrance), they may be difficult to obtain unless you purchase them at least a day ahead or book a tour that includes the ballet. **Note:** The troupe is occasionally moved to another venue, usually the National Auditorium, to accommodate visiting performing arts groups. Check with Ticketmaster regarding specific schedule information.

Theater and Cinema

Theaters are not centralized in an entertainment district but are located throughout the city. Plays are almost always presented in Spanish, but other theaters present shows in a cabaret or variety format that can be enjoyed by non-Spanish speakers.

The Insurgentes Theater (Teatro de Los Insurgentes), Av. Insurgentes Sur #1587, presents plays and musicals in a building that boasts a striking Diego Rivera mosaic on its facade. The Blanquita Theater (Teatro Blanquita), 4 blocks north of the Latin-American Tower on Avenida Lázaro Cárdenas (M: Bellas Artes, lines 2 and 8), offers variety shows performed by Mexico's top singers, dancers, comedians and magicians.

Other theaters include the Hidalgo, Av. Hidalgo #23 (M: Hidalgo, line 2); and the Virginia Fábregas Theater, Calle Velasquez de León #29, a few blocks from the Zona Rosa (M: Allende, line 2). For listings, check *Tiempo Libre.*

American and foreign films are shown in their original language with Spanish subtitles. Hollywood blockbusters and first-run films open in Mexico soon after they do in the United States, and admission is inexpensive (about $3.75 U.S.; half-price on Wednesdays). For listings, check *Tiempo Libre.*

Cineteca Nacional, Av. México-Coyoacán #389, the southern extension of Avenida Cuauhtémoc (M: Coyoacán, line 3), is a multiplex with a wide range of movie choices; phone (55) 1253-9390. Closer to the city center is Cinepolis Diana, Paseo de la Reforma #423, Colonia Cuauhtémoc; phone (55) 5511-3236. Cinemex Casa de Arte, Av. Anatole France #120 at Avenida Presidente Masaryk in the Polanco neighborhood, has four small theaters that show arthouse films from around the world; phone (55) 5257-6969.

Special Events

Mexico City residents observe many of the celebrations listed in the "Fiestas and Holidays" section beginning on page 675. The capital also gives an extra flourish to historical commemorations that helped secure independence and pave the way for modern Mexico. Several religious holidays are of special importance as well.

Flower-garlanded cows, beribboned dogs and cats and irreverent roosters are paraded on Jan. 17 for the Feast of San Antonio Abad, or the "blessing of the animals." This whimsical ceremony takes place at the Metropolitan Cathedral on the *Zócalo.* Holy Week *(Semana Santa)* celebrations take place in mid-April.

On May 1, Labor Day *(Día del Trabajo),* the president reviews a huge parade of workers from the central balcony of the National Palace. For the Feast of Corpus Christi, families dress children in native costumes or their Sunday best and gather at the Metropolitan Cathedral for a priest's blessing. The date is variable, occurring between late May and mid-June.

The fall of Tenochtitlan to Hernando Cortés and his followers is commemorated on Cuauhtémoc Day, Aug. 21, with wreath-laying ceremonies at the Plaza of the Three Cultures and the Cuauhtémoc Statue at the intersection of Paseo de la Reforma and Avenida Insurgentes.

Father Miguel Hidalgo's *"El Grito de Dolores,"* the rallying cry of Mexican independence, is repeated by the president of Mexico and echoed by hundreds of thousands on the evening of Sept. 15 in Plaza Constitución (the *Zócalo*). One of the year's biggest events, it is nationally televised. A morning military parade on Independence Day, Sept. 16, proceeds from the *Zócalo* to the Independence Monument, past buildings draped with streamers in the national colors of red, green and white.

Columbus Day *(Día de la Raza)* on Oct. 12 commemorates Christopher Columbus' discovery of the Americas. Families build altars in their homes and decorate the graves of loved ones with extravagant flower garlands to celebrate the Day of the Dead Nov. 1. Revolution Day, Nov. 20, features a spirited parade down avenidas Madero, Juárez and Reforma in commemoration of the start of the Revolution of 1910.

The venerated Virgin of Guadalupe, patron saint of the country, is the focal point of a nationwide celebration of dancing, fireworks and religious processions on Dec. 12, the Feast Day of the Virgin of Guadalupe. Devout believers from throughout the country and abroad make the journey to the Basilica of Guadalupe, in the northern suburb of Villa de Guadalupe. Mexico City is decorated in high style for Christmas and the 9 days leading up to it, during which there are traditional re-enactments of the Holy Family's search for an inn *(posada).*

National Museum of Anthropology / Nadine Markova / Mexico Tourism Board

This ends listings for Mexico City.
The following page resumes the alphabetical listings of cities in Mexico City and Vicinity.

SAN ANGEL, DISTRITO FEDERAL (B-3)

San Angel (sahn AHN-hehl) was once a small town far removed from colonial Mexico City. Like other southern suburbs, however, it has been overtaken by the capital's inexorable growth. Even so, a leisurely stroll past San Angel's elegant colonial mansions and bougainvillea-draped walls is a trip back through history and a welcome respite from downtown Mexico City's noise and congestion.

In the beautifully leafy Bombilla Park (Parque de la Bombilla), at the junction of avenidas La Paz and Insurgentes Sur, stands a granite monument honoring Gen. Alvaro Obregón. Obregón helped draft the Constitution of 1917 and was the first president of post-revolutionary Mexico. He was assassinated in San Angel by a religious fanatic in 1928.

A few blocks southwest of the park off Avenida La Paz is Plaza San Jacinto, a pleasant square bordered by cobblestone streets, tucked-away restaurants and outdoor cafés. A plaque in the square honors members of St. Patrick's Battalion, a group of Irish immigrants who deserted the U.S. Army and sided with Mexico during the Mexican-American War. Today the plaza is known for its Saturday Bazaar (Bazar del Sábado); *see description under the Mexico City Shopping section, page 306.*

West of San Angel on the Mexico-Toluca Highway (Mex. 15) is Miguel Hidalgo National Park (Parque Nacional Miguel Hidalgo), known locally as La Marquesa for the name of the small town nearby. Surrounded by mountains, the park contains picnic sites, a government trout hatchery and a man-made lake stocked with trout. Horseback rides can be arranged at several park locations.

CARRILLO GIL ART MUSEUM (Museo de Arte Carrillo Gil) is about 3 blks. n. of Plaza San Jacinto at Av. Revolución #1608 (Metro: Miguel A. de Quevedo, line 3). It displays the collection amassed by Dr. Carrillo Gil, focusing on paintings and graphics by noted 20th-century Mexican artists but including European works as well. José Clemente Orozco, Diego Rivera, David Alfaro Siqueiros and Pablo Picasso are among those represented. Tues.-Sun. 10-6. Admission 15 pesos (about $1.45 U.S.).

CASA DEL RISCO is at Plaza San Jacinto #15 (Metro: Miguel A. de Quevedo, line 3). The building contains an extensive library and one of Mexico City's finest collections of European paintings from the 14th through the 17th centuries. Don't miss the colorful, wildly abstract fountain in the patio that appears to be made primarily of broken crockery. Tues.-Sun. 10-5. Free.

DIEGO RIVERA STUDIO MUSEUM (Museo Casa Estudio Diego Rivera) is on Calle Diego Rivera, across the street from the San Angel Inn (Metro: Miguel A. de Quevedo, line 3). Designed by architect Juan O'Gorman in 1931, it was Rivera's last home, where he died in 1957. Surrounded by different kinds of cacti, it has interior and exterior staircases leading up to the artist's large studio, which contrasts sharply with the small bedrooms. A roof bridge links the house to one occupied by fellow artist and partner Frida Kahlo. Temporary exhibitions are mounted.

Tues.-Sun. 10-6. Admission about $1 (U.S.); free to all Sun. Phone (55) 5616-0996.

EL CARMEN MUSEUM (Museo del Carmen) is just s. of Av. La Paz at Av. Revolución #4 and Monasterio (Metro: Miguel A. de Quevedo, line 3). It occupies a former Carmelite convent dating from 1615. The building is distinguished by carved doors, baroque altarpieces, a fine collection of religious paintings and three domes, each tiled in a different color. The cloister's garden has a tropical look, unusual for Mexico City. Tues.-Sun. 10-5. Admission about $3.50 (U.S.); free to all Sun.

NATIONAL UNIVERSITY OF MEXICO (Universidad Nacional Autonoma de México) is s. of San Angel (M: Copilco or Universidad, line 3), roughly between avs. Insurgentes Sur and Universidad. The National University of Mexico, or UNAM, spreads over some 800 acres. Its mosaic-covered modern buildings and academic reputation have made University City (Ciudad Universitaria), as the complex is commonly referred to, world famous.

The best reason to visit is to see the murals that decorate the exterior of the main campus buildings, most of them concentrated just east of Insurgentes Sur. One of the most visually arresting is the Main Library (Biblioteca). This rectangular tower is covered with stone mosaic work, augmented in places by colored tiles.

Near the library is the Administration Building (Rectoría), dominated by a huge David Alfaro Siqueiros mural that incorporates pieces of colored glass. A mosaic that includes a three-headed mask symbolizing Indian, Spanish and *mestizo*—the three peoples of Mexico—adorns one wall of the School of Medicine.

The easiest way to get to the university is to take a taxi or line 3 of the Metro, getting off at one of the last two stops. City buses marked "Ciudad Universitaria" travel regularly down Avenida Insurgentes Sur and stop in front of the main complex of buildings. Weekends, when students are noticeably absent, are the best time to view the buildings.

TENANCINGO, MEXICO (C-2)

pop. 31,600, elev. 6,632′

Tenancingo (teh-nahn-SEEN-goh)—its name an Indian term meaning "place of little walls"—was founded in 1425. Overlooking the town from atop a hill is a large Christ statue; this vantage point provides a sweeping view. Tenancingo produces wood and palm furniture, *rebozos* (shawl-like woven garments) and fruit liqueurs, all of which are for sale at the huge open-air market held on Sundays.

MALINALCO is about 25 km (16 mi.) e. of Tenancingo via a graded road to the village of Malinalco, then approximately 2 km (1.2 mi.) w. on a good dirt road. Buses from Toluca travel to Malinalco. Partially restored, the site is hewn into a cliffside.

The Temple of the Eagles and Jaguars, one of the world's few archeological remains carved from solid stone, has a reconstructed thatch and wood roof entrance, in front of which sits a headless stone figure. The doorway resembles an open-mouthed serpent. A beautifully carved wooden drum retrieved from the Temple of the Sun (Building IV) resides in the Museum of Anthropology at the Mexiquense Cultural Center in Toluca *(see attraction listing under Toluca)*.

The staircase that leads to the site is carved into the mountainside. It's an arduous climb of more than 400 steps that takes 30 minutes, but the view of the surrounding valley is magnificent. Tues.-Sun. 9-5:30. Admission 39 pesos (about $3.80 U.S.).

SANTO DESIERTO DEL CARMEN MONASTERY NATIONAL PARK is about 12 km (7 mi.) southeast of Tenancingo on a graded road, a short distance from Malinalco. The park's main feature is a late 18th-century Carmelite monastery that sits in a lovely wooded setting.

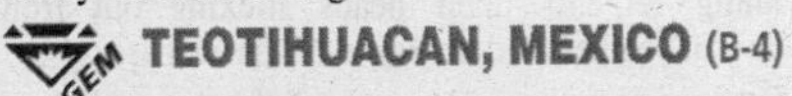

TEOTIHUACAN, MEXICO (B-4)

San Juan Teotihuacán (teh-oh-tee-wah-KAHN) is one of the most widely known and easily accessible of Mexico's major archeological zones. Very little is known about this religious center, the people who built it, or even what the city was originally called. It was designated a World Heritage Site by UNESCO in 1987.

Teotihuacán is thought to have been founded as early as 700 B.C., although it was not until around 100 B.C. that construction of its two great pyramids began. Archeologists estimate that at its height around A.D. 500, up to 200,000 people lived there, making it bigger than Rome at the time and one of the largest cities in the world. The city was burned and abandoned for unknown reasons around A.D. 750; it is believed the decline was gradual and perhaps facilitated by overpopulation and a resulting depletion of natural resources.

The area was later inhabited by the Toltecs; by the time the Aztecs discovered the site, it was in such an advanced state of ruin that they named it Teotihuacán, which means "place of the gods," or more broadly, "where men become gods." The gray stone structures seen today are to a large degree reconstructed, and the barren landscape barely hints at what the city must have looked like during its heyday some 1,500 years ago.

Exploring the Site

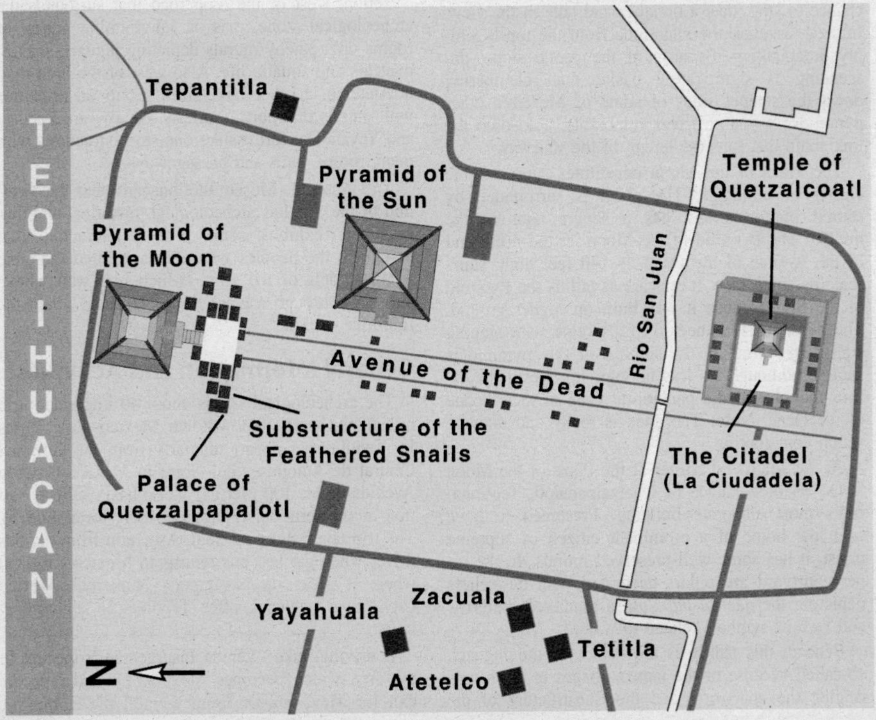

Teotihuacán was once paved with volcanic stone and mica slabs, and buildings were plastered with lime and mortar and then decorated with bas-relief sculptures and murals, often painted red; traces of the color are still discernible. The typical structural arrangement was often a courtyard surrounded by several levels of temples and rooms.

The ruins are aligned along a north-south axis traversed by the Avenue of the Dead (Avenida de Los Muertos). The name was given by the Aztecs, who believed that the low structures lining both sides of the avenue were burial sites. All similar in size and style, they accentuate the grandness of the pyramids. Touches of paint can still be detected on some of the building fragments. This wide thoroughfare (paved for today's visitors) is more than a mile long; it seems even longer when you're trekking from one building to another.

The Pyramid of the Sun, on the east side of the Avenue of the Dead, dominates the ruins and is the oldest of Teotihuacán's structures. It is the world's third-largest pyramid; only those at Cholula and Cheops, Egypt, are bigger. The structure rises in five sloping levels to a height of more than 250 feet; each side of its base measures about 735 feet.

Built of adobe brick faced with volcanic stone, the pyramid is visible for some distance from the highway approaching the site. When first discovered it was a gigantic mound covered with vegetation, but even the subsequent reconstruction fails to detract from the achievement of those who originally built this enormous monument without benefit of the wheel or metal tools.

A stairway on the west flank begins at the pyramid's base and leads to the summit, where a temple probably once stood. The 248 steps make for an arduous climb, but the five levels each provide a chance to stop, take a breather and take in the view. In clear weather, the panorama from the top is simply breathtaking. Because of the gentle slope, descending is significantly easier than clambering down the steeper sides of some of Mexico's other pyramids. If you still feel vulnerable, hold onto the link chain that runs the length of the stairway.

The Plaza of the Moon constitutes a remarkable cluster of buildings. The plaza is surrounded by staired platforms and has a square altar in the middle. The Pyramid of the Moon, at the north end of the Avenue of the Dead, is 140 feet high; stairs scale its south face. It appears as tall as the Pyramid of the Sun because it was built on higher ground. The pyramid is connected to a temple with sloping walls. The climb to the summit of this pyramid is shorter (although no less taxing). It's worth the effort, though, for the panoramic vista of the Avenue of the Dead. **Note:** The apex is rocky and uneven; watch your footing.

At the southwest corner of the Plaza of the Moon is the restored Palace of Quetzalpapalotl, Teotihuacán's most elaborate building. Presumed to have been the home of a prominent citizen or supreme priest, it has some well-preserved murals. In the inner courtyard are pillars decorated with bas-reliefs depicting the *quetzal-papalotl,* a feathered butterfly, and various symbols related to water.

Beneath this palace is the Palace of the Jaguars, so called because of the jaguar images in the rooms ringing the courtyard, and the Substructure of the Feathered Snails, part of a beautifully decorated temple beneath the Quetzalpapalotl Palace that features carvings of large snails garlanded with feathers.

In 1998 excavations uncovered a tomb and offerings inside the Pyramid of the Moon that archeologists hope will provide additional clues to help solve the riddle of the site's origination. Objects at what has initially been described as a burial site—most likely someone of high social standing—include obsidian and jade sculptures and skeleton fragments.

At the southern end of the zone is The Citadel (La Ciudadela). Teotihuacán was ruled from this vast sunken square, which encompassed nearly 17 acres and was surrounded by a low wall. The inner esplanade once held thousands of standing people.

Within the courtyard are several temples; the most elaborate is the restored Temple of Quetzalcóatl (the Feathered Serpent). The god Quetzalcóatl was worshipped by the Mayan, Toltec and Aztec civilizations, although it is unknown whether the inhabitants of Teotihuacán paid tribute to the same being. Carved stone slabs face part of the structure; writhing serpents, their heads sticking out from ruffles of feathers, adorn some of the walls.

Other structures are located off the Avenue of the Dead. Tepantitla, east of the Pyramid of the Moon, may have been the residence of a high priest. Several walls have traces of paintings showing Tláloc, the rain god, amid swimming male figures and water imagery.

Tetitla, west of the loop road that surrounds the archeological zone, has a labyrinthine maze of rooms with patchy murals depicting jaguars, snakes, quetzals and aquatic life. Also west of the loop road is Atetelco, another large-sized group of structures with murals that portray priests. Nearby are Zacuala and Yayahuala, fortresslike one-story structures with many rooms, halls and passageways.

The museum (Museo Teotihuacán) near the Pyramid of the Sun has archeological, historical and diagrammatic exhibits, some of them interactive, that pertain to the peoples who once inhabited the area. Scale models of the zone (which you walk above and view through a glass floor) will help orient the first-time visitor.

General Information and Activities

The archeological site is about 49 kilometers (30 miles) northeast of downtown Mexico City. Buses for Teotihuacán depart regularly from the Terminal Central de Autobuses del Norte in Mexico City, on Avenida de los 100 Metros; Metro has a subway station at the terminal (Autobuses del Norte, line 5). The trip takes about an hour. Ascertain from the bus driver when the last bus returns to Mexico City and where it picks up passengers. Numerous Mexico City travel agencies offer Teotihuacán sightseeing tours.

If driving, take Avenida Insurgentes Norte out of the city, which becomes Mex. 85-D, and take the exit for Mex. 132-D. From the toll plaza, the site entrance is about 22 kilometers (14 miles) east (about a 30-minute drive); signs along the way are marked "Pirámides."

Wear sturdy, nonslip walking shoes if you plan to climb the pyramids, because the rocks can be slippery. On warm, sunny days wear lightweight clothing, sunscreen and a hat. During the summer months (June through September) afternoon showers are frequent. Fall and winter days can be cloudy, chilly and breezy. The altitude is more than 7,000 feet, so walk and climb at a relaxed pace.

Note: Numerous souvenir vendors roam the site, and you will be approached on many occasions to purchase items ranging from jewelry to carved figurines to lace shawls. The vendors are persistent but usually not aggressive. If you have no intention of buying anything, keep walking; a negative shake of the head and a polite *"gracias"* will convey a "thanks, but no thanks" response. If you stop, chances are you'll never get away. But if you want to buy something, by all means bargain; a vendor will initially offer three to four times what he or she is willing to settle for.

Avoid going on weekends, which can be very crowded. Try to visit during the week and early in the day before the tour buses begin arriving.

Snacks are available at the entrance and there are a few restaurants just outside the site, but most hotels will pack a box lunch to take along on a bus tour. Bring bottled water, particularly if it's a hot day. There are very basic restrooms at the entrance. The site is open daily 8-5; the museum is open Tues.-Sun. Admission (includes museum) 48 pesos (about $4.50 U.S.). There is an additional fee of 30 pesos (about $2.90) for the use of a video camera.

TEPOTZOTLAN, MEXICO (B-2)

pop. 40,500, elev. 7,577′

Tepotzotlán (teh-poht-soh-TLAHN), about 35 kilometers (22 miles) north of Mexico City, is an easy day trip destination from the capital. From the downtown area, take Avenida Avila Camacho (Mex. 57) northwest out of the city and watch for the Tepotzotlán turn-off; the town lies about a mile west. Buses depart regularly for Tepotzotlán from the Cuatro Caminos Metro station (the western terminus of line 2); ask for the bus going to Tepotzotlán. To return, take a bus going to the Cuatro Caminos station.

The town is the perfect antidote for visitors tired of Mexico City's grinding congestion and noise: It has clear air, wonderful mountain views, colonial charm and a commercial yet laid-back atmosphere. After visiting the Church of San Francisco Xavier, Tepotzotlán's main attraction, have a relaxed lunch at one of the eateries surrounding the central plaza.

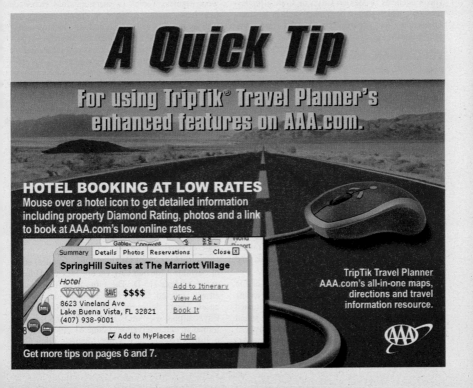

CHURCH OF SAN FRANCISCO XAVIER faces the plaza. It was founded by the Jesuits in the late 16th century, serving as a seminary for the religious training of the children of Otomí Indians. The richly detailed stone carvings of angels and saints on the building's facade—a masterful example of Mexican baroque architecture—reflect the Jesuit order's wealth and influence.

A tree-lined atrium leads to the Aljibes Cloister (Claustro de Los Aljibes), which contains paintings by Miguel Cabrera. The interior is filled with gold gilt, carvings of cherubs and saints, and five extravagant altarpieces. A highlight is the Camarín de la Virgen, or altar room, behind the Chapel of the Virgin of Loreto (Capilla de la Virgen de Loreto). This small, octagonal-shaped chamber is a jewel box of intricate interior design.

Outside the Orange Cloister (Claustro de Los Naranjos), planted with orange trees, are carefully tended gardens. Church and National Museum of the Viceroyalty open Wed.-Sun. 9-6, Tues. 10-5. Museum admission about $3.80 (U.S.), free (ages 0-13).

National Museum of the Viceroyalty (Museo Nacional del Virreinato) is adjacent to the church, within the restored monastery. It houses 3 centuries' worth of colonial and religious art. Rare 16th-century vestments and altar hangings, gold and repoussé silver monstrances from the 17th century and a painting of the Virgin attributed to Bartolomé Esteban Murillo are among its many treasures.

Pastorelas, traditional re-enactments of Christ's birth, are performed during the Christmas season. Travel agencies in Mexico City can arrange for reservations, which should be booked well in advance. Admission is charged for the *pastorela* performances.

TEPOZTLAN, MORELOS (C-3)

pop. 15,200, elev. 5,579′

Tepoztlán (teh-pos-LAHN), a name that means "place of copper," is secluded on the lush green slopes of the Sierra del Ajusco mountains and sheltered by the Sierra de Tepoztlán. The latter's scarred cliffs make up Tepozteco National Park, which surrounds the village of Tlalnepantla, northeast of Tepoztlán. This sequestered location was perfect for Emiliano Zapata, regarded locally as a folk hero, who made the village his revolutionary stronghold in 1910.

Despite proximity to urban Cuernavaca and Mexico City, some traditional customs of Tepoztlán's pre-Hispanic predecessors hang on. This is, after all, the reputed birthplace of the Aztec god Quetzalcóatl *(see sidebar p. 370)*. Older residents still speak Náhuatl, the ancient Aztec tongue, and mingle Christian and pagan religious practices.

Religious celebrations, in fact, are a way of life here, observed through somber processions to the town cathedral as well as raucous fiestas punctuated by the music of brass bands and the explosive sound of bottle rockets. During Mardi Gras, held on the 5 days preceding Ash Wednesday, people perform Aztec dances and dress as Spanish *conquistadores.* On Sept. 8 a celebration honors both the Nativity of the Virgin and the god Tepoztécatl, the town's patron saint, a Mexican version of Bacchus credited with the creation of pulque, a fermented alcoholic drink extracted from the maguey plant.

Tepoztlán also has a decidedly mystical air. The panoramic setting naturally lures artists and other creative types, and its spiritual appeal attracts devotees of meditation and yoga as well as followers of New Age philosophies. Certainly the backdrop—a lush green valley hemmed in by volcanic peaks—is inspirational. The altitude and mild year-round weather nurture both tropical and temperate vegetation; everywhere there are exuberant growths of palms, bananas, orchids and bougainvillea, as well as pine and cedar trees and rose bushes. The sandstone cliffs visible from just about any location in town emerge sharply from early morning fog and cast a mellow glow at sunset.

Tepoztlán also is well known for various health treatments, particularly its Aztec sweat lodges, or *temazcales.* These small, round stone structures, which resemble igloos, are scattered around town. An hour's immersion in sauna-like heat includes short breaks when participants rub fresh aloe, eucalyptus and rosemary leaves on their skin. *Temazcal* aficionados swear by this cleansing ritual.

Tepoztlán's vibrant Saturday and Sunday market, which sets up in and around the main square, is one of the best in the region. It overflows with locally made clothing and handicrafts—pottery, hand-carved wood figures, woolen sweaters, carvings etched on tree bark, incense, '60s-style hippie jewelry—as well as mounds of produce and an amazing variety of food stands. Natural healers and shamans (Tepoztlán and the surrounding towns have a reputation for their *brujos,* or witches) also congregate at the market, selling herbs and potions. It can get very crowded, as many Mexico City families head here on weekends.

The mystical vibe even extends to ice cream. Tepoznieves, on Avenida 5 de Mayo near the main square, offers more than 70 flavors of ice cream and sorbet, including such unusual choices as rose petal and chili. Many are made from exotic native fruits like the green, grapefruit-sized guanabana. No artificial colorings or preservatives are used, lending the different varieties a rainbow of pale, pastel hues. Ice cream made here is packed in freezers and shipped to Tepoznieves outlets all over Mexico. It's worth stopping by just to see this ice cream parlor's wildly colorful tables and counters, tile floors and yellow walls covered with fanciful artwork.

Tepoztlán is about 80 kilometers (50 miles) south of downtown Mexico City via toll Mex. 95-D to the exit for Mex. 115-D. The turn-off to Tepoztlán is clearly marked. First-class Pullman de Morelos buses depart daily for Cuernavaca from Mexico City's airport; the fare is about $9.50 (U.S.). For information and reservations phone 01 (800) 624-0360 (toll-free long distance within Mexico). From Cuernavaca, taxi fare for the 40-minute drive to Tepoztlán averages about $10.

EX-CONVENT OF DOMINICO (Ex-Convento Dominico de la Navidad) is just e. of the main plaza, off Av. Revolución 1910. Built by Dominican friars, it was completed in 1588. Some walls of this massive structure are more than 6 feet thick. It has a crumbling beauty—much of the plaster has peeled away over time—and walls covered with frescoes. Upstairs is the small Historical Museum of Tepoztlán, with interesting exhibits that depict the region's religious, ethnological and natural history. Information is in Spanish.

The cathedral adjoining the monastery has twin spires, a barrel-vaulted interior and a walled atrium filled with aromatic eucalyptus trees. Religious paintings done by local artists also are on display. Don't miss the entry gate, which features a psychedelic-looking mural with a design created entirely from seeds and dried beans. Monastery complex open Tues.-Sun. 10-5. Free.

TEPOZTECO PYRAMID (Pirámide de Tepozteco) stands high on a hill overlooking Tepoztlán and is accessible by a trail beginning at the n. end of Av. Tepozteco/Av. 5 de Mayo (the street changes names n. of the main plaza). Built around 1200 by the Tlahuica Indians, it honored the god Tepoztécatl.

The pyramid, about 35 feet tall, rises from a stone platform and can be climbed (the 13 steps are very tall). It is topped by the remains of a two-room temple, which still shows evidence of carved door jambs and pedestals; the view of the valley below is magnificent. You also may encounter some coatimundis; these long-snouted, tree-dwelling relatives of the raccoon, native to Mexico and Central America, beg for food from visitors.

Note: The hike to the pyramid is about a mile from the center of town; the steep ascent is via a winding stone staircase, ending with a climb up a metal ladder. It takes about an hour each way; wear sturdy, comfortable hiking shoes. The path is tree-shaded and beautiful, so plan on several stops to both conserve energy and admire the views. Site daily 9-5:30. Admission 35 pesos (about $3.40 U.S.).

TEQUESQUITENGO, MORELOS (D-3)

elev. 3,083′

South of Cuernavaca lies the resort area of Tequesquitengo (teh-kehs-kee-TEHN-goh), on Lake Tequesquitengo. The village was moved to its present location in 1820 when rising lake waters forced the abandonment of an earlier site. Between 1957 and 1958 the lake rose nearly 13 feet, inundating lakeside homes and the first floor of a hotel. To restore the water level, a 1.7-mile tunnel was bored through a nearby mountain rim.

The lake, about 3,000 feet above sea level, has calm, spring-fed waters ideal for water skiing; it is the site of championship exhibitions. Swimming, boating and fishing also are possible.

TLALPAN, DISTRITO FEDERAL (B-3)

Tlalpan (TLAHL-pan), south of University City, can be reached by bus from the Taxqueña Metro station (line 2). The name means "place of solid ground"; in this area south of the Valley of Mexico, regional civilizations flourished as early as 1200 B.C. The Olympic Village (Villa Olímpica), built to house athletes during the 1968 summer games, is now a residential area.

Near Plaza de la Constitución, Tlalpan's main square, is the 1532 church of San Agustín de las Cuevas, which contains paintings by Miguel Cabrera. To the southwest is the extinct 13,097-foot Volcán Ajusco. Buses that leave from Azteca Stadium on Calzada de Tlalpan travel to the volcano, which offers excellent views of the surrounding area if the weather is clear.

CUICUILCO PYRAMID is near the intersection of Av. Insurgentes Sur (Mex. 95) and the Anillo Periférico, close to Olympic Village. The city of Cuicuilco was a major urban center, believed to have developed as early as 700 B.C. It eventually had a population estimated to be 20,000, but was abandoned around the end of the fourth century after several eruptions by the volcano Xitle.

Today the site consists of a round platform, discovered in the early 1920s, and a ramp that once led to an altar at the temple's summit. The original structure was some 370 feet in diameter and 59 feet high; it was enlarged several times over the centuries. A small museum at the site has geologic exhibits and displays objects found during the excavations. Daily 9-5. Admission is charged to the museum. Phone (55) 5606-9758.

TOLUCA, MEXICO (B-2)

pop. 461,400, elev. 8,790′

Capital of the state of México, Toluca (toh-LOO-cah)—about 65 kilometers (40 miles) west of Mexico City—is a commercial center in the middle of the flat Toluca Valley. One of the highest Mexican cities in elevation, it thus enjoys cool weather despite the tropical latitude. Although it is heavily industrial, low buildings characterize Toluca's skyline, and there are many little plazas and manicured parks.

Toluca was an Indian settlement as early as 1200; the name is derived from the Náhuatl Indian expression *tollocan*, or "those who bow their heads." Spaniards under Hernando Cortés began settling the region in the early 16th century after the conqueror was granted 22 towns in central and southern Mexico by King Carlos V.

Plaza of the Martyrs (Plaza de Los Mártires), the main plaza, is between avenidas Sebastian Lerdo de Tejada and de la Independencia. It was named for a group of revolutionaries who were executed in 1811 for their part in Mexico's struggle to win freedom from Spain, an uprising started by Father Miguel Hidalgo. On the plaza's south side is the cathedral, where traditional dances are presented on various Mexican holidays. Check with the State Tourism Office *(see below)* for more information about these colorful spectacles.

Among several downtown museums is the Museum of Fine Arts (Museo de Bellas Artes), on

Avenida Santos Degollado a block north of the plaza. The collection of paintings and sculptures spans the 16th through the 19th centuries.

A block or so south of the plaza along Avenida Miguel Hidalgo is Los Portales, a pedestrian-only walkway fronting an arcade of shops and restaurants protected by arches and buzzing with sidewalk vendors. It's an interesting place to stroll. Here rows of candy stands offer Toluca's local fruit confections, and liquor stores sell an orange-flavored liqueur called *moscos.*

From Mexico City, the easiest way to reach Toluca by car is to take toll highway Mex. 15-D. This direct route is expensive but fast. Buses to Toluca depart regularly from Mexico City's Terminal de Autobuses del Poniente, the western bus terminal; to get there, take Metro to the Observatorio station (at the western end of Line 1). Buses marked "Toluca—Directo" make the trip in the least amount of time.

Several towns and villages to the east and south of Toluca offer a firsthand look at the way Mexico's rural population has engaged in manufacturing and marketing since pre-Hispanic days. Visiting these places during the morning is a good way to acquire locally made items at the various *tianguis* (open-air markets), even without benefit of bargaining expertise. East of Toluca on Mex. 15 to the paved turn-off for the village of San Pedro Cholula, then south, is appropriately named Tianguistenco. The Tuesday market fills roughly half the streets in town with baskets, *sarapes* and other crafts from throughout the Toluca Valley.

México State Tourism Office (Dirección General de Turismo): Avenida 1 de Mayo #731 at the corner of Roberto Bosch, second floor, Industrial Zone; phone (722) 275-8108 or (722) 275-8109.

What To See in and Around Town

BOTANIC GARDEN (Cosmovitral Jardín Botánico) is just e. of the main plaza at calles Lerdo de Tejada, Degollado and Ignacio Rayón. Hundreds of plant species native to Mexico are exhibited within the walls of this Art Nouveau-style building. Most impressive, however, are the magnificent stained-glass panels, which replaced the original windows. They were designed and built in 1980 by local artist Leopoldo Flores, who utilized some 45 tons of glass, 65 tons of metal and 25 tons of lead in their creation. Tues.-Sun. 10-6. Admission about $1.25 (U.S.).

CALIXTLAHUACA ARCHEOLOGICAL ZONE is 8 km (5 mi.) n. on Mex. 55 to the site turn-off, then about 3 km (2 mi.) w. The site is located on a hilltop above the village of the same name. Not much is known about its origins, although it was taken over by the Aztecs around 1476. Several buildings have been uncovered: the conical Temple of Quetzalcóatl-Ehecatl; the Pyramid of Tláloc; and the Altar of Skulls (Tzompantli), which was probably used for human sacrifice. Buses make frequent trips from Toluca to Calixtlahuaca; there is a short uphill walk to get to the site entrance. Daily 9-5. Admission about $3 (U.S.); free to all Sun.

CASA DE ARTESANIAS is at Paseo Tollocan Oriente #700, at the corner of Uracua. This government-run crafts store offers contemporary crafts produced in the state of México, including textiles, carved wood figures, ceramics and blown glass. It also is possible to watch the artisans as they work. The store is staffed with multilingual personnel. Daily 10-7.

FELIPE S. GUTIERREZ MUSEUM is downtown at Calle Nicolas Bravo #303, at the corner of Av. Lerdo de Tejada. It features works by the 19th-century portrait painter who taught figure drawing to José María Velasco. Gutiérrez was one of the first Mexican artists who rendered his subjects' Indian lineage, making no attempt to give them European features. Guided tours are available. Tues.-Sun. 10-6. Free. Phone (722) 213-2647.

JOSE MARIA VELASCO MUSEUM is at Av. Lerdo de Tejada #400, adjoining the Felipe S. Gutiérrez Museum. It exhibits paintings and sculptures by one of Mexico's most influential 19th-century painters. One of Velasco's more notable works, "Vista desde Molino del Rey," was donated to the museum by former president Ernesto Zedillo. One room contains a re-creation of the artist's workshop. Guided tours are available. Tues.-Sun. 10-6. Free. Phone (722) 213-2647.

METEPEC is about 8 km (5 mi.) s.e. of Toluca and an hour w. of Mexico City. It is best known for the Trees of Life *(Arboles de la Vida)* meticulously created by local artisans. Against a backdrop of clay trunks and branches, these delightful trees depict stories populated by a diverse cast of religious and secular characters and inanimate objects. Many families in town are engaged in the craft.

Buses depart frequently for Metepec from Toluca's central bus station. The town is an easy day trip from Mexico City as well. By car, leave the capital via Paseo de la Reforma or Avenida Constituyentes, picking up either toll Mex. 15-D or free Mex. 15 west toward Toluca. Take the Mex. 15-D exit for Taxco/Ixtapan de La Sal and follow signs for Metepec. Pottery shops line the main street; ask for directions to the artisans' workshops *(alfarerías)*, where bargaining for purchases is expected. **Note:** Many are closed from 2-4 for afternoon *siesta.*

MUSEUM OF WATERCOLOR (Museo de la Acuarela) is at Melchor Ocampo #105. It occupies one of Toluca's oldest buildings, a two-story house with a central courtyard. It is known as "El Gallito," a reference to the brand of thread that was once distributed from the building. The permanent collection of 176 paintings is displayed in six halls, each named after a popular artist from the state of México. Guided tours are available. Tues.-Sun. 10-6. Free. Phone (722) 214-7304.

NEVADO DE TOLUCA NATIONAL PARK (Parque Nacional Nevado de Toluca) is about 25 km (16 mi.) s.w. of Toluca on Mex. 134 to the junction with Mex. 10, then s. on Mex. 10 about 8 km (5 mi.) to the park entrance. From the entrance, a paved road winds about 3.5 km (2 mi.) to the main gate, then a rough, unsurfaced road ascends the 17 km (11 mi.) to the crater. This 15,032-foot-high extinct volcano is Mexico's fourth highest summit.

Nevado de Toluca's summit is snowcapped from November to March and frequently obscured by clouds. Within the crater are two deep-blue lakes, El Sol (Lake of the Sun) and La Luna (Lake of the Moon). With care and a good guide, you can drive to the top of the mountain and then hike down into the crater; on a clear day, the views are splendid. Check with the State Tourism Office in Toluca for information about guided excursions. Park admission about $1 (U.S.).

STATE OF MEXICO CULTURAL CENTER (Centro Cultural Mexiquense) is off the Paseo Tollocan loop road; from its s.w. section (between the monument to Christopher Columbus, at the junction with Mex. 134, and the University of the State of México), follow the signs about 1.6 km (1 mi.) s.w. to the cultural center. This large, spread-out complex comprises a mix of architectural styles from colonial to contemporary.

The center can be reached from downtown Toluca via bus or taxi. Guide service in English is available. Museums open daily 10-6. Admission about $2 (U.S.). Phone (722) 274-1200.

Museum of Anthropology (Museo de Antropología), within the center, exhibits artifacts from the state's archeological zones, including Malinalco and Calixtlahuaca. It was designed by Pedro Ramírez Vasquez, the architect who supervised construction of Mexico City's National Museum of Anthropology.

Museum of Modern Art (Museo de Arte Moderno), within the center, has works by Mexican muralists José Clemente Orozco, Diego Rivera and David Alfaro Siqueiros, among others.

Museum of Popular Arts (Museo de Artes Popular), within the center, is housed in a hacienda dating from the 17th century. Colorful murals decorate its walls, and a variety of regional handicrafts are on display. A huge "tree of life" sits in the front hall. The museum's exhibits of saddles, clothing and other items used by *charros* (cowboys) are considered among the best of their type in the country.

TEOTENANGO ARCHEOLOGICAL ZONE is about 25 km (16 mi.) s. of Toluca via Mex. 55, overlooking the village of Tenango de Arista. Teotenango was probably a ceremonial center for nearby Malinalco *(see Tenancingo listing)*. This walled, hilltop site covers more than 2 square miles, spread across a flat bluff. The impressive reconstructions include a good-sized ball court, large pyramids and squat temples faced with broad staircases. An uphill walk to the ruins passes a small museum displaying artifacts recovered during restoration efforts. Bus transportation is available from Toluca. Tues.-Sun. 9-5. Admission (site and museum) about $1.25 (U.S.).

ZACANGO ZOO is about 7 km (4 mi.) s.e. of the city via Mex. 55 to the Metepec exit, then approximately 6 km (3.5 mi.) w., following signs. The zoo displays more than 200 species of animals on the grounds of the former Hacienda de Zacango, home of the Order of Franciscan Priests in the 16th century. Features include an African compound with free-roaming animals, a walk-through aviary and a petting zoo. Food is available. Daily 9-5. Admission is charged.

VALLE DE BRAVO, MEXICO (C-1)

pop. 26,600, elev. 5,937′

Situated on a forested mountain slope about 140 kilometers (87 miles) west of Mexico City, Valle de Bravo (VAH-yeh deh BRAH-voh) overlooks large, man-made Lake Avándaro, part of a vast hydroelectric project serving the Valley of Mexico. The town is a popular weekend resort for well-to-do residents of Mexico City and Toluca.

Hang gliding, hiking, horseback riding, kayaking mountain biking, sailing and windsurfing are among the recreational activities available. Nearby Avándaro Reort and Spa has an 18-hole golf course. Valle de Bravo also hosts an international hang-gliding competition. Due to the elevation, the region is blessed with some of Mexico's nicest weather—mild, dry and sunny.

Buildings with whitewashed stucco walls and red-tiled roofs give the town an attractive colonial look. Further color is supplied by masses of bougainvillea cascading over walls and terraces, and—from November through March—fluttering clouds of monarch butterflies en route to and from their nearby wintering grounds *(see Angangueo listing under Central Mexico)*. In the vicinity of Plaza Independencia, the main square, are boutiques, restaurants, a two-story artisans' market and a bookstore.

XOCHIMILCO, DISTRITO FEDERAL (C-3)

Xochimilco (soh-chee-MEEL-coh) is about 24 kilometers (15 miles) southeast of downtown Mexico City, within the Federal District but outside the city limits. Designated a World Heritage Site by UNESCO in 1987, the "place where the flowers grow" was once a Chichimec Indian stronghold.

The best way to reach Xochimilco is to take Mexico City's Metro (line 2) to the Taxqueña station, then board a light rail train *(tren ligero)* and get off at the Xochimilco stop. *Peseros* (minibuses) also make the trip from the Taxqueña Metro station to Xochimilco, as do buses that travel down Avenida Insurgentes Sur and Calzada de Tlalpan to the Anillo Periférico.

By car, Xochimilco can be reached via the Periférico, exiting at Jardines del Sur. The tourist-oriented "floating gardens" area is busiest on

Sunday, when Mexican families come on their traditional day off. It's much less crowded in the middle of the week.

Xochimilco is threaded by numerous waterways, the last remains of a once-extensive lake. *Chinampas,* rafts woven from twigs, were covered with earth and planted with flowers or vegetables. The rafts often carried a small hut and were propelled about the lake with oars. The roots of willows planted around the perimeter of some rafts gradually attached to the lake bottom, and the so-called "floating gardens" became islands threaded by canals.

For a real taste of Mexican merrymaking visit on Sunday, when Xochimilco is thronged by families and a freewheeling carnival atmosphere prevails. Signs marked "Embarcadero" point the way to the boat launches. The rental rate is per boat rather than per person, so it's cheaper—and more fun—to join a group.

Restaurants and souvenir stands line the canals. Everywhere there are hawkers, ashore and afloat in canoes, peddling tacos, beer, drinks, trinkets, balloons, flowers and fruit. Music is an integral part of the fun, and some boats are occupied by mariachi bands or guitar trios, in full costume and of varying degrees of polish, who paddle up to prospective customers and serenade them for a fee.

The government sets authorized rates for the boats, called *trajineras*. If an operator tries to charge more, complain to the police, who usually patrol the principal pier. If a police officer is not available, you must resort to bargaining, at which the boat operators are uncannily skillful; many have learned some English for just this purpose. Be sure to agree on the price and the length of the ride before embarking. Most rides average about 300 pesos (about $29 U.S.).

North of the town center is a more recently developed area of canals and *chinampas* where produce is raised, most of it bound for Mexico City markets. Boats can be hired to cruise these canals as well, although the area is kept separate from the tourist-targeted floating gardens. Picnicking is permitted along the banks of a man-made lake, where there also is a visitor center.

Although the floating gardens are the reason most people come here, Xochimilco has other attractions. Facing the main square is the early 16th-century Franciscan Convent and Church of San Bernardino, one of the first in New Spain. Stone carvings of angels and flowers adorn the church's exterior. Inside are several chapels and a main altar resplendent with gold gilt, sculptures and paintings. Also in the central part of town are garden centers and the market, liveliest on Saturdays when Indians come from miles around to sell their wares.

GEM **DOLORES OLMEDO PATIÑO MUSEUM** is at Av. México #5843; take Metro line 2 to the Taxqueña station, then the *tren ligero* (light rail) to the La Noria station. The museum is several blocks from the light rail station. Since street parking is limited, it's easier to hire a hotel taxi driver for the trip. Philanthropist, art collector and benefactor of Diego Rivera, Olmedo bequeathed her hacienda, La Noria, and her outstanding art collection to the Mexican people upon Rivera's death in 1957.

Featured are Rivera paintings, drawings and engravings; paintings by Frida Kahlo (including some of her best-known works); watercolors and engravings by Russian artist Angelina Beloff; sculptures; and Mexican folk and religious art. The lovely grounds of this immense complex are alone worth a visit, with their lush gardens, orange and fig trees, Aztec and Mayan artifacts, wandering peacocks and a friendly pack of *xoloitzcuintle,* a rare, mid-size hairless dog with black skin dating from pre-Hispanic times. Children's programs, concerts and other special events take place Sat.-Sun.

Food is available. Restrooms are provided. Allow 2 hours minimum. Tues.-Sun. 10-6. Guided tours are given Wed.-Sun. at 10, noon and 4. Admission about $3 (U.S.), free (ages 0-5 and 64+); free to all Tues. Headphone and cassette player rental fee $1. Phone (55) 5555-1016.

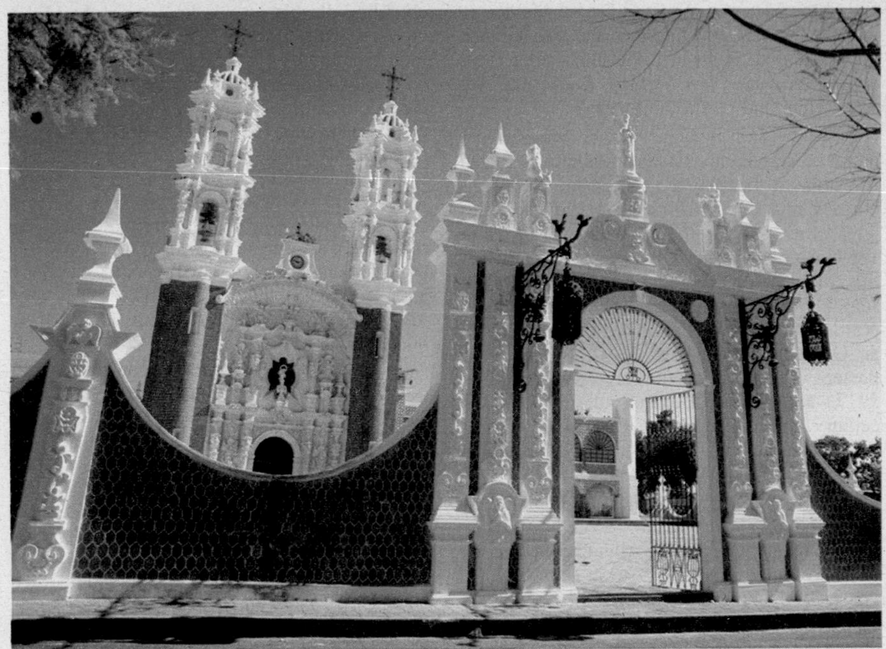

Sanctuary of the Virgin of Ocotlán, Tlaxcala, Tlaxcala / © José Fuste Raga / age fotostock

Central Mexico

The "heartland of Mexico" evokes more reminders of Spain's legacy than any other part of the country. It is in this region that Spanish explorers capitalized upon abundant mineral resources, particularly silver, and built Mexico's first colonial cities. Many of the country's grand cathedrals and historic buildings were constructed during 3 centuries of Spanish rule. But Spanish colonists put most of their effort into exploiting the natural resources of their far-flung colony rather than developing an infrastructure to improve it, and the emergence of a rigid class society that put Indians on the bottom rung had bred widespread divisiveness by the turn of the 19th century.

As a result, history figures strongly in this region. The push for independence began with secret meetings in Morelia, Querétaro and San Miguel de Allende. These revolutionarues plotted Spain's downfall to coincide with the rising of Nueva España ("New Spain"), an independent nation. It was in the town of Dolores Hidalgo that Father Miguel Hidalgo first declared Mexico's freedom from Spain in his 1810 proclamation *Grito de Dolores.*

Father Hidalgo, an intriguing mix of flawed cleric (he sired several children) and committed champion for Indian rights, became the leader of a group of like-minded intellectuals intent on securing Mexican independence. He and two of his chief officers, Ignacio Allende and Ignacio Aldama, were captured outside the city of Chihuahua and executed in 1811, and it would be 10 more long years before independence was finally achieved. Although Hidalgo died in disgrace as a failed rebel and defrocked priest, he is revered in Mexico today.

The Treaty of Guadalupe Hidalgo was signed in the city of Querétaro in 1848. It ended the Mexican War and forced Mexico to give up its territory north of the Rio Grande to the United States, an enormous area comprising Arizona, New Mexico, California, Nevada, Utah and part of Colorado.

In May 1862, invading French forces under emperor Napoleon III were soundly defeated in battle at Puebla, a triumphant event celebrated in today's *Cinco de Mayo* festivities both north and south of the border. And in 1867, Archduke Maximilian, de facto "ruler" of Mexico while then-president Benito Juárez's government was in disarray due to political turmoil, was executed by firing squad at Querétaro. Querétaro also is where the present Mexican constitution was drafted in 1917, and where Mexico's dominant 20th-century political party, the Partido Revolucionario Institucional (PRI), was organized in 1929.

Central Mexico's so-called "colonial" cities—including Guanajuato, Morelia, Puebla, Querétaro, San Miguel de Allende and Zacatecas—are noted for their historic centers. Here you'll find pretty plazas, carefully preserved old buildings, and beautiful cathedrals and churches. Puebla also is known for buildings covered with Talavera tiles arranged in geometric patterns—a Spanish import.

Guadalajara, Mexico's second city and the capital of Jalisco, offers much to see. But it also is a magnet for Mexico's poor, who pour into the city hoping for a better life, putting a strain on already overburdened public services. While visitors are likely to be enchanted by the colonial plazas and stately architecture, they must also contend with traffic jams, air pollution and other urban ills. Still, to many people Guadalajara embodies the essence of Mexico, and its residents are known for their hospitality.

Guadalajara preserves the Spanish colonial past but also celebrates such homegrown pleasures as the *jarabe,* or Mexican hat dance, the heartfelt strains of mariachi music and the flashy horsemanship that characterizes a *charreada,* or Mexican rodeo. And be sure to investigate Chapala, Ajijic and the other resort towns along the shore of nearby Lake Chapala; pleasant year-round weather plus cultural and recreational opportunities have helped make this area a major destination for U.S. and Canadian retirees.

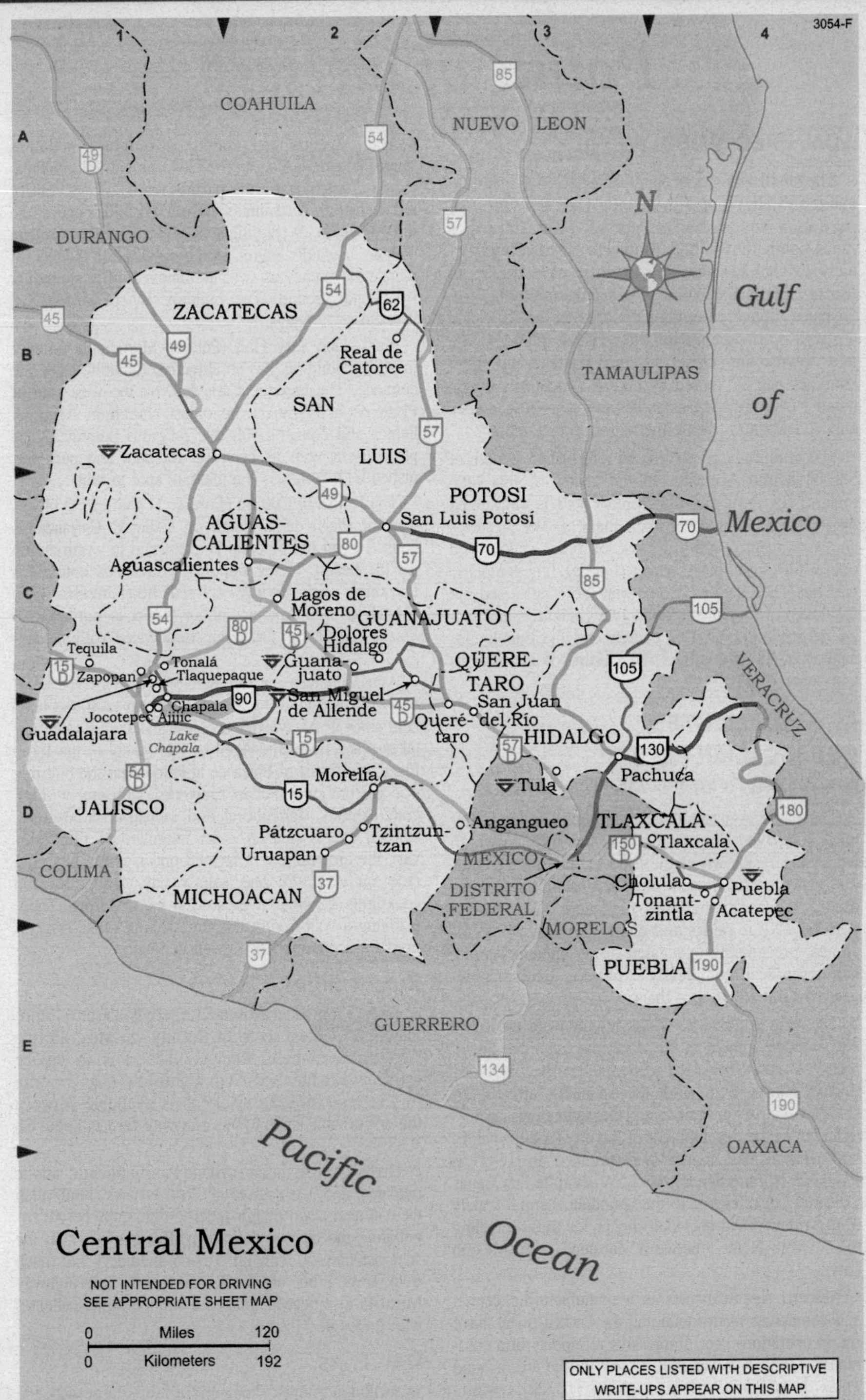
3054-F
COAHUILA
NUEVO LEON
DURANGO
ZACATECAS
Real de Catorce
SAN LUIS POTOSI
TAMAULIPAS
Gulf of Mexico
Zacatecas
San Luis Potosí
AGUAS-CALIENTES
Aguascalientes
Lagos de Moreno
GUANAJUATO
Dolores Hidalgo
Guanajuato
QUERETARO
Tequila
Tonalá
Zapopan
Tlaquepaque
San Miguel de Allende
Querétaro
San Juan del Río
Chapala
Jocotepec
Ajijic
Guadalajara
Lake Chapala
HIDALGO
Pachuca
VERACRUZ
Morelia
Tula
JALISCO
Pátzcuaro
Tzintzuntzan
Angangueo
TLAXCALA
Tlaxcala
Uruapan
MEXICO
COLIMA
MICHOACAN
DISTRITO FEDERAL
Cholula
Puebla
Tonantzintla
Acatepec
MORELOS
PUEBLA
GUERRERO
OAXACA
Pacific Ocean
Central Mexico
NOT INTENDED FOR DRIVING
SEE APPROPRIATE SHEET MAP
0 Miles 120
0 Kilometers 192
ONLY PLACES LISTED WITH DESCRIPTIVE WRITE-UPS APPEAR ON THIS MAP.
© AAA

Points of Interest

ACATEPEC, PUEBLA (D-4)

The small villages of San Francisco Acatepec (ah-kah-teh-PEHK) and Tonantzintla *(see separate listing within this region)* are just off Mex. 190 a few miles south of Cholula. Both are distinguished by baroque churches that are magnificent examples of Indian craftsmanship—local artisans employing pre-Hispanic imagery to depict Christian beliefs—and are well worth seeing for their visual splendor. The two towns are close to each other, and both churches can be visited by taking a local bus designated "Chipilo." Buses make the trip to Acatepec and Tonantzintla from either Cholula or Puebla.

The beautifully preserved and refurbished Church of San Francisco Acatepec, in the center of this little town, dates from the 18th century and is considered one of the most ornate in the Americas. The facade is an extravagantly colorful feast of blue, yellow and orange tiles fastidiously arranged in dazzling geometric patterns. The interior is somewhat more restrained but still lovely, with paneled doors, wall paintings and folk art decoration. Both this church and the one in Tonantzintla strongly reflect the culture of the Indians who labored to build them.

AGUASCALIENTES, AGUASCALIENTES (C-1)

pop. 618,400, metro area 734,400, elev. 6,193′

The name Aguascalientes (ah-guahs-ka-lee-EHN-tehs) is derived from nearby thermal springs, which were already known at the time of the city's founding. An extensive system of underground tunnels has earned Aguascalientes the nickname "La Ciudad Perforada" (the perforated city). This maze of catacombs, presumably excavated by an ancient people, has never been completely explored. Visitors, however, are not allowed in them.

The first inhabitants of this region were an indigenous people known as the Chichimecas (brave dogs), many of whom belonged to nomadic tribes with distinctive names. Soon after the Spaniards arrived, orchards began to be cultivated; the settlements around them led to the development of the city's oldest neighborhoods. Aguascalientes was founded in 1575 as "Villa de Nuestra Señora de la Asunción de Las Aguas Calientes," a reference to the abundant thermal waters in the vicinity, and provided shelter for those traveling the "Silver Route" between Zacatecas and Mexico City.

Modern Aguascalientes is a manufacturing center, and companies from Japan and the United States have set up operations here. Impressive reminders of a colonial past, however, can still be seen in the area around Plaza de la Patria, the main plaza. The city's warm, dry climate also makes it pleasant to explore on foot.

The cathedral and various government buildings flank Plaza de la Patria. The Government Palace (Palacio de Gobierno), on the plaza's south side, is built of red sandstone; it features hand-carved pillars and a fine interior patio. A highlight is the mural by Chilean painter Oswaldo Barra, which depicts all manner of mercantile scenes as well as miners grimly ascending from underground. The building is open Mon.-Sat. 9-4; closed holidays.

Next door, City Hall (Palacio Municipal), another imposing building, has an attractive fountain inside the entrance. The baroque Cathedral, on the west side of Plaza de la Patria, is the oldest church in Aguascalientes and contains valuable religious paintings. The plaza itself, with its beautiful fountain and park furnished with benches, is a pleasant spot to relax.

The House of Culture (Casa de la Cultura), 2 blocks west of Plaza de la Patria on Calle V. Carranza, is housed in an old colonial convent and is worth a stop for the beauty of the building, which has courtyards festooned with vividly colored bougainvillea. The Church of San Antonio, about 6 blocks northeast of Plaza de la Patria, has a cupola adorned with stained-glass windows.

Aguascalientes' annual San Marcos Fair (Feria de San Marcos), honoring the city's patron saint, has been held since 1604. Mexico's oldest and largest state fair takes place from mid-April to early May at the Expo Plaza, southwest of Plaza de la Patria near the bullring. The celebrations include fireworks, amusement rides, craft exhibits, agricultural and industrial expositions, cultural events (including an international film festival), the crowning of a festival queen and a huge parade on Apr. 25, the saint's day. Bullfights and cockfights generate a great deal of wagering. Those planning a visit during this time should make reservations for accommodations well in advance.

Practicalities

Jesús Terán International Airport is about 34 kilometers (21 miles) south of the city via Mex. 45 (the Aguascalientes-León Highway). There is air service to Aguascalientes via Aero California *(see Arriving by Air, page 61)*. Taxi service is available between the airport and downtown; one-way fare is about $8 (U.S.).

Highway signs in and around Aguascalientes can be outdated, and it is easy to get lost; visitors should plan their itinerary and obtain specific directions before negotiating the city on their own. Roadways within the state are narrow, with little or no shoulders and much truck traffic, but are well maintained. Toll highway Mex. 45-D proceeds southeast, linking Aguascalientes with Lagos de Moreno.

Day Trips

Although Aguascalientes is a fairly large city, the attractions of interest to tourists are concentrated around or near the main plaza. It should take no more than a day or two to see the sights. Another option is to stroll the plaza area in the morning and then arrange an afternoon excursion to a nearby winery or spa. Peñuelas Hacienda is a breeding ranch said to produce some of Mexico's most spirited bulls; make arrangements to visit beforehand, either through your hotel or the State Tourism Office.

Ojocaliente Sports Center (Centro Deportivo Ojocaliente) is about a kilometer east of downtown on Mex. 70. This spa has thermal pools, steam baths, saunas and tennis courts. Plaza Vestir, about 10 kilometers (6 miles) south on Mex. 45, is a collection of shops selling locally made clothing, embroidered items and shoes. A city bus or taxi will take you to the center.

In the nearby town of Pabellón de Hidalgo, 33 kilometers (20 miles) north of Aguascalientes on Mex. 45, then 5 kilometers (3 miles) west, is the Hacienda San Blas de Pabellón, which houses the Museum of the Insurgency. Here, after losing two important battles against the Spanish in 1811, insurgent leader Father Miguel Hidalgo y Costilla was relieved of his command and replaced by Ignacio Allende. The hacienda produces woolen goods on hand-powered looms.

The mining town of Asientos, easily reached by bus, is about 45 kilometers (28 miles) northeast. Many 16th- and 17th-century paintings are on display in the local churches, and a colonial atmosphere prevails. Encarnación de Díaz, about 42 kilometers (26 miles) south on Mex. 45, has old baroque churches and a central plaza with living trees sculpted into various shapes, including Christopher Columbus' ships the *Niña,* the *Pinta* and the *Santa María.*

Aguascalientes State Tourism Office (Coordinadora de Turismo): Calle Manuel M. Ponce #134 in the historic city center; phone 01 (800) 949-4949 (toll-free long distance within Mexico) or (449) 915-1155.

CITY MUSEUM (Museo de Aguascalientes) is about 6 blks. n.e. of Plaza de la Patria at Calle Zaragoza #507, opposite the Church of San Antonio. It exhibits 20th-century art, including a collection of paintings by Saturnino Herrán, who was born in the city. His work depicts the common people with uncommon sensitivity and fostered a sense of nationalist pride. Tues.-Sun. 11-6. Admission about $1.25 (U.S.); free to all Sun.

JOSE GUADALUPE POSADA MUSEUM is about 6 blks. s. of Plaza de la Patria on Plaza Encino, next to Encino Church (Templo del Encino). It houses a fascinating collection of works by Posada, a 19th-century Mexican engraver and cartoonist who was another native son. He was best known for his *calaveras,* skeletal-like figures that satirized events leading up to the Mexican Revolution of 1910. These humorous political scenarios influenced public opinion in their day. Tues.-Sun. 11-6. Admission about 50c (U.S.); free to all Sun.

AJIJIC, JALISCO (D-1) pop. 13,300

Ajijic (ah-hee-HEEK) is about 8 kilometers (5 miles) west of Chapala on the northern shore of Lake Chapala. This artists' and writers' colony, one of several resort/retirement communities along the lake, is populated by many former U.S. residents.

Along Calle Morelos between the main square and the waterfront are shops and boutiques selling everything from local handicrafts to designer fashions. Easily reached from Guadalajara, Ajijic has a picturesque waterfront area and cobblestone streets and is a pleasant destination for shopping, strolling and perhaps lunch. The town's Fiesta of St. Andrew, held in late November, is celebrated with parades, dancing and fireworks.

ANGANGUEO, MICHOACAN (D-3) elev. 7,997′

Angangueo (ahn-gahn-GEH-oh), which sits in a canyon carved by the Río Puerco, was a pueblo inhabited by Tarascan Indians long before the arrival of the Spanish. The name means "mouth of the cave." Towering above are the 10,000-foot peaks of Cerro de Guadalupe, El Campanario and Cerro de la Gotera.

Angangueo's heyday was in the early 20th century, when it was a mining center. Today this hamlet, dominated by two imposing Catholic churches facing each other across the main plaza, survives as a tourist departure point for trips to the surrounding monarch butterfly sanctuaries; there are more than a dozen, most of them in the state of Michoacán.

Every winter the generation of monarchs that have spent the spring and summer in Canada and the United States east of the Rockies arrive in this mountainous, forested region of Mexico as part of their remarkable migratory life cycle. Scientists do not know for sure what inner navigational system guides the insects into making this 2,500-mile journey, although one possible explanation is that more than half of North America's species of milkweed—the caterpillars' food source—are native to Mexico, indicating that the urge to migrate is passed along genetically.

After reaching their wintering grounds the monarchs hibernate, forming enormous colonies that completely cloak the tall pines and firs. In a semi-dormant state they burn almost no energy, but begin to grow more active as the weather warms, preparing for the northward migration in the spring. Several generations hatch along the way, thus continuing the monarch's life cycle for another year.

The monarch has a remarkable ability to survive decimating losses; in the winter of 2002, heavy rainstorms and freezing winter weather killed millions and millions of butterflies. However, both scientists and environmentalists worry that herbicide use in the United States and Canada, which kills milkweed plants, as well as illegal Mexican logging operations that destroy the butterflies' sanctuaries will have a devastating long-term effect on their numbers.

EL ROSARIO MONARCH BUTTERFLY SANCTUARY (Santuario de Las Mariposas Monarca, El Rosario) is about 6 km (4 mi.) n.e. of Angangueo, near the small village of El Rosario. The steep and rough dirt road to the sanctuary should be negotiated only in a truck or four-wheel-drive vehicle. An alternate entry can be made via a dirt road from the village of Ocampo, a few miles s.w. of Angangueo; this route is longer but can be made adequately in a small car.

Organized daylong bus or van tours to the sanctuary from Mexico City or Morelia can be arranged through travel agencies in those cities. But while a tour saves time and effort, it also necessitates getting up before dawn. If you're driving, leave your car in Angangueo and ride in a four-wheel-drive vehicle to the sanctuary. This is easier than it sounds; numerous freelance guides are available, and tourists are approached the moment they set foot in town. The slow, steep route to the sanctuary takes about an hour.

Another alternative is to spend the night in Angangueo. The Hotel Albergue Don Bruno, in the center of town at Calle Morelos #92, has comfortable rooms; phone (715) 156-0026.

Wear sturdy, comfortable walking shoes and bring a jacket or sweater in case the weather is chilly. Weekends are crowded with Mexico City residents;

go during the week if possible. Sanctuary open daily 9-6, Dec.-Mar. Admission about $2.25 (U.S.).

CHAPALA, JALISCO (D-1) pop. 19,600

Along with Ajijic and Jocotepec, the resort community of Chapala (chah-PAH-lah) is on the northern shore of Lake Chapala. During the early 20th century it was the summer residence of dictator Porfirio Díaz. At that time the town attracted a rich international clientele who spent weekends at lavish estates, enjoying the area's tranquil beauty and delightfully springlike weather, a bit cooler in summer and warmer in winter than Guadalajara.

Today Chapala has an established resident population of American and Canadian retirees. Commercial activity is centered along Avenida Madero, which leads to the lake and town pier. The street is lined with shops and small cafes. Near the pier is the main square, a pleasant spot to relax; band serenades are held here on Sunday evenings. Along the lakeshore is Cristiania Park, where vendors gather on the weekend.

The lake itself, some 53 miles long and 18 miles wide, is the largest natural lake in Mexico, surrounded by lushly forested mountains. It is, however, the chief source of water for the city, and because of tremendous population growth in the surrounding area, the water level has dropped by half since the turn of the 20th century. Cutting down trees has caused millions of cubic feet of mud to seep into the lake over the years, and the stench of pollution is strongly evident in some areas. Engineers and Mexican environmental groups have worked to promote reforestation programs to reverse this trend.

Mezcala Island can be reached by boat from the Chapala pier. The ruins of a fort and bastion here date from the Mexican War of Independence, when rebels successfully defended the island against the Spanish army and navy from 1812-16. Hunger and sickness finally forced these 1,500 courageous souls to surrender, but their valor prompted the Spaniards to present them with an honor guard and a military pardon.

CHOLULA, PUEBLA (D-3)
pop. 125,000, elev. 7,039′

The Cholula (choh-LOO-lah) of today is practically a suburb of ever-expanding Puebla, but at the time of its destruction in 1519 by Hernando Cortés it was a religious city built on the foundations of a ceremonial center that had flowered by the second century A.D. At its peak Cholula was inhabited by 100,000 Cholultecs—a mixture of Olmec, Toltec, Aztec, Mixtec and Mazatec Indians.

When Cortés arrived in Cholula en route to Tenochtitlán, the Aztecs mistook the conqueror for the god Quetzalcóatl, which their mythology described as being fair skinned and with light hair. Consequently, the 100,000 inhabitants showed deference to Cortés and his band of 500 men. The conqueror promptly shattered this illusion by having his second in command, Pedro de Alvarado, carry out the slaughter of 6,000 Indians and the destruction of their temples and shrines.

Following custom, the Spanish conquerors erected a church atop the rubble of each temple they razed. An example sits atop Tepanapa Pyramid, one of the New World's largest structures. Burrowing into the earth near the base of this brush-covered hill, archeologists discovered that the Cholultecs, in fact, appeared to be better builders than the Aztecs who last occupied the city. An earthquake in 1999 caused extensive damage to this church, which has since been restored by the state.

ROYAL CHAPEL (Capilla Real) faces the main square. The chapel is within the walls of the Church of San Gabriel. Originally built for defensive as well as religious purposes, it contains seven naves and has 49 domes.

TEPANAPA PYRAMID (Pirámide Tepanapa) rises near the main square. Its base length is about 1,315 feet—each side some 500 feet longer than the Pyramid of the Sun at Teotihuacán. An arduous stone trail leads to the Santuario de Los Remedios, the church that crowns the hill 230 feet above ground level. Climbers reaching the top are rewarded with excellent views. Some of the nearly 5 miles of tunnels are lighted; guides identify structures and decorative highlights.

A museum near the entrance exhibits pottery and artifacts dating from pre-Hispanic times, Indian knives and arrowheads used in sacrifices, and a scale model of the pyramid as it is believed to have appeared prior to Hernando Cortés' arrival. Site open Tues.-Sun. 9-5. Admission (includes museum) 39 pesos (about $3.80 U.S.).

DOLORES HIDALGO, GUANAJUATO
(C-2) pop. 52,100, elev. 6,517′

Known in Mexico as Cuna de la Independencia Nacional (The Cradle of National Independence) and designated a national historic monument, Dolores Hidalgo (doh-LOH-rehs ee-DAHL-goh) lies in the valley of the Río Laja. Just before midnight on Sept. 15, 1810, Father Miguel Hidalgo y Costilla called together his parishioners by ringing the village church bell. He then gave the venerated *Grito de Dolores*, a speech announcing Mexican independence that ignited the 11-year war to achieve it.

A statue of Hidalgo stands in Plaza Principal, the main plaza, where various vendors ply their wares among comfortable old benches and square-trimmed trees. The former homes of other Mexican heroes are here as well; guides are available for town tours.

The annual Independence Day celebrations held Sept. 15-16 re-create Father Hidalgo's historic rallying cry, and the president of Mexico often officiates.

HIDALGO HOUSE MUSEUM (Museo Casa de Hidalgo) is on Morelos #1 at Hidalgo, a block south of the main plaza. Miguel Hidalgo lived here when he was the town's parish priest. It contains many items relating to the life of the patriot, including paintings, portraits, books, period furniture and a room filled with wreaths and other memorials. Tues.-Sat. 10-5:30, Sun. 10-4:30. Admission about $2.50 (U.S.).

Guadalajara

City Population: 1,659,400, metropolitan area 3,847,000 (2002 estimate)
Elevation: 1,552 meters (5,091 feet)

Editor's Picks:

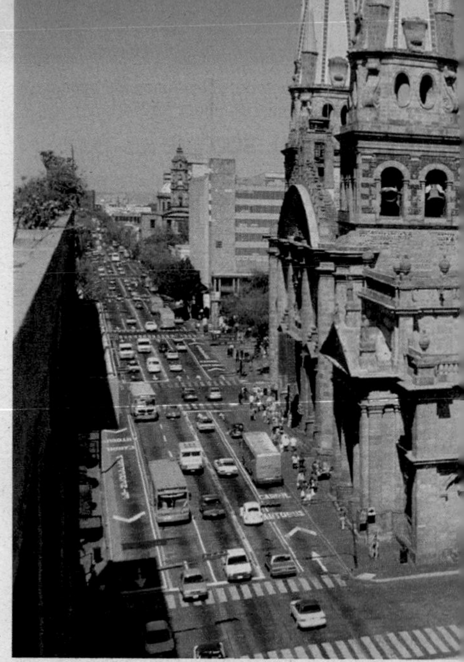

Cathedral / © age fotostock / SuperStock

Guadalajara's (gwah-dah-lah-HAH-rah) history dates to 1530, just 38 years after Christopher Columbus first reached North America and 9 years after the conquest of Mexico by Hernando Cortés. Another Spanish explorer, Nuño de Guzmán, founded the settlement.

Guzmán was a cruel conqueror; he and his soldiers slaughtered entire Indian communities in the course of exploring the lands west and north of Mexico City. He established Guadalajara—named for his hometown in Spain—at the site of present-day Nochistlán in the state of Zacatecas, about 60 miles to the northeast. Early settlers moved several times after Indian attacks before finally settling in the Valley of Atemajac in 1542. It was a wise choice, for the mile-high plateau ensured unimpeded expansion.

When the Spanish Crown learned of Guzmán's atrocities, he was deported back to Spain and the name of his self-appointed "country" was changed from La Gran España to Nuevo Galicia. Early on Guadalajara figured prominently in the history of this area. The town grew rapidly and by 1769 had become a provincial capital.

Spanish expeditions left from Guadalajara to gain control of such far-flung lands as the Philippine and Molucca Islands and the island of Guam, and to establish missions in northern Mexico and present-day California. Wealth from the surrounding farms and silver mines was channeled into the construction of lavish churches, mansions and monuments.

After abolishing slavery and launching the War of Independence in September 1810, Father Miguel Hidalgo briefly occupied the city. In the late 1850s and early 1860s Guadalajara withstood army attacks led alternately by Archduke Maximilian and Benito Juárez, who made the city the capital of his reform government for a few months during his forced exile from Mexico City.

Guadalajara today is a sprawling metropolis, Mexico's second largest. Nearly 4 million residents jam the city and its suburbs. The surrounding high plains of the Valley of Atemajac, part of Mexico's great central plateau, are noted for fine horse, cattle and grain ranches. Factories convert metals, hides and foodstuffs into many different products.

Situated as it is on a plateau a mile above sea level, the city enjoys springlike weather much of the year, along with abundant sunshine. High temperatures are normally in the 70s and 80s; uncomfortably humid days are rare. In April and May, the warmest months, it can creep into the low 90s, but always cools off in the evening. The rainy season is June through September. Air pollution is a problem, although not as severe as in Mexico City. A sweater or light jacket will come in handy on chilly nights.

Guadalajara even has its own word—*tapatío*. Reputedly derived from *tlapatiotl*, a term used to denote cacao or other small units of exchange frequently used in the Indian marketplace, it now refers to any person, thing or quality that is indisputably Guadalajaran. *Tapatío* indeed are such characteristically Mexican pleasures as the *jarabe*,

or Mexican hat dance, and the music of the mariachis.

Getting There

By Air

Miguel Hidalgo International Airport is about 17 kilometers (11 miles) southeast of the city off Mex. 23. Aeroméxico, Alaska Airlines, Continental, Delta, Mexicana and United offer direct flights from U.S. cities; Aero California serves Guadalajara from Tijuana. International connections are usually via Mexico City. Numerous half-hour flights connect Guadalajara with Puerto Vallarta. Always check with a travel agency or the airline prior to booking a flight, as routes and direct-flight availability differ depending on the time of year. For additional information about airlines *see Arriving by Air, page 61*.

Airport Transportation (Autotransportaciónes Aeropuerto) offers shared-ride shuttle van service to and from any place in the metropolitan area. Tickets are sold at a booth outside the terminal exit; fares are based on a zone system and average about $15 per person (U.S.). For details phone (33) 3812-4278. Taxis also take passengers to and from the airport; the fare to the downtown area is about $15 (U.S.).

By Car

Guadalajara's location between the Pacific coast and central Mexico makes it an ideal base from which to explore Jalisco and the surrounding states of Nayarit, Zacatecas, Aguascalientes, Guanajuato, Michoacán and Colima. Mex. 15/15-D is the major highway from the northwest; Mex. 54 from the north and northeast. Mex. 80 proceeds southwest to coastal Mex. 200, which heads south to Manzanillo or north to Puerto Vallarta. With the exception of Mex. 15-D, all of the above routes are old (free) highways.

© Jerry Driendl Photography / Panoramic Images

The Guadalajara-Manzanillo toll highway, Mex. 54-D, begins at El Cuarenta, on Mex. 15 south of the city. Although the distance to Colima is not much shorter than that traveled on free Mex. 54, the toll road avoids the latter's narrow, winding stretches.

The Mex. 15-D toll highway is a multilane route linking Guadalajara with Mexico City. It takes between 5 and 6 hours to drive the 506-kilometer (316-mile) route, which runs south of Mex. 90, Mex. 45-D and Mex. 57-D via Irapuato and Querétaro—previously the most direct route between the two cities.

South of and roughly parallel to Mex. 15-D is old Mex. 15, a winding road that hugs the southern shore of Lake Chapala and passes through the cities of Morelia, Zitácuaro and Toluca on its way to Mexico City—a scenic but much more time-consuming alternative. The road is in poor condition in places, and driving the stretch from Morelia to

The Informed Traveler

WHOM TO CALL

Police (emergency): Dial 060, 066 or 080 (emergency services) and ask to be connected to an English-speaking operator if you need immediate assistance.

Police (non-emergency): (33) 3668-0800 (English not likely to be spoken).

Hospitals: Hospital México-Americano, Calle Colomos #2110, (33) 3641-3141, and the Red Cross (Cruz Roja), (33) 3345-7777 or 065 (ambulance assistance), both provide 24-hour emergency service. Major hotels and the U.S. Consulate can provide a list of doctors who are on 24-hour call.

WHERE TO LOOK

Newspapers

English-language newspapers, including the weekly *Guadalajara Reporter,* are available at newsstands and the Best Western Hotel Fenix, downtown at avenidas Corona and López Cotilla. The monthly *Lake Chapala Review* has information about the communities around Lake Chapala.

Publications

Sandi Bookstore, Av. Tepeyac #718 in the Chapalita neighborhood west of downtown, has English-language newspapers and books. The Sanborn's restaurant chain has several area locations and also offers books, newspapers and magazines in English; the downtown branch is at avenidas Juárez and 16 de Septiembre, a block south of Plaza de Armas.

Visitor Information

Jalisco State Tourism Office (Secretaría de Turismo): Calle Morelos #102 at Plaza Tapatía (behind the Degollado Theater); phone (33) 3668-1600 or 01 (800) 363-2200 (toll-free long distance within Mexico). The office is open Mon.-Fri. 9-8, Sat.-Sun. and holidays 9-1. It has lots of information about Guadalajara and other destinations within the state, and also provides listings for hotels, restaurants and cultural events, as well as walking tour maps of the historic center. The staff speaks English.

A tourist information booth is inside the southern doorway of the Government Palace (Palacio de Gobierno), facing Plaza de Armas; it is open Mon.-Fri. 9-3 and 6-8 p.m., Sat. 9-1.

U.S. Consulate: Calle Progreso #175 at Avenida López Cotilla; phone (33) 3268-2100. The Citizens Consular Services office provides a reference list of English-speaking lawyers, doctors and translators for those in difficulty. A duty officer is available for after-hours emergencies; phone (33) 3268-2145.

WHAT TO KNOW

Currency Exchange

A number of *casas de cambio* (currency exchange offices) are located downtown along Avenida López Cotilla between calles Corona and Degollado, about 3 blocks south of the cathedral. Almost all offices post their rates, and they normally don't have the lines that banks often have. Dollars and traveler's checks can be exchanged at branches of Banamex banks Mon.-Sat. 9-1. A Banamex branch is at Calle Corona and Avenida Juárez. ATMs are the quickest and most convenient way to get cash; withdrawals are in pesos.

Staying Safe

The rules in Guadalajara are the same as those in any big city. At night, avoid urban neighborhoods that are away from the downtown core or other tourist areas; dark side streets in particular can be dangerous. If going out for the evening or taking a side trip during the day, it's a good idea to hire a taxi driver affiliated with your hotel. Keep an eye on personal items at all times, especially in the crowded shopping districts, and avoid wearing jewelry or carrying large sums of money. Women are not welcome in *cantina* bars and other bastions of heavy drinking and *machismo* attitudes.

Mexico City is not recommended because of the possibility of encounters with *banditos*.

Mex. 15-D begins east of Guadalajara near the suburb of Tonalá, bypassing cities and towns for the most part as it traverses rolling farmland and upland valleys and skirts the southern shore of Lake Cuitzeo. The route reaches its highest elevation—and also ends—near Atlacomulco in the state of México; from there Mex. 55 and Mex. 15 proceed south and east, respectively, to Mexico City. Toll charges are typically expensive, but toll highways in general are in much better condition than free roads throughout Mexico.

By Bus

Bus lines out of Guadalajara's big, modern New Bus Station (Nueva Central Camionera), about 10 kilometers (6 miles) southeast of downtown outside the suburb of Tlaquepaque (on the way to Tonalá), service all cities and most towns in the country. Several of the biggest lines are connected with Greyhound Lines Inc. Cross-country buses make frequent trips between Guadalajara and border points. First-class travel compares favorably with major U.S. lines; these buses are the standard size but carry half as many passengers. ETN is one of the lines offering first-class service.

Seven terminal buildings *(módules)* accommodate different lines. Amenities include shuttle bus service, luggage storage (referred to as *guarda equipaje*), restaurants, Ladatel long-distance telephones and hotel information. City buses and *colectivos* designated "Centro" or "Central" travel between the bus station and downtown. You also can take a taxi from the station to the downtown area. Taxi tickets are sold inside each terminal building; fares are based on a zone system.

For shorter bus trips to Tequila, the Lake Chapala suburban communities or other towns within a 60-mile radius of the city, use the Old Bus Station (Antigua Central Camionera), located off Avenida Dr. R. Michel at calles Los Angeles and 28 de Enero (just northeast of Parque Agua Azul). A convenient way to obtain route, schedule and fare information for the main Mexican lines is to stop at the Servicios Coordinados office, Calz. Independencia #254 at Plaza Tapatía. Reservations can also be made here. For additional information about buses *see Bus Service, page 72*.

Getting Around

City Layout

Sprawling Guadalajara is divided into four sectors; street names change when a new sector is entered. The major north-south routes are Calzada Independencia/Calzada Gobernador Curiel, which divides Guadalajara into east and west sectors; Avenida Alcalde/Avenida 16 de Septiembre, which passes through the Historic Center (Centro Histórico); Avenida Federalismo/Avenida Colón, which runs a few blocks west of Alcalde; and Avenida López Mateos, the main thoroughfare passing through a concentration of malls, upscale shops

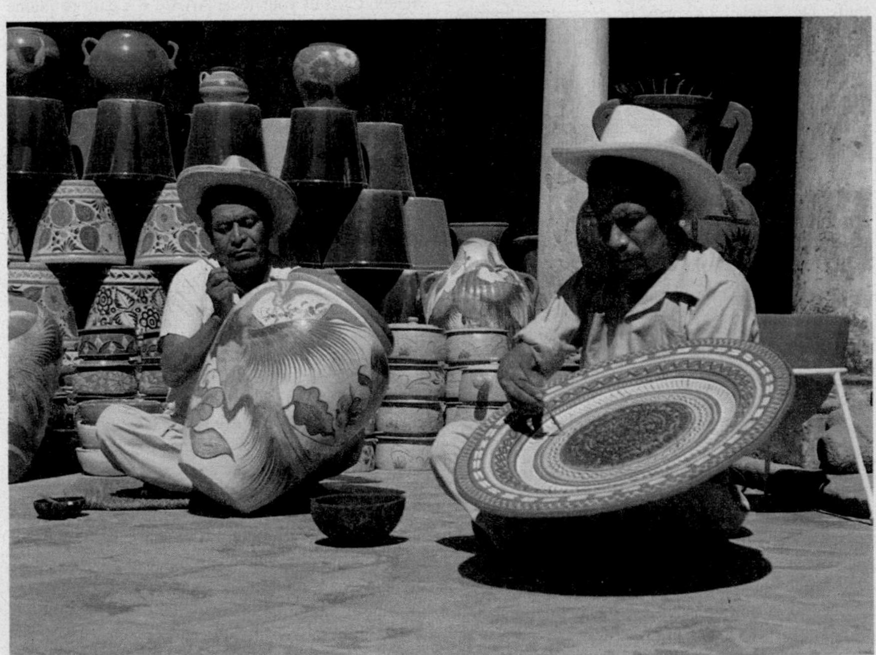

Tlaquepaque / © SuperStock

and restaurants west of downtown that cater to the city's wealthy business class.

The major east-west routes are Avenida Circunvalación, which runs north of downtown; Avenida Avila Camacho, which provides access to the northwestern suburb of Zapopan; Avenida Independencia/Avenida Industria (not to be confused with Calzada Independencia), which runs through the historic center a block north of the cathedral; Avenida Vallarta/Avenida Juárez/Avenida Javier Mina, which also runs through the historic center and divides the city into north and south sectors; and Avenida Guadalupe/Avenida Niños Héroes/Calzada González Gallo, which links points of interest in the southern part of the city.

For visitors, Guadalajara's chief attraction is the careful preservation of its downtown historic district. Forming a shape somewhat like a giant cross are four different plazas, each offering a distinct personality: Plaza Tapatía, Plaza de la Liberación, Plaza de Armas and Plaza Guadalajara. They all surround the cathedral *(see attraction listing)*, which is the heart of the old city. Centuries of history unfold along the narrow cobblestone lanes and in the weathered two- and three-story buildings that constitute the center of old Guadalajara, where street vendors and shoeshine boys are an immutable part of the urban landscape.

Plaza Tapatía *(see attraction listing)* is Guadalajara's gathering place, conveniently located close to museums, monuments and grand examples of colonial architecture. Here are tree-shaded parks, stone walkways, burbling fountains and numerous restaurants. On Sundays, throngs of dressed-up families parade up and down Plaza de la Liberación, just east of the cathedral at the western end of Plaza Tapatía. A narrow waterway runs along this plaza, bordered on both sides by shops and more restaurants. A statue of Father Miguel Hidalgo shows the priest holding a broken chain, a symbol of his call to end slavery in Mexico.

Plaza de Armas, a block south of the cathedral, is the city's traditional main square, bordered on the east side by the Government Palace *(see attraction listing)*. Plaza Guadalajara (just west of the cathedral) was formerly called Plaza de los Laureles for the Indian laurel trees that shade it. The church on the plaza's north side, built in the mid-20th century, is one of the newer buildings in the historic center.

West and south of the historic center the boulevards are wider, the buildings newer and taller. Along north-south Avenida Chapultepec between Avenida Niños Héroes and Avenida México—about 20 blocks west of the cathedral—are modern offices, fine shopping and some good restaurants. Farther west, along Avenida López Mateos between Avenida Vallarta and Avenida Mariano Otero, are many of Guadalajara's major hotels and nightlife venues as well as the big Plaza del Sol mall.

Lending a unifying appearance to this structural and human diversity are the vibrant purple of blooming jacaranda trees and the colorful cascades of bougainvillea, which seems to grow just about everywhere. Fountains, most of them delightfully ornate, also are scattered throughout the city.

Two thoroughfares loop around Guadalajara. The inner Avenida de la Patria travels around the western half of the city between Avenida de las Américas and Avenida López Mateos. The outer Anillo Periférico encircles the entire metropolitan area; navigating this two-lane route can be slow going, however, due to potholes and heavy truck traffic. **Note:** During and after the summer rainy season, roads both within the city and the state of Jalisco may develop dangerous breaks in the pavement and potholes that can cause accidents.

City traffic is heavy and moves slowly, and many streets are equipped with *topes* (speed bumps). Significant truck traffic adds to the overall congestion. *Glorietas* (traffic circles) are common at busy intersections. **Note:** Air pollution levels have risen to the point where state officials have instituted a tune-up test that all vehicles with Jalisco license plates must pass. Vehicles with out-of-state plates, however, are exempted.

Rental Cars

Hertz is one of many rental car agencies with offices at the airport and downtown. Be sure you fully understand the terms of any rental contract, especially with regard to insurance coverage. It's significantly less expensive to reserve before you leave home; make reservations at least 1 week in advance.

Note: AAA/CAA members enjoy discounts through Hertz for vehicles booked in the United States. Consult your local AAA/CAA club or phone Hertz, (800) 654-3080.

Buses

Buses are the preferred—and most economical—means of local transportation, for they cover every part of town. City buses run daily every 5 to 10 minutes from 6 a.m.-11 p.m. School bus-style vehicles are the cheapest (about 40c U.S.), but conditions tend to be substandard to what visitors are used to. They also are quite likely to be very crowded.

Tur buses (operated by Linea Turquesa), turquoise in color and with the letters "TUR" designated on the side, cost more (about 70c U.S.) but are air conditioned, do not carry standing passengers and travel to such outlying tourist destinations as Tlaquepaque, Tonalá and Zapopan. *Par Vial* buses travel a central east-west route along avenidas Independencia/Hidalgo as far west as Minerva Circle (at Avenida López Mateos); from there, they double back along Avenida Vallarta/Juárez, a few blocks south.

Privately operated *colectivos* (minivans) cost about the same as city buses; some have their destination marked on the windshield, although routes and pick-up points change frequently.

Taxis

Compared to the bus, a taxi ride in Guadalajara is expensive. Even short 10-minute rides are likely to cost at least $5 (U.S.). Rates go up at night. All cabs are equipped with a meter, but drivers can be reluctant to use them, quoting a flat fee instead; make certain you agree on a destination and a fare with the driver before entering the cab. Check at your hotel's front desk for current fares; bellboys can often assist those who don't speak Spanish.

Most cabs are found at or called from a cab stand *(sitio)*. *Sitios* are located near all the major hotels and attractions. The safest option is to stick with cab drivers who are affiliated with your hotel.

Parking

On-street parking in the city center is scarce. Public parking garages generally charge a fixed rate per hour; few are insured for customers. Parking lots charge less than garages. An underground lot is below Plaza de la Liberación, just east of the cathedral. Always avoid areas marked *"No E," "Estacionamiento Prohibido"* (No parking) or *"Exclusivo"* (Reserved). License plates are removed from illegally parked vehicles, and a fine must be paid to retrieve them.

Public Transportation

Guadalajara's *tren ligero* (light rail) rapid-transit system has two lines. Line 1 runs north-south along Avenida Federalismo-Colón for a distance of about 10 miles, between the northern and southern stretches of the Periférico. More helpful to visitors is Line 2, which runs east-west along avenidas Vallarta/Juárez and Javier Mina (the street name changes at Calzada Independencia). Trains run about every 15 minutes or so daily 6 a.m.-11 p.m.; the fare is inexpensive. Stops are marked by a "T" symbol.

Guides/Tours

Tour guides with name tags who congregate at the bus terminal are likely to be agents on commission with hotels. The major hotels usually have a list of licensed bilingual guides. Bus tours of the downtown area and nearby points of interest, including Ajijic, Lake Chapala, Tlaquepaque and Tequila, are offered by Panoramex, at Av. Federalismo Sur #944; phone (33) 3810-5109 (English spoken). For visitors without a car, this is the easiest way to explore the city and outlying suburbs.

Rides in horse-drawn *calandrias* (carriages) can be taken throughout the central downtown area for about $20 (U.S.) for up to four people and are a relaxing way to see the sights. Excursions depart from the Regional Museum of Guadalajara, Liberty Market and San Francisco Park. Few drivers speak English, so you may want to familiarize yourself with the layout of the city before embarking.

What To See

AGUA AZUL PARK (Parque Agua Azul) is at the intersection of calzadas Independencia Sur and González Gallo, about 20 blks. s. of the city center. This is the oldest of the city's parks. Trees, flowers, fountains and a man-made lake make it a popular spot for city residents and a pleasant place to while away an afternoon. On the grounds are an orchid house, an aviary and an outdoor amphitheater where band concerts take place. On the other side of Calzada González Gallo is Plaza Juárez, which has a monument encircled by the flags of other Latin American countries. Daily 8-6. Admission about $1 (U.S.), 50c (children).

Jalisco House of Handicrafts (Casa de las Artesanías de Jalisco) is just past the park entrance, with a separate entrance on Calz. Gallo. This state-run store sells fixed-price regional handicrafts, including leather saddles, furniture, blown glass, ceramics, pottery, textiles, tinwork and woodcarvings. Mon.-Fri. 10-6, Sat. 11-3, Sun. 11-2.

ARCHEOLOGICAL MUSEUM OF WESTERN MEXICO (Museo de Arqueología del Occidente de Mexico) is on Plaza Juárez (at calzadas Independencia Sur and del Campesino), across from the entrance to Agua Azul Park. It exhibits a small but select group of figurines, pottery and other artifacts from sites in Colima, Jalisco and Nayarit. Tues.-Sun. 10-2 and 5-7. Admission about 40c (U.S.).

GEM **CABAÑAS CULTURAL INSTITUTE** (Instituto Cultural Cabañas) is at the e. end of Plaza Tapatía at Cabañas #8; take a taxi, as this is a congested area. It was built in the early 19th century and financed by Bishop Juan Cruz Ruíz de Cabañas. Originally offering shelter for crippled, destitute and orphaned men, women and children, Hospicio Cabañas provided education and medical care for children through the 1970s before being renovated for use as a cultural center.

This architecturally fascinating complex encompasses 23 patios linked by pink-tiled corridors. It is the showplace for some of José Clemente Orozco's most powerful murals, particularly *"El Hombre de Fuego"* ("Man of Fire"), which graces the lofty ceiling. The art is memorable, although it depicts scenes of horrific violence from Mexico's history.

In addition to contemporary art and changing exhibitions, the institute has a movie theater, performing arts theater and an outdoor patio where ballet, music and dance performances take place. Tues.-Sat. 10-6, Sun. 10-3. Admission 10 pesos. Phone (33) 3818-2800.

CATHEDRAL faces Av. Alcalde. Begun in 1561, it was consecrated in 1618. Its twin 200-foot towers were erected in 1848 after an earthquake destroyed the original, much shorter structures. Emblazoned with yellow and blue tiles, they are a city landmark. Inside are three cavernous naves and 11 elegantly appointed altars, a gift from King Ferdinand VII of Spain. A lovely sculpture, "Our Lady of the Roses," was given to the city by the 16th-century Spanish king Carlos V. The priceless painting "The Assumption of the Virgin" in the sacristy is thought to be by Bartolomé Murillo. Open daily. Free.

CHURCH OF OUR LADY OF ARANZAZU (Iglesia de Nuestra Señora de Aranzazu) is at avs. 16 de

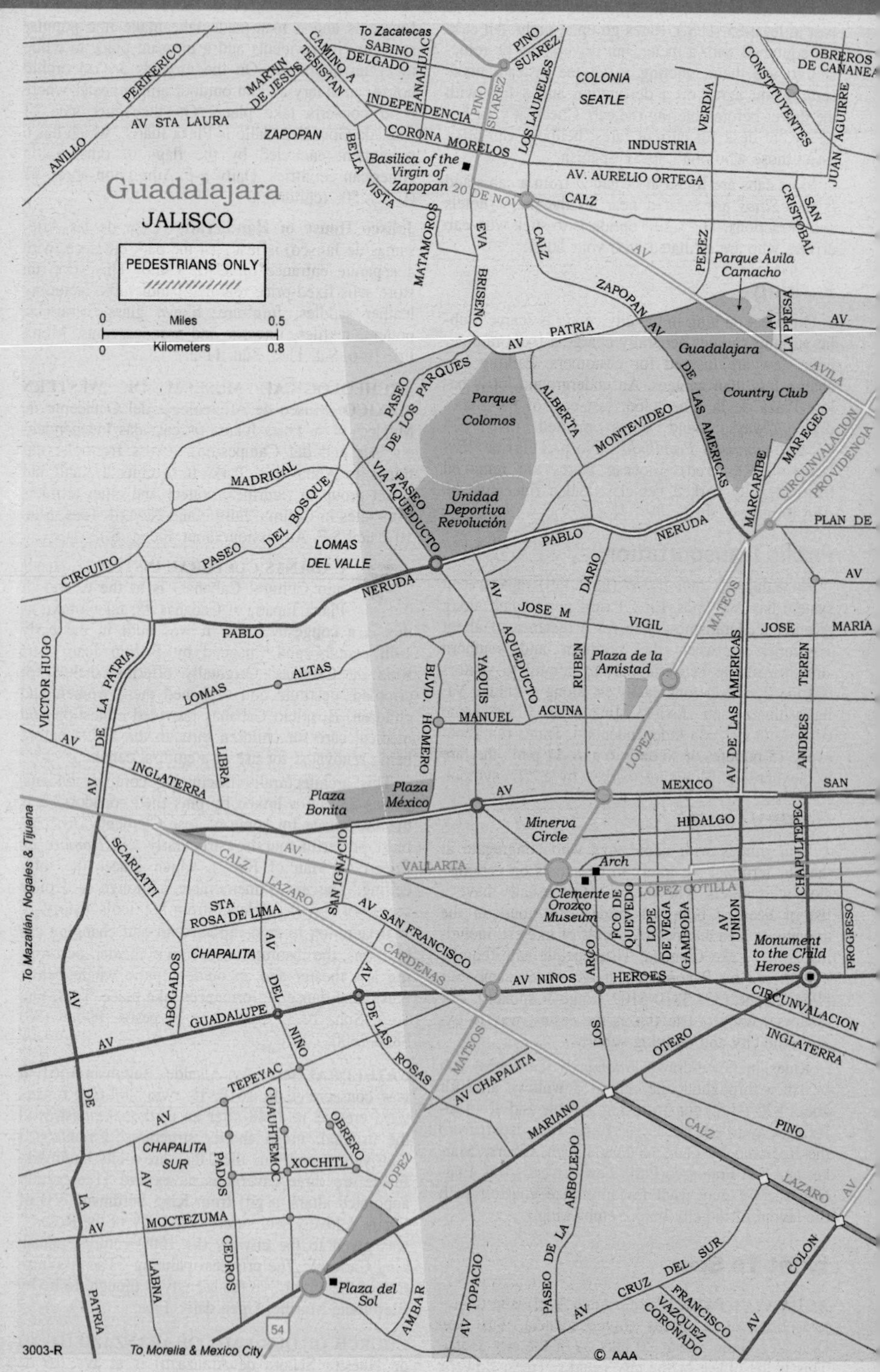
Guadalajara
JALISCO
PEDESTRIANS ONLY
0 Miles 0.5
0 Kilometers 0.8
To Zacatecas
Basilica of the Virgin of Zapopan
ZAPOPAN
COLONIA SEATLE
Parque Ávila Camacho
Guadalajara Country Club
Parque Colomos
Unidad Deportiva Revolución
LOMAS DEL VALLE
Plaza de la Amistad
Plaza Bonita
Plaza México
Minerva Circle
Arch
Clemente Orozco Museum
Monument to the Child Heroes
CHAPALITA
CHAPALITA SUR
Plaza del Sol
To Mazatlán, Nogales & Tijuana
To Morelia & Mexico City
54
3003-R
© AAA

DOWNTOWN
Guadalajara
0 Miles 0.2
0 Kilometers 0.3
Church of Santa Mónica
Rotunda of Illustrious Men
Post Office
Municipal Palace
Regional Museum of Guadalajara
Plaza de los Laureles
Cathedral
Plaza de la Liberación
Degollado Theater
Plaza Tapatía
Cabañas Cultural Institute
Government Palace
Plaza de Armas
Parque Morelos
Parque Libertad
Mercado Libertad
Church of Our Lady of Aranzazú
Parque San Francisco
Iglesia San Francisco
Coliseum
PEDESTRIANS ONLY
CLOSED TO TRAFFIC
TUNNEL
To Zacatecas
To Barranca de Oblatos
To Barranca de Oblatos, Guadalajara Zoo & I.M.S.S.
Panteón de Mezquitán Vigil
Parque Alcalde
Hospital
SEE INSET MAP FOR DETAIL
Parque Morelos
Centro Médico
City Museum
Parque Revolución
Expiatory Temple
University of Guadalajara Museum of Arts
Jaliscan Cultural Center Archeological Museum of Western México
Jalisco House of Handicrafts
Plaza Juárez
Parque Agua Azul
Railroad Station
Instituto Tecnológico
Estadio Olímpico
Parque González Gallo
To Tlaquepaque & Mexico City, DF
To Chapala &
To Miguel Hidalgo International Airport & Morelia
N

Septiembre and Prisciliano Sánchez, bordering the s. side of San Francisco Park (Parque San Francisco). It has a plain exterior, but inside is an extravagantly ornate *retablo* (altarpiece) that is a dazzling example of Spanish baroque design; its niches contain life-size statues of the saints. Also impressive are the colorful walls and ceilings.

Next to this church stands the less-ornate San Francisco Church (Iglesia de San Francisco). San Francisco Park is a starting point for horse-drawn carriage rides.

CITY MUSEUM (Museo de la Ciudad) is w. of the historic center at Av. Independencia #684 (at Av. Mariano Bárcenas) in an area with street parking only. It opened in 1992 to commemorate Guadalajara's 450th anniversary. The old stone convent housing the museum is a fine example of late 17th-century colonial architecture. *Salas* (halls) on two floors display photographs and other exhibits that present a chronological timeline of the city's history and development.

Background information is in Spanish. Allow 30 minutes minimum. Tues.-Sat. 10-5, Sun. 10-2:30; closed major holidays. Admission 7 pesos. Phone (33) 3658-2531.

JOSE CLEMENTE OROZCO MUSEUM (Casa Museo José Clemente Orozco) is at Av. Aurelio Aceves #27, just e. of Minerva Circle off Av. Vallarta. This is the former workshop and residence of José Clemente Orozco, Jalisco's leading muralist (1883-1949). Distinguished by a three-story window, it displays photographs, tools, clothing and his personal easel. The wall facing the window is covered by a huge mural entitled *"Alegoría del Vino"* ("Wine Allegory"). The museum also has a collection of documents, handwritten letters, posters, diplomas and other tributes to Orozco.

Mon.-Fri. 9-5. Free. Phone (33) 3616-8329.

DEGOLLADO THEATER (Teatro Degollado) is on Calle Belén between Calle Morelos and Av. Hidalgo, just e. of the cathedral. This impressive neoclassic structure, completed in 1866, has been compared to Milan's La Scala Opera House, although it has the grimy look of stone buildings exposed to years of vehicle exhaust. The relief above the columned entrance depicts Apollo and the Nine Muses. The plaque on the outside back wall commemorates Guadalajara's 1542 founding ceremony.

Inside are opulent red and gold balconies and a dome with murals painted by Gerardo Suárez that depict Dante's "Divine Comedy." The remodeled theater is the home of the Jalisco Philharmonic Orchestra and presents concerts, live theater performances and film festivals year-round. Performances are given by the University of Guadalajara Folkloric Ballet every Sunday at 10 a.m. If you can't attend an event, the theater is open Mon.-Sat. 10-1 for tours. Phone (33) 3614-4773 for performance and ticket information.

EXPIATORY TEMPLE (Templo Expiatorio) is w. of the historic center, bounded by avs. López Cotilla, Juárez and Enrique Díaz de León. This massive structure covers a city block. One balcony of the Gothic-style church, built at the turn of the 20th century, features mechanical representations of the 12 Apostles who make an appearance, accompanied by a carillon playing classical music, three times daily (9 a.m., noon and 6 p.m.). The clockwork figures can be viewed from the square in front of the church.

GOVERNMENT PALACE (Palacio de Gobierno) faces the e. side of Plaza de Armas. This Spanish baroque building dates from 1643 and was completed in 1774. Note the stone gargoyles, used to divert water from the roof, and the pillared front entrance. An enormous mural by José Clemente Orozco depicts Father Miguel Hidalgo, bearing a flaming torch, symbolically leading Mexico's struggle against such 20th-century forces of oppression as communism and fascism.

Two important historical events took place here: Hidalgo's decree abolishing slavery in 1810 and Guillermo Prieto's plea saving president Benito Juárez from assassination in 1858. The cannon and armor carved on the building's facade are a symbol of colonial authority. Daily 9-9.

GUADALAJARA REGIONAL MUSEUM (Museo Regional de Guadalajara) is at Av. Liceo #60, a block north of the Government Palace. Housed in a former theological seminary dating from around 1700, it has been a museum since 1918. Exhibits focus on the history of Jalisco and western Mexico, and include pre-Hispanic artifacts, ethnological displays and a 1,715-pound meteorite discovered in the state of Zacatecas in 1792.

A collection of Spanish and Mexican art on the second floor features paintings from the school of Bartolomé Murillo. Tues.-Sat. 9-5, Sun. 9-3. Admission about $3.50 (U.S.), free (ages 0-12); free to all Tues. Phone (33) 3614-9957.

GUADALAJARA ZOO (Zoológico de Guadalajara) is about 6 km (4 mi.) n. of Plaza Tapatía at the junction of Calz. Independencia Norte and Paseo del Zoológico. Overlooking Río Santiago Canyon, it contains a variety of large mammals, reptiles, monkeys and birds, including brightly colored toucans and macaws. A train and well-marked footpaths traverse the major viewing areas. There also is a children's petting zoo.

Next to the zoo is a planetarium and the Selva Mágica amusement park, which has a pool with performing dolphins. Parking is provided. Wed.-Sun. 10-6; daily during Holy Week. Admission about $3 (U.S.), $1.50 (children).

JALISCAN CULTURAL CENTER (Casa de la Cultura Jalisciense) is at avs. 16 de Septiembre and Constituyentes, near Agua Azul Park. This state-supported center houses a movie theater, two art exhibition halls, artists' studios and the offices of various culture-oriented organizations. The 300,000-volume Guadalajara Public Library also is in this building.

OBLATOS CANYON (Barranca de Oblatos) is 10 km (6 mi.) n.e. of downtown Guadalajara via Calz. Independencia Norte, near the Guadalajara Zoo. This 2,000-foot-deep gorge was cut by the Santiago and Verde rivers. Thermal rivulets plunge down the red walls (except during the dry season). The greater the depth, the more tropical the climate: Papayas, oranges, guavas, bananas, mangoes and other fruits grown at the canyon bottom are marketed in Guadalajara.

A cable car leaves the rim daily at 8 a.m. to take workers to the power plant on the canyon floor. The best views are from the Parque Huentitán el Alto Mirador lookout area at the top of the gorge.

PLAZA TAPATIA is along Av. Hidalgo. A 7-block-long pedestrian pathway connects the Degollado Theater at the west end to the Cabañas Cultural Institute at the east end. The walkway enables visitors to see several of Guadalajara's downtown attractions without having to cross major streets. Underground parking lots also are along the route.

Plaza Tapatía is a prime spot for strolling and people watching. Vendors sell everything from candy to canaries. The festive atmosphere unfolds against a backdrop of flower beds, statues, fountains and reflecting pools, and there are myriad storefronts in which to browse or window shop.

An unusual but practical service is offered by the *escritorios* who set up shop in the arcade close to the State Tourism Office. For centuries these typists, writers and editors have helped illiterate people fill out documents or write messages and correspondence, particularly love letters.

ROTUNDA OF ILLUSTRIOUS MEN (Rotonda de Los Hombres Ilustres) is on the n. side of the cathedral in a park bounded by Calle Hidalgo and avs. Alcalde, Independencia/Industria and Liceo. The mausoleum is where six of Jalisco's foremost native sons—representing artistic, philanthropic and musical fields as well as the military—are buried. Sculptures of the men, plus other Jaliscan notables, are surrounded by a circular grouping of columns.

SANTA MONICA CHURCH (Iglesia de Santa Monica) is at calles Santa Mónica and Reforma, about 4 blks. n.w. of the cathedral. It dates from around 1720. The baroque facade features exquisite stone carvings in 18th-century Spanish style. The interior is elaborate as well.

UNIVERSITY OF GUADALAJARA is on Av. Juárez at Av. Enrique Díaz de León, behind the Expiatory Temple and 4 blks. w. of Revolución Park. The main building, French Renaissance in style, contains an Orozco mural. On the north side of Avenida Vallarta is the university tower, where cultural events are held regularly.

University of Guadalajara Museum of Arts (Museo de las Artes de la Universidad de Guadalajara) is opposite the main building. It occupies a beautiful early 20th-century edifice that was once a primary school. The permanent collection consists primarily of contemporary Jaliscan and Mexican artists; traveling exhibitions are mounted regularly. Also here are early Orozco murals. Tues.-Sat. 10-8, Sun. noon-8.

What To Do

Dining

Guadalajaran restaurants offer diners a number of meaty options. Typically *tapatío* fare includes grilled steaks; *carne asada a la tampiqueña,* spicy broiled or roasted meat served with bacon and beans; *pozole,* a thick, satisfying hominy-based soup with hunks of *carnitas* (pork), tomatoes, cilantro and frequently chickpeas; and *birria* (stewed goat or pork in a thick, spicy tomato broth). But the city also has elegant Continental dining rooms, vegetarian eateries, Italian-style trattorias and *loncherías,* stand-up lunch counters offering sandwich fixings piled on a fresh *bolillo* roll. Such options should satisfy anyone's taste and pocket.

Perhaps the most authentic of the city's eateries are the *restaurantes campestres,* country-style establishments serving big steaks with such hearty Mexican side dishes as beans, quesadillas and tortillas. The food is accompanied by mariachi music and entertainment. Some establishments also present a modified form of *charreada,* or rodeo, which gives willing customers the opportunity to fight a young bull; cheers or laughs ensue depending on the outcome. *Restaurantes campestres* are located within the city and also along main highways outside the urban area.

Gastronomic adventurers will be sorely tempted by the astounding variety of street food. Numerous inexpensive *taquerías* (taco stands) operate up and down the length of Plaza Tapatía; the freshly made corn tortillas are wrapped around a wide variety of meat or vegetable fillings. The Mercado Libertad *(see Shopping below)* has hundreds of tiny stands offering full-course *comida corrida* meals, tamales, enchiladas, quesadillas and other treats. You can also find cheese, fruit and pastries. Cleanliness levels vary, however, and anyone planning to nibble their way from stall to stall should keep in mind the possibility of bacterial contamination, especially if the food has been sitting for a long time.

Travelers longing for a taste of home need not despair. Whether it's due to the many U.S. and Canadian expatriates residing in Guadalajara or the changing tastes of local residents, U.S. fast-food franchises are everywhere. And for a meal on the run, Guadalajara has a number of pizza carryouts.

Except at first-class hotels and restaurants where purified water is customarily used, be careful of drinking water; this includes the ice cubes in drinks. Avoid unpeeled raw vegetables and fruit as well as untreated milk and dairy products. *For a list of AAA-RATED dining establishments in Guadalajara, see the Lodgings & Restaurants section.*

Shopping

Fashionable shops and boutiques line Avenida Chapultepec between avenidas México and Niños Héroes, west of the historic center. This is Guadalajara's Zona Rosa (Pink Zone), an upper-class area frequented by tourists.

Malls dot the metropolitan landscape as well. La Gran Plaza is a sleek three-story collection of stores and a movie theater multiplex on Avenida Vallarta near the Camino Real Hotel. The largest is Plaza del Sol, at avenidas López Mateos Sur and Mariano Otero southwest of downtown. Restaurants and outdoor garden areas offer a break from shopping. City buses designated "Plaza del Sol" travel to the mall from Calzada Independencia in the vicinity of the Liberty Market.

Guadalajara also has an amazing number of shoe stores. Calle Esteban Alatorre, northeast of the historic center, is known locally as "shoe street." Galería del Calzado, at the corner of avenidas México and Yaquis (on the west side of town near Plaza México), is a shoe shopping center covering a square block. Shoe and boot prices at its stores are reputed to be among the best in Mexico.

If you're a first-time visitor or just want to have a quintessential Mexican shopping experience, set aside a couple of hours to wander through the Liberty Market (Mercado Libertad), just east of Calzada Independencia between avenidas Rodriguez and Javier Mina (on the south side of Plaza Tapatía; an elevated pedestrian walkway provides access from the plaza to the market). Locals often call it the Mercado San Juan de Dios, after the name of a nearby church and neighborhood, or the Mercado Taiwan because of the abundance of cheap imported electronic gadgets for sale. The building stands on the site occupied for centuries by Guadalajara's traditional *tianguis* (open-air market).

Everything under the sun is sold here: foodstuffs, clothing, housewares, handicrafts, hardware, leather good, shoes, office supplies, trinkets. Browse the hundreds of stalls featuring pottery, woven baskets, clay miniatures, papier-mâché masks, wooden toys, maracas and other hand-crafted items. The long counters selling watches and gold and silver jewelry often have rows of guitars hanging overhead. Cobblers and shoe vendors offer shoes, leather boots and *huaraches* (sandals). Clothing ranges from traditional Mexican garments and sombreros to the ubiquitous T-shirts. Vendors selling similar items tend to be grouped together, which makes locating things a bit easier; still, expect to be distracted by the market's sheer size and maze of narrow aisles and colorful stalls.

Produce vendors display an encyclopedic array of fruits and vegetables—from familiar items like dried beans, yams and spices to exotica like the chewy *zapote* fruit from the sapodilla tree. Look for stalls selling sugar skulls and other traditional Mexican sweets. There is a tremendous variety of prepared food as well, from tacos to delicately carved mango slices. Sandwich booths whip up *tortas,* various combinations of meats, cheeses and toppings piled on large, fresh rolls.

There also are things you're not likely to encounter back home, such as speckled quail eggs and herbal potions touted as cures for impotence. And the butcher stalls can be traumatizing for the squeamish. Every animal part, from cuts of meat to hanging heads, feet and intestines, is in plain view and available for purchase, and the smells emanating from the likes of *menudo* (tripe stew) can be quite strong. Avoid this part of the market if you have a weak stomach.

Note: There are restrooms in the market, but you'll need to pay an attendant to enter, and pay another small fee to use toilet paper or soap.

El Baratillo, Guadalajara's Sunday morning flea market, offers shopping that is more for fun than for serious purchasing, unless you're an expert haggler. It stretches for blocks along Avenida Javier Mina in an area east of the Liberty Market; take a local bus along Avenida Gigantes, 2 blocks south of the market, to get there. You'll find just about everything, most of it used.

Sightseeing

Guadalajara is a convenient base for day excursions to the Lake Chapala communities of Ajijic, Jocotepec and Chapala; to the suburban handicraft centers of Tlaquepaque and Tonalá; to the town of Tequila, known for the production of one of Mexico's more potent brews; and to the suburb of Zapopan, home of the revered Virgin of Zapopan.

Casual attire is suitable for almost any sightseeing excursion in the Guadalajara area; shorts are frowned upon in churches, however. For more information about these destinations *see their individual alphabetical listings under this region.*

Sports and Recreation

Bullfighting fans head for the 25,000-seat Plaza de Toros Nuevo Progreso, northeast of downtown on Avenida Pirineos between Calzada Independencia Norte and Avenida Fidel Velasqués (across from Jalisco Stadium). From October through March, bullfights *(corridas)* take place on Sunday afternoons starting at 4:30. Tickets are sold at the bullring. Spectators can opt for seats in the sun *(sol)* or shade *(sombra);* those in the shade are more expensive. For further information phone (33) 3637-9982, or ask at your hotel about dates and ticket prices.

Although similar to the Western rodeos of the United States, the ***charreada*** is unmistakably Mexican. When Spanish explorers and conquerors reintroduced the horse (which had roamed the North American plains some 45,000,000 years earlier), only noblemen were permitted to ride. By the 19th century, the development of large *haciendas* (estates) for agricultural purposes made horses an everyday necessity, and the *charro* (male rider) evolved from the requirements of livestock raising in open country.

Charros were resourceful, self-reliant men, familiar with the land and able to live off it. *Charro* contingents fought in the war to achieve Mexican independence, and *charreadas,* where native horseback riders gathered to show off their skills, became part of Mexican culture. The National Association of Charros (Asociación Nacional de Charros) was founded in Mexico City 1921, and in Guadalajara these events are still very popular.

Both *charro* and *escaramuza* (female) riders are expert at fancy horsemanship and roping. The focus is on style and finesse rather than competition, although some of the sidesaddle riding feats performed are of the daredevil variety. One of the chief pleasures of a *charreada* is viewing the elegantly ceremonial costumes on display (on both horses and riders). Men are decked out in white pleated shirts, black pants encrusted with silver buttons and a sombrero embroidered with gold or silver thread. *Charras*—often the daughters or wives of *charros*—wear lacy petticoats, brightly colored skirts decorated with lace and ribbons, and braided, beribboned hair.

The arena Lienzo Charros de Jalisco, Av. Dr. R. Michel #577 (near Agua Azul Park), presents a *charreada* Sundays at noon with different events as well as mariachi music. Admission begins at about $3 (U.S.); phone (33) 3619-0315.

Soccer *(fútbol)* is the city's most popular spectator sport. Professional teams play at Jalisco Stadium

(Estadio Jalisco), on Calzada Independencia Norte across from the bullring. Schedules vary; for ticket and other information, check with your hotel or the Jalisco State Tourism Office.

Guadalajara's year-round mild, sunny weather is ideal for **golf.** Some private courses allow visitors to play for a greens fee and proof of membership in a U.S. club; others are closed to nonmembers on weekends and holidays. Admittance to the immaculately maintained, 18-hole course at the Guadalajara Country Club is through a member, although the better hotels may be able to get their guests in. The country club is off Avenida Avila Camacho, about 8 kilometers (5 miles) northwest of the downtown historic center.

The Atlas Country Club (18 holes) is southeast of the city, on Mex. 23 just south of Tlaquepaque (on the way to Lake Chapala); phone (33) 3689-2620. The Santa Anita Golf Club is on Mex. 15, about 7 kilometers (4 miles) south of the Periférico loop road; phone (33) 3686-0962.

Some of the larger hotels, such as the Crowne Plaza Guadalajara and the Camino Real Guadalajara, permit nonguests to use their **tennis** courts for a fee. Colomos Park (Parque Colomos), south of Avenida Patria and west of the country club in the city's western sector, has a track and tree-lined paths for **jogging.**

Nightlife

Bars and clubs tend to be concentrated in two places: in the historic downtown center, and along Avenida Vallarta in the vicinity of Minerva Circle, an area of hotels and shopping west of downtown. La Maestranza, Calle Maestranza #179 at the corner of Avenida Madero (3 blocks south of the Government Palace), is a classic *cantina* that also is filled with bullfighting memorabilia. The Capitol Club, Av. Vallarta #2648 (near Minerva Circle) is a lively dance club and video bar housed in a lovely Renaissance-style building; it attracts a young, partying crowd. Inquire at the front desk or ask a bellboy what's happening in town during your stay.

The lobby bar in the Fiesta Americana Hotel, Av. Aurelio Aceves #225 on Minerva Circle, is a classy club/lounge with live music. La Diligencia in the Camino Real Hotel, Avenida Vallarta #5005, has a romantic atmosphere and music for dancing. Maxim's Disco in the Hotel Frances, downtown at Calle Maestranza #35 (near Plaza de la Liberación), has live music and a dance floor. The Frances also has an intimate lobby bar with piano music.

Several theaters show foreign and repertory films, including the Cine Cinematógrafo, Av. Vallarta #1102 (2 blocks west of the University of Guadalajara Museum of Arts), and Cine-Teatro Cabañas, in the Cabañas Cultural Institute at the eastern end of Plaza Tapatía. Malls such as Plaza del Sol have multiplexes showing the latest American releases.

Soak up the local ambience at Plaza de los Mariachis, on Calzada Independencia Sur between avenidas Javier Mina and Alvaro Obregón (on the south side of the Mercado Libertad). This pretty plaza is staked out by the roving bands of musicians. For a fee (usually about $5 U.S.) they will perform with guitar, violin, trumpet and an enthusiasm second to none. It costs nothing to listen to these serenades from another table, but if you're the one requesting a song, negotiate the price first.

The numerous sidewalk cafés clustered around the plaza are pleasant places to relax during the day; it's advisable not to linger in this area after it gets dark. Use the pedestrian overpass from the market to avoid the heavy traffic congestion. **Note:** Pickpockets frequent the plaza; keep an eye on your valuables.

On Thursday and Sunday evenings the Jalisco State Band gives free performances at Plaza de Armas, across from the Government Palace. The music starts at 6:30 p.m., but if you want a seat at one of the benches arrive at least half an hour early.

Theater and Concerts

Probably the grandest spectacle in town is the presentation of the University of Guadalajara's Ballet Folklórico in the Degollado Theater. Regional dances are complemented by *estudiantinas* or *rondallas* string ensembles, the Mexican counterpart of American high school marching bands or drum-and-bugle corps. Performances take place Sunday mornings at 10 a.m. Tickets for each performance go on sale Thursday afternoon; phone the box office at (33) 3614-4773 for more information.

The Jalisco Philharmonic Orchestra (Orquesta Filarmónica de Jalisco) performs following the Ballet Folklórico on Sundays and seasonally at other times at the Degollado Theater. National and international artists appear at the theater as well. The Cabañas Cultural Institute presents various theater, dance and musical performances throughout the year. Chamber music recitals take place in the institute's Tolsá Chapel. The English-language *Guadalajara Reporter* publishes schedules of current events.

For something a little out of the ordinary, take in a performance at the Experimental Theater of Jalisco (Teatro Experimental de Jalisco), on Calzada Independencia Sur next to the entrance to Agua Azul Park. The University of Guadalajara's theater company is headquartered here. Performances are in Spanish.

Special Events

Guadalajara's chief annual event is the October Fair, or Fiestas de Octubre. This monthlong artistic and cultural festival offers concerts, ballet, opera, theater, movies, folk art expositions and live music. Events take place at various locations, many in the vicinity of Plaza Tapatía, where outdoor stages and pavilions sprout. Hotel and ticket reservations are highly advised for the entire month of October and should be made in advance.

Guadalajarans celebrate many of the occasions listed in the "Fiestas and Holidays" section beginning on page 675. Some festivities of particular interest include Independence Day celebrations in mid-September, and the return of the Virgin of Zapopan to the Basilica of Zapopan on Oct. 12 *(see Zapopan)*. A series of cultural events take place the last 2 weeks of February before the beginning of Lent.

Other festivities with a special *tapatío* flavor are the Day of the Three Wise Men on Jan. 6; the Tlaquepaque Ceramics Fair, beginning June 15; the Day of St. James the Apostle in Tonalá on July 25, which features a mock battle between Indians and Spaniards; and Day of the Dead celebrations Nov. 1-2. Most of these are characterized by *tianguis* (open-air markets), *charreadas* (rodeos), fireworks, dancing, mariachi bands and tempting spreads of regional food.

The Christmas holidays in Guadalajara are celebrated with *pastorelas,* folk representations of the birth of Christ, and *posadas,* re-enactments of Mary and Joseph's search for an inn. The city's museums often participate, offering traditional dance programs and providing special refreshments. Families also get together to take part in candlelight processions to each other's homes, and nativity scenes are set up in churches and plazas. If you'll be visiting during December, check with your hotel, the Jalisco State Tourism Office or the bulletin boards at museums for further information.

Degollado Theater / © Martin Siepmann / age fotostock

This ends listings for Guadalajara.
The following page resumes the alphabetical listings of cities in Central Mexico.

GUANAJUATO, GUANAJUATO (C-2)

pop. 76,900, elev. 6,649′

Guanajuato (gwah-nah-HWAH-toh) is one of Mexico's most beautifully preserved colonial cities. Steeped in history, rich with culture and perched at the bottom of a delightfully scenic canyon, it offers numerous pleasures for the traveler. Leafy plazas, ornate mansions and flowerpot-bedecked alleyways add to Guanajuato's charm. So much of the city's colonial aspect endures, in fact, that it was designated a World Heritage Site by UNESCO in 1988. Guanajuato also—in an age of global information sharing and pop culture predominance—remains thoroughly Mexican in character.

Capital of the state of the same name, Guanajuato (the name means "place of frogs") was founded in 1548. Silver is its reason for being. For a while the fabulous strike at La Valenciana Mine alone supplied more than half of all the silver received by the Spanish monarchs.

This mineral wealth made Guanajuato the commercial and financial center of a region known as the Bajío, or heartland, for its green, rolling hills and fertile farmland. The establishment of a university by the Jesuits in 1732 began Guanajuato's reputation as an intellectual center and seat of learning.

Ironically, the city which had become wealthy under Spanish rule took an integral role in the struggle for Mexican independence. In 1810, Guanajuato was invaded by a motley army of peasant farmers, miners and other disenfranchised citizens under the leadership of Father Miguel Hidalgo de Costilla, venerated as the "Father of Mexican Independence."

Spanish Royalists—mining barons and the landowning elite—holed up in the massive town granary, Alhóndiga de Granaditas, which is now a museum *(see attraction listing)*. Under orders from Hidalgo, a young miner nicknamed El Pípila heroically made his way to the wooden door of the fortresslike structure, setting it on fire and allowing the insurgents to storm the interior, giving them the first major military victory of the War of Independence.

Although Guanajuato was sacked and many of the town's Spanish aristocracy massacred, the revolutionaries did not remain in control for long. In 1811, Hidalgo and three of his leaders were executed near Chihuahua and their heads sent to Guanajuato to be hung on hooks protruding from the four outside corners of the granary, grisly reminders that this particular conflict was far from over. The heads remained impaled until 1821, when Mexico finally won its independence.

Happily, those Spanish legacies that remain add immeasurably to the city's picturesque air. It crowds the slopes of a dry, narrow, rugged canyon. Houses hug the canyon's different levels, with the foundation of one house sitting at the rooftop level of the one below. The Spanish architectural influence is unmistakably evident, but because Andalusians were among the early arrivals, there is a Moorish touch to some early buildings.

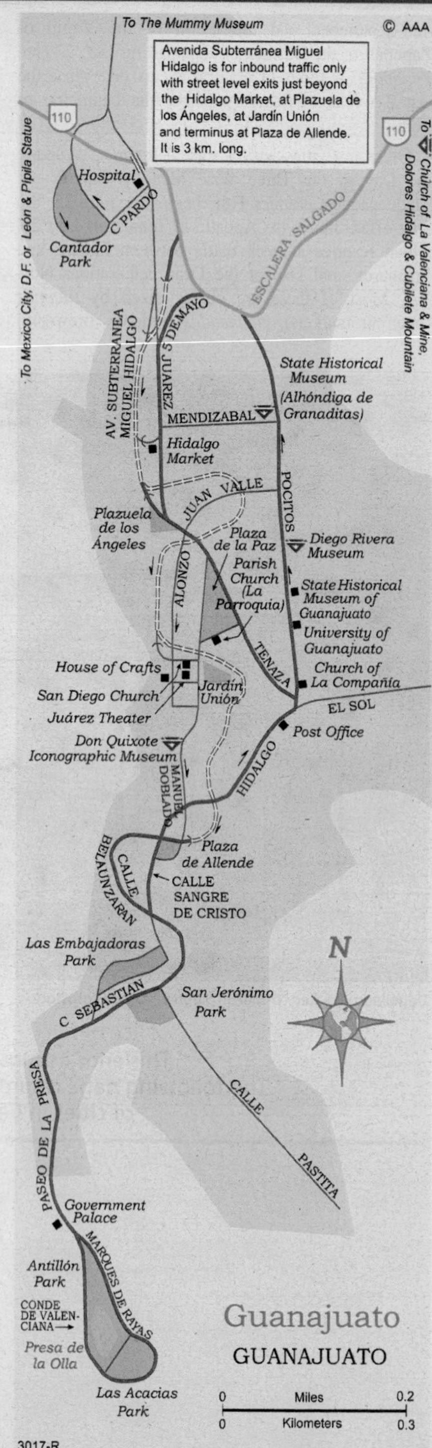

Guanajuato's downtown core maintains architectural integrity by restricting gas stations and other concessions to contemporary living to the suburbs and outlying areas. The city's twisting streets are interspersed with little plazas, perfect for relaxing on a shaded bench or perhaps chatting over coffee with one of the students who attend the prestigious University of Guanajuato.

Planning Your Stay

If you're basing a vacation in Guanajuato, plan on at least 2 days to fully appreciate the city's fine museums, colonial churches and outstanding university. A third day could be spent simply enjoying the compact city center—wandering from plaza to plaza, browsing through the Hidalgo Market and having a leisurely dinner at one of the outdoor cafes near the centrally located Jardín Unión, a park with an old-fashioned, romantic atmosphere.

Add another day for exploring attractions in the environs, such as the Church of La Valenciana, the La Valenciana Mine, Cubilete Mountain or the Mummy Museum *(see attraction listings)*. Drive the Panoramic Highway (Carretera Panoramica), the loop road that roughly encircles the city and offers several memorably scenic vantage points, or have a picnic at Olla Dam (Presa de la Olla), site of a man-made lake and the pretty gardens at Acacia Park.

Allow even more time to attend performances if your visit coincides with the International Cervantes Festival *(see Special Events)*, held from mid- to late October. Hotel reservations, however, will need to be booked up to 6 months in advance.

It's an easy trip from Guanajuato to the nearby colonial cities of San Miguel de Allende, Querétaro and Dolores Hidalgo *(see separate listings within this region)*. Northwest of Guanajuato is León. It's a sprawling industrial center, but diehard shoppers should note that it also is the country's leading producer of shoes. Spend an afternoon bargaining for footwear and leather goods at several of the many downtown shops.

For those who cannot or would rather not negotiate Guanajuato's hilly streets, Transportes Turísticos de Guanajuato offers guided tours in and around the city aboard a streetcar called "El Quijote." The office is underneath the Basilica of Our Lady of Guanajuato (Basilica Nuestra Señora de Guanajuato) on Plaza de la Paz; phone (473) 732-2134.

Practicalities

The nearest airport is in León, about 56 kilometers (35 miles) northwest. Aeroméxico offers flights from Mexico City; the taxi ride to Guanajuato takes about an hour. *For additional information about airlines see Arriving by Air, page 61.*

Central Camionera, the main bus station, is about 6 kilometers (3.5 miles) southwest of downtown. First-class bus service is offered by ETN and Omnibus de México. There is frequent service between Mexico City's Terminal del Norte (North Bus Terminal) and Guanajuato. The Flecha Amarilla line has service from Guanajuato to San Miguel de Allende several times daily. For additional information about buses *see Bus Service, page 72.*

Local buses navigate several routes. One runs from downtown east along Mex. 110, passing several hotels along the way, and heads toward the La Valenciana Church and Mine and the town of Dolores Hidalgo. Buses designated "Presa-Estación" basically travel from one end of town to the other; they use the subterranean avenue if going toward the La Olla Reservoir and above-ground streets if going toward the train station. Another line takes tourists to the popular Mummy Museum. All schedules are subject to frequent change; the State Tourism Office *(see below)* can provide helpful bus information.

The city's high altitude guarantees mild weather year-round. Daytime highs are usually in the low or mid 70s except in April and May, when they climb into the low 80s. Nighttime lows are usually in the 40s and 50s, although winter nights can be chillier. Showers or thunderstorms occur from June through September, but the weather is usually dry and sunny. Bring a couple of sweaters and a jacket or light coat if you're visiting in the fall or winter. Comfortable walking shoes are a must, not only for the cobblestoned street surfaces but for climbing the numerous hills.

Guanajuato has a large student population and an active social and cultural life. The city is small, and most establishments are casual and friendly. Tourist crime occurs infrequently, and personal safety is essentially a matter of taking the usual common sense precautions.

City Layout

Attempting to negotiate Guanajuato's narrow, congested and utterly illogical streets by car is a classic exercise in frustration. Furthermore, there are practically no local car rentals available. Most maps, including those available from the State Tourism Office, fail to show the winding, often unmarked streets in perspective. If you're staying at a hotel outside of the city, use local transportation for forays into and around downtown. Taxi stands *(sitios)* are located around Plaza de la Paz and the Jardín Unión, and taxis also can be hailed on the street. Always establish the fare before setting out.

Unlike many Mexican cities, where the streets are laid out in an orderly grid pattern radiating from a central plaza, downtown Guanajuato's twisting thoroughfares simply follow the dictates of the terrain. The two main streets, Avenida Juárez and Calle Pocitos, run one way roughly east to west. Juárez is closed to vehicular traffic east of the basilica, and past Jardín Unión its name changes to Avenida Sopeña. Pocitos runs north of Juárez and changes names from Lascuraín de Retana to Pocitos to 28 de Septiembre as it travels from east to west.

Traffic going west to east uses Avenida Subterránea Miguel Hidalgo, an antiquated tunnel which in the mid-1960s was transformed into a vehicular route for inbound traffic. It follows the original course of the Río Guanajuato under the city—roughly parallel with Avenida Juárez/Sopeña—for about 1.5 miles. Mexican engineers rerouted the river following a flood in 1905. Street-level exits are just beyond the Hidalgo Market, at Plazuela de los Angeles, at Jardín Unión and at the subway terminus at Plaza Allende. Little more than illumination and paving stones were required to turn the tunnel into a traffic artery.

A confusing network of subsidiary tunnels have since been added in a not-too-successful effort to alleviate the heavy traffic; the city's layout was never intended to accommodate automobiles. Even horse-drawn carriages cannot fully negotiate the steep streets. It's best to travel on foot whenever possible.

The best starting point for the Panoramic Highway (Carretera Panoramica), the delightfully scenic loop road that travels around Guanajuato's periphery, is from Mex. 110 just south of the Real de Minas Hotel (north of downtown). This route offers easy access to such attractions as the El Pípila Statue, Acacia Park, La Olla Dam, the Mummy Museum at the city cemetery (El Panteón) and the Church of La Valenciana.

Events

Guanajuato's biggest cultural event is the annual International Cervantes Festival (Festival Cervantino). University of Guanajuato students first began presenting *entremeses*—skits—of Spanish author Miguel de Cervantes' work in the early 1950s at the Plaza de San Roque.

The festival has grown ever since, and for 2 to 3 weeks in October, Mexican as well as international actors, dance companies and symphony orchestras perform at plazas and in theaters across the city. Theater performances are reserved, paying events, while the open-air performances in the plazas are often free. The farcical *entremeses,* presented mostly in pantomime, are easily grasped even if you don't understand Spanish.

Ballet, films, and classical, jazz and rock concerts round out the offerings. Reservations need to be made months in advance for the top events; if Guanajuato hotels are full, an alternative is to stay in San Miguel de Allende. For information about the festival, contact Festival Cervantino, Plaza San Francisquito #1, Colonia Pastita, 36000 Guanajuato, Gto.; phone (473) 731-1221. Tickets can be ordered through Ticketmaster in Mexico City; phone (55) 5325-9000.

Note: The festival draws huge crowds to the city and the already-narrow streets can become extremely congested, something to keep in mind if you're staying in Guanajuato.

Day of the Dead, or Día de Los Muertos, is celebrated Nov. 1 and 2. *Posadas,* re-enactments of Mary and Joseph's search for an inn, take place during the Christmas season. The arrival of the Virgin of Guanajuato is commemorated in late May and again on Aug. 9. These festivals usually include fireworks, regional dance groups and sometimes a parade.

Shopping

The Hidalgo Market (Mercado Hidalgo), on Avenida Juárez west of the city center, occupies a hangarlike 1910 building that resembles, with its glass windows and elaborate iron grillwork, a Victorian train station.

The market has two levels. A peripheral walkway above is roamed by souvenir vendors and contains shops selling crafts, clothing and sombreros. Below are the produce, meat and sweet stands, where local families do their marketing, and little eateries offering quick bites of typical Mexican fare. Everything from fruit to honey-laced candy is offered along row after row of these tidy stalls. In contrast to the market's timeless look are the miniature-screen TVs hidden beneath some of the counters. Flower vendors congregate on the sidewalks outside. The market is open daily.

Bargainers may want to focus their skills on pottery purchases. Numerous types are sold, including the highly glazed, pale green and blue ceramic designs known as majolica or Talavera, a style introduced by the Spaniards. Ceramic mugs and other items fashioned by Gorky González, a local artisan renowned for his Talavera-influenced work, are available at lower prices here than at his studio, which is located on Calle Pastita near Embajadoras Park (Parque de las Embajadoras).

Touring Guanajuato's Parks and Plazas

Guanajuato's meandering, often steep streets and tiny alleyways were made to be explored on foot. Several streets are closed to traffic, and those that aren't frequently are congested and filled with the fumes of idling vehicles. Strolling, therefore, is not only a more practical but a more pleasurable alternative. All you really need for a jaunt through the city's plazas is a good pair of shoes.

The Jardín Unión, in the center of town, is the city's lively focal point. This elegant park has old-fashioned lampposts, tiled, tree-shaded walkways, outdoor cafes and a band shell that is the scene of frequent musical performances. Most of Guanajuato's downtown attractions are within easy walking distance. It's just off Avenida Juárez/Sopeña, which can be used as a point of orientation when exploring the downtown area.

Facing one side of the triangle-shaped plaza are the opulent Teatro Juárez and the Church of San Diego, another of Guanajuato's picturesque colonial churches. Commissioned by Franciscan missionaries, it was almost destroyed by floodwaters and rebuilt in the late 18th century. The doorway in particular is representative of the flamboyant Churrigueresque architectural style.

Just off Jardín Unión is Plazuela del Baratillo, a peaceful spot for relaxing in the *sol* (sun) or *sombra* (shade) to the sounds of a gurgling fountain, a gift to the city from Emperor Maximilian.

West from the Jardín Unión is Plaza de la Paz, anchored by the Basilica of Our Lady of Guanajuato, or Parish Church (La Parroquia). Behind the plaza is the University of Guanajuato. Palatial private residences dating from the 18th and 19th centuries surround the plaza, recalling the days when silver poured out of the region's mines.

Continue down Avenida Juárez to Plazuela de Los Angeles, where the walls of the shops and houses are painted in bright colors. Close by is the Alley of the Kiss (Callejón del Beso), an intimate passageway narrow enough to permit a smooch from balconies on either side of the street; according to local legend, two lovers who were kept apart did just that.

Near Jardín de la Reforma, a shady park along Avenida Juárez a block or so from the Hidalgo Market, is Plaza de San Roque, a small square that is the site of many of the *entremeses* presented by university students as part of the Cervantes festival in October.

Equally engaging are the *callejoneadas* (kah-yeh-hoh-neh-AH-dahs), or serenades, that take place at Guanajuato's plazas or in the city streets on various weekend evenings. During these frolics, strolling student ensembles called *estudiantinas* dress in medieval costumes and sing songs with guitar and mandolin accompaniment. The public is welcome to join in the merriment.

The reservoir impounded by La Olla Dam (Presa de la Olla), built in the mid-18th century, provides Guanajuato's supply of drinking water as well as a recreational setting favored by local weekenders. This residential area at the east end of town can be reached via Paseo de la Presa or by taking a city bus designated "Presa."

Antillón Park is just below the dam. Flower gardens and a large statue of Father Miguel Hidalgo distinguish Acacia Park; picnicking is permitted, and rowboats can be rented for paddling around on the man-made lake.

Guanajuato State Tourism Office (Coordinadora Estatal de Turismo): Plaza de la Paz #14, across from the Basilica of Our Lady of Guanajuato. Open Mon.-Fri. 9-7, Sat. 10-4, Sun. 10-2; phone 01 (800) 714-1086 (toll-free long distance within Mexico).

What To See in and Around Town

CHURCH OF LA COMPAÑIA (Iglesia de la Compañia) is at Calle Pocitos and Navarro near the University of Guanajuato. It was built by the Jesuits 1747-65 and then abandoned when the order was expelled from New Spain. Restored in the 19th century, the church has a lovely, typically ornate Churrigueresque exterior of rose-colored stone, intricately carved wooden doors and a large dome. The interior contains paintings by 18th-century artist Miguel Cabrera.

CHURCH OF LA VALENCIANA (Iglesia de la Valenciana) is about 4 km (2.5 mi.) n.w. of downtown on Mex. 110, toward Dolores Hidalgo; some parking is available along the road by the church. The Church of San Cayetano (Iglesia de San Cayetano) is commonly referred to as La Valenciana. It dates from 1788 and was constructed by the Don Antonio de Obregón Alconcer family, wealthy owners of the La Valenciana Mine.

The pink-stone facade, with its profusion of delicate carvings, is a fine example of the florid Churrigueresque architectural style. But it is the interior that is truly breathtaking, adorned with a soaring gilt and gold-leaf, ornately carved *retablo* (wall behind the main altar), which includes many life-size statues of saints and biblical figures. Two additional *retablos,* each as tall and as magnificent as the central decoration, grace the transepts on either side. Three huge oil paintings by Luis Monray Pinto depicting biblical stories hang along the side walls of the narthex.

On Dec. 8 a fiesta honors The Immaculate Conception (La Purísima). Designated "Valenciana" buses take visitors to the church, which has operated continuously since its inception. Allow 30 minutes minimum. Mass daily at 10 a.m.; church open all day. Free; donations accepted.

CUBILETE MOUNTAIN (Cerro del Cubilete) is about 16 km (10 mi.) w. of Guanajuato off Mex. 110, on the way to Silao. It is said to be the geographical center of Mexico and draws many pilgrims. A gravel road climbs to the 9,440-foot summit, which is surmounted by a 65-foot-tall bronze statue of Christ the King (Cristo Rey). From here are superb views of the Bajío region, a fertile green plain dotted with lakes and isolated mountain peaks. City buses travel to the summit; the trip takes about 90 minutes.

DIEGO RIVERA MUSEUM (Museo Casa Diego Rivera) is at Calle Pocitos #47, 3 blks. n. of the Guanajuato State Museum; street parking is very limited. The city's most celebrated native son and one of Mexico's most esteemed muralists lived here the first 9 years of his life. The first floor of the home has been restored and is furnished with turn-of-the-20th-century antiques. The second and third floors contain more than 90 paintings, sketches and watercolors that trace the development of his style, influenced by both 20th-century Cubism and ancient Mayan techniques.

Political beliefs strongly informed Rivera's work, as evidenced by a sketch for the 1933 mural commissioned by Rockefeller Center in New York City that was destroyed because it included a portrait of Vladimir Lenin. Exhibit information is in Spanish. Restrooms are provided. Allow 1 hour minimum. Tues.-Sat. 10-6:30, Sun. 10-2:30. Admission 15 pesos (about $1.45 U.S.). Phone (473) 732-1197.

GEM **DON QUIXOTE ICONOGRAPHIC MUSEUM** (Museo Iconográfico del Quijote) is at Manuel Doblado #1, about 2 blks. s.e. of Jardín Unión in an area of very limited street parking. Housing more than 700 pieces of art, this fascinating museum provides a look at the enduring literary character created by Spanish author Miguel de Cervantes as seen through the eyes of Pedro Coronel, Salvador Dalí, Pablo Picasso and other artists.

The pieces are displayed in rooms surrounding a three-story courtyard. Quixote and trusty companion Sancho Panza are executed in a variety of media, including paintings, sculpture, stained-glass windows, clocks, painted eggs, woodcarvings and one large leaf, complete with veins, that shows Cervantes' hero in profile on horseback. There also are huge wall murals and quartz, bronze, silver and porcelain statuary.

Exhibit information is in Spanish. Restrooms are provided. Allow 1 hour minimum. Tues.-Sat. 10-6:30, Sun. 10-2:30; closed national holidays. Admission 20 pesos (about $1.95 U.S.). Phone (473) 732-6721.

GOVERNMENT PALACE (Palacio de Gobierno) is on Paseo de la Presa near the La Olla Dam. It stands on the site of the old house of the Marqués of San Clemente. The original building was destroyed by a flood; the present structure was completed in 1903. It evokes a European elegance, enhanced by the use of Guanajuato green sandstone.

GUANAJUATO STATE MUSEUM (Museo del Pueblo de Guanajuato) is at Calle Pocitos #7 near the University of Guanajuato. An art museum housed in a 17th-century mansion, it has an extensive collection of colonial-era religious paintings amassed by muralist José Chávez Morado, as well as Morado murals. Also displayed are works by contemporary Mexican artists. Tues.-Sat. 10-2 and 4-7, Sun. 10-2. Admission about $2 (U.S.). Phone (473) 732-2990.

HOTEL POSADA SANTA FE is at Plaza Principal #12 at Jardín Unión. The hotel houses a collection of paintings by Don Manuel Leal, a Guanajuatan who dramatically documented his perceptions of the city's history. The paintings hang in the hotel's lavishly appointed, colonial-style public areas. Phone (473) 732-0084.

JUAREZ THEATER (Teatro Juárez) faces Jardín Unión; street parking is very limited. Very European in appearance, it is a deliciously opulent reminder of Guanajuato's late 19th-century prosperity. The exterior is impressive, with tall columns, ascending steps, branching lampposts, bronze lions and statues of the Greek muses at the roof line.

Inside there are four levels of seating, private boxes and a smoking room with circular velvet settees, heavy drapes and a marble floor. The Moorish-style ornamentation includes dazzlingly intricate red-and-gold patterns on the walls and ceiling. Performances associated with October's International Cervantes Festival take the stage here.

Call for festival performance schedule. Tours of the facility given daily 11-2. Tour fee 15 pesos (about $1.45 U.S.). Phone (473) 732-1542.

LA VALENCIANA MINE is across the highway from the church. Discovered in 1760, it ranks as one of the greatest silver mines in history, at one point said to produce more than a fifth of the world's silver. The outer walls of the mine area are peaked to symbolize the crown of Spain. The shaft is exceptionally wide and more than 1,500 feet deep; visitors can look down it but are not permitted to descend. The mine was reactivated in the late 1960s after decades of lying in ruin, and still brings up silver, lead and nickel. Daily 8-7. Admission about 50c (U.S.).

MARFIL is about 3 km (2 mi.) s.w. of Guanajuato off Mex. 110; the old road to Marfil (Camino Antiguo a Marfil) winds into a valley. At the height of this former mining town's prosperity in the late 19th century, numerous silver mines operated and luxurious mansions lined the streets. Marfil was devastated in 1905 when La Olla Dam burst, killing many of the residents. In recent years Marfil has experienced a rebirth, with ongoing renovations sprucing up some of the long-neglected haciendas of the mine owners.

Ex-Hacienda of San Gabriel de Barrera (Museo Ex-Hacienda San Gabriel de Barrera) is at Camino Antiguo a Marfil Km marker 2.5, opposite the Hotel Misión Guanajuato. This former hacienda, which contains paintings and elegant Victorian-era furniture as well as a small chapel with an ornately carved *retablo* (decorative wall) behind the altar, offers a peek at the lifestyle enjoyed by privileged late 19th- and early 20th-century Mexicans. The gardens are a delight—more than a dozen, all beautifully maintained, whimsically named and distinctive with regard to plants and statuary.

Food is available. Allow 1 hour minimum. Daily 9-6. Admission 22 pesos (about $2.10 U.S.). The fee to use a camera is 20 pesos (about $1.95), a video camera 25 pesos (about $2.40).

MUMMY MUSEUM (Museo de Las Momias) is w. of downtown on Calzada del Panteón, next to the city cemetery (El Panteón). This is the city's ghastliest attraction. Dryness, minerals and natural salts in the soil all helped preserve some 120 corpses, which escaped decomposition to a remarkable degree.

The mummies—men, women and children, some still with shoes and hair—are displayed behind glass with various frozen expressions, giving visitors the morbid thrill of viewing them face to face. This museum is not recommended for the squeamish or the claustrophobic (it's small and often crowded). City buses and taxis that can be boarded or hailed along Avenida Juárez will stop within walking distance of the museum. Daily 9-6. Admission about $3 (U.S.); about $2 (children). The charge for using a camera is about $1, a video camera about $2. Phone (473) 732-0639.

PARISH CHURCH (La Parroquía) is on Plaza de la Paz. It also is known as the Basilica of Our Lady of Guanajuato. The church, which has a baroque facade that is an interesting yellow-orange in color, dates from 1671. The celebrated image of the Virgin of Guanajuato, brought from Granada, Spain, in 1557, was a gift from King Philip II. Mounted on a pedestal of solid silver, the jewel-bedecked wooden statue is said to date from the seventh century and is considered to be the oldest piece of Christian art in Mexico. The church also contains ornamental frescoes and Miguel Cabrera paintings.

GEM **STATE HISTORICAL MUSEUM** (Alhóndiga de Granaditas) is at Mendizábal and 28 de Septiembre (Calle Pocitos), n.w. of the city center; street parking in the immediate area is very limited. This massive 1809 structure was originally a seed and grain warehouse.

Among the varied exhibits are Indian weavings, saddles, leather clothing, hats, tools, pottery, *Carnaval* masks and a full-sized kitchen with period displays of pots and foods. Upstairs are historical exhibits and a number of pre-Columbian stone artifacts. Murals by José Chávez Morado depicting revolutionary themes embellish the Alhóndiga's stairwells. Bronze busts of War of Independence heroes Hidalgo, Jiménez, Aldama and Allende preside in a hall illuminated by an eternal flame.

Permanent and temporary exhibitions feature the work of Mexican and international artists, and a fine exhibit depicts Guanajuato's historical, social and mining importance through photographs and various artifacts. Exhibit information is in Spanish. Restrooms are provided. Allow 1 hour minimum. Tues.-Sat. 10-2 and 4-5:30, Sun. 10-2:30; closed state holidays. Admission 30 pesos (about $2.90 U.S.). Phone (473) 732-1112.

STATUE OF EL PIPILA (Estatua de El Pípila) overlooks Guanajuato from a steep hill to the e. of the Jardín Unión. It immortalizes Juan José Martínez, a miner who set fire to the front door of the Alhóndiga de Granaditas, the massive granary where Spanish Royalists took refuge in 1810 during an attack on the city by Mexican revolutionaries. The dramatic, 30-foot-high figure, bearing a torch, keeps watch over the city below. This vantage point affords an outstanding view of Guanajuato's architectural landmarks.

Buses designated "Pípila" take visitors to the monument; parking for other vehicles is free. El Pípila also is accessible by a steep climb on foot (wear sturdy walking shoes). To get there, take Calle Sopeña east to Callejón del Calvario and watch for the sign that says "Al Pípila." An incline railway (funicular) takes passengers up the hill to a terminal just below the monument. Funicular runs Mon.-Sat. 9 a.m.-10 p.m., Sun. 10-9. Monument free; funicular about $1.25 (U.S.) one way, $2.25 round trip.

UNIVERSITY OF GUANAJUATO is on Calle Pocitos/Lascurain de Retana. The school has been in almost continuous operation since it was opened by Jesuits in 1732 at the request of Spain's King Philip V. It became a state university in 1945. Ten years later a modern new addition with interconnecting patios and open-air hallways was built, complete with Moorish-style facade. The city's cultural arts showcase, it offers theater, symphonies and student performances of Cervantes' *entremeses* (short comic presentations).

JOCOTEPEC, JALISCO (D-1) pop. 15,900

Founded in 1528, Jocotepec (hoh-koh-teh-PEHK) sits at the western end of Lake Chapala. This popular retreat still manages to exude a relatively unspoiled Mexican atmosphere. It is known for handwoven items, which are still produced on old-fashioned looms. Local artisans turn out bedspreads, table coverings, wall hangings and *sarapes.* Several small shops line Calle Hidalgo, and it's possible to watch the weavers at work.

LAGOS DE MORENO, JALISCO (C-2)

pop. 81,300, elev. 5,917′

Lagos de Moreno (LAH-gos day moh-REH-noh) is an attractive town in the Jaliscan highlands, strategically situated at the intersection of two major highways, Mex. 45 and Mex. 80. Although it is an important commercial hub, Lagos de Moreno retains a sense of timelessness. Designated a national historic monument, it has a downtown riverside park, colonial mansions with central patios, streets brightened by flowers and tiny plazas in unexpected places.

Worth visiting are the Montecristo House of Antiques, downtown, and its remodeled Hacienda de Montecristo, just southwest of town on Mex. 80. Although the monastery that overlooks Lagos de Moreno from a hillside perch is not open to visitors, those who make the climb will be rewarded with beautiful views, especially around sunset.

MORELIA, MICHOACAN (D-2)

pop. 562,400, elev. 6,399′

See map page 349.

Capital of the state of Michoacán, Morelia (Moh-REH-lee-ah) was founded in 1541. It was first known as Valladolid, after the Spanish birthplace of New Spain's first viceroy, Antonio de Mendoza. In 1828, the name was changed to honor native son José María Morelos, who became a general for and hero of the Mexican War of Independence.

Morelia retains a strong Spanish flavor that has earned it the title "Aristocrat of Colonial Cities"; the historic center was designated a World Heritage Site by UNESCO in 1991. In an effort to retain this atmosphere of Old World charm, building ordinances require that all new construction conform to the architectural blueprint of the city's richly decorated 17th- and 18th-century buildings. Morelia's early planners also had the foresight to lay out wide, straight boulevards, which for the most part accommodate today's vehicle traffic.

The city's famed Boy's Choir, which has sung in Rome and at Carnegie Hall, has its base in the

Church and College of las Rosas (Templo y Colegio de las Rosas), established in the late 16th century as a Dominican convent and the home of the oldest school for liturgical music in the Western Hemisphere. Visitors are welcome to attend the rehearsals at Las Rosas, which occupies a magnificent colonial building on Avenida Santiago Tapia, 2 blocks north of the northwest corner of Plaza de Armas. A statue of Vasco de Quiroga stands opposite the statue of Cervantes in the nearby Garden of the Roses (Jardín de las Rosas).

An aqueduct (El Acueducto) dating from 1789 was once the primary means of bringing water to the city. It extends for more than a mile and is made up of 253 arches, the tallest 25 feet in height. They're impressively lit at night. Concealing small shops and private homes, some of the arches line two sides of Parque Villalongín.

Extending east from this small park is Calzada Fray Antonio de San Miguel, a tree-shaded, three-block-long pedestrian street lined on both sides with stone benches. It runs to the Guadalupe Sanctuary (Santuario de Guadalupe) on Calzada Ventura Puente. This typically lavish baroque church was built in the early 18th century, although the highly ornate interior dates from the early 20th century.

The Michoacán State Museum (Museo del Estado) is half a block west of Plaza de Armas at Av. Guillermo Prieto #176. It has some nice examples of pre-Columbian pottery, as well as a collection of clothing and household items and a few paintings of local 18th- and 19th-century notables. The building housing the museum was once the residence of self-designated Mexican emperor Agustín Iturbide. Phone (443) 313-0629.

Cultural events assume special importance in this university city. Folkloric dance performances and music recitals take place regularly at several locations around town. For schedule information, check with the State Tourism Office *(see below)* or at the Casa de Cultura. Band concerts take place at Plaza de Armas on Sundays. The Morelia Fair (Feria de Morelia), held in mid-May, is an old-fashioned state fair showcasing livestock and produce displays; it also features regional dance performances and a celebration of the city's founding in 1541.

Musicians perform at various locations during the International Music Festival (Festival Internacional de Música), which occurs in late July and early August. Michoacános also celebrate Independence Day Sept. 15-16, the Birthday of José María Morelos on Sept. 30, Day of the Dead (Día de Los Muertos) Nov. 1-2 and the Feast of the Virgin of Guadalupe, honoring Mexico's patron saint, on Dec. 12.

Practicalities

Aeroméxico offers daily flights between Mexico City and Morelia's Francisco Mújica Airport, about 30 kilometers (19 miles) north of the city. Schedules change frequently, and flight times should be confirmed in advance. Airport taxi services charge about $17 (U.S.) between the airport and the city center.

First-class bus service is offered by ETN between Morelia and Mexico City's Terminal de Autobuses del Poniente (Western Terminal), as well as to Guadalajara and Guanajuato. The central bus station is near the intersection of avenidas Eduardo Ruíz and Gomez Farias, a couple of blocks northwest of the main plaza; a newer bus station is on Periférico República, opposite the football stadium on the northwestern city outskirts.

Buses, taxicabs and *combis* (usually white VW vans) all provide public transportation. Buses can be helpful for getting to and from Cuauhtémoc Woods Park and the Aqueduct via Avenida Madero, but they move slowly along the crowded streets during rush hours. *Combi* vehicles have different-colored stripes depending on their destination. Taxis are not metered. The average in-town fare is normally about $2.50 (U.S.); agree on the amount before getting in the cab.

City Layout

Large, tree-lined Plaza de Armas, the main square, is bounded on the north by Avenida Francisco I. Madero and on the south by Calle Allende. It also is known as the Plaza of the Martyrs (Plaza de los Mártires) in honor of the rebel priests who were executed during Mexico's War of Independence. The square is surrounded by colonial-era buildings, and this part of the city is pedestrian-friendly (although congested with vehicles and vendors). Almost all of Morelia's visitor attractions are within walking distance of the plaza.

Downtown street names change north and south of Avenida Madero (Mex. 15), which is the city's principal east-west artery. Two blocks west of Plaza de Armas, Avenida López Rayón becomes Gómez Farias north of Avenida Madero. A block west of the plaza, Calzada Galeana becomes Nigromante north of Madero. Avenida Abasolo, which runs along the west side of Plaza de Armas, becomes Guillermo Prieto north of Madero; a block east of Plaza de Armas, Avenida García Obeso becomes Juárez north of Madero.

East-west thoroughfares change names at the cathedral. West of the cathedral Avenida Madero is Poniente (Pte.); to the east it is Oriente (Ote.). Calle Allende, which runs along the south side of Plaza de Armas, becomes Valladolid once east of the cathedral.

Nearby Destinations

About 32 kilometers (20 miles) north of Morelia on Mex. 43 is an unusual 19th-century causeway across Lake Cuitzeo. The town of Cuitzeo, on the lake's north shore, contains one of the region's two fortresslike 17th-century Augustinian monasteries; the other is in the city of Yuríria, north of Cuitzeo and a short distance east off Mex. 43.

Two national parks with scenic views are east of Morelia on Mex. 15. José María Morelos National Park (Parque Nacional Insurgente José María Morelos) is about 26 kilometers (16 miles) east of the city. Cerro de Garnica National Park (Parque Nacional Cerro de Garnica), which has two *miradores* (observation points) overlooking the rugged Mil Cumbres (Thousand Peaks) landscape, is another 24 kilometers (15 miles) farther east. From here, Mex. 15 continues winding through steep mountains and dense forests to the town of Ciudad Hidalgo.

Michoacán State Tourism Office (Secretaría de Turismo): adjoining Clavijero Palace, downtown at Calle Nigromante #79. In addition to maps and visitor information, the office can provide details about free guided walking tours of the city center. Open Mon.-Fri. 9-8, Sat.-Sun. 9-4; phone 01 (800) 450-2300 (toll-free long distance within Mexico).

What To See in and Around Town

BALNEARIO SPA (Balneario Cointzio) is 9 km (6 mi.) w. of Morelia on Mex. 15, then about 6 km (4 mi.) s. The spa, at the base of a cliff where mineral waters of 100 F (37 C) emerge, includes two swimming pools, a wading pool, bathhouse, refreshment facilities and bungalows. Open Wed.-Mon. Admission is charged; there are additional fees for parking, pool facilities and bungalows.

BENITO JUAREZ ZOO (Parque Zoológico Benito Juárez) is about 3 km (1.9 mi.) s. of the city center via Av. Juárez. It houses an extensive collection of animals and birds amid landscaped grounds. The

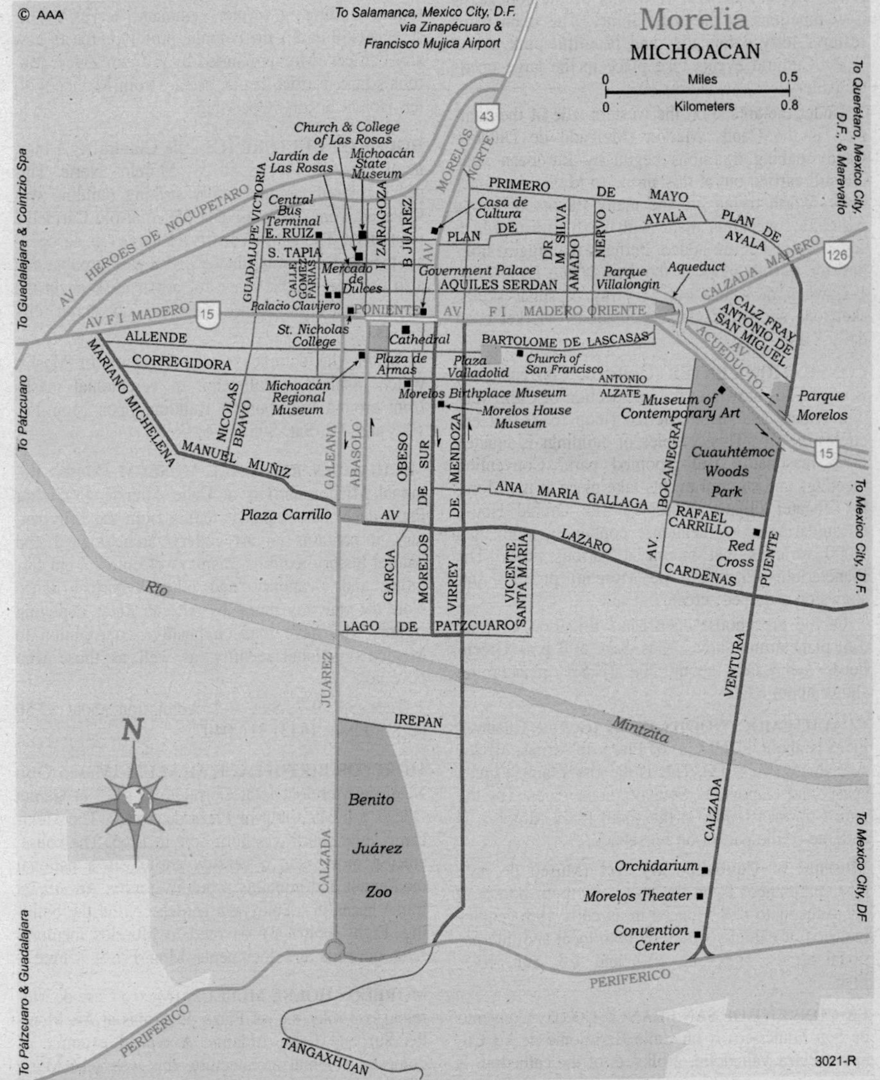

zoo also contains a small lake (rowboats are available for rent) and a children's playground. Picnicking is permitted. Daily 10-5. Admission about $1.50 (U.S.).

CATHEDRAL is on the e. side of Plaza de Armas, facing Av. Madero. One of Mexico's most beautiful churches, it took more than a century (1640-1744) to build. Exterior highlights are the rose-colored stone facade, two elaborately decorated towers, and a colonial fence and gates. Inside are religious relics and paintings as well as a magnificent three-story organ with 4,600 pipes, reputed to be one of the world's largest. The cathedral is the site of the International Organ Festival, held annually in early May.

CLAVIJERO PALACE (Palacio Clavijero) is at Calle Nigromante #79. A former Jesuit college, it now functions as the state library. The main patio features lofty colonnades and beautiful pink stonework. Cultural events take place in the large open-air gallery.

Under the arcade on the western side of the complex is the Candy Market (Mercado de Dulces). Candy-making traditions begun by European nuns are still carried out at this shrine to Mexican confections. Worth trying are the many flavors of *ate,* a pastelike concoction made with fresh fruit to which sugar and water are added. Perhaps the biggest holiday for sweets shops is the *Day of the Dead* Nov. 1-2, when they turn out an array of sugar skulls, skeletons and other ghostly creations. Market open daily 9 a.m.-10 p.m.

CONVENTION CENTER (Centro de Convenciones) is s.e. of downtown, at the intersection of Calz. Ventura Puente and the Periférico (loop road) that encircles the city. This complex of buildings is situated in a reasonably well-groomed park. Convention meetings and cultural events take place at the Morelos Theater (Teatro Morelos). The Orchid House (Orquidario) is a greenhouse containing more than 3,000 varieties that bloom at various times. The Planetarium (Planetario de Morelia) presents star shows on a domed screen.

Orchid greenhouse open Mon.-Fri. 9-6, Sat.-Sun. 3-6; planetarium shows Tues.-Sun. at 7 p.m. Greenhouse admission about 50c (U.S.), planetarium shows about $2.25.

CUAUHTEMOC WOODS PARK (Bosque Cuauhtémoc) is about 12 blks. e. of Plaza de Armas, off Av. Acueducto (Mex. 15). This is the city's largest green space and a popular Sunday picnic spot. On the park's northeast side, in the small Plaza Morelos, is a statue of the patriot on horseback.

Museum of Contemporary Art (Museo de Arte Contemporaneo) is on the park's northern border at Av. Acueducto #18. Housed in an early 19th-century mansion, it exhibits works by both local and international artists. Tues.-Sat. 10-2 and 4-8, Sun. 10-5. Free.

EX-CONVENT OF SAN FRANCISCO (Ex-Convento de San Francisco) is on Calle Bartolomé de las Casas at Plaza Valladolid, 2 blks. e. of the cathedral. It dates from 1531. The founding of Morelia took place in the square in front of the church. Closely set columns give its interior courtyard a medieval look, unlike the open archways that characterize others in the city.

House of Crafts (Casa de las Artesanías) is in the church cloister. This combination museum and workshop displays lacquerware, woodcarvings, pottery, copper items, ceramics and other crafts from throughout the state. Artisans also can be observed at work. The quality of the handicrafts is excellent, and prices are accordingly high. Daily 10-3 and 5-8; individual shop hours may vary.

GOVERNMENT PALACE (Palacio de Gobierno) faces the cathedral across Calle Allende. This baroque building, a former semniary, serves as the state capitol and is the colonial prototype for all new city edifices. Murals painted by Alfredo Zalce, Morelia's famed artist, depict scenes from Mexico's often violent history. Open daily.

HOUSE OF CULTURE (Casa de Cultura) is 4 blks. n. of Plaza de Armas on Av. Morelos Norte. This peach-colored, architecturally striking building was salvaged from the ruins of a 350-year-old Carmelite monastery. The central courtyard serves as an open-air theater for drama, dance and music groups, and also provides studio space for artists. Ask about the free monthly brochure that lists upcoming city events.

Within the complex is the Museum of Masks, which displays a collection of ceremonial masks from around the country. Building open Mon.-Fri. 10-3 and 4-8, Sat.-Sun. 10-6. Free.

MICHOACAN REGIONAL MUSEUM (Museo Regional Michoacano) is at Calle Allende #305 near Plaza de Armas. A palace dating from the 18th century, it contains an art gallery, archeological and natural history exhibits, displays of colonial-era furniture and weaponry, and other historical items. Note the stairway mural by Alfredo Zalce depicting figures who have made a positive contribution to Mexico's national identity, as well as those who have not.

Tues.-Sat. 9-7, Sun. 9-2. Admission about $2.50 (U.S.). Phone (443) 312-0407.

MORELOS BIRTHPLACE MUSEUM (Museo Casa Natal de Morelos) is at Corregidora #113 at García Obeso, a block south of Plaza de Armas. The Mexican revolutionary was born here in 1765. The house, erected more than a century earlier, is a national monument and contains a public library. An eternal flame burns in a courtyard garden behind the building. Eight rooms are devoted to Morelos memorabilia, portraits and documents. Mon.-Fri. 9-7. Free.

MORELOS HOUSE MUSEUM (Museo Casa de Morelos) is 3 blks. s.e. of Plaza de Armas at Av. Morelos Sur and Calle Aldama. A typical example of domestic colonial architecture, this was José María

Morelos' residence beginning in 1801. His descendants lived in the house until 1910, when it was converted into a museum. Inside are personal belongings, manuscripts and exhibits relating to the War of Independence. Daily 9-7. Admission about $2.50 (U.S.).

ST. NICHOLAS COLLEGE (Colegio de San Nicolas) is at the corner of Calle Nigromante and Av. Madero Poniente, a block n.w. of Plaza de Armas. This is the oldest Mexican university still in operation, and was the second educational institution to be established in the Americas. Among its distinguished alumni were War of Independence leaders José María Morelos and Father Miguel Hidalgo. Interesting frescoes decorate the inner walls of the main building's colonial patio. Open Mon.-Fri. Free.

PACHUCA, HIDALGO (D-3)

pop. 278,100, elev. 7,957′

Capital of the state of Hidalgo, Pachuca (pah-CHOO-kah) is the center of a rich mining district that produces much of the world's silver. It is believed that silver was mined before the arrival of the Spanish, who founded the city in 1534. The surrounding hills are honeycombed with tunnels and heaped with slag piles, although industrialization has increased to counteract declining mineral production. The Pachuca area also is known for the production of pulque, a mildly alcoholic drink made from the fermented juice of the maguey (mah-GAY) cactus.

Government offices are in the Red Houses (Casas Coloradas), a complex built as a school toward the end of the 18th century by the Count of Regla, who made his fortune from Pachuca's silver mines. Also of interest is the 1596 Convent of San Francisco. Housed within the convent is the Casasola Archives (Archivo Casasola), which contains an extensive collection of photographs chronicling Mexican history from the late 19th to early 20th centuries. The Mexican Revolution of 1910-20 is particularly well documented.

Nearby Destinations

Northwest of Pachuca along Mex. 85 is the town of Actópan (ahk-TOH-pahn). The name, meaning "in thick and fertile soil," is appropriate, as the town lies in a rich agricultural region. It was founded July 8, 1546, 10 years after Augustinian friars had first journeyed to the area to Christianize the indigenous people. The Toltecs, meanwhile, had arrived even earlier—perhaps as far back as the seventh century.

In the nearby mountains are rock formations known locally as "The Friars," or Los Frailes. According to legend, these rocks were formed when God, angry with two friars who fell in love with a beautiful woman, turned all three people into stone.

Actópan's St. Nicholas Church and Monastery (Templo y Convento de San Nicolas), built in 1546, is distinguished by its massive and harmonious proportions. Among the building's impressive features are its patio, Renaissance-style doorway, frescoes and Gothic cloisters.

The 125-foot-tall bell tower, between the church entrance and the door to the monastery, resembles a giant vertical prism and suggests a Moorish influence. In the chapel ruins outside the church, parts of a mural fresco painted on the walls and ceiling can still be seen. Painted to impress newly converted Indians, it depicts the various punishments their souls would receive in hell if they were not good Christians.

Farther west along Mex. 85, between Actópan and Ixmiquilpan, is El Mezquital, an Otomí Indian region known for its embroidered clothing. Ixmiquilpan (ees-mee-KEEL-pahn) was once the Otomí capital. The town's Church and Monastery of St. Michael the Archangel is a huge, medieval-style fortress/complex and former monastery dating from 1550 and founded by the Order of St. Augustine. Inside the main church are Indian frescoes depicting imaginary beasts and warriors engaged in classic combat. The Church of El Carmen, graced by gilded altars, also is noteworthy.

Monday is market day in Ixmiquilpan; beautifully worked bags, mother-of-pearl-encrusted miniatures, guitars, wine bottle racks and Otomí belts are all for sale. Maguey is an important local crop. From this versatile plant paper, vinegar, molasses, medicines, rope and thread all are made. More potent derivatives include such alcoholic drinks as aguamiel, pulque and mezcal.

About 11 kilometers (7 miles) northeast of Pachuca via Mex. 105 is Mineral Real del Monte, an old mining town that overlooks Pachuca. Its narrow, extremely steep cobblestone streets and old buildings are reminiscent of a Cornish village. Most of the houses were built more than 200 years ago, after the Count of Regla abandoned area mining operations and an English firm took over. Mex. 105 continues on to the picturesque town of Omitlán.

About 3 kilometers (1.9 miles) past Omitlán a road branches eastward off Mex. 105 to Huasca, another village, and the nearby 18th-century smelting haciendas of Santa María Regla and San Miguel Regla. The two complexes have been converted into historical lodgings, with rooms, restaurants and other facilities occupying many of the original buildings.

From Mineral Real del Monte a paved road travels northwest to another old mining town, Mineral El Chico. En route is El Chico National Park, an area of enormous rock formations and cool pine woods.

Hidalgo State Tourism Office (Secretaría de Turismo): Av. Revolución #1300. Open Mon.-Fri. 8:30-4:30; phone 01 (800) 718-2600 (toll-free long distance within Mexico).

PATZCUARO, MICHOACAN (D-2)

pop. 48,400, elev. 7,131′

Pátzcuaro (PAHTZ-kwah-roh), built on the hills sloping back from Lake Pátzcuaro, has red and cream-colored churches, mansions and other buildings erected during 3 centuries of Spanish rule. It also boasts one of Mexico's loveliest colonial plazas: Plaza Vasco de Quiroga, named for the first Spanish bishop of Michoacán, who introduced Christianity and various craft industries to the region's Tarascan Indians. A statue of "Tata Vasco" gazes down from a stone fountain in the center of the plaza.

A block north of Plaza Vasco de Quiroga is Plaza Gertrudis Bocanegra, named in honor of a woman who was executed by firing squad in 1818 for staunchly supporting the War of Independence. This is the commercial center of town; the market on the plaza's west side bustles with food, clothing and craft stalls.

Many of the colorful native dances performed throughout Mexico originated in this area. One of the most widely known is "Los Viejitos" (the little old men), a witty commentary on the manners and foibles of age.

First-class bus service is provided by the Herradura de Plata line between Mexico City's Terminal de Autobuses del Poniente (Western Terminal) and Pátzcuaro's Central Bus Station (Central Camionera), on the southwest outskirts on Avenida Circunvalación, a loop road encircling town.

Michoacán State Tourism Office: A branch office (Delegación Regional de Turismo) is at Calle Buena Vista #7, on the northwest side of Plaza de la Basilica (about 2 blocks northeast of Plaza Vasco de Quiroga, near the basilica). Open daily 9-3 and 4-7; phone (434) 342-1214 (English may not be spoken).

BASILICA (Basilica de Nuestra Señora de la Salud) is on a hill 2 blks. n.e. of Plaza Vasco de Quiroga. The church dates from 1554. The venerated Virgin of Health, on the main altar, is made from a paste of crushed cornstalks mixed with a substance extracted from orchids. On Dec. 8 a fiesta honors the Virgin.

Every morning local women set up shop in Plaza de la Basilica to serve a breakfast of *corundas.* These triangular *tamales* are made of cornmeal dough, filled with meat or beans, then wrapped in cornhusks and steamed; they are frequently served with thick cream. An accompanying beverage might be *atole,* which is made from ground cornmeal or rice, served warm and often flavored with vanilla.

HOUSE OF THE ELEVEN COURTYARDS (Casa de Los Once Patios) is about a block s.e. of Plaza Vasco de Quiroga. Once a Dominican convent, it now houses the studios and galleries of painters and artisans, whom visitors can watch at work. The building also contains small shops *(artesanías)* selling regional handicrafts. Most shops open daily 10-7.

JANITZIO ISLAND (Isla Janitzio) is in the middle of Lake Pátzcuaro. The town of the same name is built in terraced fashion. Day of the Dead ceremonies held Nov. 1-2 include an all-night candlelight vigil in the village cemetery. The island is accessible by launch and is crowded with day visitors on weekends and holidays.

Statue of Morelos is on Janitzio Island. It has been called "quite an accomplishment in ugliness." José María Morelos' raised arm tops the 130-foot-tall figure. A balcony offering a panoramic view of the lake is in the cuff of his sleeve. A spiral staircase leads to the top. The climb is arduous, but the stairway walls are adorned with more than 50 somewhat deteriorated murals depicting the life of the priest turned freedom fighter. Admission about 60c (U.S.).

LAKE PATZCUARO is north of town. This is one of the highest lakes in the country. Its placid waters are dotted with islands, and a score or more of tiny Tarascan villages ring the shoreline, many accessible only by boat. The distinctive "butterfly" nets that once were the main tool of local fishermen now appear mostly for photographers. The lake still yields the *pescado blanco,* a small, almost transparent whitefish that is a local favorite.

MUSEUM OF POPULAR ARTS (Museo de Artes Populares) is a block s. of the Basilica in the former Colegio de San Nicolás. The exhibits of Michoacán arts and crafts here include white lace *rebozos* (shawls), hand-painted ceramics and copperware. Behind the museum are the remains of some pre-Columbian stone structures. Tues.-Sat. 9-7, Sun. 9-3. Admission about $3.50 (U.S.); free to all Sun. Phone (434) 342-1029.

STIRRUP PEAK (El Estribo) is about 4 km (2.5 mi.) w. of the main plaza via Calle Ponce de León (beginning at the southwest corner of Plaza Vasco de Quiroga), following signs. Reached by a steep cobblestone road, it overlooks the lake and surrounding villages. The road can be walked or driven; if you choose to hike to the summit, which takes about an hour, it's safer to go on a weekend when there are other people around. Picnicking is permitted.

PUEBLA, PUEBLA (D-4)

pop. 1,320,600, metro area 2,500,000, elev. 7,091'

See map page 356.

Puebla (PWEH-blah), capital and commercial center of the state of Puebla, lies in a large valley flanked by four volcanoes: Popocatépetl, Iztaccíhuatl, Malinche and Citlaltépetl (Pico de Orizaba). A product of the Spanish conquest, the city was established in 1531 by colonists to whom Spain had granted land and Indian slaves. Legend maintains that one of these founders, Bishop Julian Garcés, was visited by angels who showed him where the new settlement was to be located—hence the nickname Puebla de los Angeles, or City of the Angels.

Strategically located along trade routes between the Gulf of Mexico coast and Mexico City, Puebla became a travel stopover between the coast and the interior, and also developed into a major center of the Catholic church; today's city is filled with churches and former convents. By the late 18th century it also was an important producer of pottery and textiles.

History was made at forts Loreto and Guadalupe *(see attraction listing)* on May 5, 1862, when about 4,000 poorly armed Mexicans defeated some 6,500 well-trained French troops who invaded the country as part of emperor Napoleon III's attempt to add to his empire. This rare Mexican military victory was greeted with a huge outpouring of national pride, and Gen. Ignacio Zaragoza became a hero, despite the fact that French reinforcements arrived the following year to install Archduke Maximilian as emperor of Mexico while president Benito Juárez's government was still in disarray. The event gave rise to the many *Cinco de Mayo* celebrations that take place in cities both north and south of the border.

Spain's legacy is still much evident in Puebla. Visually it is represented by the Talavera tiles *(azulejos)* that adorn buildings both old and new. These colorful hand-painted tiles were introduced from Talavera de la Reina, a town near Toledo. Spanish tile-makers settled in Puebla, which was the first city in Mexico to produce these decorative wares. You'll see Talavera tiles on church domes, fountains, rooftops and on walls in combination with red brick.

The *china poblana* dress, the national folkloric costume for women, is another *poblano* icon *(see the Church of La Compañia attraction listing)*. It is worn on occasion by little girls as well as older women. *Charras* (female rodeo riders) and dancers performing the *jarabe tapatío* (Mexican hat dance) also don the garment.

The traditional ensemble is an ankle-length, sequin-studded red flannel skirt, an embroidered white blouse and a shawl *(rebozo)* worn around the shoulders and folded across in front. Decorative accents include colorful strands of beads and a red or green head bow. The green, white and red colors replicate the Mexican flag. A monument to La China Poblana—a rather monumental statue standing atop a tiled fountain—is at the northern end of the city at the intersection of Boulevard Héroes del 5 de Mayo and Avenida Defensores de la República.

Puebla also is known for its distinctive cuisine. *Mole* (mo-LEH), the Náhuatl Indian word for sauce, comes in a variety of guises; many of these complex concoctions were painstakingly developed by Dominican convent nuns. Popular versions are *poblano*, a blend of chilies and bitter chocolate; *pipian*, which mixes chilies and pumpkin or squash seeds; and *adobo*, a pairing of cumin and a variety of regional chilies.

Another signature dish is *chilies en nogada*, created by the nuns to honor Agustín de Iturbide, emperor of Mexico 1822-23. A large green *poblano* chile pepper is filled with a mixture of cooked chicken or pork, onions, garlic, raisins and other dried or candied fruit. It is topped with a creamy white sauce made from ground walnuts and sprinkled with parsley and red pomegranate seeds, the colors again recalling the Mexican flag. Restaurant menus normally feature *chilies en nogada* seasonally (July through September).

Camotes, a confection of sweet potato paste molded into a stick shape and flavored with fruit, are sold by street vendors along with sweet potatoes and plantains baked in wood-burning stoves. Street vendors also sell *tacos arabes*, seasoned roast pork rolled into puffy wheat tortillas or pita bread.

The ubiquitous *cemita* is a big bread roll containing meat (usually ham), mild white cheese and avocado and seasoned with chilies or herbs. While these tasty snacks should all be safe to eat, it's best to avoid sno-cones, popsicles and ice cream—even on a hot day—since the water used to make them may not be purified.

Major events include Holy Week, which is observed Palm Sunday to Easter Sunday. The Huey Atlixcóyotl Fiesta is held during September. This dance and music celebration was once presented as an offering to the god Quetzalcóatl in return for a bountiful harvest season. The festivities take place in the town of Atlixco, southwest of Puebla via Mex. 190-D.

Practicalities

Hermanos Serdán International Airport is about 22 kilometers (13 miles) west of Puebla via Mex. 190, the Mexico-Puebla Highway (Carretera México-Puebla), at Km marker 91.5 near the town of Huejotzingo. Continental offers direct flights from Houston. Most travelers, however, fly into Mexico City and take a bus to Puebla, which is convenient and easy. For additional information about airlines *see Arriving by Air, page 61*. For additional information about Mexico City's Benito Juárez International Airport *see Getting There—By Air, page 285*.

Puebla-bound buses depart frequently from both the Mexico City airport and the city's eastern bus terminal, Terminal de Autobuses de Pasajeros de Oriente (TAPO). The terminal is near the airport at Calzada Ignacio Zaragoza #200; the closest Metro subway stop is San Lázaro, line 1. The Estrella Roja bus line leaves from the airport and the TAPO terminal. Autobuses de Oriente (ADO) buses also leave for Puebla from the TAPO terminal.

Estrella Roja has its own counter at the airport. The departure time is printed on the ticket; tickets are nonrefundable. The nonstop trip takes a little less than 2 hours; the fare is about $17 (U.S.). Buses arrive at Puebla's main bus station, the Central de Autobuses de Puebla (CAPU), which is located in the northwestern part of the city about 4 kilometers (2.5 miles) from the *Zócalo*. Estrella Roja buses also stop at the station at Avenida 4 Poniente near Calle 11 Norte (5 blocks west of the *Zócalo*), which is closer to the historic center.

Taxi Autorizado kiosks at the CAPU bus terminal sell government-authorized tickets for white-and-yellow CAPO taxis. The fare to specific destinations is based on a zone system; maps at the kiosks show the different zones. Pay the kiosk attendant for your ticket and tip the driver (10 percent of the fare is appropriate).

By car from Mexico City, Puebla is about a 3-hour drive via free Mex. 190; the drive time is shortened to about 90 minutes taking toll Mex. 150-D. Mex. 190 is scenic but slow, with more traffic and some bumpy stretches. To access either highway from downtown Mexico City, take the major east-west city thoroughfare Viaducto Miguel Alemán east toward Benito Juárez International Airport, exiting east at the junction with Calzada Ignacio Zaragoza; Zaragoza becomes Mex. 190. Heading east, watch for the signs to access Mex. 150-D.

Most of Puebla's museums and other tourist attractions are within a 4-block walk of the main plaza, or *Zócalo*. For getting around the city public buses are plentiful, and the fare—4 pesos—is inexpensive. Exact change is required. Hailing one of the black city cabs that cruise the streets is not recommended. Driving in the historic center also should be avoided, since traffic can be heavy and there are few public parking spaces.

City Layout

Just as Puebla was long second in importance to Mexico City in New Spain, it is bypassed by many travelers today. There is much to see here, however; the city was designated a World Heritage Site by UNESCO in 1987. A mix of old and new, Puebla has both imposing glass towers and colonial-era buildings featuring ornamental wrought iron and walls adorned with Talavera tiles.

The *Zócalo* is an island of refuge in the middle of this busy city. It used to be a marketplace *(tianguis)* and was popular for such events as bullfights and public hangings, but the look of today's tree-shaded, spacious public square dates back to an 1854 renovation. It is flanked on three sides by broad stone arches *(portales)* that shelter restaurants, sidewalk cafes and a warren of little shops.

This is a classic Mexican plaza with a bandstand, shoeshine stands and lots of iron benches on which to relax and observe passers-by. Sundays are particularly festive; dressed-up families stroll together after Mass, and in the evening there are sidewalk entertainers and vendors selling balloons and all kinds of snacks.

The surrounding narrow, cobblestone streets form a grid pattern that adheres to the classic blueprint for cities built by the Spanish in Mexico. Although they become poorer and more dilapidated as you head farther away from the city center, the streets in the vicinity of the *Zócalo* are lined with carefully preserved buildings in a mix of Churrigueresque, baroque and neoclassic architectural styles. Recurring motifs include the liberal use of Talavera tile, ornate white stucco ornamentation known as *alfeñique* (the name comes from a sweet confection made of almond paste) and gray stone carved into all sorts of curlicues, cherubs, gargoyles and other decorative accents.

Noted for its French Renaissance design is City Hall (Palacio Municipal), on the north side of the *Zócalo* at Portal Hidalgo #14. Intricate stone carvings adorn the exterior of the Theater (Teatro Principal), about 4 blocks northeast of the *Zócalo* at Avenida 8 Oriente and Calle 6 Norte. Dating from 1760, it is among the oldest theaters in the Americas (although it was rebuilt in the 1930s). The interior can be toured when performances are not taking place; for information check the Puebla State Tourism Office.

A striking contrast is provided by the William O. Jenkins Convention Center (Centro de Convenciones de Puebla), an impressive example of preserving the character of historic buildings—in this case, four ancient textile factories—while grafting on contemporary additions. The complex is worth a visit for its architecture alone. It is located at the eastern end of the historic district along Boulevard Héroes del 5 de Mayo between avenidas 4 and 10 Oriente, just south of the Church of San Francisco.

The downtown street system is based on numbers rather than names. The northwest corner of the *Zócalo* is the city center; from this point, the main thoroughfares are north-south Avenida 5 de Mayo/16 de Septiembre and east-west Avenida Palafox y Mendoza/Reforma. East-west streets are even-numbered north of the *Zócalo* and odd-numbered south of it. Likewise, north-south streets are odd-numbered west of the *Zócalo* and even-numbered east of it.

Street names also include a direction—north/*norte*, south/*sur*, east/*oriente* or west/*poniente*—based on the Avenida Reforma/Avenida 5 de Mayo axis. This makes it a bit easier to find the location of addresses, since the city is essentially divided into four quadrants.

In June 1999 an earthquake centered in the state of Oaxaca caused significant damage in Puebla and nearby Cholula. In addition to caving in the roof of the Palacio Municipal, the quake resulted in cracks and facade damage to many of the city's colonial-era churches. Restoration efforts began soon after, however, and by the end of 2001 almost every historic structure had been repaired.

Puebla State Tourism Office (Secretaría de Turismo): Avenida 5 Oriente #3, a block south of the *Zócalo* and across the street from the cathedral. Open Mon.-Sat. 9-8, Sun. 9-noon; phone (222) 246-2044. The municipal tourist office is on the north side of the *Zócalo* in the City Hall building (Palacio Municipal). Both offices have city maps and can provide information about guided tours of the historic center.

Shopping areas: Among the city's long-established Talavera workshops is Uriarte Talavera (Taller de Cerámica Uriarte), 5 blocks west of the *Zócalo* at Avenida 4 Poniente #911. Factory tours to observe the ceramics being molded, hand painted, fired and cooled are given Mon.-Fri. at 11, noon and 1. They also will ship purchases; phone (222) 232-1598.

El Parián Market, 3 blocks east of the *Zócalo* between calles 6 and 8 Norte, offers typical crafts from this part of Mexico, including Talavera pottery, trees of life and onyx jewelry. The open-air shops are in a pedestrian-only area. Bargaining is expected.

Plazuela de Los Sapos (Plaza of the Toads), bounded by avenidas 3 and 5 Oriente and calles 4 and 8 Sur, is lined with shops offering antique furniture and collectibles as well as new furniture made to look old. The Artists' Neighborhood, in a pedestrian passageway at Avenida 6 Oriente and Calle 6 Norte (behind the Theater), is a concentration of studios where local artists create and sell their work.

What To See in and Around Town

5 DE MAYO CIVIC CENTER (Centro Cívico 5 de Mayo) is about 15 blks. n.e. of the *Zócalo* in a park on top of a steep hill (Cerro de Guadalupe). It is best reached by bus. Set amid groves of eucalyptus trees, the complex includes a group of public facilities as well as Forts Loreto and Guadalupe *(see separate attraction listing).*

Museums include the Regional Museum of Anthropology and History (Museo Regional de Antropología y Historia); the Planetarium (El Planetario); the Natural History Museum (Museo de Historia Natural); Expo Puebla, an exhibition hall on the state fairgrounds; and the Relicario Bullring (Plaza de Toros El Relicario). The bubble-domed Reforma Auditorium (Auditorio de la Reforma) seats 2,000.

Museums open Tues.-Sun. 9-5. Natural History Museum admission about $2.50 (U.S.). Regional Museum of Anthropology and History admission 20 pesos (about $1.95 U.S.). Planetarium light shows about $3.

AFRICAM is about 16 km (10 mi.) s. of Puebla on the road to Valsequillo, at Km marker 16.5 (follow signs). This ecological park is a bit of Africa on the Mexican high plains, where such animals as lions, tigers, giraffes, buffaloes, deer and peacocks roam freely. Visitors can get out of their cars at certain locations for picture-taking opportunities. Guided tours are available. Buses to Africam depart Tues.-Sun. from the *Zócalo.*

Daily 10-5. Admission 150 pesos (about $14.50 U.S.), 140 pesos (children). Phone (222) 281-7000.

GEM **AMPARO MUSEUM** is 3 blks. s. of the *Zócalo* at Calle 2 Sur #708 (at Calle 9 Oriente); street parking in the vicinity is limited. It contains one of the finest collections of pre-Hispanic art in Mexico, as well as pre-Columbian, colonial and modern works. The exhibits are housed in a two-story complex with several outdoor courtyards and fountains.

Two floors are filled with Olmec art, Nayarit clay figurines and other objects, including such whimsical pieces as a figure wearing a long conical hat and another strapped to a bed while a laughing dog peers through the framed headboard. One of the museum's most delightful works is a mural, completed in 1990 by Pedro Diego de Alvarado, that depicts four angels creating the colonial town of Puebla. Colonial art *(arte virreinal)* is on the second floor. There also are frequent rotating exhibits. Information is presented in both Spanish and English; English-speaking guides can be hired as well.

Food is available. Allow 2 hours minimum. Wed.-Mon. 10-6. Admission 25 pesos (about $2.40 U.S.); 15 pesos (ages 3-12). Free to all Mon. Audio headphones with English commentary can be rented for the pre-Hispanic exhibit areas. Phone (222) 229-3850.

BELLO Y GONZALEZ MUSEUM is about 3 blks. from the *Zócalo* at Av. 3 Poniente #302. The museum's collection of art and artifacts was donated to the city by the son of José Luis Bello, a textile magnate and collector. Beautifully handcarved furniture, glassware, porcelain, gold and silver articles, paintings, ironwork from the 17th to 19th centuries and a large collection of Talavera pottery are all on display, as well as several huge ocean-going travel trunks equipped with hidden locks and latches. Guided tours are available. Allow 1 hour minimum. Tues.-Sun. 10-5. Admission 15 pesos (about $1.45 U.S.).

BELLO ZETINA MUSEUM is at 5 de Mayo #409 next to the Church of Santo Domingo. It displays turn-of-the-20th-century antiques and religious art. Open Tues.-Sun. Free. Phone (222) 232-4720.

CATHEDRAL OF THE IMMACULATE CONCEPTION (Catedral de la Nuestra Señora de la Inmaculada Concepción) stands on the s. side of the *Zócalo.* The plans for the cathedral, one of the largest in Mexico, were approved in 1562 by Philip II of Spain, but construction was not completed until 1641; it was consecrated in 1649.

The immense building is noted for its elaborately carved but severe facade, great doors, 14 chapels and two bell towers—the tallest in Mexico—that were erected in 1678. The interior features an altar of gray onyx, marble and gold designed in 1799 by Manuel Tolsá, onyx sculptures carved by Tolsá, wood inlay in the choir, lovely tapestries and a collection of rare paintings.

CHURCH OF LA COMPAÑIA (Iglesia de la Compañia) is a block e. of the *Zócalo* on Calle 4 Sur. This huge blue and white tiled, Churrigueresque-style church was built by Jesuits. Also known as the Church of the Holy Ghost (Iglesia del Espiritu Santo), it is said to be the final resting place of a local legend, La China Poblana.

Although the story has several interpretations, it is generally agreed that a young girl named Mirrha was born in the early 17th century in India, kidnapped by Portuguese pirates and sold into slavery. She was later adopted by Miguel de Sosa, a well-to-do *poblano* who had her baptized with the name

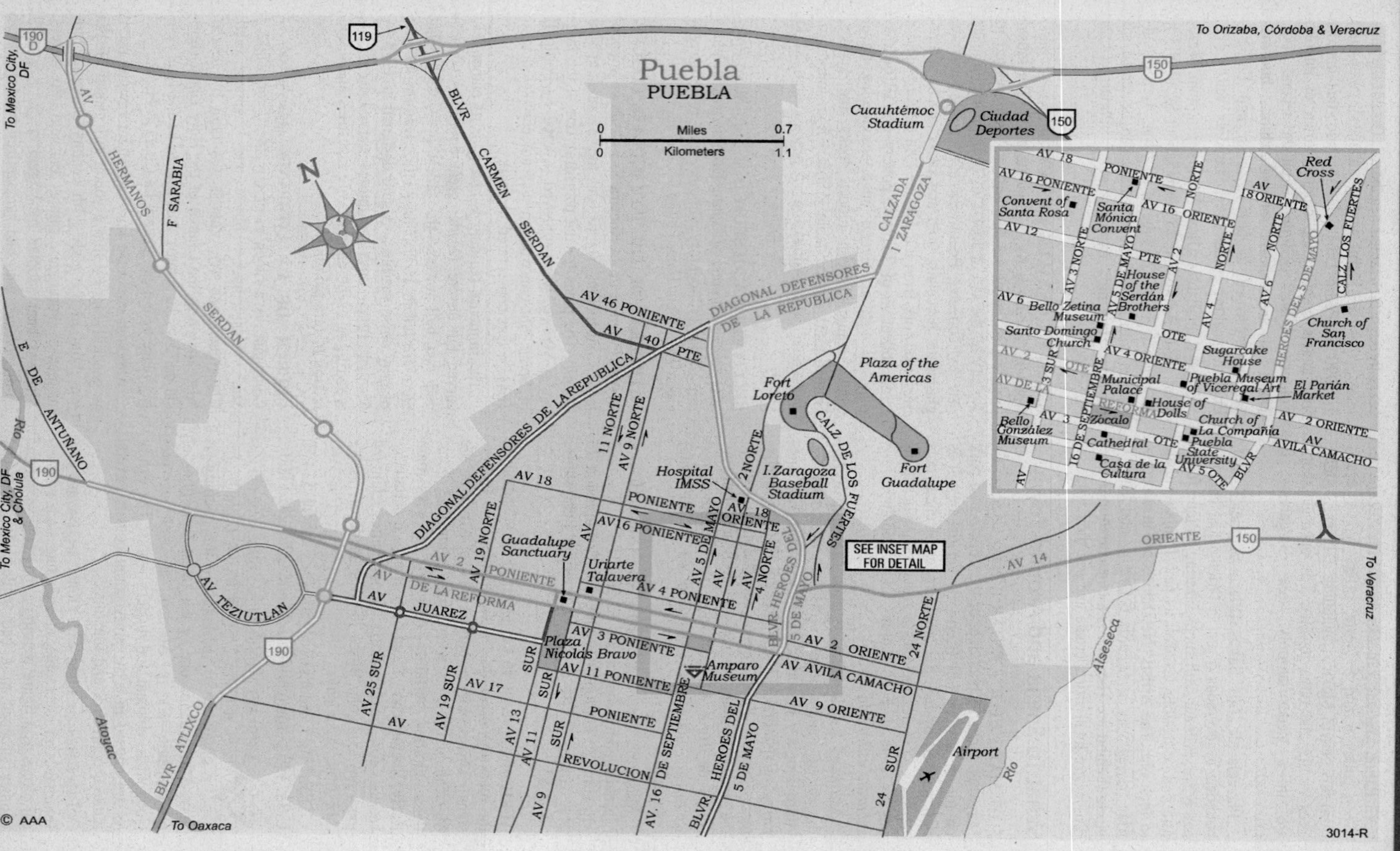
Puebla
PUEBLA
0
Miles
0.7
0
Kilometers
1.1
To Orizaba, Córdoba & Veracruz
To Veracruz
To Mexico City, DF
To Mexico City, DF & Cholula
To Oaxaca
Ciudad Deportes
Cuauhtémoc Stadium
Plaza of the Americas
Fort Guadalupe
Fort Loreto
I. Zaragoza Baseball Stadium
CALZ DE LOS FUERTES
CALZADA I ZARAGOZA
DIAGONAL DEFENSORES DE LA REPUBLICA
DIAGONAL DEFENSORES DE LA REPUBLICA
SEE INSET MAP FOR DETAIL
Hospital IMSS
Amparo Museum
Uriarte Talavera
Guadalupe Sanctuary
Plaza Nicolás Bravo
Airport
BLVR CARMEN SERDAN
AV HERMANOS SERDAN
F SARABIA
E DE ANTUÑANO
AV TEZIUTLAN
JUAREZ
BLVR ATLIXCO
BLVR HEROES DEL 5 DE MAYO
AV AVILA CAMACHO
AV. 16 DE SEPTIEMBRE
REVOLUCION
AV 2 ORIENTE
AV 9 ORIENTE
AV 14 ORIENTE
AV 46 PONIENTE
AV 40 PTE
AV 18 ORIENTE
AV 5 DE MAYO
AV 16 PONIENTE
AV 4 PONIENTE
AV 3 PONIENTE
AV 11 PONIENTE
AV 2 PONIENTE
AV DE LA REFORMA
AV 9 NORTE
11 NORTE
AV 19 NORTE
2 NORTE
4 NORTE
24 NORTE
24 SUR
AV 9 SUR
AV 11 SUR
AV 13 SUR
AV 17
AV 19 SUR
AV 25 SUR
AV 18 PONIENTE
Alseseca
Rio
Atoyac
Red Cross
Church of San Francisco
El Parián Market
Puebla Museum of Viceregal Art
Sugarcake House
House of Dolls
Church of La Compañía
Puebla State University
House of the Serdán Brothers
Santa Mónica Convent
Convent of Santa Rosa
Bello Zetina Museum
Santo Domingo Church
Municipal Palace
Zócalo
Cathedral
Casa de la Cultura
Bello González Museum
CALZ LOS FUERTES
HEROES DEL 5 DE MAYO
AV 2 ORIENTE
AV AVILA CAMACHO
BLVR
AV 5 OTE
AV 18 ORIENTE
AV 16 ORIENTE
AV 16 PONIENTE
AV 12
AV 4 ORIENTE
16 DE SEPTIEMBRE
AV 3 NORTE
AV 3 SUR
REFORMA
3014-R
© AAA

Catarina. Freed to assume a life of piety and religious devotion, Catarina married a Chinese servant named Domingo Suárez—thus earning her nickname—and was revered for her acts of charity, so much so that her characteristic style of dress became universally known as the *china poblana*.

CHURCH OF SAN FRANCISCO (Templo de San Francisco) is about 6 blks. n.e. of the *Zócalo*, just off Av. 14 Oriente at the corner of Blvd. Héroes del 5 de Mayo. The oldest church in Puebla was founded in 1535; the present edifice was completed in the 18th century. Its imposing north doorway is a good example of the decorative motif known as plateresque. The facade of brick and colorful rectangular tiles is noteworthy.

Off the main altar is a small chapel with a funerary glass box containing the remains of Franciscan friar Sebastián de Aparicio. Before taking his vows, Fray Sebastián was distinguished as one of New Spain's first roadbuilders. He was beatified for his good deeds and purported miracles, and many worshippers come to pay their respects.

CHURCH OF SANTO DOMINGO (Iglesia de Santo Domingo) is 3 blks. n. of the *Zócalo* on Av. 5 de Mayo, between avs. 4 Poniente and 6 Poniente. It was completed in the early 17th century and features colorful tile decoration.

Don't miss the spectacularly ornate Chapel of the Rosary (Capilla del Rosario), which has walls and a ceiling completely covered with gold leaf and gilded stucco figures of angels, saints, children and animals. The extravagant altar features a statue of the Virgen del Rosario, crowned and adorned with jewels.

EX-CONVENT OF SANTA MONICA (Ex-Convento de Santa Mónica) is 9 blks. n. of the *Zócalo* at Av. 18 Poniente #103, just off Av. 5 de Mayo. It was ordered closed when the 1857 Reform Laws abolished monasteries and convents in Mexico; the convent's nuns continued their work in semi-secrecy until 1934.

The museum preserves the dark corridors and austere rooms and includes a collection of religious art; the paintings on velvet by Rafael Morante have retained their brilliant colors after centuries. Guides are available. Entry to the museum is through a house and passageway. Tues.-Sun. 9-5. Admission 24 pesos (about $2.30 U.S.).

EX-CONVENT OF SANTA ROSA (Ex-Convento de Santa Rosa) is 7 blks. n.w. of the *Zócalo* at Av. 14 Poniente #305, between calles 3 and 5 Norte. This partially restored convent has a museum with handicraft exhibits and a splendid 18th-century tiled kitchen. According to legend, the traditional chocolate and chile sauce called *mole poblano* was invented here by nuns who wanted to prepare a special dish for the saint's day of their bishop.

A government-sponsored craft shop on the premises sells embroidery, lace and *poblano* craft items. Tues.-Sun. 10-5. Admission 10 pesos; 5 pesos (children).

FORTS LORETO AND GUADALUPE (Fuertes de Loreto y Guadalupe) stand on a hill (Cerro de Guadalupe) in a park about 2 km (1.2 mi.) n.e. of the *Zócalo*. They commemorate the defeat of 6,500 French troops by a force of 4,000 Mexicans led by General Ignacio Zaragoza on May 5, 1862.

Fort Loreto, at the western end of the park, contains original cannons, a chapel that dates from 1780 and the No Intervention Museum (Museo de la No Intervención), which chronicles the Battle of Puebla and the French occupation of Mexico and also has a display of uniforms. Fort Guadalupe, another key battle site, stands just 1,500 feet away across Plaza of the Americas at the park's eastern end. Mon.-Fri. 9-5. Admission to each 33 pesos (about $3.20 U.S.), free (children).

GUADALUPE SANCTUARY (Santuario de Guadalupe) is on Av. Reforma, 6 blks. w. of the *Zócalo*. This is one of the finest examples of the region's traditional architecture.

HOUSE OF CULTURE (Casa de la Cultura) is 1 blk. s. of the *Zócalo* at Av. 5 Oriente #5, facing the s. side of the Cathedral. It is housed in the former Archbishop's Palace (Palacio del Obispado), a building in the classic *poblano* style—patterned red brick interspersed with glazed blue-and-white tiles, windows framed in white stucco, and a flat roof embellished with a row of white spikes. It contains a concert and lecture hall as well as the Palafox Library. Free maps of the city can be obtained here. Daily 10-8. Phone (222) 242-1966 or (222) 246-6922.

Palafox Library (Biblioteca Palafoxiana) is on the second floor. The immense room, just 20 feet wide but more than 200 feet long, contains thousands of volumes, mostly priceless bound manuscripts in Latin. Other valuable books include a 1584 atlas printed in Antwerp, Belgium, and a 16th-century Bible in four languages. Exquisitely carved cedar bookshelves protected by wire stand in three tiers above the worn red-tile floors. The reading tables are onyx with inlaid wood. Marble busts of Aristotle, Plato and other philosophers line one wall. Open Tues.-Sun. Admission 10 pesos; 5 pesos (children).

HOUSE OF THE SERDAN BROTHERS (Casa de Aquiles Serdán) is at Av. 6 Oriente #206, between calles 2 and 4 Norte. It contains the Museum of the Revolution (Museo de la Revolución). In their *poblano*-style home, which they had turned into an arsenal, the Serdán family played an important role in launching the revolution against dictator Porfirio Díaz. On Nov. 18, 1910, the house was surrounded by 500 federal army soldiers and policemen, who were alerted to the family's plot. During a 14-hour gunfight, several members of the family were killed; the rest were imprisoned.

Bullet holes still scar the walls, floor and ceiling of the living room. Tues.-Sun. 10-4:30. Admission 11 pesos; 5 pesos (children).

NATIONAL MUSEUM OF MEXICAN RAILWAYS (Museo Nacional de Los Ferrocarriles Mexicanos) is at Calle 11 Norte #1005 (at Av. 10 Poniente), about 6 blks. n.w. of the *Zócalo;* street parking in the vicinity is limited. This large rail yard, located on station property of the former Mexican and Mexican Southern railways, contains about a dozen period locomotives hooked up to boxcars, pullmans and coal and diner rail cars. Mail rail cars have multiple "pigeon hole" slots, many containing mail with canceled stamps from the era. A featured display is the presidential train, with cars for dining, sleeping, meetings and staff. Visitors can stroll the grounds and climb aboard some of the engines for an up-close experience.

Allow 1 hour minimum. Tues.-Sun. 10-5. Admission 20 pesos (about $1.95 U.S.). Phone (222) 232-4988.

PUEBLA MUSEUM OF VICEREGAL ART (Museo Poblano de Arte Virreinal) is 2 blks. n.e. of the *Zócalo* at Calle 4 Norte #203. This museum, housed in the restored Hospital of San Pedro, exhibits paintings, sculpture, ceramics, china and glassware from the Bello Y Gonzalez collection. The second floor displays antique pharmacy jars and other vessels engraved with the names of various plants, herbs and medicines. Rotating temporary exhibitions are devoted to contemporary Mexican artists.

Guided tours are available. Allow 1 hour minimum. Tues.-Sun. 10-5. Admission 15 pesos (about $1.45 U.S.). Phone (222) 246-6618.

SUGARCAKE HOUSE (Casa de Alfeñique) is 3 blks. n.e. of the *Zócalo* at Av. 4 Oriente and Calle 6 Norte. This 17th-century colonial mansion, named for its ornate exterior, was once a residence for visiting dignitaries. Now a museum, it has an archeological and historical collection on the first two floors; the third floor is furnished in period. Tues.-Sun. 10-5. Admission about $2 (U.S.).

QUERETARO, QUERETARO (D-2)

pop. 565,400, metro area 825,500, elev. 6,078′

Querétaro (keh-REH-tah-roh) lies in a valley at the base of a hill called the Sangremal. The city was founded by Otomí Indians long before Europeans discovered the New World. It was captured by the Spanish in 1531 and developed as the headquarters for the Franciscan monks who established missions throughout Central America, Mexico and California.

Querétaro has played a pivotal role in Mexican history. The early 19th century saw the city as the center of rebellion against Spain. Doña Josefa (La Corregidora) and her husband, the local magistrate, formed the Society for the Study of Fine Arts to discuss poetry and politics; two of Mexico's greatest revolutionary heroes, Father Miguel Hidalgo and Capt. Ignacio Allende, often attended. In 1810, when budding plots for national independence were uncovered, Doña Josefa alerted the principal insurgents of their impending arrest.

The city also was Mexico's capital 37 years later when U.S. troops took over Mexico City; the Treaty of Guadalupe-Hidalgo, which ceded California, Arizona and New Mexico to the United States, was formulated in 1848 at Querétaro's Academy of Fine Arts. During the War of Reform (1857-59), President Benito Juárez made Querétaro his headquarters. Emperor Maximilian's headquarters were here as well; he ended his 3-year reign before a firing squad on the nearby Hill of the Bells (Cerro de las Campañas), thus ending Europe's dream of controlling Mexico.

Elegant colonial architecture is concentrated in the historic downtown area, which was designated a World Heritage Site by UNESCO in 1996. The cobblestone streets are narrow but well maintained, with pedestrian-only thoroughfares *(andadores)* linking several plazas.

The central plaza is called Jardín Zenea; north-south Avenida Corregidora, downtown's main street, runs along its east side. Band concerts take place at the plaza on Sunday evenings at 6 p.m. Six blocks south is the large, tree-shaded Alameda.

Two blocks east of Jardín Zenea is Plaza de Armas (also called Plaza de la Independencia). On the plaza's west side, at the Portal de Dolores (Avenida Pasteur #6), is Ecala's House (Casa de Ecala). This building has what might be the most beautiful 18th-century baroque facade in the city; note the brick and stone staircases and the small window with an elaborate ornamentation of drapes sculpted in stone. Visitors can walk around the inner courtyard during normal business hours.

Among other notable downtown buildings is the Casa de la Marquesa, at Av. Madero #41. In the 18th century this elegant mansion was the residence of a wealthy family of royal blood; it now houses a hotel. The interior courtyard is graced with Moorish-style arches. Another hotel, the Mesón de Santa Rosa (on Plaza de Armas at Av. Pasteur #17) has three spectacular courtyards; in the middle one stands an old trough that once served to water guests' horses.

A block north of the Jardín Zenea at the corner of avenidas Corregidora and Hidalgo is the Theater of the Republic (Teatro de la República), built in neoclassic style between 1850 and 1852 and embellished with accents of olive leaves, crowns and shields. The Mexican Constitution was signed there in 1917.

A block west of the Jardín Zenea at Avenida Madero and Calle Allende is the Neptune Fountain (Fuente de Neptuno). It was designed by Eduardo Tresguerras, who was responsible for a number of the city's neoclassic buildings.

Another landmark is the 6-mile-long, 50-foot-high aqueduct *(acueducto),* constructed by the Spanish more than 200 years ago and still supplying the city with water. Its 74 arches run along the center of east-west Avenida Zaragoza.

The state of Querétaro is known for its gemstones, especially opals. These should be purchased only at reputable shops; avoid sidewalk vendors. Lapidaria de Querétaro, a few blocks north of the

Jardín Zenea at Av. Corregidora Norte #149-A, sells locally mined opals and other semiprecious stones.

The Plaza de Toros Santa María, south of downtown on Avenida Constituyentes, is one of Mexico's best bullrings, drawing top matadors from Mexico and Spain. The main season runs from November through January.

Querétaro State Tourism Office (Secretaría de Turismo): Av. Luis Pasteur #4 Norte off Plaza de Armas. Open daily 9-8; phone 01 (800) 715-1742 (toll-free long distance within Mexico) or (888) 811-6130 (from the United States).

What To See

CHURCH OF SAN FRANCISCO (Iglesia de San Francisco) is opposite the Jardín Zenea on Calle 5 de Mayo. It dates from 1545 and dominates the plaza. The dome's colored tiles were brought from Spain in 1540. The church houses a collection of 17th-, 18th- and 19th-century religious paintings, and a figure of Santiago adorns the doorway.

CHURCH OF SANTA CLARA (Iglesia de Santa Clara) is on Calle Allende, just n. of the Neptune Fountain. Founded in 1633 and reconstructed during the 18th century by architect Eduardo Tresguerras, Santa Clara had one of Mexico's richest nunneries. It is noted for its ornately carved interior, gilded altarpieces and delicate exterior ironwork.

CHURCH OF SANTA ROSA DE VITERBO (Iglesia de Santa Rosa de Viterbo) is about 5 blks. s.w. of the Jardín Zenea at Av. General Arteaga and Calle Ezequiel Montes. Oriental influences are visible in this 1752 church's bell tower, fashioned after a pagoda, and in its flying buttresses, flanked by dragon faces. The interior exhibits a profusion of gilt, carved wood with inlaid marble and filigree work.

CONVENT OF SANTA CRUZ (Convento de la Santa Cruz) is e. of the city center at Av. Venustiano Carranza/Independencia and Calle Acuña. As many as 200 monks once lived in the mission compound, a well-preserved series of cloisters and cells complete with an orchard, a kitchen with a cold storage chamber, several schools and an enclosed reservoir. The monastery's gardens have trees with cross-shaped thorns.

Standing watch over the church plaza are statues of Querétaro's founders and other figures important to the city's early history. The monastery also served as Maximilian's army barracks and later, after his defeat in 1867, as his prison. The ashes of the heroine La Corregidora are encased in a monument behind the church. Guided tours are available. Open Tues.-Sat. Donations.

GOVERNMENT PALACE (Palacio Gobierno) is at the n. end of Plaza de Armas. Now housing the state of Querétaro offices, it was once the home of Doña Josefa Ortiz, or "La Corregidora" (the mayor's wife), the heroine of the 1810 War of Independence. Under house arrest, she whispered instructions through a keyhole to a messenger to warn insurgents Father Miguel Hidalgo and Capt. Ignacio Allende in the nearby town of Dolores. As a result, Hidalgo immediately issued his famous cry *(grito)* for independence. More than 50 years later, Archduke Maximilian presided over many meetings here. Open during normal business hours.

HILL OF THE BELLS (Cerro de las Campañas) is on the western outskirts of the city. It was the site of Archduke Maximilian's last battle, and it was at this location that he was executed by a firing squad on June 19, 1867.

A monument erected by the government in honor of Benito Juárez, who defeated the ill-fated "Emperor of Mexico," is at the top of a hill behind the Capilla de la Piedad. This neoclassic chapel, erected by the Austrian government in 1901, is dedicated to Maximilian. Stela mark the spots where Maximilian and his two Mexican generals, Miramón and Mejía, fell. In the small Museum of the Siege of Querétaro (Museo del Sitio de Querétaro) near the chapel are several photographs documenting the event. Museum open Tues.-Sun. 10-5. Admission about $1 (U.S.).

MUSEUM OF ART (Museo de Arte) is at Calle Allende Sur #14. It is housed in a former monastery, the Convent of San Agustín (Convento de San Agustín), an outstanding example of baroque architecture built in 1731 by Mexican architect Ignacio Mariano de las Casas. The building's exterior ornamentation is as impressive as the collection of Mexican colonial and European art inside. Tues.-Sun. 11-5. Admission about $2 (U.S.).

REGIONAL MUSEUM (Museo Regional) is on Av. Corregidora next to the Church of San Francisco. Housed in the former monastery, it displays colonial relics; uniforms and weaponry; 17th-, 18th- and 19th-century paintings by Juan Correa, Villalpando, Miguel Cabrera and Luis Rodríguez; and a library of more than 8,000 books, mostly parchment tomes from the 17th and 18th centuries. Tues.-Sun. 11-5. Admission about $3.25 (U.S.).

REAL DE CATORCE, SAN LUIS POTOSI (B-2)

Real de Catorce (ray-ALL day cah-TOR-say) is one of Mexico's most interesting old mining towns. (The literal translation of the name is "royal of 14," allegedly a reference to the killing of 14 Spanish soldiers by Indian resisters.) Situated in the Sierra de Catorce range at an altitude of 9,000 feet, it has a dry climate, extraordinarily blue skies, peerlessly starry nights and spectacular mountain vistas. The stark countryside—forested to the south, treeless and cacti-strewn to the north—has been featured in several films, including the John Huston classic "The Treasure of the Sierra Madre" and more recently "The Mexican," starring Brad Pitt and Julia Roberts.

The town's history dates back to at least the 1630s, a period when Spanish *conquistadores* were busy conquering the region that today constitutes much of northern Mexico. Silver was discovered in 1773, and Real de Catorce became one of the wealthiest mining towns in the Americas. By the late 19th century it had a population of 15,000, a bullring and shops that sold expensive items imported from Europe.

But although it was rich, the community was isolated. When Mexican dictator Porfirio Díaz journeyed here in 1896 to visit the Santa Ana Mine—the first mine in the country to install water-removing pumps that were powered by electricity—he traveled by train, mule-drawn carriage and finally on horseback in order to reach it. Several years later a tunnel was cut through solid rock to provide access into and out of town.

After an apex of prosperity at the turn of the 20th century, decline set in. The falling price of silver in 1905 initiated an exodus that was exacerbated by the subsequent political and social turmoil of the Mexican Revolution, and the town was all but abandoned. Although Real de Catorce never quite became a ghost town, by 1920 the population had dwindled to a few hundred people eking out a hardscrabble existence.

While mining never regained its importance (the last process plant shut down in 1990), a slow rebirth had begun in the 1970s as tourists began rediscovering both the glorious mountain scenery and the town's unhurried pace. Entrepreneurs began to move in, renovating crumbling buildings and opening hotels, shops and restaurants. More recently Catorce has seen an influx of artists and filmmakers.

There are a number of ex-haciendas in the surrounding region that date back to the 18th century. Built by the Spanish to supply animals and agricultural products to local mining communities, they passed through various owners after Mexico won its independence and continued to function as ranches until the end of the 19th century. Most of them then gradually fell into disrepair as the *ejido* system of community-owned land was revived in the 1930s by president Lázaro Cárdenas. Today very few of the ex-haciendas have survived intact, with collapsed roofs and weathered walls standing as mute testimony to the past.

This is a place of pilgrimage for Huichol Indians who live in the states of Durango, Jalisco, Nayarit and Zacatecas. They journey to El Quemado, a hilltop that is a revered ceremonial site, and to the surrounding desert scrublands, which make up their spiritual homeland of Wirikuta. The Huichols also come here to participate in religious rituals involving the use of peyote, the common name for a small, spineless species of cactus that grows throughout much of northern Mexcio; the buds it produces have a hallucinogenic effect when chewed.

Another important pilgrimage is made by thousands of devout Catholics every year to the Parish of the Immaculate Conception, or parish church, to pay homage to St. Francis of Assisi, the town's patron saint. The church, which dates from 1817, stands in a small plaza between calles Lanzagorta and Constitución; it replaced an older, smaller church building that had a wooden roof. The exterior is neoclassic; inside, frescoes adorn the baptistery and there are several altars. Especially notable is the St. Joseph altar, in the cross vaults under the church dome, which has its original stucco and is decorated with a painting of the Virgin of Guadalupe.

An altar devoted to St. Francis—affectionately known as "Panchito" or "El Charrito"—is in the nave. It features a wood sculpture of the saint, jointed at the arms and legs so that it can be stood on its feet and moved, as well as a painting of Our Lady of Refuge, the patron saint of miners. The image of St. Francis is said to be miraculous, and as a result the church receives a flow of pilgrims from all over northern Mexico, particularly on Oct. 4, the Day of St. Francis.

Hundreds of *retablos* (small devotional paintings) adorn the walls near the main altar. Created on tinplate by regional artisans, *retablos* can be anything from entreaties by those who are sick to thanks for health, wealth or protection—all expressions of gratitude made to a benefactor saint. They are a distinctly Mexican form of popular art.

Calle Lanzagorta, Catorce's cobblestone main street, is lined with stalls selling religious souvenirs. There are other historic sites as well. Opposite the parish church is the old mint (Casa de Moneda), where coins were made in 1865 and 1866 before it was shut down by order of Emperor Maximilian. The building, which is currently being restored, suggests the town's former opulence. Two blocks west of the mint is Plaza Hidalgo, a pleasant place to relax in the shade of aged trees. There are shops and restaurants on the plaza and along the nearby streets.

At Calle Zaragoza #3 (opposite the northwest corner of the plaza) is Galería Vega M-57, housed in a restored former residence. Real de Catorce is increasingly becoming a magnet for artists, and here you can see contemporary paintings, sculpture, jewelry and silver work by Mexican and foreign artists who live in town. The gallery is open Sat.-Sun. or by appointment; phone (488) 887-5061.

About a block northwest of the plaza via Calle Zaragoza is the Palenque de Gallos, a former cock fighting arena built in the style of a Roman amphitheater; cultural and musical events now take place here. A bit farther north on Zaragoza at the edge of town is the bullring, now used for soccer games. Across the street in the cemetery *(panteón)* stands one of the oldest buildings in town, a Franciscan chapel built around 1775. Past the cemetery hikers can follow an old mining road that ends with a view looking out over the high plains that sweep toward the west.

Visitors also can hike into the surrounding countryside. An hour's walk will bring you to the summit of El Quemado; from this hilltop vantage point there are panoramic vistas of the desert below. Another hike can be made to the ruins of the La Concepción Mine, one of many former mines in this region, located high in the hills above the Ogarrio

Tunnel. The old mine works, mills and warehouses stand in utter serenity against a backdrop of mountains. **Note:** The terrain is impressively rugged; wear sturdy hiking shoes and a hat and bring water. If you would rather not go it alone, guided horseback, jeep and walking excursions can be arranged.

There are several restaurants in town. El Cactus, on the west side of Plaza Hidalgo, serves both Mexican and Italian food, including homemade pasta. Restaurante Eucalipto, near the plaza on Calle Lerdo, also has Italian dishes as well as good steaks. La Esquina Chata, on Plaza Hidalgo at Calle Lanzagorta #2, is a cafe and bakery that serves breakfast and has excellent coffee. Street stalls along Calle Lanzagorta sell tacos, *gorditas*—thick corn tortillas with different fillings—and *chiles rellenos,* roasted green or poblano peppers stuffed with cheese or ground meat, dipped in egg batter and fried.

This is a very low-key place most of the year, with more tourists on weekends than during the week. The Semana Santa and Christmas holidays bring crowds, but the year's biggest event is the Fiesta of San Francisco from late September to mid-October. Thousands of pilgrims, many coming just for a day, descend on Real de Catorce by the busload—and every vehicle must pass through the one-way Ogarrio Tunnel. If you want peace and quiet this is not the time to visit.

Practicalities

Getting here is something of an adventure. The Real de Catorce turn-off is on Mex. 57 a little over 3 miles north of the city of Matehuala; watch for the sign that says "Cedral/Real de Catorce." The mostly paved road travels west about 28 kilometers (17 miles), passing through the town of Cedral before reaching a signed junction. At the junction a cobblestone road proceeds south about 24 kilometers (15 miles) to town. **Note:** There is a Pemex station in Cedral; there are no gas stations in Real de Catorce.

The drive is slow but spectacularly scenic, winding up a mountainside past abandoned buildings before reaching the entrance to the Ogarrio Tunnel. Opened in 1901, the tunnel is just 1.5 miles long but dark, cold and winding. It also is so narrow that vehicles can be accommodated in only one direction at a time. Highway workers at each end direct the flow, and there can be a long wait if traffic is busy. At the other end of the tunnel is a parking area, and local youngsters are likely to ask you for money to watch your car. From the parking area it's a short walk to Calle Lanzagorta, the main street.

If you'd rather have someone else do the driving, buses leave from Matehuala's central bus station (Centro de Autobuses) daily at 8 a.m., noon, 2 and 6 p.m. The station is on Avenida 5 de Mayo, just north of the junction with Mex. 57 and about 2 kilometers (1.2 miles) south of the center of town. Passengers switch to a minibus at the tunnel entrance, as the larger vehicle cannot negotiate the narrow bends. The drive takes about 2 hours; one-way fare is about $5 (U.S.). **Note:** The return trip can be very crowded on the smaller bus.

Although tourism is growing, this is still a small town, and there are no banks or currency exchange offices *(casas de cambio).* Keep pesos on hand if you intend to shop, dine or sightsee. There is an ATM in the tourist office (Dirección de Turismo), which is located inside the Presidencia Municipal building (across Calle Constitución from the parish church). Keep in mind that withdrawal charges can be steep. For visitors who want more than just a day trip, accommodations range from simple guest houses *(casas de huéspedes)* to several hotels that occupy restored old buildings.

SAN JUAN DEL RIO, QUERETARO

(D-3) pop. 105,600, elev. 6,498′

San Juan del Río (sahn hwan dehl REE-oh), noted for semiprecious stones, woodcarvings, baskets and palm furniture, is located in a prosperous agricultural region that yields corn, dairy products and wine. This picturesque city was once an important stop on the stagecoach route to Mexico City. San Juan del Río features many buildings painted white and enhanced by decorative elements of dark brown carved stone.

Also near San Juan del Río are the Trinidad opal mines. Opals and amethysts are polished in town; gems should be purchased only at established shops.

A short distance northeast of San Juan del Río via Mex. 120 is the resort town of Tequisquiapan (teh-kees-kee-AP-an). This weekend retreat was once popular for its hot-water thermal springs, but competition from local industries for the available water has hurt the spa business. It remains a pretty place to stroll, however, with narrow streets planted with flowering fruit trees and cloaked in brightly colored bougainvillea, and a quaint main plaza surrounded by arcades *(portales).*

On the plaza's north side is the neoclassic Church of Santa Maria of the Assumption (Templo de Santa María de la Asunción). A crafts market (Mercado de Artesanías) near the plaza sells rattan furniture and other locally made items.

From Tequisquiapan, continue north on Mex. 120 to Ezequiel Montes; from here, take the paved turn-off west about 10 kilometers (6 miles) to Bernal. Another popular weekend destination, this picturesque little town has craft shops offering wool and cotton clothing. The main attraction, however, is La Peña de Bernal, a huge, pyramid-shaped monolith.

About 38 kilometers (24 miles) north of Tequisquiapan on Mex. 120 is the town of Cadereyta; ask in town for directions to La Quinta Schmoll, a botanical garden devoted to cacti (more than 4,000 varieties). The garden is open daily; admission is free.

This stretch of Mex. 120 through northeastern Querétaro state traverses the Sierra Gorda, part of the eastern Sierra Madre mountain range and a green oasis at the edge of central Mexico's vast semi-desert region. The scenery is impressively rugged; forested peaks rise more than 10,000 feet, while the valleys between them are hot and humid.

Mex. 120 passes through the town of Pinal de Amoles, then makes a series of dramatic ascents and descents to Jalpan. Beginning in the 1750s, Franciscan priest Father Junípero Serra established five missions in this region to evangelize the Chichimeca Indians. These five missions—Jalpan, Concá, Landa, Tancoyol and Tilaco—were designated World Heritage Sites by UNESCO in 2003. Serra went on to found another, more famous chain of missions in Alta (upper) California.

Jalpan's old mission church, the Misión de Jalpan, is beautifully restored. Also in town is the Museum of the Sierra Gorda (Museo de la Sierra Gorda), a former military fort with exhibits offering insight into the region's Indian cultures and Father Serra's evangelical work.

SAN LUIS POTOSI, SAN LUIS POTOSI (C-2)

pop. 670,500, metro area 936,000, elev. 6,157′

See map page 363.

San Luis Potosí (sahn loo-EES poh-toh-SEE), capital of the state of the same name, dates from the late 1500s when it was established as a mining settlement. The city was seat of the national government under President Benito Juárez in 1863 and again in 1867. While here in 1854, González Bocanegra wrote the Mexican national anthem, first sung in Mexico City's Santa Ana Theater on Sept. 15 of that year. The San Luis Plan, drafted by Francisco I. Madero while he was imprisoned in the city by dictator Porfirio Díaz, set the stage for the Revolution of 1910.

A distribution point for foreign and domestic merchandise, San Luis Potosí's atmosphere is largely industrial. Tanneries, flour mills, smelters, textile mills, breweries and furniture factories are among the manufacturing concerns, and highways around the city and within the state are busy with truck traffic.

But San Luis Potosí is not all soot and smoke. It has a well-preserved colonial center, anchored by Plaza de Armas, the main square. The plaza is flanked by the city's 18th-century cathedral on the east and the Government Palace (Palacio de Gobierno) on the west.

Two blocks northwest of Plaza de Armas is Founders' Plaza (Plaza de Los Fundadores); 2 blocks east and a block south of Plaza de Armas is Plaza del Carmen. Two blocks west and 2 blocks south of Plaza de Armas is Plaza San Francisco. Each of these plazas is a pleasant spot to take in city life.

The Plaza España bullring is on Avenida Universidad, at the eastern end of downtown near the southeastern corner of Alameda Park. On the north side of this large park is the city's modern train station, where a series of Fernando Leal frescoes depict the history of transportation in Mexico.

Holy Week (Semana Santa) celebrations are among the city's most traditional as well as most solemn. Various cultural, artistic and gastronomic events lead up to Good Friday, when there is a silent procession through the historic city center. More down to earth is the San Luis Potosí National Fair (Feria Nacional Potosina), normally held the latter half of August, which features bullfights, cockfights, rodeos, and agricultural and livestock exhibitions.

About 56 kilometers (35 miles) south of the city via Mex. 57 are two spas known for their medicinal waters. Lourdes Spa, just outside Santa María del Río, has strongly alkaline, radioactive waters that purportedly benefit intestinal ailments. El Gogorrón National Park is accessible from a paved road that branches southwest off Mex. 57 to the village of Villa de Reyes; its thermal pools and many springs are reputed to alleviate circulatory problems and rheumatism.

San Luis Potosí State Tourism Office (Secretaría de Turismo): downtown at Av. Alvaro Obregón #520, less than a block west of Plaza de Los Fundadores. Open Mon.-Fri. 8-8, Sat. 9-2; phone (444) 812-9939.

Shopping areas: Among the wares on display at the huge Hidalgo Market (Mercado Hidalgo), 4 blocks north of Plaza de Armas, are prized Santa María *rebozos* (shawl-like garments), so gauzy in texture they can be pulled through a woman's wedding ring; pottery; and a candy called *queso de tuna* made from the fruit of the prickly pear cactus. Calle Hidalgo between the market and Plaza de Armas is a pedestrian-only street flanked by numerous shops and stores.

The best place in the city to shop for handicrafts is the government-run FONART store on Plaza San Francisco, which stocks items from all over Mexico. Another good place to browse is La Casa del Artesano, Av. Carranza #540 about 5 blocks west of Plaza de Armas; it sells crafts from the state of San Luis Potosí.

What To See

CERRO DE SAN PEDRO is 8 km (5 mi.) e. out of the city on Av. Universidad (Mex. 70) following signs, then 13 km (8 mi.) n. This ghost town contains the ruins of shops, churches, estates and a hospital. It was founded in 1583 after several mines in the vicinity began operations. By the late 1940s, the gold, lead, iron, manganese and mercury deposits finally began to give out. Local firms continue to extract limited quantities of minerals from the mines. Visitors can enter La Descubridora, the town's first mine. Guide service is available.

CHURCH OF OUR LADY OF EL CARMEN (Iglesia de Nuestra Señora del Carmen) is on Plaza del Carmen. This ornate church is the city's finest example of Churrigueresque architecture. Its domes are decorated with blue, green, yellow and white tiles. Also note the profusion of carved stone angels, a hallmark of indigenous craftsmanship. The interior contains a carved pulpit, a reredos by Eduardo Tresguerras, paintings by Vallejo and a baroque altar considered one of the most impressive in Mexico.

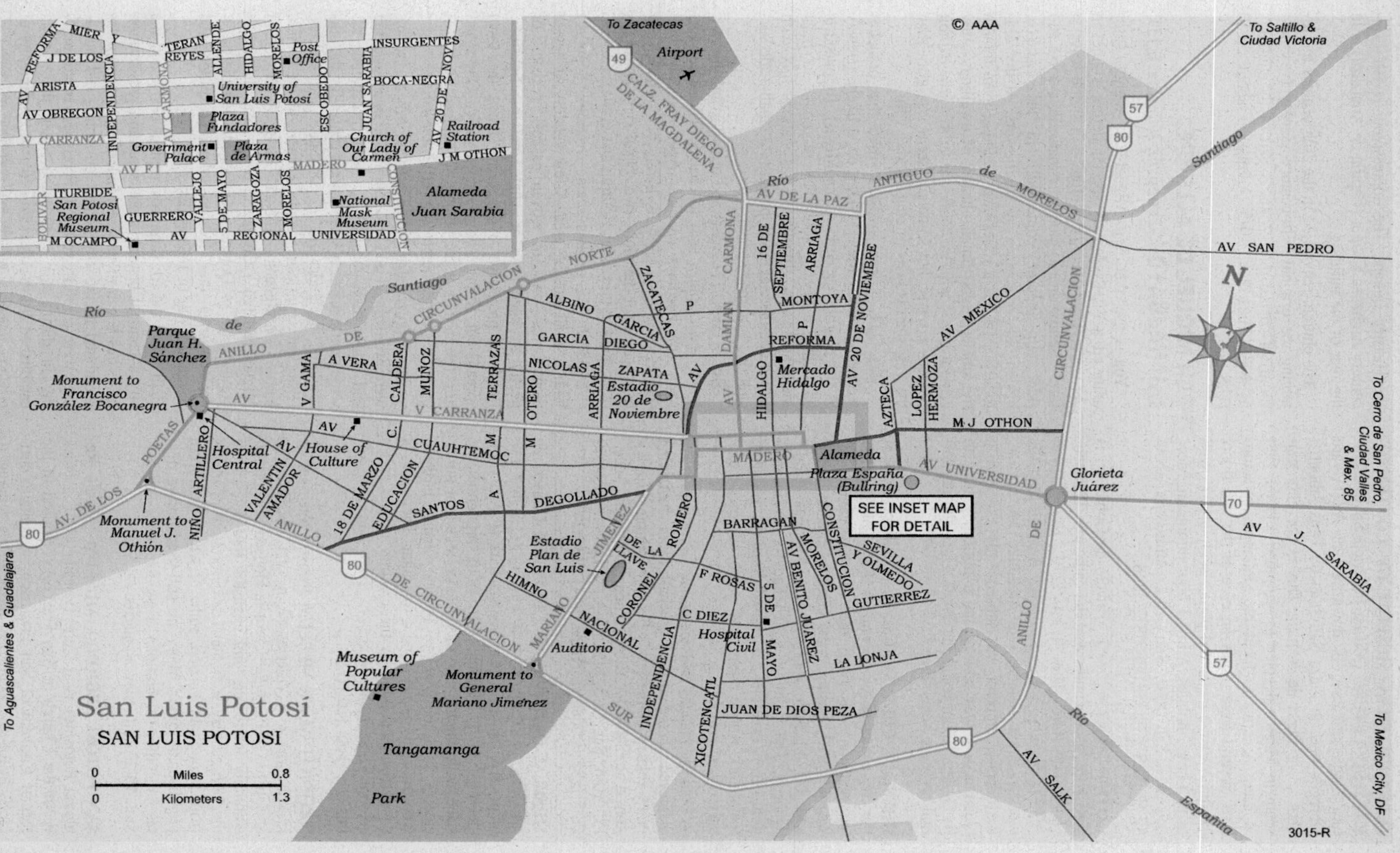
San Luis Potosí
SAN LUIS POTOSI
© AAA
3015-R
SEE INSET MAP FOR DETAIL
To Zacatecas
To Saltillo & Ciudad Victoria
To Cerro de San Pedro, Ciudad Valles & Mex. 85
To Mexico City, DF
To Aguascalientes & Guadalajara
Airport
CALZ. FRAY DIEGO DE LA MAGDALENA
Río Santiago
Río Españita
ANTIGUO de MORELOS
AV DE LA PAZ
AV SAN PEDRO
AV MEXICO
CIRCUNVALACION
NORTE
ANILLO DE CIRCUNVALACION SUR
Parque Juan H. Sánchez
Monument to Francisco González Bocanegra
Hospital Central
House of Culture
Monument to Manuel J. Othión
AV. DE LOS POETAS
Estadio 20 de Noviembre
Mercado Hidalgo
Alameda
Plaza España (Bullring)
Glorieta Juárez
AV UNIVERSIDAD
M J OTHON
AV 20 DE NOVIEMBRE
Estadio Plan de San Luis
Auditorio
Hospital Civil
Museum of Popular Cultures
Monument to General Mariano Jiménez
Tangamanga Park
AV J. SARABIA
AV SALK
AV BENITO JUAREZ
JUAN DE DIOS PEZA
Miles 0 0.8
Kilometers 0 1.3
Post Office
University of San Luis Potosí
Plaza Fundadores
Government Palace
Plaza de Armas
Church of Our Lady of Carmen
Railroad Station
Alameda Juan Sarabia
National Mask Museum
San Potosí Regional Museum

FEDERICO SILVA MUSEUM OF CONTEMPORARY SCULPTURE (Museo Federico Silva Escultura Contemporánea) is downtown at Av. Alvaro Obregón #80, at Plaza San Juan de Dios (about 3 blks. e. of Plaza de Armas). This is the only museum in Mexico devoted to sculpture, and the first in Latin America to focus on contemporary sculpture. Several large rooms on each of the two floors exhibit oversize metal and plaster sculptures as well as two large mobiles. Allow 1 hour minimum. Mon. and Wed.-Sat. 10-6, Sun. 10-2. Admission about $2.50 (U.S.). Phone (444) 812-3848.

GOVERNMENT PALACE (Palacio de Gobierno) is across Plaza de Armas from the cathedral. This neoclassic structure dates from 1770. Here Benito Juárez, despite petitions for mercy from all over the world, denied clemency to Archduke Maximilian; the deposed emperor was subsequently executed at Querétaro. A wax tableau and a portrait gallery in the Juárez Room recall the event. Open during normal business hours. Free.

HOUSE OF CULTURE (Casa de la Cultura) is w. of the city center at Av. Carranza #1815. This neoclassic mansion was once the "country house" of wealthy Irish businessman Gerardo Meade Lewis and his Spanish wife Monica Joaquina Sainz-Trapaga. The building, which had former incarnations as a hotel and a school, features beautiful woodwork, ornate doors and window frames and a carved staircase railing.

Both permanent and temporary art exhibits are displayed. There also is a small room containing items related to the city's history. Exhibit information is in Spanish. Allow 1 hour minimum. Tues.-Fri. 10-6, Sat. 10-5, Sun. 10-2. Admission about $2 (U.S.); $1 (students). Phone (444) 813-2247.

MUSEUM OF POPULAR CULTURES (Museo de las Culturas Populares) is about 2 km (1.2 mi.) s.w. of the city center in Tangamanga Park (Parque Tangamanga 1). It exhibits crafts from throughout the state, with emphasis on the Huastec region of northeastern Mexico. Displays include chairs, baskets, wooden items, pottery and a wax altar. There also is an exhibit pertaining to the creation of the area's celebrated Santa María shawls. Tues.-Sun. 9-4. Admission about 30c (U.S.).

NATIONAL MASK MUSEUM (Museo Nacional de la Máscara) is at Villerías #2, n. of Calle Guerrero and just s. of Plaza del Carmen. Housed in an architecturally interesting pink mansion that dates from the 18th century, it displays an assortment of masks from throughout Mexico, some of which date from pre-Hispanic times. Many are still used during fiestas and other celebrations. Tues.-Sat. 10-2 and 5-7, Sun. 10-2. Admission about 50c (U.S.).

SAN POTOSI REGIONAL MUSEUM (Museo Regional Potosino) is at Calle Galeana #450, a block w. of the Church of San Francisco. Housed in the former Convent of San Francisco, it contains artifacts, historical documents and exhibits relating to the Huastec Indians. The impressively lavish 17th-century Aranzazú Chapel (Capilla de Aranzazú) is in the rear of the building.

The church, remodeled in the 20th century but retaining the original 17th-century sacristy (vestment room) of carved pink stone, is part of the complex as well. Tues.-Sun. 10-5. Admission about $2.50 (U.S.).

SAN MIGUEL DE ALLENDE, GUANAJUATO (C-2) pop. 62,200, elev. 6,134′

You sense that San Miguel de Allende (pronounced a-YEHN-deh) is special before you even get there. The feeling is reinforced in subtle ways: a family selling snacks along the roadside, a horse and rider clip-clopping contentedly in the distance, brown hills brightened by wildflowers. At this altitude the air has a refreshing coolness, even though the sun is bright. Small clusters of dwellings—tiny cement cubes with tin roofs—and dirt yards exhibit obvious poverty, but somehow seem less grim than the vast shantytowns ringing Mexico City.

Mex. 111, a local two-lane road that branches west off highway Mex. 57-D, is an unlikely gateway to the charm that defines San Miguel. Its outskirts have that everyday scruffiness common to most Mexican towns—dilapidated gas stations mix with newer commercial development in a small-scale version of "suburban sprawl."

But as Mex. 111 twists and turns toward the center of town, things start to change. The street narrows and becomes cobbled. Aged buildings rub shoulders along a sidewalk barely wide enough for one pedestrian, let alone two. Open shop doorways offer quick glimpses of clothing and crafts.

Suddenly you're at a scenic overlook, a pulloff with a small parking area. A few vendors sit beside their wares—piles of woven baskets, perhaps, or neatly arranged rows of painted ceramic figurines. Below a protective wrought-iron fence the town spreads out, filling a bowl-shaped valley. One structure towers above the others: multispired La Parroquía, the parish church *(see attraction listing)*.

San Miguel began as a mission where Indians were evangelized and also taught European weaving and agricultural techniques. As it prospered, the settlement became a local market center for the surrounding haciendas trading in cattle and textiles. Historical significance made its mark as well: Here native son Ignacio Allende, along with Father Miguel Hidalgo y Costilla, a priest from the neighboring town of Dolores Hidalgo, planned the original uprising that led to Mexico's bitter and protracted War of Independence.

In 1926, the Mexican government designated the city a national historic monument, and preservation measures began in earnest. Modern construction was prohibited in the city center; crumbling old buildings were carefully restored. Foreigners began moving in during the 1930s, and today there is an established North American expatriate community of artisans, teachers, writers and part-time residents.

Practicalities

The León-Guanajuato Airport is in León, about a 90-minute drive away. Aeroméxico, American, Continental and Mexicana offer flights from selected U.S. cities, including Chicago, Los Angeles and New York. Polanco Tours, a San Miguel tour company, offers van transportation to and from the airport. One-way fare is about $72 (U.S.) for two passengers, plus $10 for each additional passenger up to six; phone (415) 152-4193. A taxi ride from Querétaro to San Miguel will run about $45. For additional information about airlines *see Arriving by Air, page 61.*

"Deluxe" bus service from Mexico City's Terminal Central de Autobuses del Norte is provided daily by ETN; Primera Plus and Pegaso Plus provide first-class service. The trip is nonstop and takes about 3 hours. Second-class service by Flecha Amarilla and Herradura de Plata takes 4 hours and includes a stop in Querétaro and local stops en route. Flecha Amarilla buses also provide frequent service between San Miguel and Guanajuato. The central bus station is on the westward extension of Calle Canal, about 1.5 kilometers (1 mile) west of the center of town. For additional information about buses *see Bus Service, page 72.*

Taxis provide flat-rate service between the bus station and downtown, as well as to other locations around the city, for about $1.50 (U.S.). There is a *sitio* (cab stand) at the main plaza.

By car, the 180-mile journey from Mexico City takes 3 to 4 hours via Mex. 57-D to the Querétaro toll bypass (watch for the San Miguel exit). The bypass highway crosses Mex. 57-D north of Querétaro and connects with Mex. 111, which proceeds northwest to San Miguel. The trip along two-lane Mex. 111 is slow but scenic, offering views of typical Mexican rural life. From Guanajuato, take Mex. 45 and 45-D south and east toward Celaya, then Mex. 51 north.

Note: Street parking is scarce in the congested historic center, and local police do not hesitate to issue violators a ticket. If driving from Mexico City or elsewhere, you may have to park several blocks from the center. If you're staying in town and have a car leave it at your hotel, since almost everything of interest is within walking distance. The altitude may initially tire visitors not used to walking at higher elevations.

Banks along Calle San Francisco exchange currency Mon.-Fri. 9-1:30, but have long lines; the *casas de cambio* (currency exchange offices) located in the vicinity of the main plaza are a quicker alternative.

For Internet access try Estación Internet, on the main square at Portal de Allende #4 (2nd floor); phone (415) 152-4465. Internet San Miguel Cyber Café, Calle Mesones #57 (entrance on Calle Reloj), 2 blocks north of the main square, offers full cyber cafe services as well as espresso and cappuccino made from organic Chiapan coffee beans. An hour of access is about $3.25 (U.S.). It's open Mon.-Sat. 9-9, Sun. 10-6.

San Miguel's weather is warm and dry most of the year, but the city rarely experiences the extremes of heat common to much of Mexico. Winter nights can be chilly, and many hotels aren't heated (although some have fireplaces). The rainy season is June through September. In May an extra splash of color is added when the jacaranda trees are covered with purple blooms.

Exploring Around Town

Some travelers complain that San Miguel's "gentrification," so to speak, has replaced authentic Mexican atmosphere with a touristy vibe—trendy restaurants, pricey boutiques and a lack of local grit. It's true that foreign investors have driven up prices, and the bright orange and red facades add a Disneyesque touch.

But a stroll through the historic center proves that these complaints are primarily quibbles. There is atmosphere to spare, from the heavy carved wooden doors to intricate stone carvings adorning the windows of handsome old buildings. Their sheltered inner patios, cool retreats filled with trees, burbling fountains, clipped hedges and flowerpot urns, have a timeless beauty.

There's a sense of discovery along the narrow streets that sparks curiosity as to what's around the next corner. You'll see other tourists but also have plenty of opportunities to mingle with locals—perhaps children who shyly ask if you want to buy some gum *("Chicle"?),* or an elderly gentleman whiling away the afternoon at El Jardín, the main plaza.

Make the plaza, located between calles San Francisco and Correo, your first stop. Shaded by Indian laurel trees, it's a great place to relax on a wrought-iron bench, listen to the tolling bells of La Parroquía and observe the local scene. Buy a cold drink and plan the day's itinerary. In the evening mariachi bands play, vendors sell *carnitas* (grilled pork) and *churros* (doughnut-like fritters), flocks of pigeons flutter and couples stroll. This is the city's heart.

Most of the city's attractions are within easy walking distance of the plaza, and the historic center is compact. **Note:** Wear comfortable shoes; most streets are cobblestoned, and some are steep.

San Miguel's reputation as an arts center was established by the opening of the Allende Institute, southwest of downtown at Calle Ancha de San Antonio #20. One of its American founders, Stirling Dickinson, came to Mexico as a tourist in the 1930s and fell in love with the city. Fountains, arcades and courtyard gardens grace the grounds of the campus, which has extensive classroom space, two art galleries, a theater and a library.

The Bellas Artes Cultural Center (Centro Cultural Bellas Artes), about 2 blocks west of the main plaza at Calle Hernández Macías #75, also is called the Centro Cultural el Nigromante (its official name) and the Centro Cultural Ignacio Ramírez. It is a branch of the well-known National Institute of Fine Arts (Instituto Nacional de Bellas Artes) in Mexico City. The impressive building dates from the mid-18th century and has an immense, tree-shaded courtyard. Several murals are exhibited, including one by David Alfaro Siqueiros.

Saturday morning "adventure" tours to local handicraft workshops and out-of-town points of interest such as haciendas, ranches, vineyards or a monastery benefit the Centro de Crecimiento, a school for children with disabilities that is supported through donations. The 3-hour tours depart from the main plaza at 10:30 a.m.; tickets can be purchased from the Casa Maxwell shop at Calle Canal #14, about half a block west of the plaza. The suggested donation is 150 pesos (about $14.50 U.S.).

The Promotion of Mexican Culture, Calle Cuna de Allende #11, sponsors city walking tours, adventure and nature tours, and field trips to colonial and archeological sites. Their offices are open Mon.-Sat. 9-7; phone (415) 152-1630. For information about local happenings, consult the weekly English-language newspaper *Atención San Miguel,* which is available at the public library *(see attraction listing)* and the El Colibri bookstore, about 2 blocks east of the main plaza at Calle Sollano #30.

Siesta Tours, Inc. specializes in guided tours of San Miguel, Guanajuato and Querétaro as well as such other colonial destinations as Morelia, Pátzcuaro and Oaxaca. For information phone (800) 679-2746 (from the United States).

Shopping

San Miguel is known for the variety and quality of its regionally produced handicrafts. Metalwork—masks, trays, lanterns, picture frames and decorative objects made of tin, copper, brass, bronze and wrought iron—and the designs of local silversmiths are particularly worth seeking out. Also available are pottery, weavings, sculpture, straw items, hand-loomed *cambaya* cloth (a material frequently used to make skirts), and folk and traditional art. The colonial furniture is some of the finest produced in Mexico.

Most craft and gift shops are open Mon.-Sat. 9-7 and close from 2-4 for the traditional *siesta;* a few may open briefly on Sunday. Many accept U.S. dollars and/or MasterCard and Visa, and some will pack and ship purchases.

The open-air City Market fills the plaza near the Church of San Felipe Neri, several blocks northeast of the main plaza, and usually spreads onto the surrounding streets. Livestock and fresh produce share space with inexpensive everyday items and souvenirs at the cheaper end of the price scale. The Crafts Market (Mercado de Artesanías) consists of vendor stalls in an alley off Calle Loreto, near the Quinta Loreto Hotel and the City Market.

Pricier boutiques are scattered throughout the historic downtown area. Casa Canal, on Calle Canal, specializes in hand-carved wooden furniture. Casa Maxwell, Calle Canal #14, has an array of Mexican and Latin American folk art. Veryka, Calle Zacateros #6A, sells indigenous art—masks, ceramics, Huichol crafts.

Casa Anguiano, at the corner of calles Canal and Hernández Macías, features embroidered fabrics and copperware. For a large selection of antiques, colonial art and home furnishings, browse through La Antigua Casa Canela, Calle Umaran #20.

Art galleries are concentrated around the main plaza, and exhibit openings are big social events. Two that showcase both regional and national talent are Galería San Miguel, Plaza Principal #14, and Galería Atenea, Calle Jesús #2.

Set aside an afternoon for a trip to Galería Atotonilco. From downtown, drive north on Calzada de la Aurora (the extension of Calle Hidalgo), which curves and becomes Mexico #51 to Dolores Hidalgo. Continue north about 8 kilometers (5 miles). At El Cortijo, just past the Escondido Spa, turn left in front of a small stone arch, then left again where the main road veers left. After approximately .65 kilometers (.4 miles), watch for two houses (one yellow and one white) next to each other. Turn right between them and follow the curving driveway to the red gallery building.

Opened in late 2006, Galería Atotonilco is located in a beautiful rural setting on the Río Laja. The extensive, high-quality selection of folk art and antiques includes art from all over Mexico. Browse among displays of ceramic jars, vases and platters, whimsical trees of life in different sizes, hand-painted animal wood carvings from Oaxaca, playful papier-mâché skeletons, *retablos* (small oil paintings of Catholic saints) and colorful baskets, country furniture and hand-forged ironwork, and vintage historical photographs. There also is a noteworthy collection of hand-woven *sarapes* from villages in Saltillo state in northern Mexico. The gallery is open by appointment only; phone (415) 185-2225 or (510) 295-4097 (from the United States).

Dining, Nightlife and Events

Despite its small size, San Miguel has a number of restaurants offering a wide range of cuisines—from reliable French and Italian to regional Mexican to such unexpected choices as Tex-Mex and vegetarian. Much of this variety has to do with the American expatriate community. Restaurants also open and close with regularity, so check with the tourism office for local favorites.

The most expensive establishments are in upscale hotels, where a jacket and tie for men may be advised. But if you want a change of pace from these restaurants' standard Continental offerings, there are plenty of options. Bella Italia, Calle Hernández Macías #59, offers spinach ravioli, risotto and other Italian standbys, plus a good tiramisu. *For a list of AAA-RATED dining establishments in San Miguel, see the Lodgings & Restaurants section.*

La Fragua, Calle Cuna de Allende #3, is a popular gathering place housed in an old colonial building. Traditional Mexican music is performed evenings in the courtyard. Rock, reggae, country and blues bands play at Pancho and Lefty's, a local institution at Calle Mesones #99 near the main plaza. Mama Mia's, a bar and restaurant at Calle Umarán #8, has live salsa and jazz bands.

San Miguel celebrates a number of festivals throughout the year. Perhaps the biggest event is the Fiesta of the Archangel San Miguel (Fiesta de San Miguel Arcángel) on Sept. 29, which honors the town's patron saint. The festivities, which extend for several days, take place around the main plaza and along the adjoining streets and include parades, fireworks and regional dance performances.

Holy Week (Semana Santa) celebrations, which begin about 2 weeks before Easter Sunday, include a lavish procession on Good Friday and the burning of Judas effigies on Easter. The traditional and very popular Festival of San Antonio de Padua (Fiesta de San Antonio de Padua) is held on June 13; it features the Los Locos (Crazy Ones) parade, when people dress up in fanciful costumes and masks and parade through the streets to the accompaniment of live music.

The Chamber Music Festival (Festival de Música de Cámara) is held the first 2 weeks of August at the Bellas Artes Cultural Center. The International Jazz Festival takes place the last week in November.

San Miguel's traditional *posadas,* with music, canticles and plays dramatizing Mary and Joseph's search for an inn, ring in the holiday season beginning Dec. 16. For schedule information about these and other event happenings, stop by the State Tourism Office.

Guanajuato State Tourism Office: The San Miguel branch is on the southeast side of the main plaza, to the left of La Parroquía. Open Mon.-Fri. 10-5, Sat.-Sun. 10-2; phone (415) 152-6565 (English spoken).

What To See

ALLENDE HOUSE MUSEUM (Museo Casa de Allende) is on Calle Cuna de Allende #1, opposite the s.w. corner of the main plaza; street parking is limited. It was the birthplace of Ignacio Allende, one of the few early leaders of the War of Independence with actual military training. Together, he and Father Miguel Hidalgo organized a ragtag army and plotted strategies for overthrowing Spanish rule. Exhibits include weapons, documents, a collection of pre-Columbian pottery and ceremonial stone pipes. Information is in Spanish.

Allow 30 minutes minimum. Tues.-Sun. 10-4. Admission 32 pesos (about $3.10 U.S.); free to all Sun.

CHURCH OF THE CONCEPTION (Iglesia de la Concepción) is a few blks. w. of the main plaza at calles Canal and Hernández Macías. It was begun in the mid-17th century, although the domed roof—one of the largest in Mexico—was not completed until 1891. While the exterior is worn, inside is a breathtaking *retablo* more than 30 feet tall, decorated with gilded wood and numerous statues. Also notable are the huge oil paintings in both transepts portraying events in the lives of Jesus and Mary. Allow 30 minutes minimum. Open daily; Sun. Mass. at 10 a.m. Free; donations accepted.

CHURCH OF SAN FELIPE NERI (Oratorio de San Felipe Neri) is at calles Insurgentes and Loreto, 2 blks. n.e. of the main plaza. It was built by San Miguel's Indian population in the early 18th century. The original structure is graced with a lovely facade of pink stone and detailed carvings of saints. The southern exterior, added later, incorporates a baroque style, and the difference is striking. Pass through the low, narrow entrance vestibule to the church's interior, replete with ancient wood benches, rich gold leaf decoration and colorful ceramic statues. The small garden courtyard is a cool and peaceful spot to relax.

Allow 1 hour minimum. Daily 8-4 when Mass is not taking place. Free; donations accepted.

CHURCH OF SAN FRANCISCO is on Calle Juárez between calles San Francisco and Mesones, 2 blks. from the main plaza. Built in the late 18th century, it is thought to be the work of Eduardo Tresguerras, who contributed to the design of many churches in central Mexico. Construction was financed through donations from wealthy families and the proceeds from bullfights.

The intricate stone carvings gracing the exterior are a fine example of the ornate Churrigueresque style. The high-ceilinged interior contains statues, paintings and more carved stone. The church's shaded outdoor courtyard, complete with stone fountain, is a pleasant spot to rest your feet. Daily 7-2; walk-in visitors are not permitted during services that begin at 7 a.m., 10 and 1. Free; donations accepted.

GEM **PARISH CHURCH** (La Parroquía) is on Calle Correo, facing the s. side of the main plaza; street parking is limited. Soaring over the plaza, La Parroquía dominates the city. Originally built in the late 17th century in a plain Franciscan style, it was given an imposing facelift 2 centuries later by a local Indian artisan, Zeferino Gutiérrez. With no formal training, he added the present facade of pink-hued sandstone, allegedly using postcard pictures of French Gothic cathedrals as his inspiration.

Inside are murals, vaulted ceilings, side chapels and statues of saints, including St. Michael the Archangel (the church's official name is Parroquía de San Miguel Arcángel). The tomb of Anastasio Bustamante, president of Mexico from 1832-33 and again from 1839-41, is open to the public on Nov. 2. The original bell, cast in 1732, begins ringing early in the morning to summon parishioners. Allow 45 minutes minimum. Church staff do not speak English. Open daily; Sun. mass 6 a.m.-1 p.m. and at 6 and 8 p.m. Free; donations accepted.

PUBLIC LIBRARY (Biblioteca Pública) is 2 blks. n. of the main plaza at Calle Insurgentes #25. A repository for some 22,000 English volumes and an equal number of books in Spanish, it is the second largest bilingual library in Latin America. Scanning the variety of notices posted at the entrance (many in English) is a good way to find out what's going on around town.

A 2-hour house and garden tour of various San Miguel homes departs from the library on Sundays at 11:30 (doors open at 11), except three specified Sundays celebrating Mexican and religious holidays; phone (415) 152-0293. A fixed donation of about $15 U.S. ($20 for the annual Christmas tour) is charged, which benefits a scholarship fund for the education of San Miguel youth. Library open Mon.-Fri. 10-2 and 4-7, Sat. 10-2.

SANCTUARY OF ATOTONILCO (Santuario de Atotonilco) is about 15 km (9 mi.) n. on Mex. 51, then about 3 km (1.9 mi.) s.w. off the highway in the village of Atotonilco. "El Santuario" minibuses make this trip, departing from the bus stop on Calle Puente Umarán (opposite the city market). The village itself is uninteresting, and the church's exterior is plain and worn. Inside, however, is true beauty—walls and arched ceilings covered with writings, poems, paintings and frescoes, most in full color. The Chapel of the Rosario, dedicated to Our Lady of Guadalupe, has an entire wall adorned with gold-framed stations of the cross surrounding a life-size statue of the saint.

Hiring a guide in San Miguel to show you around the church and explain its historical significance makes for a more rewarding experience. Allow 30 minutes minimum. Open daily. Free; donations accepted.

TABOADA SPRINGS are about 8 km (5 mi.) n. of San Miguel on Mex. 51. The mineral springs feed a thermal spa, which provides a hot soaking and reputed skin benefits. There also are two swimming pools and a large lawn area. Snacks and drinks are available. The buses that go to Atotonilco also stop within walking distance of the spa, but a more reliable means of transportation is to hire a taxi. Wed.-Mon. 9-6. Admission about $5 (U.S.).

TEQUILA, JALISCO (C-1) pop. 24,400

This typical Mexican town is about 56 kilometers (35 miles) northwest of Guadalajara, just off Mex. 15. It sits amid extensive plantations devoted to the cultivation of the agave plant, from which the same-named beverage is extracted. Local distilleries (the major one is Sauza) have obtained a patent that prohibits other producers, even those within Mexico, from calling their drink tequila.

Cultivated agave plants resemble a field of spiny blue bayonets. Although the region's indigenous peoples had long drunk the fermented sap, the Spaniards introduced the distilling process. The tough, swordlike fronds are stripped from the plant, exposing its "heart," which can weigh more than 100 pounds. The hearts are "cooked" in large copper kettles, and the resulting liquid is transferred to huge tanks. Clear tequila is bottled at once; the golden variety ages in oak casks for up to 7 years.

The Guadalajara Chamber of Commerce organizes a Tequila day trip, the "Tequila Express," in conjunction with Mexican National Railways. The train leaves the Guadalajara rail station, located at Avenida Washington and Calzada Independencia Sur (near Agua Azul Park), Saturdays around 11 a.m. en route to the Herradura distilllery in the town of Amatitán.

The trip includes mariachi music and tequila tastings on board, a tour of the distillery and a buffet-style lunch. Tickets cost 770 pesos (about $75 U.S.); 450 pesos (ages 5-12). They can be purchased at the chamber, Av. Vallarta #4095 (at the corner of Avenida Niño Obrero); phone (33) 3880-9099, or through Ticketmaster in Guadalajara, phone (33) 3818-3800. Tickets should be purchased at least 10 days in advance.

Tequila lies at the northern base of extinct, 9,797-foot Volcán de Tequila, which has a stopper of hardened lava in its crater. Shards of obsidian, a volcanic glass, are visible in cuts flanking the highway near town. La Toma, a picnic spot with a waterfall and swimming pool, is about 4 kilometers (2.5 miles) northwest of Tequila off Mex. 15; the Santiago River Canyon, through which the river winds, is particularly scenic.

TLAQUEPAQUE, JALISCO (C-1)

pop. 467,900

A southeastern suburb of Guadalajara, Tlaquepaque (tla-keh-PAH-keh) is an important crafts center. Distinctive, hand-painted Tlaquepaque pottery is prized throughout Mexico. The fragile earthenware is decorated by hand. Many artisans still use the potter's wheel, and visitors can view the work in progress at some pottery shops. Tlaquepaque also is known for blown glass, textiles, jewelry, furniture, copperware and carved wood. The town is a tourist magnet and can get very crowded, but dedicated shoppers won't want to miss out on the huge selection of high-quality handicrafts.

The word "mariachi" seems to have originated in Tlaquepaque. French soldiers garrisoned in the city in the mid-19th century noted that the strolling troubadours performed primarily at weddings, or *mariages,* hence the possible derivation of the term. Mariachi bands perform in the gazebo within Jardín Hidalgo, the main plaza (bounded by the streets Independencia, Guillermo Prieto, Morelos and Francisco I. Madero).

Browsing is easiest along pedestrian-only Calle Independencia. Many of the shops and galleries are housed in refurbished old mansions with thick stone walls and iron gates. Most of the larger shops accept U.S. dollars or payment by credit card, and will arrange to have purchases packed and shipped as well. Many are closed or open limited hours on Sunday. Under the circular roof of El Parián, a building in the middle of town, are many sidewalk cafes, pleasant spots to relax over a leisurely lunch while the shops close for afternoon *siesta* (usually between 2 and 4).

La Casa Canela, Independencia #258, has showrooms arranged around a lush garden patio. This tasteful shop offers Mexican furniture, papier-mâché artworks and antiques. Tierra Tlaquepaque, Independencia #156, offers wood sculpture, pottery and decorative objects. Sergio Bustamente's fanciful sculptures, known around the world, are featured at the Galería Sergio Bustamente, Calle Independencia #236.

Linea Turquesa (TUR) buses depart regularly for Tlaquepaque and Tonalá *(see separate listing within this region)* from downtown Guadalajara; the trip takes about half an hour. They carry only seated passengers; cheaper city buses carry standing passengers as well and are likely to be crowded. Tell the driver you want to get off at the stop nearest El Parián.

If driving, take Avenida Revolución off Calzada Independencia Sur, heading southeast away from downtown Guadalajara. This road becomes Boulevard Tlaquepaque as it heads into town. At the traffic circle, bear right onto Avenida Niños Héroes, which runs into Calle Independencia after a block.

Tourist information office: Calle Guillermo Prieto #80, across from the main plaza. Open Mon.-Fri. 9-3, Sat. 9-1; phone (33) 3635-5756.

REGIONAL MUSEUM OF CERAMICS (Museo Regional de la Cerámica) is at Calle Independencia #237, at Calle Alfareros. Housed in an 18th-century building that was formerly a private home, it contains several rooms displaying mostly modern regional pottery pieces as well as some pre-Columbian artifacts. Exhibit information is in Spanish. Mon.-Sat. 10-6, Sun. 10-3; closed Easter and Dec. 25. Free.

TLAXCALA, TLAXCALA (D-4)

pop. 77,000, elev. 7,387′

A highland city in the middle of a wooded region, Tlaxcala (tlas-KAH-lah), the state capital, is about 75 miles east of Mexico City. The Tlaxcala Indians, a Chichimec group, settled in this region after defeating the Aztecs at Lake Texcoco. Alliance with the Otomí Indians provided the military protection that gave the Tlaxcaltecs the freedom to advance their civilization. Leaders of this small, powerful nation were the second, after the Totonacs, to align their forces with Hernando Cortés.

Apparently, joining the wrong side has been forgiven. This amiable colonial town, off the usual tourist track, is one of Mexico's most picturesque and makes for a pleasant side trip from Mexico City or Puebla. The downtown area is a delightful assemblage of structures in shades of sepia, deep red and orange. Plaza Constitución, the main square, is distinguished by neatly trimmed trees, a bandstand and a burbling fountain presented to the city by King Philip III.

Most points of interest in town surround the plaza. On its north side is the Government Palace (Palacio de Gobierno), with a brick exterior punctuated by ornately decorated windows and doorways. Inside are extravagantly colorful murals depicting agricultural life and the history of the Tlaxcaltec people, painted in the early 1960s by local artist Desiderio Hernández Xochitiotzin.

Also on the plaza is the baroque Palace of Justice (Palacio de Justicia), with neoclassic touches added in the 18th century. Inside the Parish Church of St. Joseph (Parroquía de San José), a peach-colored building, is the Chapel of St. Joseph (Capilla de San José), which has an arched ceiling with plaster ornamentation and impressive altarpieces.

Perhaps the finest examples of pre-Columbian artwork in all of Mexico are the mural paintings on view at the ruins of Cacaxtla *(see attaction listing)*. Discovered only in 1975, they remain vividly colorful more than a thousand years after their execution. Archeological evidence suggests the city that once stood here reached a peak of development between A.D. 650 and 900, and was abandoned by the beginning of the 11th century.

Cacaxtla (ca-CASHT-la) is thought to have been the capital of the Olmecan-Xicalancas, one of several groups who moved into this region of Mexico during a period of widespread unrest. Their domain encompassed the Valley of Puebla and the southwestern corner of present-day Tlaxcala state. The city was built atop a rise that facilitated contact with other Mesoamerican tribes but was also vulnerable to raids. As a result, the perimeter was walled and moated to ward off attack.

Cacaxtla's earliest structures were a group of adobe edifices that over time were demolished and filled in to form a large platform. This process was repeated several times until the foundation reached its present height. Most of the structures that visitors see today are vestiges dating from the latest period of construction. Ceremonial courtyards, tombs and enclosures were repeatedly reconfigured during the site's centuries of occupation.

About 45 kilometers (28 miles) southeast of Tlaxcala is La Malinche National Park, which has as its centerpiece La Malinche, an extinct volcano 14,632 feet high. At the entrance to the park is Malintzin, a vacation resort run by the Mexican Social Security Institute (IMSS) that offers lodgings, sports facilities and medical services in a wooded setting. Malintzin lies at a 9,840-foot elevation on the northern slopes of the mountain; from a marked exit on Mex. 136 between the towns of Apizaco and Huamantla (the sign reads "Centro Vacacional Malintzi"), a road ascends 14 kilometers (9 miles) to the retreat.

Tlaxcala State Tourism Office (Secretaría de Turismo): at the intersection of avenidas Benito Juárez and Lardizábal (behind the Government Palace). The staff speaks English. Open Mon.-Fri. 9-7, Sat.-Sun. 10-6; phone 01 (800) 509-6557 (toll-free long distance within Mexico).

CACAXTLA RUINS are about 17 km (12 mi.) southwest of Tlaxcala. To reach them by car from the center of town, take the road to Nativitas (follow signs) and then watch for the sign about 1.5 km (1

The Legend of Quetzalcóatl

One of Mexican history's most intriguing mysteries surrounds Quetzalcóatl, a man known for his advocacy of peace and who was believed to have opposed the practice of human sacrifice. Over time, fact and myth have become almost impenetrably tangled, although certain events are reasonably established. The son of Toltec chieftain Mixcóatl, Quetzalcóatl took the full name Ce Acatl Quetzalcóatl (literally, "One Reed Feathered Serpent"). It is believed that he founded the Toltec city of Tollan (Tula); the plumed serpent motif is noticeably evident at this archeological site. A power struggle ensued, and according to legend Quetzalcóatl's rivals conspired to get him drunk and thereby shame him into exile. (A more likely scenario is that the continued invasion of warlike tribes caused a decline in Toltec power.) The king led his followers, it is said, out of Tula and east toward the Gulf coast, where he either sailed off, promising to return in a future era, or burned himself alive and was reincarnated as the morning star. Meanwhile, Quetzalcóatl the myth continued to be invoked, a personage described as light-skinned, blue-eyed and bearded—features different from those of any person the Indians had ever before seen. When Hernando Cortés arrived in the Aztec capital of Tenochtitlán, the emperor Moctezuma believed him to be the returning god—a case of mistaken identity the *conquistador* craftily used to his advantage.

© SuperStock

mi.) w. of that town indicating the direction to Cacaxtla and the nearby village of San Miguel del Milagro. The hillside entrance to the site is about a 1-mi. walk from the parking lot. From the Mexico City-Puebla toll road (Mex. 150-D), take the San Martín Texmelucan exit and proceed e. toward Nativitas about 6 km (4 mi.), following signs.

Climb the stairs to reach the Gran Plaza, a broad platform protected by a huge metal roof. In addition to providing rain and sun protection, boardwalks beneath this overhead run right up to the various murals and stone carvings. The largest and most dramatic of the murals is the mythological Mural of the Battle, painted between A.D. 650 and 700. It depicts two groups of warriors—one outfitted in bird-like plumage and feather headdresses, the other cloaked in the skins of jaguars. The colors—rich blues, reds, yellows and browns—and the depth of detail are startling.

Note: The ticket window is about 100 feet inside the ruins complex, which is open per the schedule below, even if the gate is closed. Food is available. Picnicking is permitted. Allow 3 hours minimum. Daily 10-5. Admission (includes Xochitécatl site) 46 pesos (about $4.50 U.S.). The fee to use a video camera is about $4.

Xochitécatl is about 2 km (1.2 mi.) from Cacaxtla on the other side of a small valley. It was not uncovered until 1994. The large, open-air site consists of three pyramids and the base of a fourth. The Pirámide de la Espiral, named for its circular shape, is thought to have been used for astronomical explorations or built in dedication to Ehecatl, the god of wind. The Pyramid of the Flowers (Pirámide de las Flores), also constructed of rounded stones, has an exceptionally wide base. Allow 3 hours minimum. Tues.-Sun. 10-5. Admission included in Cacaxtla Ruins fee.

EX-CONVENT OF THE ASSUMPTION (Ex-Convento Francisco de la Asunción) is s.e. of the main plaza and off a smaller plaza, Plaza Xicoténcatl; a cobblestone path leads up a hill to the cathedral. It dates from the early 16th century. The original chapel with its stone baptismal font can be seen. In the Franciscan church are gilded altars, 17th-century religious paintings and an intricately carved and decorated wooden ceiling in *mudéjar* (Moorish) fashion. A lovely open-air chapel features Moorish-style pointed arches.

Tlaxcala Regional Museum (Museo Regional de Tlaxcala) occupies the church's cloister. Exhibits in the whitewashed rooms depict the state's history from prehistoric times to the present. Tues.-Sun. 10-5. Admission about $3.50 (U.S.).

MUSEUM OF POPULAR ARTS AND TRADITIONS (Museo de Artes Populares y Tradiciones) is at Blvd. Sanchez and Av. 1 de Mayo, 3 blks. w. of the main plaza. This small museum exhibits such items as clay water jugs and animal skins. Tues.-Sun. 10-6. Admission about 80c (U.S.), free (ages 0-5).

SANCTUARY OF THE VIRGIN OF OCOTLAN (Santuario de la Virgen de Ocotlán) sits atop a hill about a mile e. of town. It commemorates the supposed appearance of the Virgin of Guadalupe to the Indian Juan Diego Bernardino at this site in 1541. A masterpiece of baroque architecture in the indigenous Puebla-Tlaxcalan style, the shrine has a dazzlingly white, elaborately carved stucco facade and towers supported by twin tiled bases of red clay. The interior is a riot of gilded wood ornamentation. The octagonal Dressing Room (Camarín), a chamber where the Virgin's robes were said to be changed, explodes with carvings of angels and saints.

Visitors can hike to the shrine from the center of town, or take an inexpensive *colectivo* (minivan) designated "Ocotlán"; the driver stops at the front steps and will wait while you tour the sanctuary.

SANTA ANA CHIAUTEMPAN is less than 3 km (2 mi.) from Tlaxcala; it can be reached via the paved road that branches e. from town. At this weaving center, artists fashion hand-loomed *sarapes* and beautiful bolts of cloth. The village's main street is lined with shops selling rugs and *sarapes.* Native craftwork is supplemented by the tweeds and woolen bedspreads produced in the region's modern textile plants.

TIZATLAN RUINS are about 4 km (2.5 mi.) n.e. of town via Mex. 117 to the Tizatlán turn-off. A wool-weaving settlement established by the Tlaxcaltecs in the mid-14th century, Tizatlán developed into a major trade center. The ruins include a palace built on a small platform and small sanctuaries with murals painted on the altars. These paintings depict wars with the Aztecs, who failed in their attempt to conquer the Tlaxcaltec nation. Admission 29 pesos (about $2.80 U.S.).

TONALA, JALISCO (C-1) pop. 335,900

Tonalá (toh-nah-LAH), about 7 kilometers (4 miles) east of Tlaquepaque, was the original site of Guadalajara until 1531, when the Spaniards, repeatedly harassed by hostile Indians, abandoned the area. Many homes in this noted pottery-producing center double as family-run pottery workshops, or *talleres,* and factories here produce many of the wares displayed in Tlaquepaque.

The best days to visit are Thursdays and Sundays, when there is a large open-air *tianguis* (market). Savvy shoppers can obtain excellent buys on glassware, ceramics and papier-mâché crafts, all spread out on the sidewalks in a colorful, enticing hodgepodge.

Tonalá's factories and workshops are concentrated along north-south Avenida de Los Tonaltecas, the main thoroughfare, and in the vicinity of the main plaza, at calles Juárez and Hidalgo. An excellent selection of ceramics can be found at Casa de Artesanos, Av. Tonaltecas Sur #140. The workshop of Jorge Wilmot, who combined modern technology with traditional methods to produce distinctive ceramic designs, is at Calle Morelos #88. The shop/studio of Ken Edwards, Calle Morelos #184, features lovely stoneware items.

The public buses that travel to Tlaquepaque *(see separate listing within this region)* go to Tonalá. You also can get there by taxi; one-way fare should average about $4 (U.S.) from Tlaquepaque, $7 from Guadalajara. If driving, take the Zapotlanejo Highway (Carretera Zapotlanejo) east out of Tlaquepaque.

Tourist information office: in the Casa de Artesanos, Av. Tonaltecas Sur #140. Open Mon.-Fri. 9-3, Sat. 9-1; phone (33) 3683-1740. Inquire about the free walking tours on nonmarket days (Mon.-Wed. and Fri.-Sat.) that include visits to local workshops; English-speaking guides can be requested.

NATIONAL MUSEUM OF CERAMICS (Museo Nacional de la Cerámica) is at Av. Constitución #104, 2 blks. n. of City Hall. Housed in a two-story mansion, it displays a quality collection of pieces from different regions of Mexico dating from pre-Columbian to modern times, as well as displays showing the various methods of creating and firing pottery. Exhibit information is in Spanish. Tues.-Fri. 9-5, Mon. and Sat. 9-3. Free.

TONANTZINTLA, PUEBLA (D-4)

Tonantzintla (toh-nahn-TSEEN-tlah) *(see Acatepec listing)* is worth a visit just for its amazing church, which dominates the tiny village.

CHURCH OF SANTA MARIA TONANTZINTLA is a couple of miles s. of Cholula via Blvd. Miguel Alemán, across from the main plaza. While the yellow and white exterior looks fairly disciplined, the riotously ornate interior of this church is a definitive example of the Churrigueresque architectural style. The walls and ceiling are completely covered with gilded decorations, painted cherubs and saints garlanded in plumed headdresses. The colorful motifs include fruits, flowers, birds and Christmas themes, and the faces and dress of the human figures are strongly Indian in character.

Although it was under construction for nearly 300 years—from 1607 to 1897—the church exhibits such harmonious ornamental continuity that it all appears to date from the early 17th century. Both this church and the one in neighboring Acatepec are an easy side trip from Cholula, Puebla or Mexico City. Free.

TULA, HIDALGO (D-3)
pop. 27,300, elev. 6,776′

Tula (TOO-lah) was founded by Franciscans in the early 16th century; their fortresslike church, which also dates from that time, still stands. Typical of smaller Mexican towns, it has a busy market and a quiet central plaza bordered with taco stands. Evening band concerts occasionally take place in the square. Archeologists long believed that the remains of the Toltec capital of Tollan, which means "metropolis" or "large city," were somewhere in this region; however, the exact whereabouts remained a mystery until the Tula ruins were determined to be the site in 1938.

Tula's dominance as a major city in pre-Hispanic Mexico was relatively brief—from about A.D. 950

to 1174, when the Chichimecs, forerunners of the Aztecs, attacked, sacked and burned it. The sculptural figure known as Chac Mool, first found at this site, has become an international artistic symbol of Mesoamerican culture. But the reclining figure—holding a vessel that presumably received still-beating hearts torn from victims' chests during sacrificial ceremonies—underscores the violent nature of Toltec culture.

GEM **TULA RUINS** are about 32 km (20 mi.) off Mex. 57-D (the toll highway to Querétaro) n. through the center of Tula, then 4 km (2.5 mi.) n.w. to the site, following signs. Taxis departing from Tula's main plaza drop visitors off at the ruins. They constitute what is left of the capital and chief ceremonial center of the Toltecs. The focal point of the ruins is the five-tiered pyramid with a tongue-twisting name, the Temple of Tlahuizcalpantecuitli (Lord of the House of the Morning Star Venus). It dominates the north side of a plaza flanked by colonnaded buildings.

On top of the pyramid stand four colossal figures known as the Atlantes (one is a replica). They once supported the roof of a temple that stood atop the pyramid. Each Atlantean is swaddled in a loincloth, its chest protected by stylized butterfly breastplates and its back by shields in the shape of the sun. The figures wear headdresses decorated with feathers and carry a spear-thrower in the right hand, a supply of spears in the left. This pyramid as well as several others can be climbed, but their steepness makes descending more difficult than ascending.

The museum near the entrance houses professional displays of artifacts found at the site, including huge sandal-clad feet carved from solid rock. Vendors hawking artifact replicas line the path from the museum to the ruins. Allow 1 hour minimum. Site daily 10-5, museum Tues.-Sun. 10-5. Admission 39 pesos (about $3.70 U.S.). Guided tour fees are negotiable.

TZINTZUNTZAN, MICHOACAN (D-2)

elev. 6,724'

Once the capital of a powerful Tarascan kingdom, Tzintzuntzan (tseen-TSOON-tsahn) is now a small village on the shores of Lake Pátzcuaro. The curious name means "the place of the hummingbirds" in the Tarascan Indian language.

This area is one of the largest sources of inexpensive hand-painted pottery in Mexico. Local artisans decorate their pottery with simple, childlike drawings of swans, fish and native net fishermen. They also weave figurines and table and floor mats out of reeds. Another cottage industry is woodcarving; items range from small wall decorations, dishes and flowerpots to doors, windows and columns.

The restored 16th-century Franciscan Convent of Santa Ana can be visited. The church courtyard is noted for its olive trees, which were planted by Don Vasco de Quiroga despite a Spanish injunction against planting the trees in the New World. Restored *yácatas,* ruins of Tarascan pyramids, are visible from Mex. 120; a paved side road leads to the edge of the site.

Holy Week ceremonies culminate with a series of concerts and performances of classical Spanish plays, staged by residents in the atrium of the Santa Ana Convent. The village's *pastorelas,* medieval dramas based on the Nativity, begin Dec. 16.

Tzintzuntzan also participates in Day of the Dead ceremonies Nov. 1-2. During this all-night vigil, families visit the local cemetery to bring food, drink and other *ofrendas* (offerings) to their deceased relatives. This ritual, as well as those observed during Holy Week, attract many visitors to towns on the islands of and around Lake Pátzcuaro. If you'll be visiting during either of these times, book hotel reservations in Pátzcuaro or nearby Quiroga well in advance.

URUAPAN, MICHOACAN (D-2)

pop. 229,400, elev. 5,491'

Uruapan (oo-roo-AH-pahn) means "place where the flowers bloom," and the lush vegetation seen throughout the city is a testament to the warm climate (it is nearly 2,000 feet lower in elevation than nearby Pátzcuaro). Orange groves and plantations growing coffee, bananas and especially avocados flourish in the fertile farmland that surrounds the city. Uruapan also is known for hand-painted lacquerware carved from cedar and other native woods.

Michoacán State Tourism Office (Delegación de Turismo): Av. Ayala #16, 2 blocks northwest of the main plaza. Open Mon.-Sat. 9-2 and 4-7; phone (452) 524-7199. Casa de Turista, located at Av. Emilio Carranza #20, promotes the folk art that is made throughout this region and can guide travelers to the communities where various handicrafts are produced. The center also has information about local and regional attractions. It is open daily 9-7:30; phone (452) 524-0667.

EDUARDO RUIZ PARK (Parque Eduardo Ruiz) has an entrance at the end of east-west Av. Independencia (off Calzada La Quinta), about 8 blks. w. of the main plaza. This shady subtropical park has lush vegetation along the banks of the Río Cupatitzio and fountains with dancing waters propelled by gravity alone; no pumps are used. Numerous footpaths wind along the riverbank.

The river rises at Devil's Knee (Rodilla del Diablo) spring, named—according to legend—for the spot where Lucifer left a kneeling imprint. Daily 8-6. Admission about $1 (U.S.), 50c (children).

PARICUTIN is n. on Mex. 37 for about 16 km (10 mi.) to the junction with a paved road branching w. 21 km (13 mi.) to the town of Angahuan. Paracutin (pah-ree-koo-TEEN), a now-dormant volcano, sprang from a cornfield in 1943. The blunt-topped cone rises some 1,700 feet above the surrounding valley.

During its brief period of activity, Paricutín destroyed two villages (part of a church protruding from the jumble of boulders is the only remaining evidence of their existence) and forced more than 4,000 people to abandon their homes. The volcanic cone and the weirdly blackened surrounding lava fields can be reached on horseback or by hiking on foot. Guided trips can be arranged in Angahuan, or check with the State Tourism Office in Uruapan.

REGIONAL MUSEUM OF POPULAR ART (Museo de Arte Popular) is at the corner of Calle Vasco de Quiroga, facing the n. side of Plaza Morelos. It is housed within La Huatapera, a colonnaded building that is a fine example of 16th-century architecture; built under the direction of Spanish bishop Vasco de Quiroga, it was originally a hospital. The museum exhibits artwork by the Purepecha, Mazahua, Nahua and Otomi Indians—all indigenous peoples of Michoacán—and also has two rooms featuring rotating displays. Tues.-Sun. 9:30-1:30 and 3:30-6; closed Jan. 1, May 1 and Dec. 25. Free.

TZARARACUA WATERFALL (Cascada de Tzaráracua) is just off Mex. 37 about 10 km (6 mi.) s. of town. Here the Río Cupatitzio rushes through a natural stone amphitheater, then drops about 90 feet into a pool within a cool, leafy setting. There is a fairly steep half-mile descent from the parking area down to the falls, but the trail is well marked, and handrails are provided. Buses to Tzaráracua (tsah-RAH-rah-kwah) depart from Uruapan's main plaza on weekends and drop passengers off at the parking lot; a cab ride to the falls is about $4 (U.S.).

ZACATECAS, ZACATECAS (B-1)

pop. 115,700, elev. 8,115′

Zacatecas (sah-kah-TEH-kahs), capital of the state of the same name, is built in a ravine on the slopes of Cerro de la Bufa, a rock-crowned hill 8,748 feet high. Long a mining center, the settlement was taken by the Spaniards in 1548. In 1588, it was named "The Very Noble and Loyal City of Our Lady of the Zacatecas" because of the vast quantities of silver shipped from the region to Spain. Although now surrounded by agricultural and cattle-raising lands, Zacatecas continues to be a center for silver mining. The largest mine in the region is 200-year-old El Bote, which is still in operation.

Elaborate old mansions, an aqueduct and stone steps connecting steeply inclined flagstone streets lend Zacatecas a charmingly medieval atmosphere; the historic city center was designated a World Heritage Site by UNESCO in 1993. The beautiful baroque buildings also attest to the great wealth that was generated by the mines. A magnificent cathedral *(see attraction listing)* and several excellent museums also are reasons to visit.

A wide, divided avenue 5 kilometers (3 miles) long leads east from downtown Zacatecas to the suburb of Guadalupe, the site of an early 18th-century convent. It once served as a base for Franciscan missions established to the north of Mexico in what is now the southwestern United States. The town is noted for colonial architecture as well as for marquetry (inlaid woodwork) and wool *sarapes* with portraits woven into their designs.

Trancoso, 22 kilometers (14 miles) east off Mex. 45/49, has one of the most elegant and best preserved old haciendas in Mexico. In Bracho, on the north side of the loop road encircling the city, La Morisma is celebrated the last week in August. During this fiesta, hundreds of local boys and men dressed in Moorish-style costumes act out a battle against a European army for several consecutive days.

Zacatecas State Tourism Office (Consejo Estatal de Turismo): downtown at Av. Hidalgo #403 (second floor); phone (492) 922-6751 or 01 (800) 712-4078 (toll-free long distance within Mexico).

What To See in and Around Town

CATHEDRAL is on the s. side of Plaza de Armas. Begun in 1612 and completed in 1752, it is one of the ultimate expressions of the Mexican baroque style. The extravagant exterior carvings of pink sandstone (called *cantera* in Spanish) are notable. This is still an active church, and Mass is held daily. Open for services (closes after dark); there is no tour schedule, but visitors can enter the building and look around. Free.

CERRO DE LA BUFA overlooks the city from the n.e. There are panoramic views from the summit, which can be reached by the Zacatecas Cable Car *(see attraction listing).*

Battle of Zacatecas Museum (Museo Toma de Zacatecas) is next to the chapel. It chronicles the 1914 battle led by Pancho Villa to gain control of the city, one of the decisive conflicts of the Revolution of 1910. Information is presented in Spanish. Daily 10-5. Admission about $2 (U.S.).

Patrocinio Chapel (La Capilla de la Virgen del Patrocinio) is at the summit. Erected in 1728, it is named for the patron saint of miners.

EL EDEN MINE (Mina el Edén) can be reached by car from Mex. 54; when entering the city, follow

DID YOU KNOW ?

With an estimated population of some 107,500,000, Mexico is the most populous Spanish-speaking country in the world.

signs to downtown (Centro), then signs to "Mina el Edén." The mine is just n. on Calle Dovali Jamie from the intersection with Av. Torreón; a nearby landmark is the IMSS Social Security Hospital (Seguro Social Hospital). First operated in the 16th century, El Edén produced great quantities of silver, copper and zinc during its most active period.

A small powered train takes visitors through several of the mine's tunnels before stopping at a small museum with a display of rocks and minerals from around the world. Visitors then proceed on foot while a tour guide provides information about mining processes, the mine's history and the living conditions of the original Indian miners.

Most tours are in Spanish; visitors may want to call ahead to set up a tour with an English-speaking guide. Allow 2 hours minimum. Tours daily 10-6 (noon-6 on Jan. 1 and Dec. 25). Admission 60 pesos (about $5.80 U.S.); 30 pesos (ages 4-10 and 60+). Phone (492) 922-3002.

FRANCISCO GOITIA MUSEUM (Museo Francisco Goitia) is s. of the city center at Av. Estrada #102, across from Enrique Estrada Park. Housed in the former Governor's Mansion, it exhibits works by Goitia (1882-1960) that include a dramatic self-portrait, as well as sculpture and paintings by other 20th-century Zacatecano artists. Tues.-Sun. 10-5. Admission about $2.50 (U.S.).

LA QUEMADA RUINS lie on the hillside of a valley, about 56 km (35 mi.) s.w. of Zacatecas off Mex. 54. Also known as Chicomostoc Ruins, this archeological site bears traces of narrow streets and the foundations of homes and temples of the Náhuatlac Indians, who settled the valley around 1170. Thought to be destroyed by fire, the city was already a ruin when the Spaniards discovered it in 1535.

Among the remaining structures are a restored pyramid, a palace with 11 standing columns, and the substantial surrounding walls. Since local transportation is unreliable, the ruins are much easier to reach if you have your own vehicle. From the highway it's an uphill, 30-minute walk to the site entrance. Visitors should wear comfortable hiking shoes and bring water. Daily 10-5. Admission about $3 (U.S.).

OUR LADY OF GUADALUPE CONVENT (Convento de Nuestra Señora de Guadalupe) is about 7 km (4 mi.) s.e. of Zacatecas via Mex. 45/49, in the town of Guadalupe. Local *Ruta* 13 buses depart regularly for Guadalupe from the corner of Calle Salazar and Blvd. López Mateos, near the old bus terminal in downtown Zacatecas.

This enormous convent and baroque church dates from 1707 and once housed Franciscan monks. Rows of corridors lined with paintings and portraits pass cells where the monks spent their time when not ministering to the Indians. Especially noteworthy is the church's Chapel (Capilla de Nápoles), which has a domed roof covered with beautiful gold leaf and a parquet floor elaborately inlaid with zodiac signs and scriptures. It is not always open, so a tip for the guide who grants entrance is appreciated.

Daily 10-4:30. Admission (includes Museum of Viceregal Art) about $3 (U.S.).

Museum of Viceregal Art (Museo de Arte Virreinal) is within the convent. It contains paintings of the Virgin of Guadalupe and other works of 18th-century colonial religious art by such artists as Miguel Cabrera, Juan Correa and Cristóbal de Villalpando. Guided tours are available. Exhibit information is in Spanish. Open same hours as the convent.

PEDRO CORONEL MUSEUM is on Plaza Santo Domingo, about 2 blks. w. of Plaza de Armas. It houses the outstanding private collection of noted Zacatecan artist and sculptor Pedro Coronel, which includes works by Pablo Picasso, Salvador Dalí, Joan Miró and Marc Chagall.

Other displays include Coronel's tomb and an exhibit of his own sculpture and paintings; pre-Columbian pieces and colonial-era works by Zacatecano artists; Chinese, Indian, Greek and Egyptian art; and a fine collection of Mesoamerican and African masks. Fri.-Wed. 10-5. Admission about $2.50 (U.S.). Phone (492) 922-8021.

GEM **RAFAEL CORONEL MUSEUM** (Museo Rafael Coronel) is on Calle Chevano, a short distance n. of the cathedral; from the cathedral front, walk up Av. Hidalgo 2 blks. to Calle Abasolo, proceed left at the fork for 2 short blks. to Calle Chevano, then take the right fork to the museum. It is housed in the Convento de San Francisco, a gracious 18th-century edifice abandoned as a convent in 1857, which has an exterior colored in tones of mellowed pink. Lush flowering plants fill the gardens in the interior courtyard.

On display in large, high-ceilinged galleries is an amazing collection of several thousand masks from all over Mexico, donated by Rafael Coronel, younger brother of Pedro. They depict saints as well as grotesque-looking, devilish figures, *conquistadores* and bizarrely imaginative animals. Entirely handmade and decorated with everything from human hair and glitter to steel wool and bones, the masks are a remarkable testament to Mexican artistic ingenuity. There also are impressive dioramas of puppets engaged in such activities as warfare, a bullfight and a wedding, all created by a family of puppet makers from Huamantla, Tlaxcala.

Food is available. Tues.-Sun. 10-5. Admission 20 pesos (about $1.95 U.S.). Phone (492) 922-8116.

ZACATECAS CABLE CAR (Teleférico), next to the Del Bosque Motel, can be reached from Mex. 54, following signs. Built by Swiss engineers, it connects the hills Cerro de la Bufa and Cerro Grillo, spanning the northern section of the city. The journey takes 8 minutes, covers a distance of 2,100 feet and overlooks Zacatecas from varying heights. The two enclosed cars are capable of holding 15 passengers at a time. Parking is available at either end of the run. Trips every 15 minutes, weather permitting, daily 10-6. One-way fare about $2.50 (U.S.), round trip $4.50.

ZAPOPAN, JALISCO (C-1) pop. 932,700

About 7 kilometers (4 miles) northwest of downtown Guadalajara via Avenida Avila Camacho, the sprawling "suburb" of Zapopan (sah-POH-pahn) is the home of the Virgin of Zapopan—often referred to as La Zapopanita ("Little Zapopaner") since her image, made of corn paste, stands a mere 10 inches tall.

Legend alleges that Chimalhuacano Indians, awed by a Franciscan friar's display of La Zapopanita during the heat of battle against the Spanish, surrendered and were converted to Christianity. In 1734, at the height of an epidemic, she was taken to the towns and villages around Guadalajara. Wherever the virgin appeared, sickness reputedly ceased, and many miracles were subsequently attributed to her.

Each summer the statue of the virgin is encased in a protective glass shell and embarks on a 4-month pilgrimage to the more than 100 parish churches throughout the state. Transported by special car, the virgin begins a final journey at dawn on Oct. 12 from Guadalajara's cathedral back to her home church, the massive 17th-century Basilica of the Virgin of Zapopan (Basilica de la Virgen de Zapopan), on the west side of Zapopan's central plaza.

Piety and merrymaking are both in evidence on this occasion. In addition to solemn marchers holding banners, there are marching bands, cowboys on horseback, police cars with screaming sirens, dancers in native costume and assorted revelers dressed up as if for a giant Halloween party.

Many pilgrims show their devotion by crawling the last kilometer or two on their knees, underscoring the importance of this annual event for the nation's devout Catholics. The homecoming procession from the cathedral to the basilica—a 5-mile route—often involves more than 1 million participants and spectators and is a highlight of Guadalajara's *Fiestas de Octubre* celebration *(see page 340)*.

The basilica features an ornate Plateresque exterior and a tiled *mudéjar* dome. In the church courtyard a statue commemorates Pope John Paul II, who gave a mass at the plaza during his 1979 visit. Within the Franciscan monastery next door is the small Huichol Museum (Museo Huichol), which has displays of beadwork and other handicrafts (all for sale) made by the Huichol Indians of northern Jalisco, Nayarit and Zacatecas.

Guadalajara city buses traveling northbound on Avenida 16 de Septiembre/Alcalde go to the basilica; the trip takes about half an hour.

Monte Alban Ruins, Oaxaca / © Miguel Ángel Muñoz / age fotostock

Southern Mexico

This is Mexico's poorest region economically but among its richest in cultural traditions. The states of Oaxaca and Chiapas are home to the country's largest concentration of Indian communities. Most of the people are descended from the Zapotec, Mixtec and Mayan civilizations that flourished hundreds of years before the Spanish conquest of Mexico. The Zapotecs settled in the Valley of Oaxaca and created the ceremonial center of Monte Albán, which eluded discovery by Spanish *conquistadores.* Much more recently Chiapas, Mexico's southernmost state, made international headlines with the 1994 emergence of the Zapatista National Liberation Army, a guerrilla movement that demanded greater economic opportunities for the region's Indians, or *indígenas.*

The Maya left behind the ruins of Palenque, Bonampak, Yaxchilan and Tonina, also in Chiapas. Palenque's crumbling but intricately decorated structures seem to be inhabited by ghosts of the distant past. The primordial feeling is heightened by the occasional chattering of monkeys or the shriek of an exotic bird. Similarities between the architecture at Palenque and that of palaces in southeast Asia hint at a possible link between Mexico and the Orient, although the mysteries of Mayan civilization related to this particular puzzle will probably lay forever buried beneath the rubble.

Oaxaca, meanwhile, just might be the quintessential Mexican destination. It offers excellent museums, beautiful churches, a delightfully vibrant central plaza, Indian markets overflowing with native handicrafts, and a distinctive regional cuisine incorporating everything from subtly spiced *mole* sauces to *panuchos,* pizzas made of cornmeal and topped with pork and onions.

Oaxaca state's Sierra Norte, characterized by a cool, damp climate, forested mountains and a wealth of native plant and animal species, is distinctly different from the dry central valleys and the flat, steamy Isthmus of Tehuantepec to the south. A network of Zapotec hamlets northeast of Oaxaca city called the Commonwealth of Villages (Pueblos Mancomunados) have worked together to develop this impoverished but beautiful region as an ecotourism center. Villagers have created more than 100 miles of signposted trails, some designated for hikers and others for mountain biking. You can explore on your own or take a trip led by a trained local guide.

For a different experience, head to Veracruz. It has the languid ambience of a tropical port (Mexico's oldest and largest) as well as the energy provided by lively music, folk dances and a jolt of *café con leche*—strong black coffee laced with hot milk—that can be enjoyed at one of the city's many sidewalk cafes.

The city also has played an important role in Mexican history, from the arrival of Hernando Cortés through the Mexican Revolution of 1910. In addition to coffee, Veracruz is noted for cigars, distinctive cuisine and the *quexquémetl*, a capelike garment decorated with multicolored embroidery. Totonac Indians produce some of the finest traditional designs.

Jalapa isn't on most Mexican tourist itineraries, but this little-visited city is an altogether charming blend of old and new. Built on the slopes of Macuiltépetl, a large, tiered hill, Jalapa was a Spanish stronghold and an important stagecoach stop between Veracruz and Mexico City. The colonists who followed in the wake of Hernando Cortés almost certainly found the higher altitude and cooler climate a welcome respite from steamy Veracruz, as well as a more suitable environment for the cultivation of coffee and fruit trees.

Much of Veracruz state is green, and the natural lushness makes it an ideal choice for ecotourism. More than 40 rivers flow from the Sierra mountains through the jungle to the Caribbean Sea, etching the hillsides with cascading waterfalls. Tour companies offer whitewater rafting trips down such rivers as the Antigua and the Filobobos, with fearsomely named rapids like La Brujita (The Little Witch) and Las Puertas del Infierno (The Doors to Hell) providing the thrills.

True adventurers will be enchanted by the Los Tuxtlas Biosphere Reserve. Created in 1998 in the southern part of the state, Los Tuxtlas preserves a remnant of tropical rain forest from the devastating effects of deforestation due to human activity. The reserve has a biodiversity rivaled by few other areas in Mexico: nearly 2,700 species of plants, more than 100 species of fish and some 570 species of migratory and native birds. In addition to bird watching, available tours include kayaking into the mangroves of Lake Sontecomapan and visits to Hidden Lagoon (Laguna Escondida) and Monkey Island (La Isla de los Monos).

Taxco, a delightfully picturesque old silver-mining town in the state of Guerrero, is a designated national historic monument and a popular tourist stop between Mexico City and Acapulco. Sprawled over a rugged hillside in the heart of the Sierra Madre, Taxco has changed little in appearance since the 18th century. The Mexican government prohibits the building of modern structures; older ones proliferate, in various stages of preservation, along with whitewashed houses, red-tiled roofs and cobblestoned streets.

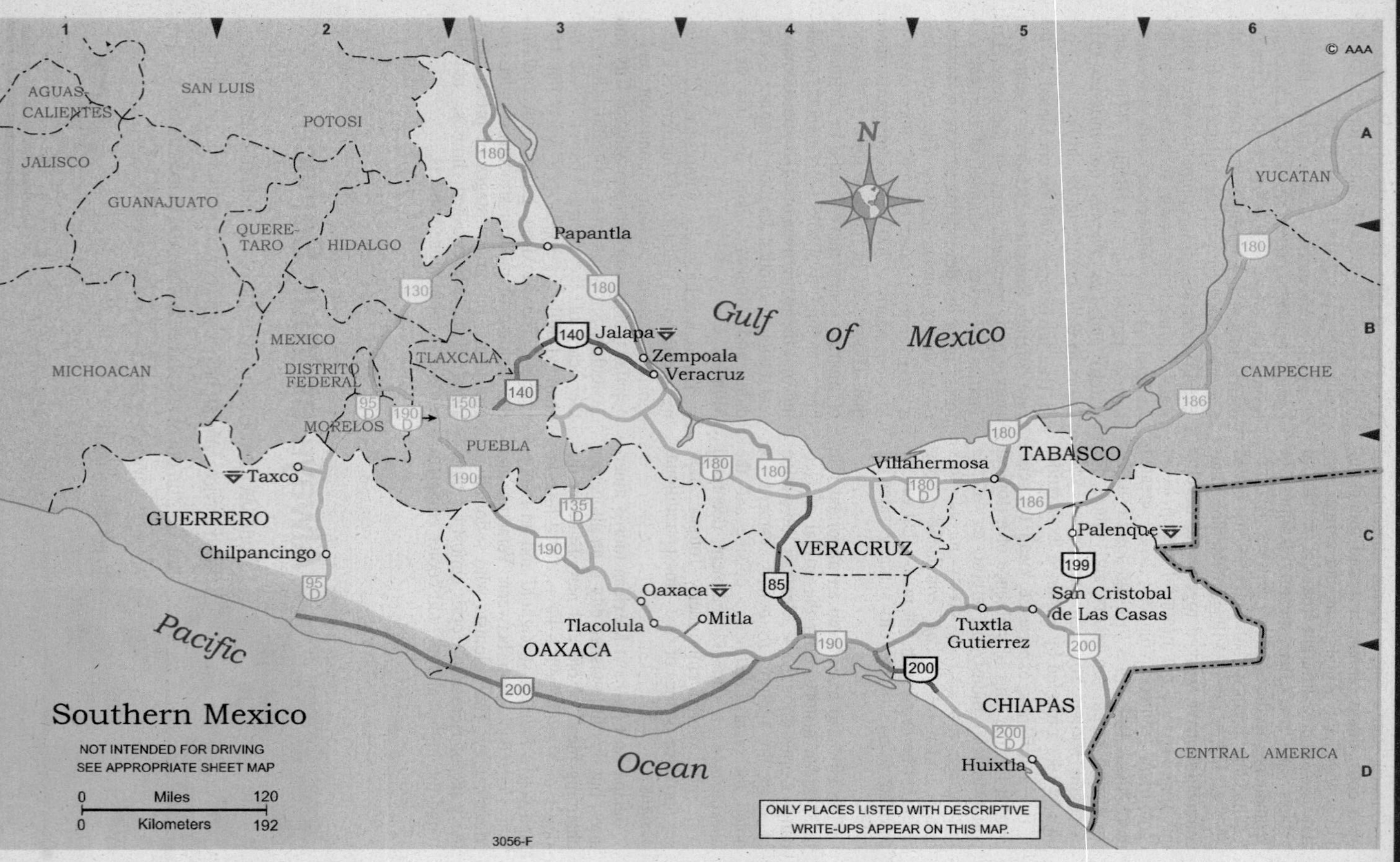

Southern Mexico
NOT INTENDED FOR DRIVING
SEE APPROPRIATE SHEET MAP
Miles 0 120
Kilometers 0 192
ONLY PLACES LISTED WITH DESCRIPTIVE WRITE-UPS APPEAR ON THIS MAP.
© AAA
3056-F
Gulf of Mexico
Pacific Ocean
N
AGUASCALIENTES
SAN LUIS POTOSI
JALISCO
GUANAJUATO
QUERETARO
HIDALGO
MEXICO
MICHOACAN
DISTRITO FEDERAL
TLAXCALA
MORELOS
PUEBLA
GUERRERO
OAXACA
VERACRUZ
TABASCO
CHIAPAS
YUCATAN
CAMPECHE
CENTRAL AMERICA
Papantla
Jalapa
Zempoala
Veracruz
Taxco
Chilpancingo
Oaxaca
Tlacolula
Mitla
Villahermosa
Palenque
San Cristobal de Las Casas
Tuxtla Gutierrez
Huixtla

Points of Interest

CHILPANCINGO, GUERRERO (C-1)

pop. 149,200, elev. 4,460′

Capital of the state of Guerrero and home to the University of Guerrero, Chilpancingo (cheel-pahn-SEEN-goh) is a bustling college town. It also has historical credentials—the first Congress of Mexico met here in 1813.

Points of interest include the House of the First Revolutionary Congress (Casa del Primer Congreso Revolucionario), La Asunción Church, the city's ancient cemetery and the State Capitol (Palacio de Gobierno), which has some fine murals. The Indian village of Acatlán, 55 kilometers (34 miles) northeast of Chilpancingo via a partially paved road, is noted for hand-loomed and embroidered shawls.

In Chilapa, 54 kilometers (33 miles) east of Chilpancingo, the Day of St. Gertrude on Nov. 16 features whimsically named native dances, including The Seven Vices, The Eight Lunatics, The Old Woman and The Mule. In Chichihualco, 33 kilometers (20 miles) northwest of Chilpancingo, the Fiesta of St. James Sept. 28-29 includes a parade, regional foods and such native dances as Fishermen and Devils.

JUXTLAHUACA CAVES are reached via a paved road that leaves Mex. 95 at Petaquillas, about 11 km (7 mi.) south of Chilpancingo. Rivaling Cacahuamilpa Caves National Park *(see Taxco listing)* in size and beauty, these caves are little known outside the region. They contain walls decorated with 3,000-year-old Olmec paintings and unusual geological formations, including translucent salt "veils" and flowerlike crystal formations.

Subterranean ponds and streams support a variety of sightless creatures. A lantern-lit guided tour takes about 5 hours. Explorers should wear comfortable, sturdy walking shoes and bring a light snack; rainwear is advised against spray from subterranean waterfalls. Admission is charged.

JALAPA, VERACRUZ (B-3)

pop. 387,900, elev. 4,681′

Capital of the state of Veracruz and home to nearly 400,000 people, Jalapa (hah-LAH-pah, but spelled Xalapa in Mexico) doesn't seem like a big city. The natural setting is breathtaking—the black volcanic peaks of the Sierra Madre Oriental rise in the distance, towered over by Pico de Orizaba, Mexico's tallest mountain. Practically every corner offers a vista of the mountainous terrain that surrounds the city.

Jalapa's colonial legacy is evident in the structures flanking its older, cobblestone avenues; their red-tiled roofs, wrought-iron balconies, carved wooden doors and window grilles are unmistakably Spanish. Shops and homes are painted in vibrant shades of white, green and deep red. The streets are steep and curving, and also change names and directions frequently; a good city map is an effective navigational aid. Taxis and local buses provide inexpensive transportation to points within the city center.

Begin a morning stroll of downtown Jalapa at the Café la Parroquía, on Calle Zaragoza near the south side of the Government Palace (Palacio de Gobierno). A local gathering place, it has an old-fashioned '50s look and attracts everyone from university professors to families. As in Veracruz, a favorite morning beverage is a *lechero,* a tall glass of strong espresso to which hot milk is added. Tapping your glass with a spoon signals the waiter, who pours the milk from a steaming kettle.

At the corner of calles Enríquez and Revolución, just north of the Government Palace, stands the city's 18th-century Cathedral. Its plain white facade is accented by Moorish-style arches and a bell tower clock transported from London. The religious paintings inside are worth a look, as is the sloping floor.

The *chipichipi,* a light but persistent winter rain, and evening mists in summer contribute to Jalapa's reputation as the "flower garden of Mexico." The warmth and moisture create a natural greenhouse effect, and the city is filled with roses, bougainvillea and pine trees. Tree-shaded Juárez Park (Parque Juárez), across Calle Enríquez from the City Hall (Palacio Municipal), is representative of the prevailing lushness. White wrought-iron benches are scattered among pruned hedges and well-tended flower beds at this park, which also is the city's central plaza.

Home to the University of Veracruz, Jalapa also has a cultural side. The Agora Arts Center, just off Juárez Park, is a hangout for students and artists and has extensive events listings. The State Theater (Teatro del Estado) on Ignacio de la Llave hosts performances by the ballet and the symphony. All Jalapa celebrates on Sept. 30, the Day of St. Jerome, when streets are bedecked with flowers and candlelight processions are held.

A few blocks south of Juárez Park on the grounds of an attractively landscaped lakeside park is the state-run Casa de Artesanías, where there are handicrafts for sale by Veracruzan artists, as well as packaged coffee beans. The indoor market on Calle Altamirano, about 2 blocks north of Juárez Park, is a typically colorful hodgepodge displaying assorted trinkets, heaps of dried chilies and beans, and containers of bubbling *mole* sauces.

Street vendors frequent Callejón Diamante, a steep little alley off Calle Enríquez (a block or so east of Juárez Park), along which are several casual restaurants specializing in regional fare. Locals and

Travel Advisory

It is recommended that visitors check on current conditions before traveling to the states of Chiapas, Guerrero (outside the established tourist destinations of Acapulco, Ixtapa/Zihuatanejo and Taxco) and Oaxaca. Although not directed specifically at tourists, sporadic outbursts of politically motivated violence continue in the more remote sections of Chiapas and Oaxaca. The most potentially dangerous areas in Guerrero are the mountainous, remote interior and undeveloped sections of the Pacific coast. For additional information, consult a Mexico Tourism Board Office *(see page 57)*, a Mexican consulate *(see page 65)* or the U.S. State Department's Bureau of Consular Affairs Web site *(see page 56)*.

visitors alike head to La Sopa, which serves a filling *comida corrida* (fixed-price lunch).

Macuiltépetl Park (Parque Macuiltépetl), north of downtown, is an ecological preserve that showcases indigenous flora and fauna. The winding paths are a bracing climb up one of Jalapa's hillsides, but the views are outstanding.

Practicalities

The nearest international airport is in Veracruz. From Veracruz, Jalapa is about a 2-hour drive north on Mex. 180 to the town of Cardel, then east on Mex. 140 past numerous coffee plantations.

The central bus station (CAXA) is on Avenida 20 de Noviembre, about a mile east of the downtown area. From this clean, modern building you can make first-class bus connections and long-distance phone calls, arrange for a taxi into town (an otherwise hilly walk) and even grab a bite to eat. It also has a tourist information booth that is open daily. First-class bus service is offered by Autobuses del Oriente (ADO).

Nearby Destinations

Formal plantings, an arboretum and a palm collection make up Clavijero Botanical Gardens, about 3 kilometers (1.5 miles) south of downtown via the road to Coatepec. En route are views of coffee and banana plantations. Coatepec, a colonial town about 8 kilometers (5 miles) south of Jalapa, is known for the raising of ornamental plants, chiefly orchids. The main plaza is surrounded by small shops selling coffee beans and *heladerías* (ice cream parlors) dishing up exotic flavors.

About 11 kilometers (7 miles) past Coatepec is Xico (HEE-coh), a village where sacks of coffee beans are one of the most common sights. Nearby Texolo Waterfall (Cascada de Texolo) has been put to good scenic use in such films as "Romancing the Stone" and parts of the Harrison Ford espionage adventure "A Clear and Present Danger." The falls cascade into a gorge surrounded by lush greenery. A restaurant is at the site, and pathways allow visitors to observe the falls from different vantage points. Local buses to Coatepec and Xico depart from Jalapa's central bus station.

Veracruz State Tourism Office (Subsecretaría de Turismo): Blvd. Cristóbal Colón #5 in the Torre Animas building, about 3 kilometers (1.9 miles) east of downtown; phone 01 (800) 712-6666 (toll-free long distance within Mexico).

What To See

GOVERNMENT PALACE (Palacio de Gobierno) is on the e. side of Plaza Juárez. Ornate fountains face this long, pink, colonial-style building, which serves as the state capitol. Inside are murals by José Chávez Morado, including "Liberation," which depicts humanity's struggle for freedom.

HACIENDA EL LENCERO is about 9 km (5.5 mi.) e. of Jalapa off the Xalapa-Veracruz toll road (Mex.

140), then follow signs 1.5 km (1 mi.) to the hacienda. A guided tour of this country estate, a former inn for stagecoaches traveling between Veracruz and Mexico City and later a sugarcane plantation, offers insight into 19th-century hacienda life, a relatively luxurious existence reserved for wealthy plantation owners. The various rooms are furnished with canopied beds, large armoires, hand-carved wood and stone angels, Mexican rugs and ornate light fixtures.

Food is available. Allow 1 hour minimum. Tues.-Sun. 10-5. Admission 20 pesos (about $1.95 U.S.). Phone (228) 820-0270.

GEM **MUSEUM OF ANTHROPOLOGY** (Museo de Antropología de Xalapa) is n.w. of downtown on Av. Xalapa, between avs. Acueducto and 10 de Mayo. It houses a superb collection of artifacts encompassing most of Mexico's gulf coast Indian groups, with an emphasis on the Olmec, Totonac and Huastec cultures. Contrasting vividly with the antiquity of the exhibits is the ultramodern museum building, which incorporates a series of tropically landscaped outdoor patios.

A massive Olmec head is stationed at the museum entrance; several other heads, the largest almost 9 feet tall, are on display in outdoor gardens and indoor galleries. Additional highlights include dramatically lifelike ceramic statues of women wearing belts in the form of writhing serpents; a carved figure in green stone holding an infant with jaguar-like facial features that are characteristically Olmec; and beautifully crafted jade and bone jewelry. The carefully organized displays are augmented by maps that note excavation sites and show where the civilizations flourished.

Information about the exhibits is presented in Spanish only, but bilingual guides are available for tours. Allow 2 hours minimum. Tues.-Sun. 9-5. Admission about $3.50 (U.S.); there is an extra fee for the use of a video camera. Phone (228) 815-0920.

MITLA, OAXACA (C-4)

The town of Mitla (MEE-tlah) is about 42 kilometers (26 miles) southeast of Oaxaca and about 1.9 kilometers (3 miles) off Mex. 190. The original city, a religious and ceremonial center, was inhabited by the Zapotecs as early as 800 B.C.; by the 11th or 12th century, the Mixtecs had expelled the Zapotecs from both Mitla and Monte Albán and began to establish their own culture. Mitla prospered up until the time of the Spanish conquest. The name means "place of rest" and refers to the catacombs beneath the Mitla ruins.

Weaving is the principal commercial activity today; woven goods can be purchased almost everywhere. Around Mitla and south along Mex. 190 are outlet stores selling mezcal, a locally produced liquor that packs a wallop. Derived from a variety of the maguey plant, mezcal is a specialty of the state of Oaxaca. The bottle often includes a pickled *gusano* (worm). If imbibed at all, mezcal is best diluted with fruit juice.

MITLA RUINS are about 1 km (.6 mi.) n. of the main plaza via Av. Morelos. This site was begun by the Zapotecs but taken over by the Mixtecs, and the architectural style of elaborate cut stonework reflects the latter group. Unlike many Mayan ruins, Mitla was never buried under encroaching jungle, and the structures are well preserved.

Rectangular patios are surrounded by buildings or long, narrow rooms. Underground chambers and cruciform tombs honeycomb the soil beneath these structures. The Hall of Columns, the most important group, is supported by six enormous pillars, each a single stone, and more than 100,000 pieces of cut stones form the intricate mosaic decorating its walls. The most common design is a zigzag pattern. What sets Mitla apart from other North American archeological sites is the lack of human, animal or mythological figures—abstract representations predominate.

Note: Vendors congregate outside the ruins, vociferously hawking fake archeological pieces and a variety of crafts. There also is a craft market near the ruins entrance. Keep in mind, however, that many of the same items can be purchased in town as well, sometimes at lower prices. Daily 8-5. Admission 35 pesos (about $3.40 U.S.). The fee to use a video camera is about $5.

OAXACA, OAXACA (C-3)

pop. 257,000, elev. 5,084′

See map page 382.

Oaxaca (wa-HAH-ka), the state capital, is situated in a high valley surrounded by the towering summits of the Sierra Madre del Sur. It also lies in the shadow of the Mixtec and Zapotec civilizations. Highly religious, these tribes erected elaborate ceremonial centers, were knowledgeable in astronomy and developed systems of writing that are reputed to be the oldest on the North American continent.

The coastal areas of Oaxaca state are steamy and the low-lying Isthmus of Tehuantepec region hot and dry, but the capital is sheltered by the encircling mountains. This fertile valley is one of Mexico's oldest continuously inhabited regions; evidence of human settlement dates back to 8,000 B.C.

Zapotec culture was at its zenith from about the third through the seventh centuries; it was challenged by the Mixtecs, who built their own center at Mitla. The two tribes fought for control of the valley until the Aztecs came and conquered in the late 15th century. The Spanish followed, and the city of Oaxaca was founded by Hernando Cortés in 1529. Today's city retains a strongly Indian character, and both the downtown historic center and the ruins of Monte Albán *(see attraction listing)* were designated World Heritage Sites by UNESCO in 1987.

Oaxaca produced two of Mexico's best known presidents. Benito Juárez was born in the nearby village of Guelatao. A Zapotec with no formal childhood education, he nevertheless entered politics, serving as governor of the state, chief justice of the Mexican Supreme Court and later as president of

Mexico (1858-72). Streets, statues and a university bear this national hero's name.

Porfirio Díaz, on the other hand, is not nearly so highly regarded. Of Mixtec rather than Zapotec heritage, Díaz embarked on a military career and assumed the presidency in 1876. The Díaz government soon took on the trappings of a dictatorship, however. Important Mexican advances in railroads, manufacturing, oil production and investment abroad were made during his regime, but at the expense of the country's poor and indigenous citizens.

Indian traditions and heritage have remained largely intact in both Oaxaca and neighboring Chiapas, encouraging richness and diversity in handicrafts, ethnic celebrations and regional cookery. Descendants of the Zapotec and Mixtec peoples live in small villages throughout the valley and in the mountains. Regional dialects abound, and for many residents—known as Oaxaqueños—Spanish is a second language.

This strong cultural identity has made Oaxaca one of Mexico's leading art centers. In the last few decades a group of artists, all native to the state, have converged here to produce artwork that is stylistically diverse but rooted in themes relating to the lives of the Indians who populate the many rural villages surrounding the city.

The setting would certainly inspire many an artist. The older buildings are constructed of an unusual greenish volcanic stone that takes on a golden tone when the sun is low on the horizon. Others are painted bright turquoise or pink. Bougainvillea and roses tumble over walls, geraniums spill out of huge clay pots, and when the jacaranda trees are in bloom they form masses of purple. Completing this colorful palette is the sky, which is most often an azure blue.

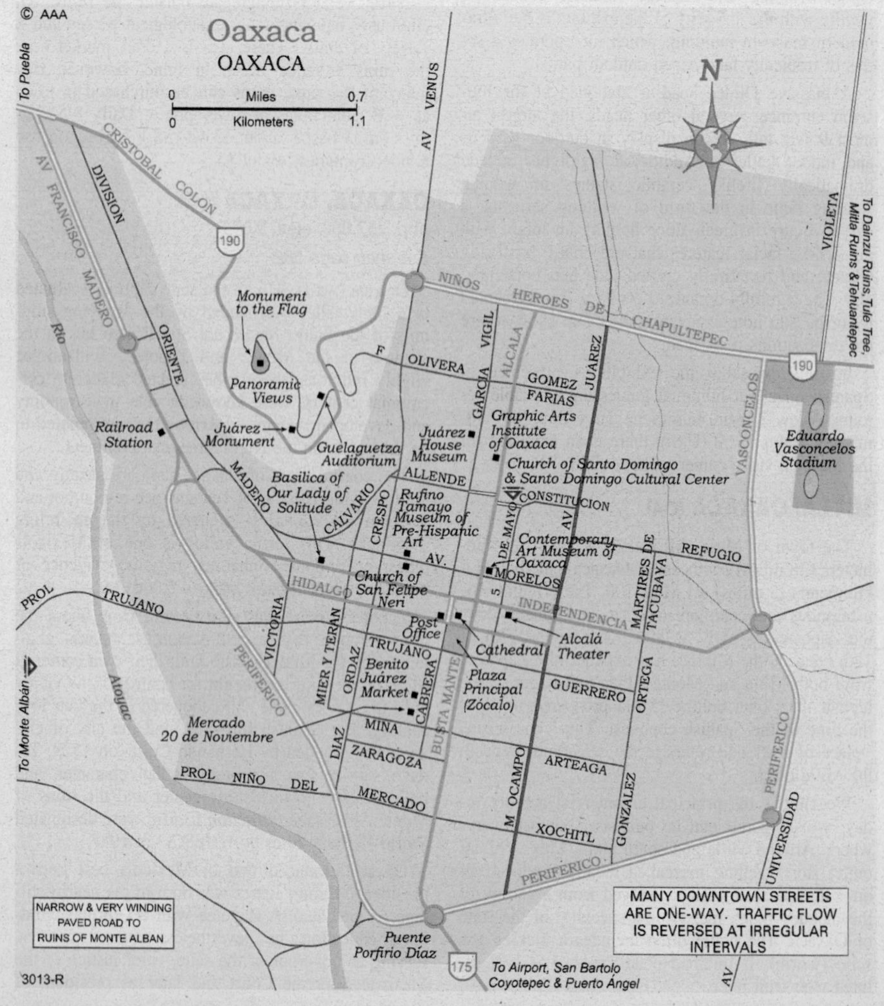

Be sure to sample the local cuisine. The state is known in particular for *mole* sauces, which incorporate a number of spices. There are distinct varieties, only *mole negro* employing the chocolate that also turns up in the *mole poblano* sauce of Puebla.

Other Oaxacan specialties include *tamales oaxaqueños,* a mixture of ground corn *(masa),* shredded chicken and Oaxacan *mole* sauce wrapped in a banana leaf and then steamed; *tlayudas,* crispy, dinner plate-sized corn tortillas topped with a wash of refried beans, meat, lettuce or cabbage, cheese, avocado slices and almost anything else; *picadillo,* spicy shredded pork; and *quesillo,* a stringy, mildly flavored white cheese. The adventurous can try *chapulines* (fried grasshoppers) with a squeeze of lime and a dash of chili powder or garlic, sold in the food markets and by vendors at Plaza Principal.

The *comida corrida,* a fixed-item midday meal available at many local restaurants, is a good way to enjoy Oaxacan cooking at reasonable prices.

Planning Your Stay

The peak tourist seasons in Oaxaca are Holy Week *(Semana Santa)* and the Christmas season. But there are so many things to see and do that visitors could easily spend 4 or 5 days at any time of year. Allow at least a day to visit the principal downtown attractions; if you have a particular interest in colonial architecture, spend a day touring the cathedral and churches and another visiting the museums.

The bustling city markets are certainly worth a visit, especially on Saturdays; spend the morning shopping and take in a few downtown attractions in the afternoon. For nighttime entertainment—music, atmosphere, people watching—there's no better place than the main plaza.

Bus tours to nearby craft villages or town markets will fill up a full day. Of the nearby archeological sites, Monte Albán and Mitla *(see place listing)* are the most significant; plan on a full day at Monte Albán and half a day at Mitla. Monte Albán is busiest on Sundays, when admission is free; while it's festive and fun, go on a weekday if you would prefer a quiet and uncrowded visit to these mysterious ruins. Excursions to each site also could be combined with a shopping expedition *(see Village Day Trips).*

Many potholed detours lead in and out of Oaxaca; if you'd rather not drive, take a guided tour. Hotels and travel agencies offer various sightseeing packages. Itineraries include nearby market villages, craft centers and archeological sites, a general tour of the city or tours of churches and museums. A more expensive option is to hire a licensed guide, available through the State Tourism Office.

Note: For much of 2006 the city of Oaxaca endured unrest from protestors determined to force state governor Ulises Ruíz to resign. There is currently no U.S. State Department cautionary advisory regarding travel to the city.

Practicalities

There are no direct U.S. flights to Oaxaca. Both Aeroméxico, phone 01 (800) 021-4010 (toll-free long distance within Mexico), and Mexicana, phone 01 (800) 509-8960 (toll-free long distance within Mexico), offer nonstop connecting flights from Mexico City. The domestic airlines Aero Caribe and Aviacsa have flights from nearby cities, including Cancún, Mérida, Tuxtla Gutiérrez and Villahermosa.

Oaxaca's Benito Juárez Airport is about 8 kilometers (5 miles) south of the city off Mex. 175. Transportes Terrestres minibus *(combi)* and taxi service between the airport and downtown hotels is easily arranged. Taxi fare averages about $8 (U.S.); *combis* are cheaper. For additional information about airlines *see Arriving by Air, page 61.*

A toll road running north to the city of Tehuacán reduces the amount of time it takes to travel by car between Oaxaca and Mexico City. The two-lane roadway features wider lanes, fewer curves and better-engineered grades than most other routes that travel through the mountains. It parallels Mex. 190 from Oaxaca northwest to the town of Nochixtlán, then travels north-northwest to Tehuacán, paralleling Mex. 131 for part of the way. Northwest of Tehuacán the road ties into Mex. 150-D, which proceeds west to Mexico City.

Bus service is available to and from Mexico City, but there are many stops along the 565-kilometer (350-mile) route. "Deluxe" service is provided by UNO and Cristóbal Colón, first-class service by ADO. The first-class bus station is about 1.5 kilometers northeast of downtown at Calzada Niños Héroes de Chapultepec #1036.

Local buses depart from the second-class bus station (about 1 kilometer west of Plaza Principal via Avenida Trujano). They're an economical way to travel to the archeological ruins and Indian villages, although trips can be excruciatingly slow along the narrow, winding mountain roads. For additional information about buses *see Bus Service, page 72.*

Taxis are another way to get around town, and the fare to nearby destinations can be shared among several riders; negotiate the rate before you set out. Fares within the city center average about $2.25 (U.S.). Taxis line up around Plaza Principal.

Personal safety in Oaxaca means using common sense—precautions such as keeping your car in a lot overnight rather than parking it on the street, storing all valuables out of sight, and staying alert in public places where smooth professional pickpockets operate, like markets and bus stations. Stick to established tourist areas, and avoid driving after dark.

Temperatures are mild to warm throughout the year, averaging in the 70s or 80s during the day and the 50s or 60s at night. May is the hottest month and the height of the dry season; the rainy season is from June through September. At this tropical latitude the sun can be quite strong; take the necessary precautions if you'll be outside all day. Sturdy, comfortable walking shoes also come in handy for exploring the ruins and trekking around the village

Hard Labor in the Cane Fields

Sugar cane, the main source for the raw sugar that is refined to produce the granulated sweetener known the world over, is a member of the grass family. This plant has tall, thick, fibrous stalks that contain a sap rich in sucrose—a sweetening agent for foods and beverages and also a major ingredient in cakes, soft drinks, alcohol, preservatives and many other products.

Sugar cane is grown in many tropical and subtropical parts of the world. Along with olive oil, rice and citrus fruits, it was one of the agricultural products introduced to Mexico by Spanish *conquistadores.* Sugar was a precious commodity during the Spanish colonial era, and sugar haciendas—plantations that were worked by Indian and African slave labor—amassed great wealth for their owners. Sugar cane, which ranks with corn and tomatoes as one of the country's most important cash crops, is grown today in northwestern Mexico with the aid of irrigation, but more commonly in the gulf coast states of Veracruz and Tabasco, where the hot, rainy climate is ideal.

markets. Avoid wearing skimpy or revealing clothing inside churches.

Special Events

Oaxaca's festivals, like the city itself, are dynamic, colorful and expansive. They draw big crowds, so hotel space should be booked well in advance for the Easter holiday and in July, November and December.

The Guelaguetza, meaning "offering," is a centuries-old festival celebrated throughout the state. Community troupes present their regional costumes, dances, songs and music in a specially designed, open-air theater (Auditorio Guelaguetza) built into the side of Cerro del Fortín, the hill in the northern part of the city. To reach the site, take Calzada Madero north to the Mex. 190 junction, then go east on Mex. 190 about 1.6 kilometers (1 mile).

A dizzying whirl of Oaxacan folk dance and musical performances comprise the Guelaguetza, as participating singers, dancers and musicians throw *guelaguetzas* (gifts) to spectators. An evening show presents the legend of Princess Donají, which includes staged re-enactments of battles between Zapotec and Mixtec warriors. Even if you have tickets, arrive early—at least by 8 a.m.—for the best seats. **Note:** Bring water, and wear a hat or appropriate headgear for protection from the strong sun.

Performances are given on the two successive Mondays following July 16. (In years when July 18—the anniversary of Benito Juárez's death—falls on a Monday, the dates are July 25 and Aug. 1.) Check in advance with a travel agency, the Oaxaca State Tourism Office or your hotel for the exact dates. Tickets, necessary for the main performances, should be reserved no later than May, preferably through a travel agent; confirm the exact festival dates when you make your reservations.

Holy Week, beginning the Friday before Easter Sunday, brings parades and communion services, and local churches sponsor fairs, concerts and other activities. Oaxaca celebrates the Day of the Dead (Día de Los Muertos) Oct. 31 and Nov. 1 and 2. The markets are ablaze with marigolds and sell all manner of offerings with which to decorate altars built to honor the deceased.

The Fiesta of the Virgen de la Soledad in mid-December is a Christmas season highlight and honors the city's patron saint with processions, fireworks, floats and dances. Dec. 23 brings the Night of the Radishes. For this competition the main plaza is filled with booths displaying local radishes carved into every conceivable shape. Sweets are served in clay dishes; after finishing the treat, fling your dish to the ground so it smashes.

Shopping

Oaxaca's markets are among Mexico's most exciting, with head-turning displays of crafts, foodstuffs, household products and curios. If you don't mind the crowds and noise, Saturdays provide the biggest spectacle, drawing Indians who come for miles around to buy and sell. Arrive unburdened so you can maintain your bearings amid the jostling, and be prepared to bargain—begin by offering to pay half the selling price for any item.

Look for leather goods, hand-loomed cottons, jewelry, carved idols and black pottery from the village of San Bartolo Coyotepec. Teotitlán and Ocotlán are weaving and pottery centers, respectively. Local artisans also create carved, brightly painted wooden animals that have whimsical or surreal expressions. Gold, silver and jade jewelry is often a reproduction of actual pieces found at Monte Albán or designed in a similar style.

The enormous Abastos Market (Mercado de Abastos), southwest of downtown off the Periférico, the loop road that encircles the city, is one of Oaxaca's busiest. It is open daily but is most active on Saturday, when villagers dressed in native garb convene to display their merchandise in a huge warehouse and across blocks of open-air lots and canopied stalls.

This market is crammed with such items as shawls, embroidered blouses, pottery, woven baskets, rugs, toys, religious ornaments, woodcarvings and jewelry. The air is filled with the smells of incense, chocolate and tortillas. Abastos also is a produce and livestock market, and there are piles of dried chilies in a rainbow of colors, mounds of garlic bulbs, herbs, unfamiliar vegetables and tropical fruits.

One block south of Plaza Principal along Calle 20 de Noviembre is the indoor Benito Juárez Market, also busiest on Saturday. There are numerous food stalls here. Use appropriate caution when deciding whether or not to sample snacks; if you can see something being cooked it's usually safe to eat. Among the clothing items for sale are coarse-weave woolen sweaters, shawls and capes. In the next block south is the Mercado 20 de Noviembre, which offers *mole* sauces, Oaxacan chocolate and other foodstuffs, as well as a few craft stalls.

The Handicrafts Market (Mercado de Artesanías), a block southwest of the Mercado 20 de Noviembre at the corner of calles J.P. García and Zaragoza, specializes in textiles. The artisans can be observed as they weave rugs, wall hangings and *sarapes* on simple looms. Expect to bargain for any purchase.

If you don't relish the give-and-take of haggling, try one of Oaxaca's many fixed-price stores. The government-run FONART store, at Cempoaltépetl #409, Colonia Volcanes, sells a variety of representative crafts from all over the country. The state-run ARIPO (Artesanías y Industrias Populares del Estado de Oaxaca), Calle García Vigil #809, has rooms filled with Oaxacan black pottery, rugs and textiles. The store has an English-speaking staff and will ship purchases.

The Galería Arte de Oaxaca, 3 blocks north and 1 block east of Plaza Principal at Calle Murguía #105, is a gallery featuring the work of noted Oaxacan painters and sculptors. Víctor Artes Regionales, Porfirio Díaz #111 between Independencia and Morelos, is housed in a 17th-century monastery and

Hard Labor in the Cane Fields (continued)

If you're traveling through the fertile farming regions around Veracruz during harvesting season (March and April) you're likely to see—in addition to bananas, cacao trees, and mango and papaya orchards—a waving green sea of sugar cane. Since harvesting cane by machine is difficult, it is still done mainly by hand in centuries-old fashion, which requires a large supply of manual labor.

Generations of *caneros*—essentially serfs toiling the land—have labored in Mexican cane fields. First the fields are burned, which destroys dead leaves and small thorns but leaves the juicy stalks intact. Then the laborers wrap their hands, ankles and feet in layers of old cloth to protect themselves from the bites of poisonous snakes not flushed out during the burning. They wade into 12-foot-tall forests of prickly, razor-sharp cane, cutting it by hand with long machetes in broiling heat and humidity before loading it high onto trucks—all for about $20 (U.S.) per truck.

© Javier Larrea
age fotostock

specializes in locally handcrafted textiles, basketry, toys, masks and ceramics.

Calle M. Alcalá between the main square and the Church of Santo Domingo is a pedestrian boulevard lined with high-quality shops. La Mano Mágica, Calle M. Alcalá #203, is a combination art gallery and crafts shop. It's known for finely woven rugs, particularly those by Teotitlán weaver Arnulfo Mendoza, and lovely pieces of regional folk art. Corazón del Pueblo, Calle M. Alcalá #307-329, stocks a distinctive collection of ceramic figurines, Huichol bead work, masks, painted wooden animals, jewelry and likenesses of Frida Kahlo by artisans from Oaxaca and elsewhere in Mexico.

If you'd like to support local artisans, visit MARO (Mujeres Artesanas de las Regiones de Oaxaca), Av. 5 de Mayo #204 between Morelos and Murguía. This cooperative benefiting women in the villages of the Oaxaca Valley offers a variety of handicrafts, including Atzompa and Coyotepec pottery, stamped tinware, leather bags, sandals, belts and toys.

Note: While it's easy to accumulate a trove of treasures, they may need to be shipped home. The better shops and stores can usually arrange for shipping, but this is not the case with items purchased at the markets or from craftspeople in the villages. The most important thing to remember in such cases is to procure a written receipt.

Village Day Trips

Excursions to area villages can be as rewarding as shopping in the city. The second-class bus station *(see Practicalities)* has bus service to most of the villages; another option is to take an inexpensive taxi from a lot near the Abastos Market. Taxis serve the local population as well and fill up quickly in the morning; a per-person rate is charged.

Tianguis (open-air markets) take place on different days. Green-glazed pottery, including bowls from which breasts or lilies unexpectedly sprout, is the specialty at Atzompa, about 6 kilometers (4 miles) northwest of Oaxaca on Mex. 190. Also look for clay dolls. Market day is Tuesday. A variety of cheeses and mole sauces can be purchased at the Wednesday market at San Pablo Etla, 14 kilometers (9 miles) northwest on Mex. 190. Thursday's market at Ejutla, 61 kilometers (38 miles) south on Mex. 175, is agriculturally oriented as well.

Zaachila, about 18 kilometers (11 miles) southwest on the road to Cuilapan, also has a Thursday market that does not target tourists but is interesting for its produce and livestock displays and slice of Mexican village life. The raucous Friday market at Ocotlán, about 40 kilometers (25 miles) south on Mex. 175, is the busiest outside of Oaxaca. *Rebozos* (scarves or shawl-like garments), produce, leather goods, cutlery and whimsical ceramic figurines of women are among the many items for sale.

Other towns are known for a particular craft in which the entire populace seems to be involved. Arrazola, a tiny village southwest of Oaxaca near the ruins of Monte Albán, is noted for carvers who fashion fanciful wooden creatures painted in vivid colors. Second-class buses travel to Arrazola, and local youngsters will take you to the artisans' homes for a small tip.

San Bartolo Coyotepec, about 16 kilometers (10 miles) south of Oaxaca on Mex. 175, is the source of the distinctive black pottery sold in many Oaxaca shops. Buses and tours travel frequently to this village. Items can be purchased at the local factory, in shops around the plaza or from the potters' homes. Friday is market day.

The village of Guelatao, 63 kilometers (39 miles) north on Mex. 175, is the birthplace of Mexican president Benito Juárez. Guelatao's monument-studded plaza honors this native son, and lively celebrations are held on his birthday, Mar. 21. Although the journey to Guelatao offers impressive views at around 7,000 feet, motorists should exercise caution when negotiating the roadway's serpentine bends and potholes. Frequent drizzle also can make the road surface slippery. To fully enjoy the scenery, take a bus.

Oaxaca State Tourism Office (Secretaría de Desarrollo Turístico): downtown at Murguía #206. Open daily 8-8; phone (951) 516-0045.

What To See in and Around Town

ALCALA THEATER (Teatro Macedonio de Alcalá) is on Av. Independencia at Calle Armienta y Lopez, 2 blks. n.e. of Plaza Principal. Built around the turn of the 20th century, the Alcalá reflects the grandiose style public buildings took under the rule of native son and dictator Porfirio Díaz. The interior in particular is plushly opulent. Open only for events; check with the State Tourism Office for schedule information.

BASILICA OF OUR LADY OF SOLITUDE (Basilica de la Soledad) is at Av. Independencia #107 (at Av. Galeana), about 5 blks. w. of Plaza Principal. This massive 17th-century structure, actually a complex of several buildings and a garden, has a richly carved exterior. The basilica is dedicated to the Virgin of Solitude (Virgen de la Soledad). A statue of the Virgin, Oaxaca's patron saint, is displayed above the altar, draped in jewel-encrusted black velvet.

The interior is an extravagant showcase of baroque ornamentation. A museum to the rear of the church displays a replica of the Virgin statue. It also contains glass panels depicting the legend of her arrival in the city and an enormous assemblage of gifts (primarily miniature glass figurines) sent in tribute. Exhibit information is in Spanish. Basilica normally open daily 7-2 and 4-9, museum Mon.-Sat. 10-2 and 4-6; hours may vary. Basilica free, admission to the museum is by donation.

CATHEDRAL faces the n. side of Plaza Principal. Begun in 1563, the church was completed about 2 centuries later. Although severely damaged by earthquakes, the rebuilt cathedral, which is constructed of the native greenish stone, still reflects much of its original grandeur. The clock, its works made of wood, was presented by a Spanish king. The facade and central panel above the door are fine examples of baroque craftsmanship. Daily 7 a.m.-9 p.m. Free.

CHURCH OF SAN FELIPE NERI (Iglesia de San Felipe Neri) is on Av. Independencia at Calle Tinoco y Palacios, about 3 blks. n.w. of Plaza Principal. The interior of this 17th-century baroque church features a lavish altar of carved, gilded wood and impressive wall frescoes. Daily 8 a.m.-10 p.m. Free.

GEM **CHURCH OF SANTO DOMINGO** (Iglesia de Santo Domingo) is at Gurrión, M. Alcalá, Berriozábal and Reforma, about 4 blks. n. of Plaza Principal. Founded by the Dominicans in the mid-16th century, it took about a century to build. Even in a city (and country) of impressive churches, Santo Domingo has a well-deserved reputation as one of the most ornate. Every square inch of the interior walls and ceilings is covered with gold leaf, polychrome reliefs and plaster statues. Try to visit in the afternoon, when sunlight pouring through the stained-glass window casts everything in a golden glow.

One particularly noteworthy decoration, on the ceiling under the raised choir loft near the entrance, depicts crowned heads appearing on the branches of the family tree of Santo Domingo de Guzmán, founder of the Dominican order. The adjoining monastery now houses the Santo Domingo Cultural Center *(see attraction listing)*. Allow 2 hours minimum. Daily 7-1 and 5-8 p.m. Free.

CONTEMPORARY ART MUSEUM OF OAXACA (Museo de Arte Contemporáneo de Oaxaca, or MACO) is at Calle M. Alcalá #202, 2 blks. n. of Plaza Principal. It occupies a turn-of-the-18th-century building also known as the House of Cortés (Casa de Cortés), so named for supposedly being a former residence of the conqueror (historians and chronology insist otherwise). Changing exhibits in this beautifully restored colonial building feature the work of contemporary artists, both regional and international. Wed.-Mon. 10:30-8. Admission about $1.25 (U.S.). Phone (951) 514-2818.

DAINZU RUINS are about 24 km (15 mi.) s.e. of Oaxaca on a paved road off Mex. 190, on the way to Mitla; watch for the signed turn-off. Believed to be one of the final evidences of Olmec civilization in the Oaxaca region, their zenith was from around 600 B.C. to A.D. 200, before the better-known Monte Albán. A pyramidal structure (Edificio A) shows artwork portraying ball players, and there are dramatic carvings of jaguars, rabbits and dancers, as well as a partially restored ball court. Some sections are still being excavated. Visitors can descend the underground connecting tunnels, but they are dark and claustrophobic, with steep stairs.

Guided tours are available. Picnicking is permitted. Allow 1 hour minimum. Daily 8-5:30. Admission 29 pesos (about $2.80 U.S.).

GRAPHIC ARTS INSTITUTE OF OAXACA (Instituto de Artes Gráficas de Oaxaca) is at M. Alcalá #507, across from the Church of Santo Domingo. It was created primarily through the efforts of celebrated Oaxacan artist Francisco Toledo. The institute has a collection of more than 5,000 engravings that includes his work, that of fellow Mexicans Rufino Tamayo and José Guadalupe Posada, and international artists. There also is an extensive library of art-related volumes. Daily 10:30-8. Donations requested. Phone (951) 516-6980.

JUAREZ HOUSE MUSEUM (Museo Casa de Juárez) is about 6 blks. n. of Plaza Principal at García Vigil #609. This 19th-century colonial home was once owned by Padre Antonio Salanueva. The Salanuevas brought a young Oaxaqueño, Benito Juárez, from the village of Guelatao to live with them; Juárez's resulting education was the springboard for his careers in law and politics. The house is furnished to reflect a typical Oaxacan middle class lifestyle in the 19th century. Tues.-Sun. 10-7. Admission about $3 (U.S.). Phone (951) 516-1860.

GEM **MONTE ALBAN RUINS** are about 10 km (6 mi.) s.w. of Oaxaca; if driving, take Calle Trujano w. out of town across the Río Atoyac; it becomes the narrow, winding road to the ruins. One of Mexico's greatest pre-Columbian sites, Monte Albán presides over the valley of Oaxaca from a mountaintop location. This major religious center was built by the Zapotecs around 600 B.C. atop a summit that was deliberately flattened. At its height around A.D. 300, Monte Albán supported 40,000 inhabitants. The city was taken over in the 10th century by the Mixtecs, who were in turn conquered by the Aztecs, and fell into ruin around the time of the Spanish conquest.

The site's focal point is the Great Plaza, a grassy area about 970 feet long and 650 feet wide, bounded by four large ceremonial platforms. It was leveled by hewing away rock outcroppings. All of the buildings are aligned on a precise north-south axis except for one, an observatory believed to be placed in relation to the stars rather than to compass directions. Many of the structures are roped off from visitors.

An I-shaped ball court dominates one corner of the plaza. One of the most fascinating buildings is the Temple of the Dancers *(danzantes),* on the west side of the plaza. The oldest building at the site, it is named for the elaborate figures carved into its stone slabs. They were first thought to be dancers but may be representations of the diseased or cadavers used for study in a school of medicine.

Some 170 subterranean tombs are scattered throughout the ruins. These contain numerous slab paintings, glyphs, frescoes and stone carvings. Tombs 104 and 105 can be entered by climbing down a ladder, but aren't always open. In 1932, Tomb 7 (near the site entrance) yielded a priceless collection of items, which are on display at the Santo Domingo Cultural Center.

Autobuses Turísticos tour buses depart for Monte Albán several times a day from the Rivera del Angel

Hotel at Calle Mina #518 (round-trip fare about $4 U.S.). The journey to the site is very slow but very scenic. There is a museum (with exhibit information in Spanish only), a bookstore and a casual restaurant at the site entrance. Licensed guide service is available for a fee.

Food is available. Allow 3 hours minimum. Daily 8-6. Admission (includes museum) 48 pesos (about $4.50 U.S.). The fee for using a video camera is about $5.

PLAZA PRINCIPAL is bordered by avs. Hidalgo, Miguel Cabrera, Guerrero and Valdivieso. Although it was rocked by demonstrations for much of 2006, an abundance of Old World charm still makes this one of Mexico's most enjoyable plazas. Indian laurel trees shade the square; fountains decorate some of the walkways, and a wrought-iron gazebo and bandstand stands at its center. Early evening, when a formal flag-lowering ceremony is performed and people start to gather, is a good time to visit.

Plaza Principal really comes alive as darkness falls. Street musicians materialize and offer impromptu performances. Vendors hawk ice cream, roast corn, pineapple chunks, *chorizo* (sausage), musical instruments, balloons, children's toys and tin skeletons dancing on the end of sticks. Band concerts—from brass to marimba to Oaxacan rock—take place regularly.

RUFINO TAMAYO MUSEUM OF PRE-HISPANIC ART (Museo Rufino Tamayo de Arte Prehispanico) is at Av. Morelos #503, 4 blks. n.w. of Plaza Principal. It spotlights the private collection of artist Rufino Tamayo, which he donated to his native city. Housed in a restored, 16th-century colonial mansion, it includes artifacts from Teotihuacán, Nayarit state, and the Olmec, Mayan, Totonac and Aztec civilizations. Figurines, sculpture and other works are handsomely displayed in the series of brightly colored rooms. Exhibit information is in Spanish.

Wed.-Sat. and Mon. 10-2 and 4-7, Sun. 10-3. Admission about $2.75 (U.S.). Phone (951) 516-4750.

GEM **SANTO DOMINGO CULTURAL CENTER** is next to the Church of Santo Domingo. Housed in a beautifully restored former Dominican convent, it charts the course of human development in the Valley of Oaxaca.

The showcase exhibits focus on some 500 pieces of priceless jewelry and art objects—goblets, urns, masks, breastplates—made of gold, turquoise, jade, amber and obsidian that were found in Tomb 7 of the Monte Albán ruins. The museum also contains fascinating, carefully organized collections of regional handicrafts, costumes worn by the different Indian groups within the state, and archeological artifacts. Information is presented in Spanish.

Tours with English-speaking guides are available; inquire at the information desk. Allow 2 hours minimum. Tues.-Sun. 10-7:45. Admission about $4.50 (U.S.); free to all Sun. Phone (951) 516-2991.

TEMPLE AND EX-CONVENT OF SANTIAGO APOSTAL is at the southern edge of the town of Cuilapan, about 16 km (10 mi.) s.w. of Oaxaca via Mex. 135. The roofless cloister at the entrance to this Dominican monastery (the ceiling was never completed) is accentuated by enormous 50-foot columns topped with parapets. Beyond the cloister is an immense complex of rooms, tunnels and hidden stairways, with enormous portals framed by ornate stonework high atop walls. A museum section displays large, intricately carved stone stela.

Next to the monastery are the remnants of a water-driven stone gristmill once used to process wheat. Vicente Guerrero, one of Mexico's first presidents, was executed at this site on Feb. 14, 1831; his remains lie in the base of the Independence Monument in Mexico City.

Picnicking is permitted. Allow 2 hours minimum. Daily 10-6. Admission about $2 (U.S.).

TULE TREE (Arbol del Tule) is in the village of Santa María del Tule, about 10 km (6 mi.) s.e. of Oaxaca on Mex. 190. This colossal specimen of a Mexican cypress, or *ahuehuete,* is believed to be at least 2,000 years old. The tree stands in the local churchyard and measures more than 150 feet both in height and around its base. Churchyard open daily 9-5. Admission about 50c (U.S.).

ZAACHILA RUINS are in Zaachila, about 18 km (11 mi.) s.w. of Oaxaca past the village of Cuilapan; the site, behind the town church on the main plaza, is marked "Zona Arqueológica." There is limited street parking in the vicinity of the plaza. The site, which means "place of the Zapoteca kings," consists of a large platform with two sets of stairs descending to tombs that contain ornate carvings very similar in detail to the zig-zag facades found at Uxmal *(see place listing under Yucatán Peninsula).*

Picnicking is permitted. Allow 2 hours minimum. Daily 8-6. Admission 29 pesos (about $2.80 U.S.).

PALENQUE, CHIAPAS (C-5) pop. 31,800

The town of Palenque, some 145 kilometers (90 miles) southeast of Villahermosa, has little to offer tourists, although there are hotels and restaurants around its main plaza. It does, however, provide access to the Mayan ruins of Palenque *(see attraction listing),* designated a World Heritage Site by UNESCO in 1987. Occupying the lower foothills of the Sierra Madre in one of Mexico's wettest, most lushly forested regions, Palenque (pah-LEHN-keh) is perhaps the most haunting archeological site in the entire country.

This ancient city most likely began as a farming settlement around 150 B.C. and flourished between A.D. 600 and 800, when it ruled an area covering much of the present-day states of Chiapas and Tabasco. Palenque was abandoned around A.D. 900 for reasons unknown but still debated by historians.

Large-scale excavations in the 1920s under the supervision of Danish explorer Frans Blom *(see San*

Cristóbal de las Casas) began clearing away centuries of earth and encroaching jungle. Subsequent excavations have brought to light significant knowledge about Palenque, its inhabitants, its culture and its central role within the Mayan empire.

Travel agencies in Villahermosa, Tuxtla Gutiérrez and San Cristóbal de Las Casas can provide information on reaching Palenque by first-class bus; the trip takes 2 to 3 hours from Villahermosa and about 6 hours from Tuxtla Gutiérrez. Although the ruins can be adequately toured in half a day, staying overnight makes for a less hurried agenda.

From Villahermosa, motorists should take Mex. 186 to Catazajá, then Mex. 199 south to the ruins. Passing through lush countryside, the roadway is generally straight, although slick during the June-through-October rainy season and potholed at any time of year.

Mex. 199 intersects Avenida Juárez about half a mile west of the town's main plaza; the junction is designated by a large statue of a Maya chieftain's head. The road to the ruins branches west off Mex. 199 less than half a mile south of this junction. If you arrive by first-class bus, *colectivo* shuttle buses and taxis run between the center of town and the ruins.

The winter months—November through February—are a better time to visit than in the summer, when it is oppressively hot and humid. Arrive early to avoid both the heat and the crowds, and wear a hat and sunblock for protection from the sun. An all-weather jacket or other rain gear will come in handy at any time. Insect repellent is necessary if you plan on doing any exploring or clambering around the ruins, particularly in the late afternoon.

Chiapas State Tourism Office: intersection of Avenida Juárez and Abasolo, a block from the main plaza; open Mon.-Sat. 9-9, Sun. 9-1. Information on transportation to the ruins can be obtained here.

AGUA AZUL WATERFALLS (Cascadas de Agua Azul) are about 68 km (42 mi.) s. of Palenque via Mex. 199, toward the town of Ocosingo; the entrance is about 4 km (2.5 mi.) w. of the highway via a signed turn-off.

Although not very high, the broad series of cascades plunge dramatically over enormous boulders into clear pools that have a jungle backdrop. Wooden deck platforms provide good views. Swimming is permitted but not recommended; currents can be strong and submerged rocks are hazardous. Several uphill walkways cover the spread-out grounds, and makeshift huts serve as market stalls and simple eateries. Intentional burning in April and May to clear the jungle can result in a thick haze of smoke. The water also is murky and silt-laden after heavy rains.

The trip to Agua Azul is as exciting as the falls themselves. The pocked, two-lane blacktop road winds sinuously through mountainous terrain; it abuts steep cliffs and there are no shoulders, but the views are spectacular. The road also bristles with *topes* (speed bumps), and there are locations where small children try to stop traffic to hawk beverages, locally grown fruit and other wares. If you don't want to make the drive yourself, travel agencies in Palenque offer day trip packages; inquire along Avenida Juárez near the main plaza.

Picnicking is permitted. Allow 2 hours minimum. Open daily. Admission 10 pesos per vehicle. Parking fee 10 pesos.

Misol-Ha is about 19 km (12 mi.) s. of Palenque off Mex. 199; watch for the signed turn-off. This waterfall is a shorter trip as well as being equally beautiful; it drops 90 feet into a wide pool. Both Misol-Ha and Agua Azul are crowded on weekends and holidays. Open daily. Admission 10 pesos.

GEM **PALENQUE RUINS** are about 8 km (5 mi.) from the Mex. 199 jct. just s. of town. The excavated section—small in relation to the city's size during its heyday more than 1,000 years ago—spreads a mile or so from east to west. The structures here are among the best preserved in Mesoamerica. Stone plaques at the individual temples offer descriptions in English, Spanish and Maya.

Next to the Temple of the Inscriptions *(see subattraction listing)* is Temple XIII, where a tomb was discovered in 1994. Just east of this temple is the Palace, a complex of stepped buildings and four courtyards connected by corridors and an extensive system of underground passageways. The exterior walls are adorned with the beautifully carved, unusually well-preserved panels and stucco reliefs for which Palenque is famous.

Other groups of structures are in various stages of restoration. Cross the Río Otolum (little more than a stream) to reach the Temple of the Cross, at the southeastern edge of the ruins. It is one of several structures ringing a spacious plaza. Projecting upward from the temple are vertical roof combs, a decorative architectural feature favored by Mayan builders. Inside the building is a small shrine.

Nearby are Temple 14, which contains more stone tablets with carved inscriptions, and the Temple of the Sun, believed to contain the tomb of King Pacal's son, Chan-Bahlum, his successor to the throne.

At the site's northern end is the Northern Group of buildings, including a ball court and the Temple of the Count, named for Frederick Waldeck, an early explorer. This structure, the best preserved of the group, is made up of five stepped tiers; its main facade faces east.

A combined museum and visitor center, located on the ruins access road about a mile before the site entrance, contains a refreshment stand and shops selling Chiapan handicrafts. The museum displays reproductions of hieroglyphic panels and other artifacts uncovered at the ruins, with explanations in both Spanish and English. Local vendors peddle souvenirs in the large parking lot at the site entrance, where the ticket booth is located.

Note: Sporadic outbursts of politically motivated violence occur from time to time in the state of Chiapas. Although these ruins are an established tourist attraction, they are in a remote location. It is a good idea to check with hotel staff, taxi drivers or tour guides regarding any local developments that could affect safety.

Food is available. Allow 3 hours minimum. Site open daily 8-5; museum daily 9-4. Admission (includes museum) 48 pesos (about $4.50 U.S.). The fee to use a video camera is $4 (U.S.).

Temple of the Inscriptions (Templo de las Inscripciones) is to the right as you enter the site. This stairstepped, 90-foot-tall pyramidal structure is one of Palenque's most impressive. The climb to the top is slow going but manageable, and well worth the effort for the panoramic view of the surrounding buildings.

The temple was the final resting place of Pacal, the king who ruled Palenque for almost 70 years beginning at the ripe old age of 12. It is believed to be one of the only temples in Mexico constructed expressly to be a tomb. The royal crypt has relief carvings on the walls and contains the massive carved stone sarcophagus lid. It is reached by descending a steep flight of stone block stairs. The steps can be slippery, and those subject to claustrophobia will want to avoid the dank, stuffy atmosphere and stay above ground.

Note: The crypt was closed for restoration work in 2001, and both it and the temple may have restricted visitor access.

PAPANTLA, VERACRUZ (B-3) pop. 48,600

Papantla (pah-PAHN-tlah) spreads out over the green foothills of the Sierra Madre Oriental, about 243 kilometers (150 miles) northwest of Veracruz. This was the capital of the Totonac kingdom in the mid-15th century, before it fell to the conquering Aztecs. The vanquished Totonacs extracted a revenge of sorts by aiding Hernando Cortés in defeating the Aztecs. The city remains a center of Totonac culture today, and visitors are likely to see locals wearing native garb: billowing white pants and sailor shirts for men, lacy skirts and embroidered white blouses for women.

This is Mexico's vanilla-producing center, and the distinctively sweet scent frequently hovers in the air. Vanilla bean pods are fashioned into small figures that are sold around town, along with textiles, embroidered clothing and baskets. Souvenir hunters also can try the Hidalgo Market (Mercado Hidalgo), on Avenida 20 de Noviembre just off the northwest corner of the main plaza, for handmade men's and women's clothing.

Papantla is celebrated for its Papantla Flyers (Voladores de Papantla), Totonac Indians who give an exciting rendition of the "Flying Pole" dance. Ropes that have been wound around a 70-foot-tall pole are tied around their waists. Four dancers jump backward off a tiny revolving platform atop the pole, whirling downwards as the ropes unwind. A fifth man, who dances while playing a flute and beating a drum, remains on top of the platform. Each performer revolves around the pole 13 times; the total number of revolutions, 52, equals the number of years in the Aztec religious life cycle.

Before it evolved into a crowd-pleasing spectacle of its own, the dance was part of a pre-Hispanic agricultural ceremony designed to secure the favor of the rain gods and to celebrate the vanilla harvest. The dancers perform up to three times a day during the Festival of Corpus Christi in late May and early June. Papantla's signature annual event, the festival is celebrated with art exhibitions, traditional dances, cockfights and fireworks displays.

Overlooking the city from a hilltop is a giant likeness of a flute-playing *volador*, a monument erected in 1988. There are good views of the surrounding countryside from the base of the statue, which can be reached by walking up Avenida Reforma from the cathedral.

The first-class Autobuses del Oriente (ADO) bus station is at the intersection of avenidas Venustiano Carranza and Benito Juárez, north of Plaza Tellez *(see attraction listing)*. From the station there is service to Jalapa and Veracruz.

Tourist information office: on Avenida 16 de Septiembre in a building opposite the cathedral.

EL TAJIN is about 13 kilometers (8 miles) w. of Papantla via a paved road. The main reason to come to Papantla is to visit El Tajín (tah-HEEN). Some of the site has been restored, although archeologists estimate that hundreds of ruined buildings remain hidden beneath the jungle growth. The ruins were discovered in the late 18th century; a major restoration project began in 1992, the same year that El Tajín was designated a World Heritage Site by UNESCO. More than 30 buildings have since been restored, although many more hidden under grassy mounds await excavation.

The excavated structures are divided into two main groups. In the main group is the most impressive structure, the Pyramid of the Niches. Its seven terraces are punctuated with a total of 365 corniced, deeply recessed square niches. A steep staircase with bordering ramps ascends the east side. A smaller pyramid, Building 5, is just south, as is the South Ball Court, the largest and best-preserved of the site's several ball courts.

North of the Pyramid of the Niches, an uphill pathway leads to a newer group of buildings called El Tajín Chico (Little Tajín). Overlooking this complex is the Building of the Columns; the six richly carved column shafts—three on each side—once supported a ceiling. A Mayan arch forms the entrance to Building A. Building C, a pyramid, features stone fretwork similar to that adorning the Pyramid of the Niches.

A museum at the entrance displays artifacts retrieved from the excavations as well as a scale model of the entire site. The flying pole dance performed in town also takes place here (the pole is near the museum) whenever there are enough tourists—usually touring groups—to form an appreciative crowd. A $2 (U.S.) donation is requested to watch the spectacle, which is not without risk to its daredevil performers.

Note: Visitors should stay on the cleared pathways between the buildings; the thick underbrush in this part of Mexico is likely to be inhabited by poisonous snakes. Climbing the pyramids is not permitted. Bring a water bottle and wear a hat and sunblock for protection, as the site has little shade.

White minibuses marked "Chote/Tajín" depart for the site from Avenida 16 de Septiembre (running along the uphill side of the cathedral) on the main plaza. The tourist information office can provide information about bus or minibus service to the ruins, although English is not likely to be spoken. It's easier to reach the site in your own vehicle or visit it as part of an organized bus tour. Daily 8-5. Admission (includes museum) 48 pesos (about $4.50 U.S.). The fee to use a video camera is $3.50.

PLAZA TELLEZ is terraced into a hillside in the center of town. White-tiled and palm-shaded, it has benches inlaid with tile mosaics. On the plaza's south side is the Cathedral of Our Lady of the Assumption (Catedral de Nuestra Señora de la Asunción). Carved into the church's north wall is the Tribute to the Totonac Culture (Homenaje a la Cultura Totonaca), a 165-foot-long stone mural. It depicts Totonac folkloric figures and is dominated by a rendering of the plumed serpent Quetzalcóatl that runs its entire length.

SAN CRISTOBAL DE LAS CASAS, CHIAPAS (C-5) pop. 118,200, elev. 6,888′

San Cristóbal (sahn krees-TOH-bahl) de Las Casas was settled in 1528 by troops of Hernando Cortés under the command of Diego de Mazariegos, who later became the governor of Cuba. It was a neglected outpost for much of the Spanish colonial era, when the state of Chiapas was a Guatemalan province. The indigenous Tzotzil and Tzeltal Indians, descendants of the ancient Maya, were subjected to forced labor in the wheat fields, losing their own farmland in the process while Spanish citizens grew rich.

The town is named for Bartolomé de Las Casas, a New World settler and Dominican priest who was appointed bishop of Chiapas in 1545 and became famous for his advocacy on behalf of the indigenous peoples of Mexico and the Caribbean—a position bolstered after he witnessed the atrocities committed by Spanish *conquistadores.* Three years after independence from Spain was won in 1821, San Cristóbal became the Chiapan state capital and remained so until 1892, when the capital was moved to Tuxtla Gutiérrez.

Isolation prevailed until the 1950s, when the first paved roads were built into town. They also brought the first tourists, and an international, bohemian community of artists and expatriates has flourished here ever since. Another major social change occurred in the 1970s, when thousands of residents from the many Indian villages in the vicinity of San Cristóbal were exiled for converting to Protestantism under the influence of foreign missionaries. These displaced people resettled in new communities ringing the city, many of them poverty-stricken due to a lack of jobs and educational opportunities.

San Cristóbal and Chiapas made international headlines in 1994, Mexico's most politically turbulent year since the 1910 Revolution. In January of that year, Indian guerrillas calling themselves the Zapatista National Liberation Army (in honor of revolutionary leader Emiliano Zapata) occupied San Cristóbal and several other mountain towns, demanding more land and a measure of self-rule for their communities. The rebellion, which left more than 100 dead over 12 days, was a violent reminder that large numbers of poor Indian farmers were not sharing in the country's prosperity.

Peace talks between the government and Zapatista guerrilla leader Subcomandante Marcos sputtered on and off through the remainder of the 1990s and into the first half of the 2000s. Occasional military roadblocks and several political assassinations have served to underscore the social injustices Mexico's *indígenas*—natives who speak a primary language other than Spanish—have historically endured.

While these issues are understandably taken very seriously in Mexico, visitors aren't likely to see evidence of political tension in San Cristóbal outside of the occasional demonstration or graffiti-scrawled wall. Tourism contributes greatly to the local income, and visitors come from around the world; street vendors sell ski-masked Subcomandante Marcos dolls (a popular souvenir) along with the usual trinkets.

San Cristóbal—designated a national historic monument—is a beautiful city, nestled in a highland valley where the surrounding pine and oak forests are sprinkled with orchids and ferns. It has the whitewashed walls and cobblestone streets of other Mexican colonial cities, with an added mystical backdrop of cloud-shrouded mountain peaks. In the evening the air is redolent with the smoky fragrance of burning *ocote,* a pitch-pine kindling sold in local markets.

Although well into the tropics, the altitude, cool weather and frequent fog lend San Cristóbal a decidedly nontropical feeling. This also is where Central America begins, culturally if not politically; the border with Guatemala lies little more than 160 kilometers (100 miles) southeast.

Practicalities

Getting to remote San Cristóbal takes some planning. The easiest way is to fly into the Tuxtla Gutiérrez or Villahermosa airports. Continental, phone 01 (800) 900-5000 (toll-free long distance within Mexico), offers direct service to Villahermosa from Houston. Aeroméxico, phone 01 (800) 021-4010 (toll-free long distance within Mexico), and Mexicana, phone 01 (800) 509-8960 (toll-free long distance within Mexico), fly to Villahermosa from Mexico City. The regional airline Aviacsa flies to Tuxtla Gutiérrez from Mexico City. For additional information about airlines *see Arriving by Air, page 61*.

A taxi ride from Tuxtla Gutiérrez to San Cristóbal will cost about $50 (U.S.). The drive from Tuxtla east to San Cristóbal takes about 1.5 hours via Mex. 190. It winds for some 83 kilometers (51 miles) in a series of S-curves around high mountain peaks, frequently above cloud level. The elevation ascends some 5,000 feet between the two cities. The two-lane road passes through beautiful, unspoiled scenery, but slippery pavement during the June-through-October rainy season can make the surface dangerous.

Note: If you're unfamiliar with mountain driving, exercise caution. Never drive at a faster speed than conditions warrant, downshift to a lower gear when climbing or going down steep grades, and use particular caution when negotiating curves. Also keep in mind that high elevations often experience changeable weather and can cause headaches or shortness of breath if you're not used to the altitude.

"Deluxe" and first-class bus service to and from Tuxtla Gutiérrez, Palenque, Villahermosa, Oaxaca and Mérida is offered by Autotransportes Cristóbal Colón and ADO. These two lines share a bus terminal at the intersection of Mex. 190 and Avenida Insurgentes, about 9 blocks south of the main plaza. Bus tickets can be purchased at the terminal or at the Ticket Bus agency in downtown San Cristóbal, at Avenida Belisario Domínguez #8 (a block northeast of the main plaza).

Most of San Cristóbal's visitor-related attractions, restaurants and shopping areas are within walking distance of the main plaza. For trips to Indian villages in the vicinity *(see Nearby Destinations)*, passenger vans *(colectivos)* and taxis depart from locations along Mex. 190 in the vicinity of the first-class bus terminal. *Combis* (Volkswagen vans) make regular runs from Mex. 190 (pickup is by the main bus terminal) north to downtown via Avenida Crescencio Rosas. Taxi rides within town average about $1.50 (U.S.); a knowledge of Spanish will be helpful when determining the exact fare.

Chiapas, Mexico's southernmost state, is largely mountainous and forested, and the stunning natural scenery—from mist-shrouded peaks and cascading waterfalls to steamy jungles inhabited by many kinds of wildlife—makes it a fascinating place to explore. ATC Tours conducts a variety of regional eco-oriented adventures, including bird-watching trips, hikes to observe butterflies and orchids, and hiking and white-water rafting excursions. The San Cristóbal office is at Av. 16 de Septiembre #16 at Calle 5 de Febrero, a block northwest of the main plaza; for information phone (967) 678-2550.

City Layout

Plaza 31 de Marzo, the main plaza, is downtown San Cristóbal's focal point and thus a good starting point for exploring. Musicians normally play on weekend evenings at the gazebo in the center of the plaza. The many colonial-era buildings surrounding it are stylistically Spanish, although the atmosphere is unmistakably Indian. If you stop here to relax and observe daily life, you'll likely be approached by street vendors (mostly women and children).

On the north side of the plaza stands San Cristóbal's 16th-century Cathedral. It was constructed in 1528 and rebuilt in 1693. Some of the exterior carvings of saints are missing their heads. The bright yellow exterior is particularly lovely in the late afternoon sun. The west side is dominated by the neoclassic, yellow-and-white Municipal Palace, distinguished by its numerous arcades. At the plaza's southeast corner is the House of Diego Mazariegos (Casa de Diego Mazariegos), which is now occupied by a hotel. Dating from the 16th century, the building's detailed exterior stonework is an example of the plateresque architectural style.

The narrow streets of the historic center are laid out in an easy-to-navigate grid pattern. As in other Mexican cities, street names change depending on geographical orientation to the main plaza. The principal north-south thoroughfare is called Avenida Insurgentes south of the plaza and General M. Utrilla north of it; Calle Madero, the principal east-west thoroughfare, becomes Diego Mazariegos west of the plaza. Similarly, north-south Avenida 16 de Septiembre changes to Crescencio Rosas south of the plaza; east-west Calle M.A. Flores is named 5 de Febrero west of the plaza.

Opposite the plaza's northwest corner on Avenida 16 de Septiembre is the Museum of Jade (Museo del Jade), which exhibits jewelry and reproductions of Olmec carvings. The highlight is a painstaking replica of the sarcophagus lid from the tomb of King Pacal, the ruler of Palenque for more than 70 years.

Three blocks south of the plaza, just off Avenida Miguel Hidalgo, is the 1587 Church of El Carmen (Templo del Carmen); a street passes through the middle of its four-story arch. Crowning one of the rolling hills east of the center of town (about 7 blocks east of the plaza via Calle Real de Guadalupe) is the Church of the Virgin of Guadalupe. The view from the top takes in the entire city.

Surrounding the downtown core is a patchwork quilt of neighborhoods *(barrios)* that originally developed around specific trades—carpenters, blacksmiths, candle makers. Today *ladinos*—Mexicans of non-Indian descent—live in these neighborhoods, where the one-story, pastel-colored stucco houses have red-tiled roofs and windows are grilled with wrought iron.

Mex. 190, the Pan-American Highway, runs through the southern part of town on its way to the Guatemalan border. The official name is Boulevard Juan Sabines, but it's known locally as "El Bulevar."

Dining, Nightlife and Events

Chiapanecan cuisine incorporates such reliable Mexican standbys as *tamales,* enchiladas and tacos, although they're often enhanced with distinctively flavored herbs and hot sauces. A popular local beverage is *atole,* a lightly sweetened drink made from cornmeal, and vendors outside the cathedral sell corn on the cob and other snacks from their carts. San Cristóbal restaurants also offers numerous vegetarian options.

El Fogón de Jovel, a block west of the main plaza at Av. 16 de Septiembre #11 (at Calle Guadalupe Victoria), has a courtyard and live music, all the better to enjoy such specialties as chicken in *pipián,* a traditional *mole* sauce made from ground pumpkin seeds, chile peppers and other seasonings. Another restaurant close to the main plaza—and a popular local hangout—is Emiliano's Moustache, Calle Crescensio Rosas #7 (at Avenida Mazariegos). The tacos come with various fillings, and tortillas are handmade.

La Paloma, just south of the main plaza at Calle Hidalgo #3, is a hip little cafe with good Mexican choices: quesadillas, *albondigas* (meatballs) in a sauce made from chilies, steak *tampiqueña* with rice, beans and guacamole, and chicken in mushroom sauce *(pollo con huitlacoche y maiz).* For something non-Mexican try Restaurant El Edén, 2 blocks northwest of the main plaza at Calle 5 de Febrero (in the Hotel El Paraíso). The menu features Swiss-inspired dishes, including raclette (melted cheese draped over potatoes) and fondue.

Businesses on Real de Guadalupe cater to tourists, and this also is a convenient place to have breakfast. Cafetería del Centro has two locations on the street, one a block east of the main plaza, where you can fuel up on eggs, tortillas, toast, jam, fruit juice and coffee. La Casa del Pan, Calle Dr. Navarro #10 at Avenida Belisario Domínguez (near the Temple and Ex-Convent of Santo Domingo), emphasizes healthy vegetarian dishes made with regionally grown grains and beans. The bread is fresh-baked, and the coffee is a good reason to linger. The shop in the restaurant sells organic coffee beans, raw chocolate and other local products.

Hotel bars and several nightclubs, all in the historic downtown area, offer live music ranging from salsa and jazz to reggae, rock and cover versions of old top 40 hits. The choice is greatest on weekends, but there is something going on almost every night of the week. Musicians play most evenings at El Cocodrilo, in the Hotel Santa Clara (on Avenida Insurgentes across from the south side of the main plaza). Latino's, a block east of the main plaza at Av. Francisco I. Madero #23, features Latin music. Just east of the plaza on Madero is Las Velas, where raucous rock bands attract a young crowd of locals and visiting tourists.

San Cristóbal's Spring Fair (Feria de la Primavera y de la Paz) takes place the week after Easter. The festivities include parades, bullfights, band concerts, handicraft exhibits, amusement rides and stalls serving an array of regional foods.

The Feast of San Cristóbal, held July 17-25, honors the town's patron saint. Pilgrims carrying torches climb the steep hill to the Church of San Cristóbal *(see attraction listing)* to attend special services. Chiapanecos also celebrate—along with the rest of Mexico—the Days of the Dead Nov. 1 and 2, the Feast Day of the Virgin of Guadalupe Dec. 12 and celebrations of Jesus' birth during the Christmas season.

The Indian village of San Juan Chamula is noted for its religious observances, particularly those celebrated during Holy Week (between Palm Sunday and Easter Sunday). A blend of Christian and pagan rites, the ceremonies take place both inside the village church and on the plaza in front of it. On June 24, a Catholic priest visits the village to baptize newborn children.

Carnaval celebrations, featuring a parade of vivid costumes, are held just before Lent. The Feast of St. John the Baptist (San Juan Bautista), the patron saint of San Juan Chamula, is observed June 22-25 with much merriment.

Nearby Destinations

The ethnic peoples populating the nearby communities north of San Cristóbal are among the most resilient in the country. They have managed to maintain their cultural identity over hundreds of years and also in the face of drastic modernization. Although almost all are members of the Tzeltal, Tzotzil and Chamula tribes, the more than 80,000 inhabitants of these mountain villages retain a striking variety of differences in manner of dress, dialect, and religious customs and ceremonies.

Among the handicrafts produced by village artisans are wooden musical instruments, leather goods, ceramics, furniture and woven baskets. The best time to visit is during a fiesta or on Sunday morning, when most of the villages have their own market and tourists are most welcomed.

Daily dress varies according to the village. In San Juan Chamula, men wear short or long white trousers secured by a leather belt and a black, gray or white wool *jorongo* (a sort of sleeveless tunic). Standard garb for women, regardless of the village, is the *huipil* (a white blouse with colorful embroidery), a black wool skirt and a blue or red shawl. Village leaders can be recognized by their somewhat more elaborate costumes, which often feature a woven straw hat brimming with colorful ribbons.

Men frequently leave the villages to find work; women tend to the cornfields, take care of the children and run the market stalls. You'll often see women trudging up and down hills bent under a load of firewood, which is balanced on their backs with the aid of a strap fitted across the forehead.

San Juan Chamula, about 10 kilometers (6 miles) northwest of San Cristóbal via a paved road, is the best-known village. Spanish is not spoken, and English is rarely heard. Daily life centers on the town church (Iglesia de San Juan Bautista) and its religious rituals, which are a fascinating blend of Christian and non-Christian. The church is named for St. John the Baptist, a religious figure who in this region takes precedence over Jesus Christ.

The white stucco structure, which stands next to the main plaza, has a beautifully carved wooden door. Inside the dimness is illuminated by a sea of flickering candles, the tile floor is strewn with pine needles and the smell of incense wafts throughout. There are no pews; people sit on the floor. Statues of saints line the walls, swaddled in layers of brightly colored cloth. While worshipers chant and pray in front of these statues, they figure in church rituals in name only; Catholicism is not observed by the villagers.

You must obtain a 10-peso ticket (about 90c U.S.) to enter the church; tickets are available at the local tourist office on the main plaza. Visitors may stand and observe quietly in the background while prayer or curing rituals are being performed, which often involve rubbing the bodies of the sick with eggs or chicken bones. People also drink from bottles of Coca-Cola—the resultant burping is thought to expel evil spirits from the body—and some imbibe *posh,* a more potent beverage made from fermented sugarcane. Photography is strictly forbidden. Do not wear a hat inside.

Near the church is Ora Ton, a small museum that displays musical instruments and examples of traditional clothing. The ticket allowing admittance to the church includes admission to the museum.

Zinacantán is about 11 kilometers (7 miles) northwest of San Cristóbal; the road to this village forks west off the road to San Juan Chamula and descends into a valley. It's a bit more prosperous than Chamula; villagers' clothing often incorporates the colors pink and purple and is adorned with tassels. Zinacantán's side-by-side churches also have floors covered in pine needles, but the rituals here incorporate Catholicism to a greater degree. Photography, both inside and out, is strictly prohibited, and you may be escorted in rather than being allowed to enter on your own. A small fee also is charged.

Unless you feel comfortable assimilating into an unfamiliar culture, a guided trip is the best way to experience a bit of daily life in these villages. Small group tours with an English-speaking guide depart daily around 10 a.m. from the Na-Bolom Museum *(see attraction listing).* The fee is about $11 (U.S.) per person.

Note: A visit to any local village involves sensitivity and respect, as you are an outsider and may well be made to feel like one. Picture taking is forbidden at most events, particularly so inside churches, and residents may not take kindly to being stared at. Photography of any sort is generally objected to, so keep cameras packed. Youthful vendors in San Juan Chamula, many of whom live in desperate poverty, will hawk tourists aggressively.

Chiapas State Tourism Office (Secretaría de Turismo): Av. Hidalgo #1B, just south of the main plaza. Open Mon.-Sat. 8-8, Sun. 9-2; phone (967) 678-6570. The municipal tourist office is located at the north end of the City Hall (Palacio Municipal) building, on the west side of the main plaza. Open Mon.-Sat. 9-8, Sun. 9-2; phone (967) 678-0665.

Check the bulletin board at the municipal tourist office for notices pertaining to cultural events and guided tours, and at each office about arranging excursions to points of interest in and around San Cristóbal. There usually is at least one English-speaking staff member on hand at each office.

Shopping areas: The Municipal Market, 8 blocks north of the main plaza between avenidas General M. Utrilla and Belisario Domínguez, spreads out over blocks and is worth visiting just to observe the colorfully attired merchants and customers. It's open every day but Sunday, when the local village markets take over; Saturday morning is the best time to visit. Produce, flower stands, Chiapan coffee beans and household items dominate the open-air portion; butcher stalls are within the covered section. Be very discreet about taking photographs of vendors or shoppers (or better yet, don't take them at all), and watch out for pickpockets.

If you're searching for handicrafts, try the shops along Calle Real de Guadalupe in the blocks just east of the main plaza. The quality is evident in the lovely woollen shawls, *huipiles* (white cotton dresses embroidered with flower and geometric designs), bolts of fabric, leather goods, woven blankets and amber jewelry. Women and children will often approach tourists on the street selling dolls, bracelets and other handmade items.

The government-run House of Crafts (Casa de las Artesanías), 2 blocks south of the main plaza at Calle Niñoes Héroes and Avenida Hidalgo, stocks a representative selection of woollen vests, embroidered blouses and other clothing, amber jewelry, ceramics and textiles. An exhibition room showcases the native dress of villagers in the surrounding Indian communities.

Sna Jolobil, on Calzada Lázaro Cardenas within the Temple and Ex-Convent of Santo Domingo *(see attraction listing),* is a crafts cooperative run by Tzeltal and Tzotzil Indians, who also handcraft the high-quality merchandise on display. The name means "weaver's house." Another cooperative effort is Taller Leñateros, east of the main plaza at Calle Flavio A. Paniagua #54. In addition to crafts, the workshop—where artisans can be observed on the job—creates ingenious postcards, book binders and writing paper.

La Galeria, Calle Hidalgo #3, spotlights well-known artists and also sells turquoise and silver jewelry. The restaurant above the gallery features live music in the evening.

About 37 kilometers (23 miles) southeast of San Cristóbal via Mex. 190 is the Tzeltal village of Amatenango del Valle, known for its women potters. The pottery is fired by wood rather than in a kiln. You can buy directly from local families, whose wares include simple jugs and pots as well as *animalito* (animal) figures. The women wear *huipiles* embroidered in distinctive red and yellow patterns.

What To See

AMBER MUSEUM (Museo del Ambar) is 4 blks. w. of the main plaza on Av. Diego Mazariegos. Housed in a restored section of the former Ex-Convento de la Merced, this is perhaps the only museum in Mexico devoted to amber, a brownish-yellow, translucent fossil resin that is mined in the nearby Simojovel Valley. On view are sculpted amber pieces carved by local artisans, as well as ancient chunks with fossilized insects inside. Background information is in Spanish.

Tues.-Sun. 10-2 and 4-7. Admission 10 pesos. Phone (967) 678-9716.

CHURCH OF SAN CRISTOBAL (Templo de San Cristóbal) perches atop a hill at the end of Calle Hermanos Domínguez; walk 3 blks. s. of the main plaza along Av. Miguel Hidalgo, then turn right. Although you'll have to climb what seems like an endless series of steps up the hill to reach the church, the view of the city from the lookout point *(mirador)* at the top is worth it.

NA-BOLOM MUSEUM (Casa Na-Bolom) is about 10 blks. n.e. of the main plaza at Av. Vicente Guerrero #33. It celebrates the work of Danish explorer and ethnologist Frans Blom. The colonial-style building, dating from 1891 and now a museum, was purchased by Blom in 1950.

Blom conducted extensive research at the Mayan ruins around Palenque and oversaw some of the first excavations at Uxmal *(see separate listing under Yucatán Peninsula)*. His wife Gertrude, a journalist and photographer, devoted herself to preserving the rain forest homeland of the reclusive Lacandón Indians. Na-Bolom continues to operate as a private, nonprofit institute dedicated to the preservation of the environment and native cultures.

Guided group tours of the home take in a collection of pre-Hispanic artifacts put together by Blom; the library, with thousands of volumes about the Maya and Chiapas; a walk through the extensive gardens; and a showing of the film "La Reina de la Selva," about the Lacandón forest and its inhabitants. Tours in English are offered Tues.-Sun. at 11:30 and 4:30. Tour fee about $5 U.S. Phone (967) 678-1418.

TEMPLE AND EX-CONVENT OF SANTO DOMINGO is about 5 blks. n. of the main plaza, entered from Av. 20 de Noviembre. Construction of the church was begun in 1547; the extravagantly detailed carvings of saints, angels and decorative accents on its baroque exterior have weathered to a dusty pink. Note the double-headed Hapsburg eagle over the doorway, a symbol of the Spanish monarchy added in the 17th century. The interior features a lavishly ornate pulpit, a gilded altarpiece and gilt-framed *retablos* (religious paintings).

The adjacent convent houses Sna Jolobil, a handicraft showroom selling wool capes, clothing, woven goods and other Indian-made items. Church complex open Tues.-Sun. 10-5. Showroom open Tues.-Sat. 9-2 and 4-7. Church admission free.

Altos Cultural Center (Centro Cultural de Los Altos) is within the church complex. This museum (the name means "highlands") has displays pertaining to San Cristóbal and Mayan history as well as changing cultural exhibits, with rooms set around a courtyard overlooked by wide balconies. Background information is in Spanish. Tues.-Sun. 10-5. Admission 30 pesos (about $2.90 U.S.).

TAXCO, GUERRERO (C-2)

pop. 51,500, elev. 5,897′

See map page 396.

Probably the oldest mining town in North America, Taxco (TAHS-coh) originated as the Indian village of Tlachco (meaning "place of ball game") when Hernando Cortés' captains discovered rich gold deposits. The restored Hacienda del Chorrillo, where they handled smelted silver shipments, is now the governor's guest house and can be visited. Bermeja Hill still bears the scar of a cavernous mining shaft called the King's Shaft, reputed to be the oldest on the continent. The town's real development dates from the time of José de la Borda, a French miner who arrived in 1716 and amassed an immense fortune.

Borda's initial impact on the mining industry was carried on by a young American named William Spratling, who came to Taxco in 1929 to write a book. Stranded in Mexico after his publisher went broke, Spratling turned to the silver business. He opened a retail outlet and found apprentices among the local youth, many of whom went on to become proprietors of Taxco's silver shops.

Plaza Borda, Taxco's main square, is typical of those in other old Mexican towns, shaded by trees, offering benches for relaxation and providing a bandstand for musical performances. The shops in and around the plaza specialize in silver, and shopping for it is undoubtedly the most popular tourist activity in town. The range of items in Taxco's more than 300 silver shops covers everything from inexpensive trinkets to artistic pieces selling for hundreds of dollars.

The price of most pieces is determined primarily by weight, and many shops sell both retail *(menudeo)* and wholesale *(mayoreo)*. Always check for the stamp bearing the numerals ".925," which certifies that it is at least 92.5 percent sterling silver, and for the two-letter initials signifying the manufacturer. If you're looking for items at the less expensive end of the scale, try the Silver Market (Mercado de Artesanías Plata), a block or so southeast of Plaza Borda; the stalls here carry a huge selection of rings, chains and other jewelry.

Much pageantry is associated with Holy Week (Semana Santa). On Palm Sunday an image of Christ on a donkey departs the nearby village of Tehuilotepec, east of town, for a processional to Taxco. Candlelit processions by *penitentes* take place nightly, culminating on Holy Thursday, when the Last Supper is staged in front of the Church of Santa Prisca *(see attraction listing)*. The Resurrection re-enactment takes place on Saturday evening, and another processional occurs on Easter Sunday. If you plan on being in town during Holy Week, make hotel reservations in advance.

The weeklong National Silver Fair (Feria Nacional de la Plata), held the last week in November or the first week in December, is Mexico's most important silversmithing contest. Each year judges confer international recognition to artisans whose designs and workmanship are deemed superior.

Another annual event of interest to visitors is Alarcón Days (Jornadas Alarconianas). This cultural and artistic festival offers painting expositions, band serenades in Plaza Borda and musical performances during the last three weekends in May; check with the State Tourism Office *(see below)* for exact dates. Presentations of plays by Juan Ruiz de Alarcón, a Taxco native born of noble Spanish parentage who wrote his works during the same period as Miguel de Cervantes, are given in plazas and city streets.

Steep, narrow roads, infrequent street name designations and many one-way streets make driving in Taxco difficult. Walking is the best way to explore. *Combis* are a convenient and inexpensive means of local transportation; rides in these white Volkswagen minibuses are about 30c (U.S.) in town. Taxi fares in town average about $1.50; taxis also are available for visiting points of interest in the surrounding area.

"Tour guides" will eagerly approach visitors around Plaza Borda. Ask to see their credentials, and beware of freelance guides who are not federally licensed or government sponsored. The State Tourism Office can recommend a reliable licensed guide. The Hotel Loma Linda, at the southern end of town at Av. de Los Plateros #52, organizes city walking tours; for information phone (762) 622-0206 or (762) 622-0753.

Malasia Tours, a local travel agency, offers guided tours to Cacahuamilpa Caves National Park *(see attraction listing)* and the Xochicalco Ruins *(see Cuernavaca listing under Mexico City and Vicinity)*. The agency is located at Plazuela de San Juan #5; phone (762) 622-3808 (English spoken).

Guerrero State Tourism Office (Secretaría de Fomento Turístico): Av. J.F. Kennedy #1 (Mex. 95), at the north end of town where the aqueduct arches cross the highway. Open daily 9-8; phone (762) 622-6616.

CACAHUAMILPA CAVES NATIONAL PARK (Parque Nacional Grutas de Cacahuamilpa) is at the intersection of Mex. 166 and Mex. 55, about 32 km (20 mi.) n.e. of Taxco. Spelunkers have burrowed more than 8 miles through the passageways of Grutas de Cacahuamilpa (kah-kah-wah-MEEL-pah) and still haven't reached the end. About half a mile of

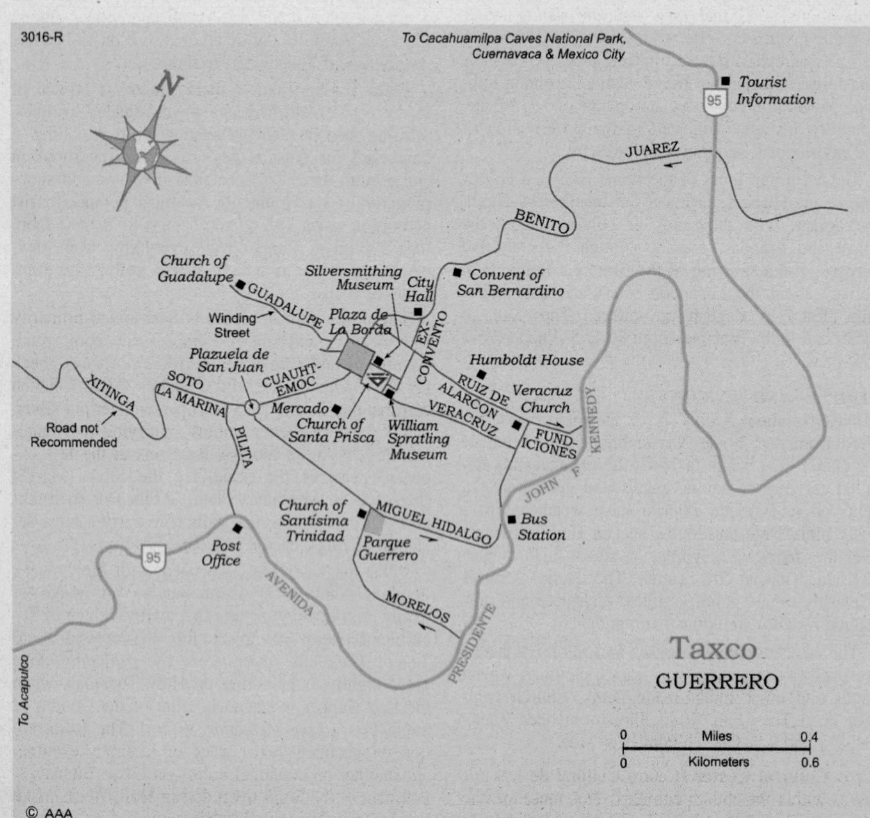

the vast labyrinth can be viewed from wide, paved pathways.

Huge chambers—100 feet high, 200 feet long and nearly as wide—hold an array of fantastic formations, some of which are enhanced by lighting. Comfortable walking shoes are recommended. Spanish-speaking guides lead regularly scheduled, 90-minute tours of the caverns. Daily 10-6. Admission about $3.50 (U.S.), about $2.25 (children).

GEM **CHURCH OF SANTA PRISCA** (Iglesia de Santa Prisca) faces the main square. It was funded by José de la Borda in gratitude for his good fortune in mining. Begun in 1751 and completed 7 years later, the church has a beautifully carved facade with twin 130-foot spires flanking a tiled dome. The interior is even more elaborate, a breathtaking profusion of gold-leaf saints and cherubs, 12 highly decorated altars and lovely paintings by Miguel Cabrera, one of Mexico's most celebrated colonial-era artists; Borda spared no expense in making this a beautifully appointed church.

Guides approach visitors outside offering tours. For a few pesos you'll receive some enlightening background information, but determine whether the fee applies to an individual or group tour and make sure the guide speaks understandable English. Allow 1 hour minimum. Daily 6:30 a.m.-8 p.m. Free. Phone (762) 622-0184.

CONVENT OF SAN BERNARDINO is off Plaza del Convento. It was founded in 1592. The Plan of Iguala was drafted here in 1821 by Agustín de Iturbide, a pivotal character in the battle for Mexican independence from Spain. The plan drew the various Mexican social classes into the freedom movement, consolidating previously ineffective efforts. Mexico finally achieved independence several months later.

HUMBOLDT HOUSE (Casa Humboldt) is at Calle Juan Ruíz de Alarcón #12. It dates from the 16th century. German naturalist Baron Alexander von Humboldt spent the night in April 1803 while on a scientific journey that included South America and Cuba, hence the name. The restored house, boasting a rich Moorish facade, has also served as a convent, hospital and Taxco's first movie theater. It now houses the Museum of Viceregal Art (Museo de Arte Virreinal), which displays a small but interesting collection of religious paintings.

Tues.-Sat. 10-6. Admission about $1.75 (U.S.). Phone (762) 622-5501.

SILVERSMITHING MUSEUM (Museo de la Platería) is in the Patio de las Artesanías building on Plaza Borda, next to the Church of Santa Prisca; after entering turn left, go down the hallway and then down the stairs. It houses a collection of exquisite silver items that have won prizes in national contests, and seeing them may whet your appetite to do some shopping. Exhibit information is in Spanish. Tues.-Sun. 10-5:30. Admission about $1.50 (U.S.).

WILLIAM SPRATLING MUSEUM (Museo Guillermo Spratling) is directly behind the Church of Santa Prisca at Av. Porfirio A. Delgado #1. On display are pre-Columbian art and artifacts, many from Spratling's private collection. Tues.-Sat. 9-6, Sun. 9-3. Admission about $3.50 (U.S.), free (ages 0-12).

TLACOLULA, OAXACA (C-3) pop. 11,400

Tlacolula (tlah-coh-LOO-lah), dating from around 1250, is an important market center for the surrounding Indian communities and the area's mezcal and castor oil producers. Its 16th-century *mudéjar* (Moorish-style) chapel is one of the most ornate in the state of Oaxaca. Known as the Chapel of Silver, it is built of cut stone and decorated with intricate carvings.

Tlacolula's Sunday market is notable for its size and selection, and all kinds of intriguing items turn up among the mundane housewares and utilitarian clothing. In mid-October a regional festival is held, with celebrants dancing from Tlacolula to nearby villages.

YAGUL RUINS are about 2.75 km (1.7 mi.) e. of town on Mex. 190 (Km marker 35.5), then 2 km (1.2 mi.) n. of Mex. 190 via a paved road; watch for the signed turn-off. The ruins, which cover the base and side of a large hill, consist of the Triple Tombs (Tumbas Triples), four patios (one a complex of six separate patios), the Room of Consultations and the Palace of Creatures. Dramatic face carvings guard the entrances to the tombs. The ball court here is large and in excellent condition. A marked path leads to the top of the hill; climb it for views that take in the valley and surrounding mountains.

Allow 2 hours minimum. Daily 8-5:30. Admission 35 pesos (about $3.40 U.S.).

TUXTLA GUTIERREZ, CHIAPAS (C-5) pop. 445,100

Tuxtla Gutiérrez (TOOX-tlah goo-TYEH-rehs) replaced San Cristóbal de Las Casas as the capital of the state of Chiapas in 1892. The discovery of vast oil reserves brought an influx of people and wealth to this prosperous commercial hub, which is lower in elevation and therefore steamier than many of the surrounding mountain communities. Tuxtla Gutiérrez also is a distribution point for the region's coffee and tobacco plantations.

Mex. 190 passes through the city; its approach from the west is cluttered with hotels. The hectic downtown area is divided by Avenida Central, the principal thoroughfare, which runs east-west. The main square constitutes two plazas separated by Avenida Central. It is fronted by imposing government buildings, shaded by manicured trees and filled with benches. In the marketplace and in shops near the plaza, such articles as appliqued scarves, gold filigree jewelry, boxes of inlaid wood and brightly painted gourds are sold.

At Blvd. Belisario Domínguez #2035 is the government-run Casa de las Artesanías, which has Chiapan handicrafts on display and for sale. First-class bus service is provided by Autotransportes

Cristóbal Colón. The first-class bus station is 2 blocks west of the main plaza at Avenida 2 Norte and 2 Poniente.

This is Chiapas' economic and transportation center, and there is little for tourists to see. If you're touring this part of Mexico, however, you may need to spend the night here. The surrounding countryside is noted for lush scenery, including mountains, canyons, forests and such waterfalls as El Chorreadero.

Chiapas State Tourism Office (Secretaría de Turismo): in the western part of the city at Blvd. Belisario Domínguez #950 (in the Plaza de las Instituciones building); phone (961) 602-5299 or 01 (800) 280-3500 (toll-free long distance within Mexico).

SUMIDERO CANYON (Cañon del Sumidero), about 23 km (14 mi.) n. of the city, is reached by a paved mountain road. It features five different lookout points that provide spectacular views of the canyon's sheer walls as they plunge to the Río Grijalva below. Boat tours can be arranged in the town of Chiapa de Corzo, east of Tuxtla Gutiérrez, to observe not only the canyon's gaping cliffs but the river's murky green waters and the surrounding forest's alligators, exotic birds and colorful butterflies.

ZOOMAT (Zoológico Miguel Alvarez del Toro) is about 8 km (5 mi.) s.e. of downtown; a taxi ride is about $3 (U.S.). This is one of Mexico's most noteworthy zoos. On exhibit is an impressive collection of more than 150 animal species native to Chiapas, including monkeys, tapirs, toucans, anteaters, eagles, boa constrictors, iguanas, scorpions and jaguars. The animals are housed in simulated habitats so roomy they appear to roam free through the lush vegetation. Tues.-Sun. 8:30-5. Admission 20 pesos (about $1.95 U.S.).

VERACRUZ, VERACRUZ (B-3)

pop. 544,800, metro area 607,000

Veracruz (veh-rah-CROOS) has traditionally served as a doorway leading to the heart of Mexico as well as Mexico's gateway to the world. Its long history has been a tumultuous one, inextricably tied to the fortunes and misfortunes of Spain's presence in the New World and enduring the suffering borne out of conquest, war and subjugation. That Veracruz not only survived but blossomed into the festive, culturally vibrant city it is today is no small feat.

From around 800 to 400 B.C.—more than 2,000 years before the 1519 arrival of Spaniard Hernando Cortés—the Olmecs had created the first advanced civilization in Mesoamerica, an area archeologists designate as stretching from Mexico's central plateau south to Costa Rica. Olmec culture particularly flourished along the Gulf of Mexico coast in what is now the states of Veracruz and Tabasco. Little is known about the people, although they did produce an early calendar, developed a written language and

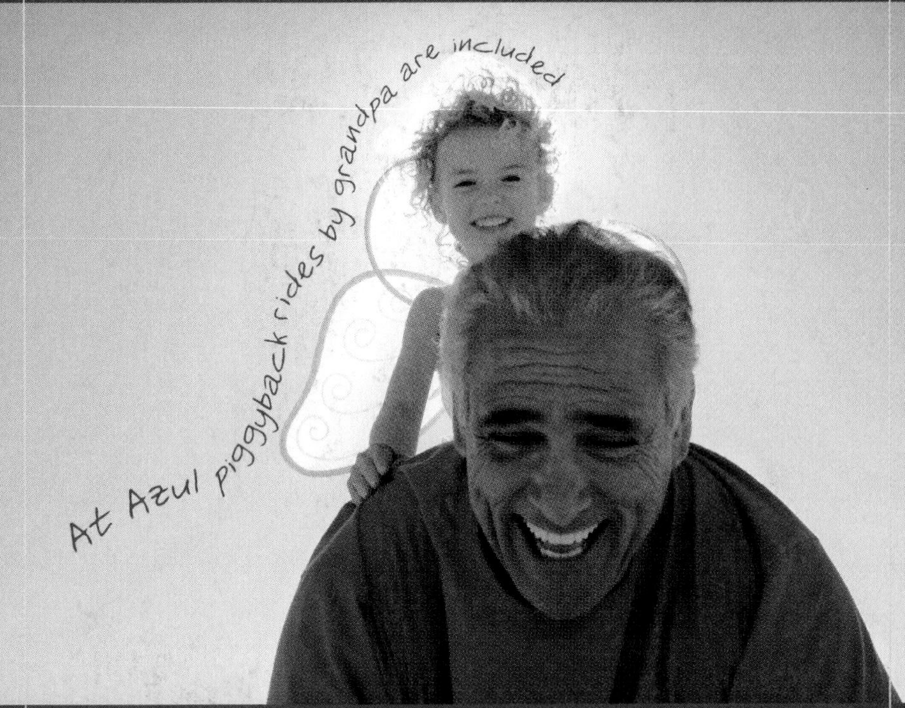

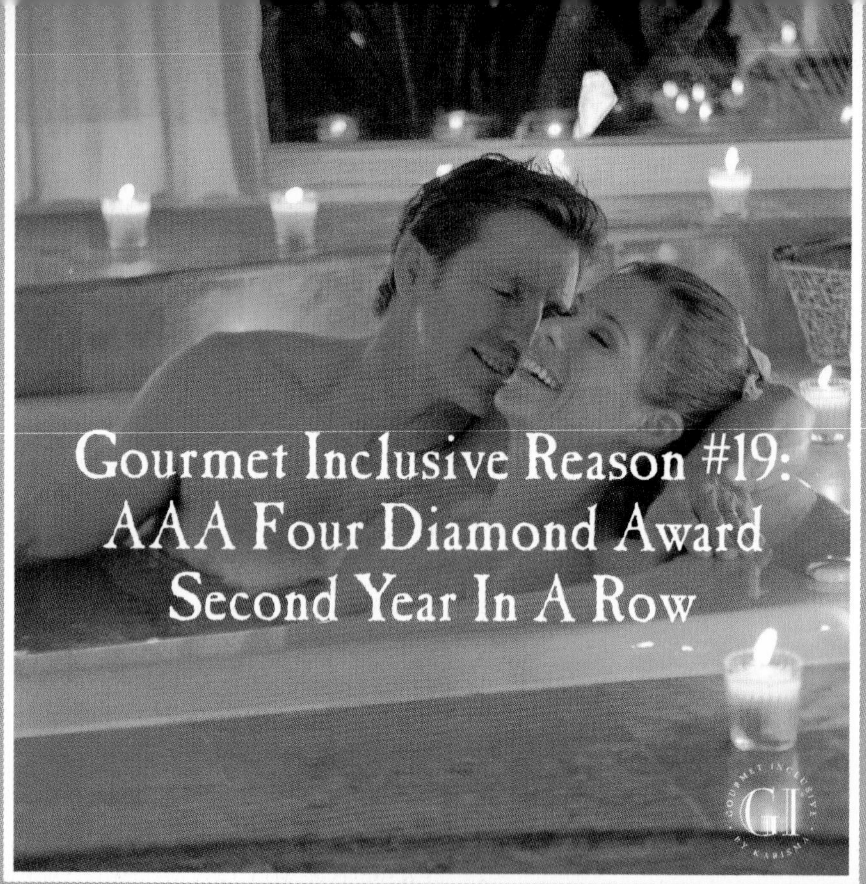

carved monumental stone heads with features that resembled both a jaguar and a human infant.

Later the coast was inhabited by other pre-Hispanic cultures, primarily the Totonac Indians. By the late 15th and early 16th centuries Spanish explorers were beginning to make inroads, discovering Caribbean islands and points along the North and South American coasts. In 1518 Juan de Grijalva explored the Mexican coastline from the Yucatán Peninsula west to the vicinity of Veracruz. He was followed by Hernando Cortés.

Cortés was a 34-year-old colonist and landowner living in Cuba. In 1519 he set out on an expedition to conquer this uncharted territory, no doubt intrigued by tales of fabulous riches waiting to be plundered. His expedition party—several hundred Spanish soldiers, gunpowder, horses and a contingent of Cuban Indians to bear supplies—landed on the little island of San Juan de Ulúa, in the harbor along which Veracruz later was established.

Cortés founded the first Spanish settlement in México a bit farther up the coast at La Antigua *(see attraction listing)* before marching inland to the Aztec capital of Tenochtitlan and launching the brutal military campaign that resulted in the colonization of the continental Americas. The name he bestowed upon Veracruz—La Villa Rica de la Vera Cruz (Rich Town of the True Cross)—turned out to be prophetic, as the port soon became the main point of departure for Spanish galleons loaded with silver from Mexican mines.

From the beginning Veracruz was bedeviled by pirate raids. Celebrated English privateer John Hawkins met his only defeat here in 1568; attempting to sell slaves in defiance of the Spanish trade monopoly, his powerful fleet was thwarted by a surprise attack. Hawkins' nephew sir Francis Drake was aboard one of two ships that escaped; he went on to a swashbuckling career raiding Spanish ships. One of the most vicious pirate attacks occurred in 1683, when the city was looted and its citizens terrorized by French buccaneer Laurent de Gaff. The construction of mighty Fort San Juan de Ulúa *(see attraction listing)* was a response to the constant danger.

During the colonial era Veracruz was the point of arrival for African slaves brought to Mexico, served as a supply base for Spain's forays into Florida and weathered rampant epidemics of malaria and yellow fever. Ironically, Spanish rule ended in the city as well: Three centuries after Cortés' landfall, the Spanish flag was lowered at Fort San Juan de Ulúa.

The city's strategic location also destined it to be invaded by foreign powers. After Spain's expulsion, Veracruz was occupied by the French navy in 1838 as a result of the whimsically named Pastry War, which arose from a French baker's demands for restitution after claiming that his Mexico City shop had been looted. When the Mexican president balked at paying the outrageous amount the French king dispatched a fleet to blockade all Mexican ports (war was declared on France as a result).

U.S. forces under Gen. Winfield Scott overtook Veracruz in 1847 on their way to Mexico City during the Mexican-American War; the city was bombarded for a week before it surrendered. In 1862 French, Spanish and British troops occupied Veracruz to enforce payment of debts Mexico owed. Intending to conquer the country, the French forces stayed and marched inland to prepare for the installation of Archduke Maximilian as emperor.

The United States again took over the city in 1914 to protest the actions of the Mexican military under dictator Victoriano Huerta—who had seized the presidency after having President Francisco I. Madero assassinated—and again it played a key role in Mexico's defense. It's little wonder, then, that Veracruz has earned the title *"cuatro veces heroica"* ("four times heroic").

Although this is one of Mexico's most historically significant cities, the sultry, laid-back setting is what really lures vacationers. Mexicans love Veracruz, but it seems to be off the radar of many foreign travelers—which is unfortunate, because there is a seductive charm as well as a bracing energy. You'll feel it just taking a walk along waterfront Paseo de Malecón, where cargo ships, ocean liners and all manner of fishing vessels attest to this seaport's continuing importance.

City Layout

Central Veracruz is fairly compact and easily negotiated, with streets laid out in a grid pattern. Street names often are posted on the corner buildings at intersections. Since it's hard to get lost, seeing the sights on foot can be a leisurely affair—and you'll want to take it easy from April through October, which is hot and humid. The city also tends to get lots of rain during these months, so an umbrella is a handy item to bring along.

A logical starting point is Plaza de Armas (also called the *Zócalo*). Veracruz's main square is the city's hub and one of the oldest Spanish plazas in North America. Facing its east side is the 17th-century City Hall (Palacio Municipal). On the south side stands the Cathedral (Catedral de Nuestra Señora de la Asunción), built in 1721, which has a loudly tolling bell tower.

Palm trees and black and white-tiled walkways give the plaza an appropriately tropical look, and the arched arcades, or *portales,* are a distinctive Spanish touch. The arches shelter a series of open-air cafes that are popular places to meet and socialize over coffee in the morning, but it's evenings—after the sun has set and the heat takes a bit of a breather—that the plaza really starts to hum. Vendors hawk their wares and bars offer the regional libation *menjulep,* rum and vermouth mixed with sugar and crushed mint leaf.

Veracruz's coastal location gives it an appropriately maritime air, and nowhere is this more evident than along the seawall *(malecón),* a promenade that runs east from Plaza de Armas, hugging the harbor before turning south to follow the gulf shore. Lined with benches, it offers views of bustling port activity as well as massive Fort San Juan de Ulúa across the harbor.

The doglegged concrete breakwater piers along the *malecón* are lined with people fishing, their lines wrapped around small pieces of wood. Intertwined couples, families and sailors on shore leave all stroll along the walkway as vendors hawking *volvones* (puff pastry filled with tuna or chopped beef) exuberantly call out *"Guerro!"* or *"Guerra!"* to attract potential customers of both sexes.

Facing the harbor at the corner of avenidas Xicotencatl and Aquiles Serdán is the Carranza Lighthouse (Faro Carranza). Mexican president Venustiano Carranza lived in this ornate-looking building during the drafting of the 1917 Mexican constitution; it now contains naval offices.

Elongated Plaza de la República, just north and west of the *malecón,* also faces the harbor. The public buildings along this plaza include the turn-of-the-19th-century Customs House (Aduana Marítima) and the pastel yellow facades of the main post office and the telegraph office.

Downtown Veracruz has a venerable feel; most of the buildings and churches are more than 150 years old. The city once was surrounded by a defensive wall that incorporated nine fortresses, all protection against pirates. The only one that remains is the Baluarte de Santiago (Santiago Bulwark), on Calle Canal between avenidas Gomez Farías and 16 de Septiembre (about 5 blocks south of the harbor). Standing at what was then the waterfront, it dates from 1635. Inside the remnants of the fortress is a museum displaying a collection of pre-Hispanic gold jewelry. Museum open Tues.-Sun.; admission is charged.

The Fish Market, on Avenida Landero y Cos just north of Avenida Mariano Arista (2 blocks south of the harbor), is two stories tall and covers an entire block. It displays rows and rows of fresh seafood, live crabs with their red claws neatly tied with green seaweed grass and neatly stacked mountains of fish. Food stands offer seafood cocktails *(cócteles)* made with shrimp, oysters or octopus.

Past the *malecón* Boulevard M. Avila Camacho continues on to Playa Villa del Mar, about 4 kilometers (2.5 miles) south of downtown Veracruz. This and the other beaches closest to the city are not the stuff of tourist brochures; the sand is a brownish color and the gulf water is a dull green rather than an inviting turquoise. During the week fishermen mend nets or make repairs to their boats. On weekends the pace is livelier, with families getting together, vendors selling fresh seafood and cold beer, and a backdrop of almost nonstop band music.

En route to Playa Villa del Mar on Boulevard Camacho (at the Plaza Acuario Mall) is the Veracruz Aquarium (Acuario de Veracruz). A large, doughnut-shaped viewing tank contains sea turtles, rays, sharks, barracudas and other marine creatures, while smaller tanks display species found in the gulf waters. There also is a manatee exhibit. Open daily; admission is charged. Phone (229) 932-7984.

Music, Dance and Cuisine

Veracruzans, descended from hardy seafaring stock, are electric with life, passion and happiness. And since this is a fiercely cultural city, artistic expression—most notably in the form of music and dance—is as much a part of the city's character as the balmy breezes blowing off the gulf.

Music is a major contributor to the Veracruz scene. "La Bamba"—popularized by Hispanic pop singer Ritchie Valens in 1959 and remade into an even bigger hit in 1987 by the East Los Angeles band Los Lobos—is actually a Veracruzan folk song. Music also underscores this region's African, Cuban, Spanish and Indian roots.

Plaza de Armas is the site of strolling mariachi players, frequent band concerts and string trios playing guitar, harp and *jarana,* a guitar-shaped, five-stringed instrument unique to the Veracruz region. In addition to the ubiquitous mariachis, you're likely to hear the lilting sound of the marimba (a relative of the xylophone), which has wooden keys that the musicians deftly strike with mallets.

The *son jarocho* is quintessentially Veracruzan. Set to a fast, syncopated percussion beat, it features a vigorous strumming of stringed instruments accented by a rhythmically pounded tambourine. The accompanying dance steps are a fandango-derived staccato movement of the heels known as *zapateado. Son jarocho* originated in the 17th and 18th centuries during a time when slaves were imported for plantation agriculture, and many *jarocho* musicians today are of African-Mexican heritage.

A more refined dance is the *danzón,* a Cuban import that itself was influenced by European ballroom dancing. Less frenetic than the *son jarocho,* it features more gliding movements as the partners promenade arm in arm and women wave their fans—maneuvers that don't work up as much of a sweat in this hot and humid city. On Wednesday and Sunday evenings you can see everyone from young children to elderly couples dance the *danzón* at Zamora Park (Parque Zamora), about 7 blocks inland from the waterfront between avenidas Independencia and 5 de Mayo.

The state of Veracruz is known for good coffee, and rival establishments within several blocks of each other are two of the best places to sample the brew. The Gran Café de la Parroquia, on Paseo del Malecón just west of Avenida 16 de Septiembre, is a Veracruz institution that faces the bustling harbor. This huge, white-tiled space is especially popular for breakfast, which you should accompany with a *café con leche* served in a tall glass. A concentrated shot of inky black coffee is augmented by hot milk, which the waiters pour with great flair from silver kettles. For a refill, simply clink your spoon against the glass.

Café con leche also is served at the Gran Café del Portal, on Avenida Independencia across from the southwest corner of Plaza de Armas. (It used to be called the Gran Café de la Parroquia until a change in ownership.) Equally cavernous—it covers a city block—the Portal has more meal choices than the Parroquia, including a very good version of the city's signature dish, *huauchinango a la Veracruzana*. For the best atmosphere try to get a table under one of the namesake arches. In the evening it is almost taken over by strolling mariachis and marimba players.

As delectable as the coffee is Veracruzan cuisine, with its emphasis on fresh seafood. *Salsa Veracruzana*—a piquant combination of tomatoes, chilies, onions, garlic, pimentos, capers and green olives sauteed in olive oil—is a perfect accompaniment to fish (or chicken or pasta, for that matter). Broiled red snapper awash in this sauce is *huachinango a la Veracruzana*, which is on almost every restaurant menu in town.

Specialties like *torta de mariscos* (a fluffy omelet) or *filetes relleno* (stuffed fish filets) have rich fillings of oysters, crab and shrimp enlivened with fresh lime juice and herbs. Plantains, sweet potatoes and peanuts (which were introduced by African slaves) are other essential ingredients in Veracruzan cookery. Peanuts are ground to make sauces for pork or chicken (such as spicy *salsa macha,* which also includes garlic, chilies and olive oil) and even turn up in ice cream. Plantains are fried and served with rice and beans or mashed with garlic and rolled around fillings of cheese or crabmeat.

Nearby Destinations

The gulf beaches become more attractive the farther out of town you go. About 10 kilometers (6 miles) south of downtown via Boulevard Camacho is Playa Mocambo. Beyond Playa Mocambo, at the mouth of the Río Jamapa, is Boca del Río, a small fishing village known for its open-air seafood restaurants.

Drives into the surrounding countryside pass large ranches and pastures, tropical fruit orchards and fields of sugar cane *(see sidebar)*. The change in topography can be dramatic—from mangrove swamps and mazes of lagoons and estuaries to lush, mountainous country ideal for growing coffee.

Toll highway Mex. 150-D west from the gulf coast toward Puebla is a spectacularly scenic drive that begins in flat cane fields and ascends through pine forests to elevations as high as 9,000 feet. The route passes snowcapped Pico de Orizaba, at 18,555 feet Mexico's loftiest peak. Highway conditions are excellent, and there are plenty of gas stations. Quaint hamlets as well as larger cities like Córdoba, Fortín de las Flores and Orizaba offer plenty of opportunities for sightseeing, shopping or just taking in the mountain views.

Events

Veracruz's party of the year is Carnaval. The celebration rivals New Orleans' Mardi Gras in spectacle and enthusiasm, if not in size. The Veracruz version begins with the "burning of ill humor" and concludes with the funeral of Juan Carnaval. Parades wend their way down waterfront Boulevard Avila Camacho during the 9 days prior to Ash Wednesday, replete with lavishly decorated floats and outrageously attired revelers. Other events, including fireworks, folkloric dance shows and plenty of salsa and other music, take place around Plaza de Armas. Local hotels are booked solid for Carnaval, so if you plan on attending make reservations well in advance.

Veracruz State Tourism Office: on the ground floor of City Hall (Palacio Municipal), on the east side of Plaza de Armas. Open Mon.-Sat. 9-8, Sun. 10-6; phone (229) 989-8817 (English may not be spoken).

Shopping areas: The Hidalgo Market (Mercado Hidalgo) is between avenidas Madero and Hidalgo a block west of Zamora Park (about 7 blocks south of the *Zócalo*). This is one of those Mexican markets that is fascinating to wander through for the sheer variety of wares—everything from live parrots to bushels of produce to animal parts guaranteed to induce squirms.

If you're looking for a trinket to take home, the place to go is Paseo del Malecón; the waterfront boulevard is lined with shops and stalls selling every imaginable type of seashell knickknack, along with embroidered blouses, men's *guayabera* shirts—lightweight, short-sleeved garments worn untucked—coral jewelry, crucifixes and of course, T-shirts. Plaza de las Artesanías, on Paseo del Malecón 2 blocks east of Plaza de Armas, has a mix of souvenirs and more high-quality merchandise.

FORT SAN JUAN DE ULUA (Castillo San Juan de Ulúa) is in the harbor on Gallega Island; to get there by car, take the free causeway that runs n. from avs. Morelos and de la República. This massive fort was built by the Spanish to protect their New World interests. Construction began in the 1530s but was not completed until the late 18th century. It later served as a place of incarceration for political prisoners; even Mexican president Benito Juárez was held here. The maze of stairways, ramparts, barracks and dank prison cells can all be explored.

"San Juan de Ulúa" buses depart for the fort from the east side of Plaza de la República, in front of the Customs House. English-speaking guides give tours for a fee. Tues.-Sun. 9-5. Admission about $3.25 (U.S.). Phone (229) 938-5151.

LA ANTIGUA is about 32 km (20 mi.) n. of the city via Mex. 180. This small village, shaded by big trees, was the original site of Veracruz. It contains a ruined 16th-century customs house (Casa de Cortés) as well as the Hermitage (La Ermita del Rosario), reputed to be the oldest church on the American mainland. This is a popular day trip, and there are a couple of small seafood eateries in the vicinity.

NAVAL HISTORY MUSEUM (Museo Histórico Naval) is about 4 blks. s.e. of Plaza de Armas on Calle Arista. This impressively restored late 19th-century building once housed Mexico's naval academy. Displays include model ships, weapons and nautical apparatus, and there are exhibits on the American occupation of Veracruz in 1914 and the history of the naval academy. Exhibit information is in Spanish only. Guided tours are available. Tues.-Sun. 9-5. Free.

VERACRUZ CITY MUSEUM (Museo de la Ciudad de Veracruz) is at Calle Zaragoza #397 at Calle Morales, 5 blks. s. of Plaza de Armas. Exhibits focus on historical and social themes, including slavery, the colonial era and the Revolution of 1910. Exhibit information is in Spanish only. Wed.-Sun. 10-6. Admission about $2.50 (U.S.).

VILLAHERMOSA, TABASCO (C-4)

pop. 342,200, metro area 625,500

Villahermosa (vee-yah-ehr-MOH-sah) was founded in 1519 under the name Santa María de la Victoria. Hernando Cortés established the settlement to commemorate his defeat of an army of Indian warriors who had attacked him during his march toward the Aztec capital of Tenochtitlan. In tribute to their conqueror, the Indians gave Cortés an Indian princess. Baptized Doña Marina, she became Cortés' mistress and trusted translator, an invaluable asset in his conquest of Mexico.

Villahermosa's strategic location on the banks of the navigable Río Grijalva, which flows northward out of rubber, cacao and coffee country, makes it an important distribution center. This river and the Río Usumacinta carry the largest volumes of water in a country not known for extensive river systems.

The 1970s discovery of some of the world's richest oil fields, as well as the development of extensive hydroelectric projects and successful agricultural programs, energized this hot, humid port. Today Villahermosa is a booming business city and the regional hub for Chiapas, Campeche, Tabasco and eastern Veracruz. It also makes a convenient base from which to explore points of interest in these states.

The city's central downtown area of stores, hotels and restaurants is known as the Zona Luz. It extends from Juárez Park (Parque Juárez) south to Plaza de Armas, the main plaza, and is roughly bounded by Avenida Zaragoza on the north, Avenida 5 de Mayo on the west, Avenida Allende on the south and waterfront Calle Madrazo (the *malecón*) on the east. Many of the streets are brick-paved pedestrian malls, closed to traffic.

The newer hotel and shopping district, Tabasco 2000, is about 6 kilometers (4 miles) northwest of the Zona Luz; it can be reached via Avenida Ruiz Cortines (Mex. 180), the main east-west thoroughfare. The wealth generated by oil is evident in this complex's contemporary government buildings, upscale hotels and sleek Galerías Tabasco 2000 mall. The Tabasco 2000 area also has the city's nicest accommodations.

First-class bus service to Campeche, Mérida, Mexico City, Palenque, San Cristóbal de Las Casas, Veracruz and other cities is offered by ADO. The ADO bus terminal is at Calle Javier Mina #297 at Calle Lino Merino, about 10 blocks northwest of the Zona Luz and 3 blocks south of Avenida Ruiz Cortines. Taxi fares within the area encompassing the city center north to Avenida Ruiz Cortines average about $1.50 (U.S.) in shared *colectivo* taxis, about $2 in *especial* taxis. Villahermosa's streets, unlike those in other Mexican cities, are well marked, with arrows indicating the direction of traffic flow—a boon for navigating the hectic, congested downtown area.

West of the city are prosperous cacao plantations and the important archeological site of Comalcalco *(see attraction listing)*. A driving tour of this region reveals lush countryside that contrasts sharply with Mexico's more common arid expanses. Along Mex. 180 toward Cárdenas are masses of banana plants laden with clusters of fruit, which is sold at roadside stands.

Cárdenas itself is a cacao processing center, and some chocolate plantations and factories offer guided tours (check with travel agencies in Villahermosa). The cacao tree grows everywhere; its large, elliptical pods bear the seeds from which cocoa and chocolate are made. The harvesting season is November through April. Small family-run operations throughout this region grow and process cacao beans that end up as boxes of chocolate. You'll also see mounds of the beans for miles along the highway, drying in the sun.

Tabasco State Tourism Office (Subsecretaría de Turismo): Avenida de Los Ríos at the corner of Calle 13 in the Tabasco 2000 complex, past the La Venta Museum and heading west out of downtown. Open Mon.-Fri. 9-3 and 6-8 p.m.; phone (993) 316-5134.

What To See

COMALCALCO RUINS are w. on Mex. 180 to the town of Cárdenas, then n. about 35 km (22 mi.) on Mex. 187 to the town of Comalcalco; the site is about 3 km (2 mi.) farther on the right. There are no informational highway signs en route from Villahermosa; watch for signs in Comalcalco that direct you to the ruins.

This large site consists of several tall pyramids spread out over grassy meadows and small hills. The structures here were constructed of thin, flat bricks called *tabiques*, covered with a plaster made from ground seashells, rather than the stone used elsewhere in pre-Hispanic Mexico. Heed the signs warning *No Subir* (Do Not Climb). A small one-room museum contains carved stone figures.

Descendants of the Chontal Maya, who originally inhabited Comalcalco around A.D. 600-900, still live in the area and earn a livelihood as their ancestors did by processing cacao and raising bananas and other fruits. **Note:** This is one of Mexico's hottest regions; visit early in the day and bring a hat or umbrella as a sunscreen. Daily 9-5. Admission 39 pesos (about $3.80 U.S.), free (ages 0-7).

LA VENTA MUSEUM (Parque Museo La Venta) is w. of downtown off Av. Ruiz Cortines (Mex. 180), just e. of the Tabasco 2000 complex. This open-air park-museum spreads along the shores of man-made Lake of the Illusions (Laguna de las Ilusiones). Its 30 monuments, some weighing as much as 30 tons, were discovered in the late 1930s at the ruins of La Venta, an Olmec ceremonial center in the river country near the Veracruz state line. When oil exploration threatened to destroy the archeological zone, most of the artifacts were transported to this site.

Three colossal stone heads wear war helmets and display the characteristic facial features of Olmec art: wide noses, infantile expressions and full, downward-turning lips resembling the mouth of a jaguar. Other artifacts include sculptures, stone altars, stela (carved stone tablets) and a tomb. All are scattered along a trail through junglelike grounds inhabited by free-roaming monkeys and deer, twittering birds, crocodiles (confined to a moat) and some caged animals.

This lush sanctuary should be toured in the morning before it gets too hot. Insect repellent is strongly advised. Daily 8-4. Admission 39 pesos (about $3.80 U.S.). Phone (993) 314-1652.

GEM **MUSEUM OF ANTHROPOLOGY** (Museo Regional de Antropología) is s. of downtown at Periférico Carlos Pellicer #511, along the w. bank of the Río Grijalva within the Investigation Center for the Olmec and Mayan Cultures, or CICOM (Investigaciones de Culturas Olmeca y Maya).

Exhibit halls contain representative pieces from Teotihuacán and the Aztec, Totonac, Mixtec and Zapotec cultures, as well as artifacts from the states of Nayarit and Colima. Featured are jade, ceramic and clay figurines, stela (carved stone tablets), burial urns and gold objects. Special attention is given to the Olmec and Mayan civilizations. The displays are complemented by photographs and maps of the archeological sites from which they were taken; descriptions are in Spanish. Tues.-Sun. 9-7:30. Admission about $3 (U.S.). Phone (993) 312-6344.

ZEMPOALA, VERACRUZ (B-3)

About 40 kilometers (25 miles) north of Veracruz off Mex. 180, Zempoala (sehm-poh-AH-lah), also known as Cempoala, is the site of remains that once comprised the ceremonial center and fortress of the Totonac Indians. Zempoala was a Classic Period contemporary of El Tajín *(see Papantla)*, although it continued to thrive after the latter's abandonment sometime during the 13th century.

It was here that Hernando Cortés gained the first Indian allies in his 1519 campaign to conquer the Aztecs. The *conquistadores* took note of the city because the white stucco buildings, gleaming in the tropical sun, most likely reminded them of silver. He gained the trust of the Totonac chief (reputedly celebrated for his enormous girth) and his followers, who had been under Aztec rule for the previous 50 years.

ZEMPOALA RUINS are on the northern edge of town. The site is about a 45-minute drive from Veracruz; watch for the sign indicating the Zempoala turn-off about 7 km (4 mi.) n. of the town of Cardel.

Six major structures remain. The Main Temple (Templo Mayor), constructed of riverbed stones, rises on 13 platforms to about 35 feet and probably resembled similar temples in the Aztec capital of Tenochtitlan. The Temple of the Chimneys (Templo de las Chimeneas) derives its name from a series of semicircular pillars. The Little Faces (Las Caritas), a three-story edifice of boulders and cement, is adorned with niches that once contained small carved faces. At the west end of the site is the Great Pyramid (La Gran Pirámide), which has two staircases that climb to a three-level platform.

First-class buses travel regularly from Veracruz north to Cardel; from Cardel, *colectivos* (minivans) or a taxi can take you to the ruins. Daily 9-5. Admission 35 pesos (about $3.40 U.S.).

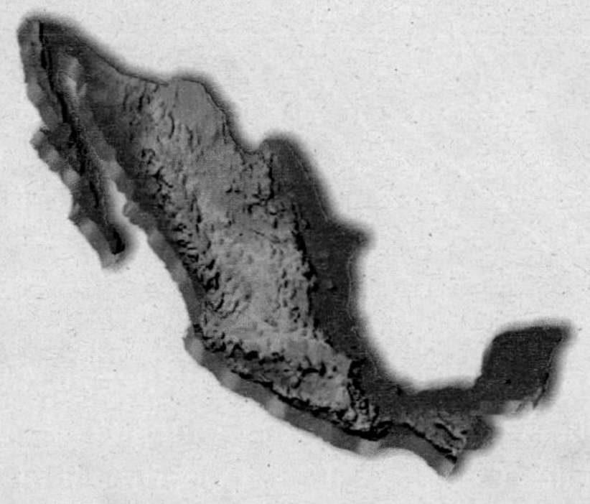

America on the Move is made possible by generous support from General Motors Corporation, AAA, State Farm Companies Foundation, The History Channel, United States Congress, U.S. Department of Transportation, Exxo Mobil, American Public Transportation Association, American Road & Transportation Builders Association, Association of American Railroads, National Asphalt Pavement Association, The UPS Foundation.

Smithsonian
National Museum of American History
Kenneth E. Behring Center
9:51
See how we got here.
Immerse yourself in the newly renovated museum and explore how transportation has changed America. National Museum of American History, Washington, D.C.
http://americanhistory.si.edu/onthemove
AMERIC

Ships' Registry: The Bahamas

Mexico

Xochimilco, Distrito Federal, Mexico City

YUCATAN PENINSULA

AKUMAL, QUINTANA ROO

WHERE TO STAY

The following lodgings were either not evaluated or did not meet AAA rating requirements but are listed for your information only.

BAHIA PRINCIPE AKUMAL **Phone:** 984/875-5000

fyi Not evaluated. **Address:** KM 250 Carr Chetumal, Benito Juarez **Location:** KM 250 Carr Chetumal Benito Juarez Local B. Facilities, services, and decor characterize a mid-scale property.

GRAND OASIS RIVIERA MAYAN **Phone:** 984/875-7300

fyi Not evaluated. **Address:** Carr Chetumal P Juarez KM 25 **Location:** Just w off Mex 307. Facilities, services, and decor characterize an upscale property.

HACIENDA DE LA TORTUGA **Phone:** 984/875-9068

fyi Not evaluated. **Address:** Carr Chetumal P Juarez KM 30. Facilities, services, and decor characterize a mid-scale property.

HOTEL AKUMAL CARIBE **Phone:** 984/206-3500

fyi Not evaluated. **Address:** Carr Chetumal P Juarez KM 21 **Location:** Just e of Mex 307. Facilities, services, and decor characterize an economy property.

VISTA DEL MAR **Phone:** 984/875-9060

fyi Not evaluated. **Address:** Carr Chetumal P Juarez KM 32 **Location:** Just n of city limit. Facilities, services, and decor characterize an economy property.

CAMPECHE, CAMPECHE pop. 216,897

WHERE TO STAY

The following lodgings were either not evaluated or did not meet AAA rating requirements but are listed for your information only.

HACIENDA UAYAMON **Phone:** 198/1829-7527

fyi Not evaluated. **Address:** KM 20 Carr Uayamon-China-Edzna **Location:** In northern Campeche. Facilities, services, and decor characterize an upscale property.

HOTEL DEL MAR **Phone:** 981/811-9191

fyi Not evaluated. **Address:** Ave Ruiz Cortines #51 **Location:** Center; facing the gulf. Facilities, services, and decor characterize a mid-scale property.

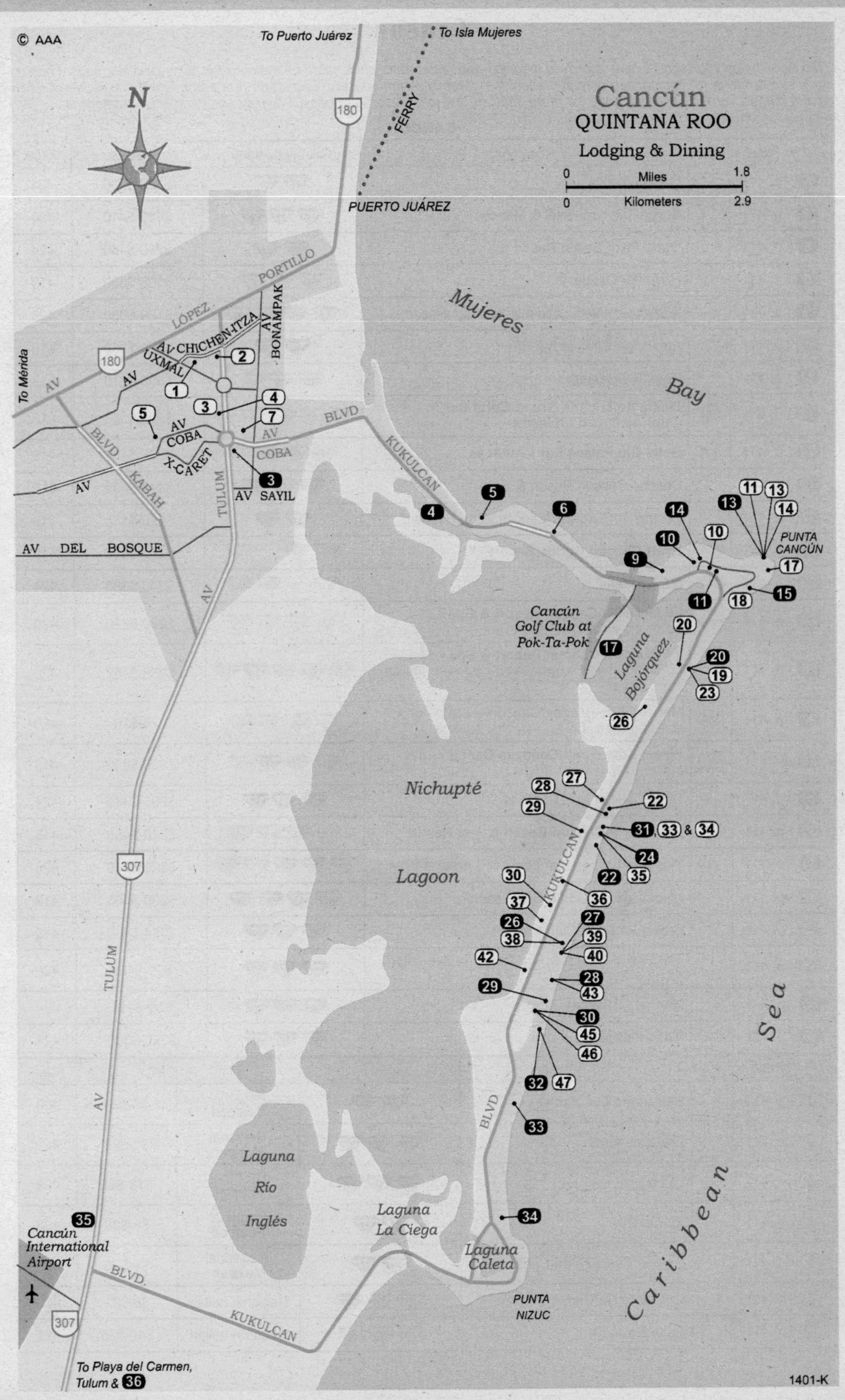
© AAA
To Puerto Juárez
To Isla Mujeres
Cancún
QUINTANA ROO
Lodging & Dining
0 Miles 1.8
0 Kilometers 2.9
FERRY
PUERTO JUÁREZ
N
Mujeres
Bay
PORTILLO
LÓPEZ
AV CHICHEN-ITZA
AV BONAMPAK
UXMAL
AV
To Mérida
AV COBA
X-CARET
BLVD KABAH
AV TULUM
AV SAYIL
AV DEL BOSQUE
BLVD KUKULCAN
PUNTA CANCÚN
Cancún Golf Club at Pok-Ta-Pok
Laguna Bojórquez
Nichupté
Lagoon
Sea
Caribbean
Laguna Río Inglés
Laguna La Ciega
Laguna Caleta
PUNTA NIZUC
Cancún International Airport
To Playa del Carmen, Tulum & 36
1401-K

Cancun

This index helps you "spot" where approved lodgings and restaurants are located on the corresponding detailed maps. Lodging daily rate range is for comparison only and show the property's high season. Restaurant rate range is a combination of lunch and/or dinner. Turn to the listing page for more detailed rate information and consult display ads for special promotions.

CANCUN

Map Page	OA	Lodgings	Diamond Rated	High Season	Page
3 / p. 411		Oasis America	◆◆	$320-$400	424
4 / p. 411		Sunset Lagoon Hotel & Marina	◆◆◆	$280-$410	426
5 / p. 411		Oasis Palm Beach Resort	◆◆	$260-$480	424
6 / p. 411		Hotel Riu Caribe	◆◆◆	$165-$330	419
9 / p. 411		Presidente InterContinental Cancun Resort	◆◆◆◆	$180-$680	426
10 / p. 411		Ambiance Villas at Kin-Ha	◆◆	$220-$360	415
11 / p. 411		Hotel Riu Cancun	◆◆◆	$305-$610	419
13 / p. 411	AAA	**Fiesta Americana Grand Coral Beach** - see color ad p 416, on insert	◆◆◆◆◆	$285-$560	415
14 / p. 411	AAA	**Hotel Riu Palace Las Americas**	◆◆◆◆	$196-$439	419
15 / p. 411		Dreams Cancun Resort & Spa	◆◆◆	$310-$495	415
17 / p. 411		Holiday Inn Express Cancun Zona Hotelera	◆◆	$120-$150	419
20 / p. 411	AAA	**Hyatt Cancun Caribe Resort**	◆◆◆◆	$119-$538	419
22 / p. 411	AAA	**ME by Melia**	◆◆◆◆	$240-$380	424
24 / p. 411	AAA	**Le Meridien Cancun Resort & Spa** - see color ad p 421, on insert	◆◆◆◆	$280-$620	420
26 / p. 411	AAA	**JW Marriott Cancun Resort & Spa** - see color ad inside front cover, opposite inside front cover	◆◆◆◆◆	$256-$462	420
27 / p. 411	AAA	**Marriott CasaMagna Cancun** - see color ad starting on p 422	◆◆◆◆	$174-$267	420
28 / p. 411	AAA	**Fiesta Americana Condesa Cancun** - see color ad p 418, on insert	◆◆◆◆	$230-$340	415
29 / p. 411		Omni Cancun Hotel & Villas	◆◆◆	$295-$485	424
30 / p. 411	AAA	**Gran Melia Cancun Beach & Spa Resort**	◆◆◆◆	$240-$450	415
31 / p. 411	AAA	**The Ritz-Carlton Cancun** - see color ad p 4	◆◆◆◆◆	$329-$748	426
32 / p. 411		Hilton Cancun Golf & Spa Resort	◆◆◆◆	$230-$465	419
33 / p. 411		Crown Paradise Club Cancun	◆◆◆	$384-$450	415
34 / p. 411		The Westin Resort & Spa Cancun - see color ad on insert	◆◆◆	$99-$459	426
35 / p. 411		Marriott Courtyard Cancun	◆◆◆	$99-$115	424
36 / p. 411		Moon Palace - see color ad on insert	◆◆◆	$380-$390	424

Map Page	OA	Restaurants	Diamond Rated	Cuisine	Meal Range	Page
1 / p. 411		Restaurant El Calamar	◆◆	Regional Seafood	$8-$20	430
2 / p. 411		Los Almendros	◆◆◆	Regional Mexican	$7-$28	429
3 / p. 411		La Habichuela	◆◆◆	Regional Mexican	$18-$35	429
4 / p. 411		El Pescador	◆◆	Regional Seafood	$8-$28	428
5 / p. 411		Pericos Restaurante-Cantina	◆◆	Traditional Mexican	$8-$35	430
7 / p. 411		La Dolce Vita Centro	◆◆◆	Regional Italian	$8-$21	429
10 / p. 411		Casa Rolandi's	◆◆◆	Northern Italian	$10-$25	427

Map Page	OA	Restaurants (cont'd)	Diamond Rated	Cuisine	Meal Range	Page
11 / p. 411		Le Basilic	◆◆◆◆◆	Regional Mediterranean	$23-$35	429
13 / p. 411		Isla Contoy	◆◆◆	Regional Caribbean	$18-$45	428
14 / p. 411		La Joya Restaurant	◆◆◆◆	New Mexican	$30-$50	429
17 / p. 411		Paloma Bonita	◆◆◆	Regional Mexican	$15-$38	430
18 / p. 411		Hacienda El Mortero Restaurante	◆◆◆	Mexican	$18-$40	428
19 / p. 411		Cafe Cocay	◆◆◆	Regional International	$5-$22	427
20 / p. 411		Lorenzillo's	◆◆◆	Seafood	$12-$50	429
22 / p. 411		Ruth's Chris Steak House	◆◆◆	Steak	$30-$60	430
23 / p. 411		Blue Bayou	◆◆◆	Regional International	$18-$30	427
26 / p. 411		La Madonna	◆◆◆	Italian	$15-$55	429
27 / p. 411	AAA	**La Casa de Las Margaritas Restaurant**	◆◆◆	Mexican	$14-$37	428
28 / p. 411		Cenacola Il Ristorante Italiano	◆◆◆	Italian	$14-$22	427
29 / p. 411		La Destileria	◆◆◆	Mexican	$8-$14	428
30 / p. 411		Puerto Madero Steakhouse and Fish Marina	◆◆◆	International	$18-$46	430
33 / p. 411	AAA	**The Club Grill**- see color ad p 4	◆◆◆◆◆	International	$35-$49	427
34 / p. 411	AAA	**Fantino**- see color ad p 4	◆◆◆◆◆	Mediterranean	$43-$80	428
35 / p. 411	AAA	**Aioli**	◆◆◆◆	Regional Mediterranean	$10-$65	427
36 / p. 411		Crab House Restaurant & Bar	◆◆	Regional Seafood	$10-$30	427
37 / p. 411		La Dolce Vita	◆◆◆	Italian	$12-$28	429
38 / p. 411		Gustino Italian Beachside Grill	◆◆◆◆	Regional Italian	$20-$50	428
39 / p. 411		La Capilla Argentina	◆◆◆	Argentine	$15-$30	428
40 / p. 411		Mikado	◆◆◆	Asian	$18-$30	429
42 / p. 411		Captain's Cove	◆◆	Seafood	$10-$33	427
43 / p. 411		Rosato Ristorante	◆◆◆◆	Regional New World	$28-$52	430
45 / p. 411		TEMPO	◆◆◆◆	Regional Mediterranean	$25-$65	431
46 / p. 411		Ku-Nah	◆◆◆◆	Regional Mexican	$28-$66	428
47 / p. 411		Mitachi	◆◆◆	Regional Japanese	$10-$35	430

▼ See AAA listing p 444 ▼

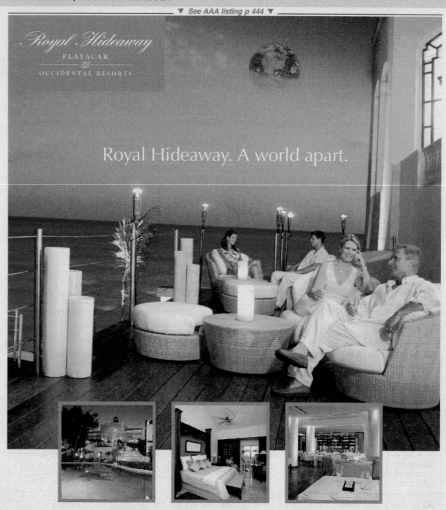

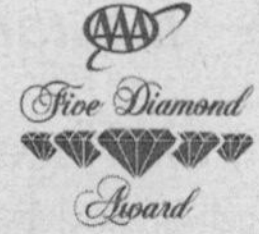

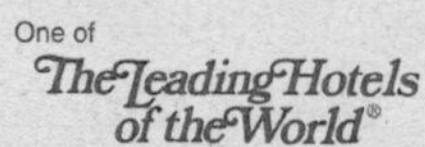

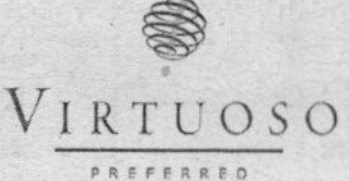

CANCUN, QUINTANA ROO pop. 167,700 (See map and index starting on p. 411)

WHERE TO STAY

AMBIANCE VILLAS AT KIN-HA **Phone:** (998)891-5400 10

Hotel
$220-$360 All Year

Address: Blvd Kukulcan KM 8.5, Zona Hotelera **Location:** Oceanfront. On north beach. **Facility:** 132 units. 76 one-bedroom standard units. 56 one-bedroom suites with kitchens. 3-4 stories, interior corridors. *Bath:* shower only. **Parking:** on-site. **Terms:** 3 day cancellation notice. **Amenities:** safes, hair dryers. **Pool(s):** outdoor. **Leisure Activities:** *Fee:* sailboats, windsurfing, scuba diving, snorkeling, fishing, massage. **Guest Services:** coin laundry. **Business Services:** meeting rooms, fax (fee). **Cards:** AX, MC, VI.

/ SOME UNITS

CROWN PARADISE CLUB CANCUN **Phone:** (998)848-9000 33

Resort Hotel
$384-$450 All Year

Address: Blvd Kukulcan KM 18.5 **Location:** Oceanfront. On beach; windward side of Cancun Island. **Facility:** Among Cancun's ultimate family spots, the all-inclusive resort includes plentiful activities: Find kids theater, arts and crafts and an indoor pool. 508 units. 500 one-bedroom standard units, some with whirlpools. 8 one-bedroom suites with whirlpools. 7-8 stories, interior corridors. **Parking:** on-site. **Terms:** 30 day cancellation notice, in season. **Amenities:** high-speed Internet (fee), voice mail, safes, irons, hair dryers. *Some:* CD players, honor bars. **Pool(s):** 3 outdoor, 2 heated outdoor. **Leisure Activities:** whirlpools, steamroom, waterslide, canoeing, paddleboats, windsurfing, 2 lighted tennis courts, recreation programs, playground, exercise room, sports court, basketball, shuffleboard, volleyball. *Fee:* scuba diving, snorkeling, charter fishing, massage. **Guest Services:** valet laundry, wireless Internet. **Business Services:** meeting rooms. *Fee:* PC, fax. **Cards:** AX, MC, VI.

24 D / SOME UNITS

DREAMS CANCUN RESORT & SPA *Book at AAA.com* **Phone:** (998)848-7000 15

Resort Hotel
$310-$495 All Year

Address: Punta Cancun S/N **Location:** Oceanfront. On the beach at Punta Cancun. **Facility:** Set in a scenic area featuring Mayan ruins and palm-tree-shaded beaches, this hotel offers rooms with balconies and ocean or lagoon view. 380 units. 355 one-bedroom standard units. 25 one-bedroom suites with whirlpools. 5-16 stories, interior/exterior corridors. *Bath:* shower only. **Parking:** on-site (fee) and valet. **Terms:** 7 day cancellation notice. **Amenities:** video library, DVD players, high-speed Internet (fee), voice mail, safes, honor bars, irons, hair dryers. **Dining:** Paloma Bonita, see separate listing. **Pool(s):** heated outdoor. **Leisure Activities:** whirlpool, limited beach access, sailboats, windsurfing, 2 lighted tennis courts, exercise room. *Fee:* massage. **Guest Services:** valet laundry, area transportation (fee), wireless Internet. **Business Services:** business center. **Cards:** AX, MC, VI. Affiliated with A Preferred Hotel.

S D / SOME UNITS

FIESTA AMERICANA CONDESA CANCUN *Book great rates at AAA.com* **Phone:** (998)881-4200 28

AAA
Resort Hotel
$230-$340 All Year

Address: Blvd Kukulcan KM 16.5 **Location:** Oceanfront. On the beach; windward side of Cancun Island. **Facility:** Accented by a Mediterranean-style exterior, lush landscaping and refined public areas, this property features ocean views from all rooms. 502 units. 476 one-bedroom standard units. 25 one- and 1 three-bedroom suites, some with whirlpools. 7-8 stories, exterior corridors. **Parking:** on-site and valet. **Terms:** 3 day cancellation notice-fee imposed. **Amenities:** high-speed Internet (fee), dual phone lines, voice mail, safes, honor bars, irons, hair dryers. *Some:* CD players. **Dining:** 3 restaurants, also, Rosato Ristorante, see separate listing, entertainment. **Pool(s):** outdoor, heated outdoor. **Leisure Activities:** sauna, steamroom, recreation programs. *Fee:* scuba diving, snorkeling, fishing, charter fishing, 2 lighted tennis courts, exercise room, massage. **Guest Services:** valet laundry, wireless Internet. *Fee:* airport transportation-Cancun International Airport, area transportation. **Business Services:** conference facilities, business center. **Cards:** AX, DC, JC, MC, VI.
(See color ad p 418 & on insert)

FEE 24 CALL D / SOME UNITS

FIESTA AMERICANA GRAND CORAL BEACH *Book great rates at AAA.com* **Phone:** (998)881-3200 13

AAA
Resort Hotel
$285-$560 All Year

Address: Blvd Kukulcan KM 9.5 **Location:** Oceanfront. On the beach; leeward side of Cancun Island. **Facility:** Large rooms with balconies overlook the Caribbean at this hotel offering sophisticated common areas and an extensive beachfront pool. 602 units. 519 one-bedroom standard units. 83 one-bedroom suites with whirlpools. 11 stories, interior corridors. *Bath:* combo or shower only. **Parking:** valet. **Amenities:** CD players, dual phone lines, voice mail, safes, honor bars, irons, hair dryers. *Fee:* video games, high-speed Internet. *Some:* DVD players. **Dining:** 5 restaurants, also, Isla Contoy, La Joya Restaurant, Le Basilic, see separate listings, entertainment. **Pool(s):** 3 outdoor, heated outdoor. **Leisure Activities:** saunas, steamrooms, lifeguard on duty, rental boats, rental canoes, pool & ocean sun decks, golf privileges, recreation programs, fiesta kids club, playground, spa. *Fee:* sailboats, windsurfing, waterskiing, scuba diving, snorkeling, fishing, charter fishing, personal watercraft, 3 lighted indoor tennis courts, game room. **Guest Services:** valet laundry, wireless Internet. *Fee:* airport transportation-Cancun International Airport, area transportation. **Business Services:** conference facilities, business center. **Cards:** AX, CB, DC, JC, MC, VI.
(See color ad starting on p 416 & on insert)

FEE 24 D / SOME UNITS

GRAN MELIA CANCUN BEACH & SPA RESORT *Book great rates at AAA.com* **Phone:** (998)881-1100 30

AAA
Resort Hotel
$240-$450 All Year

Address: Blvd Kukulcan KM 16.5 **Location:** Oceanfront. Blvd Kukulcan KM 16.5. **Facility:** One of the largest hotels in the Zona Hotelera, the property offers extensive beach and water activities as well as several restaurants. 674 units. 605 one-bedroom standard units. 68 one- and 1 three-bedroom suites, some with kitchens and/or whirlpools. 6-9 stories, interior corridors. **Parking:** on-site and valet. **Amenities:** high-speed Internet, voice mail, safes, honor bars, irons, hair dryers. *Some:* DVD players. **Dining:** 7 restaurants, also, Ku-Nah, TEMPO, see separate listings, entertainment. **Pool(s):** 2 outdoor. **Leisure Activities:** sauna, whirlpools, steamroom, rental sailboats, rental sailboards, scuba equipment rental, snorkeling equipment rental, fishing, kayak, recreation programs, playground, exercise room, spa, volleyball. **Guest Services:** valet and coin laundry, wireless Internet. **Business Services:** conference facilities, business center. **Cards:** AX, JC, MC, VI.

24 CALL D / SOME UNITS VCR

▼ See AAA listing p 415 ▼

▼ See AAA listing p 415 ▼

(See map and index starting on p. 411)

HILTON CANCUN GOLF & SPA RESORT — Phone: (998)881-8000 32

Resort Hotel
$230-$465 All Year

Address: Blvd Kukulcan KM 17, Zona Hotelera **Location:** On the beach; windward side of Cancun Island. **Facility:** This dramatic pyramid building with extensive pool areas features secluded villas on a spectacular beach; rooms offer dramatic views of the Caribbean. 426 units. 384 one-bedroom standard units. 36 one- and 6 two-bedroom suites, some with whirlpools. 2-9 stories, interior/exterior corridors. **Parking:** on-site and valet. **Terms:** 3 day cancellation notice. **Amenities:** video games, CD players, high-speed Internet, voice mail, safes, honor bars, irons, hair dryers. *Some:* DVD players. **Dining:** Mitachi, see separate listing. **Pool(s):** 7 heated outdoor. **Leisure Activities:** whirlpools, scuba diving, snorkeling, recreation programs, jogging, spa, volleyball. *Fee:* sailboats, windsurfing, charter fishing, golf-18 holes, 2 lighted tennis courts. **Guest Services:** valet laundry, area transportation (fee), wireless Internet. **Business Services:** conference facilities, business center. **Cards:** AX, CB, DC, MC, VI.

FEE / SOME UNITS

HOLIDAY INN EXPRESS CANCUN ZONA HOTELERA — Book at AAA.com — Phone: (998)883-2200 17

Hotel
$120-$150 All Year

Address: Paseo Pok-Ta-Pok 21/22 **Location:** On north side of Cancun Island, off Blvd Kukulcan; 4.2 mi (7 km) from downtown; next to Pok-Ta-Pok Golf Club House. Located in a quiet area. **Facility:** 119 one-bedroom standard units. 2 stories (no elevator), interior corridors. *Bath:* combo or shower only. **Parking:** on-site. **Terms:** cancellation fee imposed. **Amenities:** high-speed Internet, irons, hair dryers. *Some:* CD players. **Pool(s):** outdoor. **Guest Services:** valet laundry, area transportation, wireless Internet. **Business Services:** meeting rooms, PC, fax (fee). **Cards:** AX, DC, MC, VI.

/ SOME UNITS

HOTEL RIU CANCUN — Phone: 998/848-7151 11

Resort Hotel
$305-$610 All Year

Address: Blvd Kukulcan, KM 8.5, Manz 50, Lote 5 **Location:** Oceanfront. 6 mi (10 km) from downtown; in Corazone area. **Facility:** The ultra-all-inclusive resort includes elegant lobby areas, modern, well-equipped guest rooms, multiple dining outlets and extensive pool activities. 569 one-bedroom standard units. 5-14 stories, interior corridors. **Parking:** on-site. **Terms:** 3 night minimum stay, 3 day cancellation notice-fee imposed. **Amenities:** voice mail, safes, honor bars, irons, hair dryers. **Pool(s):** 3 outdoor. **Leisure Activities:** sauna, whirlpools, beach access, canoeing, sailboats, windsurfing, snorkeling, lighted tennis court, recreation programs, playground, spa, volleyball. *Fee:* scuba diving, charter fishing, bicycles. **Guest Services:** valet laundry. **Business Services:** PC (fee). **Cards:** AX, MC, VI.

HOTEL RIU CARIBE — Phone: 998/848-7850 6

Resort Hotel
$165-$330 All Year

Address: Blvd Kukulcan KM 5.5, Lote 6-C **Location:** Oceanfront. 2.6 mi (4.5 km) from downtown; 12.6 mi (21 km) from Cancun International Airport. **Facility:** This ultra-all-inclusive resort is centered around a grand strand of beach and boasts an Aztec pyramid-style lobby; rooms feature Spanish decor. 541 one-bedroom standard units. 9 stories, interior corridors. **Parking:** on-site. **Terms:** 3 night minimum stay, 3 day cancellation notice-fee imposed. **Amenities:** voice mail, safes, honor bars, hair dryers. **Pool(s):** 2 outdoor. **Leisure Activities:** whirlpool, steamroom, beach access, canoeing, sailboats, windsurfing, snorkeling, 2 lighted tennis courts, recreation programs, spa, sports court, volleyball, game room. *Fee:* scuba diving. **Guest Services:** valet laundry. **Business Services:** meeting rooms, PC (fee). **Cards:** AX, MC, VI.

HOTEL RIU PALACE LAS AMERICAS — Phone: 998/891-4300 14

AAA

Hotel
$196-$439 All Year

Address: Blvd Kukulcan KM 8.5, Manz 50, Lote 4 **Location:** Oceanfront. Windward side of Cancun Island; in Corazone. **Facility:** Large guest rooms, ample dining choices and a renowned spa draw visitors to the property from around the world. 372 units. 348 one-bedroom standard units. 24 one-bedroom suites, some with whirlpools. 8 stories, interior corridors. **Parking:** on-site. **Terms:** 3 night minimum stay, 3 day cancellation notice-fee imposed. **Amenities:** safes, honor bars, irons, hair dryers. **Dining:** 6 restaurants, entertainment. **Pool(s):** 2 outdoor. **Leisure Activities:** saunas, whirlpools, snorkeling, tennis privileges, recreation programs, table tennis, playground, spa. *Fee:* scuba diving. **Guest Services:** valet laundry, beauty salon, wireless Internet. **Business Services:** meeting rooms, business center. **Cards:** AX, MC, VI.

HYATT CANCUN CARIBE RESORT — Book great rates at AAA.com — Phone: (998)848-7800 20

AAA

Contemporary Hotel
$119-$538 All Year

Address: Blvd Kukulcan KM 10.5, Zona Hotelera **Location:** Oceanfront. On the beach; windward side of Cancun Island. **Facility:** Rooms at the contemporary hotel face the Caribbean, most offer balconies and spectacular views; pool and beachside massages are available. 296 units. 200 one-bedroom standard units. 96 one-bedroom suites with whirlpools. 3-7 stories, interior/exterior corridors. **Parking:** on-site and valet. **Terms:** 3 day cancellation notice-fee imposed. **Amenities:** high-speed Internet, voice mail, safes, honor bars, irons, hair dryers. *Some:* DVD players, CD players. **Dining:** Blue Bayou, Cafe Cocay, see separate listings, entertainment. **Pool(s):** 3 outdoor. **Leisure Activities:** whirlpools, 3 tennis courts (1 lighted), jogging, playground, exercise room, volleyball. *Fee:* scuba diving, snorkeling, charter fishing, massage. **Guest Services:** valet laundry, wireless Internet. **Business Services:** conference facilities, business center. **Cards:** AX, DC, JC, MC, VI.

(See map and index starting on p. 411)

JW MARRIOTT CANCUN RESORT & SPA Book great rates at AAA.com **Phone:** (998)848-9600 26

Resort Hotel
$256-$462 All Year

JW MARRIOTT
HOTELS & RESORTS
AAA Benefit:
A deluxe level of comfort and a Member rate.

Address: Blvd Kukulcan KM 14.5 **Location:** Oceanfront. Adjacent to Marriott CasaMagna Cancun; 2 mi (3.2 km) s of Cancun Convention Center. **Facility:** Lavish public areas, extensive resort facilities, multiple dining outlets, a world-class spa and excellent service comprise the property. Meets AAA guest room security requirements. Smoke free premises. 448 units. 374 one-bedroom standard units. 74 one-bedroom suites. 14 stories, interior corridors. **Parking:** valet. **Terms:** check-in 4 pm, 7 day cancellation notice-fee imposed. **Amenities:** video games, CD players, high-speed Internet (fee), dual phone lines, voice mail, safes, honor bars, irons, hair dryers. **Dining:** 3 restaurants, also, Gustino Italian Beachside Grill, see separate listing, entertainment. **Pool(s):** 2 outdoor, heated indoor. **Leisure Activities:** whirlpools, steamrooms, beach access, 2 lighted tennis courts, paddle board court, spa. *Fee:* saunas, scuba diving, snorkeling, charter fishing. **Guest Services:** valet laundry. *Fee:* airport transportation-Cancun International Airport, area transportation. **Business Services:** conference facilities, business center. **Cards:** AX, CB, DC, DS, MC, VI.
(See color ad inside front cover & opposite inside front cover)

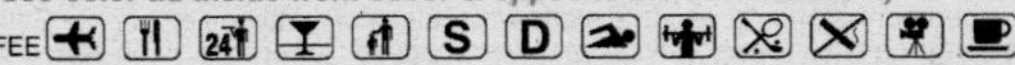

LE MERIDIEN CANCUN RESORT & SPA Book great rates at AAA.com **Phone:** (998)881-2200 24

Contemporary Hotel
$280-$620 All Year

Le MERIDIEN
AAA Benefit:
Members get up to 15% off, plus Starwood Preferred Guest® bonuses.

Address: KM 14 Retorno del Rey **Location:** Oceanfront. Off Blvd Kukulcan; windward side of Cancun Island. **Facility:** Sophisticated French resort. All rooms with view of Caribbean. Expansive pool/beach area with occasionally strong, dramatic surf. 213 units. 188 one-bedroom standard units. 19 one- and 6 two-bedroom suites, some with whirlpools. 7 stories, interior corridors. **Parking:** on-site and valet. **Terms:** 7 day cancellation notice-fee imposed. **Amenities:** CD players, high-speed Internet, dual phone lines, voice mail, safes, honor bars, irons, hair dryers. *Some:* DVD players. **Dining:** 2 restaurants, also, Aioli, see separate listing, entertainment. **Pool(s):** 2 outdoor. **Leisure Activities:** whirlpool, steamroom, lifeguard on duty, scuba diving & rental equipment, snorkeling & rental equipment, recreation programs, kids club, spa, volleyball. *Fee:* sauna, charter fishing, 2 lighted tennis courts, tennis instruction. **Guest Services:** valet laundry, wireless Internet. **Business Services:** conference facilities, business center. **Cards:** AX, DC, JC, MC, VI.
(See color ad p 421, on insert)

MARRIOTT CASAMAGNA CANCUN **Phone:** (998)881-2000 27

Resort Hotel
$174-$267 All Year

Marriott
HOTELS & RESORTS
AAA Benefit:
Members save a minimum 5% off the best available rate.

Address: Manzana 23, Lote 41, Secc A, 2A Etapa **Location:** Oceanfront. Blvd Kukulcan KM 16; on the beach; windward side of Cancun Island. **Facility:** A spacious, luxurious lobby and a large oceanfront pool with an activity area complement the stylish rooms at the resort hotel. Smoke free premises. 450 units. 426 one-bedroom standard units. 24 one-bedroom suites, some with whirlpools. 6 stories, interior corridors. **Parking:** on-site. **Terms:** 7 day cancellation notice-fee imposed. **Amenities:** voice mail, safes, honor bars, irons, hair dryers. *Some:* CD players. *Fee:* DVD players. **Dining:** 2 restaurants, also, La Capilla Argentina, Mikado, see separate listings, entertainment. **Pool(s):** outdoor. **Leisure Activities:** saunas, whirlpools, beach access, recreation programs, playground, exercise room, basketball, volleyball. *Fee:* waterskiing, scuba diving, snorkeling, charter fishing, personal watercraft, parasailing, scuba instructions, 2 lighted tennis courts, kids club, massage. **Guest Services:** valet laundry. **Business Services:** conference facilities. **Cards:** AX, CB, DC, MC, VI.
(See color ad starting on p 422)

FEE CALL S D / SOME UNITS FEE VCR FEE

▼ See AAA listing p 420 ▼

▼ See AAA listing p 420 ▼

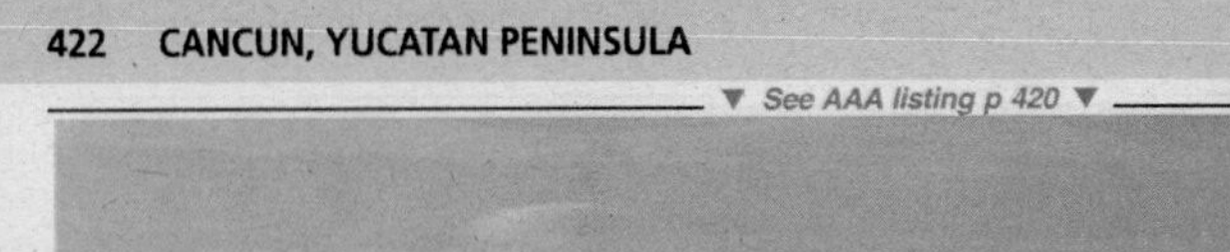

(See map and index starting on p. 411)

MARRIOTT COURTYARD CANCUN Book great rates at AAA.com Phone: (998)287-2200 35

Hotel
$99-$115 All Year

Address: Blvd Luis Donaldo Colosio KM 12.5 **Location:** 0.5 mi (0.8 km) n of jct Mex 307, exit airport. **Facility:** Smoke free premises. 201 units. 195 one-bedroom standard units. 6 one-bedroom suites. 4 stories, interior corridors. **Parking:** on-site. **Amenities:** high-speed Internet, irons, hair dryers. **Pool(s):** outdoor. **Leisure Activities:** whirlpool, exercise room. **Guest Services:** valet and coin laundry, area transportation, wireless Internet. **Business Services:** meeting rooms, business center. **Cards:** AX, MC, VI.

CALL S D

AAA Benefit:
Members save a minimum 5% off the best available rate.

ME BY MELIA Book great rates at AAA.com Phone: (998)881-2500 22

Contemporary Hotel
$240-$380 All Year

Address: Blvd Kukulcan KM 12 **Location:** Oceanfront. **Facility:** Through high-tech equipment, state-of-the-art guest rooms and a relaxed ambiance, the hotel strives to make your visit memorable. Meets AAA guest room security requirements. 448 units. 406 one-bedroom standard units. 42 one-bedroom suites, some with whirlpools. 11 stories, interior corridors. *Bath:* shower only. **Parking:** on-site and valet. **Terms:** age restrictions may apply, 7 day cancellation notice. **Amenities:** video library, DVD players, CD players, dual phone lines, voice mail, safes, irons, hair dryers. **Dining:** 3 restaurants, entertainment. **Pool(s):** 4 outdoor. **Leisure Activities:** sauna, whirlpools, spa. *Fee:* charter fishing. **Guest Services:** valet laundry, wireless Internet. *Fee:* airport transportation-Cancun International Airport, area transportation. **Business Services:** conference facilities, business center. **Cards:** AX, CB, DC, DS, JC, MC, VI.

FEE 24 CALL S D / SOME UNITS

MOON PALACE Phone: (998)881-6000 36

Resort Hotel
$380-$390 All Year

Address: Carr Cancun-Chetumal KM 340 **Location:** Oceanfront. Mex 307, 5 mi (8 km) s of Cancun International Airport exit. **Facility:** This very large complex has two sections offering everything from multiple restaurants to all types of water and beach activities. 1982 one-bedroom standard units with whirlpools. 3 stories, interior/exterior corridors. **Parking:** on-site and valet. **Terms:** 3 night minimum stay, 21 day cancellation notice-fee imposed. **Amenities:** voice mail, safes, irons, hair dryers. **Pool(s):** 2 outdoor. **Leisure Activities:** whirlpools, beach access, sailboats, windsurfing, boat dock, scuba equipment rental, golf-27 holes, miniature golf, 6 lighted tennis courts, bicycles, exercise room, spa, basketball. *Fee:* game room. **Guest Services:** valet laundry, area transportation (fee). **Business Services:** conference facilities, business center. **Cards:** AX, CB, DC, DS, JC, MC, VI. ***(See color ad on insert)***

FEE 24 / SOME UNITS

OASIS AMERICA Phone: (998)848-8600 3

Hotel
$320-$400 All Year

Address: Ave Tulum y Calle Brisa SM 4 CP **Location:** Off Cancun Island; on Ave Tulum, jct highway to beaches. Located in Old Town Cancun. **Facility:** 167 one-bedroom standard units. 6 stories, interior corridors. *Bath:* shower only. **Parking:** on-site. **Terms:** 14 day cancellation notice-fee imposed. **Amenities:** safes (fee), honor bars, hair dryers. **Pool(s):** outdoor. **Guest Services:** valet laundry, area transportation, wireless Internet. **Business Services:** conference facilities, business center. **Cards:** AX, DC, MC, VI.

D / SOME UNITS

OASIS PALM BEACH RESORT Book at AAA.com Phone: (998)848-7500 5

Resort Hotel
$260-$480 All Year

Address: Blvd Kukulcan, Seccion C, Lote 1 **Location:** Oceanfront. On Playa Linda; at leeward side of Cancun Island. Located on the beach. **Facility:** Modern pyramid-shaped high-rise, colorful rooms; few with balcony. Recently remodeled. Wide, tranquil beach with palapas. Meets AAA guest room security requirements. 470 one-bedroom standard units. 8 stories, interior corridors. *Bath:* shower only. **Parking:** on-site. **Terms:** 10 day cancellation notice-fee imposed. **Amenities:** voice mail, safes, hair dryers. **Pool(s):** 2 outdoor. **Leisure Activities:** sauna, steamroom, rental boats, rental sailboats, rental sailboards, scuba diving, snorkeling, lighted tennis court. *Fee:* marina, waterskiing, fishing, massage. **Guest Services:** valet laundry, wireless Internet. **Business Services:** meeting rooms. **Cards:** AX, MC, VI.

FEE / SOME UNITS

OMNI CANCUN HOTEL & VILLAS Phone: (998)881-0600 29

Resort Hotel
$295-$485 All Year

Address: Blvd Kukulcan L-48, M-53, KM 16.5 **Location:** Oceanfront. Windward side of Cancun Island. Located on the beach. **Facility:** A beachfront location and a range of recreational facilities add appeal to this property, which offers both traditional rooms and full villas. 351 units. 310 one-bedroom standard units. 21 one-bedroom suites, some with whirlpools. 20 houses. 3-12 stories, interior corridors. **Parking:** on-site. **Terms:** 3 day cancellation notice. **Amenities:** voice mail, safes, irons, hair dryers. *Some:* DVD players (fee). **Pool(s):** 3 outdoor. **Leisure Activities:** whirlpools, steamroom, scuba diving & rental equipment, snorkeling & rental equipment, recreation programs, exercise room, spa, sports court. *Fee:* paddleboats, sailboats, waterskiing, charter fishing, 2 lighted tennis courts. **Guest Services:** valet laundry, wireless Internet. **Business Services:** conference facilities, business center. **Cards:** AX, CB, DC, MC, VI.

24 D / SOME UNITS

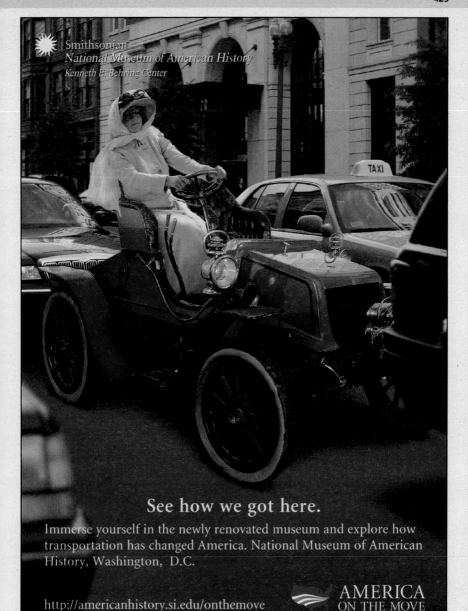

(See map and index starting on p. 411)

PRESIDENTE INTERCONTINENTAL CANCUN RESORT *Book at AAA.com* **Phone:** (998)848-8700 9

Resort Hotel
$180-$680 All Year

Address: Blvd Kukulcan KM 7.5 **Location:** Oceanfront. On the beach; north side of Cancun Island. **Facility:** Lagoon or Caribbean views. Striking pyramid-shaped pool area with whirlpools. Superb, wide beach area with palapas; usually a tranquil surf. Meets AAA guest room security requirements. 299 units. 296 one-bedroom standard units. 3 one-bedroom suites with whirlpools. 6-10 stories, interior corridors. **Parking:** on-site and valet. **Terms:** 7 day cancellation notice-fee imposed. **Amenities:** high-speed Internet (fee), voice mail, safes, honor bars, irons, hair dryers. *Some:* CD players. **Pool(s):** outdoor, heated outdoor. **Leisure Activities:** whirlpools, rental boats, rental sailboats, rental sailboards, scuba diving & rental equipment, snorkeling & rental equipment, lighted tennis court, recreation programs, jogging, playground, exercise room, basketball. *Fee:* waterskiing, charter fishing, massage. **Guest Services:** valet laundry, wireless Internet. **Business Services:** conference facilities, business center. **Cards:** AX, DC, JC, MC, VI.

D / SOME UNITS VCR

THE RITZ-CARLTON CANCUN *Book great rates at AAA.com* **Phone:** (998)881-0808 31

AAA
Resort Hotel
$329-$748 All Year

Address: Retorno del Rey #36, Zona Hotelera **Location:** Oceanfront. Blvd Kukulcan KM 17.5. **Facility:** Impressive common areas and a refined ambiance enhance this hotel's location on a prime section of beach in the middle of the hotel zone. Meets AAA guest room security requirements. Smoke free premises. 364 units. 309 one-bedroom standard units. 55 one-bedroom suites, some with whirlpools. 9 stories, interior corridors. **Parking:** on-site and valet. **Terms:** 7 day cancellation notice. **Amenities:** CD players, dual phone lines, voice mail, safes, honor bars, irons, hair dryers. *Fee:* video games, high-speed Internet. **Dining:** 2 restaurants, also, The Club Grill, Fantino, see separate listings, entertainment. **Pool(s):** 2 outdoor. **Leisure Activities:** saunas, whirlpool, steamrooms, beach access, recreation programs, kids club, playground, exercise room, spa, cooking school. *Fee:* scuba diving, snorkeling, fishing, charter fishing, 3 lighted tennis courts. **Guest Services:** valet laundry, wireless Internet. *Fee:* airport transportation-Cancun International Airport, area transportation. **Business Services:** conference facilities, business center. **Cards:** AX, CB, DC, JC, MC, VI. *(See color ad p 4)*

FEE S D

SUNSET LAGOON HOTEL & MARINA **Phone:** 998/881-4500 4

Hotel
$280-$410 All Year

Address: Blvd Kukulcan KM 5.8 **Location:** Oceanfront. On north side of Cancun Island; facing lagoon. **Facility:** 100 one-bedroom standard units with kitchens, some with whirlpools. 3 stories, exterior corridors. *Bath:* shower only. **Parking:** on-site and valet. **Terms:** check-in 4 pm, 3 day cancellation notice. **Amenities:** safes, honor bars, irons, hair dryers. **Pool(s):** outdoor. **Leisure Activities:** whirlpool, boating, paddleboats, sailboats, windsurfing, scuba equipment rental, snorkeling equipment rental, recreation programs, playground. *Fee:* marina, waterskiing, charter fishing, massage. **Guest Services:** valet laundry, wireless Internet. **Business Services:** *Fee:* PC, fax. **Cards:** AX, MC, VI.

THE WESTIN RESORT & SPA CANCUN *Book great rates at AAA.com* **Phone:** (998)848-7400 34

Resort Hotel
$99-$459 All Year

Address: Blvd Kukulcan KM 20 Lote 70 y Zona Hotel **Location:** Oceanfront. On beach; windward side of Cancun Island. **Facility:** Ocean and lagoon views, excellent public, pool and beach areas. Bright colors, open areas; some units with private balcony. Smoke free premises. 379 units. 373 one-bedroom standard units. 6 one-bedroom suites, some with whirlpools. 6 stories, interior corridors. **Parking:** on-site and valet. **Amenities:** high-speed Internet (fee), dual phone lines, voice mail, safes, honor bars, irons, hair dryers. *Some:* DVD players, CD players. **Pool(s):** 5 outdoor. **Leisure Activities:** sauna, whirlpools, steamroom, paddleboats, windsurfing, boat dock, recreation programs. *Fee:* waterskiing, scuba diving, snorkeling, charter fishing, 2 lighted tennis courts, massage. **Guest Services:** valet laundry, area transportation, beauty salon, wireless Internet. **Business Services:** conference facilities, business center. **Cards:** CB, DC, DS, JC. *(See color ad on insert)*

FEE CALL M / SOME UNITS

The following lodgings were either not evaluated or did not meet AAA rating requirements but are listed for your information only.

AQUA **Phone:** 998/881-7600

fyi

Not evaluated. **Address:** Blvd Kukulcan KM 14.5 **Location:** On the beach; windward side of Cancun Island. Facilities, services, and decor characterize an upscale property. ***(See color ad on insert & back cover)***

BEACH PALACE RESORT **Phone:** 998/891-4110

fyi

Not evaluated. **Address:** Blvd Kukulcan KM 11.5. Facilities, services, and decor characterize an upscale property.

CANCUN PALACE **Phone:** 998/881-3600

fyi

Not evaluated. **Address:** Blvd Kukulcan KM 14.5 **Location:** Blvd Kukulcan; windward side of Cancun Island. Facilities, services, and decor characterize an upscale property.

LE BLANC SPA RESORT **Phone:** 998/881-4740

fyi

Not evaluated. **Address:** Blvd Kukulcan KM 10. Facilities, services, and decor characterize an upscale property. ***(See color ad on insert)***

(See map and index starting on p. 411)

OASIS VIVA — **Phone:** 998/883-0800

fyi — Not evaluated. **Address:** Blvd Kukulcan KM 8.5 **Location:** Blvd Kukulcan; in Zona Hotelera. Facilities, services, and decor characterize a mid-scale property.

SUN PALACE RESORT — **Phone:** 998/891-4100

fyi — Not evaluated. **Address:** Blvd Kukulcan KM 20. Facilities, services, and decor characterize an upscale property.

WHERE TO DINE

AIOLI — **Phone:** 998/881-2260 (35)

Regional Mediterranean
$10-$65

Ocean views are exceptional from either the large terrace or the dramatic floor-to-ceiling windows inside this distinctively designed dining room. Specialty Mediterranean entrees include duck breast with potato galette, served with a honey lavender sauce, or pan-seared grouper with a paste of black olives, crushed potato and tomato. Lighter fare also is available, particularly on the lunch bistro menu. The "fifth element" dessert is renowned. Dressy casual. Entertainment. **Bar:** Full bar. **Reservations:** suggested. **Hours:** 6:30 am-11:30 & 1-11 pm. **Address:** KM 14 Retorno del Rey **Location:** Off Blvd Kukulcan; windward side of Cancun Island; in Le Meridien Cancun Resort & Spa. **Parking:** on-site and valet. **Cards:** AX, DC, MC, VI.

CALL

BLUE BAYOU — **Phone:** 998/848-7800 (23)

Regional International
$18-$30

Distinctive bayou decor is fitting at this semi-formal restaurant, which specializes in Cajun preparations. Dressy casual. Entertainment. **Bar:** Full bar. **Reservations:** suggested. **Hours:** 6 pm-11 pm. **Address:** Blvd Kukulcan KM 10.5, Zona Hotelera **Location:** On the beach; windward side of Cancun Island; in Hyatt Cancun Caribe Resort. **Parking:** on-site and valet. **Cards:** AX, DC, DS, MC, VI.

CAFE COCAY — **Phone:** 998/848-7800 (19)

Regional International
$5-$22

On the ground level of a boutique resort, the dining room displays colorful yet elegant Caribbean decor. Breakfast includes a vast buffet, including omelets made on-the-spot, as well as a la carte selections. Casual dress. **Bar:** Full bar. **Reservations:** accepted. **Hours:** 6:30 am-1 & 6-10 pm. Closed: Mon. **Address:** Blvd Kukulcan KM 10.5, Zona Hotelera **Location:** On the beach; windward side of Cancun Island; in Hyatt Cancun Caribe Resort. **Parking:** on-site and valet. **Cards:** AX, CB, DC, JC, MC, VI.

CAPTAIN'S COVE — **Phone:** 998/885-0016 (42)

Seafood
$10-$33

In the Zona Hotelera, the restaurant overlooks the lagoon side of the island. A nautical theme with a Mexican flair sets the atmosphere for the seafood restaurant. Views of the sunset across the lagoon are excellent. Casual dress. **Bar:** Full bar. **Reservations:** accepted. **Hours:** 2 pm-11 pm. **Address:** Blvd Kukulcan KM 16.5 **Location:** Blvd Kukulcan KM 16.5. **Parking:** street. **Cards:** MC, VI.

CASA ROLANDI'S — **Phone:** 998/883-2557 (10)

Northern Italian
$10-$25

In the heart of a popular mall, this local favorite is well known for its grotto walls, attentive servers and tasty dishes prepared with fresh ingredients and pasta. Casual dress. **Bar:** Full bar. **Reservations:** accepted. **Hours:** 1 pm-2 am, Sun-11:30 pm. **Address:** Site 32-34 Plaza Caracol Shopping Mall **Location:** On lagoon side of Blvd Kukulcan; in Plaza Caracol Shopping Mall. **Parking:** on-site and street. **Cards:** AX, MC, VI.

CENACOLA IL RISTORANTE ITALIANO — **Phone:** 998/885-3603 (28)

Italian
$14-$22

A Cancun flair punctuates preparations of fine Italian cuisine. In addition to traditional gourmet pizzas and homemade pasta, the menu incorporates exotic choices, such as sea salt gulf shrimp. There is a choice of elegant indoor seating, where guests are surrounded by large European wall murals, as well as space on the patio, where candlelit tables and robust Italian music set a decidedly romantic tone. Service is detailed and attentive. Casual dress. **Bar:** Full bar. **Reservations:** suggested. **Hours:** 1 pm-11:30 pm; hours may vary in season. **Address:** Blvd Kukulcan KM 13 **Location:** In Plaza Kukulcan. **Parking:** on-site. **Cards:** AX, MC, VI.

THE CLUB GRILL — **Phone:** 998/881-0808 (33)

International
$35-$49

The lavish, club-like setting sets the stage for a refined, romantic dining experience. Seafood, steak and game dishes are vividly presented and augmented by local Yucatan and Caribbean flavors. Service is formal and precise. The adjoining lounge is ideal for dancing or enjoying a Cuban cigar. Dressy casual. Entertainment. **Bar:** Full bar. **Reservations:** suggested. **Hours:** 6:30 pm-11 pm. Closed: Mon. **Address:** Retorno del Rey #36, Zona Hotelera **Location:** Blvd Kukulcan KM 17.5; in The Ritz-Carlton Cancun. **Parking:** valet. **Cards:** AX, CB, DC, DS, JC, MC, VI. *(See color ad p 4)*

CRAB HOUSE RESTAURANT & BAR — **Phone:** 998/193-0350 (36)

Regional Seafood
$10-$30

In addition to the fabulous seafood selections featuring crab and lobster, the menu also offers pastas, steaks and a fun children's menu. Casual dress. **Bar:** Full bar. **Hours:** noon-11:30 pm. **Address:** Blvd Kukulcan KM 14.8 **Location:** On Blvd Kukulcan; across from Marriott Complex. **Parking:** on-site. **Cards:** AX, MC, VI.

(See map and index starting on p. 411)

EL PESCADOR **Phone:** 998/884-2673 (4)

Regional Seafood
$8-$28

This downtown restaurant (the name translates to "The Fisherman") offers fresh seafood in an open, casual atmosphere. Casual dress. **Bar:** Full bar. **Hours:** 1 pm-11 pm. **Address:** Talipanes #28, SM 22 **Location:** 4 blks e of jct Blvd Kukulcan and Ave Tulum; in Tulipanes outdoor pedestrian mall (Callejon Tulipanes). **Parking:** on-site. **Cards:** MC, VI.

FANTINO **Phone:** 998/881-0808 (34)

Mediterranean
$43-$80

The specialty restaurant features surprising presentations and refined service. Caribbean flavors lend a distinctive taste to Italian dishes. Dressy casual. Entertainment. **Bar:** Full bar. **Reservations:** suggested. **Hours:** 7 pm-11 pm. Closed: Sun. **Address:** Retorno del Rey #36 , Zona Hotelera **Location:** Blvd Kukulcan KM 17.5; in The Ritz-Carlton Cancun. **Parking:** valet. **Cards:** AX, CB, DC, JC, MC, VI. *(See color ad p 4)*

GUSTINO ITALIAN BEACHSIDE GRILL **Phone:** 998/848-9600 (38)

Regional Italian
$20-$50

Terraced seating provides great views at the classic Italian restaurant, which has a wine cellar and an immense antipasto bar with cured meats, imported cheeses and marinated vegetables. Menu favorites include thick bone-in chops, freshly made ravioli and sweet desserts. Dressy casual. **Bar:** Full bar. **Reservations:** suggested. **Hours:** 6 pm-10:30 pm. **Address:** Blvd Kukulcan KM 14.5 **Location:** Adjacent to Marriott CasaMagna Cancun; 2 mi (3.2 km) s of Cancun Convention Center; in JW Marriott Cancun Resort & Spa. **Parking:** on-site and valet. **Cards:** AX, CB, DC, DS, JC, MC, VI.

CALL

HACIENDA EL MORTERO RESTAURANTE **Phone:** 998/883-1133 (18)

Mexican
$18-$40

For true Mexican flavor in both food and atmosphere, this cozy restaurant is a great choice. Wandering mariachis entertain diners as they feast on homemade, tasty meals in the bright, festive atmosphere of a center courtyard. Menu highlights include fresh fish, seafood, Mexican crepes and more traditional favorites along the lines of ranch steaks and sizzling fajitas. Casual dress. Entertainment. **Bar:** Full bar. **Reservations:** suggested. **Hours:** 5:30 pm-11:30 pm. **Address:** Blvd Kukulcan KM 9 **Location:** Next to Cancun Convention Center. **Parking:** street. **Cards:** AX, MC, VI.

ISLA CONTOY **Phone:** 998/881-3200 (13)

Regional Caribbean
$18-$45

Facing the Caribbean, this indoor/outdoor restaurant features a seafood and pasta market where guests select fresh items to be prepared a la minute. The laid-back atmosphere contrasts well with the elevated cuisine and attentive service. Casual dress. **Bar:** Full bar. **Hours:** 11:30 am-5 & 6:30-11 pm. Closed: for dinner Tues. **Address:** Blvd Kukulcan KM 9.5 **Location:** On the beach; leeward side of Cancun Island; in Fiesta Americana Grand Coral Beach. **Parking:** on-site and valet. **Cards:** AX, CB, DC, DS, JC, MC, VI.

KU-NAH **Phone:** 998/881-1100 (46)

Regional Mexican
$28-$66

Ku-Nah is Mayan for "temple of nutrition," and this place follows through with authentic Mexican sopes made from freshly ground cornmeal, stacked with marinated pulled pork, chicken or beef and topped with queso asadero. Another must-try item is seafood bisque presented with diced scallops, shrimp and calamari and finished with a shimmering broth. Casual dress. **Bar:** Full bar. **Reservations:** suggested. **Hours:** 6:30 pm-midnight. **Address:** Blvd Kukulcan KM 16.5 **Location:** Blvd Kukulcan KM 16.5; in Gran Melia Cancun Beach & Spa Resort. **Parking:** on-site. **Cards:** AX, MC, VI.

LA CAPILLA ARGENTINA **Phone:** 998/881-2000 (39)

Argentine
$15-$30

Among the comfortable restaurant's decor touches are a Spanish tile floor and Mexican fountain. However, the food is the clear highlight. Servers display fresh cuts of beef and tempting starters such as gaucho sausage to enhance the experience. Expect huge portions of freshly prepared and perfectly spiced cuisine with an Argentine flair. Casual dress. **Bar:** Full bar. **Reservations:** suggested. **Hours:** 6:30 am-11 & 5:30-11 pm. **Address:** Manzana 23, Lote 41, Seccion A **Location:** Blvd Kukulcan KM 16; on the beach; windward side of Cancun Island; in Marriott CasaMagna Cancun. **Parking:** on-site and valet. **Cards:** AX, CB, DC, DS, JC, MC, VI.

LA CASA DE LAS MARGARITAS RESTAURANT **Phone:** 998/883-3222 (27)

Mexican
$14-$37

The upscale Mexican restaurant is in the middle of one of the town's premier shopping areas. The interior resembles a typical street scene, with walls depicting shop windows displaying Mexican wares. Colorful and elaborate tile walls, chairs and decorations enhance the atmosphere. Friendly and efficient staff combined with tasty cuisine contribute to a delightful dining experience. Casual dress. **Bar:** Full bar. **Reservations:** accepted. **Hours:** 1 pm-10 pm. **Address:** Blvd Kukulcan KM 12 **Location:** In La Isla Shopping Village. **Parking:** on-site (fee). **Cards:** AX, MC, VI.

LA DESTILERIA **Phone:** 998/885-1086 (29)

Mexican
$8-$14

Resembling a turn-of-the-20th-century tequila-making ranch, the restaurant is reminiscent of another time. The menu centers on Mexican fare. Guests are told their satisfaction is guaranteed. Casual dress. **Bar:** Full bar. **Reservations:** suggested. **Hours:** 1 pm-10 pm. **Address:** Blvd Kukulcan KM 13 **Location:** Blvd Kukulcan; in Zona Hotelera. **Parking:** on-site. **Cards:** AX, MC, VI.

(See map and index starting on p. 411)

LA DOLCE VITA **Phone:** 998/885-0161 (37)

Italian

$12-$28

Overlooking the beautiful Nichupte Lagoon, the 18-year-old establishment features Italian specialties in a contemporary setting. The ample wine list includes a good selection of by-the-glass choices. Recommended is the tripasta dolce vita, consisting of cannelloni, ravioli and gnocchi. For a touch of the Caribbean, try tagliolini with lobster medallions. Seating is available indoors or on the terrace. Casual dress. Entertainment. **Bar:** Full bar. **Reservations:** suggested, for dinner. **Hours:** noon-11:30 pm. Closed: 1/1. **Address:** Blvd Kukulcan KM 14.6 **Location:** Across from Marriott CasaMagna Cancun and JW Marriott Cancun Resort & Spa; facing lagoon. **Parking:** on-site. **Cards:** AX, MC, VI.

LA DOLCE VITA CENTRO **Phone:** 998/884-3393 (7)

Regional Italian

$8-$21

Located in Old Town Cancun, just off the island proper, this is one of Cancun's earliest Italian restaurants brought back to life after 30 years. Casual dress. **Bar:** Full bar. **Reservations:** suggested. **Hours:** noon-11 pm, Sun from 2:30 pm. **Address:** Ave Coba 87, SM 3 **Location:** 1 blk w from bridge to Cancun Island. **Parking:** street. **Cards:** AX, MC, VI.

LA HABICHUELA **Phone:** 998/884-3158 (3)

Regional Mexican

$18-$35

Mayan stone relief carvings complement the tropical garden setting where patrons dine on Caribbean dishes under the stars. Food is prepared using fresh fruit sauces, such as mango, guava and guanabana. Good choices include the specialty "cocobichuela" entree, a light curry with chunks of lobster and shrimp served in a coconut with tropical fruits, and jumbo shrimp in a ginger/mushroom sauce. For a wonderful ending, try strawberries flambe with a "cafe maya" prepared tableside. Casual dress. **Bar:** Full bar. **Reservations:** suggested, for dinner. **Hours:** noon-midnight. **Address:** Margaritas 25 **Location:** 2 blks n of Ave Tulum at Calle Azucenas; downtown; behind theater. **Parking:** on-site and street. **Cards:** AX, MC, VI.

LA JOYA RESTAURANT **Phone:** 998/881-3200 (14)

New Mexican

$30-$50

Those who dine in the main plaza of this quaint place can discover authentic Mexican haute cuisine. Distinctive and artistic dishes combine national and classic flavors. Live mariachi music enhances the splendid dining atmosphere. Dressy casual. Entertainment. **Bar:** Full bar. **Reservations:** suggested. **Hours:** 6:30 pm-11 pm. Closed: Mon. **Address:** KM 9.5 Blvd Kukulcan **Location:** On the beach; leeward side of Cancun Island; in Fiesta Americana Grand Coral Beach. **Parking:** valet. **Cards:** AX, CB, DC, DS, JC, MC, VI.

LA MADONNA **Phone:** 998/883-4837 (26)

Italian

$15-$55

Homemade rich pasta, gourmet pizzas, live lobster and fresh local seafood are just some of the menu highlights. Huge statues, floor-to-ceiling murals and ornate decor enhance the distinctive European setting. Overlooking activities at the shopping venue, the small patio area on the ground or second level is a nice spot for drinks. Casual dress. **Bar:** Full bar. **Reservations:** suggested. **Hours:** noon-midnight. **Address:** Blvd Kukulcan KM 12.5 **Location:** At La Isla Shopping Village. **Parking:** street. **Cards:** AX, MC, VI.

LE BASILIC **Phone:** 998/881-3200 (11)

Regional Mediterranean

$23-$35

The newest arrival in Cancun is where Mediterranean creations meet with subtle undertones of French haute cuisine. The elegant dining room, with its pianist and attentive service, encourages romance and celebration. After dinner, diners can step out to the lounge for a nightcap and live nightly entertainment. Semi-formal attire. **Bar:** Full bar. **Reservations:** suggested. **Hours:** 6:30 pm-11 pm. Closed: Sun. **Address:** Blvd Kukulcan KM 9.5 **Location:** On the beach; leeward side of Cancun Island; in Fiesta Americana Grand Coral Beach. **Parking:** valet. **Cards:** AX, CB, DC, DS, JC, MC, VI. ***(See ad starting on p 416)***

CALL

LORENZILLO'S **Phone:** 998/883-1254 (20)

Seafood

$12-$50

Named after legendary French pirate Lorenzillo, who came to Mexico in 1683, the long-established restaurant is built over the water on Nichupte Lagoon. The specialty, live lobster, can be selected from the water-filled boat moored in the dining room. Seafood dishes can be cooked in several ways. Seating is available outside or inside in the open-air dining room under the large palapa (thatched) roof. Casual dress. **Bar:** Full bar. **Reservations:** suggested, for dinner. **Hours:** 1 pm-midnight. **Address:** Blvd Kukulcan KM 10.5 **Location:** Opposite Hotel Porto Real. **Parking:** valet. **Cards:** AX, MC, VI.

LOS ALMENDROS **Phone:** 998/887-1332 (2)

Regional Mexican

$7-$28

The restaurant offers classic Yucatan cuisine using citrus juices, tropical leaves and Old World spices. Pibil-style shredded pork, tikin-xic-style fish, fried eggs with ham, peas, fried plantains, beans and soft tortillas are Motuleno-style. Casual dress. Entertainment. **Bar:** Full bar. **Reservations:** accepted. **Hours:** 11 am-10 pm. **Address:** Ave Tulum Lote 66 Manz 32; SM 23 **Location:** 1 mi (1.6 km) n of jct Ave Tulum and Blvd Kukulcan; 1 blk s of fire station (Bomberos). **Parking:** street. **Cards:** AX, MC, VI.

MIKADO **Phone:** 998/881-2000 (40)

Asian

$18-$30

Near the entrance of the hotel, the restaurant enables diners to choose from both Japanese and Thai selections amid sleek, contemporary Asian decor. Choices include tempura, yellow and green curries, Pad Thai and extensive sushi varieties. Also available are teppan-style grill seating and sunset dinners. Dressy casual. **Bar:** Full bar. **Reservations:** suggested. **Hours:** 5:30 pm-11 pm. **Address:** Mnz 23, Lote 41, Secc A, 2A Etapa **Location:** Blvd Kukulcan KM 16; on beach; windward side of Cancun Island; in Marriott CasaMagna Cancun. **Parking:** on-site and valet. **Cards:** AX, CB, MC, VI.

(See map and index starting on p. 411)

MITACHI

Phone: 998/881-8000 (47)

Regional Japanese
$10-$35

Authentic Japanese creations are served in a relaxed, inviting dining room located steps from the turquoise Caribbean. Casual dress. Entertainment. **Bar:** Full bar. **Reservations:** suggested. **Hours:** noon-11 pm. **Address:** Blvd Kukulcan KM 17, Zona Hotelera **Location:** On beach; windward side of Cancun Island; in Hilton Cancun Golf & Spa Resort. **Parking:** on-site and valet. **Cards:** AX, CB, DC, JC, MC, VI.

PALOMA BONITA

Phone: 998/848-7000 (17)

Regional Mexican
$15-$38

This high-energy, family-oriented restaurant takes diners on a fun-filled gastronomical tour through Mexican regions, customs, foods and people. Strolling musicians enliven the atmosphere. Authentic, colorfully presented Mexican dishes—including the smoked marlin appetizer, the chef's specialty of chicken almond mole and the delicious poblano chilies stuffed with lobster and seafood—are made with fresh, quality ingredients. Casual dress. Entertainment. **Bar:** Full bar. **Reservations:** required. **Hours:** 6 pm-midnight. **Address:** Punta Cancun Lote 17 **Location:** On beach at Punta Cancun; in Dreams Cancun Resort & Spa. **Parking:** on-site and valet. **Cards:** AX, CB, DC, MC, VI.

PERICOS RESTAURANTE-CANTINA

Phone: 998/884-3152 (5)

Traditional Mexican
$8-$35

This not-to-be-missed cantina features live marimba and mariachi music in an eclectic, high-energy atmosphere. On the menu are several styles of brochettes flambeed with orange liqueur, as well as sizzling fajitas, fresh seafood ceviche and other Mexican favorites. The wait staff—also known as the bandoleros—serves up food and plenty of entertainment. Casual dress. Entertainment. **Bar:** Full bar. **Reservations:** accepted. **Hours:** noon-1 am. **Address:** Ave Yaxchilan 61 **Location:** In town; near jct aves Uxmal and Yaxchilan. **Parking:** street. **Cards:** AX, MC, VI.

PUERTO MADERO STEAKHOUSE AND FISH MARINA

Phone: 998/885-2829 (30)

International
$18-$46

Overlooking a lagoon, the steakhouse appeals to well-heeled locals. An extensive wine list complements choices such as ahi tuna, empanadas, Kobe beef and New Zealand lamb. The rugged masculine decor incorporates leather placemats on wood tables and nautical artifacts on the walls. Casual dress. **Bar:** Full bar. **Reservations:** accepted. **Hours:** 1 pm-1 am. **Address:** Blvd Kukulcan KM 14 **Location:** In Marina Barracuda. **Parking:** on-site and valet. **Cards:** AX, MC, VI.

RESTAURANT EL CALAMAR

Phone: 998/884-0190 (1)

Regional Seafood
$8-$20

For the past 25 years, fresh seafood and Mexican dishes have been served at this simple cantina. The tradition continues today, with fish being brought to the table for approval prior to being cooked and several dishes prepared in the tasty tikin-xic style. For starters, diners can munch on assorted bocadillos. Fresh ceviches, including caracol (conch), and desserts such as coconut flan round out the menu nicely. Casual dress. **Bar:** Full bar. **Reservations:** accepted. **Hours:** noon-10 pm. **Address:** Margaritas Retorno 2 **Location:** From North/South Monument, 0.3 mi (0.5 km) e to Revolution Monument, left on Ave Uxmal, then just e of jct; near bus terminal. **Parking:** street. **Cards:** MC, VI.

ROSATO RISTORANTE

Phone: 998/881-4200 (43)

Regional New World
$28-$52

Patrons can relax in a comfortable dining room while enjoying an excellent variety of Italian-based dishes presented with artistic flair. Nice touches include a wide variety of imported cheeses and a focused wine list with some by-the-glass selections. Dressy casual. **Bar:** Full bar. **Reservations:** suggested. **Hours:** 6:30 pm-11 pm. Closed: Tues. **Address:** Blvd Kukulcan KM 16.5 **Location:** On the beach; windward side of Cancun Island; in Fiesta Americana Condesa Cancun. **Parking:** on-site and valet. **Cards:** AX, DC, MC, VI.

RUTH'S CHRIS STEAK HOUSE

Phone: 998/885-0500 (22)

Steak
$30-$60

The main fare is steak, which is prepared from several cuts of prime beef and cooked to perfection, but the menu also lists lamb, chicken and seafood dishes. Guests should come hungry because the side dishes, which are among the a la carte offerings, could make a meal in themselves. Casual dress. **Bar:** Full bar. **Reservations:** suggested. **Hours:** 1 pm-11:30 pm. **Address:** Blvd Kukulcan KM 13.5 **Location:** Blvd Kukulcan; in Kukulcan Plaza Mall. **Parking:** on-site. **Cards:** AX, MC, VI.

SANBORN'S

Phone: 998/884-7818

Regional Mexican
$8-$28

Restaurants in the casual chain, which includes more than 100 locations throughout Mexico, offer a good selection of American-style sandwiches, salads, soups and both Mexican and American entrees. The selection of desserts is impressive. Casual dress. **Bar:** Full bar. **Hours:** 7 am-1 am. **Address:** Ave Tulum Sur #260, Plaza Las Americas **Location:** Just s of jct Blvd Kukulcan. **Parking:** on-site. **Cards:** AX, MC, VI.

SENOR FROG'S

Phone: 998/883-1092

International
$7-$16

Part of the chain of Mexican restaurants that also includes Carlos 'n Charlie's, the fun and festive eatery is a great place to eat with the family or rendezvous with friends. The menu is lined with Tex-Mex, American and Mexican favorites, such as Buffalo wings, quesadillas, fajitas and burritos. After hours, a bar atmosphere prevails. Casual dress. **Bar:** Full bar. **Hours:** noon-3 am. **Address:** Blvd Kukulcan KM 9.5 **Location:** Blvd Kukulcan KM 9.5, Frente a La Playa Chac Mool, Zona Hotelera. **Parking:** on-site. **Cards:** AX, MC, VI.

(See map and index starting on p. 411)

TEMPO **Phone:** 998/881-1100 (45)

Regional Mediterranean
$25-$65

Visit fun and elegant Italy while in Cancun at this ristorante, which features white starched linens, candles and comfortable seating, plus an excitingly imaginative menu. Start with mussels poached in wine, diced olives, shallots and tomatoes; follow with fresh raviolis stuffed with lobster and dressed in a lobster bisque reduction. Casual dress. **Bar:** Full bar. **Reservations:** suggested. **Hours:** 6:30 pm-midnight. Closed: Mon. **Address:** Blvd Kukulcan KM 16.5 **Location:** Blvd Kukulcan KM 16.5; in Gran Melia Cancun Beach & Spa Resort. **Parking:** on-site (fee) and valet. **Cards:** AX, MC, VI.

The following restaurants have not been evaluated by AAA but are listed for your information only.

MB'S **Phone:** 998/881-7600

fyi

Not evaluated. Light, fresh and flavorful are the hallmarks of the menu at this restaurant, featuring Haute Mexican Caribbean cuisine and an indoor theater kitchen or terrace dining overlooking an azure sea. **Address:** Blvd Kukulcan KM 14.5 **Location:** On the beach; windward side of Cancun Island; in Aqua Hotel.

SIETE **Phone:** 998/881-7600

fyi

Not evaluated. Amongst the newest of the town's hot dining spots, Siete offers guests haute Mexican/Caribbean cuisine in a relaxed atmosphere served by an attentive and well-trained staff. Try the flavorful and lightly grilled fish tacos. **Address:** Blvd Kukulcan KM 14.5 **Location:** On the beach; windward side of Cancun Island; in Aqua Hotel.

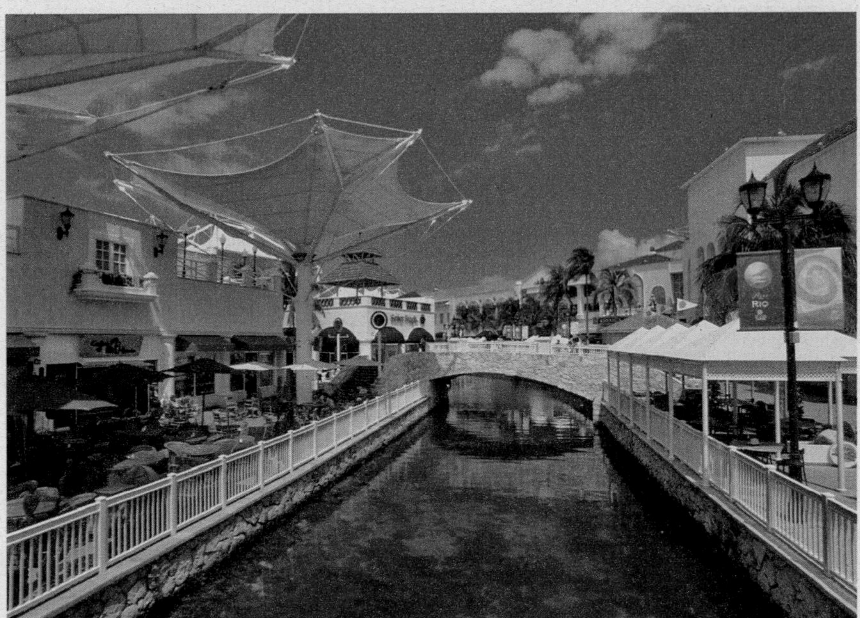

This ends listings for Cancun.
The following page resumes the alphabetical listings of cities in Yucatan Peninsula.

CHICHEN ITZA, YUCATAN pop. 1,000

WHERE TO STAY

HACIENDA CHICHEN RESORT — **Phone:** (985)851-0045

Classic Historic Country Inn
$110-$180 All Year

Address: KM 120 Merida-Puerto Juarez Hwy **Location:** 6 mi (10 km) s of Cancun-Merida Toll Hwy, exit Chichen Itza/Piste. Located adjacent to the main archeological area. **Facility:** Within walking distance of the grand Chichen Itza archaeological zone, this hotel's rooms are spread out among lush jungle gardens. 28 one-bedroom standard units. 1 story, exterior corridors. *Bath:* combo or shower only. **Parking:** on-site. **Amenities:** honor bars, hair dryers. **Dining:** Restaurante Hacienda Chichen, see separate listing. **Pool(s):** outdoor. **Leisure Activities:** hiking trails, jogging. **Business Services:** meeting rooms, fax. **Cards:** AX, MC, VI.

/ SOME UNITS

HOTEL MAYALAND AND BUNGALOWS — **Phone:** (985)851-0100

Hotel
$100-$180 All Year

Address: KM 120 Carr 180 **Location:** 6 mi (10 km) s of Cancun-Merida Toll Hwy, exit Chichen Itza/Piste. Located adjacent to the main archaeological zone. **Facility:** 89 one-bedroom standard units, some with whirlpools. 3 stories, interior/exterior corridors. *Bath:* combo or shower only. **Parking:** on-site. **Terms:** 15 day cancellation notice-fee imposed. **Amenities:** hair dryers. **Dining:** Restaurante Mayaland, see separate listing. **Pool(s):** 2 outdoor. **Leisure Activities:** jogging, playground, spa. *Fee:* horseback riding. **Guest Services:** valet laundry. **Business Services:** conference facilities, PC. **Cards:** AX, MC, VI.

/ SOME UNITS

VILLAS ARQUEOLOGICAS — **Phone:** (985)856-6000

Hotel
$80-$170 All Year

Address: KM 120 Carr Merida-Valladolid **Location:** 6 mi (10 km) s of Cancun-Merida Toll Hwy, exit Chichen Itza/Piste. Located adjacent to the main archaeological area. **Facility:** 40 one-bedroom standard units. 2 stories (no elevator), exterior corridors. *Bath:* shower only. **Parking:** on-site. **Amenities:** safes, hair dryers. **Pool(s):** outdoor. **Guest Services:** valet laundry. **Business Services:** fax (fee). **Cards:** AX, MC, VI.

D

WHERE TO DINE

RESTAURANTE HACIENDA CHICHEN — **Phone:** 985/851-0045

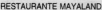

Regional Mexican
$4-$13

In addition to traditional American selections, the menu lists classic Mayan offerings. Seating is offered in the air-conditioned dining room or on the spectacular garden terrace. Casual dress. **Bar:** Full bar. **Hours:** 7 am-10 pm. **Address:** KM 120 Merida-Puerto Juarez Hwy **Location:** 6 mi (10 km) s of Cancun-Merida Toll Hwy, exit Chichen Itza/Piste; in Hacienda Chichen Resort. **Parking:** on-site. **Cards:** AX, MC, VI.

RESTAURANTE MAYALAND — **Phone:** 985/851-0100

International
$10-$25

Deep in the Yucatan village but well worth seeking out, the large restaurant is adjacent to the Chichen-Itza Mayan ruins. A few American selections pop up on a menu of mostly Mayan dishes, such as sweet and sour pork pibil and lime soup. Casual dress. **Bar:** Full bar. **Reservations:** suggested. **Hours:** 7 am-9 pm. **Address:** KM 120 Merida-Puerto Juarez Hwy **Location:** 6 mi (10 km) s of Cancun-Merida Toll Hwy, exit Chichen Itza/Piste. **Parking:** on-site. **Cards:** AX, MC, VI.

COZUMEL, QUINTANA ROO pop. 64,100

WHERE TO STAY

EL CID LA CEIBA *Book at AAA.com* — **Phone:** (987)872-0844

Hotel
$280-$360 All Year

Address: Carr Chankanaab KM 4.5 **Location:** Oceanfront. 0.3 mi (0.5 km) s of municipal ferry landing. **Facility:** 60 units. 52 one- and 8 two-bedroom standard units, some with efficiencies. 9 stories, interior corridors. **Parking:** on-site. **Amenities:** hair dryers. *Some:* DVD players, irons. **Pool(s):** outdoor. **Leisure Activities:** exercise room, massage. **Guest Services:** valet laundry, wireless Internet. **Business Services:** meeting rooms, business center. **Cards:** AX, MC, VI.

D / SOME UNITS

PLAYA AZUL HOTEL — **Phone:** 987/869-5160

Hotel
$185-$295 All Year

Address: Carr San Juan KM 4 **Location:** Oceanfront. Zona Hotelera Norte. Located on a quiet beach. **Facility:** 50 units. 45 one-bedroom standard units. 4 one- and 1 three-bedroom suites, some with kitchens and/or whirlpools. 3 stories, interior corridors. **Parking:** on-site. **Amenities:** high-speed Internet, safes (fee). **Pool(s):** outdoor. **Leisure Activities:** scuba equipment rental, snorkeling. *Fee:* charter fishing. **Guest Services:** wireless Internet. **Business Services:** meeting rooms, fax (fee). **Cards:** AX, MC, VI.

PRESIDENTE INTERCONTINENTAL COZUMEL RESORT AND SPA

Book at AAA.com

Contemporary Resort Hotel

$280-$670 All Year

Phone: (987)872-9500

Address: Carr Chankanaab KM 6.5 **Location:** Oceanfront. 3.9 mi (6.5 km) s of San Miguel on beach road; at La Caleta Yacht Basin. **Facility:** Find tropically landscaped grounds, a tranquil beach area and on-site snorkeling at this property, where most rooms have ocean views. Meets AAA guest room security requirements. 220 units. 208 one-bedroom standard units. 12 one-bedroom suites, some with kitchens and/or whirlpools. 2-5 stories, interior/exterior corridors. *Bath:* combo or shower only. **Parking:** on-site and valet. **Terms:** 14 day cancellation notice-fee imposed. **Amenities:** high-speed Internet, voice mail, safes, honor bars, irons, hair dryers. *Some:* CD players. **Dining:** Alfredo di Roma, see separate listing. **Pool(s):** 2 heated outdoor. **Leisure Activities:** rental boats, boat dock, scuba diving & rental equipment, snorkeling & rental equipment, putting green, 2 lighted tennis courts, playground, exercise room, spa. *Fee:* paddleboats, sailboats, windsurfing, waterskiing, charter fishing. **Guest Services:** valet laundry, wireless Internet. **Business Services:** conference facilities, business center. **Cards:** AX, DC, JC, MC, VI.

24 D / SOME UNITS FEE VCR

The following lodgings were either not evaluated or did not meet AAA rating requirements but are listed for your information only.

HOTEL AGUILAR

fyi

Phone: 987/872-0307

Not evaluated. **Address:** Calle 3 Sur con Ave 5 **Location:** 1 blk e of ferry landing. Facilities, services, and decor characterize an economy property.

HOTEL BARRACUDA

fyi

Phone: 987/872-0002

Not evaluated. **Address:** Carr Chankanaab KM 5.2 **Location:** 1.2 mi (2 km) n of ferry landing. Facilities, services, and decor characterize an economy property.

HOTEL EL MARQUES

fyi

Phone: 987/872-0677

Not evaluated. **Address:** No 180 Ave 5 Sur **Location:** 4 blks s of ferry landing. Facilities, services, and decor characterize an economy property.

LA CASONA REAL

fyi

Phone: 987/872-5471

Not evaluated. **Address:** No 501 Ave Juarez **Location:** Between 25th and 30th N sts. Facilities, services, and decor characterize an economy property.

OCCIDENTAL GRAND COZUMEL

fyi

Resort Hotel

Phone: 987/872-9730

Did not meet all AAA rating requirements for locking devices in some guest rooms at time of last evaluation. **Address:** Carr Sur Cozumel KM 17.5 **Location:** 10.5 mi (17.5 km) s of Main City Pier. Facilities, services, and decor characterize an upscale property.

PALMA DORADA HOTEL

fyi

Phone: 987/872-0330

Not evaluated. **Address:** No 44 Calle Dr A R Salas. Facilities, services, and decor characterize a mid-scale property.

SCUBA CLUB COZUMEL

fyi

Phone: 987/872-1800

Not evaluated. **Address:** Waterfront **Location:** 1.6 mi (2.6 km) s of San Miguel on beach road. Facilities, services, and decor characterize an economy property.

WHERE TO DINE

ALFREDO DI ROMA

Italian

$30-$70

Phone: 987/872-9500

Newly built after Hurricane Wilma, the upscale dining room features floor-to-ceiling plate-glass windows that afford views of the Caribbean. Tables settings include Villeroy & Boch, Frette and high-quality flatware. Live classical guitar music enhances the atmosphere. The signature fettuccine dish is prepared tableside. Dressy casual. Entertainment. **Bar:** Full bar. **Reservations:** accepted. **Hours:** 6 pm-midnight. **Address:** Carr Chankanaab KM 6.5 **Location:** 3.9 mi (6.5 km) s of San Miguel on beach road; at La Caleta Yacht Basin; in Presidente InterContinental Cozumel Resort and Spa. **Parking:** on-site and valet. **Cards:** AX, MC, VI.

CARLOS 'N CHARLIE'S

American

$7-$12

Phone: 987/869-1646

Overlooking the main pier and busy seafront promenade, the second-floor restaurant boasts a high-spirited crowd. On the menu are "gringo" favorites—hamburgers, barbecued ribs and shrimp—as well as Mexican favorites, including enchiladas, fajitas and the house specialty, molcajete served in a lava-style pot. Beer and drinks are served by the yard. Casual dress. **Bar:** Full bar. **Reservations:** accepted. **Hours:** 10 am-1 am, Sun from 5 pm. Closed: 1/1; also 12/24. **Address:** Punta Langosta **Location:** In mall centro commercial, next to city cruise line pier. **Parking:** on-site. **Cards:** AX, MC, VI.

EL CAPI NAVIGANTE
Phone: 987/872-1730

Seafood
$8-$18

Casual, fun and authentic, this local favorite tucked into a corner of the city is where Cozumelenos dine on fish, shellfish, squid, seafood, soup and fillets wrapped in banana leaves. Casual dress. **Bar:** Full bar. **Reservations:** accepted. **Hours:** noon-10:30 pm. **Address:** Ave 10 Sur #312 **Location:** Ave 10 Sur at Calle 3 Sur; 3 blks e of downtown pier. **Parking:** street. **Cards:** MC, VI.

FRENCH QUARTER
Phone: 987/872-6321

Regional Cajun
$15-$25

A surprising find on the island—typical New Orleans dining on the second level of an open-air restaurant, with a refreshing evening breeze. A wide selection of classic New Orleans-style cuisine is offered. Casual dress. **Bar:** Full bar. **Hours:** 5 pm-10:30 pm. Closed: Tues. **Address:** Ave 5 Sur **Location:** 4 blks e of Ave Rafael Melgar. **Parking:** street. **Cards:** AX, MC, VI.

LA CHOZA
Phone: 987/872-0958

Regional Mexican
$6-$15

Featuring authentic Mexico island dishes, the local favorite offers a fun and casual experience under the open breeze palapa. Casual dress. **Bar:** Full bar. **Hours:** 7:30 am-10:30 pm. **Address:** Ave 10 Sur esq con Ave Rosando Salas **Location:** 3 blks e of Ave Rafael Melgar. **Parking:** street. **Cards:** AX, MC, VI.

PEPE'S GRILL
Phone: 987/872-0213

Continental
$15-$35

A longtime island favorite, the eatery features quality steaks, chops, seafood, pasta and more. Many dishes are prepared at your table, which offers a great view of Cozumel's promenade. Casual dress. **Bar:** Full bar. **Reservations:** suggested. **Hours:** 5 pm-11 pm. **Address:** Ave Rafael Melgar esq con Rosando Salas **Location:** On malecon; opposite ferry pier. **Parking:** street. **Cards:** AX, MC, VI.

SENOR FROG'S
Phone: 987/869-1651

International
$7-$16

Part of the chain of Mexican restaurants that also includes Carlos 'n Charlie's, the fun and festive eatery is a great place to eat with the family or rendezvous with friends. The menu is lined with Tex-Mex, American and Mexican favorites, such as Buffalo wings, quesadillas, fajitas and burritos. After hours, a bar atmosphere prevails. Casual dress. **Bar:** Full bar. **Reservations:** accepted. **Hours:** 10 am-11 pm. Closed: Sun. **Address:** Ave Rafael Melgar #551, Loc AD-1 **Location:** On Main Ave, across from beach. **Parking:** on-site. **Cards:** AX, MC, VI.

The following restaurants have not been evaluated by AAA but are listed for your information only.

CASA DENIS
Phone: 987/872-3749

fyi

Not evaluated. This 90-year-old restaurant has served authentic Mexican seafood and Yucatecan specialties to locals and international celebrities such as Placido Domingo and Jacqueline Kennedy. Made-in-house specialties include tangy shrimp or conch seviche, empanadas and soups such as Mayan lime, avocado cream and bouillabaisse. **Address:** Calle 4 Norte No 22 **Location:** 1 blk n of ferry landing.

CASA MISSION RESTAURANT
Phone: 987/872-3248

fyi

Not evaluated. The old world island mansion features extensive gardens and exotic fauna and flora and offers good selections of Mayan and regional dishes. **Address:** Ave Juarez con 55 Ave **Location:** 5 blks e at downtown pier.

COCO'S
Phone: 987/872-0241

fyi

Not evaluated. Known locally for early breakfast and brunch, this spot in the main plaza prepares both typical Mexican dishes, such as tacos and huevos rancheros, and American favorites, including pancakes, eggs and ham-filled croissants. Credit cards are not accepted. **Address:** No 180 Ave 5 Sur **Location:** 4 blks s of ferry landing; under Hotel El Marques.

LA COCAY
Phone: 987/872-5533

fyi

Not evaluated. Featured in The New York Times, this modern restaurant serves distinctive Mediterranean dishes along the lines of artichoke salads, cheese-filled phyllo rolls and spinach manicotti topped with tomato basil sauce. The back patio provides a more casual setting. **Address:** No 20 Calle 8 **Location:** 4 blks s of ferry landing.

LA VERANDA
Phone: 987/872-4132

fyi

Not evaluated. This converted home has a relaxing ambience. Open only for dinner, including Sundays, the restaurant enables patrons to sample choices such as carpaccio, quesadillas, shrimp curry or seafood-filled chili poblanos. **Address:** Calle 4 entre Ave 5 y 10 Sur **Location:** 2 blks s of ferry landing.

ISLA HOLBOX, QUINTANA ROO

WHERE TO STAY

The following lodging was either not evaluated or did not meet AAA rating requirements but is listed for your information only.

CASA SANDRA
Phone: 984/875-2171

fyi

Not evaluated. **Address:** 40 Oriente Playa Norte **Location:** North beach. Facilities, services, and decor characterize a mid-scale property.

WHERE TO DINE

The following restaurant has not been evaluated by AAA but is listed for your information only.

BUENA VISTA GRILL **Phone:** 984/875-2102

fyi

Not evaluated. Featured in a 2006 CNN.com Coastal Living column raving about its seviche, this casual restaurant behind the Hotel Faro Viejo serves lunch and dinner. Seafood abounds; conch, lobster, octopus, shrimp and, of course, seviche make up the menu. **Address:** No. 10 Porfirio Diax **Location:** North beach; just w of main plaza.

ISLA MUJERES, QUINTANA ROO pop. 11,313

WHERE TO STAY

AVALON REEF CLUB **Phone:** (998)999-2050

Resort Hotel
$214-$360 All Year

Address: Calle Zaziltla S/N 7 Islote Yunque **Location:** Oceanfront. On Yunque Islet, across wood bridge from Isla Mujeres northern tip. Located on its own island. **Facility:** Situated on a private island and connected by a wooden bridge, the hotel features wide beaches, tranquil surfs and ample resort activities. 136 units. 130 one-bedroom standard units. 6 one-bedroom suites. 1-6 stories, interior/exterior corridors. *Bath:* shower only. **Parking:** no self-parking. **Terms:** 14 day cancellation notice, in season. **Amenities:** CD players, safes, honor bars, hair dryers. **Pool(s):** outdoor. **Leisure Activities:** saunas, canoeing, paddleboats, sailboats, windsurfing, boat dock, snorkeling, exercise room. *Fee:* charter fishing, massage. **Guest Services:** valet laundry. **Business Services:** meeting rooms, fax. **Cards:** AX, MC, VI.

D / SOME UNITS

HOTEL NA BALAM **Phone:** 998/877-0279

Hotel
$136-$208 All Year

Address: Calle Zazil Ha 118 **Location:** Oceanfront. Northern end of island; on the beach. **Facility:** 35 units. 30 one-bedroom standard units. 5 one-bedroom suites. 2 stories (no elevator), exterior corridors. *Bath:* shower only. **Parking:** on-site. **Terms:** office hours 7 am-11 pm, 14 day cancellation notice. **Amenities:** safes. **Dining:** Restaurant Zazil-Ha, see separate listing. **Pool(s):** outdoor. **Leisure Activities:** *Fee:* scuba diving, snorkeling, fishing, charter fishing, massage. **Guest Services:** valet laundry, wireless Internet. **Cards:** AX, MC, VI.

/ SOME UNITS

HOTEL SECRETO **Phone:** (998)877-1039

Contemporary Hotel
$225-$320 All Year

Address: Secc Rocas, Lote 11, Punta Norte **Location:** On north beach. Located in a quiet secluded area. **Facility:** As the name infers, this trendy, stylish property is hidden on a sandy back street near the island's small convention center; it's worth the search. 9 one-bedroom standard units. 3 stories (no elevator), interior corridors. *Bath:* shower only. **Parking:** on-site. **Terms:** 5 night minimum stay - seasonal and/or weekends, cancellation fee imposed. **Amenities:** DVD players, CD players, safes, honor bars, irons, hair dryers. **Pool(s):** outdoor. **Leisure Activities:** *Fee:* massage. **Guest Services:** wireless Internet. **Business Services:** fax (fee). **Cards:** MC, VI.

D

VILLA VERA PUERTO ISLA MUJERES **Phone:** 998/287-3340

Contemporary Hotel
$180-$300 All Year

Address: Laguna Makax S/N **Location:** Towards southern end of island; south of airstrip. **Facility:** Specializing in marina services, this small hotel has wide lawn and pool areas, an upscale restaurant and many all-inclusive leisure activities. 26 units. 22 one-bedroom standard units with whirlpools. 4 one-bedroom suites with efficiencies and whirlpools. 2 stories, exterior corridors. *Bath:* shower or tub only. **Parking:** on-site. **Terms:** 21 day cancellation notice, in season. **Amenities:** video library, CD players, safes, honor bars, hair dryers. **Pool(s):** heated outdoor. **Leisure Activities:** scuba diving & rental equipment, snorkeling & rental equipment, massage. *Fee:* marina, charter fishing, lighted tennis court. **Guest Services:** valet laundry. **Business Services:** meeting rooms, PC, fax (fee). **Cards:** AX, MC, VI.

D / SOME UNITS VCR

The following lodgings were either not evaluated or did not meet AAA rating requirements but are listed for your information only.

CABANAS MARIA DEL MAR **Phone:** 998/877-0179

fyi

Not evaluated. **Address:** No. 18 Ave Arq. C. Lazaro. Facilities, services, and decor characterize an economy property.

CASA DE LOS SUENOS **Phone:** 998/877-0651

fyi

Not evaluated. **Address:** Carr Garrafon KM 6. Facilities, services, and decor characterize an upscale property.

CRISTALMAR RESORT BEACH CLUB **Phone:** 998/877-0398

fyi

Not evaluated. **Address:** Fracc Paraiso Laguna Mar s/n. Facilities, services, and decor characterize an economy property.

ELEMENTS OF THE ISLAND **Phone:** 998/877-0736

fyi

Not evaluated. **Address:** No. 64 Ave B. Juarez. Facilities, services, and decor characterize a mid-scale property.

HOTEL BELMAR

Phone: 998/877-0430

fyi

Not evaluated. **Address:** Ave Hidalgo No 110 **Location:** On Ave Hidalgo; between Calle Madero and Abasolo. Facilities, services, and decor characterize an economy property.

ROLANDI GOURMET BEACH CLUB

Phone: 998/877-0700

fyi

Not evaluated. **Address:** Lotes 15 y 16 Carr Sac-bajo **Location:** Laguna Mar section of Sac-bajo. Facilities, services, and decor characterize an upscale property.

WHERE TO DINE

PIZZA ROLANDI

Phone: 998/877-0429

Italian
$8-$35

Focusing on Northern Italian cuisine served in a fun, spirited atmosphere and located within walking distance of the main city pier, the restaurant is a longtime island favorite. Casual dress. **Bar:** Full bar. **Hours:** 11 am-midnight, Sun-10 pm. **Address:** Ave Hidalgo 110 **Location:** On Ave Hidalgo walk-way, 3 blks e from ferry landing. **Parking:** no self-parking. **Cards:** AX, MC, VI.

RESTAURANT ZAZIL-HA

Phone: 998/877-0279

Regional Mexican
$7-$25

Hidden on the beach and covered with palapas, this casual restaurant offers local favorites; ask for the fish tacos. Casual dress. **Bar:** Full bar. **Hours:** 7:30 am-11 pm. **Address:** Calle Zazil-Ha 118 **Location:** Northern end of island; on beach; in Hotel Na Balam. **Parking:** street. **Cards:** AX, MC, VI.

The following restaurants have not been evaluated by AAA but are listed for your information only.

CAFE CITO

Phone: 998/877-1470

fyi

Not evaluated. Open only for breakfast and lunch, Cafe Cito ("little coffee") specializes in varied coffee beverages that accompany choices such as pan dulce and typical Mexican breakfasts. Recommended choices include huevos rancheros, fried and topped with spicy tomato sauce, and huevos a la Mexicana, scrambled with diced chiles, onions and tomatoes. **Address:** Ave Benito Juarez #202 **Location:** 4 blks e of ferry landing.

CASA O

Phone: 998/888-0170

fyi

Not evaluated. Visitors can take a taxi on the road south to Garrafon to discover this secluded, palapa-topped restaurant, which serves fresh seafood, arrachera, kebabs, chops and bisques. Reservations are suggested. **Address:** Rueda Medina Sur s/n **Location:** On southern end towards EL Garrafon.

EL PINGUINO

Phone: 998/877-0044

fyi

Not evaluated. In the Posada del Mar hotel just blocks from the main ferry landing, this restaurant is open all day. Patrons can enjoy views of the Caribbean as they wake up to Mexican-style eggs or later indulge in a seafood platter right on the beach. **Address:** Ave Rueda Medina esq con Morelos.

LA PALAPA HUINIC

Phone: 998/877-0398

fyi

Not evaluated. As the name implies, La Palapa Huinic's open-air setting is palapa-topped and appointed in colorful tablecloths and lush surroundings. In the Cristalmar Resort and Beach Club, this place presents a menu of burgers, tacos, spaghetti and arroz con pollo (rice and chicken). **Address:** Fracc Paraiso Laguna Mar s/n.

IZAMAL, YUCATAN pop. 23,006

WHERE TO DINE

KINICH KAKMO

Phone: 988/954-0489

Regional Mexican
$5-$10

Within walking distance of the pyramid that bears its name, this local favorite is well known for its Yucatan and Mayan specialties. Casual dress. **Bar:** Full bar. **Hours:** 10 am-6 pm, Fri & Sat-9 pm. **Address:** Calle 27 #299 **Location:** 1 blk s of Kinich Kakmo Pyramid. **Parking:** street. **Cards:** MC, VI.

KANTENAH, QUINTANA ROO

WHERE TO STAY

The following lodging was either not evaluated or did not meet AAA rating requirements but is listed for your information only.

EL DORADO SEASIDE SUITES BY KARISMA

Phone: 984/875-1910

fyi

Not evaluated. **Address:** KM 95 Carr Cancun-Tulum **Location:** In lush Yucatan jungle near Akumas; off Mex 307; 20.4 mi (34 km) s of Playa del Carmen. Facilities, services, and decor characterize an upscale property.

MERIDA, YUCATAN pop. 705,055

WHERE TO STAY

DEL GOBERNADOR HOTEL — **Phone:** (999)930-4141

Hotel
$65-$130 All Year

Address: 535 Calle 59 **Location:** Jct calles 59 and 66. Located in a quiet area. **Facility:** 86 one-bedroom standard units, some with whirlpools. 3 stories (no elevator), exterior corridors. *Bath:* shower only. **Parking:** on-site. **Terms:** cancellation fee imposed. **Amenities:** voice mail. *Some:* high-speed Internet, irons, hair dryers. **Pool(s):** 2 outdoor. **Guest Services:** valet laundry, wireless Internet. **Business Services:** meeting rooms, business center. **Cards:** AX, DC, DS, MC, VI.

/ SOME UNITS

FIESTA AMERICANA MERIDA — **Phone:** (999)942-1111

Hotel
$145-$285 All Year

Address: Paseo de Montejo #451 **Location:** Paseo de Montejo at Ave Colon; 0.6 mi (1 km) n of main plaza. Facing historic Paseo de Montejo. **Facility:** Set just off Paseo de Montejo, this large-scale hotel offers a refined atmosphere, full service and a striking atrium lobby. 350 units. 327 one-bedroom standard units. 22 one- and 1 two-bedroom suites, some with whirlpools. 5 stories, interior corridors. **Parking:** on-site. **Terms:** 3 day cancellation notice. **Amenities:** video games (fee), high-speed Internet, voice mail, safes, honor bars, irons, hair dryers. **Dining:** 2 restaurants, also, Sanborn's, see separate listing. **Pool(s):** heated outdoor. **Leisure Activities:** sauna, whirlpool, steamroom, tennis court, exercise room, spa. **Guest Services:** valet laundry, area transportation (fee), wireless Internet. **Business Services:** conference facilities, business center. **Cards:** AX, DC, MC, VI.
(See color ad on insert)

FEE / SOME UNITS

HACIENDA XCANATUN CASA DE PIEDRA — **Phone:** (999)941-0213

Classic Historic Country Inn
$240-$305 All Year

Address: KM 12 Carr Merida-Progreso **Location:** Just e of Mex 261 at KM 12 Merida-Progreso Hwy. Adjacent to Xcanatun hamlet. **Facility:** The beautifully restored former hacienda features Mayan relics, lush gardens and luxurious accommodations in the midst of the Yucatan jungle. Meets AAA guest room security requirements. 18 one-bedroom suites, some with whirlpools. 1-2 stories (no elevator), exterior corridors. **Parking:** on-site. **Amenities:** CD players, high-speed Internet, safes, honor bars, hair dryers. **Dining:** Casa de Piedra, see separate listing. **Pool(s):** 2 outdoor. **Leisure Activities:** hiking trails, spa. **Guest Services:** valet laundry, wireless Internet. *Fee:* airport transportation-Merida International Airport, area transportation. **Business Services:** meeting rooms, fax (fee). **Cards:** AX, MC, VI.

FEE / SOME UNITS

HOLIDAY INN *Book great rates at AAA.com* — **Phone:** (999)942-8800

Hotel
$115-$185 All Year

Address: Ave Colon 498 **Location:** 0.6 mi (1 km) n of main plaza; jct Calle 60 and Ave Colon; just off Paseo de Montejo. Located behind the US Consulate. **Facility:** Meets AAA guest room security requirements. 212 one-bedroom standard units. 4 stories, interior corridors. **Parking:** on-site. **Amenities:** high-speed Internet, voice mail, irons, hair dryers. *Some:* safes. **Dining:** La Veranda, see separate listing, entertainment. **Pool(s):** outdoor. **Leisure Activities:** exercise room, spa. *Fee:* lighted tennis court. **Guest Services:** valet laundry, wireless Internet. **Business Services:** conference facilities, business center. **Cards:** AX, DC, MC, VI.

/ SOME UNITS

HOTEL CASA DEL BALAM — **Phone:** (999)924-8844

Historic Hotel
$100-$180 All Year

Address: Calle 60 #488 **Location:** 2 blks n of main plaza; jct calles 60 and 57. **Facility:** Simple yet distinguished, this is a Colonial-style hotel with an interior courtyard/pool area, traditional Mayan cuisine and a friendly staff. 52 units. 49 one-bedroom standard units. 3 one-bedroom suites. 6 stories, exterior corridors. **Parking:** on-site. **Terms:** 3 day cancellation notice. **Amenities:** honor bars, hair dryers. **Pool(s):** outdoor. **Guest Services:** valet laundry. **Business Services:** meeting rooms, PC, fax (fee). **Cards:** AX, CB, DC, MC, VI.

/ SOME UNITS

HOTEL EL CONQUISTADOR — **Phone:** (999)940-6400

Hotel
$115-$180 All Year

Address: Paseo de Montejo #458 **Location:** On Paseo de Montejo, just s of Calle 33. **Facility:** 159 one-bedroom standard units. 8 stories, interior corridors. **Parking:** on-site. **Amenities:** high-speed Internet, safes (fee), honor bars, irons, hair dryers. **Dining:** 2 restaurants, entertainment. **Pool(s):** outdoor. **Leisure Activities:** recreation programs. **Guest Services:** valet laundry, wireless Internet. **Business Services:** conference facilities, business center. **Cards:** AX, CB, DC, MC, VI.

FEE / SOME UNITS

HOTEL LOS ALUXES *Book at AAA.com* — **Phone:** (999)924-2199

Hotel
$90-$175 All Year

Address: Calle 60 #444 **Location:** 5 blks n of main plaza; jct calles 60 and 49. **Facility:** 155 units. 137 one-bedroom standard units, some with whirlpools. 18 one-bedroom suites. 3-5 stories, interior corridors. **Parking:** on-site. **Terms:** 3 day cancellation notice. **Amenities:** voice mail, hair dryers. *Some:* honor bars. **Pool(s):** outdoor. **Guest Services:** valet laundry. **Business Services:** conference facilities, business center. **Cards:** AX, MC, VI.

HOTEL PRESIDENTE INTERCONTINENTAL VILLA MERCEDES *Book at AAA.com* — **Phone:** (999)942-9000

Hotel
$180-$240 All Year

Address: Ave Colon 500 **Location:** 0.6 mi (1 km) n of main plaza; jct Calle 60 and Ave Colon; just off Paseo de Montejo. **Facility:** A former hacienda and French Consulate, the hotel offers stylish guest rooms with spacious bathrooms; rotating art displays are featured in the lobby. Meets AAA guest room security requirements. 127 units. 121 one-bedroom standard units. 6 one-bedroom suites, some with whirlpools. 5 stories, interior corridors. **Parking:** on-site and valet. **Amenities:** video games, high-speed Internet, dual phone lines, voice mail, safes, honor bars, irons, hair dryers. *Some:* CD players. **Pool(s):** outdoor. **Leisure Activities:** whirlpool, exercise room. *Fee:* massage. **Guest Services:** valet laundry. **Business Services:** meeting rooms, business center. **Cards:** AX, MC, VI.

/ SOME UNITS

HOTEL RESIDENCIAL **Phone:** (999)924-3099

Hotel
$85-$150 All Year

Address: Calle 59 #589 **Location:** Jct calles 59 and 76. **Facility:** Meets AAA guest room security requirements. 66 units. 64 one-bedroom standard units. 2 one-bedroom suites with whirlpools. 5 stories, interior/exterior corridors. *Bath:* shower only. **Parking:** on-site. **Terms:** 3 day cancellation notice. **Amenities:** hair dryers. **Dining:** entertainment. **Pool(s):** outdoor. **Guest Services:** valet laundry, wireless Internet. **Business Services:** meeting rooms, fax (fee). **Cards:** AX, MC, VI.

HYATT REGENCY MERIDA Book great rates at AAA.com **Phone:** (999)942-1234

Hotel
$95-$149 All Year

Address: Calle 60 #344 **Location:** 0.6 mi (1 km) n of main plaza; jct Calle 60 and Ave Colon; just off Paseo de Montejo. **Facility:** This striking high-rise just off Paseo de Montejo features elegant rooms, modern public areas and two dining outlets. Meets AAA guest room security requirements. 289 units. 285 one-bedroom standard units. 4 one-bedroom suites with whirlpools. 17 stories, interior corridors. **Parking:** on-site and valet. **Terms:** 3 day cancellation notice-fee imposed. **Amenities:** high-speed Internet (fee), voice mail, safes, honor bars, irons, hair dryers. **Dining:** Spasso, see separate listing, entertainment. **Pool(s):** outdoor. **Leisure Activities:** whirlpool, steamroom, 2 lighted tennis courts, exercise room, spa. **Guest Services:** valet laundry, area transportation (fee), wireless Internet. **Business Services:** conference facilities, business center. **Cards:** AX, MC, VI.

FEE / SOME UNITS

HYATT HOTELS & RESORTS
AAA Benefit:
Ask for the AAA rate and save 10%.

LA MISION DE FRAY DIEGO Book at AAA.com **Phone:** (999)924-1111

Country Inn
$90-$160 All Year

Address: Calle 61 #524 **Location:** 2 blks w of main city plaza; between calles 64 and 66. **Facility:** 26 units. 24 one-bedroom standard units. 2 one-bedroom suites with whirlpools. 2-3 stories (no elevator), exterior corridors. *Bath:* shower or tub only. **Parking:** on-site and valet. **Amenities:** safes, honor bars, hair dryers. **Pool(s):** outdoor. **Guest Services:** valet laundry, wireless Internet. **Business Services:** fax (fee). **Cards:** AX, MC, VI.

WHERE TO DINE

ALBERTO'S CONTINENTAL PATIO **Phone:** 999/928-5367

Regional International
$6-$20

Lebanese specialties are among the international dishes prepared in this converted 17th-century home. Decorated with artifacts from the city's rich colonial past, the museum-like restaurant offers seating in the open-air patio or the air-conditioned dining room. Tour groups occasionally flood this place. Casual dress. **Bar:** Full bar. **Reservations:** accepted. **Hours:** 1 pm-11 pm; from 6 pm 12/25, 1/1 & Sun. Closed: Mardi Gras & Good Friday. **Address:** Calle 64 #482 **Location:** Corner of calles 57 and 64. **Parking:** street. **Cards:** MC, VI. **Historic**

CASA DE PIEDRA **Phone:** 999/941-0213

Regional International
$10-$45

The restaurant offers haute cuisine, featuring regional and European dishes artisticaly presented by highly trained staff in an upscale dining room. Dressy casual. **Bar:** Full bar. **Reservations:** suggested. **Hours:** 7:30 am-11 pm. **Address:** KM 12 Carr Merida-Progreso **Location:** Just e of Mex 261 at KM 12 Merida-Progreso Hwy; in Hacienda Xcanatun Casa de Piedra. **Parking:** on-site and valet. **Cards:** AX, MC, VI.

HACIENDA TEYA RESTAURANTE **Phone:** 999/928-1885

Regional Mexican
$6-$18

On the main highway to Chichen Itza, the restored henequen hacienda has original furnishings and specializes in Mayan cuisine. Casual dress. **Bar:** Full bar. **Reservations:** suggested. **Hours:** noon-6 pm. **Address:** KM 12.5 Carr Merida-Cancun **Location:** On Merida-Cancun Hwy. **Parking:** on-site. **Cards:** AX, CB, DC, DS, JC, MC, VI.

LA BELLA EPOCA **Phone:** 999/928-1928

Regional Mexican
$12-$25

The Yucatan is the focus of traditional Mexican dishes. Most distinctive grilled dishes are a worthy first choice. The setting is casual on several floors, but second-floor balcony tables offer the best views and cool breezes. Casual dress. **Bar:** Full bar. **Reservations:** suggested. **Hours:** 4 pm-1 am. **Address:** Calle 60 #497 **Location:** 2 blks n of main plaza; between calles 57 and 59. **Parking:** street. **Cards:** AX, MC, VI.

LA PARRILLA **Phone:** 999/944-3999

Regional Mexican
$7-$18

Young at heart, this fun, casual restaurant serves a wide assortment of Yucatan specialities; don't miss the combo plates with beef fajitas, mole enchiladas and side of beans. Casual dress. **Bar:** Full bar. **Hours:** 1 pm-midnight, Fri & Sat-2 am. **Address:** Calle 60 esq con Calle 59 **Location:** In historic downtown area. **Parking:** street. **Cards:** AX, MC, VI.

LA PIGUA **Phone:** 999/920-3605

Regional Seafood
$7-$20

Widely varied fresh seafood is prepared using both classic and innovative approaches. The service staff is knowledgeable. Dressy casual. **Bar:** Full bar. **Reservations:** suggested. **Hours:** noon-6 pm. **Address:** Calle Cupules #505 **Location:** 2 blks w of Fiesta Americana Merida; at Cupules Ave and Calle 35. **Parking:** on-site. **Cards:** AX, MC, VI.

LA VERANDA **Phone:** 999/942-8800

Regional Mexican
$15-$28

Undecided diners will find a varied choice of Yucatecan dishes and American favorites, which can be chosen from the large buffet or ordered a la carte. The menu standout is botana Yucateca, which offers grilled link Valladolid sausage, mini volcanoes and panuchos, but guests can play it safe with burgers, pasta or steaks imported from the United States. Casual dress. **Bar:** Full bar. **Reservations:** not accepted. **Hours:** 7 am-10 pm. **Address:** Ave Colon 498 **Location:** 0.6 mi (1 km) n of main plaza; jct Calle 60 and Ave colon; just off Paseo de Montejo; in Holiday Inn. **Parking:** on-site and valet. **Cards:** AX, MC, VI.

LOS ALMENDROS **Phone:** 999/928-5459

Regional Mexican
$7-$18

Classic Yucatan cuisine includes pibil-style dishes, fried plantains, pork and chicken marinated in citrus fruits. A favorite choice is a plate of tender, oversized tamales wrapped in banana leaves. Leon beer is popular. Casual dress. **Bar:** Full bar. **Reservations:** accepted. **Hours:** 10 am-11 pm. **Address:** Calle 50 #493 **Location:** 7 blks n of main plaza. **Parking:** street. **Cards:** AX, MC, VI.

PANCHO'S RESTAURANT AND PATIO BAR **Phone:** 999/923-0942

Regional Mexican
$10-$30

Mexico comes alive in the drinks, food and dancing at the high-energy dining choice. Casual dress. **Bar:** Full bar. **Reservations:** accepted. **Hours:** 6 pm-2 am. **Address:** Calle 59 #509 **Location:** 1 blk n of main plaza. **Parking:** no self-parking. **Cards:** AX, MC, VI.

RESTAURANTE FRUTAS Y FLORES **Phone:** 999/942-9000

Regional New World
$7-$24

Must-try specialties at the casual eatery include the Motul-style eggs, Huevos Motulenos and the fresh-made pizzas. The menu space is also shared with other worldly dishes. The breakfast or lunch buffet, complete with a carving and a pasta station, is ideal for those in a hurry. Casual dress. **Bar:** Full bar. **Hours:** 7 am-10 pm, Fri & Sat-midnight. **Address:** Ave Colon 500 **Location:** 0.6 mi (1 km) n of main plaza; jct Calle 60 and Ave Colon, just off Paseo de Montejo; in Hotel Presidente InterContinental Villa Mercedes. **Parking:** on-site and valet. **Cards:** AX, MC, VI.

SANBORN'S **Phone:** 999/941-8214

Regional Mexican
$8-$28

Restaurants in the casual chain, which includes more than 100 locations throughout Mexico, offer a good selection of American-style sandwiches, salads, soups and both Mexican and American entrees. The selection of desserts is impressive. Casual dress. **Bar:** Full bar. **Hours:** 7 am-1 am. **Address:** Calle 50 Diagonal No 460 **Location:** In Gran Plaza Shopping Complex. **Parking:** on-site. **Cards:** AX, MC, VI.

SANBORN'S **Phone:** 999/925-6177

Mexican
$6-$22

Restaurants in the casual chain, which includes more than 100 locations throughout Mexico, offer a good selection of American-style sandwiches, salads, soups and both Mexican and American entrees. The selection of desserts is impressive. Casual dress. **Bar:** Full bar. **Hours:** 7:30 am-1 am. **Address:** Paseo de Montejo #451 **Location:** Paseo de Montejo at Ave Colon; 0.6 mi (1 km) n of main plaza; in Fiesta Americana Merida. **Parking:** on-site (fee) and street. **Cards:** AX, MC, VI.

SPASSO **Phone:** 999/942-1234

Italian
$22-$38

Diners might not expect Italian fine dining in the Yucatan jungle, but the recently remodeled restaurant delivers just that. Authentic fare is served in a dining room marked by rich wood-paneled walls and soft music. Selections from a fully stocked wine case complement porcini lobster risotto, sole in lemon-butter sauce, chops and an array of pasta dishes. Casual dress. **Bar:** Full bar. **Reservations:** suggested. **Hours:** 6 pm-2 am. Closed: Sun. **Address:** Calle 60 #344 **Location:** 0.6 mi (1 km) n of main plaza; jct Calle 60 and Ave Colon; just off Paseo de Montejo; in Hyatt Regency Merida. **Parking:** on-site and valet. **Cards:** AX, MC, VI.

PLAYA DEL CARMEN, QUINTANA ROO pop. 47,200

WHERE TO STAY

CARIBBEAN PARADISE **Phone:** 984/803-2032

Hotel
$120-$200 All Year

Address: Ave 5, corner of Constituyentes **Location:** Northwest corner of jct Constituyentes and Ave 5. **Facility:** 45 one-bedroom standard units. 3 stories, interior corridors. *Bath:* shower only. **Parking:** street. **Amenities:** safes (fee). **Pool(s):** outdoor. **Guest Services:** valet laundry. **Business Services:** fax (fee). **Cards:** MC, VI.

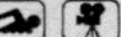

DESEO HOTEL & LOUNGE

Hotel
$265 All Year

Phone: 984/879-3620

Address: Ave 5A y Calle 12 **Location:** Southwest corner of jct Calle 12 and Ave 5 walkway. **Facility:** 15 one-bedroom standard units. 2 stories (no elevator), interior corridors. *Bath:* combo or shower only. **Parking:** street. **Terms:** age restrictions may apply, 7 day cancellation notice. **Amenities:** high-speed Internet, safes, honor bars. **Pool(s):** heated outdoor. **Leisure Activities:** whirlpool. **Guest Services:** valet laundry, wireless Internet. **Business Services:** PC, fax (fee). **Cards:** AX, MC, VI.

/ SOME UNITS

FAIRMONT MAYAKOBA *Book great rates at AAA.com*

Resort Hotel
$240-$2700 All Year

Phone: (984)206-3000

Address: Carr Federal KM 298 **Location:** Oceanfront. On Mex 307, KM 298 (Carr Federal), 25.8 mi (43 km) s of Cancun. **Facility:** Expansive grounds house many pools, gardens and casitas. You may ride bikes, be driven in a cart or take a boat to your room, restaurant, spa or beach. Meets AAA guest room security requirements. 401 units. 367 one-bedroom standard units. 33 one- and 1 two-bedroom suites. 2-4 stories, exterior corridors. **Parking:** valet. **Terms:** check-in 4 pm, 3 day cancellation notice. **Amenities:** CD players, dual phone lines, voice mail, safes, irons, hair dryers. *Fee:* video games, high-speed Internet. **Dining:** 4 restaurants, also, El Puerto, La Laguna, Las Brisas, see separate listings. **Pool(s):** 5 heated outdoor. **Leisure Activities:** saunas, whirlpools, steamrooms, waterslide, limited beach access, 2 tennis courts, bicycles, jogging, spa, volleyball. *Fee:* golf-18 holes. **Guest Services:** airport transportation (fee)-Cancun International Airport, wireless Internet. **Business Services:** conference facilities, business center. **Cards:** AX, MC, VI.
(See color ad on insert)

FEE S D FEE / SOME UNITS

THE GRAND MAYAN RIVIERA MAYA WYNDHAM ALLIANCE RESORT

Resort Hotel
$475-$785 All Year

Phone: (984)206-4000

Address: KM 48 Carr Federal Cancun **Location:** Oceanfront. Mex 307 KM 48. **Facility:** This lodging shares many of its restaurants and outdoor activities with its sister property next door. 376 units. 188 one-bedroom standard units. 188 one-bedroom suites with efficiencies. 3 stories, interior corridors. **Parking:** on-site and valet. **Terms:** check-in 5 pm, 3-7 night minimum stay - seasonal and/or weekends, 21 day cancellation notice-fee imposed. **Amenities:** voice mail, safes, irons, hair dryers. **Pool(s):** outdoor. **Leisure Activities:** whirlpools, lifeguard on duty, rental paddleboats, rental sailboats, scuba diving & rental equipment, snorkeling & rental equipment, recreation programs, bicycles, volleyball. *Fee:* charter fishing, golf-18 holes, 2 lighted tennis courts, massage. **Guest Services:** valet and coin laundry, area transportation (fee), wireless Internet. **Business Services:** meeting rooms. *Fee:* PC, fax. **Cards:** AX, MC, VI.

FEE D / SOME UNITS

HOTEL AVENTURA MEXICANA

Hotel
$140-$230 All Year

Phone: 984/873-1876

Address: Ave 10 & Calle 22 **Location:** Northeast corner. **Facility:** 48 units. 46 one-bedroom standard units. 2 one-bedroom suites with efficiencies. 3 stories, interior corridors. *Bath:* combo or shower only. **Parking:** on-site. **Terms:** 3 day cancellation notice. **Amenities:** safes, hair dryers. *Some:* CD players. **Pool(s):** 2 outdoor. **Leisure Activities:** whirlpool. *Fee:* massage. **Guest Services:** area transportation (fee), wireless Internet. **Business Services:** PC, fax (fee). **Cards:** MC, VI.

FEE / SOME UNITS

HOTEL RIU PALACE MEXICO

Resort Hotel
$220-$490 All Year

Phone: 984/877-4200

Address: Ave Xaman-Ha, Mz 3, Lote 2 **Location:** Oceanfront. E of Mex 307, on beach; in Playacar development. **Facility:** Elegant lobby areas, modern, well-equipped guest rooms, multiple dining outlets and extensive pool activities comprise the ultra-all-inclusive resort. 434 units. 426 one-bedroom standard units, some with whirlpools. 8 one-bedroom suites. 3 stories, interior/exterior corridors. **Parking:** on-site. **Amenities:** safes (fee), honor bars, irons, hair dryers. **Dining:** 5 restaurants, entertainment. **Pool(s):** 2 outdoor. **Leisure Activities:** beach access, scuba equipment rental, snorkeling equipment rental, 2 lighted tennis courts, rental bicycles. *Fee:* scooters. **Guest Services:** valet laundry, wireless Internet. **Business Services:** conference facilities, PC (fee), fax. **Cards:** AX, CB, DC, DS, JC, MC, VI.

D / SOME UNITS

HOTEL RIU PLAYACAR

Resort Hotel
$210-$390 All Year

Phone: 984/877-2300

Address: Ave Xaman-Ha, Mz 3 Lote 0 **Location:** Oceanfront. E of Mex 307, on the beach; in Playacar development. **Facility:** A very nice beach and pool area, with extensive water sports available for guests, give this property appeal. 396 one-bedroom standard units. 3 stories (no elevator), interior/exterior corridors. **Parking:** on-site. **Terms:** 3 night minimum stay, 3 day cancellation notice-fee imposed. **Amenities:** safes, honor bars, hair dryers. **Pool(s):** 2 outdoor. **Leisure Activities:** beach access, scuba equipment rental, snorkeling equipment rental, 2 lighted tennis courts, spa. **Guest Services:** valet laundry, wireless Internet. **Business Services:** PC, fax. **Cards:** AX, MC, VI.

S D

HOTEL RIU TEQUILA

Resort Hotel
$124-$288 All Year

Phone: 984/873-4300

Address: Ave Xaman-Ha, Mz 3, Lote 19 **Location:** Oceanfront. E of Mex 307, near beach; in Playacar development. **Facility:** Set across the road from its sister properties, the hotel offers extensive manicured grounds and an array of activities. 664 one-bedroom standard units. 2 stories (no elevator), interior corridors. **Parking:** on-site. **Terms:** 3 night minimum stay, 3 day cancellation notice-fee imposed. **Amenities:** safes (fee), honor bars, irons, hair dryers. **Pool(s):** 2 outdoor. **Leisure Activities:** beach access, 2 lighted tennis courts, rental bicycles, playground, spa, volleyball. **Guest Services:** valet laundry. **Business Services:** PC, fax. **Cards:** AX, MC, VI.

HOTEL RIU YUCATAN

Phone: 984/873-1300

Resort Hotel

$168-$348 All Year

Address: Ave Xaman-Ha, Mz 3 **Location:** Oceanfront. E of Mex 307, on beach; in Playacar development. **Facility:** One of four sister properties located in Playacar, this lodging offers rooms with plenty of space as well as an array of available activities. 507 one-bedroom standard units. 3 stories (no elevator), interior/exterior corridors. **Parking:** on-site. **Terms:** 3 night minimum stay, 3 day cancellation notice-fee imposed. **Amenities:** safes (fee), honor bars, hair dryers. **Pool(s):** outdoor. **Leisure Activities:** beach access, scuba equipment rental, snorkeling equipment rental, 2 lighted tennis courts, rental bicycles, spa. **Guest Services:** valet laundry, area transportation (fee). **Business Services:** PC (fee), fax. **Cards:** AX, MC, VI.

FEE

IBEROSTAR QUETZAL

Phone: (984)877-2000

Resort Hotel

$300-$390 All Year

Address: Ave Xaman-Ha, Lote Hotelero #2 **Location:** Oceanfront. E off Mex 307; in Playacar development. **Facility:** Along with several restaurants to make each night's dining different, the hotel also offers guests a range of outdoor activities. 700 one-bedroom standard units. 3 stories, interior/exterior corridors. *Bath:* shower only. **Parking:** on-site. **Amenities:** hair dryers. **Pool(s):** 3 outdoor. **Leisure Activities:** whirlpool, beach access, rental boats, rental sailboards, scuba equipment rental, snorkeling equipment rental, exercise room, spa, volleyball. **Guest Services:** valet laundry, wireless Internet. **Business Services:** conference facilities. *Fee:* PC, fax. **Cards:** AX, MC, VI.

(See color ad starting on p 440)

D

MANDARIN ORIENTAL RIVIERA MAYA

Phone: 984/877-3888

fyi

Resort Hotel

$560-$3150 All Year

Too new to rate. **Address:** Carr Federal KM 298.8 **Location:** On Mex 307, KM 298.8 (Carr Federal). **Amenities:** 128 units, restaurant, pool. **Cards:** AX, MC, VI.

MAYAN PALACE RIVIERA MAYA WYNDHAM ALLIANCE RESORT

Phone: (984)206-4000

Resort Hotel

$370-$630 All Year

Address: Carr Federal Cancun KM 48 **Location:** Oceanfront. Mex 307 KM 48. **Facility:** Newly completed, the complex has the Caribbean on one side and 18 holes of rolling turf on the other; rooms are well-appointed and generous in size. 336 units. 168 one-bedroom standard units. 168 one-bedroom suites with efficiencies. 3 stories, interior corridors. **Parking:** on-site and valet. **Terms:** check-in 5 pm, 3-7 night minimum stay - seasonal and/or weekends, 21 day cancellation notice-fee imposed. **Amenities:** voice mail, safes, hair dryers. *Some:* irons. **Pool(s):** outdoor. **Leisure Activities:** whirlpools, lifeguard on duty, rental paddleboats, rental sailboats, windsurfing, scuba diving & rental equipment, snorkeling & rental equipment, recreation programs, bicycles, volleyball. *Fee:* charter fishing, golf-18 holes, 2 lighted tennis courts, massage. **Guest Services:** valet and coin laundry, area transportation (fee), wireless Internet. **Business Services:** meeting rooms. *Fee:* PC, fax. **Cards:** AX, MC, VI.

FEE 24 D / SOME UNITS

MOSQUITO BLUE

Phone: (984)873-1335

Hotel

$120-$325 All Year

Address: Calle 12 **Location:** Between aves 5 and 10. **Facility:** 45 units. 44 one-bedroom standard units. 1 two-bedroom suite with whirlpool. 2 stories, interior corridors. *Bath:* shower only. **Parking:** street. **Terms:** 4 night minimum stay - weekends. **Amenities:** safes, irons, hair dryers. **Pool(s):** 2 outdoor. **Guest Services:** valet laundry, wireless Internet. **Business Services:** PC, fax (fee). **Cards:** AX, MC, VI.

OCCIDENTAL GRAND FLAMENCO XCARET

Book at AAA.com

Phone: (984)871-5400

Resort Hotel

$320-$530 All Year

Address: Carr Chetumal-Puerto Juarez KM 282 **Location:** Oceanfront. Mex 307, KM 282; on the grounds of Xcaret archeological park. **Facility:** Adjacent to Xcaret eco-archeological park, the all-inclusive resort offers an abundance of recreational activities and public areas. 769 units. 762 one-bedroom standard units, some with whirlpools. 7 one-bedroom suites with whirlpools. 3 stories, interior/exterior corridors. **Parking:** on-site and valet. **Terms:** check-in 4 pm, 15 day cancellation notice. **Amenities:** safes, irons, hair dryers. **Pool(s):** 2 outdoor. **Leisure Activities:** canoeing, paddleboats, sailboats, windsurfing, scuba diving & rental equipment, snorkeling & rental equipment, 2 lighted tennis courts, recreation programs, bicycles, playground, exercise room, spa, sports court, volleyball, game room. *Fee:* boats, charter fishing. **Guest Services:** coin laundry, area transportation (fee), wireless Internet. **Business Services:** conference facilities, business center. **Cards:** AX, MC, VI.

FEE D / SOME UNITS

OCCIDENTAL ROYAL HIDEAWAY RESORT & SPA *Book great rates at AAA.com* **Phone:** (984)873-4500

Resort Hotel
$589-$1360 All Year

Address: Lote Hotelera #6 Fracc Playacar **Location:** Oceanfront. E off Mex 307; in Playacar development. Located in a modern upscale area. **Facility:** This all-inclusive resort offers luxurious rooms, full concierge service, elegant dining and an abundance of resort activities. Designated smoking area. 200 units. 192 one-bedroom standard units with whirlpools. 8 one-bedroom suites with whirlpools. 2-3 stories (no elevator), exterior corridors. **Parking:** on-site and valet. **Terms:** age restrictions may apply. **Amenities:** video library, DVD players, video games (fee), CD players, voice mail, safes, irons, hair dryers. *Some:* fax. **Dining:** 7 restaurants, also, Azia, see separate listing, entertainment. **Pool(s):** 5 outdoor, heated outdoor. **Leisure Activities:** whirlpools, rental boats, canoeing, paddleboats, sailboats, windsurfing, marina, snorkeling, poolside aerobics, introductory scuba instruction, 2 lighted tennis courts, recreation programs, library, non-motorized sports, table tennis, theater, bicycles, exercise room, spa, basketball. *Fee:* scuba diving, charter fishing, tennis lessons. **Guest Services:** valet laundry, wireless Internet. **Business Services:** conference facilities, business center. **Cards:** AX, CB, JC, MC, VI. *(See color ad p 414)*

THE REEF PLAYACAR **Phone:** (984)873-4120

Resort Hotel
$325-$500 All Year

Address: Ave Xaman-Ha Retorno Sayil S/N **Location:** Oceanfront. E off Mex 307, on beach; in Playacar development. **Facility:** Located in the Riviera Maya, this impressive beachfront hotel offers a complete array of outdoor and water activities. 202 one-bedroom standard units. 3 stories (no elevator), exterior corridors. **Parking:** on-site. **Terms:** 3 day cancellation notice. **Amenities:** irons, hair dryers. *Fee:* high-speed Internet, safes. **Pool(s):** 2 outdoor. **Leisure Activities:** whirlpool, boating, sailboats, windsurfing, scuba equipment rental, snorkeling equipment rental, lighted tennis court, exercise room, spa, volleyball. *Fee:* charter fishing. **Guest Services:** valet laundry, wireless Internet. **Business Services:** *Fee:* PC, fax. **Cards:** AX, MC, VI.

RIU PALACE RIVIERA MAYA *Book at AAA.com* **Phone:** 984/877-2280

Resort Hotel
$320-$480 All Year

Address: Xaman-Ha, Mzn 9 y 10, Lote 1 **Location:** Oceanfront. Off Mex 307, just s of Playa del Carmen; in Playacar development. **Facility:** One glance around the public areas and guest rooms and you'll think you have entered a palace; guest rooms feature a sunken sitting area. 460 units. 422 one-bedroom standard units. 38 one-bedroom suites. 3-4 stories, interior corridors. **Parking:** on-site. **Terms:** 14 day cancellation notice. **Amenities:** safes, irons, hair dryers. **Pool(s):** 3 outdoor. **Leisure Activities:** saunas, whirlpools, canoeing, paddleboats, windsurfing, scuba diving & rental equipment, snorkeling & rental equipment, 2 lighted tennis courts, exercise room. *Fee:* boats, waterskiing, charter fishing, massage. **Guest Services:** valet laundry, wireless Internet. **Business Services:** meeting rooms, business center. **Cards:** AX, MC, VI.

FEE / SOME UNITS

ROSEWOOD MAYAKOBA **Phone:** 984/875-8000

fyi
Resort Hotel
$790-$8000 All Year

Too new to rate. **Address:** Carr Federal KM 298 **Location:** On Mex 307, 25.8 mi (43 km) s of Cancun. **Amenities:** 128 units, restaurant, pool. **Cards:** AX, MC, VI.

SECRETS CAPRI RIVIERA CANCUN **Phone:** (984)873-4880

Resort Hotel
$504-$828 All Year

Address: Carr Cancun-Chetumal KM 299 **Location:** Oceanfront. 2 mi (3.2 km) n of Playa del Carmen; just e off Mex 307, follow signs. **Facility:** This modern, all-inclusive resort built in 2005 offers upscale public areas, comfortable guest rooms, multiple dining outlets and pool activities. 291 units. 280 one-bedroom standard units with whirlpools. 11 one-bedroom suites with whirlpools. 2-3 stories, interior/exterior corridors. **Parking:** on-site and valet. **Terms:** age restrictions may apply, 14 day cancellation notice. **Amenities:** video library, DVD players, CD players, high-speed Internet, voice mail, safes, honor bars, irons, hair dryers. **Pool(s):** 2 outdoor. **Leisure Activities:** whirlpool, paddleboats, sailboats, windsurfing, snorkeling, 3 lighted tennis courts, recreation programs, bicycles, jogging, exercise room, spa, volleyball, game room. *Fee:* waterskiing, scuba diving, charter fishing. **Guest Services:** valet laundry, area transportation (fee), wireless Internet. **Business Services:** conference facilities, business center. **Cards:** AX, CB, DC, DS, JC, MC, VI. Affiliated with A Preferred Hotel.

FEE / SOME UNITS

VIVA WYNDHAM AZTECA **Phone:** (984)877-4100

Resort Hotel
$290-$500 All Year

Address: Ave Xaman-Ha, Mz #8, Lote 1 **Location:** Oceanfront. E off Mex 307, on beach; in Playacar development. **Facility:** Offering an excellent selection of water activities, with a very nice beach, this property is in the Zona Hotelera area. 234 one-bedroom standard units, some with efficiencies. 3 stories (no elevator), interior/exterior corridors. **Parking:** on-site and valet. **Terms:** 7 day cancellation notice. **Amenities:** safes, irons, hair dryers. **Pool(s):** outdoor. **Leisure Activities:** whirlpool, rental boats, rental sailboards, scuba equipment rental, snorkeling equipment rental, 2 lighted tennis courts, rental bicycles, exercise room, volleyball. *Fee:* charter fishing, massage. **Guest Services:** valet laundry, wireless Internet. **Business Services:** *Fee:* PC, fax. **Cards:** AX, DS, MC, VI.

/ SOME UNITS

VIVA WYNDHAM MAYA

Resort Hotel

$280-$390 All Year

Phone: (984)873-4600

Address: Ave Xaman-Ha, Lote Hotelera #5 **Location:** Oceanfront. E of Mex 307, on beach; in Playacar development. **Facility:** With extensive activities and a very nice beach area, the property offers good-size guest rooms and well-maintained public areas. 400 one-bedroom standard units. 3 stories (no elevator), interior/exterior corridors. **Parking:** on-site and valet. **Terms:** 7 day cancellation notice. **Amenities:** safes, irons, hair dryers. **Pool(s):** outdoor. **Leisure Activities:** whirlpool, rental boats, rental sailboards, scuba equipment rental, snorkeling equipment rental, fishing, 2 lighted tennis courts, rental bicycles, exercise room, spa. **Guest Services:** valet laundry, wireless Internet. **Business Services:** meeting rooms. *Fee:* PC, fax. **Cards:** AX, DS, MC, VI.

CALL / SOME UNITS

The following lodgings were either not evaluated or did not meet AAA rating requirements but are listed for your information only.

ACANTO SUITES

fyi

Phone: 984/873-1252

Not evaluated. **Address:** Calle 16 Norte s/n **Location:** Just e of 5th Ave and jct calle 16 business norte. Facilities, services, and decor characterize an economy property.

AVENTURA SPA PALACE

fyi

Phone: 984/875-1100

Not evaluated. **Address:** Rancho El Trebol **Location:** KM 72 Carr Cancun-Tulum. Facilities, services, and decor characterize an upscale property.

EL DORADO MAROMA, A BEACHFRONT RESORT BY KARISMA

fyi

Phone: 984/206-3470

Not evaluated. **Location:** Off Mex 307; in Maroma Development. Facilities, services, and decor characterize an upscale property.

GRAN PORTO REAL RESORT AND SPA

fyi

Phone: 984/873-4000

Not evaluated. **Address:** Constituyentes #1 **Location:** On the beach; in town; just off Mex 307. Facilities, services, and decor characterize a mid-scale property.

ROYAL PORTO REAL RESORT & SPA

fyi

Phone: 984/873-4000

Not evaluated. **Address:** Constituyentes #2 **Location:** On the beach; just off Mex 307. Facilities, services, and decor characterize a mid-scale property.

WHERE TO DINE

AZIA

Asian

$80

Phone: 984/873-4500

From the Zen garden entry to your table is a trip into a new world of food. Attentive staff assist you while sushi and Teppan grill chefs prepare succulent dishes such as pad thai or seabass satay with spicy lime sauce. Casual dress. **Bar:** Full bar. **Reservations:** required. **Hours:** 6 pm-10:30 pm. Closed: Tues. **Address:** Lote Hotelera #6 Fracc Playacar **Location:** E off Mex 307; in Playacar development; in Occidental Royal Hideaway Resort & Spa. **Parking:** on-site and valet. **Cards:** AX, CB, DC, DS, JC, MC, VI.

CALL

EL PUERTO

Seafood

$24-$60

Phone: 984/206-3000

The restaurant overlooks the lagoon, mangroves and jungle. Before guests are seated, staff members show off the fresh fish on ice, which can be prepared several ways. Steaks and other local seafood also are nice choices. Selections from the grill include blackened tuna with oyster mushroom and white wine sauce, Alaskan king crab legs grilled with mushroom au vermouth and glazed chicken breast with sauteed vegetables, caramelized apples and potato puree. Dressy casual. **Bar:** Full bar. **Reservations:** suggested. **Hours:** 6 pm-10:30 pm. Closed: Mon-Wed. **Address:** Carr Federal KM 298 **Location:** On Mex 307, KM 298 (Carr Federal), 25.8 mi (43 km) s of Cancun; in Fairmont Mayakoba. **Parking:** valet. **Cards:** AX, CB, DC, DS, JC, MC, VI.

CALL

LA CASA DEL AGUA **Phone:** 984/803-0232

Regional Mexican
$10-$30

A charming restaurant offering ocean views and a varied menu of European, Mexican and seafood selections. Casual dress. **Bar:** Full bar. **Reservations:** suggested, for dinner. **Hours:** noon-1 am. **Address:** Ave 5 esq 2 Norte, Col Centro **Location:** On Ave 5 walkway. **Parking:** no self-parking. **Cards:** MC, VI.

LA LAGUNA **Phone:** 984/206-3000

Regional Mexican
$10-$29

Dine on the patio overlooking the pool, or inside where vaulted wooden ceilings soar. Foods have local flavors: Try the "prehistoric" chicken with chilatole sauce, grilled and seasoned as by pre-Spanish natives. Thanks to the use of many, varied chiles found in the countryside, richly flavored sauces enhance your meal. Casual dress. **Bar:** Full bar. **Reservations:** accepted. **Hours:** 7 am-10:30 pm. **Address:** Carr Federal KM 298 **Location:** On Mex 307, KM 298 (Carr Federal), 25.8 mi (43 km) s of Cancun; in Fairmont Mayakoba. **Parking:** valet. **Cards:** AX, MC, VI.

LAS BRISAS **Phone:** 984/206-3000

International
$18-$32

This sophisticated restaurant features a high thatched roof ceiling and a refined atmosphere created by glowing candles throughout the dining room. At dinner, a band plays elegant traditional music. The menu features a fine mix of international fare marked by creative and innovative presentations. Dressy casual. Entertainment. **Bar:** Full bar. **Reservations:** suggested. **Hours:** 6 pm-10:30 pm. **Address:** Carr Federal KM 298 **Location:** On Mex 307, KM 298 (Carr Federal), 25.8 mi (43 km) s of Cancun; in Fairmont Mayakoba. **Parking:** valet. **Cards:** AX, MC, VI.

PALAPA HEMINGWAY **Phone:** 984/803-0003

Regional Mexican
$8-$35

A lively ambience and a distinctly Cuban menu make this a popular choice with tourists and locals alike. Casual dress. **Bar:** Full bar. **Reservations:** accepted. **Hours:** noon-midnight. **Address:** Ave 5 #230 **Location:** On Ave 5 walkway; between 12th and 14th sts. **Parking:** no self-parking. **Cards:** MC, VI.

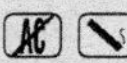

PEZ VELA **Phone:** 984/873-0999

Mexican
$7-$20

In the city's main shopping area, the restaurant is open to the street and under a large tree in the entrance. In the large bar on one side, swings hanging from the ceiling beams are an alternative to chairs. Lending to the Mexican/Caribbean atmosphere are a high thatched ceiling and roof and live music daily. Although Mexican food is the main draw, a few American dishes appeal to the less daring. Casual dress. Entertainment. **Bar:** Full bar. **Hours:** 8 am-10:30 pm. **Address:** Ave 5 esq Calle 2 Nte **Location:** On Ave 5 walkway. **Parking:** street. **Cards:** AX, DC, MC, VI.

SENOR FROG'S **Phone:** 984/873-0930

International
$7-$16

Part of the chain of Mexican restaurants that also includes Carlos 'n Charlie's, the fun and festive eatery is a great place to eat with the family or rendezvous with friends. The menu is lined with Tex-Mex, American and Mexican favorites, such as Buffalo wings, quesadillas, fajitas and burritos. After hours, a bar atmosphere prevails. Casual dress. **Bar:** Full bar. **Reservations:** accepted. **Hours:** 10 am-11 pm; closing hours may vary, call ahead to confirm. **Address:** Centro Comercial Plaza Mavina **Location:** On the beach. **Parking:** street. **Cards:** AX, DC, MC, VI.

SUR ARGENTINE GRILL BAR LOUNGE **Phone:** 984/803-3285

Steak
$10-$22

The restaurant is in the central shopping area that is open only to walking traffic. Open on two sides, the dining area looks out onto the street. The specialty is Argentinean-grilled beef, but chicken and fish dishes also appear on the menu. Casual dress. **Bar:** Full bar. **Reservations:** accepted. **Hours:** noon-11:30 pm. **Address:** Ave 5 **Location:** On Ave 5 walkway; between 12th and 14th sts. **Parking:** street. **Cards:** AX, DS, MC, VI.

YAXCHE-MAYA CUISINE **Phone:** 984/873-2502

Regional Mexican
$9-$15

For a true ancient Mexican experience, dine at Yaxche, where both the menu and decor take diners back in time. Casual dress. **Bar:** Full bar. **Reservations:** accepted. **Hours:** noon-11:30 pm. **Address:** Calle 8 Norte entre aves 5 & 10 **Location:** Just n off Ave 5. **Parking:** no self-parking. **Cards:** AX, MC, VI.

The following restaurants have not been evaluated by AAA but are listed for your information only.

BIG LOBSTER RESTAURANT **Phone:** 984/873-2026

fyi

Not evaluated. Known for all things lobster, this fun and colorful spot features lobster bisque, surf and turf, carpaccio, seviche, seafood casserole, spaghetti lobster and typical chicken and chops. **Address:** Ave 5 con Calle 4 Norte **Location:** On 5th Ave; between Calle 4 and 6 Norte.

CAFE ANDRADE **Phone:** 984/873-3035

fyi

Not evaluated. At the corner of Calle 8 and Ave 20, the casual family restaurant puts forth a menu of economically priced food. Open 24 hours, it features daily specials comprising several courses. At the country's main meal time — 2 pm — guests can enjoy a featured special for about $6. **Address:** Ave 20 esq Calle 8 Norte **Location:** On 20th Ave at Calle 8 Norte; in front of municipal palace.

TARRAYA — **Phone:** 984/873-2040

fyi

Not evaluated. Said to be one of the city's oldest restaurants, this place is one not to miss. Guests must walk on sand to get to the open-air, palapa-topped spot, which is literally on the beach. Cool sea breezes wash over the Bohemian-style dining area, from which views of the Caribbean are spectacular. Credit cards are not accepted. **Address:** 101 Calle 2 Norte **Location:** At the beach.

PUERTO AVENTURAS, QUINTANA ROO

WHERE TO STAY

The following lodgings were either not evaluated or did not meet AAA rating requirements but are listed for your information only.

SUNSCAPE PUERTO AVENTURAS — **Phone:** 984/875-3000

fyi

Not evaluated. **Address:** KM 269 Carr Cancun-Chetumal. Facilities, services, and decor characterize a mid-scale property.

XPU-HA PALACE RESORT — **Phone:** 984/875-1010

fyi

Not evaluated. **Address:** Carr Chetumal-Puerto Juarez KM 265. Facilities, services, and decor characterize an upscale property.

PUERTO MORELOS, QUINTANA ROO pop. 800

WHERE TO STAY

AZUL FIVES HOTEL BY KARISMA

fyi

Hotel

Rates not provided

Too new to rate, opening scheduled for December 2008. **Address:** Predio El Limonar Fracc 2 **Location:** I-307. **Amenities:** 360 units, restaurant, coffeemakers, microwaves, refrigerators, pool, tennis. ***(See color ad on insert)***

AZUL SENSATORI HOTEL BY KARISMA — **Phone:** 998/872-8080

fyi

Hotel

Rates not provided

Too new to rate, opening scheduled for October 2008. **Address:** Carr Federal Cancun, KM 27.5, Lote 5 **Location:** I-307. **Amenities:** 438 units, restaurant, coffeemakers, refrigerators, pool, tennis. ***(See color ad on insert)***

CEIBA DEL MAR SPA RESORT — **Phone:** (998)872-8060

Contemporary Hotel

$305-$445 All Year

Address: Costera Norte Lote 1, SM 10, Mz 26 **Location:** Oceanfront. Off Mex 307, 3.7 mi (6 km) e. **Facility:** Tucked into Puerto Morelos, this upscale, all-inclusive, beachside mini-resort has well-appointed rooms, modern public areas and leisure activities. 88 units. 48 one-bedroom standard units. 33 one- and 7 two-bedroom suites. 3 stories (no elevator), exterior corridors. **Parking:** on-site and valet. **Terms:** 14 day cancellation notice, in season. **Amenities:** video library, DVD players, high-speed Internet, voice mail, safes, honor bars, hair dryers. *Some:* CD players. **Pool(s):** 2 outdoor. **Leisure Activities:** sauna, whirlpool, steamroom, scuba equipment rental, snorkeling, 2 lighted tennis courts, bicycles, exercise room, spa. *Fee:* charter fishing. **Guest Services:** valet laundry, wireless Internet. **Business Services:** meeting rooms, PC, fax (fee). **Cards:** AX, MC, VI. Affiliated with A Preferred Hotel.

24 D VCR / SOME UNITS

EL DORADO ROYALE A SPA RESORT *Book great rates at AAA.com* — **Phone:** (998)872-8030

Contemporary Hotel

$360-$500 All Year

Address: Carr Federal Cancun-Tulum KM 45 **Location:** Oceanfront. KM 45 Cancun-Tulu Hwy, Mex 307 at KM 314. **Facility:** Stretching a half-mile along the beach, this all-inclusive resort has spacious rooms, an attentive staff and a wide variety of recreational options. 644 units. 602 one-bedroom standard units with whirlpools. 42 two-bedroom suites with whirlpools. 3-4 stories (no elevator), exterior corridors. **Parking:** on-site and valet. **Terms:** age restrictions may apply, 15 day cancellation notice. **Amenities:** video library, voice mail, safes, irons, hair dryers. *Some:* DVD players, high-speed Internet. **Dining:** 10 restaurants, entertainment. **Pool(s):** 13 outdoor. **Leisure Activities:** saunas, whirlpools, kayaks, 2 lighted tennis courts, recreation programs, bicycles, jogging, exercise room, spa, volleyball. *Fee:* scuba diving, snorkeling. **Guest Services:** valet laundry, airport transportation (fee)-Cancun International Airport, wireless Internet. **Business Services:** conference facilities, business center. **Cards:** AX, CB, DC, DS, JC, MC, VI. *(See color ad on insert)*

FEE 24 CALL D / SOME UNITS

EXCELLENCE RIVIERA CANCUN **Phone:** (998)872-8500

Contemporary Resort Hotel

$408-$880 All Year

Address: KM 328 Carr Cancun-Chetumal **Location:** Oceanfront. Mex 307, 28 mi (44 km) s of Cancun International Airport; 1.5 mi (2.4 km) n of town. **Facility:** The adults-only, all-inclusive resort features a wide array of leisure activities, like yoga, dance and cooking lessons, basketball and archery. Meets AAA guest room security requirements. 440 units. 434 one-bedroom standard units, some with whirlpools. 6 one-bedroom suites with whirlpools, some with kitchens. 4 stories, exterior corridors. **Parking:** on-site and valet. **Terms:** age restrictions may apply, 7 day cancellation notice-fee imposed. **Amenities:** video library, DVD players, CD players, high-speed Internet, voice mail, safes, irons, hair dryers. *Some:* honor bars. **Dining:** 8 restaurants, nightclub, entertainment. **Pool(s):** 5 outdoor, 2 heated outdoor. **Leisure Activities:** whirlpools, rental boats, canoeing, paddleboats, sailboats, windsurfing, boat dock, scuba diving & rental equipment, snorkeling & rental equipment, 2 lighted tennis courts, recreation programs, bicycles, spa, volleyball, game room. *Fee:* waterskiing, charter fishing. **Guest Services:** valet laundry, beauty salon, wireless Internet. *Fee:* airport transportation-Cancun International Airport, area transportation. **Business Services:** conference facilities, business center. **Cards:** AX, DS, MC, VI.

FEE 24 D / SOME UNITS

PARADISUS RIVIERA CANCUN **Phone:** (998)872-8383

Resort Hotel

$726-$1120 All Year

Address: SM 11, Mz 9, Lote 10 **Location:** Oceanfront. Off Mex 307, 1.8 mi (3 km) n, follow signs. **Facility:** The upscale all-inclusive resort's open air lobby, Mayan theme and beautiful beach activities area make it a special destination for families. 496 units. 458 one-bedroom standard units, some with whirlpools. 38 one-bedroom suites with whirlpools. 2-3 stories, exterior corridors. **Parking:** on-site and valet. **Terms:** 4 day cancellation notice. **Amenities:** voice mail, safes, honor bars, irons, hair dryers. *Some:* high-speed Internet. **Dining:** 6 restaurants, also, L' Hermitage Restaurante, see separate listing, entertainment. **Pool(s):** 4 outdoor. **Leisure Activities:** limited beach access, paddleboats, sailboats, snorkeling, spa. *Fee:* scuba diving, charter fishing. **Guest Services:** valet laundry, wireless Internet. *Fee:* airport transportation-Cancun International Airport, area transportation. **Business Services:** meeting rooms, business center. **Cards:** AX, DS, JC, MC, VI.

FEE 24 S D / SOME UNITS

PARAISO DE LA BONITA RESORT AND THALASSO **Phone:** (998)872-8300

Boutique Hotel

$634-$822 All Year

Address: Carr Chetumal-Cancun KM 328 **Location:** Oceanfront. Mex 307. **Facility:** The small, secluded resort is comprised of palatial guest rooms and public areas, a world-class spa and highly personalized service. 90 units. 82 one- and 8 two-bedroom suites. 2-3 stories (no elevator), exterior corridors. **Parking:** on-site and valet. **Terms:** age restrictions may apply, cancellation fee imposed. **Amenities:** video library, DVD players, CD players, voice mail, safes, hair dryers. **Dining:** 4 restaurants, also, La Canoa, see separate listing, entertainment. **Pool(s):** heated outdoor. **Leisure Activities:** saunas, whirlpools, steamrooms, beach access, windsurfing, boat dock, snorkeling, lighted tennis court, exercise room, spa. *Fee:* boats, sailboats, charter fishing, helicopter, Thalasso Therapy Center & Anti-Aging Center. **Guest Services:** valet laundry, airport transportation-Cancun International Airport, area transportation (fee)-within 20 mi (33 km), wireless Internet. **Business Services:** meeting rooms, business center. **Cards:** AX, DC, MC, VI.

24 D / SOME UNITS

The following lodgings were either not evaluated or did not meet AAA rating requirements but are listed for your information only.

CASA DE LOS ANGELES **Phone:** 998/871-0238

fyi

Not evaluated. **Address:** Punta Bravo, Lote 15 **Location:** Just e of Mex 307. Facilities, services, and decor characterize an economy property.

HOTEL ACAMAYA **Phone:** 998/871-0131

fyi

Not evaluated. **Address:** Super Manzana 11 Lote 5. Facilities, services, and decor characterize an economy property.

HOTEL INGLATERRA **Phone:** 998/671-6418

fyi

Not evaluated. **Address:** Ave Nino Heroes No. 29 **Location:** 2 blks s from main plaza. Facilities, services, and decor characterize a mid-scale property.

WHERE TO DINE

LA CANOA **Phone:** 998/872-8300

International

$22-$35

The flavors of North Africa, France and Mexico gracefully collide at the top-notch eatery, making for a dining adventure. Those who are unsure of what to have should ask the chef as he passes the table, and maybe a surprise will be whipped up in their honor. Dressy casual. **Bar:** Full bar. **Reservations:** suggested. **Hours:** 6 pm-11 pm. Closed: Sun & Wed. **Address:** Carr Chetumal-Cancun KM 328 **Location:** Mex 307; in Paraiso de la Bonita Resort and Thalasso. **Parking:** valet. **Cards:** AX, DC, JC, MC, VI.

L' HERMITAGE RESTAURANTE **Phone:** 998/872-8383

French

$70

The elegant room appreat to float on the water and outdoor fountains add charm. Attentive staff serve a selection of classic dishes such as escargot, and grilled beef tenderloin with potatoes and grilled asparagus. Dressy casual. **Bar:** Full bar. **Reservations:** suggested. **Hours:** 6 pm-10:30 pm. **Address:** SM 11, Mz 9, Lote 10 **Location:** Off Mex 307, 1.8 mi (3 km) n, follow signs; in Paradisus Riviera Cancun. **Parking:** on-site and valet. **Cards:** AX, MC, VI.

The following restaurants have not been evaluated by AAA but are listed for your information only.

AFRICA BY NIGHT **Phone:** 998/937-6445

fyi

Not evaluated. On Ave J.R. Gomez between Cozumel and Isla Mujeres streets, this Mediterranean restaurant uses olive-infused ingredients to prepare specialty seafood dishes. Noteworthy choices include pasta seafood and bisques. **Address:** No. 604 Ave Javier Rojo **Location:** Between Isla Mujeres and Cozumel sts.

BODO'S GERMAN RESTAURANT **Phone:** 998/871-0613

fyi

Not evaluated. Schnitzel and strudel aren't what patrons expect to find in the Mexican Caribbean, but this spot two blocks south of the main plaza on the beach surprises with authentic German fare. **Address:** No. 300 Oriente Ave Ninos Heroes **Location:** 3 blks e of main plaza.

POSADA DE AMOR **Phone:** 998/871-0033

fyi

Not evaluated. Said to be among the oldest restaurants in Puerto Morelos, this 30-year-old palapa-covered restaurant is casual and fun with homemade wooden benches and tables, real Mexican food and distinctive interpretations of dishes such as seafood bisque. Sunday brunch is a daylong affair. **Address:** Ave J. R. Gomez s/n **Location:** Just e of Mex 307.

TEMOZON, YUCATAN pop. 12,274

WHERE TO STAY

The following lodging was either not evaluated or did not meet AAA rating requirements but is listed for your information only.

HACIENDA TEMOZON **Phone:** 999/923-8089

fyi

Not evaluated. **Address:** KM 182 Carr Merida-Uxmal **Location:** Off Mex 281, Merida-Uxmal Hwy. Facilities, services, and decor characterize an upscale property.

WHERE TO DINE

RESTAURANTE HACIENDA TEMOZON **Phone:** 999/923-8089

Regional Mexican
$8-$18

The secluded restaurant overlooks the lush gardens of world-famous Hacienda Temozon and features authentic Yucatan dishes. Casual dress. **Bar:** Full bar. **Reservations:** suggested. **Hours:** 9 am-5 pm. **Address:** KM 183 Carr Merida-Uxmal **Location:** Off Mex 281, Merida-Uxmal Hwy; in Hacienda Temozon. **Parking:** on-site. **Cards:** AX, DC, MC, VI.

TIXKOKOB, YUCATAN pop. 15,281

WHERE TO STAY

The following lodging was either not evaluated or did not meet AAA rating requirements but is listed for your information only.

HACIENDA SAN JOSE **Phone:** 999/910-4617

fyi

Not evaluated. **Address:** KM 30 Carr Tixkokob-Tekanto. Facilities, services, and decor characterize an upscale property.

TULUM, QUINTANA ROO

WHERE TO STAY

CATALONIA ROYAL TULUM — **Phone:** 984/875-1800

Resort Hotel
$247-$345 All Year

Address: Carr Cancun-Chetumal **Location:** Oceanfront. Mex 307 at KM 264.5. **Facility:** The large, all-inclusive resort includes lavish public areas, modern rooms, excellent service and a wide Caribbean beach. 288 one-bedroom standard units. 3 stories (no elevator), exterior corridors. *Bath:* shower only. **Parking:** on-site. **Terms:** age restrictions may apply. **Amenities:** voice mail, safes, irons, hair dryers. **Pool(s):** heated outdoor. **Leisure Activities:** whirlpools, recreation programs, bicycles, exercise room. *Fee:* scuba diving, snorkeling. **Guest Services:** valet laundry, wireless Internet. **Business Services:** meeting rooms, PC (fee). **Cards:** AX, MC, VI.

D / SOME UNITS

The following lodgings were either not evaluated or did not meet AAA rating requirements but are listed for your information only.

DREAMS TULUM — **Phone:** 984/871-3333

fyi

Not evaluated. **Address:** Carr Cancun Chetumal KM 238 **Location:** 1.8 mi (3 km) n of Tulum, off Mex 307. Facilities, services, and decor characterize an upscale property.

GRAN PRINCIPE TULUM — **Phone:** 984/875-5000

fyi

Not evaluated. **Address:** KM 250 Carr Chetumal, Benito Juarez **Location:** KM 250 Carr Cancun-Chetumal, Benito Juarez Local B. Facilities, services, and decor characterize a mid-scale property.

SUNSCAPE TULUM — **Phone:** 984/871-3333

fyi

Not evaluated. **Address:** Riviera Mayan KM 234. Facilities, services, and decor characterize a mid-scale property.

UMAN, YUCATAN pop. 49,145

WHERE TO STAY

The following lodging was either not evaluated or did not meet AAA rating requirements but is listed for your information only.

HACIENDA SANTA ROSA — **Phone:** 999/910-4852

fyi

Not evaluated. **Address:** KM 129 Carr Merida Campeche **Location:** 25.2 mi (42 km) s on Mex 180. Facilities, services, and decor characterize an upscale property.

UXMAL, YUCATAN pop. 2,200

WHERE TO STAY

HOTEL HACIENDA UXMAL — **Phone:** (997)976-2013

Hotel
$89-$194 All Year

Address: Mex 261 **Location:** 51 mi (85 km) s of Merida. Located at main entrance to archaeological zone. **Facility:** 72 one-bedroom standard units, some with whirlpools. 3 stories (no elevator), interior/exterior corridors. **Parking:** on-site. **Terms:** 7 day cancellation notice-fee imposed. **Amenities:** honor bars. **Pool(s):** 2 outdoor. **Guest Services:** valet laundry, area transportation (fee). **Business Services:** meeting rooms, fax (fee). **Cards:** AX, MC, VI.

FEE / SOME UNITS

THE LODGE AT UXMAL — **Phone:** (997)976-2031

Classic Country Inn
$134-$285 All Year

Address: Mex 261 **Location:** 51.3 mi (85.5 km) s of Merida. Located at main entrance to archaeological zone. **Facility:** Handmade furniture and stained-glass windows reveal a Mayan theme at this property located at the Uxmal ruins. 62 units. 40 one-bedroom standard units, some with whirlpools. 22 one-bedroom suites with whirlpools. 2 stories (no elevator), exterior corridors. **Parking:** on-site. **Terms:** 7 day cancellation notice-fee imposed. **Amenities:** honor bars. **Pool(s):** 2 outdoor. **Guest Services:** valet laundry, area transportation (fee). **Business Services:** fax (fee). **Cards:** AX, MC, VI.

FEE

BAJA CALIFORNIA

BUENAVISTA, BAJA CALIFORNIA SUR pop. 5,000

WHERE TO STAY

HOTEL BUENA VISTA BEACH RESORT Book at AAA.com Phone: (624)141-0033

Resort Hotel
$135-$265 All Year

Address: KM 105 Carr al Sur **Location:** Oceanfront. On shore of Bahia de Palmas off Mex 1. **Facility:** One-story buildings down the hillside to the beach with lush gardens, flowers and fountains. Meets AAA guest room security requirements. 60 one-bedroom standard units. 1 story, exterior corridors. *Bath:* shower only. **Parking:** on-site. **Terms:** office hours 6 am-10 pm, 14 day cancellation notice-fee imposed. **Pool(s):** outdoor. **Leisure Activities:** whirlpools, boat ramp, scuba diving, snorkeling, fishing. *Fee:* boats, canoes, charter fishing, massage. **Guest Services:** valet laundry, wireless Internet. **Business Services:** conference facilities. **Cards:** AX, MC, VI.

FEE / SOME UNITS

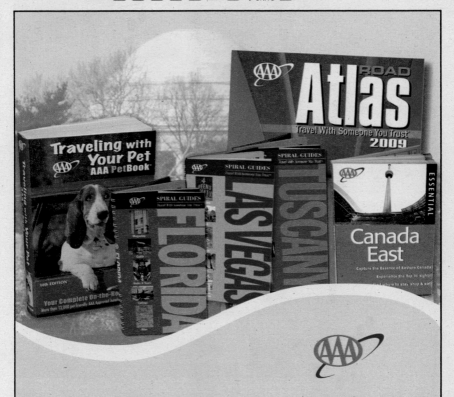

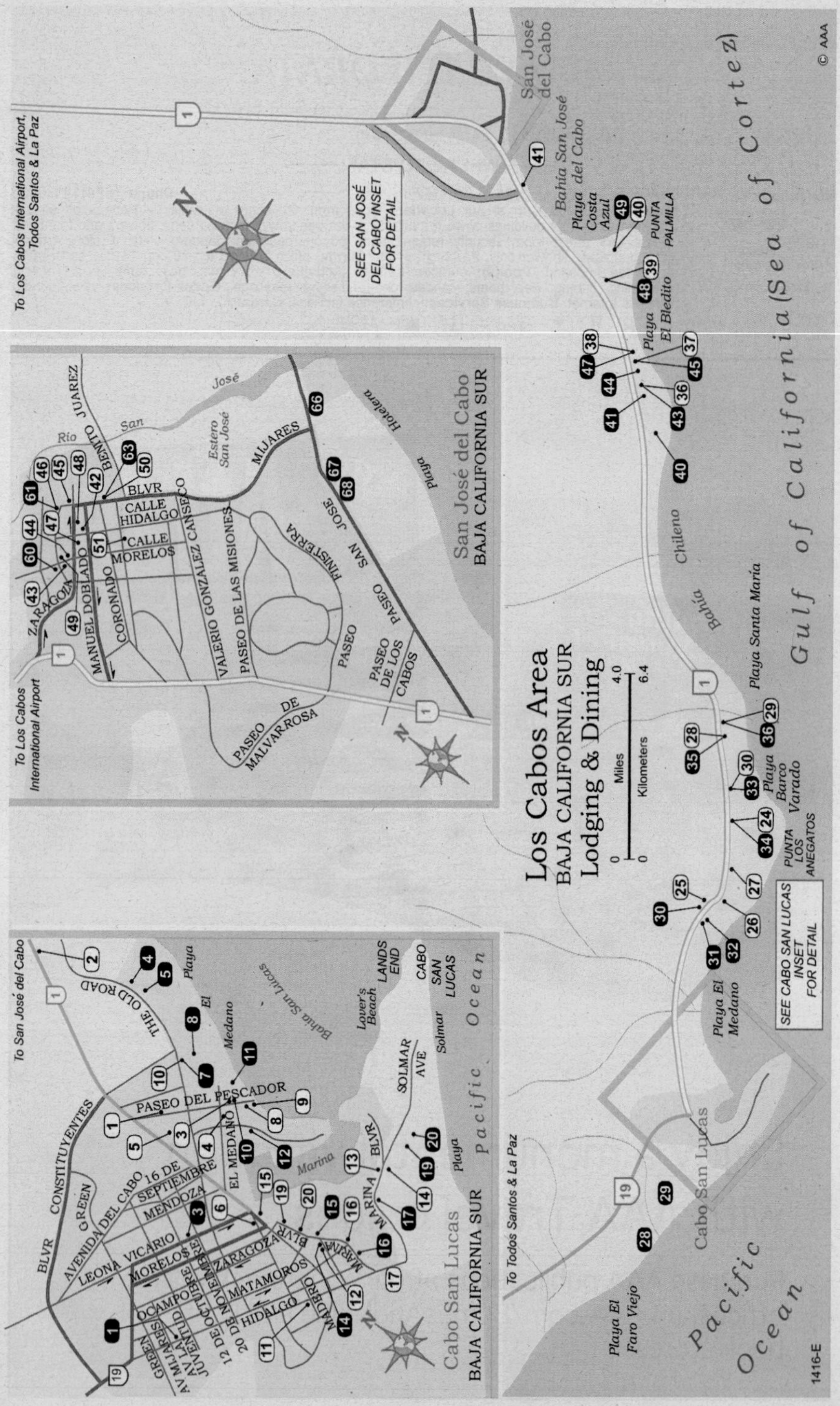

Cabo San Lucas
BAJA CALIFORNIA SUR

To San José del Cabo
BLVR CONSTITUYENTES
AVENIDA DEL CABO
GREEN
LEONA VICARIO
MORELOS
16 DE SEPTIEMBRE
MENDOZA
THE OLD ROAD
PASEO DEL PESCADOR
EL MEDANO
AV MIJARES
AV LA JUVENTUD
OCAMPO
12 DE OCTUBRE
20 DE NOVIEMBRE
ZARAGOZA
HIDALGO
MATAMOROS
MADERO
MARINA BLVR
SOLMAR AVE
Playa El Medano
Bahía San Lucas
Marina
Lover's Beach
LANDS END
CABO SAN LUCAS
Solmar
Playa
Pacific Ocean

San José del Cabo
BAJA CALIFORNIA SUR

To Los Cabos International Airport
ZARAGOZA
MANUEL DOBLADO
CORONADO
MORELOS
CALLE MORELOS
CALLE HIDALGO
BLVR MIJARES
BENITO JUAREZ
Río San José
VALERIO GONZALEZ CANSECO
PASEO DE LAS MISIONES
PASEO DE MALVARROSA
PASEO FINISTERRA
PASEO SAN JOSE
PASEO DE LOS CABOS
Estero San José
Playa Hotelera

To Los Cabos International Airport, Todos Santos & La Paz
SEE SAN JOSÉ DEL CABO INSET FOR DETAIL

Los Cabos Area
BAJA CALIFORNIA SUR
Lodging & Dining

Miles 0 – 4.0
Kilometers 0 – 6.4

To Todos Santos & La Paz
Playa El Faro Viejo
Cabo San Lucas
Pacific Ocean
Playa El Medano
SEE CABO SAN LUCAS INSET FOR DETAIL
PUNTA LOS ANEGATOS
Playa Barco Varado
Playa Santa María
Bahía Chileno
Playa El Bledito
PUNTA PALMILLA
Playa Costa Azul
Playa del Cabo
Bahía San José
San José del Cabo
Gulf of California (Sea of Cortez)

1416-E

Los Cabos Area, Baja California Sur

This index helps you "spot" where approved lodgings and restaurants are located on the corresponding detailed maps. Lodging daily rate range is for comparison only and show the property's high season. Restaurant rate range is a combination of lunch and/or dinner. Turn to the listing page for more detailed rate information and consult display ads for special promotions.

CABO SAN LUCAS

Map Page	OA	Lodgings	Diamond Rated	High Season	Page
1 / p. 452		Casa Pablito	◆◆	$75-$100	456
3 / p. 452		Comfort Inn Los Cabos	◆	$85-$110	456
4 / p. 452		Villa del Palmar Beach Resort & Spa	◆◆◆	$277-$677	461
5 / p. 452		Villa La Estancia	◆◆◆	$330-$650	461
7 / p. 452		Pueblo Bonito Rose	◆◆◆	$245-$345	458
8 / p. 452		Pueblo Bonito Los Cabos	◆◆◆	$225-$360	458
10 / p. 452	AAA	**Me Cabo By Melia**	◆◆◆◆	$406-$975	457
11 / p. 452		Casa Dorada Los Cabos	◆◆◆	$150-$800	456
12 / p. 452		Marina Fiesta Resort & Spa	◆◆	$344-$540	457
14 / p. 452		Siesta Suites Hotel	◆	$65-$85	460
15 / p. 452		Plaza Nautica Condominiums	◆◆◆	$80-$250	457
16 / p. 452	AAA	**Tesoro Los Cabos** - see color ad p 460	◆◆	$143-$199	460
17 / p. 452		Hotel Finisterra	◆◆	$140-$367	456
19 / p. 452		Playa Grande Resort	◆◆◆	$273-$395	457
20 / p. 452		Solmar Suites Resort	◆◆◆	$189-$265	460
28 / p. 452		Pueblo Bonito Pacifica	◆◆◆	$385-$680	458
29 / p. 452		Pueblo Bonito Sunset Beach	◆◆◆	$295-$995	458
30 / p. 452		Los Patios Hotel	◆◆	$110-$145	457
31 / p. 452		Hotel Riu Palace Cabo San Lucas-All Inclusive	◆◆◆	$217-$367	457
32 / p. 452		Hotel Riu Sante Fe - All Inclusive	◆◆◆	$199-$250	457
33 / p. 452		Hacienda Encantada Resort & Spa	◆◆◆	$480-$1025	456
34 / p. 452		Esperanza An Auberge Resort	◆◆◆◆	$475-$2000	456
35 / p. 452		Sheraton Hacienda del Mar Resort & Spa - see color ad p 459	◆◆◆◆	$290-$750	459
36 / p. 452	AAA	**Fiesta Americana Grand Los Cabos** - see color ad on insert	◆◆◆	$280-$750	456

Map Page	OA	Restaurants	Diamond Rated	Cuisine	Meal Range	Page
1 / p. 452		La Golondrina	◆◆	Mexican	$14-$62	462
2 / p. 452		La Casona	◆◆◆	Steak	$25-$50	462
3 / p. 452		Peacocks Restaurant	◆◆◆	Mediterranean	$20-$35	463
4 / p. 452		Casa Rafael's	◆◆◆	Continental	$16-$41	461
5 / p. 452		La Panga Antigua	◆◆◆	Mexican	$20-$42	462
6 / p. 452		Stop Light Bar & Grill	◆◆	Mexican	$9-$24	464
8 / p. 452		Edith's	◆◆	Seafood	$13-$65	461
9 / p. 452		The Office	◆◆	Mexican	$8-$54	462
10 / p. 452		Fellini's Restaurant	◆◆◆◆	Italian	$30-$70	461
11 / p. 452		Mi Casa	◆◆	Mexican	$12-$40	462
12 / p. 452		Pancho's Restaurant & Tequila Bar	◆◆	Mexican	$10-$25	463

Map Page	OA	Restaurants (cont'd)	Diamond Rated	Cuisine	Meal Range	Page
13 / p. 452		Senor Greenberg's Mexicatessen	2 Diamonds	Deli	$9-$15	463
14 / p. 452		Galeon Italian Restaurant	2 Diamonds	Italian	$12-$29	462
15 / p. 452		Ruth's Chris Steak House	3 Diamonds	Steak	$22-$50	463
16 / p. 452		Sancho Panza Wine Bistro	3 Diamonds	Mediterranean	$17-$32	463
17 / p. 452		Romeo y Julieta Ristorante	2 Diamonds	Italian	$10-$25	463
19 / p. 452		Hard Rock Cafe	2 Diamonds	American	$12-$24 SAVE	462
20 / p. 452		O Mole Mio	2 Diamonds	Mexican	$10-$34	463
21 / p. 452		Bohai - Asian Bistro	3 Diamonds	Asian	$19-$35	461
24 / p. 452		El Restaurante at Esperanza	4 Diamonds	International	$34-$52	461
25 / p. 452		Latitude 22+ Roadhouse	2 Diamonds	American	$8-$30	462
26 / p. 452		Sunset Da Mona Lisa	3 Diamonds	Italian	$22-$49	464
27 / p. 452		French Rivera Restaurant	3 Diamonds	Mediterranean	$18-$69	461
28 / p. 452		Pitahayas	4 Diamonds	Pacific Rim	$25-$41	463
29 / p. 452		Rosato	4 Diamonds	Northern Italian	$18-$42	463
30 / p. 452		Las Marias	3 Diamonds	Mexican	$12-$32	462

SAN JOSE DEL CABO

Map Page	OA	Lodgings	Diamond Rated	High Season	Page
40 / p. 452		Dreams Los Cabos Resort & Spa	3 Diamonds	$250-$850	475
41 / p. 452		Casa del Mar Suites Golf & Spa Resort	4 Diamonds	$450-$1000	475
43 / p. 452		Las Ventanas al Paraiso	5 Diamonds	$650-$6000	476
44 / p. 452		Melia Cabo Real Beach & Golf Resort, All Inclusive	3 Diamonds	$338-$446	476
45 / p. 452		Hilton Los Cabos Beach & Golf Resort	4 Diamonds	$130-$600	476
47 / p. 452		Marquis Los Cabos Beach, Golf, Spa & Casitas Resort	4 Diamonds	$380-$1250	476
48 / p. 452	AAA	**The Westin Resort & Spa Los Cabos** - see color ad on insert	4 Diamonds	$500-$1000	477
49 / p. 452		One & Only Palmilla	4 Diamonds	$500-$2600	476
60 / p. 452		El Encanto Inn	2 Diamonds	$114-$288	475
61 / p. 452		Casa Natalia	3 Diamonds	$250-$565	475
63 / p. 452		Tropicana Inn	2 Diamonds	$90	477
66 / p. 452	AAA	**Presidente InterContinental All Inclusive Resort Los Cabos**	3 Diamonds	$287-$789	477
67 / p. 452		Royal Solaris Los Cabos- All Inclusive Resort & Spa	3 Diamonds	$265-$370	477
68 / p. 452		Crowne Plaza Los Cabos Grand Faro All Inclusive Resort	3 Diamonds	$244-$731	475

Map Page	OA	Restaurants	Diamond Rated	Cuisine	Meal Range	Page
36 / p. 452		The Restaurant	4 Diamonds	Mexican	$21-$49	478
37 / p. 452		Restaurant Fenicia	3 Diamonds	International	$24-$65	479
38 / p. 452		Canto Del Mar Restaurant	4 Diamonds	International	$75-$95	478
39 / p. 452		Arrecifes	4 Diamonds	International	$35-$50	477
40 / p. 452		C	4 Diamonds	Continental	$30-$50	477
41 / p. 452		Restaurante Mama Mia	2 Diamonds	Mexican	$7-$20	478
42 / p. 452		La Panga Antigua	3 Diamonds	Mexican	$20-$48	478

Map Page	OA	Restaurants (cont'd)	Diamond Rated	Cuisine	Meal Range	Page
43 / p. 452		Baan Thai	♦♦	Asian	$9-$27	477
44 / p. 452		Morgan's Encore	♦♦♦	Mediterranean	$18-$40	478
45 / p. 452		Damiana	♦♦	Mexican	$10-$50	478
46 / p. 452		Mi Cocina	♦♦♦	International	$18-$50	478
47 / p. 452		Morgan's Restaurant & Cellar	♦♦♦	International	$25-$48	478
48 / p. 452		Tequila Restaurante	♦♦♦	Mediterranean	$20-$42	479
49 / p. 452		Voila	♦♦♦	Mediterranean	$10-$35	479
50 / p. 452		Tropicana Bar & Grill	♦♦	Seafood	$8-$45	479
51 / p. 452		El Chilar	♦♦♦	Mexican	$14-$28	478

CABO SAN LUCAS, BAJA CALIFORNIA SUR pop. 40,300 (See map and index starting on p. 452)

WHERE TO STAY

CASA DORADA LOS CABOS — Phone: 624/163-5757 — 11

Resort Hotel — $150-$800 All Year

Address: Av El Pescador S/N Col El Medano **Location:** Oceanfront. 0.7 mi (1.1 km) e of Mex 1 via Paseo del Pescador, just e. **Facility:** An open-air lobby provides grand views of Medano Beach and the Cabo Rocks; guest rooms are elegantly appointed. Meets AAA guest room security requirements. 186 units. 60 one-bedroom standard units with efficiencies. 81 one-, 43 two- and 2 three-bedroom suites. 7 stories, exterior corridors. **Parking:** valet. **Terms:** 3 night minimum stay - seasonal, cancellation fee imposed. **Amenities:** video library, DVD players, CD players, voice mail, safes, honor bars, irons, hair dryers. **Pool(s):** outdoor, 2 heated outdoor. **Leisure Activities:** whirlpool, recreation programs, exercise room, spa. *Fee:* scuba diving, snorkeling, fishing. **Guest Services:** wireless Internet. **Business Services:** business center. **Cards:** AX, MC, VI.

/ SOME UNITS

CASA PABLITO — Phone: 624/143-1971 — 1

Bed & Breakfast — $75-$100 All Year

Address: 1906 Ave Miguel Hidalgo esq Con Felix Ortega **Location:** Mex 1, 0.9 mi (1.5 km) s. **Facility:** Meets AAA guest room security requirements. Smoke free premises. 14 one-bedroom standard units with efficiencies. 1 story, exterior corridors. *Bath:* shower only. **Parking:** on-site. **Terms:** office hours 7 am-10 pm, check-in 4 pm, 10 day cancellation notice-fee imposed. **Pool(s):** heated outdoor. **Leisure Activities:** whirlpool. **Guest Services:** wireless Internet. **Cards:** MC, VI.

COMFORT INN LOS CABOS — *Book at AAA.com* — Phone: (624)143-7501 — 3

Hotel — $85-$110 All Year

Address: Leona Vicario at 20 Noviembre y Rev **Location:** Just n of Lazaro Cardenas. **Facility:** 103 one-bedroom standard units. 3 stories (no elevator), exterior corridors. *Bath:* shower only. **Parking:** on-site. **Terms:** 5 day cancellation notice-fee imposed. **Amenities:** safes, hair dryers. **Pool(s):** outdoor. **Guest Services:** wireless Internet. **Business Services:** meeting rooms, PC. **Cards:** AX, MC, VI.

/ SOME UNITS

ESPERANZA AN AUBERGE RESORT — *Book at AAA.com* — Phone: (624)145-6400 — 34

Resort Hotel — $475-$2000 All Year

Address: Carr Transpeninsular KM 7, Punta Ballena **Location:** Oceanfront. On Mex 1, 3.6 mi (6 km) n of town. **Facility:** This intimate, luxury, seaside resort offers rooms of 925 square feet and larger, all with indoor and outdoor living spaces. Designated smoking area. 54 units. 44 one-bedroom standard units. 7 one- and 3 two-bedroom suites, some with kitchens and/or whirlpools. 3-4 stories, exterior corridors. **Parking:** on-site and valet. **Terms:** 28 day cancellation notice-fee imposed. **Amenities:** video library, DVD players, CD players, high-speed Internet, dual phone lines, voice mail, safes, honor bars, irons, hair dryers. **Dining:** El Restaurante at Esperanza, see separate listing. **Pool(s):** 4 heated outdoor. **Leisure Activities:** saunas, whirlpools, steamrooms, 2 lighted tennis courts, exercise room, spa. **Guest Services:** valet laundry, wireless Internet. **Business Services:** meeting rooms, business center. **Cards:** AX, DC, MC, VI.

/ SOME UNITS FEE

FIESTA AMERICANA GRAND LOS CABOS — *Book great rates at AAA.com* — Phone: (624)145-6200 — 36

AAA

Resort Hotel — $280-$750 All Year

Address: Carr Transpeninsular KM 10.3, Lote A-1 **Location:** Oceanfront. On Mex 1, 6 mi (10 km) e of town. Located at Cabo del Sol. **Facility:** On a hillside facing the sea, this resort is well-suited for groups and offers large guest rooms, ocean-view balconies and marble bathrooms. Meets AAA guest room security requirements. 250 units. 230 one-bedroom standard units. 10 one-, 7 two- and 3 three-bedroom suites with kitchens and whirlpools. 1-6 stories, exterior corridors. **Parking:** valet. **Terms:** 3 day cancellation notice-fee imposed. **Amenities:** CD players, dual phone lines, voice mail, safes, honor bars, irons, hair dryers. **Dining:** 2 restaurants, also, Rosato, see separate listing. **Pool(s):** 5 heated outdoor. **Leisure Activities:** whirlpools, steamrooms, recreation programs, spa. *Fee:* saunas, golf-18 holes, exercise room. **Guest Services:** valet laundry, wireless Internet. **Business Services:** conference facilities, business center. **Cards:** AX, MC, VI. *(See color ad on insert)*

/ SOME UNITS

HACIENDA ENCANTADA RESORT & SPA — Phone: (624)163-5555 — 33

Resort Hotel — $480-$1025 All Year

Address: Carr Transpeninsular 7.3 KM **Location:** Oceanfront. On Mex 1, 3.7 mi (6 km) ne of town. **Facility:** Rooms overlook the rocks at the edge of the Sea of Cortez; elegant furnishings remind one of Colonial Mexico with poster beds and attractive artwork. Meets AAA guest room security requirements. Designated smoking area. 58 units. 29 one-bedroom standard units with efficiencies. 29 one-bedroom suites with kitchens and whirlpools. 4 stories, exterior corridors. *Bath:* combo or shower only. **Parking:** on-site and valet. **Terms:** 3 day cancellation notice-fee imposed. **Amenities:** DVD players, CD players, voice mail, safes, irons, hair dryers. **Pool(s):** 3 heated outdoor. **Leisure Activities:** whirlpool, spa. *Fee:* scuba diving, snorkeling. **Guest Services:** area transportation (fee), wireless Internet. **Business Services:** PC. **Cards:** AX, MC, VI.

HOTEL FINISTERRA — *Book at AAA.com* — Phone: (624)143-3333 — 17

Resort Hotel — $140-$367 All Year

Address: Domicilio Conocido **Location:** Oceanfront. 0.6 mi (1 km) s of town via Blvd Marina. Located at Land's End. **Facility:** Palapa-style thatched umbrellas and large free-form pools bring the tropical touch to this hotel set amid sand and cliffs at the water's edge. 286 units. 236 one-bedroom standard units. 38 one- and 12 two-bedroom suites. 1-8 stories, interior/exterior corridors. *Bath:* combo or shower only. **Parking:** on-site. **Terms:** check-in 4 pm, 3 day cancellation notice-fee imposed. **Amenities:** voice mail, safes, irons, hair dryers. *Some:* honor bars. **Pool(s):** 3 outdoor. **Leisure Activities:** sauna, whirlpools, exercise room. *Fee:* 2 lighted tennis courts, massage. **Guest Services:** valet laundry, wireless Internet. **Business Services:** conference facilities, business center. **Cards:** AX, MC, VI.

/ SOME UNITS

(See map and index starting on p. 452)

HOTEL RIU PALACE CABO SAN LUCAS-ALL INCLUSIVE Book great rates at AAA.com Phone: (624)146-7160 31

Resort Hotel

$217-$367 All Year

Address: Camino Viejo A San Jose Del Cabo **Location:** Oceanfront. Mex 1, 2.7 mi (4.5 km) e of town via eastbound lateral/access road. **Facility:** Within easy access of the beach, the property offers elegant guest rooms, multiple restaurants and live entertainment at several of the pool areas. Meets AAA guest room security requirements. 642 one-bedroom standard units, some with whirlpools. 1-4 stories, exterior corridors. *Bath:* combo or shower only. **Parking:** on-site. **Terms:** 3 night minimum stay, 3 day cancellation notice-fee imposed. **Amenities:** safes, honor bars, irons, hair dryers. **Pool(s):** 4 heated outdoor. **Leisure Activities:** whirlpools, 2 lighted tennis courts, recreation programs, playground, exercise room, spa, basketball, volleyball. *Fee:* game room. **Guest Services:** valet laundry, wireless Internet. **Business Services:** conference facilities, business center. **Cards:** AX, MC, VI.

/ SOME UNITS

HOTEL RIU SANTE FE - ALL INCLUSIVE Phone: 624/163-6150 32

Resort Hotel

$199-$250 12/1-5/31
$108-$131 6/1-11/30

Address: Camino Viejo A San Jose Del Cabo **Location:** Oceanfront. On Mex 1, 2.7 mi (4.5 km) e of town via eastbound access/lateral road. **Facility:** Guest rooms are well appointed with marble baths; public areas are expansive and include easy access to Medano Beach. Meets AAA guest room security requirements. 902 one-bedroom standard units, some with whirlpools. 3-4 stories (no elevator), exterior corridors. *Bath:* combo or shower only. **Parking:** on-site. **Terms:** 3 day cancellation notice. **Amenities:** safes, honor bars, irons, hair dryers. **Pool(s):** 3 outdoor, 4 heated outdoor. **Leisure Activities:** saunas, whirlpools, steamrooms, 2 lighted tennis courts, playground, exercise room, spa. **Guest Services:** wireless Internet. **Business Services:** business center. **Cards:** AX, MC, VI.

FEE / SOME UNITS

LOS PATIOS HOTEL Phone: (624)145-6070 30

Hotel

$110-$145 All Year

Address: Carr Transpeninsular KM 4 **Location:** Mex 1, 2.7 mi (4.5 km) e of town via westbound lateral/access road. **Facility:** Meets AAA guest room security requirements. 76 one-bedroom standard units. 2 stories (no elevator), exterior corridors. *Bath:* shower only. **Parking:** on-site. **Terms:** 3 day cancellation notice-fee imposed. **Amenities:** safes, irons, hair dryers. **Pool(s):** heated outdoor. **Leisure Activities:** whirlpool. **Guest Services:** wireless Internet. **Business Services:** meeting rooms, PC. **Cards:** AX, MC, VI.

/ SOME UNITS

MARINA FIESTA RESORT & SPA Book at AAA.com Phone: (624)145-6020 12

Condominium

$344-$540 All Year

Address: Col La Marina Lote 37 y 38 **Location:** On east side of marina. **Facility:** Meets AAA guest room security requirements. 155 units. 60 one-bedroom standard units with efficiencies. 93 one- and 2 two-bedroom suites with kitchens. 4-7 stories, exterior corridors. *Bath:* combo or shower only. **Parking:** on-site and valet. **Terms:** check-in 4 pm, 2 night minimum stay - seasonal, 3 day cancellation notice-fee imposed. **Amenities:** voice mail, irons, hair dryers. *Some:* safes. **Pool(s):** outdoor, heated outdoor. **Leisure Activities:** whirlpools, playground, exercise room, spa. *Fee:* saunas, steamrooms. **Guest Services:** valet laundry, wireless Internet. **Business Services:** meeting rooms, PC (fee). **Cards:** AX, MC, VI.

ME CABO BY MELIA Book great rates at AAA.com Phone: (624)145-7800 10

AAA

Boutique Hotel

$406-$975 All Year

Address: Playa El Medano S/N Zona Hotelera **Location:** Oceanfront. 0.6 mi (1 km) e of Mex 1 via Paseo del Pescador. Located at El Medano Beach. **Facility:** Catering to the young, hip crowd, the pueblo-style buildings feature high-tech, updated and comfortable guest rooms with modern baths. 150 units. 146 one-bedroom standard units, some with whirlpools. 4 one-bedroom suites with whirlpools. 6 stories, exterior corridors. *Bath:* combo or shower only. **Parking:** on-site and valet. **Terms:** age restrictions may apply, 3 day cancellation notice. **Amenities:** DVD players, CD players, high-speed Internet, voice mail, safes, honor bars, irons, hair dryers. **Dining:** 3 restaurants. **Pool(s):** 2 heated outdoor. **Leisure Activities:** exercise room, spa. **Guest Services:** valet laundry, wireless Internet. **Business Services:** conference facilities, business center. **Cards:** AX, MC, VI.

24 / SOME UNITS FEE

PLAYA GRANDE RESORT Phone: (624)145-7575 19

Resort Condominium

$273-$395 All Year

Address: Ave Playa Grande #1 **Location:** Oceanfront. 0.9 mi (1.5 km) s of town via Blvd Marina. Located at Land's End. **Facility:** Resembling a colorful seaside village, this resort sits on the sands at the tip of the peninsula; expansion is ongoing. Designated smoking area. 358 units. 42 one-bedroom standard units with efficiencies. 255 one-, 59 two- and 2 three-bedroom suites with kitchens, some with whirlpools. 4-8 stories, exterior corridors. **Parking:** on-site. **Terms:** check-in 4 pm, 3 night minimum stay - seasonal, 7 day cancellation notice. **Amenities:** voice mail, safes, irons, hair dryers. **Dining:** Galeon Italian Restaurant, see separate listing. **Pool(s):** 7 outdoor. **Leisure Activities:** whirlpools, waterslide, spa. *Fee:* miniature golf, lighted tennis court, exercise room. **Guest Services:** valet and coin laundry, wireless Internet. **Business Services:** conference facilities, business center. **Cards:** AX, MC, VI.

/ SOME UNITS

PLAZA NAUTICA CONDOMINIUMS Phone: (624)143-1788 15

Condominium

$80-$250 All Year

Address: Blvd Marina Plaza Nautica **Location:** In town; at marina. Located in a shopping complex. **Facility:** This high-rise is conveniently located in the downtown shopping district with a 24-hour deli, restaurants and a marina. Meets AAA guest room security requirements. 33 units. 3 one-, 26 two- and 4 three-bedroom suites with kitchens. 8 stories, exterior corridors. *Bath:* combo or shower only. **Parking:** on-site. **Terms:** office hours 9 am-6 pm, 3 night minimum stay - weekends, 30 day cancellation notice-fee imposed. **Amenities:** DVD players, CD players, irons. *Some:* safes. **Pool(s):** outdoor. **Leisure Activities:** whirlpool. *Fee:* massage. **Guest Services:** complimentary laundry. **Cards:** MC, VI.

FEE / SOME UNITS

(See map and index starting on p. 452)

PUEBLO BONITO LOS CABOS

Resort Condominium
$225-$360 All Year

Phone: (624)142-9797 8

Address: Playa El Medano s/n **Location:** Oceanfront. Mex 1, 0.6 mi (1 km) n of town to Mex 19, 0.5 mi w to the "Old Road", then just s. **Facility:** Mediterranean in style and painted all white, this property is on sandy grounds near town; units have a balcony, living room and kitchen. 147 units. 30 one-bedroom standard units with efficiencies. 110 one-, 4 two- and 3 three-bedroom suites with kitchens. 5 stories, exterior corridors. **Parking:** on-site and valet. **Terms:** check-in 4 pm, 14 day cancellation notice. **Amenities:** voice mail, safes, irons, hair dryers. **Pool(s):** heated outdoor. **Leisure Activities:** recreation programs, exercise room, volleyball. *Fee:* massage. **Guest Services:** valet laundry, wireless Internet. **Business Services:** business center. **Cards:** AX, MC, VI.

PUEBLO BONITO PACIFICA

Resort Hotel
$385-$680 All Year

Phone: 624/142-9696 28

Address: Predio Paraiso Escondido S/N **Location:** Oceanfront. Marina Blvd, 1.1 mi (1.8 km) w via Lazaro Cardenas and Miguel Herrera. **Facility:** Located outside Cabo San Lucas on Sunset Beach, this newest Pueblo Bonito property boasts elegant guest rooms, spacious baths and upscale bedding. Meets AAA guest room security requirements. Designated smoking area. 154 units. 140 one-bedroom standard units. 14 one-bedroom suites. 3-5 stories, exterior corridors. *Bath:* combo or shower only. **Parking:** on-site and valet. **Terms:** check-in 4 pm, age restrictions may apply, 14 day cancellation notice. **Amenities:** voice mail, safes, honor bars, irons, hair dryers. **Pool(s):** 2 heated outdoor. **Leisure Activities:** saunas, whirlpools, steamrooms, 2 lighted tennis courts, exercise room, spa. **Guest Services:** valet laundry, area transportation, wireless Internet. **Business Services:** meeting rooms, business center. **Cards:** AX, MC, VI.

PUEBLO BONITO ROSE

Resort Condominium
$245-$345 All Year

Phone: (624)142-9898 7

Address: Playa El Medano s/n **Location:** Oceanfront. Mex 1, 0.6 mi (1 km) n of town to Mex 19, 0.5 mi (0.8 km) w to the "Old Road", then just s. **Facility:** The elegant lobby and grounds feature classic Italian sculptures, a large reflection pool, a giant free-form pool, koi ponds and tropical birds. Meets AAA guest room security requirements. Designated smoking area. 260 units. 147 one-bedroom standard units with efficiencies. 93 one-, 14 two- and 6 three-bedroom suites with efficiencies. 6 stories, interior corridors. *Bath:* combo or shower only. **Parking:** on-site and valet. **Terms:** check-in 4 pm, 14 day cancellation notice. **Amenities:** voice mail, safes, irons, hair dryers. **Pool(s):** heated outdoor. **Leisure Activities:** spa. *Fee:* sauna, whirlpool, steamroom, lighted tennis court. **Guest Services:** valet laundry, wireless Internet. **Business Services:** meeting rooms, business center. **Cards:** AX, MC, VI.

FEE

PUEBLO BONITO SUNSET BEACH *Book at AAA.com*

Resort Hotel
$295-$995 All Year

Phone: (624)142-9999 29

Address: Predio Paraiso Escondido S/N **Location:** Oceanfront. Marina Blvd, 1.1 mi (1.8 km) w via Lazaro Cardenas and Miguel Herrera. **Facility:** The resort's hacienda-style buildings are terraced on the hillside, providing all rooms with a sunset view over the Pacific and a beachside pool. Meets AAA guest room security requirements. 583 units. 179 one-bedroom standard units, some with efficiencies. 282 one-, 112 two- and 10 three-bedroom suites, some with whirlpools. 2-6 stories, exterior corridors. *Bath:* combo or shower only. **Parking:** valet. **Terms:** check-in 4 pm, 15 day cancellation notice. **Amenities:** voice mail, safes, honor bars, irons, hair dryers. **Pool(s):** 5 heated outdoor. **Leisure Activities:** whirlpools, spa, kids club. *Fee:* saunas, steamrooms, 2 lighted tennis courts, exercise room. **Guest Services:** valet laundry, area transportation, wireless Internet. **Business Services:** conference facilities, business center. **Cards:** AX, MC, VI.

/ SOME UNITS

(See map and index starting on p. 452)

SHERATON HACIENDA DEL MAR RESORT & SPA *Book great rates at AAA.com* **Phone:** (624)145-8000 

Resort Hotel

$290-$750 All Year

Address: Corredor Touristico KM 10, Lote D **Location:** Oceanfront. On Mex 1, 6 mi (10 km) e of town. Located at Cabo del Sol. **Facility:** Nestled on the beach, tree-shaded mosaic patios offer guests an oasis from the sun and sand; guest rooms are large and comfortable. 270 units. 242 one-bedroom standard units with whirlpools. 15 one- and 13 three-bedroom suites, some with kitchens and/or whirlpools. 2-5 stories, exterior corridors. **Parking:** valet and street. **Terms:** 3 day cancellation notice-fee imposed. **Amenities:** high-speed Internet (fee), voice mail, safes, honor bars, irons, hair dryers. **Dining:** Pitahayas, see separate listing. **Pool(s):** 4 outdoor. **Leisure Activities:** saunas, whirlpools, steamrooms, recreation programs, exercise room, spa. *Fee:* golf-36 holes. **Guest Services:** area transportation, wireless Internet. **Business Services:** conference facilities, business center. **Cards:** AX, DC, MC, VI. ***(See color ad below & on insert)***

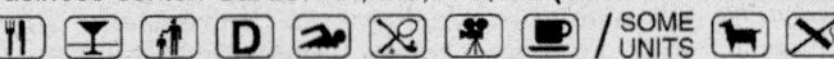

AAA Benefit:
Members get up to 15% off, plus Starwood Preferred Guest® bonuses.

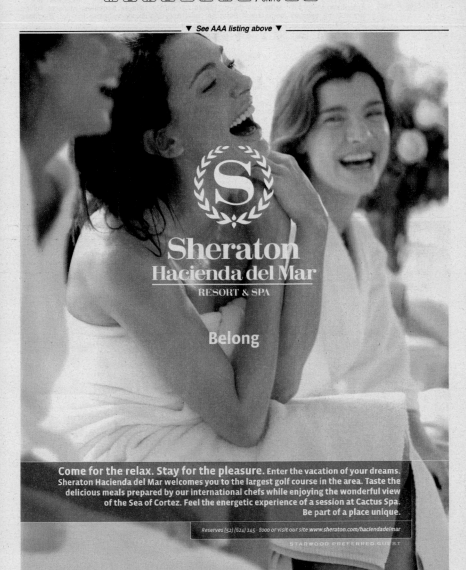

▼ *See AAA listing above* ▼

(See map and index starting on p. 452)

SIESTA SUITES HOTEL — **Phone:** (624)143-2773 14

Hotel

$65-$85 All Year

Address: Calle E Zapata y Guerrero **Location:** Just n of Marina Blvd and Miguel Hidalgo; downtown. **Facility:** Designated smoking area. 20 units. 5 one-bedroom standard units. 15 one-bedroom suites with kitchens. 4 stories (no elevator), exterior corridors. *Bath:* shower only. **Parking:** street. **Terms:** 15 day cancellation notice-fee imposed. **Pool(s):** outdoor. **Guest Services:** wireless Internet. **Business Services:** PC (fee). **Cards:** MC, VI.

SOLMAR SUITES RESORT — **Phone:** (624)146-7700 20

Resort Hotel

$189-$265 All Year

Address: Ave Solmar #1 **Location:** Oceanfront. 0.9 mi (1.5 km) s of town via Blvd Marina. Located at Land's End. **Facility:** This beachfront resort features expansive grounds and ample lounging areas; rooms and suites each have a private patio or balcony. 190 units. 135 one-bedroom standard units, some with kitchens. 53 one- and 2 two-bedroom suites with kitchens. 2-5 stories, exterior corridors. *Bath:* combo or shower only. **Parking:** on-site. **Terms:** check-in 4 pm, 7 day cancellation notice. **Amenities:** voice mail, safes, hair dryers. **Pool(s):** 3 outdoor. **Leisure Activities:** whirlpool, lighted tennis court, exercise room. **Guest Services:** valet and coin laundry, wireless Internet. **Business Services:** meeting rooms, business center. **Cards:** AX, MC, VI.

TESORO LOS CABOS — **Phone:** (624)173-9300 16

Hotel

$143-$199 All Year

Address: Blvd Marina Lote 9 y 10 **Location:** In town; at marina. **Facility:** 286 units. 283 one-bedroom standard units, some with efficiencies. 3 one-bedroom suites with kitchens. 5 stories, interior corridors. *Bath:* shower only. **Parking:** on-site. **Terms:** 15 day cancellation notice-fee imposed. **Amenities:** voice mail, safes, honor bars, hair dryers. **Dining:** 2 restaurants. **Pool(s):** outdoor. **Leisure Activities:** whirlpool. *Fee:* massage. **Guest Services:** valet laundry, area transportation-Medano Beach. **Business Services:** conference facilities, business center. **Cards:** AX, MC, VI. *(See color ad below)*

▼ See AAA listing above ▼

(See map and index starting on p. 452)

VILLA DEL PALMAR BEACH RESORT & SPA Book at AAA.com Phone: (624)145-7000 4

Resort Condominium
$277-$677 All Year

Address: KM 0.5 Camino Viejo a San Jose **Location:** Oceanfront. Mex 1, 0.6 mi (1 km) n of town to Mex 19, 0.6 mi (1 km) e to the "Old Road", then just n. **Facility:** Notable features include a seashell chandelier, a nine-story atrium lobby, waterfalls, two tiered pools and a waterslide. Meets AAA guest room security requirements. 465 units. 230 one-bedroom standard units with kitchens. 169 one-, 56 two- and 10 three-bedroom suites, some with whirlpools. 7-8 stories, interior corridors. **Parking:** on-site and valet. **Terms:** 14 day cancellation notice-fee imposed. **Amenities:** high-speed Internet (fee), voice mail, safes, honor bars, irons, hair dryers. **Dining:** La Casona, see separate listing. **Pool(s):** 3 heated outdoor. **Leisure Activities:** whirlpools, waterslide, miniature golf, 2 lighted tennis courts, recreation programs, spa, shuffleboard. **Guest Services:** valet and coin laundry, wireless Internet. **Business Services:** meeting rooms. **Cards:** AX, MC, VI.

VILLA LA ESTANCIA Book at AAA.com Phone: (624)145-6900 5

Resort Condominium
$330-$650 All Year

Address: KM 0.5 Camino Viejo a San Jose **Location:** Oceanfront. Mex 1, 0.6 mi (1 km) n of town to Mex 19, 0.3 mi (0.5 km) e to the "Old Road", then just n. **Facility:** A luxury complex on Medano Beach with private balconies and views of the ocean and Land's End. 299 units. 146 one-bedroom standard units. 146 one-, 1 two- and 6 three-bedroom suites with kitchens and whirlpools. 7 stories, interior/exterior corridors. **Parking:** on-site and valet. **Terms:** check-in 4 pm, 14 day cancellation notice-fee imposed. **Amenities:** high-speed Internet, voice mail, safes, irons, hair dryers. *Some:* DVD players. **Pool(s):** heated outdoor. **Leisure Activities:** saunas, whirlpools, steamrooms, 2 lighted tennis courts, exercise room, spa. **Guest Services:** valet and coin laundry, wireless Internet. **Business Services:** meeting rooms, business center. **Cards:** AX, MC, VI.

/ SOME UNITS

WHERE TO DINE

BOHAI - ASIAN BISTRO Phone: 624/144-4731 21

Asian
$19-$35

This new restaurant's upscale decor includes wall fountains and magical lighting. Among Asian dishes are the freshest sushi, spicy curries and creative blends of flavors from Thailand, Japan and China. Although Bohai was an area in China that existed for only a few decades, diners would be well served if the bistro enjoys a long run. Casual dress. **Bar:** Full bar. **Reservations:** accepted. **Hours:** 4 pm-10:30 pm, Sun from 2 pm. Closed major holidays. **Address:** Ave Cabo San Lucas entre Blvd Marina **Location:** Jct Cabo San Lucas and Blvd Marina; center. **Parking:** street. **Cards:** MC, VI.

CASA RAFAEL'S Phone: 624/143-0739 4

Continental
$16-$41

Skilled staff members at this quaint Mexican-colonial inn provide refined service to guests in the garden room, ocean room or poolside. Chicken Allison is a house specialty on a menu that also includes chiote red snapper, scampi, ribs and steak. Dressy casual. **Bar:** Full bar. **Reservations:** suggested. **Hours:** 6:30 pm-10 pm. Closed: 1/1; also 9/1-10/1. **Address:** Playa El Medano and Camino Pescador **Location:** 0.6 mi (1 km) s of Mex 1 via Paseo de la Marina. **Parking:** street. **Cards:** MC, VI.

EDITH'S Phone: 624/143-0801 8

Seafood
$13-$65

Affording an impressive view of Land's End, the popular palapa dining room is a favorite for seafood. Steaks, lamb and chicken are also on the menu. As patrons enter, they pick up the aroma of the mesquite grill and see tortillas being made. Casual dress. **Bar:** Full bar. **Reservations:** suggested. **Hours:** Open 12/1-8/15 & 10/2-11/30; 5 pm-10:30 pm. **Address:** Camino A Playa El Medano S/N **Location:** 0.7 mi (1.1 km) s of Mex 1. **Parking:** street. **Cards:** MC, VI.

EL RESTAURANTE AT ESPERANZA Phone: 624/145-6400 24

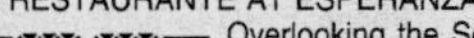

International
$34-$52

Overlooking the Sea of Cortez, the restaurant showcases the talent of Chef Howland, who creates magic with food. Appetizers such as lobster agnolotti with butternut squash and sage-scented homemade ricotta lead into entrees such as roasted sea bream with banana-orange puree and black olive powder. Desserts tantalize with delicate flavors and enchanting eye appeal. Dressy casual. **Bar:** Full bar. **Reservations:** required. **Hours:** 7 am-4 & 6:30-10:30 pm. **Address:** Carr Transpeninsular KM 7, Punta Ballena **Location:** On Mex 1, 3.6 mi (6 km) n of town; in Esperanza An Auberge Resort. **Parking:** valet. **Cards:** AX, DC, MC, VI.

FELLINI'S RESTAURANT Phone: 624/142-9898 10

Italian
$30-$70

Terrace seats afford the best view of the bay and famous rocks of Cabo San Lucas. The accomplished staff carries out attentive and expert service. Chef de Livier is apt to come out to say hello and check on diners' preferences. The tasting menu typically lines up choices such as stuffed pasta, grilled sea bass, organic greens salad and delicately flavored panna cotta. Casual dress. **Bar:** Full bar. **Reservations:** required. **Hours:** 6 pm-11 pm. Closed: Mon & 9/8-9/25. **Address:** Pueblo Bonito S/N **Location:** Mex 1, 0.6 mi (1 km) n of town to Mex 19, 0.5 mi (0.8 km) w to the "Old Road", then just s; in Pueblo Bonito Rose. **Parking:** on-site and valet. **Cards:** AX, MC, VI.

FRENCH RIVERA RESTAURANT Phone: 624/104-3125 27

Mediterranean
$18-$69

Enjoy dining with a view of the Sea of Cortez at this restaurant, where the chef creates fine French dishes with ingredients fresh from their garden. The menu is ever-changing with dishes like grilled frog legs, braised red snapper and roasted Sonora beef, or create your own lunch from a selection of appetizers. Casual dress. **Bar:** Full bar. **Reservations:** suggested. **Hours:** 6 pm-10 pm. **Address:** Carr Transpeninsular KM 6.3 Loc 10 y 11 **Location:** On Mex 1, 3.8 mi (6.3 km) e; in Plaza Del Rey. **Parking:** on-site. **Cards:** AX, MC, VI.

(See map and index starting on p. 452)

GALEON ITALIAN RESTAURANT **Phone:** 624/143-0443 (14)

Italian
$12-$29

Overlooking the town and bay, the restaurant offers seating in the relaxed dining room and on the balcony. Offered is a nice selection of seafood, pasta, veal and pizza. Casual dress. **Bar:** Full bar. **Reservations:** accepted. **Hours:** 4 pm-11 pm. **Address:** Blvd Marina S/N **Location:** 0.6 mi (1 km) s of town. **Parking:** on-site. **Cards:** AX, MC, VI.

HARD ROCK CAFE **Phone:** 624/143-3779 (19)

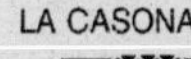

American
$12-$24

Rock 'n' roll memorabilia decorates the walls of the popular theme restaurant. Live music on the weekends contributes to the bustling atmosphere. On the menu is a wide variety of American cuisine—from burgers and sandwiches to seafood, steaks and pasta. Casual dress. **Bar:** Full bar. **Hours:** 11 am-11 pm. Closed major holidays. **Address:** Blvd Marina L 17L28C Plaza Bonita **Location:** Center; in Plaza Bonita. **Parking:** street. **Cards:** AX, DS, JC, MC, VI.

LA CASONA **Phone:** 624/145-7000 (2)

Steak
$25-$50

Patrons order fresh and innovative dishes that are prepared to their request. Dressy casual. Entertainment. **Bar:** Full bar. **Reservations:** suggested. **Hours:** 6 pm-10:30 pm. **Address:** KM 0.5 Camino Viejo a San Jose **Location:** Mex 1, 0.6 mi (1 km) s of town to Mex 19, 0.5 mi (0.8 km) e to the "Old Road," then just n; between the Villa del Palmar and Villa La Estancia hotels. **Parking:** on-site and valet. **Cards:** AX, DC, MC, VI.

LA GOLONDRINA **Phone:** 624/143-0542 (1)

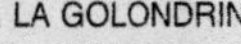

Mexican
$14-$62

At a historic trading post, this popular restaurant lets diners relax on the patio while savoring Mexican-style combination plates of seafood, chicken and beef. Casual dress. **Bar:** Full bar. **Reservations:** suggested. **Hours:** 5 pm-10:30 pm. Closed: 1/1, 12/24, 12/25. **Address:** Paseo del Pescador S/N **Location:** Just e of Mex 1; next to City Club. **Parking:** street. **Cards:** MC, VI. **Historic**

LA PANGA ANTIGUA **Phone:** 624/143-6898 (5)

Mexican
$20-$42

The open-roofed hacienda setting evokes Old Mexico. Star-shaped lights are replicated with a lighted, glass mosaic star in the floor. Freshly caught seafood, including shellfish from the Sea of Cortez, as well as steaks are offered. Whole snapper with guajillo pepper marinade is a house specialty. Casual dress. **Bar:** Full bar. **Reservations:** accepted. **Hours:** noon-4 & 5-10 pm. Closed: 4/12. **Address:** Camino Viejo a San Jose esq **Location:** Center. **Parking:** street. **Cards:** AX, MC, VI.

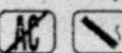

LAS MARIAS **Phone:** 624/163-5555 (30)

Mexican
$12-$32

In Hacienda Encantada, the oceanfront restaurant affords spectacular views over the bay to the Cabo rocks. Elegant open-air surroundings and fine foods such as mahi mahi in citrus cream sauce satisfy. Casual dress. **Bar:** Full bar. **Reservations:** required. **Hours:** 7 am-10 pm. **Address:** Carr Transpeninsular KM 7.3 **Location:** On Mex 1, 3.7 mi (6 km) ne of town; in Hacienda Encantada Resort & Spa. **Parking:** valet. **Cards:** AX, MC, VI.

LATITUDE 22+ ROADHOUSE **Phone:** 624/143-9282 (25)

American
$8-$30

The small cafe and bar can boast great food and attitude. Funky memorabilia is pinned to the walls and ceiling. On the menu are not only great hamburgers and barbecue sandwiches, but also ribs, prime rib, chicken-fried steak and pasta dishes. Fishermen can bring in their catch for preparation. Casual dress. **Bar:** Full bar. **Hours:** 9 am-11 pm. Closed: Tues. **Address:** KM 4.5 Carr Transpeninsular **Location:** 2.4 mi (4 km) e on Mex 1; next to Costco; behind power plant. **Parking:** on-site. **Cards:** MC, VI.

MI CASA **Phone:** 624/143-1933 (11)

Mexican
$12-$40

Colorful murals surround the enchanting courtyard, a place best experienced after dark. Authentic regional dishes from throughout Mexico include such popular choices as mole poblano fish, roasted pork, filet of beef and grilled chicken. Casual dress. **Bar:** Full bar. **Reservations:** suggested. **Hours:** 10 am-3 & 5:30-10:30 pm, Sun from 5:30 pm. **Address:** Ave Cabo San Lucas **Location:** 0.6 mi (1 km) w of Blvd Marina via Lazaro Cardenas; in town. **Parking:** street. **Cards:** AX, MC, VI.

THE OFFICE **Phone:** 624/143-3464 (9)

Mexican
$8-$54

This is a prototype casual restaurant, with tables and chairs on the sand. Stop in for breakfast after a morning walk or sunset as the shadows fall on the "Arch." Office assistants serve fun with an assortment of special beverages, hamburgers, chicken enchiladas and Tampiquena top sirloin. Party favors and entertainment enliven theme nights on Monday, Thursday and Sunday at 6:30 pm. Casual dress. **Bar:** Full bar. **Reservations:** suggested. **Hours:** Open 12/1-8/31 & 10/2-11/30; 7 am-10 pm. **Address:** Playa El Medano S/N **Location:** 0.8 mi (1.2 km) se of Mex 1 via Paseo del Pescador. **Parking:** street. **Cards:** MC, VI.

(See map and index starting on p. 452)

O MOLE MIO — **Phone:** 624/143-7577 (20)

Mexican
$10-$34

Just a short walk off the Cabo marina, the small creatively decorated eatery features a custom metal sculpture stairway, fun barstools and shelves covered in Day of the Dead pottery sculptures. The margaritas are cold and the hearty portions of regional Mexican dishes filling. Particularly noteworthy are red or green chicken mole dishes and fish in sweet guajillo pepper sauce. Casual dress. **Bar:** Full bar. **Hours:** 8 am-5 & 6-11 pm. **Address:** Blvd Marina S/N Lote 23 y 24 **Location:** Blvd Marina Plaza del Sol; center. **Parking:** street. **Cards:** MC, VI.

PANCHO'S RESTAURANT & TEQUILA BAR — **Phone:** 624/143-0973 (12)

Mexican
$10-$25

The colorfully decorated restaurant treats diners to friendly service and more than 250 selections of tequila. Tender pork posole, pico de gallo salad, shredded-beef omelet and large hamburgers are a sampling of the comfort foods offered. Casual dress. Entertainment. **Bar:** Full bar. **Reservations:** suggested. **Hours:** 7 am-10:30 pm. Closed: 1/1. **Address:** Miguel Hildago at Calle Zapata **Location:** Just w of Blvd Marina; in town. **Parking:** street. **Cards:** MC, VI.

PEACOCKS RESTAURANT — **Phone:** 624/143-1858 (3)

Mediterranean
$20-$35

European cuisine is served in the palapa dining room and on the patio. Boned Chilean salmon in cream sauce, baked whole red snapper and cabo dorado in pecan crust are among seafood dishes. Other dishes include grilled New York steak in peppercorn sauce and New Zealand rack of lamb in a mustard crust. Dressy casual. **Bar:** Full bar. **Reservations:** suggested. **Hours:** 6 pm-10:30 pm. **Address:** Paseo del Pescador s/n **Location:** 0.3 mi (0.5 km) e of Mex 1. **Parking:** street. **Cards:** AX, MC, VI.

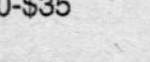

PITAHAYAS — **Phone:** 624/145-8010 (28)

Pacific Rim
$25-$41

Overlooking the beach and the Sea of Cortez, the restaurant allows patrons to relax under the stars as they sample well-presented fresh local seafood and organic vegetables prepared in a variety of styles—from blackened catch of the day to whole steamed snapper with ying-yang sauce. Also meriting consideration is the "shaked" Angus tenderloin with wasabi mashed potatoes. Dressy casual. **Bar:** Beer only. **Reservations:** suggested. **Hours:** 5 pm-10:30 pm. **Address:** Corredor Touristico KM 10, Lote D **Location:** On Mex 1, 6 mi (10 km) e of town; in Sheraton Hacienda del Mar Resort & Spa. **Parking:** valet. **Cards:** AX, DC, MC, VI.

ROMEO Y JULIETA RISTORANTE — **Phone:** 624/143-0225 (17)

Italian
$10-$25

Pasta, seafood and specialty pizzas are served in this quaint, family-friendly hacienda. Dressy casual. **Bar:** Full bar. **Reservations:** accepted. **Hours:** 4 pm-11 pm. **Address:** Camino del Cerro **Location:** 0.3 mi (0.5 km) s of town via Blvd Marina. **Parking:** street. **Cards:** AX, MC, VI.

ROSATO — **Phone:** 624/145-6200 (29)

Northern Italian
$18-$42

Overlooking the resort and the Sea of Cortez, the sophisticated dining room incorporates subdued lighting, candles and soft music into its intimate setting. Delicious examples of Northern Italian cooking include a variety of risottos, tuna with wine cream sauce and rack of lamb. Jazz brightens the atmosphere on Thursday evenings. Dressy casual. **Bar:** Full bar. **Reservations:** suggested. **Hours:** 6 pm-11 pm. **Address:** Carr Transpeninsular KM 10.3, Lote A-1 **Location:** On Mex 1, 6 mi (10 km) e of town; in Fiesta Americana Grand Los Cabos. **Parking:** valet. **Cards:** AX, DC, DS, MC, VI.

RUTH'S CHRIS STEAK HOUSE — **Phone:** 624/144-3232 (15)

Steak
$22-$50

The main fare is steak, which is prepared from several cuts of prime beef and cooked to perfection, but the menu also lists lamb, chicken and seafood dishes. Guests should come hungry because the side dishes, which are among the a la carte offerings, could make a meal in themselves. Casual dress. **Bar:** Full bar. **Reservations:** accepted. **Hours:** 11 am-11 pm. Closed major holidays. **Address:** Lazaro Cardenas s/n, Local 41 CP **Location:** Center; in Plaza Paraiso. **Parking:** on-site. **Cards:** AX, CB, DC, DS, JC, MC, VI.

SANCHO PANZA WINE BISTRO — **Phone:** 624/143-3212 (16)

Mediterranean
$17-$32

The art deco and Cuban art hangings are what stand out when you enter the restaurant, along with the aroma of Mediterranean cuisine with a Latin twist and eclectic blend of everything. Offering an extensive wine list. Entrees vary from osso bucco and liver mousse to a tasteful ribeye Florentine. You will be tempted to try their homemade desserts. Live jazz and blues nightly. Casual dress. **Bar:** Full bar. **Reservations:** suggested. **Hours:** 4 pm-11 pm. **Address:** Blvd Marina **Location:** Next to Tesoro Los Cabos Hotel By the Marina. **Parking:** street. **Cards:** MC, VI.

SENOR GREENBERG'S MEXICATESSEN — **Phone:** 624/143-6772 (13)

Deli
$9-$15

Right on the marina, the delicatessen is as popular for its vantage point, which allows for great people-watching, as for its coffee and pastries. Hot dogs, burritos, baked meatloaf and barbecue ribs are ordered as often as the corned beef and pastrami. Breakfast is served around the clock, and boxed lunches can be prepared to go. Casual dress. **Bar:** Full bar. **Hours:** 24 hours. **Address:** Blvd Marina, Plaza Gali **Location:** In town, on marina. **Parking:** on-site. **Cards:** MC, VI.

(See map and index starting on p. 452)

STOP LIGHT BAR & GRILL **Phone:** 624/143-4740 (6)

Mexican
$9-$24

Simple dishes, such as hamburgers, tamales and tacos, share menu space with fresh seafood plates, steaks, pork chops and chicken. On the main drag, the open, streetside restaurant always offers daily specials. Casual dress. **Bar:** Full bar. **Hours:** 8 am-1 am. **Address:** Blvd Lazaro Cardenas **Location:** Just e of Calle Zaragoza; in town. **Parking:** street. **Cards:** MC, VI.

SUNSET DA MONA LISA **Phone:** 624/145-8160 (26)

Italian
$22-$49

The impressive, open-air, palapa-covered restaurant affords views of the ocean and Land's End. The menu centers on pasta, seafood and pizza. Casual dress. **Bar:** Full bar. **Reservations:** suggested. **Hours:** 5 pm-10 pm. **Address:** Carr Transpeninsular KM 6.5 **Location:** 3.1 mi (5 km) e on Mex 1, then 0.6 (1 km) s; past Misiones del Cabo. **Parking:** on-site. **Cards:** MC, VI.

CATAVINA, BAJA CALIFORNIA pop. 1,500

WHERE TO STAY

The following lodging was either not evaluated or did not meet AAA rating requirements but is listed for your information only.

DESERT INN **Phone:** 200/124-9123

fyi

Not evaluated. **Address:** KM 178 **Location:** On Mex 1. Facilities, services, and decor characterize an economy property.

EL ROSARIO, BAJA CALIFORNIA

WHERE TO DINE

The following restaurant has not been evaluated by AAA but is listed for your information only.

MAMA ESPINOSA'S **Phone:** 616/165-8770

fyi

Not evaluated. Baja-influenced lobster, fish and beef dishes are served in this historic restaurant, the home of Dona Anita. **Address:** KM 55 Carr Transpeninsular **Location:** On Mex 1; town center.

ENSENADA, BAJA CALIFORNIA pop. 764,602

WHERE TO STAY

AMERICAS BEST VALUE INN/POSADA EL REY SOL **Phone:** 646/178-1601

Motel
$82-$95 All Year

Address: Ave Blancarte #130 **Location:** Just n of Ave Lopez Mateos; center. Located in the tourist area. **Facility:** Meets AAA guest room security requirements. 52 units. 51 one-bedroom standard units, some with whirlpools. 1 one-bedroom suite with whirlpool. 3 stories, exterior corridors. *Bath:* combo or shower only. **Parking:** on-site. **Amenities:** high-speed Internet, safes, hair dryers. **Dining:** El Rey Sol Restaurant, see separate listing. **Pool(s):** outdoor. **Leisure Activities:** whirlpool. **Guest Services:** valet laundry, wireless Internet. **Business Services:** meeting rooms, fax. **Cards:** AX, MC, VI. Affiliated with Americas Best Value Inn.

D / SOME UNITS FEE

BEST WESTERN EL CID Book great rates at AAA.com **Phone:** (646)178-2401

Hotel
$52-$92 All Year

Address: Ave Lopez Mateos #993 **Location:** Just w of Ave Blancarte; center. Located in the tourist area. **Facility:** Meets AAA guest room security requirements. 52 units. 50 one-bedroom standard units. 2 one-bedroom suites with whirlpools. 3 stories (no elevator), interior corridors. *Bath:* combo or shower only. **Parking:** on-site. **Terms:** 3 day cancellation notice-fee imposed. **Amenities:** high-speed Internet, voice mail, hair dryers. **Pool(s):** outdoor. **Guest Services:** valet and coin laundry, wireless Internet. **Business Services:** meeting rooms. **Cards:** AX, DC, DS, MC, VI.

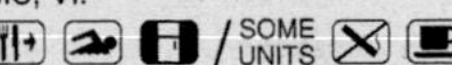

AAA Benefit:
Members save up to 20%, plus 10% bonus points with rewards program.

CASA DEL SOL MOTEL **Phone:** 646/178-1570

Motel
$60-$85 All Year

Address: Ave Lopez Mateos #1001 **Location:** At Ave Blancarte; center. Located in the tourist area. **Facility:** Meets AAA guest room security requirements. 40 one-bedroom standard units. 2 stories (no elevator), exterior corridors. *Bath:* shower only. **Parking:** on-site. **Amenities:** high-speed Internet. **Pool(s):** outdoor. **Leisure Activities:** spa. **Guest Services:** wireless Internet. **Cards:** AX, MC, VI.

CASA NATALIE HOTEL & SPA **Phone:** 646/174-7373

Hotel
$180-$395 All Year

Address: Carr Tijuana KM 103.3 **Location:** On Mex 1, 4.8 mi (8 km) n of town. **Facility:** 8 one-bedroom standard units. 2 stories (no elevator), interior corridors. *Bath:* combo or shower only. **Parking:** on-site. **Terms:** 2 night minimum stay - weekends, age restrictions may apply. **Amenities:** CD players, safes, irons, hair dryers. **Pool(s):** heated outdoor. **Leisure Activities:** whirlpools. *Fee:* massage. **Guest Services:** valet laundry, wireless Internet. **Cards:** AX, MC, VI.

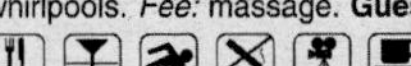

CORONA HOTEL **Phone:** 646/176-0901

Hotel
$64-$150 All Year

Address: Blvd Lazaro Cardenas #1442 **Location:** 0.6 mi (1 km) s. **Facility:** Meets AAA guest room security requirements. 92 units. 90 one-bedroom standard units. 2 one-bedroom suites, some with whirlpools. 4 stories, interior corridors. **Parking:** on-site. **Terms:** 3 day cancellation notice-fee imposed. **Amenities:** high-speed Internet, safes, irons, hair dryers. **Pool(s):** heated outdoor. **Leisure Activities:** whirlpool, exercise room, spa. **Guest Services:** valet laundry, wireless Internet. **Business Services:** meeting rooms. **Cards:** AX, DC, DS, MC, VI.

ESTERO BEACH RESORT HOTEL **Phone:** 646/176-6230

Resort Hotel
$60-$140 All Year

Address: 482 W San Ysidro Blvd **Location:** 7 mi (10.5 km) s of town on Mex 1, 1 mi (1.5 km) w on Ave Jose Moreles and Lupita Novelo O. **Facility:** A family-oriented resort on several acres of beachfront grounds. Units are located in several buildings, from modest to upscale. 99 units. 90 one-bedroom standard units. 4 two-bedroom suites, some with efficiencies and/or whirlpools. 5 cottages. 2 stories (no elevator), exterior corridors. *Bath:* combo or shower only. **Parking:** on-site. **Terms:** 3 day cancellation notice-fee imposed. **Amenities:** irons, hair dryers. *Some:* DVD players, CD players. **Pool(s):** heated outdoor. **Leisure Activities:** whirlpools, boat ramp, banana rides, personal watercraft, kayak, 3 tennis courts, BMX track, rental bicycles, playground, volleyball. *Fee:* horseback riding, massage. **Guest Services:** valet laundry. **Cards:** MC, VI.

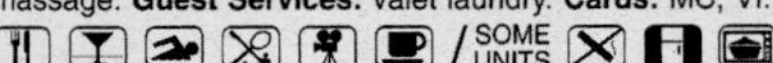

HACIENDA BAJAMAR **Phone:** 646/155-0151

Resort Hotel
$154-$287 All Year

Address: Carr Escenica Tijuana KM 77.5 **Location:** On Mex 1-D (toll road), exit Baja Mar; 19.8 mi (33 km) n of town. **Facility:** A golf resort located along a picturesque and peaceful coastline, this Mexican colonial-style hotel surrounds a secluded courtyard. 81 units. 71 one-bedroom standard units. 10 one-bedroom suites with efficiencies. 2 stories (no elevator), interior/exterior corridors. **Parking:** on-site. **Terms:** check-in 4 pm, 3 day cancellation notice-fee imposed. **Amenities:** safes, hair dryers. **Pool(s):** outdoor. **Leisure Activities:** whirlpool, 2 lighted tennis courts, playground, exercise room. *Fee:* golf-27 holes, massage. **Guest Services:** valet laundry. **Business Services:** meeting rooms, PC. **Cards:** AX, MC, VI.

HOTEL CORAL & MARINA RESORT **Phone:** (646)175-0000

Hotel
$105-$150 All Year

Address: Carr Tijuana-Ensenada #3421 **Location:** On Mex 1-D (toll road), 1.8 mi (3 km) n of town at KM 103. **Facility:** Meets AAA guest room security requirements. 147 units. 20 one-bedroom standard units. 122 one-, 4 two- and 1 three-bedroom suites, some with efficiencies (no utensils). 6 stories, interior corridors. *Bath:* combo or shower only. **Parking:** on-site. **Terms:** 3 day cancellation notice-fee imposed. **Amenities:** high-speed Internet, safes, irons, hair dryers. **Pool(s):** outdoor, heated indoor. **Leisure Activities:** saunas, whirlpools, steamrooms, fishing, 2 lighted tennis courts, playground, basketball, volleyball, game room. *Fee:* boats, sailboats, marina, charter fishing, massage. **Guest Services:** valet laundry, wireless Internet. **Business Services:** meeting rooms, PC (fee). **Cards:** AX, MC, VI.

HOTEL CORTEZ *Book great rates at AAA.com* **Phone:** (646)178-2307

Hotel
$80-$100 All Year

Address: Ave Lopez Mateos #1089 **Location:** At Ave Castillo; center. Located in the tourist area. **Facility:** Meets AAA guest room security requirements. 80 units. 73 one-bedroom standard units. 7 one-bedroom suites. 2 stories (no elevator), interior/exterior corridors. *Bath:* combo or shower only. **Parking:** on-site. **Terms:** 3 day cancellation notice-fee imposed. **Pool(s):** heated outdoor. **Leisure Activities:** limited exercise equipment, basketball. **Guest Services:** valet laundry, wireless Internet. **Business Services:** meeting rooms, business center. **Cards:** AX, MC, VI.

/ SOME UNITS

LAS ROSAS HOTEL **Phone:** 646/174-4310

Hotel
$80-$250 All Year

Address: Carr Tijuana-Ensenada KM 105.5 **Location:** On Mex 1, 4.3 mi (7 km) n of town. **Facility:** Meets AAA guest room security requirements. 48 units. 47 one-bedroom standard units, some with whirlpools. 1 cottage. 4 stories, exterior corridors. *Bath:* combo or shower only. **Parking:** on-site. **Terms:** 3 day cancellation notice-fee imposed. **Amenities:** irons, hair dryers. **Pool(s):** heated outdoor. **Leisure Activities:** sauna, whirlpool, exercise room. *Fee:* lighted tennis court, massage. **Guest Services:** valet laundry. **Business Services:** meeting rooms, business center. **Cards:** MC, VI.

D / SOME UNITS

PUNTA MORRO RESORT **Phone:** (646)178-3507

Hotel
$155-$395 All Year

Address: KM 106 Carr Tijuana-Ensenada **Location:** 3.1 mi (5 km) n of town on Mex 1, 0.3 mi (0.5 km) w. **Facility:** Meets AAA guest room security requirements. 24 units. 3 one-bedroom standard units. 9 one-, 9 two- and 3 three-bedroom suites. 3 stories, exterior corridors. *Bath:* shower only. **Parking:** on-site. **Terms:** 7 day cancellation notice-fee imposed. **Amenities:** high-speed Internet, safes, irons, hair dryers. **Dining:** The Restaurant at Punta Morro, see separate listing. **Pool(s):** heated outdoor. **Leisure Activities:** whirlpool. *Fee:* massage. **Guest Services:** valet laundry, wireless Internet. **Business Services:** meeting rooms. **Cards:** AX, MC, VI.

/ SOME UNITS

VILLA FONTANA INN **Phone:** 646/178-3434

Motel
$54-$95 All Year

Address: Ave Lopez Mateos #1050 **Location:** Just w of Ave Blancarte; center. Located in the tourist area. **Facility:** Meets AAA guest room security requirements. 69 one-bedroom standard units, some with whirlpools. 2 stories, exterior corridors. *Bath:* combo or shower only. **Parking:** on-site. **Terms:** 2 night minimum stay - seasonal, 3 day cancellation notice. **Amenities:** *Some:* hair dryers. **Pool(s):** outdoor. **Leisure Activities:** whirlpool. **Guest Services:** wireless Internet. **Cards:** AX, DC, DS, MC, VI.

/ SOME UNITS

WHERE TO DINE

BRONCO'S STEAKHOUSE **Phone:** 646/176-4900

Continental
$8-$26

Great mesquite grilled steaks are served in this popular local cantina; a Mexican breakfast buffet is offered Saturdays and Sundays and a lunch buffet on Wednesdays. Casual dress. **Bar:** Full bar. **Hours:** 8 am-10:30 pm, Sun from 9 am. Closed: 1/1, 12/25; also 5/1 & 11/20. **Address:** Ave Lopez Mateos #1525 **Location:** 0.6 mi (1 km) s of town on Ave Lopez Mateos, cross Ave Guadalupe. **Parking:** on-site. **Cards:** AX, DS, MC, VI.

EL CID **Phone:** 646/178-1809

Mexican
$8-$28

Nestled on the main strip in downtown with indoor and outdoor seating. The variety of menu selections depicts the flavor of Mexican delicacies starting off with chips and homemade salsa. Try their combination platter if you can't make up your mind. Flan is a typical Mexican dessert which will satisfy any sweet tooth. Casual dress. **Bar:** Full bar. **Hours:** 7 am-11 pm. **Address:** Ave Lopez Mateos #995-A Zona Centro **Location:** Just w of Ave Blancarte; center; next to Best Western El Cid. **Parking:** street. **Cards:** MC, VI.

EL REY SOL RESTAURANT **Phone:** 646/178-1733

French
$9-$35

Family-operated since 1947, the award-winning French restaurant offers formal dining, fresh baked pastries and a tea room. The extensive menu includes swordfish with cilantro sauce, fish and shrimp broiled with butter and garlic and chicken chipotle. Casual dress. **Hours:** 7:30 am-10:30 pm. **Address:** Ave Lopez Mateos 1000 **Location:** Just n of Ave Lopez Mateos; center; in Americas Best Value Inn/Posada El Rey Sol. **Parking:** street. **Cards:** AX, MC, VI.

HALIOTIS **Phone:** 646/176-3720

Seafood
$10-$35

Popular with locals, the family-operated restaurant is just outside the tourist area. Spacious dining rooms are appointed with nautical decor and family pictures. The menu centers on fresh seafood, including the specialty: pacifico abalone grilled in a wine and butter sauce. Other choices include scallops in garlic sauce, fish stuffed with cheese, broiled clams and lobster tacos. Casual dress. **Bar:** Full bar. **Hours:** noon-10 pm. Closed: 1/1, 12/25. **Address:** Calle Delante 179 **Location:** Mex 1, 0.6 mi (1 km) e; south end of town. **Parking:** on-site. **Cards:** AX, DS, MC, VI.

LA EMBOTELLADORA VIEJA RESTAURANTE **Phone:** 646/174-0807

Mediterranean
$8-$18

At the Bodegas de Santo Tomas Winery, the restaurant has a large dining room—formerly the bottling room—with brick pillars and massive wine barrels. Well matched with wine list recommendations, menu selections include fish filet with scallions, salmon in cream sauce, veal and mushrooms and pasta with shrimp. Service is attentive. Diners can take the winery tour for no additional fee. Casual dress. **Bar:** Beer & wine. **Hours:** 3 pm-11 pm, Sun 1 pm-10 pm. Closed: 1/1, 12/25; also Mon. **Address:** Ave Miramar #666 **Location:** 0.3 mi (0.5 km) n of downtown. **Parking:** street. **Cards:** AX, MC, VI.

LAS CAZUELAS RESTAURANT **Phone:** 646/176-1044

Mexican
$6-$38

Fast, friendly service and generous portions of comfort food attract business and family diners all day long to the busy dining room. Breakfast is a special draw. Lobster, abalone, jumbo shrimp stuffed with lobster, chicken adobo, chillaques with chicken and grilled or baked fish with garlic are a few of the dishes. Casual dress. **Bar:** Full bar. **Hours:** 7 am-11 pm. **Address:** Ave Sangines #6 **Location:** 1.2 mi (2 km) s of town on blvds Lazaro Cardenas and Costero, just e. **Parking:** on-site. **Cards:** MC, VI.

THE RESTAURANT AT PUNTA MORRO **Phone:** 646/178-3507

International
$15-$35

Set atop a rock overlooking the ocean, this restaurant offers sunset views across the ocean and views of the city lights. The waves lap beneath the dining room, which offers calamari steak with "Pinguica" sauce scented with lime-leafed sage, New Zealand rack of lamb with sangrita sauce, prime rib with a poblanas corn basket and chicken breast marinated in balsamic vinegar and virgin olive oil. The large wine list and the flan with Irish cream will complete any meal. Dressy casual. **Bar:** Full bar. **Reservations:** accepted. **Hours:** noon-11 pm, Sat & Sun from 9 am. **Address:** KM 106 Carr Tijuana-Ensenada **Location:** 3.1 mi (5 km) n of town on Mex 1, 0.3 mi (0.5 km) w; in Punta Morro Resort. **Parking:** on-site. **Cards:** MC, VI.

RESTAURANT CASAMAR **Phone:** 646/174-0417

Seafood
$9-$20

This long-established restaurant, patronized by loyal diners, prepares such steak and seafood dishes as grilled sea bass, salmon with cilantro sauce and steak rinconada. Dressy casual. **Bar:** Full bar. **Reservations:** accepted. **Hours:** noon-11 pm. **Address:** Blvd Lazaro Cardenas #987 **Location:** Across from marina. **Parking:** street. **Cards:** MC, VI.

GUERRERO NEGRO, BAJA CALIFORNIA SUR pop. 10,900

WHERE TO STAY

The following lodging was either not evaluated or did not meet AAA rating requirements but is listed for your information only.

DESERT INN **Phone:** 615/157-1304

fyi

Not evaluated. **Address:** 28th Parallel **Location:** 4.6 mi (7.5 km) ne of town on Mex 1. Facilities, services, and decor characterize an economy property.

WHERE TO DINE

The following restaurant has not been evaluated by AAA but is listed for your information only.

MALARRIMO RESTAURANT **Phone:** 615/157-0250

fyi

Not evaluated. The long-established restaurant counts its specialties as preparations of local seafood and beef. **Address:** Blvd Emiliano Zapata **Location:** 0.6 mi (1 km) w of Mex 1; east edge of town.

LA PAZ, BAJA CALIFORNIA SUR pop. 196,907

WHERE TO STAY

ARAIZA PALMIRA *Book at AAA.com* **Phone:** (612)121-6200

Hotel
$97-$130 All Year

Address: Blvd Alberto Alvarado Aramburo S/N **Location:** 1.5 mi (2.5 km) n of town on Carr a Pichilingue. **Facility:** Meets AAA guest room security requirements. 120 one-bedroom standard units. 3 stories (no elevator), interior corridors. *Bath:* shower only. **Parking:** on-site. **Terms:** 3 day cancellation notice-fee imposed. **Amenities:** hair dryers. *Some:* irons. **Pool(s):** outdoor. **Leisure Activities:** lighted tennis court, playground, exercise room. **Guest Services:** valet laundry, wireless Internet. **Business Services:** conference facilities, business center. **Cards:** AX, MC, VI.

/ SOME UNITS

CABANAS DE LOS ARCOS **Phone:** (612)122-2744

Hotel
$90-$113 All Year

Address: Paseo Alvaro Obregon 498 **Location:** Just off Paseo Alvaro Obregon; opposite the malecon; center; adjacent to Hotel Los Arcos. **Facility:** Meets AAA guest room security requirements. 52 units. 50 one- and 2 two-bedroom standard units. 1-4 stories, interior/exterior corridors. *Bath:* shower only. **Parking:** on-site. **Terms:** cancellation fee imposed. **Amenities:** voice mail, safes, honor bars, irons, hair dryers. **Pool(s):** heated outdoor. **Leisure Activities:** *Fee:* massage. **Guest Services:** valet laundry, wireless Internet. **Business Services:** meeting rooms. **Cards:** AX, MC, VI.

/ SOME UNITS

CASA TUSCANY INN **Phone:** 425/367-4918

Bed & Breakfast
$105-$145 All Year

Address: Calle Nicolas Bravo 110 **Location:** Paseo Alvaro Obregon, just past Hotel Los Arcos, just e on Rosales, 1 blk n on Revolution, then just w. **Facility:** Designated smoking area. 4 one-bedroom standard units. 2 stories (no elevator), exterior corridors. *Bath:* shower only. **Parking:** street. **Terms:** office hours 8 am-7:30 pm, 30 day cancellation notice. **Amenities:** video library. **Leisure Activities:** *Fee:* massage. **Guest Services:** wireless Internet.

D / SOME UNITS VCR

CLUB EL MORO **Phone:** (612)122-4084

Hotel
$80-$160 All Year

Address: KM 2 Carr a Pichilingue **Location:** Oceanfront. 1.2 mi (2 km) n of town. **Facility:** 28 units. 10 one-bedroom standard units. 15 one- and 3 two-bedroom suites, some with kitchens. 2 stories (no elevator), exterior corridors. *Bath:* shower only. **Parking:** on-site. **Terms:** office hours 7 am-11 pm, 15 day cancellation notice-fee imposed. **Amenities:** hair dryers. *Some:* CD players. **Pool(s):** outdoor. **Leisure Activities:** whirlpools, fishing. **Guest Services:** wireless Internet. **Business Services:** PC. **Cards:** MC, VI.

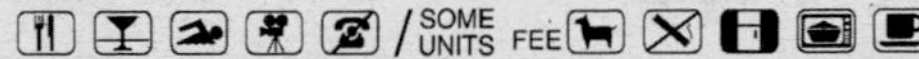

FIESTA INN Book great rates at AAA.com **Phone:** (612)123-6000

Contemporary Resort Hotel
$198-$305 All Year

Address: KM 7.5 Carr Pichilinque **Location:** 4.5 mi (7.5 km) n of town; adjacent to Marina Costa Baja. **Facility:** Ocean and bay front views grace the multi-story building; recently re-decorated guest rooms have luxurious bedding and spacious baths. Meets AAA guest room security requirements. 120 units. 114 one-bedroom standard units. 6 one-bedroom suites. 4 stories, exterior corridors. *Bath:* shower only. **Parking:** on-site and valet. **Terms:** 3 day cancellation notice-fee imposed. **Amenities:** high-speed Internet, voice mail, irons, hair dryers. **Pool(s):** 2 heated outdoor. **Leisure Activities:** limited beach access, rental boats, scuba diving & rental equipment, snorkeling equipment rental, fishing, playground, exercise room. *Fee:* marina, charter fishing. **Guest Services:** valet laundry, area transportation-downtown, wireless Internet. **Business Services:** meeting rooms, business center. **Cards:** AX, DC, DS, JC, MC, VI. *(See color ad on insert)*

/ SOME UNITS

GRAND PLAZA LA PAZ HOTEL AND SUITES Book at AAA.com **Phone:** (612)124-0830

Hotel
$185-$336 All Year

Address: Lote A Marina Norte Fidepaz **Location:** 3.3 mi (5.5 km) sw on Mex 1 (Abasolo). **Facility:** Meets AAA guest room security requirements. 54 units. 24 one-bedroom standard units. 19 one-, 10 two- and 1 three-bedroom suites, some with whirlpools. 2-3 stories (no elevator), exterior corridors. **Parking:** on-site. **Terms:** cancellation fee imposed. **Amenities:** CD players, safes, irons, hair dryers. **Pool(s):** 3 outdoor. **Leisure Activities:** sauna, whirlpool, playground, exercise room, sports court. **Guest Services:** valet laundry, wireless Internet. **Business Services:** conference facilities, PC. **Cards:** AX, DC, DS, MC, VI.

/ SOME UNITS

HOTEL LOS ARCOS Book at AAA.com **Phone:** (612)122-2744

Hotel
$113-$153 All Year

Address: Paseo Alvaro Obregon 498 **Location:** Center. **Facility:** Meets AAA guest room security requirements. 130 one-bedroom standard units. 3 stories, interior corridors. *Bath:* shower only. **Parking:** on-site. **Terms:** cancellation fee imposed. **Amenities:** voice mail, safes, honor bars, irons, hair dryers. **Dining:** Restaurant Bermejo, see separate listing. **Pool(s):** heated outdoor. **Leisure Activities:** *Fee:* sauna, massage. **Guest Services:** valet laundry, wireless Internet. **Business Services:** meeting rooms, business center. **Cards:** AX, MC, VI.

/ SOME UNITS

HOTEL MARINA **Phone:** (612)121-6254

Hotel
$115-$210 All Year

Address: KM 2.5 Carr a Pichilingue **Location:** 1.5 mi (2.5 km) n of town. **Facility:** Meets AAA guest room security requirements. 89 units. 84 one-bedroom standard units, some with efficiencies. 5 one-bedroom suites, some with kitchens. 5 stories, exterior corridors. *Bath:* combo or shower only. **Parking:** on-site. **Terms:** 3 day cancellation notice. **Amenities:** hair dryers. *Some:* safes, honor bars, irons. **Pool(s):** outdoor. **Leisure Activities:** whirlpool, lighted tennis court, spa. *Fee:* marina, charter fishing. **Guest Services:** valet laundry, wireless Internet. **Business Services:** conference facilities, PC. **Cards:** AX, JC, MC, VI.

/ SOME UNITS

HOTEL MEDITERRANE **Phone:** (612)125-1195

Hotel
$80-$96 All Year

Address: Allende #36 **Location:** Just e of Paseo Alvaro Obregon; in town. **Facility:** Designated smoking area. 9 one-bedroom standard units. 2 stories (no elevator), exterior corridors. *Bath:* shower only. **Parking:** street. **Terms:** office hours 7 am-11 pm, 7 day cancellation notice. **Amenities:** *Some:* CD players. **Dining:** La Pazta Restaurante, see separate listing. **Guest Services:** wireless Internet. **Business Services:** PC. **Cards:** AX, MC, VI.

HOTEL PERLA Book at AAA.com **Phone:** (612)122-0777

Hotel
$70-$95 All Year

Address: Paseo Alvaro Obregon #1570 **Location:** In town. **Facility:** 109 one-bedroom standard units. 4 stories, interior corridors. *Bath:* shower only. **Parking:** on-site and valet. **Amenities:** irons, hair dryers. **Dining:** Restaurant La Terraza, see separate listing. **Pool(s):** outdoor. **Leisure Activities:** whirlpool, playground. **Guest Services:** valet laundry, wireless Internet. **Business Services:** meeting rooms, PC (fee). **Cards:** AX, MC, VI.

/ SOME UNITS

HOTEL SEVEN CROWN **Phone:** (612)128-7788

Hotel
$109-$154 All Year

Address: Paseo Alvaro Obregon y Lerdo de Tejada **Location:** In town. **Facility:** 54 one-bedroom standard units, some with efficiencies. 6 stories, interior corridors. *Bath:* shower only. **Parking:** valet. **Terms:** 3 day cancellation notice-fee imposed. **Amenities:** hair dryers. *Some:* high-speed Internet. **Dining:** El Aura, see separate listing. **Leisure Activities:** whirlpool. *Fee:* massage. **Guest Services:** valet laundry, wireless Internet. **Business Services:** meeting rooms, PC. **Cards:** AX, MC, VI.

/ SOME UNITS

LA CASA JALISCO Book great rates at AAA.com **Phone:** (612)128-4311

Hotel
$69-$88 All Year

Address: Jalisco 480 esq I Ramirez Col Pueblo Nuevo **Location:** 2 mi (3.3 km) s of town on Mex 1 (Abasolo), just e. **Facility:** Designated smoking area. 10 units. 9 one- and 1 two-bedroom standard units. 3 stories (no elevator), interior corridors. **Parking:** on-site (fee). **Terms:** office hours 8 am-8 pm, check-in 4 pm, age restrictions may apply, 3 day cancellation notice. **Amenities:** video library (fee), hair dryers. *Some:* irons. **Pool(s):** outdoor. **Leisure Activities:** *Fee:* massage. **Guest Services:** wireless Internet. **Business Services:** meeting rooms, PC. **Cards:** AX, CB, DC, DS, JC, MC, VI.

LA CASA MEXICANA INN — **Phone:** 612/125-2748

Bed & Breakfast

$75-$135 12/1-4/1 & 11/15-11/30

Address: Calle Bravo #106 **Location:** Paseo Alvaro Obregon, turn e, just past Hotel Los Arcos, just e on Rosales, 1 blk n on Revolution, then just w. **Facility:** A Spanish-deco home, steps from the bay and tourist area, the inn has individually themed rooms featuring art, antiques and hand-woven textiles. Smoke free premises. 5 one-bedroom standard units, some with kitchens. 2 stories (no elevator), interior corridors. *Bath:* combo or shower only. **Parking:** street. **Terms:** open 12/1-4/1 & 11/15-11/30, office hours 8 am-7:30 pm, age restrictions may apply, 30 day cancellation notice. **Guest Services:** wireless Internet.

/ SOME UNITS

POSADA DE LAS FLORES LA PAZ — **Phone:** 612/125-5871

Bed & Breakfast

$171-$282 All Year

Address: Paseo Alvaro Obregon, # 440 **Location:** Oceanfront. On northern end of town along the malecon. **Facility:** Not too far from the romantic walkway, this reddish brick-colored hotel sits fronting stunning views of the sunrise and sunset. This antique Mexican house exemplifies authenticity in its furnishings and decor, tapered by crafted workmanship and tile floors. The lovely inner courtyards offer a serene ambience with an opportunity to relax, read and comtemplate the sun or enjoy short walks to nearby shops and restaurants. Designated smoking area. 8 units. 7 one-bedroom standard units. 1 one-bedroom suite. 3 stories (no elevator), exterior corridors. *Bath:* combo or shower only. **Parking:** street. **Terms:** office hours 7 am-11 pm, check-in 4 pm, age restrictions may apply, 15 day cancellation notice-fee imposed. **Amenities:** honor bars, hair dryers. **Pool(s):** outdoor. **Guest Services:** wireless Internet. **Cards:** MC, VI.

WHERE TO DINE

CAFFE MILANO — **Phone:** 612/125-9981

Italian

$10-$20

Filtered down from Mamma Milano, the generations of fine recipes the kitchen prepares include an array of homemade pastas, fresh seafood and fine cuts of beef with nicely complementing sauces. Freshly baked breads and homemade pastries are another lure. Casual dress. **Bar:** Full bar. **Hours:** 1 pm-11 pm. Closed: 1/1, 12/25; also Sun. **Address:** Esquerro 15, Col Centro **Location:** Paseo Alvaro Obregon, just e on Lerdo de Gollado, then just n. **Parking:** street. **Cards:** MC, VI.

EL AURA — **Phone:** 612/128-7787

International

$8-$30

On the fourth floor of the hotel, the restaurant is made of glass walls and offers a spectacular view of the bay. The young chef creates new and artfully prepared dishes with touches of Mexican, Italian and Continental influence. The setting is also popular for breakfast. Casual dress. **Bar:** Full bar. **Hours:** 7 am-11 pm, Sun-10 pm. **Address:** Paseo Alvaro #1710 Obregon y Lerdo **Location:** In town; in Hotel Seven Crown. **Parking:** street. **Cards:** AX, MC, VI.

EL PATRON BAYSIDE RESTAURANT & CANTINA — **Phone:** 612/125-9977

International

$14-$29

At the end of Coral Marina Wharf with strings of lights that match the city view back across the bay, the restaurant provides attentive service in a circular dining room, on the patio and waterside on the wharf. Among menu choices are quality steaks, fresh seafood and pizza. Casual dress. **Bar:** Full bar. **Reservations:** accepted. **Hours:** 1 pm-11 pm. **Address:** Marquez de Leon y Topete 2415 **Location:** Paseo Alvaro Obregon, just w via Marquez de Leon; in The Plaza Vista Coral. **Parking:** on-site. **Cards:** AX, DC, MC, VI.

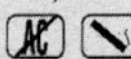

EL TASTE — **Phone:** 612/122-8121

Mexican

$7-$26

On the popular malecon, the open-air restaurant overlooks the bay. Guests watch such sights as boats navigating the harbor, sunsets and street activity. Lining the menu are good, basic dishes: breaded or grilled fish or shrimp in garlic butter, T-bone or pepper steak, carne asada and grilled lobster. Casual dress. **Bar:** Full bar. **Hours:** 8 am-midnight. Closed: 1/1. **Address:** Paseo Alvaro Obregon #780 **Location:** In town. **Parking:** street. **Cards:** MC, VI.

LA BOHEME — **Phone:** 612/125-6080

French

$8-$20

Paintings, sculptures and wall murals in the historic building give patrons the feeling of dining in a gallery. Seating in the garden also can be requested. The relocated French family has created a menu of traditional dishes, such as crepes polo, lamb chops with capers and fresh seafood, shrimp and lobster served steamed or flambeed. Casual dress. **Bar:** Full bar. **Hours:** 10:30 am-11 pm. Closed: 12/24, 12/25. **Address:** Calle Esquerro #10 **Location:** Paseo Alvaro Obregon, just e on Lerdo Degollado, just n. **Parking:** street. **Cards:** AX, MC, VI.

LA PAZ-LAPA DE CARLOS 'N CHARLIE'S — **Phone:** 612/122-9290

Mexican

$9-$20

Many factors contribute to the restaurant's boisterous atmosphere: the upbeat streetside patio and sidewalk, the festive dining room, lively music and comedic waiters. Guests can survey the town while enjoying such menu offerings as hamburgers, tacos, rellenos or full dinners of grilled beef filet, ribs, chicken or fish. Casual dress. **Bar:** Full bar. **Hours:** noon-midnight. Closed: 12/24, 12/25. **Address:** Paseo Alvaro Obregon **Location:** On the malecon at Calle 16 de Septiembre. **Parking:** street. **Cards:** AX, MC, VI.

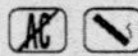

LA PAZTA RESTAURANTE **Phone:** 612/125-1195

Italian
$8-$19

In front of the hotel, the converted house has black and white tile floors, open walls and contemporary decor. Guests can sit in one of several rooms or on the front patio. Made fresh daily on the premises, pasta is used in such preparations as pasta with squid in wine and cream sauce. Other favorites include chicken with lemon cream sauce, mushroom-stuffed ravioli and pizza. Casual dress. **Bar:** Full bar. **Reservations:** accepted. **Hours:** 3 pm-10:45 pm. Closed: 1/1, 12/25; also Tues. **Address:** Allende 36 **Location:** Just e of Paseo Alvaro Obregon; in town; in Hotel Mediterrane. **Parking:** street. **Cards:** AX, MC, VI.

LOS MAGUEYES RESTAURANT **Phone:** 612/128-7846

Mexican
$7-$27

Los Magueyes means "cactus," and patrons find the real thing growing outside. However, the fresh salsas, crisp salads, tender beef and classic Mexican food are anything but prickly. Good choices include chicken mole and flank steak grilled with onions. Classic guitar music kicks up the atmosphere on the weekend. Casual dress. **Bar:** Full bar. **Hours:** 8 am-10 pm. Closed: Mon. **Address:** I Allende 512 e/Gmo Prieto Ramirez **Location:** Central; jct Allende and Prieto. **Parking:** on-site. **Cards:** MC, VI.

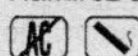

RESTAURANT BERMEJO **Phone:** 612/122-2744

Mexican
$7-$18

Brick columns, arches and windows overlooking bobbing sailboats on the bay lend to the pleasant atmosphere in the hotel dining room. Formal servers present a selection of steaks and seafood. Chicken breast stuffed with lobster over a demi-glace sauce and brandy is a signature item. Dressy casual. **Bar:** Full bar. **Reservations:** accepted. **Hours:** 7 am-midnight, Sun from 8 am. **Address:** Paseo Alvaro Obregon 498 **Location:** Center; in Hotel Los Arcos. **Parking:** street. **Cards:** AX, MC, VI.

RESTAURANT LA COSTA **Phone:** 612/122-8808

Mexican
$10-$35

Right on the beach, the charming restaurant has sandy floors and a palapa roof to prove it. Exceptionally fresh seafood dishes include manta ray or shrimp soup, thick with fish and veggies, and Veracruz-style preparations of fish and shellfish. Casual dress. **Bar:** Full bar. **Hours:** 10 am-10 pm. Closed: 1/1, 12/25. **Address:** Navarro y Bahia de La Paz **Location:** Central; just nw of jct Abasolo; on the beach. **Parking:** street. **Cards:** MC, VI.

RESTAURANT LA TERRAZA **Phone:** 612/122-0777

Mexican
$6-$20

Popular for its window to the bay and streetside views, the coffee shop-style restaurant offers good food and prompt service. The varied menu lists Mexican favorites, chicken cordon bleu, T-bone steak and filet mignon. Casual dress. **Bar:** Full bar. **Hours:** 7 am-10:30 pm. **Address:** Paseo Alvaro Obregon #1570 **Location:** In town; in Hotel Perla. **Parking:** street. **Cards:** AX, MC, VI.

LORETO, BAJA CALIFORNIA SUR pop. 11,812

—— WHERE TO STAY ——

DESERT INN-LA PINTA HOTELES **Phone:** 613/135-0025

Hotel
$90-$124 All Year

Address: Calle Davis S/N **Location:** Oceanfront. Mex 1, 0.9 mi (1.5 km) e to Calle Indepencia, 0.9 mi (1.5 km) n to Calle Pinta, then just e. **Facility:** Meets AAA guest room security requirements. 48 one-bedroom standard units. 2 stories (no elevator), exterior corridors. *Bath:* shower only. **Parking:** on-site. **Terms:** 3 day cancellation notice. **Amenities:** *Some:* hair dryers. **Pool(s):** outdoor. **Leisure Activities:** whirlpool. **Guest Services:** valet laundry. **Business Services:** meeting rooms. **Cards:** AX, MC, VI.

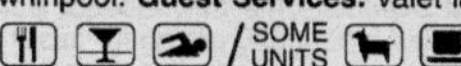

HACIENDA SUITES **Phone:** 613/135-0202

Hotel
$95-$125 All Year

Address: Salvatierra #152 **Location:** 0.6 mi (1 km) e of Mex 1; at town entrance. **Facility:** 42 units. 39 one-bedroom standard units. 3 one-bedroom suites. 2 stories (no elevator), exterior corridors. *Bath:* shower only. **Parking:** on-site. **Terms:** 7 day cancellation notice. **Amenities:** safes. **Pool(s):** outdoor. **Leisure Activities:** exercise room. **Guest Services:** wireless Internet. **Business Services:** meeting rooms. **Cards:** MC, VI.

/ SOME UNITS

INN AT LORETO BAY *Book at AAA.com* **Phone:** (613)133-0010

Resort Hotel
$175-$330 All Year

Address: Blvd Mision de Loreto S/N Fracc Napolo **Location:** Oceanfront. 4.8 mi (8 km) s on Mex 1, 0.6 mi (1 km) e on Mision San Ignacio, then 0.6 mi (1 km) s; in Nopolo. **Facility:** This hotel is on the beach, with a large swimming pool, palapas in the sand and an adjacent golf course; all rooms face the ocean. Meets AAA guest room security requirements. 155 one-bedroom standard units, some with whirlpools. 2-3 stories, exterior corridors. *Bath:* shower only. **Parking:** on-site and valet. **Amenities:** voice mail, safes, irons, hair dryers. **Pool(s):** outdoor. **Leisure Activities:** whirlpool, snorkeling, bicycles, hiking trails, jogging, exercise room, spa, basketball, volleyball. *Fee:* golf-18 holes, 2 lighted tennis courts. **Guest Services:** valet laundry, wireless Internet. **Business Services:** meeting rooms, PC. **Cards:** AX, MC, VI.

POSADA DE LAS FLORES LORETO

Bed & Breakfast
$180-$280 All Year

Phone: 613/135-1162

Address: Salvatierra esq Madero Col Centro **Location:** Mex 1, 0.9 mi (1.5 km) e to Calle Indepencia, just n to Blvd Benito Juarez, then 0.3 mi (0.5 km) s. **Facility:** Colorful walls, heavy wood furniture and stone floors accent this hacienda; a glass-bottomed rooftop swimming pool forms the lobby ceiling. Designated smoking area. 15 one-bedroom standard units. 3 stories (no elevator), exterior corridors. *Bath:* shower only. **Parking:** street. **Terms:** office hours 7 am-11 pm, age restrictions may apply. **Amenities:** honor bars, hair dryers. **Pool(s):** outdoor. **Leisure Activities:** spa. **Guest Services:** valet laundry, wireless Internet. **Cards:** MC, VI.

WHERE TO DINE

DOMINGO'S PLACE

Steak
$5-$25

Phone: 613/135-2445

Rough brick walls, heavy wood doors and tables with wagon wheel lights contribute to the hacienda-style, ranch atmosphere. The aromas of mesquite-grilled steaks fill the air. Also offered are pork chops, fish and shrimp with garlic butter, tacos, chiles rellenos and hamburgers. Casual dress. **Bar:** Full bar. **Hours:** 1 pm-10 pm. **Address:** Salvatierra #154 **Location:** 0.6 mi (1 km) e of El Nido Mex 1; at town entrance. **Parking:** on-site.

MEDITERRANEO

Seafood
$8-$50

Phone: 613/135-2577

Patrons who sit upstairs on the deck are afforded a great view across the malecon. Fresh fish, shellfish and pasta dishes are specialties here. Casual dress. **Bar:** Full bar. **Hours:** Open 12/1-8/31 & 9/16-11/30; noon-10 pm. Closed: 1/1. **Address:** Malecon Lopez mateos e/ Salvatierra **Location:** Mex 1, 1.2 mi (2.0 km) e on Salvatierra towards Malecon, then just n. Malecon Lopez Mateos el Salvatierra e Hidalgo. **Parking:** on-site and street. **Cards:** MC, VI.

PACHAMAMA

Argentine
$8-$21

Phone: 613/135-2219

Locally a favorite, the restaurant serves hearty portions that satisfy any appetite. Casual dress. **Bar:** Full bar. **Hours:** 5 pm-10 pm. Closed: 1/1, 12/24, 12/25; also Tue & 9/1-9/15. **Address:** Zapata #3 **Location:** Mex 1, 0.8 mi (1.5 km) e to Ave Miguel Hidalgo, then 0.3 mi n; near Mision Nuestra Senora de Loreto. **Parking:** street. **Cards:** MC, VI.

LOS BARRILES, BAJA CALIFORNIA SUR

WHERE TO STAY

LOS BARRILES HOTEL

Hotel
$60-$70 All Year

Phone: (624)141-0024

Address: 20 de Noviembre **Location:** 0.6 mi (1 km) e of Mex 1, 0.6 mi (1 km) n. **Facility:** 20 one-bedroom standard units. 2 stories (no elevator), exterior corridors. *Bath:* shower only. **Parking:** on-site. **Pool(s):** outdoor. **Leisure Activities:** whirlpool. **Cards:** MC, VI.

/ SOME UNITS

WHERE TO DINE

OTRA VEZ RESTAURANT

American
$8-$20

Phone: 624/141-0249

The local cafe, with indoor and patio seating, serves American-style dishes with a Mexican accent. The menu lists such items as fish and chips, hamburgers, blackened fish and spicy Thai chicken. At breakfast, look for prime rib hash or an omelet. Casual dress. **Bar:** Full bar. **Hours:** Open 12/1-8/15 & 10/15-11/30; 5 pm-10 pm. Closed: Sun. **Address:** 20 de Noviembre **Location:** 0.6 mi (1 km) e of Mex 1, 0.9 mi (1.5 km) n. **Parking:** on-site. **Cards:** MC, VI.

TIO PABLO'S BAR & GRILL

American
$6-$21

Phone: 624/141-0330

Diners who visit the local-favorite gathering place unwind in the large palapa or on the garden patio. The casual setting and service match the menu, which lists such choices as hamburgers, sandwiches, fajitas, pasta, pizza, ribeye steak, Santa Fe chicken and vegetarian enchiladas. Casual dress. **Bar:** Full bar. **Hours:** 11 am-10 pm. Closed major holidays. **Address:** Camino al Cardonal S/N **Location:** 0.6 mi (1 km) e of Mex 1, just n; in town. **Parking:** on-site. **Cards:** MC, VI.

MEXICALI, BAJA CALIFORNIA pop. 764,602

WHERE TO STAY

ARAIZA HOTEL

Hotel
$129-$199 All Year

Phone: (686)564-1100

Address: Blvd Benito Juarez #2220 **Location:** From border, 2.6 mi (4.5 km) e on Ave Cristobal Colon, 1.9 mi (3 km) s on Calzada Justo Sierra and Blvd Benito Juarez. **Facility:** Meets AAA guest room security requirements. 270 units. 221 one-bedroom standard units. 49 one-bedroom suites. 3-6 stories, interior corridors. *Bath:* combo or shower only. **Parking:** on-site. **Terms:** cancellation fee imposed. **Amenities:** high-speed Internet, voice mail, irons, hair dryers. *Some:* safes. **Pool(s):** 2 outdoor, heated outdoor. **Leisure Activities:** whirlpool, exercise room. **Guest Services:** valet laundry, wireless Internet. **Business Services:** meeting rooms. **Cards:** AX, MC, VI.

CALAFIA HOTEL AND CONVENTION CENTER *Book at AAA.com* **Phone:** (686)568-3311

Hotel

$86-$106 All Year

Address: Calzada Justo Sierra #1495 **Location:** From border, 2.6 mi (4.5 km) e on Ave Cristobal Colon, 1.4 mi (2.4 km) s. **Facility:** Meets AAA guest room security requirements. 172 units. 163 one-bedroom standard units. 9 one-bedroom suites. 2-4 stories (no elevator), exterior corridors. *Bath:* combo or shower only. **Parking:** on-site. **Amenities:** high-speed Internet, voice mail, hair dryers. *Some:* irons. **Pool(s):** outdoor. **Leisure Activities:** exercise room. **Guest Services:** valet laundry, wireless Internet. **Business Services:** meeting rooms. **Cards:** AX, MC, VI.

FEE / SOME UNITS

CITY EXPRESS HOTELES **Phone:** 686/564-1650

Hotel

$55-$64 All Year

Address: Blvd Benito Juarez #1342 **Location:** From border, 2.6 mi (4.5 km) e on Ave Cristobal Colon, 1.9 mi (3.1 km) s on Calzada Justo Sierra and Blvd Benito Juarez. **Facility:** 117 units. 113 one-bedroom standard units. 4 one-bedroom suites. 7 stories, interior corridors. *Bath:* shower only. **Parking:** on-site. **Leisure Activities:** exercise room. **Guest Services:** valet laundry, area transportation, wireless Internet. **Business Services:** meeting rooms, business center. **Cards:** AX, MC, VI.

/ SOME UNITS

CROWNE PLAZA HOTEL AND RESORT *Book at AAA.com* **Phone:** (686)557-3600

Hotel

$127-$176 All Year

Address: Ave de los Heroes #201 **Location:** 2.6 mi (4.5 km) s of border on Blvd Lopez Mateos, just w. **Facility:** Meets AAA guest room security requirements. 158 units. 151 one-bedroom standard units. 7 one-bedroom suites. 8 stories, interior corridors. **Parking:** on-site. **Terms:** 3 day cancellation notice. **Amenities:** CD players, high-speed Internet, voice mail, irons, hair dryers. **Dining:** The Premiere, see separate listing. **Pool(s):** outdoor. **Leisure Activities:** exercise room. **Guest Services:** valet laundry, wireless Internet. **Business Services:** meeting rooms, business center. **Cards:** AX, DC, DS, MC, VI.

/ SOME UNITS

FIESTA INN MEXICALI *Book great rates at AAA.com* **Phone:** (686)837-3300

Hotel

$90-$158 All Year

Address: Blvd Adolfo Lopez Mateos #1029 **Location:** 2.6 mi (4.5 km) s of border on Blvd Lopez Mateos, then just w. **Facility:** 150 units. 147 one-bedroom standard units. 3 one-bedroom suites. 4 stories, interior corridors. **Parking:** on-site. **Amenities:** high-speed Internet, voice mail, irons, hair dryers. **Pool(s):** outdoor. **Leisure Activities:** playground, limited exercise equipment. **Guest Services:** valet laundry, wireless Internet. **Business Services:** meeting rooms, business center. **Cards:** AX, CB, DC, DS, MC, VI. *(See color ad on insert)*

/ SOME UNITS

HOTEL COLONIAL **Phone:** (686)556-1312

Motel

$80-$100 All Year

Address: Blvd Adolfo Lopez Mateos #1048 **Location:** 2.6 mi (4.5 km) s of border. **Facility:** Meets AAA guest room security requirements. 150 one-bedroom standard units. 2 stories (no elevator), exterior corridors. **Parking:** on-site. **Terms:** 3 day cancellation notice. **Amenities:** high-speed Internet. *Some:* irons, hair dryers. **Pool(s):** outdoor. **Leisure Activities:** limited exercise equipment. **Guest Services:** valet laundry, wireless Internet. **Business Services:** meeting rooms, business center. **Cards:** AX, MC, VI.

/ SOME UNITS

HOTEL LUCERNA *Book great rates at AAA.com* **Phone:** (686)564-7000

Hotel

$152-$162 All Year

Address: Blvd Benito Juarez #2151 **Location:** From border, 2.6 mi (4.5 km) e on Ave Cristobal Colon, 2.3 mi (3.8 km) s on Calzada Justo Sierra and Blvd Benito Juarez. **Facility:** Meets AAA guest room security requirements. 176 units. 169 one-bedroom standard units. 7 one-bedroom suites. 1-6 stories, interior/exterior corridors. *Bath:* combo or shower only. **Parking:** on-site. **Terms:** cancellation fee imposed. **Amenities:** high-speed Internet, voice mail, irons, hair dryers. *Some:* safes, honor bars. **Dining:** 2 restaurants, also, Mezzosole Restaurante Italiano, see separate listing. **Pool(s):** 2 outdoor. **Leisure Activities:** sauna, exercise room. **Guest Services:** valet laundry, wireless Internet. **Business Services:** meeting rooms, business center. **Cards:** AX, MC, VI.

/ SOME UNITS

HOTEL POSADA INN **Phone:** 686/558-6100

Motel

$69-$73 All Year

Address: Lopez Mateos y Torneros No 939 **Location:** 2.4 mi (4 km) s of border on Blvd Lopez Mateos y Torneros. **Facility:** 49 one-bedroom standard units. 2 stories (no elevator), exterior corridors. *Bath:* combo or shower only. **Parking:** on-site. **Amenities:** high-speed Internet, safes, irons, hair dryers. **Guest Services:** wireless Internet. **Cards:** AX, MC, VI.

/ SOME UNITS

WHERE TO DINE

CASINO DE MEXICALI **Phone:** 686/552-9966

International

$7-$25

A local favorite for special occasions, the stylish restaurant has a stone entrance, white linen tablecloths, a sprig of greens on each table, designer lighting and a display kitchen. On the menu are prime steaks, chicken parmigiana, fresh fish with herbs, gourmet hamburgers, tacos and burritos. Dressy casual. **Bar:** Full bar. **Reservations:** accepted. **Hours:** 8 am-11 pm, Sun 10 am-6 pm. **Address:** Pino Suarez #2001 **Location:** 2.4 mi (4 km) e of border on Ave Francisco Madero, 0.3 mi (0.5 km) s on Calle K, then just e to Calle L. **Parking:** street. **Cards:** MC, VI.

EL ACUEDUCTO **Phone:** 686/564-7000

Mediterranean

$16-$37

The atmosphere is defined by an elegant yet casual ambiance that's enhanced by personable staff that go the extra mile to accommodate your needs. Menu selections range from fresh seafood to savory meats but you can't go wrong with any of the Mexican specialty entrees to get a real taste of their flavorful culture. Casual dress. **Hours:** 7 am-midnight. **Address:** Blvd Benito Juarez #2151 **Location:** From Border; 2.6 mi (4.5 km) e on Ave Cristobal Colon, 2.3 mi (3.8 km) s on Calzada Justo Sierra and Blvd Benito Juarez; in Hotel Lucerna. **Parking:** on-site. **Cards:** AX, MC, VI.

EL RINCON DE PANCHITO RESTAURANT **Phone:** 686/567-7718

Chinese
$7-$20

A great place to accommodate large parties or family celebrations. Offering authentic Cantonese dishes, specialty items include seafood and pork entrees, healthy items such as vegetables steamed or fried are also a popular mix. Portions are fit to share so come with a hardy appetite. Casual dress. **Bar:** Full bar. **Hours:** 11 am-midnight, Sun-11 pm. **Location:** From border, 2.6 mi (4.5 km) e on Ave Cristobal Colon, 1.8 mi (3 km) s on Calzada Justo Sierra and Blvd Benito Juarez. **Parking:** on-site. **Cards:** MC, VI.

LOS ARCOS RESTAURANT **Phone:** 686/556-0903

Seafood
$9-$21

Festively decorated with fish netting, sculptures and bright colors, the restaurant has lively servers to match. Fresh fish from local waters is the specialty. Open-faced fish tacos with lime are a treat, as is the seafood fiesta for two, which includes a variety of stews of squid and octopus, shredded fish, smoked fish and shrimp, stuffed peppers and perch. Steaks also are available. Top dessert choices are bananas flambe and crepes Suzette. Casual dress. **Bar:** Full bar. **Hours:** 11 am-10 pm, Thurs-Sat to 11 pm. **Address:** Calle Calafia #454 **Location:** 2.6 mi (4.5 km) s of border via Blvd Lopez Mateos, just w. **Parking:** on-site. **Cards:** MC, VI.

MEZZOSOLE RESTAURANTE ITALIANO **Phone:** 686/564-7000

Italian
$13-$26

A cool and relaxing atmosphere exudes through the intimate dining room, which has wall and ceiling murals and overlooks a swimming pool. Popular dishes on a menu of pasta, pizza and seafood entrees include seafood linguine, Gorgonzola and beef and chicken prosciutto. Dressy casual. **Reservations:** suggested. **Hours:** noon-11 pm, Sun 2 pm-10 pm. **Address:** Blvd Benito Juarez #2151 **Location:** From border, 2.6 mi (4.5 km) e on Ave Cristobal Colon, 2.3 mi (3.8 km) s on Calzada Justo Sierra and Blvd Benito Juarez; in Hotel Lucerna. **Parking:** on-site. **Cards:** AX, MC, VI.

THE PREMIERE **Phone:** 686/557-3600

International
$15-$24

The refined staff contributes to an elegant dining experience. Examples of artfully presented dishes include filet mignon in braised mushroom sauce, seared ahi, grilled shrimp with scallions, rosemary chicken and made-to-order pasta. Flaming desserts and gourmet coffees top off the meal. Dressy casual. **Bar:** Full bar. **Reservations:** suggested. **Hours:** 11 am-11 pm. Closed: Sun. **Address:** Ave de los Heroes #201 **Location:** 2.6 mi (4.5 km) s of border on Blvd Lopez Mateos, just w; in Crowne Plaza Hotel and Resort. **Parking:** on-site. **Cards:** AX, MC, VI.

SAKURA RESTAURANT **Phone:** 686/566-4848

Japanese
$7-$35

The large complex houses a video bar and karaoke club. Wood paneling, bridges and a rock and water garden with live turtles decorate the dining room. The sushi bar and teppanyaki tables occupy separate areas. Locals frequent the buffet lunch from noon-4 pm daily. Dressy casual. **Bar:** Full bar. **Reservations:** accepted. **Hours:** 11 am-11 pm, Sun-10 pm. Closed: 1/1, 12/25. **Address:** Blvd Lazaro Cardenas y Calz Fco L Monte **Location:** 2.6 mi (4.5 km) s of border on Blvd Lopez Mateos, just w. **Parking:** on-site. **Cards:** AX, MC, VI.

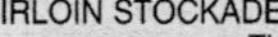

SIRLOIN STOCKADE **Phone:** 686/554-8447

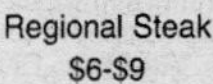

Regional Steak
$6-$9

The steakhouse lines up buffet items, including pizza, tacos, soups, salads and desserts, providing both excellent variety and a good value. Rotating theme nights might allow for the sampling of sushi, barbecue and seafood. The buffet also may serve to complement a quality steak. Rolls are baked several times daily. Casual dress. **Bar:** Beer & wine. **Hours:** 8 am-8 pm, Sat & Sun from 9 am. Closed: 12/25. **Address:** Blvd Lopez Mateos Esq Calle Compresora **Location:** In Colonia Industrial District. **Parking:** on-site. **Cards:** DS, MC, VI.

VIPS **Phone:** 686/562-9002

Regional Mexican
$6-$22

Owned by Wal-Mart of Mexico and found in most major cities, the budget-friendly chain serves a good variety of Mexican and American dishes, including burgers, sandwiches, salads, spaghetti and enchiladas, as well as a fine selection of desserts. Casual dress. **Bar:** Beer & wine. **Hours:** 7 am-11 pm. **Address:** Blvd Lazaro Cardenas No 1801 **Location:** In Colonia Ex-Ejido de Zacatecas. **Parking:** on-site. **Cards:** AX, MC, VI.

MULEGE, BAJA CALIFORNIA SUR pop. 45,989

WHERE TO DINE

LAS CASITAS RESTAURANT **Phone:** 615/153-0019

Mexican
$5-$23

Popular for breakfast and lunch, the casual patio setting gets lively Friday night, when a mariachi band and folkloric dancers accompany the fiesta buffet. Grilled lobster, fried or ranchero-style garlic chicken, baby back pork ribs and breaded, charcoal-broiled or grilled fish or shrimp are among tried-and-true entrees. Casual dress. **Bar:** Full bar. **Hours:** 7 am-10 pm. **Address:** Madero #50 **Location:** Callejon de los Estudiantes and Ave Independencia; center. **Parking:** street. **Cards:** MC, VI.

PUNTA CHIVATO, BAJA CALIFORNIA SUR

WHERE TO STAY

POSADA DE LAS FLORES PUNTA CHIVATO **Phone:** 615/155-5600

Hotel
$120-$400 All Year

Address: Domicilio Conocido **Location:** Mex 1 at Palo Verde, 10.2 mi (17 km) e on gravel and dirt road. Located in a remote area. **Facility:** Designated smoking area. 25 units. 21 one- and 2 two-bedroom standard units. 2 two-bedroom suites. 1 story, exterior corridors. *Bath:* shower only. **Parking:** on-site. **Terms:** check-in 4 pm, age restrictions may apply. **Amenities:** hair dryers. **Pool(s):** outdoor. **Leisure Activities:** snorkeling, fishing, tennis court, bicycles, hiking trails. *Fee:* boats. **Guest Services:** wireless Internet. **Business Services:** meeting rooms, PC. **Cards:** MC, VI.

ROSARITO, BAJA CALIFORNIA pop. 63,420

WHERE TO STAY

LAS ROCAS RESORT & SPA *Book great rates at AAA.com* **Phone:** (661)614-9850

Hotel
$79-$389 All Year

Address: KM 38.5 Carr Libre Tijuana-Ensenada **Location:** On Mex 1, 6.2 mi (10 km) s of town. **Facility:** Meets AAA guest room security requirements. 74 one-bedroom standard units. 4 stories (no elevator), exterior corridors. **Parking:** on-site. **Terms:** 2-3 night minimum stay - seasonal and/or weekends, 3 day cancellation notice. **Amenities:** hair dryers. *Some:* irons. **Dining:** 2 restaurants. **Pool(s):** 2 outdoor. **Leisure Activities:** whirlpools, spa, volleyball. *Fee:* exercise room. **Guest Services:** wireless Internet. **Cards:** MC, VI.

/ SOME UNITS

ROSARITO BEACH HOTEL & SPA **Phone:** (661)612-0144

fyi
Resort Hotel
$79-$519 All Year

Under major renovation, scheduled to be completed December 2008. Last rated: **Address:** Blvd Benito Juarez #31 **Location:** On Mex 1-D (toll road), exit south end of town, just prior to toll station, circle right, then just n. **Facility:** In town, the historic resort continues to re-build to provide modern accommodations. Units are modest to upscale in high-rise and one-story buildings. 495 units. 190 one-bedroom standard units, some with whirlpools. 226 one-, 65 two- and 14 three-bedroom suites, some with efficiencies, kitchens and/or whirlpools. 1-17 stories, interior/exterior corridors. **Parking:** on-site (fee). **Terms:** check-in 4 pm, 4 day cancellation notice, 75% penalty fee if less than 4 days-fee imposed. **Amenities:** voice mail, hair dryers. *Some:* CD players, high-speed Internet, safes, irons. **Dining:** Azteca Restaurant, Chabert's Restaurant, see separate listings. **Pool(s):** 4 heated outdoor. **Leisure Activities:** whirlpools, fishing, tennis court, racquetball courts, recreation programs, pool tables, jogging, playground, spa, basketball. **Guest Services:** valet laundry, wireless Internet. **Business Services:** meeting rooms. **Cards:** MC, VI.

WHERE TO DINE

AZTECA RESTAURANT *Menu on AAA.com* **Phone:** 661/612-0144

Mexican
$5-$22

Enjoy the picturesque view from the dining room where your taste buds will water with Mexican delicacies flavored with fresh herbs. Typical local dishes are prepared to reflect the local culture and ambience with their new tile decor and fireplace setting. Try their seafood Baja omelette stuffed with shrimp and lobster. Machaca (shredded beef) is always a favorite. Ceviche, diced filet of fish marinated in lemon, tomato and chiles and a tortilla, is a meal in itself. Casual dress. **Bar:** Full bar. **Hours:** 7:30 am-10 pm. **Address:** Blvd Benito Juarez #31 **Location:** On Mex 1-D (toll road), exit south end of town, just prior to toll station, circle right, then just n; in Rosarito Beach Hotel & Spa. **Parking:** on-site. **Cards:** MC, VI.

CHABERT'S RESTAURANT *Menu on AAA.com* **Phone:** 661/612-0144

International
$5-$32

In the stately mansion of the founder of the hotel, the elegant dining room is well-attended by formal servers. Food preparations reflect European and Mexican influences. Shining examples are New York and pepper steaks, salmon medallions, Puerto Nuevo lobster, chicken Mediterranean and guindas duck. Caesar and spinach salads are prepared tableside. Dressy casual. **Bar:** Full bar. **Hours:** 5 pm-midnight. Closed: Tues & Wed; Mon in winter. **Location:** On Mex 1-D (toll road), exit south end of town, just prior to toll station, circle right, then just n; in Rosarito Beach Hotel & Spa. **Parking:** on-site. **Cards:** MC, VI.

EL NIDO STEAKHOUSE **Phone:** 661/612-1430

Steak
$7-$27

Rough brick walls, heavy wood doors and tables with wagon wheel lights contribute to the hacienda-style, ranch atmosphere. The aromas of mesquite-grilled steaks fill the air. Also offered are pork chops, fish and shrimp with garlic butter, tacos, chiles rellenos and hamburgers. Casual dress. **Bar:** Full bar. **Hours:** 8 am-11:30 pm. **Address:** Blvd Benito Juarez 67 **Location:** Center. **Parking:** street.

LOS PELICANOS **Phone:** 661/612-1757

Steak
$7-$27

Mesquite-broiled steaks and seafood are served in the dining room or on the patio, both of which overlook the ocean. Casual dress. **Bar:** Full bar. **Hours:** 8 am-11:30 pm. **Address:** Calle Ebano 113 **Location:** Just w of Blvd Benito Juarez; on the beach. **Parking:** on-site. **Cards:** AX, MC, VI.

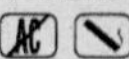

SAN IGNACIO, BAJA CALIFORNIA SUR pop. 800

WHERE TO STAY

The following lodging was either not evaluated or did not meet AAA rating requirements but is listed for your information only.

DESERT INN — **Phone:** 615/154-0300

fyi

Not evaluated. **Address:** KM 74 **Location:** 1.6 mi (2.5 km) w of jct Mex 1, towards town plaza. Facilities, services, and decor characterize an economy property.

SAN JOSE DEL CABO, BAJA CALIFORNIA SUR pop. 33,000 (See map and index starting on p. 452)

WHERE TO STAY

CASA DEL MAR SUITES GOLF & SPA RESORT *Book at AAA.com* — **Phone:** (624)145-7700 41

Resort Hotel

$450-$1000 All Year

Address: Carr Transpeninsular KM 19.5 **Location:** Oceanfront. 6.9 mi (11.5 km) w on Mex 1. Located at Cabo Real. **Facility:** With its stone archways, massive wooden doors, courtyard, and verdant garden, the resort calls to mind a classic Mexican hacienda. 31 units. 25 one-bedroom standard units with whirlpools. 6 one-bedroom suites with whirlpools. 1-3 stories (no elevator), exterior corridors. **Parking:** on-site. **Terms:** 14 day cancellation notice-fee imposed. **Amenities:** CD players, voice mail, safes, irons, hair dryers. **Pool(s):** 5 outdoor. **Leisure Activities:** whirlpools, steamrooms, 4 lighted tennis courts, exercise room, spa. *Fee:* saunas, golf-18 holes. **Guest Services:** valet laundry, wireless Internet. **Business Services:** meeting rooms, business center. **Cards:** AX, MC, VI.

S D

CASA NATALIA *Book at AAA.com* — **Phone:** (624)146-7100 61

Boutique Hotel

$250-$565 All Year

Address: Blvd Mijares 4-B, Centro **Location:** Downtown; at town plaza. **Facility:** An intimate Mexican-contemporary style inn on palm filled grounds, waterfalls, and fireplaces. Rooms are individually theme-decorated with private terraces and hammocks. 16 one-bedroom standard units. 2-3 stories (no elevator), interior corridors. *Bath:* shower only. **Parking:** street. **Terms:** office hours 6:30 am-11 pm, age restrictions may apply, 14 day cancellation notice-fee imposed. **Amenities:** video library, DVD players, CD players, high-speed Internet, voice mail, safes, hair dryers. **Dining:** Mi Cocina, see separate listing. **Pool(s):** heated outdoor. **Leisure Activities:** *Fee:* massage. **Guest Services:** valet laundry, area transportation, wireless Internet. **Business Services:** PC. **Cards:** AX, MC, VI.

/ SOME UNITS

CROWNE PLAZA LOS CABOS GRAND FARO ALL INCLUSIVE RESORT *Book at AAA.com* — **Phone:** (624)142-9292 68

Resort Hotel

$244-$731 All Year

Address: Blvd San Jose S/N Secc Hoteles **Location:** Oceanfront. 0.6 mi (1 km) e off Mex 1; in Hotelera Fonatur. **Facility:** Whether for business or families, this all-inclusive resort offers an abundance of activities with numerous restaurants, bars and swimming pools. Meets AAA guest room security requirements. 333 units. 320 one-bedroom standard units, some with whirlpools. 12 one- and 1 two-bedroom suites. 5 stories, interior corridors. *Bath:* combo or shower only. **Parking:** on-site. **Terms:** 3 day cancellation notice-fee imposed. **Amenities:** voice mail, safes, irons, hair dryers. *Some:* CD players. **Pool(s):** 4 heated outdoor. **Leisure Activities:** whirlpool, 2 lighted tennis courts, racquetball court, recreation programs, bicycles, jogging, exercise room, spa. **Guest Services:** valet laundry, wireless Internet. **Business Services:** conference facilities, business center. **Cards:** AX, MC, VI.

24 D / SOME UNITS

DREAMS LOS CABOS RESORT & SPA *Book at AAA.com* — **Phone:** (624)145-7600 40

Resort Hotel

$250-$850 All Year

Address: KM 18.5 Carr Transpeninsular **Location:** Oceanfront. 7.2 mi (12 km) w on Mex 1. Located at Cabo Real. **Facility:** Wide arches open this Spanish hacienda-style resort's airy lobby to a free-form pool, a sandy beach and the sea. Meets AAA guest room security requirements. 213 units. 143 one-bedroom standard units. 70 one-bedroom suites. 4-6 stories, exterior corridors. *Bath:* combo or shower only. **Parking:** on-site and valet. **Terms:** 2-7 night minimum stay - seasonal, 15 day cancellation notice. **Amenities:** video library, DVD players, voice mail, safes, irons, hair dryers. *Some:* honor bars. **Pool(s):** 3 heated outdoor. **Leisure Activities:** whirlpools, waterslide, recreation programs, exercise room, spa, basketball. *Fee:* saunas, steamrooms, lighted tennis court. **Guest Services:** valet laundry, area transportation (fee), wireless Internet. **Business Services:** meeting rooms, PC. **Cards:** AX, MC, VI. Affiliated with A Preferred Hotel.

24 S D / SOME UNITS

EL ENCANTO INN — **Phone:** 624/142-0388 60

Hotel

$114-$288 All Year

Address: Calle Morelos #133 **Location:** Just n of Zaragosa and town square; at jct Comonfort. **Facility:** Designated smoking area. 28 units. 26 one-bedroom standard units, some with efficiencies. 1 one- and 1 two-bedroom suites, some with efficiencies. 2 stories (no elevator), exterior corridors. *Bath:* combo or shower only. **Parking:** street. **Terms:** office hours 8 am-11 pm, 14 day cancellation notice. **Amenities:** hair dryers. *Some:* honor bars. **Pool(s):** heated outdoor. **Leisure Activities:** spa. **Guest Services:** wireless Internet. **Business Services:** PC. **Cards:** AX, MC, VI.

/ SOME UNITS FEE

(See map and index starting on p. 452)

HILTON LOS CABOS BEACH & GOLF RESORT *Book great rates at AAA.com* **Phone:** (624)145-6500 45

Resort Hotel
$130-$600 All Year

Address: Carr Transpeninsular KM 19.5 **Location:** Oceanfront. 6.6 mi (11 km) w on Mex 1. Located at Cabo Real. **Facility:** This large resort on a hillside overlooks an infinity swimming pool and the sea and is adjacent to two world-class golf courses. Meets AAA guest room security requirements. 375 units. 344 one-bedroom standard units, some with whirlpools. 30 one- and 1 two-bedroom suites with whirlpools, some with kitchens. 5-6 stories, interior corridors. **Parking:** valet. **Terms:** 3 day cancellation notice-fee imposed. **Amenities:** CD players, high-speed Internet (fee), dual phone lines, voice mail, safes, honor bars, irons, hair dryers. *Some:* DVD players. **Dining:** Restaurant Fenicia, see separate listing. **Pool(s):** 2 heated outdoor. **Leisure Activities:** saunas, whirlpools, steamrooms, 2 lighted tennis courts, exercise room, spa. *Fee:* golf-18 holes. **Guest Services:** valet laundry, area transportation, wireless Internet. **Business Services:** conference facilities, business center. **Cards:** AX, DC, MC, VI.

/ SOME UNITS

LAS VENTANAS AL PARAISO **Phone:** (624)144-2800 43

Resort Hotel
$650-$6000 All Year

Address: KM 19.5 Carr Transpeninsular **Location:** Oceanfront. 6.9 mi (11.5 km) w on Mex 1. Located at Cabo Real. **Facility:** Accenting this elegant and serene oceanfront resort are native-specimen plants and waterways; all rooms have a fireplace, patio and whirlpool. 71 units. 56 one-bedroom standard units with whirlpools. 6 one-, 7 two- and 2 three-bedroom suites with whirlpools, some with kitchens. 2 stories (no elevator), exterior corridors. **Parking:** on-site and valet. **Terms:** 5 night minimum stay - weekends, 28 day cancellation notice-fee imposed. **Amenities:** video library, DVD players, CD players, high-speed Internet, dual phone lines, voice mail, safes, honor bars, irons, hair dryers. **Dining:** The Restaurant, see separate listing. **Pool(s):** outdoor, 6 heated outdoor. **Leisure Activities:** saunas, whirlpools, steamrooms, 2 lighted tennis courts, spa. **Guest Services:** valet laundry, wireless Internet. **Business Services:** meeting rooms, PC. **Cards:** AX, MC, VI.

/ SOME UNITS

MARQUIS LOS CABOS BEACH, GOLF, SPA & CASITAS RESORT *Book at AAA.com* **Phone:** (624)144-2000 47

Resort Hotel
$380-$1250 All Year

Address: Carr Transpeninsular KM 21.5 **Location:** Oceanfront. 6.6 mi (11 km) w on Mex 1. Located at Cabo Real. **Facility:** The resort is designed with an open-air arch and a 36-foot waterfall splashing through the lobby into the pool bar; rooms have contemporary decor. Meets AAA guest room security requirements. 237 units. 204 one-bedroom standard units with whirlpools. 33 one-bedroom suites with whirlpools. 2-5 stories, interior corridors. *Bath:* combo or shower only. **Parking:** valet. **Terms:** 15 day cancellation notice-fee imposed. **Amenities:** CD players, high-speed Internet, dual phone lines, voice mail, safes, honor bars, hair dryers. *Some:* DVD players, irons. **Dining:** Canto Del Mar Restaurant, see separate listing. **Pool(s):** 3 heated outdoor. **Leisure Activities:** whirlpools, steamrooms, exercise room, spa. *Fee:* golf-18 holes. **Guest Services:** valet laundry, wireless Internet. **Business Services:** meeting rooms, business center. **Cards:** AX, DC, DS, JC, MC, VI.

/ SOME UNITS

MELIA CABO REAL BEACH & GOLF RESORT, ALL INCLUSIVE *Book at AAA.com* **Phone:** (624)144-2222 44

Resort Hotel
$338-$446 12/1-4/19
$311-$392 4/20-11/30

Address: KM 19.5 Carr Transpeninsular **Location:** Oceanfront. 6.6 mi (11 km) w on Mex 1. Located at Cabo Real. **Facility:** Wrapping around palm-shaded grounds and a large free-form pool, these recently remodeled units have marble floors and light, airy decor. Meets AAA guest room security requirements. 305 units. 290 one-bedroom standard units. 15 one-bedroom suites. 1-5 stories, exterior corridors. **Parking:** on-site. **Terms:** 7 day cancellation notice-fee imposed. **Amenities:** voice mail, safes, honor bars, irons, hair dryers. **Pool(s):** outdoor. **Leisure Activities:** saunas, whirlpool, steamrooms, 2 tennis courts, exercise room, spa. **Guest Services:** valet laundry, area transportation, wireless Internet. **Business Services:** conference facilities, business center. **Cards:** AX, MC, VI.

ONE & ONLY PALMILLA *Book at AAA.com* **Phone:** (624)146-7000 49

Resort Hotel
$500-$2600 All Year

Address: 7.5 KM Carr Transpeninsular **Location:** Oceanfront. 2.4 mi (4 km) w on Mex 1. **Facility:** Nine hundred acres of lush, palm-covered grounds surround this long-established Colonial Mexican-style property. Meets AAA guest room security requirements. Designated smoking area. 172 units. 152 one-bedroom standard units. 20 one-bedroom suites. 1-3 stories (no elevator), exterior corridors. *Bath:* combo or shower only. **Parking:** valet. **Terms:** 3 night minimum stay - weekends, 21 day cancellation notice-fee imposed. **Amenities:** video library, DVD players, CD players, high-speed Internet, dual phone lines, voice mail, safes, honor bars, hair dryers. **Dining:** C, see separate listing. **Pool(s):** 2 heated outdoor. **Leisure Activities:** whirlpool, 2 lighted tennis courts, recreation programs, bicycles, hiking trails, jogging, exercise room, spa. *Fee:* scuba diving, snorkeling, charter fishing, golf-27 holes. **Guest Services:** valet laundry, wireless Internet. **Business Services:** meeting rooms, business center. **Cards:** AX, MC, VI.

FEE / SOME UNITS FEE

(See map and index starting on p. 452)

PRESIDENTE INTERCONTINENTAL ALL INCLUSIVE RESORT LOS CABOS

Phone: (624)142-9229 66

Resort Hotel

$287-$789 All Year

Address: Blvd Mijares s/n, Zona Hotelera **Location:** Oceanfront. 1.5 mi (2.5 km) e of Mex 1. **Facility:** 23400Next to a fresh-water estuary and natural park, this property accents its scenic setting with pools, organized sports and numerous buffets. Meets AAA guest room security requirements. 390 units. 383 one-bedroom standard units. 7 one-bedroom suites, some with whirlpools. 3 stories, exterior corridors. *Bath:* combo or shower only. **Parking:** on-site. **Terms:** 3 night minimum stay - seasonal, 3 day cancellation notice-fee imposed. **Amenities:** voice mail, irons, hair dryers. *Some:* CD players, safes, honor bars. **Dining:** 5 restaurants. **Pool(s):** 3 heated outdoor. **Leisure Activities:** 3 lighted tennis courts, recreation programs, kids club, bicycles, exercise room, volleyball. *Fee:* massage. **Guest Services:** valet laundry, area transportation (fee)-Cabo San Lucas, wireless Internet. **Business Services:** conference facilities, business center. **Cards:** AX, DS, MC, VI.

CALL / SOME UNITS

ROYAL SOLARIS LOS CABOS- ALL INCLUSIVE RESORT & SPA *Book at AAA.com*

Phone: (624)145-6800 67

Resort Hotel

$265-$370 All Year

Address: Blvd San Jose, Lote 10 Campo De Golf **Location:** Oceanfront. 0.4 mi (0.6 km) e. **Facility:** Themed parties are among the many activities organized at this family-friendly resort located on the beach. Meets AAA guest room security requirements. 389 one-bedroom standard units. 6 stories, interior corridors. *Bath:* shower only. **Parking:** on-site. **Terms:** 3 day cancellation notice-fee imposed. **Amenities:** voice mail, safes, irons, hair dryers. **Pool(s):** 2 heated outdoor. **Leisure Activities:** whirlpools, steamrooms, scuba diving, lighted tennis court, recreation programs, bicycles, exercise room, spa, basketball, game room. **Guest Services:** valet laundry, wireless Internet. **Business Services:** meeting rooms, business center. **Cards:** AX, DC, DS, MC, VI.

/ SOME UNITS

TROPICANA INN

Phone: (624)142-2311 63

Hotel

$90 12/1-4/30

$81 5/1-11/30

Address: Blvd Mijares #30 **Location:** In town. **Facility:** Meets AAA guest room security requirements. 40 one-bedroom standard units. 2-3 stories (no elevator), exterior corridors. *Bath:* combo or shower only. **Parking:** on-site. **Terms:** 3 day cancellation notice-fee imposed. **Amenities:** hair dryers. **Dining:** Tropicana Bar & Grill, see separate listing. **Pool(s):** heated outdoor. **Guest Services:** wireless Internet. **Cards:** AX, JC, MC, VI.

/ SOME UNITS

THE WESTIN RESORT & SPA LOS CABOS *Book great rates at AAA.com*

Phone: (624)142-9000 48

Resort Hotel

$500-$1000 All Year

Address: Carr Transpeninsular KM 22.5 **Location:** Oceanfront. 6 mi (10 km) w on Mex 1. **Facility:** Extraordinary architecture creating a window to the sea is the signature of this resort, providing private ocean views from every room. Meets AAA guest room security requirements. Smoke free premises. 243 units. 229 one-bedroom standard units. 14 one-bedroom suites, some with whirlpools. 3-9 stories, exterior corridors. **Parking:** on-site. **Terms:** cancellation fee imposed. **Amenities:** high-speed Internet, dual phone lines, voice mail, safes, honor bars, irons, hair dryers. *Some:* DVD players, CD players. **Dining:** 4 restaurants, also, Arrecifes, see separate listing. **Pool(s):** 7 heated outdoor. **Leisure Activities:** whirlpool, 2 lighted tennis courts, recreation programs, spa. *Fee:* saunas, steamrooms, golf privileges, exercise room. **Guest Services:** valet laundry, wireless Internet. **Business Services:** conference facilities, business center. **Cards:** AX, DC, MC, VI.

(See color ad on insert)

/ SOME UNITS

WHERE TO DINE

ARRECIFES

Phone: 624/142-9000 39

International

$35-$50

Diners should visit just prior to sunset to enjoy the dramatic views from this cliffside location. Upscale table settings and attentive servers complement a sophisticated menu of Continental- and Mexican-influenced dishes. Grilled scallops, salmon with cream cheese and red snapper on a bed of bell peppers are among seafood specialties. Dressy casual. **Bar:** Full bar. **Reservations:** suggested. **Hours:** 6 pm-11 pm. Closed: Wed. **Address:** Carr Transpeninsular KM 22.5 **Location:** 6 mi (10 km) w on Mex 1; in The Westin Resort & Spa Los Cabos. **Parking:** on-site and valet. **Cards:** AX, MC, VI.

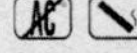

BAAN THAI

Phone: 624/142-3344 43

Asian

$9-$27

Asian teak and bamboo furnishings add to the relaxing effect of the dining room and patio. Seafood curry, pad thai, lamb shank with herbs, green papaya salad and lettuce-wrapped chicken soon are among crisply flavored Thai- and Asian-influenced dishes. Casual dress. **Bar:** Full bar. **Reservations:** accepted. **Hours:** noon-10:30 pm, Sun from 4 pm. Closed: 12/25; also 9/16. **Address:** Morelos at Alvaro Obregon **Location:** Just n of Zaragosa and town square. **Parking:** street. **Cards:** AX, MC, VI.

C

Phone: 624/146-7000 40

Continental

$30-$50

Specializing in seafood, this off-shoot of Charlie Trotter's of Chicago has brought the metropolitan heartbeat to southern Baja. The contemporary decor matches a menu that features seared wahoo with prosciutto, watermelon, watercress and mango or herb crusted grouper with lemon basil couscous and saffron sauce. Dressy casual. **Bar:** Full bar. **Reservations:** required. **Hours:** 7 am-11 & 6-11 pm. **Address:** Carr Transpeninsular KM 7.5 **Location:** 2.4 mi (4 km) w on Mex 1; in One & Only Palmilla. **Parking:** on-site and valet. **Cards:** AX, DC, DS, MC, VI.

(See map and index starting on p. 452)

CANTO DEL MAR RESTAURANT **Phone:** 624/144-2000 (38)

International
$75-$95

The intimate restaurant is the perfect location for that special occasion. The prix fixe dinners are created to match each guest with the recommendation from the chef. A sample dinner includes smoked duck breast salad with foie gras, celery cream soup with shell fish broth and black caviar, lamb fillet in pistachio custard with couscous and coriander spicy Mexican sausage butter and ginger sauce, and tatin tart of pear with caramel ice cream with rosemary. Dressy casual. **Bar:** Full bar. **Reservations:** suggested. **Hours:** 6 pm-11 pm. **Address:** Carr Transpeninsular KM 21.5 **Location:** 6.6 mi (11 km) w on Mex 1; in Marquis Los Cabos Beach, Golf, Spa & Casitas Resort. **Parking:** valet. **Cards:** AX, DC, DS, JC, MC, VI.

DAMIANA **Phone:** 624/142-0499 (45)

Mexican
$10-$50

Traditional Mexican seafood and regional dishes are served on the garden patio and in the quaint, colorful dining room. Chayote salad is a menu specialty. Omelets are served with shrimp, fish, lobster or chicken. Brunch is offered daily until 5 pm. Casual dress. **Bar:** Full bar. **Reservations:** accepted. **Hours:** Open 12/1-8/31 & 10/1-11/30; 10:30 am-10:30 pm. **Address:** Blvd Mijares 8 **Location:** Downtown; at town plaza. **Parking:** street. **Cards:** AX, MC, VI.

EL CHILAR **Phone:** 624/142-2544 (51)

Mexican
$14-$28

Chef Montano changes the menu monthly, using chili for flavor, not heat. In the simple, comfortable, candlelit dining room, guests can sample imaginative dishes such as zucchini blossom quesadilla, green mole enchilada, marinated flank steak with cumin and chili, and chicken breast over polenta. Casual dress. **Bar:** Full bar. **Reservations:** suggested. **Hours:** Open 12/1-9/1 & 10/1-11/30; 3 pm-10 pm. Closed: 1/1, 12/25; also Sun. **Address:** Blvd Benito Juarez #1515 Col 8 de Oct **Location:** Just w of Blvd Mijares; downtown. **Parking:** street.

LA PANGA ANTIGUA **Phone:** 624/142-4041 (42)

Mexican
$20-$48

The hacienda setting evokes Old Mexico from a century ago. Star-shaped lights hang from courtyard trees to cast a soft glow over the dining area. Fresh seafood, including shellfish from the Sea of Cortez, as well as steaks are offered. Casual dress. **Bar:** Full bar. **Reservations:** accepted. **Hours:** noon-10:30 pm. Closed: 4/12. **Address:** Zaragoza #20 **Location:** Just w of Hidalgo; center. **Parking:** street. **Cards:** AX, MC, VI.

MI COCINA **Phone:** 624/146-7100 (46)

International
$18-$50

A casual, yet sophisticated ambience sets the stage for nouvelle Mexican-Euro cuisine. International wines accompany such dishes as grilled shrimp with risotto, pan-seared sea bass on buckwheat soba, grilled lamb with pasta and spinach saffron, and filet mignon on potato leek galette. Dressy casual. **Bar:** Full bar. **Reservations:** suggested. **Hours:** 6 pm-10 pm. Closed: Tues 6/1-11/1. **Address:** Blvd Mijares 4-B, Centro **Location:** Downtown; at town plaza; in Casa Natalia. **Parking:** street. **Cards:** AX, MC, VI.

MORGAN'S ENCORE **Phone:** 624/142-4737 (44)

Mediterranean
$18-$40

Indoor seating offers a glimpse into the open kitchen, but folks may prefer seats on the enchantingly lit patio or on the rooftop, which has a fireplace and soft lights. This offshoot from the well-established Morgan's Restaurant presents an ever-changing Italian menu. Casual dress. **Bar:** Full bar. **Reservations:** suggested. **Hours:** Open 12/1-7/31 & 10/16-11/30; 6 pm-10:30 pm. **Address:** Morelos at Obregon **Location:** Just n of Zaragosa and town square; corner of Morelos and Obregon. **Parking:** street. **Cards:** AX, MC, VI.

MORGAN'S RESTAURANT & CELLAR **Phone:** 624/142-3825 (47)

International
$25-$48

Twinkling lights, a fountain, soft music and an open kitchen set the stage for an enchanting experience in the open-air courtyard. The highly trained staff serves dishes with a Mexican touch, including tuna mignon with risotto, grilled prawns, beef tenderloin and rack of lamb with herbs. Among specialties are fish in Veracruz sauce and rice with raisins and curry. Dressy casual. **Bar:** Full bar. **Reservations:** suggested. **Hours:** Open 12/1-7/31 & 9/15-11/30; 6 pm-10:30 pm. **Address:** Manuel Doblado #107 **Location:** In town; 1 blk from center; corner of Hidalgo and Doblado. **Parking:** street. **Cards:** AX, MC, VI.

THE RESTAURANT **Phone:** 624/144-2800 (36)

Mexican
$21-$49

Patrons can enjoy elegant dining under the palapa roof or on the open-air patio, which affords views of the sea. A private wine room and beach dining in the sand are also available. Attentive service complements the menu, which lists high-quality dishes prepared with fresh ingredients and a Mexican flair. Steamed parrot fish, roasted cabrilla, Parmesan gnocchi and tender braised short ribs are a few of the items on the ever-changing menu. Dressy casual. **Bar:** Full bar. **Reservations:** required. **Hours:** 7 am-10 pm. **Address:** KM 19.5 Carr Transpeninsular **Location:** 6.9 mi (11.5 km) w on Mex 1; in Las Ventanas al Paraiso. **Parking:** valet. **Cards:** AX, CB, DC, DS, MC, VI.

RESTAURANTE MAMA MIA **Phone:** 624/142-3939 (41)

Mexican
$7-$20

Serving authentic Mexican food, international dishes and wood oven pizza, the restaurant features live entertainment and theme dinners served in a casual setting with an ocean view at the beach. Casual dress. **Bar:** Full bar. **Hours:** 8 am-10:30 pm. **Address:** Carr Transpeninsular KM 29.5 **Location:** On Mex 1, 1.8 mi (3 km) w of town; in The Coral Baja Resort. **Parking:** on-site. **Cards:** AX, DC, DS, MC, VI.

(See map and index starting on p. 452)

RESTAURANT FENICIA **Phone:** 624/145-6500 (37)

International
$24-$65

The pleasant hotel setting overlooks the pool and sea. Although the Mediterranean menu specializes in seafood, it also lists well-presented preparations of steaks and lamb. Dressy casual. **Bar:** Full bar. **Reservations:** suggested. **Hours:** 6 pm-10:30 pm. **Address:** Carr Transpeninsular KM 19.5 **Location:** 6.6 mi (11 km) w on Mex 1; in Hilton Los Cabos Beach & Golf Resort. **Parking:** valet. **Cards:** AX, DC, MC, VI.

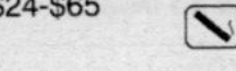

TEQUILA RESTAURANTE **Phone:** 624/142-1155 (48)

Mediterranean
$20-$42

Mexican and Asian flavors punctuate Mediterranean-influenced cuisine on a limited menu. The pleasant garden setting occasionally bustles with groups. Dressy casual. **Bar:** Full bar. **Reservations:** accepted. **Hours:** 6 pm-11 pm. **Address:** Manuel Doblado #1011 **Location:** Just w of Blvd Mijares; in town. **Parking:** street. **Cards:** AX.

TROPICANA BAR & GRILL **Phone:** 624/142-1580 (50)

Seafood
$8-$45

Fresh seafood and friendly service abound in the large palapa dining room, the comfortable palapa bar and the sidewalk seating area. Specialties are lobster, mahi mahi, ahi tuna and whole red snapper. Breakfasts are popular. Casual dress. **Bar:** Full bar. **Reservations:** accepted. **Hours:** 8 am-10:30 pm. **Address:** Blvd Mijares #30 **Location:** In town; in Tropicana Inn. **Parking:** street. **Cards:** AX, MC, VI.

VOILA **Phone:** 624/130-7569 (49)

Mediterranean
$10-$35

Romantic decor makes this place a perfect choice for special occasion dinners. Casual dress. **Bar:** Full bar. **Hours:** Open 12/1-8/31 & 9/16-11/30; noon-10 pm, Sun from 3 pm. Closed: 12/24, 12/25. **Address:** Esq Calle Morelos y Comonfort **Location:** Just n of Zaragosa and town square; across from El Encanto Inn & Suites. **Parking:** street. **Cards:** MC, VI.

SAN QUINTIN, BAJA CALIFORNIA pop. 2,000

WHERE TO STAY

The following lodging was either not evaluated or did not meet AAA rating requirements but is listed for your information only.

DESERT INN **Phone:** 616/165-9008

fyi

Not evaluated. **Address:** Playa Santa Maria In San Quintin **Location:** 9.9 mi (16 km) s on Mex 1, 2.8 mi (4.5 km) w to outer San Quintin Bay. Facilities, services, and decor characterize an economy property.

TECATE, BAJA CALIFORNIA pop. 77,795

WHERE TO DINE

LA MISION **Phone:** 665/654-2105

Mexican
$5-$16

Known locally for friendly service and good food. A variety of sandwiches, soups and salads are offered with seafood, steaks and chicken entrees prepard with a choice of traditional Mexican sauces. A Sunday brunch buffet is available. Casual dress. **Bar:** Full bar. **Reservations:** required. **Hours:** 10 am-10 pm, Fri & Sat-10:30 pm, Sun 9:30 am-7:30 pm. **Address:** Ave Juarez #1110 **Location:** 0.6 mi (1 km) w of town center. **Parking:** on-site. **Cards:** MC, VI.

TIJUANA, BAJA CALIFORNIA pop. 1,210,820

WHERE TO STAY

CAMINO REAL TIJUANA **Phone:** (664)633-4000

Hotel
$150-$230 All Year

Address: Paseo de los Heroes #10305, Zona **Location:** 1.6 mi (2.5 km) se of the border. **Facility:** Meets AAA guest room security requirements. 263 units. 256 one-bedroom standard units. 7 one-bedroom suites, some with whirlpools. 7 stories, interior corridors. *Bath:* combo or shower only. **Parking:** on-site and valet. **Terms:** cancellation fee imposed. **Amenities:** high-speed Internet, dual phone lines, voice mail, safes, irons, hair dryers. *Some:* honor bars. **Leisure Activities:** exercise room. **Guest Services:** valet laundry, wireless Internet. **Business Services:** conference facilities, business center. **Cards:** AX, MC, VI.

24 D / SOME UNITS

FIESTA INN *Book great rates at AAA.com* **Phone:** (664)636-0000

AAA

Hotel
$98-$150 All Year

Address: Paseo de los Heroes #18818, Zona Rio **Location:** 1.8 mi (3 km) se of the border on Paseo de los Heroes to Ave Rodriguez, just n to Poniente, then 0.3 mi (0.5 km) e. **Facility:** 127 units. 123 one-bedroom standard units. 4 one-bedroom suites. 4 stories, interior corridors. *Bath:* combo or shower only. **Parking:** on-site. **Amenities:** high-speed Internet, voice mail, irons, hair dryers. **Pool(s):** outdoor. **Leisure Activities:** whirlpool, limited exercise equipment, spa. **Guest Services:** valet laundry, wireless Internet. **Business Services:** meeting rooms, business center. **Cards:** AX, DC, MC, VI. *(See color ad on insert)*

D / SOME UNITS

FIESTA INN TIJUANA OTAY

Hotel
$98-$150 All Year

Phone: 664/979-1900
Address: Rampa Aeropuerto #16000 **Location:** From Otay Mesa border crossing, 1.8 mi (3 km) s via Carr al Aeropuerto and Calsada Tezhnologico. Located in front of Universidad of Baja California. **Facility:** Meets AAA guest room security requirements. 142 one-bedroom standard units. 6 stories, interior corridors. **Parking:** on-site. **Terms:** cancellation fee imposed. **Amenities:** high-speed Internet, voice mail, irons, hair dryers. **Pool(s):** heated outdoor. **Leisure Activities:** recreation programs, playground, exercise room. **Guest Services:** complimentary laundry, wireless Internet. **Business Services:** meeting rooms, business center. **Cards:** AX, MC, VI. ***(See color ad on insert)***

S D / SOME UNITS

GRAND HOTEL TIJUANA *Book great rates at AAA.com*

Hotel
$79-$126 All Year

Phone: (664)681-7000
Address: Blvd Agua Caliente #4500 **Location:** 1.8 mi (3 km) se of the border via Paseo de los Heroes, 0.3 mi (0.5 km) s on Ave Rodriguez, then just e. Located in a commercial area. **Facility:** Meets AAA guest room security requirements. 422 units. 402 one-bedroom standard units. 20 one-bedroom suites. 22 stories, interior corridors. **Parking:** on-site and valet. **Terms:** cancellation fee imposed. **Amenities:** high-speed Internet, voice mail, honor bars, irons, hair dryers. *Some:* DVD players, safes. **Dining:** 3 restaurants. **Pool(s):** heated outdoor. **Leisure Activities:** saunas, whirlpool, steamrooms, 2 tennis courts, exercise room. **Guest Services:** valet laundry, airport transportation-Abelardo L. Rodriguez International Airport, wireless Internet. **Business Services:** conference facilities, business center. **Cards:** AX, MC, VI.

24 D / SOME UNITS

HOTEL BUGAMBILIAS

Hotel
$75-$95 All Year

Phone: (664)973-7600
Address: Ave Tijuana 1600; CD Industrial **Location:** From Otay Mesa border crossing, 1.8 mi (3 km) sw via Carr al Aeropuerto and Calle 16. **Facility:** 140 units. 135 one-bedroom standard units. 5 one-bedroom suites. 4 stories, interior corridors. **Parking:** on-site. **Terms:** cancellation fee imposed. **Amenities:** high-speed Internet, irons, hair dryers. **Pool(s):** heated outdoor. **Leisure Activities:** sauna, whirlpool, exercise room. **Guest Services:** valet laundry, area transportation, wireless Internet. **Business Services:** meeting rooms, business center. **Cards:** AX, MC, VI.

D / SOME UNITS

HOTEL HACIENDA DEL RIO

Motel
$90-$110 All Year

Phone: (664)684-8644
Address: Blvd Rodolfo Sanchez Taboada #10606 **Location:** 1.8 mi (3 km se) of the border on Paseo de los Heroes to Ave Rodriguez, just s, then just w. **Facility:** 131 units. 126 one-bedroom standard units. 5 one-bedroom suites. 3 stories (no elevator), exterior corridors. *Bath:* combo or shower only. **Parking:** on-site. **Amenities:** irons, hair dryers. **Pool(s):** outdoor. **Leisure Activities:** exercise room. **Guest Services:** valet laundry. **Business Services:** meeting rooms, business center. **Cards:** AX, MC, VI.

/ SOME UNITS

HOTEL LA MESA INN

Motel
$90-$110 All Year

Phone: 664/681-6522
Address: Blvd Diaz Ordaz esq con Cardenias #50 **Location:** 1.8 mi (3 km) se of the border on Paseo de los Heroes, 0.3 mi (0.5 km) s on Ave Rodriguez, then 1.6 mi (2.5 km) e on Blvd Agua Caliente (Blvd Diaz Ordaz). Located in the La Mesa area. **Facility:** 139 units. 137 one-bedroom standard units. 2 one-bedroom suites. 1-3 stories, interior/exterior corridors. *Bath:* combo or shower only. **Parking:** on-site. **Terms:** cancellation fee imposed. **Amenities:** *Some:* hair dryers. **Pool(s):** heated outdoor. **Leisure Activities:** limited exercise equipment. **Guest Services:** wireless Internet. **Business Services:** meeting rooms, PC. **Cards:** AX, MC, VI.

/ SOME UNITS

HOTEL LUCERNA *Book great rates at AAA.com*

Hotel
$95-$160 All Year

Phone: (664)633-3900
Address: Paseo de los Heroes #10902, Zona **Location:** 1.8 mi (3 km) se of the border. **Facility:** Meets AAA guest room security requirements. 168 units. 163 one-bedroom standard units. 5 one-bedroom suites, some with whirlpools. 2-6 stories, interior/exterior corridors. *Bath:* combo or shower only. **Parking:** on-site and valet. **Amenities:** high-speed Internet, voice mail, irons, hair dryers. **Dining:** Rivoli's, see separate listing. **Pool(s):** outdoor. **Leisure Activities:** limited exercise equipment. **Guest Services:** valet laundry, wireless Internet. **Business Services:** meeting rooms, business center. **Cards:** AX, MC, VI.

D / SOME UNITS

HOTEL PALACIO AZTECA *Book great rates at AAA.com*

Hotel
$100-$193 All Year

Phone: (664)681-8100
Address: Blvd Cuauhtemoc Sur #213 Col Davila **Location:** 1.6 mi (2.2 km) s of the border on Paseo de los Heroes, 0.3 mi (0.6 km) s on Ave Cuauhtemoc (Ave 16 de Septiembre) to Ibarrq, just e, then just n. **Facility:** 204 one-bedroom standard units, some with whirlpools. 7 stories, interior corridors. **Parking:** on-site and valet. **Terms:** cancellation fee imposed. **Amenities:** high-speed Internet, safes, irons, hair dryers. **Pool(s):** outdoor. **Leisure Activities:** limited exercise equipment. **Guest Services:** valet laundry, airport transportation-Abelardo L. Rodriguez International Airport, wireless Internet. **Business Services:** meeting rooms, business center. **Cards:** AX, CB, DS, JC, MC, VI.

D / SOME UNITS

HOTEL REAL DEL RIO *Book great rates at AAA.com*

Hotel
$76-$113 All Year

Phone: (664)634-3100
Address: Jose Ma Velasco 1409-A, Zona Rio **Location:** 1.6 mi (2.5 km) se of the border on Paseo de los Heroes to Diego Rivera, just n to Poniente, just e, then just s. **Facility:** Meets AAA guest room security requirements. 105 units. 103 one-bedroom standard units. 2 one-bedroom suites with whirlpools, 5 stories, interior/exterior corridors. **Parking:** on-site. **Terms:** 3 day cancellation notice. **Amenities:** high-speed Internet, voice mail, safes, irons, hair dryers. **Guest Services:** wireless Internet. **Business Services:** meeting rooms. **Cards:** MC, VI.

D / SOME UNITS

MARRIOTT TIJUANA **Phone:** (664)622-6600

Hotel
$208-$223 All Year

Address: Blvd Agua Caliente #11553 **Location:** 1.8 mi (3 km) se of the border on Paseo de los Heroes, 0.3 mi (0.5 km) s on Ave Rodriguez, then 0.6 mi (1 km) e. **Facility:** Smoke free premises. 209 units. 206 one-bedroom standard units. 1 one- and 2 two-bedroom suites, some with kitchens. 10 stories, interior corridors. *Bath:* combo or shower only. **Parking:** on-site and valet. **Terms:** cancellation fee imposed. **Amenities:** high-speed Internet, voice mail, safes, honor bars, irons, hair dryers. *Some:* DVD players. **Pool(s):** heated outdoor. **Leisure Activities:** whirlpools, exercise room. **Guest Services:** valet laundry, area transportation, wireless Internet. **Business Services:** conference facilities, business center. **Cards:** AX, CB, DC, DS, MC, VI.

Marriott HOTELS & RESORTS

AAA Benefit:
Members save a minimum 5% off the best available rate.

PUEBLO AMIGO HOTEL *Book at AAA.com* **Phone:** (664)624-2700

Hotel
$140-$150 All Year

Address: Via Oriente 9211 **Location:** 0.5 mi (0.8 km) se of border, 1st right after border, veer left under bridge to Paseo de Tijuana, just e to Alfonso Reyes, then just s. **Facility:** Meets AAA guest room security requirements. 106 units. 104 one-bedroom standard units. 2 one-bedroom suites with whirlpools. 7 stories, interior corridors. *Bath:* combo or shower only. **Parking:** on-site. **Terms:** cancellation fee imposed. **Amenities:** *Some:* safes, hair dryers. **Leisure Activities:** exercise room. **Guest Services:** valet laundry, wireless Internet. **Business Services:** meeting rooms, business center. **Cards:** AX, MC, VI.

/SOME UNITS

RESIDENCE INN BY MARRIOTT-REAL DEL MAR **Phone:** (664)631-3670

Hotel
$109-$129 All Year

Address: KM 19.5 Carr Cuota **Location:** Mex 1-D (toll road), exit Real Del Mar, just e; 11.8 mi (19.5 km) s of the border. **Facility:** Meets AAA guest room security requirements. Smoke free premises. 76 units. 18 one-bedroom standard units with efficiencies, some with whirlpools. 58 one-bedroom suites with efficiencies. 2 stories (no elevator), exterior corridors. **Parking:** on-site. **Terms:** 3 day cancellation notice-fee imposed. **Amenities:** high-speed Internet, voice mail, safes, irons, hair dryers. **Pool(s):** heated outdoor. **Leisure Activities:** saunas, whirlpool, steamrooms, 2 lighted tennis courts, exercise room, spa, basketball, volleyball. *Fee:* golf-18 holes. **Guest Services:** valet and coin laundry, wireless Internet. **Business Services:** meeting rooms, PC, fax (fee). **Cards:** AX, DS, MC, VI.

AAA Benefit:
Members save a minimum 5% off the best available rate.

/SOME UNITS FEE

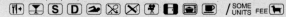

WHERE TO DINE

BICE BISTRO **Phone:** 664/633-4000

Italian
$10-$30

An open kitchen affords patrons views of the talented staff preparing delicious creations of pasta dishes, seafood entrees and grilled meats, poultry and fish items. A trendy ambiance helps define the fun and entertaining atmosphere while high window panels frame awesome views of the statuesque turnstile. The lounge is the ideal spot to gather with friends for a drink and light appetizer. Casual dress. **Bar:** Full bar. **Hours:** noon-midnight. **Address:** Paseo de los Heroes #10305, Zona **Location:** 1.6 mi (2.5 km) se of the Border; in Camino Real Tijuana. **Parking:** on-site. **Cards:** AX, MC, VI.

CAFE LA ESPECIAL **Phone:** 664/685-6654

Mexican
$5-$20

Operating since 1952, the festive, friendly restaurant offers a convenient stop during shopping. The menu is full of familiar dishes, including tamales, enchiladas and chiles rellenos, but charbroiled steaks are the specialty. Casual dress. **Bar:** Full bar. **Hours:** 9 am-10:30 pm. Closed: 1/1, 12/25. **Address:** Ave Revolucion #718 **Location:** 0.6 mi (1 km) from the border via Carrillo Puerto Calle #3A (downtown), just s; lower level below Hotel Lafayette. **Parking:** no self-parking. **Cards:** MC, VI.

CASA PLASENCIA **Phone:** 664/686-3604

Spanish
$8-$25

Attentive servers attend to guests in the comfortable dining room. Traditional Spanish recipes are used to prepare numerous tapas and paellas, as well as such dishes as shredded beef with chiles and seasoned chicken breast. Casual dress. **Bar:** Full bar. **Reservations:** accepted. **Hours:** noon-11 pm, Sun-10 pm. **Address:** Calle Robirosa #250 **Location:** 1.8 mi (3 km) se of border via Paseo de los Heroes, 0.3 mi (0.5 km) s on Ave Rodriquez to Blvd Agua Caliente, 0.3 mi (0.5 km) e, then just s. **Parking:** on-site and valet. **Cards:** AX, MC, VI.

CHAN'S CUISINE **Phone:** 664/634-2766

Sichuan
$15-$30

Offering a selection of tasty platters of Szechuan and Mandarin cuisine, the restaurant features ambience that befits the artwork, and Asian porcelain vases displayed throughout the restaurant. The variety of authentic Oriental selections ranges from mild to spicy dishes. Each dish has its own individual flavor which will water your palate and can be served as combinations dinners or on their own. You will be sure to leave with leftovers in hand. Casual dress. **Bar:** Full bar. **Hours:** noon-11:30 pm. **Address:** Blvd Sanchez Taboada 10880 **Location:** 1.8 mi (3 km) se of border on Paseo de los Heroes to Ave Rodriguez, just s, then just e. **Parking:** on-site. **Cards:** AX, MC, VI.

EL POTRERO **Phone:** 664/686-3626

Mexican
$6-$15

Shaped like a large hat, the popular restaurant has walls covered with cultural artifacts and pictures. Service is thoughtful and informal. Ribeye steak, New York cut and carne Asada are popular steak choices. Chicken can be marinated in polano, conejo or parrilla sauce. Samplings of seafood dishes include poached salmon and fish filet in Veracruz sauce. Casual dress. **Bar:** Full bar. **Hours:** 7 am-11 pm. Closed: 12/25. **Address:** Blvd Salinas #4700, Col Aviacion **Location:** 1.8 mi (3 km) se of border on Paseo de los Heroes, 0.3 mi (0.5 km) s on Ave Rodriguez to Blvd Agua Caliente, 0.6 mi (1 km) e, then circle left. **Parking:** on-site. **Cards:** AX, MC, VI.

EL RODEO — **Phone:** 664/686-5640

Steak
$5-$30

The steak house, which has been serving guests since 1972, specializes in Sonora-style cooking and charcoal-broiled meats. Meals include marinated vegetables, beans, beef broth, a salad and dessert. Casual dress. **Bar:** Full bar. **Hours:** 11 am-11 pm. **Address:** Blvd Salinas #1647 **Location:** 1.8 mi (3 km) se of border on Paseo de los Heroes, 0.3 mi (0.5) km s on Ave Rodriguez, just e on Ave Gustavo Salinas. **Parking:** on-site. **Cards:** MC, VI.

LA ESPANADA — **Phone:** 664/634-1488

Mexican
$7-$25

A friendly village-feeling envelops the hacienda-style mission building. Popular for families and business companions, the energetic restaurant provides fast service, but there sometimes can be a wait for seating. Among reliable menu offerings are chiles rellenos, chicken with mole sauce, pork ribs, grilled beef, enchiladas and fresh pastries. Breakfast is a favorite time. Casual dress. **Bar:** Full bar. **Hours:** 7:30 am-11 pm, Sun-10 pm. Closed: 12/25. **Address:** Blvd Sanchez Taboada #10813, Zona Rio **Location:** 1.8 mi (3 km) se of border on Paseo de los Heroes to Ave Rodriguez, just s, then just e. **Parking:** on-site. **Cards:** MC, VI.

LOS ARCOS RESTAURANT — **Phone:** 664/686-3171

Seafood
$10-$25

Festively decorated with fish netting, sculptures and bright colors, the restaurant has lively servers to match. Fresh fish from local waters is the specialty. Open-faced fish tacos with lime are a treat, as is the seafood fiesta for two, which includes stews of squid and octopus, shredded fish, smoked fish and shrimp, stuffed peppers and perch. Steaks also are available. Top dessert choices are bananas flambe and crepes Suzette. Dressy casual. **Bar:** Full bar. **Hours:** 11 am-10 pm, Sat & Sun-midnight. Closed: 12/25. **Address:** Blvd Salinas #1000 **Location:** 1.8 mi (3 km) se of the border on Paseo de los Heroes, 0.3 mi (0.5 km) s on Ave Rodriguez, just e on Blvd Agua Caliente, then just n on Calle Escuadron. **Parking:** on-site and valet. **Cards:** MC, VI.

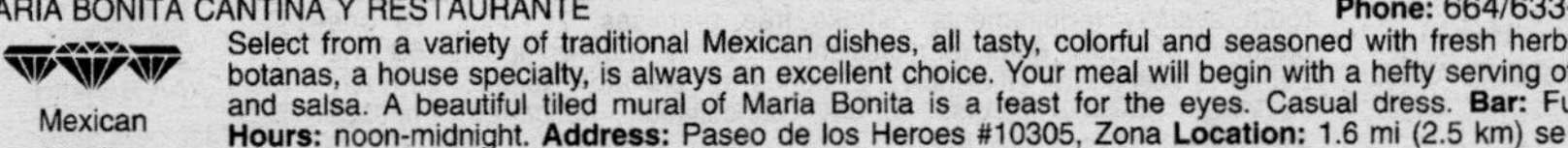

MARIA BONITA CANTINA Y RESTAURANTE — **Phone:** 664/633-4000

Mexican
$14-$20

Select from a variety of traditional Mexican dishes, all tasty, colorful and seasoned with fresh herbs. The botanas, a house specialty, is always an excellent choice. Your meal will begin with a hefty serving of chips and salsa. A beautiful tiled mural of Maria Bonita is a feast for the eyes. Casual dress. **Bar:** Full bar. **Hours:** noon-midnight. **Address:** Paseo de los Heroes #10305, Zona **Location:** 1.6 mi (2.5 km) se of the border; in Camino Real Tijuana. **Parking:** on-site. **Cards:** AX, MC, VI.

RESTAURANTE LA COSTA — **Phone:** 664/685-8494

Seafood
$12-$30

Near jai alai and shopping areas, the long-established restaurant is popular for business meetings and family gatherings. The nautical theme is matched by "old time" service from the staff. The menu lists many types of seafood: shrimp, fish kebabs, stone crabs, abalone, squid, salt cod and Alaskan king crab. Meals include soup, salad and rice. Casual dress. **Bar:** Full bar. **Hours:** 10 am-10 pm, Sat & Sun-midnight. Closed: 12/25. **Address:** Calle 7A #150 **Location:** 0.6 mi (1 km) from the border on Carrillo Puerto Calle #3A (downtown) to Ave Revolucion, just s, then just w. **Parking:** on-site. **Cards:** DC, DS, MC, VI.

RINCON SAN ROMAN — **Phone:** 664/631-2241

International
$8-$30

In the hillside center at Real Del Mar, the intimate dining room overlooks red-tile roofs, the golf course and the ocean. White tablecloths and candelabra lights set a sophisticated mood, which attentive servers continue to foster. The ever-changing menu might include such choices as filet of beef with rosemary, salmon in a bed of scallions and chiles rellenos with cheese. Dressy casual. **Bar:** Full bar. **Hours:** 1 pm-10 pm, Fri & Sat-11 pm. **Address:** KM 19.5 Carr Cuota **Location:** 11.8 mi (19.5 km) s of the border on Mex 1-D (toll road), exit Real Del Mar, just e. **Parking:** on-site. **Cards:** MC, VI.

RIVOLI'S — **Phone:** 664/633-3900

International
$8-$18

Mural-painted walls decorate the pleasant, peaceful dining room, which has a wall of glass overlooking the courtyard. The well-trained staff serves from a menu offering duck in fig sauce with aromatic lavender, shrimp or lobster with coconut and mango chutney, beef filet Singapore with pureed sweet potato sauce and wasabi. Penne with Gorgonzola, ricotta and mozzarella cheeses and ginger linguine with chicken and shrimp are among pastas. Dressy casual. **Bar:** Full bar. **Hours:** 7 am-11 pm, Sun-1 pm. Closed: 1/1. **Address:** Paseo de los Heroes #10902, Zona **Location:** 1.8 mi (3 km) se of border; in Hotel Lucerna. **Parking:** on-site and valet. **Cards:** AX, MC, VI.

CALL

SANBORN'S — **Phone:** 664/688-1433

Regional Mexican
$8-$28

Restaurants in the casual chain, which includes more than 100 locations throughout Mexico, offer a good selection of American-style sandwiches, salads, soups and both Mexican and American entrees. The selection of desserts is impressive. Casual dress. **Bar:** Full bar. **Hours:** 7:30 am-1 am. **Address:** Ave Revolucion No 1102 **Location:** In downtown district. **Parking:** on-site. **Cards:** AX, MC, VI.

SIRLOIN STOCKADE — **Phone:** 664/686-0803

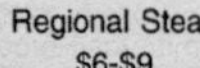

Regional Steak
$6-$9

The steakhouse lines up buffet items, including pizza, tacos, soups, salads and desserts, providing both excellent variety and a good value. Rotating theme nights might allow for the sampling of sushi, barbecue and seafood. The buffet also may serve to complement a quality steak. Rolls are baked several times daily. Casual dress. **Bar:** Beer & wine. **Hours:** 11 am-10 pm, Sat from 9 am, Sun 9 am-9 pm. Closed: 12/25. **Address:** Ave Ramon Alarid Cardenas No 15601 **Location:** Jct Blvd Federico Benitez. **Parking:** on-site. **Cards:** DS, MC, VI.

VILLA SAVERIOS

Italian
$14-$40

Phone: 664/686-6502

An attractive, modern, Italian-style building houses the large, aroma-filled dining room. Italian and Greek influences are evident in delicious pasta, chicken, beef and seafood dishes. The extensive wine collection surrounds a private dining room in the cellar. Dressy casual. **Bar:** Full bar. **Reservations:** accepted. **Hours:** noon-11 pm. Closed: Sun. **Address:** Escuadron #201, Rio Zona **Location:** 1.8 mi (3 km) se of the border on Paseo de los Heroes, 0.3 mi (0.5 km) s on Ave Rodriguez, just e on Blvd Agua Caliente, then just n. **Parking:** on-site. **Cards:** AX, MC, VI.

TODOS SANTOS, BAJA CALIFORNIA SUR pop. 2,400

WHERE TO STAY

POSADA LA POZA

Boutique Hotel
$195-$380 All Year

Phone: (612)145-0400

Address: Colonia La Poza **Location:** Mex 19, 1.14 mi (1.9 km) s via Olachea; southside of town; at La Poza. **Facility:** Set in a secluded location, above a lagoon and palm grove well-suited for bird watching, this beachfront property offers a retreatlike ambience. Designated smoking area. 7 one-bedroom standard units, some with whirlpools. 2 stories, exterior corridors. *Bath:* combo or shower only. **Parking:** on-site. **Terms:** office hours 7 am-10 pm, age restrictions may apply, 30 day cancellation notice. **Amenities:** CD players, safes, honor bars, hair dryers. *Some:* irons. **Dining:** El Gusto! Restaurant, see separate listing. **Pool(s):** outdoor. **Leisure Activities:** whirlpool, beach access, fishing, bicycles, hiking trails. *Fee:* massage. **Guest Services:** wireless Internet. **Business Services:** PC. **Cards:** MC, VI.

FEE

TODOS SANTOS INN

Bed & Breakfast
$125-$225 All Year

Phone: (612)145-0040

Address: Calle Legaspi #33 **Location:** Mex 19, just w on Hidalgo, just n; in town. **Facility:** Within the town's historic district, this restored inn has tastefully furnished rooms with tranquil gardens; a gallery is on the premises. Designated smoking area. 8 units. 6 one-bedroom standard units. 2 one-bedroom suites. 1 story, exterior corridors. *Bath:* combo or shower only. **Parking:** street. **Terms:** office hours 7:30 am-midnight, age restrictions may apply, 30 day cancellation notice-fee imposed. **Amenities:** hair dryers. **Pool(s):** heated outdoor. **Leisure Activities:** *Fee:* massage. **Guest Services:** wireless Internet. **Cards:** MC, VI.

/ SOME UNITS

The following lodging was either not evaluated or did not meet AAA rating requirements but is listed for your information only.

HOTEL CALIFORNIA

fyi

Phone: 612/145-0525

Not evaluated. **Address:** Benito Juarez S/N Col Centro **Location:** Center. Facilities, services, and decor characterize a mid-scale property.

WHERE TO DINE

CAFE SANTA FE

Italian
$19-$39

Phone: 612/145-0340

Refined Italian dishes are served in an attractively decorated dining room and on the lush, tropical patio. Casual dress. **Bar:** Full bar. **Reservations:** suggested. **Hours:** Open 12/1-9/1 & 11/1-11/30; noon-9 pm. Closed: 1/1, 12/25; also Tues. **Address:** Calle Centenario #4 **Location:** Center. **Parking:** street. **Cards:** MC, VI.

EL GUSTO! RESTAURANT

International
$12-$32

Phone: 612/145-0400

Mexican gourmet cuisine is prepared with an International flair. The full-size bar is spacious. The restaurant sits high enough to offer a breathtaking view of the sunset and is ideal for memorable weddings and private events. The wine list comprises a nice selection of local bottled and by-the-glass choices. Poultry, fish and meat entrees are pleasantly decorated with fresh vegetables and herbs. An European influence is seen in the presentations of homemade desserts. Dressy casual. **Bar:** Full bar. **Reservations:** suggested. **Hours:** 11:30 am-9 pm. Closed: Thurs. **Address:** Colonia La Poza **Location:** Mex 19, 1.14 mi (1.9 km) s via Olachea; southside of town; at La Poza; in Posada La Poza. **Parking:** on-site. **Cards:** MC, VI.

LA CORONELA

Regional Mexican
$11-$22

Phone: 612/145-0525

The restaurant prepares creative takes on regional Mexican fare, including shrimp-stuffed rellenos, chicken mole and mesquite-grilled fresh fish. Patrons can relax in the bar or dine on the garden terrace while soaking up the atmosphere and peace of this area. Casual dress. **Bar:** Full bar. **Reservations:** accepted. **Hours:** 7 am-11 pm. **Address:** Benito Juarez y Marques de Leon **Location:** Center; in Hotel California. **Parking:** street. **Cards:** MC, VI.

LOS ADOBES DE TODOS SANTOS

Mexican
$8-$22

Phone: 612/145-0203

Regional dishes from throughout Mexico have been given a light new touch. Fresh local ingredients enhance such dishes as white fish with cilantro, amaretto and garlic or herbs, chicken mole poblano and pork loin stuffed with mushroom in plum sauce. The kitchen is in a restored historic house, and seating is on the patio. Also on the premises are an internet cafe with coffee and lighter fare, and a wine and tequila bar set in the garden. Casual dress. **Bar:** Full bar. **Reservations:** accepted. **Hours:** Open 12/1-9/1 & 10/1-11/30; 11 am-9 pm; 11 am-6:30 pm 4/1-9/1. Closed: Sun. **Address:** Calle Hidalgo between Juarez & Militar **Location:** Between Juarez and Militar; in town. **Parking:** on-site. **Cards:** MC, VI.

NORTHWESTERN MEXICO

ALAMOS, SONORA pop. 25,152

WHERE TO STAY

CASA DE LOS TESOROS — **Phone:** (647)428-0010

Historic Country Inn
$88-$125 All Year

Address: Calle Obregon 10 **Location:** Just se of Plaza de Armas. **Facility:** Unique 18th-century converted convent. Period furniture; fireplaces. Indian dances every Saturday night in season. Strolling musicians in the evening. 15 one-bedroom standard units. 1 story, exterior corridors. *Bath:* combo or shower only. **Parking:** on-site. **Terms:** 14 day cancellation notice. **Pool(s):** outdoor. **Guest Services:** valet laundry, wireless Internet. **Cards:** AX, MC, VI.

/ SOME UNITS FEE

CASA ENCANTADA DE LOS TESOROS — **Phone:** 647/428-0482

Historic Bed & Breakfast
$88-$140 All Year

Address: Ave Juarez 20 **Location:** Next to Palacio Municipal. **Facility:** This is a converted 280-year-old hacienda, large rooms, high ceilings and attractive inner courtyard. Smoke free premises. 10 one-bedroom standard units. 1 story, exterior corridors. *Bath:* shower only. **Parking:** on-site. **Terms:** 14 day cancellation notice. **Guest Services:** valet laundry, wireless Internet. **Cards:** AX, MC, VI.

/ SOME UNITS FEE

HACIENDA DE LOS SANTOS RESORT & SPA — **Phone:** 647/428-0222

Hotel
$250-$1400 All Year

Address: Calle Molina #8 **Location:** 2 blks s of main plaza. **Facility:** Built in the late 17th century, this beautifully restored stately hacienda offers manicured, Mexican gardens; all units have fireplaces. Smoke free premises. 27 units. 21 one-bedroom standard units. 5 one- and 1 two-bedroom suites. 1-2 stories (no elevator), exterior corridors. *Bath:* combo or shower only. **Parking:** on-site. **Amenities:** CD players, safes, honor bars, irons, hair dryers. *Some:* DVD players. **Dining:** restaurant, see separate listing. **Pool(s):** 2 outdoor, 2 heated outdoor. **Leisure Activities:** whirlpool, exercise room, spa. **Guest Services:** valet laundry, wireless Internet. **Business Services:** meeting rooms, business center. **Cards:** AX, MC, VI.

D / SOME UNITS VCR

LA MANSION — **Phone:** 647/428-0221

Bed & Breakfast
$88-$140 All Year

Address: Calle Obregon 2 **Location:** Just se of Plaza de Armas; center. **Facility:** 11 one-bedroom standard units. 1 story, exterior corridors. *Bath:* shower only. **Parking:** on-site. **Guest Services:** valet laundry, wireless Internet. **Cards:** AX, MC, VI.

/ SOME UNITS FEE

LA PUERTA ROJA INN — **Phone:** 647/428-0142

Bed & Breakfast
$94-$115 All Year

Address: Calle Galeana #46 **Location:** 4 blks w of Plaza de Armas. **Facility:** Modern yet intimate, the inn offers comfortable guest rooms complete with antiques, decorated archways and large picture windows. 5 one-bedroom standard units. 1 story, interior/exterior corridors. *Bath:* combo or shower only. **Parking:** street. **Guest Services:** valet laundry, area transportation (fee), wireless Internet. **Cards:** MC, VI.

/ SOME UNITS

WHERE TO DINE

HACIENDA DE LOS SANTOS RESTAURANT — **Phone:** 647/428-0222

International
$12-$30

Featuring fine dining in an elegant cantina-style dining room, the restaurant offers well-prepared Mexican and Continental fare and attentive service. Dressy casual. **Bar:** Full bar. **Reservations:** suggested. **Hours:** 7 am-11 pm. **Address:** Calle Molina #8 **Location:** 2 blks s of main plaza; in Hacienda de los Santos Resort & Spa. **Parking:** on-site and street. **Cards:** AX, MC, VI.

BAHIA KINO, SONORA pop. 3,100

WHERE TO DINE

JORGE'S RESTAURANT — **Phone:** 662/242-0049

Seafood
$9-$27

The restaurant serves fresh seafood, as well as beef and chicken, with a nice view of the beach and sea, especially from the available outside seating; lobster is available in season. Casual dress. **Bar:** Full bar. **Reservations:** accepted. **Hours:** 8 am-10 pm. **Address:** Mar de Cortez y Alicantes **Location:** 4.8 mi (8 km) nw on beach highway; just w of Kino Bay RV Park. **Parking:** on-site. **Cards:** MC, VI.

CEROCAHUI, CHIHUAHUA pop. 2,100

WHERE TO STAY

HOTEL MISION — **Phone:** 668/818-7046

Hotel
$225-$285 All Year

Address: Bahuichivo Station **Location:** 10.8 mi (18 km) from Bahuichivo Station. Located in a remote area; accessible only by train. **Facility:** 41 one-bedroom standard units. 1 story, interior/exterior corridors. *Bath:* shower only. **Parking:** on-site. **Terms:** 20 day cancellation notice. **Pool(s):** heated indoor. **Leisure Activities:** game room. *Fee:* horseback riding. **Guest Services:** area transportation. **Business Services:** meeting rooms. **Cards:** AX, MC, VI.

The following lodging was either not evaluated or did not meet AAA rating requirements but is listed for your information only.

MARGARITAS CEROCAHUI WILDERNESS LODGE **Phone:** 635/456-0245

fyi

Not evaluated. **Address:** Bahuichivo Station **Location:** 13.2 mi (22 km) from town. Facilities, services, and decor characterize an economy property.

CHIHUAHUA, CHIHUAHUA pop. 671,790

WHERE TO STAY

BEST WESTERN MIRADOR MOTOR INN *Book great rates at AAA.com* **Phone:** (614)432-2200

Hotel
$67-$110 All Year

Address: Ave Universidad 1309 **Location:** On Mex 45; 6 blks s of Pancho Villa Monument. **Facility:** 87 units. 83 one-bedroom standard units. 4 one-bedroom suites. 2 stories, exterior corridors. *Bath:* shower only. **Parking:** on-site. **Terms:** 3 day cancellation notice. **Amenities:** voice mail, safes, irons, hair dryers. **Pool(s):** indoor. **Guest Services:** valet laundry, wireless Internet. **Business Services:** meeting rooms, business center. **Cards:** AX, MC, VI.

/ SOME UNITS

AAA Benefit:
Members save up to 20%, plus 10% bonus points with rewards program.

CASA GRANDE HOTELES BUSINESS PLUS *Book at AAA.com* **Phone:** (614)439-4444

Hotel
$72-$106 All Year

Address: Ave Tecnologico 4702 **Location:** 4.2 mi (7 km) n on Mex 45. **Facility:** Meets AAA guest room security requirements. 115 units. 109 one-bedroom standard units. 6 one-bedroom suites, some with efficiencies. 2 stories (no elevator), interior corridors. **Parking:** on-site. **Terms:** cancellation fee imposed. **Amenities:** voice mail, irons, hair dryers. **Pool(s):** outdoor. **Leisure Activities:** tennis court, exercise room, sports court, basketball, game room. **Guest Services:** valet laundry, wireless Internet. **Business Services:** meeting rooms, business center. **Cards:** AX, MC, VI.

/ SOME UNITS

FIESTA INN *Book great rates at AAA.com* **Phone:** (614)429-0100

Hotel
$97-$145 All Year

Address: 2801 Blvd Ortiz Mena **Location:** 1.2 mi (2 km) w on Blvd Ortiz Mena at Minnesota St. Located in a commercial area. **Facility:** Meets AAA guest room security requirements. 152 units. 145 one-bedroom standard units. 7 one-bedroom suites. 7 stories, interior corridors. **Parking:** on-site. **Amenities:** high-speed Internet, dual phone lines, voice mail, irons, hair dryers. **Pool(s):** heated outdoor. **Leisure Activities:** exercise room. **Guest Services:** valet laundry, wireless Internet. **Business Services:** meeting rooms, business center. **Cards:** AX, MC, VI. *(See color ad on insert)*

S D / SOME UNITS

HOLIDAY INN EXPRESS *Book at AAA.com* **Phone:** (614)442-2200

Hotel
$96 All Year

Address: Ave Cristobal Colon 11390 **Location:** 4.8 mi (8 km) n on Mex 45. Located next to Denny's Restaurant. **Facility:** Meets AAA guest room security requirements. 153 one-bedroom standard units. 2 stories (no elevator), interior corridors. **Parking:** on-site. **Pool(s):** heated outdoor. **Leisure Activities:** whirlpool, exercise room. **Guest Services:** valet and coin laundry, wireless Internet. **Business Services:** meeting rooms, business center. **Cards:** AX, MC, VI.

D / SOME UNITS

HOLIDAY INN HOTEL & SUITES CHIHUAHUA *Book at AAA.com* **Phone:** (614)439-0000

Hotel
$100-$145 All Year

Address: Escudero 702 **Location:** On Mex 45; 6 blks s of Pancho Villa Monument. **Facility:** 74 units. 60 one- and 14 two-bedroom standard units with kitchens. 2 stories (no elevator), exterior corridors. **Parking:** on-site. **Amenities:** high-speed Internet, dual phone lines, voice mail, safes, irons, hair dryers. **Pool(s):** heated outdoor, heated indoor. **Leisure Activities:** sauna, whirlpool, exercise room, sports court. **Guest Services:** valet and coin laundry. **Business Services:** meeting rooms, business center. **Cards:** AX, DC, DS, JC, MC, VI.

D / SOME UNITS

HOTEL DIVISADERO BARRANCAS **Phone:** 614/415-1199

Hotel
$165-$180 All Year

Address: Divisadero Station **Location:** Near Divisadero Train Station. **Facility:** 48 one-bedroom standard units. 2 stories (no elevator), interior corridors. *Bath:* shower only. **Parking:** on-site. **Terms:** cancellation fee imposed. **Cards:** AX, MC, VI.

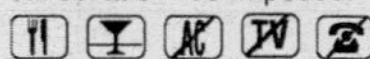

HOTEL HAMPTON INN CHIHUAHUA **Phone:** (614)439-8000

Hotel
$89-$119 All Year

Address: Periferico de la Juventud #6100 **Location:** Jct Mex 16 to Ave Cuauhtemoc. **Facility:** 139 one-bedroom standard units. 4 stories, interior corridors. **Parking:** on-site. **Terms:** 1-30 night minimum stay, cancellation fee imposed. **Amenities:** high-speed Internet, dual phone lines, voice mail, irons, hair dryers. **Pool(s):** heated outdoor. **Leisure Activities:** exercise room. **Guest Services:** valet and coin laundry, area transportation, wireless Internet. **Business Services:** meeting rooms, business center. **Cards:** AX, DC, DS, MC, VI.

/ SOME UNITS

AAA Benefit:
Members save up to 10% everyday!

HOTEL PALACIO DEL SOL **Phone:** 614/412-3456

Hotel
$155-$175 All Year

Address: Ave Independencia 116 **Location:** Just n of Plaza de Armas; downtown. **Facility:** 183 one-bedroom standard units, some with efficiencies. 17 stories, interior corridors. **Parking:** on-site. **Amenities:** irons, hair dryers. **Dining:** Restaurante & Bar Las Truffas, see separate listing. **Leisure Activities:** exercise room. **Guest Services:** valet and coin laundry, wireless Internet. **Business Services:** meeting rooms, business center. **Cards:** AX, MC, VI.

/ SOME UNITS

HOTEL SICOMORO *Book at AAA.com* **Phone:** (614)214-2500

Hotel
$60-$120 All Year

Address: Blvd Ortiz Mena 411 **Location:** 2 mi (3.2 km) nw on Ave Universidad to VW dealer, 0.2 mi (0.3 km) sw on Americas to Pemex Station, then 1 mi (1.6 km) s. **Facility:** 128 one-bedroom standard units. 2 stories (no elevator), interior corridors. *Bath:* shower only. **Parking:** on-site. **Amenities:** high-speed Internet, dual phone lines, voice mail. *Some:* irons, hair dryers. **Dining:** Restaurant del Hotel Sicomorro, see separate listing. **Pool(s):** outdoor. **Guest Services:** valet laundry, wireless Internet. **Business Services:** meeting rooms, business center. **Cards:** AX, MC, VI.

/ SOME UNITS

MICROTEL INN & SUITES CHIHUAHUA *Book at AAA.com* **Phone:** (614)432-2525

Hotel
$80-$103 All Year

Address: Periferico de la Juventud, #3304 **Location:** Jct Polytecnico. **Facility:** 108 one-bedroom standard units. 3 stories, interior corridors. *Bath:* combo or shower only. **Parking:** on-site. **Amenities:** voice mail. **Leisure Activities:** exercise room. **Guest Services:** valet laundry, wireless Internet. **Business Services:** meeting rooms, business center. **Cards:** AX, MC, VI.

/ SOME UNITS

POSADA TIERRA BLANCA **Phone:** (614)415-0000

Hotel
$75 All Year

Address: Ninos Heroes #102 **Location:** Just n of Plaza de Armas. **Facility:** 94 one-bedroom standard units. 3 stories (no elevator), interior/exterior corridors. *Bath:* shower only. **Parking:** on-site. **Terms:** 3 day cancellation notice. **Pool(s):** outdoor. **Leisure Activities:** limited exercise equipment. **Guest Services:** wireless Internet. **Business Services:** meeting rooms, PC. **Cards:** AX, MC, VI.

/ SOME UNITS

QUALITY INN SAN FRANCISCO CHIHUAHUA *Book at AAA.com* **Phone:** (614)439-9000

Hotel
$85-$130 All Year

Address: Calle Victoria 409 **Location:** Just off main plaza; center of downtown. **Facility:** Meets AAA guest room security requirements. 123 one-bedroom standard units. 4 stories, interior corridors. **Parking:** on-site. **Amenities:** dual phone lines, voice mail, irons, hair dryers. **Dining:** Restaurante Dega, see separate listing. **Leisure Activities:** exercise room. **Guest Services:** valet laundry, wireless Internet. **Business Services:** meeting rooms, business center. **Cards:** AX, MC, VI.

/ SOME UNITS

THE WESTIN SOBERANO CHIHUAHUA *Book great rates at AAA.com* **Phone:** (614)429-2929

Hotel
$154-$195 All Year

Address: Barranca del Cobre #3211 **Location:** 4.8 mi (8 km) nw on Cuauhtemoc Bypass. **Facility:** Meets AAA guest room security requirements. Smoke free premises. 204 units. 194 one-bedroom standard units. 10 one-bedroom suites, some with whirlpools. 5 stories, interior corridors. **Parking:** on-site. **Terms:** cancellation fee imposed. **Amenities:** high-speed Internet, dual phone lines, voice mail, safes, honor bars, irons, hair dryers. **Dining:** Los Candiles, see separate listing. **Pool(s):** heated outdoor. **Leisure Activities:** whirlpool, steamroom, 2 tennis courts, racquetball court, exercise room. *Fee:* massage. **Guest Services:** valet laundry, wireless Internet. **Business Services:** meeting rooms, business center. **Cards:** AX, CB, DC, DS, JC, MC, VI.

/ SOME UNITS

WESTIN HOTELS & RESORTS

AAA Benefit:
Enjoy up to 15% off your next stay, plus Starwood Preferred Guest® bonuses.

WHERE TO DINE

EL RETABLO **Phone:** 614/415-5545

Mexican
$7-$26

This is a favorite lunch stop for the local folks who enjoy traditional northern Mexican cuisine, such as green chile salsa with a real kick to it. Slow-cooked pork melts in the mouth. The restaurant is an archetypical example of the genre. Casual dress. **Bar:** Full bar. **Reservations:** accepted. **Hours:** 11 am-midnight. **Address:** Blvd Ortiz Mena 1810 **Location:** 2 mi (3.2 km) nw. **Parking:** on-site. **Cards:** AX, MC, VI.

GARUFA RESTAURANTE ARGENTINO **Phone:** 614/430-0417

Argentine
$28-$44

You'll enjoy the excellent quality, well-prepared beef at this eating establishment serving Argentinian-style food. Casual dress. **Bar:** Full bar. **Reservations:** suggested. **Hours:** 1 pm-midnight, Sun-9 pm. Closed: 12/25. **Address:** Periferico de la Juventud #3108 **Location:** On Periferico de la Juventud, jct Mex 16 to Ave Cuauhtemoc. **Parking:** on-site. **Cards:** AX, MC, VI.

CALL

LOS CANDILES **Phone:** 614/429-2929

International
$19-$27

The elegant, fine dining restaurant is appointed in upscale decor and affords commanding city views. Features on the eclectic menu include beef, seafood and fowl prepared in a blend of International and Mexican styles. Dressy casual. **Bar:** Full bar. **Reservations:** accepted. **Hours:** 1 pm-11 pm. Closed: Sun. **Address:** Barranca del Cobre #3211 **Location:** 4.8 mi (8 km) nw on Cuauhtemoc Bypass; in The Westin Soberano Chihuahua. **Parking:** on-site. **Cards:** AX, DC, MC, VI.

LOS VITRALES **Phone:** 614/437-1200

International
$8-$25

Elegant, refined dining in a gracefully restored, colonial-style home with stained glass windows, or vitrales. Specializing in seafood, steaks, poultry and Mexican dishes, the restaurant also offers upstairs dining and outside dining on the second floor terrace in season. Dressy casual. **Bar:** Full bar. **Reservations:** suggested. **Hours:** noon-11 pm, Fri & Sat-midnight, Sun-6 pm. **Address:** Ave Juarez #3116 **Location:** Jct aves Juarez and Cristobol Colon; 1.1 mi (1.8 km) e on Mex 45. **Parking:** on-site and valet. **Cards:** AX, MC, VI.

MARIA CHUCHENA **Phone:** 614/200-0875

Mexican
$12-$26

This eatery features haute mexican cuisine, so don't expect to find here what you normally see north of the border..stylish night club atmosphere..salsas are made in a traditional "molcajete" (mortar and pestle) tableside. Casual dress. **Bar:** Full bar. **Reservations:** suggested. **Hours:** 8 am-11 pm, Fri & Sat-midnight. Closed: 12/25. **Address:** Ave de la Empresa, #3110 **Location:** Off of Periferico de la Juventud, jct Mex 16 to Ave Cuauhtemoc. **Parking:** on-site. **Cards:** AX, DS, MC, VI.

RESTAURANT DEL HOTEL SICOMORRO **Phone:** 614/413-5445

International
$6-$15

Popular with both locals and visitors, the colorful eatery builds a menu on Continental dishes and Mexican fare. Quick, competent servers add to the friendly feel of the busy, lively dining room. Casual dress. **Bar:** Full bar. **Reservations:** accepted. **Hours:** 6:30 am-11 pm. **Address:** Blvd Ortiz Mena 411 **Location:** 2 mi (3.2 km) nw on Ave Universidad to VW dealer, 0.2 mi (0.3 km) sw on Americas to Pemex Station, then 1 mi (1.6 km) s; in Hotel Sicomoro. **Parking:** on-site. **Cards:** AX, MC, VI.

RESTAURANTE & BAR LAS TRUFFAS **Phone:** 614/416-6000

International
$10-$21

Operating as the dining room of a downtown hotel, the restaurant prepares a number of Continental selections as well as traditional Mexican dishes. This place can be quite busy at lunchtime. Casual dress. **Bar:** Full bar. **Reservations:** accepted. **Hours:** 6 am-midnight. **Address:** Ave Independencia 116 **Location:** Just n of Plaza de Armas; downtown; in Hotel Palacio del Sol. **Parking:** on-site. **Cards:** AX, MC, VI.

RESTAURANTE BAR LA CALESA **Phone:** 614/416-0222

International
$10-$32

Uniformed staff circulate through the semi-formal dining room, which is appointed with crisp linens. On the menu is a fine selection of steaks, Mexican food and delectable desserts. Dressy casual. Entertainment. **Bar:** Full bar. **Reservations:** accepted. **Hours:** noon-midnight. **Address:** Ave Juarez 3300 Col Centro **Location:** 1.1 mi (1.8 km) e on Mex 45. **Parking:** on-site. **Cards:** AX, MC, VI.

RESTAURANTE DEGA **Phone:** 614/439-9000

Regional Mexican
$8-$21

Inside a popular downtown hotel, the dining room is usually busy with local business people and patrons from the hotel. The cuisine is a mix of Continental and Mexican dishes. Casual dress. **Bar:** Full bar. **Reservations:** accepted. **Hours:** 7 am-11 pm. **Address:** Calle Victoria 409 **Location:** Just off main plaza; center of downtown; in Quality Inn San Francisco Chihuahua. **Parking:** on-site. **Cards:** AX, MC, VI.

VIPS **Phone:** 614/423-2142

Mexican
$5-$9

Owned by Wal-Mart of Mexico and found in most major cities, the budget-friendly chain serves a good variety of Mexican and American dishes, including burgers, sandwiches, salads, spaghetti and enchiladas, as well as a fine selection of desserts. Casual dress. **Hours:** 7 am-midnight. **Address:** Periferico de la Juventud #2200 D **Location:** Jct Periferico de la Juventud and Mirador, just s. **Parking:** on-site. **Cards:** MC, VI.

YI HE YUAN **Phone:** 614/425-6965

Chinese
$7-$11

The all-you-can-eat Chinese buffet lines up all the favorite dishes, including sweet and sour pork, Chinese fried chicken, beef with vegetables and chicken with bamboo shoots, as well as such American-style desserts as apple pie. Casual dress. **Bar:** Full bar. **Reservations:** accepted. **Hours:** noon-9 pm. Closed: 12/25. **Address:** Ave Francisco Villa #5514 **Location:** Just e of jct Periferico de la Juventud. **Parking:** on-site. **Cards:** MC, VI.

CIUDAD JUAREZ, CHIHUAHUA pop. 1,218,817

WHERE TO STAY

FIESTA INN CIUDAD JUAREZ — **Phone:** (656)686-0700

Hotel
$104-$148 All Year

Address: Paseo Triunfo de la Republica 3451 **Location:** 2.2 mi (3.7 km) e on Chihuahua Hwy (Mex 45). **Facility:** Meets AAA guest room security requirements. 166 one-bedroom standard units. 9 stories, interior corridors. **Parking:** on-site. **Terms:** 5 day cancellation notice. **Amenities:** voice mail, irons, hair dryers. **Pool(s):** heated indoor. **Leisure Activities:** whirlpool, exercise room. **Guest Services:** valet laundry, wireless Internet. **Business Services:** conference facilities, business center. **Cards:** AX, DC, MC, VI. *(See color ad on insert)*

S D / SOME UNITS

HAMPTON INN-CIUDAD JUAREZ *Book great rates at AAA.com* — **Phone:** (656)227-1717

Hotel
$82-$99 All Year

Address: Blvd Tomas Fernandez #7770 **Location:** Jct Tomas Fernandez and Vicente Guerero, just e. **Facility:** Meets AAA guest room security requirements. 137 one-bedroom standard units. 5 stories, interior corridors. **Parking:** on-site. **Terms:** 1-30 night minimum stay, cancellation fee imposed. **Amenities:** high-speed Internet, dual phone lines, voice mail, irons, hair dryers. **Pool(s):** heated outdoor. **Leisure Activities:** exercise room. **Guest Services:** valet laundry, airport transportation-Gonzales International Airport, area transportation, wireless Internet. **Business Services:** meeting rooms, business center. **Cards:** AX, CB, DC, DS, MC, VI.

/ SOME UNITS

HILTON GARDEN INN *Book great rates at AAA.com* — **Phone:** (656)629-0994

Hotel
$80-$116 All Year

Address: Ave Tecnologico 3750 **Location:** 6 mi (10 km) e on Chihuahua Hwy (Mex 45). **Facility:** Meets AAA guest room security requirements. 120 one-bedroom standard units. 4 stories, interior corridors. **Parking:** on-site. **Terms:** 1-30 night minimum stay, cancellation fee imposed. **Amenities:** high-speed Internet, voice mail, irons, hair dryers. **Pool(s):** heated indoor. **Leisure Activities:** whirlpool, exercise room. **Guest Services:** valet laundry, area transportation, wireless Internet. **Business Services:** meeting rooms, business center. **Cards:** AX, DC, DS, JC, MC, VI.

S D / SOME UNITS

HOLIDAY INN EXPRESS *Book at AAA.com* — **Phone:** (656)629-6000

Hotel
$98-$144 All Year

Address: 3745 Paseo Triunfo de la Republica **Location:** 2.4 mi (4 km) e on Chihuahua Hwy (Mex 45). **Facility:** Meets AAA guest room security requirements. 147 one-bedroom standard units. 4 stories, interior corridors. **Parking:** on-site. **Terms:** 3 day cancellation notice. **Amenities:** high-speed Internet, voice mail, safes, irons, hair dryers. **Pool(s):** heated indoor. **Leisure Activities:** exercise room. **Guest Services:** valet and coin laundry, wireless Internet. **Business Services:** meeting rooms, business center. **Cards:** AX, MC, VI.

S D / SOME UNITS

HOLIDAY INN LINCOLN CIUDAD JUAREZ — **Phone:** (656)613-1310

Hotel
$72-$169 All Year

Address: Avenida Lincoln #722, Zona Pronaf **Location:** 2.1 mi (3.5 km) s of Bridge of the Americas. **Facility:** 162 one-bedroom standard units, some with efficiencies (no utensils). 2 stories (no elevator), exterior corridors. **Parking:** on-site. **Amenities:** voice mail, irons, hair dryers. **Pool(s):** heated outdoor. **Leisure Activities:** exercise room. **Guest Services:** valet and coin laundry, wireless Internet. **Business Services:** meeting rooms, business center. **Cards:** AX, MC, VI.

D / SOME UNITS

HOTEL COLONIAL *Book at AAA.com* — **Phone:** (656)613-5050

Hotel
$65-$93 All Year

Address: 1355 S Lincoln Ave **Location:** 1.8 mi (3 km) s of Bridge of the Americas. **Facility:** Meets AAA guest room security requirements. 140 one-bedroom standard units. 2 stories (no elevator), exterior corridors. **Parking:** on-site. **Pool(s):** 2 heated outdoor. **Guest Services:** area transportation, wireless Internet. **Business Services:** conference facilities, business center. **Cards:** AX, MC, VI.

/ SOME UNITS

HOTEL LUCERNA *Book great rates at AAA.com* — **Phone:** (656)629-9900

Hotel
$80-$165 All Year

Address: Paseo Triunfo de la Republica 3976 **Location:** 2.3 mi (3.9 km) e on Chihuahua Hwy (Mex 45). **Facility:** Meets AAA guest room security requirements. 138 one-bedroom standard units. 8 stories, interior corridors. **Parking:** on-site. **Terms:** cancellation fee imposed. **Amenities:** voice mail, irons, hair dryers. **Pool(s):** outdoor. **Leisure Activities:** whirlpool, exercise room. **Guest Services:** valet laundry, wireless Internet. **Business Services:** meeting rooms, business center. **Cards:** AX, DC, MC, VI.

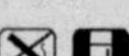 / SOME UNITS

RADISSON HOTEL CASA GRANDE CIUDAD JUAREZ *Book at AAA.com* **Phone:** (656)629-4000

Hotel

$40-$113 All Year

Address: Ave Tecnologico 3620 **Location:** 6.2 mi (10 km) e on Chihuahua Hwy (Mex 45). **Facility:** Meets AAA guest room security requirements. 145 one-bedroom standard units. 4 stories, interior corridors. **Parking:** on-site. **Amenities:** high-speed Internet, dual phone lines, voice mail, irons, hair dryers. **Pool(s):** heated outdoor. **Leisure Activities:** exercise room. **Guest Services:** valet laundry, wireless Internet. **Business Services:** meeting rooms, business center. **Cards:** AX, DC, MC, VI.

/ SOME UNITS

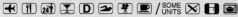

WHERE TO DINE

SANBORN'S **Phone:** 656/648-2181

Mexican

$8-$18

Restaurants in the casual chain, which includes more than 100 locations throughout Mexico, offer a good selection of American-style sandwiches, salads, soups and both Mexican and American entrees. The selection of desserts is impressive. Casual dress. **Bar:** Full bar. **Hours:** 7 am-11 pm. **Address:** Centro Comercial Las Misiones **Location:** In Misiones Shopping Center. **Parking:** on-site (fee). **Cards:** MC, VI.

SANBORN'S **Phone:** 656/616-9024

Mexican

$8-$18

Restaurants in the casual chain, which includes more than 100 locations throughout Mexico, offer a good selection of American-style sandwiches, salads, soups and both Mexican and American entrees. The selection of desserts is impressive. Casual dress. **Bar:** Full bar. **Hours:** 7 am-1 am, Sun-midnight. **Address:** Paseo Triumfo de La Republica 3809 **Location:** In Pronaf shopping zone. **Parking:** on-site (fee). **Cards:** AX, MC, VI.

SHANGRI-LA RESTAURANT **Phone:** 656/613-0033

Chinese

$10-$25

A popular dining spot for tourists, local business people and El Paso residents who live just across the border, the restaurant serves authentic Chinese dishes in a semi-formal setting. Dressy casual. **Bar:** Full bar. **Reservations:** suggested. **Hours:** 11:30 am-midnight, Fri & Sat-2 am, Sun-11 pm. **Address:** Ave de las Americas 133 **Location:** 2.7 mi (4.5 km) sw of Bridge of the Americas. **Parking:** on-site. **Cards:** AX, MC, VI.

VIPS **Phone:** 656/623-2168

Mexican

$5-$9

Owned by Wal-Mart of Mexico and found in most major cities, the budget-friendly chain serves a good variety of Mexican and American dishes, including burgers, sandwiches, salads, spaghetti and enchiladas, as well as a fine selection of desserts. Casual dress. **Hours:** 7 am-midnight. **Address:** Ave Pase o Triunfo de la Republica #6308 **Location:** Jct Ave Lopez Mateos and Paseo Triunfo de la Republica, just w. **Parking:** on-site. **Cards:** MC, VI.

VIPS **Phone:** 666/623-5158

Mexican

$5-$9

Owned by Wal-Mart of Mexico and found in most major cities, the budget-friendly chain serves a good variety of Mexican and American dishes, including burgers, sandwiches, salads, spaghetti and enchiladas, as well as a fine selection of desserts. Casual dress. **Hours:** 7 am-midnight. **Address:** Ave Ejercito Nacional #7051 **Location:** Jct Ave Ejercito Nacional and Camino San Jose, just e. **Parking:** on-site. **Cards:** MC, VI.

CIUDAD OBREGON, SONORA pop. 220,000

WHERE TO STAY

HOLIDAY INN CUIDAD OBREGON **Phone:** 644/410-5090

Hotel

$76-$115 All Year

Address: Ave Miguel Aleman 200 Norte y Allende **Location:** Center. Located in a commercial area. **Facility:** 89 one-bedroom standard units. 3 stories, exterior corridors. *Bath:* shower only. **Parking:** on-site. **Amenities:** irons, hair dryers. **Pool(s):** outdoor. **Leisure Activities:** exercise room. **Guest Services:** valet laundry, wireless Internet. **Business Services:** meeting rooms, business center. **Cards:** AX, DS, MC, VI.

/ SOME UNITS

HOTEL VALLE GRANDE OBREGON **Phone:** 644/410-6500

Hotel

$85-$105 All Year

Address: Ave Miguel Aleman y Tetabiate **Location:** 0.8 mi (1.2 km) n on Mex 15. **Facility:** 135 units. 131 one-bedroom standard units. 4 one-bedroom suites. 2 stories (no elevator), exterior corridors. *Bath:* combo or shower only. **Parking:** on-site. **Amenities:** high-speed Internet, voice mail, safes, irons, hair dryers. *Some:* honor bars. **Pool(s):** outdoor. **Leisure Activities:** exercise room. **Guest Services:** valet laundry, wireless Internet. **Business Services:** meeting rooms, business center. **Cards:** AX, MC, VI.

/ SOME UNITS

WHERE TO DINE

VIPS **Phone:** 644/413-0025

Mexican

$5-$9

Owned by Wal-Mart of Mexico and found in most major cities, the budget-friendly chain serves a good variety of Mexican and American dishes, including burgers, sandwiches, salads, spaghetti and enchiladas, as well as a fine selection of desserts. Casual dress. **Hours:** 7 am-11 pm. **Address:** Carr Internacional #1073 Norte **Location:** Center; on main highway through town. **Parking:** on-site. **Cards:** MC, VI.

CREEL, CHIHUAHUA pop. 3,100

WHERE TO STAY

BEST WESTERN THE LODGE AT CREEL — **Phone:** (635)456-0071

Country Inn
$96-$130 All Year

Address: Calle Lopez Mateos 61 **Location:** Center. **Facility:** 40 units. 39 one-bedroom standard units, some with whirlpools. 1 one-bedroom suite with kitchen. 1-2 stories, exterior corridors. *Bath:* combo or shower only. **Parking:** on-site. **Terms:** cancellation fee imposed. **Amenities:** video library (fee), voice mail, irons, hair dryers. **Dining:** Sierra Madre Restaurant, see separate listing. **Leisure Activities:** sauna, whirlpool, playground, exercise room. *Fee:* bicycles, massage. **Guest Services:** valet and coin laundry, area transportation, wireless Internet. **Business Services:** meeting rooms, PC, fax (fee). **Cards:** AX, MC, VI.

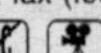

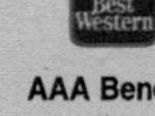

AAA Benefit:
Members save up to 20%, plus 10% bonus points with rewards program.

MARGARITA'S PLAZA MEXICANA — **Phone:** (635)456-0538

Hotel
$75 All Year

Address: Elefido Batista S/N **Location:** Center. **Facility:** 29 units. 27 one-bedroom standard units. 2 cabins. 2 stories, exterior corridors. *Bath:* combo or shower only. **Parking:** on-site. **Leisure Activities:** *Fee:* bicycles.

/ SOME UNITS

MOTEL PARADOR DE LA MONTANA — **Phone:** 635/456-0023

Hotel
$76-$98 All Year

Address: Calle Lopez Mateos 44 **Location:** Center. **Facility:** 50 one-bedroom standard units. 2 stories, exterior corridors. *Bath:* shower only. **Parking:** on-site. **Guest Services:** wireless Internet. **Business Services:** meeting rooms. **Cards:** AX, MC, VI.

/ SOME UNITS

VILLA MEXICANA

Vacation Rental Cabin
$85-$145 All Year

Phone: (635)456-0666

Address: Calle Lopez Mateos S/N **Location:** 0.6 mi (1 km) se. Located adjacent to RV park. **Facility:** Rustic log cabins with heaters; each with picnic table and charcoal grill. 36 cabins. 1 story, exterior corridors. *Bath:* shower only. **Parking:** on-site. **Terms:** 3 day cancellation notice. **Amenities:** high-speed Internet. **Leisure Activities:** playground, basketball, volleyball. **Guest Services:** coin laundry, area transportation, wireless Internet. **Business Services:** meeting rooms, PC. **Cards:** AX, MC, VI.

/ SOME UNITS

WHERE TO DINE

SIERRA MADRE RESTAURANT

Mexican
$9-$27

Phone: 635/456-0071

Tasty food, such as roasted pork served with grilled apples, is served in a lodge-style atmosphere that includes a fireplace. Casual dress. **Bar:** Full bar. **Reservations:** accepted. **Hours:** 7:30-11:30 am, 1:30-5:30 & 6:30-10:30 pm. **Address:** Calle Lopez Mateos 61 **Location:** Center; in Best Western The Lodge at Creel. **Parking:** on-site. **Cards:** AX, MC, VI.

CULIACAN, SINALOA pop. 745,537

WHERE TO STAY

FIESTA INN *Book great rates at AAA.com*

Hotel
$94-$212 All Year

Phone: (667)759-5900

Address: Blvd Jose Diego Valadez #1676 Pte **Location:** 1.2 mi (2 km) n of historic centro; in Plaza Forum Center Mall. **Facility:** Meets AAA guest room security requirements. 142 one-bedroom standard units. 6 stories, interior corridors. **Parking:** on-site. **Amenities:** dual phone lines, voice mail, irons, hair dryers. **Pool(s):** outdoor. **Leisure Activities:** exercise room. **Guest Services:** valet laundry, wireless Internet. **Business Services:** meeting rooms, business center. **Cards:** AX, MC, VI.

(See color ad on insert)

/ SOME UNITS

HOLIDAY INN CULIACAN

Hotel
$70-$120 All Year

Phone: (667)716-5850

Address: Ave Juan Carrasco 606 N Cross Rosa **Location:** Jct aves Juan Carrasco and Rosales. **Facility:** Meets AAA guest room security requirements. 116 one-bedroom standard units. 10 stories, interior corridors. *Bath:* combo or shower only. **Parking:** on-site. **Amenities:** irons, hair dryers. **Leisure Activities:** limited exercise equipment. **Guest Services:** wireless Internet. **Business Services:** meeting rooms, business center. **Cards:** AX, MC, VI.

FEE / SOME UNITS

HOTEL EXECUTIVO *Book at AAA.com*

Hotel
$90-$120 All Year

Phone: (667)713-9300

Address: Blvd Fco Madero & Ave Obregon **Location:** Just n of jct Blvd Francisco I Madero and Ave Alvaro Obregon; center. **Facility:** 229 one-bedroom standard units. 6 stories, interior corridors. **Parking:** on-site. **Amenities:** high-speed Internet, voice mail. *Some:* irons, hair dryers. **Leisure Activities:** exercise room. **Guest Services:** valet laundry, wireless Internet. **Business Services:** meeting rooms, business center. **Cards:** AX, MC, VI.

/ SOME UNITS

HOTEL SAN LUIS LINDA VISTA

Hotel
$109-$138 All Year

Phone: 667/716-7010

Address: Rio Sinaloa #1 **Location:** 1.1 mi (1.8 km) s on Ave Alvaro Obregon. **Facility:** 90 units. 85 one- and 5 two-bedroom standard units. 2-5 stories, interior corridors. *Bath:* combo or shower only. **Parking:** on-site. **Amenities:** high-speed Internet, hair dryers. **Dining:** El Mirador, see separate listing. **Pool(s):** outdoor. **Guest Services:** valet laundry. **Business Services:** meeting rooms, PC, fax. **Cards:** AX, MC, VI.

/ SOME UNITS

The following lodging was either not evaluated or did not meet AAA rating requirements but is listed for your information only.

HOTEL LUCERNA CULIACAN

fyi

Phone: 667/759-0000

Not evaluated. **Address:** Blvd Carlos Salinas #99 **Location:** 1.2 mi (2 km) n of historic town center; adjacent to Forum Mall Shopping Center. Facilities, services, and decor characterize a mid-scale property.

WHERE TO DINE

EL MIRADOR

International
$10-$18

Phone: 667/716-7010

Perched atop the hotel, the well-known restaurant provides not only traditional Mexican food but also a splendid view of the city below. The setting is casual. Casual dress. **Bar:** Full bar. **Reservations:** suggested. **Hours:** 7 am-11 pm. **Address:** Ave Las Palmas #1 **Location:** 0.8 mi (1.8 km) s on Ave Alvaro Obregon; in Hotel San Luis Linda Vista. **Parking:** on-site. **Cards:** AX, MC, VI.

SANBORN'S

Mexican
$8-$18

Phone: 667/713-6601

Restaurants in the casual chain, which includes more than 100 locations throughout Mexico, offer a good selection of American-style sandwiches, salads, soups and both Mexican and American entrees. The selection of desserts is impressive. Casual dress. **Bar:** Full bar. **Hours:** 7:30 am-1 am. **Address:** Blvd Carlos Salinas de Gortari #1676 Pte **Location:** Downtown. **Parking:** on-site (fee). **Cards:** MC, VI.

VIPS

Mexican
$5-$9

Phone: 667/712-7500

Owned by Wal-Mart of Mexico and found in most major cities, the budget-friendly chain serves a good variety of Mexican and American dishes, including burgers, sandwiches, salads, spaghetti and enchiladas, as well as a fine selection of desserts. Casual dress. **Hours:** 7 am-11 pm. **Address:** Avenida Alvaro Obregon #1880 Sur **Location:** On Mex 86; jct Mex 86 and Alvaro Obregon, just s. **Parking:** on-site. **Cards:** MC, VI.

VIPS

Mexican
$5-$9

Phone: 667/750-9502

Owned by Wal-Mart of Mexico and found in most major cities, the budget-friendly chain serves a good variety of Mexican and American dishes, including burgers, sandwiches, salads, spaghetti and enchiladas, as well as a fine selection of desserts. Casual dress. **Hours:** 7 am-11 pm. **Address:** Avenida Regional 1330 Norte Projecto Tres **Location:** In Tres Rios Shopping Mall. **Parking:** on-site. **Cards:** MC, VI.

DELICIAS, CHIHUAHUA pop. 116,426

WHERE TO STAY

HOTEL CASA GRANDE

Hotel
$91-$121 All Year

Phone: (639)474-0404

Address: Ave 6 Oriente 601 **Location:** 6 blks e of center; just w of Mex 45. **Facility:** 89 one-bedroom standard units. 3 stories, interior corridors. **Parking:** on-site. **Amenities:** voice mail, irons. **Dining:** Los Nogales Restaurante, see separate listing. **Pool(s):** heated outdoor. **Leisure Activities:** exercise room. **Guest Services:** valet laundry, wireless Internet. **Business Services:** meeting rooms, business center. **Cards:** AX, MC, VI.

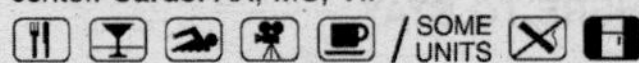

WHERE TO DINE

LOS NOGALES RESTAURANTE

International
$8-$15

Phone: 639/474-0404

Featured here are well-prepared Mexican specialties, as well as a good selection of meat, poultry and seafood selections. The well-appointed dining room is in the covered atrium of the hotel. Casual dress. **Bar:** Full bar. **Hours:** 7 am-11 pm. **Address:** Ave 6 Oriente 601 **Location:** 6 blks e of center; just w of Mex 45; in Hotel Casa Grande. **Parking:** on-site. **Cards:** AX, MC, VI.

DURANGO, DURANGO pop. 491,436

WHERE TO DINE

SANBORN'S

Mexican
$7-$18

Phone: 618/825-4780

Restaurants in the casual chain, which includes more than 100 locations throughout Mexico, offer a good selection of American-style sandwiches, salads, soups and both Mexican and American entrees. The selection of desserts is impressive. Casual dress. **Bar:** Full bar. **Hours:** 7 am-11 pm. **Address:** Ave 20 de Noviembre, #506 PTE **Location:** Center. **Parking:** on-site (fee). **Cards:** MC, VI.

EL FUERTE, SINALOA pop. 89,515

WHERE TO STAY

The following lodging was either not evaluated or did not meet AAA rating requirements but is listed for your information only.

HOTEL POSADA DEL HIDALGO

fyi

Phone: 698/893-1194

Not evaluated. **Address:** Hidalgo 101 **Location:** Mex 15, just s of KM 55, 33 mi (55 km) e on rural paved road; just ne of main plaza. Facilities, services, and decor characterize an economy property.

GOMEZ PALACIO, DURANGO pop. 273,315

WHERE TO STAY

HOTEL POSADA DEL RIO BEST WESTERN

Hotel
$65-$89 All Year

Phone: 871/714-3399

Address: Ave Fransisco I Madero 144 Sur **Location:** 2.4 mi (4 km) s on Mex 49 (becomes Fco Madero) to Ave Juarez; downtown. **Facility:** 100 one-bedroom standard units. 2 stories (no elevator), interior/exterior corridors. *Bath:* shower only. **Parking:** on-site. **Amenities:** high-speed Internet, hair dryers. *Some:* honor bars. **Dining:** El Parador, see separate listing. **Pool(s):** outdoor. **Leisure Activities:** exercise room. **Guest Services:** wireless Internet. **Business Services:** meeting rooms, business center. **Cards:** AX, MC, VI.

AAA Benefit:
Members save up to 20%, plus 10% bonus points with rewards program.

WHERE TO DINE

EL PARADOR

Continental
$8-$17

Phone: 871/714-3399

Well-prepared meat, poultry and seafood specialties are at the heart of a menu that also includes soup, sandwiches and some Mexican specialties. Casual dress. **Bar:** Full bar. **Hours:** 7 am-11 pm. **Address:** Fco Madero y Ave Juarez 144 Sur **Location:** 2.4 mi (4 km) s on Mex 49 (becomes Fco Madero) to Ave Juarez; downtown; in Hotel Posada del Rio Best Western. **Parking:** on-site. **Cards:** AX, MC, VI.

GUAMUCHIL, SINALOA pop. 34,000

WHERE TO STAY

MOTEL YORK SA DE CV

Hotel
$50-$73 All Year

Phone: 673/732-5611
Address: Carr Internacional KM 1528 **Location:** 0.9 mi (1.5 km) n. **Facility:** 80 units. 78 one-bedroom standard units. 1 one- and 1 two-bedroom suites with whirlpools. 2 stories, exterior corridors. *Bath:* shower only. **Parking:** on-site. **Pool(s):** outdoor. **Leisure Activities:** playground. **Guest Services:** valet laundry, wireless Internet. **Business Services:** meeting rooms, business center. **Cards:** AX, MC, VI.

/ SOME UNITS

HERMOSILLO, SONORA pop. 609,829

WHERE TO STAY

FIESTA INN *Book great rates at AAA.com*

Hotel
$135-$150 All Year

Phone: (662)289-2200
Address: Blvd Eusebio Kino 375 **Location:** 2.7 mi (4.5 km) n on Mex 15. **Facility:** 155 units. 72 one-bedroom standard units. 83 one-bedroom suites. 4 stories, interior corridors. **Parking:** on-site. **Amenities:** hair dryers. **Pool(s):** heated indoor. **Leisure Activities:** exercise room. **Guest Services:** valet laundry, wireless Internet. **Business Services:** conference facilities, business center. **Cards:** AX, DC, MC, VI. *(See color ad on insert)*

/ SOME UNITS

HOLIDAY INN HERMOSILLO *Book at AAA.com*

Hotel
$59-$115 All Year

Phone: (662)289-1700
Address: Blvd Eusebio Kino y Ramon Corral **Location:** 2.3 mi (3.8 km) ne on Mex 15. **Facility:** 133 units. 126 one-bedroom standard units. 7 one-bedroom suites. 3 stories, interior/exterior corridors. *Bath:* combo or shower only. **Parking:** on-site. **Terms:** cancellation fee imposed. **Amenities:** voice mail, safes, irons, hair dryers. **Pool(s):** outdoor. **Leisure Activities:** exercise room. **Guest Services:** valet laundry, wireless Internet. **Business Services:** meeting rooms, business center. **Cards:** AX, MC, VI.

/ SOME UNITS

HOTEL ARAIZA

Hotel
$88-$90 All Year

Phone: (662)210-2717
Address: Blvd Eusebio Kino 353 **Location:** 2.4 mi (4 km) ne on Mex 15. Located in a commercial area. **Facility:** 159 units. 153 one-bedroom standard units. 6 one-bedroom suites. 4 stories, interior/exterior corridors. **Parking:** on-site. **Amenities:** high-speed Internet, irons, hair dryers. **Pool(s):** outdoor. **Leisure Activities:** exercise room. **Guest Services:** valet and coin laundry, wireless Internet. **Business Services:** meeting rooms, business center. **Cards:** AX, MC, VI.

/ SOME UNITS

HOTEL BUGAMBILIA

Hotel
$52-$67 All Year

Phone: 662/289-1600
Address: Blvd Eusebio Kino 712 **Location:** 2.3 mi (3.8 km) ne on Mex 15. Located in a commercial area. **Facility:** 103 one-bedroom standard units. 1-3 stories (no elevator), exterior corridors. *Bath:* shower only. **Parking:** on-site. **Terms:** 3 day cancellation notice. **Pool(s):** heated outdoor. **Guest Services:** valet laundry, wireless Internet. **Business Services:** meeting rooms, business center. **Cards:** AX, MC, VI.

/ SOME UNITS

HOTEL FIESTA AMERICANA HERMOSILLO *Book great rates at AAA.com*

Hotel
$155-$191 All Year

Phone: (662)259-6000
Address: Blvd Eusebio Kino 369 **Location:** 2.7 mi (4.5 km) n on Mex 15. **Facility:** 221 one-bedroom standard units. 9 stories, interior corridors. **Parking:** on-site. **Terms:** cancellation fee imposed. **Amenities:** high-speed Internet (fee), safes, honor bars, irons, hair dryers. **Dining:** 2 restaurants, also, El Rincon, see separate listing, entertainment. **Pool(s):** outdoor. **Leisure Activities:** lighted tennis court, exercise room. **Guest Services:** valet laundry, wireless Internet. **Business Services:** conference facilities, business center. **Cards:** AX, DC, MC, VI. *(See color ad on insert)*

/ SOME UNITS

HOTEL PLAZA DEL SOL

Hotel
$40-$70 All Year

Phone: (662)215-5958
Address: Blvd Eusebio Kino #197 **Location:** 2.2 mi (3.6 km) ne on Mex 15. Located in a commercial area. **Facility:** 59 one-bedroom standard units, some with whirlpools. 5 stories, interior corridors. **Parking:** on-site. **Terms:** 3 day cancellation notice. **Amenities:** high-speed Internet. **Pool(s):** outdoor. **Guest Services:** valet laundry, wireless Internet. **Business Services:** meeting rooms. **Cards:** MC, VI.

/ SOME UNITS

WHERE TO DINE

EL RINCON

Mexican
$18-$27

Phone: 662/259-6000
Patrons who visit this high-end dining room can expect an extensive selection of prime Sonoran steaks cooked to order over a wood fire. Casual dress. **Bar:** Full bar. **Reservations:** accepted. **Hours:** 1 pm-midnight. **Address:** Blvd Eusebio Kino 369 **Location:** 2.7 mi (4.5 km) n on Mex 15; in Hotel Fiesta Americana Hermosillo. **Parking:** on-site. **Cards:** AX, MC, VI.

SONORA STEAK **Phone:** 662/210-0313

Steak
$12-$22

At Sonora Steak you'll find jumbo steaks cut from premium local beef, charcoal grilled to perfection "al carbon." The New York cut is particularly flavorful, and makes for a grand meal when accompanied by one of their tasty, decoratively prepared salads. Casual dress. **Bar:** Full bar. **Hours:** noon-1 am. Closed: 1/1, 12/24, 12/25; also Thurs, Fri & Holy Week. **Address:** Blvd Eusebio Kino 914 **Location:** On Mex 15; in Zona Hotelera. **Parking:** on-site. **Cards:** AX, MC, VI.

VIPS **Phone:** 662/212-7625

Mexican
$5-$9

Owned by Wal-Mart of Mexico and found in most major cities, the budget-friendly chain serves a good variety of Mexican and American dishes, including burgers, sandwiches, salads, spaghetti and enchiladas, as well as a fine selection of desserts. Casual dress. **Hours:** 7 am-11 pm. **Address:** Ave Rosales #116 **Location:** Jct aves Rosales and Serdan, just s. **Parking:** on-site. **Cards:** MC, VI.

VIPS **Phone:** 662/213-9189

Mexican
$5-$9

Owned by Wal-Mart of Mexico and found in most major cities, the budget-friendly chain serves a good variety of Mexican and American dishes, including burgers, sandwiches, salads, spaghetti and enchiladas, as well as a fine selection of desserts. Casual dress. **Hours:** 7 am-11 pm. **Address:** Oaseo Rio Sunora Sur #37. **Parking:** on-site. **Cards:** MC, VI.

LOS MOCHIS, SINALOA pop. 204,900

WHERE TO STAY

EL DORADO HOTEL Y MOTEL **Phone:** (668)815-1111

Hotel
$73-$112 All Year

Address: Ave Gabriel Leyva y H Valdez **Location:** 2.1 mi (3.5 km) w of Mex 15. Secure parking in a commercial area. **Facility:** 98 one-bedroom standard units. 2-3 stories, interior/exterior corridors. *Bath:* shower only. **Parking:** on-site. **Terms:** 8 day cancellation notice-fee imposed. **Pool(s):** outdoor. **Leisure Activities:** playground. **Guest Services:** valet laundry, wireless Internet. **Business Services:** meeting rooms. **Cards:** AX, MC, VI.

/ SOME UNITS

HOTEL SANTA ANITA **Phone:** 668/818-7046

Hotel
$131 All Year

Address: Ave Gabriel Leyva y Hidalgo **Location:** Downtown. **Facility:** 116 units. 115 one-bedroom standard units. 1 one-bedroom suite. 5 stories, interior corridors. *Bath:* shower only. **Parking:** on-site. **Terms:** 10 day cancellation notice-fee imposed. **Amenities:** hair dryers. **Dining:** restaurant, see separate listing. **Guest Services:** valet laundry, wireless Internet. **Business Services:** meeting rooms, business center. **Cards:** AX, MC, VI.

/ SOME UNITS

PLAZA INN HOTEL & CONVENTION CENTER **Phone:** (668)816-0800

Hotel
$90-$270 All Year

Address: Aves Gabriel Leyva y L Cardenas S/N **Location:** 0.3 mi (0.5 km) e. **Facility:** Meets AAA guest room security requirements. 123 units. 113 one-bedroom standard units. 10 one-bedroom suites, some with whirlpools. 5 stories, interior/exterior corridors. *Bath:* combo or shower only. **Parking:** on-site. **Amenities:** high-speed Internet, dual phone lines, voice mail, irons, hair dryers. *Some:* safes. **Dining:** Mr Owen's Restaurant & Bar, see separate listing. **Pool(s):** indoor. **Leisure Activities:** exercise room. **Guest Services:** valet laundry, wireless Internet. **Business Services:** conference facilities, business center. **Cards:** AX, MC, VI.

/ SOME UNITS

WHERE TO DINE

MR OWEN'S RESTAURANT & BAR **Phone:** 668/816-0800

Steak & Seafood
$10-$15

Although this place is decorated much like an American coffee shop, the service and cuisine it offers are more refined. In addition to a fine breakfast selection, food choices include a wide variety of steaks. At dinner, service is semi-formal. Casual dress. **Bar:** Full bar. **Reservations:** suggested, 11/1-3/31. **Hours:** 6 am-1 am. **Address:** Aves Gabriel Leyva y L Cardenas S/N **Location:** 0.3 mi (0.5 km) e; in Plaza Inn Hotel & Convention Center. **Parking:** on-site. **Cards:** AX, MC, VI.

RESTAURANTE SANTA ANITA **Phone:** 668/818-7046

International
$8-$25

Mexican charm prevails at this hotel restaurant. The food represents a good selection of International cuisine, as well as some pleasing Mexican selections. Casual dress. Entertainment. **Bar:** Full bar. **Reservations:** accepted. **Hours:** 7 am-11 pm. **Address:** Ave Gabriel Leyva & Hidalgo **Location:** Downtown; in Hotel Santa Anita. **Parking:** on-site. **Cards:** AX, DC, MC, VI.

VIPS **Phone:** 668/815-5148

Mexican
$5-$9

Owned by Wal-Mart of Mexico and found in most major cities, the budget-friendly chain serves a good variety of Mexican and American dishes, including burgers, sandwiches, salads, spaghetti and enchiladas, as well as a fine selection of desserts. Casual dress. **Hours:** 7 am-11 pm. **Address:** Blvd Jiquil Pan 112 PTE **Location:** Center. **Parking:** on-site. **Cards:** MC, VI.

NAVOJOA, SONORA pop. 140,650

WHERE TO STAY

BEST WESTERN HOTEL DEL RIO **Phone:** 642/425-5300

Hotel
$70-$83 All Year

Address: Pesqueira Norte S/N **Location:** On Mex 15; at south end of bridge over Rio Mayo. **Facility:** Meets AAA guest room security requirements. 77 units. 74 one- and 1 two-bedroom standard units. 2 one-bedroom suites. 2 stories (no elevator), exterior corridors. *Bath:* shower only. **Parking:** on-site. **Terms:** 7 day cancellation notice. **Amenities:** voice mail, hair dryers. **Pool(s):** outdoor. **Leisure Activities:** sauna, tennis privileges. **Guest Services:** valet laundry, airport transportation (fee)-Obregon Airport, wireless Internet. **Business Services:** meeting rooms, business center. **Cards:** AX, DS, MC, VI.

FEE / SOME UNITS

AAA Benefit:
Members save up to 20%, plus 10% bonus points with rewards program.

MOTEL DEL MAYO **Phone:** 642/422-6828

Hotel
$52-$98 All Year

Address: Otero y Jimenez **Location:** Just s of jct Mex 15 and Son 13 to Otero y Jimenez, just e. **Facility:** Meets AAA guest room security requirements. 48 units. 45 one-bedroom standard units, some with efficiencies and/or whirlpools. 3 one-bedroom suites with efficiencies. 2 stories, exterior corridors. *Bath:* combo or shower only. **Parking:** on-site. **Terms:** 7 day cancellation notice. **Amenities:** video library, DVD players, high-speed Internet. *Some:* hair dryers. **Pool(s):** heated outdoor. **Leisure Activities:** whirlpool, exercise room. **Guest Services:** valet laundry, area transportation (fee), wireless Internet. **Business Services:** meeting rooms, business center. **Cards:** AX, MC, VI.

FEE / SOME UNITS

WHERE TO DINE

TIP'S RESTAURANTE **Phone:** 642/422-9028

Mexican
$6-$10

Although it resembles a US coffee shop, the restaurant offers mostly Mexican cuisine. Patrons find all the traditional dishes, such as enchiladas, tacos and burritos. Try the carne adobada plate; it's exceptional. Casual dress. **Bar:** Beer only. **Hours:** 7 am-11 pm. Closed: 1/1, 12/25. **Address:** Pesquiera y J O de Dominguez **Location:** On Mex 15 through town; 2 blks s of Alamos turn off; center. **Parking:** on-site. **Cards:** DC, MC, VI.

POSADA BARRANCA, CHIHUAHUA pop. 1,000

WHERE TO STAY

HOTEL POSADA BARRANCA MIRADOR **Phone:** (668)818-7046

Hotel
$250-$295 All Year

Address: Estacion Posada Barranca **Location:** Just s of Posada Barranca Train Station. **Facility:** 65 one-bedroom standard units. 3 stories, exterior corridors. *Bath:* shower only. **Parking:** on-site. **Terms:** 5 day cancellation notice. **Leisure Activities:** hiking trails. *Fee:* horseback riding. **Guest Services:** area transportation. **Business Services:** meeting rooms. **Cards:** AX, MC, VI.

RANCHO POSADA BARRANCA **Phone:** 668/818-7046

Hotel
$217 All Year

Address: Estacion Posada Barranca **Location:** Just n of Posada Barranca Train Station. **Facility:** 23 one-bedroom standard units. 2 stories, exterior corridors. *Bath:* shower only. **Parking:** on-site. **Terms:** 5 day cancellation notice-fee imposed. **Leisure Activities:** hiking trails. *Fee:* bicycles, horseback riding. **Business Services:** conference facilities, business center. **Cards:** AX, MC, VI.

PUERTO PENASCO, SONORA pop. 31,157

WHERE TO STAY

HOTEL PENASCO DEL SOL **Phone:** 638/383-0300

Hotel
$119-$259 All Year

Address: Paseo Las Glorias #1 **Location:** Oceanfront. Center; at the west end of 13th St. **Facility:** Meets AAA guest room security requirements. Smoke free premises. 203 units. 157 one-bedroom standard units. 44 one- and 2 three-bedroom suites, some with whirlpools. 5 stories, exterior corridors. *Bath:* combo or shower only. **Parking:** on-site. **Terms:** check-in 4 pm, cancellation fee imposed. **Amenities:** safes, irons, hair dryers. **Dining:** Miguel's, see separate listing. **Pool(s):** 2 outdoor. **Leisure Activities:** whirlpool. **Guest Services:** valet laundry, wireless Internet. **Business Services:** meeting rooms. **Cards:** AX, MC, VI.

D / SOME UNITS

HOTEL PLAYA BONITA **Phone:** 638/383-2586

Hotel
$95-$300 All Year

Address: Paseo Balboa #100 **Location:** Oceanfront. Center; east end of Sandy Beach. Located on Playa Bonita. **Facility:** 124 units. 118 one-bedroom standard units, some with efficiencies and/or whirlpools. 4 one- and 2 two-bedroom suites, some with efficiencies. 4 stories, interior corridors. *Bath:* combo or shower only. **Parking:** on-site. **Amenities:** irons, hair dryers. **Pool(s):** 2 heated outdoor. **Leisure Activities:** whirlpool. **Guest Services:** wireless Internet. **Business Services:** PC (fee). **Cards:** AX, MC, VI.

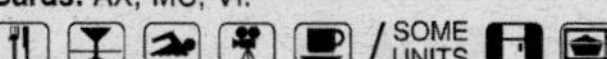

HOTEL PLAYA INN — **Phone:** 638/383-0250

Hotel
$70-$125 All Year

Address: Calle Sinaloa #18 **Location:** Jct Juarez Blvd, 0.5 mi (0.8 km) e on Fremont Blvd, just s; center. **Facility:** 80 units. 58 one-bedroom standard units. 22 one-bedroom suites with efficiencies (no utensils). 2 stories (no elevator), exterior corridors. *Bath:* shower only. **Parking:** on-site. **Terms:** check-in 4 pm. **Amenities:** hair dryers. *Some:* irons. **Pool(s):** outdoor. **Leisure Activities:** whirlpool. **Guest Services:** wireless Internet. **Business Services:** business center. **Cards:** AX, DC, MC, VI.

/ SOME UNITS

HOTEL SENORIAL — **Phone:** 638/383-2120

Hotel
$45-$95 All Year

Address: Calle Trece #81 **Location:** Center; just w of Blvd Benito Juarez. **Facility:** 70 one-bedroom standard units. 2 stories (no elevator), exterior corridors. *Bath:* shower only. **Parking:** on-site. **Pool(s):** outdoor. **Guest Services:** coin laundry, wireless Internet. **Cards:** DC, DS, MC, VI.

LAS PALOMAS BEACH & GOLF RESORT — *Book great rates at AAA.com* — **Phone:** (638)108-1000

Resort Condominium
$148-$718 All Year

Address: Blvd Costero #150 Col Sandy Beach **Location:** Oceanfront. Jct Blvd SG Brown, 1.2 mi (2 km) w on Cholla Blvd, then 0.6 mi (1 km) s. **Facility:** Upscale furnishings and appointments in the luxurious rooms invite you to settle in, relax and enjoy the beautiful beach along the Sea of Cortez. Meets AAA guest room security requirements. 377 units. 121 one-, 164 two- and 92 three-bedroom suites with efficiencies. 11-12 stories, exterior corridors. *Bath:* combo or shower only. **Parking:** on-site. **Terms:** check-in 4 pm. **Amenities:** DVD players, high-speed Internet, voice mail, irons, hair dryers. **Dining:** 2 restaurants, also, Citron Fine Cuisine, La Maria Bistro, see separate listings. **Pool(s):** 2 outdoor, 2 heated outdoor. **Leisure Activities:** whirlpools, waterslide, 2 lazy rivers, putting green, exercise room, volleyball. *Fee:* golf-18 holes. **Guest Services:** complimentary laundry, wireless Internet. **Business Services:** conference facilities, business center. **Cards:** AX, MC, VI.

/ SOME UNITS

MAYAN PALACE WYNDHAM PUERTO PENASCO — **Phone:** (638)383-0400

Resort Hotel
$370-$630 All Year

Address: KM 24 Carr Puerto Penasco Caborca **Location:** Oceanfront. Jct Sonora Hwy 8, 14.4 mi (24 km) e, 3.4 mi (5.7 km). **Facility:** In addition to well-appointed rooms and striking public areas, this luxury resort features a really fine beach. Meets AAA guest room security requirements. 258 units. 96 one-bedroom standard units. 162 one-bedroom suites with efficiencies. 3-8 stories, interior corridors. **Parking:** on-site and valet. **Terms:** check-in 5 pm, 2-7 night minimum stay - seasonal and/or weekends, 21 day cancellation notice-fee imposed. **Amenities:** voice mail, safes, hair dryers. *Some:* DVD players (fee), irons. **Pool(s):** heated outdoor, heated indoor. **Leisure Activities:** saunas, steamrooms, putting green, exercise room, spa, volleyball, game room. *Fee:* boats, scuba diving, snorkeling, fishing, charter fishing, golf-18 holes, 3 lighted tennis courts. **Guest Services:** valet and coin laundry, wireless Internet. **Business Services:** PC. **Cards:** AX, MC, VI.

/ SOME UNITS

PRINCESA DE PENASCO — **Phone:** 638/382-8020

Condominium
$138-$425 All Year

Address: Blvd Costero KM 3.7 S/N, Camina a la Cho **Location:** Oceanfront. Jct blvds Benito Juarez and SG Brown, 3.7 mi (5.9 km) w on Blvd SG Brown through roundabout at Pemex via Cholla Bay Rd, then just sw. **Facility:** One of the first condos on Sandy Beach, built in 2001, the older property has spacious units, attractive furnishings and some master baths with windows overlooking the beach. Smoke free premises. 166 units. 26 one-, 126 two- and 14 three-bedroom suites with efficiencies. 6 stories, exterior corridors. *Bath:* combo or shower only. **Parking:** on-site. **Terms:** check-in 4 pm, 2-3 night minimum stay, 10 day cancellation notice-fee imposed. **Amenities:** irons. *Some:* DVD players, hair dryers. **Pool(s):** outdoor, 2 heated outdoor. **Leisure Activities:** whirlpools, exercise room, volleyball. **Guest Services:** complimentary laundry, wireless Internet. **Cards:** MC, VI.

/ SOME UNITS

SONORAN SEA RESORT — **Phone:** 638/382-8253

Condominium
$129-$380 All Year

Address: Camino de la Cholla KM 3.7 S/N **Location:** Oceanfront. Jct Blvd S G Brown and Cholla Bay Rd, 2.2 mi (3.7 km) w, follow signs. Located on Sandy Beach. **Facility:** Set on a great stretch of beach, amenities are bountiful at the luxury, vacation resort; each unit sports a unique decor. 158 units. 59 one-, 68 two- and 31 three-bedroom suites with kitchens, some with whirlpools. 10 stories, exterior corridors. **Parking:** on-site. **Terms:** check-in 4 pm. **Amenities:** DVD players, CD players, irons, hair dryers. **Pool(s):** outdoor, heated outdoor. **Leisure Activities:** whirlpools, snorkeling, tennis court, exercise room. **Guest Services:** complimentary laundry, wireless Internet. **Business Services:** meeting rooms, PC. **Cards:** MC, VI.

/ SOME UNITS

SONORAN SKY RESORT — **Phone:** 638/108-2100

Condominium
$161-$412 All Year

Address: Camino Costero #600 Col Ferr Playa **Location:** Oceanfront. Jct Blvd SG Brown, 1.2 mi (2 km) w on Cholla Blvd, 0.8 mi (1.1 km) s through roundabout, then just sw. **Facility:** Opened in December 2007, the facilities are stunning and offer upscale, attractive guest units with up-to-date kitchens, some with a wine fridge. Designated smoking area. 50 units. 19 one-, 18 two- and 13 three-bedroom suites with efficiencies, some with whirlpools. 14 stories, exterior corridors. *Bath:* combo or shower only. **Parking:** on-site. **Terms:** check-in 4 pm, 2-3 night minimum stay, 14 day cancellation notice-fee imposed. **Amenities:** DVD players, irons. *Some:* voice mail. **Pool(s):** 3 outdoor, heated outdoor. **Leisure Activities:** whirlpools, playground, exercise room, spa. **Guest Services:** complimentary laundry, wireless Internet. **Business Services:** meeting rooms, business center. **Cards:** MC, VI.

VCR

SONORAN SPA RESORT

Condominium
$115-$318 All Year

Phone: 638/382-8060

Address: Camino de la Cholla KM 3.7 S/N **Location:** Oceanfront. Jct Blvd S G Brown and Cholla Bay Rd, 2.2 mi (3.7 km) w, follow signs. Located on Sandy Beach. **Facility:** A sister property to the adjacent Sonoran Sea Resort, the well-appointed, beachside accommodations offer ample amenities including pools and a gym. 145 units. 48 one-, 82 two- and 15 three-bedroom suites with kitchens. 8 stories, interior corridors. *Bath:* combo or shower only. **Parking:** on-site. **Terms:** check-in 4 pm. **Amenities:** video library, DVD players, irons, hair dryers. **Dining:** Sonoran Grill Restaurant & Bar, see separate listing. **Pool(s):** outdoor, heated outdoor. **Leisure Activities:** whirlpool, snorkeling, tennis court, exercise room, spa, horseshoes. **Guest Services:** complimentary laundry, wireless Internet. **Business Services:** PC. **Cards:** MC, VI.

D / SOME UNITS

SONORAN SUN RESORT

Condominium
$142-$390 All Year

Phone: 638/383-0200

Address: Camino de la Cholla KM 3.7 S/N **Location:** Oceanfront. Jct Blvd SG Brown and Cholla Bay Rd, 2.7 mi (4 km) w, follow signs. **Facility:** Opened in 2005, the rooms, including some five-bedroom units, are gorgeous with attractive marble baths and ocean views from the patio or balcony. 180 units. 52 one-, 105 two- and 23 three-bedroom suites with efficiencies. 10 stories, exterior corridors. **Parking:** on-site. **Terms:** check-in 4 pm. **Amenities:** DVD players. *Some:* irons, hair dryers. **Pool(s):** outdoor, heated outdoor. **Leisure Activities:** whirlpools, lighted tennis court, exercise room. **Guest Services:** complimentary laundry, wireless Internet. **Cards:** MC, VI.

D / SOME UNITS

WHERE TO DINE

CASA DEL CAPITAN

Seafood
$9-$18

Phone: 638/383-5698

Marvelous ocean and bay views abound from the setting atop a hill overlooking the harbor. The abundant local seafood is the specialty here, and it's prepared in the Mexican style. Bacon-wrapped shrimp is memorable. Casual dress. **Bar:** Full bar. **Reservations:** accepted. **Hours:** 10 am-10 pm. **Address:** Lote 1 y 2 Fracc del Cerro **Location:** Center; on hill above Old Port. **Parking:** on-site. **Cards:** MC, VI.

CHANGO'S RESTAURANT & BAR

AAA

American
$7-$14

Phone: 638/382-8648

Resembling a tiki hut on the beach, the restaurant entices patrons with nice breezes under its palapa roof. Selections including peanut butter and jelly, mac 'n' cheese, hearty burgers and chicken dinners appeal to guests from child to adult. The bar tempts with frozen margaritas, and live music is offered Thursday through Saturday nights. Casual dress. **Bar:** Full bar. **Hours:** 11:30 am-10 pm, Sat & Sun from 7:30 am. Closed: Tues. **Address:** Camino de la Cholla KM 3.7 S/N **Location:** Jct Blvd SG Brown and Cholla Bay Rd, 2.2 mi (3.7 km) w, just sw. **Parking:** on-site. **Cards:** MC, VI.

CITRON FINE CUISINE

French
$16-$54

Phone: 638/108-1000

A charming lounge with fieldstone walls and comfortable chairs welcomes the diner here. Attentive and polished servers lend guidance through a meal of classic dishes such as escargots or veal. Among innovative choices are ratatouille of mushrooms and zucchini risotto. Dressy casual. **Bar:** Full bar. **Reservations:** suggested. **Hours:** 7 am-11 pm. **Address:** Blvd Costero #150, Col Sandy Beach **Location:** Jct Blvd SG Brown, 1.2 mi (2 km) w on Cholla Blvd, then 0.6 mi (1 km) s; in Las Palomas Beach & Golf Resort. **Parking:** on-site. **Cards:** AX, MC, VI.

CALL

HACIENDA LAS FUENTES

Mexican
$9-$19

Phone: 638/388-0056

The charming building is reminiscent of an old hacienda, with bodega brick ceilings and a large fountain. The food—from crisp salads to classics such as chicken or shrimp fajitas or beef enchiladas—is freshly prepared. Casual dress. **Bar:** Full bar. **Reservations:** accepted. **Hours:** noon-10 pm, Fri & Sat-11 pm. **Address:** Blvd Fremont y Calle Sinaloa S/N **Location:** Jct Blvd B Juarez, 0.6 mi (1 km) e. **Parking:** on-site. **Cards:** MC, VI.

LA MARIA BISTRO

Continental
$14-$30

Phone: 638/108-1000

This bistro has a casually elegant setting, an expertly trained staff and food that will entice your taste buds. Choose from such soups as light zucchini flower cream soup to minestrone—and if selection is difficult, the chef offers tastings of them all. Pasta dishes like mushroom ravioli with clams in orange butter or grilled shrimp tamarind served with potato have such rich flavors, it is indeed hard to pick one. Casual dress. **Bar:** Full bar. **Reservations:** suggested. **Hours:** 7 am-11, noon-4 & 5-11 pm. **Address:** Blvd Costero #150 Col Sandy Beach **Location:** Jct Blvd SG Brown, 1.2 mi (2 km) w on Cholla Blvd, then 0.6 mi (1 km) s; in Las Palomas Beach & Golf Resort. **Parking:** on-site. **Cards:** AX, MC, VI.

LAPA-LAPA RESTAURANT BAR

Mexican
$10-$18

Phone: 638/388-0599

Located upstairs over a curio shop, the restaurant's open doors and balcony overlooking a wharf to the Sea of Cortez invite you to relax and enjoy good food and expansive views. Fresh seafood is prepared in a variety of sauces highlighting the region. The shrimp tamarind has a rich, deeply flavored sauce, and the flounder in mango is scrumptious. Casual dress. **Bar:** Full bar. **Reservations:** accepted. **Hours:** 10 am-11 pm. Closed: 1/1, 12/25. **Address:** Malecon Kino S/N Esq Zaragoza **Location:** On wharf at Old Port; center. **Parking:** street. **Cards:** MC, VI.

THE LIGHTHOUSE RESTAURANT BAR

International
$12-$18

Phone: 638/383-2389

Patrons can dine by rock 'n' roll or jazz music at the lively eatery and lounge, which overlooks the town and the harbor. Local seafood and beef are prepared in a variety of International styles. Casual dress. **Bar:** Full bar. **Reservations:** accepted. **Hours:** 4 pm-10 pm; to 9 pm in summer. Closed: 12/25; also Mon 7/4-9/5. **Address:** Fracc del Cerro Lotes 2 y 2Bis **Location:** Center; on top of hill at Old Port. **Parking:** on-site. **Cards:** MC, VI.

MAX'S CAFE — **Phone:** 638/383-1011

American
$5-$14

A pleasant, informal atmosphere prevails at the cafe, which serves a great breakfast burrito and a fine selection of espressos, coffee and lattes. Lunch guests can choose from a good selection of sandwiches and a daily soup special. Wireless internet access allows patrons to log on while enjoying a meal. Casual dress. **Bar:** Full bar. **Reservations:** accepted. **Hours:** 8 am-10 pm. Closed: 12/25. **Address:** Calle Trece #15 **Location:** Center; across from Hotel Penasco del Sol. **Parking:** on-site.

MIGUEL'S — **Phone:** 638/383-0300

Mexican
$8-$18

Overlooking the pool area, the restaurant lays out a sumptuous breakfast buffet and also serves hearty lunches and dinners with wine and fine foods. The chef provides plates that look as lovely as they taste wonderful. Local and American dishes, including shrimp enchiladas and margarita pizza, share space on the menu. Casual dress. **Bar:** Full bar. **Reservations:** accepted. **Hours:** 7 am-11 pm. **Address:** Paseo Las Glorias #1 **Location:** Center; at west end of 13th St; in Hotel Penasco del Sol. **Parking:** on-site. **Cards:** MC, VI.

CALL

PORTOFINO ITALIAN RESTAURANT & BAR — **Phone:** 638/383-6838

Italian
$13-$27

This restaurant comes alive in the evening, serving succulent local seafood prepared Italian style. Casual dress. **Bar:** Full bar. **Reservations:** accepted. **Hours:** 11 am-10 pm, Fri & Sat-11 pm. **Address:** Malecon Kino y 1 de Junio S/N **Location:** Center; on the Malecon Kino. **Parking:** street. **Cards:** MC, VI.

THE REEF RESTAURANT & PIANO BAR — **Phone:** 638/383-0656

Continental
$10-$27

Directly on the ocean in Sandy Beach, the restaurant's huge windows offer stunning views of the Sea of Cortez. Chef Reynoso, who has cooked for queens and popes, delights patrons with extravagant presentations of all the dishes. Casual dress. **Bar:** Full bar. **Reservations:** accepted. **Hours:** 8 am-10:30 pm. Closed: 12/25. **Address:** Camino a la Cholla KM 7.5 **Location:** Jct Mex 8 and La Cholla Rd, 2.3 mi (3.7 km) w, then 0.6 mi (1 km) s at sign. **Parking:** on-site. **Cards:** MC, VI.

The following restaurant has not been evaluated by AAA but is listed for your information only.

SONORAN GRILL RESTAURANT & BAR — **Phone:** 638/382-8089

fyi

Not evaluated. The eatery's owners are expatriate Americans and the cuisine is a mixture of the best of Mexican and American food. **Address:** Camino de la Cholla KM 3.7 S/N **Location:** Jct Blvd S G Brown and Cholla Bay Rd, 2.2 mi (3.7 km) w, follow signs; in Sonoran Spa Resort.

SAN CARLOS, SONORA pop. 4,000

WHERE TO STAY

BEST WESTERN HACIENDA TETA KAWI — **Phone:** (622)226-0248

Hotel
$62-$95 All Year

Address: Blvd M F Beltrones KM 9.5 **Location:** 6.4 mi (10.7 km) nw on Mex 15, 5.6 mi (9.3 km) w on San Carlos turn-off. Located across from the beach. **Facility:** 22 one-bedroom standard units. 3 stories (no elevator), exterior corridors. *Bath:* shower only. **Parking:** on-site. **Terms:** 3 day cancellation notice. **Amenities:** high-speed Internet, hair dryers. **Pool(s):** outdoor. **Guest Services:** wireless Internet. **Cards:** AX, DC, DS, JC, MC, VI.

/ SOME UNITS

AAA Benefit:
Members save up to 20%, plus 10% bonus points with rewards program.

WHERE TO DINE

The following restaurants have not been evaluated by AAA but are listed for your information only.

BLACKIE'S RESTAURANT & BAR — **Phone:** 622/226-1525

fyi

Not evaluated. Just the place for a fun evening; dine on sumptuous local seafood, chicken, or fine beef cuts, or try some of the international flavors on the menu. You'll also find a good selection of cocktails, wine and beer to liven up your meal. **Address:** Blvd M F Beltrones KM 10.3 S/N **Location:** 6.4 mi (10.7 km) nw on Mex 15, 6.2 mi (10.3 km) w on San Carlos turn-off.

CHARLY'S ROCK — **Phone:** 622/226-1805

fyi

Not evaluated. This quaint establishment provides a spectacular view of the sea. Enjoy grilled lobster in season, seafood salads, soups and fresh fish prepared in several ways. **Address:** Blvd M F Beltrones KM 9 **Location:** 6.4 mi (10.7 km) nw on Mex 15, 5.6 mi (9.3 km) w on San Carlos turn-off.

NORTHEASTERN MEXICO

MATAMOROS, TAMAULIPAS pop. 418,141

WHERE TO DINE

SANBORN'S

Regional Mexican

$8-$28

Phone: 868/817-3452

Restaurants in the casual chain, which includes more than 100 locations throughout Mexico, offer a good selection of American-style sandwiches, salads, soups and both Mexican and American entrees. The selection of desserts is impressive. Casual dress. **Bar:** Full bar. **Hours:** 7 am-10 pm, Fri-Sun to 1 am. **Address:** Ave Pedro Cardenas Gonzales No 10 **Location:** In front of Plaza Fiesta, just off Ave Longoria. **Parking:** on-site. **Cards:** AX, MC, VI.

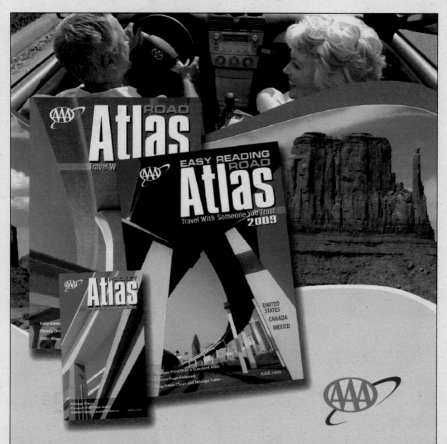

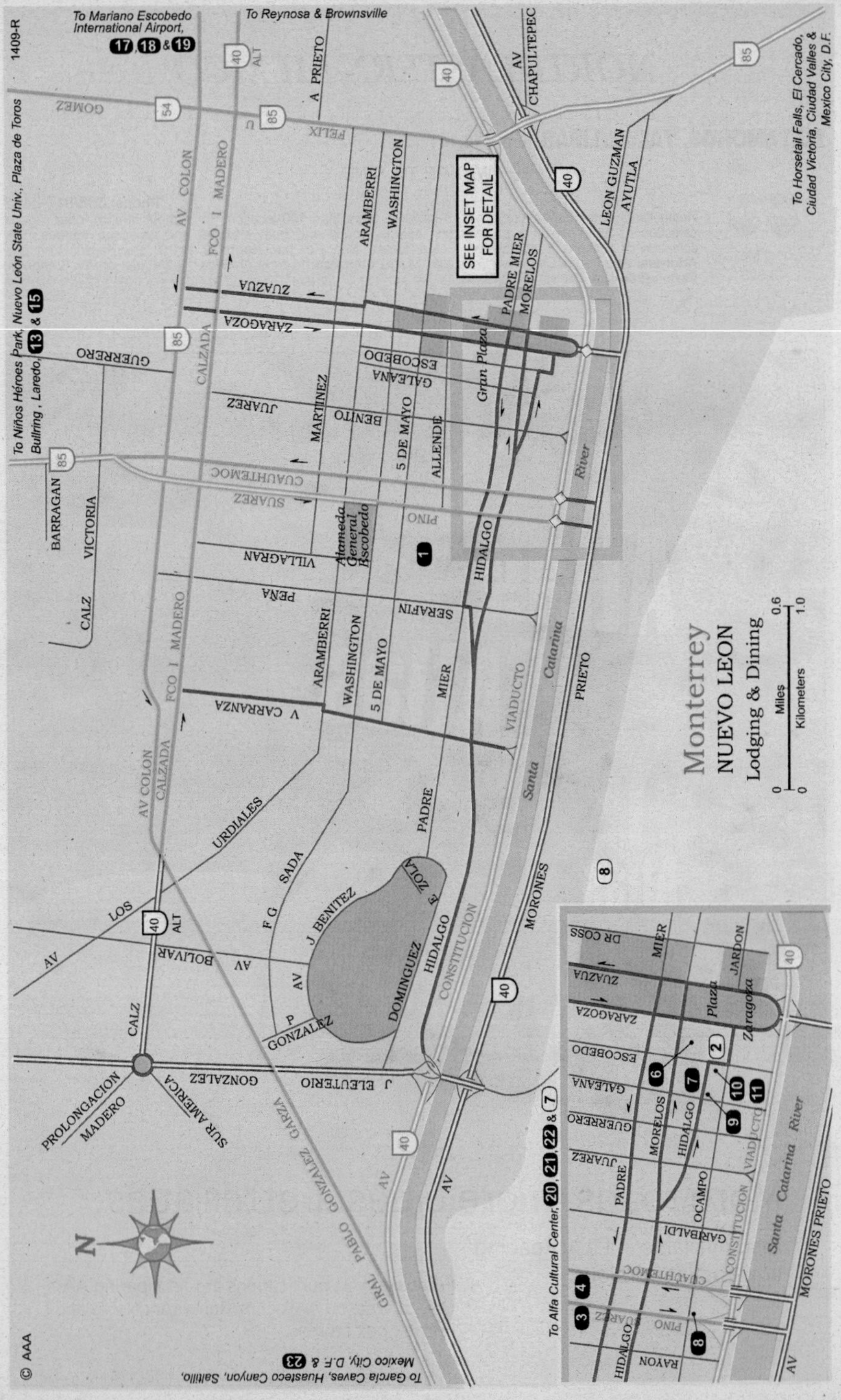

Monterrey
NUEVO LEON
Lodging & Dining

Miles 0 0.6
Kilometers 0 1.0

1409-R

© AAA

SEE INSET MAP FOR DETAIL

To Mariano Escobedo International Airport, 17, 18 & 19

To Reynosa & Brownsville

To Niños Héroes Park, Nuevo León State Univ., Plaza de Toros Bullring, Laredo, 13 & 15

To Horsetail Falls, El Cercado, Ciudad Victoria, Ciudad Valles & Mexico City, D.F.

To García Caves, Huasteco Canyon, Saltillo, Mexico City, D.F. & 23

To Alfa Cultural Center, 20, 21, 22 & 7

GOMEZ
FELIX U
A PRIETO
AV COLON
FCO I MADERO
ZUAZUA
ZARAGOZA
GUERRERO
CALZADA
ESCOBEDO
GALEANA
JUAREZ
BENITO
MARTINEZ
ARAMBERRI
WASHINGTON
5 DE MAYO
ALLENDE
BARRAGAN
VICTORIA
CUAUHTEMOC
SUAREZ
PINO
Alameda General Escobedo
VILLAGRAN
PEÑA
SERAFIN
CALZ
HIDALGO
Gran Plaza
PADRE MIER
MORELOS
AV CHAPULTEPEC
LEON GUZMAN
AYUTLA
River
Santa Catarina
VIADUCTO
PRIETO
MIER
V CARRANZA
PADRE
AV COLON CALZADA
FCO I MADERO
URDIALES
AV LOS
SADA
F G
J BENITEZ
ZOLA
E
AV BOLIVAR
AV
P GONZALEZ
DOMINGUEZ
HIDALGO
CONSTITUCION
MORONES
CALZ
PROLONGACION MADERO
SUR AMERICA
GONZALEZ
J ELEUTERIO
GRAL PABLO GONZALEZ GARZA
AV
N

DR COSS
MIER
JARDON
ZUAZUA
ZARAGOZA
Plaza Zaragoza
ESCOBEDO
GALEANA
GUERRERO
JUAREZ
PADRE
MORELOS
HIDALGO
OCAMPO
GARIBALDI
CUAUHTEMOC
SUAREZ
PINO
HIDALGO
RAYON
VIADUCTO
CONSTITUCION
Santa Catarina River
MORONES PRIETO
AV

Airport Accommodations

Map Page	OA	GENERAL MARIANO ESCOBEDO	Diamond Rated	High Season	Page
17 / p. 500		Courtyard by Marriott Monterrey Aeropuerto, 0.9 mi (1.5 km) n of main terminal entrance	◆◆◆	$147-$158	502
19 / p. 500		Fairfield Inn by Marriott, 1.5 km n of main terminal entrance	◆◆	$97	502
18 / p. 500	AAA	**Hampton Inn Monterrey Aeropuerto, 0.9 mi (1.5 km) n of main terminal entrance**	◆◆◆	$90-$139	503

Monterrey

This index helps you "spot" where approved lodgings and restaurants are located on the corresponding detailed maps. Lodging daily rate range is for comparison only and show the property's high season. Restaurant rate range is a combination of lunch and/or dinner. Turn to the listing page for more detailed rate information and consult display ads for special promotions.

MONTERREY

Map Page	OA	Lodgings	Diamond Rated	High Season	Page
1 / p. 500		Hampton Inn Monterrey Galerias Obispado	◆◆◆	$112-$130	503
3 / p. 500		Safi Monterrey	◆◆◆	$90-$160	504
4 / p. 500		Days Inn Alameda-Monterrey	◆◆	$80-$150	502
6 / p. 500		Hotel Howard Johnson Macroplaza Monterrey	◆◆	$110-$239	503
7 / p. 500	AAA	**Fiesta Americana Centro Monterrey** - see color ad on insert	◆◆◆	$134-$232	502
8 / p. 500	AAA	**Fiesta Inn Centro** - see color ad on insert	◆◆◆	$120	502
9 / p. 500	AAA	**Sheraton Ambassador Monterrey Hotel**	◆◆◆◆	$99-$249	504
10 / p. 500		Gran Hotel Ancira	◆◆◆	$105-$140	503
11 / p. 500		Crowne Plaza Monterrey	◆◆◆	$110-$175	502
13 / p. 500		Best Western Royal Courts	◆◆	$70-$110	502
15 / p. 500	AAA	**Hampton Inn & Suites Monterrey Norte**	◆◆◆	$75-$95	503
17 / p. 500		Courtyard by Marriott Monterrey Aeropuerto	◆◆◆	$147-$158	502
18 / p. 500	AAA	**Hampton Inn Monterrey Aeropuerto**	◆◆◆	$90-$139	503
19 / p. 500		Fairfield Inn by Marriott	◆◆	$97	502
20 / p. 500		Radisson Hotel Casa Grande	◆◆◆◆	$88-$200	504
21 / p. 500		Holiday Inn Express Galerias-San Jeronimo	◆◆◆	$106-$135	503
22 / p. 500		Hotel Quinta Real Monterrey - see color ad p 8	◆◆◆◆	$170-$270	504
23 / p. 500	AAA	**Presidente InterContinental Monterrey**	◆◆◆◆	$277-$330	504

Map Page	OA	Restaurants	Diamond Rated	Cuisine	Meal Range	Page
2 / p. 500		Luisiana Restaurant	◆◆◆	Continental	$18-$40	505
7 / p. 500		Wall St. Steakhouse	◆◆◆	Regional Steak & Seafood	$15-$45	506
8 / p. 500		Los Arcos	◆◆	Regional Seafood	$10-$25	504

MONTERREY, NUEVO LEON pop. 110,997 (See map and index starting on p. 500)

WHERE TO STAY

BEST WESTERN ROYAL COURTS Phone: (81)8305-1900 13

Hotel
$70-$110 All Year

Address: Ave Universidad 314 **Location:** On Mex 85, 5.1 mi (8.5 km) s of toll road to Nuevo Laredo; on northern city outskirts. Located in a busy commercial area. **Facility:** 82 one-bedroom standard units. 2-3 stories (no elevator), exterior corridors. *Bath:* shower only. **Parking:** on-site. **Terms:** 3 day cancellation notice. **Amenities:** safes, irons, hair dryers. **Pool(s):** heated outdoor. **Guest Services:** valet laundry, area transportation, wireless Internet. **Business Services:** meeting rooms, business center. **Cards:** AX, MC, VI.

/ SOME UNITS

AAA Benefit: Members save up to 20%, plus 10% bonus points with rewards program.

COURTYARD BY MARRIOTT MONTERREY AEROPUERTO Phone: (81)8196-7900 17

Hotel
$147-$158 All Year

Address: Carr Miguel Aleman KM 23.8 **Location:** At entrance to General Mariano Escobedo International Airport. **Facility:** Smoke free premises. 205 units. 197 one-bedroom standard units. 8 one-bedroom suites. 5 stories, interior corridors. *Bath:* combo or shower only. **Parking:** on-site. **Terms:** cancellation fee imposed. **Amenities:** high-speed Internet, dual phone lines, voice mail, irons, hair dryers. **Pool(s):** outdoor. **Leisure Activities:** exercise room. **Guest Services:** valet and coin laundry, area transportation, wireless Internet. **Business Services:** meeting rooms, business center. **Cards:** AX, CB, DC, MC, VI.

S D / SOME UNITS 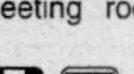

AAA Benefit: Members save a minimum 5% off the best available rate.

CROWNE PLAZA MONTERREY *Book at AAA.com* Phone: (81)8319-6000 11

Hotel
$110-$175 All Year

Address: Ave Constitution Ote 300 **Location:** Just w of Plaza Hidalgo. Located adjacent to downtown historic center. **Facility:** Meets AAA guest room security requirements. 403 units. 398 one-bedroom standard units. 5 one-bedroom suites. 15 stories, interior corridors. **Parking:** on-site (fee) and valet. **Amenities:** video games (fee), high-speed Internet, dual phone lines, voice mail, safes, honor bars, irons, hair dryers. **Pool(s):** heated indoor. **Leisure Activities:** sauna, whirlpool, exercise room. *Fee:* lighted tennis court, massage. **Guest Services:** valet laundry, wireless Internet. **Business Services:** conference facilities, business center. **Cards:** AX, DC, MC, VI.

24 S D / SOME UNITS

DAYS INN ALAMEDA-MONTERREY *Book at AAA.com* Phone: (81)8150-7100 4

Hotel
$80-$150 All Year

Address: Ave Pino Suarez 343 Sur Col Centro **Location:** On Ave Pino Suarez, jct 5 de Mayo. **Facility:** 70 units. 68 one-bedroom standard units. 2 one-bedroom suites. 5 stories, interior corridors. **Parking:** on-site. **Leisure Activities:** exercise room. **Guest Services:** valet laundry. **Business Services:** meeting rooms, business center. **Cards:** AX, MC, VI.

S D / SOME UNITS

FAIRFIELD INN BY MARRIOTT Phone: (81)8196-8900 19

Hotel
$97 All Year

Address: Ave Rogelio Gonzalez Caballero #150 **Location:** At entrance to General Mariano Escobedo International Airport on Carr Miguel Aleman. **Facility:** Smoke free premises. 206 one-bedroom standard units. 3 stories, interior corridors. *Bath:* combo or shower only. **Parking:** on-site. **Amenities:** high-speed Internet, voice mail, irons. **Pool(s):** outdoor. **Leisure Activities:** exercise room. **Guest Services:** valet laundry, area transportation, wireless Internet. **Business Services:** business center. **Cards:** AX, CB, DC, DS, MC, VI.

S D / SOME UNITS

AAA Benefit: Members save a minimum 5% off the best available rate.

FIESTA AMERICANA CENTRO MONTERREY Phone: (81)8319-0900 7

Hotel
$134-$232 All Year

Address: Corregidora 519 Zona Rosa **Location:** In downtown historic Zona Rosa. **Facility:** Meets AAA guest room security requirements. 207 units. 189 one-bedroom standard units. 18 one-bedroom suites. 13 stories, interior corridors. **Parking:** on-site (fee). **Terms:** cancellation fee imposed. **Amenities:** video games (fee), high-speed Internet, voice mail, safes, honor bars, irons, hair dryers. **Dining:** entertainment. **Pool(s):** heated indoor. **Leisure Activities:** exercise room. *Fee:* massage. **Guest Services:** valet laundry, wireless Internet. **Business Services:** conference facilities, business center. **Cards:** AX, DS, MC, VI. *(See color ad on insert)*

24 S D / SOME UNITS

FIESTA INN CENTRO *Book great rates at AAA.com* Phone: (81)8150-2200 8

Hotel
$120 All Year

Address: Ave Pino Suarez #1001, Col Centro **Location:** Jct aves Pino Suarez and Ocampo. **Facility:** 231 one-bedroom standard units. 13 stories, interior corridors. **Parking:** on-site. **Amenities:** high-speed Internet, voice mail, irons, hair dryers. **Pool(s):** indoor. **Leisure Activities:** exercise room. **Guest Services:** valet laundry, wireless Internet. **Business Services:** meeting rooms, business center. **Cards:** AX, MC, VI. *(See color ad on insert)*

24 / SOME UNITS

(See map and index starting on p. 500)

GRAN HOTEL ANCIRA — **Phone:** (81)8150-7000 **10**

Historic Hotel
$105-$140 All Year

Address: Ocampa #443 Ote **Location:** Southwest corner of Plaza Hidalgo; entrance only by one-way eastbound Ave Hidalgo. Located in the historic main plaza. **Facility:** Neoclassic landmark boasting a grand marbled lobby combined with contemporary amenities and service. 267 units. 262 one-bedroom standard units. 5 one-bedroom suites, some with whirlpools. 5 stories, interior corridors. **Parking:** on-site (fee) and valet. **Terms:** 5 day cancellation notice. **Amenities:** high-speed Internet, voice mail, honor bars, irons, hair dryers. **Pool(s):** heated outdoor. **Leisure Activities:** sauna, whirlpool, exercise room. **Guest Services:** valet laundry, wireless Internet. **Business Services:** conference facilities, business center. **Cards:** AX, DC, MC, VI.

/ SOME UNITS

HAMPTON INN & SUITES MONTERREY NORTE — **Phone:** (81)8305-2400 **15**

Hotel
$75-$95 All Year

Address: Ave Universidad 501 Norte **Location:** 4.8 mi (8 km) s of Mex 85 and Monterrey-Nuevo Laredo toll road; 1 mi (1.7 km) n of Universidad de Nuevo Leon. **Facility:** Meets AAA guest room security requirements. 235 units. 217 one-bedroom standard units. 18 one-bedroom suites. 6 stories, interior corridors. *Bath:* combo or shower only. **Parking:** on-site. **Terms:** 1-30 night minimum stay, cancellation fee imposed. **Amenities:** high-speed Internet, voice mail, irons, hair dryers. **Pool(s):** outdoor. **Leisure Activities:** exercise room. **Guest Services:** valet laundry, area transportation-within 6.2 mi (10 km), wireless Internet. **Business Services:** meeting rooms, business center. **Cards:** AX, CB, DC, DS, JC, MC, VI.

AAA Benefit:
Members save up to 10% everyday!

HAMPTON INN MONTERREY AEROPUERTO *Book great rates at AAA.com* — **Phone:** (81)8196-8500 **18**

Hotel
$90-$139 All Year

Address: Carr Miguel Aleman KM 23.7 **Location:** At entrance to General Mariano Escobedo International Airport. **Facility:** 181 one-bedroom standard units. 5 stories, interior corridors. *Bath:* combo or shower only. **Parking:** on-site. **Terms:** 15 day cancellation notice-fee imposed. **Amenities:** high-speed Internet, dual phone lines, voice mail, irons, hair dryers. **Pool(s):** outdoor. **Leisure Activities:** exercise room, sports court. **Guest Services:** valet and coin laundry, airport transportation-Monterrey International Airport, area transportation-within 9.3 mi (15 km), wireless Internet. **Business Services:** meeting rooms, business center. **Cards:** AX, DS, MC, VI.

AAA Benefit:
Members save up to 10% everyday!

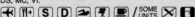

HAMPTON INN MONTERREY GALERIAS OBISPADO *Book great rates at AAA.com* — **Phone:** (81)8625-2450 

Hotel
$112-$130 All Year

Address: Ave Gonzalitos 415 S **Location:** Across from Galerias Mall. Located in modern Galerias District. **Facility:** Meets AAA guest room security requirements. 223 one-bedroom standard units. 7 stories, interior corridors. *Bath:* combo or shower only. **Parking:** on-site. **Terms:** 1-30 night minimum stay, 3 day cancellation notice-fee imposed. **Amenities:** high-speed Internet, dual phone lines, voice mail, irons, hair dryers. **Pool(s):** outdoor. **Leisure Activities:** exercise room. **Guest Services:** valet laundry, area transportation, wireless Internet. **Business Services:** meeting rooms, business center. **Cards:** AX, DC, JC, MC, VI.

FEE / SOME UNITS

AAA Benefit:
Members save up to 10% everyday!

HOLIDAY INN EXPRESS GALERIAS-SAN JERONIMO *Book at AAA.com* — **Phone:** (81)8389-6000 **21**

Hotel
$106-$135 All Year

Address: 1082 Ave San Jeronimo **Location:** Just w of Galerias Mall. **Facility:** 170 units. 166 one-bedroom standard units. 4 one-bedroom suites with whirlpools. 5 stories, interior corridors. *Bath:* combo or shower only. **Parking:** on-site and valet. **Amenities:** high-speed Internet, voice mail, honor bars, irons, hair dryers. **Pool(s):** heated outdoor. **Leisure Activities:** exercise room. **Guest Services:** valet and coin laundry, wireless Internet. **Business Services:** meeting rooms, business center. **Cards:** AX, MC, VI.

/ SOME UNITS

HOTEL HOWARD JOHNSON MACROPLAZA MONTERREY — **Phone:** (81)8380-6000 **6**

Hotel
$110-$239 All Year

Address: Morelos 574 Ote **Location:** In front of Plaza Zaragoza; in downtown historic center. Located in a busy commercial area. **Facility:** Meets AAA guest room security requirements. 203 units. 202 one-bedroom standard units. 1 one-bedroom suite. 9 stories, interior corridors. *Bath:* combo or shower only. **Parking:** on-site. **Amenities:** safes, irons, hair dryers. **Pool(s):** heated indoor. **Leisure Activities:** sauna, steamroom, exercise room. **Guest Services:** valet and coin laundry, area transportation (fee), wireless Internet. **Business Services:** conference facilities, business center. **Cards:** AX, MC, VI.

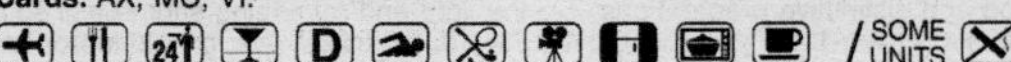

(See map and index starting on p. 500)

HOTEL QUINTA REAL MONTERREY — Phone: (81)8368-1000 — 22

Hotel
$170-$270 All Year

Address: Diego Rivera #500 **Location:** Across from Plaza Fiesta San Agustin. Located in an upscale financial district. **Facility:** Colonial architecture and upscale decor enhance the property, which features a rotunda registration area, life-size artwork and palatial furnishings. 165 units. 160 one-bedroom standard units, some with whirlpools. 5 one-bedroom suites with whirlpools. 5 stories, interior corridors. **Parking:** on-site. **Amenities:** high-speed Internet, dual phone lines, voice mail, safes, honor bars, irons, hair dryers. **Pool(s):** heated indoor. **Leisure Activities:** whirlpool, jogging, exercise room. *Fee:* massage. **Guest Services:** valet laundry, wireless Internet. **Business Services:** conference facilities, business center. **Cards:** AX, MC, VI. Affiliated with A Preferred Hotel. ***(See color ad p 8)***

CALL / SOME UNITS FEE VCR

PRESIDENTE INTERCONTINENTAL MONTERREY — Phone: (81)8368-6000 — 23

AAA
Hotel
$277-$330 All Year

Address: Ave Vasconcelos 300 Ote **Location:** In financial district. Located in upscale Valle District. **Facility:** A modern high-rise, the hotel has expansive public areas, tastefully decorated guest rooms and an outdoor courtyard area with waterfalls. Meets AAA guest room security requirements. 305 units. 248 one-bedroom standard units. 57 one-bedroom suites, some with kitchens (no utensils). 10 stories, interior corridors. **Parking:** on-site. **Terms:** cancellation fee imposed. **Amenities:** high-speed Internet (fee), voice mail, safes, honor bars, irons, hair dryers. **Dining:** 2 restaurants, also, Wall St. Steakhouse, see separate listing, entertainment. **Pool(s):** heated indoor. **Leisure Activities:** whirlpool, lighted tennis court. *Fee:* tennis instruction, massage. **Guest Services:** valet laundry, wireless Internet. **Business Services:** conference facilities, business center. **Cards:** AX, DC, DS, JC, MC, VI.

S D / SOME UNITS

RADISSON HOTEL CASA GRANDE — Phone: (81)8133-0808 — 20

Hotel
$88-$200 All Year

Address: Ave Lazaro Cardenas #2305 **Location:** In upscale Valle District. **Facility:** This elegant new hotel in Monterrey is known for modern rooms and excellent services, including menus for pillows, CDs, books and room service. 198 one-bedroom standard units. 7 stories, interior corridors. **Parking:** on-site and valet. **Amenities:** high-speed Internet, voice mail, safes, irons, hair dryers. **Pool(s):** heated outdoor. **Leisure Activities:** exercise room. *Fee:* massage. **Guest Services:** valet laundry, area transportation (fee), wireless Internet. **Business Services:** meeting rooms, business center. **Cards:** AX, MC, VI.

24 D / SOME UNITS

SAFI MONTERREY — Phone: 81/8399-7000 — 3

Hotel
$90-$160 All Year

Address: Ave Pino Suarez 444 Sur **Location:** From Monterrey-Nuevo Laredo toll road, s on Ave Universidad to Ave Pino Suarez, then s to northern edge of downtown. Located adjacent to Alameda Park. **Facility:** Meets AAA guest room security requirements. 162 units. 151 one-bedroom standard units. 11 one-bedroom suites. 7 stories, interior/exterior corridors. **Parking:** on-site. **Amenities:** safes, irons, hair dryers. *Some:* high-speed Internet. **Pool(s):** heated outdoor. **Leisure Activities:** whirlpool, exercise room. **Guest Services:** valet laundry, wireless Internet. **Business Services:** meeting rooms, business center. **Cards:** AX, MC, VI.

24 D / SOME UNITS

SHERATON AMBASSADOR MONTERREY HOTEL — *Book great rates at AAA.com* — Phone: (81)8380-7000 — 9

AAA
Historic Hotel
$99-$249 All Year

Address: Hidalgo 310 Oriente **Location:** Just w of Plaza Hidalgo at Ave Hidalgo and E Carranza. Located in the heart of the historic area. **Facility:** Find turn-of-the-20th-century ambience at this hotel, which offers elegantly furnished public areas, spacious units, suites and 24-hour room service. Meets AAA guest room security requirements. 229 units. 213 one-bedroom standard units. 15 one- and 1 two-bedroom suites, some with whirlpools. 11 stories, interior corridors. **Parking:** valet. **Amenities:** high-speed Internet, dual phone lines, voice mail, safes, honor bars, irons, hair dryers. *Some:* DVD players, CD players. **Dining:** entertainment. **Pool(s):** outdoor. **Leisure Activities:** whirlpool, tennis court, racquetball court, racquetball equipment. *Fee:* massage. **Guest Services:** valet laundry, wireless Internet. **Business Services:** conference facilities, business center. **Cards:** AX, CB, DC, DS, JC, MC, VI.

Sheraton Hotels & Resorts
AAA Benefit:
Members get up to 15% off, plus Starwood Preferred Guest® bonuses.

24 D / SOME UNITS

The following lodging was either not evaluated or did not meet AAA rating requirements but is listed for your information only.

HOLIDAY INN MONTERREY CENTRO — Phone: 81/8228-6000

fyi

Not evaluated. **Address:** Padre Mier 194 Pte **Location:** 0.4 mi (0.7 km) w of Grand Plaza; jct Padre Mier and Ave Garibaldi. Located in a busy commercial area. Facilities, services, and decor characterize a mid-scale property.

WHERE TO DINE

LOS ARCOS — Phone: 81/8347-2301 — 8

Regional Seafood
$10-$25

A well-known local favorite, the casual Monterrey-style seafood house prepares a wide selection of excellent seafood and distinctive preparations. Try the light and refreshing shrimp ball soup. Casual dress. **Bar:** Full bar. **Hours:** 11 am-11:30 pm. Closed: 4/9 & 4/10. **Address:** Ave Ignacio Morones Prieta #2414 **Location:** In financial district. **Parking:** on-site. **Cards:** AX, MC, VI.

(See map and index starting on p. 500)

LUISIANA RESTAURANT **Phone:** 81/8343-1561 (2)

Continental
$18-$40

Diners who patronize this classic establishment get a feel for the true meaning of the word restaurant: to restore. Soft piano music, a quiet dining room and formally attired staff members with crisp, white napkins draped perfectly over their forearms invite those who dine here to relax and rejuvenate. The mood is distinctly European. Dressy casual. Entertainment. **Bar:** Full bar. **Reservations:** suggested. **Hours:** noon-midnight, Sun-5 pm. Closed major holidays; also Holy Week. **Address:** Plaza Hidalgo 530 **Location:** In downtown historic center. **Parking:** on-site. **Cards:** AX, MC, VI.

SANBORN'S **Phone:** 81/8486-0093

Regional Mexican
$8-$28

Restaurants in the casual chain, which includes more than 100 locations throughout Mexico, offer a good selection of American-style sandwiches, salads, soups and both Mexican and American entrees. The selection of desserts is impressive. Casual dress. **Bar:** Full bar. **Hours:** 7 am-11 pm, Fri & Sat-1 am. **Address:** Ave Laza ro Cardenas No 1000 Col Valle del M **Location:** In Valle Financial District. **Parking:** on-site. **Cards:** AX, MC, VI.

SANBORN'S **Phone:** 81/8363-2280

Regional Mexican
$8-$28

Restaurants in the casual chain, which includes more than 100 locations throughout Mexico, offer a good selection of American-style sandwiches, salads, soups and both Mexican and American entrees. The selection of desserts is impressive. Casual dress. **Bar:** Full bar. **Hours:** 7 am-midnight, Fri & Sat-1 am. **Address:** Ave Lazaro Cardenas No 314 Centro Comer **Location:** Jct Ave Jose Vasconcelos Oriente. **Parking:** on-site. **Cards:** AX, MC, VI.

SANBORN'S **Phone:** 81/8358-9632

Regional Mexican
$8-$28

Restaurants in the casual chain, which includes more than 100 locations throughout Mexico, offer a good selection of American-style sandwiches, salads, soups and both Mexican and American entrees. The selection of desserts is impressive. Casual dress. **Bar:** Full bar. **Hours:** 7 am-midnight, Fri & Sat-1 am. **Address:** Ave Eugenio Garza Sada No 3367 Loc 1 Co **Location:** Jct Cerro Verde St. **Parking:** on-site. **Cards:** AX, MC, VI.

SANBORN'S **Phone:** 81/8333-2720

Regional Mexican
$8-$28

Restaurants in the casual chain, which includes more than 100 locations throughout Mexico, offer a good selection of American-style sandwiches, salads, soups and both Mexican and American entrees. The selection of desserts is impressive. Casual dress. **Bar:** Full bar. **Hours:** 7 am-midnight, Fri & Sat-1 am. **Address:** Ave Insurgentes No 2500, Col Vista **Location:** Just n of jct Pierre Lofi St. **Parking:** on-site (fee). **Cards:** AX, MC, VI.

SANBORN'S **Phone:** 81/8343-1834

Regional Mexican
$8-$28

Restaurants in the casual chain, which includes more than 100 locations throughout Mexico, offer a good selection of American-style sandwiches, salads, soups and both Mexican and American entrees. The selection of desserts is impressive. Casual dress. **Bar:** Full bar. **Hours:** 7 am-11 pm, Fri & Sat-1 am. **Address:** Ave Mariano Escobedo Sur No 920, Col **Location:** Jct Ave Reforma. **Parking:** no self-parking. **Cards:** AX, MC, VI.

SIRLOIN STOCKADE **Phone:** 81/8363-3318

Regional Steak
$6-$9

The steakhouse lines up buffet items, including pizza, tacos, soups, salads and desserts, providing both excellent variety and a good value. Rotating theme nights might allow for the sampling of sushi, barbecue and seafood. The buffet also may serve to complement a quality steak. Rolls are baked several times daily. Casual dress. **Bar:** Beer & wine. **Hours:** noon-9 pm, Fri & Sat-11 pm. Closed: 12/25. **Address:** Ave Lazaro Cardenas Pte 2510 **Location:** On Ave Lazaro Cardenas at Diego Rivera St. **Parking:** on-site. **Cards:** DS, MC, VI.

SIRLOIN STOCKADE **Phone:** 81/8352-9902

Steak
$6-$9

The steakhouse lines up buffet items, including pizza, tacos, soups, salads and desserts, providing both excellent variety and a good value. Rotating theme nights might allow for the sampling of sushi, barbecue and seafood. The buffet also may serve to complement a quality steak. Rolls are baked several times daily. Casual dress. **Bar:** Beer & wine. **Hours:** noon-11 pm, Fri & Sat-midnight, Sun 11 am-11 pm. Closed: 12/25. **Address:** Ave Alfonso Reyes 110 Nte, Col Anahuac **Location:** Just n of Ciudad Universitaria; next to HEB Shopping Complex. **Parking:** on-site. **Cards:** DS, MC, VI.

VIPS **Phone:** 81/8333-5272

Regional Mexican
$6-$22

Owned by Wal-Mart of Mexico and found in most major cities, the budget-friendly chain serves a good variety of Mexican and American dishes, including burgers, sandwiches, salads, spaghetti and enchiladas, as well as a fine selection of desserts. Casual dress. **Bar:** Beer & wine. **Hours:** 7 am-midnight, Fri & Sat-2 am. **Address:** Ave Paseo de los Leones No 610, Col **Location:** Just e of jct Paseo de Los Insurgentes. **Parking:** on-site (fee). **Cards:** AX, MC, VI.

(See map and index starting on p. 500)

VIPS

Phone: 81/8334-0035

Regional Mexican
$6-$22

Owned by Wal-Mart of Mexico and found in most major cities, the budget-friendly chain serves a good variety of Mexican and American dishes, including burgers, sandwiches, salads, spaghetti and enchiladas, as well as a fine selection of desserts. Casual dress. **Bar:** Beer & wine. **Hours:** 7 am-midnight, Fri & Sat-2 am. **Address:** Carr Miguel Aleman No 7000, Col Torres **Location:** Jct Ave Altagarcia Cantu. **Parking:** on-site. **Cards:** AX, MC, VI.

VIPS

Phone: 81/8369-1640

Regional Mexican
$6-$22

Owned by Wal-Mart of Mexico and found in most major cities, the budget-friendly chain serves a good variety of Mexican and American dishes, including burgers, sandwiches, salads, spaghetti and enchiladas, as well as a fine selection of desserts. Casual dress. **Bar:** Beer & wine. **Hours:** 7 am-midnight, Fri & Sat-2 am. **Address:** Ave Eugiono Garza Sada No 427, Col **Location:** Jct Ave Luis. **Parking:** on-site. **Cards:** AX, MC, VI.

VIPS

Phone: 81/8335-0423

Regional Mexican
$6-$22

Owned by Wal-Mart of Mexico and found in most major cities, the budget-friendly chain serves a good variety of Mexican and American dishes, including burgers, sandwiches, salads, spaghetti and enchiladas, as well as a fine selection of desserts. Casual dress. **Bar:** Beer & wine. **Hours:** 7 am-midnight, Fri & Sat 24 hours. **Address:** Calz San Pedro No 110 Nte, Col Fuentes de **Location:** Just w of jct Ave Rio Mississippi. **Parking:** on-site. **Cards:** AX, MC, VI.

VIPS

Phone: 81/8369-1957

Regional Mexican
$6-$22

Owned by Wal-Mart of Mexico and found in most major cities, the budget-friendly chain serves a good variety of Mexican and American dishes, including burgers, sandwiches, salads, spaghetti and enchiladas, as well as a fine selection of desserts. Casual dress. **Bar:** Beer & wine. **Hours:** 7 am-midnight, Fri & Sat-2 am. **Address:** Ave Eugenio Garza Sada No 3755, Col **Location:** Between aves Country and Alfonso Reyes. **Parking:** on-site. **Cards:** AX, MC, VI.

VIPS

Phone: 81/8370-8976

Regional Mexican
$6-$22

Owned by Wal-Mart of Mexico and found in most major cities, the budget-friendly chain serves a good variety of Mexican and American dishes, including burgers, sandwiches, salads, spaghetti and enchiladas, as well as a fine selection of desserts. Casual dress. **Bar:** Beer & wine. **Hours:** 7 am-midnight, Fri & Sat-2 am. **Address:** Ave Jose E Gonzales No 400, Col Mitras Norte **Location:** In Gonzalitos Shopping District. **Parking:** on-site. **Cards:** AX, MC, VI.

VIPS

Phone: 81/8340-8347

Regional Mexican
$6-$22

Owned by Wal-Mart of Mexico and found in most major cities, the budget-friendly chain serves a good variety of Mexican and American dishes, including burgers, sandwiches, salads, spaghetti and enchiladas, as well as a fine selection of desserts. Casual dress. **Bar:** Beer & wine. **Hours:** 7 am-1 am. **Address:** Calle Miguel Hidalgo No 401, Col Centro **Location:** Between aves Emilio Carranca and Escobedo. **Parking:** on-site (fee). **Cards:** AX, MC, VI.

VIPS

Phone: 81/8332-2095

Regional Mexican
$8-$18

Owned by Wal-Mart of Mexico and found in most major cities, the budget-friendly chain serves a good variety of Mexican and American dishes, including burgers, sandwiches, salads, spaghetti and enchiladas, as well as a fine selection of desserts. Casual dress. **Bar:** Beer & wine. **Hours:** 7 am-midnight, Fri & Sat-2 am. **Address:** Ave Universidad Norte 407 Col Roble **Location:** Jct Ave Universidad at Ave Central; 1 mi (1.6 km) n of Universidad de Nuevo Leon. **Parking:** on-site. **Cards:** AX, MC, VI.

WALL ST. STEAKHOUSE

Phone: 81/8368-6000 (7)

Regional Steak & Seafood
$15-$45

The classic New York-style steak house features rich woods, starched white linens and sparkling glassware. Attentive, well-trained staffers serve large portions of high-quality imported steaks, chops and seafood. Dressy casual. **Bar:** Full bar. **Reservations:** suggested. **Hours:** 8:30-11 am, 1-4 & 6-1 am, Sat 6 pm-2 am. **Address:** Ave Vasconcelos 300 Ote **Location:** In financial district; in Presidente InterContinental Monterrey. **Parking:** on-site (fee) and valet. **Cards:** AX, CB, DC, JC, MC, VI.

NUEVO LAREDO, TAMAULIPAS pop. 310,915

WHERE TO STAY

The following lodging was either not evaluated or did not meet AAA rating requirements but is listed for your information only.

HILTON GARDEN INN

Phone: 867/711-4600

fyi

Not evaluated. **Address:** Ave Reforma 5102 **Location:** 4 mi (6.4 km) s of International Bridge. Facilities, services, and decor characterize a mid-scale property.

AAA Benefit:
Members save 5% or more everyday!

REYNOSA, TAMAULIPAS pop. 420,463

WHERE TO DINE

VIPS

Phone: 899/922-9747

Regional Mexican
$7-$25

Owned by Wal-Mart of Mexico and found in most major cities, the budget-friendly chain serves a good variety of Mexican and American dishes, including burgers, sandwiches, salads, spaghetti and enchiladas, as well as a fine selection of desserts. Casual dress. **Bar:** Beer & wine. **Hours:** 7 am-midnight, Fri & Sat-1 am. **Address:** Ave Emil io Portes Gil No 803, Col del Prado **Location:** Jct Calle Colon. **Parking:** no self-parking. **Cards:** AX, MC, VI.

SALTILLO, COAHUILA pop. 578,046

WHERE TO STAY

AMERICAN EUROTEL

Phone: (844)438-8888

Hotel
$80-$105 All Year

Address: Blvd V Carranza #4100 **Location:** 0.6 mi (1 km) s from Glorieta; at N Ortiz G and Blvd V Carranza. Located in a modern commercial area. **Facility:** 182 units. 179 one-bedroom standard units. 3 one-bedroom suites. 3 stories, interior corridors. **Parking:** on-site. **Amenities:** voice mail, safes, honor bars, irons, hair dryers. *Some:* dual phone lines. **Pool(s):** heated indoor. **Leisure Activities:** sauna, whirlpool, playground, exercise room. **Guest Services:** valet laundry, wireless Internet. **Business Services:** conference facilities, business center. **Cards:** AX, MC, VI.

D

AMERICAN HOTEL EXPRESS

Phone: (844)438-8800

Hotel
$98-$173 All Year

Address: Carr Saltillo-Monterrey #9000 **Location:** 10.8 mi (18 km) on Saltillo to Monterrey Hwy (libre). Located in far north greater Saltillo near Saltillo Airport. **Facility:** 120 one-bedroom standard units. 2 stories (no elevator), interior corridors. **Parking:** on-site. **Amenities:** high-speed Internet, dual phone lines, voice mail, safes, irons, hair dryers. **Pool(s):** heated indoor. **Leisure Activities:** whirlpools, exercise room. **Guest Services:** valet and coin laundry, area transportation (fee), wireless Internet. **Business Services:** meeting rooms, business center. **Cards:** AX, DC, DS, MC, VI.

/ SOME UNITS

AMERICAN SUITES RESORT & SPA *Book at AAA.com*

Phone: (844)438-7000

Hotel
$79-$150 All Year

Address: Blvd Venustiano Carranza 8800 **Location:** 10.8 mi (18 km) n on Saltillo to Monterrey Hwy (libre). Located in north greater Saltillo near Saltillo Airport. **Facility:** 76 units. 39 one-bedroom standard units. 26 one- and 11 two-bedroom suites. 4 stories, interior corridors. **Parking:** on-site. **Amenities:** high-speed Internet, safes, irons, hair dryers. **Pool(s):** indoor. **Leisure Activities:** whirlpool, playground, exercise room. **Guest Services:** valet laundry, area transportation (fee), wireless Internet. **Business Services:** meeting rooms, business center. **Cards:** AX, DS, MC, VI.

D / SOME UNITS

CAMINO REAL SALTILLO

Phone: (844)438-0000

AAA

Hotel
$128-$245 All Year

Address: Blvd Los Fundadores #2000, Col Los Cerritos **Location:** 3.6 mi (6 km) se on Mex 57 from Mex 40; on eastern city outskirts. Located in a quiet area. **Facility:** Located on a mountain slope overlooking Saltillo Valley, this motor inn features modern rooms, an excellent staff and extensive landscaped gardens. 164 units. 161 one-bedroom standard units. 2 one- and 1 two-bedroom suites with whirlpools. 1-2 stories (no elevator), exterior corridors. **Parking:** on-site. **Amenities:** voice mail, safes, honor bars, irons, hair dryers. *Some:* high-speed Internet. **Dining:** 2 restaurants. **Pool(s):** heated outdoor. **Leisure Activities:** 2 lighted tennis courts, playground, exercise room. **Guest Services:** valet laundry, wireless Internet. **Business Services:** conference facilities, business center. **Cards:** AX, DC, MC, VI.

/ SOME UNITS

HAMPTON INN ZONA AEROPUERTO *Book great rates at AAA.com* **Phone:** (844)450-4500

Hotel
$79-$99 All Year

Address: 6580 Carr Saltillo-Monterrey **Location:** 11.4 mi (19 km) n on Saltillo to Monterrey Hwy (libre). Located in far north greater Saltillo near Saltillo Airport. **Facility:** 227 units. 219 one-bedroom standard units. 8 one-bedroom suites. 4 stories, interior corridors. **Parking:** on-site. **Terms:** 1-30 night minimum stay, cancellation fee imposed. **Amenities:** high-speed Internet, dual phone lines, voice mail, irons, hair dryers. **Pool(s):** outdoor. **Leisure Activities:** exercise room. **Guest Services:** valet and coin laundry, airport transportation-Aeropuerto Ramos Arizpe, wireless Internet. **Business Services:** meeting rooms, business center. **Cards:** AX, DC, DS, MC, VI.

S D / SOME UNITS

AAA Benefit:
Members save up to 10% everyday!

WHERE TO DINE

RESTAURANT LA CANASTA **Phone:** 844/415-8050

Regional Mexican
$7-$28

Fireplaces lend to the restaurant's elegant, yet informal, country-style decor. Ample parking is offered behind this place, which is north of downtown. Among examples of popular regional Mexican dishes is the house specialty: mole poblano. Casual dress. **Bar:** Full bar. **Reservations:** suggested. **Hours:** noon-midnight. **Address:** Blvd V Carranza 2485 **Location:** 0.8 mi (1.3 km) from Glorieta; at N Ortiz G and Blvd V Carranza. **Parking:** on-site and valet. **Cards:** AX, MC, VI.

SANBORN'S **Phone:** 844/416-6689

Regional Mexican
$8-$28

Restaurants in the casual chain, which includes more than 100 locations throughout Mexico, offer a good selection of American-style sandwiches, salads, soups and both Mexican and American entrees. The selection of desserts is impressive. Casual dress. **Bar:** Full bar. **Hours:** 7 am-1 am. **Address:** Blvd L Echeverria No 686, Col Republica **Location:** 0.3 mi (0.5 km) n of downtown Saltillo, on Blvd Luis Echeverria. **Parking:** on-site. **Cards:** AX, MC, VI.

VIPS **Phone:** 844/410-3056

Regional Mexican
$7-$25

Owned by Wal-Mart of Mexico and found in most major cities, the budget-friendly chain serves a good variety of Mexican and American dishes, including burgers, sandwiches, salads, spaghetti and enchiladas, as well as a fine selection of desserts. Casual dress. **Bar:** Beer & wine. **Hours:** 7 am-11 pm. **Address:** Calz Emilio Carranza No 1094, Col Centro **Location:** Jct Ave Presidente Cardenas. **Parking:** on-site. **Cards:** AX, MC, VI.

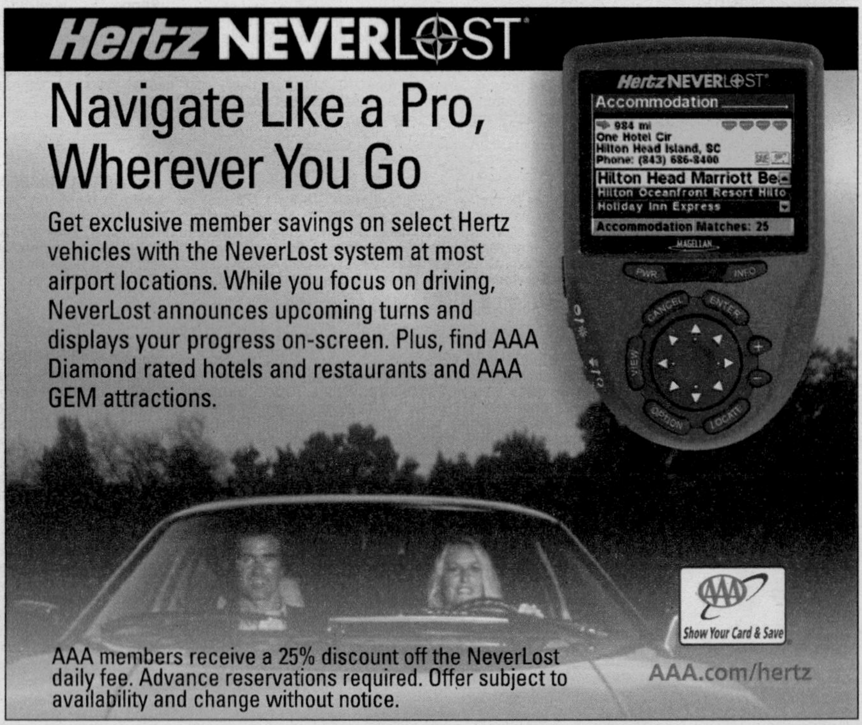

TAMPICO, TAMAULIPAS pop. 295,442

WHERE TO DINE

SANBORN'S — **Phone:** 833/224-5559

Regional Mexican
$8-$28

Restaurants in the casual chain, which includes more than 100 locations throughout Mexico, offer a good selection of American-style sandwiches, salads, soups and both Mexican and American entrees. The selection of desserts is impressive. Casual dress. **Bar:** Full bar. **Hours:** 7 am-1 am. **Address:** Prolonga cion Ave Hidalgo No 5107, Col. Flam **Location:** 0.4 mi (0.6 km) n of downtown. **Parking:** on-site. **Cards:** AX, MC, VI.

TORREON, COAHUILA pop. 439,400

WHERE TO STAY

CROWNE PLAZA TORREON *Book at AAA.com* — **Phone:** (871)729-9600

Hotel
$119-$155 All Year

Address: Blvd Torreon Matamoros #4050 **Location:** Off Diagonal Reforma; center. **Facility:** 193 units. 188 one-bedroom standard units. 5 one-bedroom suites. 11 stories, interior corridors. **Parking:** on-site. **Amenities:** high-speed Internet, dual phone lines, voice mail, safes, honor bars, irons, hair dryers. **Pool(s):** heated indoor. **Leisure Activities:** sauna, whirlpool, exercise room, spa. **Guest Services:** valet laundry, wireless Internet. **Business Services:** conference facilities, business center. **Cards:** AX, MC, VI.

24 S D / SOME UNITS

FIESTA INN TORREON GALERIAS — **Phone:** 871/749-3300

Hotel
$115-$173 All Year

Address: Periferico Raul Lopez Sanchez #6000 **Location:** On Mex 40; in Galerias Shopping Center. **Facility:** Meets AAA guest room security requirements. 146 one-bedroom standard units. 9 stories, interior corridors. **Parking:** on-site. **Amenities:** high-speed Internet, dual phone lines, voice mail, irons, hair dryers. **Pool(s):** heated outdoor. **Leisure Activities:** exercise room. **Guest Services:** valet laundry, wireless Internet. **Business Services:** meeting rooms, business center. **Cards:** AX, MC, VI.
(See color ad on insert)

S D / SOME UNITS

FIESTA INN TORREON-LA ROSITA — **Phone:** (871)729-4300

Hotel
$78-$89 All Year

Location: Jct Paseo de las Rositas and Diagonal de los Fuentes, just w. Paseo de las Rositas #910, Col Campestre la Rosita. **Facility:** 149 units. 146 one-bedroom standard units. 3 one-bedroom suites, some with whirlpools. 8 stories, interior corridors. **Parking:** on-site. **Amenities:** video games (fee), voice mail, irons, hair dryers. **Pool(s):** outdoor. **Leisure Activities:** exercise room. **Guest Services:** valet laundry, wireless Internet. **Business Services:** meeting rooms, PC (fee). **Cards:** AX, MC, VI.
(See color ad on insert)

D / SOME UNITS

HAMPTON INN TORREON AEROPUERTO GALERIAS — **Phone:** (871)705-1550

Hotel
$85-$120 All Year

Address: Periferico Raul Lopez Sanchez 10995 **Location:** Just nw of jct Carretera Santa Fe. **Facility:** 152 units. 145 one-bedroom standard units. 7 one-bedroom suites. 7 stories, interior corridors. **Parking:** on-site. **Terms:** 1-30 night minimum stay, cancellation fee imposed. **Amenities:** high-speed Internet, dual phone lines, voice mail, irons, hair dryers. **Pool(s):** outdoor. **Leisure Activities:** exercise room. **Guest Services:** valet laundry, area transportation, wireless Internet. **Business Services:** meeting rooms, business center. **Cards:** AX, DC, DS, MC, VI.

CALL S D / SOME UNITS

AAA Benefit:
Members save up to 10% everyday!

HOLIDAY INN EXPRESS TORREON *Book at AAA.com* — **Phone:** (871)729-6000

Hotel
$82-$148 All Year

Address: Blvd Independencia 1133 Ote **Location:** Just ne on Mex 30. Located in a financial district. **Facility:** Meets AAA guest room security requirements. 165 one-bedroom standard units. 5 stories, interior corridors. **Parking:** on-site. **Amenities:** high-speed Internet, voice mail, safes, irons, hair dryers. **Dining:** Martin's Restaurant, see separate listing. **Pool(s):** indoor. **Leisure Activities:** exercise room. **Guest Services:** valet and coin laundry, wireless Internet. **Business Services:** meeting rooms, business center. **Cards:** AX, DS, MC, VI.

S D / SOME UNITS

MARRIOTT TORREON — **Phone:** (871)895-0000

Hotel
$75-$98 All Year

Address: Blvd Independencia 100 Pte **Location:** 1.2 mi (2 km) ne on Mex 30. **Facility:** Smoke free premises. 152 one-bedroom standard units, some with whirlpools. 4-6 stories, interior corridors. **Parking:** on-site. **Amenities:** high-speed Internet, voice mail, safes, honor bars, irons, hair dryers. **Pool(s):** outdoor. **Leisure Activities:** whirlpool, steamroom, exercise room. *Fee:* massage. **Guest Services:** valet and coin laundry, wireless Internet. **Business Services:** meeting rooms, business center. **Cards:** AX, MC, VI.

24 S D VCR

Marriott HOTELS & RESORTS

AAA Benefit:
Members save a minimum 5% off the best available rate.

The following lodging was either not evaluated or did not meet AAA rating requirements but is listed for your information only.

BEST WESTERN HOTEL POSADA DEL RIO EXPRESS

Phone: 871/750-7500

fyi

Not evaluated. **Address:** Blvd Independencia #3837 **Location:** On Mex 40; near Industrial City turn off. Facilities, services, and decor characterize a mid-scale property.

AAA Benefit:
Members save up to 20%, plus 10% bonus points with rewards program.

WHERE TO DINE

MARTIN'S RESTAURANT

Phone: 871/729-6000

Mexican
$8-$30

Locally popular, the coffee shop-style restaurant serves a good selection of reasonably priced American sandwiches, soups and Mexican food, in addition to some luscious desserts. Casual dress. **Bar:** Full bar. **Hours:** 7 am-midnight. **Address:** Blvd Independencia 1133 Ote **Location:** Just ne on Mex 30; in Holiday Inn Express Torreon. **Parking:** on-site. **Cards:** AX, MC, VI.

SANBORN'S

Phone: 871/750-7941

Mexican
$8-$18

Restaurants in the casual chain, which includes more than 100 locations throughout Mexico, offer a good selection of American-style sandwiches, salads, soups and both Mexican and American entrees. The selection of desserts is impressive. Casual dress. **Bar:** Full bar. **Hours:** 7 am-11 pm, Wed-Sat to 1 am. **Address:** Periferico Rall Lopez Sanchez #6000 **Location:** In Galerias La Laguna Shopping Mall. **Parking:** on-site (fee). **Cards:** MC, VI.

VIPS

Phone: 871/717-0458

Mexican
$5-$9

Owned by Wal-Mart of Mexico and found in most major cities, the budget-friendly chain serves a good variety of Mexican and American dishes, including burgers, sandwiches, salads, spaghetti and enchiladas, as well as a fine selection of desserts. Casual dress. **Hours:** 7 am-midnight. **Address:** Boulevard Independencia 1300 Ote **Location:** Jct Rio Nazas and Blvd Independencia. **Parking:** on-site. **Cards:** MC, VI.

VIPS

Phone: 871/712-8724

Mexican
$5-$9

Owned by Wal-Mart of Mexico and found in most major cities, the budget-friendly chain serves a good variety of Mexican and American dishes, including burgers, sandwiches, salads, spaghetti and enchiladas, as well as a fine selection of desserts. Casual dress. **Hours:** 7 am-midnight. **Address:** Calzon Colon #210 **Location:** Just w of jct Ocampo St. **Parking:** on-site. **Cards:** MC, VI.

THE PACIFIC COAST

Acapulco

This index helps you "spot" where approved lodgings and restaurants are located on the corresponding detailed maps. Lodging daily rate range is for comparison only and show the property's high season. Restaurant rate range is a combination of lunch and/or dinner. Turn to the listing page for more detailed rate information and consult display ads for special promotions.

ACAPULCO

Map Page	OA	Lodgings	Diamond Rated	High Season	Page
1 / p. 512	AAA	**Hotel Emporio Acapulco**		$300	514
3 / p. 512		Ritz Acapulco Hotel de Playa		$228-$297	517
4 / p. 512		Hotel Crowne Plaza Acapulco		$170-$250	514
5 / p. 512		Park Royal Acapulco		$220-$440	517
6 / p. 512		Hotel Acapulco Tortuga		$75-$100	514
7 / p. 512	AAA	**Fiesta Americana Villas Acapulco** - see color ad on insert		$145-$236	513
8 / p. 512	AAA	**Fiesta Inn Acapulco** - see color ad on insert		$136-$227	513
10 / p. 512		Villa Vera Hotel Spa & Racquet Club Acapulco		$100-$315	517
11 / p. 512		Quinta Real Acapulco - see color ad p 8		$370-$500	517
12 / p. 512		Hotel Elcano		$350	514
13 / p. 512		Copacabana Beach Hotel Acapulco		$80-$230	513
14 / p. 512		Hotel Las Hamacas		$50-$100	516
16 / p. 512		El Mirador Acapulco		$75-$170	513
18 / p. 512	AAA	**Hyatt Regency Acapulco**		$79-$315	516
21 / p. 512	AAA	**Hotel Las Brisas Acapulco** - see color ad p 515		$240-$515	515
23 / p. 512		Camino Real Acapulco Diamante		$280-$475	513
24 / p. 512		The Fairmont Acapulco Princess		$179-$259	513
25 / p. 512		The Fairmont Pierre Marques		$284	513
27 / p. 512		Mayan Palace Acapulco Wyndham Alliance Resort		$520	516
28 / p. 512		Mayan Sea Garden Acapulco		$366-$637	516
29 / p. 512		The Grand Mayan Acapulco Wyndham Alliance Resort		$475-$785	514

Map Page	OA	Restaurants	Diamond Rated	Cuisine	Meal Range	Page
1 / p. 512		La Mansion		International	$14-$27	518
2 / p. 512		Sunset		International	$12-$35	519
3 / p. 512		El Olvido		Continental	$18-$30	518
4 / p. 512		El Fogon Mexican Restaurant		Mexican	$4-$10	518
5 / p. 512		Suntory Acapulco		Japanese	$11-$36	519
6 / p. 512		Su Casa		Continental	$14-$32	519
7 / p. 512		Coyuca 22		Continental	$20-$38	518
8 / p. 512		Kookaburra		Seafood	$6-$40	518
9 / p. 512		Baikal		International	$19-$55	517
10 / p. 512		CasaNova		Northern Italian	$20-$35	517
11 / p. 512		La Hacienda		Mexican	$20-$30	518
12 / p. 512		Tabachin		French	$20-$40	519
13 / p. 512		Bellavista		International	$23-$55	517
14 / p. 512		El Pescador		International	$15-$30	518
15 / p. 512		La Trattoria		Italian	$15-$22	518
17 / p. 512		Sonora Steaks Bar and Grill		Steak	$15-$25	519
18 / p. 512		La Veranda		Italian	$12-$25	518
19 / p. 512		Restaurant Buena Vista		International	$13-$37	519

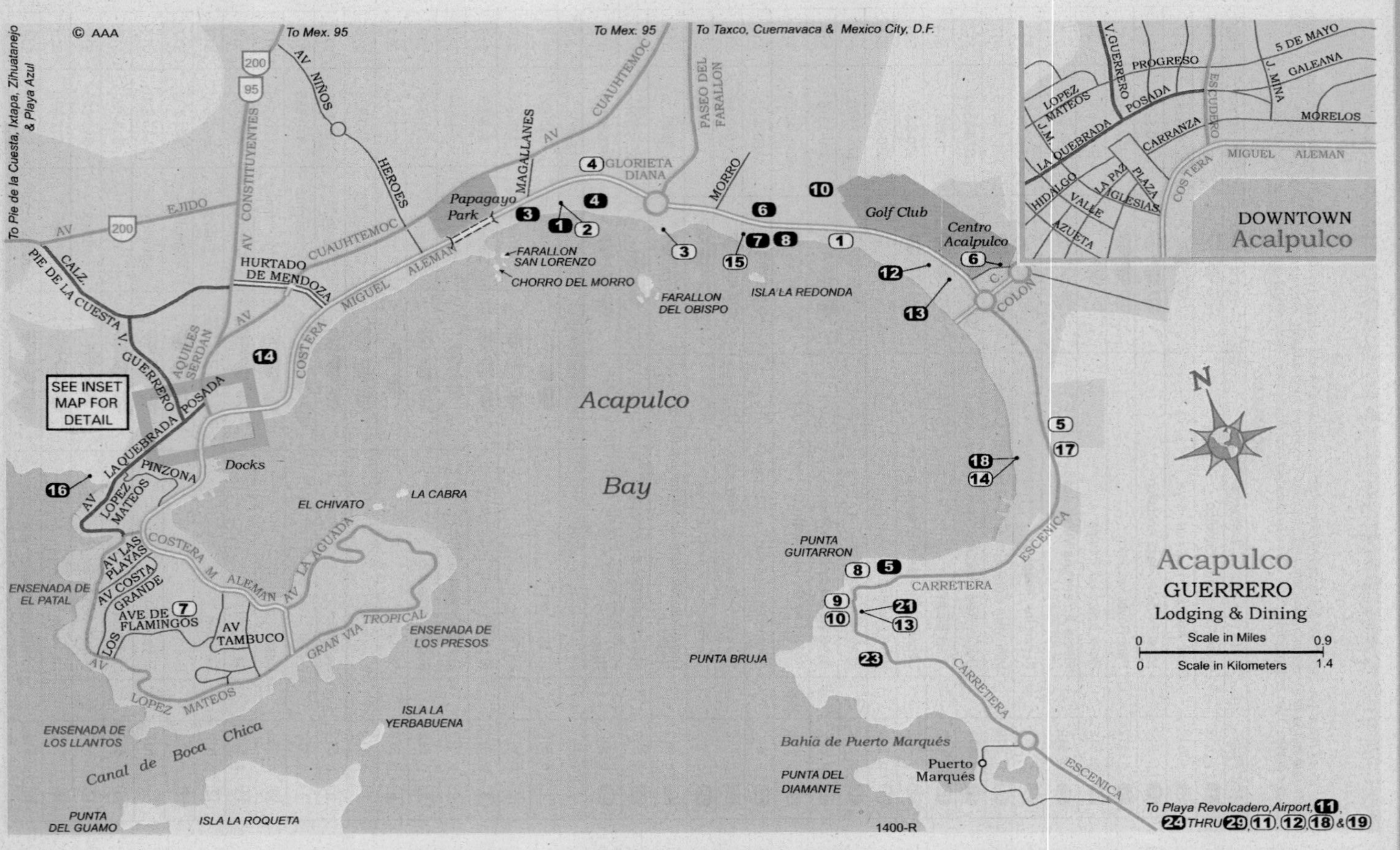

© AAA
To Pie de la Cuesta, Ixtapa, Zihuatanejo & Playa Azul
To Mex. 95
To Mex. 95
To Taxco, Cuernavaca & Mexico City, D.F.
DOWNTOWN
Acalpulco
5 DE MAYO
GALEANA
MORELOS
J. MINA
PROGRESO
V.GUERRERO
LOPEZ MATEOS
J.M.
LA QUEBRADA
POSADA
CARRANZA
ESCUDERO
MIGUEL ALEMAN
COSTERA
HIDALGO
VALLE
LA PAZ
PLAZA
IGLESIAS
AZUETA
200
95
AV NIÑOS
HEROES
AV CUAUHTEMOC
MAGALLANES
GLORIETA DIANA
PASEO DEL FARALLON
MORRO
Papagayo Park
Golf Club
Centro Acalpulco
C. COLON
AV EJIDO
AV CONSTITUYENTES
CALZ. PIE DE LA CUESTA
V. GUERRERO
HURTADO DE MENDOZA
AQUILES SERDAN
AV
COSTERA MIGUEL ALEMAN
FARALLON SAN LORENZO
CHORRO DEL MORRO
FARALLON DEL OBISPO
ISLA LA REDONDA
SEE INSET MAP FOR DETAIL
POSADA
LA QUEBRADA
PINZONA
Docks
AV LOPEZ MATEOS
Acapulco
Bay
EL CHIVATO
LA CABRA
AV LAS PLAYAS
AV COSTA GRANDE
AVE DE FLAMINGOS
AV LOS
AV TAMBUCO
COSTERA M. ALEMAN
AV LA AGUADA
GRAN VIA TROPICAL
ENSENADA DE EL PATAL
ENSENADA DE LOS PRESOS
LOPEZ MATEOS
ENSENADA DE LOS LLANTOS
Canal de Boca Chica
ISLA LA YERBABUENA
PUNTA DEL GUAMO
ISLA LA ROQUETA
PUNTA GUITARRON
PUNTA BRUJA
CARRETERA
CARRETERA ESCENICA
ESCENICA
Bahía de Puerto Marqués
PUNTA DEL DIAMANTE
Puerto Marqués
1400-R
N
Acapulco
GUERRERO
Lodging & Dining
Scale in Miles
0
0.9
Scale in Kilometers
0
1.4
To Playa Revolcadero, Airport, 11, 24 THRU 29, 11, 12, 18 & 19

ACAPULCO, GUERRERO pop. 722,499 (See map and index starting on p. 512)

WHERE TO STAY

CAMINO REAL ACAPULCO DIAMANTE — Phone: (744)435-1010 — 23

Hotel
$280-$475 All Year

Address: Carr Escencia KM 14 **Location:** 8.1 mi (13 km) se on Mex 200 (Airport Hwy); overlooking Bahia de Puerto Marques. Located in a secluded residential area. **Facility:** 157 units. 146 one-bedroom standard units. 11 one-bedroom suites, some with whirlpools. 5 stories, interior corridors. **Parking:** on-site and valet. **Terms:** 7 day cancellation notice-fee imposed. **Amenities:** high-speed Internet (fee), safes, honor bars, hair dryers. *Some:* irons. **Pool(s):** 3 outdoor. **Leisure Activities:** exercise room, spa. **Guest Services:** valet laundry, beauty salon, wireless Internet. **Business Services:** conference facilities, business center. **Cards:** AX, DC, MC, VI.

/ SOME UNITS

COPACABANA BEACH HOTEL ACAPULCO — Phone: (744)484-3260 — 13

Hotel
$80-$230 All Year

Address: Tabachines #2 Fracc Club Deportivo **Location:** 3.8 mi (6 km) e of downtown; off Costera Miguel Aleman. Located on the bay. **Facility:** 430 one-bedroom standard units. 18 stories, interior corridors. *Bath:* shower only. **Parking:** on-site (fee). **Terms:** 7 day cancellation notice, in season. **Amenities:** high-speed Internet (fee), voice mail, safes, hair dryers. *Some:* irons. **Pool(s):** outdoor. **Leisure Activities:** whirlpools, recreation programs, exercise room. *Fee:* massage, game room. **Guest Services:** valet laundry, beauty salon, wireless Internet. **Business Services:** conference facilities, business center. **Cards:** AX, DC, MC, VI.

/ SOME UNITS

EL MIRADOR ACAPULCO — Phone: (744)483-1155 — 16

Hotel
$75-$170 All Year

Address: Plazoleta de la Quebraoa #74 **Location:** 0.6 mi (1 km) w; on La Quebrada Cliffs. Located in a commercial area. **Facility:** 133 units. 130 one- and 3 two-bedroom standard units with efficiencies (utensils extra charge), some with whirlpools. 1-4 stories (no elevator), exterior corridors. *Bath:* combo or shower only. **Parking:** on-site. **Terms:** 7 day cancellation notice, 3 day off season. **Pool(s):** 3 outdoor. **Guest Services:** valet laundry. **Cards:** AX, MC, VI.

THE FAIRMONT ACAPULCO PRINCESS — Book at AAA.com — Phone: (744)469-1000 — 24

Resort Hotel
$179-$259 All Year

Address: Playa Revolcadero S/N **Location:** 12.1 mi (19.3 km) se, off Mex 200 (Airport Hwy). Located in a quiet area. **Facility:** An enormous hotel with beautiful, sprawling, tropical grounds, this property is oceanfront, away from the hustle and bustle of downtown. 1017 units. 975 one-bedroom standard units. 40 one- and 2 two-bedroom suites, some with kitchens and/or whirlpools. 10-14 stories, interior corridors. **Parking:** on-site and valet. **Terms:** cancellation fee imposed. **Amenities:** voice mail, safes, irons, hair dryers. *Some:* DVD players, CD players, high-speed Internet (fee). **Dining:** La Hacienda, La Veranda, see separate listings. **Pool(s):** 4 outdoor. **Leisure Activities:** lifeguard on duty, limited beach access, spa, basketball, volleyball. *Fee:* golf-36 holes, 8 tennis courts (2 indoor, 8 lighted), exercise room, game room. **Guest Services:** valet laundry, wireless Internet. **Business Services:** conference facilities, business center. **Cards:** AX, MC, VI.

/ SOME UNITS

THE FAIRMONT PIERRE MARQUES — Book at AAA.com — Phone: (744)435-2600 — 25

Resort Hotel
$284 All Year

Address: Playa Revolcadero S/N **Location:** 10.9 mi (17.5 km) se, off Mex 200 (Airport Hwy). Located in a quiet beachside setting. **Facility:** On sprawling grounds, the property offers a variety of elegant room types including bungalows and villas, some with ocean views. 335 units. 326 one-bedroom standard units. 9 one-bedroom suites. 1-5 stories, exterior corridors. *Bath:* combo or shower only. **Parking:** on-site and valet. **Amenities:** voice mail, safes. *Some:* DVD players, CD players, high-speed Internet (fee), irons, hair dryers. **Dining:** Tabachin, see separate listing. **Pool(s):** 3 outdoor. **Leisure Activities:** lifeguard on duty, playground, basketball, volleyball. *Fee:* golf-36 holes, 5 lighted tennis courts. **Guest Services:** valet laundry, wireless Internet. **Business Services:** conference facilities, business center. **Cards:** AX, MC, VI.

FEE / SOME UNITS

FIESTA AMERICANA VILLAS ACAPULCO — Book great rates at AAA.com — Phone: (744)435-1600 — 7

AAA
Hotel
$145-$236 All Year

Address: Costera Miguel Aleman 97 **Location:** 3.3 mi (5.3 km) e. Located on the bay in a busy commercial area. **Facility:** 324 one-bedroom standard units. 19 stories, interior corridors. **Parking:** on-site (fee) and valet. **Terms:** 14 day cancellation notice, 3 day off season-fee imposed. **Amenities:** DVD players, high-speed Internet (fee), voice mail, safes, irons, hair dryers. **Dining:** 3 restaurants, also, La Trattoria, see separate listing. **Pool(s):** 3 outdoor. **Leisure Activities:** kids club. *Fee:* steamrooms, massage. **Guest Services:** valet laundry, wireless Internet. **Business Services:** business center. **Cards:** AX, MC, VI. *(See color ad on insert)*

FEE / SOME UNITS

FIESTA INN ACAPULCO — Book great rates at AAA.com — Phone: (744)435-0500 — 8

AAA
Hotel
$136-$227 All Year

Address: Costera Miguel Aleman #2311 **Location:** 3.4 mi (5.4 km) e. Located on the bay in a heavy-commercial area. **Facility:** 220 units. 216 one-bedroom standard units. 4 one-bedroom suites. 15 stories, interior corridors. **Parking:** valet. **Terms:** 3 day cancellation notice. **Amenities:** video games (fee), voice mail, irons, hair dryers. **Pool(s):** 2 outdoor. **Leisure Activities:** kids club, exercise room. **Guest Services:** valet laundry, wireless Internet. **Business Services:** conference facilities, business center. **Cards:** AX, DC, MC, VI. *(See color ad on insert)*

/ SOME UNITS

(See map and index starting on p. 512)

THE GRAND MAYAN ACAPULCO WYNDHAM ALLIANCE RESORT

Resort Hotel

$475-$785 All Year

Phone: (744)469-6000 29

Address: Ave Costera de las Palmas #1121 **Location:** 13.8 mi (22 km) se, off Mex 200 (Airport Hwy). **Facility:** The hotel shares facilities with the Mayan Palace and features large, luxurious rooms with eclectic decor, a terrace and a small plunge-pool. 354 units. 97 one-bedroom standard units with whirlpools. 257 one-bedroom suites with kitchens. 10 stories, interior corridors. **Parking:** on-site and valet. **Terms:** check-in 5 pm, 3-7 night minimum stay - seasonal and/or weekends, 21 day cancellation notice-fee imposed. **Amenities:** voice mail, safes, hair dryers. *Some:* irons. **Pool(s):** 2 outdoor. **Leisure Activities:** whirlpool, steamrooms, lifeguard on duty, recreation programs, spa, volleyball. *Fee:* canoes, golf-18 holes, 12 lighted tennis courts. **Guest Services:** valet and coin laundry. **Business Services:** business center. **Cards:** AX, MC, VI.

FEE / SOME UNITS

HOTEL ACAPULCO TORTUGA *Book at AAA.com*

Hotel

$75-$100 All Year

Phone: (744)484-8889 6

Address: Costera Miguel Aleman 132, Fracc Farallon **Location:** 3.1 mi (5 km) e. Located in a busy commercial area. **Facility:** 252 one-bedroom standard units. 7 stories, interior corridors. **Parking:** on-site (fee). **Pool(s):** outdoor. **Leisure Activities:** limited exercise equipment. **Guest Services:** valet laundry, wireless Internet. **Business Services:** meeting rooms, business center. **Cards:** AX, MC, VI.

HOTEL CROWNE PLAZA ACAPULCO

Hotel

$170-$250 All Year

Phone: (744)440-5555 4

Address: Costera Miguel Aleman 123, Fracc Magallanes **Location:** 2.8 mi (4.5 km) w. Located on the bay in a busy commercial area. **Facility:** 506 units. 427 one-bedroom standard units, some with whirlpools. 79 one-bedroom suites, some with whirlpools. 28 stories, interior corridors. **Parking:** valet. **Terms:** 3 day cancellation notice-fee imposed. **Amenities:** CD players, voice mail, safes, irons, hair dryers. *Some:* honor bars. **Pool(s):** 8 outdoor. **Leisure Activities:** limited beach access, 2 tennis courts (Fee: 2 lighted), recreation programs, exercise room, basketball. **Guest Services:** valet laundry, wireless Internet. **Business Services:** conference facilities, business center. **Cards:** AX, MC, VI.

D / SOME UNITS

HOTEL ELCANO *Book at AAA.com*

Hotel

$350 All Year

Phone: (744)435-1500 12

Address: Costera Miguel Aleman 75 **Location:** 3.8 mi (6 km) e. Located on the bay in a commercial area. **Facility:** 180 units. 163 one-bedroom standard units. 16 one- and 1 two-bedroom suites with whirlpools. 10 stories, interior corridors. **Parking:** on-site. **Terms:** 3 day cancellation notice. **Amenities:** safes, honor bars, hair dryers. **Pool(s):** outdoor. **Leisure Activities:** sauna, limited beach access, exercise room, volleyball. *Fee:* massage. **Guest Services:** valet laundry, wireless Internet. **Business Services:** meeting rooms, business center. **Cards:** AX, MC, VI.

HOTEL EMPORIO ACAPULCO *Book great rates at AAA.com*

AAA

Hotel

$300 All Year

Phone: (744)469-0505 1

Address: Ave Costera Miguel Aleman #121 **Location:** Oceanfront. 2.6 mi (4.5 km) w. Located on the bay in busy commercial area. **Facility:** Meets AAA guest room security requirements. 419 one-bedroom standard units. 11-14 stories, exterior corridors. **Parking:** on-site (fee) and valet. **Amenities:** safes, irons, hair dryers. *Some:* honor bars. **Dining:** 3 restaurants, also, Sunset, see separate listing. **Pool(s):** 3 heated outdoor. **Leisure Activities:** waterslide, beach access, playground, exercise room, spa, volleyball. *Fee:* tennis court, kids club. **Guest Services:** valet laundry, wireless Internet. **Business Services:** meeting rooms, business center. **Cards:** AX, CB, DC, DS, JC, MC, VI.

/ SOME UNITS

(See map and index starting on p. 512)

HOTEL LAS BRISAS ACAPULCO *Book great rates at AAA.com* **Phone:** (744)469-6900 **21**

Resort Hotel

$240-$515 All Year

Address: Carr Escenica 5255 **Location:** 7.1 mi (11.3 km) se on Mex 200 (Airport Hwy). Located on a mountainside in a residential area. **Facility:** Picturesque location with commanding view. Duplex cottages with private or semi-private swimming pools. 263 units. 216 one-bedroom standard units. 47 one-bedroom suites, some with whirlpools. 1 story, exterior corridors. *Bath:* combo or shower only. **Parking:** on-site. **Terms:** 7 day cancellation notice, 3 day off season-fee imposed. **Amenities:** DVD players, CD players, voice mail, safes, honor bars, irons, hair dryers. **Dining:** 2 restaurants, also, Bellavista, see separate listing. **Pool(s):** outdoor. **Leisure Activities:** exercise room, spa. *Fee:* 5 lighted tennis courts. **Guest Services:** valet laundry, beauty salon, wireless Internet. **Business Services:** conference facilities, business center. **Cards:** AX, MC, VI. *(See color ad below)*

/ SOME UNITS

▼ See AAA listing above ▼

(See map and index starting on p. 512)

HOTEL LAS HAMACAS **Phone:** 744/483-7006 14

Hotel

$50-$100 All Year

Address: Costera Miguel Aleman #239 **Location:** 0.6 mi (1 km) e, just n of beach. Located in a busy commercial area. **Facility:** 127 units. 122 one-bedroom standard units. 5 one-bedroom suites. 3-5 stories, exterior corridors. *Bath:* shower only. **Parking:** on-site. **Terms:** 7 day cancellation notice. **Pool(s):** outdoor. **Leisure Activities:** playground. **Guest Services:** valet laundry, wireless Internet. **Business Services:** meeting rooms. **Cards:** AX, MC, VI.

HYATT REGENCY ACAPULCO Book great rates at AAA.com **Phone:** (744)469-1234 18

Hotel

$79-$315 All Year

Address: Costera Miguel Aleman 1 **Location:** 5 mi (8 km) e. Located on the bay next to the Icacos Naval Base. **Facility:** 640 units. 603 one-bedroom standard units. 37 one-bedroom suites. 23 stories, interior corridors. **Parking:** on-site (fee) and valet. **Terms:** 3 day cancellation notice-fee imposed. **Amenities:** voice mail, hair dryers. *Some:* safes, honor bars. **Dining:** 3 restaurants, also, El Pescador, see separate listing. **Pool(s):** 2 outdoor. **Leisure Activities:** lifeguard on duty, spa, game room. *Fee:* exercise room. **Guest Services:** valet laundry, wireless Internet. **Business Services:** meeting rooms, business center. **Cards:** AX, MC, VI.

SOME UNITS

HYATT HOTELS & RESORTS

AAA Benefit:

Ask for the AAA rate and save 10%.

MAYAN PALACE ACAPULCO WYNDHAM ALLIANCE RESORT **Phone:** (744)469-6000 27

Resort Hotel

$520 All Year

Address: Ave Costera de las Palmas #1121 **Location:** 13.8 mi (22 km) se, off Mex 200 (Airport Hwy). Located in a quiet beachside setting. **Facility:** An enormous resort on the beach with unique Aztec construction, the property features lush gardens and has a huge reflecting pool in the lobby. 166 one-bedroom suites with efficiencies. 7 stories, interior corridors. **Parking:** on-site and valet. **Terms:** check-in 5 pm, 3-7 night minimum stay - seasonal and/or weekends, 21 day cancellation notice-fee imposed. **Amenities:** voice mail, safes, irons, hair dryers. **Pool(s):** 6 outdoor. **Leisure Activities:** whirlpool, steamrooms, lifeguard on duty, recreation programs, exercise room, spa, volleyball. *Fee:* canoes, paddleboats, golf-18 holes, 12 lighted tennis courts. **Guest Services:** valet laundry. **Business Services:** PC (fee). **Cards:** AX, MC, VI.

FEE

MAYAN SEA GARDEN ACAPULCO **Phone:** 744/466-1850 28

Hotel

$366-$637 All Year

Address: Ave Costera de las Palmas #1121 **Location:** 13.8 mi (22 km) se, off Mex 200 (Airport Hwy). Located adjacent to the beach. **Facility:** 112 units. 23 one-bedroom standard units. 89 one-bedroom suites with kitchens. 2-3 stories (no elevator), interior corridors. **Parking:** on-site. **Terms:** check-in 5 pm. **Amenities:** voice mail, safes (fee), irons, hair dryers. **Pool(s):** outdoor. **Leisure Activities:** lifeguard on duty, playground. *Fee:* golf-18 holes. **Guest Services:** valet laundry. **Business Services:** PC (fee). **Cards:** AX, MC, VI.

SOME UNITS

(See map and index starting on p. 512)

PARK ROYAL ACAPULCO Book at AAA.com Phone: (744)440-6565 5

Resort Hotel
$220-$440 All Year

Address: Costera Guitarron 110 Fracc Playa Guitarron **Location:** 5.9 mi (9.5 km) se off Carr Escencia, follow signs. Located on the bay in a residential area. **Facility:** Perched on the side of a mountain, the hotel overlooks Acapulco Bay and has an elegant lobby and a unique trolley system to take guests to their rooms. 207 units. 191 one-bedroom standard units. 12 one- and 4 two-bedroom suites. 4-7 stories, interior/exterior corridors. **Amenities:** voice mail, safes (fee), irons, hair dryers. **Pool(s):** 2 outdoor. **Leisure Activities:** limited beach access, recreation programs, spa, volleyball. *Fee:* exercise room. **Guest Services:** valet laundry, wireless Internet. **Business Services:** meeting rooms, PC (fee). **Cards:** AX, MC, VI.

/ SOME UNITS

QUINTA REAL ACAPULCO Book at AAA.com Phone: (744)469-1500 11

Hotel
$370-$500 All Year

Address: Paseo de la Quinta #6 Fracc Real Diamante **Location:** 1.3 mi (2 km) off Mex 200 (Airport Hwy); in Punta Diamante. Located in a quiet cliffside area. **Facility:** Located in an upscale area, the hotel is built into the side of a cliff and offers spectacular views of Acapulco Bay. 74 one-bedroom standard units, some with whirlpools. 5 stories, exterior corridors. **Parking:** on-site and valet. **Terms:** 2 night minimum stay - weekends, 3 day cancellation notice-fee imposed. **Amenities:** voice mail, honor bars, irons, hair dryers. *Some:* CD players, safes. **Dining:** Restaurant Buena Vista, see separate listing. **Pool(s):** outdoor. **Leisure Activities:** lifeguard on duty, exercise room, spa. **Guest Services:** valet laundry, wireless Internet. **Business Services:** conference facilities. **Cards:** AX, DC, DS, MC, VI. Affiliated with A Preferred Hotel. ***(See color ad p 8)***

24 / SOME UNITS

RITZ ACAPULCO HOTEL DE PLAYA Phone: (744)469-3500 3

Resort Hotel
$228-$297 All Year

Address: Costera Miguel Aleman 159 **Location:** 2.6 mi (4.2 km) e. Located on the bay in a busy commercial area. **Facility:** High-rise towers on beachfront. Average-size rooms with contemporary decor. Most with balcony and ocean view. 240 one-bedroom standard units. 11-14 stories, interior corridors. *Bath:* combo or shower only. **Parking:** on-site and valet. **Terms:** 7 day cancellation notice, in season-fee imposed. **Amenities:** voice mail, safes (fee). **Pool(s):** outdoor. **Leisure Activities:** recreation programs, exercise room. *Fee:* snorkeling. **Guest Services:** valet laundry, wireless Internet. **Business Services:** meeting rooms, PC (fee). **Cards:** AX, MC, VI.

D / SOME UNITS

VILLA VERA HOTEL SPA & RACQUET CLUB ACAPULCO Book at AAA.com Phone: (744)109-0570 10

Hotel
$100-$315 All Year

Address: Lomas del Mar 35 Fracc Club **Location:** 4 mi (6 km) e, 5 blks opposite from Beach Blvd. Located in a residential area. **Facility:** 70 one-bedroom standard units, some with whirlpools. 1-3 stories (no elevator), exterior corridors. **Parking:** on-site. **Terms:** check-in 4 pm, 3 day cancellation notice-fee imposed. **Amenities:** high-speed Internet (fee), voice mail, safes, honor bars, irons, hair dryers. *Some:* CD players. **Pool(s):** 5 outdoor. **Leisure Activities:** sauna, whirlpool, racquetball courts, spa. *Fee:* 2 lighted tennis courts, exercise room. **Guest Services:** valet laundry, wireless Internet. **Business Services:** meeting rooms, business center. **Cards:** AX, MC, VI.

The following lodging was either not evaluated or did not meet AAA rating requirements but is listed for your information only.

CALINDA BEACH ACAPULCO Phone: 744/435-0600

fyi

Not evaluated. **Address:** Costera Miguel Aleman, #1260 **Location:** 3.5 mi (5.6 km) e. Located on the bay in a heavy-commercial area. Facilities, services, and decor characterize a mid-scale property.

WHERE TO DINE

BAIKAL Phone: 744/446-6845 9

International
$19-$55

The visually stunning fine dining restaurant is set on a cliff overlooking Acapulco Bay. From the glass enclosed lobby surrounded by a reflecting pool to the spiral staircase, marble floors, large white columns, lovely art pieces and fabulous views, Baikal introduces a unique dining experience for its guests. Fresh fish, seafood, poultry, pasta and prime beef cuts make up some of the changing menu choices. A video light show is featured during dinner along with live music. Dressy casual. **Bar:** Full bar. **Reservations:** suggested. **Hours:** 7 pm-1 am, Fri & Sat-2 am. Closed: Mon off season. **Address:** Carr Escenica #16 & #22 Playa Guitarron **Location:** 5.9 mi (9.5 km) se. **Parking:** valet. **Cards:** AX, MC, VI.

CALL M

BELLAVISTA Phone: 744/469-6900 13

International
$23-$55

The restaurant offers creative cuisine in an elegant atmosphere. Enjoy dining outside, where every table has a spectacular view of Acapulco Bay. The menu consists of lobster, shrimp, duck, beef, chicken, and pasta dishes. Dressy casual. **Bar:** Full bar. **Reservations:** suggested, for dinner. **Hours:** 7 pm-11 pm. **Address:** Carr Escenica 5255 **Location:** 7.1 mi (11.3 km) se on Mex 200 (Airport Hwy); in Hotel Las Brisas Acapulco. **Parking:** on-site. **Cards:** AX, MC, VI.

CASANOVA Phone: 744/446-6237 10

Northern Italian
$20-$35

Both indoors and on the outdoor patio, the atmosphere is elegant and the hilltop vantage point ideal for looking out on Acapulco Bay. The attentive wait staff is dressed in semi-formal attire. The menu features varieties of veal, shrimp, fresh fish, beef, lamb and pasta, as well as traditional antipasto and desserts. Dressy casual. Entertainment. **Bar:** Full bar. **Reservations:** suggested. **Hours:** 7 pm-11 pm, Fri & Sat-midnight. Closed: Sun. **Address:** Escenica Las Brisas 5256 **Location:** 7.5 mi (12 km) se on Mex 200 (Airport Hwy). **Parking:** on-site and valet. **Cards:** AX, MC, VI.

(See map and index starting on p. 512)

COYUCA 22 **Phone:** 744/482-3468 (7)

Continental
$20-$38

In an open-air setting on the mountainside, the attractive restaurant affords a panoramic view of Acapulco Bay. Menu features include succulent lobster and prime rib. Dressy casual. **Bar:** Full bar. **Reservations:** suggested. **Hours:** 7 pm-11 pm. **Address:** Coyuca 22 **Location:** From Caleta Beach, follow signs. **Parking:** street. **Cards:** AX, DC, DS, MC, VI.

EL FOGON MEXICAN RESTAURANT **Phone:** 744/484-3607 (4)

Mexican
$4-$10

A casual eatery set along Acapulco's busiest thoroughfares, this open-air restaurant features an enormous menu of classic Mexican comfort food. The service is laid back and friendly. Casual dress. **Bar:** Full bar. **Hours:** 24 hours. **Address:** Costera Miguel Aleman S/N **Location:** 2.9 mi (4.6 km) e; near Diana Glorieta traffic circle. **Parking:** on-site. **Cards:** AX, MC, VI.

EL OLVIDO **Phone:** 744/481-0214 (3)

Continental
$18-$30

Dishes reflect a fusion of French and Mexican styles at this open-breezeway restaurant on Acapulco Bay. Mood lighting lends a romantic feel to multi-tiered terraces among palm trees. Tabletop candles flicker to the soothing sound of crashing waves. Dressy casual. **Bar:** Full bar. **Reservations:** accepted. **Hours:** 6 pm-1 am. **Address:** Costera Miguel Aleman S/N **Location:** 3.1 mi (5 km) e of Zocalo; adjacent to Diana Glorieta traffic circle. **Parking:** on-site and street. **Cards:** AX, MC, VI.

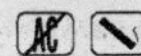

EL PESCADOR **Phone:** 744/469-1234 (14)

International
$15-$30

This romantic and casual open-air restaurant offers stunning views of Acapulco Bay from most of the tables. Grilled fish and other seafood—as well as meats, pasta and lighter fare such as burgers and entree salads—are prepared with international influences. Casual dress. **Bar:** Full bar. **Reservations:** suggested. **Hours:** noon-11 pm. **Address:** Costera Miguel Aleman 1 **Location:** 5 mi (8 km) e; in Hyatt Regency Acapulco. **Parking:** on-site (fee). **Cards:** AX, MC, VI.

KOOKABURRA **Phone:** 744/446-6020 (8)

Seafood
$6-$40

Perched on a hill beside Acapulco Bay, the open-air restaurant presents creative preparations of quail, duck, local red snapper and beef filet, many tinged with citrus flavorings. Desserts are fun and tempting. The staff is gracious and friendly. Casual dress. Entertainment. **Bar:** Full bar. **Reservations:** suggested. **Hours:** noon-5 & 6-midnight. **Address:** Carr Escenica S/N **Location:** 6.3 mi (10 km) e; 1.8 mi (3 km) s of Costera Miguel Aleman. **Parking:** valet. **Cards:** MC, VI.

LA HACIENDA **Phone:** 744/469-1000 (11)

Mexican
$20-$30

Guests dine amid the sounds of the lovely ballads sung by the mariachi singers and the peaceful echoes of the ocean waves rolling ashore. The menu has an excellent variety ranging from the more traditional Mexican cuisine to plenty of fish, seafood and steak options. The wait staff are welcoming and are dressed in traditional Mexican clothing. Dressy casual. **Bar:** Full bar. **Reservations:** suggested. **Hours:** 7 pm-11 pm, Sun noon-6 pm. Closed: Mon. **Address:** Playa Revolcadero S/N **Location:** 12.1 mi (19.3 km) se, off Mex 200 (Airport Hwy); in The Fairmont Acapulco Princess. **Parking:** on-site and valet. **Cards:** AX, MC, VI.

LA MANSION **Phone:** 744/481-0796 (1)

International
$14-$27

Prime beef cuts are the main attraction at the restaurant, which counts sharply dressed servers and tables draped in white cloths among the features lending to its upscale ambience. Those wanting traditional Mexican food will find suitable selections on the large menu. Steaks are served on heavy wood plates with handles. Dressy casual. **Bar:** Full bar. **Reservations:** accepted. **Hours:** 2 pm-midnight. **Address:** Costera Miguel Aleman 81-26 **Location:** 3.8 mi (6 km) e. **Parking:** valet. **Cards:** AX, MC, VI.

LA TRATTORIA **Phone:** 744/435-1600 (15)

Italian
$15-$22

Italian and Continental dishes come together on the menu at the upbeat restaurant, which is appointed in contemporary decor. On weekends, many explore the extensive buffet, which includes a wide selection of meats and vegetables, a made-to-order pasta station and an extensive choice of desserts. Before or after their meals, diners can head to the outdoor lounge for drinks and great views of Acapulco Bay. Casual dress. **Bar:** Full bar. **Reservations:** suggested. **Hours:** 6 pm-midnight. **Address:** Costera Miguel Aleman #2311 **Location:** 3.1 mi (5.3 km) e; in Fiesta Americana Villas Acapulco. **Parking:** on-site (fee). **Cards:** AX, MC, VI.

LA VERANDA **Phone:** 744/469-1000 (18)

Italian
$12-$25

A broad selection of Italian fare includes freshly prepared pasta dishes, gourmet pizzas, grilled meats and seafood options. The large air-conditioned dining room features a pleasant decor and is tended by warm, personal servers. Casual dress. **Reservations:** suggested. **Hours:** 7 pm-11 pm. **Address:** Playa Revolcadero S/N **Location:** 12.1 mi (19.3 km) se, off Mex 200 (Airport Hwy); in The Fairmont Acapulco Princess. **Parking:** on-site (fee). **Cards:** AX, MC, VI.

(See map and index starting on p. 512)

RESTAURANT BUENA VISTA **Phone:** 744/469-1500 (19)

International
$13-$37

Perched high on a hill, the restaurant affords outstanding views, particularly from its elegant dining room, which is appointed with upscale artwork. Guests can sit here or on the romantic outdoor terrace to explore the international menu. Semi-formal attire. **Bar:** Full bar. **Reservations:** suggested. **Hours:** 7 am-noon & 6-11:30 pm. **Address:** Paseo de la Quinta #6 **Location:** 1.3 mi (2 km) off Mex 200 (Airport Hwy); in Punta Diamante; in Quinta Real Acapulco. **Parking:** on-site. **Cards:** AX, DC, DS, MC, VI.

SANBORN'S **Phone:** 744/481-2426

Mexican
$8-$18

Restaurants in the casual chain, which includes more than 100 locations throughout Mexico, offer a good selection of American-style sandwiches, salads, soups and both Mexican and American entrees. The selection of desserts is impressive. Casual dress. **Bar:** Full bar. **Hours:** 7 am-1 am, Sun-midnight. **Address:** Costera Miguel Aleman, #1260 **Location:** 3.5 mi (5.6 km) e; in Calinda Beach Acapulco. **Parking:** on-site. **Cards:** AX, MC, VI.

SANBORN'S **Phone:** 744/482-6169

Mexican
$8-$18

Restaurants in the casual chain, which includes more than 100 locations throughout Mexico, offer a good selection of American-style sandwiches, salads, soups and both Mexican and American entrees. The selection of desserts is impressive. Casual dress. **Bar:** Full bar. **Hours:** 7:30 am-11 pm. **Address:** Costera Miguel Aleman, #209 **Location:** In downtown area. **Parking:** on-site. **Cards:** AX, MC, VI.

SANBORN'S **Phone:** 744/484-2025

Mexican
$8-$18

Restaurants in the casual chain, which includes more than 100 locations throughout Mexico, offer a good selection of American-style sandwiches, salads, soups and both Mexican and American entrees. The selection of desserts is impressive. Casual dress. **Bar:** Full bar. **Hours:** 7 am-1 pm, Sun-midnight. **Address:** Costera Miguel Aleman, #3111 **Location:** Jct El Morro and Costern Miguel Aleman. **Parking:** on-site. **Cards:** AX, MC, VI.

SENOR FROG'S **Phone:** 744/446-5734

International
$10-$16

Part of the chain of Mexican restaurants that also includes Carlos 'n Charlie's, the fun and festive eatery is a great place to eat with the family or rendezvous with friends. The menu is lined with Tex-Mex, American and Mexican favorites, such as Buffalo wings, quesadillas, fajitas and burritos. After hours, a bar atmosphere prevails. Casual dress. **Bar:** Full bar. **Reservations:** accepted. **Hours:** 1 pm-1 am. Closed: 1/1. **Address:** Carretera Escenica No 28 **Location:** Carret Excenica No 28 Fracc. **Parking:** valet. **Cards:** AX, MC, VI.

SONORA STEAKS BAR AND GRILL **Phone:** 744/481-1404 (17)

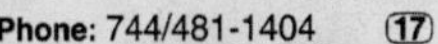

Steak
$15-$25

In a residential area removed from the tourist traffic along the bustling strip, the casual open-air eatery features a good selection of grilled steaks and tasty Mexican fare. Casual dress. **Bar:** Full bar. **Hours:** 5 pm-2 am. **Address:** Horacio Nelson 3206 **Location:** Just n of Ave Custera M Aleman. **Parking:** on-site. **Cards:** MC, VI.

SU CASA **Phone:** 744/484-4350 (6)

Continental
$14-$32

Perched on a mountainside, this intimate restaurant offers fabulous views of Acapulco Bay. The dining area is on a large open-air terrace with archways that are lined with twinkling lights and flower baskets. The ambience is romantic and the food is well-prepared. While Su Casa offers a wide variety of Continental cuisine, the adjoining dining room and sister restaurant, La Margarita, offers the more traditional Mexican food. Dressy casual. **Bar:** Full bar. **Reservations:** suggested, in season. **Hours:** 5 pm-11:30 pm. **Address:** Anahuac #110, Lomas de Costa Azul **Location:** Jct Costera Miguel Aleman and Calle Cristobal Colon, 0.6 mi (1 km) nw. **Parking:** on-site. **Cards:** MC, VI.

SUNSET **Phone:** 744/469-0505 (2)

International
$12-$35

The open-air restaurant's covered terrace overlooks the pool and beachfront. A peaceful feel envelops the upscale tropical setting. Distinct Asian influences flavor the varied international dishes. This place affords a nice change from the normal bustle of Acapulco. Casual dress. **Bar:** Full bar. **Reservations:** suggested. **Hours:** 1 pm-midnight. Closed: Mon. **Address:** Ave Costera Miguel Aleman #121 **Location:** 2.6 mi (4.5 km) w; in Hotel Emporio Acapulco. **Parking:** on-site (fee). **Cards:** AX, CB, DC, DS, JC, MC, VI.

SUNTORY ACAPULCO **Phone:** 744/484-8088 (5)

Japanese
$11-$36

Dishes are prepared tableside at the Japanese restaurant, which features combinations of fresh seafood, poultry and beef, as well as sushi and rice. Dining room windows look over a manicured garden. The dining room is a nice spot for groups and conversation. Casual dress. **Bar:** Full bar. **Reservations:** accepted. **Hours:** 2 pm-midnight. **Address:** Costera Miguel Aleman #36 **Location:** 4.7 mi (7.5 km) e. **Parking:** valet. **Cards:** AX, MC, VI.

TABACHIN **Phone:** 744/435-2600 (12)

French
$20-$40

It is daring. It is exciting. It is French fusion and Asian-inspired cuisine. It is Tabachin! It is out of the ordinary! And, it is one of Acapulco's best and most 'civilized' restaurants. Dressy casual. Entertainment. **Bar:** Full bar. **Reservations:** suggested. **Hours:** 7 pm-midnight. **Address:** Playa Revolcadero S/N **Location:** 10.9 mi (17.5 km) se, off Mex 200 (Airport Hwy); in The Fairmont Pierre Marques. **Parking:** on-site and valet. **Cards:** AX, MC, VI.

(See map and index starting on p. 512)

VIPS

Mexican
$5-$9

Phone: 744/486-8572

Owned by Wal-Mart of Mexico and found in most major cities, the budget-friendly chain serves a good variety of Mexican and American dishes, including burgers, sandwiches, salads, spaghetti and enchiladas, as well as a fine selection of desserts. Casual dress. **Hours:** 7 am-midnight, Fri & Sat-2 am. **Address:** Costera Miguel Aleman #1626 **Location:** On Gran Plaza, jct aves Costera Miguel Aleman and Wilfrido Massiew. **Parking:** on-site. **Cards:** MC, VI.

VIPS

Mexican
$5-$9

Phone: 744/484-7871

Owned by Wal-Mart of Mexico and found in most major cities, the budget-friendly chain serves a good variety of Mexican and American dishes, including burgers, sandwiches, salads, spaghetti and enchiladas, as well as a fine selection of desserts. Casual dress. **Hours:** 7 am-midnight, Fri & Sat-1 am. **Address:** Costera Miguel Aleman #1252 **Location:** Jct Ave Wilfrido Massiau Perez. **Parking:** on-site. **Cards:** MC, VI.

VIPS

Mexican
$5-$9

Phone: 744/481-3165

Owned by Wal-Mart of Mexico and found in most major cities, the budget-friendly chain serves a good variety of Mexican and American dishes, including burgers, sandwiches, salads, spaghetti and enchiladas, as well as a fine selection of desserts. Casual dress. **Hours:** 7 am-midnight. **Address:** Vincente Xanez de Pizon #L30 **Location:** Just w of Glorieta La Diana. **Parking:** on-site. **Cards:** MC, VI.

VIPS

Mexican
$5-$9

Phone: 744/484-9509

Owned by Wal-Mart of Mexico and found in most major cities, the budget-friendly chain serves a good variety of Mexican and American dishes, including burgers, sandwiches, salads, spaghetti and enchiladas, as well as a fine selection of desserts. Casual dress. **Hours:** 7 am-midnight. **Address:** Costera Miguel Aleman #500 **Location:** Jct Calle Horacio Nelson and Costera Miguel Aleman, just e. **Parking:** on-site. **Cards:** MC, VI.

This ends listings for Acapulco.
The following page resumes the alphabetical listings of cities in The Pacific Coast.

BAHIAS DE HUATULCO, OAXACA pop. 28,237

WHERE TO STAY

BARCELO HUATULCO BEACH *Book at AAA.com* **Phone:** (958)581-0055

Resort Hotel
$154-$290 All Year

Address: Blvd Benito Juarez **Location:** In Tangolunda Hotel Zone. **Facility:** Wide sandy beach. All rooms with balcony view of the Pacific Ocean. In-season entertainment and social activities. 351 units. 346 one-bedroom standard units. 5 one-bedroom suites. 6 stories, interior corridors. **Parking:** on-site. **Terms:** 3 day cancellation notice. **Amenities:** safes, honor bars, irons, hair dryers. **Dining:** Don Quijote, El Agave, see separate listings. **Pool(s):** 2 outdoor. **Leisure Activities:** putting green, 3 lighted tennis courts, recreation programs, playground, exercise room, sports court, volleyball. *Fee:* sailboats, windsurfing, waterskiing, charter fishing, massage. **Guest Services:** valet laundry, wireless Internet. **Business Services:** conference facilities. *Fee:* PC, fax. **Cards:** AX, MC, VI.

SOME UNITS

BEST WESTERN POSADA CHAHUE *Book great rates at AAA.com* **Phone:** (958)587-0945

Hotel
$120-$155 All Year

Address: Mixie y Mixteco, Bahia de Chahue **Location:** 4.9 mi (8 km) from center. **Facility:** 20 one-bedroom standard units, some with whirlpools. 3 stories (no elevator), exterior corridors. *Bath:* combo or shower only. **Parking:** on-site. **Amenities:** safes, honor bars, irons, hair dryers. **Pool(s):** outdoor. **Guest Services:** wireless Internet. **Business Services:** meeting rooms. **Cards:** AX, DS, MC, VI.

AAA Benefit: Members save up to 20%, plus 10% bonus points with rewards program.

CAMINO REAL ZAASHILA *Book at AAA.com* **Phone:** (958)583-0300

Resort Hotel
$220-$380 All Year

Address: Blvd Benito Juarez 5 **Location:** In Tangolunda Hotel Zone. **Facility:** Spacious guest rooms sport a bright Mexican decor; some units feature a balcony with ocean views or a private plunge pool. 148 units. 120 one-bedroom standard units. 20 one- and 8 two-bedroom suites with efficiencies (no utensils). 2-4 stories (no elevator), exterior corridors. **Parking:** valet. **Amenities:** high-speed Internet (fee), voice mail, safes, honor bars, irons, hair dryers. **Dining:** Azul Profundo Restaurant, see separate listing. **Pool(s):** outdoor. **Leisure Activities:** whirlpool, limited beach access, tennis court (Fee: 1 lighted), exercise room. *Fee:* bicycles, massage. **Guest Services:** valet laundry, wireless Internet. **Business Services:** meeting rooms, PC. **Cards:** AX, MC, VI.

SOME UNITS

CROWN PACIFIC HUATULCO **Phone:** 958/581-0044

Resort Hotel
$300-$460 All Year

Address: Blvd Benito Juarez #8 **Location:** In Tangolunda Hotel Zone. **Facility:** Lavish, built on terraced hillside overlooking the ocean. Flamboyant design. Some rooms reached by funicular. Large, attractive suites. Meets AAA guest room security requirements. 135 one-bedroom standard units, some with whirlpools. 2-3 stories, exterior corridors. **Parking:** on-site. **Terms:** 20 day cancellation notice-fee imposed. **Amenities:** safes, honor bars, hair dryers. *Some:* DVD players, CD players, irons. **Pool(s):** 2 outdoor. **Leisure Activities:** steamrooms, recreation programs, playground, exercise room, game room. *Fee:* lighted tennis court, massage. **Guest Services:** valet laundry, area transportation, wireless Internet. **Business Services:** conference facilities, PC, fax. **Cards:** AX, MC, VI.

SOME UNITS

HOTEL MEICER PALMIER **Phone:** 985/587-0307

Hotel
$140 All Year

Address: Blvd Santa Cruz 201 **Location:** In Santa Cruz Bay area. **Facility:** 165 one-bedroom standard units. 2 stories (no elevator), interior corridors. *Bath:* shower only. **Parking:** on-site. **Amenities:** safes. **Pool(s):** outdoor. **Guest Services:** area transportation, wireless Internet. **Cards:** AX, MC, VI.

HOTEL VILLABLANCA **Phone:** 958/587-0606

Hotel
$68-$145 All Year

Address: Blvd Benito Juarez S/N **Location:** In Bahia Chahue. **Facility:** 40 units. 34 one- and 6 two-bedroom standard units. 3 stories (no elevator), interior/exterior corridors. *Bath:* shower only. **Parking:** on-site. **Terms:** check-in 4 pm. **Amenities:** safes, hair dryers. **Pool(s):** outdoor. **Guest Services:** wireless Internet. **Business Services:** meeting rooms, PC. **Cards:** AX, MC, VI.

SOME UNITS

LAS BRISAS HUATULCO *Book at AAA.com* **Phone:** (958)583-0200

Resort Hotel
$244-$332 All Year

Address: Bahia de Tangolunda Lote 1 **Location:** In Tangolunda Hotel Zone. **Facility:** Nestled on a cliff overlooking a peaceful bay, the property's guest rooms are tastefully decorated; select from all-inclusive or European plans. 484 one-bedroom standard units. 3 stories (no elevator), exterior corridors. *Bath:* shower only. **Parking:** on-site. **Amenities:** voice mail, safes, honor bars, hair dryers. **Pool(s):** 3 outdoor. **Leisure Activities:** limited beach access, 12 lighted tennis courts, playground, basketball, volleyball. **Guest Services:** valet laundry, wireless Internet. **Business Services:** conference facilities. **Cards:** AX, MC, VI.

QUINTA REAL HUATULCO

Hotel
$290-$509 All Year

Phone: 958/581-0428

Address: Blvd Benito Juarez Lote 2 **Location:** Oceanfront. In Tangolunda Hotel Zone. **Facility:** Units feature a Mexican decor with cobblestone floors and stunning views of the bay; some units include a private balcony with a plunge-pool. 28 one-bedroom standard units with whirlpools. 2-3 stories, exterior corridors. **Parking:** on-site. **Amenities:** safes, honor bars, irons, hair dryers. **Dining:** Las Cupulas Restaurant, see separate listing. **Pool(s):** outdoor. **Leisure Activities:** limited beach access, lighted tennis court. **Guest Services:** valet laundry, wireless Internet. **Business Services:** meeting rooms. **Cards:** AX, MC, VI. ***(See color ad p 8)***

WHERE TO DINE

AZUL PROFUNDO RESTAURANT

International
$18-$30

Phone: 958/581-0460

This elegant restaurant features tables directly on the beach, as well as others on an open-air patio. A path of candles leading to the dining area lends to the romantic ambience. On the menu is a creative mix of Mexican and international fare. Casual dress. **Reservations:** suggested. **Hours:** 7 pm-midnight. Closed: Tues & Sat. **Address:** Blvd Benito Jurez 5 **Location:** In Tangolunda Hotel Zone; in Camino Real Zaashila. **Parking:** valet. **Cards:** AX, MC, VI.

DON QUIJOTE

Spanish
$15-$25

Phone: 958/581-0055

Sophistication characterizes the Spanish-style dining room, where a pianist performs as patrons savor a good variety of fresh fish and other seafood, in addition to meat and poultry prepared with a spicy flair. Tasty starters include Spanish sausages and a variety of homemade soups and salads. Servers in formal attire do their best to make the evening memorable. Dressy casual. **Bar:** Full bar. **Reservations:** required. **Hours:** 7 pm-11 pm. **Address:** Blvd Benito Juarez **Location:** In Tangolunda Hotel Zone; in Barcelo Huatulco Beach. **Parking:** on-site. **Cards:** AX, MC, VI.

EL AGAVE

Mexican
$10-$18

Phone: 958/581-0055

Comfortable decor marks this Mexican restaurant, where the nice menu selection includes local and regional cuisine. Starters, including tortilla soup and stuffed peppers, get the taste buds primed for entrees such as chicken with mole and tequila shrimp. Homemade desserts taste great with Mexican coffee. Casual dress. **Bar:** Full bar. **Reservations:** required. **Hours:** 7 pm-11 pm. **Address:** Blvd Benito Juarez **Location:** In Tangolunda Hotel Zone; in Barcelo Huatulco Beach. **Parking:** on-site. **Cards:** AX, MC, VI.

LAS CUPULAS RESTAURANT

International
$17-$28

Phone: 958/581-0428

This elegant restaurant offers diners the choice of open-air patio or air-conditioned indoor seating. Luxurious decor and fine Mexican artwork characterize the inside tables, while romance prevails on the candlelit patio. On the menu is a good mix of Mexican and international fare. Roaming mariachis play requests tableside. Casual dress. **Bar:** Full bar. **Reservations:** suggested. **Hours:** 7:30-noon & 7-11 pm. **Address:** Blvd Benito Juarez Lote 2 **Location:** In Tangolunda Hotel Zone; in Quinta Real Huatulco. **Parking:** valet. **Cards:** AX, MC, VI.

BUCERIAS, NAYARIT pop. 2,000

WHERE TO STAY

ROYAL DECAMERON COMPLEX

Resort
Hotel
$240 All Year

Phone: 329/298-0226

Address: Lazaro Cardenas 150 **Location:** Oceanfront. On Mex 200, exit n through the Decameron gates; center. **Facility:** The all-inclusive resort features comfortable rooms with a bright Mexican decor, a good choice of dining options and various entertainment programs. 620 one-bedroom standard units. 4-5 stories (no elevator), exterior corridors. *Bath:* shower only. **Parking:** on-site. **Amenities:** safes (fee), hair dryers. **Pool(s):** 5 outdoor. **Leisure Activities:** limited beach access, windsurfing, snorkeling, 3 tennis courts, recreation programs, bicycles, playground, exercise room, spa, shuffleboard, volleyball, game room. *Fee:* scuba diving. **Business Services:** meeting rooms, PC (fee). **Cards:** MC, VI.

The following lodgings were either not evaluated or did not meet AAA rating requirements but are listed for your information only.

HOTEL PALMERAS

fyi

Phone: 329/298-1288

Not evaluated. **Address:** Calle Lazaro Cardenas #35 **Location:** 0.3 mi (0.5 km) s of central plaza. Facilities, services, and decor characterize a mid-scale property.

SUITES COSTA DORADA

fyi

Phone: 329/298-0046

Not evaluated. **Address:** Lazaro Cardenas #156 Sur **Location:** Center. Facilities, services, and decor characterize an economy property.

WHERE TO DINE

ADAUTO'S ON THE BEACH

Seafood
$13-$36

Phone: 329/298-2790

Diners can sit right on the beach with their toes touching the sand or in the indoor dining room, which has a high palapa roof. Seafood is a specialty on a menu of local and regional fare. Highlights include shrimp fajitas, fresh local lobster, combination platters and homemade Mexican dishes. Casual dress. **Bar:** Full bar. **Reservations:** accepted. **Hours:** 11:30 am-10 pm. Closed: Mon. **Address:** Ave del Pacifico #11A **Location:** Center. **Parking:** street. **Cards:** MC, VI.

ADRIATICO **Phone:** 329/298-6038

Italian
$12-$32

Lush tropical plants and tranquil water fountains surround the open-air dining area, which tucks under a high palapa roof. Freshly prepared Italian dishes include innovative pasta, meat, lamb and fish and other seafood selections. Live music is featured Tuesday through Saturday. Dressy casual. **Bar:** Full bar. **Reservations:** suggested. **Hours:** 5:30 pm-10:30 pm. **Address:** Lazarco Cardenas S/N **Location:** Center. **Parking:** street. **Cards:** MC, VI.

CLAUDIO'S MESON BAY RESTAURANT **Phone:** 329/298-1634

Seafood
$4-$15

At the beachside eatery, patrons can watch the breakers while dining on fresh seafood. Shrimp, lobster and fresh red snapper are perfectly baked. There's a bar here, too, with giant margaritas that demand quick attention. Casual dress. **Bar:** Full bar. **Reservations:** accepted. **Hours:** 11 am-11 pm. **Address:** Calle Lazaro Cardenas #17 **Location:** Center. **Parking:** street.

EL BRUJO **Phone:** 329/298-0406

Seafood
$8-$15

This casual and comfortable eatery's covered open-air terrace overlooks the ocean. Fresh seafood and traditional Mexican dishes share space on the menu. Freshly prepared tortillas and a showy flaming presentation of fajitas appeal. Credit cards are not accepted. Casual dress. **Bar:** Full bar. **Reservations:** not accepted. **Hours:** noon-9 pm. **Address:** Ave Pacifico No 202A **Location:** Center. **Parking:** no self-parking.

KAREN'S PLACE BEACHFRONT RESTAURANT **Phone:** 329/298-3176

International
$12-$25

In the evening, candlelit tables enhance the feeling of romance at this open-air restaurant, where guests enjoy beach views as they dine on fresh pasta, seafood or fine steak. Casual dress. **Bar:** Full bar. **Reservations:** suggested. **Hours:** 9 am-9 pm, Sun-3 pm. **Address:** Lazaro Cardenas #156 Sur **Location:** Center. **Parking:** street. **Cards:** MC, VI.

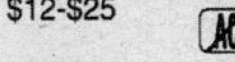

MARK'S BAR AND GRILL **Phone:** 329/298-0303

International
$15-$31

Reservations are highly recommended for this popular establishment, which presents an innovative menu in an upscale yet comfortable setting. Offerings include hot and cold appetizers, including fresh flat-bread selections, and fire-baked pizzas as well as fresh pasta dishes, seafood and grilled meats. Stuffed whole baby chicken is a popular choice. Homemade desserts provide a decadent indulgence. Patrons can sit indoor or on the patio. Casual dress. **Bar:** Full bar. **Reservations:** suggested. **Hours:** 5 pm-11 pm. **Address:** Lazaro Cardenas 56 **Location:** Center. **Parking:** street. **Cards:** MC, VI.

MEZZOGIORNO RISTORANTE ITALIANO **Phone:** 329/298-0350

Italian
$9-$20

This popular eatery attracts both loyal locals and the tourist market. Several tables in the stunning setting directly overlook the beach. Ocean breezes blow through the open-air dining room, which has a thatched palapa roof. Homemade pasta combines with seafood, chicken and rich sauces. Casual dress. **Bar:** Full bar. **Reservations:** required. **Hours:** 6 pm-11 pm. Closed: Mon. **Address:** Ave del Pacifico #33 **Location:** Center. **Parking:** street. **Cards:** DS, MC, VI.

COLIMA, COLIMA pop. 129,958

WHERE TO STAY

FIESTA INN COLIMA **Phone:** 312/316-4444

Hotel
$87-$148 All Year

Address: Prolongacion Blvd Camino Real 1101 **Location:** Next to the University of Colima. Located across from the Convention Centre. **Facility:** 104 one-bedroom standard units. 3 stories, interior corridors. *Bath:* shower only. **Parking:** on-site. **Amenities:** hair dryers. **Pool(s):** heated outdoor. **Leisure Activities:** exercise room. **Guest Services:** wireless Internet. **Business Services:** meeting rooms, PC (fee). **Cards:** AX, MC, VI. *(See color ad on insert)*

/ SOME UNITS

MOTEL LOS CANDILES SA **Phone:** (312)312-3212

Hotel
$80-$105 All Year

Address: Blvd Camino Real #399 **Location:** 0.9 mi (1.5 km) ne on Mex 54. **Facility:** 75 units. 73 one-bedroom standard units. 2 one-bedroom suites. 3 stories (no elevator), interior/exterior corridors. *Bath:* combo or shower only. **Parking:** on-site. **Amenities:** *Some:* safes. **Pool(s):** outdoor. **Business Services:** meeting rooms, PC. **Cards:** AX, MC, VI.

The following lodgings were either not evaluated or did not meet AAA rating requirements but are listed for your information only.

BEST WESTERN HOTEL CEBALLOS — **Phone:** 312/312-4444

fyi

Not evaluated. **Address:** Portal Medellin No 12 **Location:** Centre. Facilities, services, and decor characterize a mid-scale property.

AAA Benefit: Members save up to 20%, plus 10% bonus points with rewards program.

HACIENDA DE SAN ANTONIO — **Phone:** 312/314-3143

fyi

Not evaluated. **Address:** Municipio Comala. Facilities, services, and decor characterize a mid-scale property.

WHERE TO DINE

VIPS — **Phone:** 312/312-0083

Mexican
$5-$9

Owned by Wal-Mart of Mexico and found in most major cities, the budget-friendly chain serves a good variety of Mexican and American dishes, including burgers, sandwiches, salads, spaghetti and enchiladas, as well as a fine selection of desserts. Casual dress. **Hours:** 7 am-11 pm, Fri & Sat-midnight. **Address:** Pedro A Galvan Norte #120 **Location:** Jct Calzon Pedro A Galvan Norte and Ave Allende, just s. **Parking:** on-site. **Cards:** MC, VI.

IXTAPA, GUERRERO pop. 1,000

WHERE TO STAY

BARCELO IXTAPA BEACH *Book at AAA.com* — **Phone:** (755)555-2000

Hotel
$234-$324 All Year

Address: Blvd Ixtapa S/N **Location:** South end of hotel zone. **Facility:** 390 units. 340 one-bedroom standard units. 50 one-bedroom suites with efficiencies. 12 stories, interior corridors. **Parking:** on-site. **Terms:** 7 day cancellation notice-fee imposed. **Amenities:** voice mail, safes, honor bars, irons, hair dryers. **Pool(s):** 2 outdoor. **Leisure Activities:** whirlpool, 3 tennis courts (1 lighted), recreation programs, bicycles, playground, exercise room, volleyball. *Fee:* massage. **Guest Services:** valet laundry, wireless Internet. **Business Services:** meeting rooms, PC (fee). **Cards:** AX, MC, VI.

SOME UNITS

BEST WESTERN POSADA REAL IXTAPA — **Phone:** (755)553-1745

Hotel
$140 All Year

Address: Blvd Ixtapa S/N **Location:** Oceanfront. North end of hotel zone. **Facility:** 110 one-bedroom standard units. 4 stories, interior corridors. *Bath:* shower only. **Parking:** on-site. **Amenities:** voice mail, safes, hair dryers. **Pool(s):** 2 outdoor. **Leisure Activities:** limited beach access. **Guest Services:** valet laundry, wireless Internet. **Business Services:** meeting rooms. **Cards:** AX, MC, VI.

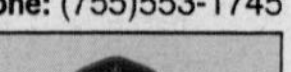

AAA Benefit: Members save up to 20%, plus 10% bonus points with rewards program.

DORADO PACIFICO IXTAPA *Book at AAA.com* — **Phone:** (755)553-2025

Hotel
$170-$210 All Year

Address: Paseo de Ixtapa S/N Lote 3-A **Location:** Oceanfront. North end of hotel zone. **Facility:** 285 one-bedroom standard units. 11 stories, interior corridors. **Parking:** on-site. **Amenities:** voice mail, safes, honor bars, hair dryers. **Dining:** La Terraza del Mar, see separate listing. **Pool(s):** outdoor. **Leisure Activities:** waterslide, limited beach access, 2 tennis courts (Fee: 2 lighted), recreation programs, playground. *Fee:* massage. **Guest Services:** valet laundry, wireless Internet. **Business Services:** meeting rooms, PC (fee). **Cards:** AX, MC, VI.

SOME UNITS

EMPORIO IXTAPA *Book at AAA.com* — **Phone:** (755)553-1066

Hotel
$169 All Year

Address: Blvd Ixtapa S/N **Location:** In center of hotel zone. **Facility:** 219 units. 196 one-bedroom standard units. 17 one- and 6 two-bedroom suites. 11 stories, interior corridors. *Bath:* shower only. **Parking:** on-site. **Terms:** 3 day cancellation notice. **Amenities:** safes, honor bars, hair dryers. **Pool(s):** outdoor. **Leisure Activities:** sauna, whirlpool, recreation programs, exercise room, spa. *Fee:* 2 lighted tennis courts. **Guest Services:** valet laundry, wireless Internet. **Business Services:** meeting rooms, business center. **Cards:** AX, MC, VI.

SOME UNITS

HOLIDAY INN IXTAPA — **Phone:** 755/555-0500

Hotel
$130-$191 All Year

Address: Paseo del Palmar Mz 1 L 1 **Location:** South end of hotel zone; across from beach. **Facility:** 153 one-bedroom standard units. 6 stories, interior corridors. *Bath:* combo or shower only. **Parking:** on-site. **Terms:** 3 day cancellation notice. **Amenities:** high-speed Internet, voice mail, safes, irons, hair dryers. **Pool(s):** outdoor. **Leisure Activities:** whirlpool, playground, exercise room. **Guest Services:** wireless Internet. **Business Services:** meeting rooms, business center. **Cards:** AX, MC, VI.

/ SOME UNITS

HOTEL FONTAN IXTAPA BEACH RESORT — Book at AAA.com — **Phone:** (755)553-1666

Hotel
$153-$202 All Year

Address: Blvd Ixtapa S/N **Location:** In center of hotel zone. **Facility:** 472 units. 464 one-bedroom standard units. 8 one-bedroom suites. 8 stories, interior corridors. *Bath:* shower only. **Parking:** on-site. **Terms:** check-in 4 pm, cancellation fee imposed. **Pool(s):** 2 outdoor. **Leisure Activities:** recreation programs, bicycles, exercise room, volleyball. *Fee:* massage. **Guest Services:** valet laundry, wireless Internet. **Business Services:** meeting rooms. **Cards:** AX, MC, VI.

LAS BRISAS IXTAPA — Book great rates at AAA.com — **Phone:** (755)553-2121

Hotel
$297-$555 All Year

Address: Playa Vistahermosa S/N **Location:** On beach at Playa Vistahermosa. **Facility:** All rooms at this architecturally rich property feature ocean views and private balconies with hammocks; some rooms have private pools. 416 one-bedroom standard units, some with whirlpools. 12 stories, interior corridors. **Parking:** on-site and valet. **Terms:** check-in 4 pm, 3 day cancellation notice-fee imposed. **Amenities:** voice mail, safes, honor bars, irons, hair dryers. **Dining:** 6 restaurants, also, La Brisa II, Portofino Ristorante, Restaurant El Mexicano, see separate listings, entertainment. **Pool(s):** 3 outdoor. **Leisure Activities:** exercise room. *Fee:* 4 lighted tennis courts, massage. **Guest Services:** valet laundry, beauty salon, wireless Internet. **Business Services:** conference facilities, business center. **Cards:** AX, DC, MC, VI.

/ SOME UNITS

MELIA AZUL IXTAPA ALL INCLUSIVE BEACH RESORT AND CONVENTION CENTER — Book at AAA.com — **Phone:** (755)555-0000

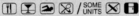

Resort Hotel
$440 All Year

Address: Paseo Punta Ixtapa Lote 2 **Location:** Oceanfront. At Playa Linda; across from Ixtapa Island. **Facility:** Expect to find huge swimming pools, a swim-up bar and dining choices at this activity-oriented, all-inclusive resort. 340 units. 310 one-bedroom standard units. 30 one-bedroom suites, some with whirlpools. 9 stories, interior corridors. **Parking:** on-site and valet. **Amenities:** high-speed Internet (fee), safes, irons, hair dryers. **Pool(s):** 2 outdoor. **Leisure Activities:** whirlpools, limited beach access, snorkeling, 2 tennis courts (Fee: 2 lighted), recreation programs, bicycles, playground, exercise room, childrens club, soccer. *Fee:* miniature golf, massage. **Guest Services:** valet laundry, wireless Internet. **Business Services:** conference facilities, business center. **Cards:** AX, MC, VI.

/ SOME UNITS

NH KRYSTAL IXTAPA — Book at AAA.com — **Phone:** (755)555-0510

Hotel
$133-$190 All Year

Address: Blvd Ixtapa S/N **Location:** North end of hotel zone. **Facility:** 255 units. 252 one-bedroom standard units. 3 two-bedroom suites, some with kitchens. 11 stories, interior corridors. **Parking:** on-site. **Terms:** 3 day cancellation notice. **Amenities:** safes, honor bars, hair dryers. *Some:* CD players. **Dining:** Bogarts, La Parillada - Las Velas, see separate listings. **Pool(s):** outdoor. **Leisure Activities:** recreation programs, playground, volleyball. *Fee:* exercise room, massage. **Guest Services:** valet laundry, wireless Internet. **Business Services:** meeting rooms, business center. **Cards:** AX, MC, VI.

/ SOME UNITS

PARK ROYAL HOTELS — **Phone:** (755)555-0550

Hotel
$320-$400 All Year

Address: Blvd Ixtapa S/N Lote #5-A **Location:** North end of hotel zone. **Facility:** 228 one-bedroom standard units. 12 stories, interior corridors. **Parking:** on-site. **Terms:** 7 day cancellation notice. **Amenities:** voice mail, irons, hair dryers. **Pool(s):** outdoor. **Leisure Activities:** sauna, recreation programs, playground, basketball, volleyball, game room. *Fee:* massage. **Guest Services:** valet laundry. **Business Services:** meeting rooms, business center. **Cards:** AX, MC, VI.

/ SOME UNITS

PRESIDENTE INTERCONTINENTAL-IXTAPA, AN ALL INCLUSIVE RESORT — Book great rates at AAA.com — **Phone:** (755)553-0018

Hotel
$360-$430 All Year

Address: Blvd Ixtapa S/N **Location:** In center of hotel zone. **Facility:** 420 one-bedroom standard units. 3-11 stories, interior/exterior corridors. **Parking:** on-site. **Terms:** 3 day cancellation notice-fee imposed. **Amenities:** voice mail. *Some:* safes, irons, hair dryers. **Dining:** entertainment. **Pool(s):** 2 outdoor. **Leisure Activities:** sauna, steamroom, 2 lighted tennis courts, recreation programs, exercise room. *Fee:* massage. **Guest Services:** valet laundry, beauty salon, wireless Internet. **Business Services:** meeting rooms, business center. **Cards:** AX, DC, JC, MC, VI.

/ SOME UNITS

QUALTON CLUB IXTAPA ALL INCLUSIVE — **Phone:** (755)552-0080

Resort Motel
$300 All Year

Address: Carr Escenica S/N **Location:** At Playa Linda; across from Ixtapa Island. **Facility:** All rooms have balcony or terrace, spacious grounds. 150 one-bedroom standard units. 1-2 stories (no elevator), exterior corridors. *Bath:* shower only. **Parking:** on-site. **Terms:** 3 day cancellation notice. **Amenities:** safes. **Pool(s):** 2 outdoor. **Leisure Activities:** windsurfing, snorkeling, recreation programs, bicycles, exercise room, basketball, volleyball, game room. *Fee:* 2 lighted tennis courts, massage. **Business Services:** meeting rooms, PC (fee). **Cards:** AX, MC, VI.

TESORO IXTAPA *Book great rates at AAA.com* **Phone:** 755/553-0600

Hotel
$175-$185 All Year

Address: Blvd Ixtapa S/N Lote #5 **Location:** North end of hotel zone. **Facility:** 203 one-bedroom standard units. 7 stories, interior corridors. *Bath:* combo or shower only. **Parking:** on-site. **Terms:** 5 day cancellation notice-fee imposed. **Amenities:** safes, honor bars, hair dryers. **Dining:** 2 restaurants, entertainment. **Pool(s):** outdoor. **Leisure Activities:** recreation programs, exercise room, volleyball. *Fee:* golf club privileges, massage. **Guest Services:** valet laundry, wireless Internet. **Business Services:** meeting rooms. **Cards:** AX, MC, VI. *(See color ad below)*

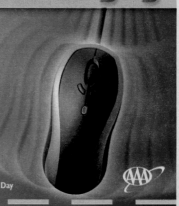

/ SOME UNITS

▼ See AAA listing above ▼

The following lodging was either not evaluated or did not meet AAA rating requirements but is listed for your information only.

LOMA DEL MAR **Phone:** 755/555-0460

fyi

Not evaluated. **Address:** Calle Fragatas F-17 Seccion. Facilities, services, and decor characterize an upscale property.

WHERE TO DINE

BECCOFINO RESTAURANT AND BAR **Phone:** 755/553-1770

Northern Italian
$10-$30

A Mediterranean atmosphere pervades the seaside dining room and the beautiful teak wood deck, which perches right on the water. Plentiful seafood is well-prepared in Continental-style dishes. Casual dress. **Bar:** Full bar. **Reservations:** suggested. **Hours:** 9 am-midnight. **Location:** 0.9 mi (1.5 km) n of hotel zone, via Blvd Ixtapa; at marina. **Parking:** on-site. **Cards:** AX, MC, VI.

BOGARTS **Phone:** 755/555-0510

International
$20-$30

Appointments reflect a theme based on the movie "Casablanca," complete with a staff costumed in North African garb. Among creative menu choices are seafood, steaks and several flambeed selections prepared tableside, as well as attractive desserts. Dressy casual. Entertainment. **Bar:** Full bar. **Reservations:** suggested. **Hours:** 6 pm-midnight. **Address:** Blvd Ixtapa S/N **Location:** North end of hotel zone; in NH Krystal Ixtapa. **Parking:** on-site. **Cards:** AX, MC, VI.

BUCANERO'S RESTAURANT **Phone:** 755/553-0916

International
$8-$40

With outdoor dining overlooking the marina, the popular dining spot presents a creative, Italian-based menu. Featured are many preparations of abundant local seafood, such as fresh shrimp and sea bass, as well as pasta dishes. A light luncheon menu also is available. **Bar:** Full bar. **Reservations:** suggested. **Hours:** 8 am-11 pm. **Location:** 1 mi (1.5 km) n of hotel zone, via Blvd Ixtapa; at marina. **Parking:** on-site. **Cards:** AX, MC, VI.

CAFE SALSA **Phone:** 755/553-0939

International
$8-$20

This large dining room features covered patio dining and a casual relaxed ambience. The menu is varied and caters to all cravings, offering pizzas, pasta, kebobs and grilled meats and seafoods. Mexican specialties are also featured with quite an extensive fajita list. Come hungry, as portions are hearty and the desserts are tempting. It's also a popular spot for breakfast, within easy walking distance of most hotels in the zone. Casual dress. **Bar:** Full bar. **Reservations:** accepted. **Hours:** 8 am-11 pm. **Address:** Blvd Ixtapa S/N **Location:** South end of hotel zone; across from Barcelo Hotel. **Parking:** no self-parking. **Cards:** AX, MC, VI.

CARLOS 'N CHARLIE'S **Phone:** 755/553-0085

International
$8-$14

In the hotel area along the beach, the lively and busy beach club, which incorporates a bar and restaurant, serves a variety of American and Mexican dishes and scores of popular drinks, including this place's classic margarita. Casual dress. **Bar:** Full bar. **Hours:** 11 am-4 am. Closed: 12/25. **Address:** Blvd Ixtapa S/N **Location:** North end of hotel zone; Posada Real. **Parking:** on-site. **Cards:** AX, MC, VI.

CASA MORELOS **Phone:** 755/553-0578

Mexican
$7-$30

Authentic Mexican fare in an open-air, cantina-like setting keeps the tourists and locals coming back. Situated in the shopping area/restaurant row of the hotel zone, this popular eatery attracts diners for breakfast, lunch and dinner with a menu mixing the flavors of Mexico with some of the favorites from back home. Whether it's hot and spicy fajitas, enchiladas or simply broiled steak and seafood, you are sure to be pleased, as they cater to all taste buds here. Casual dress. **Bar:** Full bar. **Reservations:** accepted. **Hours:** 8 am-11:30 pm. **Address:** Zona Commercial, La Puerta Local 18 **Location:** In center of hotel zone. **Parking:** no self-parking. **Cards:** MC, VI.

CHIMICHANGA **Phone:** 755/553-1705

International
$15-$29

Diners savor hearty portions of fine cuts of beef and fresh seafood prepared on a large open charcoal grill. Even the baked potatoes taste better prepared to order in foil. The menu also features full-course meals for two, such as the Caribbean mix with lobster, shrimp and fish fillet with salad and potatoes and the Mexican combo with quesadillas, enchiladas, tacos and chili. Casual dress. **Bar:** Full bar. **Reservations:** accepted. **Hours:** 5:30 pm-11 pm. Closed: Mon & Tues. **Address:** Blvd Ixtapa Manzana 1 Lote 8 **Location:** In hotel zone; 2nd Floor of Ixtapa Plaza, across from Emporio Ixtapa. **Parking:** no self-parking. **Cards:** MC, VI.

DA BAFFONE **Phone:** 755/553-1122

Italian
$9-$20

In a center of shopping activity, the bustling eatery features a wide mix of casual Italian fare and grilled meats. Diners enjoy the open-air dining room's bright decor and the tasty menu options. Casual dress. **Bar:** Full bar. **Hours:** 4 pm-midnight. **Address:** La Puerto Loc 3,4,7y8 CP **Location:** At La Puerto Shopping Mall. **Parking:** no self-parking. **Cards:** MC, VI.

DEBORAHS CHILI BEANS

Phone: 755/553-3313

Mexican
$4-$22

Bright Mexican appointments decorate the casual eatery's bi-level open-air dining room. Chili peppers pop up in interesting photographs and pictures showing the different types of peppers and their degree of heat. The menu lists many Mexican and American dishes, not to mention well-priced breakfasts. Casual dress. **Bar:** Full bar. **Hours:** 7:30 am-11 pm. **Address:** Ixtapa Blvd S/N **Location:** Across from Emporio Ixtapa. **Parking:** street.

EL FARO RESTAURANTE

Phone: 755/555-2500

International
$18-$30

Diners are treated to an outstanding view of Ixtapa from this prime hilltop location. The open-air dining room provides a truly romantic setting complete with live entertainment. Making up the menu are international preparations of fresh seafood, pasta, meat and poultry. Semi-formal attire. Entertainment. **Bar:** Full bar. **Reservations:** suggested. **Hours:** 8 am-noon & 6-10:30 pm. **Address:** Paseo de la Colinas S/N **Location:** Adjacent to Las Brisas Resort. **Parking:** on-site. **Cards:** MC, VI.

EL GALEON

Phone: 755/553-2150

Seafood
$7-$17

The distinctive, open-air restaurant resembles a Spanish galleon, parked pierside, and affords a good view of the many yachts and boats housed at the marina. The menu includes pasta, seafood, chicken and beef selections, prepared in the Continental style, as well as some Mexican dishes. Casual dress. **Bar:** Full bar. **Reservations:** suggested. **Hours:** 4 pm-11 pm. **Location:** 1 mi (1.5 km) n of hotel zone, via Blvd Ixtapa; at marina. **Parking:** on-site. **Cards:** AX, MC, VI.

LA BRISA II

Phone: 755/553-2121

Continental
$14-$35

The romantic terrace overlooks the sea below. On the menu are delicious fresh seafood, steaks and pasta. Some items—such as shrimp with garlic and white wine and the mango fruit dessert—are flambeed tableside. Casual dress. **Bar:** Full bar. **Reservations:** accepted. **Hours:** Open 12/15-4/15; 6 pm-11:30 pm. **Address:** Playa Vistahermosa S/N **Location:** On beach at Playa Vistahermosa; in Las Brisas Ixtapa. **Parking:** on-site and valet. **Cards:** AX, DC, MC, VI.

LAGUNA RESTAURANT AND AMERICAN BAR

Phone: 755/553-1103

Steak & Seafood
$10-$20

This open-air dining room features a display case of meats and fish at the entrance to entice diners. The thatched roof creates a real holiday feel, and the ambience is loud and bustling. Casual dress. **Bar:** Full bar. **Reservations:** accepted. **Hours:** noon-midnight. **Address:** Paseo de Ixtapa S/N **Location:** In center of hotel zone; adjacent to Senor Frogs. **Parking:** no self-parking. **Cards:** AX, MC, VI.

LA PARILLADA - LAS VELAS

Phone: 755/555-0510

Steak
$15-$18

A stunning oceanfront setting and relaxed vibe make the restaurant a perfect spot for a casual romantic dinner. The chef char-broils fine cuts of meat, chicken and seafood to order. Fresh, tasty items on the salad bar complement all meals. Casual dress. **Bar:** Full bar. **Hours:** 6 pm-midnight. **Address:** Blvd Ixtapa S/N **Location:** North end of hotel zone; in NH Krystal Ixtapa. **Parking:** on-site. **Cards:** AX, MC, VI.

LA TERRAZA DEL MAR

Phone: 755/553-2025

Steak & Seafood
$16-$30

Diners hear the sounds of the ocean as they dine in a delightful open-air restaurant facing the beach. The menu lists preparations of freshly grilled meat and seafood, which guests can enjoy with the fresh salad and dessert bar. Mexican entertainment enhances the festive feel most nights. Casual dress. **Bar:** Full bar. **Hours:** 6 pm-midnight. **Address:** Paseo de Ixtapa S/N Lote 3-A **Location:** North end of hotel zone; in Dorado Pacifico Ixtapa. **Parking:** on-site. **Cards:** AX, MC, VI.

LOBSTER HOUSE

Phone: 755/553-0621

Seafood
$10-$30

This well-established eatery has been keeping diners happy since 1985. Located on the second level, it features a covered open-air setting in a dining room filled with greenery. In addition to the lobster, the menu also specializes in fresh shrimp prepared in a variety of ways, as well as many other seafood, steak and pasta options. It offers a casual, relaxed dining experience. Casual dress. **Bar:** Full bar. **Reservations:** accepted. **Hours:** 3 pm-10:30 pm. **Address:** Centro Comercial Galerias Altus (Terraza) **Location:** In center of hotel zone. **Parking:** no self-parking. **Cards:** MC, VI.

LOS BIGOTES DE ZAPATA

Phone: 755/553-2496

Mexican
$7-$18

The menu features a wide mix of tasty homemade local classics, as well as the popular fresh shrimp, which is cooked in a variety of ways. In the midst of a busy tourist and shopping zone, the casual open-air setting allows for great people-watching. Casual dress. **Bar:** Full bar. **Hours:** 8 am-10:30 pm. **Address:** La Puerto Loc 12 **Location:** Centro Commercial; across from hotel zone. **Parking:** no self-parking. **Cards:** MC, VI.

LOS MADRIGALES

Phone: 755/553-1740

Mexican
$15-$30

This festive restaurant's open-air patio affords great views of the Ixtapa Marina. Strolling mariachis and plenty of people-watching enhance the experience here. The menu focuses on creative and upscale dishes prepared with a strong local influence. Particularly tasty among the appetizers is shrimp casserole, which features a rich and outstanding cheese and chili sauce. Casual dress. **Bar:** Full bar. **Reservations:** accepted. **Hours:** 4 pm-midnight. **Address:** Marina Ixtapa **Location:** 1 mi (1.5 km) n of hotel zone via Blvd Ixtapa; at marina. **Parking:** no self-parking. **Cards:** MC, VI.

MAMMA NORMA AND DEBORAH — **Phone:** 755/553-0274

American
$7-$23

A casual covered patio and a menu featuring wholesome home-cooked cuisine make this a popular favorite with locals and tourists alike for breakfast, lunch and dinner. Menu highlights include homemade soups, salads and sandwiches, as well as some Mexican specialties and grilled items such as chicken, steak and seafood. Desserts are homemade and tasty; the chocolate cake is just like mom's. Casual dress. **Bar:** Full bar. **Reservations:** accepted. **Hours:** 8 am-11 pm. **Address:** Ixtapa Plaza Local 5 **Location:** In center of hotel zone; across from Presidente InterContinental-Ixtapa, An All Inclusive Resort. **Parking:** street. **Cards:** MC, VI.

PORTOFINO RISTORANTE — **Phone:** 755/553-2121

AAA

Italian
$15-$33

The formal, fine dining restaurant is characterized by an elegant dining room, tuxedoed maitre d' and imaginatively prepared Italian cuisine. Dressy casual. **Bar:** Full bar. **Reservations:** suggested. **Hours:** 6 pm-11:30 pm. Closed: Tues, Thurs & Sun. **Address:** Playa Vistahermosa S/N **Location:** On beach at Playa Vistahermosa; in Las Brisas Ixtapa. **Parking:** on-site and valet. **Cards:** AX, DC, MC, VI.

RAFFAELLO RISTORANTE — **Phone:** 755/553-2386

Italian
$7-$18

This popular spot features casual sidewalk cafe dining and an extensive menu offering casual Italian fare. In addition to the tasty pizzas and pastas, grilled items such as steak, chicken and seafood are also offered. The location is great: within easy walking distance of the major hotels and in the heart of the shopping area. Casual dress. **Bar:** Full bar. **Hours:** 5 pm-midnight. **Address:** Paseo de Ixtapa #6 **Location:** In hotel zone. **Parking:** no self-parking. **Cards:** AX, MC, VI.

RESTAURANT EL MEXICANO — **Phone:** 755/553-2121

Mexican
$13-$28

The moderately upscale spot prepares steaks, chicken and seafood in a traditional Mexican style. The atmosphere is reflective of a 16th-century colonial hacienda. Casual dress. **Bar:** Full bar. **Reservations:** required. **Hours:** 6 pm-11:30 pm. Closed: Mon, Wed, Fri & Sat. **Address:** Playa Vistahermosa S/N **Location:** On beach at Playa Vistahermosa; in Las Brisas Ixtapa. **Parking:** on-site and valet. **Cards:** AX, DC, MC, VI.

RUBEN'S HAMBURGERS — **Phone:** 755/553-0027

American
$5-$10

Folks who notice the lack of fast food restaurants in this area yet crave a good old-fashioned burger will find out quickly why this place has been popular for years. Hearty homemade burgers can be ordered with tasty fries and other sides. A take-out counter allows for grab-and-go dining. Casual dress. **Bar:** Beer only. **Hours:** noon-midnight. **Address:** Centro Commercial Flamboyant **Location:** In hotel zone. **Parking:** no self-parking. **Cards:** MC, VI.

SENOR FROG'S — **Phone:** 755/553-2282

International
$7-$16

Part of the chain of Mexican restaurants that also includes Carlos 'n Charlie's, the fun and festive eatery is a great place to eat with the family or rendezvous with friends. The menu is lined with Tex-Mex, American and Mexican favorites, such as Buffalo wings, quesadillas, fajitas and burritos. After hours, a bar atmosphere prevails. Casual dress. **Bar:** Full bar. **Hours:** 6 pm-midnight. **Address:** Paseo de Ixtapa s/n Mza 11 Lote 15 **Location:** Downtown. **Parking:** on-site. **Cards:** AX, MC, VI.

VILLA DE LA SELVA — **Phone:** 755/553-0362

International
$25-$30

Soft music, formal service and a breathtaking, cliffside view of the ocean add to the inviting atmosphere of this moderately upscale spot, a favorite with knowledgeable tourists. The menu centers on well-prepared Continental and Mexican cuisine. Dressy casual. **Bar:** Full bar. **Reservations:** suggested. **Hours:** 7 pm-midnight. **Address:** Paseo de la Roca Lote D S/N **Location:** On beach at Playa Vistahermosa; next to Las Brisas Ixtapa. **Parking:** on-site. **Cards:** AX, MC, VI.

MANZANILLO, COLIMA pop. 125,143

WHERE TO STAY

BARCELO KARMINA PALACE *Book at AAA.com* — **Phone:** (314)331-1300

Resort Hotel
$298-$328 All Year

Address: Ave Vistahermosa #13 **Location:** On Mex 200, Peninsula de Santiago. **Facility:** The resort has seven connected pools that eventually lead down to a private sheltered lagoon and lots of ocean activities. 324 units. 226 one-bedroom standard units. 98 one-bedroom suites. 7 stories, interior corridors. **Parking:** on-site and valet. **Amenities:** high-speed Internet (fee), voice mail, safes, irons, hair dryers. **Pool(s):** 6 outdoor. **Leisure Activities:** steamroom, waterslide, snorkeling, recreation programs, playground, exercise room, spa, volleyball, game room. *Fee:* scuba diving. **Guest Services:** valet laundry, wireless Internet. **Business Services:** meeting rooms, business center. **Cards:** AX, MC, VI.

24 D / SOME UNITS

BLUE BAY CLUB LOS ANGELES LOCOS — **Phone:** 315/351-5020

Resort Hotel
$160-$260 All Year

Address: Carr Federal #200 KM 20 **Location:** Mex 200, KM 20, follow signs 1.9 mi (3 km). **Facility:** Located in a remote area on a lovely beach, the family-oriented resort offers tons of activities including nightly entertainment and a boat cruise. 204 one-bedroom standard units. 3 stories (no elevator), exterior corridors. *Bath:* combo or shower only. **Parking:** on-site. **Amenities:** safes (fee). **Pool(s):** outdoor. **Leisure Activities:** sauna, steamroom, limited beach access, snorkeling, 3 tennis courts (Fee: 3 lighted), recreation programs, horseback riding, playground, exercise room, shuffleboard, volleyball, game room. *Fee:* scuba diving. **Guest Services:** valet laundry, wireless Internet. **Business Services:** meeting rooms, PC (fee). **Cards:** AX, MC, VI.

CAMINO REAL MANZANILLO **Phone:** 314/331-1740

Classic Historic Resort Hotel
$425-$670 All Year

Address: Paraisoll Col Residencial Salagua **Location:** Oceanfront. 0.9 mi (1.5 km) off Mex 200, follow signs. **Facility:** The oceanfront hotel, with a large pool and intimate spa, features very spacious suites and bi-level units, each with a contemporary Mexican flair. 50 units. 36 two- and 14 three-bedroom suites, some with whirlpools. 4 stories, exterior corridors. *Bath:* combo or shower only. **Parking:** valet. **Amenities:** safes, honor bars, hair dryers. **Dining:** Azulejos Restaurante, see separate listing. **Pool(s):** 2 outdoor. **Leisure Activities:** exercise room, spa. **Guest Services:** valet laundry, wireless Internet. **Business Services:** meeting rooms. **Cards:** AX, DC, MC, VI.

/ SOME UNITS

CLUB MAEVA **Phone:** 314/331-0875

Resort Hotel
$250 All Year

Address: KM 12.5 Carbet **Location:** Directly across from Miramar Beach. **Facility:** A huge complex directly across the street from Miramar Beach, the activity-oriented resort caters to families; rooms are on a cliff with steep stairs. 444 units. 49 one-bedroom standard units. 205 one- and 190 two-bedroom suites, some with efficiencies. 4 stories (no elevator), exterior corridors. *Bath:* shower only. **Parking:** on-site. **Terms:** check-in 4 pm. **Amenities:** safes. **Pool(s):** 4 outdoor. **Leisure Activities:** recreation programs, bicycles, playground, exercise room, shuffleboard, volleyball, game room. *Fee:* 11 lighted tennis courts, massage. **Guest Services:** valet and coin laundry. **Business Services:** meeting rooms, PC (fee). **Cards:** MC, VI.

/ SOME UNITS

EL CAREYES BEACH RESORT AND SPA *Book at AAA.com* **Phone:** (315)351-0000

Resort Hotel
$315-$625 All Year

Address: KM 53.5 Carr Barra de Navidad **Location:** Mex 200, KM 53.5, 1.3 mi (2 km) w, follow signs. **Facility:** A scenic beach, a pool, an open-air fine-dining restaurant and luxury rooms with private hot tubs all help make this secluded resort a standout. 51 units. 30 one-bedroom standard units, some with whirlpools. 13 one- and 5 two-bedroom suites, some with efficiencies and/or whirlpools. 3 houses. 3 stories (no elevator), interior/exterior corridors. *Bath:* combo or shower only. **Parking:** on-site. **Amenities:** video library, DVD players, CD players, safes, honor bars, irons, hair dryers. **Dining:** La Lantana, see separate listing. **Pool(s):** outdoor. **Leisure Activities:** saunas, whirlpools, steamrooms, hiking trails, exercise room, spa, volleyball, game room. *Fee:* boats, scuba diving, snorkeling, fishing, 2 lighted tennis courts, bicycles, horseback riding. **Guest Services:** valet laundry, wireless Internet. **Business Services:** meeting rooms, PC (fee). **Cards:** AX, MC, VI.

FEE

GRAND BAY HOTEL-ISLA NAVIDAD RESORT-A WYNDHAM LUXURY RESORT *Book great rates at AAA.com* **Phone:** (314)331-0500

Resort Hotel
$339-$549 All Year

Address: Circuito de los Marinos S/N **Location:** Mex 200, 3.8 mi (6 km) n of Cihuatlan, 11.3 mi (18 km) w. **Facility:** An extremely impressive, luxurious resort hotel complex that features golf, beach and spa facilities, it also offers excellent, refined service. 199 units. 158 one-bedroom standard units. 40 one- and 1 three-bedroom suites, some with whirlpools. 10 stories, interior/exterior corridors. **Parking:** valet. **Amenities:** high-speed Internet (fee), voice mail, safes, honor bars, irons, hair dryers. *Some:* DVD players, CD players. **Dining:** 4 restaurants, also, Antonio's, Terrace Restaurant, see separate listings, entertainment. **Pool(s):** 2 outdoor, heated outdoor. **Leisure Activities:** whirlpools, waterslide, jogging, exercise room, spa, volleyball. *Fee:* boats, sailboats, windsurfing, marina, scuba diving, snorkeling, fishing, golf-27 holes, 3 lighted tennis courts, bicycles. **Guest Services:** valet laundry, area transportation (fee)-Manzanillo area, wireless Internet. **Business Services:** conference facilities, business center. **Cards:** AX, MC, VI.

FEE / SOME UNITS

HOTEL EJECUTIVO *Book at AAA.com* **Phone:** (314)333-2265

Hotel
$85-$95 All Year

Address: Blvd Costero Miguel de la Madrid **Location:** Off Mex 200, 1.9 mi (3 km); on Playa Azul. **Facility:** 24 one-bedroom standard units. 3 stories (no elevator), interior/exterior corridors. **Parking:** no self-parking. **Amenities:** safes. **Dining:** La Pergola, see separate listing. **Pool(s):** outdoor. **Leisure Activities:** exercise room. **Business Services:** PC. **Cards:** MC, VI.

HOTEL LA POSADA **Phone:** (314)333-1899

Motel
$78 12/1-5/1
$58 5/2-11/30

Address: Lazaro Cardenas 201 **Location:** 1.9 mi (3 km) off Mex 200; in Las Brisas; on Playa Azul. **Facility:** Meets AAA guest room security requirements. 23 one-bedroom standard units. 1-2 stories (no elevator), exterior corridors. *Bath:* shower only. **Parking:** on-site. **Terms:** 10 day cancellation notice. **Pool(s):** outdoor. **Guest Services:** coin laundry. **Business Services:** PC (fee). **Cards:** MC, VI.

/ SOME UNITS

LAS ALAMANDAS **Phone:** 322/285-5500

Hotel
$360-$1990 All Year

Address: KM 83.5 Carr Barra de Navidad **Location:** Mex 200, KM 83.5; entry to property, follow signs. **Facility:** Set on 1,500 acres of a private reserve, this exclusive resort features a private airstrip and three beaches. 14 units. 11 one-bedroom standard units, some with whirlpools. 3 one-bedroom suites. 1-2 stories (no elevator), exterior corridors. **Parking:** on-site. **Terms:** office hours 8 am-11 pm, check-in 4 pm, 2 night minimum stay, 30 day cancellation notice. **Amenities:** safes, honor bars, hair dryers. *Some:* DVD players, CD players. **Pool(s):** outdoor. **Leisure Activities:** snorkeling, lighted tennis court, bicycles, hiking trails, playground, exercise room, basketball, horseshoes. *Fee:* massage. **Guest Services:** coin laundry. **Business Services:** meeting rooms, business center. **Cards:** AX, MC, VI. Affiliated with A Preferred Hotel.

FEE / SOME UNITS

LAS HADAS GOLF RESORT & MARINA *Book great rates at AAA.com* **Phone:** (314)331-0101

Resort Hotel

$150-$240 All Year

Address: Ave Vistahermosa S/N **Location:** 7.2 mi (11.5 km) nw on Mex 200, 1.5 mi (2.5 km) s on Peninsula Santiago. **Facility:** Arabesque buildings set in a private cove at the base of rugged hills form a striking sight at this property complete with beach and marina. 234 units. 230 one-bedroom standard units, some with whirlpools. 1 one- and 3 two-bedroom suites, some with whirlpools. 2-5 stories, interior/exterior corridors. *Bath:* combo or shower only. **Parking:** on-site and valet. **Terms:** 7 day cancellation notice-fee imposed. **Amenities:** high-speed Internet (fee), voice mail, safes, honor bars, irons, hair dryers. *Some:* DVD players, CD players. **Dining:** 5 restaurants, also, Los Delfines, Restaurant Legazpi, see separate listings, entertainment. **Pool(s):** 2 outdoor. **Leisure Activities:** limited beach access, kayaking, exercise room, spa, volleyball. *Fee:* sailboats, marina, waterskiing, scuba diving, snorkeling, fishing, golf-18 holes, 10 lighted tennis courts. **Guest Services:** valet and coin laundry, area transportation-Casa Club & Golf Course, wireless Internet. **Business Services:** meeting rooms. *Fee:* PC, fax. **Cards:** AX, CB, DC, MC, VI.

/ SOME UNITS

MESON DONA PAZ **Phone:** 314/337-9000

Country Inn

$300-$350 All Year

Address: Rinconada del Capitan S/N **Location:** Mex 200, 3.8 mi (6 km) n of Cihuatlan, 11.3 mi (18 km) w on Circuito de los Marinos, then just s. **Facility:** The former luxury residence of a wealthy family, this inn has manicured grounds, a beach and a fine-dining restaurant. 13 units. 11 one-bedroom standard units. 2 one-bedroom suites, some with whirlpools. 3 stories, exterior corridors. **Parking:** on-site. **Amenities:** safes, honor bars, hair dryers. *Some:* DVD players. **Pool(s):** outdoor. **Leisure Activities:** whirlpool, limited beach access, lighted tennis court. *Fee:* fishing, massage. **Guest Services:** valet laundry, area transportation (fee). **Business Services:** meeting rooms. **Cards:** AX, MC, VI.

FEE / SOME UNITS

PUNTA SERENA VILLAS AND SPA **Phone:** 315/351-5020

Hotel

$320-$360 All Year

Address: Carr Federal #200, KM 20 **Location:** Mex 200, KM 20, then follow signs 1.9 mi (3 km). **Facility:** 24 one-bedroom standard units. 2 stories, exterior corridors. *Bath:* combo or shower only. **Parking:** on-site. **Terms:** age restrictions may apply. **Amenities:** safes, hair dryers. **Pool(s):** outdoor. **Leisure Activities:** saunas, whirlpools, steamrooms, limited beach access, exercise room, spa, shared facilities with Blue Bay Club Los Angeles Locos. **Guest Services:** valet laundry, wireless Internet. **Business Services:** meeting rooms. **Cards:** MC, VI.

TESORO MANZANILLO **Phone:** (314)331-2200

Resort Hotel

$220-$418 All Year

Address: Ave de La Audencia #1 **Location:** 7.2 mi (11.5 km) nw on Mex 200, 1.6 mi (2.5 km) s on Peninsula Santiago. **Facility:** Frequented by tourists from the United States and Canada, this resort has lively entertainment as well as fine beaches. 331 units. 314 one-bedroom standard units. 17 one-bedroom suites. 19 stories, interior corridors. **Parking:** on-site. **Terms:** 3 day cancellation notice. **Amenities:** safes, hair dryers. **Dining:** 3 restaurants, entertainment. **Pool(s):** outdoor. **Leisure Activities:** sauna, whirlpool, steamroom, fishing, recreation programs, playground, exercise room, spa, shuffleboard, volleyball. *Fee:* boats, windsurfing, waterskiing, 2 lighted tennis courts, childrens waterslide, kids club, game room. **Guest Services:** valet laundry. **Business Services:** meeting rooms, business center. **Cards:** AX, MC, VI. *(See color ad below)*

/ SOME UNITS

▼ See AAA listing above ▼

The following lodgings were either not evaluated or did not meet AAA rating requirements but are listed for your information only.

DOLPHIN COVE INN — **Phone:** 314/334-1689

fyi

Not evaluated. **Address:** Ave Vista Hermosa S/N **Location:** Manzanillo Bay. Facilities, services, and decor characterize a mid-scale property.

EL TAMARINDO GOLF RESORT — **Phone:** 315/351-5031

fyi

Not evaluated. **Address:** KM 7.5 Carr Barra de Navidad **Location:** Mex 200, KM 7.5, 5 mi (8 km) w, follow signs. Facilities, services, and decor characterize a mid-scale property.

HOTEL TENISOL — **Phone:** 314/335-0412

fyi

Not evaluated. **Address:** Playa de Santiago S/N. Facilities, services, and decor characterize a mid-scale property.

WHERE TO DINE

ANTONIO'S — **Phone:** 314/331-0500

International
$15-$35

The fine-dining restaurant of the hotel, Antonio's features several table-side preparations of salad, delectable seafood dishes and desserts such as cherries jubilee. It's appropriate that in this hacienda-style setting, the bar would feature over 200 tequilas from which to choose. Dressy casual. **Bar:** Full bar. **Reservations:** required. **Hours:** 7 pm-midnight. **Address:** Circuito de los Marinos S/N **Location:** Mex 200, 3.8 mi (6 km) n of Cihuatlan, 11.3 mi (18 km) w; in Grand Bay Hotel-Isla Navidad Resort-A Wyndham Luxury Resort. **Parking:** valet. **Cards:** AX, MC, VI.

AZULEJOS RESTAURANTE — **Phone:** 314/331-1740

International
$7-$29

Diners enjoy stunning views of the ocean and mountains from the covered open terrace. The menu centers on international and Mexican fare. At night, romantic candlelit tables complement the lights of the skyline. Semi-formal attire. **Bar:** Full bar. **Hours:** 7 am-midnight. **Address:** Paraiso II Col Residencial Salagua **Location:** 9 mi (1.5 km) off Mex 200, follow signs; in Camino Real Manzanillo. **Parking:** on-site. **Cards:** AX, DC, MC, VI.

LA HIGUERA RESTAURANT — **Phone:** 315/351-5031

Mexican
$10-$38

The open-air restaurant is the perfect spot to stop for a wonderful lunch on the drive between Puerto Vallarta and Manzanillo. In the jungle setting of the resort, the restaurant occupies a stunning oceanfront location. The daily changing menu of fine, freshly prepared Mexican cuisine offers a touch of local flavor. Casual dress. **Bar:** Full bar. **Reservations:** required, for non-hotel guests. **Hours:** 7:30 am-10:30 pm. **Address:** KM 7.5 Carr Barra de Navidad **Location:** Mex 200, KM 7.5, 5 mi (8 km) w, follow signs; in El Tamarindo Golf Resort. **Parking:** on-site. **Cards:** AX, MC, VI.

LA LANTANA — **Phone:** 315/351-0000

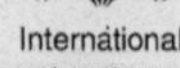

International
$10-$25

A peaceful atmosphere attracts diners to the relaxing restaurant at El Careyes Resort, en route between Puerto Vallarta and Manzanillo. The open-air dining room affords lovely views of the ocean in the day and a wonderful sea breeze and romantic ambience at night. Mexican and international dishes mingle on the varied menu. Casual dress. **Bar:** Full bar. **Reservations:** required, for non-hotel guests. **Hours:** 7:30 am-10:30 pm. **Address:** KM 53.5 Carr Barra de Navidad **Location:** Mex 200, KM 53.5, 1.3 mi (2 km) w, follow signs; in El Careyes Beach Resort and Spa. **Parking:** on-site. **Cards:** AX, MC, VI.

LA PERGOLA — **Phone:** 314/333-2265

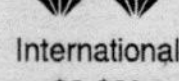

International
$9-$20

This casual eatery gives guests a choice of seating indoors or on the outdoor terrace. The varied menu includes Locals often gather at the comfortable bar to soak up the laid-back atmosphere. Casual dress. **Bar:** Full bar. **Hours:** 5 pm-11:30 pm. **Address:** Blvd Costero Miguel de la Madrid KM 11.5 **Location:** Off Mex 200, 1.9 mi (3 km); on Playa Azul; in Hotel Ejecutivo. **Parking:** street. **Cards:** MC, VI.

LA TOSCANA — **Phone:** 314/333-2515

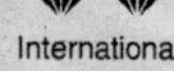

International
$9-$20

While the name has changed from Willy's, the food and staff are still the same. Diners walk past the open outdoor kitchen as they enter the restaurant and then wait at their table for other guests to finish ordering so they can have the dry erase board brought over that proclaims the night's dining selection of Mexican and seafood choices. Most seating is on the outdoor patio where a live band plays and the sound of crashing waves can be heard. Casual dress. **Bar:** Full bar. **Reservations:** accepted. **Hours:** 6 pm-midnight. **Address:** Blvd Miguel de la Madrid KM 7 **Location:** 1.9 mi (3 km) off Mex 200; on Playa Azul. **Parking:** on-site. **Cards:** MC, VI.

LOS DELFINES — **Phone:** 314/331-0101

Seafood
$10-$35

A stunning oceanfront setting perfectly complements the fine menu of freshly prepared seafood. The covered, open-air dining room features a cool ocean breeze and a relaxed, romantic ambience. Casual dress. **Bar:** Full bar. **Reservations:** suggested. **Hours:** noon-midnight. **Address:** Ave Vistahermosa S/N **Location:** 7.2 mi (11.5 km) nw on Mex 200, 1.5 mi (2.5 km) s on Peninsula Santiago; in Las Hadas Golf Resort & Marina. **Parking:** on-site (fee). **Cards:** AX, CB, DC, MC, VI.

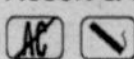

RESTAURANT LEGAZPI **Phone:** 314/331-0101

Continental
$20-$35

A new fine-dining restaurant at the hotel that shows promise. An extensive Continental menu, as well as local favorites, are offered in an opulent setting. Dressy casual. **Bar:** Full bar. **Reservations:** suggested. **Hours:** 6 pm-midnight. Closed: Tues. **Address:** Ave Vistahermosa S/N **Location:** 7.2 mi (11.5 km) nw on Mex 200, 1.5 mi (2.5 km) s on Peninsula Santiago; in Las Hadas Golf Resort & Marina. **Parking:** on-site (fee). **Cards:** AX, CB, DC, DS, MC, VI.

RESTAURANT L'RECIF **Phone:** 314/335-0900

International
$15-$30

A must try classic, this treasure is a ways out of town so if arriving by taxi, ask the driver to wait while you dine. When making your reservation, the best seats are on the outer edge of a stone terrace where flood lights illuminate the crashing waves and rock outcropping far below while softly lit palm fronds dance overhead with the stars. The International menu is well-rounded with items like chicken breast in mango sauce, mahi mahi with dill sauce, beef brochette and tamarindo shrimp. Casual dress. **Bar:** Full bar. **Reservations:** suggested. **Hours:** 5 pm-11 pm. **Address:** Cerro del Cenicero S/N **Location:** On Peninsula de Juluapan; in Vida del Mar Complex. **Parking:** on-site. **Cards:** MC, VI.

TERRACE RESTAURANT **Phone:** 314/331-0500

International
$19-$38

Candlelit tables and live guitarist entertainment enhance the romantic atmosphere at the open-air restaurant. Patrons enjoy stunning views of the bay as they explore the chef's seasonally changing menu of innovative fare. Casual dress. Entertainment. **Bar:** Full bar. **Reservations:** required. **Hours:** Open 12/20-4/21; 7 pm-11 pm. **Address:** Circuito de los Marinos S/N **Location:** Mex 200, 3.8 mi (6 km) n of Cihuatlan, 11.3 mi (18 km) w; in Grand Bay Hotel-Isla Navidad Resort-A Wyndham Luxury Resort. **Parking:** valet. **Cards:** AX, MC, VI.

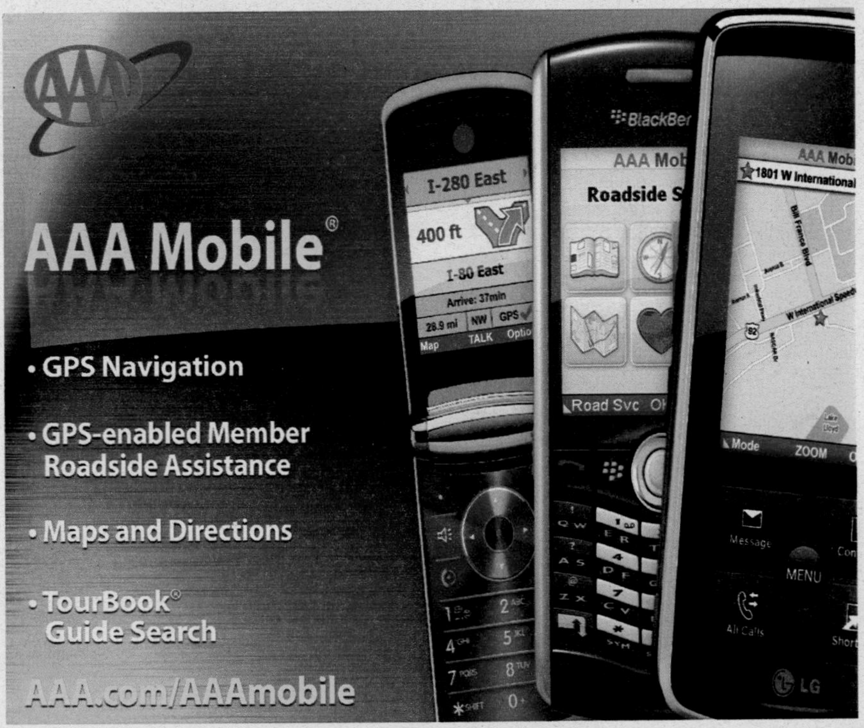

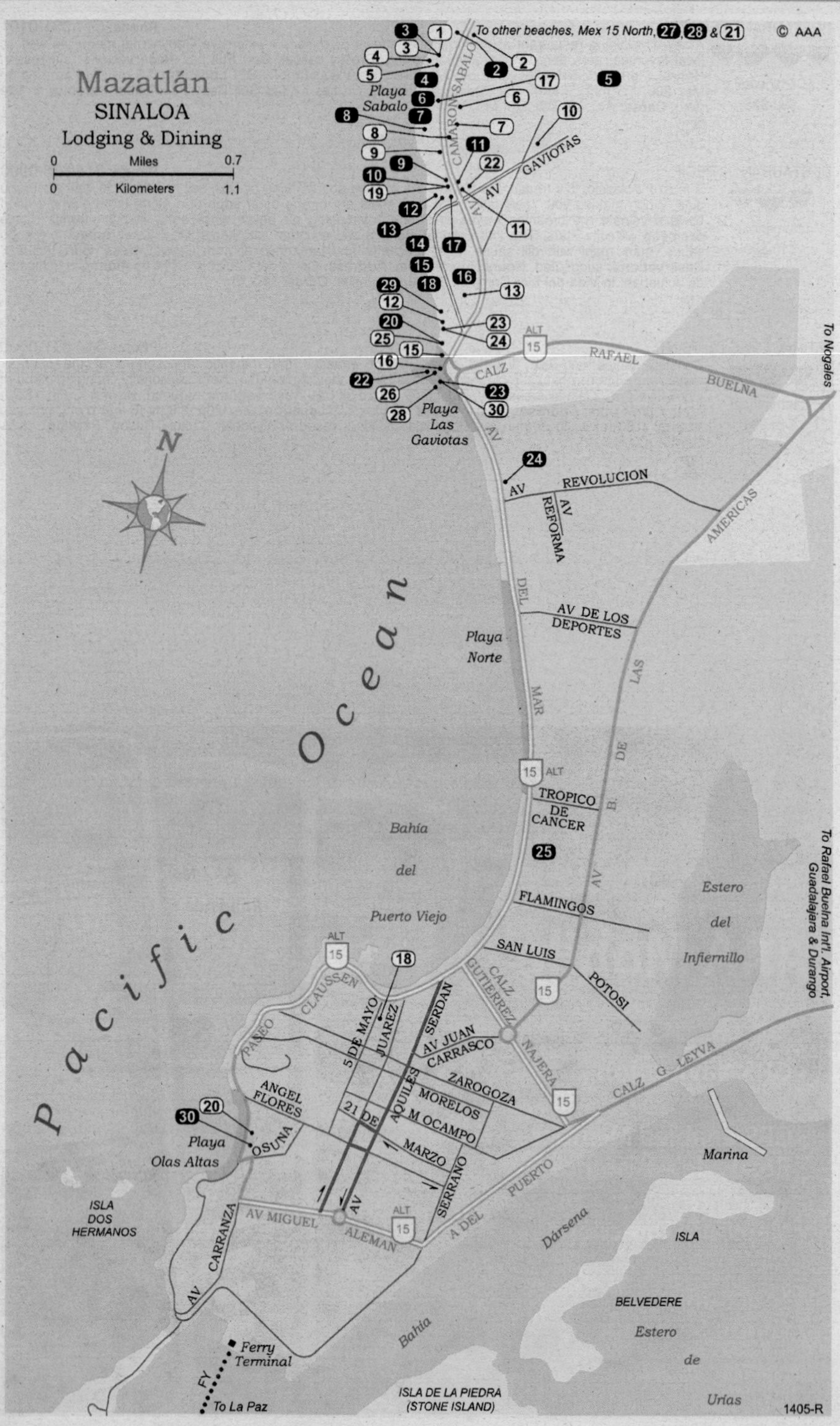
Mazatlán
SINALOA
Lodging & Dining
0 Miles 0.7
0 Kilometers 1.1
© AAA
To other beaches, Mex 15 North, 27, 28 & 21
Playa Sabalo
Playa Las Gaviotas
AV CAMARON SABALO
AV GAVIOTAS
CALZ RAFAEL BUELNA
To Nogales
AV REVOLUCION
AV REFORMA
AV DE LAS AMERICAS
AV DEL MAR
AV DE LOS DEPORTES
Playa Norte
Pacific Ocean
Bahía del Puerto Viejo
TROPICO DE CANCER
AV B. DE LAS
FLAMINGOS
SAN LUIS POTOSI
Estero del Infiernillo
To Rafael Buelna Int'l. Airport, Guadalajara & Durango
CLAUSSEN
PASEO
5 DE MAYO
JUAREZ
SERDAN
AV JUAN CARRASCO
CALZ GUTIERREZ NAJERA
ZAROGOZA
MORELOS
M OCAMPO
21 DE MARZO
AQUILES
ANGEL FLORES
OSUNA
SERRANO
CALZ G LEYVA
Marina
Playa Olas Altas
ISLA DOS HERMANOS
AV CARRANZA
AV MIGUEL ALEMAN
AV DEL PUERTO
Dársena
ISLA BELVEDERE
Estero de Urías
Bahía
Ferry Terminal
FY
To La Paz
ISLA DE LA PIEDRA (STONE ISLAND)
1405-R

Mazatlan

This index helps you "spot" where approved lodgings and restaurants are located on the corresponding detailed maps. Lodging daily rate range is for comparison only and show the property's high season. Restaurant rate range is a combination of lunch and/or dinner. Turn to the listing page for more detailed rate information and consult display ads for special promotions.

MAZATLAN

Map Page	OA	Lodgings	Diamond Rated	High Season	Page
2 / p. 534		Faro Mazatlan Beach Resort	◆◆◆	$150-$200	539
3 / p. 534		Hotel Pueblo Bonito	◆◆◆	$230-$395	540
4 / p. 534		Suites Luna Palace	◆◆◆	$148-$155	541
5 / p. 534	AAA	**Pueblo Bonito at Emerald Bay**	◆◆◆◆	$205-$485	541
6 / p. 534		Oceano Palace	◆◆	$112-$117	541
7 / p. 534	AAA	**Fiesta Inn** - see color ad on insert	◆◆◆	$81-$145	539
8 / p. 534		Holiday Inn SunSpree Resort Mazatlan	◆◆◆	$120-$140	539
9 / p. 534		El Cid El Moro Beach Hotel	◆◆◆	$151-$232	539
10 / p. 534		Royal Villas Resort	◆◆◆	$150-$349	541
11 / p. 534		El Cid Granada Country Club	◆◆	$73-$200	539
12 / p. 534		Hotel Costa de Oro	◆◆◆	$150	539
13 / p. 534		El Cid Castilla Beach Hotel	◆◆◆	$105-$176	538
14 / p. 534		Motel Marley	◆◆	$83-$95	541
15 / p. 534		Suites Lindamar	◆◆	$90	541
16 / p. 534		Azteca Inn	◆◆	$50-$70	537
17 / p. 534		Best Western Hotel Posada Freeman-Golden Zone	◆◆◆	$140-$190	537
18 / p. 534		Motel Los Arcos	◆	$90-$120	540
20 / p. 534		Hotel Playa Mazatlan	◆◆◆	$101-$124	540
21 / p. 534	AAA	**D' Gala Mazatlan Hotel** - see color ad p 538	◆◆◆	$85-$145	538
22 / p. 534		Los Sabalos Mazatlan Hotel	◆◆◆	$120-$150	540
23 / p. 534		Emporio Mazatlan	◆◆◆	$130-$180	539
24 / p. 534		Howard Johnson Don Pelayo	◆◆	$70-$120	540
25 / p. 534		Hotel Aguamarina-Mazatlan	◆◆	$65-$100	539
27 / p. 534		Marina El Cid Hotel & Yacht Club	◆◆◆	$116-$202	540
28 / p. 534		Mayan Sea Garden Mazatlan	◆◆◆	$297-$360	540
29 / p. 534		Las Flores Beach Resort	◆◆	$137-$199	540
30 / p. 534		Best Western Hotel Posada Freeman Express	◆◆◆	$95-$120	537

Map Page	OA	Restaurants	Diamond Rated	Cuisine	Meal Range	Page
1 / p. 534		Cilantro's	◆◆	International	$6-$25	542
2 / p. 534		Sr Pepper	◆◆◆	Steak	$20-$35	544
3 / p. 534		Angelo's Restaurant	◆◆◆	Italian	$20-$35	541
4 / p. 534		La Costa Marinera	◆◆	Seafood	$12-$25	542
5 / p. 534		The Place	◆	International	$8-$20	543
6 / p. 534		Villa Italia	◆◆	Italian	$11-$18	544
7 / p. 534		La Casa Country Restaurant	◆◆	Steak	$10-$30	542
8 / p. 534		El Parador Espanol	◆◆◆	Spanish	$15-$30	542

Map Page	OA	Restaurants (cont'd)	Diamond Rated	Cuisine	Meal Range	Page
9 / p. 534		Carlos & Lucia's Restaurant Bar & Grill	◆◆	Cuban	$7-$17	541
10 / p. 534		Restaurant Casa Loma	◆◆◆	International	$15-$22	543
11 / p. 534		Tequila's Pub	◆◆	American	$6-$12	544
12 / p. 534		Terraza Playa	◆◆	International	$8-$17	544
13 / p. 534		The Shrimp Factory	◆◆	Seafood	$8-$16	544
15 / p. 534		Vittore	◆◆◆	Italian	$10-$20	544
16 / p. 534		Cowboy Restaurant and Sports Bar	◆◆	Steak	$7-$22	542
17 / p. 534		Chili's Pepper	◆◆	Mexican	$7-$16	541
18 / p. 534		Restaurant Mamucas	◆◆	Seafood	$7-$18	543
19 / p. 534	AAA	**La Hacienda de la Flor**	◆◆◆	Continental	$9-$28	543
20 / p. 534		El Shrimp Bucket	◆◆	Seafood	$7-$20	542
21 / p. 534		Restaurante La Marina	◆◆◆	International	$7-$24	543
22 / p. 534		Mister Ace Restaurant and Bar	◆◆	Steak	$8-$35	543
23 / p. 534		Ernie Tomato's Restaurant and Bar	◆◆	American	$7-$20	542
24 / p. 534		Gringo Lingo Bar and Grill	◆◆	American	$12-$16	542
25 / p. 534	AAA	**Las Lupitas Restaurante**	◆◆◆	International	$16-$28	543
26 / p. 534		Panchos Restaurant	◆◆	International	$7-$16	543
28 / p. 534		Restaurant El Captino	◆◆	Seafood	$8-$20	543
30 / p. 534		Condimento	◆◆◆	International	$7-$20	542

MAZATLAN, SINALOA pop. 380,509 (See map and index starting on p. 534)

WHERE TO STAY

AZTECA INN — **Phone:** (669)913-4477 **16**

Motel
$50-$70 All Year

Address: Ave Playa Gaviotas #307 **Location:** 4.6 mi (7.3 km) nw. **Facility:** 74 one-bedroom standard units. 3 stories (no elevator), exterior corridors. *Bath:* shower only. **Parking:** on-site. **Terms:** 5 day cancellation notice. **Pool(s):** heated outdoor. **Leisure Activities:** whirlpool. **Guest Services:** valet laundry, wireless Internet. **Business Services:** PC, fax (fee). **Cards:** AX, MC, VI.

BEST WESTERN HOTEL POSADA FREEMAN EXPRESS *Book great rates at AAA.com* — **Phone:** (669)985-6060 **30**

Hotel
$95-$120 All Year

Address: Ave Olas Atlas #79 **Location:** In historic centre. **Facility:** 72 one-bedroom standard units. 12 stories, interior corridors. *Bath:* shower only. **Parking:** on-site. **Terms:** cancellation fee imposed. **Amenities:** high-speed Internet, safes, hair dryers. **Pool(s):** outdoor. **Guest Services:** valet laundry, wireless Internet. **Business Services:** meeting rooms, PC. **Cards:** AX, CB, DC, DS, MC, VI.

/ SOME UNITS

AAA Benefit:
Members save up to 20%, plus 10% bonus points with rewards program.

BEST WESTERN HOTEL POSADA FREEMAN-GOLDEN ZONE *Book great rates at AAA.com* — **Phone:** (669)989-4400 **17**

Hotel
$140-$190 12/1-4/30
$120-$140 5/1-11/30

Address: Ave Camaron Sabalo 777 **Location:** Oceanfront. 5.3 mi (8.5 km) nw; in Zona Dorado. **Facility:** 50 one-bedroom standard units. 5 stories, interior corridors. **Parking:** on-site. **Terms:** 2-5 night minimum stay - seasonal and/or weekends, cancellation fee imposed. **Amenities:** high-speed Internet, safes, hair dryers. **Pool(s):** outdoor. **Leisure Activities:** limited beach access. **Guest Services:** wireless Internet. **Business Services:** meeting rooms, PC. **Cards:** AX, MC, VI.

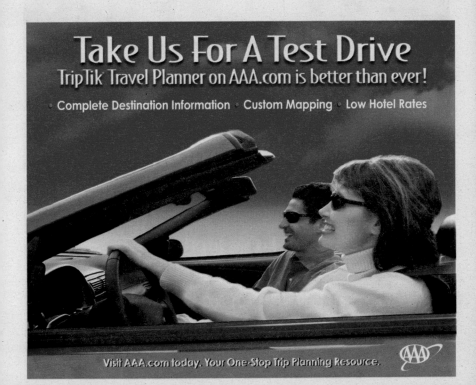   / SOME UNITS

AAA Benefit:
Members save up to 20%, plus 10% bonus points with rewards program.

(See map and index starting on p. 534)

D' GALA MAZATLAN HOTEL — **Phone:** 669/913-4496 — 21

Hotel

$85-$145 All Year

Address: Bugambilias #100 **Location:** In the Golden Zone. **Facility:** 89 one-bedroom standard units, some with whirlpools. 3 stories, interior corridors. *Bath:* combo or shower only. **Parking:** on-site. **Amenities:** high-speed Internet, safes, irons, hair dryers. **Pool(s):** 2 heated outdoor. **Guest Services:** valet laundry, wireless Internet. **Business Services:** meeting rooms, PC. **Cards:** AX, MC, VI. *(See color ad below)*

/ SOME UNITS

EL CID CASTILLA BEACH HOTEL *Book at AAA.com* — **Phone:** (669)913-3333 — 13

Resort Hotel

$105-$176 All Year

Address: Ave Camaron Sabalo S/N **Location:** 5.4 mi (8.7 km) nw; in Camaron Sabalo Hotel Zone. **Facility:** Part of the massive El Cid Resort Complex, this mid-level high-rise property offers a huge lobby and ample public areas. 500 one-bedroom standard units. 4-15 stories, interior corridors. **Parking:** on-site and valet. **Amenities:** safes, irons, hair dryers. **Pool(s):** heated outdoor. **Leisure Activities:** sauna, whirlpool, recreation programs, exercise room, spa, basketball, volleyball. *Fee:* golf-27 holes, 9 tennis courts (5 lighted). **Business Services:** conference facilities, business center. **Cards:** AX, MC, VI.

▼ See AAA listing above ▼

(See map and index starting on p. 534)

EL CID EL MORO BEACH HOTEL — **Phone:** 669/913-3333 — 9

Resort Hotel
$151-$232 All Year

Address: Ave Camaron Sabalo S/N **Location:** 5.4 mi (8.7 km) nw; in Camaron Sabalo Hotel Zone. **Facility:** Next to El Cid Castilla Beach Hotel, this impressive tower property has a mall with fine shops, as well as a beach, swimming pools and restaurants. 310 units. 40 one-bedroom standard units. 270 one-bedroom suites with kitchens. 28 stories, interior corridors. *Bath:* combo or shower only. **Parking:** on-site. **Amenities:** safes, irons, hair dryers. **Pool(s):** 2 outdoor. **Leisure Activities:** whirlpool, recreation programs, spa, basketball, volleyball. *Fee:* golf-27 holes, 9 tennis courts (5 lighted), exercise room. **Guest Services:** valet laundry. **Business Services:** conference facilities, business center. **Cards:** AX, MC, VI.

EL CID GRANADA COUNTRY CLUB — *Book at AAA.com* — **Phone:** (669)913-3333 — 11

Resort Hotel
$73-$200 All Year

Address: Ave Camaron Sabalo S/N **Location:** 5.4 mi (8.7 km) nw; in Camaron Sabalo Hotel Zone; across from El Moro Tower. **Facility:** Next to a golf course and across the street from the beach, the property offers modest guest units designed to accommodate families. 120 one-bedroom standard units, some with efficiencies. 3 stories, interior corridors. **Parking:** on-site and valet. **Amenities:** safes, irons. **Pool(s):** outdoor. **Leisure Activities:** sauna, whirlpool, spa. *Fee:* golf-27 holes, 9 tennis courts (5 lighted), exercise room. **Guest Services:** valet laundry, wireless Internet. **Cards:** AX, MC, VI.

EMPORIO MAZATLAN — *Book at AAA.com* — **Phone:** (669)983-4822 — 23

Hotel
$130-$180 All Year

Address: Ave Camaron Sabalo 51 **Location:** 4.1 mi (6.5 km) nw. **Facility:** 134 one-bedroom standard units. 4 stories, exterior corridors. *Bath:* shower only. **Parking:** on-site. **Amenities:** safes, irons, hair dryers. *Some:* DVD players. **Dining:** Condimento, see separate listing. **Pool(s):** 2 heated outdoor. **Leisure Activities:** whirlpool. **Guest Services:** valet laundry, wireless Internet. **Business Services:** meeting rooms. *Fee:* PC, fax. **Cards:** AX, MC, VI.

/ SOME UNITS

FARO MAZATLAN BEACH RESORT —  *Book at AAA.com* — **Phone:** (669)913-1111 — 2

Resort Hotel
$150-$200 All Year

Address: Punta del Sabalo S/N **Location:** 8.1 mi (13 km) nw; on north end of Zona Hotelera. **Facility:** On promontory. Some rooms with oceanview. 165 one-bedroom standard units. 4 stories, interior corridors. **Parking:** on-site. **Terms:** 7 day cancellation notice. **Amenities:** *Some:* safes. **Pool(s):** outdoor. **Leisure Activities:** recreation programs, exercise room, volleyball. **Guest Services:** valet laundry, wireless Internet. **Business Services:** meeting rooms. *Fee:* PC, fax. **Cards:** AX, MC, VI.

/ SOME UNITS

FIESTA INN — *Book great rates at AAA.com* — **Phone:** (669)989-0100 — 7

AAA

Hotel
$81-$145 All Year

Address: Ave Camaron Sabalo 1927 **Location:** Oceanfront. 6.3 mi (10 km) nw. **Facility:** 117 one-bedroom standard units. 2-9 stories, interior corridors. **Parking:** on-site. **Amenities:** voice mail, irons, hair dryers. *Some:* high-speed Internet. **Dining:** 2 restaurants. **Pool(s):** heated outdoor. **Leisure Activities:** limited beach access, exercise room. **Guest Services:** valet laundry, wireless Internet. **Business Services:** meeting rooms, business center. **Cards:** AX, MC, VI. *(See color ad on insert)*

S D / SOME UNITS

HOLIDAY INN SUNSPREE RESORT MAZATLAN — **Phone:** (669)913-2222 — 8

Hotel
$120-$140 All Year

Address: Ave Camaron Sabalo 696 **Location:** 5.8 mi (9.2 km) nw. **Facility:** 190 units. 167 one-bedroom standard units, some with efficiencies. 23 one-bedroom suites with efficiencies. 6 stories, interior corridors. *Bath:* shower only. **Parking:** on-site and valet. **Terms:** 4 day cancellation notice. **Amenities:** safes (fee), irons, hair dryers. **Pool(s):** heated outdoor. **Leisure Activities:** exercise room, shuffleboard, volleyball. *Fee:* tennis court. **Guest Services:** valet and coin laundry, wireless Internet. **Business Services:** meeting rooms, business center. **Cards:** AX, MC, VI.

D / SOME UNITS

HOTEL AGUAMARINA-MAZATLAN — **Phone:** (669)981-7080 — 25

Hotel
$65-$100 All Year

Address: Ave del Mar 110 **Location:** 2.1 mi (3.3 km) nw. **Facility:** 111 units. 103 one-bedroom standard units. 8 one-bedroom suites with efficiencies. 3 stories (no elevator), interior/exterior corridors. *Bath:* shower only. **Parking:** on-site. **Terms:** 3 day cancellation notice-fee imposed. **Amenities:** *Some:* hair dryers. **Pool(s):** heated outdoor. **Guest Services:** valet laundry, wireless Internet. **Business Services:** meeting rooms, PC. **Cards:** AX, MC, VI.

/ SOME UNITS

HOTEL COSTA DE ORO — **Phone:** 669/913-5344 — 12

Resort Hotel
$150 All Year

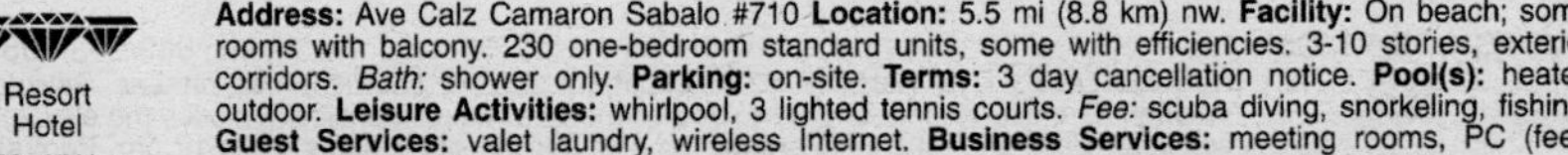

Address: Ave Calz Camaron Sabalo #710 **Location:** 5.5 mi (8.8 km) nw. **Facility:** On beach; some rooms with balcony. 230 one-bedroom standard units, some with efficiencies. 3-10 stories, exterior corridors. *Bath:* shower only. **Parking:** on-site. **Terms:** 3 day cancellation notice. **Pool(s):** heated outdoor. **Leisure Activities:** whirlpool, 3 lighted tennis courts. *Fee:* scuba diving, snorkeling, fishing. **Guest Services:** valet laundry, wireless Internet. **Business Services:** meeting rooms, PC (fee). **Cards:** AX, DS, MC, VI.

/ SOME UNITS

(See map and index starting on p. 534)

HOTEL PLAYA MAZATLAN — Resort Hotel — $101-$124 All Year — **Phone:** (669)989-0555 — 20

Address: Ave Playa Gaviotas #202 **Location:** 4.6 mi (7.3 km) nw; on Las Gaviotas Beach. **Facility:** Well-appointed rooms, many with ocean view. Balcony or patio. Very attractive grounds, beach and restaurant facilities. 408 units. 405 one-bedroom standard units. 3 one-bedroom suites. 3-5 stories, interior/exterior corridors. *Bath:* shower only. **Parking:** on-site. **Terms:** 7 day cancellation notice-fee imposed. **Amenities:** hair dryers. *Some:* irons. **Dining:** Terraza Playa, see separate listing. **Pool(s):** 3 outdoor. **Leisure Activities:** whirlpools, recreation programs, exercise room, spa, volleyball. **Guest Services:** valet laundry, wireless Internet. **Business Services:** meeting rooms, business center. **Cards:** AX, MC, VI.

/ SOME UNITS

HOTEL PUEBLO BONITO — Resort Hotel — $230-$395 All Year — **Phone:** (669)989-8900 — 3

Address: Ave Camaron Sabalo 2121 **Location:** 7.8 mi (12.5 km) nw. **Facility:** A feature of some of the rooms at this well-maintained facility is beach-view balconies. 247 units. 149 one-bedroom standard units with efficiencies. 98 one-bedroom suites with efficiencies. 4-5 stories, exterior corridors. **Parking:** on-site. **Terms:** check-in 4 pm. **Amenities:** voice mail, safes, irons, hair dryers. **Dining:** Angelo's Restaurant, Cilantro's, see separate listings. **Pool(s):** 2 heated outdoor. **Leisure Activities:** whirlpool, recreation programs, exercise room, volleyball. *Fee:* massage. **Guest Services:** valet laundry. **Business Services:** meeting rooms, business center. **Cards:** AX, MC, VI.

HOWARD JOHNSON DON PELAYO — Hotel — $70-$120 All Year — **Phone:** 669/983-1888 — 24

Address: Ave del Mar #1111, Col Flamingos **Location:** 2.5 mi (4 km) nw. **Facility:** 162 one-bedroom standard units, some with efficiencies (utensils extra charge). 5-10 stories, interior/exterior corridors. *Bath:* shower only. **Parking:** on-site. **Amenities:** *Some:* high-speed Internet (fee). **Pool(s):** outdoor. **Leisure Activities:** whirlpool, exercise room, game room. **Guest Services:** valet laundry, wireless Internet. **Business Services:** meeting rooms, PC. **Cards:** AX, MC, VI.

D / SOME UNITS

LAS FLORES BEACH RESORT — Book at AAA.com — Resort Hotel — $137-$199 All Year — **Phone:** (669)913-5100 — 29

Address: Ave Playa Gaviotas 212 **Location:** Oceanfront. 4.6 mi (7.3 km) nw; on Las Gaviotas Beach. **Facility:** Most rooms with balcony and ocean view. 117 units. 75 one-bedroom standard units, some with efficiencies. 42 one-bedroom suites with efficiencies. 11 stories, interior/exterior corridors. *Bath:* combo or shower only. **Parking:** on-site. **Terms:** check-in 4 pm, 3 day cancellation notice. **Amenities:** *Some:* hair dryers. **Pool(s):** 2 outdoor. **Leisure Activities:** whirlpool, limited beach access. **Guest Services:** valet laundry, wireless Internet. **Business Services:** PC, fax (fee). **Cards:** AX, MC, VI.

/ SOME UNITS

LOS SABALOS MAZATLAN HOTEL — Book at AAA.com — Resort Hotel — $120-$150 All Year — **Phone:** (669)983-5333 — 22

Address: Ave Playa Gaviotas #100 **Location:** 4.4 mi (7 km) nw; on Las Gaviotas Beach. **Facility:** This mid-level Mexican hotel features well-tended grounds, a swimming pool and a beach-view restaurant. 200 units. 158 one- and 28 two-bedroom standard units. 14 one-bedroom suites. 8 stories, exterior corridors. *Bath:* combo or shower only. **Parking:** on-site. **Terms:** 4 day cancellation notice. **Amenities:** safes, hair dryers. **Pool(s):** outdoor. **Leisure Activities:** exercise room, spa, volleyball. *Fee:* sauna, whirlpool, scuba diving, snorkeling. **Guest Services:** valet laundry, wireless Internet. **Business Services:** meeting rooms, business center. **Cards:** AX, MC, VI.

/ SOME UNITS

MARINA EL CID HOTEL & YACHT CLUB — Book at AAA.com — Resort Hotel — $116-$202 All Year — **Phone:** (669)913-3333 — 27

Address: Ave Camaron Sabalo S/N **Location:** 8.4 mi (13.5 km) nw; on north end of Zona Hotelera. **Facility:** Situated around a private marina, the resort consists of many smaller buildings, so it feels more residential than hotel in scope. 204 units. 83 one-bedroom standard units with efficiencies. 114 one-, 1 two- and 6 three-bedroom suites with efficiencies, some with whirlpools. 3-7 stories, exterior corridors. *Bath:* shower only. **Parking:** on-site. **Terms:** check-in 4 pm. **Amenities:** safes, irons, hair dryers. **Dining:** Restaurante La Marina, see separate listing. **Pool(s):** outdoor, heated outdoor. **Leisure Activities:** whirlpool, recreation programs, playground, spa, shuffleboard, volleyball. *Fee:* marina, golf-27 holes, miniature golf, 9 tennis courts (4 lighted). **Guest Services:** valet and coin laundry, wireless Internet. **Business Services:** meeting rooms. *Fee:* PC, fax. **Cards:** AX, MC, VI.

MAYAN SEA GARDEN MAZATLAN — Book at AAA.com — Hotel — $297-$360 All Year — **Phone:** (669)989-4000 — 28

Address: Calz Sabalo-Cerritos S/N **Location:** 0.6 mi (1 km) n of marina. **Facility:** 350 one-bedroom suites, some with efficiencies. 4-12 stories, exterior corridors. *Bath:* combo or shower only. **Parking:** on-site. **Terms:** check-in 5 pm. **Amenities:** safes, hair dryers. **Pool(s):** outdoor, 2 heated outdoor. **Leisure Activities:** limited beach access, exercise room, game room. **Guest Services:** valet and coin laundry. **Business Services:** business center. **Cards:** AX, MC, VI.

CALL M

MOTEL LOS ARCOS — Hotel — $90-$120 All Year — **Phone:** 669/913-5066 — 18

Address: Ave Playa Gaviotas #214 **Location:** 4.7 mi (7.5 km) nw; on Las Gaviotas Beach. **Facility:** 22 units. 13 one- and 9 two-bedroom suites with efficiencies. 2 stories (no elevator), exterior corridors. *Bath:* shower only. **Parking:** on-site. **Terms:** office hours 7 am-10 pm. **Pool(s):** outdoor. **Leisure Activities:** limited beach access. **Business Services:** fax. **Cards:** MC, VI.

/ SOME UNITS FEE

(See map and index starting on p. 534)

MOTEL MARLEY Phone: 669/913-5533 14

Motel
$83-$95 All Year

Address: Ave Playa Gaviotas #226 **Location:** 4.7 mi (7.5 km) nw; on Las Gaviotas Beach. **Facility:** 16 units. 12 one- and 4 two-bedroom suites with efficiencies. 2 stories (no elevator), exterior corridors. *Bath:* shower only. **Parking:** on-site. **Terms:** office hours 7 am-10 pm, 7 day cancellation notice. **Pool(s):** outdoor. **Leisure Activities:** limited beach access. **Business Services:** PC. **Cards:** MC, VI.

OCEANO PALACE Phone: (669)913-0666 6

Resort Hotel
$112-$117 All Year

Address: Ave Camaron Sabalo S/N **Location:** Oceanfront. 7.5 mi (12 km) nw. **Facility:** Many rooms with ocean view and balcony. 200 one-bedroom standard units. 6 stories, interior corridors. *Bath:* combo or shower only. **Parking:** on-site. **Amenities:** safes (fee). **Pool(s):** outdoor. **Leisure Activities:** limited beach access. **Business Services:** meeting rooms. *Fee:* PC, fax. **Cards:** AX, MC, VI.

/ SOME UNITS

PUEBLO BONITO AT EMERALD BAY Book great rates at AAA.com Phone: (669)989-0525 5

Resort Hotel
$205-$485 All Year

Address: Ave Ernesto Coppel Campana S/N **Location:** In Zona Mueva de Mazatlan; just n of Culiacan turn off, on Mex 15. **Facility:** A luxury beach hotel in a recently developed area, this property features an impressive marble lobby, gardens and an upscale restaurant and lounge. Meets AAA guest room security requirements. 280 units. 120 one-bedroom standard units with efficiencies. 160 one-bedroom suites, some with efficiencies. 2-4 stories, interior corridors. **Parking:** on-site and valet. **Terms:** check-in 4 pm. **Amenities:** high-speed Internet, voice mail, safes, irons, hair dryers. **Dining:** 2 restaurants. **Pool(s):** 2 heated outdoor. **Leisure Activities:** whirlpools, steamroom, 2 tennis courts (Fee: 2 lighted), recreation programs, kids club, spa, basketball, horseshoes, volleyball. *Fee:* snorkeling, fishing, exercise room. **Guest Services:** valet laundry. **Business Services:** meeting rooms, business center. **Cards:** AX, DS, MC, VI.

/ SOME UNITS

ROYAL VILLAS RESORT Phone: 669/916-6161 10

Hotel
$150-$349 All Year

Address: Ave Camaron Sabalo 500 **Location:** Oceanfront. 5.3 mi (8.5 km) nw; in Camaron Sabalo Hotel Zone. **Facility:** 125 units. 65 one-bedroom standard units with efficiencies. 20 one-, 38 two- and 2 three-bedroom suites, some with efficiencies and/or whirlpools. 12 stories, interior corridors. **Parking:** on-site. **Amenities:** high-speed Internet, voice mail, irons, hair dryers. **Dining:** La Hacienda de la Flor, see separate listing. **Pool(s):** heated outdoor. **Leisure Activities:** whirlpool, waterslide, limited beach access, recreation programs, exercise room, game room. *Fee:* massage. **Guest Services:** valet and coin laundry, wireless Internet. **Business Services:** meeting rooms, PC. **Cards:** AX, MC, VI.

/ SOME UNITS

SUITES LINDAMAR Phone: 669/913-5533 15

Motel
$90 All Year

Address: Ave Playa Gaviotas #222 **Location:** 4.7 mi (7.5 km) nw; on Las Gaviotas Beach. **Facility:** 12 one-bedroom suites with kitchens. 3 stories (no elevator), exterior corridors. *Bath:* shower only. **Parking:** on-site. **Terms:** office hours 7 am-10 pm, 7 day cancellation notice. **Leisure Activities:** limited beach access. **Cards:** MC, VI.

SUITES LUNA PALACE Phone: (669)914-6366 4

Resort Hotel
$148-$155 All Year

Address: Ave Camaron Sabalo S/N **Location:** Oceanfront. 7.5 mi (12 km) nw. **Facility:** This property is on attractive grounds with secure parking; some rooms include a balcony with ocean views. 71 units. 47 one-bedroom standard units with efficiencies (no utensils). 24 one-bedroom suites with efficiencies. 8 stories, interior corridors. **Parking:** on-site. **Amenities:** safes, hair dryers. **Pool(s):** heated outdoor. **Guest Services:** wireless Internet. **Business Services:** fax (fee). **Cards:** AX, MC, VI.

WHERE TO DINE

ANGELO'S RESTAURANT Phone: 669/989-8900 3

Italian
$20-$35

The popular restaurant features Italian specialties, as well as great, cooked-to-order steaks. The setting is casual yet refined. Casual dress. Entertainment. **Bar:** Full bar. **Reservations:** required. **Hours:** 6 pm-11 pm. **Address:** Ave Camaron Sabalo 2121 Norte Fracc **Location:** 7.8 mi (12.5 km) nw; in Hotel Pueblo Bonito. **Parking:** no self-parking. **Cards:** AX, MC, VI.

CARLOS & LUCIA'S RESTAURANT BAR & GRILL Phone: 669/913-5677 9

Cuban
$7-$17

Cuban cuisine is served in a relaxed, pleasant atmosphere. Guests can sit on the patio or in the indoors dining room. The Cuban sandwich is a must-try, and imperial shrimp is fabulous. Casual dress. **Bar:** Full bar. **Reservations:** accepted. **Hours:** 8:30 am-10 pm. Closed: Mon. **Address:** Camaron Sabalo S/N **Location:** On Ave Camaron Sabalo; just s of Holiday Inn SunSpree Resort Mazatlan. **Parking:** street.

CHILI'S PEPPER Phone: 669/916-7939 17

Mexican
$7-$16

This casual beachfront eatery is the perfect spot to relax and unwind with a jumbo margarita and some tasty Mexican fare. The open-air dining room offers fabulous ocean views, and the staff provides warm and friendly service. In addition to Mexican specialties, the menu lists preparations of grilled meats and fresh seafood, including shrimp, as well as some American fare. Casual dress. **Bar:** Full bar. **Hours:** 8 am-midnight. **Address:** Ave Camaron Sabalo **Location:** 6.3 mi (10 km) nw; directly overlooking the beach. **Parking:** street. **Cards:** MC, VI.

(See map and index starting on p. 534)

CILANTRO'S **Phone:** 669/989-8900 (1)

International
$6-$25

A great spot for a casual meal, the open-air restaurant's spectacular oceanfront setting lends to its popularity with tourists and locals alike. Because reservations are not accepted, diners should be prepared to wait, but heading to the bar for a decadent cocktail and complimentary chips and salsa helps bide the time. The menu lists a good variety of freshly grilled items, including lobster, beef and seafood. Casual dress. **Bar:** Full bar. **Reservations:** not accepted. **Hours:** 10:30 am-10:30 pm. **Address:** Ave Camaron Sabalo 2121 Norte Fracc **Location:** 7.8 mi (12.5 km) nw; in Hotel Pueblo Bonito. **Parking:** no self-parking. **Cards:** AX, MC, VI.

CONDIMENTO **Phone:** 669/983-4822 (30)

International
$7-$20

Regardless of whether they're sitting on the outdoor terrace or in the brightly decorated dining room, diners enjoy a wonderful setting overlooking the beach and ocean. The menu lists a fine selection of regional Mexican and international dishes, available both a la carte and from the expansive buffet, which is set up during high season. Casual dress. **Bar:** Full bar. **Reservations:** suggested. **Hours:** 7 am-11 pm. **Address:** Ave Camaron Sabalo 51 **Location:** 4.1 mi (6.5 km) nw; in Emporio Mazatlan. **Parking:** on-site. **Cards:** AX, MC, VI.

COWBOY RESTAURANT AND SPORTS BAR **Phone:** 669/983-5333 (16)

Steak
$7-$22

Located in the heart of the Golden Zone, this restaurant is popular with the tourists looking for a good down-home steak in a relaxed setting. Many like to start their meal with a fresh local shrimp cocktail and then move on to a sizzling steak with a huge baked potato. The open air dining room offers a relaxed setting and features a big screen television in the back section so diners can keep up to date with sporting events. Casual dress. **Bar:** Full bar. **Hours:** 8 am-midnight. **Address:** Ave Playa Gaviotos #100 **Location:** 4.4 mi (7 km) nw; in Las Gaviotas beach area; across from Los Sabalos Resort Hotel. **Parking:** street. **Cards:** AX, MC, VI.

EL PARADOR ESPANOL **Phone:** 669/913-0767 (8)

Spanish
$15-$30

If you're not sure what you want for dinner, the tapas menu is sure to please with small portions and plenty of variety from which to choose. If you're looking for something really light, then perhaps try the tortilla soup with lemon broth and chicken or maybe the white fish ceviche. Casual dress. **Bar:** Full bar. **Reservations:** accepted. **Hours:** 11 am-11:30 pm. **Address:** Ave Camaron Sabalo 714 **Location:** 5.6 mi (9 km) nw. **Parking:** street. **Cards:** MC, VI.

EL SHRIMP BUCKET **Phone:** 669/981-6350 (20)

Seafood
$7-$20

Shrimp served in a clay bucket with fries is the signature dish at the popular cafe, which features an outdoor sidewalk section that affords fine views of the malecon and ocean. Sunsets here are a treat. Casual dress. **Bar:** Full bar. **Reservations:** accepted. **Hours:** 6 am-11 pm, Thurs-Sat to 2 am. Closed: 5/1. **Address:** Olas Atlas #11 **Location:** 5 blks sw of Plaza de la Republica. **Parking:** street. **Cards:** AX, MC, VI.

ERNIE TOMATO'S RESTAURANT AND BAR **Phone:** 669/914-2474 (23)

American
$7-$20

Colorful wall and ceiling murals brighten this casual eatery, where patrons explore a varied menu of tasty appetizers, pizza, pasta dishes and some casual Mexican fare. Casual dress. **Bar:** Full bar. **Reservations:** accepted. **Hours:** 1 pm-1 am. **Address:** Ave Playa Gaviotas No. 403 **Location:** In the Golden Zone. **Parking:** no self-parking. **Cards:** MC, VI.

GRINGO LINGO BAR AND GRILL **Phone:** 669/913-7737 (24)

American
$12-$16

This bustling eatery features bright Mexican decor and a lively atmosphere. The all-you-can-eat a la carte concept has guests order as many courses as they like, both at lunch and at dinner. The menu lists a wide choice, with fresh shrimp—prepared in many ways—a highlight. Pasta dishes, ribs, chicken and Mexican specialties also tempt. Casual dress. **Bar:** Full bar. **Reservations:** accepted. **Hours:** 11 am-11 pm. **Address:** Ave Playa Gaviotas #313 **Location:** In the Golden Zone. **Parking:** no self-parking. **Cards:** MC, VI.

LA CASA COUNTRY RESTAURANT **Phone:** 669/916-5300 (7)

Steak
$10-$30

A great place for a hearty steak dinner and a wild Western atmosphere, this restaurant is a favorite with the locals and tourists alike, as evidenced by the usual wait for seating. However, diners don't seem to mind as the wait pays off when they are served up some heaping portions of fine steaks, corn on the cob and a steaming baked potato. In season they have festive cowboy entertainment to add to the fun. Casual dress. **Bar:** Full bar. **Hours:** noon-2 am. **Address:** Ave Camaron Sabalo S/N **Location:** 5.9 mi (9.5 km) nw. **Parking:** on-site. **Cards:** AX, MC, VI.

LA COSTA MARINERA **Phone:** 669/916-1599 (4)

Seafood
$12-$25

If you're looking for a fun beach shack environment set just above the sand where venders can still lean through the windows with trinkets and the setting sun can be enjoyed over a margarita and prawns Bombay, then this is for you! Casual dress. **Bar:** Full bar. **Reservations:** accepted. **Hours:** 10 am-11 pm. **Address:** Privada del Camaron y Privada de la Florida **Location:** 7.5 mi (12 km) nw; on the beach; between Oceano Palace and Luna Palace hotels. **Parking:** street. **Cards:** MC, VI.

(See map and index starting on p. 534)

LA HACIENDA DE LA FLOR **Phone:** 669/916-6161 (19)

Continental
$9-$28

Lending to the cozy restaurant's festive feel are distinctive Mexican decor and live music each evening. Staff members are skilled at tableside and flambe presentations. The menu incorporates a good mix of Mexican and international fare. **Bar:** Full bar. **Reservations:** suggested. **Hours:** noon-11 pm. **Address:** Ave Camaron Sabalo #500 **Location:** 5.3 mi (8.5 km) nw; in Camaron Sabalo Hotel Zone; in Royal Villas Resort. **Parking:** on-site. **Cards:** AX, MC, VI.

LAS LUPITAS RESTAURANTE **Phone:** 669/989-2309 (25)

International
$16-$28

Upscale contemporary design, both indoors and out, characterizes this chic restaurant. Mood lighting and modern music enhance the dining room, while candlelit tables on the terrace face the city street. The fine mix of innovative international fare pleases a wide range of tastes. Semi-formal attire. **Bar:** Full bar. **Hours:** 7 am-11 pm. **Address:** Bugambilias No. 100 **Location:** In the heart of the Golden Zone. **Parking:** street. **Cards:** MC, VI. *(See color ad p 538)*

LOS ARCOS RESTAURANT **Phone:** 669/913-9577

Seafood
$6-$20

A shrimp lover's paradise, this popular restaurant delights locals and tourists alike with its fine selection of fresh local shrimps and seafood cooked in every way imaginable. From fresh tasty starters such as a traditional chilled shrimp cocktail to coconut, garlic, Mexican spiced or Hawaiian pineapple jumbo shrimps, diners are sure to be satisfied. The dining room is brightly decorated with a district Mexican theme and features pleasant evening entertainment. Casual dress. **Bar:** Full bar. **Hours:** 11 am-10 pm. **Address:** Ave Camaron Sabalo #1019 **Location:** Between Hotel El Cid and Holiday Inn; 5.6 mi (9 km) nw. **Parking:** on-site. **Cards:** MC, VI.

MISTER ACE RESTAURANT AND BAR **Phone:** 669/914-4948 (22)

Steak
$8-$35

Guests relax in the bustling dining room with a fine menu of steak, seafood and some Mexican specialties. Servers are skilled in tableside and flambe presentation and delight diners with their showmanship. Nightly entertainment and a choice of inside or outdoor patio seating enhance the experience. Casual dress. **Bar:** Full bar. **Hours:** 8 am-11 pm. **Address:** Gabriel Ruiz #3 **Location:** At Ave Camoron Sabalo. **Parking:** no self-parking. **Cards:** MC, VI.

PANCHOS RESTAURANT **Phone:** 669/914-0911 (26)

International
$7-$16

This popular eatery offers sweeping views of the ocean from its main and second-floor dining areas. The lower level features covered patio seating, while upstairs has large panoramic windows and bright, festive decor. The menu features a good mix of casual fare, including Mexican, seafood and American specialties. This place is always busy, and it's common to wait for seating. Casual dress. **Bar:** Full bar. **Hours:** 7 am-1 am. **Address:** Ave Playa Gaviotas No 408 **Location:** 4.4 mi (7 km) nw; on Las Gaviotas Beach. **Parking:** no self-parking. **Cards:** AX, MC, VI.

THE PLACE **Phone:** 669/916-1301 (5)

International
$8-$20

This is the place where "all you can eat & drink" is taken seriously with bottomless margaritas, platters of ribs and a dinner special that includes three lobsters. Set right on the sidewalk, diners can take in the petalumas rumbling by and do some great people watching. Festive music and a friendly staff make for a very relaxed and fun meal. Casual dress. **Bar:** Full bar. **Reservations:** accepted. **Hours:** 7 am-10:30 pm. **Address:** Ave Camaron Sabalo 5504 **Location:** 7.5 mi (12 km) nw. **Parking:** street. **Cards:** DS, MC, VI.

RESTAURANT CASA LOMA **Phone:** 669/913-5398 (10)

International
$15-$22

In a quiet residential neighborhood, the popular restaurant blends well-prepared Italian cuisine and some Mexican dishes on its diverse menu. Casual dress. **Bar:** Full bar. **Reservations:** suggested. **Hours:** Open 12/1-8/7 & 9/21-11/30; 1:30 pm-10:30 pm. **Address:** Ave Playa Gaviotas, #104 Fracc Gaviotas **Location:** 4.9 mi (7.8 km) nw. **Parking:** on-site. **Cards:** MC, VI.

RESTAURANTE LA MARINA **Phone:** 669/913-3333 (21)

International
$7-$24

A stylish dining experience awaits. From the open patio, patrons are treated to a marvelous view of white yachts in the marina. Seafood, as well as fowl and meats, is skillfully prepared and attractively presented. Dressy casual. **Bar:** Full bar. **Reservations:** accepted. **Hours:** 7 am-11 pm. **Address:** Punta del Sabalo S/N **Location:** 8.4 mi (13.5 km) nw; on north end of Zona Hotelera; in Marina El Cid Hotel & Yacht Club. **Parking:** on-site and valet. **Cards:** AX, MC, VI.

RESTAURANT EL CAPTINO **Phone:** 669/913-1191 (28)

Seafood
$8-$20

By day, diners enjoy great ocean views from this beachfront open-air restaurant, while at night they enjoy the festive Mexican entertainment. On the menu is a good selection of fresh local seafood and tasty Mexican fare, including combination platters with grilled chicken, beef and local lobster. Casual dress. **Bar:** Full bar. **Hours:** 10 am-11 pm. **Address:** Marina Ave #104 **Location:** North end of hotel zone; just n of marina. **Parking:** street. **Cards:** MC, VI.

RESTAURANT MAMUCAS **Phone:** 669/981-3490 (18)

Seafood
$7-$18

First-timers shouldn't let the modest looks of the cafe fool them; this is where local folks go for seafood. Jumbo shrimp grilled with butter is absolutely fantastic, and this place serves everything available on the local seafood market. Octopus is a standout. Casual dress. **Bar:** Full bar. **Reservations:** accepted. **Hours:** 10:30 am-9:30 pm. **Address:** Simon Bolivar #404 Pte **Location:** Jct Paseo Claussen and Ave Nelson, just e, then just s; in Old Mazatlan. **Parking:** street. **Cards:** MC, VI.

(See map and index starting on p. 534)

SENOR FROG'S **Phone:** 669/985-1110

International
$8-$16

Part of the chain of Mexican restaurants that also includes Carlos 'n Charlie's, the fun and festive eatery is a great place to eat with the family or rendezvous with friends. The menu is lined with Tex-Mex, American and Mexican favorites, such as Buffalo wings, quesadillas, fajitas and burritos. After hours, a bar atmosphere prevails. Casual dress. **Bar:** Full bar. **Reservations:** accepted. **Hours:** 11 am-2 am. **Address:** Ave del Mar #882, Zona Costera **Location:** On the malecon; between aves Insurgentes and de los Deportes. **Parking:** street. **Cards:** AX, MC, VI.

THE SHRIMP FACTORY **Phone:** 669/916-5318 (13)

Seafood
$8-$16

A pleasant outdoor cafe setting in the heart of the Golden Zone and a fresh menu featuring local shrimps, seafood and lobster make this a worthwhile choice for a tasty meal. In addition to the very popular peel and eat shrimp, the chef also features tasting-style menus that offer a sample of most of the popular varieties of shrimp including chilled cocktail, breaded, garlic spiced and Mexican style. A great choice for the undecided diner. Casual dress. **Bar:** Full bar. **Hours:** noon-10 pm. **Address:** Ave Playa Gaviotas #14 **Location:** In the heart of Golden Zone. **Parking:** street. **Cards:** MC, VI.

SR PEPPER **Phone:** 669/914-0101 (2)

Steak
$20-$35

Gilded mirrors and polished brass are visible throughout the dining room so as to reflect the rich wood paneling, linen-draped tables and tuxedo-attired staff, which all create an atmosphere that makes this a perfect stop for a special occasion or just a super night out. The menu has a few seafood selections but focuses primarily on select cuts of fresh beef that are brought to the table for viewing prior to ordering. Live music and dancing Tuesday through Sunday. Casual dress. **Bar:** Full bar. **Reservations:** accepted. **Hours:** 5:30 pm-11 pm. **Address:** Ave Camaron Sabalo Norte S/N **Location:** 8.1 mi (13 km) nw; on north end of Zona Hotelera. **Parking:** on-site. **Cards:** MC, VI.

TEQUILA'S PUB **Phone:** 669/913-5344 (11)

American
$6-$12

At the lively sports bar and eatery, diners can nibble on tasty American and Mexican dishes while viewing sporting events on a big-screen television. Casual dress. **Bar:** Full bar. **Reservations:** accepted. **Hours:** 11 am-10 pm. **Address:** Ave Camaron Sabalo S/N **Location:** 5.5 mi (8.8 km) nw; across from Hotel Costa de Oro. **Parking:** on-site. **Cards:** AX, MC, VI.

TERRAZA PLAYA **Phone:** 669/989-0555 (12)

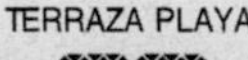

International
$8-$17

On beachside terrace. Casual dress. Entertainment. **Bar:** Full bar. **Hours:** 7 am-11 pm. **Address:** Ave Playa Gaviotas #202 **Location:** 4.6 mi (7.3 km) nw; on Las Gaviotas Beach; in Hotel Playa Mazatlan. **Parking:** on-site. **Cards:** AX, MC, VI.

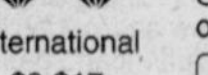

VILLA ITALIA **Phone:** 669/913-0311 (6)

Italian
$11-$18

Casual, well-prepared Italian specialties are served indoors and on the casual patio. The outdoor brick oven is used to prepare bread and pizza. Casual dress. **Bar:** Full bar. **Reservations:** suggested. **Hours:** noon-midnight. **Address:** Ave Camaron Sabalo S/N **Location:** 5 mi (8 km) nw; in front of Hotel El Cid. **Parking:** on-site. **Cards:** MC, VI.

VIPS **Phone:** 669/914-0754

Mexican
$5-$9

Owned by Wal-Mart of Mexico and found in most major cities, the budget-friendly chain serves a good variety of Mexican and American dishes, including burgers, sandwiches, salads, spaghetti and enchiladas, as well as a fine selection of desserts. Casual dress. **Hours:** 7 am-midnight, Fri & Sat-2 am. **Address:** Ave Lomas de Mazatlan #101 **Location:** Jct Lomas de Mazatlan and Sierrade Venados, just s. **Parking:** on-site. **Cards:** MC, VI.

VITTORE **Phone:** 669/986-2424 (15)

Italian
$10-$20

A wood-burning pizza oven, trattoria ambience, open dining room and pleasant patio all add up to an enjoyable Italian dining experience. Casual dress. **Bar:** Full bar. **Reservations:** suggested. **Hours:** noon-1 am. **Address:** Ave Playa Gaviotas #100 **Location:** 4.4 mi (7 km) nw; on Las Gaviotas Beach; across from Los Sabalos Resort Hotel. **Parking:** on-site. **Cards:** AX, MC, VI.

NUEVO VALLARTA, NAYARIT pop. 4,000

WHERE TO STAY

CLUB HOTEL RIU JALISCO *Book great rates at AAA.com* **Phone:** (322)226-6600

Resort Hotel
$208-$257 All Year

Address: Paseo de los Cocoteros S/N Lote K **Location:** Mex 200, exit Nuevo Vallarta, 1.3 mi (2 km) n. **Facility:** This huge all-inclusive resort features a prime beachfront location and a variety of dining options; there is an abundance of activities for all ages. 726 units. 700 one-bedroom standard units. 26 one-bedroom suites. 6 stories, exterior corridors. *Bath:* combo or shower only. **Parking:** on-site. **Terms:** 3 night minimum stay, 3 day cancellation notice-fee imposed. **Amenities:** safes, honor bars, hair dryers. **Dining:** 5 restaurants, nightclub, entertainment. **Pool(s):** 2 outdoor. **Leisure Activities:** saunas, whirlpools, snorkeling, 2 lighted tennis courts, recreation programs, exercise room, spa, basketball, volleyball. *Fee:* scuba diving. **Guest Services:** valet laundry. **Business Services:** PC (fee). **Cards:** AX, MC, VI.

THE GRAND MAYAN NUEVO VALLARTA WYNDHAM ALLIANCE RESORT — **Phone:** (322)226-4000

Resort Hotel
$475-$785 All Year

Address: Paseo de las Moras S/N **Location:** Mex 200, 1.3 mi (2 km) n via Nuevo Vallarta exit. **Facility:** This huge resort complex features outstanding public facilities; a train and boat on site transport guests throughout the grounds and waterways. 781 units. 329 one-bedroom standard units, some with whirlpools. 452 one-bedroom suites with efficiencies. 9 stories, interior corridors. **Parking:** on-site (fee) and valet. **Terms:** check-in 5 pm, 3-7 night minimum stay - seasonal and/or weekends, 21 day cancellation notice-fee imposed. **Amenities:** voice mail, safes (fee), irons, hair dryers. **Dining:** Punta Arena, Samba Restaurant, Tramonto, see separate listings. **Pool(s):** heated outdoor. **Leisure Activities:** whirlpools, waterslide, limited beach access, lazy river, wave pool, recreation programs. *Fee:* scuba diving, snorkeling, golf-18 holes. **Guest Services:** valet laundry. **Cards:** AX, MC, VI.

FEE FEE / SOME UNITS

GRAND VELAS ALL SUITES & SPA RESORT *Book great rates at AAA.com* — **Phone:** (322)226-8000

Resort Hotel
$920-$1100 All Year

Address: Ave Cocoteros Sur #98 **Location:** Mex 200, 1.3 mi (2 km) n via Nuevo Vallarta exit. **Facility:** This luxurious spa retreat offers outstanding facilities and a prime beachfront setting; it is an all-inclusive facility. 267 units. 158 one-bedroom standard units, some with whirlpools. 95 one- and 14 two-bedroom suites, some with whirlpools. 9 stories, interior corridors. **Parking:** valet. **Terms:** 21 day cancellation notice. **Amenities:** video library, DVD players, CD players, high-speed Internet (fee), dual phone lines, voice mail, safes, honor bars, irons, hair dryers. **Dining:** 5 restaurants, also, Lucca, Piaf, see separate listings. **Pool(s):** outdoor, 2 heated outdoor. **Leisure Activities:** saunas, whirlpools, steamrooms, 2 lighted tennis courts, recreation programs, table tennis, kids club, bicycles, spa. *Fee:* scuba diving, snorkeling. **Guest Services:** valet laundry, wireless Internet. **Business Services:** conference facilities, business center. **Cards:** AX, MC, VI.
(See color ad p 560 & opposite title page)

FEE / SOME UNITS

HOTEL RIU VALLARTA — **Phone:** 322/226-7250

Resort Hotel
$446 All Year

Address: Avenida de lost Cocteros S/N Lote K **Location:** Mex 200, exit Nuevo Vallarta, 1.3 mi (2 km) n. **Facility:** The all-inclusive resort is situated beachfront and features a lush, tropical pool area; well-planned activity programs cater to all ages. 550 one-bedroom standard units. 9 stories, interior corridors. *Bath:* combo or shower only. **Parking:** on-site. **Terms:** 3 night minimum stay, 3 day cancellation notice-fee imposed. **Amenities:** safes, honor bars, hair dryers. *Some:* irons. **Pool(s):** 2 outdoor. **Leisure Activities:** limited beach access, snorkeling, exercise room, spa. *Fee:* scuba diving. **Guest Services:** valet laundry, wireless Internet. **Business Services:** meeting rooms, PC (fee). **Cards:** AX, MC, VI.

MARIVAL RESORT AND SUITES — **Phone:** 322/226-8200

Resort Hotel
$230-$380 All Year

Address: Blvd Nuevo Vallarta y Paseo Cocoter S/N **Location:** Oceanfront. Mex 200, 1.2 mi (2 km) n via Nuevo Vallarta exit. **Facility:** Set on a lovely stretch of beach, this all-inclusive resort is very activity oriented. 495 units. 374 one-bedroom standard units. 77 one-, 39 two- and 5 three-bedroom suites. 3-6 stories, interior corridors. **Parking:** on-site. **Amenities:** safes (fee), hair dryers. *Some:* irons. **Dining:** 6 restaurants, entertainment. **Pool(s):** 4 heated outdoor. **Leisure Activities:** limited beach access, snorkeling, 4 lighted tennis courts, exercise room, spa. *Fee:* scuba diving. **Guest Services:** valet and coin laundry, wireless Internet. **Business Services:** meeting rooms, business center. **Cards:** AX, MC, VI.

/ SOME UNITS

MAYAN PALACE NUEVO VALLARTA WYNDHAM ALLIANCE RESORT — **Phone:** (322)226-4000

Resort Hotel
$405-$682 All Year

Address: Paseo de las Moras S/N **Location:** Mex 200, 1.3 mi (2 km) n via Nuevo Vallarta exit. **Facility:** Guests are transported to their rooms via a water taxi on the lagoon or a small train service; the impressive resort's huge pool overlooks the ocean. 523 units. 174 one-bedroom standard units. 349 one-bedroom suites with efficiencies. 4-7 stories, interior corridors. *Bath:* combo or shower only. **Parking:** on-site (fee) and valet. **Terms:** check-in 5 pm, 3-7 night minimum stay - seasonal and/or weekends, 21 day cancellation notice-fee imposed. **Amenities:** voice mail, irons, hair dryers. *Fee:* high-speed Internet, safes. **Dining:** 3 restaurants, also, Cafe del Lago, Punta Arena, Rouge Wine Bar, see separate listings, entertainment. **Pool(s):** heated outdoor. **Leisure Activities:** steamroom, recreation programs, spa. *Fee:* whirlpool, kayaks, golf-18 holes, game room. **Guest Services:** valet and coin laundry, wireless Internet. **Business Services:** meeting rooms. **Cards:** AX, MC, VI.

FEE / SOME UNITS

MAYAN SEA GARDEN NUEVO VALLARTA *Book great rates at AAA.com* — **Phone:** (322)226-4000

Hotel
$395-$535 4/15-10/31

Address: Paseo de las Moras S/N **Location:** Mex 200, 1.3 mi (2 km) n via Nuevo Vallarta exit. **Facility:** 182 units. 78 one-bedroom standard units. 104 one-bedroom suites with efficiencies. 7 stories, exterior corridors. **Parking:** on-site and valet. **Terms:** open 4/15-10/31, check-in 5 pm, 3 night minimum stay - seasonal and/or weekends, 30 day cancellation notice. **Amenities:** voice mail, safes (fee), hair dryers. **Dining:** 2 restaurants. **Pool(s):** heated outdoor. **Leisure Activities:** limited beach access, recreation programs. **Guest Services:** valet and coin laundry. **Cards:** AX, MC, VI.

FEE / SOME UNITS

OCCIDENTAL ALLEGRO NUEVO VALLARTA ALL INCLUSIVE Book great rates at AAA.com

Phone: (322)297-0400

Resort Hotel
$260 All Year

Address: Paseo de los Cocoteros #18 **Location:** Oceanfront. Mex 200, exit Nuevo Vallarta, 1.3 mi (2 km) n. **Facility:** Well-appointed guest rooms at the large, modern facility offer a comfortable retreat; the property's beach and pool areas are very nice. 292 one-bedroom standard units. 7 stories, interior corridors. *Bath:* shower only. **Parking:** on-site. **Terms:** 14 day cancellation notice-fee imposed. **Amenities:** safes, irons, hair dryers. **Dining:** 3 restaurants, entertainment. **Pool(s):** outdoor. **Leisure Activities:** sailboats, kayak, 2 lighted tennis courts, recreation programs, badminton, bocci, table tennis, kids club, bicycles, playground, exercise room, horseshoes, shuffleboard, volleyball. *Fee:* boats, scuba diving, snorkeling, fishing, massage. **Guest Services:** valet laundry. **Business Services:** meeting rooms. **Cards:** AX, MC, VI.

D / SOME UNITS

PARADISE VILLAGE BEACH RESORT & SPA Book great rates at AAA.com

Phone: (322)226-6770

Resort Hotel
$157-$572 All Year

Address: Paseo de los Cocoteros #1 **Location:** Mex 200, 1.3 mi (2 km) n via Nuevo Vallarta exit. **Facility:** Even a zoo is featured at this large-scale resort with all the amenities; there are also three pools, a fine beach, five restaurants and many shops. 711 units. 264 one-bedroom standard units with efficiencies. 199 one-, 177 two- and 71 three-bedroom suites with kitchens. 8 stories, interior corridors. **Parking:** on-site. **Terms:** check-in 4 pm. **Amenities:** safes, irons, hair dryers. **Dining:** 4 restaurants, also, El Faro de Tulum, Il Pescatore Ristorante, Mayapan, see separate listings, entertainment. **Pool(s):** 3 heated outdoor. **Leisure Activities:** limited beach access, kids club, playground, spa, basketball, shuffleboard, volleyball. *Fee:* windsurfing, scuba diving, snorkeling, fishing, charter fishing, kayaks, golf-18 holes, 2 lighted tennis courts, bicycles, exercise room. **Business Services:** conference facilities. **Cards:** AX, MC, VI.

24 S D / SOME UNITS

PLAYA DEL SOL GRAND

Phone: 322/226-1050

Hotel
$150-$249 All Year

Address: Blvd Costero 800 SUR **Location:** Oceanfront. Mex 200, exit Nuevo Vallarta, 1.3 mi (2 km) n. **Facility:** 160 units. 118 one-bedroom standard units, some with whirlpools. 42 one-bedroom suites. 7 stories, exterior corridors. *Bath:* combo or shower only. **Parking:** on-site. **Terms:** check-in 4 pm. **Amenities:** video library, DVD players, CD players, safes, irons, hair dryers. **Dining:** Cardinalli's Fine Italian Dining, Palm Terrace at Grand, see separate listings. **Pool(s):** heated outdoor. **Leisure Activities:** limited beach access, exercise room, spa. *Fee:* scuba diving, bicycles. **Guest Services:** valet laundry, wireless Internet. **Business Services:** PC (fee). **Cards:** AX, MC, VI.

/ SOME UNITS

SAMBA VALLARTA BY PUEBLO BONITA Book at AAA.com

Phone: (322)226-8250

Hotel
$270 All Year

Address: Ave Costera y la Playa S/N **Location:** Oceanfront. Mex 200, exit Nuevo Vallarta, 1.3 mi (2 km) n. **Facility:** 183 units. 160 one-bedroom standard units. 23 one-bedroom suites. 4 stories, interior corridors. *Bath:* combo or shower only. **Parking:** on-site. **Amenities:** safes. *Some:* irons, hair dryers. **Pool(s):** 3 outdoor. **Leisure Activities:** limited beach access, windsurfing, bicycles, playground, exercise room, volleyball, game room. *Fee:* scuba diving, fishing, charter fishing, massage. **Guest Services:** valet laundry. **Business Services:** PC (fee). **Cards:** AX, MC, VI.

/ SOME UNITS

VALLARTA PALACE Book great rates at AAA.com

Phone: (322)226-8470

Resort Hotel
$586-$740 All Year

Address: Paseo de las Cocteros 19 Villa 8 **Location:** Mex 200, 1.3 mi (2 km) n via Nuevo Vallarta exit. **Facility:** The beachfront, all-inclusive resort features many dining options, Flambe coffee presentations, a huge tropical pool and nightly entertainment. 348 units. 325 one-bedroom standard units with whirlpools. 23 one-bedroom suites with whirlpools. 6-8 stories, interior corridors. **Parking:** on-site. **Amenities:** video games (fee), high-speed Internet, voice mail, safes, honor bars, irons, hair dryers. **Dining:** 5 restaurants, entertainment. **Pool(s):** outdoor, heated outdoor. **Leisure Activities:** whirlpools, limited beach access, windsurfing, kayaks, boogie boards, putting green, lighted tennis court, pool table, kids club, soccer field, spa, basketball, shuffleboard. *Fee:* scuba diving. **Guest Services:** valet laundry, wireless Internet. **Business Services:** conference facilities, PC (fee). **Cards:** AX, MC, VI.

24 D / SOME UNITS

VILLA DEL PALMAR FLAMINGO BEACH RESORT AND SPA Book at AAA.com

Phone: (322)226-8100

Hotel
$345-$446 All Year

Address: Paseo Cocoteros 750 Sur **Location:** Oceanfront. Mex 200, exit Nuevo Vallarta, 1.3 mi (2 km) n. **Facility:** Designated smoking area. 282 units. 136 one-bedroom standard units. 131 one-, 12 two- and 3 three-bedroom suites, some with whirlpools. 8 stories, exterior corridors. **Parking:** valet. **Terms:** check-in 4 pm. **Amenities:** safes, irons, hair dryers. **Dining:** Bella Vista Restaurant, see separate listing. **Pool(s):** heated outdoor. **Leisure Activities:** saunas, whirlpools, steamrooms, limited beach access, spa. **Guest Services:** valet laundry, wireless Internet. **Business Services:** meeting rooms, PC (fee). **Cards:** AX, DS, MC, VI.

WHERE TO DINE

ANGELO'S ITALIAN CUISINE STEAKS

Phone: 322/297-6130

Italian
$10-$20

Grilled meats and Italian favorites make up the menu at the casual eatery, which is within easy walking distance of many hotels from its spot in the Paradise Village mall. Casual dress. **Bar:** Full bar. **Hours:** 4 pm-10 pm. **Address:** Paradise Plaza J-2 **Location:** At Paradise Plaza, 2nd floor. **Parking:** on-site. **Cards:** MC, VI.

BELLA VISTA RESTAURANT — **Phone:** 322/226-8100

International
$10-$45

Guests can sit indoors or on the terrace, where ocean breezes and pianist entertainment enhance the romantic atmosphere on many evenings. Mexican influences infuse offerings of international fare. **Bar:** Full bar. **Reservations:** suggested. **Hours:** 7 am-11 pm, Sun-5 pm. **Address:** Paseo Cocoteros 750 SUR **Location:** Mex 200, exit Nuevo Vallarta, 1.3 mi (2 km) n; in Villa del Palmar Flamingos Beach Resort and Spa. **Parking:** valet. **Cards:** AX, DS, MC, VI.

CAFE DEL LAGO — **Phone:** 322/226-4000

International
$7-$23

Changing theme buffets and a simple a la carte menu of lighter fare—such as entree salads, sandwiches, burgers, Mexican dishes and cooked-to-order fish and shrimp—make up the offerings at the comfortable cafe. Diners can sit under a large palapa roof in the dining room or look out over the lagoon from the spacious open-air terrace. Casual dress. **Bar:** Full bar. **Reservations:** suggested. **Hours:** 7 am-noon & 6-midnight. **Address:** Paseo de las Moras S/N **Location:** Mex 200, 1.3 mi (2 km) n via Nuevo Vallarta exit; in Mayan Palace Nuevo Wyndham Puerto Vallarta. **Parking:** on-site (fee) and valet. **Cards:** AX, MC, VI.

CARDINALLI'S FINE ITALIAN DINING — **Phone:** 322/226-1050

Italian
$9-$20

Diners have a choice of seating under a huge palapa roof in the elegant dining room or on the romantic patio. Included in a selection of fine Italian cuisine are fresh pasta dishes, grilled meats and seafood and made-to-order gourmet pizzas. Decadent desserts merit an indulgence. Casual dress. **Bar:** Full bar. **Reservations:** suggested. **Hours:** 6 pm-10:30 pm. Closed: Sun. **Address:** Blvd Costero 800 SUR **Location:** Mex 200, exit Nuevo Vallarta, 1.3 mi (2 km) n; in Playa del Sol Grand. **Parking:** on-site. **Cards:** AX, MC, VI.

EL FARO DE TULUM — **Phone:** 322/226-6770

International
$10-$25

Open-air dining and an oceanfront setting attract diners to the lovely restaurant, but tasty and creative dishes keep them coming back. The menu blends contemporary Mexican cuisine and seafood specialties. Service is warm and personable, and the setting is comfortable. Casual dress. **Bar:** Full bar. **Reservations:** suggested. **Hours:** 7 am-10:30 pm. **Address:** Paseo de los Cocoteros #1 **Location:** Mex 200, 1.3 mi (2 km) n via Nuevo Vallarta exit; in Paradise Village Beach Resort & Spa. **Parking:** on-site. **Cards:** AX, MC, VI.

IL PESCATORE RISTORANTE — **Phone:** 322/226-6670

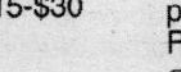

Italian
$15-$30

Set on the peaceful side of the marina, the open-air restaurant boasts a romantic setting and a fine menu of freshly prepared Italian cuisine. The chef features fresh local seafood, including a particularly popular grilled lobster entree served with a side of tasty pasta. The eatery proves to be a wonderful spot to linger over a glass of wine and a fine meal. Casual dress. **Bar:** Full bar. **Reservations:** suggested. **Hours:** 5 pm-10:30 pm. **Address:** Paseo de los Cocoteros #1 **Location:** Mex 200, 1.3 mi (2 km) n via Nuevo Vallarta exit; in Paradise Village Beach Resort & Spa. **Parking:** on-site. **Cards:** AX, MC, VI.

THE JUNGLE — **Phone:** 322/226-6770

International
$10-$25

Fun, casual decor revolves around a jungle theme at the family-oriented restaurant, which has a live snake tank and many stuffed jungle animals. Guests can sample hearty portions of tasty Mexican and Mediterranean cuisine with a strong focus on fresh local seafood. At night after the kitchen closes, this place transforms into a lively disco. Casual dress. **Bar:** Full bar. **Reservations:** suggested. **Hours:** 5 pm-9 pm. **Address:** Paseo de los Cocoteros #1 **Location:** Mex 200, 1.3 mi (2 km) n on Nuevo Vallarta exit, follow signs; at Paradise Plaza. **Parking:** on-site. **Cards:** AX, MC, VI.

LA CASONA — **Phone:** 322/226-9700

Steak
$32-$45

Live music boosts the atmosphere on the open-air terrace and in the semi-enclosed dining room. Tropical night breezes cool diners as they savor succulent steaks and fine international fare. **Bar:** Full bar. **Reservations:** suggested. **Hours:** 7 am-1 & 5-10:30 pm. **Address:** Paseo Los Cocoteros 750 Sur **Location:** Mex 200, exit Nuevo Vallarta, 1.3 mi (2 km) n; in Villa La Estancia. **Parking:** valet. **Cards:** AX, DS, MC, VI.

LUCCA — **Phone:** 322/226-8000

Italian
$12-$20

A pianist entertains guests who sit down in the elegant dining room to a fine meal of classic Italian cuisine. Dressy casual. **Bar:** Full bar. **Reservations:** required, for non guests. **Hours:** 6 pm-10:30 pm. **Address:** Ave Cocoteros #98 SUR **Location:** Mex 200, 1.3 mi (2 km) n via Nuevo Vallarta exit; in Grand Velas All Suites & Spa Resort. **Parking:** valet. **Cards:** AX, MC, VI.

MAYAPAN — **Phone:** 322/226-6770

International
$12-$25

Sea breezes wash over the large open-air terrace, where patrons sit down to international dishes prepared with Mexican influences. Live entertainment enhances the atmosphere most evenings. It's a good idea to phone ahead for information about theme nights, which may include barbecue or Western nights. Casual dress. **Bar:** Full bar. **Reservations:** suggested. **Hours:** 6 pm-10 pm. Closed: Mon. **Address:** Paseo de los Cocoteros #1 **Location:** Mex 200, 1.3 mi (2 km) n via Nuevo Vallarta exit; in Paradise Village Beach Resort & Spa. **Parking:** on-site. **Cards:** AX, MC, VI.

PALM TERRACE AT GRAND — **Phone:** 322/226-1050

International
$7-$20

On many evenings, the sounds of live harp music drift through the patio, where diners savor diverse choices while looking out over the ocean. The patio sometimes transforms into a grill where fine cuts of beef, chicken and seafood are prepared to order. On cooler evenings, the elegant indoor dining area offers seating. Casual dress. **Bar:** Full bar. **Reservations:** suggested. **Hours:** 7:30 am-10:30 pm. **Address:** Blvd Costero 800 SUR **Location:** Mex 200, exit Nuevo Vallarta, 1.3 mi (2 km) n; in Playa del Sol Grand. **Parking:** on-site. **Cards:** AX, MC, VI.

PIAF **Phone:** 322/226-8000

French
$28-$50

Classic French cuisine presented in a serene room with sunset views over the ocean. The attentive staff will see to your every need, offering dishes such as foie gras terrine, escargot and veal kidneys with Dijon mustard sauce. You may choose to end your meal with the peach melba which is a cool delight or the saffron creme brulee may be more enticing. Dressy casual. **Bar:** Full bar. **Reservations:** required, for non hotel guests. **Hours:** 6 pm-10:30 pm. **Address:** Ave Cocoteras 98 Sur **Location:** Mex 200, 1.3 mi (2 km) n via Nuevo Vallarta exit; in Grand Velas All Suites & Spa Resort. **Parking:** valet. **Cards:** AX, MC, VI.

PUNTA ARENA **Phone:** 322/226-4000

Seafood
$16-$29

Diners here enjoy the sea breeze from the open air dining room and the swaying of the palm trees. At night the tables are candlelit, setting a romantic tone. The service is warm and personable and the waiters go out of their way to provide a wonderful dining experience. Menu highlights include fresh soups, a variety of hot and cold appetizers, pastas and a selection of fresh seafood and grilled meats. Casual dress. **Bar:** Full bar. **Reservations:** accepted. **Hours:** 11 am-11 pm. **Address:** Paseo de las Moras S/N **Location:** Mex 200, 1.3 mi (2 km) n via Nuevo Vallarta exit; in The Grand Mayan Wyndham Nuevo Vallarta Resort. **Parking:** on-site. **Cards:** AX, MC, VI.

ROUGE WINE BAR **Phone:** 322/226-4000

International
$12-$20

Patrons of the chic wine bar have the option of ordering a la carte or indulging in the chef's tasting menu, complete with wine pairings. Floor-to-ceiling wine cases surround the upscale lounge setting, which offers an alternative to the limited seating on the patio. The well-trained staff adeptly finds the perfect wine to complement the chef's tasty offerings. Semi-formal attire. **Bar:** Full bar. **Reservations:** suggested. **Hours:** 3 pm-11 pm. Closed: Mon. **Address:** Paseo de las Moras S/N **Location:** Mex 200, 1.3 mi (2 km) n via Nuevo Vallarta exit ; in Mayan Palace Nuevo Wyndham Puerto Vallarta. **Parking:** valet. **Cards:** AX, MC, VI.

SAMBA RESTAURANT **Phone:** 322/226-4000

International
$12-$30

This open-air restaurant overlooks the Grand Mayan Resort's pool and fountain. In the evening, entertainment adds to the casual ambiance. The menu features a nice mix of International fare with grilled meats and seafood. Casual dress. **Bar:** Full bar. **Reservations:** suggested. **Hours:** 7 am-12:45 am. **Address:** Paseo de las Moras S/N **Location:** Mex 200, 1.3 mi (2 km) n via Nuevo Vallarta exit; in The Grand Mayan Wyndham Nuevo Vallarta Resort. **Parking:** on-site (fee) and valet. **Cards:** AX, MC, VI.

TRAMONTO **Phone:** 322/226-4000

International
$15-$30

Chic contemporary design characterizes both main dining room, while a breezier feel prevails on several covered patio areas. The innovative menu incorporates fine Italian and international fare. Semi-formal attire. **Bar:** Full bar. **Reservations:** suggested. **Hours:** 8 am-noon & 6-11 pm. **Address:** Paseo de los Moras S/N **Location:** Mex 200, 1.3 mi (2 km) n via Nuevo Vallarta exit; in The Grand Mayan Wyndham Nuevo Vallarta Resort. **Parking:** on-site (fee). **Cards:** AX, MC, VI.

PUERTO ESCONDIDO, OAXACA pop. 19,000

WHERE TO STAY

CASAMAR **Phone:** 954/582-2593

Motel
$46-$151 All Year

Address: Calle Puebla #407 **Location:** 2 mi s of town off Mex 200. **Facility:** Designated smoking area. 12 units. 9 one-bedroom standard units with efficiencies. 1 one- and 2 two-bedroom suites with kitchens. 2-4 stories (no elevator), exterior corridors. *Bath:* combo or shower only. **Parking:** on-site. **Pool(s):** outdoor. **Guest Services:** TV in common area, wireless Internet. **Business Services:** meeting rooms. **Cards:** MC, VI.

/ SOME UNITS

HOTEL BEST WESTERN POSADA REAL PUERTO ESCONDIDO **Phone:** 954/582-0133

Hotel
$220-$290 All Year

Address: Blvd Benito Juarez S/N **Location:** 1.4 mi (2.2 km) n of jct Mex 200 and 131; just w of tourist information booth. **Facility:** Meets AAA guest room security requirements. 100 one-bedroom standard units. 3 stories (no elevator), interior/exterior corridors. *Bath:* shower only. **Parking:** on-site. **Terms:** 3 day cancellation notice-fee imposed. **Amenities:** voice mail, hair dryers. **Dining:** Coco's, Hacienda Restaurant, see separate listings. **Pool(s):** 2 outdoor. **Leisure Activities:** putting green, sports court. *Fee:* tennis court, game room. **Guest Services:** valet laundry, area transportation, wireless Internet. **Business Services:** fax (fee). **Cards:** AX, DC, MC, VI.

/ SOME UNITS

AAA Benefit:

Members save up to 20%, plus 10% bonus points with rewards program.

HOTEL SANTA FE **Phone:** 954/582-0170

Hotel
$126-$162 All Year

Address: Calle del Morro S/N **Location:** At Playa Zicatela, off Mex 200; at south end of town. **Facility:** 69 units. 53 one-bedroom standard units. 10 one- and 6 two-bedroom suites with kitchens, some with whirlpools. 3 stories (no elevator), exterior corridors. *Bath:* combo or shower only. **Parking:** on-site. **Terms:** 30 day cancellation notice. **Amenities:** honor bars. *Some:* safes. **Pool(s):** 3 outdoor. **Leisure Activities:** *Fee:* massage. **Guest Services:** valet laundry, wireless Internet. **Business Services:** *Fee:* PC, fax. **Cards:** AX, MC, VI.

/ SOME UNITS

WHERE TO DINE

COCO'S

Phone: 954/582-0133

International

$8-$15

Lush tropical gardens surround this beachfront eatery's lovely setting, which overlooks the pool and ocean. The menu features a mix of light and international fare, including burgers, sandwiches and nachos, as well as grilled fish, seafood and chicken. A children's menu is also offered. Casual dress. **Bar:** Full bar. **Reservations:** not accepted. **Hours:** 10 am-6 pm. **Address:** Blvd Benito Juarez S/N **Location:** 1.4 mi (2.2 km) n of jct Mex 200 and 131; just w of tourist information booth; in Hotel Best Western Posada Real Puerto Escondido. **Parking:** on-site. **Cards:** AX, DC, MC, VI.

HACIENDA RESTAURANT

Phone: 954/582-0133

International

$7-$16

A peaceful feel marks the covered open-air dining room, which overlooks a tropical pool and gardens. The menu focuses on simple fare, including Mexican and international specialties such as shrimp cocktail filled with fresh shrimp and chopped avocado, tortilla soup and preparations of pasta, grilled chicken and seafood. Casual dress. **Bar:** Full bar. **Reservations:** accepted. **Hours:** 7 am-10:30 pm. **Address:** Blvd Benito Juarez S/N **Location:** 1.4 mi (2.2 km) n of jct Mex 200 and 131; just w of tourist information booth; in Hotel Best Western Posada Real Puerto Escondido. **Parking:** on-site. **Cards:** AX, DC, MC, VI.

HOTEL SANTA FE RESTAURANT

Phone: 954/582-0170

International

$8-$18

This open-air restaurant features a thatched roof, leather tables and chairs and an outstanding view of the ocean from its raised balcony. The menu has a strong focus on vegetarian fare but also lists pasta dishes, Mexican specialties and made-to-order shrimp, fish and other seafood. Casual dress. **Bar:** Full bar. **Reservations:** accepted. **Hours:** 7 am-10:30 pm. **Address:** Calle del Morro S/N **Location:** Off Mex 200; at Playa Zicatela; at south end of town; in Hotel Santa Fe. **Parking:** street. **Cards:** AX, MC, VI.

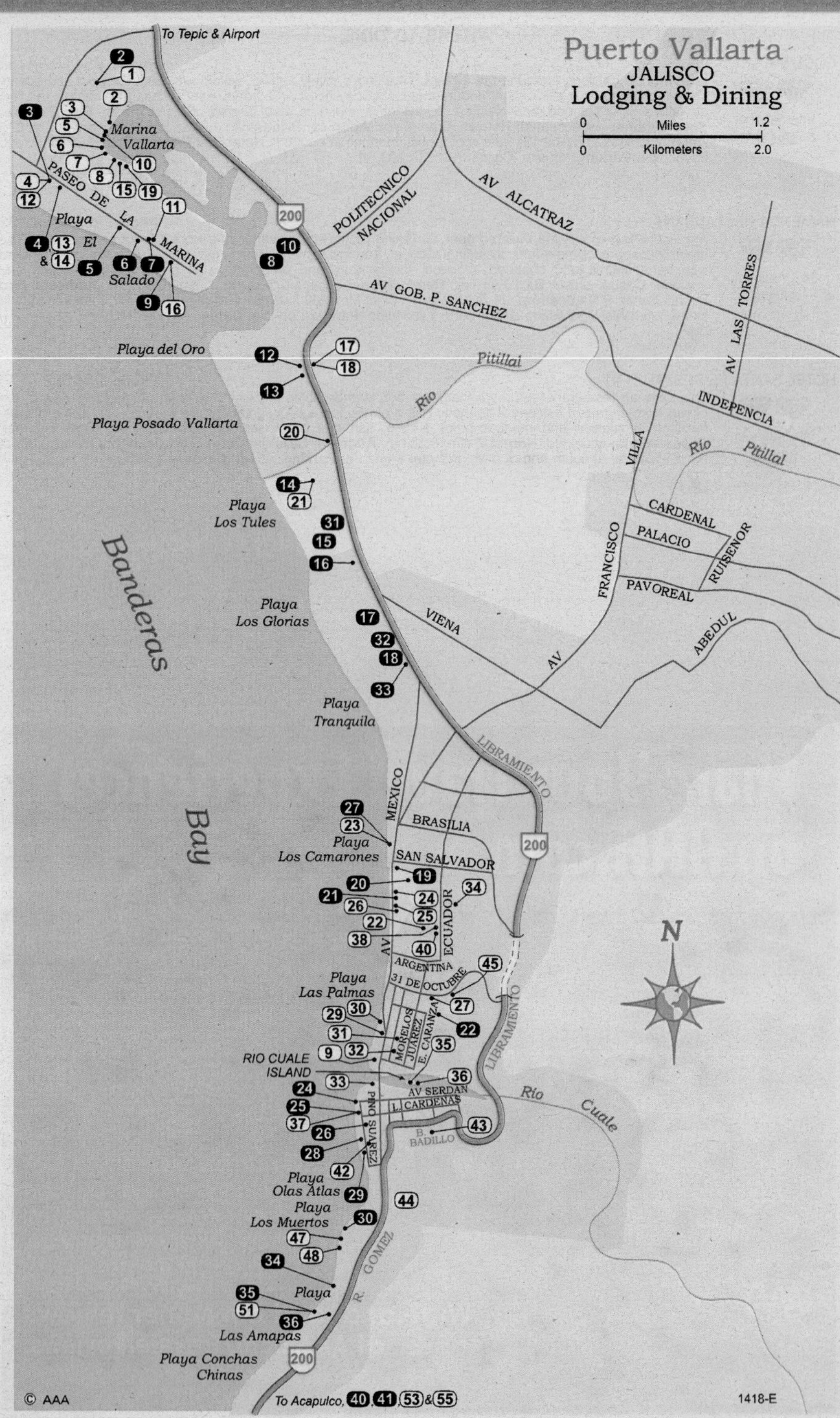
Puerto Vallarta
JALISCO
Lodging & Dining
0 Miles 1.2
0 Kilometers 2.0
To Tepic & Airport
Marina Vallarta
PASEO DE LA MARINA
Playa El Salado
Playa del Oro
Playa Posado Vallarta
Playa Los Tules
Playa Los Glorias
Playa Tranquila
Banderas Bay
Playa Los Camarones
Playa Las Palmas
RIO CUALE ISLAND
Playa Olas Atlas
Playa Los Muertos
Playa Las Amapas
Playa Conchas Chinas
POLITECNICO NACIONAL
AV ALCATRAZ
AV GOB. P. SANCHEZ
AV LAS TORRES
INDEPENCIA
Rio Pitillal
VILLA
CARDENAL
PALACIO
RUISENOR
PAVOREAL
FRANCISCO
AV
ABEDUL
VIENA
LIBRAMIENTO
MEXICO
BRASILIA
SAN SALVADOR
ECUADOR
AV
ARGENTINA
31 DE OCTUBRE
MORELOS
JUAREZ
E. CARANZA
AV SERDAN
L. CARDENAS
PINO SUAREZ
B. BADILLO
Rio Cuale
R. GOMEZ
200
N
To Acapulco, 40, 41, 53 & 55
© AAA
1418-E

Puerto Vallarta, Jalisco

This index helps you "spot" where approved lodgings and restaurants are located on the corresponding detailed maps. Lodging daily rate range is for comparison only and show the property's high season. Restaurant rate range is a combination of lunch and/or dinner. Turn to the listing page for more detailed rate information and consult display ads for special promotions.

PUERTO VALLARTA

Map Page	OA	Lodgings	Diamond Rated	High Season	Page
2 / p. 550	AAA	**Casa Velas Hotel Boutique** - see color ad p 561	◆◆◆◆	$610-$720	555
3 / p. 550		Velas Vallarta Suite Resort and Convention Center - see color ad p 561	◆◆◆	$300-$380	562
4 / p. 550	AAA	**CasaMagna Marriott Puerto Vallarta Resort & Spa** - see color ad starting on p 556	◆◆◆◆	$184-$462	554
5 / p. 550		Melia Puerto Vallarta All Inclusive Beach Resort	◆◆◆	$190-$272	559
6 / p. 550		Mayan Palace Puerto Vallarta Wyndham Alliance Resort	◆◆◆	$395-$525	559
7 / p. 550		Embarcadero Pacifico Hotel and Villas All Inclusive Resort	◆◆	$170-$220	555
8 / p. 550		Crown Paradise Club	◆◆◆	$290-$450	555
9 / p. 550	AAA	**The Westin Resort and Spa Puerto Vallarta** - see color ad on insert	◆◆◆◆	$119-$529	564
10 / p. 550		Golden Crown Paradise Resort-Adults All Inclusive	◆◆◆	$300-$460	555
12 / p. 550		Hacienda Hotel & Spa	◆◆	$184-$230	558
13 / p. 550		NH Krystal Puerto Vallarta	◆◆◆	$139-$186	559
14 / p. 550	AAA	**Holiday Inn Puerto Vallarta**	◆◆◆	$150-$220	558
15 / p. 550		Hola Puerto Vallarta Club & Spa	◆◆◆	$174-$248	558
16 / p. 550	AAA	**Fiesta Americana Puerto Vallarta** - see color ad on insert	◆◆◆◆	$379	555
17 / p. 550		Las Palmas by the Sea	◆◆	$200-$215	558
18 / p. 550	AAA	**Sheraton Buganvilias Resort and Convention Center** - see color ad on insert	◆◆◆	$95-$584	562
19 / p. 550	AAA	**Buenaventura Grand Hotel and Spa Puerto Vallarta**	◆◆◆	$260-$450	554
20 / p. 550		Hotel El Pescador	◆◆	$72-$115	558
21 / p. 550		Hotel Rosita	◆◆	$72-$115	558
22 / p. 550		Hacienda San Angel	◆◆◆◆	$260-$620	558
24 / p. 550		Casa Dona Susana	◆◆	$63-$98	554
25 / p. 550	AAA	**Playa Los Arcos Beach Resort & Spa** - see color ad p 559	◆◆	$85-$152	562
26 / p. 550		Los Arcos Suites	◆◆	$87-$92	558
27 / p. 550	AAA	**Villa Premiere Hotel & Spa** - see color ad p 563	◆◆◆◆	$575-$1250	563
28 / p. 550		Hotel San Marino	◆◆	$149-$299	558
29 / p. 550		Casa Andrea	◆◆◆	$75-$215	554
30 / p. 550		Club Meza del Mar An All Inclusive Hotel	◆	$88-$229	555
31 / p. 550		Villa del Palmar	◆◆	$106-$219	562
32 / p. 550		Plaza Pelicanos Grand Beach Resort	◆◆◆	$260-$320	562
33 / p. 550		Buganvilias Resort	◆◆◆	$255-$319	554
34 / p. 550	AAA	**Dreams Puerto Vallarta Resort and Spa**	◆◆◆◆	$450-$550	555
35 / p. 550	AAA	**Presidente InterContinental Puerto Vallarta**	◆◆◆◆	$104-$504	562
36 / p. 550		Playa Del Sol Costa SUR	◆◆	$150-$179	559

PUERTO VALLARTA (cont'd)

Map Page	OA	Lodgings (cont'd)	Diamond Rated	High Season	Page
40 / p. 550		Barcelo La Jolla de Mismaloya	◆◆◆◆	$375-$540	554
41 / p. 550		Casa Iguana Hotel de Mismaloya	◆◆	$84-$99	554

Map Page	OA	Restaurants	Diamond Rated	Cuisine	Meal Range	Page
1 / p. 550	AAA	**Emiliano**	◆◆◆	Continental	$12-$34	566
2 / p. 550		Suzie Wong's Chinese Cuisine	◆◆	Chinese	$8-$28	569
3 / p. 550		Rincon de Buenos Aires	◆◆	Argentine	$10-$30	568
4 / p. 550		La Ribera Restaurant	◆◆	Steak	$12-$24	567
5 / p. 550		Terrazza di Roma Ristorante Italiano	◆◆	Italian	$7-$18	569
6 / p. 550		Fajita Banana Tropical Grill & Bar	◆◆	American	$7-$14	566
7 / p. 550		Las Palomas Doradas	◆◆	International	$8-$20	567
8 / p. 550		Porto Bello Ristorante Italiano	◆◆◆	Italian	$13-$40	568
9 / p. 550		Vitea Oceanfront Bistro	◆◆◆	Continental	$8-$25	569
10 / p. 550		Restaurant Las Palomas Marinas	◆◆	Seafood	$6-$20	568
11 / p. 550		La Casitas	◆◆◆	International	$15-$28	566
12 / p. 550		Andrea Gourmet	◆◆◆	Continental	$10-$35	564
13 / p. 550		Mikado	◆◆◆	Japanese	$17-$33	567
14 / p. 550		La Estancia	◆◆◆	Mexican	$8-$20	566
15 / p. 550		Morgan's Steak House	◆◆	Steak	$10-$30	567
16 / p. 550		Nikki Beach Restaurant and Bar	◆◆◆	International	$12-$35	568
17 / p. 550		La Petite France	◆◆◆	French	$7-$35	567
18 / p. 550		La Hacienda	◆◆◆	International	$18-$24	566
19 / p. 550		Tikul Pacific Cuisine	◆◆◆	International	$20-$40	569
20 / p. 550		Thierry's Prime Steakhouse	◆◆◆	Steak	$20-$48	569
21 / p. 550	AAA	**Restaurante Mariaches**	◆◆	Mexican	$14-$20	568
22 / p. 550		Azul 96 Restaurant	◆◆◆	International	$14-$30	565
23 / p. 550		Murales	◆◆◆	Mexican	$11-$23	568
24 / p. 550		La Dolce Vita Ristorante Bar	◆◆	Italian	$10-$29	566
25 / p. 550		Paradise Burger	◆◆	American	$7-$15	568
26 / p. 550		La Chata de Guadalajara	◆◆	Mexican	$7-$20	566
27 / p. 550		Cafe des Artistes	◆◆◆	French	$20-$25	565
29 / p. 550		Hard Rock Cafe	◆◆	American	$12-$24 SAVE	566
30 / p. 550		Z tai Restaurant	◆◆◆	International	$15-$25	570
31 / p. 550		Trio Restaurant	◆◆◆	Mediterranean	$16-$18	569
32 / p. 550		The Blue Shrimp Restaurant	◆◆◆	Seafood	$18-$40	565
33 / p. 550		Oscar's Fine Cuisine	◆◆◆	International	$9-$30	568
34 / p. 550	AAA	**El Arrayan**	◆◆◆	Mexican	$16-$24	565
35 / p. 550		The River Cafe	◆◆◆	International	$8-$30	568
36 / p. 550		Le Bistro Jazz Cafe	◆◆◆	International	$15-$40	567
37 / p. 550		Kaiser Maximilian	◆◆◆	Austrian	$15-$27	566
38 / p. 550	AAA	**Cilantro's**	◆◆◆	International	$18-$25	565

Map Page	OA	Restaurants (cont'd)	Diamond Rated	Cuisine	Meal Range	Page
40 / p. 550		Mestizo Restaurant	◆◆◆	International	$19-$25	567
42 / p. 550		Daiquiri Dick's	◆◆◆	Continental	$16-$28	565
43 / p. 550		Boca Bento	◆◆◆	Asian	$12-$20	565
44 / p. 550	AAA	**Vista Grill**	◆◆◆◆	Continental	$20-$30	569
45 / p. 550		Si Senor	◆◆◆	Mexican	$18-$35	569
47 / p. 550	AAA	**La Palapa Restaurante and Bar**	◆◆◆	International	$20-$50	567
48 / p. 550		El Dorado	◆◆◆	International	$8-$30	565
51 / p. 550		Alfredo Di Roma	◆◆◆◆	Italian	$15-$25	564
53 / p. 550		Le Kliff Restaurante and Bar	◆◆◆	Seafood	$15-$45	567
55 / p. 550		Don Quijote	◆◆◆	Spanish	$14-$20	565

PUERTO VALLARTA, JALISCO pop. 184,728 (See map and index starting on p. 550)

WHERE TO STAY

BARCELO LA JOLLA DE MISMALOYA — **Phone:** (322)226-0660 — 40

Resort Hotel
$375-$540 All Year

Address: Zona Hotelera Sur KM 11.5 No. 4900 **Location:** 7.2 mi (11.5 km) s of town center. **Facility:** This resort is loaded with recreational activities, guest room amenities and a great view of Los Arcos. 318 units. 108 two-bedroom standard units. 206 one- and 4 two-bedroom suites, some with whirlpools. 9 stories, exterior corridors. *Bath:* combo or shower only. **Parking:** on-site. **Terms:** 15 day cancellation notice-fee imposed. **Amenities:** high-speed Internet (fee), dual phone lines, voice mail, safes, honor bars, irons, hair dryers. *Some:* DVD players, CD players. **Dining:** Don Quijote, see separate listing. **Pool(s):** 4 heated outdoor. **Leisure Activities:** whirlpools, steamrooms, paddleboats, snorkeling, lighted tennis court, recreation programs, playground, spa, volleyball. *Fee:* boats, scuba diving, fishing, charter fishing, horseback riding, game room. **Guest Services:** valet laundry, wireless Internet. **Business Services:** conference facilities, business center. **Cards:** AX, MC, VI.

/ SOME UNITS

BUENAVENTURA GRAND HOTEL AND SPA PUERTO VALLARTA *Book great rates at AAA.com* — **Phone:** (322)226-7000 — 19

AAA
Resort Hotel
$260-$450 All Year

Address: Ave Mexico 1301, Col 5 de Diciembre **Location:** 0.6 mi (1 km) n on Airport Hwy (Mex 200). **Facility:** Near downtown. Traditional room decor. 236 units. 232 one-bedroom standard units, some with whirlpools. 4 one-bedroom suites with efficiencies. 5 stories, interior corridors. *Bath:* combo or shower only. **Parking:** street. **Terms:** 21 day cancellation notice, 7 day off season-fee imposed. **Amenities:** high-speed Internet, safes, honor bars, irons, hair dryers. **Dining:** 3 restaurants, entertainment. **Pool(s):** outdoor, 2 heated outdoor. **Leisure Activities:** whirlpool, recreation programs, kids club. *Fee:* massage. **Guest Services:** valet laundry, wireless Internet. **Business Services:** business center. **Cards:** AX, MC, VI.

/ SOME UNITS

BUGANVILIAS RESORT — **Phone:** 322/226-0404 — 33

Hotel
$255-$319 All Year

Address: Blvd Fco Medina Ascencio 999 **Location:** Just n of town center. **Facility:** 150 one-bedroom standard units, some with efficiencies. 15 stories, interior corridors. *Bath:* combo or shower only. **Parking:** on-site. **Amenities:** safes, irons, hair dryers. **Pool(s):** heated outdoor. **Leisure Activities:** exercise room, spa, shared facilities privileges with Sheraton Buganvilias Resort & Convention Center. **Business Services:** business center. **Cards:** AX, MC, VI.

/ SOME UNITS

CASA ANDREA — **Phone:** 322/222-1213 — 29

Bed & Breakfast
$75-$215 All Year

Address: Francisca Rodriguez #174 **Location:** Just e of Olas Altas St; center; in Zona Romantica. Located a block from the beach. **Facility:** A pleasant, well-decorated and well-maintained lodging choice, Andrea's is close to the beach and restaurants. 11 units. 8 one- and 3 two-bedroom suites with kitchens. 2 stories (no elevator), exterior corridors. *Bath:* shower only. **Parking:** on-site. **Terms:** office hours 9 am-5 pm, age restrictions may apply. **Pool(s):** outdoor. **Leisure Activities:** whirlpool. **Guest Services:** TV in common area, wireless Internet. **Business Services:** PC.

/ SOME UNITS

CASA DONA SUSANA — **Phone:** 322/222-1583 — 24

Hotel
$63-$98 All Year

Address: Manuel M Diguec #171 **Location:** Center; in Zona Romantica. **Facility:** 42 one-bedroom standard units, some with efficiencies. 4 stories, interior corridors. *Bath:* shower only. **Parking:** on-site. **Terms:** age restrictions may apply, 7 day cancellation notice. **Amenities:** high-speed Internet (fee), safes, hair dryers. **Pool(s):** heated outdoor. **Guest Services:** valet laundry. **Cards:** AX, MC, VI.

/ SOME UNITS

CASA IGUANA HOTEL DE MISMALOYA — **Phone:** 322/228-0186 — 41

Motel
$84-$99 All Year

Address: Ave 5 de Mayo #455 **Location:** 7.2 mi (11.5 km) s of centre. **Facility:** 53 units. 50 two- and 3 three-bedroom suites with efficiencies. 4 stories (no elevator), exterior corridors. *Bath:* shower only. **Parking:** on-site. **Terms:** 3 day cancellation notice. **Amenities:** high-speed Internet. **Pool(s):** heated outdoor. **Leisure Activities:** whirlpool. **Guest Services:** wireless Internet. **Business Services:** meeting rooms, PC (fee). **Cards:** AX, MC, VI.

/ SOME UNITS

CASAMAGNA MARRIOTT PUERTO VALLARTA RESORT & SPA *Book great rates at AAA.com* — **Phone:** (322)226-0000 — 4

AAA
Resort Hotel
$184-$462 All Year

Address: Paseo de la Marina 5 **Location:** Oceanfront. 3.1 mi (5 km) n on Mex 200; at Marina Vallarta. **Facility:** Fine location, very attractive grounds and public facilities. Pleasant, well-appointed rooms. Smoke free premises. 433 units. 405 one-bedroom standard units. 28 one-bedroom suites, some with whirlpools. 5-9 stories, interior corridors. **Parking:** on-site. **Terms:** check-in 4 pm, 7 day cancellation notice-fee imposed. **Amenities:** high-speed Internet (fee), voice mail, safes, honor bars, irons, hair dryers. *Some:* CD players. **Dining:** 4 restaurants, also, La Casitas, La Estancia, Mikado, see separate listings, entertainment. **Pool(s):** heated outdoor, heated indoor. **Leisure Activities:** saunas, whirlpool, limited beach access, recreation programs, exercise room, spa. *Fee:* 2 lighted tennis courts, kids club. **Guest Services:** valet laundry, wireless Internet. **Business Services:** conference facilities, business center. **Cards:** AX, CB, DC, DS, JC, MC, VI.
(See color ad starting on p 556)

/ SOME UNITS

(See map and index starting on p. 550)

CASA VELAS HOTEL BOUTIQUE Phone: 322/226-6688 2

Resort Hotel
$610-$720 All Year

Address: 311 Pelicanos Marina Vallarta **Location:** At Marina Vallarta Golf Course. **Facility:** This gated resort features private villas or spacious guestrooms, many with private dip pool and views of the adjoining golf course. 80 units. 64 one-bedroom standard units, some with whirlpools. 8 one-, 4 two- and 4 three-bedroom suites with whirlpools. 4 stories, interior/exterior corridors. *Bath:* combo or shower only. **Parking:** valet. **Amenities:** DVD players, CD players, dual phone lines, voice mail, safes, honor bars, irons, hair dryers. **Dining:** Emiliano, see separate listing. **Pool(s):** heated outdoor. **Leisure Activities:** saunas, whirlpools, steamrooms, beach club privileges, golf privileges, 2 lighted tennis courts, bicycles, exercise room, spa. **Guest Services:** valet laundry, wireless Internet. **Business Services:** PC. **Cards:** AX, MC, VI. *(See color ad p 561)*

/ SOME UNITS

CLUB MEZA DEL MAR AN ALL INCLUSIVE HOTEL Phone: (322)222-4888 30

Hotel
$88-$229 All Year

Address: Amapas 380, Col E Zapata **Location:** 0.6 mi (1 km) s, on Playa de los Muertos. **Facility:** 128 units. 74 one-bedroom standard units. 41 one- and 13 three-bedroom suites. 4-8 stories, interior corridors. *Bath:* shower only. **Parking:** street. **Terms:** office hours 9 am-6 pm, 3 day cancellation notice-fee imposed. **Amenities:** safes (fee). **Pool(s):** 2 outdoor. **Leisure Activities:** whirlpool, tennis court. **Guest Services:** valet laundry. **Cards:** MC, VI.

/ SOME UNITS

CROWN PARADISE CLUB *Book at AAA.com* Phone: (322)226-6868 8

Resort Hotel
$290-$450 All Year

Address: Ave Las Garzas #1 **Location:** Oceanfront. 3 mi (4.8 km) n off Airport Hwy (Mex 200). **Facility:** Attractive grounds. Pleasant rooms, some with ocean view; balcony. 253 one-bedroom standard units, some with whirlpools. 4 stories, exterior corridors. *Bath:* combo or shower only. **Parking:** on-site. **Terms:** 3 day cancellation notice-fee imposed. **Amenities:** safes, irons, hair dryers. **Pool(s):** heated outdoor. **Leisure Activities:** whirlpool, rental boats, windsurfing, snorkeling, recreation programs, playground, exercise room, sports court, shuffleboard, volleyball, game room. *Fee:* waterskiing, scuba diving, fishing, 2 lighted tennis courts, massage. **Guest Services:** valet laundry, wireless Internet. **Business Services:** meeting rooms. *Fee:* PC, fax. **Cards:** AX, MC, VI.

/ SOME UNITS

DREAMS PUERTO VALLARTA RESORT AND SPA Phone: 322/226-5000 34

Resort Hotel
$450-$550 All Year

Address: Playa Las Estacas S/N KM 3.5 **Location:** 2.2 mi (3.5 km) s on Mismaloya Hwy (Mex 200). **Facility:** Private cove and beach. Fine public facilities. All rooms with ocean views; some with balcony. Excellent staff. 337 units. 326 one-bedroom standard units, some with whirlpools. 11 one-bedroom suites. 11 stories, interior/exterior corridors. **Parking:** on-site and valet. **Terms:** 3 day cancellation notice. **Amenities:** video library, DVD players, CD players, voice mail, safes, honor bars, irons, hair dryers. **Dining:** 5 restaurants, entertainment. **Pool(s):** 2 outdoor, heated outdoor. **Leisure Activities:** whirlpools, rental boats, snorkeling, 2 lighted tennis courts, kid's club, playground, exercise room, spa. *Fee:* waterskiing, scuba diving, fishing. **Guest Services:** valet laundry, wireless Internet. **Business Services:** meeting rooms, business center. **Cards:** AX, MC, VI.

D / SOME UNITS

EMBARCADERO PACIFICO HOTEL AND VILLAS ALL INCLUSIVE RESORT *Book at AAA.com* Phone: (322)221-1177 7

Hotel
$170-$220 All Year

Address: Ave Paseo de la Marina Sur S/N Marina **Location:** 3.1 mi (5 km) n on Mex 200; in Marina District. **Facility:** 253 units. 154 one-bedroom standard units. 22 one-, 42 two- and 35 three-bedroom suites with efficiencies. 3-9 stories, exterior corridors. *Bath:* combo or shower only. **Parking:** on-site. **Terms:** check-in 4 pm. **Amenities:** safes. **Pool(s):** 4 outdoor. **Leisure Activities:** limited beach access, snorkeling, recreation programs, bicycles, playground, spa, kids club, basketball, volleyball. *Fee:* saunas, steamrooms, scuba diving, 2 lighted tennis courts. **Guest Services:** valet and coin laundry, wireless Internet. **Business Services:** meeting rooms. **Cards:** AX, MC, VI.

/ SOME UNITS

FIESTA AMERICANA PUERTO VALLARTA *Book great rates at AAA.com* Phone: (322)226-2100 16

Hotel
$379 All Year

Address: Blvd Fco Medina Ascencio KM 2.5 **Location:** 2.5 mi (4 km) n on Paseo de las Palmas, off Airport Hwy (Mex 200). **Facility:** All rooms with ocean view from balcony. 291 units. 288 one-bedroom standard units. 3 one-bedroom suites, some with whirlpools. 9 stories, interior corridors. *Bath:* combo or shower only. **Parking:** on-site. **Terms:** 15 day cancellation notice. **Amenities:** voice mail, safes, honor bars, irons, hair dryers. *Fee:* video games, high-speed Internet. **Dining:** 3 restaurants, also, La Hacienda, see separate listing, entertainment. **Pool(s):** heated outdoor. **Leisure Activities:** recreation programs, spa. **Guest Services:** valet laundry, wireless Internet. **Business Services:** conference facilities, PC (fee). **Cards:** AX, MC, VI. *(See color ad on insert)*

FEE / SOME UNITS

GOLDEN CROWN PARADISE RESORT-ADULTS ALL INCLUSIVE Phone: 322/226-6800 10

Resort Hotel
$300-$460 All Year

Address: Paseo de las Garzas, #3 **Location:** 3 mi (4.8 km) n off Airport Hwy (Mex 200). **Facility:** This all-inclusive, adults-only resort on a lovely stretch of beach welcomes guests who are 18 and over; rooms are spacious and well appointed. 214 one-bedroom standard units, some with efficiencies and/or whirlpools. 7-8 stories, exterior corridors. **Parking:** on-site. **Terms:** age restrictions may apply. **Amenities:** safes, irons, hair dryers. *Some:* honor bars. **Pool(s):** heated outdoor. **Leisure Activities:** whirlpool, limited beach access, windsurfing, snorkeling. *Fee:* scuba diving, charter fishing, 2 lighted tennis courts, massage. **Guest Services:** valet laundry, wireless Internet. **Business Services:** meeting rooms, PC (fee). **Cards:** AX, MC, VI.

▼ See AAA listing p 554 ▼

(See map and index starting on p. 550)

HACIENDA HOTEL & SPA — **Phone:** 322/226-6667 12

Hotel
$184-$230 All Year

Address: Blvd Fco Medina Ascencio 2699 **Location:** 3 mi (4.8 km) n; just off Airport Hwy (Mex 200). **Facility:** 155 one-bedroom standard units. 2-4 stories (no elevator), interior corridors. *Bath:* combo or shower only. **Parking:** on-site. **Terms:** 5 day cancellation notice, in season. **Amenities:** *Some:* safes. **Pool(s):** heated outdoor. **Leisure Activities:** whirlpool, beach access, spa, shuffleboard. **Guest Services:** valet laundry, wireless Internet. **Business Services:** meeting rooms, fax (fee). **Cards:** AX, MC, VI.

/ SOME UNITS

HACIENDA SAN ANGEL *Book at AAA.com* — **Phone:** (322)222-2692 22

Hotel
$260-$620 All Year

Address: Miramar 336 **Location:** 3 blks e of town square; center. **Facility:** Set high on a hill, guests will delight in this fine Hacienda, a hidden treasure in the heart of Puerto Vallarta. The luxurious rooms are spread throughout this charming series of connected villas with many open courtyard terraces and 2 pool areas for outdoor lounging. The many open air living rooms are also favorite places for guests to relax and the gracious staff will serve meals in any of these areas. Designated smoking area. 16 one-bedroom standard units, some with whirlpools. 2-3 stories (no elevator), interior/exterior corridors. *Bath:* combo or shower only. **Parking:** street. **Terms:** office hours 8 am-11 pm, 3 night minimum stay, age restrictions may apply, 45 day cancellation notice-fee imposed. **Amenities:** video library, DVD players, CD players, safes, honor bars, hair dryers. **Pool(s):** 3 heated outdoor. **Leisure Activities:** whirlpool. **Guest Services:** wireless Internet. **Business Services:** PC. **Cards:** AX, MC, VI.

/ SOME UNITS

HOLA PUERTO VALLARTA CLUB & SPA — **Phone:** (322)226-4600 15

Resort Hotel
$174-$248 All Year

Address: KM 2.5 Blvd Fco Medina Ascencio S/N **Location:** 2.5 mi (4 km) n on Ave de las Palmas, off Airport Hwy (Mex 200). **Facility:** Extensive spa facilities. 218 one-bedroom standard units, some with whirlpools. 5-14 stories, interior corridors. **Parking:** valet. **Terms:** 3 day cancellation notice. **Amenities:** voice mail, safes, hair dryers. **Pool(s):** outdoor. **Leisure Activities:** saunas, whirlpools, steamrooms, paddleboats, windsurfing, recreation programs, spa. *Fee:* scuba diving, lighted tennis court. **Guest Services:** valet laundry. **Business Services:** meeting rooms. *Fee:* PC, fax. **Cards:** AX, MC, VI.

/ SOME UNITS

HOLIDAY INN PUERTO VALLARTA *Book great rates at AAA.com* — **Phone:** (322)226-1700 14

Hotel
$150-$220 All Year

Address: Blvd Fco Medina Ascencio S/N KM 3.5 **Location:** 2.5 mi (4 km) n on Airport Hwy (Mex 200). **Facility:** 300 one-bedroom standard units. 9 stories, interior corridors. *Bath:* combo or shower only. **Parking:** on-site. **Terms:** cancellation fee imposed. **Amenities:** high-speed Internet, voice mail, safes, irons, hair dryers. **Dining:** 3 restaurants, also, Restaurante Mariaches, see separate listing, entertainment. **Pool(s):** 2 outdoor. **Leisure Activities:** whirlpools, steamrooms, rental boats, fishing, exercise room, game room. *Fee:* waterskiing, scuba diving, charter fishing, 2 lighted tennis courts, childrens club, massage. **Guest Services:** valet laundry, wireless Internet. **Business Services:** meeting rooms, business center. **Cards:** AX, MC, VI.

/ SOME UNITS

HOTEL EL PESCADOR *Book at AAA.com* — **Phone:** (322)222-1884 20

Hotel
$72-$115 All Year

Address: Paraguay #1117 Col S de Diciembre **Location:** 2 blks n of malecon. **Facility:** 103 one-bedroom standard units. 3 stories, exterior corridors. *Bath:* shower only. **Parking:** no self-parking. **Pool(s):** outdoor. **Guest Services:** wireless Internet. **Business Services:** PC (fee). **Cards:** MC, VI.

/ SOME UNITS

HOTEL ROSITA — **Phone:** 322/223-2000 21

Hotel
$72-$115 All Year

Address: Paseo Diaz Ordaz #901 **Location:** Downtown; at beginning of malecon. **Facility:** 114 one-bedroom standard units. 4 stories, exterior corridors. *Bath:* combo or shower only. **Parking:** no self-parking. **Pool(s):** outdoor. **Guest Services:** wireless Internet. **Business Services:** PC (fee). **Cards:** MC, VI.

/ SOME UNITS

HOTEL SAN MARINO — **Phone:** 322/222-3050 28

Hotel
$149-$299 All Year

Address: Rodolfo Gomez #111 Col E Zapata **Location:** Center; in Zona Romantica. **Facility:** 167 one-bedroom standard units. 5-8 stories, exterior corridors. *Bath:* shower only. **Parking:** street. **Terms:** 7 day cancellation notice. **Amenities:** safes (fee). **Pool(s):** 2 outdoor. **Leisure Activities:** limited beach access. *Fee:* windsurfing. **Guest Services:** valet laundry. **Cards:** AX, MC, VI.

/ SOME UNITS

LAS PALMAS BY THE SEA — **Phone:** (322)226-1220 17

Resort Hotel
$200-$215 All Year

Address: Blvd Fco Medina Ascencio KM 2.5 **Location:** 1.6 mi (2.5 km) n off Airport Hwy (Mex 200). **Facility:** Balconies and patios. Beachfront dining. 225 one-bedroom standard units. 4 stories, interior/exterior corridors. *Bath:* shower only. **Parking:** street. **Amenities:** voice mail. *Some:* safes (fee). **Pool(s):** 2 outdoor. **Leisure Activities:** whirlpool, recreation programs, playground, volleyball. *Fee:* boats, windsurfing, waterskiing, scuba diving, snorkeling. **Guest Services:** valet laundry. **Business Services:** *Fee:* PC, fax. **Cards:** AX, MC, VI.

/ SOME UNITS

LOS ARCOS SUITES — **Phone:** 322/222-1583 26

Hotel
$87-$92 All Year

Address: Manuel M Diguec #164 **Location:** Center; in Zona Romantica. **Facility:** 44 one-bedroom suites with efficiencies. 4 stories, exterior corridors. *Bath:* shower only. **Parking:** on-site. **Amenities:** safes, hair dryers. **Pool(s):** heated outdoor. **Guest Services:** valet laundry. **Cards:** AX, MC, VI.

/ SOME UNITS

(See map and index starting on p. 550)

MAYAN PALACE PUERTO VALLARTA WYNDHAM ALLIANCE RESORT **Phone:** (322)226-6000 6

Resort Hotel

$395-$525 All Year

Address: Paseo de la Marina Sur 220 **Location:** 3.1 mi (5 km) off Mex 200; in Marina District. **Facility:** Authentic Mexican decor is found throughout this resort, which features a peaceful lagoon in addition to a huge pool, all in an oceanfront setting. 213 units. 83 one-bedroom standard units. 130 one-bedroom suites with efficiencies. 5-7 stories, interior corridors. *Bath:* combo or shower only. **Parking:** on-site (fee). **Terms:** check-in 5 pm, 3-7 night minimum stay - seasonal and/or weekends, 21 day cancellation notice-fee imposed. **Amenities:** safes (fee), hair dryers. *Some:* irons. **Pool(s):** 2 heated outdoor. **Leisure Activities:** whirlpool, recreation programs, volleyball. *Fee:* boats, charter fishing, exercise room. **Business Services:** meeting rooms, PC (fee). **Cards:** AX, MC, VI.

/ SOME UNITS

MELIA PUERTO VALLARTA ALL INCLUSIVE BEACH RESORT *Book at AAA.com* **Phone:** (322)226-3000 5

Resort Hotel

$190-$272 All Year

Address: Paseo de la Marina Sur Lote #7 **Location:** 3.1 mi (5 km) n off Mex 200; in Marina District. **Facility:** Very good recreational facilities. Modern, well-appointed rooms, attractive grounds. 321 one-bedroom standard units. 4-9 stories, interior corridors. *Bath:* combo or shower only. **Parking:** on-site. **Terms:** 7 day cancellation notice. **Amenities:** voice mail, safes, irons, hair dryers. **Pool(s):** outdoor. **Leisure Activities:** windsurfing, 2 lighted tennis courts, recreation programs, playground, exercise room, shuffleboard, volleyball, game room. *Fee:* sailboats, waterskiing, scuba diving. **Guest Services:** valet laundry, wireless Internet. **Business Services:** meeting rooms, PC (fee). **Cards:** AX, MC, VI.

D / SOME UNITS

NH KRYSTAL PUERTO VALLARTA **Phone:** 322/226-0700 13

Resort Hotel

$139-$186 All Year

Address: Av de las Garzas S/N Zona Hotelera **Location:** Oceanfront. 2.8 mi (4.5 km) n off Mex 200. **Facility:** A huge, beachfront resort on acres of tropical landscaping offers standard hotel rooms, beachfront units or ground-level villas with private pools. 312 units. 301 one-bedroom standard units. 11 one-bedroom suites. 1-4 stories, interior/exterior corridors. **Parking:** on-site. **Terms:** 7 day cancellation notice. **Amenities:** high-speed Internet, safes, honor bars, irons, hair dryers. **Pool(s):** 4 heated outdoor. **Leisure Activities:** whirlpools, waterslide, limited beach access, scuba diving, racquetball courts, playground, exercise room. *Fee:* snorkeling, 2 lighted tennis courts, massage. **Guest Services:** valet laundry, wireless Internet. **Business Services:** meeting rooms, PC (fee). **Cards:** AX, MC, VI.

/ SOME UNITS

PLAYA DEL SOL COSTA SUR **Phone:** 322/226-8050 36

Hotel

$150-$179 All Year

Address: Barra de Navidad KM 4.5 **Location:** Oceanfront. KM 4.5 Carr Puerto Vallarta a Barra de Navidad. **Facility:** 208 units. 158 one-bedroom standard units. 42 one- and 8 two-bedroom suites. 9-14 stories, interior/exterior corridors. *Bath:* shower only. **Parking:** on-site. **Terms:** check-in 4 pm. **Amenities:** safes, irons. **Pool(s):** outdoor, heated outdoor. **Leisure Activities:** limited beach access, exercise room, spa. **Guest Services:** valet laundry. **Business Services:** PC. **Cards:** AX, MC, VI.

▼ See AAA listing p 562 ▼

▼ See AAA listing p 545 ▼

(See map and index starting on p. 550)

PLAYA LOS ARCOS BEACH RESORT & SPA **Phone:** (322)222-1583 25

Hotel
$85-$152 All Year

Address: Olas Altas 380 **Location:** Center; in Zona Romantica. **Facility:** 171 units. 156 one-bedroom standard units. 15 one-bedroom suites with kitchens. 4 stories, interior/exterior corridors. *Bath:* shower only. **Parking:** on-site. **Terms:** 7 day cancellation notice-fee imposed. **Amenities:** safes, hair dryers. **Pool(s):** 2 heated outdoor. **Leisure Activities:** whirlpool, recreation programs, spa. **Guest Services:** valet laundry. **Business Services:** fax (fee). **Cards:** AX, MC, VI. *(See color ad p 559)*

/ SOME UNITS

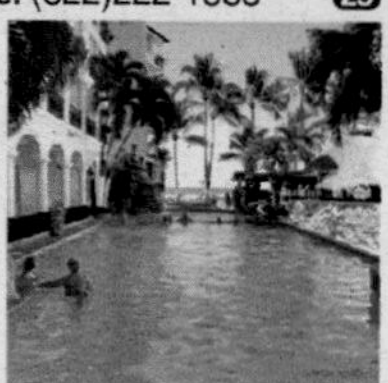

PLAZA PELICANOS GRAND BEACH RESORT *Book at AAA.com* **Phone:** (322)226-2700 32

Hotel
$260-$320 All Year

Address: Diego Rivera No120 Hotel Zone Las Glorias **Location:** 1.6 mi (2.5 km) n off Airport Hwy (Mex 200). **Facility:** 262 one-bedroom standard units. 3 stories (no elevator), interior/exterior corridors. **Parking:** on-site. **Amenities:** high-speed Internet (fee), safes. *Some:* hair dryers. **Pool(s):** 3 outdoor, heated outdoor. **Leisure Activities:** exercise room. *Fee:* scuba diving, snorkeling. **Guest Services:** valet laundry, wireless Internet. **Business Services:** meeting rooms. **Cards:** AX, MC, VI.

/ SOME UNITS

PRESIDENTE INTERCONTINENTAL PUERTO VALLARTA *Book great rates at AAA.com* **Phone:** (322)228-0191 35

Hotel
$104-$504 All Year

Address: KM 8.5 Mex 200, Carr Puerto Vallarta **Location:** On Mex 200, 5.3 mi (8.5 km) s. **Facility:** Fine location on pretty beach. Beautiful landscaping. All guest rooms have balcony overlooking the ocean. 120 units. 116 one-bedroom standard units, some with whirlpools. 4 two-bedroom suites with whirlpools. 10 stories, exterior corridors. **Parking:** on-site. **Terms:** 3 day cancellation notice-fee imposed. **Amenities:** video library (fee), DVD players, CD players, voice mail, honor bars, irons, hair dryers. *Some:* high-speed Internet, safes. **Dining:** 2 restaurants, also, Alfredo Di Roma, see separate listing. **Pool(s):** heated outdoor. **Leisure Activities:** exercise room. *Fee:* scuba diving, snorkeling, fishing, kayaks, lighted tennis court, massage. **Guest Services:** valet laundry, wireless Internet. **Business Services:** meeting rooms, business center. **Cards:** AX, MC, VI.

/ SOME UNITS

SHERATON BUGANVILIAS RESORT AND CONVENTION CENTER **Phone:** (322)226-0404 18

Resort Hotel
$95-$584 All Year

Address: 999 Medina Ascencio Blvd **Location:** Just n of town center. **Facility:** This large complex features two large pools with swim-up bars and a fine oceanfront location; it is walking distance from the popular downtown area. 477 units. 473 one-bedroom standard units. 4 one-bedroom suites with whirlpools. 13 stories, interior corridors. **Parking:** on-site. **Terms:** 3 day cancellation notice-fee imposed. **Amenities:** high-speed Internet (fee), voice mail, safes, honor bars, irons, hair dryers. **Dining:** 4 restaurants, entertainment. **Pool(s):** heated outdoor. **Leisure Activities:** whirlpool, recreation programs, shared facilities with Bujanvilias Resort, spa. *Fee:* 2 lighted tennis courts. **Guest Services:** wireless Internet. **Business Services:** conference facilities, business center. **Cards:** AX, CB, DC, MC, VI. *(See color ad on insert)*

/ SOME UNITS

Sheraton
HOTELS & RESORTS

AAA Benefit:
Members get up to 15% off, plus Starwood Preferred Guest® bonuses.

VELAS VALLARTA SUITE RESORT AND CONVENTION CENTER **Phone:** 322/221-0091 3

Resort Hotel
$300-$380 All Year

Address: Ave Custera S/N LH-2 Marina Vallarta **Location:** 3.1 mi (5 km) n on Mex 200; in Marina District. **Facility:** Interlocking pools are set around lush tropical gardens at this all-inclusive resort on a lovely stretch of beach; choose a suite or studio unit. 344 units. 124 one-bedroom standard units with efficiencies. 150 one-, 36 two- and 34 three-bedroom suites, some with efficiencies. 8 stories, exterior corridors. *Bath:* combo or shower only. **Parking:** valet. **Terms:** check-in 4 pm. **Amenities:** voice mail, safes, honor bars, irons, hair dryers. **Dining:** Andrea Gourmet, La Ribera Restaurant, see separate listings. **Pool(s):** 2 heated outdoor. **Leisure Activities:** limited beach access, 3 lighted tennis courts, recreation programs, bicycles, exercise room, spa, basketball. **Guest Services:** valet laundry, wireless Internet. **Business Services:** meeting rooms, PC (fee). **Cards:** AX, MC, VI. ***(See color ad p 561)***

VILLA DEL PALMAR **Phone:** 322/226-1400 31

Hotel
$106-$219 All Year

Address: Blvd Fco Medina Ascencio KM 2.5 **Location:** Oceanfront. 2.5 mi (4 km) n on Airport Hwy (Mex 200). **Facility:** 560 units. 281 one-bedroom standard units with efficiencies (no utensils). 220 one- and 59 two-bedroom suites. 4-8 stories, interior/exterior corridors. *Bath:* combo or shower only. **Parking:** on-site. **Terms:** check-in 4 pm, 7 day cancellation notice, 3 day off season. **Amenities:** safes, irons, hair dryers. **Pool(s):** 3 outdoor. **Leisure Activities:** exercise room, spa. *Fee:* 3 tennis courts (2 lighted). **Guest Services:** coin laundry, wireless Internet. **Business Services:** meeting rooms, PC (fee). **Cards:** AX, DC, MC, VI.

(See map and index starting on p. 550)

VILLA PREMIERE HOTEL & SPA *Book great rates at AAA.com* **Phone:** (322)226-7040 27

Hotel

$575-$1250 All Year

Address: San Salvador 117, Col 5 Diciembre **Location:** 0.6 mi (1 km) n on Airport Hwy (Mex 200). **Facility:** This luxurious hotel offers highly personalized service and is adult oriented. Guests are welcomed with a complimentary beverage and neck massage on arrival. Their rooms are then customized to an aroma of their choice, such as mint, basil or eucalyptus to add to the ambiance. All rooms are ocean view with a balcony and have a luxurious Mexican decor. 83 units. 65 one-bedroom standard units, some with whirlpools. 18 one-bedroom suites with whirlpools. 7 stories, interior corridors. **Parking:** on-site and valet. **Terms:** age restrictions may apply, 14 day cancellation notice. **Amenities:** DVD players, high-speed Internet, safes, honor bars, irons, hair dryers. *Some:* CD players. **Dining:** 3 restaurants, also, Murales, see separate listing, entertainment. **Pool(s):** 2 heated outdoor. **Leisure Activities:** saunas, steamrooms, limited beach access, spa, shared facilities with Buenaventura Grand Hotel & Spa. **Guest Services:** valet laundry, wireless Internet. **Business Services:** meeting rooms, PC (fee). **Cards:** AX, MC, VI. Affiliated with A Preferred Hotel. *(See color ad below)*

  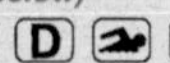 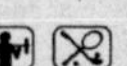 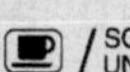 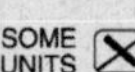  / SOME UNITS

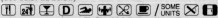

▼ See AAA listing above ▼

(See map and index starting on p. 550)

THE WESTIN RESORT AND SPA PUERTO VALLARTA *Book great rates at AAA.com* **Phone:** (322)226-1100 9

Resort Hotel
$119-$529 All Year

Address: Paseo de la Marina Sur #205 Marina Vallarta **Location:** 3.1 mi (5 km) n on Mex 200; in Marina Vallarta. **Facility:** Handsome beachfront hotel with excellent facilities and very attractive rooms. Smoke free premises. 280 units. 266 one-bedroom standard units, some with whirlpools. 14 one-bedroom suites, some with whirlpools. 14 stories, interior corridors. **Parking:** on-site. **Terms:** 7 day cancellation notice-fee imposed. **Amenities:** high-speed Internet (fee), dual phone lines, voice mail, safes, honor bars, irons, hair dryers. *Some:* DVD players. **Dining:** 4 restaurants, also, Nikki Beach Restaurant and Bar, see separate listing, entertainment. **Pool(s):** 4 outdoor. **Leisure Activities:** saunas, whirlpools, steamrooms, recreation programs, playground, spa. *Fee:* 3 lighted tennis courts, golf privileges. **Guest Services:** valet laundry, wireless Internet. **Business Services:** conference facilities, business center. **Cards:** CB, DC, DS, JC.
(See color ad on insert)

WESTIN HOTELS & RESORTS
AAA Benefit:
Enjoy up to 15% off your next stay, plus Starwood Preferred Guest® bonuses.

The following lodgings were either not evaluated or did not meet AAA rating requirements but are listed for your information only.

CANTO DEL SOL PLAZA VALLARTA **Phone:** 322/226-0123

fyi

Not evaluated. **Address:** Jose Clemente Orozco #125 **Location:** Zone Hotelera Norte. Facilities, services, and decor characterize a mid-scale property.

LOS TULES RESORT **Phone:** 322/224-5425

fyi

Not evaluated. **Address:** Francisco Medina Ascencio S/N **Location:** 2.5 mi (4 km) n on Paseo de las Palmas, off Mex 200. Facilities, services, and decor characterize an economy property.

WHERE TO DINE

ALFREDO DI ROMA **Phone:** 322/228-0191 51

Italian
$15-$25

An elegant dining room with live piano entertainment and views overlooking the ocean sets the stage. The romantic restaurant presents diners a menu of freshly prepared fine Italian cuisine. Service is professional and polished. **Bar:** Full bar. **Reservations:** suggested. **Hours:** 6 pm-11 pm. Closed: Mon. **Address:** KM 8.5 Mex 200, Carr Puerto Vallarta **Location:** On Mex 200, 5.3 mi (8.5 km) s; in Presidente InterContinental Puerto Vallarta. **Parking:** on-site. **Cards:** AX, MC, VI.

ANDREA GOURMET **Phone:** 322/221-0091 12

Continental
$10-$35

The elegant dining room features candlelit tables and both indoor and outdoor terrace seating. Mexico-influenced contemporary decor complements a fine menu of Continental and Italian cuisine. Casual dress. **Bar:** Full bar. **Reservations:** suggested. **Hours:** 7:30 am-noon, 12:30-5 & 6-10:30 pm. **Address:** Paseo de la Marina **Location:** 3.1 mi (5 km) n of Mex 200; in Marina Vallarta; in Hotel Velas Vallarta. **Parking:** street. **Cards:** AX, MC, VI.

(See map and index starting on p. 550)

AZUL 96 RESTAURANT Phone: 322/222-1022 (22)

International
$14-$30

Diners sit down to innovative international choices in an upscale contemporary setting. Brightly colored lights and high vaulted ceilings add to the grandeur. Many enjoy an after-dinner drink in the open-air rooftop lounge, which features a sand-covered floor and a funky atmosphere. Dressy casual. **Bar:** Full bar. **Reservations:** suggested. **Hours:** 6 pm-midnight. **Address:** Morelos #696 **Location:** Center of downtown; e of Malecon. **Parking:** street. **Cards:** AX, MC, VI.

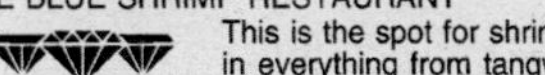

THE BLUE SHRIMP RESTAURANT Phone: 322/222-4246 (32)

Seafood
$18-$40

This is the spot for shrimp lovers. As the name suggests, the popular restaurant specializes in fresh shrimp in everything from tangy cocktails to pay-by-the-pound options. The chef cooks them in a variety of ways, including tequila, freshly breaded coconut and the often-ordered garlic-seasoned. Also featured are fresh local lobsters of huge proportions, some meat options and a tasty salad bar. After dinner, guests can head upstairs to the Martini Bar, which has live entertainment. Casual dress. **Bar:** Full bar. **Reservations:** suggested. **Hours:** noon-1 am. **Address:** Morelos #779 Col Centro **Location:** Center of downtown; e of Malecon. **Parking:** street. **Cards:** AX, MC, VI.

BOCA BENTO Phone: 322/222-9108 (43)

Asian
$12-$20

This funky restaurant features an innovative mix of Asian and Latino cuisine on its menu and a sleek contemporary decor. Diners enjoy arriving early for their reservation to have a pre-dinner drink in the upscale lounge. The prime location in the heart of Old Town Vallarta is another plus. The chef recommends diners try a variety of dishes so he has the menu offer two portion sizes and a wonderful mix of flavors. Casual dress. **Bar:** Full bar. **Reservations:** suggested. **Hours:** 6 pm-11 pm, Fri & Sat-11:30 pm. **Address:** Basilio Badillo 180 **Location:** In old section of Vallarta; in Zona Romantica. **Parking:** street. **Cards:** MC, VI.

CAFE DES ARTISTES Phone: 322/222-3228 (27)

French
$20-$25

Innovative cuisine combines French and Mexican preparation styles. For a real treat, try the custom-prepared "menu de degustacion." Piano performances are offered nightly on the deck, where the secluded atmosphere is romantic. Dressy casual. Entertainment. **Bar:** Full bar. **Reservations:** required. **Hours:** 6 pm-11:30 pm. **Address:** Guadalupe Sanchez 740 **Location:** Center. **Parking:** on-site. **Cards:** AX, MC, VI.

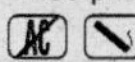

CILANTRO'S Phone: 322/222-7147 (38)

International
$18-$25

This bright and cheerful restaurant presents a menu of international dishes prepared with an innovative touch. Among starters are pear and Brie quesadillas, prawn and cilantro fritters, and cream of cilantro soup. Mains include salmon flambe, Brie-stuffed chicken and beef medallions in tequila sauce. Freshly prepared desserts are tempting. Casual dress. **Bar:** Full bar. **Reservations:** suggested. **Hours:** 5:30 pm-1 am. Closed: Sun. **Address:** Abasolo 169 **Location:** 1 blk from Malecon; center. **Parking:** no self-parking. **Cards:** AX, MC, VI.

DAIQUIRI DICK'S Phone: 322/222-0566 (42)

Continental
$16-$28

Diners appreciate not only the prime beachfront location but also the contemporary design of the trendy dining room. Such innovative dishes as grilled asparagus, pork chops with espresso sauce and lobster tacos complement the decor. Key lime pie finishes a meal with style. Casual dress. **Bar:** Full bar. **Reservations:** suggested. **Hours:** 8:30 am-11 pm. Closed: Tues 5/1-10/30. **Address:** Olas Atlas 314, South Side **Location:** In the Romantic Zone. **Parking:** no self-parking. **Cards:** MC, VI.

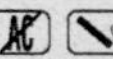

DON QUIJOTE Phone: 322/226-0660 (55)

Spanish
$14-$20

A distinct Spanish ambience characterizes the decor at the inviting spot, which offers a fine menu selection and a self-serve tapas bar, not to mention a wonderful selection of flambe coffees to end each evening. Semi-formal attire. Entertainment. **Bar:** Full bar. **Reservations:** required. **Hours:** 6 pm-10:30 pm. **Address:** Zona Hotelera Sur KM 11.5 **Location:** 7.2 mi (11.5 km) s of Puerto Vallarta; at Barcelo La Jolla de Mismaloya. **Parking:** on-site. **Cards:** AX, MC, VI.

EL ARRAYAN Phone: 322/221-7195 (34)

Mexican
$16-$24

This bright, festive restaurant features an authentic Mexican feel both in decor and menu options. All courses are made to order, and great care has been taken to offer choices with a wide array of flavors and spice levels. Casual dress. **Bar:** Full bar. **Reservations:** required. **Hours:** 6 pm-11 pm. Closed: Tues. **Address:** Allende #344 El Centro **Location:** Center; just e of Matamoros. **Parking:** no self-parking. **Cards:** MC, VI.

EL DORADO Phone: 322/222-1511 (48)

International
$8-$30

A prime beachfront location and a mixed menu of casual fare make this a popular choice for diners both day and night. In the day, in addition to the fully serviced dining room, the restaurant also features a beach club, where diners can enjoy meals while relaxing in their lounge chairs. The menu features such light fare favorites as burgers, clubhouse sandwiches and salads, as well as a good variety of fresh local seafood. Shrimp dishes, offered in several sauces, are superb. Casual dress. **Bar:** Full bar. **Reservations:** accepted. **Hours:** 8:30 am-11 pm. Closed: 5/1. **Address:** Pulpito #102 Playa de los Muertos **Location:** On Playa de los Muertos. **Parking:** street. **Cards:** AX, DS, MC, VI.

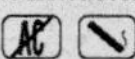

(See map and index starting on p. 550)

EMILIANO **Phone:** 322/226-6688 (1)

Continental
$12-$34

Guests enter through secured gates and graceful lobby of the hotel before being awed by cascading waters leading to a midnight blue pool, which will be the backdrop for an enjoyable meal. Menu options might include sweet plantain and black bean turnover in a sweet cream sauce, a salad of tender lobster and sliced pineapple in a citric vinaigrette or maybe beef medallions in a blue agave sauce with cracked black pepper. Dressy casual. **Bar:** Full bar. **Reservations:** accepted, for non hotel guests. **Hours:** 7 am-11 pm. **Address:** 311 Pelicanos Marina Vallarta **Location:** At Marina Vallarta Golf Course; in Casa Velas Hotel Boutique. **Parking:** valet. **Cards:** AX, MC, VI.

FAJITA BANANA TROPICAL GRILL & BAR **Phone:** 322/221-3154 (6)

American
$7-$14

US-style ribs, burgers and, of course, fajitas, are served at the eatery, which lets guests sit in an open-air setting and view the boats in the marina. Indoors is a bar and lounge. Patrons might overindulge on the all-you-can-eat ribs. Casual dress. **Bar:** Full bar. **Reservations:** accepted. **Hours:** 9 am-11 pm. **Address:** Puesta del Sol Loc 17 Marina Vallarta **Location:** In Marina Vallarta. **Parking:** street. **Cards:** MC, VI.

HARD ROCK CAFE **Phone:** 322/222-5532 (29)

American
$12-$24

Rock 'n' roll memorabilia decorates the walls of the popular theme restaurant. Live music on the weekends contributes to the bustling atmosphere. On the menu is a wide variety of American cuisine—from burgers and sandwiches to seafood, steaks and pasta. Casual dress. Entertainment. **Bar:** Full bar. **Hours:** 11 am-11 pm. **Address:** Ave Presidente Diaz Ordaz #652 **Location:** Center; on Malecon. **Parking:** no self-parking. **Cards:** AX, DS, JC, MC, VI.

KAISER MAXIMILIAN **Phone:** 322/223-0760 (37)

Austrian
$15-$27

European decor and ambience punctuate the indoor dining room and the sidewalk area. A few Austrian specialties stand out on the menu. Coffee and pastries are served at a separate coffee bar. Casual dress. **Bar:** Full bar. **Reservations:** suggested. **Hours:** 6 pm-11 pm. Closed: Sun. **Address:** Olas Altas #38 B **Location:** In older part of town. **Parking:** on-site. **Cards:** AX, MC, VI.

LA CASITAS **Phone:** 322/226-0000 (11)

International
$15-$28

This oceanfront open-air dining room serves as a perfect setting for a casual and romantic dining experience. The chef showcases innovation in preparations and presentations of starters and grilled-to-order meats and seafood. Casual dress. **Bar:** Full bar. **Reservations:** suggested. **Hours:** 8 am-11 pm. **Address:** Paseo de la Marina S **Location:** 3.1 mi (5 km) n on Mex 200; at Marina Vallarta; in CasaMagna Marriott Puerto Vallarta Resort & Spa. **Parking:** on-site. **Cards:** AX, MC, VI.

LA CHATA DE GUADALAJARA **Phone:** 322/222-5529 (26)

Mexican
$7-$20

In a great location overlooking the Malecon, this well-established restaurant presents a menu of home-style Mexican cuisine for breakfast, lunch and dinner. Diners sit down to hearty portions of freshly prepared cuisine. Strolling mariachi players often enhance the festive atmosphere. Casual dress. **Bar:** Full bar. **Reservations:** accepted. **Hours:** 8 am-midnight. **Address:** Paseo Diaz Ordaz #708 **Location:** On Malecon. **Parking:** no self-parking. **Cards:** MC, VI.

LA DOLCE VITA RISTORANTE BAR **Phone:** 322/222-3852 (24)

Italian
$10-$29

The beachfront cafe serves traditional pasta dishes, as well as fresh, well-prepared Italian-style seafood. Views of the busy malecon can be enjoyed from most tables. Casual dress. **Bar:** Full bar. **Reservations:** not accepted. **Hours:** noon-2 & 6-midnight. **Address:** Ave P Diaz Ordaz #674 **Location:** On Malecon, along beachfront road; center. **Parking:** street. **Cards:** AX, MC, VI.

LA ESTANCIA **Phone:** 322/226-0000 (14)

Mexican
$8-$20

High ceilings, marble floors and lots of tropical plants add to the perfect setting for an enjoyable meal. Service is friendly and personable. Among options are items on a daily changing buffet and selections of fine Mexican fare from the a la carte menu. For a tasty local food adventure, try tortilla soup and shrimp fajitas. Casual dress. **Bar:** Full bar. **Reservations:** suggested. **Hours:** 6:30 am-11 pm. **Address:** Paseo de la Marina 5 **Location:** 3.1 mi (5 km) n on Mex 200; at Marina Vallarta; in CasaMagna Marriott Puerto Vallarta Resort & Spa. **Parking:** on-site. **Cards:** AX, DC, MC, VI.

LA HACIENDA **Phone:** 322/226-2100 (18)

International
$18-$24

Lending to the Mexican atmosphere are wonderful displays of hand-painted pottery and festive artwork. Diners can peruse the fine Continental menu at candlelit tables in the main dining room or on the romantic patio. Dressy casual. **Bar:** Full bar. **Reservations:** suggested. **Hours:** 6 pm-midnight. **Address:** Blvd Fco Medina Ascencio KM 2.5 **Location:** 2.5 mi (4 km) n on Paseo de las Palmas, off Airport Hwy (Mex 200); in Fiesta Americana Puerto Vallarta. **Parking:** on-site. **Cards:** AX, MC, VI.

(See map and index starting on p. 550)

LA PALAPA RESTAURANTE AND BAR **Phone:** 322/222-5225 (47)

International
$20-$50

Casual elegance and a prime beachfront setting are the main attractions. During the day, diners can take a break from the sun and have a wonderful light or full entree lunch on the sand or in the main dining room. At night, the setting is romantic as diners hear the roar of the waves. Live entertainment is featured in the lounge day and night. The menu features a range of local and International fare including fresh seafood, fajitas and beef selections. Casual dress. **Bar:** Full bar. **Reservations:** suggested, for dinner. **Hours:** 8 am-4 & 6-11 pm. Closed: 5/1. **Address:** Pulpito 103 **Location:** On Playa de los Muertos. **Parking:** no self-parking. **Cards:** AX, DC, DS, MC, VI.

LA PETITE FRANCE **Phone:** 322/293-0901 (17)

French
$7-$35

A European feel is re-created in the large but cozy dining room. Pictures of old-day Paris adorn the walls. Fine French cuisine is prepared with wonderful sauces. Whether choosing tableside-prepared Caesar salad, traditional French onion soup or mussels in wine or cream sauce, guests are sure to have a wonderful beginning. Among entrees are duck a l'orange, coq au vin and varied meat and seafood selections. Dressy casual. **Bar:** Full bar. **Reservations:** accepted. **Hours:** 8 am-midnight. **Address:** Blvd Fco Medina Ascencio KM 2.5 **Location:** 2.5 mi (4 km) n on Paseo de las Palmas, off Airport Hwy (Mex 200). **Parking:** street. **Cards:** AX, MC, VI.

LA RIBERA RESTAURANT **Phone:** 322/221-0091 (4)

Steak
$12-$24

Reservations are not taken at the casual open-air restaurant, which overlooks the ocean. Diners who don't opt for the daily buffet can order such a la carte dishes as the tasty specialty grilled steaks. Casual dress. **Bar:** Full bar. **Reservations:** not accepted. **Hours:** 7:30 am-10:30 pm. **Address:** Ave Costera S/N LH-2 Marina Vallarta **Location:** 3.1 mi (5 km) n on Mex 200; in Marina District; in Velas Vallarta Suite Resort and Convention Center. **Parking:** valet. **Cards:** AX, MC, VI.

LAS PALOMAS DORADAS **Phone:** 322/221-0470 (7)

International
$8-$20

Close to the sailboats and yachts in the marina, the boardwalk cafe serves fresh fish, US-style steaks and Mexican cuisine. Margaritas are enormous, and the food is deftly prepared. Casual dress. **Bar:** Full bar. **Reservations:** accepted. **Hours:** Open 12/1-8/15 & 9/15-11/30; 8 am-11 pm. Closed: 12/25. **Address:** Club de Tenis, Puesta Local Marina Vallarta **Location:** In Marina Vallarta. **Parking:** street. **Cards:** AX, MC, VI.

LE BISTRO JAZZ CAFE **Phone:** 322/222-0283 (36)

International
$15-$40

Outdoor and covered dining available. Casual dress. **Bar:** Full bar. **Reservations:** suggested, for dinner. **Hours:** 9 am-4 & 5-11 pm. Closed: Sun. **Address:** Rio Cuale Island 16A **Location:** On Rio Cuale Island; center. **Parking:** on-site. **Cards:** AX, DC, DS, MC, VI.

LE KLIFF RESTAURANTE AND BAR **Phone:** 322/228-0666 (53)

Seafood
$15-$45

On a cliff overlooking the ocean, the restaurant is known for its spectacular views. Many patrons reserve a table so they can dine while watching the sunset. Marriage proposals are common in this romantic setting. The menu lists a wonderful selection of fine Continental cuisine, with fresh local seafood a specialty. Casual dress. **Bar:** Full bar. **Reservations:** required. **Hours:** 1 pm-10:30 pm. **Address:** Carr A Barra de Navidad KM 17.5 S/N **Location:** On Carr A Barra de Navidad KM 17.5. **Parking:** on-site. **Cards:** AX, DS, MC, VI.

MESTIZO RESTAURANT **Phone:** 322/222-1333 (40)

International
$19-$25

Large tropical trees and a Mexican-style water fountain add character to the restaurant's lovely courtyard setting. Candlelit tables lend a touch of romance. The menu features international and gourmet Mexican dishes, including highlights of cream of squash blossom soup, grilled marinated shrimp and lamb chops seasoned with rosemary. Desserts are a must-try specialty. Casual dress. **Bar:** Full bar. **Reservations:** suggested. **Hours:** 5 pm-11 pm. Closed: Sun. **Address:** Abasolo 233 **Location:** 2 blks e from Malecon; centre. **Parking:** no self-parking. **Cards:** AX, MC, VI.

MIKADO **Phone:** 322/221-0004 (13)

Japanese
$17-$33

The restaurant incorporates a Japanese sushi bar and teppanyaki tableside cooking done by entertaining chefs. Dressy casual. **Bar:** Full bar. **Reservations:** suggested. **Hours:** 6 pm-11 pm, Sat & Sun from 1 pm. **Address:** Paseo de la Marina 5 **Location:** 3.1 mi (5 km) n on Mex 200; at Marina Vallarta; in CasaMagna Marriott Puerto Vallarta Resort & Spa. **Parking:** on-site. **Cards:** AX, DC, MC, VI.

MORGAN'S STEAK HOUSE **Phone:** 322/221-3319 (15)

Steak
$10-$30

At the popular Marina Vallarta, this casual restaurant features both indoor and outdoor terrace seating. Representative of traditional fare are shrimp cocktail, Caesar salad and thick, juicy cuts of beef. Casual dress. **Bar:** Full bar. **Reservations:** not accepted. **Hours:** noon-11 pm, Sun from 3 pm. **Address:** Puesta del Sol Local 20 **Location:** At Marina Vallarta. **Parking:** no self-parking. **Cards:** MC, VI.

(See map and index starting on p. 550)

MURALES **Phone:** 322/226-7040 (23)

Mexican
$11-$23

Overlooking the pool, the fine Mexican restaurant gives patrons the choice of indoor or terrace seating, the latter of which overlooks the pool. The menu blends innovative Mexican and regional dishes, with a focus on fresh fish and other seafood. Fine Mexican artwork enhances the appeal of the dining room. **Bar:** Full bar. **Reservations:** required, for non hotel guests. **Hours:** 6:30 pm-11 pm. Closed: Sun. **Address:** San Salvador 117 Col 5 de Diciembre **Location:** 0.6 mi (1 km) n on Airport Hwy (Mex 200); in Villa Premiere Hotel & Spa. **Parking:** on-site. **Cards:** AX, MC, VI.

NIKKI BEACH RESTAURANT AND BAR **Phone:** 322/226-1150 (16)

International
$12-$35

By day, diners have a fabulous view of the beach and ocean and at night the restaurant transforms into a candlelit delight offering a very romantic setting. The open air dining room is surrounded inside and on the beach by an upscale lounge where diners can enjoy drinks before or after dinner on candlelit, cushioned beach beds. The menu features a nice mix of seafood and meats as well as a full sushi selection. Casual dress. **Bar:** Full bar. **Reservations:** suggested. **Hours:** 10:30 am-midnight. **Address:** Paseo de la Marina Sur 205 **Location:** 3.1 mi (5 km) n on Mex 200; in Marina Vallarta; in The Westin Resort and Spa Puerto Vallarta. **Parking:** on-site. **Cards:** AX, MC, VI.

OSCAR'S FINE CUISINE **Phone:** 322/223-0789 (33)

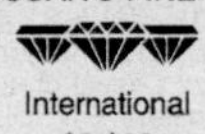

International
$9-$30

On Isla Rio Cuale and overlooking the ocean, the covered open-air restaurant serves as a great setting for a romantic meal. Freshly grilled steaks, fish and other seafood share menu space with several pasta selections. Live entertainment often enhances the atmosphere at night. After dinner, patrons can stroll on the nearby pier. Casual dress. **Bar:** Full bar. **Reservations:** suggested. **Hours:** 9 am-11 pm. **Address:** Isla Rio Cuale Local 1 **Location:** At Isla Rio Cuale. **Parking:** no self-parking. **Cards:** AX, MC, VI.

PARADISE BURGER **Phone:** 322/223-2328 (25)

American
$7-$15

In the mood for a juicy burger or some tasty onion rings? This eatery fills the bill. Also on the menu are wings, fish and chips, hearty sandwiches, salads and ribs. The great location has some balcony seating offering a great view. Casual dress. **Bar:** Full bar. **Hours:** 10:30 am-midnight. **Address:** Paseo Diaz Ordaz #740 **Location:** On Malecon, facing ocean. **Parking:** street. **Cards:** DS, MC, VI.

PORTO BELLO RISTORANTE ITALIANO **Phone:** 322/221-0003 (8)

Italian
$13-$40

This elegant restaurant offers diners a choice of indoor or outdoor patio in the relaxed, yet sophisticated style that is so common in the area. The menu features a wide variety of fine Italian cuisine with antipasto platters for sharing, fresh homemade pastas, veal and seafood offerings. Although portions are hearty, try to save room for the fabulous selection of homemade desserts, the ultimate in decadence. Casual dress. **Bar:** Full bar. **Reservations:** suggested, for dinner. **Hours:** noon-11 pm. **Address:** Marina del Sol Local 7 Marina Vallarta **Location:** In Marina Vallarta. **Parking:** street. **Cards:** AX, MC, VI.

RESTAURANTE MARIACHES **Phone:** 322/226-1700 (21)

Mexican
$14-$20

Servers dressed in traditional mariachi costumes and bright Mexican decor enhance the festive feel of the casual restaurant. Examples of traditional favorites include fajitas with corn tortillas and grilled seafood with rich sauces. Meals come with fresh salsa and tortilla chips. Servers can bring by hats from a colorful collection for diners to wear for a photographic memory. Casual dress. **Bar:** Full bar. **Reservations:** suggested. **Hours:** 6 pm-11 pm. Closed: Fri. **Address:** Blvd Fco Medina Ascencio S/N KM 3.5 **Location:** 2.5 mi (4 km) n on Airport Hwy (Mex 200); in Holiday Inn Puerto Vallarta. **Parking:** on-site. **Cards:** AX, MC, VI.

RESTAURANT LAS PALOMAS MARINAS **Phone:** 322/221-3147 (10)

Seafood
$6-$20

This casual open-air eatery prepares international dishes with a Mexican flair. Guests enjoy the marina's pleasant location, which affords nice views of the water. The menu lists many fresh seafood selections, including a wide range of shrimp selections. Musicians perform nightly. Casual dress. **Bar:** Full bar. **Hours:** 8 am-11 pm. **Address:** Paseo de la Marina 245 **Location:** At Marina Vallarta. **Parking:** no self-parking. **Cards:** AX, MC, VI.

RINCON DE BUENOS AIRES **Phone:** 322/221-2260 (3)

Argentine
$10-$30

This casual eatery features hearty portions of prime beef. Servers will display the huge cuts of meat tableside to help diners make their selection. Kebobs, seafood, and poultry are also featured. The chefs grill all meals to order over a wood fire, making the flavor sensational. Casual dress. **Bar:** Full bar. **Reservations:** suggested. **Hours:** 5 pm-11 pm. Closed: 12/24. **Address:** Malecon de la Marina Royal Pacific Local 12 **Location:** In Marina Vallarta. **Parking:** street. **Cards:** AX, MC, VI.

THE RIVER CAFE **Phone:** 322/223-0788 (35)

International
$8-$30

A tranquil setting awaits diners who wish to escape from the bustling city streets to a peaceful oasis overlooking the river. Lucky diners may spot some large iguanas sunning themselves in the heat of the day. At night, a romantic atmosphere is created with candlelit tables and pleasant background music. The menu offers light and full lunch entrees and a sophisticated dinner menu featuring fine Continental cuisine. Dressy casual. **Bar:** Full bar. **Reservations:** suggested, for dinner. **Hours:** 9 am-11:30 pm. **Address:** Isla Rio Cuale Local 4 **Location:** Center; at Isla Rio Cuale. **Parking:** no self-parking. **Cards:** AX, MC, VI.

(See map and index starting on p. 550)

SENOR FROG'S
Phone: 322/222-5177

International
$7-$16

Part of the chain of Mexican restaurants that also includes Carlos 'n Charlie's, the fun and festive eatery is a great place to eat with the family or rendezvous with friends. The menu is lined with Tex-Mex, American and Mexican favorites, such as Buffalo wings, quesadillas, fajitas and burritos. After hours, a bar atmosphere prevails. Casual dress. **Bar:** Full bar. **Hours:** noon-midnight. **Address:** Venustiano Carranza No 218 **Location:** In Old Town Vallarta. **Parking:** street. **Cards:** AX, MC, VI.

SI SENOR
Phone: 322/113-0064 (45)

Mexican
$18-$35

This cantina serves freshly prepared Mexican fare in a bright and festive atmosphere. Diners start off their meals with fresh tortillas and spicy salsa, compliments of the house, and then proceed to the main course of flaming fajitas, tasty tacos or grilled meats or seafood. Fresh tortillas are always available. Casual dress. **Bar:** Full bar. **Reservations:** suggested. **Hours:** 11 am-11 pm. **Address:** Josefa Ortiz de Dominguez #274 **Location:** Jct Calle Guadalupe Sanchez; centre. **Parking:** no self-parking. **Cards:** MC, VI.

SUZIE WONG'S CHINESE CUISINE
Phone: 322/221-2057 (2)

Chinese
$8-$28

The casual restaurant features both indoor and outdoor patio seating. Tropical foliage, a fish pond and a water fountain lend to a tranquil setting. The menu lists a selection of tasty Chinese cuisine, and daily lunch specials offer excellent value. Casual dress. **Bar:** Full bar. **Reservations:** accepted. **Hours:** noon-11 pm. **Address:** Condominio Royal Pacific #124 **Location:** At Marina Vallarta; close to lighthouse. **Parking:** street. **Cards:** AX, MC, VI.

TERRAZZA DI ROMA RISTORANTE ITALIANO
Phone: 322/221-0871 (5)

Italian
$7-$18

A charming, awning-covered pier at the water's edge is part of the setting at this restaurant. The menu lists pizza and a full range of Italian pasta and meat dishes, as well as both American and Mexican breakfast selections. Casual dress. **Bar:** Full bar. **Hours:** 8:30 am-11 pm. **Address:** Condominio Puesta del Sol Local 2 **Location:** In Marina Vallarta. **Parking:** street. **Cards:** AX, MC, VI.

THIERRY'S PRIME STEAKHOUSE
Phone: 322/221-1212 (20)

Steak
$20-$48

This chic restaurant features prime beef, which is cooked to order with a wide range of sauces. Servers take pride in tableside descriptions of fine cuts from the beef trolley. Diners can select indoor or outdoor patio seating and enjoy a pre- or post-dinner cocktail in the contemporary lounge. Casual dress. **Bar:** Full bar. **Reservations:** suggested. **Hours:** 1 pm-11:30 pm. **Address:** Peninsula Plaza **Location:** At Peninsula Plaza, 2nd Floor. **Parking:** on-site (fee). **Cards:** MC, VI.

TIKUL PACIFIC CUISINE
Phone: 322/209-2010 (19)

International
$20-$40

The terrace overlooks the marina, while the chic, upscale dining room brings in live entertainment most evenings. The chef creates innovative dishes including soft-shell crab, slow-braised short ribs with caramelized onions, baked red snapper and seared rack of lamb. Freshly prepared desserts are excellent. Dressy casual. **Bar:** Full bar. **Reservations:** suggested. **Hours:** 5 pm-11:30 pm. **Address:** Paseo de la Marina 245 **Location:** At Marina Vallarta. **Parking:** no self-parking. **Cards:** MC, VI.

TRIO RESTAURANT
Phone: 322/222-2196 (31)

Mediterranean
$16-$18

Fine European cuisine is what you'll find at this very popular dining spot located in the central part of the city. It also features a pleasant mix of local and bistro decor, live music and generous drinks. It is popular with the American and European expatriate communities. Dressy casual. **Bar:** Full bar. **Reservations:** suggested. **Hours:** 6 pm-11:30 pm. **Address:** Guerrero #264 **Location:** 3 blks n of the Malecon; center. **Parking:** street. **Cards:** AX, MC, VI.

VIPS
Phone: 322/209-1280

Mexican
$5-$9

Owned by Wal-Mart of Mexico and found in most major cities, the budget-friendly chain serves a good variety of Mexican and American dishes, including burgers, sandwiches, salads, spaghetti and enchiladas, as well as a fine selection of desserts. Casual dress. **Hours:** 7 am-midnight, Fri & Sat-2 am. **Address:** Blvd Francisco Medina Ascencio #2900 **Location:** in Zone Hotelera; jct Ave Prisciliano Sanchez and Blvd Francisco Medina Ascencio #2900. **Parking:** on-site. **Cards:** MC, VI.

VISTA GRILL
Phone: 322/222-3570 (44)

AAA

Continental
$20-$30

In addition to the tantalizing menu, diners here enjoy an outstanding view of Puerto Vallarta from the restaurant's prime hilltop location. The contemporary decor and live entertainment from the open air lounge complement the chef's innovative menu. Highlights include fresh seafood, slow roasted pork and freshly grilled meats complemented with exotic sauces. A great spot to watch the sunset. Semi-formal attire. Entertainment. **Reservations:** suggested. **Hours:** 5:30 pm-11:30 pm. **Address:** Pulpeto #377 **Location:** Just s of town, follow signs from Mex 200. **Parking:** street. **Cards:** AX, MC, VI.

VITEA OCEANFRONT BISTRO
Phone: 322/222-8703 (9)

Continental
$8-$25

Overlooking the New Malecon area of town, the bustling oceanfront eatery sports a bright and airy decor. A European Riviera theme weaves through the innovative menu, which incorporates grilled items, seafood, meats and poultry. The excellent desserts merit at least a few bites. Casual dress. **Bar:** Full bar. **Reservations:** suggested. **Hours:** 11 am-midnight. **Address:** Liberatad 2 and Malecon Centro **Location:** At Malecon Centro; oceanfront. **Parking:** no self-parking. **Cards:** MC, VI.

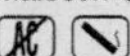

(See map and index starting on p. 550)

Z TAI RESTAURANT Phone: 322/222-0306 (30)

International
$15-$25

Guests get a delightful surprise when they enter the large contemporary lounge and sunken garden patio at this upbeat restaurant and lounge: Candlelit stairways and waterfalls take the atmosphere to a higher level. More traditional decor characterizes the indoor dining area. Asian and international dishes come together on the varied menu of creative fare. Casual dress. **Bar:** Full bar. **Reservations:** suggested. **Hours:** 6 pm-11 pm. **Address:** Morelos 737/Malecon 732-A **Location:** Center; off Malecon. **Parking:** no self-parking. **Cards:** AX, MC, VI.

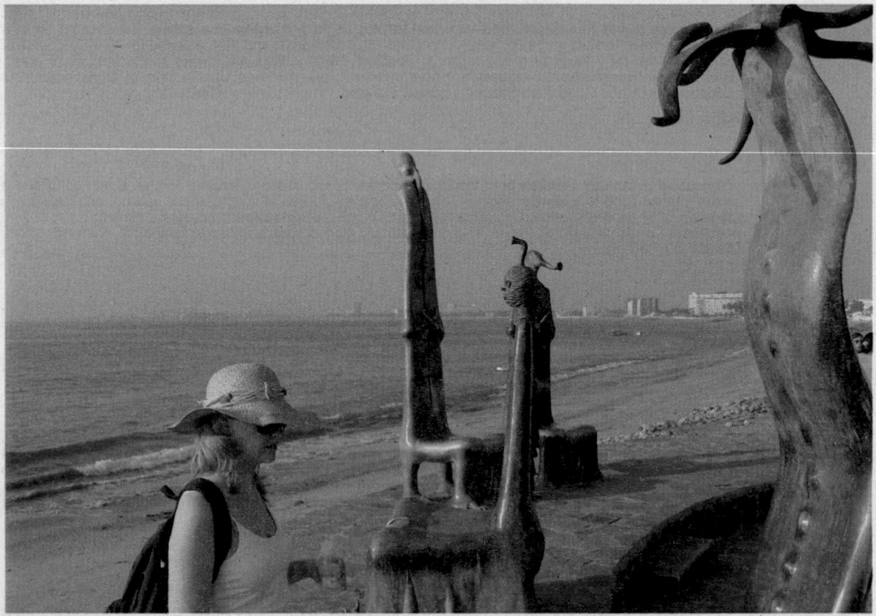

Malecón / © Ryan J. Hollander

This ends listings for Puerto Vallarta.
The following page resumes the alphabetical listings of cities in The Pacific Coast.

PUNTA MITA, NAYARIT

WHERE TO STAY

BRISAS DE MITA — **Phone:** 329/298-4114

Bed & Breakfast
$485-$615 All Year

Address: Calle Playa Caneyeras S/N **Location:** Mex 200, 11.3 mi (18 km) on Punta Mita Rd, Higuena Blanco turn off, 1.1 mi (1.8 km) w to bridge Puente Cauyeros, then 0.7 mi (1.1 km) on beach access road. **Facility:** This property is an exclusive, luxury, seaside B&B where the included meals emphasize fine dining. Designated smoking area. 8 one-bedroom standard units. 2 stories (no elevator), exterior corridors. *Bath:* shower only. **Parking:** on-site. **Terms:** office hours 8 am-11 pm, age restrictions may apply. **Amenities:** video library, safes, honor bars. **Pool(s):** heated outdoor. **Leisure Activities:** snorkeling, limited exercise equipment. *Fee:* massage. **Guest Services:** valet laundry, wireless Internet. **Business Services:** PC. **Cards:** AX, MC, VI.

FEE / SOME UNITS

FOUR SEASONS RESORT PUNTA MITA, MEXICO *Book great rates at AAA.com* — **Phone:** (329)291-6000

Resort Hotel
$535-$1065 12/1-4/20
$405-$1000 4/21-11/30

Address: Punta Mita Bahia de Banderas **Location:** Puerto Vallarta Airport, 29.2 mi (46.7 km) n. **Facility:** This exclusive resort overlooks the ocean and a beach. It caters to couples and families who enjoy outdoor activities rather than nightlife. 173 units. 143 one-bedroom standard units. 30 one-bedroom suites, some with whirlpools. 1-3 stories (no elevator), exterior corridors. **Parking:** valet. **Terms:** 30 day cancellation notice-fee imposed. **Amenities:** video library, DVD players, CD players, high-speed Internet (fee), dual phone lines, voice mail, safes, honor bars, irons, hair dryers. **Dining:** 4 restaurants, also, Aramara Restaurant, Bahia Ocean Grill and Bar, see separate listings, entertainment. **Pool(s):** 4 heated outdoor. **Leisure Activities:** whirlpools, steamrooms, limited beach access, paddleboats, windsurfing, snorkeling, fishing, kayaks, golf & tennis instruction, recreation programs, ATV, kids club, hiking trails, jogging, playground, spa, volleyball, game room. *Fee:* boats, sailboats, scuba diving, charter fishing, swim with dolphins, yacht, golf-19 holes, 4 lighted tennis courts, canopy tours, horseback riding. **Guest Services:** complimentary and valet laundry, wireless Internet. **Business Services:** conference facilities, business center. **Cards:** AX, DC, MC, VI.

FEE 24 S D / SOME UNITS

PALLADIUM VALLARTA RESORT AND SPA — **Phone:** 329/226-9900

Resort Hotel
$280 All Year

Address: Costa Banderas KM 11.5 **Location:** Mex 200, exit Punta Mita Rd, 6.9 mi (11 km) s to entrance. **Facility:** This all-inclusive resort offers a relaxing, fun atmosphere and a stunning oceanfront location; activities are available for all ages. 420 one-bedroom standard units. 3 stories (no elevator), exterior corridors. *Bath:* combo or shower only. **Parking:** on-site. **Amenities:** safes, irons, hair dryers. **Dining:** 6 restaurants, entertainment. **Pool(s):** 2 outdoor. **Leisure Activities:** saunas, whirlpool, windsurfing, snorkeling, kayaks, boogie boards, recreation programs, kids club, spa, volleyball, game room. *Fee:* scuba diving, 2 lighted tennis courts. **Guest Services:** wireless Internet. **Business Services:** meeting rooms, PC (fee). **Cards:** AX, MC, VI.

/ SOME UNITS

THE ROYAL SUITES BY PALLADIUM — **Phone:** 329/226-9900

Hotel
$340 All Year

Address: Costa Banderas KM 11.5 **Location:** Mex 200, exit Punta Mita Rd, 6.9 mi (11 km) s to entrance. **Facility:** 100 one-bedroom standard units with whirlpools. 3 stories (no elevator), interior/exterior corridors. **Parking:** on-site. **Terms:** age restrictions may apply. **Amenities:** safes, irons, hair dryers. **Pool(s):** heated outdoor. **Guest Services:** wireless Internet. **Business Services:** PC. **Cards:** AX, MC, VI.

FEE 24 D / SOME UNITS

WHERE TO DINE

ARAMARA RESTAURANT — **Phone:** 329/291-6000

International
$21-$35

This elegant dining room features both indoor and outdoor terrace dining. The chef has created an innovative menu referred to as "Chino Latino" cuisine, which is a Latin American menu infused with Asian influences, and it's a big hit with diners. Take for example the cold prawn and rice noodle spring roll, the rack of lamb with sake sauce or the tangerine-glazed cornish hen with stir-fry vegetables. Every visit is a night to remember. Dressy casual. **Bar:** Full bar. **Reservations:** suggested. **Hours:** 6:30 pm-11 pm. **Address:** Punta Mita Bahia de Banderas **Location:** Puerto Vallarta Airport, 29.2 mi (46.7 km) n; in Four Seasons Resort Punta Mita, Mexico. **Parking:** valet. **Cards:** AX, DC, MC, VI.

BAHIA OCEAN GRILL AND BAR — **Phone:** 329/291-6000

Steak
$21-$45

This open-air restaurant's beachfront location affords great views of the ocean. Patrons combine simple grilled foods with exotic and creative dipping sauces in self-made creations. The chef tempts guests to be adventuresome. Casual dress. **Bar:** Full bar. **Reservations:** suggested. **Hours:** noon-3:30 & 6-11:30 pm. **Address:** Punta Mita Bahia de Banderas **Location:** Puerto Vallarta Airport, 29.2 mi (46.7 km) n; in Four Seasons Resort Punta Mita, Mexico. **Parking:** valet. **Cards:** AX, DC, MC, VI.

RINCON DE GUAYABITOS, NAYARIT pop. 1,800

WHERE TO STAY

VILLA CORONA DEL MAR BED AND BREAKFAST — **Phone:** (327)274-0912

Bed & Breakfast
$100 All Year

Address: 15 Retorno Gaviotas **Location:** From Mex 200, exit w at Rincon de Guayabitus, then 0.6 mi (1 km) n. **Facility:** Situated across from the beach, the inn offers guest rooms, many with a balcony and ocean view, brightly decorated with a distinct local flair. Designated smoking area. 10 units. 7 one-bedroom standard units. 1 two-bedroom suite with whirlpool. 2 cottages. 1-3 stories (no elevator), interior/exterior corridors. *Bath:* combo or shower only. **Parking:** on-site. **Terms:** office hours 7 am-7 pm, 7 day cancellation notice-fee imposed. **Pool(s):** 2 outdoor. **Leisure Activities:** whirlpool, tennis court. *Fee:* massage. **Guest Services:** valet laundry, wireless Internet. **Business Services:** PC.

/ SOME UNITS

The following lodging was either not evaluated or did not meet AAA rating requirements but is listed for your information only.

DECAMERON LOS COCOS — **Phone:** 327/274-0191

fyi

Not evaluated. **Address:** Retorno Las Palmas **Location:** Center. Facilities, services, and decor characterize a mid-scale property.

TEPIC, NAYARIT pop. 305,176

WHERE TO STAY

HOTEL LAS PALOMAS — *Book at AAA.com* — **Phone:** (311)214-0239

Hotel
$96 All Year

Address: Ave Insurgentes 2100 Ote **Location:** 1.9 mi (3 km) w on Mex 15. **Facility:** 61 one-bedroom standard units. 2 stories, exterior corridors. *Bath:* combo or shower only. **Parking:** on-site. **Terms:** 7 day cancellation notice-fee imposed. **Amenities:** hair dryers. **Pool(s):** outdoor. **Leisure Activities:** whirlpool. **Guest Services:** valet laundry, wireless Internet. **Business Services:** fax (fee). **Cards:** AX, MC, VI.

/ SOME UNITS

HOTEL MELANIE — **Phone:** (311)214-2310

Hotel
$90 All Year

Address: Blvd Tepic-Xalixco 109 **Location:** 1.3 mi (2 km) se on Tepic-Puerto Vallarta Hwy. **Facility:** 56 units. 55 one-bedroom standard units. 1 one-bedroom suite. 4 stories, interior corridors. *Bath:* combo or shower only. **Parking:** on-site. **Guest Services:** valet laundry, wireless Internet. **Business Services:** meeting rooms. **Cards:** AX, DC, MC, VI.

HOTEL NEKIE TEPIC — **Phone:** 311/211-8450

Hotel
$85 All Year

Address: Ave Tecnologico 2261 **Location:** On Mex 15, east end of town. **Facility:** 182 units. 180 one-bedroom standard units. 2 two-bedroom suites. 3 stories (no elevator), interior corridors. *Bath:* combo or shower only. **Parking:** on-site. **Amenities:** high-speed Internet (fee), honor bars. **Pool(s):** outdoor. **Guest Services:** valet laundry. **Business Services:** conference facilities. **Cards:** AX, MC, VI.

/ SOME UNITS

WHERE TO DINE

VIPS — **Phone:** 311/210-5811

Mexican
$5-$9

Owned by Wal-Mart of Mexico and found in most major cities, the budget-friendly chain serves a good variety of Mexican and American dishes, including burgers, sandwiches, salads, spaghetti and enchiladas, as well as a fine selection of desserts. Casual dress. **Hours:** 7 am-midnight. **Address:** Ave Insurgentes #1254 **Location:** Jct aves Insurgentes and Universidad; center. **Parking:** on-site. **Cards:** MC, VI.

ZIHUATANEJO, GUERRERO pop. 37,300

WHERE TO STAY

CATALINA BEACH RESORT Book at AAA.com **Phone:** (755)554-2137

Hotel
$79-$188 All Year

Address: Playa La Ropa S/N **Location:** Playa La Ropa, 5.6 mi (9 km) n of airport. **Facility:** 46 one-bedroom standard units, some with efficiencies. 1-4 stories (no elevator), exterior corridors. *Bath:* shower only. **Parking:** on-site. **Amenities:** *Some:* safes. **Pool(s):** outdoor. **Guest Services:** valet laundry. **Cards:** AX, DC, DS, MC, VI.

/ SOME UNITS

LA CASA QUE CANTA Book at AAA.com **Phone:** (755)555-7030

Hotel
$490-$1200 All Year

Address: Camino Escenico S/N Playa La Ropa **Location:** Playa La Ropa, 5.6 mi (9 km) n of airport; Mirador sector. **Facility:** On a cliff with bay views. Elegance with Mexican folk art. Requires stair climbing to reach most areas of hotel. Only a few rooms with elevator access. Designated smoking area. 33 one-bedroom standard units. 3-6 stories, exterior corridors. *Bath:* shower only. **Parking:** on-site. **Terms:** age restrictions may apply, 30 day cancellation notice, 60 day in season-fee imposed. **Amenities:** voice mail, safes, honor bars, hair dryers. *Some:* DVD players, CD players. **Pool(s):** 2 outdoor. **Leisure Activities:** whirlpool, beach access, exercise room, spa. **Guest Services:** valet laundry, wireless Internet. **Business Services:** meeting rooms, PC. **Cards:** AX, MC, VI.

/ SOME UNITS

SOTAVENTO BEACH RESORT Book at AAA.com **Phone:** (755)554-2032

Hotel
$65-$185 All Year

Address: Camino Escenico, S/N Playa La Ropa **Location:** Playa La Ropa, 5.6 mi (9 km) n of airport. **Facility:** 91 units. 86 one- and 5 two-bedroom standard units. 5-8 stories (no elevator), exterior corridors. *Bath:* shower only. **Parking:** on-site. **Terms:** 20 day cancellation notice. **Dining:** El Panoramic, see separate listing. **Pool(s):** outdoor. **Leisure Activities:** beach access. **Guest Services:** valet laundry, wireless Internet. **Business Services:** business center. **Cards:** DC, MC, VI.

/ SOME UNITS

THE TIDES Book at AAA.com **Phone:** (755)555-5500

Hotel
$330-$970 All Year

Address: Playa La Ropa S/N **Location:** 6.3 mi (10 km) n of airport. **Facility:** Palms and tropical gardens surround this service-oriented hotel, which features a fine restaurant; 40 rooms have private plunge pools. 70 units. 62 one-bedroom standard units. 1 one- and 7 two-bedroom suites. 1-3 stories (no elevator), exterior corridors. *Bath:* shower only. **Parking:** on-site and valet. **Terms:** age restrictions may apply, 30 day cancellation notice, 15 day in summer-fee imposed. **Amenities:** DVD players, CD players, high-speed Internet, safes, honor bars, hair dryers. **Dining:** La Villa, see separate listing. **Pool(s):** 3 outdoor. **Leisure Activities:** exercise room, spa. *Fee:* 2 lighted tennis courts. **Guest Services:** valet laundry, wireless Internet. **Business Services:** meeting rooms, business center. **Cards:** AX, MC, VI.

/ SOME UNITS

VILLA VERA PUERTO MIO ZIHUATANEJO **Phone:** (755)553-8165

Hotel
$140-$300 All Year

Address: Paseo del Morro #5 Col El Almacen **Location:** 1.9 mi (3 km) w of Mex 200 interchange; follow Morelos. **Facility:** 21 units. 20 one- and 1 two-bedroom standard units, some with whirlpools. 4 stories (no elevator), interior/exterior corridors. *Bath:* combo or shower only. **Parking:** street. **Terms:** check-in 4 pm, 3 day cancellation notice. **Amenities:** safes, honor bars, irons, hair dryers. **Dining:** Altura, see separate listing. **Pool(s):** outdoor. **Leisure Activities:** *Fee:* massage. **Guest Services:** valet laundry, wireless Internet. **Business Services:** PC (fee). **Cards:** AX, MC, VI.

/ SOME UNITS

The following lodgings were either not evaluated or did not meet AAA rating requirements but are listed for your information only.

CASA KAU-KAN **Phone:** 755/554-8446

fyi

Not evaluated. **Address:** Playa Largo S/N. Facilities, services, and decor characterize a mid-scale property.

CLUB INTRAWEST **Phone:** 755/555-0375

fyi

Not evaluated. **Address:** Carr Escenica La Ropa **Location:** Oceanfront. Playa La Ropa, 5.6 mi (9 km) n of airport. Facilities, services, and decor characterize a mid-scale property.

HOTEL IRMA **Phone:** 755/554-2105

fyi

Not evaluated. **Address:** Adelita S/N Playa La Madera **Location:** On Playa La Madera. Facilities, services, and decor characterize an economy property.

VILLA MEXICANA

fyi

Not evaluated. **Address:** Playa La Ropa S/N. Facilities, services, and decor characterize an economy property.

WHERE TO DINE

ALTURA — **Phone:** 755/553-8165

International
$8-$20

With a spectacular view overlooking a private cove, the restaurant prepares Mexican-inspired cuisine. Casual dress. **Bar:** Full bar. **Reservations:** accepted. **Hours:** 7 am-11 pm. **Address:** Paseo del Morro #5 Col El Almacen **Location:** 1.9 mi (3 km) w of Mex 200 interchange; follow Morelos; in Villa Vera Puerto Mio Zihuatanejo. **Parking:** on-site. **Cards:** AX, MC, VI.

BAY CLUB RESTAURANT AND BAR — **Phone:** 755/554-4844

Continental
$15-$30

Views of Zihuatanejo Bay are spectacular from the open-air dining room's outstanding hilltop setting. The menu lists a fine mix of international fare and some Mexican specialties. Highlights include fresh fish in mango sauce, shrimp in cilantro sauce and Chateaubriand for two. The terrace is a great spot for an after-dinner drink. Casual dress. **Bar:** Full bar. **Reservations:** suggested. **Hours:** 5 pm-midnight. **Address:** Carr Escenica a Playa La Ropa S/N **Location:** On road to Playa La Ropa Beach Rd. **Parking:** no self-parking. **Cards:** MC, VI.

CASA BAHIA RESTAURANT-BAR — **Phone:** 755/554-8666

Steak & Seafood
$20-$40

Patrons can fill up on casual fare—including such Mexican favorites as nachos, quesadillas and fajitas, as well as home-style burgers, freshly grilled meats and seafood dishes—while looking out over Zihuatanejo Bay. Casual dress. **Bar:** Full bar. **Reservations:** suggested. **Hours:** 3 pm-10 pm. **Address:** Zihuatanejo Bay S/N **Location:** Just outside of town, overlooking Zihuatanejo Bay. **Parking:** street. **Cards:** MC, VI.

CASA ELVIRA RESTAURANT — **Phone:** 755/554-2061

Seafood
$4-$13

The eatery has been in operation for almost 50 years. Fish tacos are terrific, and quesadillas are well worth trying. Casual dress. **Bar:** Full bar. **Reservations:** accepted. **Hours:** 1 pm-10:30 pm. **Address:** Paseo del Pescador #32 **Location:** Center; on waterfront; just e of town pier. **Parking:** street. **Cards:** MC, VI.

COCONUTS — **Phone:** 755/554-2518

International
$15-$32

This cozy restaurant occupies the delightful open courtyard of a historic building. The patio is filled with lush trees and fairy lights that set a romantic tone. The chef's international menu incorporates dishes prepared from fine cuts of meat, fresh fish and other seafood, pasta and some Mexican fare. Live entertainment most nights adds to the ambience. Casual dress. **Bar:** Full bar. **Reservations:** suggested. **Hours:** Open 12/1-6/30 & 9/1-11/30; 11:30 am-4:30 & 6-11 pm. **Address:** Pasaje Agustin Ramirez I **Location:** Center. **Parking:** no self-parking. **Cards:** MC, VI.

EL PANORAMIC — **Phone:** 755/554-2032

International
$6-$13

This casual open-air eatery's hilltop location affords outstanding views of the bay. On the menu is a nice selection of simple dishes, including finger foods, grilled meats, shrimp and pasta. The atmosphere is comfortable and relaxing. Casual dress. **Bar:** Full bar. **Hours:** 7:30 am-11 pm. **Address:** Camino Escencio S/N Playa La Rupa **Location:** Playa La Ropa, 5.6 mi (9 km) n of airport; in Sotavento Beach Resort. **Parking:** on-site. **Cards:** DS, MC, VI.

KAU KAN — **Phone:** 755/554-8446

International
$12-$18

A romantic view of the bay is available from the rooftop patio, where patrons can watch the sun set as they dine. A fine selection of wine and spirits complements a menu of great seafood. Dressy casual. **Bar:** Full bar. **Reservations:** accepted. **Hours:** Open 12/1-8/31 & 10/1-11/30; 5 pm-10:30 pm. **Address:** Carr Escencia Lote #7 Cd La Madera S/N **Location:** On La Ropa Beach Rd; at taxi stand. **Parking:** no self-parking. **Cards:** AX, MC, VI.

LA PERLA — **Phone:** 755/554-2700

Seafood
$8-$17

Right on the beach, the eatery prepares fresh seafood a la minute. Jumbo shrimp is plentiful, and patrons can order it cooked the way they like it. Casual dress. **Bar:** Full bar. **Reservations:** accepted. **Hours:** 9 am-11 pm. **Address:** Playa La Ropa S/N **Location:** Playa La Ropa. **Parking:** on-site. **Cards:** AX, MC, VI.

LA VILLA — **Phone:** 755/554-2239

Continental
$12-$50

Under a giant palapa, a thatched roof supported by wooden timbers, the classy outdoor restaurant features fine Continental and Mexican cuisine in a beachside setting. Dressy casual. **Bar:** Full bar. **Reservations:** suggested. **Hours:** 8 am-10:30 pm. **Address:** Playa La Ropa S/N **Location:** 6.3 mi (10 km) n of airport; in The Tides. **Parking:** on-site. **Cards:** AX, MC, VI.

ZI THE RESTAURANT AT CLUB INTRAWEST — **Phone:** 755/555-0375

Continental
$16-$36

High on a cliff overlooking Playa la Ropa, the open-air spot treats guests to sweeping views of the ocean. Candlelit tables are set elegantly, lending to a romantic ambience. The menu lists international dishes, as well as rich, decadent desserts. Casual dress. **Bar:** Full bar. **Reservations:** suggested. **Hours:** 6 pm-10 pm. **Address:** Carr Escenica La Rupa **Location:** Playa La Rupa, 5.6 mi (9 km) n of airport. **Parking:** on-site. **Cards:** AX, MC, VI.

MEXICO CITY AND VICINITY

AMACUZAC, MORELOS pop. 16,482

WHERE TO STAY

HACIENDA SAN GABRIEL DE LAS PALMAS Book at AAA.com Phone: (751)348-0113

Classic Historic Country Inn
$173-$483 All Year

Address: Carr Cuernavaca-Chilpancingo KM 41.8 **Location:** 25.1 mi (41.8 km) s of Cuernavaca. **Facility:** Located just north of Cuernavaca, this hacienda is a large, historic lodging featuring buildings from the 1500s, lavish gardens and theme guest rooms. Smoke free premises. 17 units. 5 one-bedroom standard units, some with whirlpools. 12 one-bedroom suites, some with whirlpools. 2 stories, interior corridors. **Parking:** on-site. **Terms:** age restrictions may apply. **Amenities:** hair dryers. **Pool(s):** 2 outdoor. **Leisure Activities:** 2 tennis courts, exercise room, spa. **Guest Services:** valet laundry. **Business Services:** conference facilities. **Cards:** AX, MC, VI.

/ SOME UNITS

Cuernavaca & Vicinity

This index helps you "spot" where approved lodgings and restaurants are located on the corresponding detailed maps. Lodging daily rate range is for comparison only and show the property's high season. Restaurant rate range is a combination of lunch and/or dinner. Turn to the listing page for more detailed rate information and consult display ads for special promotions.

CUERNAVACA

Map Page	OA	Lodgings	Diamond Rated	High Season	Page
1 / p. 576		Racquet Club Cuernavaca	3 diamonds	$195-$281	577
2 / p. 576		Hotel Argento	3 diamonds	$156-$198	577
3 / p. 576		Hotel Vista Hermosa	3 diamonds	$134-$202	577
4 / p. 576		Hotel Hacienda de Cortez	2 diamonds	$235-$352	577
5 / p. 576		Camino Real Sumiya, Cuernavaca	4 diamonds	$150-$245	577
6 / p. 576		Las Mananitas Hotel Garden & Restaurant	4 diamonds	$270-$480	577
7 / p. 576		Hosteria Las Quintas	3 diamonds	$145-$195	577

Map Page	OA	Restaurants	Diamond Rated	Cuisine	Meal Range	Page
1 / p. 576		Restaurante Hacienda de Cortez	2 diamonds	Regional Mexican	$8-$30	578
2 / p. 576		Restaurant Sumiya	3 diamonds	Japanese	$8-$17	578
3 / p. 576		Las Mananitas Restaurant	4 diamonds	Mexican	$16-$45	578
5 / p. 576		La Adelita	1 diamond	Mexican	$5-$9	578
6 / p. 576		Restaurante Jade	3 diamonds	Regional Continental	$10-$19	578

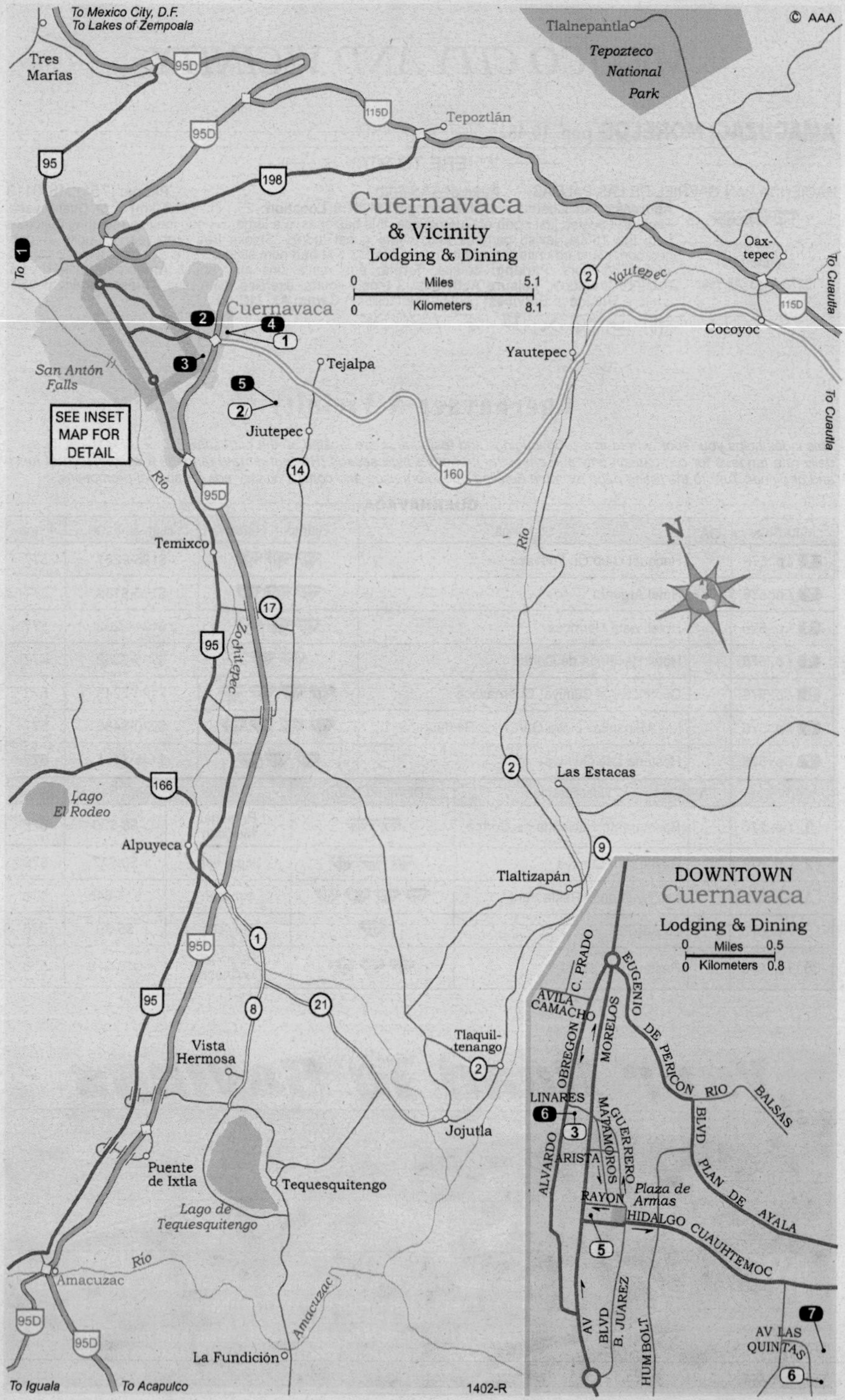

Cuernavaca & Vicinity Lodging & Dining

0 Miles 5.1
0 Kilometers 8.1

© AAA

To Mexico City, D.F.
To Lakes of Zempoala
Tres Marías
Tlalnepantla
Tepozteco National Park
Tepoztlán
Oax-tepec
To Cuautla
Cocoyoc
Yautepec
Cuernavaca
Tejalpa
Jiutepec
San Antón Falls
SEE INSET MAP FOR DETAIL
Temixco
Zochitepec
Río
Las Estacas
Lago El Rodeo
Alpuyeca
Tlaltizapán
Vista Hermosa
Tlaquil-tenango
Jojutla
Puente de Ixtla
Tequesquitengo
Lago de Tequesquitengo
Amacuzac
La Fundición
To Iguala
To Acapulco
1402-R

DOWNTOWN Cuernavaca Lodging & Dining

0 Miles 0.5
0 Kilometers 0.8

C. PRADO
AVILA CAMACHO
OBREGON
MORELOS
EUGENIO DE PERICON
RIO BALSAS
BLVD PLAN DE AYALA
LINARES
MATAMOROS
GUERRERO
ALVARDO
ARISTA
RAYON
Plaza de Armas
HIDALGO
CUAUHTEMOC
AV BLVD B. JUAREZ
HUMBOLT
AV LAS QUINTAS

CUERNAVACA, MORELOS pop. 338,706 (See map and index starting on p. 576)

WHERE TO STAY

CAMINO REAL SUMIYA, CUERNAVACA Book at AAA.com Phone: (777)329-9888 5

Resort Hotel
$150-$245 All Year

Address: Interior de Fracc Sumiya **Location:** 1.8 mi (3 km) se of Mex 95-D (toll road), exit Mex 160 (Cuernavaca-Cuautla Rd), follow signs. **Facility:** Authentic Japanese architecture, gardens and artwork are featured on the expansive grounds of this property located in a private, residential area. 163 units. 157 one-bedroom standard units. 6 one-bedroom suites. 4 stories, exterior corridors. **Parking:** on-site. **Amenities:** voice mail, safes, honor bars, irons, hair dryers. *Some:* CD players. **Dining:** Restaurant Sumiya, see separate listing. **Pool(s):** 2 heated outdoor. **Leisure Activities:** sauna, steamroom, playground, exercise room. *Fee:* 8 tennis courts (6 lighted), massage. **Guest Services:** valet laundry, wireless Internet. **Business Services:** conference facilities, business center. **Cards:** AX, CB, MC, VI.

/ SOME UNITS VCR

HOSTERIA LAS QUINTAS Book at AAA.com Phone: (777)318-3949 7

Country Inn
$145-$195 All Year

Address: Diaz Ordaz 9 **Location:** 1.8 mi (3 km) e of Cortez Palace, off Ave Cuauhtemoc at Ave Las Quintas 107. Located in a quiet residential area. **Facility:** Spacious, tropical grounds. Colonial-style inn. Some rooms with fireplace. All rooms with ceiling fans. Variety of suites and junior suites available. 93 units. 89 one-bedroom standard units. 4 one-bedroom suites with whirlpools. 2 stories, interior/exterior corridors. *Bath:* combo or shower only. **Parking:** on-site and valet. **Amenities:** high-speed Internet, voice mail, safes, honor bars, irons, hair dryers. **Dining:** Restaurante Jade, see separate listing. **Pool(s):** 3 heated outdoor. **Leisure Activities:** saunas, whirlpool, steamrooms, exercise room, spa. **Guest Services:** valet laundry, wireless Internet. **Business Services:** conference facilities, business center. **Cards:** AX, MC, VI.

/ SOME UNITS

HOTEL ARGENTO Phone: 777/316-3282 2

Hotel
$156-$198 All Year

Address: Ave Rio Mayo 1001 **Location:** Mex 95-D (toll road), exit Ave Rio Mayo, 0.8 mi (1.9 km) w. **Facility:** Meets AAA guest room security requirements. 51 one-bedroom standard units. 2 stories, interior corridors. *Bath:* shower only. **Parking:** on-site. **Amenities:** voice mail, safes, irons, hair dryers. **Pool(s):** 2 heated outdoor. **Leisure Activities:** exercise room. **Guest Services:** valet laundry, wireless Internet. **Business Services:** meeting rooms, PC, fax (fee). **Cards:** AX, MC, VI.

HOTEL HACIENDA DE CORTEZ Phone: (777)315-8844 4

Classic Historic Country Inn
$235-$352 All Year

Address: Plaza Kennedy #90 **Location:** Mex 95-D (toll road), exit Jojutla, just e to 1st traffic light, then 1.3 mi (2 km) s to Jiutepec, follow signs; in Atlacomulco Colonia of Jiutepec. **Facility:** Said to be the first sugar mill in North America, this long-standing property boasts lush gardens, rich history and massive stone walls. 23 units. 20 one-bedroom standard units. 3 one-bedroom suites with whirlpools. 1 story, exterior corridors. *Bath:* combo or shower only. **Parking:** on-site. **Amenities:** safes. **Dining:** restaurant, see separate listing. **Pool(s):** outdoor. **Leisure Activities:** playground. **Guest Services:** valet laundry, wireless Internet. **Business Services:** meeting rooms, fax (fee). **Cards:** AX, MC, VI.

/ SOME UNITS AC

HOTEL VISTA HERMOSA Phone: 777/315-2374 3

Country Inn
$134-$202 All Year

Address: Rio Panuco #600 **Location:** Mex 95-D (toll road), exit Ave Rio Mayo, 0.6 mi (1 km) sw on Calle Diana, sw on Ave Rio Mayo, then 0.7 mi (1.2 km) s; corner of Rio Papaloapan. Located in a quiet residential area. **Facility:** Colonial in style, the inn has a large, tranquil courtyard garden; guest rooms have tile floors and some feature private garden terraces. 40 units. 34 one- and 1 two-bedroom standard units. 5 one-bedroom suites. 2 stories (no elevator), interior/exterior corridors. *Bath:* combo or shower only. **Parking:** no self-parking. **Amenities:** high-speed Internet, voice mail, safes. **Pool(s):** heated outdoor. **Leisure Activities:** playground. **Guest Services:** valet laundry, wireless Internet. **Business Services:** meeting rooms, business center. **Cards:** AX, MC, VI.

FEE / SOME UNITS

LAS MANANITAS HOTEL GARDEN & RESTAURANT Book at AAA.com Phone: (777)314-1466 6

Classic Country Inn
$270-$480 All Year

Address: Ricardo Linares 107 Col Centro **Location:** Just e of Mex 95. **Facility:** Colonial-style inn. Tropical gardens. Few fireplaces. Large meeting facility adjacent to the inn with extensive landscaping including a waterfall. 25 units. 24 one-bedroom standard units. 1 two-bedroom suite. 2 stories, interior/exterior corridors. **Parking:** valet. **Terms:** age restrictions may apply, 7 day cancellation notice. **Amenities:** high-speed Internet, safes, irons, hair dryers. **Dining:** Las Mananitas Restaurant, see separate listing. **Pool(s):** heated outdoor. **Guest Services:** valet laundry. **Business Services:** meeting rooms, fax (fee). **Cards:** AX, MC, VI.

RACQUET CLUB CUERNAVACA Book at AAA.com Phone: (777)101-0350 1

Hotel
$195-$281 All Year

Address: Francisco Villa 100 **Location:** 0.5 mi (0.8 km) n of Zapata's monument, follow signs. **Facility:** 50 units. 37 one-bedroom standard units. 13 one-bedroom suites. 4 stories, interior/exterior corridors. **Parking:** on-site. **Terms:** 3 day cancellation notice-fee imposed. **Amenities:** high-speed Internet, safes (fee), honor bars, irons, hair dryers. **Pool(s):** heated outdoor. **Leisure Activities:** 9 tennis courts (4 lighted), exercise room, game room. *Fee:* massage. **Guest Services:** valet laundry, wireless Internet. **Business Services:** conference facilities, business center. **Cards:** AX, MC, VI.

S D / SOME UNITS

(See map and index starting on p. 576)

WHERE TO DINE

LA ADELITA — **Phone:** 777/312-3943 (5)

Mexican
$5-$9

This centrally located restaurant is a perfect way to enjoy a respite from sightseeing; ample sidewalk sitting and a menu of classic Mexican dishes with reasonable prices are offered. Casual dress. **Bar:** Full bar. **Reservations:** accepted. **Hours:** 7:30 am-midnight. **Address:** Ave Hidalgo #1 (Colonia Centro) **Location:** Downtown; facing Cortez Palace. **Parking:** street. **Cards:** MC, VI.

LAS MANANITAS RESTAURANT — **Phone:** 777/314-1466 (3)

Mexican
$16-$45

In a colonial country inn, the restaurant offers upscale dining on the terrace or amid meticulously manicured lawns and gardens. Extensive selections line the daily-changing menu. Semi-formal attire. **Bar:** Full bar. **Reservations:** suggested. **Hours:** 8 am-11 pm, Fri & Sat-midnight. **Address:** Ricardo Linares 107 Col Centro **Location:** Just e of Mex 95; in Las Mananitas Hotel Garden & Restaurant. **Parking:** valet. **Cards:** AX, DC, MC, VI.

RESTAURANTE HACIENDA DE CORTEZ — **Phone:** 777/315-8844 (1)

Regional Mexican
$8-$30

Established in the 1500s, the famous hacienda offers a quiet dining respite in its cool garden courtyard or inside the historic restaurant. Casual dress. **Bar:** Full bar. **Reservations:** accepted. **Hours:** 8 am-10 pm, Fri & Sat-midnight. **Address:** Plaza Kennedy #90 **Location:** Mex 95-D (toll road), exit Jojutla, just e to 1st traffic light, then 1.3 mi (2 km) s to Jiutepec, follow signs; in Atlacomulco Colonia of Jiutepec; in Hotel Hacienda de Cortez. **Parking:** on-site and valet. **Cards:** AX, CB, DC, MC, VI.

RESTAURANTE JADE — **Phone:** 777/362-3949 (6)

Regional Continental
$10-$19

In the city of "eternal spring," the restaurant is renowned for its lush, tropical gardens and refined colonial setting. Lining the menu is a combination of authentic regional preparations and Continental dishes. Dressy casual. Entertainment. **Bar:** Full bar. **Reservations:** suggested, for dinner. **Hours:** 7 am-11 pm. **Address:** Diaz Ordaz 9 **Location:** 1.8 mi (3 km) e of Cortez Palace, off Ave Cuauhtemoc at Ave Las Quintas 107; in Hosteria Las Quintas. **Parking:** on-site and valet. **Cards:** AX, MC, VI.

RESTAURANT SUMIYA — **Phone:** 777/320-9199 (2)

Japanese
$8-$17

Overlooking expansive gardens, the restaurant replicates Japan's Imperial Palace. A detour here is well worth the effort. Although the menu centers on Japanese fare, it also features some regional Mexican cuisine. Casual dress. **Bar:** Full bar. **Reservations:** accepted. **Hours:** 1 pm-midnight, Sun from 10 am. Closed: Mon & Tues. **Location:** 1.8 mi (3 km) se of Mex 95-D (toll road), exit Mex 160 (Cuernavaca-Cuautla Rd), follow signs; in Camino Real Sumiya, Cuernavaca. **Parking:** on-site. **Cards:** AX, DC, MC, VI.

SANBORN'S — **Phone:** 777/316-4802

Regional Mexican
$8-$28

Restaurants in the casual chain, which includes more than 100 locations throughout Mexico, offer a good selection of American-style sandwiches, salads, soups and both Mexican and American entrees. The selection of desserts is impressive. Casual dress. **Bar:** Full bar. **Hours:** 7 am-1 am, Fri & Sat-2 am. **Address:** Ave Plande Ayala No 629, Col Lomas **Location:** Just w of Calle Ignacio Alderma. **Parking:** on-site. **Cards:** AX, MC, VI.

SANBORN'S — **Phone:** 777/316-4206

Regional Mexican
$8-$28

Restaurants in the casual chain, which includes more than 100 locations throughout Mexico, offer a good selection of American-style sandwiches, salads, soups and both Mexican and American entrees. The selection of desserts is impressive. Casual dress. **Bar:** Full bar. **Hours:** 7 am-1 am, Fri & Sat-2 am. **Address:** Ave De Los Cincuenta Metros, Col Flores Ma **Location:** Just off Mex 95. Ave De Los Cincuenta Metros, Col Flores Magon. **Parking:** on-site (fee). **Cards:** AX, MC, VI.

VIPS — **Phone:** 777/312-8342

Regional Mexican
$7-$25

Owned by Wal-Mart of Mexico and found in most major cities, the budget-friendly chain serves a good variety of Mexican and American dishes, including burgers, sandwiches, salads, spaghetti and enchiladas, as well as a fine selection of desserts. Casual dress. **Bar:** Beer & wine. **Hours:** 7 am-11 pm, Fri & Sat-2 am. **Address:** Blvd Benito Juarez No 3, Col Centro **Location:** Between calles Las Casas and Abasolo. **Parking:** on-site. **Cards:** AX, MC, VI.

The following restaurant has not been evaluated by AAA but is listed for your information only.

CASA HIDALGO — **Phone:** 777/312-2749

Not evaluated. This stylish restaurant is easy to spot with its yellow exterior and lovely ironwork around the windows and balcony areas. Its central location makes it a suitable stop for those in the downtown area. **Address:** Jardin de los Ninos Heroes #6 **Location:** Downtown; facing Cortez Palace.

ECATEPEC DE MORELOS, MEXICO

WHERE TO DINE

SANBORN'S — Phone: 552/486-4022

Regional Mexican
$8-$28

Restaurants in the casual chain, which includes more than 100 locations throughout Mexico, offer a good selection of American-style sandwiches, salads, soups and both Mexican and American entrees. The selection of desserts is impressive. Casual dress. **Bar:** Full bar. **Hours:** 7 am-1 am. **Address:** Lote 2 Mnz 4 Conjunto Urbano Col El Salado **Location:** Off Mex 85. **Parking:** on-site (fee). **Cards:** AX, MC, VI.

HUIXQUILUCAN, MEXICO pop. 193,468

WHERE TO DINE

SANBORN'S — Phone: 55/5291-9352

Regional Mexican
$8-$28

Restaurants in the casual chain, which includes more than 100 locations throughout Mexico, offer a good selection of American-style sandwiches, salads, soups and both Mexican and American entrees. The selection of desserts is impressive. Casual dress. **Bar:** Full bar. **Hours:** 7 am-1 am. **Address:** Blvd Int erlomas Mz 111 Lt 1 Col Centro Urba **Location:** Just w of jct Ave Magocentro. **Parking:** on-site. **Cards:** AX, MC, VI.

IXTAPAN DE LA SAL, MEXICO pop. 16,600

WHERE TO STAY

The following lodgings were either not evaluated or did not meet AAA rating requirements but are listed for your information only.

HOTEL BUNGALOWS LOLITA — Phone: 721/143-0016

fyi

Not evaluated. **Address:** Blvd Arturo San Roman 33 **Location:** 0.9 mi (1.5 km) n on Mex 55. Facilities, services, and decor characterize a mid-scale property.

HOTEL VILLA VERGEL — Phone: 721/143-0349

fyi

Not evaluated. **Address:** Blvd Arturo San Roman y Ave Juarez S/N **Location:** 0.9 mi (1.5 km) n on Mex 55. Facilities, services, and decor characterize a mid-scale property.

IXTAPAN DE LA SAL MARRIOTT HOTEL & SPA — Phone: 721/143-2010

fyi

Not evaluated; located in remote area. **Address:** Jose Ma Morelos S/N Fracc Bugambilias **Location:** Just w of Mex 55. Facilities, services, and decor characterize a mid-scale property.

IZTAPALAPA, DISTRITO FEDERAL pop. 1,773,343

WHERE TO DINE

VIPS — Phone: 55/5632-6686

Regional Mexican
$7-$25

Owned by Wal-Mart of Mexico and found in most major cities, the budget-friendly chain serves a good variety of Mexican and American dishes, including burgers, sandwiches, salads, spaghetti and enchiladas, as well as a fine selection of desserts. Casual dress. **Bar:** Beer & wine. **Hours:** 7 am-11 pm, Fri & Sat-midnight. **Address:** Ave Tlah uac No 4431, Col Lomas Estrellas **Location:** Between calles Siracusa and Tecnicos. **Parking:** no self-parking. **Cards:** AX, MC, VI.

VIPS — Phone: 55/5581-2655

Regional Mexican
$7-$25

Owned by Wal-Mart of Mexico and found in most major cities, the budget-friendly chain serves a good variety of Mexican and American dishes, including burgers, sandwiches, salads, spaghetti and enchiladas, as well as a fine selection of desserts. Casual dress. **Bar:** Beer & wine. **Hours:** 7 am-11 pm. **Address:** Ave Ermi ta Iztapalapa No 907 Col Sta Isabel **Location:** Just e of Ave Tlahuac. **Parking:** on-site. **Cards:** AX, MC, VI.

VIPS

Phone: 55/5612-1192

Regional Mexican
$7-$25

Owned by Wal-Mart of Mexico and found in most major cities, the budget-friendly chain serves a good variety of Mexican and American dishes, including burgers, sandwiches, salads, spaghetti and enchiladas, as well as a fine selection of desserts. Casual dress. **Bar:** Beer & wine. **Hours:** 7 am-11 pm, Fri & Sat-midnight. **Address:** Ave Ermi ta Iztapalopa No 2013,Col Los Angel **Location:** Jct Ave Margaritas. **Parking:** on-site. **Cards:** AX, MC, VI.

VIPS

Phone: 55/5845-5665

Regional Mexican
$7-$25

Owned by Wal-Mart of Mexico and found in most major cities, the budget-friendly chain serves a good variety of Mexican and American dishes, including burgers, sandwiches, salads, spaghetti and enchiladas, as well as a fine selection of desserts. Casual dress. **Bar:** Beer & wine. **Hours:** 7 am-midnight, Fri & Sat-1 am. **Address:** Ave Tlahuac No 5662, Col San Lorenzo **Location:** Jct Ave Ejido; across from Plaza Tlahuac. **Parking:** on-site. **Cards:** AX, MC, VI.

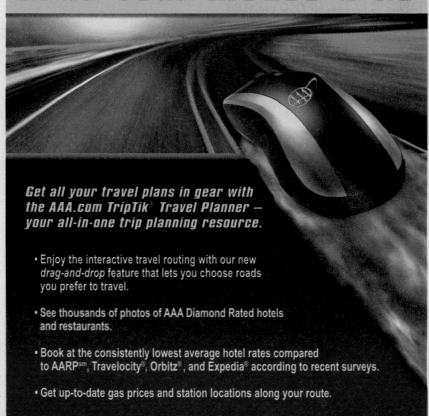

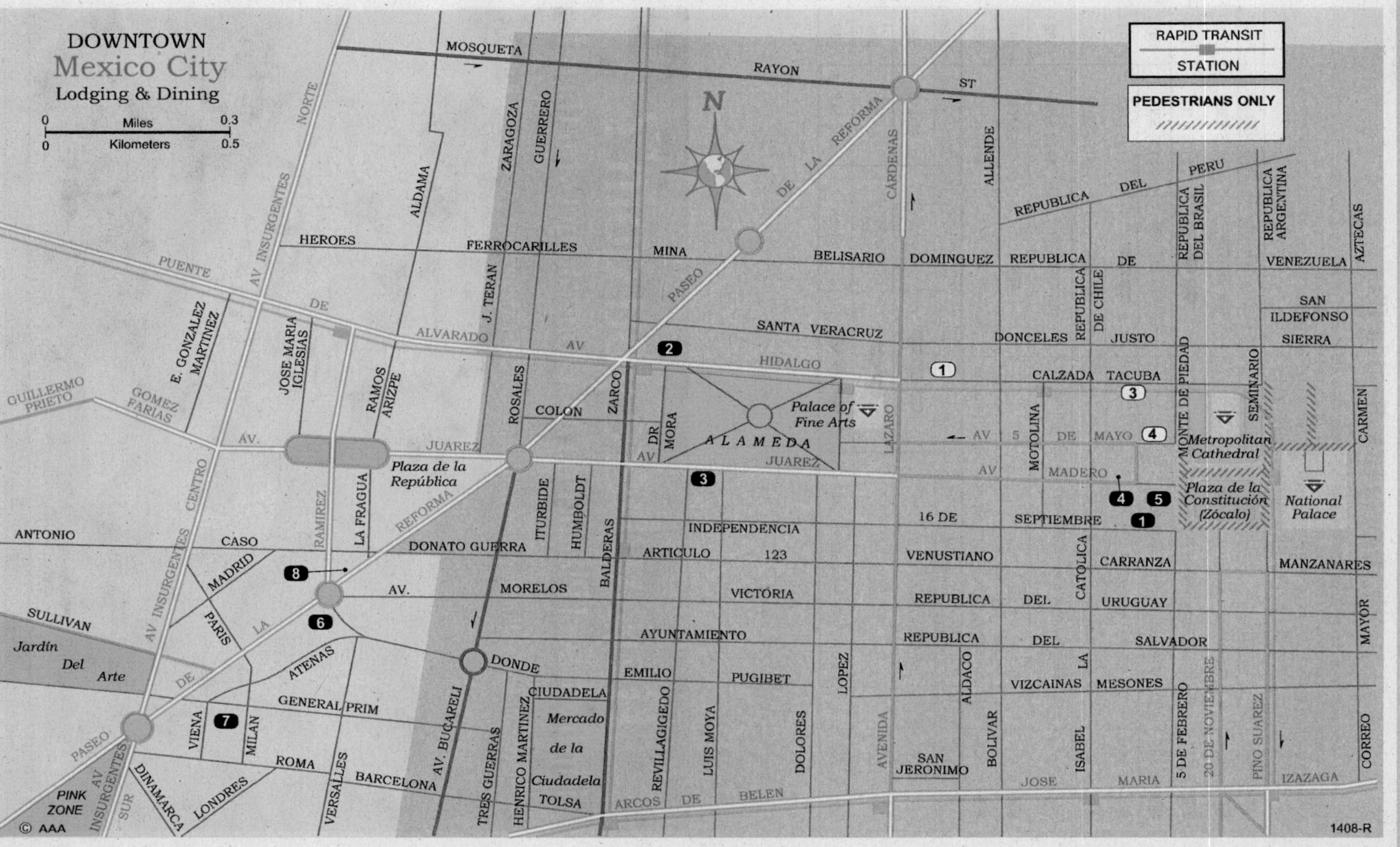
DOWNTOWN
Mexico City
Lodging & Dining
0 Miles 0.3
0 Kilometers 0.5
RAPID TRANSIT
STATION
PEDESTRIANS ONLY
National Palace
Metropolitan Cathedral
Plaza de la Constitución (Zócalo)
Palace of Fine Arts
ALAMEDA
Plaza de la República
Mercado de la Ciudadela
Jardín Del Arte
PINK ZONE
PASEO DE LA REFORMA
AV INSURGENTES NORTE
AV INSURGENTES CENTRO
AV INSURGENTES SUR
AV. BUCARELI
AV JUAREZ
AV 5 DE MAYO
AV MADERO
AV HIDALGO
PUENTE DE ALVARADO
MOSQUETA
RAYON
ST
CARDENAS
ALLENDE
REPUBLICA DEL PERU
REPUBLICA DEL BRASIL
REPUBLICA ARGENTINA
AZTECAS
VENEZUELA
SAN ILDEFONSO
SIERRA
HEROES
FERROCARILLES
MINA
BELISARIO DOMINGUEZ
REPUBLICA DE
REPUBLICA DE CHILE
SANTA VERACRUZ
DONCELES
JUSTO
CALZADA TACUBA
MONTE DE PIEDAD
SEMINARIO
CARMEN
ALDAMA
ZARAGOZA
GUERRERO
J. TERAN
E. GONZALEZ MARTINEZ
JOSE MARIA IGLESIAS
RAMOS ARIZPE
GUILLERMO PRIETO
GOMEZ FARIAS
ROSALES
COLON
ZARCO
DR MORA
LAZARO
MOTOLINA
ANTONIO CASO
RAMIREZ
LA FRAGUA
DONATO GUERRA
ITURBIDE
HUMBOLDT
BALDERAS
INDEPENDENCIA
ARTICULO 123
16 DE SEPTIEMBRE
VENUSTIANO CARRANZA
CATOLICA
MANZANARES
MADRID
AV. MORELOS
VICTORIA
REPUBLICA DEL URUGUAY
SULLIVAN
PARIS
LA
AYUNTAMIENTO
REPUBLICA DEL SALVADOR
MAYOR
ATENAS
DONDE
EMILIO
PUGIBET
LOPEZ
ALDACO
LA
VIZCAINAS
MESONES
GENERAL PRIM
CIUDADELA
VIENA
MILAN
ROMA
VERSALLES
BARCELONA
TRES GUERRAS
HENRICO MARTINEZ
TOLSA
REVILLAGIGEDO
LUIS MOYA
DOLORES
AVENIDA
SAN JERONIMO
BOLIVAR
ISABEL
5 DE FEBRERO
20 DE NOVIEMBRE
PINO SUAREZ
CORREO
JOSE MARIA IZAZAGA
ARCOS DE BELEN
DINAMARCA
LONDRES
© AAA
1408-R

Downtown Mexico City

This index helps you "spot" where approved lodgings and restaurants are located on the corresponding detailed maps. Lodging daily rate range is for comparison only and show the property's high season. Restaurant rate range is a combination of lunch and/or dinner. Turn to the listing page for more detailed rate information and consult display ads for special promotions.

MEXICO CITY

Map Page	OA	Lodgings	Diamond Rated	High Season	Page
1 / p. 581		Gran Hotel Ciudad de Mexico	3 diamonds	$175-$385	592
2 / p. 581		Best Western Hotel De Cortes	2 diamonds	$105-$165	591
3 / p. 581	AAA	**Sheraton Centro Historico**	4 diamonds	$195-$300	596
4 / p. 581		Holiday Inn Zocalo	2 diamonds	$125-$150	593
5 / p. 581		Best Western-Hotel Majestic	2 diamonds	$110-$200	591
6 / p. 581	AAA	**Fiesta Americana Reforma** - see color ad on insert	3 diamonds	$132-$205	592
7 / p. 581		Suites Mi Casa	1 diamond	$75-$105	597
8 / p. 581	AAA	**Embassy Suites Hotel Mexico City - Reforma**	4 diamonds	$180-$219	592

Map Page	OA	Restaurants	Diamond Rated	Cuisine	Meal Range	Page
1 / p. 581		Los Girasoles	3 diamonds	Regional Mexican	$7-$15	599
3 / p. 581		Cafe de Tacuba	2 diamonds	Regional Mexican	$6-$20	598
4 / p. 581		Restaurante Mercaderes Cafe	3 diamonds	Steak	$7-$20	599

Highway Signs

Stop

No Passing

Horizontal Clearance

Maximum Weight (Metric Tons)

No Pedestrians

Parking Limit

One-Hour Parking

No Left Turn

No U Turn

No Parking

Keep to the Right

Inspection

No Trucks

Pedestrians Keep Left

Speed Limit (In K.P.H.)

Right Turn on Red Permitted

No Bicycles

Keep Right

Do Not Enter

Road Signs In Spanish	*Descriptions In English*
Topes, Vibradores	Speed Bumps
Un Solo Carril	One Lane
Pavimento Derrapante	Pavement Slippery
Prohibido Seguir de Frente	Do Not Enter
Vado	Dip

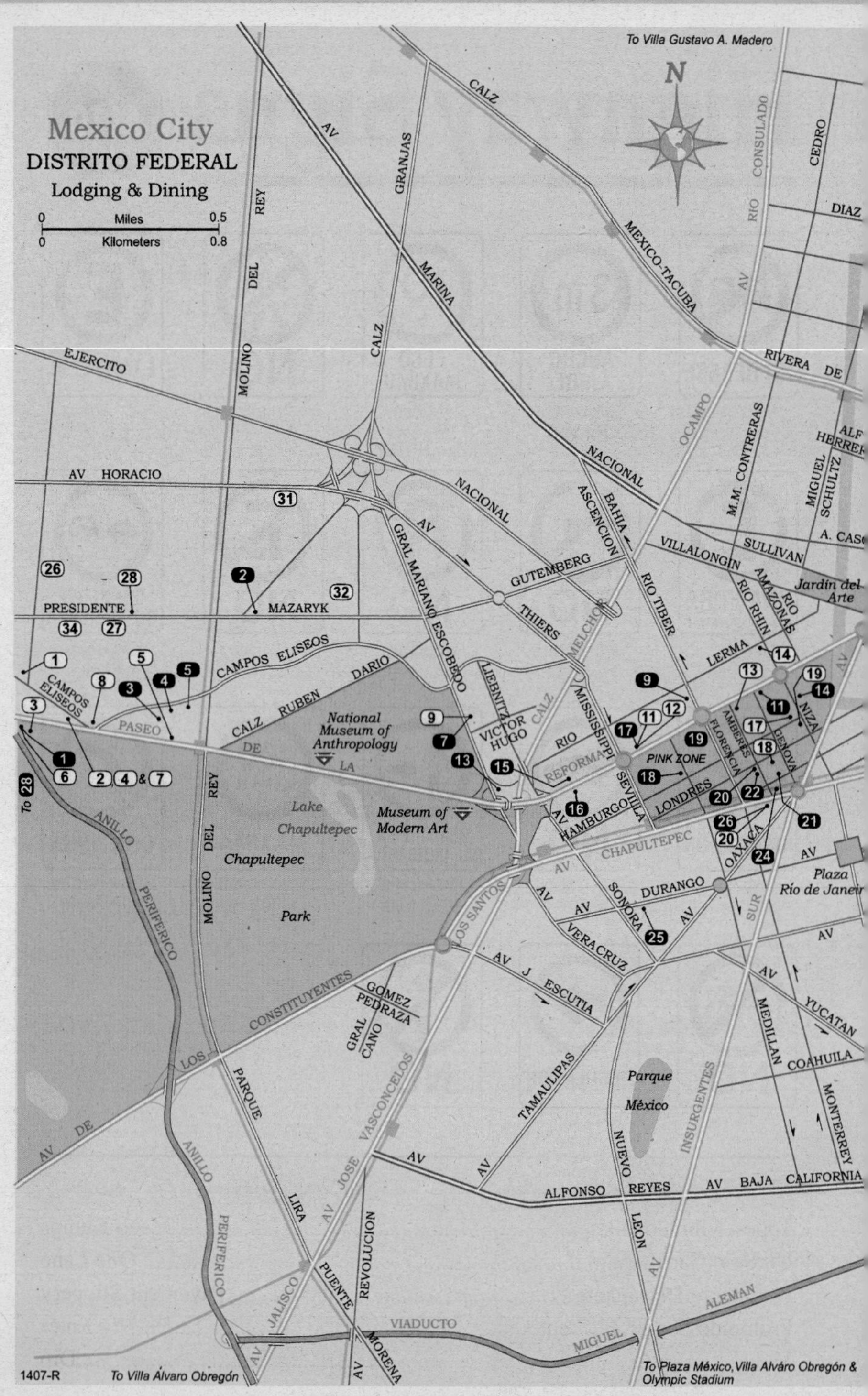
Mexico City
DISTRITO FEDERAL
Lodging & Dining
0 Miles 0.5
0 Kilometers 0.8
To Villa Gustavo A. Madero
N
National Museum of Anthropology
Lake Chapultepec
Museum of Modern Art
Chapultepec Park
PINK ZONE
Jardín del Arte
Plaza Río de Janeiro
Parque México
To 28
1407-R
To Villa Álvaro Obregón
To Plaza México, Villa Alváro Obregón & Olympic Stadium

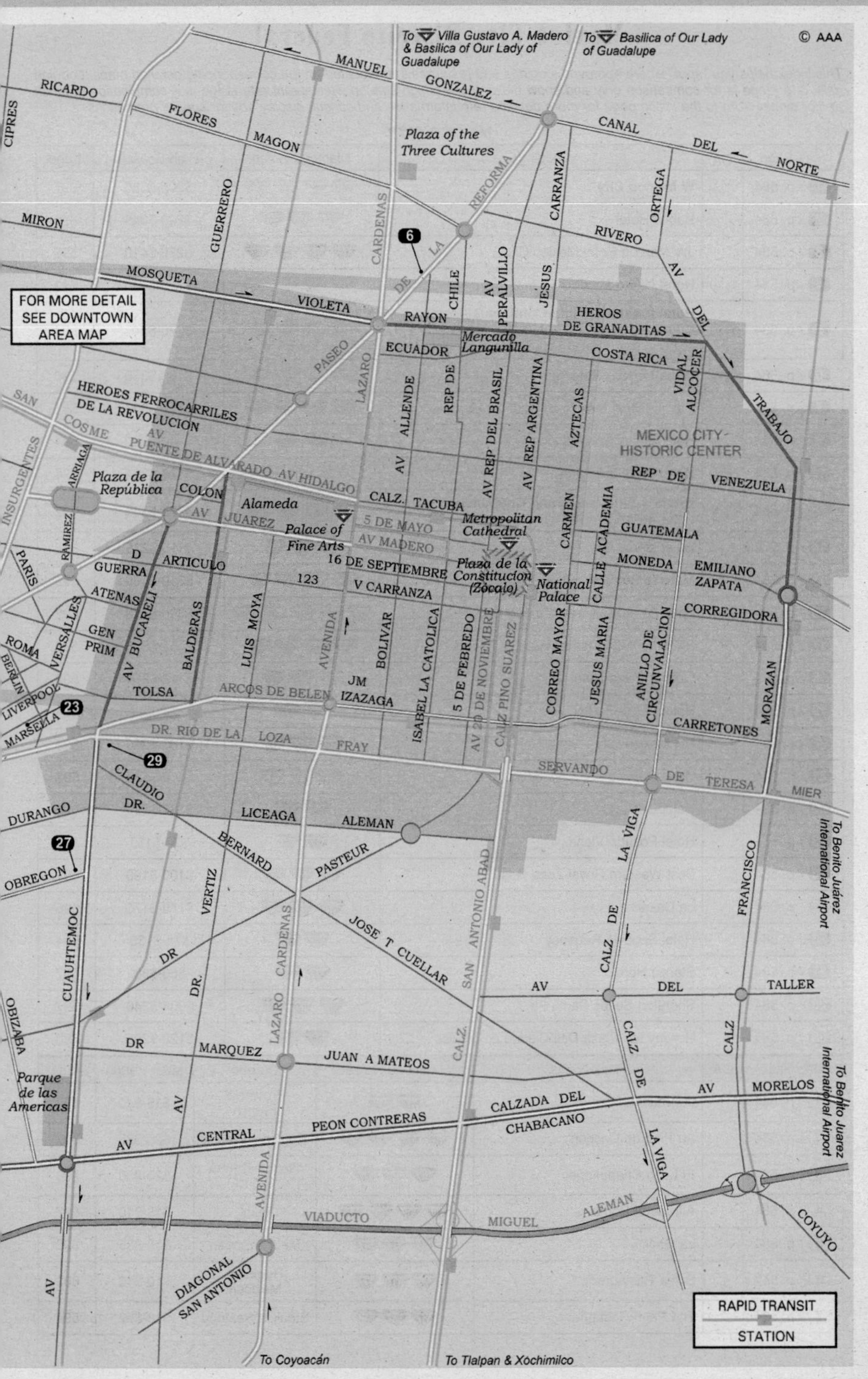

© AAA
To Villa Gustavo A. Madero & Basilica of Our Lady of Guadalupe
To Basilica of Our Lady of Guadalupe
FOR MORE DETAIL SEE DOWNTOWN AREA MAP
Plaza of the Three Cultures
Mercado Langunilla
MEXICO CITY HISTORIC CENTER
Plaza de la República
Alameda
Palace of Fine Arts
Metropolitan Cathedral
Plaza de la Constitucion (Zocalo)
National Palace
Parque de las Americas
To Benito Juárez International Airport
To Coyoacán
To Tlalpan & Xochimilco
RAPID TRANSIT STATION

Mexico City Distrito Federal

This index helps you "spot" where approved lodgings and restaurants are located on the corresponding detailed maps. Lodging daily rate range is for comparison only and show the property's high season. Restaurant rate range is a combination of lunch and/or dinner. Turn to the listing page for more detailed rate information and consult display ads for special promotions.

MEXICO CITY

Map Page	OA	Lodgings	Diamond Rated	High Season	Page
1 / p. 584	AAA	**W Mexico City**	4	$200-$535	597
2 / p. 584		Habita Hotel	3	$220-$345	593
3 / p. 584		JW Marriott Hotel Mexico City	4	$275-$410	595
4 / p. 584	AAA	**Hotel Nikko Mexico**	4	$320-$400	593
5 / p. 584	AAA	**Hotel Presidente InterContinental Mexico City** - see color ad opposite inside back cover	4	$270-$345	594
6 / p. 584	AAA	**Melia Mexico Reforma**	4	$180-$350	596
7 / p. 584		Camino Real Mexico City	4	$190-$330	591
9 / p. 584		Hotel Suites San Marino	2	$140-$220	594
11 / p. 584	AAA	**Hotel Sevilla Palace**	3	$176-$264	594
13 / p. 584	AAA	**Fiesta Americana Grand Chapultepec** - see color ad on insert	4	$275-$345	592
14 / p. 584		Hotel Marco Polo	3	$115-$275	593
15 / p. 584		Marquis Reforma Hotel	4	$310-$400	595
16 / p. 584	AAA	**Four Seasons Hotel Mexico D.F.**	5	$396-$479	592
17 / p. 584		Sheraton Maria Isabel Hotel & Towers	4	$155-$315	596
18 / p. 584		Galeria Plaza Hotel	3	$112-$214	592
19 / p. 584		Hotel Plaza Florencia	2	$200	594
20 / p. 584		NH Mexico City	3	$180-$260	596
21 / p. 584		Hotel Geneve	3	$110-$170	593
22 / p. 584		Hotel Century	2	$132-$200	593
23 / p. 584		Hotel Posada Viena	2	$70-$110	594
24 / p. 584		Best Western Royal Zona Rosa	3	$100-$190	591
25 / p. 584		La Casona	3	$140-$175	595
26 / p. 584		Hotel Segovia Regency	2	$75-$135	594
27 / p. 584		Stanza Hotel	2	$60-$88	597
28 / p. 584		Sheraton Suites Santa Fe	3	$205-$340	597
29 / p. 584		Holiday Inn Plaza Dali Ciudad de Mexico	2	$128-$205	593

Map Page	OA	Restaurants	Diamond Rated	Cuisine	Meal Range	Page
1 / p. 584		Le Bouchon	2	Provincial French	$15-$40	598
2 / p. 584		Au Pied de Cochon	4	Regional French	$25-$85	597
3 / p. 584		El Lago Chapultepec	3	Regional New World	$20-$30	598
4 / p. 584		Alfredo di Roma	4	Italian	$18-$40	597
5 / p. 584		La Griglia	3	Mediterranean	$16-$35	598
6 / p. 584		Solea Restaurant	3	Regional Mexican	$10-$15	603
7 / p. 584		The Palm Restaurant	3	Steak & Seafood	$13-$52	599

Map Page	OA	Restaurants (cont'd)	Diamond Rated	Cuisine	Meal Range	Page
8 / p. 584		Los Almendros	◆◆◆	Regional Mexican	$15-$30	599
9 / p. 584		Le Cirque	◆◆◆◆	Regional New World	$25-$50	598
11 / p. 584		Manhattan Deli	◆◆	American	$12-$30	599
12 / p. 584		Ristorante Amici	◆◆◆	Italian	$10-$25	600
13 / p. 584		Passy	◆◆	Traditional Continental	$12-$35	599
14 / p. 584		Les Moustaches	◆◆◆	French	$7-$15	598
17 / p. 584		Los Tres Soles Focolare Restaurant	◆◆	Regional Mexican	$8-$18	599
18 / p. 584		Restaurante Fonda El Refugio	◆◆	Regional Mexican	$13-$20	599
19 / p. 584		Chalet Suizo	◆◆	Continental	$12-$22	598
20 / p. 584		Restaurante Tezka	◆◆◆◆	Basque	$16-$35	600
26 / p. 584		Torre d Castilla	◆◆◆	Spanish	$9-$20	603
27 / p. 584		Bondy Restaurant y Pasteleria	◆◆	Breads/Pastries	$8-$18	598
28 / p. 584		Rincon Argentino	◆◆	Argentine	$15-$45	600
31 / p. 584		Beluz International Cuisine & Bar	◆◆◆	International	$10-$30	598
32 / p. 584	AAA	**Pujol Restaurante**	◆◆◆◆	New Mexican	$20-$30	599
34 / p. 584		Izote	◆◆◆	Mexican	$15-$25	598

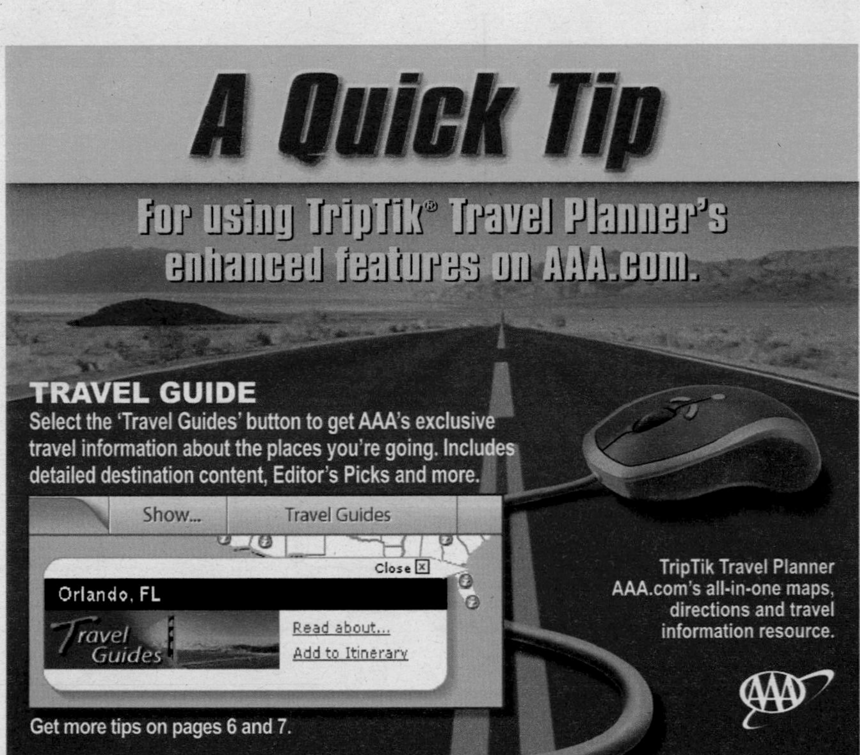
A Quick Tip
For using TripTik® Travel Planner's enhanced features on AAA.com.
TRAVEL GUIDE
Select the 'Travel Guides' button to get AAA's exclusive travel information about the places you're going. Includes detailed destination content, Editor's Picks and more.
Show...
Travel Guides
Close
Orlando, FL
Travel Guides
Read about...
Add to Itinerary
TripTik Travel Planner
AAA.com's all-in-one maps, directions and travel information resource.
AAA
Get more tips on pages 6 and 7.

1406-R
To Querétaro & Monterrey
© AAA
To Pachuca
Mexico City
& Vicinity
0
Miles
3.7
0
Kilometers
6.0
N
57D
Tepotzotlán
57
Cuautitlán
VIA LOPEZ PORTILLO
Coacalco
Tecámac
85
85D
Lechería
San Cristóbal
Ecatepec
Venta de Carpio
132D
132
Tepexpan
To San Martín de las Pirámides
QUEBRADA
Atizapán
de
Zaragoza
146
LA
CHAMAPA
Tequesquinahua
85
Ecatepec
de Morelos
VIA JOSE M MORALES
Tulpetlac
Santa Clara
85D
To Veracruz via
Tlaxcala & Jalapa
136
To Mex. 136
Santa
Cecilia
Santa Cecilia
Pyramid
San Andrés Atenco
Tlalnepantla
12
Tenayuca
Pyramid
Tepetlacalco
ANILLO
AV
Xocoyahualco
CALZ
VALLEJO
Ciudad Satélite
57
Naucalpan
16
AQUILES
SERDAN
CALZ
CAMARONES
NORTE
CALZ MISTERIOS
Basilica
Our Lady of
Guadalupe
SAN JUAN
DE ARAG
PERIFERICO
Fondo del
Lago de Texcoco
AUTOPISTA MEXICO-TEXCOCO
Texcoco
Huexotla
Ruins
Chapingo
Coatlinchán

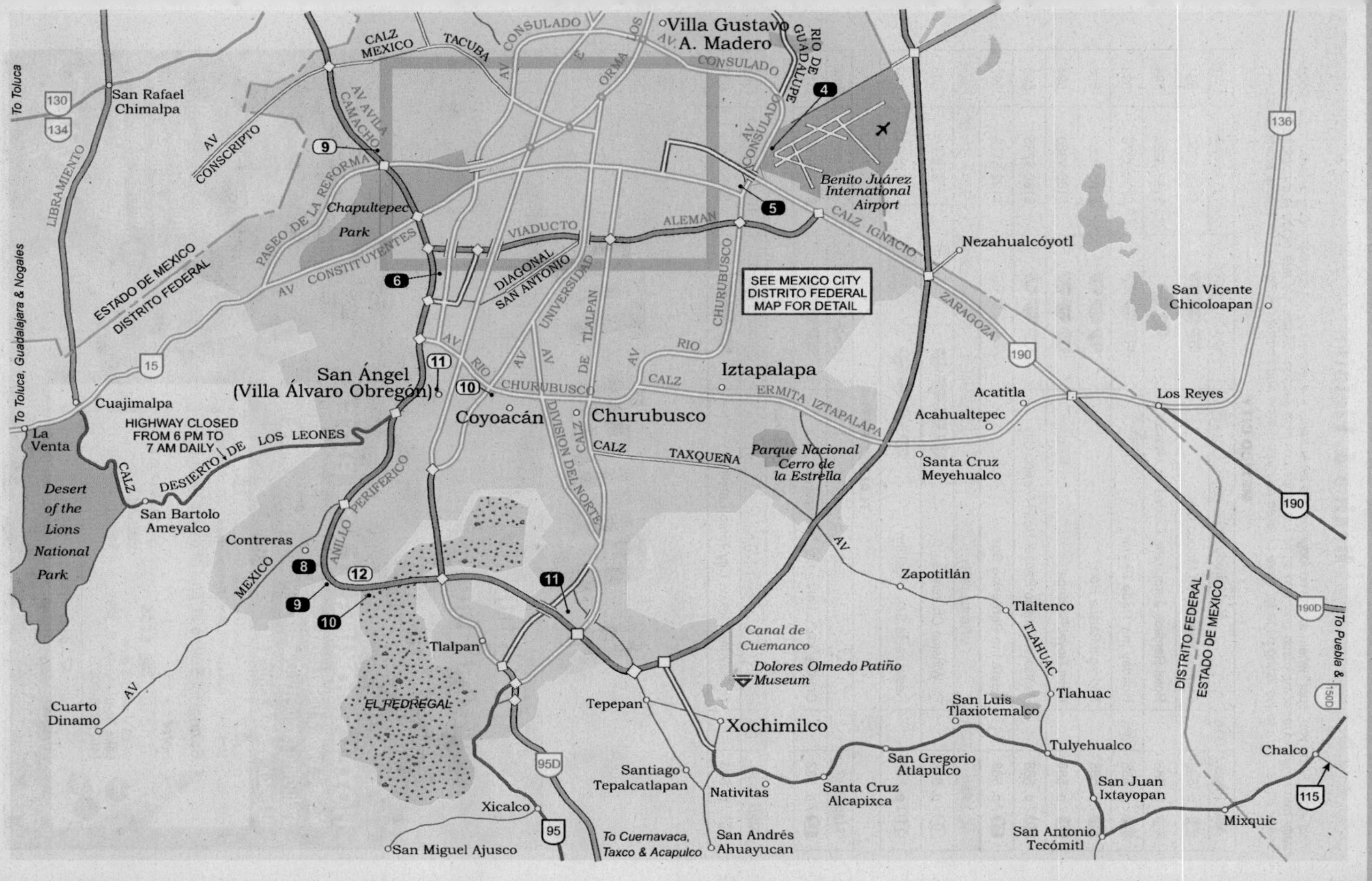
To Toluca
130
134
San Rafael Chimalpa
LIBRAMIENTO
AV CONSCRIPTO
CALZ MEXICO
TACUBA
AV CONSULADO
Villa Gustavo A. Madero
RIO DE GUADALUPE
CONSULADO
AV AVILA CAMACHO
9
4
Benito Juárez International Airport
136
PASEO DE LA REFORMA
Chapultepec Park
5
VIADUCTO
ALEMAN
CALZ IGNACIO
Nezahualcóyotl
ESTADO DE MEXICO
DISTRITO FEDERAL
AV CONSTITUYENTES
6
DIAGONAL SAN ANTONIO
AV UNIVERSIDAD
CALZ DE TLALPAN
CHURUBUSCO
SEE MEXICO CITY DISTRITO FEDERAL MAP FOR DETAIL
ZARAGOZA
San Vicente Chicoloapan
To Toluca, Guadalajara & Nogales
15
AV RIO CHURUBUSCO
190
Iztapalapa
San Ángel (Villa Álvaro Obregón)
11
10
CALZ ERMITA IZTAPALAPA
Acatitla
Los Reyes
Cuajimalpa
Coyoacán
Churubusco
Acahualtepec
La Venta
HIGHWAY CLOSED FROM 6 PM TO 7 AM DAILY
CALZ DESIERTO DE LOS LEONES
AV DIVISION DEL NORTE
CALZ TAXQUEÑA
Parque Nacional Cerro de la Estrella
Santa Cruz Meyehualco
Desert of the Lions National Park
ANILLO PERIFERICO
San Bartolo Ameyalco
Contreras
AV MEXICO
8
12
9
10
AV
Zapotitlán
Tlaltenco
TLAHUAC
Canal de Cuemanco
Dolores Olmedo Patiño Museum
Tlalpan
EL PEDREGAL
Tepepan
Xochimilco
San Luis Tlaxiotemalco
Tlahuac
DISTRITO FEDERAL
ESTADO DE MEXICO
190D
To Puebla &
150D
Cuarto Dinamo
AV
95D
Santiago Tepalcatlapan
Nativitas
San Gregorio Atlapulco
Santa Cruz Alcapixca
Tulyehualco
San Juan Ixtayopan
Chalco
115
Xicalco
95
San Miguel Ajusco
To Cuernavaca, Taxco & Acapulco
San Andrés Ahuayucan
San Antonio Tecómitl
Mixquic

Mexico & Vicinity

This index helps you "spot" where approved lodgings and restaurants are located on the corresponding detailed maps. Lodging daily rate range is for comparison only and show the property's high season. Restaurant rate range is a combination of lunch and/or dinner. Turn to the listing page for more detailed rate information and consult display ads for special promotions.

MEXICO CITY

Map Page	OA	Lodgings	Diamond Rated	High Season	Page
4 / p. 588		Camino Real Airport Mexico City	◆◆◆	$198-$330	591
5 / p. 588		Hotel Ramada Aeropuerto Ciudad de Mexico	◆◆	$132-$220	594
6 / p. 588	AAA	**Holiday Inn Trade Center**	◆◆◆	$170-$270	593
8 / p. 588		Pedregal Palace Hotel	◆◆◆	$165-$250	596
9 / p. 588		Hotel Royal Pedregal	◆◆◆	$180-$320	594
10 / p. 588		Radisson Paraiso Perisur Hotel Mexico City	◆◆◆	$160-$235	596
11 / p. 588	AAA	**Fiesta Inn Periferico Sur**	◆◆◆	$132-$175	592

Map Page	OA	Restaurants	Diamond Rated	Cuisine	Meal Range	Page
9 / p. 588		Sir Winston Churchill's	◆◆◆◆	British	$16-$54	603
11 / p. 588		Restaurante San Angel Inn	◆◆◆◆	Traditional Continental	$19-$45	600

TLALNEPANTLA

Map Page	OA	Lodging	Diamond Rated	High Season	Page
12 / p. 588		Crowne Plaza Lancaster Tlalnepantla	◆◆◆	$135-$275	610

NAUCALPAN

Map Page	OA	Lodging	Diamond Rated	High Season	Page
16 / p. 588		Holiday Inn Mexico City Toreo-Satelite	◆◆◆	$95-$140	609

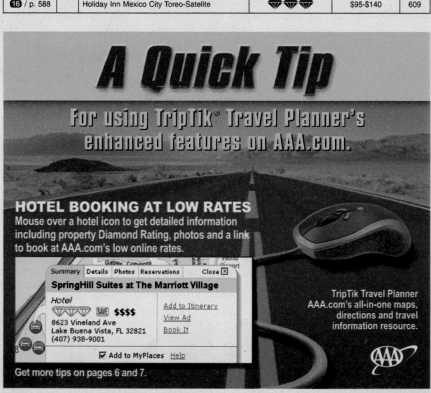

MEXICO CITY, DISTRITO FEDERAL pop. 8,605,239 (See maps and indexes p. 581-582, 584-586, 588-590)

WHERE TO STAY

BEST WESTERN HOTEL DE CORTES — Phone: (55)5518-2182 — 2

Historic Hotel
$105-$165 All Year

Address: Ave Hidalgo 85, Col Centro **Location:** Across from Alameda Park; in historic downtown. **Facility:** Authentic 18th-century guest house with beautiful patio featuring rooms with fans, windows that open and disposable slippers. 29 units. 20 one-bedroom standard units. 2 one- and 7 two-bedroom suites. 2 stories (no elevator), exterior corridors. *Bath:* combo or shower only. **Parking:** on-site. **Terms:** 3 day cancellation notice. **Amenities:** safes, hair dryers. *Some:* high-speed Internet. **Guest Services:** valet laundry, wireless Internet. **Business Services:** meeting rooms, fax (fee). **Cards:** AX, DC, MC, VI.

/ SOME UNITS

AAA Benefit:
Members save up to 20%, plus 10% bonus points with rewards program.

BEST WESTERN-HOTEL MAJESTIC *Book great rates at AAA.com* — Phone: (55)5521-8600 — 5

Historic Hotel
$110-$200 All Year

Address: Madero 73 Col Centro **Location:** In heart of Old Mexico City. Located adjacent to the Zocalo. **Facility:** Colonial-style hotel. Old World atmosphere. Public areas decorated with hand-painted ceramic tiles from the 1700s. Teeming with Mexican diversity. 85 one-bedroom standard units. 7 stories, interior corridors. **Parking:** no self-parking. **Terms:** cancellation fee imposed. **Amenities:** high-speed Internet, safes. *Some:* hair dryers. **Guest Services:** valet laundry, wireless Internet. **Business Services:** meeting rooms, business center. **Cards:** AX, MC, VI.

AAA Benefit:
Members save up to 20%, plus 10% bonus points with rewards program.

BEST WESTERN ROYAL ZONA ROSA *Book great rates at AAA.com* — Phone: (55)9149-3000

Hotel
$100-$190 All Year

Address: Amberes No. 78 **Location:** In Pink Zone; jct Ave Chapultepec and Liverpool St. **Facility:** 162 units. 161 one-bedroom standard units. 1 one-bedroom suite with whirlpool. 20 stories, interior corridors. *Bath:* combo or shower only. **Parking:** valet. **Amenities:** video games (fee), high-speed Internet, safes, honor bars, hair dryers. **Dining:** Restaurante Tezka, see separate listing. **Pool(s):** heated outdoor. **Leisure Activities:** sauna, steamroom, exercise room. *Fee:* massage. **Guest Services:** valet laundry, wireless Internet. **Business Services:** meeting rooms, business center. **Cards:** AX, DC, MC, VI.

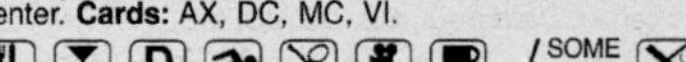

AAA Benefit:
Members save up to 20%, plus 10% bonus points with rewards program.

CAMINO REAL AIRPORT MEXICO CITY *Book at AAA.com* — Phone: (55)3003-0033 — 4

Hotel
$198-$330 All Year

Address: Puerto Mexico 80, Col Penon de los Banos **Location:** Adjacent to airport; connected via skywalk in front of Terminal B. **Facility:** Meets AAA guest room security requirements. 600 units. 599 one-bedroom standard units. 1 one-bedroom suite. 8-9 stories, interior corridors. **Parking:** on-site (fee) and valet. **Amenities:** high-speed Internet (fee), voice mail, safes, honor bars, irons, hair dryers. **Pool(s):** heated indoor. **Leisure Activities:** steamroom. *Fee:* massage. **Guest Services:** valet laundry, beauty salon, wireless Internet. **Business Services:** conference facilities, business center. **Cards:** AX, DC, MC, VI.

24 CALL S D / SOME UNITS

CAMINO REAL MEXICO CITY *Book at AAA.com* — Phone: (55)5263-8881 — 7

Classic Historic Hotel
$190-$330 All Year

Address: Mariano Escobedo 700 **Location:** Between Victor Hugo and Kent, just n of Diana Cir; Periferico, exit Ave Presidente Masaryk, then w. **Facility:** Distinguished atmosphere. Expansive public areas. Very large rooms and bathrooms. Multi-lingual staff. 712 units. 667 one-bedroom standard units. 36 one- and 9 two-bedroom suites, some with kitchens (utensils extra charge) and/or whirlpools. 5 stories, interior corridors. *Bath:* some combo or shower only. **Parking:** on-site (fee) and valet. **Terms:** cancellation fee imposed. **Amenities:** voice mail, safes, honor bars, irons, hair dryers. *Fee:* video games, high-speed Internet. *Some:* CD players, dual phone lines. **Dining:** Le Cirque, see separate listing. **Pool(s):** heated outdoor. **Leisure Activities:** *Fee:* massage. **Guest Services:** valet laundry, area transportation (fee), wireless Internet. **Business Services:** conference facilities, business center. **Cards:** AX, CB, DC, MC, VI.

FEE 24 D / SOME UNITS

(See maps and indexes p. 581-582, 584-586, 588-590)

EMBASSY SUITES HOTEL MEXICO CITY - REFORMA *Book great rates at AAA.com* **Phone:** (55)5061-3000 8

Hotel
$180-$219 All Year

Address: Paseo de la Reforma #69, Col Tabacalera **Location:** On Paseo de la Reforma at the Monumento Colon. **Facility:** Located on a bustling and attractive boulevard; rooms are modern and contemporary with a spacious seating area. Meets AAA guest room security requirements. 160 one-bedroom suites. 19 stories, interior corridors. **Parking:** valet. **Amenities:** dual phone lines, voice mail, safes, honor bars, irons, hair dryers. *Fee:* video games, high-speed Internet. **Pool(s):** heated indoor. **Leisure Activities:** whirlpool, exercise room. **Guest Services:** valet and coin laundry, wireless Internet. **Business Services:** meeting rooms, business center. **Cards:** AX, CB, DC, DS, JC, MC, VI.

FEE CALL S D / SOME UNITS

FIESTA AMERICANA GRAND CHAPULTEPEC **Phone:** (55)2581-1500 13

Hotel
$275-$345 All Year

Address: Mariano Escobedo 756 Col Anzures **Location:** On Mariano Escobedo, jct Paseo de la Reforma. **Facility:** Overlooking famed Chapultepec Park, these contemporary guest rooms feature jewel-tone color schemes; 14 corner rooms offer sweeping views of the park. 203 units. 189 one-bedroom standard units. 14 one-bedroom suites, some with efficiencies. 20 stories, interior corridors. **Parking:** on-site (fee). **Amenities:** CD players, dual phone lines, voice mail, safes, honor bars, irons, hair dryers. *Fee:* video games, high-speed Internet. **Leisure Activities:** whirlpool, spa. **Guest Services:** valet laundry, wireless Internet. *Fee:* airport transportation-Benito Juarez International Airport, area transportation. **Business Services:** meeting rooms, business center. **Cards:** AX, MC, VI. *(See color ad on insert)*

FEE / SOME UNITS

FIESTA AMERICANA REFORMA *Book great rates at AAA.com* **Phone:** (55)5140-4100 6

Hotel
$132-$205 All Year

Address: Paseo de la Reforma 80 **Location:** Southwest quarter of Glorieta Cristobal Colon. **Facility:** 616 units. 594 one-bedroom standard units. 22 one-bedroom suites. 25 stories, interior corridors. **Parking:** on-site. **Amenities:** video games, high-speed Internet (fee), dual phone lines, voice mail, safes, honor bars, irons, hair dryers. **Dining:** 2 restaurants, nightclub, entertainment. **Leisure Activities:** sauna, steamroom, exercise room. *Fee:* massage. **Guest Services:** valet laundry, wireless Internet. *Fee:* airport transportation-Benito Juarez International Airport, area transportation. **Business Services:** conference facilities, business center. **Cards:** AX, DC, DS, MC, VI. *(See color ad on insert)*

FEE D / SOME UNITS

FIESTA INN PERIFERICO SUR **Phone:** (55)5096-9300 11

Hotel
$132-$175 All Year

Location: On Periferico Sur, just s of Tlalpan Ave. Periferico Sur 5530 Col Pedregal de Carrasco. **Facility:** 212 one-bedroom standard units. 12 stories, interior corridors. **Parking:** on-site and valet. **Amenities:** video games (fee), high-speed Internet, voice mail, hair dryers. **Pool(s):** heated indoor. **Leisure Activities:** whirlpool, exercise room. **Guest Services:** valet laundry, wireless Internet. *Fee:* airport transportation-Benito Juarez International Airport, area transportation. **Business Services:** meeting rooms, business center. **Cards:** AX, CB, DC, JC, MC, VI. *(See color ad on insert)*

FEE S D / SOME UNITS

FOUR SEASONS HOTEL MEXICO D.F. *Book great rates at AAA.com* **Phone:** (55)5230-1818 16

Hotel
$396-$479 All Year

Address: Paseo de la Reforma 500 **Location:** On Paseo de la Reforma. Located adjacent to Chapultepec Park. **Facility:** Elegant and refined public areas. Spacious, tastefully appointed units. Most units overlook beautifully landscaped courtyard. Meets AAA guest room security requirements. 240 units. 200 one-bedroom standard units. 40 one-bedroom suites. 8 stories, interior corridors. **Parking:** valet. **Terms:** cancellation fee imposed. **Amenities:** video library, DVD players, CD players, dual phone lines, voice mail, safes, honor bars, irons, hair dryers. *Fee:* video games, high-speed Internet. *Some:* fax. **Dining:** Reforma 500, see separate listing, entertainment. **Pool(s):** heated outdoor. **Leisure Activities:** saunas, whirlpool. *Fee:* massage. **Guest Services:** valet laundry, wireless Internet. *Fee:* airport transportation-Benito Juarez International Airport, area transportation-within city limits. **Business Services:** conference facilities, business center. **Cards:** AX, CB, DC, DS, JC, MC, VI.

FEE S D / SOME UNITS

GALERIA PLAZA HOTEL **Phone:** (55)5230-1717 18

Hotel
$112-$214 All Year

Address: Hamburgo #195 Col Juarez **Location:** In Pink Zone. **Facility:** 434 units. 415 one-bedroom standard units. 19 one-bedroom suites. 12 stories, interior corridors. **Parking:** on-site (fee) and valet. **Amenities:** high-speed Internet, dual phone lines, voice mail, safes, honor bars, irons, hair dryers. **Pool(s):** heated outdoor. **Leisure Activities:** exercise room. **Guest Services:** valet laundry, area transportation (fee), wireless Internet. **Business Services:** meeting rooms, business center. **Cards:** AX, DC, MC, VI.

S D / SOME UNITS

GRAN HOTEL CIUDAD DE MEXICO *Book at AAA.com* **Phone:** (55)1083-7700 1

Classic Historic Hotel
$175-$385 All Year

Address: 16 de Septiembre No 82 **Location:** Just w of the Zocalo; in historic center. **Facility:** Recently renovated, this historic landmark features a spectacular 1908 Tiffany stained glass atrium ceiling in the lobby. Smoke free premises. 60 one-bedroom standard units. 4 stories, interior corridors. **Parking:** on-site (fee). **Amenities:** high-speed Internet, safes, honor bars, irons, hair dryers. **Leisure Activities:** exercise room. **Guest Services:** valet laundry, wireless Internet. **Business Services:** conference facilities, business center. **Cards:** AX, MC, VI.

D

(See maps and indexes p. 581-582, 584-586, 588-590)

HABITA HOTEL Book at AAA.com Phone: (55)5282-3100 2

Hotel
$220-$345 All Year

Address: Ave Presidente Masaryk 201 **Location:** Jct La Martine; in Polanco Zone. **Facility:** 36 one-bedroom standard units. 6 stories, interior corridors. *Bath:* combo or shower only. **Parking:** valet. **Amenities:** video library (fee), DVD players, high-speed Internet, voice mail, safes, honor bars, irons, hair dryers. **Leisure Activities:** sauna, whirlpool, exercise room. *Fee:* massage. **Guest Services:** valet laundry, area transportation (fee), wireless Internet. **Business Services:** meeting rooms, business center. **Cards:** AX, MC, VI.

FEE / SOME UNITS

HOLIDAY INN PLAZA DALI CIUDAD DE MEXICO Phone: (55)5036-0990 29

Hotel
$128-$205 All Year

Address: Viaducto Rio de la Piedad, Col Magdalena Mix **Location:** On Viaducto Rio de la Piedad, 0.4 mi (0.8 km) n of Congreso de la Union Ave. **Facility:** Smoke free premises. 150 units. 140 one-bedroom standard units. 10 one-bedroom suites, some with whirlpools. 6 stories, interior corridors. *Bath:* combo or shower only. **Parking:** on-site. **Terms:** 3 day cancellation notice-fee imposed. **Amenities:** high-speed Internet, safes, honor bars, irons, hair dryers. **Leisure Activities:** sauna, whirlpool, exercise room. **Guest Services:** valet laundry, area transportation (fee), wireless Internet. **Business Services:** meeting rooms, business center. **Cards:** AX, JC, MC, VI.

D

HOLIDAY INN TRADE CENTER Book great rates at AAA.com Phone: (55)5278-9950 6

AAA
Hotel
$170-$270 All Year

Address: Ave Revolucion 583 **Location:** Colonia San Pedro de los Pinos; Ave Revolucion S at Calle 23. **Facility:** 188 units. 180 one-bedroom standard units. 8 one-bedroom suites. 7 stories, interior corridors. **Parking:** on-site (fee). **Terms:** 7 day cancellation notice. **Amenities:** high-speed Internet, dual phone lines, voice mail, safes, honor bars, irons, hair dryers. **Dining:** entertainment. **Leisure Activities:** exercise room, spa. **Guest Services:** valet and coin laundry, airport transportation-Benito Juarez International Airport, wireless Internet. **Business Services:** conference facilities, business center. **Cards:** AX, MC, VI.

D / SOME UNITS

HOLIDAY INN ZOCALO Phone: (55)5521-2121 4

Hotel
$125-$150 All Year

Address: Cinco de Mayo y Zocalo Centro Historica **Location:** Just w of Zocalo. **Facility:** 118 units. 108 one-bedroom standard units. 10 one-bedroom suites, some with whirlpools. 7 stories, interior corridors. *Bath:* shower only. **Parking:** on-site (fee) and valet. **Amenities:** high-speed Internet, voice mail, safes, irons, hair dryers. **Leisure Activities:** exercise room. *Fee:* massage. **Guest Services:** valet laundry, area transportation (fee), wireless Internet. **Business Services:** meeting rooms, business center. **Cards:** AX, MC, VI.

FEE D / SOME UNITS

HOTEL CENTURY Phone: (55)5726-9911 22

Hotel
$132-$200 All Year

Address: Liverpool St 152 **Location:** In Pink Zone. **Facility:** 140 one-bedroom standard units. 21 stories, interior corridors. **Parking:** on-site and valet. **Terms:** cancellation fee imposed. **Amenities:** video games (fee), safes, honor bars. *Some:* hair dryers. **Pool(s):** heated outdoor. **Leisure Activities:** exercise room. **Guest Services:** valet laundry. **Business Services:** meeting rooms, PC (fee). **Cards:** AX, DC, MC, VI.

/ SOME UNITS

HOTEL GENEVE Book at AAA.com Phone: (55)5080-0800 21

Historic Hotel
$110-$170 All Year

Address: Londres 130 **Location:** In Pink Zone; 0.3 mi (0.5 km) s of Paseo de la Reforma. **Facility:** This 100 year-old property, featuring hand-carved antiques and original artwork, offers a refined, Old World atmosphere in the heart of the Zona Rosa. Meets AAA guest room security requirements. 270 one-bedroom standard units. 5 stories, interior corridors. **Parking:** on-site (fee). **Terms:** cancellation fee imposed. **Amenities:** high-speed Internet (fee), voice mail, safes, honor bars, irons, hair dryers. **Leisure Activities:** saunas, steamrooms, exercise room. *Fee:* massage. **Guest Services:** valet laundry, area transportation (fee), tanning facilities, wireless Internet. **Business Services:** meeting rooms, business center. **Cards:** AX, DC, MC, VI.

FEE D / SOME UNITS

HOTEL MARCO POLO Phone: (55)5080-0063 14

Hotel
$115-$275 All Year

Address: Amberes 27 **Location:** In Pink Zone; 4 blks s of Paseo de la Reforma. **Facility:** Meets AAA guest room security requirements. 77 units. 63 one-bedroom standard units with efficiencies. 14 one-bedroom suites with kitchens, some with whirlpools. 12 stories, interior corridors. **Parking:** on-site (fee) and valet. **Amenities:** high-speed Internet, safes, honor bars, hair dryers. *Some:* fax. **Leisure Activities:** exercise room. **Guest Services:** valet laundry, wireless Internet. **Business Services:** meeting rooms, business center. **Cards:** AX, DC, MC, VI.

D / SOME UNITS VCR

HOTEL NIKKO MEXICO Book great rates at AAA.com Phone: (55)5283-8700 4

AAA
Hotel
$320-$400 All Year

Address: Campos Eliseos 204 Col Polanco **Location:** In Polanco Zone; jct Campos Eliseos and Andres Bello St; 1 blk from National Museum of Anthropology. **Facility:** A rotating art exhibit occupies the lobby of this Mexico City high-rise, which provides a full array of business and tourism facilities. 752 one-bedroom standard units, some with kitchens. 38 stories, interior corridors. **Parking:** on-site and valet. **Amenities:** dual phone lines, voice mail, safes, honor bars, irons, hair dryers. *Fee:* video games, high-speed Internet. *Some:* DVD players, CD players. **Dining:** 4 restaurants, entertainment. **Pool(s):** heated indoor. **Leisure Activities:** saunas, steamrooms, putting green, 3 lighted tennis courts, spa. *Fee:* rooftop golf driving range. **Guest Services:** valet laundry, wireless Internet. **Business Services:** conference facilities, business center. **Cards:** AX, CB, DC, JC, MC, VI.

S D / SOME UNITS VCR

(See maps and indexes p. 581-582, 584-586, 588-590)

HOTEL PLAZA FLORENCIA

Phone: 55/5242-4700 19

Hotel
$200 All Year

Address: Florencia St 61 **Location:** In Pink Zone; just s of Paseo de la Reforma. **Facility:** Meets AAA guest room security requirements. Smoke free premises. 142 units. 106 one-bedroom standard units. 36 one-bedroom suites. 13 stories, interior corridors. *Bath:* combo or shower only. **Parking:** on-site (fee) and valet. **Terms:** 7 day cancellation notice. **Amenities:** voice mail, honor bars, hair dryers. *Some:* high-speed Internet. **Leisure Activities:** exercise room. **Guest Services:** valet laundry, wireless Internet. **Business Services:** meeting rooms, business center. **Cards:** AX, MC, VI.

/ SOME UNITS

HOTEL POSADA VIENA

Phone: (55)5566-0700 23

Hotel
$70-$110 All Year

Address: Marsella No. 28 **Location:** Just off Dinamarca. Located in a quiet area. **Facility:** 88 units. 71 one-bedroom standard units. 11 one- and 6 two-bedroom suites. 4-5 stories, interior corridors. *Bath:* shower only. **Parking:** on-site. **Terms:** 3 day cancellation notice. **Amenities:** voice mail. **Guest Services:** valet laundry, wireless Internet. **Business Services:** meeting rooms, business center. **Cards:** AX, MC, VI.

/ SOME UNITS

HOTEL PRESIDENTE INTERCONTINENTAL MEXICO CITY *Book great rates at AAA.com*

Phone: (55)5327-7700 5

Hotel
$270-$345 All Year

Address: Campo Eliseos 218 Col Pol **Location:** In Polanco Zone; on Paseo de la Reforma, 0.8 mi (1.3 km) w of Periferico; opposite Chapultepec Park and the National Auditorium. **Facility:** Welcoming such visiting heads of state as President Clinton, the modern hotel across from Chapultepec Park offers impressive views from most rooms. Meets AAA guest room security requirements. 662 units. 605 one-bedroom standard units. 55 one- and 2 two-bedroom suites, some with kitchens (utensils extra charge). 42 stories, interior corridors. **Parking:** on-site (fee) and valet. **Terms:** cancellation fee imposed. **Amenities:** voice mail, honor bars, irons, hair dryers. *Fee:* video games, high-speed Internet. *Some:* DVD players, CD players, fax. **Dining:** 4 restaurants, also, Alfredo di Roma, Au Pied de Cochon, The Palm Restaurant, see separate listings, entertainment. **Leisure Activities:** exercise room. *Fee:* massage. **Guest Services:** valet laundry, wireless Internet. *Fee:* airport transportation-Benito Juarez International Airport, area transportation. **Business Services:** conference facilities, business center. **Cards:** AX, DC, JC, MC, VI. *(See color ad opposite inside back cover)*

FEE / SOME UNITS

HOTEL RAMADA AEROPUERTO CIUDAD DE MEXICO *Book at AAA.com*

Phone: (55)5785-5200 5

Hotel
$132-$220 All Year

Address: Blvd Puerto Aereo 390 **Location:** Opposite international airport. **Facility:** 100 units. 91 one-bedroom standard units. 9 one-bedroom suites with whirlpools. 4 stories, interior corridors. **Parking:** valet. **Amenities:** high-speed Internet, irons, hair dryers. **Leisure Activities:** sauna, whirlpool, exercise room. **Guest Services:** valet laundry, wireless Internet. **Business Services:** meeting rooms, fax (fee). **Cards:** AX, CB, DC, DS, MC, VI.

/ SOME UNITS

HOTEL ROYAL PEDREGAL *Book at AAA.com*

Phone: (55)5449-4000 9

Hotel
$180-$320 All Year

Address: Periferico Sur 4363 **Location:** Adjacent to main Periferico; in southern part of city; 0.3 mi (0.5 km) n from Perisur Mall. Located near Six Flags and hospitals. **Facility:** 314 units. 313 one-bedroom standard units, some with whirlpools. 1 two-bedroom suite with whirlpool. 5 stories, interior corridors. *Bath:* combo or shower only. **Parking:** valet. **Terms:** cancellation fee imposed. **Amenities:** video games (fee), voice mail, safes, honor bars, irons, hair dryers. **Pool(s):** heated outdoor, heated indoor. **Leisure Activities:** sauna, whirlpool, spa. **Guest Services:** valet laundry, area transportation, beauty salon, wireless Internet. **Business Services:** conference facilities, business center. **Cards:** AX, DC, MC, VI.

FEE / SOME UNITS

HOTEL SEGOVIA REGENCY

Phone: 55/5208-8454 26

Hotel
$75-$135 All Year

Address: Ave Chapultepec 328 **Location:** Jct aves Monterrey and Oaxaca; adjacent to Pink Zone. **Facility:** 120 one-bedroom standard units. 7 stories, interior corridors. *Bath:* shower only. **Parking:** on-site. **Amenities:** safes, hair dryers. **Guest Services:** valet laundry. **Business Services:** meeting rooms, fax (fee). **Cards:** AX, DC, MC, VI.

HOTEL SEVILLA PALACE

Phone: (55)5705-2800 11

Hotel
$176-$264 All Year

Address: Paseo de la Reforma 105 **Location:** Southwest quarter of Glorieta Cristobal Colon; center. **Facility:** Meets AAA guest room security requirements. Smoke free premises. 413 one-bedroom standard units, some with whirlpools. 23 stories, interior corridors. *Bath:* combo or shower only. **Parking:** valet. **Terms:** cancellation fee imposed. **Amenities:** voice mail, safes, honor bars, irons, hair dryers. **Dining:** 2 restaurants, nightclub, entertainment. **Pool(s):** heated indoor. **Leisure Activities:** whirlpool, steamroom, exercise room. *Fee:* massage. **Guest Services:** valet laundry, beauty salon, wireless Internet. **Business Services:** conference facilities, business center. **Cards:** AX, MC, VI.

HOTEL SUITES SAN MARINO

Phone: 55/5525-4886 9

Hotel
$140-$220 All Year

Address: Tiber 107 **Location:** Just n of Paseo de la Reforma; in Pink Zone. **Facility:** 75 units. 73 one-bedroom standard units with efficiencies. 1 one- and 1 two-bedroom suites with kitchens. 12 stories, interior corridors. *Bath:* combo or shower only. **Parking:** valet. **Amenities:** high-speed Internet, safes, irons, hair dryers. **Leisure Activities:** sauna, exercise room. **Guest Services:** valet laundry, area transportation (fee), wireless Internet. **Business Services:** meeting rooms, business center. **Cards:** AX, DC, MC, VI.

FEE / SOME UNITS

(See maps and indexes p. 581-582, 584-586, 588-590)

JW MARRIOTT HOTEL MEXICO CITY *Book great rates at AAA.com* **Phone:** (55)5999-0000 3

Hotel
$275-$410 All Year

Address: Andres Bello #29 **Location:** On Paseo de la Reforma; opposite Chapultepec Park and National Auditorium. **Facility:** This hotel has a large entrance with 3 huge columns, handsomely appointed public areas and a state-of-the-art spa. Smoke free premises. 312 units. 299 one-bedroom standard units. 10 one- and 3 two-bedroom suites, some with whirlpools. 26 stories, interior corridors. *Bath:* combo or shower only. **Parking:** on-site (fee) and valet. **Terms:** cancellation fee imposed. **Amenities:** dual phone lines, voice mail, safes, honor bars, irons, hair dryers. *Fee:* video games, high-speed Internet. *Some:* CD players, fax. **Dining:** La Griglia, see separate listing. **Pool(s):** heated outdoor. **Leisure Activities:** saunas, whirlpool, steamrooms, spa. **Guest Services:** valet laundry, area transportation (fee), wireless Internet. **Business Services:** conference facilities, business center. **Cards:** AX, CB, DC, DS, JC, MC, VI.

FEE

JW MARRIOTT.
HOTELS & RESORTS
AAA Benefit:
A deluxe level of comfort and a Member rate.

LA CASONA *Book at AAA.com* **Phone:** (55)5286-3001 25

Country Inn
$140-$175 All Year

Address: Durango 280 Colonia Roma **Location:** Corner of Durango and Cozumel. **Facility:** This is a large, almost mansionlike, older house with large rooms, period furnishings and plenty of artwork set in a quiet, older residential area. 29 one-bedroom standard units, some with whirlpools. 2 stories (no elevator), interior corridors. *Bath:* combo or shower only. **Parking:** on-site (fee) and valet. **Terms:** 3 day cancellation notice-fee imposed. **Amenities:** safes, hair dryers. **Leisure Activities:** steamroom, exercise room. **Guest Services:** valet laundry, wireless Internet. **Business Services:** meeting rooms, PC. **Cards:** AX, DC, MC, VI.

/SOME UNITS

MARQUIS REFORMA HOTEL *Book at AAA.com* **Phone:** (55)5229-1200 15

Hotel
$310-$400 All Year

Address: Paseo de la Reforma 465 **Location:** 0.5 mi (0.8 km) sw of jct Insurgentes; opposite Chapultepec Park. **Facility:** Dramatic exterior of pink granite and blue glass. Expensive furnishings in public areas. Well-appointed rooms. Meets AAA guest room security requirements. 209 units. 123 one-bedroom standard units. 86 one-bedroom suites, some with whirlpools. 11 stories, interior corridors. **Parking:** valet. **Amenities:** dual phone lines, voice mail, fax, safes, honor bars, hair dryers. *Fee:* video games, high-speed Internet. *Some:* DVD players, CD players. **Pool(s):** heated indoor. **Leisure Activities:** saunas, whirlpools, exercise room, spa. **Guest Services:** valet laundry, wireless Internet. **Business Services:** conference facilities, business center. **Cards:** AX, DC, MC, VI.

/SOME UNITS

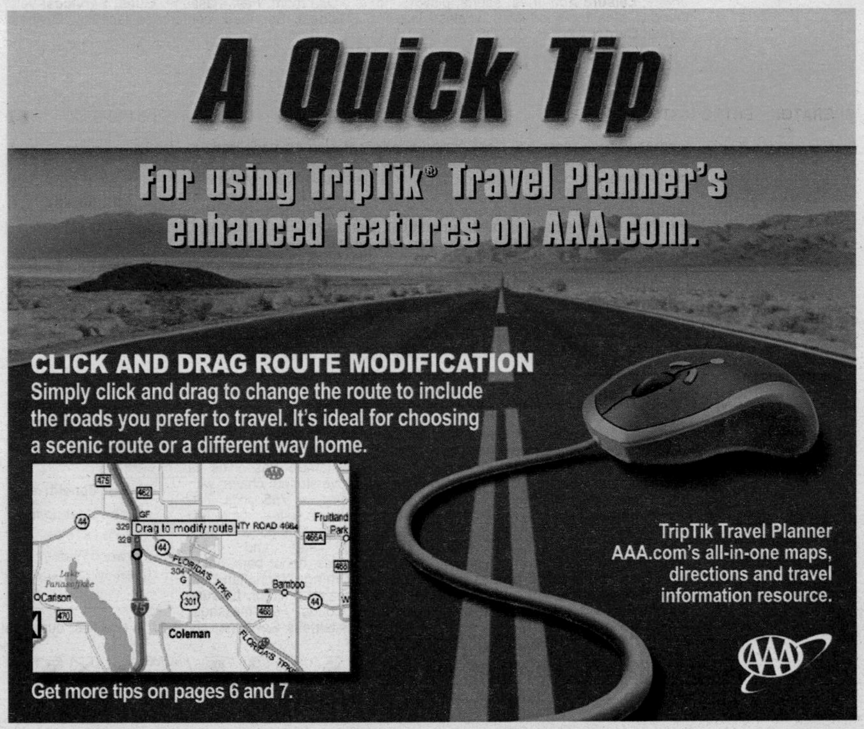

(See maps and indexes p. 581-582, 584-586, 588-590)

MELIA MEXICO REFORMA — **Phone:** (55)5063-1000 — 6

Hotel
$180-$350 All Year

Address: Paseo de la Reforma #1 **Location:** Jct Ave de la Republica. **Facility:** Located in the heart of the financial district, the hotel meets the needs of the guests expecting well-appointed rooms and refined service. Meets AAA guest room security requirements. 489 units. 457 one-bedroom standard units. 32 one-bedroom suites, some with whirlpools. 20 stories, interior corridors. **Parking:** valet. **Dining:** 3 restaurants, entertainment. **Pool(s):** heated indoor. **Leisure Activities:** saunas, whirlpools, steamrooms, exercise room, spa. *Fee:* performance theater. **Guest Services:** valet laundry, beauty salon, wireless Internet. *Fee:* airport transportation-Benito Juarez International Airport, area transportation. **Business Services:** conference facilities, business center. **Cards:** AX, MC, VI.

FEE / SOME UNITS FEE

NH MEXICO CITY — *Book at AAA.com* — **Phone:** (55)5228-9928 — 20

Hotel
$180-$260 All Year

Address: Liverpool St 155, Zona Rosa **Location:** In Pink Zone. **Facility:** 302 units. 292 one-bedroom standard units. 9 one- and 1 two-bedroom suites, some with kitchens (utensils extra charge) and/or whirlpools. 17 stories, interior corridors. **Parking:** on-site (fee). **Terms:** cancellation fee imposed. **Amenities:** dual phone lines, voice mail, safes, honor bars. **Pool(s):** heated outdoor. **Leisure Activities:** exercise room. **Guest Services:** valet laundry, wireless Internet. **Business Services:** conference facilities, business center. **Cards:** AX, DC, DS, MC, VI.

/ SOME UNITS

PEDREGAL PALACE HOTEL — **Phone:** 55/5681-6855 — 8

Hotel
$165-$250 All Year

Address: 3487 Periferico Sur **Location:** Just off Periferico Sur, exit Luis Cabrera. **Facility:** Meets AAA guest room security requirements. 64 units. 57 one-bedroom standard units. 7 one-bedroom suites, some with whirlpools. 7 stories, interior corridors. *Bath:* shower only. **Parking:** on-site and valet. **Amenities:** voice mail, safes, honor bars, hair dryers. *Some:* high-speed Internet, irons. **Leisure Activities:** whirlpool, steamroom, exercise room. **Guest Services:** valet laundry, wireless Internet. **Business Services:** meeting rooms, business center. **Cards:** AX, DC, MC, VI.

/ SOME UNITS

RADISSON PARAISO PERISUR HOTEL MEXICO CITY — *Book at AAA.com* — **Phone:** (55)5927-5959 — 10

Hotel
$160-$235 All Year

Address: Cuspide 53 Parques del Pedregal **Location:** Adjacent to main Periferico in southern part of city. Located across from Perisur Mall. **Facility:** Meets AAA guest room security requirements. 237 units. 235 one-bedroom standard units. 2 one-bedroom suites with whirlpools. 10 stories, interior corridors. *Bath:* combo or shower only. **Parking:** on-site (fee) and valet. **Terms:** 3 day cancellation notice. **Amenities:** video games (fee), dual phone lines, voice mail, safes, honor bars, irons, hair dryers. **Leisure Activities:** sauna, playground, exercise room. *Fee:* massage. **Guest Services:** valet laundry, area transportation, wireless Internet. **Business Services:** conference facilities, business center. **Cards:** AX, CB, DC, DS, JC, MC, VI.

/ SOME UNITS

SHERATON CENTRO HISTORICO — **Phone:** (55)5130-5300 — 3

Hotel
$195-$300 All Year

Address: Ave Juarez #70 Col Centro **Location:** Facing Alameda Park; in historic center. **Facility:** The downtown high-rise features upscale, contemporary decor; the upper rooms offer a spectacular view of the city. 457 units. 422 one-bedroom standard units. 34 one- and 1 two-bedroom suites, some with kitchens and/or whirlpools. 20 stories, interior corridors. **Parking:** on-site (fee) and valet. **Amenities:** dual phone lines, voice mail, safes, honor bars, irons, hair dryers. *Fee:* video games, high-speed Internet. *Some:* CD players. **Dining:** 2 restaurants. **Pool(s):** heated indoor. **Leisure Activities:** exercise room. *Fee:* massage. **Guest Services:** valet laundry, wireless Internet. *Fee:* airport transportation-Benito Juarez International Airport, area transportation. **Business Services:** conference facilities, business center. **Cards:** AX, CB, DC, DS, JC, MC, VI.

Sheraton HOTELS & RESORTS
AAA Benefit:
Members get up to 15% off, plus Starwood Preferred Guest® bonuses.

FEE / SOME UNITS

SHERATON MARIA ISABEL HOTEL & TOWERS — *Book great rates at AAA.com* — **Phone:** (55)5242-5555 — 17

Hotel
$155-$315 All Year

Address: Paseo de la Reforma 325 Col Cuauhtemoc **Location:** Next to US Embassy, opposite Angel de la Independencia Monument. **Facility:** This long-time four-diamond is on the famed Paseo de la Reforma; executive rooms feature comfortable, overstuffed chairs with ottomans. Meets AAA guest room security requirements. 755 units. 730 one-bedroom standard units. 24 one- and 1 two-bedroom suites, some with efficiencies, kitchens (utensils extra charge) and/or whirlpools. 19-22 stories, interior corridors. **Parking:** on-site (fee) and valet. **Amenities:** high-speed Internet (fee), voice mail, safes, honor bars, irons, hair dryers. *Some:* DVD players, CD players, fax. **Dining:** Manhattan Deli, Ristorante Amici, see separate listings. **Pool(s):** heated outdoor. **Leisure Activities:** saunas, steamrooms, 2 lighted tennis courts. *Fee:* massage. **Guest Services:** valet laundry, wireless Internet. **Business Services:** conference facilities, business center. **Cards:** AX, CB, DC, DS, JC, MC, VI.

Sheraton HOTELS & RESORTS
AAA Benefit:
Members get up to 15% off, plus Starwood Preferred Guest® bonuses.

CALL / SOME UNITS

(See maps and indexes p. 581-582, 584-586, 588-590)

SHERATON SUITES SANTA FE *Book great rates at AAA.com* **Phone:** (55)5258-8500 28

Hotel
$205-$340 All Year

Address: 200 Guillermo Gonzalez Camarena **Location:** In the Santa Fe District; 7.2 mi (12 km) w of Paseo de la Reforma. **Facility:** 194 one-bedroom suites, some with whirlpools. 10 stories, interior corridors. **Parking:** valet. **Amenities:** high-speed Internet (fee), dual phone lines, voice mail, safes, honor bars, irons, hair dryers. *Some:* fax. **Leisure Activities:** steamrooms, exercise room. *Fee:* massage. **Guest Services:** valet laundry, wireless Internet. **Business Services:** conference facilities, business center. **Cards:** AX, CB, DC, DS, JC, MC, VI.

/ SOME UNITS FEE

STANZA HOTEL *Book at AAA.com* **Phone:** (55)5208-0052 27

Hotel
$60-$88 All Year

Address: Ave Alvaro Obregon 13 **Location:** Colonia Roma; jct aves Cuahutemoc y Alvaro Obregon; downtown. **Facility:** 130 one-bedroom standard units. 7 stories, interior corridors. *Bath:* shower only. **Parking:** on-site and valet. **Amenities:** safes, hair dryers. **Leisure Activities:** exercise room. **Guest Services:** valet laundry, wireless Internet. **Business Services:** meeting rooms, business center. **Cards:** AX, MC, VI.

/ SOME UNITS

SUITES MI CASA **Phone:** 55/5566-6711 7

Hotel
$75-$105 All Year

Address: General Prim 106 **Location:** At General Prim and Milan St; just s of Paseo de la Reforma. **Facility:** 28 units. 26 one-bedroom standard units, some with kitchens. 2 two-bedroom suites with kitchens. 7 stories, interior corridors. *Bath:* combo or shower only. **Parking:** on-site. **Terms:** 4 day cancellation notice-fee imposed. **Amenities:** safes. **Guest Services:** valet laundry. **Cards:** AX, MC, VI.

W MEXICO CITY *Book great rates at AAA.com* **Phone:** (55)9138-1800 1

AAA

Hotel
$200-$535 All Year

Address: Campos Eliseos 252 Col Polanco **Location:** Just off Ave Paseo de la Reforma; in Polanco District. **Facility:** One of the newest hotels in a tony neighborhood, the W has spacious, high-tech rooms with urban, hip decor and an accommodating, high-energy staff. 237 units. 228 one-bedroom standard units. 9 one-bedroom suites. 25 stories, interior corridors. *Bath:* combo or shower only. **Parking:** valet. **Amenities:** DVD players, CD players, dual phone lines, voice mail, safes, honor bars, irons, hair dryers. *Fee:* video library, high-speed Internet. *Some:* fax. **Dining:** Solea Restaurant, see separate listing. **Leisure Activities:** sauna, whirlpool, steamroom, spa. **Guest Services:** valet laundry, wireless Internet. *Fee:* airport transportation-Benito Juarez International Airport, area transportation. **Business Services:** conference facilities, business center. **Cards:** AX, CB, DC, JC, MC, VI.

FEE / SOME UNITS FEE

The following lodgings were either not evaluated or did not meet AAA rating requirements but are listed for your information only.

N H CENTRO HISTORICO **Phone:** 55/5130-1850

fyi

Not evaluated. **Address:** Palma 42 Centro. Facilities, services, and decor characterize a mid-scale property.

RADISSON FLAMENCO **Phone:** 52/5627-0220

fyi

Not evaluated. **Address:** Ave Revolucion #333. Facilities, services, and decor characterize an upscale property.

WHERE TO DINE

ALFREDO DI ROMA **Phone:** 55/5327-7700 4

Italian
$18-$40

Servers navigate knowingly through the elegant dining room, bringing authentic Italian dishes to appreciative diners. House specialties include imported prosciutto and fettuccine Alfredo prepared tableside. The wine list is extensive. Hedonistic desserts are a sweet way to amplify the experience. Casual dress. **Bar:** Full bar. **Reservations:** suggested. **Hours:** 1 pm-midnight. **Address:** Campos Eliseos 218 **Location:** In Polanco Zone; on Paseo de la Reforma, 0.8 mi (1.3 km) w of Periferico; opposite Chapultepec Park and the National Auditorium; in Hotel Presidente InterContinental Mexico City. **Parking:** on-site (fee) and valet. **Cards:** AX, CB, DC, DS, JC, MC, VI.

AU PIED DE COCHON **Phone:** 55/5377-7700 2

Regional French
$25-$85

Elegant French dining can be enjoyed 24 hours a day. The menu comprises the highest-quality seafood, shellfish, pasta, rich livers and sumptuous breakfast dishes. The hot spot is usually jam-packed with the avant garde of the capital. Dressy casual. **Bar:** Full bar. **Reservations:** suggested. **Hours:** 24 hours. **Address:** Campos Eliseos 218 Col Pol **Location:** In Polanco Zone; on Paseo de la Reforma, 0.8 mi (1.3 km) w of Periferico; opposite Chapultepec Park and the National Auditorium; in Hotel Presidente InterContinental Mexico City. **Parking:** on-site (fee) and valet. **Cards:** AX, CB, DC, JC, MC, VI.

(See maps and indexes p. 581-582, 584-586, 588-590)

BELUZ INTERNATIONAL CUISINE & BAR **Phone:** 55/5280-5086 (31)

International
$10-$30

Fresh ingredients are used to prepare the high-quality menu offerings at this contemporary-style eatery. Dressy casual. **Bar:** Full bar. **Reservations:** suggested. **Hours:** 1 pm-11 pm. Closed major holidays; also Sun. **Address:** Monte Elbruz #132 Polanco Lomas **Location:** At Paso a desnivel Peatonal (pedestrian tunnel); enter Periferico and Moliere. **Parking:** valet. **Cards:** AX, MC, VI.

BONDY RESTAURANT Y PASTELERIA **Phone:** 55/5281-1818 (27)

Breads/Pastries
$8-$18

Since 1948, this restaurant has been a tradition in Polanco. The restaurant and bakery serves many European-inspired dishes, including a few Hungarian specialties and daily specials in small, cozy dining rooms (outdoor seating also is available). Breakfast is another option. Save room for a choice from the tempting dessert tray. Casual dress. **Bar:** Beer & wine. **Reservations:** suggested. **Hours:** 9 am-10 pm. Closed: Mon & 4/5-4/11. **Address:** Galileo 38 **Location:** In Polanco Zone; just off Paseo de la Reforma; enter Presidente Masarik and Newton. **Parking:** valet. **Cards:** MC, VI.

CAFE DE TACUBA **Phone:** 55/5518-4950 (3)

Regional Mexican
$6-$20

The eatery is tremendously popular with tourists but is still not to be missed. The menu offers a variety of traditional Mexican dishes; the Oaxacan tamale is a treat. Casual dress. **Bar:** Full bar. **Reservations:** accepted. **Hours:** 8 am-11:30 pm. **Address:** Tacuba #28 **Location:** Downtown; near Zocalo; in historic area. **Parking:** valet. **Cards:** AX, MC, VI.

CHALET SUIZO **Phone:** 55/5511-8807 (19)

Continental
$12-$22

A variety of well-prepared German and Swiss food is offered in an authentic Swiss setting with low ceilings and Tudor-style wood accents. The owners usually visit each table to look after diners' needs. Casual dress. **Bar:** Full bar. **Reservations:** accepted. **Hours:** 1:30 pm-10 pm, Fri & Sat-11 pm. **Address:** Niza 37 **Location:** In Pink Zone; just s of Paseo de la Reforma. **Parking:** street. **Cards:** AX, MC, VI.

EL LAGO CHAPULTEPEC **Phone:** 55/5515-9586 (3)

Regional New World
$20-$30

Elegant dining spot overlooking the lake. Sunday buffet. Semi-formal attire. Entertainment. **Bar:** Full bar. **Reservations:** suggested. **Hours:** 7:30 am-11 pm, Fri & Sat-11:30 pm; Sunday brunch. Closed major holidays. **Address:** Lago Mayor 2 da, Chapultepec Park **Location:** In new section of Chapultepec Park; near National Museum of Natural History. **Parking:** on-site (fee) and valet. **Cards:** AX, CB, DC, MC, VI.

IZOTE **Phone:** 55/5280-1671 (34)

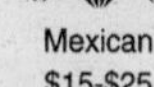

Mexican
$15-$25

The menu offers superbly prepared Mexican cuisine done with a very contemporary spin. The dining room is understated with reminders of the country's indigenous roots subtly presented on its walls. Even with minimal knowledge of the Spanish language you can feel confident, as this restaurant is heavily patronized by foreign tourists. Dressy casual. **Bar:** Full bar. **Reservations:** suggested. **Hours:** 1 pm-midnight, Sun-6 pm. Closed: 1/1, 12/24-12/26; also 1/2. **Address:** Ave Presidente Masarik #513 Local 3 **Location:** In Polanco Zone. **Parking:** valet. **Cards:** AX, MC, VI.

LA GRIGLIA **Phone:** 55/5999-0065 (5)

Mediterranean
$16-$35

This grill prepares upscale casual Italian fare with Mediterranean flavors. A variety of antipastos and risottos are featured, and diners will find pastas (of course) as well as poultry, steak and seafood offerings. Dressy casual. **Bar:** Full bar. **Reservations:** accepted. **Hours:** 7 am-11 pm; Sunday brunch. **Address:** Andres Bello #29 **Location:** On Paseo de la Reforma; opposite Chapultepec Park and National Auditorium; in JW Marriott Hotel Mexico City. **Parking:** valet. **Cards:** AX, MC, VI.

LE BOUCHON **Phone:** 55/5281-7902 (1)

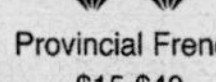

Provincial French
$15-$40

This popular restaurant features a cozy setting with indoor and outdoor patio dining and a menu of Country French cuisine. Casual dress. **Bar:** Full bar. **Reservations:** accepted. **Hours:** 1:30 pm-1 am, Sun-5:30 pm. Closed: 1/1, 12/25. **Address:** Julio Verne 102 **Location:** In Polanco Zone; jct Ave Virgilio. **Parking:** on-site. **Cards:** AX, MC, VI.

LE CIRQUE **Phone:** 55/5263-8884 (9)

Regional New World
$25-$50

The whimsical yet upscale circus decor includes chrome monkeys gazing down on guests from their rosewood perches. Dishes are complex and created with the very best ingredients from around the world, all presented in unique, dazzling compositions for an indubitably world-class experience. Semi-formal attire. **Bar:** Full bar. **Reservations:** suggested. **Hours:** 1 pm-midnight, Sat 7 pm-1 am, Sun noon-5 pm. Closed: 4/6-4/10. **Address:** Mariano Escobedo 700 **Location:** Between Victor Hugo and Kent, just n of Diana Cir; Periferico, exit Ave Presidente Masarik, then w; in Camino Real Mexico City. **Parking:** on-site (fee) and valet. **Cards:** AX, CB, DC, DS, JC, MC, VI.

LES MOUSTACHES **Phone:** 55/5533-3390 (14)

French
$7-$15

Elegant surroundings and a refined atmosphere are hallmarks of the sophisticated restaurant, in business for more than 35 years. Distinctive presentations add to the appeal of international and French menu offerings. Diners can request seating in the main dining room, garden courtyard or in a private upstairs area of the 100-year-old house. Sample delicious flambeed desserts and choose from a variety of dessert souffles—pistachio or mandarin stand out. Coats and ties are required on weekdays, but attire is casual on Saturday. Dressy casual. **Bar:** Full bar. **Reservations:** suggested. **Hours:** 1 pm-11:30 pm, Sun & Mon-6 pm. Closed: 1/1, 12/25; also 5/1. **Address:** 88 Rio Sena **Location:** Jct Rio Lerma; just off the Paseo de la Reforma. **Parking:** on-site and valet. **Cards:** AX, MC, VI.

(See maps and indexes p. 581-582, 584-586, 588-590)

LOS ALMENDROS **Phone:** 55/5531-7307 (8)

Regional Mexican
$15-$30

Known for Mayan-influenced cuisine, the restaurant transports diners to the Yucatan. A must on any tourist's itinerary, this spot offers an unforgettable experience. A well-rounded meal might start with savory, but not spicy, panuchos de cochinita pibil; center on arroz con pollo con platanos fritos; and end with cerveza Leon. Dressy casual. Entertainment. **Bar:** Full bar. **Reservations:** suggested. **Hours:** 7:30 am-11 pm, Sun 8 am-10:30 pm. **Address:** #164 Campos Eliseos **Location:** In Polanco Zone; corner of Campos Eliseos and Arquimedes, just e. **Parking:** valet and street. **Cards:** AX, DC, MC, VI.

LOS GIRASOLES **Phone:** 55/5510-0630 (1)

Regional Mexican
$7-$15

Created as a place to serve pre-Columbian recipes that have been handed down for generations, the restaurant is conveniently near museums and the Zocalo. Menu items range from traditional tortilla soup and duckling in blackberry sauce to such adventurous items as fried worms, ant eggs and grasshoppers. The cilantro soup and the tamarind mole sauce with turkey come highly recommended. Third-floor seating offers views of historic buildings, and outside dining is available. Casual dress. **Bar:** Full bar. **Reservations:** accepted. **Hours:** 1 pm-midnight, Sun & Mon-8:30 pm. Closed: 1/1. **Address:** Calle de Tacuba **Location:** Between calles 8 and 10; in front of Plaza Manuel Tolsa; in historic downtown district. **Parking:** valet. **Cards:** AX, MC, VI.

LOS TRES SOLES FOCOLARE RESTAURANT **Phone:** 55/5207-8055 (17)

Regional Mexican
$8-$18

From the large, festive dining room, diners can hear the cocks crow as they select excellent regional specialties from Puebla, Yucatan and Veracruz. A nightly folkloric show begins at 9 pm. Casual dress. Entertainment. **Bar:** Full bar. **Reservations:** suggested, for dinner. **Hours:** 7:30 am-2 am, Sat & Sun from 9 am. **Address:** Hamburgo 87, just off Niza **Location:** In Pink Zone. **Parking:** valet. **Cards:** AX, CB, DC, MC, VI.

MANHATTAN DELI **Phone:** 55/5242-5555 (11)

American
$12-$30

Finding a New York-style deli in the heart of Mexico City is quite a surprise, but this one is located directly beside the U.S. Embassy, so it fits right in. In addition to the traditional deli fare, diners will also find such Mexican influences as tacos, quesadillas and jalapeño poppers. An extensive salad bar is also offered, along with soup, entree and dessert bars. You can also opt to order a la carte from the menu, which lists a variety of baguettes, bagel and croissant sandwiches. Note: The entry to the restaurant is usually through the hotel. Casual dress. **Bar:** Full bar. **Hours:** 6:30 am-midnight. **Address:** Paseo de la Reforma 325 **Location:** Next to US Embassy, opposite Angel de la Independencia Monument; in Sheraton Maria Isabel Hotel & Towers. **Parking:** on-site (fee) and valet. **Cards:** AX, CB, DC, JC, MC, VI.

THE PALM RESTAURANT **Phone:** 55/5327-7700 (7)

Steak & Seafood
$13-$52

This bustling restaurant is noted for prime, dry-aged steaks and Nova Scotia lobsters, huge portions are delivered by an attentive staff in an atmosphere that is fun and lively. At the end of the meal, servers present tempting pastries tableside. Caricature-lined walls lend to the feeling that patrons are dining in an art gallery. Even if you bring a big appetite you still may leave with a doggy bag. Dressy casual. **Bar:** Full bar. **Reservations:** suggested. **Hours:** 1 pm-midnight. Closed major holidays; also Sun. **Address:** Campo Eliseos 218 **Location:** In Polanco Zone; on Paseo de la Reforma, 0.8 mi (1.3 km) w of Periferico; opposite Chapultepec Park and the National Auditorium; in Hotel Presidente InterContinental Mexico City. **Parking:** on-site (fee) and valet. **Cards:** AX, CB, DC, DS, JC, MC, VI.

PASSY **Phone:** 55/5207-3747 (13)

Traditional Continental
$12-$35

Find classic continental selections that include fish, chicken, steaks and chops served in what was once a residence. (Use the small side bar entrance to gain entry to the restaurant if the main doors are closed.). Dressy casual. **Bar:** Full bar. **Reservations:** suggested. **Hours:** 1 pm-6 pm. Closed major holidays; also Sun. **Address:** Amberes 10 **Location:** Just s of Paseo de la Reforma; in Pink Zone. **Parking:** valet. **Cards:** AX, DC, MC, VI.

PUJOL RESTAURANTE **Phone:** 55/5545-4111 (32)

New Mexican
$20-$30

Pujol features an upscale contemporary dining room, an interesting, contemporary Mexican menu and an extensive wine list. You may want to bring a Spanish dictionary to translate the fabulous creative menu, as you won't want to miss out on its tempting choices. Innovative starters and main courses include seafood and duck selections. The wine list offers wine flights for the inquisitive diner. Dressy casual. **Bar:** Full bar. **Reservations:** suggested. **Hours:** 1:30 pm-11:30 pm. Closed major holidays; also Sun. **Address:** F Petrarca 254 Polanco **Location:** Between Horacio and Homero; in Polanco District. **Parking:** valet. **Cards:** AX, MC, VI.

REFORMA 500 **Phone:** 55/5230-1818

Mediterranean
$15-$35

Mediterranean concepts employ premium local ingredients. Preparations are complex and presentations distinctive. Patrons can dine in the elegant dining room or on the outdoor terrace overlooking the refined courtyard. Dressy casual. **Bar:** Full bar. **Reservations:** suggested. **Hours:** 6:30 am-11:30 pm, Sat & Sun from 7 am. **Address:** Paseo de la Reforma 500 **Location:** On Paseo de la Reforma; in Four Seasons Hotel Mexico D.F. **Parking:** valet. **Cards:** AX, CB, DC, DS, JC, MC, VI.

RESTAURANTE FONDA EL REFUGIO **Phone:** 55/5525-8128 (18)

Regional Mexican
$13-$20

Quaint countryside decor lends to the informal atmosphere at this long-time local favorite restaurant. Excellent preparation marks dishes that journey through the culinary regions of Mexico. Casual dress. **Bar:** Full bar. **Reservations:** accepted. **Hours:** 1 pm-11 pm. Closed: 1/1. **Address:** Liverpool 166 **Location:** In Pink Zone. **Parking:** valet. **Cards:** AX, DC, MC, VI.

RESTAURANTE MERCADERES CAFE **Phone:** 55/5510-2213 (4)

Steak
$7-$20

A great location a few blocks from the Palace of Fine Arts makes this the perfect spot to break or end your sightseeing day. Although the menu is in Spanish only, the waiters will display the various cuts of steaks that are the featured specialty. They are grilled to order and arrive in hearty portions. Also offered are seafood, pasta and Mexican selections. Dressy casual. **Bar:** Full bar. **Reservations:** accepted. **Hours:** 8 am-9 pm. Closed: 1/1, 12/25. **Address:** Ave Cinco de Mayo #57 Centro Historico **Location:** In historic center; across from cathedral. **Parking:** valet. **Cards:** AX, MC, VI.

(See maps and indexes p. 581-582, 584-586, 588-590)

RESTAURANTE SAN ANGEL INN — **Phone:** 55/5616-2222 (11)

Traditional Continental
$19-$45

In a renovated 18th-century hacienda, the renowned dining room is surrounded by gardens and patios. Sip a beverage in any of the courtyard gardens or elegant rooms, then unwind in the large ornate main dining room and appreciate the excellent service. The menu focus is on haute Mexican cuisine. Dressy casual. Entertainment. **Bar:** Full bar. **Reservations:** required. **Hours:** 1 pm-1 am, Sun-10 pm. Closed: 1/1, 12/25. **Address:** Diego Rivera #50 esq Altavista **Location:** 7 blks w of Insurgentes Sur; 5 blks e of Annillo Periferico; in Col San Angel Inn. **Parking:** valet. **Cards:** AX, CB, DC, MC, VI. **Historic**

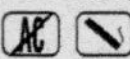

RESTAURANTE TEZKA — **Phone:** 55/5228-9918 (20)

Basque
$16-$35

Continental, sophisticated Basque cuisines are elaborately prepared and infused with fresh regional ingredients at this well-known local favorite, where attentive, knowledgeable and well-trained servers present food in an elegant, refined dining room. Dressy casual. **Bar:** Full bar. **Reservations:** suggested. **Hours:** 1 pm-11 pm, Sat-7 pm. Closed: Sun & 12/25-1/1. **Address:** 78 Amberes St **Location:** In Pink Zone; jct Ave Chapultepec and Liverpool St; in Best Western Royal Zona Rosa. **Parking:** valet. **Cards:** AX, DC, MC, VI.

RINCON ARGENTINO — **Phone:** 55/5254-8744 (28)

Argentine
$15-$45

The name translates into 'corner of Argentina,' which manifests as a bohemian atmosphere, tender cuts of beef and attentive personalized service. Casual dress. **Bar:** Full bar. **Reservations:** required. **Hours:** 12:30 pm-midnight. **Address:** Ave Presidente Masaryk #177 **Location:** In Polanco Zone. **Parking:** on-site (fee) and valet. **Cards:** AX, MC, VI.

RISTORANTE AMICI — **Phone:** 55/5242-5555 (12)

Italian
$10-$25

A contemporary look throughout the dining room complements the innovative menu at this popular spot, which specializes in fine Italian cuisine. Menu highlights include fresh tomato and mozzarella cheese salads, Caesar salads or homemade soups, followed by an extensive array of rich pastas, veal, poultry or fish selections. The desserts are a menu highlight worth saving room for. Dressy casual. **Bar:** Full bar. **Reservations:** suggested. **Hours:** 6:30 am-midnight, Sat from 6 pm. Closed: Sun. **Address:** Paseo de la Reforma 325 **Location:** Next to US Embassy, opposite Angel de la Independencia Monument; in Sheraton Maria Isabel Hotel & Towers. **Parking:** on-site (fee) and valet. **Cards:** AX, CB, DC, MC, VI.

SANBORN'S — **Phone:** 55/5616-3267

Regional Mexican
$8-$28

Restaurants in the casual chain, which includes more than 100 locations throughout Mexico, offer a good selection of American-style sandwiches, salads, soups and both Mexican and American entrees. The selection of desserts is impressive. Casual dress. **Bar:** Full bar. **Hours:** 7 am-1 am, Fri & Sat-2 am. **Address:** Altamira No 46, Col Barrio Loreto **Location:** Jct Ave Revolucion. **Parking:** on-site. **Cards:** AX, MC, VI.

SANBORN'S — **Phone:** 55/5871-4131

Regional Mexican
$8-$28

Restaurants in the casual chain, which includes more than 100 locations throughout Mexico, offer a good selection of American-style sandwiches, salads, soups and both Mexican and American entrees. The selection of desserts is impressive. Casual dress. **Bar:** Full bar. **Hours:** 7 am-1 am. **Address:** Auto Mex - Qro KM 37 Loc C25, Col Arcos de A **Location:** KM 37 Mexico City-Queretaro toll road. **Parking:** on-site. **Cards:** AX, MC, VI.

SANBORN'S — **Phone:** 55/5663-1577

Regional Mexican
$8-$28

Restaurants in the casual chain, which includes more than 100 locations throughout Mexico, offer a good selection of American-style sandwiches, salads, soups and both Mexican and American entrees. The selection of desserts is impressive. Casual dress. **Bar:** Full bar. **Hours:** 7 am-1 am. **Location:** Just n of jct Calle Barranca del Muerto. Ave Insurgentes Sur No 1605, Col San Jose Insurgentes. **Parking:** on-site (fee). **Cards:** AX, MC, VI.

SANBORN'S — **Phone:** 55/5635-2289

Regional Mexican
$8-$28

Restaurants in the casual chain, which includes more than 100 locations throughout Mexico, offer a good selection of American-style sandwiches, salads, soups and both Mexican and American entrees. The selection of desserts is impressive. Casual dress. **Bar:** Full bar. **Hours:** 7 am-11 pm, Fri & Sat-1 am. **Address:** Calz de las Aguilas No 1350 Col Puente Colo **Location:** Jct Calzada Los Petrelles. **Parking:** on-site (fee). **Cards:** AX, MC, VI.

SANBORN'S — **Phone:** 55/5660-2010

Regional Mexican
$8-$28

Restaurants in the casual chain, which includes more than 100 locations throughout Mexico, offer a good selection of American-style sandwiches, salads, soups and both Mexican and American entrees. The selection of desserts is impressive. Casual dress. **Bar:** Full bar. **Hours:** 7 am-midnight, Fri & Sat 24 hours. **Address:** Barranca del Muerto No 479 Col Merced Gomez **Location:** Jct Periferico. **Parking:** on-site (fee). **Cards:** AX, MC, VI.

(See maps and indexes p. 581-582, 584-586, 588-590)

SANBORN'S **Phone:** 55/5396-1355

Regional Mexican
$8-$28

Restaurants in the casual chain, which includes more than 100 locations throughout Mexico, offer a good selection of American-style sandwiches, salads, soups and both Mexican and American entrees. The selection of desserts is impressive. Casual dress. **Bar:** Full bar. **Hours:** 7 am-1 am. **Address:** Ave Cama rones No 108, Col Salvador Xochiman **Location:** Jct Ave Biologo Maximiliano Martinez. **Parking:** on-site (fee). **Cards:** AX, MC, VI.

SANBORN'S **Phone:** 55/5211-6451

Regional Mexican
$8-$28

Restaurants in the casual chain, which includes more than 100 locations throughout Mexico, offer a good selection of American-style sandwiches, salads, soups and both Mexican and American entrees. The selection of desserts is impressive. Casual dress. **Bar:** Full bar. **Hours:** 7 am-1 am, Fri & Sat 24 hours. **Address:** Paseo de la Reforma No 504, Col Juarez **Location:** Just e of jct Calzada Melchor Ocampo. **Parking:** no self-parking. **Cards:** AX, MC, VI.

SANBORN'S **Phone:** 55/5592-5451

Regional Mexican
$8-$28

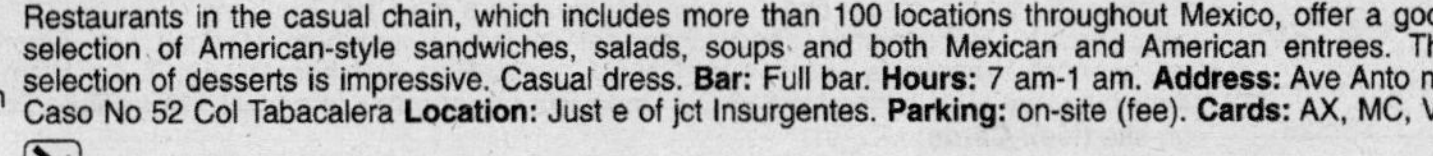

Restaurants in the casual chain, which includes more than 100 locations throughout Mexico, offer a good selection of American-style sandwiches, salads, soups and both Mexican and American entrees. The selection of desserts is impressive. Casual dress. **Bar:** Full bar. **Hours:** 7 am-1 am. **Address:** Ave Anto nio Caso No 52 Col Tabacalera **Location:** Just e of jct Insurgentes. **Parking:** on-site (fee). **Cards:** AX, MC, VI.

SANBORN'S **Phone:** 55/5255-3334

Regional Mexican
$8-$28

Restaurants in the casual chain, which includes more than 100 locations throughout Mexico, offer a good selection of American-style sandwiches, salads, soups and both Mexican and American entrees. The selection of desserts is impressive. Casual dress. **Hours:** 7 am-1 am, Fri & Sat-2 am. **Address:** Hegel No 345, Col Chapultepec Morales **Location:** In Polanco Zone; just e of Ave Emerson. **Parking:** on-site (fee). **Cards:** AX, MC, VI.

SANBORN'S **Phone:** 55/5616-3687

Regional Mexican
$8-$28

Restaurants in the casual chain, which includes more than 100 locations throughout Mexico, offer a good selection of American-style sandwiches, salads, soups and both Mexican and American entrees. The selection of desserts is impressive. Casual dress. **Bar:** Full bar. **Hours:** 7 am-midnight, Fri & Sat-2 am. **Location:** Just e of jct Ave Revolucion. Ave Desierto de los Leones No 52, Col San Angel. **Parking:** on-site (fee). **Cards:** AX, MC, VI.

SANBORN'S **Phone:** 55/5510-9399

Regional Mexican
$8-$28

Restaurants in the casual chain, which includes more than 100 locations throughout Mexico, offer a good selection of American-style sandwiches, salads, soups and both Mexican and American entrees. The selection of desserts is impressive. Casual dress. **Bar:** Full bar. **Hours:** 7:30 am-11 pm, Fri & Sat-1 am. **Address:** Isabel LaCatolica #35, Col Centro **Location:** Jct 16 de Septiembre; in historical area of downtown. **Parking:** no self-parking. **Cards:** AX, MC, VI.

SANBORN'S **Phone:** 55/5571-0164

Regional Mexican
$8-$20

Restaurants in the casual chain, which includes more than 100 locations throughout Mexico, offer a good selection of American-style sandwiches, salads, soups and both Mexican and American entrees. The selection of desserts is impressive. Casual dress. **Bar:** Full bar. **Hours:** 7 am-1 am. **Address:** Blvd Puerto Aereo No 123, Col Moctezuma **Location:** Across street from Mexico City International Airport. **Parking:** on-site (fee). **Cards:** AX, MC, VI.

SANBORN'S **Phone:** 55/5534-7626

Regional Mexican
$8-$28

Restaurants in the casual chain, which includes more than 100 locations throughout Mexico, offer a good selection of American-style sandwiches, salads, soups and both Mexican and American entrees. The selection of desserts is impressive. Casual dress. **Bar:** Full bar. **Hours:** 7 am-midnight, Fri & Sat-1 am. **Address:** Parroquia No 179, Col Del Valle **Location:** 0.3 mi (0.5 km) n of jct Ave Rio Mixcoac. **Parking:** on-site (fee). **Cards:** AX, MC, VI.

SANBORN'S **Phone:** 55/5684-9392

Regional Mexican
$8-$28

Restaurants in the casual chain, which includes more than 100 locations throughout Mexico, offer a good selection of American-style sandwiches, salads, soups and both Mexican and American entrees. The selection of desserts is impressive. Casual dress. **Bar:** Full bar. **Hours:** 7 am-1 am, Fri & Sat-2 am. **Address:** Calzada del Hueso No 519, Residencial Coapa **Location:** Jct Ave Canal de Miramontes. **Parking:** on-site (fee). **Cards:** AX, MC, VI.

(See maps and indexes p. 581-582, 584-586, 588-590)

SANBORN'S **Phone:** 55/5605-4818

Regional Mexican
$8-$28

Restaurants in the casual chain, which includes more than 100 locations throughout Mexico, offer a good selection of American-style sandwiches, salads, soups and both Mexican and American entrees. The selection of desserts is impressive. Casual dress. **Bar:** Full bar. **Hours:** 7 am-1 am, Fri & Sat-2 am. **Address:** Ave Coyocan No 2000, Col Xoco **Location:** Jct Ave Rio Churubusco. **Parking:** on-site (fee). **Cards:** AX, MC, VI.

SANBORN'S **Phone:** 55/5705-0032

Regional Mexican
$8-$28

Restaurants in the casual chain, which includes more than 100 locations throughout Mexico, offer a good selection of American-style sandwiches, salads, soups and both Mexican and American entrees. The selection of desserts is impressive. Casual dress. **Bar:** Beer & wine. **Hours:** 7:30 am-11 pm, Fri & Sat-1 am. **Address:** Paseo de la Reforma #45, Col Tabacalera **Location:** Jct Ave Jose Maria La Fragua. **Parking:** no self-parking. **Cards:** AX, MC, VI.

SANBORN'S **Phone:** 55/5752-1681

Regional Mexican
$8-$28

Restaurants in the casual chain, which includes more than 100 locations throughout Mexico, offer a good selection of American-style sandwiches, salads, soups and both Mexican and American entrees. The selection of desserts is impressive. Casual dress. **Bar:** Full bar. **Hours:** 7 am-1 am, Fri & Sat-2 am. **Address:** Ave Montevideo No 313 Col Lindavista **Location:** Just n of jct Ave Instituto Politecnico. **Parking:** on-site (fee). **Cards:** MC, VI.

SANBORN'S **Phone:** 55/5574-7302

Regional Mexican
$8-$28

Restaurants in the casual chain, which includes more than 100 locations throughout Mexico, offer a good selection of American-style sandwiches, salads, soups and both Mexican and American entrees. The selection of desserts is impressive. Casual dress. **Bar:** Full bar. **Hours:** 7 am-1 am, Fri & Sat-2 am. **Address:** Insurgentes Sur No 421, Coly **Location:** Just n of jct Ave Baja California. **Parking:** on-site (fee). **Cards:** AX, MC, VI.

SANBORN'S **Phone:** 55/5259-1083

Regional Mexican
$8-$28

Restaurants in the casual chain, which includes more than 100 locations throughout Mexico, offer a good selection of American-style sandwiches, salads, soups and both Mexican and American entrees. The selection of desserts is impressive. Casual dress. **Bar:** Full bar. **Hours:** 7 am-midnight, Fri & Sat-2 am. **Address:** Prol Bosques Reforma No 1813 **Location:** In Bosques de Vista Hermosa District. **Parking:** on-site. **Cards:** AX, MC, VI.

SANBORN'S **Phone:** 55/5525-4338

Regional Mexican
$8-$28

Restaurants in the casual chain, which includes more than 100 locations throughout Mexico, offer a good selection of American-style sandwiches, salads, soups and both Mexican and American entrees. The selection of desserts is impressive. Casual dress. **Bar:** Full bar. **Hours:** 7 am-10 pm, Fri & Sat-2 am. **Address:** Londres No 130, Col Juarez **Location:** Jct Ave Varsovia. **Parking:** on-site (fee). **Cards:** AX, MC, VI.

SANBORN'S **Phone:** 55/5574-5729

Regional Mexican
$8-$28

Restaurants in the casual chain, which includes more than 100 locations throughout Mexico, offer a good selection of American-style sandwiches, salads, soups and both Mexican and American entrees. The selection of desserts is impressive. Casual dress. **Bar:** Full bar. **Hours:** 7 am-1 am, Fri & Sat-2 am. **Address:** Ave Cuauhtemoc #287, Col Roma **Location:** Just e of jct Ave Yucatan. **Parking:** on-site. **Cards:** AX, MC, VI.

SANBORN'S **Phone:** 55/5532-0660

Regional Mexican
$8-$28

Restaurants in the casual chain, which includes more than 100 locations throughout Mexico, offer a good selection of American-style sandwiches, salads, soups and both Mexican and American entrees. The selection of desserts is impressive. Casual dress. **Bar:** Full bar. **Hours:** 7 am-1 am. **Address:** Ave Plutario Elias Calles No 1897, Col **Location:** Just e of Calzada de Tlalpan. **Parking:** on-site (fee). **Cards:** AX, MC, VI.

SANBORN'S **Phone:** 55/5573-7308

Regional Mexican
$8-$28

Restaurants in the casual chain, which includes more than 100 locations throughout Mexico, offer a good selection of American-style sandwiches, salads, soups and both Mexican and American entrees. The selection of desserts is impressive. Casual dress. **Bar:** Full bar. **Hours:** 7 am-11 pm, Fri & Sat-1 am. **Address:** Ave Insurgentes Sur No 396, Col Tlalpan **Location:** 0.3 mi (0.5 km) n of jct Ave 5 de Mayo. **Parking:** on-site (fee). **Cards:** AX, MC, VI.

(See maps and indexes p. 581-582, 584-586, 588-590)

SANBORN'S

Regional Mexican
$8-$28

Phone: 55/5259-3698
Restaurants in the casual chain, which includes more than 100 locations throughout Mexico, offer a good selection of American-style sandwiches, salads, soups and both Mexican and American entrees. The selection of desserts is impressive. Casual dress. **Bar:** Full bar. **Hours:** 7 am-10 pm. **Address:** Carr Mex Toluca No 1725, Col Lomas de Palo **Location:** Between Palo Alto and Fresnos sts. **Parking:** on-site (fee). **Cards:** AX, MC, VI.

SANBORN'S

Regional Mexican
$8-$28

Phone: 55/5561-4311
Restaurants in the casual chain, which includes more than 100 locations throughout Mexico, offer a good selection of American-style sandwiches, salads, soups and both Mexican and American entrees. The selection of desserts is impressive. Casual dress. **Bar:** Full bar. **Hours:** 7 am-11 pm, Fri & Sat-2 am. **Address:** Ave Azcapotzalco No 527, Col Azcapotzal **Location:** Se of Ave Aquiles Serdan; jct 16 de Septiembre. **Parking:** no self-parking. **Cards:** AX, MC, VI.

SANBORN'S

Regional Mexican
$8-$28

Phone: 55/5293-1991
Restaurants in the casual chain, which includes more than 100 locations throughout Mexico, offer a good selection of American-style sandwiches, salads, soups and both Mexican and American entrees. The selection of desserts is impressive. Casual dress. **Bar:** Full bar. **Hours:** 7 am-10 pm, Fri & Sat-1 am. **Location:** At jct Blvd Pipila. Ave Del Conscripto, No 311 Col Lomas de Sotelo. **Parking:** on-site (fee). **Cards:** AX, MC, VI.

SANBORN'S

Regional Mexican
$8-$28

Phone: 55/5665-3339
Restaurants in the casual chain, which includes more than 100 locations throughout Mexico, offer a good selection of American-style sandwiches, salads, soups and both Mexican and American entrees. The selection of desserts is impressive. Casual dress. **Bar:** Full bar. **Hours:** 7 am-midnight, Fri & Sat-2 am. **Address:** Calz de Tlalpan No 4737 **Location:** Just ne of jct Ave San Fernando. **Parking:** on-site (fee). **Cards:** AX, MC, VI.

SANBORN'S

Regional Mexican
$8-$28

Phone: 55/5533-0715
Restaurants in the casual chain, which includes more than 100 locations throughout Mexico, offer a good selection of American-style sandwiches, salads, soups and both Mexican and American entrees. The selection of desserts is impressive. Casual dress. **Bar:** Full bar. **Hours:** 7 am-1 am, Fri & Sat-2 am. **Address:** Hamburgo #70, Col Juarez **Location:** 2 blks s off Paseo de la Reforma; in Pink Zone. **Parking:** on-site (fee). **Cards:** AX, MC, VI.

SANBORN'S

Regional Mexican
$8-$28

Phone: 55/5669-0887
Restaurants in the casual chain, which includes more than 100 locations throughout Mexico, offer a good selection of American-style sandwiches, salads, soups and both Mexican and American entrees. The selection of desserts is impressive. Casual dress. **Bar:** Full bar. **Hours:** 7 am-1 am. **Address:** Ave Adolfo Prieto #202, Col Del Valle **Location:** Just s of jct Ave Xola. **Parking:** on-site. **Cards:** AX, MC, VI.

SIRLOIN STOCKADE

Regional Steak
$6-$9

Phone: 55/5679-7610
The steakhouse lines up buffet items, including pizza, tacos, soups, salads and desserts, providing both excellent variety and a good value. Rotating theme nights might allow for the sampling of sushi, barbecue and seafood. The buffet also may serve to complement a quality steak. Rolls are baked several times daily. Casual dress. **Bar:** Beer & wine. **Hours:** 1 pm-9 pm, Sat & Sun from noon. Closed: 12/25. **Address:** Ave Cana de Miramontes 2053 Local 4 Planta **Location:** Jct Calzada de las Bombas. **Parking:** on-site (fee). **Cards:** DS, MC, VI.

SIR WINSTON CHURCHILL'S

British
$16-$54

Phone: 55/5280-6070 (9)
Sir Winston's offers fine English and international cuisine, including Churchill's favorite—roast prime rib of beef served with Yorkshire pudding and fresh horseradish. Graced with lovely gardens, the atmosphere is Anglo-Saxon, elegant and refined. Live piano music plays daily from 1 pm-5 pm. Dressy casual. Entertainment. **Bar:** Full bar. **Reservations:** suggested. **Hours:** 1 pm-1 am. Closed major holidays; also Sun. **Address:** Blvd M Avila Camacho 67 **Location:** Jct Volcan; enter Paseo and Palmas; in Polanco District. **Parking:** valet. **Cards:** AX, MC, VI.

SOLEA RESTAURANT

Regional Mexican
$10-$15

Phone: 55/9138-1800 (6)
Reserve the private room or dine at the communal table at this hip, contemporary restaurant, which serves steak and seafood prepared with fresh ingredients and a Mexican twist. Dressy casual. **Bar:** Full bar. **Reservations:** suggested. **Hours:** 6:30 am-1 am; Saturday & Sunday brunch. **Address:** Campos Eliseos 252 **Location:** Just off Ave Paseo de la Reforma; in Polanco District; in W Mexico City. **Parking:** valet. **Cards:** AX, CB, DC, DS, JC, MC, VI.

TORRE D CASTILLA

Spanish
$9-$20

Phone: 55/5281-0906 (26)
Set in a castle, this restaurant gives diners a true sense of medieval Europe with its distressed wood floors, wall murals and stone walls. The menu features a wonderful mixture of fine Spanish cuisine, complete with an extensive selection of hot and cold appetizers, or "tapas," and a good selection of meat, poultry and seafood. The jumbo shrimp in garlic sauce is a popular selection. The menu is in Spanish so be sure to bring your language book and a sense of adventure. Dressy casual. **Bar:** Full bar. **Reservations:** suggested. **Hours:** 1 pm-11 pm, Sun-7 pm. **Address:** Esopo 31 Polanco **Location:** Jct Ave Presidente Masaryk; opposite Cuban Embassy. **Parking:** valet. **Cards:** AX, CB, DC, MC, VI.

(See maps and indexes p. 581-582, 584-586, 588-590)

VIPS **Phone:** 55/5611-7195

Regional Mexican
$7-$25

Owned by Wal-Mart of Mexico and found in most major cities, the budget-friendly chain serves a good variety of Mexican and American dishes, including burgers, sandwiches, salads, spaghetti and enchiladas, as well as a fine selection of desserts. Casual dress. **Bar:** Beer & wine. **Hours:** 7 am-10 pm. **Address:** Ave Patriotismo No 671, Col Mixcoac **Location:** Just s of jct Blvd Holbein. **Parking:** on-site. **Cards:** AX, MC, VI.

VIPS **Phone:** 55/5598-1824

Regional Mexican
$7-$25

Owned by Wal-Mart of Mexico and found in most major cities, the budget-friendly chain serves a good variety of Mexican and American dishes, including burgers, sandwiches, salads, spaghetti and enchiladas, as well as a fine selection of desserts. Casual dress. **Bar:** Beer & wine. **Hours:** 7 am-1 am, Fri & Sat 24 hours. **Address:** Ave Insurgentes 1581, Col Sn Js **Location:** Jct Ave Mercaderess. Ave Insurgentes 1581, Col Sn Js Insurgentes. **Parking:** on-site. **Cards:** AX, MC, VI.

VIPS **Phone:** 55/5536-2414

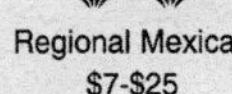

Regional Mexican
$7-$25

Owned by Wal-Mart of Mexico and found in most major cities, the budget-friendly chain serves a good variety of Mexican and American dishes, including burgers, sandwiches, salads, spaghetti and enchiladas, as well as a fine selection of desserts. Casual dress. **Bar:** Beer & wine. **Hours:** 7 am-1 am, Fri & Sat-2 am, Sun-midnight. **Address:** Calle Alabama No 7, Col Napoles **Location:** Between calles Arkansas and Louisiana. **Parking:** on-site. **Cards:** AX, MC, VI.

VIPS **Phone:** 55/5598-1132

Regional Mexican
$7-$25

Owned by Wal-Mart of Mexico and found in most major cities, the budget-friendly chain serves a good variety of Mexican and American dishes, including burgers, sandwiches, salads, spaghetti and enchiladas, as well as a fine selection of desserts. Casual dress. **Bar:** Beer & wine. **Hours:** 7 am-midnight, Fri & Sat-2 am. **Location:** Between Ave San Antonio and Calle Tintoreto. Ave Revolucion No 682, Col San Pedro de los Pinos. **Parking:** on-site. **Cards:** AX, MC, VI.

VIPS **Phone:** 55/5532-7816

Regional Mexican
$7-$25

Owned by Wal-Mart of Mexico and found in most major cities, the budget-friendly chain serves a good variety of Mexican and American dishes, including burgers, sandwiches, salads, spaghetti and enchiladas, as well as a fine selection of desserts. Casual dress. **Bar:** Beer & wine. **Hours:** 7 am-midnight, Fri & Sat-1 am. **Address:** Eugenia Sur No 194 **Location:** Just e of jct Ave Zempoala. **Parking:** on-site. **Cards:** AX, MC, VI.

VIPS **Phone:** 55/5260-4544

Regional Mexican
$7-$25

Owned by Wal-Mart of Mexico and found in most major cities, the budget-friendly chain serves a good variety of Mexican and American dishes, including burgers, sandwiches, salads, spaghetti and enchiladas, as well as a fine selection of desserts. Casual dress. **Bar:** Beer & wine. **Hours:** 7 am-11 pm. **Location:** Jct Ave Marina Nacional. Ave Melchor Ocampo No 193, Col Anahuac. **Parking:** on-site. **Cards:** AX, MC, VI.

VIPS **Phone:** 55/5595-0886

Regional Mexican
$7-$25

Owned by Wal-Mart of Mexico and found in most major cities, the budget-friendly chain serves a good variety of Mexican and American dishes, including burgers, sandwiches, salads, spaghetti and enchiladas, as well as a fine selection of desserts. Casual dress. **Bar:** Beer & wine. **Hours:** 7 am-1 am, Fri & Sat 24 hours. **Location:** Jct Blvd AL Mateos. Ave Contreras No 32, Col San Jeronimo. **Parking:** on-site (fee). **Cards:** AX, MC, VI.

VIPS **Phone:** 55/5554-6100

Regional Mexican
$7-$25

Owned by Wal-Mart of Mexico and found in most major cities, the budget-friendly chain serves a good variety of Mexican and American dishes, including burgers, sandwiches, salads, spaghetti and enchiladas, as well as a fine selection of desserts. Casual dress. **Bar:** Beer & wine. **Hours:** 7 am-10 pm. **Address:** Ave Copilco No 164, Col Oxtopulco **Location:** Jct Ave Universidad. **Parking:** on-site. **Cards:** AX, MC, VI.

VIPS **Phone:** 55/5510-3765

Regional Mexican
$7-$25

Owned by Wal-Mart of Mexico and found in most major cities, the budget-friendly chain serves a good variety of Mexican and American dishes, including burgers, sandwiches, salads, spaghetti and enchiladas, as well as a fine selection of desserts. Casual dress. **Bar:** Beer & wine. **Hours:** 7 am-10 pm. **Address:** Republic a de Uruguay No 53, Col Centro **Location:** Between Ave Bolivar and Isabel La Catolica. **Parking:** on-site (fee). **Cards:** AX, MC, VI.

(See maps and indexes p. 581-582, 584-586, 588-590)

VIPS

Phone: 55/5514-6009

Regional Mexican
$7-$25

Owned by Wal-Mart of Mexico and found in most major cities, the budget-friendly chain serves a good variety of Mexican and American dishes, including burgers, sandwiches, salads, spaghetti and enchiladas, as well as a fine selection of desserts. Casual dress. **Bar:** Beer & wine. **Hours:** 7 am-midnight, Fri & Sat-2 am. **Address:** Ave Insurgentes Sur No 180, Col Roma **Location:** Jct Aves Puebla and Tonala. **Parking:** on-site. **Cards:** AX, MC, VI.

VIPS

Phone: 55/5207-6434

Regional Mexican
$7-$25

Owned by Wal-Mart of Mexico and found in most major cities, the budget-friendly chain serves a good variety of Mexican and American dishes, including burgers, sandwiches, salads, spaghetti and enchiladas, as well as a fine selection of desserts. Casual dress. **Bar:** Beer & wine. **Hours:** 7 am-11 pm, Fri & Sat-1 am. **Address:** Ave Cuauhtmeoc No 19, Col Roma **Location:** Just s of jct Calle Puebla. **Parking:** on-site (fee). **Cards:** MC, VI.

VIPS

Phone: 55/5207-2680

Regional Mexican
$7-$25

Owned by Wal-Mart of Mexico and found in most major cities, the budget-friendly chain serves a good variety of Mexican and American dishes, including burgers, sandwiches, salads, spaghetti and enchiladas, as well as a fine selection of desserts. Casual dress. **Bar:** Beer & wine. **Hours:** 7 am-11 pm, Fri & Sat-1 am. **Address:** Calle Hamburgo No 126, Col Juarez **Location:** Between calles Amberes and Genova; in Zona Rosa. **Parking:** on-site. **Cards:** MC, VI.

VIPS

Phone: 55/5654-7500

Regional Mexican
$7-$25

Owned by Wal-Mart of Mexico and found in most major cities, the budget-friendly chain serves a good variety of Mexican and American dishes, including burgers, sandwiches, salads, spaghetti and enchiladas, as well as a fine selection of desserts. Casual dress. **Bar:** Beer & wine. **Hours:** 7 am-midnight, Fri & Sat-1 am. **Address:** Ave Rio Churubusco No 1120, Col Infonavit **Location:** Between aves Canal de Tezontle and Canal de Apatlaco. **Parking:** on-site. **Cards:** AX, MC, VI.

VIPS

Phone: 55/5705-1673

Regional Mexican
$7-$25

Owned by Wal-Mart of Mexico and found in most major cities, the budget-friendly chain serves a good variety of Mexican and American dishes, including burgers, sandwiches, salads, spaghetti and enchiladas, as well as a fine selection of desserts. Casual dress. **Bar:** Beer & wine. **Hours:** 24 hours. **Address:** Ave Insurgentes Sur No 14 Col Juarez **Location:** Jct Paseo de la Reforma and Dinamarca. **Parking:** no self-parking. **Cards:** AX, MC, VI.

VIPS

Phone: 55/5521-6170

Regional Mexican
$7-$25

Owned by Wal-Mart of Mexico and found in most major cities, the budget-friendly chain serves a good variety of Mexican and American dishes, including burgers, sandwiches, salads, spaghetti and enchiladas, as well as a fine selection of desserts. Casual dress. **Bar:** Beer & wine. **Hours:** 7 am-11 pm. **Location:** Jct Isabella la Catolica. Francisco I Madero No 53, Col Centro. **Parking:** no self-parking. **Cards:** AX, MC, VI.

VIPS

Phone: 55/5661-1414

Regional Mexican
$7-$25

Owned by Wal-Mart of Mexico and found in most major cities, the budget-friendly chain serves a good variety of Mexican and American dishes, including burgers, sandwiches, salads, spaghetti and enchiladas, as well as a fine selection of desserts. Casual dress. **Bar:** Beer & wine. **Hours:** 7 am-11 pm, Fri & Sat-1 am. **Location:** Jct Ave Universidad. Miguel Angel de Quevedo No 175, Col Oxtopuko. **Parking:** on-site. **Cards:** AX, MC, VI.

VIPS

Phone: 55/5658-5786

Regional Mexican
$7-$25

Owned by Wal-Mart of Mexico and found in most major cities, the budget-friendly chain serves a good variety of Mexican and American dishes, including burgers, sandwiches, salads, spaghetti and enchiladas, as well as a fine selection of desserts. Casual dress. **Bar:** Beer & wine. **Hours:** 7 am-midnight, Fri & Sat-2 am. **Location:** Jct Ave Pacifico. Miguel Angel de Quevado No 870, Col B de la Concepcion. **Parking:** on-site. **Cards:** AX, MC, VI.

VIPS

Phone: 55/5719-4116

Regional Mexican
$7-$25

Owned by Wal-Mart of Mexico and found in most major cities, the budget-friendly chain serves a good variety of Mexican and American dishes, including burgers, sandwiches, salads, spaghetti and enchiladas, as well as a fine selection of desserts. Casual dress. **Bar:** Beer & wine. **Hours:** 7 am-11 pm. **Address:** Ave Cuit lahuac No 367, Col Defensores de **Location:** Just e of Calzada Vallejo. **Parking:** on-site. **Cards:** AX, MC, VI.

(See maps and indexes p. 581-582, 584-586, 588-590)

VIPS

Phone: 55/5752-9506

Regional Mexican
$7-$25

Owned by Wal-Mart of Mexico and found in most major cities, the budget-friendly chain serves a good variety of Mexican and American dishes, including burgers, sandwiches, salads, spaghetti and enchiladas, as well as a fine selection of desserts. Casual dress. **Bar:** Beer & wine. **Hours:** 7 am-11 pm, Fri & Sat-1 am. **Address:** Ave Miguel othon de Mendizabal Ote **Location:** Jct Calle Juan de Dios Batiz. **Parking:** on-site. **Cards:** AX, MC, VI.

VIPS

Phone: 55/5517-2000

Regional Mexican
$7-$25

Owned by Wal-Mart of Mexico and found in most major cities, the budget-friendly chain serves a good variety of Mexican and American dishes, including burgers, sandwiches, salads, spaghetti and enchiladas, as well as a fine selection of desserts. Casual dress. **Bar:** Beer & wine. **Hours:** 7 am-11 pm, Fri & Sat-1 am. **Address:** Calz de Guadalupe No 431, Col Gde Tepeyac **Location:** Just s of Ave Victoria. **Parking:** on-site. **Cards:** AX, MC, VI.

VIPS

Phone: 55/5514-7989

Regional Mexican
$7-$25

Owned by Wal-Mart of Mexico and found in most major cities, the budget-friendly chain serves a good variety of Mexican and American dishes, including burgers, sandwiches, salads, spaghetti and enchiladas, as well as a fine selection of desserts. Casual dress. **Bar:** Beer & wine. **Hours:** 7 am-1 am, Fri & Sat 24 hours. **Address:** Ave Insurgentes Sur No 866, Col Del **Location:** Jct Calzada Ameyalco. **Parking:** on-site. **Cards:** AX, MC, VI.

VIPS

Phone: 55/5676-5564

Regional Mexican
$7-$25

Owned by Wal-Mart of Mexico and found in most major cities, the budget-friendly chain serves a good variety of Mexican and American dishes, including burgers, sandwiches, salads, spaghetti and enchiladas, as well as a fine selection of desserts. Casual dress. **Bar:** Beer & wine. **Hours:** 7 am-11 pm, Fri & Sat-1 am. **Location:** Between Calzada Tlalpan and Ave B Juarez. Ave Division del Norte No 3651, Col San Pablo. **Parking:** on-site. **Cards:** AX, MC, VI.

VIPS

Phone: 55/5259-4574

Regional Mexican
$7-$25

Owned by Wal-Mart of Mexico and found in most major cities, the budget-friendly chain serves a good variety of Mexican and American dishes, including burgers, sandwiches, salads, spaghetti and enchiladas, as well as a fine selection of desserts. Casual dress. **Bar:** Beer & wine. **Hours:** 7 am-11 pm. **Location:** Just n of jct Ave Bosque de Alisos. Paseo de las Lilas No 92, Col Bosques de las Lomas. **Parking:** on-site. **Cards:** AX, MC, VI.

VIPS

Phone: 55/5533-3187

Regional Mexican
$7-$25

Owned by Wal-Mart of Mexico and found in most major cities, the budget-friendly chain serves a good variety of Mexican and American dishes, including burgers, sandwiches, salads, spaghetti and enchiladas, as well as a fine selection of desserts. Casual dress. **Bar:** Beer & wine. **Hours:** 7 am-midnight, Fri & Sat-1 am. **Address:** Calle Lancaster No 20, Col Juarez **Location:** Across from Angel of Independance monument, off Paseo del la Reforma. **Parking:** no self-parking. **Cards:** AX, MC, VI.

VIPS

Phone: 55/5282-0822

Regional Mexican
$7-$25

Owned by Wal-Mart of Mexico and found in most major cities, the budget-friendly chain serves a good variety of Mexican and American dishes, including burgers, sandwiches, salads, spaghetti and enchiladas, as well as a fine selection of desserts. Casual dress. **Bar:** Beer & wine. **Hours:** 7 am-10 pm. **Address:** Calle Arquimedes No 130, Col Polanco **Location:** Jct Calle Horacio. **Parking:** no self-parking. **Cards:** AX, MC, VI.

VIPS

Phone: 55/5768-4660

Regional Mexican
$7-$25

Owned by Wal-Mart of Mexico and found in most major cities, the budget-friendly chain serves a good variety of Mexican and American dishes, including burgers, sandwiches, salads, spaghetti and enchiladas, as well as a fine selection of desserts. Casual dress. **Bar:** Beer & wine. **Hours:** 7 am-10 pm. **Address:** Calz de la Viga No 136, Lorenzo Boturini **Location:** Just s of Callejon Cuitlahuac. **Parking:** on-site. **Cards:** AX, MC, VI.

VIPS

Phone: 55/5702-7671

Regional Mexican
$7-$25

Owned by Wal-Mart of Mexico and found in most major cities, the budget-friendly chain serves a good variety of Mexican and American dishes, including burgers, sandwiches, salads, spaghetti and enchiladas, as well as a fine selection of desserts. Casual dress. **Bar:** Beer & wine. **Hours:** 7 am-11 pm. **Location:** Jct Calle Albaniles. Calle Vulcanizacion No 5, Col 20 de Noviembre. **Parking:** on-site. **Cards:** AX, MC, VI.

(See maps and indexes p. 581-582, 584-586, 588-590)

VIPS

Regional Mexican
$7-$25

Phone: 55/5577-1993

Owned by Wal-Mart of Mexico and found in most major cities, the budget-friendly chain serves a good variety of Mexican and American dishes, including burgers, sandwiches, salads, spaghetti and enchiladas, as well as a fine selection of desserts. Casual dress. **Bar:** Beer & wine. **Hours:** 7 am-11 pm. **Address:** Ave Montevideo No 109, Col GA Madero **Location:** Jct Ave Insurgentes Norte. **Parking:** no self-parking. **Cards:** AX, MC, VI.

VIPS

Regional Mexican
$7-$25

Phone: 55/5703-0356

Owned by Wal-Mart of Mexico and found in most major cities, the budget-friendly chain serves a good variety of Mexican and American dishes, including burgers, sandwiches, salads, spaghetti and enchiladas, as well as a fine selection of desserts. Casual dress. **Bar:** Beer & wine. **Hours:** 7 am-11 pm. **Location:** Jct Ave Insurgentes. Ave Rivera de San Cosme No 8, Col San Rafel. **Parking:** on-site (fee). **Cards:** AX, MC, VI.

VIPS

Regional Mexican
$7-$25

Phone: 55/5740-3198

Owned by Wal-Mart of Mexico and found in most major cities, the budget-friendly chain serves a good variety of Mexican and American dishes, including burgers, sandwiches, salads, spaghetti and enchiladas, as well as a fine selection of desserts. Casual dress. **Bar:** Beer & wine. **Hours:** 7 am-midnight, Fri & Sat-1 am, Sun-11 pm. **Location:** Just w of Calz Chabanaco. Calle Jose Antonio Torres No 647, Col Asturio. **Parking:** on-site (fee). **Cards:** AX, MC, VI.

VIPS

Regional Mexican
$7-$25

Phone: 55/5761-9274

Owned by Wal-Mart of Mexico and found in most major cities, the budget-friendly chain serves a good variety of Mexican and American dishes, including burgers, sandwiches, salads, spaghetti and enchiladas, as well as a fine selection of desserts. Casual dress. **Bar:** Beer & wine. **Hours:** 7 am-11 pm. **Address:** Fray Servando Teresa de Mier 45, Col **Location:** Between Eje Central and Ave Bolivar. **Parking:** on-site. **Cards:** AX, MC, VI.

VIPS

Regional Mexican
$7-$25

Phone: 55/5115-1812

Owned by Wal-Mart of Mexico and found in most major cities, the budget-friendly chain serves a good variety of Mexican and American dishes, including burgers, sandwiches, salads, spaghetti and enchiladas, as well as a fine selection of desserts. Casual dress. **Bar:** Beer & wine. **Hours:** 7 am-11 pm. **Address:** Calz I Zaragoza No 1090 Col Agricola **Location:** Between Calles 3 and 4. **Parking:** on-site. **Cards:** AX, MC, VI.

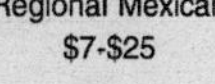

VIPS

Regional Mexican
$7-$25

Phone: 55/5535-6738

Owned by Wal-Mart of Mexico and found in most major cities, the budget-friendly chain serves a good variety of Mexican and American dishes, including burgers, sandwiches, salads, spaghetti and enchiladas, as well as a fine selection of desserts. Casual dress. **Bar:** Beer & wine. **Hours:** 7 am-11 pm, Fri & Sat-1 am. **Address:** Ignacio Ramirez #20, Col San Rafael **Location:** Just off Paseo de la Reforma; across from Fiesta American Reforma hotel. **Parking:** street. **Cards:** AX, MC, VI.

VIPS

Regional Mexican
$7-$25

Phone: 55/5666-8548

Owned by Wal-Mart of Mexico and found in most major cities, the budget-friendly chain serves a good variety of Mexican and American dishes, including burgers, sandwiches, salads, spaghetti and enchiladas, as well as a fine selection of desserts. Casual dress. **Bar:** Beer & wine. **Hours:** 7 am-11 pm, Fri & Sat-midnight. **Address:** Ave Insurgentes Sur No 3195, Col **Location:** Jct Ave Arboledas. **Parking:** on-site. **Cards:** AX, MC, VI.

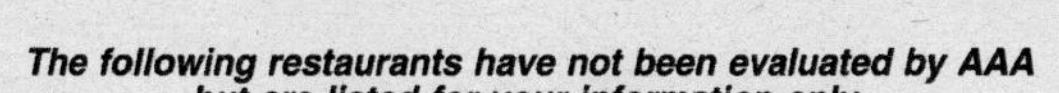

The following restaurants have not been evaluated by AAA but are listed for your information only.

AURA RESTAURANTE

fyi

Phone: 55/5282-3100

Not evaluated. Find contemporary cuisine and ambience at this casual restaurant. **Address:** Ave Presidente Masaryk #201 **Location:** Jct La Martine; in Polanco Zone; in Habita Hotel.

COMO

fyi

Phone: 55/5250-1596

Not evaluated. Diners here enjoy the casual ambience and the good menu selection featuring an extensive pasta selection, as well as meat and poultry offerings. **Address:** Horacio 253 Polanco.

LA HACIENDA DE LOS MORALES

fyi

Phone: 55/5096-3055

Not evaluated. Surrounded by beautiful gardens with fountains, the restored hacienda boasts large courtyards and dining rooms suited to relaxing, refined dining. Excellent quality ingredients go into dishes that are served in ample portions. The staff is formal. **Address:** Vazquez de Mella 525 **Location:** Just s of Ejercito Nacional; in Polanco District.

LA PIGUA

fyi

Phone: 55/5281-1302

Not evaluated. This pleasant restaurant features an interesting seafood menu which highlights specialties from the Gulf Coast and the Yucatan Peninsula. **Address:** Alejandro Dumas #16.

(See maps and indexes p. 581-582, 584-586, 588-590)

MERIDIEM **Phone:** 55/5273-3599

fyi Not evaluated. The eatery offers contemporary cuisine and an attractive patio dining area. **Address:** Margen Izquierdo Lago Mayor, 2 da **Location:** In new section of Chapultepec Park; near National Museum of History.

MESON DEL CID **Phone:** 55/5512-7629

fyi Not evaluated. Since 1972, this distinguished Mexico City favorite has been preparing classic and contemporary Spanish cuisine, the hallmarks of its menu. Medieval dinners are offered on Saturdays. **Address:** Humbolt #61 **Location:** In downtown historic center; in Articulo 123 and Morelos.

National Museum of Anthropology / Nadine Markova / Mexico Tourism Board

This ends listings for Mexico City.
The following page resumes the alphabetical listings
of cities in Mexico City and Vicinity.

NAUCALPAN, DISTRITO FEDERAL (See map and index starting on p. 588)

— WHERE TO STAY —

HOLIDAY INN MEXICO CITY TOREO-SATELITE **Phone:** 55/5312-9760 16

Hotel
$95-$140 All Year

Address: San Luis Tlatilco #2 **Location:** Corner of San Luis Tlatilco and Gustavo Bas; center. **Facility:** 114 units. 110 one-bedroom standard units. 4 one-bedroom suites with whirlpools. 6 stories, interior corridors. *Bath:* combo or shower only. **Parking:** on-site and valet. **Amenities:** high-speed Internet, voice mail, irons, hair dryers. *Some:* DVD players. **Leisure Activities:** sauna, whirlpool, steamroom, playground, exercise room, sports court. *Fee:* massage. **Guest Services:** valet and coin laundry, area transportation, wireless Internet. **Business Services:** meeting rooms, business center. **Cards:** AX, DC, MC, VI.

/ SOME UNITS

— WHERE TO DINE —

SANBORN'S **Phone:** 55/5343-5133

Regional Mexican
$8-$28

Restaurants in the casual chain, which includes more than 100 locations throughout Mexico, offer a good selection of American-style sandwiches, salads, soups and both Mexican and American entrees. The selection of desserts is impressive. Casual dress. **Bar:** Full bar. **Hours:** 7 am-1 am. **Location:** Just n of jct Ave Pierre Lyonnet. Ave Lomas Verdes No. 545, Col Lomas Verdes. **Parking:** on-site. **Cards:** AX, MC, VI.

SANBORN'S **Phone:** 55/5373-2212

Regional Mexican
$8-$28

Restaurants in the casual chain, which includes more than 100 locations throughout Mexico, offer a good selection of American-style sandwiches, salads, soups and both Mexican and American entrees. The selection of desserts is impressive. Casual dress. **Bar:** Full bar. **Hours:** 7 am-1 am, Sun-10 pm. **Address:** Ave Gustavo Baz No 226, Col Hdade **Location:** Just s of jct Calzada San Agustin. **Parking:** on-site (fee). **Cards:** AX, MC, VI.

TEOTIHUACAN, MEXICO

— WHERE TO STAY —

CLUB MED VILLAS ARQUEOLOGICAS **Phone:** (594)956-0909

Hotel
$92-$180 All Year

Address: Periferico Sur S/N **Location:** Adjacent to main archeological zone, off Mex 132. **Facility:** 42 units. 39 one-bedroom standard units. 3 one-bedroom suites. 2 stories (no elevator), exterior corridors. *Bath:* shower or tub only. **Parking:** on-site. **Terms:** 3 day cancellation notice, seasonal. **Amenities:** safes, hair dryers. **Pool(s):** outdoor. **Leisure Activities:** lighted tennis court, playground. **Guest Services:** valet laundry, wireless Internet. **Business Services:** meeting rooms, fax (fee). **Cards:** AX, CB, DC, JC, MC, VI.

/ SOME UNITS

QUINTO SOL HOTEL **Phone:** 594/956-1881

Hotel
$55-$100 All Year

Address: Ave Hidalgo #26, Barrio Purificacion **Location:** On road leading to pyramids. **Facility:** 34 one-bedroom standard units, some with whirlpools. 2 stories, interior corridors. *Bath:* shower only. **Parking:** on-site. **Amenities:** hair dryers. **Pool(s):** outdoor. **Guest Services:** area transportation (fee). **Business Services:** business center. **Cards:** AX, MC, VI.

/ SOME UNITS

— WHERE TO DINE —

RESTAURANT LA GRITA **Phone:** 594/956-0104

Regional Mexican
$15-$30

At the entrance to the pyramids, the restaurant occupies an immense cave at the foot of the mountain. Casual dress. **Bar:** Full bar. **Hours:** 11 am-7 pm. **Address:** Zona Arqueologica Teotihuacan S/N **Location:** Adjacent to main archeological zone. **Parking:** on-site. **Cards:** AX, MC, VI.

TEPOZTLAN, MORELOS pop. 32,921

— WHERE TO STAY —

POSADA DEL TEPOZTECO **Phone:** 739/395-0010

Historic Country Inn
$140-$430 All Year

Address: Paraiso #3 **Location:** Just w of main plaza. **Facility:** Situated in a village that dates back to pre-conquest Mexico, the inn's clay floor pavers, arched entries and hand-pained accents evoke ol' Mexico. 20 units. 18 one-bedroom standard units. 2 one-bedroom suites, some with whirlpools. 2 stories, exterior corridors. *Bath:* combo or shower only. **Parking:** on-site. **Amenities:** safes, irons, hair dryers. **Pool(s):** heated outdoor. **Guest Services:** valet laundry, wireless Internet. **Business Services:** meeting rooms, PC. **Cards:** AX, MC, VI.

/ SOME UNITS

— WHERE TO DINE —

RESTAURANT AXITLA **Phone:** 739/395-0519

Regional Mexican
$9-$15

Hidden in the steep hills of this ancient Aztec town, the restaurant's lush gardens provide a relaxed dining retreat. Patrons enjoy beautiful views as they savor authentic Mexican dishes such as mole, chicken enchiladas or even the classic trout amandine. Refreshing aguas frescas, such as agua de Jamaica or tamarindo, are made from exotic fruit and flowers. Casual dress. **Bar:** Full bar. **Hours:** 10 am-7 pm, Sat & Sun from 9 am. **Address:** Ave del Tepozteco S/N **Location:** At far north end of Ave del Tepozteco. **Parking:** on-site. **Cards:** MC, VI.

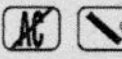

The following restaurant has not been evaluated by AAA but is listed for your information only.

LOS COLORINES **Phone:** 739/395-0198

fyi

Not evaluated. Located on the town's main boulevard, this informal Mexican restaurant has a festive decor with multi-colored flags draped from the ceiling. The menu includes classic Mexican dishes as well some American selections. **Address:** Ave de Tepozteco #13 **Location:** Center.

TEQUESQUITENGO, MORELOS pop. 2,800

WHERE TO STAY

The following lodging was either not evaluated or did not meet AAA rating requirements but is listed for your information only.

HOTEL HACIENDA VISTA HERMOSA **Phone:** 734/345-5361

fyi

Not evaluated. **Address:** KM 7 Carr Alpuyeca **Location:** 5.1 mi (8.5 km) se of Alpuyeca interchange off Mex 95 and 95-D (toll road); 0.9 mi (1.5 km) n of Lake Tequesquitengo. Facilities, services, and decor characterize a mid-scale property.

TLALNEPANTLA, MEXICO pop. 721,415 (See map and index starting on p. 588)

WHERE TO STAY

CROWNE PLAZA LANCASTER TLALNEPANTLA *Book at AAA.com* **Phone:** (55)5228-9500 12

Hotel
$135-$275 All Year

Address: Ave Roberto Fulton 2-A **Location:** Just 0.5 mi (0.8 km) e of jct MEX 57 at Tlalnepantla de Baz; n of Mexico City limits. **Facility:** Meets AAA guest room security requirements. 126 units. 119 one-bedroom standard units. 7 one-bedroom suites with whirlpools. 7 stories, interior corridors. **Parking:** on-site. **Terms:** cancellation fee imposed. **Amenities:** high-speed Internet, voice mail, safes, honor bars, irons, hair dryers. **Leisure Activities:** sauna, whirlpool, steamroom, lighted tennis court, jogging, exercise room. **Guest Services:** valet laundry, wireless Internet. **Business Services:** conference facilities, business center. **Cards:** AX, DC, DS, MC, VI.

24 D / SOME UNITS

TOLUCA, MEXICO pop. 666,596

WHERE TO STAY

DEL REY INN HOTEL **Phone:** (722)277-1010

Hotel
$132-$165 All Year

Address: Carr Mex Toluca KM 63.5 **Location:** 2.4 mi (4 km) e on Mex 15. **Facility:** 253 one-bedroom standard units, some with whirlpools. 2-5 stories, interior corridors. **Parking:** on-site. **Terms:** 3 day cancellation notice. **Amenities:** high-speed Internet, voice mail, safes, irons, hair dryers. *Some:* honor bars. **Dining:** entertainment. **Pool(s):** heated indoor. **Leisure Activities:** sauna, whirlpool, playground, exercise room, game room. *Fee:* massage. **Guest Services:** valet laundry, wireless Internet. **Business Services:** meeting rooms, business center. **Cards:** AX, MC, VI.

/ SOME UNITS

QUINTA DEL REY **Phone:** 722/275-8000

Hotel
$159-$234 All Year

Address: Paseo del Tollacan Ote KM 5 **Location:** 5.7 mi (9.5 km) e on Mex 15. **Facility:** 66 units. 63 one- and 3 two-bedroom standard units. 3 stories, interior corridors. **Parking:** on-site. **Amenities:** high-speed Internet, voice mail, safes, irons, hair dryers. **Dining:** entertainment. **Pool(s):** heated indoor. **Leisure Activities:** sauna, whirlpool, exercise room, spa, game room. **Guest Services:** valet laundry, airport transportation-Toluca Airport, area transportation-within 5 mi (8 km), wireless Internet. **Business Services:** meeting rooms, business center. **Cards:** AX, DC, MC, VI.

/ SOME UNITS

The following lodgings were either not evaluated or did not meet AAA rating requirements but are listed for your information only.

CROWNE PLAZA HOTEL TOLUCA LANCASTER **Phone:** 722/477-1000

fyi

Not evaluated. **Address:** Paseo del Tollocan 750 Ote. Facilities, services, and decor characterize an upscale property.

EL GRAN HOTEL **Phone:** 722/213-9888

fyi

Not evaluated; located in remote area. **Address:** Ave Allende #124 Col Centro **Location:** Center. Facilities, services, and decor characterize a mid-scale property.

WHERE TO DINE

SANBORN'S **Phone:** 722/212-6773

Regional Mexican
$8-$28

Restaurants in the casual chain, which includes more than 100 locations throughout Mexico, offer a good selection of American-style sandwiches, salads, soups and both Mexican and American entrees. The selection of desserts is impressive. Casual dress. **Bar:** Full bar. **Hours:** 7 am-1 am. **Address:** Paseo Colon No 200, Col Residencial Colon **Location:** Jct Ave Venustiano Carranza. **Parking:** on-site. **Cards:** AX, MC, VI.

SANBORN'S

Regional Mexican
$8-$28

Phone: 722/232-5690

Restaurants in the casual chain, which includes more than 100 locations throughout Mexico, offer a good selection of American-style sandwiches, salads, soups and both Mexican and American entrees. The selection of desserts is impressive. Casual dress. **Bar:** Full bar. **Hours:** 7 am-1 am. **Location:** Just s of jct Ave Pedro Ascencio. Blvd Toluca Ixtapan No 126 Norte, Centro Comercial Galerias. **Parking:** on-site (fee). **Cards:** AX, MC, VI.

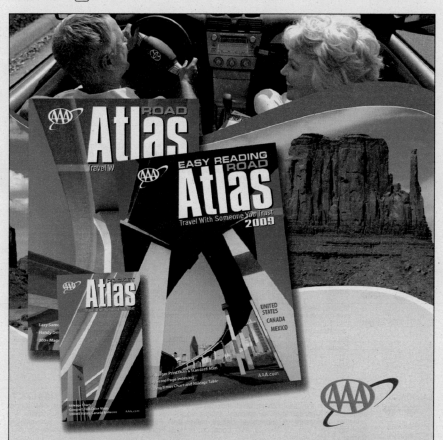

XOCHIMILCO, DISTRITO FEDERAL pop. 369,787

WHERE TO DINE

VIPS

Regional Mexican
$7-$25

Phone: 55/5675-3118

Owned by Wal-Mart of Mexico and found in most major cities, the budget-friendly chain serves a good variety of Mexican and American dishes, including burgers, sandwiches, salads, spaghetti and enchiladas, as well as a fine selection of desserts. Casual dress. **Bar:** Beer & wine. **Hours:** 7 am-midnight, Fri & Sat-1 am. **Address:** Prol Division del Norte No 4901 Col San **Location:** Jct Rincon del Rio. **Parking:** valet. **Cards:** AX, MC, VI.

CENTRAL MEXICO

ABASOLO, GUANAJUATO pop. 79,093

WHERE TO STAY

The following lodging was either not evaluated or did not meet AAA rating requirements but is listed for your information only.

HOTEL BALNEARIO SPA LA CALDERA — **Phone:** 429/693-0020

fyi

Not evaluated. **Address:** Tibramiento Carretera KM 29 **Location:** On Mex 90. Facilities, services, and decor characterize an economy property.

AGUASCALIENTES, AGUASCALIENTES pop. 643,419

WHERE TO STAY

FIESTA INN AGUASCALIENTES — **Phone:** (449)149-0200

Hotel

$140-$160 All Year

Address: Mahatma Gandhi 302 Sur **Location:** 0.6 mi (1 km) s on Leon Hwy (Mex 45). Located adjacent to a large shopping center. **Facility:** 125 one-bedroom standard units. 3 stories (no elevator), interior corridors. **Parking:** on-site. **Amenities:** irons, hair dryers. *Some:* high-speed Internet. **Pool(s):** heated outdoor. **Leisure Activities:** swing set, exercise room. **Guest Services:** valet laundry, wireless Internet. **Business Services:** meeting rooms, business center. **Cards:** AX, DC, MC, VI. *(See color ad on insert)*

/ SOME UNITS

HOTEL DE ANDREA ALAMEDA — **Phone:** (449)970-3800

Hotel

$110-$145 All Year

Address: Alameda 821 **Location:** On east side, 3 blks e of Ave de la Convencion. Located in a quiet residential area. **Facility:** 48 units. 46 one-bedroom standard units. 2 one-bedroom suites. 2 stories (no elevator), interior corridors. *Bath:* combo or shower only. **Parking:** on-site. **Amenities:** honor bars, hair dryers. **Pool(s):** heated outdoor. **Leisure Activities:** limited exercise equipment. **Guest Services:** wireless Internet. **Business Services:** meeting rooms, business center. **Cards:** AX, MC, VI.

/ SOME UNITS

HOTEL FRANCIA AGUASCALIENTES — **Phone:** 449/918-7300

Hotel

$85 All Year

Address: Ave Fco I Madero #113-A **Location:** Center. **Facility:** 74 units. 72 one-bedroom standard units. 2 two-bedroom suites. 7 stories, interior corridors. *Bath:* combo or shower only. **Parking:** valet. **Amenities:** voice mail, safes, honor bars, hair dryers. **Dining:** Sanborn's, see separate listing. **Guest Services:** valet laundry, wireless Internet. **Business Services:** meeting rooms, business center. **Cards:** AX, MC, VI.

D / SOME UNITS

QUINTA REAL AGUASCALIENTES *Book at AAA.com* — **Phone:** (449)978-5818

Hotel

$131-$335 All Year

Address: Ave Aguascalientes Sur 601 **Location:** On south side, just e of jct Blvd Jos Chavez and Ave Aguascalientes, on highway to Leon. Located along a busy boulevard. **Facility:** This stylish hotel features elegantly decorated rooms with unique art and a fountained courtyard that provides a fine level of colonial charm. 85 units. 79 one-bedroom standard units, some with whirlpools. 4 one-, 1 two- and 1 three-bedroom suites. 3 stories, interior/exterior corridors. **Parking:** on-site and valet. **Terms:** cancellation fee imposed. **Amenities:** honor bars, irons, hair dryers. **Pool(s):** heated outdoor. **Guest Services:** valet laundry, wireless Internet. **Business Services:** meeting rooms, business center. **Cards:** AX, MC, VI. Affiliated with A Preferred Hotel. ***(See color ad p 8)***

D / SOME UNITS

WHERE TO DINE

SANBORN'S — **Phone:** 449/915-8774

Mexican

$8-$18

Restaurants in the casual chain, which includes more than 100 locations throughout Mexico, offer a good selection of American-style sandwiches, salads, soups and both Mexican and American entrees. The selection of desserts is impressive. Casual dress. **Bar:** Full bar. **Hours:** 7 am-1 am, Sun-midnight. **Address:** Ave Francisco Madero, #111 **Location:** In Hotel Francia Aguascalientes. **Parking:** on-site (fee). **Cards:** AX, MC, VI.

SANBORN'S — **Phone:** 449/912-4002

Mexican

$8-$18

Restaurants in the casual chain, which includes more than 100 locations throughout Mexico, offer a good selection of American-style sandwiches, salads, soups and both Mexican and American entrees. The selection of desserts is impressive. Casual dress. **Bar:** Full bar. **Hours:** 7 am-1 am, Sun-midnight. **Address:** Ave Universidad, #1001 **Location:** Jct Ave Universidad and Ave Aguascalientes Norte, just n. **Parking:** on-site (fee). **Cards:** AX, MC, VI.

VIPS — **Phone:** 449/914-8857

Mexican

$5-$9

Owned by Wal-Mart of Mexico and found in most major cities, the budget-friendly chain serves a good variety of Mexican and American dishes, including burgers, sandwiches, salads, spaghetti and enchiladas, as well as a fine selection of desserts. Casual dress. **Hours:** 7 am-11 pm, Fri & Sat-1 am. **Address:** Ave Independencia #2351 **Location:** Jct blvds Aguascalientes and Independencia, just e; in Galerias Shopping Mall. **Parking:** on-site. **Cards:** MC, VI.

VIPS

Mexican
$5-$11

Phone: 449/914-1514

Owned by Wal-Mart of Mexico and found in most major cities, the budget-friendly chain serves a good variety of Mexican and American dishes, including burgers, sandwiches, salads, spaghetti and enchiladas, as well as a fine selection of desserts. Casual dress. **Hours:** 7 am-midnight, Fri & Sat-1 am. **Address:** Centro Comercial Expo Plaza Loc 152 **Location:** In Expo Plaza Shopping Mall. **Parking:** on-site. **Cards:** MC, VI.

AJIJIC, JALISCO pop. 13,300

WHERE TO STAY

AJIJIC INN

Bed & Breakfast
$74-$114 All Year

Phone: 376/766-1752

Address: O' Campo 54 **Location:** Jct Pedro Morenos. **Facility:** The delightful inn features spacious rooms with a distinct Mexican decor, including cupboards with hand-painted murals and etchings on the walls. 7 units. 5 one-bedroom standard units. 2 one-bedroom suites with kitchens. 1 story, exterior corridors. *Bath:* combo or shower only. **Parking:** on-site. **Terms:** age restrictions may apply. **Pool(s):** outdoor.

/ SOME UNITS

AJIJIC PLAZA SUITES

Motel
$45-$55 All Year

Phone: 376/766-0383

Address: Calle Colon 33 **Location:** Center. Located across from the main plaza. **Facility:** 10 one-bedroom standard units. 1 story, exterior corridors. *Bath:* shower only. **Parking:** street. **Terms:** 3 day cancellation notice. **Pool(s):** outdoor. **Leisure Activities:** *Fee:* massage. **Guest Services:** valet laundry. **Cards:** MC, VI.

/ SOME UNITS

HOTEL REAL DE CHAPALA

Hotel
$110-$120 All Year

Phone: 376/766-0014

Address: Paseo del Prado #20 **Location:** In La Floresta area; between Blvd Ajijic and Chapala. **Facility:** 85 units. 80 one-bedroom standard units. 5 one-bedroom suites with whirlpools. 2 stories (no elevator), interior/exterior corridors. *Bath:* combo or shower only. **Parking:** on-site. **Amenities:** safes. **Pool(s):** 2 heated outdoor. **Leisure Activities:** volleyball. *Fee:* 2 lighted tennis courts. **Guest Services:** valet laundry, wireless Internet. **Business Services:** meeting rooms, PC (fee). **Cards:** AX, MC, VI.

/ SOME UNITS

LA NUEVA POSADA

Country Inn
$91-$115 All Year

Phone: 376/766-1344

Address: Donato Guerra #9 **Location:** Just se of main plaza. **Facility:** The inn overlooks Lake Chapala. Some rooms have balconies, all display Mexican-Colonial decor, colorful artwork, and comfortable furnishings. 23 units. 21 one- and 2 two-bedroom standard units. 3 stories (no elevator), interior corridors. *Bath:* shower or tub only. **Parking:** on-site. **Terms:** 21 day cancellation notice. **Amenities:** *Some:* irons. **Dining:** Restaurante La Rusa, see separate listing. **Pool(s):** outdoor. **Guest Services:** wireless Internet. **Business Services:** meeting rooms, PC. **Cards:** MC, VI.

/ SOME UNITS

LOS ARTISTAS BED & BREAKFAST

Bed & Breakfast
$69-$89 All Year

Phone: 376/766-1027

Address: Constitucion #105 **Location:** Center. **Facility:** An eclectically decorated guest lounge is adorned with the owner's art collection, and a manicured garden offers outside interest. 6 one-bedroom standard units. 1 story, interior/exterior corridors. *Bath:* shower only. **Parking:** on-site. **Pool(s):** outdoor. **Guest Services:** wireless Internet.

/ SOME UNITS

VILLA EUCALIPTOS BED AND BREAKFAST

Bed & Breakfast
$68-$88 All Year

Phone: 376/766-1400

Address: 16 de Septiembre #127 **Location:** Just e of Aldama. **Facility:** 5 one-bedroom standard units. 2 stories (no elevator), exterior corridors. *Bath:* shower only. **Parking:** on-site and street. **Terms:** 28 day cancellation notice. **Pool(s):** heated outdoor. **Leisure Activities:** whirlpool. **Guest Services:** wireless Internet. **Business Services:** PC.

/ SOME UNITS

WHERE TO DINE

JOHANNA'S AUSTRIAN CUISINE

Continental
$8-$11

Phone: 376/766-0437

Austrian and German food is the specialty. Noteworthy are the fine schnitzels and the wonderful Leipziger filet with Dijon sauce. Apfelstrudel is magnificent. Guests can choose from a fine selection of wines and imported German beers. Casual dress. **Bar:** Beer & wine. **Reservations:** accepted. **Hours:** 12:30 pm-8 pm. Closed: 12/25; also Mon. **Address:** Blvd Ajijic 118-A **Location:** Center; along Main St through town. **Parking:** street.

PEDRO'S GOURMET

Continental
$4-$15

Phone: 376/766-4747

The open-air cafe serves US-style fare melded with Mexican accents. Attractively priced daily specials reflect the best of both cuisines. Casual dress. **Bar:** Full bar. **Reservations:** accepted. **Hours:** noon-9 pm. Closed: 4/12; also Sun & Mon. **Address:** Ocampo #71 **Location:** Jct Ocampo and Aquiles Serdan, just e; center. **Parking:** street.

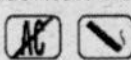

RESTAURANTE LA RUSA **Phone:** 376/766-1344

Continental
$10-$19

Popular with the town's American residents, the restaurant features Continental, American and Mexican cuisine. Some tables in the elegantly furnished dining room offer views of the garden and patio. Casual dress. **Bar:** Full bar. **Reservations:** accepted. **Hours:** 8 am-9 pm, Fri & Sat-10 pm. **Address:** Donato Guerra #9 **Location:** Just se of main plaza; in La Nueva Posada. **Parking:** on-site. **Cards:** MC, VI.

CELAYA, GUANAJUATO pop. 382,958

WHERE TO DINE

SANBORN'S **Phone:** 461/609-0600

Regional Mexican
$8-$28

Restaurants in the casual chain, which includes more than 100 locations throughout Mexico, offer a good selection of American-style sandwiches, salads, soups and both Mexican and American entrees. The selection of desserts is impressive. Casual dress. **Bar:** Full bar. **Hours:** 7 am-1 am. **Address:** Blvd Adolfo Lopez Mateos 809 Pte **Location:** At jct Ave Emetria Valencia. **Parking:** street. **Cards:** AX, MC, VI.

CIUDAD VALLES, SAN LUIS POTOSI pop. 146,604

WHERE TO STAY

The following lodging was either not evaluated or did not meet AAA rating requirements but is listed for your information only.

COUNTRY INN & SUITES BY CARLSON **Phone:** 481/813-8230

fyi

Not evaluated. **Address:** Blvd Don Antonio 151. Facilities, services, and decor characterize a mid-scale property.

DOLORES HIDALGO, GUANAJUATO pop. 128,994

WHERE TO STAY

HOTEL HIDALGO **Phone:** 418/182-2683

Hotel
$40 All Year

Address: Hidalgo #15 Centro **Location:** 2 blks e of main plaza. Located across from a hospital and half a block from bus terminal. **Facility:** 30 units. 28 one-bedroom standard units. 2 one-bedroom suites. 3 stories (no elevator), interior corridors. *Bath:* combo or shower only. **Parking:** on-site and street. **Amenities:** safes. **Leisure Activities:** steamroom, exercise room. **Guest Services:** coin laundry, wireless Internet. **Business Services:** fax. **Cards:** MC, VI.

WHERE TO DINE

EL CARUAJE DEL CAUDILLO **Phone:** 418/182-0474

Regional International
$4-$15

Facing historic Dolores Hidalgo Plaza, the family restaurant specializes in provincial dishes served with flair. Casual dress. **Bar:** Full bar. **Hours:** 8 am-11 pm. **Address:** Plaza Principal #8 **Location:** Across from east side of main plaza. **Parking:** street. **Cards:** AX, DC, DS, MC, VI.

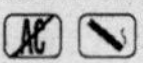

PARADOR AMIGO **Phone:** 418/185-9008

Regional Mexican
$4-$10

Located just outside of town on the highway to San Miguel, this casual family restaurant features buffet and an a carte dining in a relaxed and friendly atmosphere. Casual dress. **Bar:** Beer only. **Hours:** 8 am-7 pm, Sat & Sun from 2 pm. Closed: 12/25. **Address:** KM 6 Carr D Hidalgo S L de la Paz **Location:** On highway to San Luis de la Paz, 0.4 mi (0.6 km) from Dolores Hidalgo city limits. **Parking:** on-site. **Cards:** MC, VI.

RESTAURANTE PLAZA **Phone:** 418/182-0259

Regional Mexican
$5-$15

Facing the plaza and church made famous by "El Grito" of Padre Hidalgo, the restaurant offers a focused menu, homemade dishes and friendly service; also great for breakfast. Casual dress. **Bar:** Full bar. **Hours:** 8:30 am-10 pm. **Address:** Plaza Principal #17B **Location:** Opposite south side of main plaza. **Parking:** street. **Cards:** AX, MC, VI.

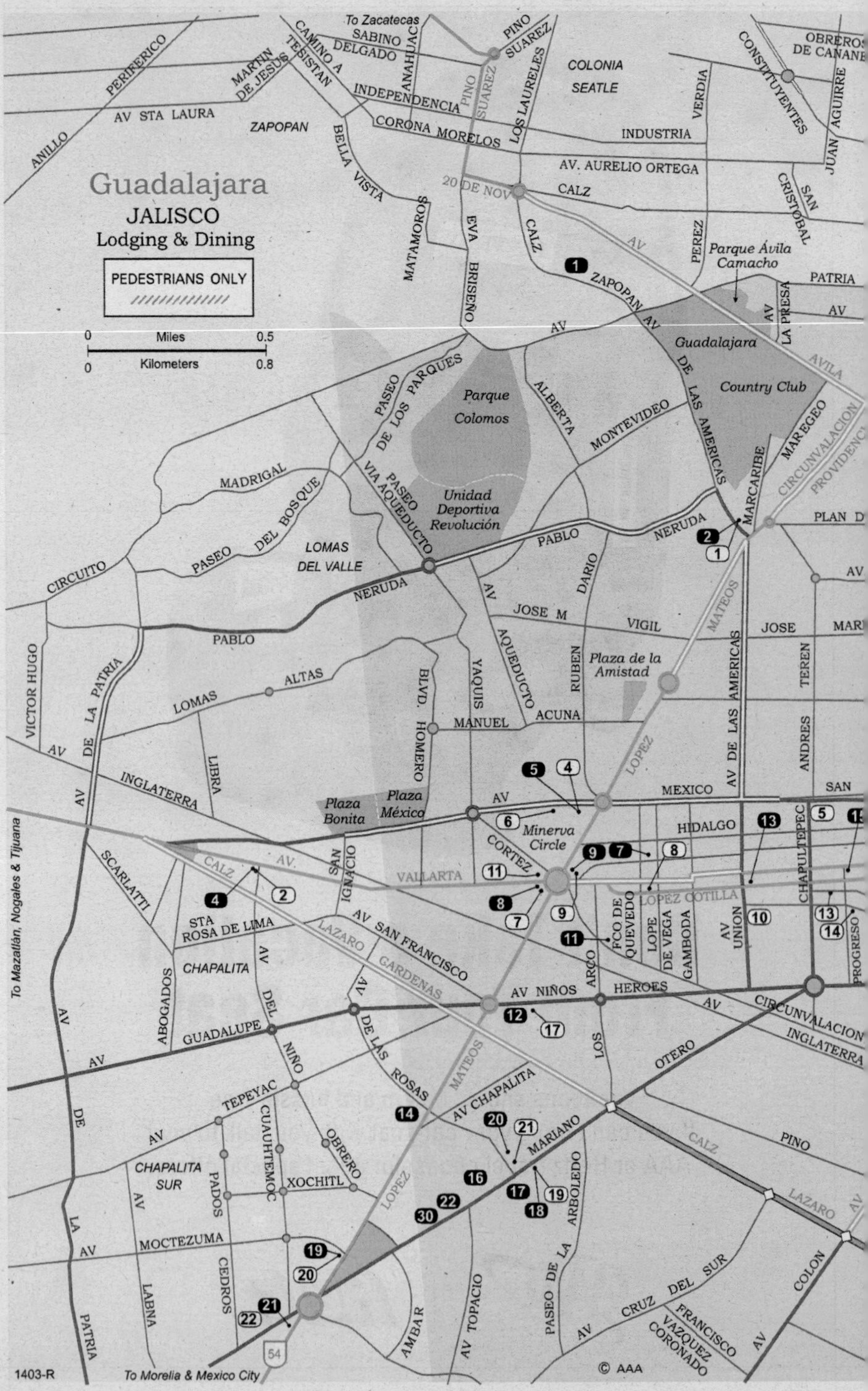

Guadalajara
JALISCO
Lodging & Dining

PEDESTRIANS ONLY

0 Miles 0.5
0 Kilometers 0.8

To Zacatecas
To Mazatlán, Nogales & Tijuana
To Morelia & Mexico City

ZAPOPAN
COLONIA SEATLE
Parque Ávila Camacho
Guadalajara Country Club
Parque Colomos
Unidad Deportiva Revolución
LOMAS DEL VALLE
Plaza de la Amistad
Plaza Bonita
Plaza México
Minerva Circle
CHAPALITA
CHAPALITA SUR

ANILLO PERIFERICO
AV STA LAURA
MARTIN DE JESUS
CAMINO A TESISTAN
SABINO DELGADO
ANAHUAC
INDEPENDENCIA
PINO SUAREZ
LOS LAURELES
CORONA MORELOS
BELLA VISTA
INDUSTRIA
VERDIA
CONSTITUYENTES
OBREROS DE CANANEA
JUAN AGUIRRE
AV. AURELIO ORTEGA
20 DE NOV
CALZ
SAN CRISTOBAL
MATAMOROS
EVA BRISEÑO
CALZ AV ZAPOPAN
PEREZ
PATRIA
AV LA PRESA
AV DE LAS AMERICAS
AVILA
PASEO DE LOS PARQUES
ALBERTA
MONTEVIDEO
MAREGEO
CIRCUNVALACION PROVIDENCIA
MARCARIBE
PLAN D
MADRIGAL
PASEO DEL BOSQUE
PASEO VIA AQUEDUCTO
PABLO NERUDA
CIRCUITO
AV
JOSE M VIGIL
RUBEN DARIO
JOSE MAR
MATEOS
LOMAS ALTAS
AV DE LA PATRIA
VICTOR HUGO
BLVD. HOMERO
YAQUIS
AV AQUEDUCTO
MANUEL ACUNA
TEREN
ANDRES
AV INGLATERRA
LIBRA
LOPEZ
AV MEXICO
SAN
HIDALGO
CHAPULTEPEC
CORTEZ
SAN IGNACIO
CALZ AV. VALLARTA
SCARLATTI
LOPEZ COTILLA
STA ROSA DE LIMA
AV SAN FRANCISCO
LAZARO GARDENAS
FCO DE QUEVEDO
LOPE DE VEGA
GAMBOA
AV UNION
PROGRESO
ABOGADOS
AV DEL NIÑO
AV DE LAS ROSAS
AV NIÑOS HEROES
ARCO
AV CIRCUNVALACION
AV GUADALUPE
INGLATERRA
LOS
OTERO
TEPEYAC
CUAUHTEMOC
OBRERO
MATEOS
AV CHAPALITA
MARIANO
CALZ
PINO
PADOS
XOCHITL
LOPEZ
ARBOLEDO
PASEO DE LA
LAZARO
AV
MOCTEZUMA
CEDROS
LABNA
AMBAR
AV TOPACIO
AV CRUZ DEL SUR
FRANCISCO VAZQUEZ CORONADO
COLON
AV DE LA PATRIA
54

1 2 4 5 7 8 9 11 12 13 14 16 17 18 19 20 21 22 30

1403-R

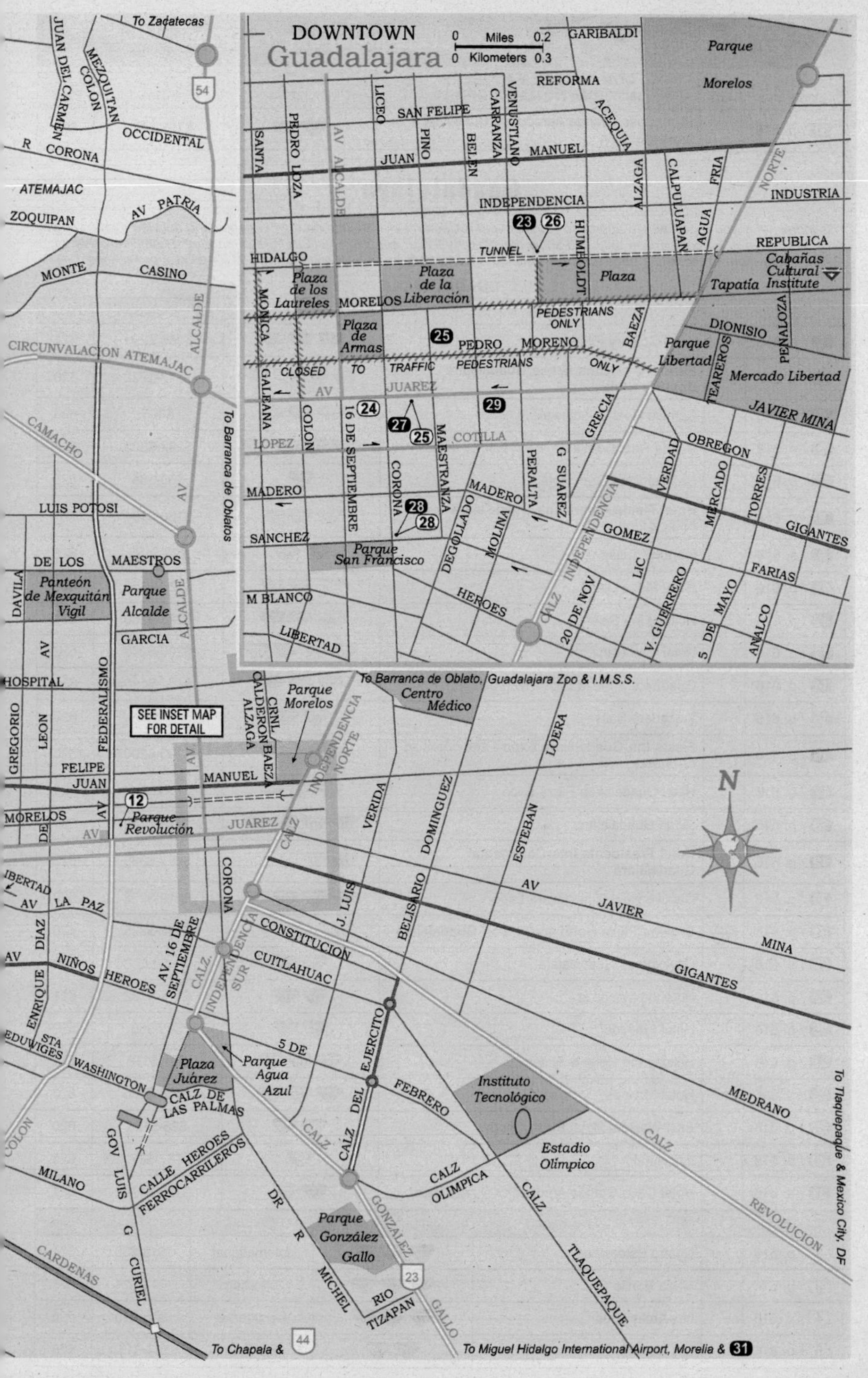
DOWNTOWN
Guadalajara
0 Miles 0.2
0 Kilometers 0.3
To Zacatecas
To Barranca de Oblatos
SEE INSET MAP FOR DETAIL
To Barranca de Oblato, Guadalajara Zoo & I.M.S.S.
To Tlaquepaque & Mexico City, DF
To Chapala &
To Miguel Hidalgo International Airport, Morelia &
Parque Morelos
Plaza de los Laureles
Plaza de la Liberación
Plaza de Armas
Plaza Tapatía
Cabañas Cultural Institute
Parque Libertad
Mercado Libertad
Parque San Francisco
Panteón de Mexquitán
Parque Alcalde
Vigil
Parque Revolución
Centro Médico
Plaza Juárez
Parque Agua Azul
Instituto Tecnológico
Estadio Olímpico
Parque González Gallo
PEDESTRIANS ONLY
CLOSED TO TRAFFIC
TUNNEL
CIRCUNVALACION ATEMAJAC
AV JAVIER MINA
GIGANTES
CALZ INDEPENDENCIA NORTE
CALZ INDEPENDENCIA SUR
CALZ REVOLUCION
CALZ TLAQUEPAQUE
CALZ OLIMPICA
CALZ DEL EJERCITO
CALZ GONZALEZ GALLO
CALZ DE LAS PALMAS
AV NIÑOS HEROES
AV LA PAZ
AV. 16 DE SEPTIEMBRE
CONSTITUCION
CUITLAHUAC
5 DE FEBRERO
MEDRANO
WASHINGTON
MILANO
CALLE HEROES FERROCARRILEROS
DR R MICHEL
RIO TIZAPAN
GOV LUIS G CURIEL
CARDENAS
ESTEBAN LOERA
BELISARIO DOMINGUEZ
J. LUIS VERIDA
JUAN MANUEL
FELIPE
MORELOS
AV JUAREZ
LIBERTAD
HOSPITAL
GREGORIO DAVILA
LEON
FEDERALISMO
ENRIQUE DIAZ DE LEON
STA EDUWIGES
COLON
CORONA
GARCIA
MAESTROS
LUIS POTOSI
CAMACHO
MONTE CASINO
ZOQUIPAN
AV PATRIA
ATEMAJAC
R CORONA
OCCIDENTAL
JUAN DEL CARMEN
MEZQUITAN
AV ALCALDE
CRNL CALDERON
BAEZA ALZAGA
GARIBALDI
REFORMA
SAN FELIPE
ACEQUIA
INDEPENDENCIA
INDUSTRIA
REPUBLICA
HIDALGO
DIONISIO
PENALOZA
TEAREROS
JAVIER MINA
OBREGON
MERCADO
TORRES
VERDAD
GOMEZ FARIAS
LIC V. GUERRERO
5 DE MAYO
ANALCO
20 DE NOV
HEROES
MADERO
SANCHEZ
M BLANCO
LOPEZ COTILLA
PEDRO MORENO
SANTA MONICA
GALEANA
PEDRO LOZA
LICEO
PINO
BELEN
VENUSTIANO CARRANZA
HUMBOLDT
ALZAGA
CALPULUAPAN
AGUA FRIA
GRECIA
DEGOLLADO
MOLINA
PERALTA
G SUAREZ
MAESTRANZA
16 DE SEPTIEMBRE
N

Airport Accommodations

Map Page	OA	DON MIGUEL Y HIDALGO INTERNATIONAL AIRPORT	Diamond Rated	High Season	Page
31 / p. 616		Hotel Casa Grande Aeropuerto Guadalajara, at airport terminal	◆◆	$125-$170	621

Guadalajara

This index helps you "spot" where approved lodgings and restaurants are located on the corresponding detailed maps. Lodging daily rate range is for comparison only and show the property's high season. Restaurant rate range is a combination of lunch and/or dinner. Turn to the listing page for more detailed rate information and consult display ads for special promotions.

GUADALAJARA

Map Page	OA	Lodgings	Diamond Rated	High Season	Page
1 / p. 616		Hotel Country Plaza	◆◆◆	$130-$220	621
2 / p. 616	AAA	**Fiesta Americana Grand Guadalajara Country Club**	◆◆◆◆	$173-$272	620
4 / p. 616		Camino Real Guadalajara	◆◆◆	$305	620
5 / p. 616		Quinta Real Guadalajara - see color ad p 8	◆◆◆◆	$292-$302	623
7 / p. 616		Las Pergolas Gran Hotel	◆	$60-$85	623
8 / p. 616	AAA	**Hotel Fiesta Americana Guadalajara** - see color ad on insert	◆◆◆	$186-$194	621
9 / p. 616		Moralva Suites	◆◆	$97-$135	623
11 / p. 616		Hotel Plaza Diana	◆◆◆	$120-$160	622
12 / p. 616		Holiday Inn Select	◆◆◆	$228-$260	621
13 / p. 616		Hotel Villa Ganz	◆◆◆◆	$200-$260	622
14 / p. 616		Guadalajara Plaza Lopez Mateos	◆◆◆	$150-$190	621
15 / p. 616		Trocadero Suites	◆◆	$80-$100	623
16 / p. 616	AAA	**Fiesta Inn Guadalajara Expo** - see color ad on insert	◆◆◆	$120-$200	620
17 / p. 616		Hotel Guadalajara Plaza Expo	◆◆◆	$170	622
18 / p. 616		Hilton Guadalajara	◆◆◆◆	$119-$249	621
19 / p. 616	AAA	**Hotel Presidente InterContinental Guadalajara**	◆◆◆◆	$150-$335	622
20 / p. 616		Camino Real Guadalajara Expo	◆◆◆◆	$219-$279	620
21 / p. 616	AAA	**Crowne Plaza Hotel and Resort Guadalajara**	◆◆◆	$195-$225	620
22 / p. 616		Cityexpress Guadalajara	◆◆	$69	620
23 / p. 616		Hotel de Mendoza	◆◆	$114-$132	621
25 / p. 616		Hotel Frances	◆◆	$65-$82	622
27 / p. 616		Holiday Inn Hotel & Suites	◆◆◆	$91-$112	621
28 / p. 616		Hotel Morales	◆◆◆	$130-$200	622
29 / p. 616		Best Western Hotel Plaza Genova	◆◆	$85-$125	620
30 / p. 616		Ibis Hotel	◆	$67-$87	623
31 / p. 616		Hotel Casa Grande Aeropuerto Guadalajara	◆◆	$125-$170	621

Map Page	OA	Restaurants	Diamond Rated	Cuisine	Meal Range	Page
1 / p. 616		Cuatro Estaciones	◆◆◆	International	$13-$30	624
2 / p. 616		Maria Bonita	◆◆◆	Mexican	$13-$24	625
4 / p. 616		Los Arcangeles	◆◆◆	Continental	$15-$40	625
5 / p. 616		Los Itacates	◆◆	Mexican	$7-$15	625

Map Page	OA	Restaurants (cont'd)	Diamond Rated	Cuisine	Meal Range	Page
6 / p. 616		La Matera	2 diamonds	International	$9-$19	625
7 / p. 616		La Franda	2 diamonds	International	$8-$25	624
8 / p. 616		Hard Rock Cafe	2 diamonds	American	$12-$24 SAVE	624
9 / p. 616		Chez Pierre	3 diamonds	International	$12-$25	624
10 / p. 616		Santo Coyote	3 diamonds	Mexican	$15-$25	626
11 / p. 616		Cocina 88	3 diamonds	International	$15-$35	624
12 / p. 616		El Sacromonte	3 diamonds	Mexican	$9-$16	624
13 / p. 616		Recco Restaurant	2 diamonds	Italian	$9-$20	625
14 / p. 616		Suehiro	2 diamonds	Japanese	$15-$24	626
17 / p. 616		La Trattoria Pomodoro de Guadalajara	2 diamonds	Italian	$6-$11	625
19 / p. 616		Angus Butcher House Restaurant and Bar	2 diamonds	Steak	$10-$30	623
20 / p. 616		Alfredo Di Roma	4 diamonds	Italian	$9-$20	623
21 / p. 616		Bice Ristorante	3 diamonds	Italian	$8-$22	623
22 / p. 616		Restaurant Jacarandas	4 diamonds	Continental	$24-$35	625
24 / p. 616		La Chata de Guadalajara	2 diamonds	Mexican	$4-$7	624
25 / p. 616		Las Carretas	2 diamonds	Continental	$7-$16	625
26 / p. 616		La Forja	2 diamonds	International	$8-$20	624
28 / p. 616		El Ruedo	2 diamonds	International	$6-$14	624

GUADALAJARA, JALISCO pop. 1,646,319 (See map and index starting on p. 616-618)

WHERE TO STAY

BEST WESTERN HOTEL PLAZA GENOVA *Book great rates at AAA.com* **Phone:** (33)3613-7500 29

Hotel
$85-$125 All Year

Address: Ave Juarez 123 **Location:** Center. **Facility:** 197 units. 196 one- and 1 two-bedroom standard units, some with whirlpools. 7 stories, interior corridors. *Bath:* combo or shower only. **Parking:** on-site (fee). **Terms:** 5 day cancellation notice. **Amenities:** high-speed Internet, honor bars, irons, hair dryers. **Leisure Activities:** steamrooms, exercise room. **Guest Services:** valet laundry, wireless Internet. **Business Services:** meeting rooms, business center. **Cards:** AX, DC, MC, VI.

D / SOME UNITS

AAA Benefit: Members save up to 20%, plus 10% bonus points with rewards program.

CAMINO REAL GUADALAJARA *Book at AAA.com* **Phone:** (33)3134-2424 4

Hotel
$305 All Year

Address: Ave Vallarta 5005 **Location:** 3.8 mi (6 km) nw on Mex 15. **Facility:** 205 one-bedroom standard units. 2 stories (no elevator), exterior corridors. *Bath:* some combo or shower only. **Parking:** on-site and valet. **Terms:** cancellation fee imposed. **Amenities:** high-speed Internet (fee), voice mail, safes, honor bars, irons, hair dryers. **Dining:** Maria Bonita, see separate listing. **Pool(s):** outdoor, 3 heated outdoor. **Leisure Activities:** putting green, playground, exercise room. *Fee:* lighted tennis court, massage. **Guest Services:** valet laundry, wireless Internet. **Business Services:** meeting rooms, business center. **Cards:** AX, DC, MC, VI.

24 D / SOME UNITS

CAMINO REAL GUADALAJARA EXPO *Book at AAA.com* **Phone:** (33)3880-7700 20

Hotel
$219-$279 All Year

Address: Mariano Otero 1326 **Location:** Opposite Expo and World Trade Center. **Facility:** Located near the expo center, guest rooms and public areas offer a contemporary decor with a Mexican twist and innovative flair. 163 units. 157 one-bedroom standard units. 6 one-bedroom suites, some with whirlpools. 9 stories, interior corridors. *Bath:* combo or shower only. **Parking:** on-site and valet. **Amenities:** high-speed Internet (fee), voice mail, safes, honor bars, irons, hair dryers. **Leisure Activities:** exercise room. **Guest Services:** valet laundry, wireless Internet. **Business Services:** meeting rooms, business center. **Cards:** AX, DC, MC, VI.

S D / SOME UNITS

CITYEXPRESS GUADALAJARA **Phone:** 33/3880-3700 22

Hotel
$69 All Year

Address: Ave Mariano Otero #1390 **Location:** 2.1 mi (3.5 km) w; near Expo Center. **Facility:** 145 one-bedroom standard units. 8 stories, interior corridors. *Bath:* shower only. **Parking:** on-site. **Amenities:** voice mail. **Leisure Activities:** exercise room. **Guest Services:** wireless Internet. **Business Services:** meeting rooms, PC. **Cards:** AX, MC, VI.

D / SOME UNITS

CROWNE PLAZA HOTEL AND RESORT GUADALAJARA *Book great rates at AAA.com* **Phone:** (33)3634-1034 21

AAA
Hotel
$195-$225 All Year

Address: Ave Lopez Mateos Sur #2500 **Location:** 4.5 mi (7.2 km) s on Mex 15 and 80; off Glorieta Mariana Otero. **Facility:** 294 units. 289 one- and 5 two-bedroom standard units. 2-9 stories, interior/exterior corridors. **Parking:** on-site (fee) and valet. **Terms:** cancellation fee imposed. **Amenities:** high-speed Internet (fee), dual phone lines, voice mail, safes, honor bars, irons, hair dryers. **Dining:** 2 restaurants, also, Restaurant Jacarandas, see separate listing, entertainment. **Pool(s):** heated outdoor. **Leisure Activities:** sauna, whirlpool, playground, exercise room. *Fee:* massage. **Guest Services:** valet laundry, beauty salon, wireless Internet. **Business Services:** conference facilities, business center. **Cards:** AX, DC, MC, VI.

24 / SOME UNITS

FIESTA AMERICANA GRAND GUADALAJARA COUNTRY CLUB **Phone:** 33/3648-3500 2

AAA
Hotel
$173-$272 All Year

Address: Ave Americas No 1551 **Location:** Directly accross from the Country Club at jct Ave Lopez Mateos. **Facility:** Guest rooms are well-equipped with a flat-screen television, fluffy bedding and fine furnishings; the lounge and dining room are a local favorite. 208 one-bedroom standard units. 19 stories, interior corridors. *Bath:* shower only. **Parking:** on-site (fee) and valet. **Amenities:** high-speed Internet (fee), dual phone lines, voice mail, safes, honor bars, irons, hair dryers. **Leisure Activities:** exercise room, spa. **Guest Services:** valet laundry, wireless Internet. **Business Services:** meeting rooms, business center. **Cards:** AX, MC, VI.

24 S D / SOME UNITS

FIESTA INN GUADALAJARA EXPO *Book great rates at AAA.com* **Phone:** (33)3669-3200 16

AAA
Hotel
$120-$200 All Year

Address: Mariano Otero 1550 **Location:** 2.1 mi (3.5 km) w; near Expo Center. **Facility:** 158 one-bedroom standard units. 8 stories, interior corridors. **Parking:** on-site. **Terms:** cancellation fee imposed. **Amenities:** high-speed Internet, irons, hair dryers. **Pool(s):** heated outdoor. **Leisure Activities:** exercise room. **Guest Services:** valet laundry, wireless Internet. **Business Services:** meeting rooms, business center. **Cards:** AX, DC, MC, VI. *(See color ad on insert)*

(See map and index starting on p. 616)

GUADALAJARA PLAZA LOPEZ MATEOS *Book at AAA.com* **Phone:** (33)3208-4400 **14**

Hotel
$150-$190 All Year

Address: Ave Lopez Mateos Sur 2128 **Location:** 4.2 mi (7 km) s on Mex 15 and 80. **Facility:** 142 units. 112 one-bedroom standard units. 30 one-bedroom suites. 2-7 stories, interior/exterior corridors. *Bath:* combo or shower only. **Parking:** valet. **Amenities:** high-speed Internet (fee), irons, hair dryers. **Pool(s):** heated outdoor. **Guest Services:** wireless Internet. **Business Services:** meeting rooms, business center. **Cards:** AX, DC, DS, MC, VI.

/ SOME UNITS

HILTON GUADALAJARA *Book great rates at AAA.com* **Phone:** (33)3678-0505 **18**

Hotel
$119-$249 All Year

Address: Ave de las Rosas 2933 **Location:** At Expo and World Trade Center. **Facility:** A spacious lobby, meeting and dining facilities, shopping area and attentive service contribute to the upscale ambience of this big-city hotel. 450 units. 435 one-bedroom standard units. 15 one-bedroom suites, some with whirlpools. 20 stories, interior corridors. **Parking:** on-site (fee) and valet. **Terms:** cancellation fee imposed. **Amenities:** dual phone lines, voice mail, safes, honor bars, irons, hair dryers. *Fee:* video games, high-speed Internet. **Dining:** Angus Butcher House Restaurant and Bar, see separate listing. **Pool(s):** heated outdoor. **Leisure Activities:** steamroom, exercise room. *Fee:* massage. **Guest Services:** valet laundry, wireless Internet. **Business Services:** conference facilities, business center. **Cards:** AX, MC, VI.

AAA Benefit:
Members save 5% or more everyday!

/ SOME UNITS

HOLIDAY INN HOTEL & SUITES *Book at AAA.com* **Phone:** (33)3560-1200 **27**

Hotel
$91-$112 All Year

Address: Ave Juarez 211-103 **Location:** Center. Located in a historic area of the city. **Facility:** Meets AAA guest room security requirements. 90 one-bedroom standard units, some with efficiencies and/or whirlpools. 5 stories, interior corridors. *Bath:* shower only. **Parking:** on-site. **Terms:** cancellation fee imposed. **Amenities:** safes, honor bars, irons, hair dryers. **Dining:** Las Carretas, see separate listing. **Leisure Activi ties:** limited exercise equipment. **Guest Services:** valet and coin laundry, wireless Internet. **Business Services:** meeting rooms, business center. **Cards:** AX, MC, VI.

/ SOME UNITS

HOLIDAY INN SELECT *Book at AAA.com* **Phone:** (33)3122-2020 **12**

Hotel
$228-$260 All Year

Address: Ave Ninos Heroes 3089 **Location:** 0.3 mi (0.5 km) s of Minerva Fountain. **Facility:** Meets AAA guest room security requirements. 220 one-bedroom standard units, some with whirlpools. 14 stories, interior corridors. **Parking:** on-site (fee). **Amenities:** high-speed Internet (fee), voice mail, safes, honor bars, irons, hair dryers. **Pool(s):** heated outdoor. **Leisure Activities:** steamroom, exercise room. **Guest Services:** valet laundry, wireless Internet. **Business Services:** meeting rooms, business center. **Cards:** AX, MC, VI.

/ SOME UNITS

HOTEL CASA GRANDE AEROPUERTO GUADALAJARA *Book at AAA.com* **Phone:** (33)3678-9000 **31**

Hotel
$125-$170 All Year

Address: Calle Interior Aeropuerto **Location:** At Guadalajara International Airport. **Facility:** 177 units. 175 one-bedroom standard units. 1 one- and 1 two-bedroom suites with whirlpools. 4 stories, interior corridors. *Bath:* combo or shower only. **Parking:** on-site (fee) and valet. **Amenities:** video library, voice mail, irons, hair dryers. *Some:* safes. **Pool(s):** heated outdoor. **Leisure Activities:** saunas, whirlpools, steamrooms, exercise room. **Guest Services:** valet laundry, area transportation, wireless Internet. **Business Services:** meeting rooms, business center. **Cards:** AX, DC, MC, VI.

/ SOME UNITS

HOTEL COUNTRY PLAZA **Phone:** (33)3208-4633 **1**

Hotel
$130-$220 All Year

Address: Prolonguacion Ave Americas 1170 **Location:** 5 mi (8 km) w. **Facility:** 119 units. 114 one-bedroom standard units. 5 one-bedroom suites, some with whirlpools. 4 stories, interior corridors. *Bath:* combo or shower only. **Parking:** on-site. **Terms:** cancellation fee imposed. **Amenities:** voice mail, irons, hair dryers. *Some:* safes, honor bars. **Pool(s):** heated indoor. **Leisure Activities:** whirlpool, exercise room. **Guest Services:** valet laundry, wireless Internet. **Business Services:** meeting rooms, business center. **Cards:** AX, MC, VI.

/ SOME UNITS

HOTEL DE MENDOZA *Book at AAA.com* **Phone:** (33)3942-5151 **23**

Hotel
$114-$132 All Year

Address: Venustiano Carranza 16 **Location:** In historic district; opposite Degollado Theatre. **Facility:** 104 one-bedroom standard units. 5 stories, interior corridors. *Bath:* combo or shower only. **Parking:** on-site (fee). **Amenities:** high-speed Internet, voice mail, safes, hair dryers. *Some:* irons. **Dining:** La Forja, see separate listing. **Pool(s):** outdoor. **Leisure Activities:** whirlpool, exercise room. **Guest Services:** valet laundry, wireless Internet. **Business Services:** meeting rooms, business center. **Cards:** AX, MC, VI.

/ SOME UNITS

HOTEL FIESTA AMERICANA GUADALAJARA *Book great rates at AAA.com* **Phone:** (33)3818-1400 **8**

AAA

Hotel
$186-$194 1/1-11/30
$169-$176 12/1-12/31

Address: Aurelio Aceves 225 **Location:** On Minerva Cir; jct aves Vallarta and Lopez Mateos. Located in a busy commercial area. **Facility:** 391 one-bedroom standard units, some with kitchens (no utensils) and/or whirlpools. 22 stories, interior corridors. **Parking:** on-site and valet. **Terms:** cancellation fee imposed. **Amenities:** voice mail, safes, honor bars, irons, hair dryers. *Fee:* video games, high-speed Internet. **Leisure Activities:** exercise room. **Guest Services:** valet laundry, wireless Internet. **Business Services:** conference facilities, business center. **Cards:** AX, DC, MC, VI.

(See color ad on insert)

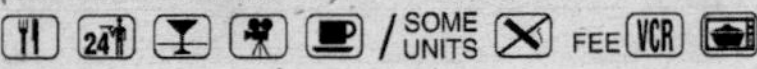

(See map and index starting on p. 616)

HOTEL FRANCES — Book at AAA.com — Phone: (33)3613-1190 — 25

Classic Historic Hotel
$65-$82 All Year

Address: Maestranza 35 **Location:** Center; in historic district. **Facility:** Constructed in 1610. Old World charm. All rooms with ceiling fan. 60 units. 55 one- and 5 two-bedroom standard units, some with whirlpools. 4 stories, interior corridors. *Bath:* combo or shower only. **Parking:** on-site. **Terms:** 3 day cancellation notice. **Business Services:** meeting rooms. **Cards:** AX, MC, VI.

/ SOME UNITS

HOTEL GUADALAJARA PLAZA EXPO — Book at AAA.com — Phone: (33)3669-0215 — 17

Hotel
$170 All Year

Address: Mariano Otero 3261 **Location:** At Expo and World Trade Center. **Facility:** 204 one-bedroom standard units. 5 stories, interior corridors. **Parking:** on-site and valet. **Amenities:** high-speed Internet (fee), voice mail, irons, hair dryers. **Pool(s):** heated outdoor. **Leisure Activities:** jogging, exercise room. **Guest Services:** valet laundry, wireless Internet. **Business Services:** meeting rooms, PC. **Cards:** AX, DC, DS, MC, VI.

D / SOME UNITS

HOTEL MORALES — Phone: 33/3658-5232 — 28

Boutique Hotel
$130-$200 All Year

Address: Ave Ramon Corona No 243 **Location:** Jct Priscilano Sanchez; in historic center. **Facility:** A large atrium welcomes guests to this truly authentic Mexican hotel, where you'll find guest rooms with high ceilings and elegant wood furnishings. Smoke free premises. 64 one-bedroom standard units, some with whirlpools. 4 stories, interior corridors. *Bath:* combo or shower only. **Parking:** no self-parking. **Amenities:** high-speed Internet, safes, irons, hair dryers. *Some:* honor bars. **Dining:** El Ruedo, see separate listing. **Leisure Activities:** limited exercise equipment. **Guest Services:** valet laundry, wireless Internet. **Business Services:** meeting rooms, PC. **Cards:** AX, MC, VI.

D

HOTEL PLAZA DIANA — Book at AAA.com — Phone: (33)3540-9700 — 11

Hotel
$120-$160 All Year

Address: Agustin Yanez 2760 **Location:** 3 mi (5 km) n. **Facility:** 152 units. 141 one-bedroom standard units. 11 one-bedroom suites. 5 stories, interior corridors. *Bath:* combo or shower only. **Parking:** on-site and valet. **Terms:** 7 day cancellation notice. **Amenities:** high-speed Internet, hair dryers. *Fee:* video games, safes. **Pool(s):** heated indoor. **Leisure Activities:** whirlpool, exercise room. **Guest Services:** valet laundry, area transportation, wireless Internet. **Business Services:** meeting rooms, business center. **Cards:** AX, DC, MC, VI.

/ SOME UNITS

HOTEL PRESIDENTE INTERCONTINENTAL GUADALAJARA — Book great rates at AAA.com — Phone: (33)3678-1234 — 19

AAA
Hotel
$150-$335 All Year

Address: Ave Lopez Mateos Sur y Moctezuma **Location:** 4.2 mi (7 km) s on Mex 15 and 80; across from Plaza del Sol. **Facility:** This large, upscale, city hotel features impressive marble-trimmed public areas, secured parking and proximity to a high-end shopping mall. 409 units. 385 one-bedroom standard units. 24 one-bedroom suites with whirlpools. 13 stories, interior corridors. **Parking:** on-site (fee) and valet. **Amenities:** dual phone lines, voice mail, safes, honor bars, irons, hair dryers. *Fee:* video games, high-speed Internet. *Some:* CD players. **Dining:** 2 restaurants, also, Alfredo Di Roma, see separate listing, entertainment. **Pool(s):** heated outdoor. **Leisure Activities:** *Fee:* saunas, whirlpools, steamroom, exercise room, massage. **Guest Services:** valet laundry, wireless Internet. **Business Services:** conference facilities, business center. **Cards:** AX, DC, JC, MC, VI.

24 S D / SOME UNITS

HOTEL VILLA GANZ — Phone: 33/3120-1416 — 13

Bed & Breakfast
$200-$260 All Year

Address: Lopez Cotilla #1739, Col Lafayette **Location:** Between Union and Chapoltepec. **Facility:** A beautifully restored home which offers guests a chance to stay in an authentic Mexican hacienda in a central location. 10 one-bedroom standard units, some with whirlpools. 2 stories (no elevator), interior corridors. *Bath:* combo or shower only. **Parking:** on-site. **Terms:** age restrictions may apply. **Amenities:** high-speed Internet, safes, hair dryers. *Some:* DVD players. **Guest Services:** wireless Internet. **Business Services:** meeting rooms, PC. **Cards:** AX, MC, VI.

/ SOME UNITS

(See map and index starting on p. 616)

IBIS HOTEL — **Phone:** 33/3880-9600 30

Hotel
$67-$87 All Year

Address: Ave Mariano Otero 1400 **Location:** 2.1 mi (3.5 km) w; near Expo Center. **Facility:** 159 one-bedroom standard units. 4 stories, interior corridors. *Bath:* shower only. **Parking:** on-site. **Pool(s):** outdoor. **Guest Services:** wireless Internet. **Business Services:** meeting rooms, PC. **Cards:** AX, DC, MC, VI.

/ SOME UNITS

LAS PERGOLAS GRAN HOTEL — **Phone:** 33/3630-1727 7

Hotel
$60-$85 All Year

Address: Ave Morelos 2244 **Location:** 3 blks e of Minerva Cir; just n of Ave Vallarta. **Facility:** 158 one-bedroom standard units. 4 stories, interior corridors. *Bath:* shower only. **Parking:** on-site. **Terms:** 30 day cancellation notice. **Amenities:** DVD players. *Some:* safes. **Pool(s):** heated outdoor. **Leisure Activities:** playground, exercise room, game room. *Fee:* sauna. **Guest Services:** valet laundry, wireless Internet. **Business Services:** PC (fee). **Cards:** MC, VI.

/ SOME UNITS

MORALVA SUITES — **Phone:** 33/3615-4805 9

Vacation Rental Condominium
$97-$135 All Year

Address: Ave Vallarta 2477 **Location:** Just e of Minerva Cir. **Facility:** Centrally located in a busy area, the small-scale property features very spacious suites with a fully-equipped kitchen. 20 units. 2 one- and 18 two-bedroom suites, some with efficiencies or kitchens. 10 stories, interior corridors. *Bath:* combo or shower only. **Parking:** on-site. **Amenities:** high-speed Internet, safes, hair dryers. *Some:* irons. **Guest Services:** wireless Internet. **Cards:** AX, MC, VI.

/ SOME UNITS

QUINTA REAL GUADALAJARA — **Phone:** (33)3669-0600 5

Hotel
$292-$302 All Year

Address: Ave Mexico 2727 **Location:** 2 blks n of Minerva Fountain; near Ave Lopez Mateos. **Facility:** Fine art, well-appointed rooms and manicured grounds add an elegant sophistication to this property. 76 units. 75 one-bedroom standard units, some with whirlpools. 1 three-bedroom suite with whirlpool. 3-5 stories, interior corridors. **Parking:** on-site and valet. **Terms:** cancellation fee imposed. **Amenities:** high-speed Internet, voice mail, safes, honor bars, irons, hair dryers. *Some:* CD players. **Dining:** Los Arcangeles, see separate listing. **Pool(s):** heated outdoor. **Leisure Activities:** whirlpool, exercise room. **Guest Services:** valet laundry, wireless Internet. **Business Services:** meeting rooms, business center. **Cards:** AX, DC, MC, VI. Affiliated with A Preferred Hotel. ***(See color ad p 8)***

/ SOME UNITS

TROCADERO SUITES — **Phone:** 33/3120-1416 15

Hotel
$80-$100 All Year

Address: Lopez Cotilla #1188, Col Americana **Location:** Between Atenas and Robles Gil. **Facility:** Smoke free premises. 6 units. 3 one-bedroom standard units. 3 one-bedroom suites. 1 story, exterior corridors. *Bath:* shower only. **Parking:** on-site. **Amenities:** high-speed Internet, safes, irons. **Cards:** AX, MC, VI.

/ SOME UNITS

The following lodging was either not evaluated or did not meet AAA rating requirements but is listed for your information only.

CLARUM 101 — **Phone:** 33/1201-7507

fyi

Not evaluated. **Address:** Parque Juan Diego 101. Facilities, services, and decor characterize a mid-scale property.

WHERE TO DINE

ALFREDO DI ROMA — **Phone:** 33/3678-1234 20

Italian
$9-$20

This upscale restaurant is very popular with the locals who seek fine Italian cuisine. The dining room offers a true European flavor with its delightful wall murals and glass showcase of pastas, and the wine cellar is one of the finest in the city. Diners enjoy a wide range of freshly-prepared Italian cuisine, sophisticated service and live Mexican music. Dressy casual. **Bar:** Full bar. **Reservations:** suggested. **Hours:** 1 pm-11:30 pm, Sun-5 pm. **Address:** Ave Moctezuma 3515 Cd del Sol **Location:** 4.2 mi (7 km) s on Mex 15 and 80; across from Plaza del Sol; in Hotel Presidente InterContinental Guadalajara. **Parking:** on-site (fee) and valet. **Cards:** AX, DC, MC, VI.

ANGUS BUTCHER HOUSE RESTAURANT AND BAR — **Phone:** 33/3671-4627 19

Steak
$10-$30

A true Western atmosphere with a Mexican flair sets the tone in the popular steakhouse, where staffers in full Western attire serve hearty steaks. Although beef is the main draw, the menu also lists some Mexican dishes and a good selection of hot and cold appetizers. **Bar:** Full bar. **Reservations:** suggested. **Hours:** 1 pm-1 am, Sun-6 pm. Closed major holidays. **Address:** Ave de las Rosas #2933 **Location:** At Expo and World Trade Center; in Hilton Guadalajara. **Parking:** on-site (fee). **Cards:** AX, DC, MC, VI.

BICE RISTORANTE — **Phone:** 33/3880-7705 21

Italian
$8-$22

Bright, contemporary decor and an innovative menu make this the perfect spot for a meal of any size. The menu offers a wide selection of tasty tapas and freshly prepared soups and salads, as well as gourmet pasta dishes, pizza and grilled meats. Casual dress. **Bar:** Full bar. **Reservations:** suggested. **Hours:** 6 am-2 am. **Address:** Mariano Otero 1326 **Location:** Opposite Expo and World Trade Center; in Camino Real Guadalajara Expo. **Parking:** on-site (fee). **Cards:** AX, DC, MC, VI.

(See map and index starting on p. 616)

CHEZ PIERRE — **Phone:** 33/3615-6645 (9)

International
$12-$25

Wall murals of Paris, stone waterfalls and fresh flowers lend visual appeal to the dining room, while the pianist adds an auditory element. French and international dishes mingle on the menu, where traditional favorites include French onion soup, escargots and mussels, as well as preparations of fine meats, seafood and poultry. Homemade crepes are a popular dessert option. Dressy casual. **Bar:** Full bar. **Reservations:** suggested. **Hours:** 1 pm-1 am, Sun-7 pm. **Address:** Espana #2095 **Location:** Adjacent to Monumento Ninos Heros. **Parking:** no self-parking. **Cards:** MC, VI.

COCINA 88 — **Phone:** 33/3827-5996 (11)

International
$15-$35

In a converted chateau, this popular restaurant features an excellent selection of fresh cuts of meat and seafood. Diners are taken to the "market" section of the restaurant, where cuts are displayed in a glass case. Servers describe the menu items, and guests select their preference and order the sides to complement it. Dressy casual. **Bar:** Full bar. **Reservations:** suggested. **Hours:** 1:30 pm-1 am, Sun 2 pm-10 pm. **Address:** Ave Vallarta 1342 **Location:** Jct Colonias. **Parking:** no self-parking. **Cards:** MC, VI.

CUATRO ESTACIONES — **Phone:** 33/3648-3500 (1)

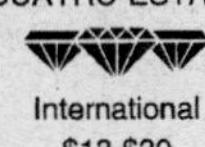

International
$13-$30

Upbeat contemporary design marks the large dining room, where patrons peruse a fine international menu. Locals frequent the featured buffet breakfast, which winds up around noon, but also take advantage of the varied a la carte options at lunch and dinner. Casual dress. **Bar:** Full bar. **Reservations:** suggested. **Hours:** 7 am-11 pm. **Address:** Ave Americas No 1551 **Location:** Jct Ave Lopez Mateos; across from Country Club. **Parking:** on-site (fee). **Cards:** AX, DC, MC, VI.

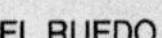

EL RUEDO — **Phone:** 33/3658-5232 (28)

International
$6-$14

Just off the lobby of the Hotel Morales, the delightful dining room has fine stone archways and a Mexican water fountain. Grilled meats and chicken share menu space with lighter fare, including burgers and sandwiches, and some tasty Mexican selections. Casual dress. **Bar:** Full bar. **Reservations:** suggested. **Hours:** 7 am-10:30 pm. **Address:** Ave Ramon Corona No 243 **Location:** Jct Priscilano Sanchez; in historic center; in Hotel Morales. **Parking:** street. **Cards:** AX, MC, VI.

EL SACROMONTE — **Phone:** 33/3825-5447 (12)

Mexican
$9-$16

Billowy fabric drapes the ceiling, while the soft glow of candlelight emanating from punctured-tin light fixtures reflects off small mirrors along yellow and ochre stucco courtyard walls. Locals and a few knowledgeable international visitors love both the casual pace and the honest Nuevo Mexican cuisine in the neighborhood restaurant. Dressy casual. **Bar:** Full bar. **Reservations:** accepted. **Hours:** 1 pm-midnight, Sun-6 pm. Closed major holidays. **Address:** Pedro Moreno #1398 Col Americana **Location:** Just e of Ave Chapultepac. **Parking:** valet. **Cards:** AX, MC, VI.

HARD ROCK CAFE — **Phone:** 33/3616-4560 (8)

SAVE

American
$12-$24

Rock 'n' roll memorabilia decorates the walls of the popular theme restaurant. Live music on the weekends contributes to the bustling atmosphere. On the menu is a wide variety of American cuisine—from burgers and sandwiches to seafood, steaks and pasta. Casual dress. **Bar:** Full bar. **Reservations:** accepted. **Hours:** 11 am-11 pm. **Address:** Ave Vallarta 2425 Col Americana **Location:** In Centro Magno center; near Minerva Circle. **Parking:** on-site (fee). **Cards:** AX, DS, JC, MC, VI.

LA CHATA DE GUADALAJARA — **Phone:** 33/3613-0588 (24)

Mexican
$4-$7

While it may be difficult to find bilingual staff members, the menu of traditional favorites—from fresh guacamole and zesty chiles rellenos to spicy meat dishes—enables guests and servers alike to speak a common language. Hand-painted tile accents decorate the cheerful, bright yellow dining room, a block from Place d'Arms and a nice respite from the crowds in the historic town center. Casual dress. **Bar:** Full bar. **Hours:** 8 am-midnight. **Address:** Ave Ramon Corona #126 **Location:** Jct aves Juarez and Ramon Corona; center. **Parking:** street. **Cards:** AX, MC, VI.

CALL

LA FORJA — **Phone:** 33/3942-5151 (26)

International
$8-$20

Guests enjoy the Old World atmosphere of the elegant restaurant, which is just off the lobby of the Hotel De Mendoza. On the menu is a good mix of Continental fare, including preparations of beef, seafood and spicy Mexican fare. The convenient spot in the historic section of town is directly opposite the Degollado Theatre. Casual dress. **Bar:** Full bar. **Reservations:** suggested. **Hours:** 7 am-10:30 pm. **Address:** Venustiano Carranza 16 **Location:** In historic district; opposite Degollado Theatre; in Hotel de Mendoza. **Parking:** on-site (fee). **Cards:** AX, MC, VI.

LA FRANDA — **Phone:** 33/3818-1400 (7)

International
$8-$25

This casual restaurant is well known for its extensive daily breakfast buffet, which is like an upscale brunch. At lunch and dinner, patrons order from an a la carte menu of excellent steaks and grilled dishes. The decor is simple and comfortable. Casual dress. **Bar:** Full bar. **Reservations:** accepted. **Hours:** 7 am-midnight. **Address:** Aurelio Aceves 225 **Location:** On Minerva Cir; jct aves Vallarta and Lopez Mateos; in Hotel Fiesta Americana Guadalajara. **Parking:** on-site (fee). **Cards:** AX, DC, MC, VI.

(See map and index starting on p. 616)

LA MATERA **Phone:** 33/3616-1626 (6)

International
$9-$19

A fun and bustling atmosphere and a diverse menu make this a place where locals love to dine. In addition to a good mix of wood-fire-baked pizzas and tasty pasta dishes, patrons can order meats and seafood cooked over an open grill. Hearty portions leave diners stuffed and satisfied. Casual dress. **Bar:** Full bar. **Reservations:** suggested. **Hours:** 11:30 am-10 pm. **Address:** Ave Mexico #2891 **Location:** Just n of Mineva Fountain, near Ave Lopez Mateos. **Parking:** no self-parking. **Cards:** MC, VI.

LAS CARRETAS **Phone:** 33/3560-1200 (25)

Continental
$7-$16

On the second floor of the Holiday Inn and Suites in the city's historic zone, the dining room is a popular choice for its hearty buffet breakfast and a la carte lunch and dinner choices. The terrace overlooks the active city streets and the elegant hotel lobby. Entertainment adds to the atmosphere. Representative of the light, casual fare are burgers, sandwiches and salads, but guests also will find spicy Mexican dishes and grilled meats and seafood. Casual dress. **Bar:** Full bar. **Hours:** 7 am-noon & 1:30-11 pm, Sun-10:30 pm. **Address:** Ave Juarez 211-103 **Location:** Center; in Holiday Inn Hotel & Suites. **Parking:** on-site. **Cards:** AX, MC, VI.

LA TRATTORIA POMODORO DE GUADALAJARA **Phone:** 33/3122-1817 (17)

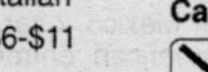

Italian
$6-$11

Popular with locals and tourists alike, the restaurant features authentic Italian entrees and an accomplished selection of appetizers and wines. Casual dress. **Bar:** Full bar. **Hours:** 1 pm-midnight, Sun-9 pm. Closed: 12/25. **Address:** Ave Ninos Heroes 3051 **Location:** Just e of jct Ave Lopez Mateos. **Parking:** on-site. **Cards:** AX, MC, VI.

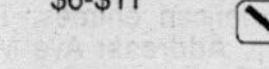

LOS ARCANGELES **Phone:** 33/3669-0600 (4)

Continental
$15-$40

The high-quality, fine-dining establishment enjoys a good reputation for its imaginatively prepared and presented food and smooth, professional service. Dressy casual. Entertainment. **Bar:** Full bar. **Reservations:** suggested. **Hours:** 7 am-midnight. **Address:** Ave Mexico 2727 **Location:** 2 blks n of Minerva Fountain; near Ave Lopez Mateos; in Quinta Real Guadalajara. **Parking:** on-site and valet. **Cards:** AX, MC, VI.

LOS ITACATES **Phone:** 33/3825-1106 (5)

Mexican
$7-$15

Mexican traditional "campestre" (country cooking) is the specialty at the friendly, colorfully decorated Guadalajara cafe. Expect a terrific meal. Casual dress. **Bar:** Full bar. **Reservations:** accepted. **Hours:** 8 am-11 pm, Fri & Sat-midnight, Sun-7 pm. Closed: 1/1, 12/25. **Address:** Ave Chapultapec Norte #110 **Location:** Jct aves Chapultapec and Mexico, just s. **Parking:** street. **Cards:** MC, VI.

MARIA BONITA **Phone:** 33/3134-2434 (2)

Mexican
$13-$24

This upscale Mexican restaurant features a distinctive contemporary design with a huge mosaic tile wall featuring pictures of the famous Maria Bonita. Large flat-screen TVs are tuned to sporting events in the bustling dining area, where patrons indulge in hearty portions of tasty regional fare. **Bar:** Full bar. **Reservations:** suggested. **Hours:** 1 pm-midnight. **Address:** Ave Vallarta 5005 **Location:** 3.8 mi (6 km) nw on Mex 15; in Camino Real Guadalajara. **Parking:** on-site (fee). **Cards:** AX, DC, MC, VI.

RECCO RESTAURANT **Phone:** 33/3825-0724 (13)

Italian
$9-$20

The Italian restaurant provides a nice change of pace, with such choices as hearty servings of lasagna and tasty osso buco. The Caesar salad is "magnifico," as are the desserts. Dressy casual. **Bar:** Full bar. **Reservations:** suggested. **Hours:** 2 pm-11 pm. Closed major holidays. **Address:** Libertad 1981 **Location:** Just e of Ave Chapultepec. **Parking:** on-site. **Cards:** AX, MC, VI.

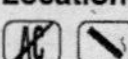

RESTAURANT JACARANDAS **Phone:** 33/3634-1034 (22)

Continental
$24-$35

The panoramic city view is a highlight of this restaurant, atop the hotel. Elegance is evident in the dining room, where imaginative salads, appetizers, high-quality beef entrees and desserts are served. Cuisine preparation styles range from local to International. Dressy casual. Entertainment. **Bar:** Full bar. **Reservations:** suggested. **Hours:** 8 am-1 am. Closed: Sun. **Address:** Ave Lopez Mateos Sur 2500 **Location:** 4.5 mi (7.2 km) s on Mex 15 and 80; off Glorieta Mariana Otero; in Crowne Plaza Hotel and Resort Guadalajara. **Parking:** on-site (fee) and valet. **Cards:** AX, DC, MC, VI.

SANBORN'S **Phone:** 33/3817-4427

Mexican
$8-$18

Restaurants in the casual chain, which includes more than 100 locations throughout Mexico, offer a good selection of American-style sandwiches, salads, soups and both Mexican and American entrees. The selection of desserts is impressive. Casual dress. **Bar:** Full bar. **Hours:** 7 am-1 am. **Address:** Ave De Las Americas, #1619 **Location:** Jct Ave de Las Americas and Blvd Filadelphia. **Parking:** on-site (fee). **Cards:** MC, VI.

SANBORN'S **Phone:** 33/3615-5899

Mexican
$8-$18

Restaurants in the casual chain, which includes more than 100 locations throughout Mexico, offer a good selection of American-style sandwiches, salads, soups and both Mexican and American entrees. The selection of desserts is impressive. Casual dress. **Bar:** Full bar. **Hours:** 7 am-1 am. **Address:** Ave Vallarta No 1600 **Location:** On Ave Vallarta; between aves Union and Chapultapec. **Parking:** on-site (fee). **Cards:** MC, VI.

(See map and index starting on p. 616)

SANBORN'S

Phone: 33/3613-6680

Mexican
$8-$18

Restaurants in the casual chain, which includes more than 100 locations throughout Mexico, offer a good selection of American-style sandwiches, salads, soups and both Mexican and American entrees. The selection of desserts is impressive. Casual dress. **Bar:** Full bar. **Hours:** 7 am-1 am, Sun-midnight. **Address:** Ave 16 de Septiembre, #127 **Location:** In historic center of town. **Parking:** on-site (fee). **Cards:** AX, MC, VI.

SANBORN'S

Phone: 33/3122-5826

Mexican
$8-$18

Restaurants in the casual chain, which includes more than 100 locations throughout Mexico, offer a good selection of American-style sandwiches, salads, soups and both Mexican and American entrees. The selection of desserts is impressive. Casual dress. **Bar:** Full bar. **Hours:** 7:30 am-1 am. **Address:** Ave Vallarta #3958 R-2-7 **Location:** In Gran Plaza Shopping Mall; Zapopan. **Parking:** on-site (fee). **Cards:** MC, VI.

SANBORN'S

Phone: 33/3121-3675

Mexican
$8-$22

Restaurants in the casual chain, which includes more than 100 locations throughout Mexico, offer a good selection of American-style sandwiches, salads, soups and both Mexican and American entrees. The selection of desserts is impressive. Casual dress. **Bar:** Full bar. **Hours:** 7 am-1 am. **Address:** Ave Lopez Mateos 2718 **Location:** 4.4 mi (7 km) s on Mex 15 and 80; across from Plaza del Sol Mall. **Parking:** on-site. **Cards:** AX, MC, VI.

SANBORN'S

Phone: 33/3813-2062

Mexican
$8-$18

Restaurants in the casual chain, which includes more than 100 locations throughout Mexico, offer a good selection of American-style sandwiches, salads, soups and both Mexican and American entrees. The selection of desserts is impressive. Casual dress. **Bar:** Full bar. **Hours:** 7 am-1 am. **Address:** Ave Mex 3370 **Location:** 1.3 mi (2 km) w of Minerva Fountain. **Parking:** on-site. **Cards:** AX, MC, VI.

SANTO COYOTE

Phone: 33/3616-6978 (10)

Mexican
$15-$25

In the former US Consul General's residence, the Nuevo Mexican eatery features several open-air rooms with hand-painted murals, romantic pixie and candle lighting and views of a courtyard garden. Cabrito (goat) and excellent baby back ribs, topped with tamarind and pepper sauce, are roasted over a wood fire in the open kitchen and grill. Dressy casual. **Bar:** Full bar. **Reservations:** accepted. **Hours:** 1 pm-1 am. **Address:** Lerdo de Tejada #2379 **Location:** Just e of Ave Chapultepec. **Parking:** valet. **Cards:** AX, MC, VI.

CALL

SUEHIRO

Phone: 33/3826-0094 (14)

Japanese
$15-$24

Japanese-style tableside preparation is the specialty of this ethnic restaurant. Table grills are skillfully employed to give diners wonderfully flavorful, freshly cooked beef, shrimp and chicken dishes. **Bar:** Full bar. **Reservations:** suggested. **Hours:** 1:30 pm-6 & 7-11 pm. Closed: 1/1, 12/25; also 05/01. **Address:** Ave La Paz 1701 **Location:** 4 blks e of Ave Chapultepec. **Parking:** valet. **Cards:** AX, MC, VI.

VIPS

Phone: 33/3817-2084

Mexican
$5-$9

Owned by Wal-Mart of Mexico and found in most major cities, the budget-friendly chain serves a good variety of Mexican and American dishes, including burgers, sandwiches, salads, spaghetti and enchiladas, as well as a fine selection of desserts. Casual dress. **Hours:** 7 am-midnight, Fri & Sat-2 am. **Address:** Ave Mar Baltico #2240 **Location:** Jct Ave Americas just e of Glorieta Colon. **Parking:** on-site. **Cards:** MC, VI.

VIPS

Phone: 33/3631-1258

Mexican
$5-$9

Owned by Wal-Mart of Mexico and found in most major cities, the budget-friendly chain serves a good variety of Mexican and American dishes, including burgers, sandwiches, salads, spaghetti and enchiladas, as well as a fine selection of desserts. Casual dress. **Hours:** 7 am-midnight, Sun-11 pm. **Address:** Ave Patria #1199 **Location:** Across from University Plaza. **Parking:** on-site. **Cards:** MC, VI.

VIPS

Phone: 33/3631-0554

Mexican
$5-$9

Owned by Wal-Mart of Mexico and found in most major cities, the budget-friendly chain serves a good variety of Mexican and American dishes, including burgers, sandwiches, salads, spaghetti and enchiladas, as well as a fine selection of desserts. Casual dress. **Hours:** 7 am-midnight. **Address:** Ave Mariano Otero #3450 **Location:** Jct ave Mariano Otero. **Parking:** on-site. **Cards:** MC, VI.

VIPS

Phone: 33/3280-1342

Mexican
$5-$9

Owned by Wal-Mart of Mexico and found in most major cities, the budget-friendly chain serves a good variety of Mexican and American dishes, including burgers, sandwiches, salads, spaghetti and enchiladas, as well as a fine selection of desserts. Casual dress. **Hours:** 7 am-11 pm, Fri & Sat-midnight. **Location:** Jct Ave Circunvalacion Division del Norte and Ave Felix Palaviccini. Ave Circunvalacion Division del Norte #1041. **Parking:** on-site. **Cards:** MC, VI.

VIPS

Phone: 33/3647-1724

Mexican
$5-$9

Owned by Wal-Mart of Mexico and found in most major cities, the budget-friendly chain serves a good variety of Mexican and American dishes, including burgers, sandwiches, salads, spaghetti and enchiladas, as well as a fine selection of desserts. Casual dress. **Hours:** 7 am-1 am. **Address:** Ave Lopez Mateos Sur #2375 **Location:** In Plaza del Sol Shopping Mall. **Parking:** on-site. **Cards:** MC, VI.

(See map and index starting on p. 616)

VIPS

Mexican
$5-$9

Phone: 33/3812-6602

Owned by Wal-Mart of Mexico and found in most major cities, the budget-friendly chain serves a good variety of Mexican and American dishes, including burgers, sandwiches, salads, spaghetti and enchiladas, as well as a fine selection of desserts. Casual dress. **Hours:** 7 am-11 pm, Fri & Sat-midnight. **Address:** Ave Arbuledas #2500 Local 1 Zone H **Location:** Jct Ave Arboledus and Calle Nunez, just w. **Parking:** on-site. **Cards:** MC, VI.

VIPS

Mexican
$5-$9

Phone: 33/3813-0394

Owned by Wal-Mart of Mexico and found in most major cities, the budget-friendly chain serves a good variety of Mexican and American dishes, including burgers, sandwiches, salads, spaghetti and enchiladas, as well as a fine selection of desserts. Casual dress. **Hours:** 7 am-1 am. **Address:** Ave Mexico #3300 Local H **Location:** Jct Ave Mexico and Ave Homero; in Plaza Mexico. **Parking:** on-site. **Cards:** MC, VI.

VIPS

Mexican
$5-$9

Phone: 33/3673-3129

Owned by Wal-Mart of Mexico and found in most major cities, the budget-friendly chain serves a good variety of Mexican and American dishes, including burgers, sandwiches, salads, spaghetti and enchiladas, as well as a fine selection of desserts. Casual dress. **Hours:** 7 am-midnight. **Address:** Ave Vallarta #5455 **Location:** Jct aves Rafael Sancio and Vallarta, just s; in Zapopan. **Parking:** on-site. **Cards:** MC, VI.

VIPS

Mexican
$5-$9

Phone: 33/3683-6295

Owned by Wal-Mart of Mexico and found in most major cities, the budget-friendly chain serves a good variety of Mexican and American dishes, including burgers, sandwiches, salads, spaghetti and enchiladas, as well as a fine selection of desserts. Casual dress. **Hours:** 7 am-11 pm. **Address:** Ave Rio Nilo #8096 **Location:** In Tonala; jct Paseo Loma Andrade and Paseo Loma Sur, just n. **Parking:** on-site. **Cards:** MC, VI.

VIPS

Mexican
$5-$9

Phone: 33/3616-8553

Owned by Wal-Mart of Mexico and found in most major cities, the budget-friendly chain serves a good variety of Mexican and American dishes, including burgers, sandwiches, salads, spaghetti and enchiladas, as well as a fine selection of desserts. Casual dress. **Hours:** 7 am-midnight, Fri-1 am, Sat 7 am-1 am. **Address:** Ave Vallanta #2425 Local B-5 **Location:** In Centro Magno Shopping Mall. **Parking:** on-site. **Cards:** MC, VI.

Degollado Theater / © Martin Siepmann / age fotostock

This ends listings for Guadalajara.
The following page resumes the alphabetical listings of cities in Central Mexico.

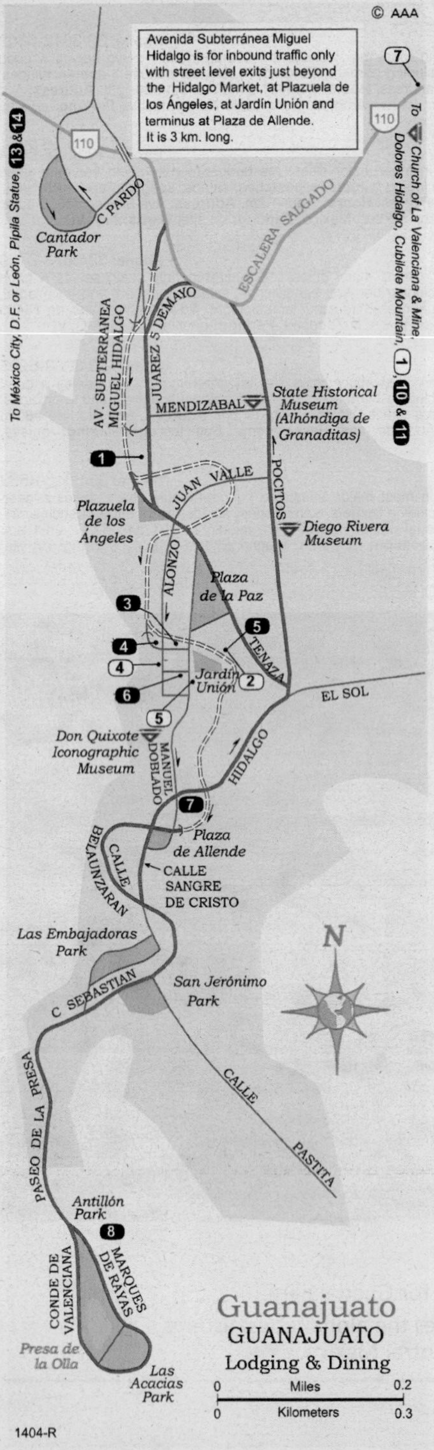

© AAA

Avenida Subterránea Miguel Hidalgo is for inbound traffic only with street level exits just beyond the Hidalgo Market, at Plazuela de los Ángeles, at Jardín Unión and terminus at Plaza de Allende. It is 3 km. long.

To México City, D.F. or León, Pipila Statue, 13 & 14

To Church of La Valenciana & Mine, Dolores Hidalgo, Cubilete Mountain, 1, 10 & 11

7

110

C PARDO

Cantador Park

ESCALERA SALGADO

AV. SUBTERRANEA MIGUEL HIDALGO

JUAREZ

5 DE MAYO

MENDIZABAL

State Historical Museum (Alhóndiga de Granaditas)

1

JUAN VALLE

POCITOS

Plazuela de los Ángeles

Diego Rivera Museum

ALONZO

Plaza de la Paz

3

4

4

5

TENAZA

Jardín Unión

2

6

5

EL SOL

Don Quixote Iconographic Museum

MANUEL DOBLADO

HIDALGO

7

Plaza de Allende

CALLE BELAUNZARAN

CALLE SANGRE DE CRISTO

Las Embajadoras Park

N

C SEBASTIAN

San Jerónimo Park

CALLE PASTITA

PASEO DE LA PRESA

Antillón Park

8

CONDE DE VALENCIANA

MARQUES DE RAYAS

Presa de la Olla

Las Acacias Park

Guanajuato
GUANAJUATO
Lodging & Dining

0 Miles 0.2
0 Kilometers 0.3

1404-R

Guanajuato

This index helps you "spot" where approved lodgings and restaurants are located on the corresponding detailed maps. Lodging daily rate range is for comparison only and show the property's high season. Restaurant rate range is a combination of lunch and/or dinner. Turn to the listing page for more detailed rate information and consult display ads for special promotions.

GUANAJUATO

Map Page	OA	Lodgings	Diamond Rated	High Season	Page
1 / p. 628		Suites Casa de las Manrique	◆	$80-$89	631
3 / p. 628	AAA	**Hotel San Diego**	◆◆	$100-$126	631
4 / p. 628		El Meson de los Poetas	◆◆	$95-$200	630
5 / p. 628		Hotel Posada Santa Fe	◆◆	$100-$165	630
6 / p. 628		Hosteria del Frayle	◆	$105-$125	630
7 / p. 628		Hotel Hostel Cantarranas	◆	$69	630
8 / p. 628	AAA	**Quinta Las Acacias**	◆◆◆◆	$200-$400	631
10 / p. 628		Casa Estrella de la Valenciana	◆◆◆	$179-$265	630
11 / p. 628		Camino Real Guanajuato	◆◆◆	$110-$185	630
13 / p. 628		Hotel Hacienda Mision Guanajuato	◆◆	$120-$220	630
14 / p. 628		Holiday Inn Express Guanajuato	◆◆◆	$110-$135	630

Map Page	OA	Restaurants	Diamond Rated	Cuisine	Meal Range	Page
1 / p. 628		Restaurant Real de la Esperanza	◆◆◆	Continental	$7-$25	631
2 / p. 628		Restaurante Hotel Posada Santa Fe	◆◆	Mexican	$6-$15	631
4 / p. 628		El Gallo Pitagorico	◆◆	Mediterranean	$6-$15	631
5 / p. 628		Casa Valadez	◆◆	Mexican	$6-$18	631
7 / p. 628		Casa del Conde de la Valenciana	◆◆◆	Regional Mexican	$8-$16	631

GUANAJUATO, GUANAJUATO pop. 141,426 (See map and index starting on p. 628)

WHERE TO STAY

CAMINO REAL GUANAJUATO Book at AAA.com **Phone:** (473)102-1500 **11**

Historic Hotel
$110-$185 All Year

Address: Alhondiga #100 **Location:** 1.2 mi (2 km) ne on Mex 110 (Dolores Hidalgo Hwy). **Facility:** Old hacienda. Modern colonial style units, a few older ones with fireplace. Very attractive grounds and pool area. Colorful building with antique carriages in garden and public areas. 105 units. 94 one-bedroom standard units. 9 one- and 2 two-bedroom suites. 6 stories, interior/exterior corridors. *Bath:* combo or shower only. **Parking:** on-site (fee) and valet. **Amenities:** high-speed Internet, dual phone lines, voice mail, safes, honor bars, irons, hair dryers. **Pool(s):** heated outdoor. **Leisure Activities:** waterslide, exercise room. **Guest Services:** valet laundry, wireless Internet. **Business Services:** meeting rooms, business center. **Cards:** AX, DC, MC, VI.

/ SOME UNITS

CASA ESTRELLA DE LA VALENCIANA **Phone:** 473/732-1784 **10**

Bed & Breakfast
$179-$265 All Year

Address: Callejon Jalisco #10 **Location:** 2.1 mi (3.5 km) nw on Mex 110 to Dolores Hidalgo Hwy, just w, follow signs. **Facility:** Across from the noted Valenciana church, the property overlooks a valley and offers elegant accommodations. Designated smoking area. 8 units. 6 one-bedroom standard units, some with whirlpools. 2 one-bedroom suites. 2 stories (no elevator), interior/exterior corridors. *Bath:* combo or shower only. **Parking:** on-site. **Terms:** check-in 4 pm, age restrictions may apply, 5 day cancellation notice-fee imposed. **Amenities:** video library, DVD players, CD players, high-speed Internet, irons, hair dryers. **Pool(s):** outdoor. **Leisure Activities:** whirlpool. *Fee:* massage. **Guest Services:** valet laundry, wireless Internet. **Business Services:** meeting rooms, PC, fax (fee). **Cards:** AX, DS, MC, VI.

D VCR / SOME UNITS

EL MESON DE LOS POETAS **Phone:** 473/732-0705 **4**

Hotel
$95-$200 All Year

Address: Positos #35 Esq con Juan Valle **Location:** Just w of Jardin a la Union; center. **Facility:** 31 units. 27 one-bedroom standard units, some with efficiencies or kitchens (no utensils). 4 one-bedroom suites with kitchens (no utensils). 9 stories (no elevator), interior corridors. *Bath:* combo or shower only. **Parking:** street. **Guest Services:** valet laundry. **Business Services:** fax (fee). **Cards:** MC, VI.

HOLIDAY INN EXPRESS GUANAJUATO Book at AAA.com **Phone:** (473)735-2000 **14**

Hotel
$110-$135 All Year

Address: Euquerio Guerrero #120 **Location:** On Mex 110 (toll road); at entrance to town; sw on Mex 10 (non toll), 0.6 mi (1 km) e on GT067. **Facility:** 165 units. 159 one-bedroom standard units. 6 one-bedroom suites. 5 stories, interior corridors. **Parking:** on-site. **Amenities:** high-speed Internet, dual phone lines, voice mail, irons, hair dryers. **Pool(s):** heated indoor. **Leisure Activities:** exercise room. **Guest Services:** valet and coin laundry, area transportation, wireless Internet. **Business Services:** conference facilities, business center. **Cards:** AX, MC, VI.

S D / SOME UNITS

HOSTERIA DEL FRAYLE **Phone:** 473/732-1179 **6**

Historic Hotel
$105-$125 All Year

Address: Sopena #3 **Location:** Center. **Facility:** Hotel converted from 17th-century gold and silver coin mint; some very steep steps. 37 units. 34 one-bedroom standard units. 3 one-bedroom suites. 4 stories (no elevator), interior corridors. *Bath:* shower only. **Parking:** no self-parking. **Terms:** 15 day cancellation notice. **Amenities:** safes. **Guest Services:** beauty salon. **Business Services:** fax (fee). **Cards:** MC, VI.

HOTEL HACIENDA MISION GUANAJUATO Book at AAA.com **Phone:** (473)732-3980 **13**

Historic Hotel
$120-$220 All Year

Address: Camino Antiguo A Marfil KM 2.5 **Location:** 1.6 mi (2.5 km) w; at entrance to town on Mex 110 (Dolores Hidalgo Hwy). **Facility:** On 'libriamineto' city bypass, the historic hacienda has thick stone walls, clay tile floors, period furnishings and austere, yet older, rooms. 138 units. 137 one-bedroom standard units. 1 one-bedroom suite with whirlpool. 2-3 stories (no elevator), interior corridors. *Bath:* combo or shower only. **Parking:** on-site. **Terms:** 3 day cancellation notice. **Amenities:** *Some:* safes, honor bars, hair dryers. **Pool(s):** outdoor. **Leisure Activities:** lighted tennis court. **Guest Services:** valet laundry, area transportation. **Business Services:** meeting rooms, PC, fax (fee). **Cards:** AX, MC, VI.

D / SOME UNITS

HOTEL HOSTEL CANTARRANAS **Phone:** (473)732-5241 **7**

Hotel
$69 All Year

Address: Calle Cantarranas 50 **Location:** Center. **Facility:** 8 units. 4 one-bedroom standard units. 4 one-bedroom suites with efficiencies. 3 stories (no elevator), exterior corridors. *Bath:* shower only. **Parking:** street. **Terms:** 15 day cancellation notice. **Business Services:** fax (fee).

/ SOME UNITS

HOTEL POSADA SANTA FE Book at AAA.com **Phone:** (473)732-0084 **5**

Historic Hotel
$100-$165 All Year

Address: Jardin de la Union 12 **Location:** Center at Jardin de la Union. **Facility:** Restored 1862 building. 50 one-bedroom standard units. 3 stories (no elevator), interior corridors. *Bath:* combo or shower only. **Parking:** on-site. **Terms:** 15 day cancellation notice. **Dining:** restaurant, see separate listing. **Leisure Activities:** whirlpools. **Guest Services:** valet laundry, wireless Internet. **Business Services:** meeting rooms, fax (fee). **Cards:** AX, MC, VI.

/ SOME UNITS

(See map and index starting on p. 628)

HOTEL SAN DIEGO Phone: 473/732-1300 3

Hotel
$100-$126 All Year

Address: Jardin de la Union #1 **Location:** Center. Located in a historic commercial district. **Facility:** 43 units. 41 one-bedroom standard units. 1 one- and 1 two-bedroom suites. 5 stories, interior corridors. *Bath:* shower only. **Parking:** on-site. **Terms:** 10 day cancellation notice. **Guest Services:** valet laundry, wireless Internet. **Business Services:** meeting rooms, fax. **Cards:** MC, VI.

QUINTA LAS ACACIAS Phone: (473)731-1517 8

Country Inn
$200-$400 All Year

Address: Paseo de la Presa #168 **Location:** Across from Acacia Park; center. **Facility:** This property offers two room styles: traditional New England with hardwood floors and antiques or one with a Mexican Colonial motif. 17 units. 9 one-bedroom standard units with whirlpools. 8 one-bedroom suites, some with whirlpools. 5 stories (no elevator), interior/exterior corridors. *Bath:* combo or shower only. **Parking:** street. **Terms:** age restrictions may apply, 7 day cancellation notice. **Amenities:** high-speed Internet, safes, hair dryers. **Leisure Activities:** whirlpool. *Fee:* massage. **Guest Services:** valet laundry, wireless Internet. **Business Services:** meeting rooms, fax (fee). **Cards:** AX, MC, VI.

SUITES CASA DE LAS MANRIQUE Phone: 473/732-7678 1

Historic Hotel
$80-$89 All Year

Address: Ave Juarez 116 **Location:** Center. Located across from the Mercado Hidalgo. **Facility:** Converted 1882 home. 8 one-bedroom suites, some with whirlpools. 3 stories (no elevator), interior corridors. *Bath:* shower only. **Parking:** on-site. **Terms:** 15 day cancellation notice. **Amenities:** safes. **Guest Services:** valet laundry. **Cards:** MC, VI.

/ SOME UNITS

WHERE TO DINE

CASA DEL CONDE DE LA VALENCIANA Phone: 473/732-2550 7

Regional Mexican
$8-$16

In the garden courtyard of a count's former home, the historic restaurant prepares haute cuisine from around the world. Worthy choices include decorative smoked salmon and tenderloin medallions. Casual dress. **Bar:** Full bar. **Reservations:** accepted. **Hours:** 10 am-6 pm. Closed: 1/1, 12/24; also Sun. **Address:** Plaza de Valenciana #11 **Location:** On Mex 110 to Dolores Hidalgo; across from Templo San Cayetano. **Parking:** street. **Cards:** MC, VI.

CASA VALADEZ Phone: 473/732-1157 5

Mexican
$6-$18

Attentive staff members welcome guests to this eatery across from Jardin de la Union and the Teatro Juarez. Homemade watermelon juice tastes great with dishes from the crowd-pleasing menu of sandwiches, Mexican specialties, pastas, steaks and salads. Casual dress. **Bar:** Full bar. **Hours:** 8:30 am-11 pm. **Address:** Jardin de la Union #3 **Location:** Center. **Parking:** street. **Cards:** AX, MC, VI.

EL GALLO PITAGORICO Phone: 473/732-9489 4

Mediterranean
$6-$15

Climbing the steps of the cobalt blue edifice up to the dining room, which is perched above the city center, allows for wonderful views. Offerings include fresh salads, meats in rich sauces, fish, seafood, chicken, beef and pasta dishes. Casual dress. **Bar:** Full bar. **Reservations:** accepted. **Hours:** 2 pm-11 pm, Fri & Sat-midnight. Closed: 1/1, 12/25. **Address:** Constancia 10-A **Location:** Just w of Jardin de la Union; center. **Parking:** street. **Cards:** MC, VI.

RESTAURANTE HOTEL POSADA SANTA FE Phone: 473/732-0084 2

Mexican
$6-$15

In the heart of the main "jardin," the restaurant has a relaxed ambience that invites diners to spend countless hours just people-watching. Most seating is on the sidewalk, a cozy place to unwind and savor traditional Mexican dishes. Casual dress. **Bar:** Full bar. **Hours:** 8 am-11:30 pm. **Address:** Jardin de la Union 12 **Location:** Center at Jardin de la Union; in Hotel Posada Santa Fe. **Parking:** street. **Cards:** AX, MC, VI.

RESTAURANT REAL DE LA ESPERANZA Phone: 473/732-1041 1

Continental
$7-$25

On the outskirts of the city, the eatery is well worth the short drive. Examples of the traditional Mexican fare include milanesa (breaded steak), arrachera (marinated skirt steak) and fideo (Mexican pasta soup). Room should be left to enjoy the delicious crepes with "cajeta," a sweet creamy sauce popular with the locals. Casual dress. **Bar:** Full bar. **Hours:** 1 pm-9 pm. **Address:** Carr A Dolores Hidalgo KM 5 **Location:** 3.3 mi (5.5 km) on Dolores Hidalgo Hwy. **Parking:** on-site. **Cards:** AX, MC, VI.

IRAPUATO, GUANAJUATO pop. 440,134

WHERE TO DINE

VIPS Phone: 462/624-3825

Regional Mexican
$7-$25

Owned by Wal-Mart of Mexico and found in most major cities, the budget-friendly chain serves a good variety of Mexican and American dishes, including burgers, sandwiches, salads, spaghetti and enchiladas, as well as a fine selection of desserts. Casual dress. **Bar:** Beer & wine. **Hours:** 7 am-11 pm, Fri & Sat-midnight. **Address:** Blvd Vil las de Irapuato No 229, Col 1 de M **Location:** Just w of jct Blvd Paseo de Irapuato. **Parking:** on-site. **Cards:** AX, MC, VI.

LAZARO CARDENAS, MICHOACAN pop. 171,100

WHERE TO STAY

NH LAZARO CARDENAS Book at AAA.com Phone: (753)533-2900

Hotel
$77-$150 All Year

Address: Circuito de las Universidades #60 **Location:** 3.8 mi (6 km) w on Mex 200. **Facility:** 118 one-bedroom standard units. 4 stories, interior corridors. **Parking:** on-site. **Amenities:** dual phone lines, voice mail. *Some:* honor bars, hair dryers. **Pool(s):** heated outdoor. **Leisure Activities:** whirlpool, exercise room. **Guest Services:** valet laundry, wireless Internet. **Business Services:** meeting rooms, business center. **Cards:** AX, MC, VI.

/ SOME UNITS

LEON, GUANAJUATO pop. 1,134,842

WHERE TO STAY

FIESTA INN LEON Book great rates at AAA.com Phone: (477)710-0500

Hotel
$159-$189 All Year

Address: Blvd Adolfo Lopez Mateos 2702 Ote **Location:** On Mex 45; jct Blvd M Escobedo. **Facility:** 160 one-bedroom standard units. 3 stories, interior corridors. **Parking:** on-site. **Amenities:** video games (fee), high-speed Internet, voice mail, irons, hair dryers. **Pool(s):** outdoor. **Leisure Activities:** exercise room. **Guest Services:** valet laundry, wireless Internet. **Business Services:** meeting rooms, business center. **Cards:** AX, DC, MC, VI. *(See color ad on insert)*

/ SOME UNITS

HOLIDAY INN CENTRO DE CONVENCIONES Book at AAA.com Phone: (477)710-0040

Hotel
$115-$169 All Year

Address: Blvd Lopez Mateos #1501 **Location:** On Mex 45, jct Blvd Chichimecas. **Facility:** Meets AAA guest room security requirements. 177 units. 171 one-bedroom standard units. 6 one-bedroom suites. 5 stories, interior corridors. *Bath:* combo or shower only. **Parking:** on-site. **Amenities:** voice mail, safes, irons, hair dryers. **Pool(s):** heated indoor. **Leisure Activities:** exercise room. **Guest Services:** valet laundry, wireless Internet. **Business Services:** meeting rooms, business center. **Cards:** AX, DC, DS, MC, VI.

/ SOME UNITS

HOLIDAY INN LEON MEXICO Book at AAA.com Phone: (477)710-0003

Hotel
$95-$107 All Year

Address: Ave Lopez Mateos 1308 **Location:** 2.2 mi (3.5 km) se on Mex 45. **Facility:** Meets AAA guest room security requirements. 170 units. 166 one-bedroom standard units. 4 one-bedroom suites. 5 stories, interior corridors. **Parking:** on-site. **Amenities:** voice mail, safes, irons, hair dryers. **Pool(s):** heated indoor. **Leisure Activities:** exercise room. **Guest Services:** valet laundry, wireless Internet. **Business Services:** meeting rooms, business center. **Cards:** AX, MC, VI.

/ SOME UNITS

HOTEL FIESTA AMERICANA-LEON Book great rates at AAA.com Phone: (477)719-8000

Hotel
$130-$245 All Year

Address: Blvd Adolfo Lopez Mateos 1102 **Location:** On Mex 45; between Merida and Pampas sts. Located across from Centro Estrella. **Facility:** This hotel houses not only well-appointed rooms, but shares its space with boutiques and retail stores. 211 units. 177 one-bedroom standard units, some with whirlpools. 34 one-bedroom suites. 8 stories, interior corridors. **Parking:** on-site. **Terms:** cancellation fee imposed. **Amenities:** video games (fee), high-speed Internet, voice mail, safes, honor bars, irons, hair dryers. **Dining:** entertainment. **Pool(s):** heated outdoor. **Leisure Activities:** saunas, whirlpool, 2 lighted tennis courts, children's playhouse, exercise room. *Fee:* tennis instruction, massage. **Guest Services:** valet laundry, area transportation (fee), wireless Internet. **Business Services:** conference facilities, business center. **Cards:** AX, DC, MC, VI. *(See color ad on insert)*

/ SOME UNITS FEE

WHERE TO DINE

FRASCATI RISTORANTE-PIZZERIA Phone: 477/773-7154

Italian
$8-$18

Pasta, pizza and other Italian staples can be sampled in a casually upscale atmosphere. Recently relocated to a standalone building outside Plaza Mayor mall, the new home to this local favorite features modern design with hardwood floors, a brick boveda ceiling, limestone walls and a hip bar area. The kitchen takes some surprising liberties with Italian cuisine. Casual dress. **Bar:** Full bar. **Reservations:** suggested. **Hours:** 2 pm-11:30 pm, Fri-midnight, Sun-6 pm. Closed: 1/1, 12/25. **Address:** Ave Cerro Gordo 201A **Location:** At Plaza Mayor Mall. **Parking:** valet and street. **Cards:** AX, MC, VI.

RESTAURANTE BAR LOS AGAVES Phone: 477/772-5588

Regional Continental
$8-$20

Midway between the airport and town, the pleasant restaurant has attractive rooms and an attentive staff. Among well-prepared regional dishes are salmon with mango and guajillo chili sauce and quesadillas with squash blossoms and cheese. Casual dress. **Bar:** Full bar. **Hours:** 1 pm-11 pm, Sun-6 pm. **Address:** Blvd Aeropuerto KM 8 **Location:** 5.6 mi (8 km) w on Leon Hwy to Silao International Airport. **Parking:** on-site. **Cards:** MC, VI.

SANBORN'S Phone: 477/713-6264

Regional Mexican
$8-$28

Restaurants in the casual chain, which includes more than 100 locations throughout Mexico, offer a good selection of American-style sandwiches, salads, soups and both Mexican and American entrees. The selection of desserts is impressive. Casual dress. **Bar:** Full bar. **Hours:** 7 am-1 am. **Address:** Blvd Adolfo Mateos No 1102, Col Centro **Location:** In historic district. **Parking:** on-site (fee). **Cards:** AX, MC, VI.

SANBORN'S **Phone:** 477/773-1316

Regional Mexican $8-$28

Restaurants in the casual chain, which includes more than 100 locations throughout Mexico, offer a good selection of American-style sandwiches, salads, soups and both Mexican and American entrees. The selection of desserts is impressive. Casual dress. **Bar:** Full bar. **Hours:** 7 am-midnight, Fri & Sat-2 am. **Address:** Blvd Juan Alonso de Torres No 3002, Col **Location:** In Plaza Mayor Shopping Complex. **Parking:** on-site (fee). **Cards:** AX, MC, VI.

SIRLOIN STOCKADE **Phone:** 477/718-4689

Steak $6-$9

The steakhouse lines up buffet items, including pizza, tacos, soups, salads and desserts, providing both excellent variety and a good value. Rotating theme nights might allow for the sampling of sushi, barbecue and seafood. The buffet also may serve to complement a quality steak. Rolls are baked several times daily. Casual dress. **Bar:** Beer & wine. **Hours:** noon-11 pm, Fri & Sat-midnight, Sun 9 am-11 pm. Closed: 12/25. **Address:** Blvd Los Torres #2002, Plaza Mayor **Location:** Jct Blvd Manuel J Clouthier; in Plaza Mayor Shopping Complex. **Parking:** on-site. **Cards:** DS, MC, VI.

VIPS **Phone:** 477/718-7032

Regional Mexican $7-$25

Owned by Wal-Mart of Mexico and found in most major cities, the budget-friendly chain serves a good variety of Mexican and American dishes, including burgers, sandwiches, salads, spaghetti and enchiladas, as well as a fine selection of desserts. Casual dress. **Bar:** Beer & wine. **Hours:** 7 am-midnight, Fri & Sat-2 am. **Address:** Blvd A L Mateos Pte No 1902, Col Penitas **Location:** In Centro Comercial Gran Plaza. **Parking:** no self-parking. **Cards:** AX, MC, VI.

The following restaurant has not been evaluated by AAA but is listed for your information only.

ARGENTILIA RESTAURANT **Phone:** 477/718-3394

fyi

Not evaluated. Meat lovers will enjoy this steak house. Cuts of beef are prepared Argentine-style and grilled over mesquite wood. **Address:** Ave Cerro Gordo #12 **Location:** 1.2 mi (2 km) w on Ave Lopez Mateos to Ave Campestre, then 1.3 mi (2.1 km) s to dead-end with Ave Cerro Gordo.

MATEHUALA, SAN LUIS POTOSI pop. 78,187

WHERE TO STAY

The following lodging was either not evaluated or did not meet AAA rating requirements but is listed for your information only.

LAS PALMAS MIDWAY INN **Phone:** 488/882-0002

fyi

Not evaluated. **Address:** Hwy 57 KM 617 **Location:** On Mex 57, by north jct entrance road to town. Facilities, services, and decor characterize an economy property.

WHERE TO DINE

The following restaurant has not been evaluated by AAA but is listed for your information only.

LAS PALMAS RESTAURANT **Phone:** 488/882-0001

fyi

Not evaluated. Diners take to the relaxing atmosphere to unwind and replenish, with the help of the well-trained staff. The menu centers on Continental fare. **Location:** On Mex 57, by north jct entrance road to town; in Las Palmas Midway Inn.

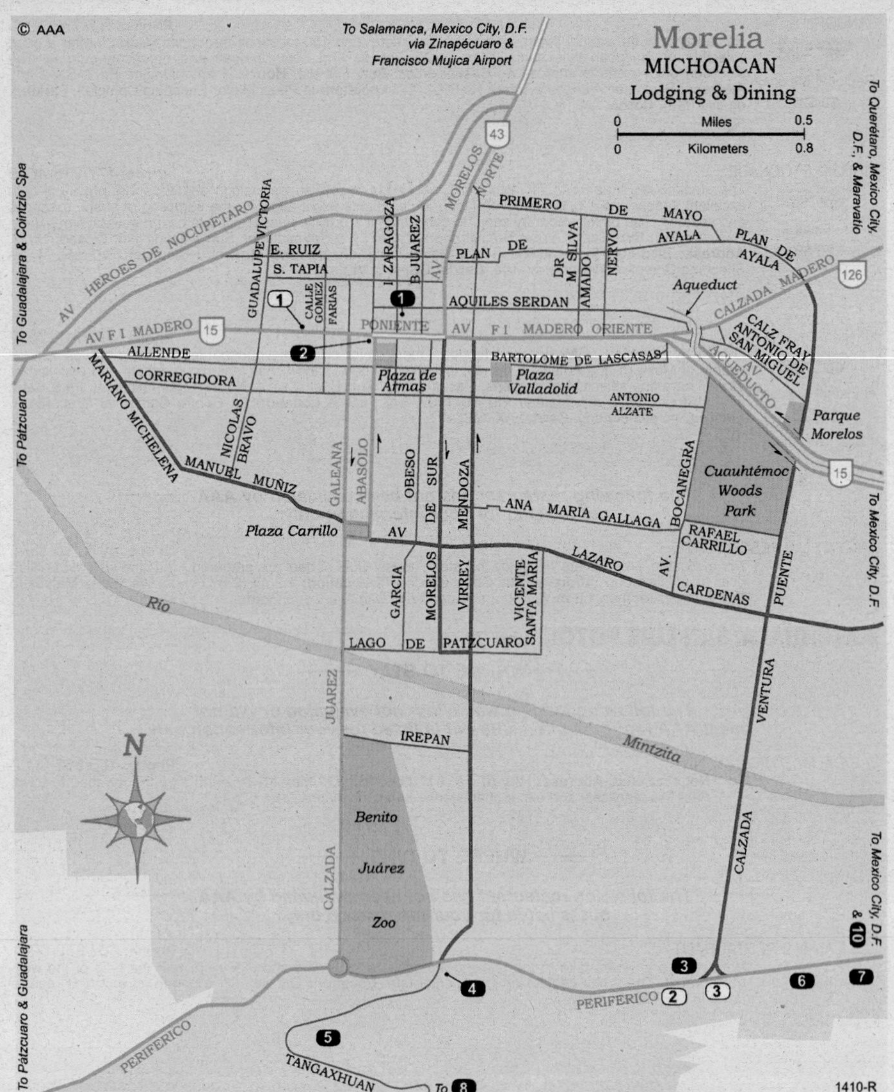
© AAA
To Salamanca, Mexico City, D.F. via Zinapécuaro & Francisco Mujica Airport
Morelia
MICHOACAN
Lodging & Dining
0 Miles 0.5
0 Kilometers 0.8
To Querétaro, Mexico City, D.F., & Maravatio
To Guadalajara & Cointzio Spa
To Pátzcuaro
To Mexico City, D.F.
To Mexico City, D.F. & 10
To Pátzcuaro & Guadalajara
AV HEROES DE NOCUPETARO
AV F I MADERO PONIENTE
AV F I MADERO ORIENTE
PRIMERO DE MAYO
PLAN DE AYALA
AQUILES SERDAN
ALLENDE
CORREGIDORA
BARTOLOME DE LASCASAS
ANTONIO ALZATE
Aqueduct
CALZADA MADERO
CALZ FRAY ANTONIO DE SAN MIGUEL
AV ACUEDUCTO
Parque Morelos
Plaza de Armas
Plaza Valladolid
Cuauhtémoc Woods Park
Plaza Carrillo
MARIANO MICHELENA
MANUEL MUÑIZ
ANA MARIA GALLAGA
AV LAZARO CARDENAS
RAFAEL CARRILLO
LAGO DE PATZCUARO
IREPAN
Río Mintzita
Benito Juárez Zoo
CALZADA JUAREZ
CALZADA VENTURA PUENTE
PERIFERICO
TANGAXHUAN
To 8
1410-R

Morelia

This index helps you "spot" where approved lodgings and restaurants are located on the corresponding detailed maps. Lodging daily rate range is for comparison only and show the property's high season. Restaurant rate range is a combination of lunch and/or dinner. Turn to the listing page for more detailed rate information and consult display ads for special promotions.

MORELIA

Map Page	OA	Lodgings	Diamond Rated	High Season	Page
1 / p. 634		Hotel de la Soledad	◆◆	$93-$200	636
2 / p. 634		Hotel Virrey de Mendoza	◆◆◆	$225-$435	636
3 / p. 634	AAA	**Hotel Fiesta Inn Morelia** - see color ad on insert	◆◆	$110-$153	636
4 / p. 634		CasaCamelinas	◆◆	$75-$95	636
5 / p. 634		Villa Montana Hotel & Spa	◆◆◆◆	$210-$490	636
6 / p. 634		Holiday Inn-Morelia	◆◆◆	$121	636
7 / p. 634		Holiday Inn Express Morelia	◆◆◆	$111-$123	636
8 / p. 634		Villa San Jose Hotel & Suites	◆◆◆	$190-$374	637
10 / p. 634		Turotel	◆◆◆	$120	636

Map Page	OA	Restaurants	Diamond Rated	Cuisine	Meal Range	Page
1 / p. 634		Fonda Las Mercedes	◆◆◆	Mexican	$8-$20	637
2 / p. 634		Las Trojes Restaurant-Bar	◆◆◆	Mexican	$11-$21	637
3 / p. 634		San Miguelito Restaurante	◆◆	Mexican	$7-$18	637

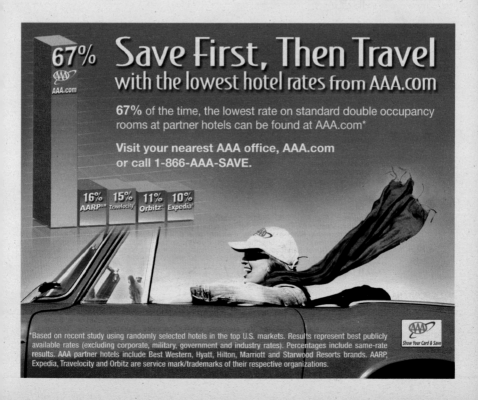

MORELIA, MICHOACAN pop. 620,532 (See map and index starting on p. 634)

WHERE TO STAY

CASACAMELINAS — Phone: 443/324-5194 — 4

Bed & Breakfast
$75-$95 All Year

Address: Jacarandas #172, Col Nueva Jacaran **Location:** 2 mi (3.3 km) s off Mex 15 via Periferico, just s. Located on terraced slope in a residential area. **Facility:** Designated smoking area. 5 one-bedroom standard units, some with kitchens. 3 stories (no elevator), exterior corridors. *Bath:* combo or shower only. **Parking:** on-site. **Amenities:** hair dryers. *Some:* irons. **Leisure Activities:** Spanish language studies.

D / SOME UNITS

HOLIDAY INN EXPRESS MORELIA — Book at AAA.com — Phone: (443)315-7100 — 7

Motel
$111-$123 All Year

Address: Ave Camelinas 5000 **Location:** 4 mi (6.7 km) se on Periferico. **Facility:** Meets AAA guest room security requirements. 133 one-bedroom standard units. 2 stories (no elevator), interior corridors. *Bath:* combo or shower only. **Parking:** on-site. **Terms:** 7 day cancellation notice-fee imposed. **Amenities:** high-speed Internet, voice mail, irons, hair dryers. **Pool(s):** heated outdoor. **Leisure Activities:** exercise room. **Guest Services:** valet laundry, wireless Internet. **Business Services:** meeting rooms, PC, fax (fee). **Cards:** AX, MC, VI.

CALL / SOME UNITS

HOLIDAY INN-MORELIA — Phone: (443)314-3111 — 6

Hotel
$121 All Year

Address: Ave Camelinas No 3466 **Location:** 3.8 mi (6.3 km) se on Periferico. Located opposite Plaza Las Americas. **Facility:** Meets AAA guest room security requirements. 123 units. 120 one-bedroom standard units. 3 one-bedroom suites. 3 stories, interior corridors. *Bath:* combo or shower only. **Parking:** on-site. **Amenities:** high-speed Internet, voice mail, safes, irons, hair dryers. **Pool(s):** heated outdoor. **Leisure Activities:** whirlpool, tennis court, jogging, exercise room, basketball, volleyball. **Guest Services:** valet laundry, wireless Internet. **Business Services:** meeting rooms, business center. **Cards:** AX, MC, VI.

D / SOME UNITS

HOTEL DE LA SOLEDAD — Phone: (443)312-1888 — 1

Hotel
$93-$200 All Year

Address: Zaragoza 90 y Melchor Ocampo **Location:** Just n of cathedral. **Facility:** 58 units. 49 one-bedroom standard units. 9 one-bedroom suites. 2 stories, exterior corridors. *Bath:* combo or shower only. **Parking:** valet. **Amenities:** safes. **Guest Services:** valet laundry, wireless Internet. **Business Services:** meeting rooms, PC. **Cards:** AX, CB, DC, MC, VI.

HOTEL FIESTA INN MORELIA — Phone: 443/322-8000 — 3

AAA

Hotel
$110-$153 All Year

Address: Aves Camelinas & Ventura Puente **Location:** On Periferico, just w of jct Calzada Ventura; at convention center. **Facility:** 253 one-bedroom standard units. 5 stories, interior corridors. **Parking:** on-site (fee). **Amenities:** voice mail, irons, hair dryers. **Pool(s):** heated outdoor. **Leisure Activities:** 2 lighted tennis courts, exercise room. **Guest Services:** valet laundry, wireless Internet. **Business Services:** conference facilities, business center. **Cards:** AX, DC, MC, VI. *(See color ad on insert)*

S D / SOME UNITS

HOTEL VIRREY DE MENDOZA — Phone: (443)312-0633 — 2

Historic Hotel
$225-$435 All Year

Address: Ave Madero Poniente 310, Colonia Cen **Location:** Just w of cathedral; center. **Facility:** From a stained-glass ceiling to original art, Old World elegance imbues this hotel built in the 17th century; some units furnished in superb antiques. 55 one-bedroom standard units. 3 stories, interior corridors. **Parking:** valet. **Terms:** 7 day cancellation notice. **Amenities:** voice mail, hair dryers. **Guest Services:** valet laundry, wireless Internet. **Business Services:** meeting rooms, business center. **Cards:** AX, MC, VI.

/ SOME UNITS

TUROTEL — Book at AAA.com — Phone: (443)333-1300 — 10

Hotel
$120 All Year

Address: Ave Aqueducto #3805 **Location:** Jct aves Aqueducto and Camelinas (Periferico). **Facility:** Meets AAA guest room security requirements. 32 one-bedroom standard units. 5 stories, interior corridors. *Bath:* shower only. **Parking:** on-site. **Amenities:** high-speed Internet, dual phone lines, voice mail, safes, irons, hair dryers. **Pool(s):** outdoor. **Leisure Activities:** limited exercise equipment. **Guest Services:** valet and coin laundry, wireless Internet. **Business Services:** meeting rooms, business center. **Cards:** AX, CB, DC, DS, JC, MC, VI.

24 D / SOME UNITS

VILLA MONTANA HOTEL & SPA — Phone: (443)314-0231 — 5

Hotel
$210-$490 All Year

Address: Patzimba 201, Vista Bella **Location:** 2 mi (3.3 km) s off Mex 15 via Periferico, s on Tangaxhuan. **Facility:** The villa's accommodations, terraced on a mountain slope above the city, feature tasteful interiors with colonial antiques. 36 units. 24 one-bedroom standard units. 8 one- and 4 two-bedroom suites. 2 stories (no elevator), exterior corridors. **Parking:** on-site. **Terms:** 7 day cancellation notice-fee imposed. **Amenities:** high-speed Internet, voice mail, safes, hair dryers. **Pool(s):** heated outdoor. **Leisure Activities:** saunas, steamrooms, tennis court, exercise room, spa. **Guest Services:** valet laundry. **Business Services:** meeting rooms, business center. **Cards:** AX, MC, VI.

/ SOME UNITS FEE

(See map and index starting on p. 634)

VILLA SAN JOSE HOTEL & SUITES Book at AAA.com Phone: (443)324-4545 8

Motel
$190-$374 All Year

Address: 77 Patzimba Col Vista Bella **Location:** 1.9 mi (3.3 km) s off Mex 15 via Periferico, s on Tangaxhuan. **Facility:** 43 units. 39 one- and 2 two-bedroom standard units. 2 two-bedroom suites. 2 stories (no elevator), exterior corridors. *Bath:* combo or shower only. **Parking:** on-site. **Terms:** 3 day cancellation notice. **Amenities:** *Some:* hair dryers. **Pool(s):** heated outdoor. **Leisure Activities:** tennis court. **Guest Services:** valet laundry, wireless Internet. **Business Services:** meeting rooms, business center. **Cards:** AX, MC, VI.

/ SOME UNITS FEE

WHERE TO DINE

FONDA LAS MERCEDES Phone: 443/312-6113 1

Mexican
$8-$20

A great starting or ending point for exploring the beautiful historic center of town, the downtown restaurant serves local specialties and some Continental dishes. The menu includes oysters, salmon, chicken, pasta, beef and Mexican specialties. Distinctively decorated dining rooms mix Colonial and contemporary styles. Numerous pots adorn the lounge ceiling. Casual dress. **Bar:** Full bar. **Reservations:** suggested. **Hours:** 1:30 pm-midnight, Sun-6 pm. Closed: 12/25; also 5/1. **Address:** Leon Guzman #47 **Location:** Just w of cathedral; corner of Ave Madero Pte; in historic district. **Parking:** street. **Cards:** MC, VI. **Historic**

LAS TROJES RESTAURANT-BAR Phone: 443/324-3283 2

Mexican
$11-$21

Named after the traditional housing of the indigenous people of Morelia, rustic yet sophisticated Las Trojes welcomes families to dine on steak, soups and salads prepared Mexican style. Complimentary starters might include tangy cucumber salad or homemade salsa, and it's all but impossible to get a bad meal here. Service is attentive and somewhat formal. Casual dress. **Bar:** Full bar. **Reservations:** accepted. **Hours:** 1 pm-midnight, Sun-6 pm. Closed: 1/1, 12/25. **Address:** Juan Sebastian Bach #51 **Location:** 1.9 mi (3.3 km) s off Mex 15 via Periferico, just s on Mozart, then just e. **Parking:** valet. **Cards:** AX, MC, VI.

SANBORN'S Phone: 443/317-8472

Mexican
$8-$18

Restaurants in the casual chain, which includes more than 100 locations throughout Mexico, offer a good selection of American-style sandwiches, salads, soups and both Mexican and American entrees. The selection of desserts is impressive. Casual dress. **Bar:** Full bar. **Hours:** 7:30 am-midnight. **Address:** Portal Galenna #171 **Location:** Jct Ave Francisco Madero and Guillermo Prieto, just ne; in historic center of town. **Parking:** on-site (fee). **Cards:** MC, VI.

SANBORN'S Phone: 443/315-1049

Mexican
$7-$18

Restaurants in the casual chain, which includes more than 100 locations throughout Mexico, offer a good selection of American-style sandwiches, salads, soups and both Mexican and American entrees. The selection of desserts is impressive. Casual dress. **Bar:** Full bar. **Hours:** 7 am-11 pm. **Address:** Camelinas 5030-26 **Location:** 3.8 mi (6.3 km) se on Periferico; in Plaza Las Americas. **Parking:** on-site. **Cards:** MC, VI.

SAN MIGUELITO RESTAURANTE Phone: 443/324-4411 3

Mexican
$7-$18

A lively crowd gathers at the colonial-styled cafe for lunch in the afternoon. On the menu is a good selection of steaks, chicken dishes and salads, reinforced by tasty margaritas. Casual dress. **Bar:** Full bar. **Hours:** 2 pm-11 pm, Thurs-Sat to midnight, Sun-5 pm. Closed: 1/1, 12/25. **Address:** Ave Camelinnas S/N Centro **Location:** 2.1 mi (3.5 km) off Mex 15 via Periferico; across from convention center. **Parking:** valet. **Cards:** AX, MC, VI.

VIPS Phone: 443/317-6332

Mexican
$5-$9

Owned by Wal-Mart of Mexico and found in most major cities, the budget-friendly chain serves a good variety of Mexican and American dishes, including burgers, sandwiches, salads, spaghetti and enchiladas, as well as a fine selection of desserts. Casual dress. **Hours:** 7 am-11 pm, Fri & Sat-midnight. **Address:** Avenida Francisco I Madero Oriente #58 **Location:** Just e of Central Plaza; in historic downtown area. **Parking:** on-site. **Cards:** MC, VI.

VIPS Phone: 443/324-2187

Mexican
$5-$9

Owned by Wal-Mart of Mexico and found in most major cities, the budget-friendly chain serves a good variety of Mexican and American dishes, including burgers, sandwiches, salads, spaghetti and enchiladas, as well as a fine selection of desserts. Casual dress. **Hours:** 7 am-1 am. **Address:** Ave Camelinas #3151 **Location:** In Las Americas Shopping Center. **Parking:** on-site. **Cards:** MC, VI.

VIPS Phone: 443/326-8085

Mexican
$5-$9

Owned by Wal-Mart of Mexico and found in most major cities, the budget-friendly chain serves a good variety of Mexican and American dishes, including burgers, sandwiches, salads, spaghetti and enchiladas, as well as a fine selection of desserts. Casual dress. **Hours:** 7 am-midnight, Fri & Sat-1 am. **Address:** Calzada La Huerta #3000 **Location:** Just e of the turn off for Patzcuato Hwy. **Parking:** on-site. **Cards:** MC, VI.

The following restaurant has not been evaluated by AAA but is listed for your information only.

630 RESTAURANT-GALLERY Phone: 443/313-9779

fyi

Not evaluated. Upscale and formal 630 Restaurant-Gallery occupies an art gallery, and you can buy a lot more than food—including the chair you're sitting on—here. **Address:** Ave Madero Pte #630 **Location:** Center.

PACHUCA, HIDALGO pop. 245,208

WHERE TO DINE

SANBORN'S

Regional Mexican
$8-$28

Phone: 771/718-7145

Restaurants in the casual chain, which includes more than 100 locations throughout Mexico, offer a good selection of American-style sandwiches, salads, soups and both Mexican and American entrees. The selection of desserts is impressive. Casual dress. **Bar:** Full bar. **Hours:** 7 am-1 am, Sun-10 pm. **Location:** Just s of jct Ave Revolucion. Blvd Everardo Marquez No. 100, Col Periodistas. **Parking:** on-site. **Cards:** AX, MC, VI.

VIPS

Regional Mexican
$7-$25

Phone: 771/718-7190

Owned by Wal-Mart of Mexico and found in most major cities, the budget-friendly chain serves a good variety of Mexican and American dishes, including burgers, sandwiches, salads, spaghetti and enchiladas, as well as a fine selection of desserts. Casual dress. **Bar:** Beer & wine. **Hours:** 7 am-midnight, Fri & Sat-2 am. **Location:** Just w of jct Blvd Everando Marquez. Ave Revolucion No 1307, Col Periodista. **Parking:** on-site. **Cards:** AX, MC, VI.

PATZCUARO, MICHOACAN pop. 77,872

WHERE TO STAY

LA MANSION DE LOS SUENOS *Book at AAA.com*

Country Inn
$242-$484 All Year

Phone: (434)342-5708

Address: Ibarra #15, Centro **Location:** Center. **Facility:** Luxurious rooms full of local art and beautifully carved furniture will impress, and the restaurant is a gem in itself. Designated smoking area. 12 one-bedroom standard units. 1-2 stories (no elevator), exterior corridors. **Parking:** valet and street. **Amenities:** honor bars, hair dryers. **Dining:** Priscillas, see separate listing. **Leisure Activities:** whirlpool. *Fee:* massage. **Guest Services:** valet laundry. **Cards:** AX, MC, VI.

FEE

POSADA DE DON VASCO-BEST WESTERN

Hotel
$68-$120 All Year

Phone: (434)342-0227

Address: Ave de Lazaro Cardenas #450 **Location:** 1.5 mi (2.5 km) n on Calz de las Americas. **Facility:** 103 units. 101 one-bedroom standard units. 2 one-bedroom suites with whirlpools. 2 stories (no elevator), exterior corridors. *Bath:* combo or shower only. **Parking:** on-site. **Terms:** 3 day cancellation notice. **Amenities:** hair dryers. **Pool(s):** heated outdoor. **Leisure Activities:** tennis court, playground, game room. **Guest Services:** valet laundry, wireless Internet. **Business Services:** meeting rooms, PC. **Cards:** AX, MC, VI.

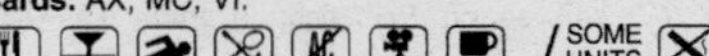

/ SOME UNITS

AAA Benefit:
Members save up to 20%, plus 10% bonus points with rewards program.

WHERE TO DINE

PRICILLAS

Regional International
$11-$16

Phone: 434/342-5708

Menu offerings are presented in an elegant, refined dining room or in the more casual setting of a courtyard under the stars. Dressy casual. **Bar:** Full bar. **Reservations:** suggested. **Hours:** 8 am-10:30 pm. **Address:** Ibarra #15, Centro **Location:** Center; in La Mansion de los Suenos. **Parking:** street. **Cards:** AX, MC, VI.

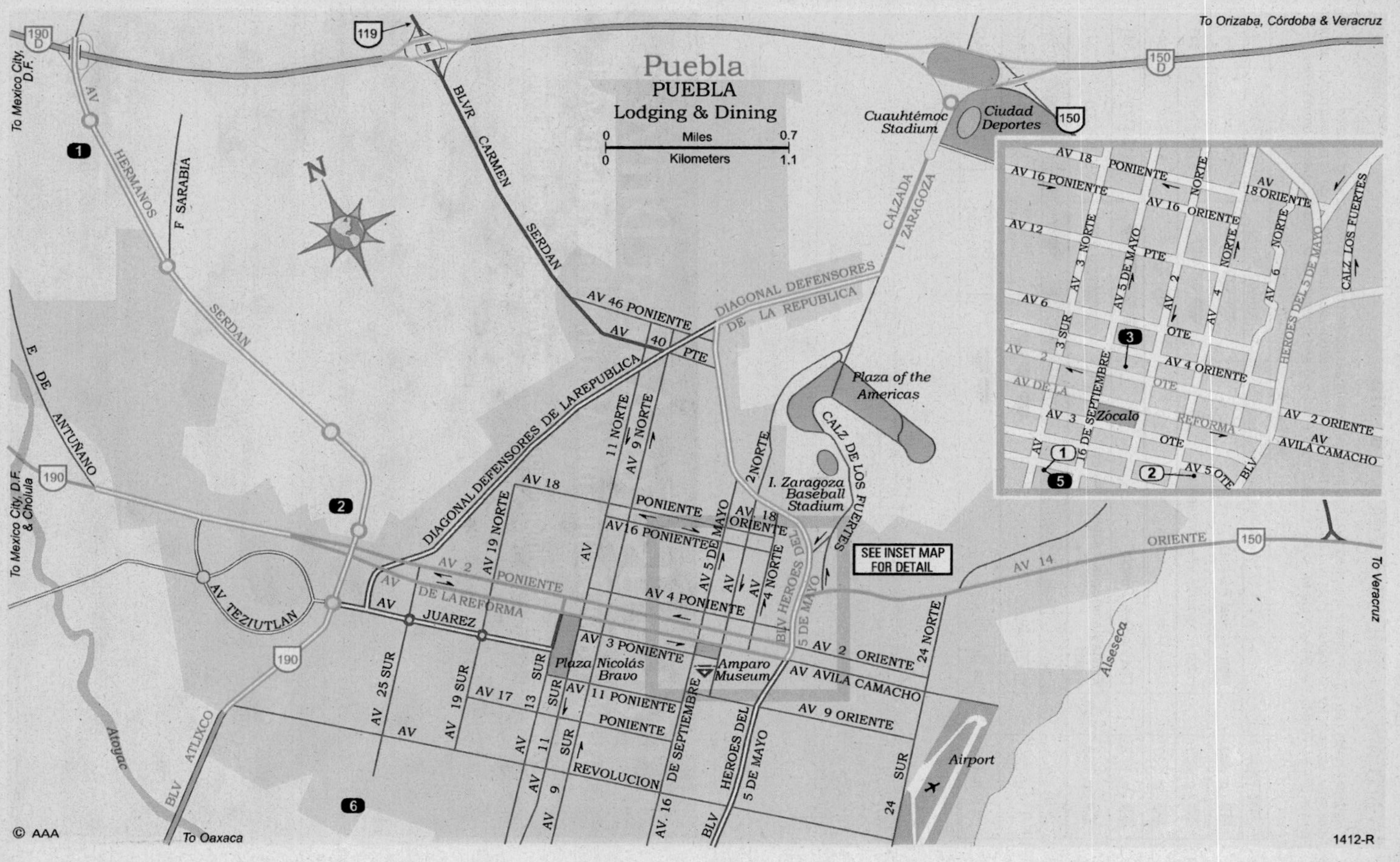
Puebla
PUEBLA
Lodging & Dining
0
Miles
0.7
0
Kilometers
1.1
N
To Mexico City, D.F.
To Mexico City, D.F. & Cholula
To Orizaba, Córdoba & Veracruz
To Veracruz
To Oaxaca
Cuauhtémoc Stadium
Ciudad Deportes
Plaza of the Americas
I. Zaragoza Baseball Stadium
SEE INSET MAP FOR DETAIL
Plaza Nicolás Bravo
Amparo Museum
Airport
Alseseca
Atoyac
Zócalo
AV HERMANOS SERDAN
F SARABIA
BLVR CARMEN SERDAN
E DE ANTUÑANO
AV TEZIUTLAN
BLV ATLIXCO
CALZADA I ZARAGOZA
DIAGONAL DEFENSORES DE LA REPUBLICA
DIAGONAL DEFENSORES DE LAREPUBLICA
AV 46 PONIENTE
AV 40 PTE
CALZ DE LOS FUERTES
CALZ LOS FUERTES
AV 18
AV 18 PONIENTE
AV 16 PONIENTE
AV 18 ORIENTE
AV 16 ORIENTE
AV 12
AV 6
AV 2 PONIENTE
AV DE LA REFORMA
AV 4 PONIENTE
AV 3 PONIENTE
AV 11 PONIENTE
PONIENTE
REVOLUCION
AV JUAREZ
AV 2 ORIENTE
AV AVILA CAMACHO
AV 9 ORIENTE
AV 4 ORIENTE
AV 5 OTE
AV 14 ORIENTE
11 NORTE
AV 9 NORTE
AV 19 NORTE
2NORTE
AV 5 DE MAYO
AV 4 NORTE
AV 3 NORTE
24 NORTE
AV 25 SUR
AV 19 SUR
AV 17
13 SUR
AV 11 SUR
AV 9
3 SUR
24 SUR
16 DE SEPTIEMBRE
AV. 16 DE SEPTIEMBRE
BLV HEROES DEL 5 DE MAYO
HEROES DEL 5 DE MAYO
119
150
150 D
190
190 D
1
2
3
5
6
© AAA
1412-R

Puebla

This index helps you "spot" where approved lodgings and restaurants are located on the corresponding detailed maps. Lodging daily rate range is for comparison only and show the property's high season. Restaurant rate range is a combination of lunch and/or dinner. Turn to the listing page for more detailed rate information and consult display ads for special promotions.

PUEBLA

Map Page	OA	Lodgings	Diamond Rated	High Season	Page
1 / p. 639		Marriott Real Puebla	◆◆◆	$80-$100	641
2 / p. 639		Hotel Presidente Intercontinental	◆◆◆	$104-$179	641
3 / p. 639		Gilfer Hotel	◆◆	$56-$72	641
5 / p. 639		Camino Real Puebla	◆◆◆◆	$115-$170	641
6 / p. 639	AAA	**Fiesta Americana Puebla** - see color ad on insert	◆◆◆◆	$130-$200	641

Map Page	OA	Restaurants	Diamond Rated	Cuisine	Meal Range	Page
1 / p. 639		El Convento	◆◆◆	Regional Continental	$16-$28	641
2 / p. 639		La Guadalupana	◆◆	Regional Mexican	$7-$20	642

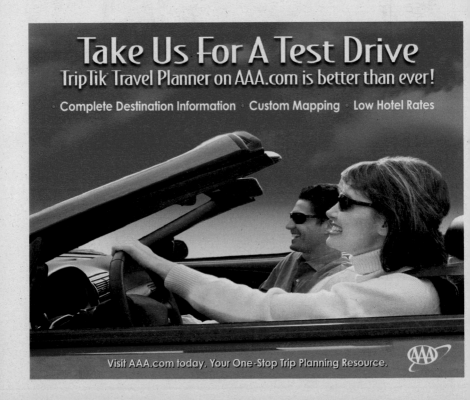

PUEBLA, PUEBLA pop. 1,346,916 (See map and index starting on p. 639)

WHERE TO STAY

CAMINO REAL PUEBLA *Book at AAA.com* **Phone:** (222)229-0909 5

Classic Historic Hotel
$115-$170 All Year

Address: 7 Poniente 105 Centro Historico **Location:** Just sw of plaza. **Facility:** A courtyard accents this handsome 16th-century convent; large rooms feature high ceilings, carved wooden headboards and talavera tile baths. 84 units. 82 one-bedroom standard units. 2 one-bedroom suites. 4 stories, interior/exterior corridors. *Bath:* combo or shower only. **Parking:** on-site (fee) and valet. **Amenities:** high-speed Internet, honor bars, irons, hair dryers. **Dining:** El Convento, see separate listing. **Guest Services:** valet laundry, wireless Internet. **Business Services:** conference facilities, business center. **Cards:** AX, DC, MC, VI.

/ SOME UNITS

FIESTA AMERICANA PUEBLA **Phone:** (222)225-9300 6

Hotel
$130-$200 All Year

Address: KM 5 Blvd Atlixcayotl **Location:** Fracc La Vista in Atlixcayotl. **Facility:** Located in upscale La Vista Atlixcayotl, this full-service hotel features fine detailing from Puebla, a Poblano restaurant and beautiful rooms. Meets AAA guest room security requirements. 153 units. 147 one-bedroom standard units. 6 one-bedroom suites. 5 stories, interior corridors. **Parking:** on-site. **Amenities:** high-speed Internet (fee), dual phone lines, voice mail, safes, irons, hair dryers. **Pool(s):** outdoor. **Leisure Activities:** exercise room. **Guest Services:** valet laundry, area transportation (fee), wireless Internet. **Business Services:** meeting rooms, business center. **Cards:** AX, MC, VI. *(See color ad on insert)*

24 S D / SOME UNITS

GILFER HOTEL **Phone:** (222)309-9800 3

Hotel
$56-$72 All Year

Address: Calle 2 Oriente Noll, Centro Historico **Location:** 2 blks e of main plaza Zocalo. **Facility:** 97 one-bedroom standard units. 8 stories, interior corridors. **Parking:** on-site. **Amenities:** high-speed Internet. **Guest Services:** valet laundry, area transportation (fee), wireless Internet. **Business Services:** PC. **Cards:** AX, MC, VI.

FEE D

HOTEL PRESIDENTE INTERCONTINENTAL **Phone:** (222)213-7070 2

Hotel
$104-$179 All Year

Address: Ave Hermanos Serdan 141 **Location:** S of Mex 190-D (toll road). **Facility:** Meets AAA guest room security requirements. 168 units. 166 one-bedroom standard units. 2 one-bedroom suites with whirlpools. 5 stories, interior/exterior corridors. *Bath:* shower only. **Parking:** on-site and valet. **Terms:** cancellation fee imposed. **Amenities:** CD players, high-speed Internet, voice mail, honor bars, irons, hair dryers. **Pool(s):** heated outdoor. **Leisure Activities:** playground, exercise room. **Guest Services:** valet laundry, beauty salon, wireless Internet. **Business Services:** conference facilities, business center. **Cards:** AX, DC, MC, VI.

24 / SOME UNITS

MARRIOTT REAL PUEBLA **Phone:** (222)141-2000 1

Hotel
$80-$100 All Year

Address: Ave Hermanos Serdan 807 **Location:** S of Mex 190-D (toll road). **Facility:** Meets AAA guest room security requirements. Smoke free premises. 192 units. 181 one-bedroom standard units, some with whirlpools. 11 one-bedroom suites. 2-3 stories (no elevator), interior/exterior corridors. **Parking:** on-site. **Terms:** cancellation fee imposed. **Amenities:** high-speed Internet (fee), voice mail, safes, honor bars, irons, hair dryers. **Pool(s):** outdoor, heated outdoor. **Leisure Activities:** tennis court, playground, exercise room. **Guest Services:** valet laundry, wireless Internet. **Business Services:** conference facilities, business center. **Cards:** AX, MC, VI.

The following lodging was either not evaluated or did not meet AAA rating requirements but is listed for your information only.

BEST WESTERN REAL DE PUEBLA **Phone:** 222/230-0122

fyi

Not evaluated. **Address:** 5 Ptc 2522, Col La Paz **Location:** Between aves Reforma and Juarez. Facilities, services, and decor characterize a mid-scale property.

WHERE TO DINE

EL CONVENTO **Phone:** 222/229-0909 1

Regional Continental
$16-$28

The elegant specialty restaurant, a 16th-century convent, serves international fare. Surrounding walls and arches are adorned with beautiful, hand-painted frescoes. Some seating faces the courtyard. The lunch buffet may help those on a budget. **Bar:** Full bar. **Reservations:** required. **Hours:** 2 pm-midnight. Closed: Mon. **Address:** 7 Poniente 105 Centro Historico **Location:** Just sw of plaza; in Camino Real Puebla. **Parking:** valet. **Cards:** AX, DC, MC, VI.

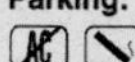

(See map and index starting on p. 639)

LA GUADALUPANA **Phone:** 222/242-4886 (2)

Regional Mexican
$7-$20

Locals often cite this place as the one not to miss when visiting Puebla. Known not only for its authentic Poblano-style cuisine, the restaurant also is where Salma Hayek filmed parts of "Frida." On the menu are mole, gorditas, skirt steak and several soups and salads. In the older section of a historic area, this converted old home, which is inside a larger building, is accessed via several small, narrow doors. Old photographs and artifacts cover the walls. Casual dress. **Bar:** Full bar. **Hours:** 8 am-9 pm, Sun-6 pm. **Address:** Calle 5 Oriente #605 **Location:** 5 blks e of main plaza Zocalo. **Parking:** no self-parking. **Cards:** AX, MC, VI.

SANBORN'S **Phone:** 222/243-4547

Regional Mexican
$8-$28

Restaurants in the casual chain, which includes more than 100 locations throughout Mexico, offer a good selection of American-style sandwiches, salads, soups and both Mexican and American entrees. The selection of desserts is impressive. Casual dress. **Bar:** Full bar. **Hours:** 7 am-10 pm, Fri & Sat-1 am. **Location:** Just n of jct Ave 31 Oriente. Blvd Heroes 5 de Mayo No 8 Col Huexotitla. **Parking:** on-site. **Cards:** AX, MC, VI.

SANBORN'S **Phone:** 222/225-0446

Regional Mexican
$8-$28

Restaurants in the casual chain, which includes more than 100 locations throughout Mexico, offer a good selection of American-style sandwiches, salads, soups and both Mexican and American entrees. The selection of desserts is impressive. Casual dress. **Bar:** Full bar. **Hours:** 7 am-midnight, Fri & Sat-1 am. **Location:** Jct Hwy Puebla to Atlixco. Blvd Nino Poblano No 2510, Centro Comercial Angelopolis. **Parking:** on-site (fee). **Cards:** AX, MC, VI.

SANBORN'S **Phone:** 222/242-3961

Regional Mexican
$8-$28

Restaurants in the casual chain, which includes more than 100 locations throughout Mexico, offer a good selection of American-style sandwiches, salads, soups and both Mexican and American entrees. The selection of desserts is impressive. Casual dress. **Bar:** Full bar. **Hours:** 7 am-11 pm, Fri & Sat-1 am. **Address:** Ave 2 Oriente No 6, Col Centro **Location:** Jct Calle 3 Norte. **Parking:** on-site (fee). **Cards:** AX, MC, VI.

VIPS **Phone:** 222/232-3819

Regional Mexican
$7-$25

Owned by Wal-Mart of Mexico and found in most major cities, the budget-friendly chain serves a good variety of Mexican and American dishes, including burgers, sandwiches, salads, spaghetti and enchiladas, as well as a fine selection of desserts. Casual dress. **Bar:** Beer & wine. **Hours:** 7 am-2 am, Fri & Sat 24 hours. **Address:** Ave B Juarez No 2502, Col La Paz **Location:** Jct Calle 25 Sur. **Parking:** on-site. **Cards:** AX, MC, VI.

VIPS **Phone:** 222/248-9930

Regional Mexican
$7-$25

Owned by Wal-Mart of Mexico and found in most major cities, the budget-friendly chain serves a good variety of Mexican and American dishes, including burgers, sandwiches, salads, spaghetti and enchiladas, as well as a fine selection of desserts. Casual dress. **Bar:** Beer & wine. **Hours:** 7 am-midnight. **Address:** Blvd Heroes del 5 de Mayo No 3676 **Location:** Across from central bus station. **Parking:** on-site. **Cards:** AX, MC, VI.

VIPS **Phone:** 222/232-7575

Regional Mexican
$7-$25

Owned by Wal-Mart of Mexico and found in most major cities, the budget-friendly chain serves a good variety of Mexican and American dishes, including burgers, sandwiches, salads, spaghetti and enchiladas, as well as a fine selection of desserts. Casual dress. **Bar:** Beer & wine. **Hours:** 7 am-1 am, Fri & Sat-2 am. **Address:** Ave 2 Oriente No 201, Col Centro **Location:** Jct Ave 2 Norte; 1 blk w of Zocalo. **Parking:** on-site. **Cards:** AX, MC, VI.

VIPS **Phone:** 222/249-2909

Regional Mexican
$7-$25

Owned by Wal-Mart of Mexico and found in most major cities, the budget-friendly chain serves a good variety of Mexican and American dishes, including burgers, sandwiches, salads, spaghetti and enchiladas, as well as a fine selection of desserts. Casual dress. **Bar:** Beer & wine. **Hours:** 7 am-1 am. **Address:** Blvd Atlixco No 3125, Col Nueva Antequer **Location:** Jct Circuito Interior; across from Wal-Mart. **Parking:** on-site. **Cards:** AX, MC, VI.

QUERETARO, QUERETARO pop. 641,386

WHERE TO STAY

HOLIDAY INN-QUERETARO

Book at AAA.com

Phone: (442)192-0202

Hotel

$110-$175 All Year

Address: Ave 5 de Febrero 110 Col Ninos Heroes **Location:** On Mex 57, 0.6 mi (1 km) n of jct Mex 45 and 45-D (toll road), exit Ave 5 de Febrero. **Facility:** Meets AAA guest room security requirements. 217 units. 208 one-bedroom standard units. 9 one-bedroom suites. 3 stories, interior corridors. *Bath:* combo or shower only. **Parking:** on-site. **Terms:** cancellation fee imposed. **Amenities:** high-speed Internet, voice mail, safes, irons, hair dryers. *Some:* honor bars. **Pool(s):** heated outdoor. **Leisure Activities:** whirlpools, 2 lighted tennis courts, playground, exercise room, sports court. **Guest Services:** valet laundry, wireless Internet. **Business Services:** conference facilities, business center. **Cards:** AX, DC, MC, VI.

/ SOME UNITS

HOTEL DONA URRACA

Phone: 442/238-5400

Boutique Hotel

$250-$280 All Year

Address: Ave 5 de Mayo #117 **Location:** In historic downtown; just e of Plaza de Armas. **Facility:** Earthy-tones, natural fibers and comfortable seating adorn the spacious guest rooms, creating an inviting, cozy retreat. 24 one-bedroom standard units, some with whirlpools. 2 stories, interior corridors. *Bath:* combo or shower only. **Parking:** on-site and valet. **Terms:** 3 day cancellation notice-fee imposed. **Amenities:** CD players, voice mail, safes, honor bars, irons, hair dryers. **Pool(s):** heated outdoor. **Leisure Activities:** whirlpool, spa. **Guest Services:** valet laundry, wireless Internet. **Business Services:** meeting rooms. **Cards:** AX, MC, VI.

HOTEL HACIENDA JURICA QUERETARO

Book at AAA.com

Phone: (442)218-0022

Historic Hotel

$130-$265 All Year

Address: Paseo Jurica esq Paseo del Meson **Location:** Mex 57, exit Jurica, 2.5 mi (4 km) w; at end of Jurica development. **Facility:** The converted 17th-century hacienda boasts period structures and furnishings, attractive landscaping and artistic cobblestone walkways. 182 units. 176 one-bedroom standard units. 6 one-bedroom suites, some with whirlpools. 2 stories (no elevator), interior corridors. *Bath:* shower or tub only. **Parking:** on-site. **Terms:** 5 day cancellation notice. **Amenities:** high-speed Internet, safes, honor bars, irons, hair dryers. **Dining:** Los Hules, see separate listing. **Pool(s):** heated outdoor. **Leisure Activities:** playground, exercise room. *Fee:* golf-18 holes, miniature golf, 2 lighted tennis courts, bicycles, horseback riding, massage. **Guest Services:** valet laundry, wireless Internet. **Business Services:** conference facilities, business center. **Cards:** AX, DC, MC, VI.

/ SOME UNITS

HOTEL MESON DE SANTA ROSA

Phone: 442/441-5000

Classic Historic Country Inn

$110-$175 All Year

Address: Pasteur Sur #17 **Location:** Center. Located on Plaza de Independencia. **Facility:** This restored 18th-century guest house sits on the main plaza; spacious rooms, a few with private balconies, overlook an inner courtyard. Meets AAA guest room security requirements. 21 one-bedroom standard units. 2 stories (no elevator), interior corridors. **Parking:** valet. **Amenities:** safes, honor bars, hair dryers. **Pool(s):** heated outdoor. **Guest Services:** valet laundry, wireless Internet. **Business Services:** meeting rooms. *Fee:* PC, fax. **Cards:** AX, MC, VI.

/ SOME UNITS

HOTEL REAL DE MINAS TRADICIONAL

Phone: (442)216-0444

Hotel

$77-$130 All Year

Address: Ave Constituyentes 124 Pte **Location:** On Mex 45 (Celaya Libre), just w of jct Mex 57. Located next to the bull ring. **Facility:** 200 one-bedroom standard units. 2 stories (no elevator), interior corridors. *Bath:* combo or shower only. **Parking:** on-site. **Amenities:** hair dryers. **Pool(s):** heated outdoor. **Leisure Activities:** tennis court, exercise room, volleyball. *Fee:* miniature golf. **Guest Services:** valet laundry, wireless Internet. **Business Services:** meeting rooms, business center. **Cards:** AX, MC, VI.

/ SOME UNITS

LA CASA DE LA MARQUESA

Book at AAA.com

Phone: (442)212-0092

Classic Historic Country Inn

$145-$378 All Year

Address: Madero 41 Esq Allende **Location:** Downtown. Located in a historic district. **Facility:** Beautiful courtyards and luxurious rooms characterize this stunning 1700s country inn, formerly home to emperors and presidents. 25 one-bedroom standard units, some with whirlpools. 3 stories (no elevator), exterior corridors. *Bath:* combo or shower only. **Parking:** valet and street. **Terms:** 3 day cancellation notice-fee imposed. **Amenities:** hair dryers. **Dining:** El Comedor de la Marquesa, see separate listing. **Guest Services:** valet laundry, wireless Internet. **Business Services:** meeting rooms, PC, fax (fee). **Cards:** AX, MC, VI.

PLAZA CAMELINAS

Phone: 442/192-3900

Hotel

$110-$159 All Year

Address: Ave 5 de Febrero #28 **Location:** Between aves Zaragoza and Constituyentes. **Facility:** 156 units. 155 one-bedroom standard units. 1 one-bedroom suite with whirlpool. 3 stories (no elevator), interior corridors. *Bath:* combo or shower only. **Parking:** on-site and valet. **Amenities:** voice mail, safes, irons, hair dryers. **Pool(s):** heated outdoor. **Leisure Activities:** exercise room. **Guest Services:** valet laundry, wireless Internet. **Business Services:** meeting rooms, business center. **Cards:** AX, MC, VI.

/ SOME UNITS

QUINTA ZOE

Phone: 442/212-3187

Bed & Breakfast

$75-$165 All Year

Address: Vergara Sur 22, Col Centro **Location:** In historic center; 1 blk from Plaza de Armas. **Facility:** Designated smoking area. 5 one-bedroom standard units, some with efficiencies. 2 stories (no elevator), exterior corridors. *Bath:* shower only. **Parking:** on-site (fee). **Terms:** age restrictions may apply, 30 day cancellation notice. **Amenities:** *Some:* high-speed Internet, safes. **Leisure Activities:** rooftop terrace. **Guest Services:** wireless Internet.

/ SOME UNITS

WHERE TO DINE

EL COMEDOR DE LA MARQUESA — **Phone:** 442/212-0092

Continental
$10-$25

Although the menu is Mexican, it exhibits notable European influences in such dishes such as lamb chops with mint sauce and fusilli Alfredo. Dressy casual. Entertainment. **Bar:** Full bar. **Reservations:** suggested. **Hours:** 7 am-10:45 pm. **Address:** Madero 41 Esquina Allende **Location:** Downtown; in La Casa de la Marquesa. **Parking:** valet and street. **Cards:** AX, MC, VI. **Historic**

EMILIA — **Phone:** 442/218-8455

Regional Italian
$10-$28

On the outskirts of town, the casually upscale restaurant focuses on Italian fare, including pizza cooked in a wood-burning oven, pasta and chicken dishes and steak. However, it also whips up some Mexican specialties. High ceilings and brick arches characterize the interior, which is reminiscent of an old hacienda. Casual dress. **Bar:** Full bar. **Reservations:** accepted. **Hours:** 1:30 pm-11 pm, Sun-6 pm. **Address:** Priv de los Indistriales No 105 **Location:** Just n of entrance to Hacienda Jurica; in Jurica Industrial Zone. **Parking:** on-site. **Cards:** AX, MC, VI.

JOSECHO — **Phone:** 442/216-0201

Regional International
$10-$50

The restaurant, popular among the business class, features Continental and Mexican dishes served by well-trained staff in a modern, stylish dining room. Menu offerings include New Zealand lamb chops, Kobe beef, Dover sole and medallions of beef with huitlacoche topping. Dressy casual. **Bar:** Full bar. **Reservations:** accepted. **Hours:** 1 pm-11 pm, Fri & Sat-1 am, Sun 1 pm-6 pm. Closed: 9/7. **Address:** Dalia #1, Fracc Orquideas **Location:** Mex 57, exit Ave Constituyentes, 0.9 mi (1.5 km) w; across from bull ring. **Parking:** valet. **Cards:** AX, CB, DC, MC, VI.

LOS HULES — **Phone:** 442/218-0022

Regional Mexican
$8-$20

Overlooking the majestic grounds of a 1600s former hacienda, the restaurant lets guests savor Mexican cuisine indoors or on a garden terrace. Casual dress. **Bar:** Full bar. **Reservations:** accepted. **Hours:** 7 am-midnight. **Location:** Mex 57, exit Jurica, 2.5 mi (4 km) w; at end of Jurica development; in Hotel Hacienda Jurica Queretaro. **Parking:** on-site and valet. **Cards:** AX, MC, VI.

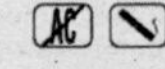

RESTAURANTE BAR 1810 — **Phone:** 442/214-3324

International
$6-$8

International and Mexican specialties are served in a lively atmosphere. On the varied menu are pasta dishes, glazed duck, steaks, fish and shrimp. Chile en nogada—poblano peppers stuffed with sweetly seasoned ground beef and topped with walnut sauce and pomegranate seeds—serves as a good introduction to regional cuisine. The outdoor patio is on the main city plaza and provides prime opportunities for interesting people-watching. Casual dress. **Bar:** Full bar. **Reservations:** suggested. **Hours:** 8 am-11 pm, Fri & Sat-midnight, Sun-10 pm. Closed: 12/24, 12/25. **Address:** Andador La Libertad 62 **Location:** Plaza de Independencia; in historic district. **Parking:** street. **Cards:** AX, MC, VI.

SANBORN'S — **Phone:** 442/220-6625

Regional Mexican
$8-$28

Restaurants in the casual chain, which includes more than 100 locations throughout Mexico, offer a good selection of American-style sandwiches, salads, soups and both Mexican and American entrees. The selection of desserts is impressive. Casual dress. **Bar:** Full bar. **Hours:** 7 am-11 pm, Fri & Sat-1 am. **Location:** Jct Mex 57. Prol Corregidora No. 691, Col Parque Industrial. **Parking:** on-site (fee). **Cards:** AX, MC, VI.

SANBORN'S — **Phone:** 442/223-6516

Regional Mexican
$8-$28

Restaurants in the casual chain, which includes more than 100 locations throughout Mexico, offer a good selection of American-style sandwiches, salads, soups and both Mexican and American entrees. The selection of desserts is impressive. Casual dress. **Bar:** Full bar. **Hours:** 7 am-10 pm, Fri & Sat-midnight. **Location:** Just w of jct Blvd Bernardo Quintana Arriola. Ave Constituyentes Oriente No 172 Col Los Arquito. **Parking:** on-site (fee). **Cards:** AX, MC, VI.

SANBORN'S — **Phone:** 442/242-9246

Regional Mexican
$6-$20

Restaurants in the casual chain, which includes more than 100 locations throughout Mexico, offer a good selection of American-style sandwiches, salads, soups and both Mexican and American entrees. The selection of desserts is impressive. Casual dress. **Bar:** Beer & wine. **Hours:** 7:30 am-11 pm, Fri & Sat-1 am. **Address:** Ave 5 de Febrero # 95, Col Virreyes **Location:** Just w of Mex 57 at exit Ave 5 de Febrero; in Centro Commercial Shopping Complex. **Parking:** on-site (fee). **Cards:** AX, MC, VI.

SUSHI ITTO — **Phone:** 442/215-6048

Japanese
$8-$20

Featuring Japanese food served fast in a casual setting, the restaurant boasts an extensive menu, a full bar and both indoor and outdoor seating. Casual dress. **Bar:** Full bar. **Hours:** 1 pm-11 pm, Sun-9 pm. **Address:** Ave Constituyentes Poniente #180 **Location:** Mex 57, exit Ave Constituyentes, 0.9 mi (1.5 km) w. **Parking:** on-site and street. **Cards:** AX, CB, DC, JC, MC, VI.

VIPS — **Phone:** 442/217-9376

Regional Mexican
$7-$25

Owned by Wal-Mart of Mexico and found in most major cities, the budget-friendly chain serves a good variety of Mexican and American dishes, including burgers, sandwiches, salads, spaghetti and enchiladas, as well as a fine selection of desserts. Casual dress. **Bar:** Beer & wine. **Hours:** 7 am-midnight, Fri & Sat-1 am. **Location:** Just e of Camino a San Jose. Blvd Bernardo Quintana No 4115, Col Industriales. **Parking:** on-site. **Cards:** AX, MC, VI.

VIPS

Regional Mexican
$7-$25

Phone: 442/214-0282

Owned by Wal-Mart of Mexico and found in most major cities, the budget-friendly chain serves a good variety of Mexican and American dishes, including burgers, sandwiches, salads, spaghetti and enchiladas, as well as a fine selection of desserts. Casual dress. **Bar:** Beer & wine. **Hours:** 7 am-11 pm, Fri & Sat-1 am. **Address:** Ave F I Madero Ote No 2, Col Centro **Location:** Across from Jardin Senca, just e of Calle Juarez. **Parking:** no self-parking. **Cards:** AX, MC, VI.

SAN JUAN DEL RIO, QUERETARO pop. 179,668

WHERE TO STAY

FIESTA AMERICANA HACIENDA GALINDO

Classic Historic Hotel
$120-$265 All Year

Phone: (427)271-8200

Address: Carr a Amealco Galindo KM 5 **Location:** On Mex 45 and 57, exit KM 172, 3.8 mi (6 km) s on Mex 120 toward Galindo, exit Amealco Galindo. Located in the country. **Facility:** The large, 16th-century hacienda has been converted and is extensively decorated with period art; beautiful grounds encompass stables and a chapel. 168 units. 161 one-bedroom standard units, some with whirlpools. 7 one-bedroom suites. 3 stories (no elevator), interior corridors. **Parking:** on-site (fee). **Amenities:** high-speed Internet, voice mail, safes, honor bars, irons, hair dryers. **Pool(s):** heated outdoor. **Leisure Activities:** miniature golf, tennis instruction, mini farm, soccer, hiking trails, jogging, playground, exercise room. *Fee:* 6 tennis courts (3 lighted), horseback riding. **Guest Services:** valet laundry, wireless Internet. **Business Services:** conference facilities, business center. **Cards:** AX, DC, MC, VI.
(See color ad on insert)

/ SOME UNITS

HOTEL MISION SAN GIL *Book at AAA.com*

Historic Hotel
$130-$250 All Year

Phone: (427)271-0030

Address: KM 172 Carr Mex-Qro **Location:** On Mex 45 and 57, 23 mi (37 km) e at KM 172. Located in a rural area. **Facility:** Located just off Hwy. 57, this sprawling 16th-century hacienda has period furnishings and extensive landscaped gardens. 134 units. 112 one-bedroom standard units. 21 one- and 1 two-bedroom suites, some with kitchens and/or whirlpools. 2 stories (no elevator), interior corridors. *Bath:* combo or shower only. **Parking:** on-site. **Terms:** cancellation fee imposed. **Amenities:** honor bars. *Some:* safes, hair dryers. **Pool(s):** heated outdoor. **Leisure Activities:** 2 tennis courts, jogging, playground, basketball. *Fee:* golf-18 holes. **Guest Services:** valet laundry. **Business Services:** conference facilities, business center. **Cards:** AX, DC, DS, MC, VI.

/ SOME UNITS

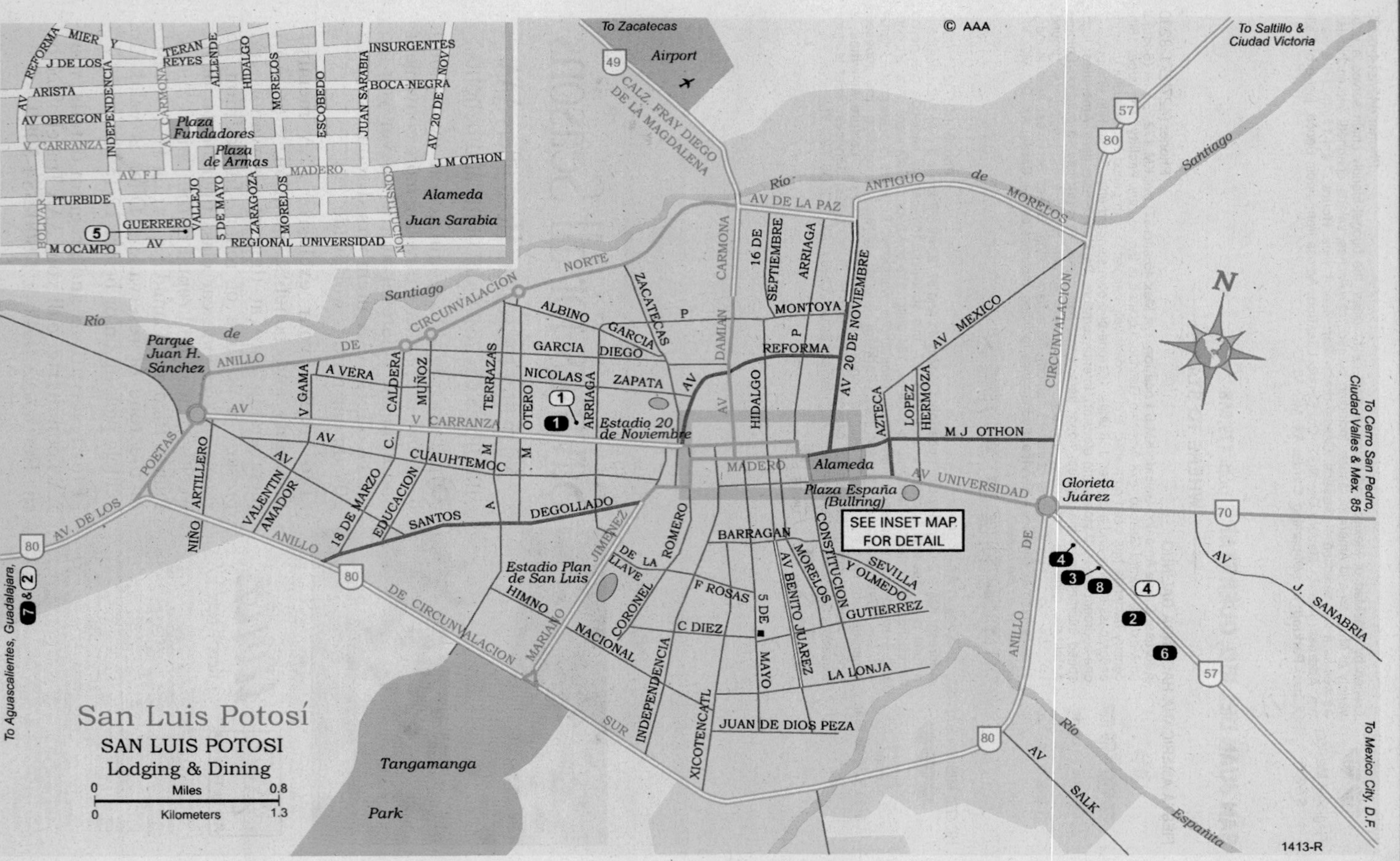
San Luis Potosí
SAN LUIS POTOSI
Lodging & Dining
0 Miles 0.8
0 Kilometers 1.3
To Zacatecas
Airport
© AAA
To Saltillo & Ciudad Victoria
To Cerro San Pedro, Ciudad Valles & Mex. 85
To Mexico City, D.F.
To Aguascalientes, Guadalajara,
1413-R
SEE INSET MAP FOR DETAIL
Alameda
Alameda Juan Sarabia
Plaza Fundadores
Plaza de Armas
Plaza España (Bullring)
Glorieta Juárez
Estadio 20 de Noviembre
Estadio Plan de San Luis
Parque Juan H. Sánchez
Tangamanga Park
CALZ. FRAY DIEGO DE LA MAGDALENA
AV DE LA PAZ
ANTIGUO de MORELOS
CIRCUNVALACION
AV 20 DE NOVIEMBRE
AV MEXICO
M J OTHON
AV UNIVERSIDAD
AV BENITO JUAREZ
JUAN DE DIOS PEZA
AV SALK
J. SANABRIA

San Luis Potosi

This index helps you "spot" where approved lodgings and restaurants are located on the corresponding detailed maps. Lodging daily rate range is for comparison only and show the property's high season. Restaurant rate range is a combination of lunch and/or dinner. Turn to the listing page for more detailed rate information and consult display ads for special promotions.

SAN LUIS POTOSI

Map Page	OA	Lodgings	Diamond Rated	High Season	Page
1 / p. 646		Hotel Real Plaza	◆◆	$65-$100	648
2 / p. 646		Country Inn & Suites By Carlson	◆◆◆	$85-$190	648
3 / p. 646		Holiday Inn Express San Luis Potosi	◆◆◆	$110-$165	648
4 / p. 646		Hotel Real de Minas	◆◆	$65-$90	648
6 / p. 646		Holiday Inn Quijote	◆◆◆	$145-$330	648
7 / p. 646		The Westin San Luis Potosi	◆◆◆◆	$180-$250	648
8 / p. 646		Courtyard by Marriott	◆◆◆	$91-$165	648

Map Page	OA	Restaurants	Diamond Rated	Cuisine	Meal Range	Page
1 / p. 646		Restaurante La Virreina	◆◆◆	International	$8-$22	649
2 / p. 646		Restaurante Westin	◆◆◆◆	International	$10-$25	649
4 / p. 646		Los Cabos Seafood Restaurant	◆◆	Regional Seafood	$8-$28	649
5 / p. 646		El Rincon de San Francisco	◆◆	Mexican	$8-$14	649

SAN LUIS POTOSI, SAN LUIS POTOSI pop. 670,532 (See map and index starting on p. 646)

WHERE TO STAY

COUNTRY INN & SUITES BY CARLSON *Book at AAA.com* **Phone:** (444)826-9900 **2**

Hotel
$85-$190 All Year

Address: Carr 57 #1530, Zona Industrial **Location:** On Mex 57, 0.6 mi (1 km) se. **Facility:** Meets AAA guest room security requirements. 120 units. 100 one-bedroom standard units. 20 one-bedroom suites. 4 stories, interior corridors. **Parking:** on-site. **Amenities:** high-speed Internet, dual phone lines, voice mail, irons, hair dryers. **Pool(s):** heated indoor. **Leisure Activities:** whirlpool, exercise room. **Guest Services:** valet laundry, area transportation (fee), wireless Internet. **Business Services:** meeting rooms, business center. **Cards:** AX, DS, MC, VI.

S D / SOME UNITS

COURTYARD BY MARRIOTT *Book great rates at AAA.com* **Phone:** (444)834-5700 **8**

Hotel
$91-$165 All Year

Address: Ave Benito Juarez No 1220 **Location:** 1.8 mi (3 km) s on Mex 57. **Facility:** Smoke free premises. 161 units. 148 one-bedroom standard units. 13 one-bedroom suites. 6 stories, interior corridors. **Parking:** on-site. **Amenities:** video games (fee), high-speed Internet, dual phone lines, voice mail, safes, irons, hair dryers. **Pool(s):** heated indoor. **Leisure Activities:** whirlpool, exercise room. **Guest Services:** valet laundry, wireless Internet. **Business Services:** meeting rooms, business center. **Cards:** AX, MC, VI.

CALL S D

COURTYARD Marriott
AAA Benefit:
Members save a minimum 5% off the best available rate.

HOLIDAY INN EXPRESS SAN LUIS POTOSI *Book at AAA.com* **Phone:** 444/499-9000 **3**

Hotel
$110-$165 All Year

Address: Ave Benito Juarez #1270 **Location:** 1.8 mi (3 km) s on Mex 57. **Facility:** 124 one-bedroom standard units, some with whirlpools. 7 stories, interior corridors. *Bath:* shower only. **Parking:** on-site. **Amenities:** video games (fee), high-speed Internet, dual phone lines, voice mail, safes, irons, hair dryers. **Pool(s):** heated outdoor. **Leisure Activities:** whirlpool, exercise room. **Guest Services:** valet laundry, area transportation, wireless Internet. **Business Services:** meeting rooms, business center. **Cards:** AX, MC, VI.

S D / SOME UNITS FEE FEE

HOLIDAY INN QUIJOTE *Book at AAA.com* **Phone:** (444)834-4100 **6**

Hotel
$145-$330 All Year

Address: Carr Central S/N Zona Ind'l **Location:** 3 mi (5 km) se on Mex 57. **Facility:** Meets AAA guest room security requirements. 208 units. 198 one-bedroom standard units, some with whirlpools. 10 one-bedroom suites with whirlpools. 2-3 stories, interior/exterior corridors. *Bath:* combo or shower only. **Parking:** on-site. **Amenities:** high-speed Internet, voice mail, safes, honor bars, irons, hair dryers. *Some:* CD players. **Pool(s):** heated outdoor. **Leisure Activities:** lighted tennis court, jogging, playground, exercise room. **Guest Services:** valet laundry, area transportation (fee), wireless Internet. **Business Services:** conference facilities, business center. **Cards:** AX, MC, VI.

24 / SOME UNITS

HOTEL REAL DE MINAS **Phone:** 444/499-8400 **4**

Hotel
$65-$90 All Year

Address: Carr Central KM 426.6 **Location:** On Mex 57; 0.6 mi (1 km) se of Glorieta Juarez; 0.3 mi (0.5 km) s of Distribuidora Juarez. **Facility:** Meets AAA guest room security requirements. 165 units. 162 one-bedroom standard units. 3 one-bedroom suites, some with whirlpools. 2 stories (no elevator), interior/exterior corridors. *Bath:* combo or shower only. **Parking:** on-site. **Amenities:** hair dryers. *Some:* irons. **Pool(s):** outdoor. **Guest Services:** valet laundry, wireless Internet. **Business Services:** meeting rooms, business center. **Cards:** AX, MC, VI.

/ SOME UNITS

HOTEL REAL PLAZA **Phone:** (444)814-6055 **1**

Hotel
$65-$100 All Year

Address: Ave Venustiano Carranza 890 **Location:** In heart of downtown. Located in a busy commercial area. **Facility:** 268 one-bedroom standard units. 10 stories, interior corridors. *Bath:* shower only. **Parking:** on-site and street. **Terms:** 3 day cancellation notice. **Amenities:** high-speed Internet. **Pool(s):** outdoor. **Leisure Activities:** exercise room. **Business Services:** meeting rooms, business center. **Cards:** AX, MC, VI.

THE WESTIN SAN LUIS POTOSI *Book great rates at AAA.com* **Phone:** (444)825-0125 **7**

Hotel
$180-$250 All Year

Address: Real de Lomas 1000 **Location:** 2.1 mi (3.5 km) sw on Carr SLP-Guadalajara. **Facility:** In the upscale Lomas District, the posh Colonial hotel evokes the sense of a rich hacienda with artwork, fine detailing and elegant guest rooms. Smoke free premises. 123 units. 78 one-bedroom standard units. 45 one-bedroom suites. 3 stories, exterior corridors. **Parking:** on-site and valet. **Terms:** cancellation fee imposed. **Amenities:** voice mail, safes, honor bars, irons, hair dryers. **Dining:** Restaurante Westin, see separate listing. **Pool(s):** heated outdoor. **Leisure Activities:** exercise room. **Guest Services:** valet laundry, wireless Internet. **Business Services:** conference facilities, fax. **Cards:** AX, DC, MC, VI.

FEE 24 D / SOME UNITS

WESTIN HOTELS & RESORTS
AAA Benefit:
Enjoy up to 15% off your next stay, plus Starwood Preferred Guest® bonuses.

(See map and index starting on p. 646)

WHERE TO DINE

EL RINCON DE SAN FRANCISCO — **Phone:** 444/812-4508 (5)

Mexican
$8-$14

Tucked into a tight side street of this colonial city, this small local favorite is worth seeking out. Menu includes classic regional dishes such as enchiladas Potosinas and arrechera skirt steak. Casual dress. **Bar:** Full bar. **Reservations:** accepted. **Hours:** 6 pm-midnight, Sat from 2 pm. Closed: 1/1, 12/25; also Sun. **Address:** Callejon de Lozada No 1 **Location:** Center. **Parking:** street. **Cards:** AX, MC, VI.

LOS CABOS SEAFOOD RESTAURANT — **Phone:** 444/822-7648 (4)

Regional Seafood
$8-$28

Just south of the city on Hwy 57, the informal restaurant tempts patrons with fresh seafood at economical prices. Favorites include steaming seafood soup and grilled red fish with toasted diced garlic and olive oil. Casual dress. **Bar:** Full bar. **Hours:** 11:30 am-7:30 pm. **Address:** Ave Florencia #1299 **Location:** 1.5 mi (2.5 km) s on Mex 57 northbound access road. **Parking:** street. **Cards:** AX, MC, VI.

RESTAURANTE LA VIRREINA — **Phone:** 444/812-3750 (1)

International
$8-$22

The Maximilian-period mansion is a refined spot for classic, Old World dining. Traditional Continental dishes make up the menu. Service is sophisticated. Casual dress. Entertainment. **Bar:** Full bar. **Reservations:** suggested, for dinner. **Hours:** 1:30 pm-midnight, Sun-6 pm. Closed: Mon. **Address:** Ave Venustiano Carranza 830 **Location:** 0.6 mi (1 km) w on Mex 80; center of downtown. **Parking:** street. **Cards:** AX, MC, VI. **Historic**

RESTAURANTE WESTIN — **Phone:** 444/825-0125 (2)

International
$10-$25

This elegant dining room is in an upscale boutique hotel. A formal staff serves distinctive preparations of fish, steak, pasta and a few Mexican favorites that incorporate fresh, quality ingredients. At lunch, the buffet is among options. Semi-formal attire. **Bar:** Full bar. **Reservations:** suggested. **Hours:** 6:30 am-11 pm. **Address:** Real de Lomas 1000 **Location:** 2.1 mi (3.5 km) sw on Carr SLP-Guadalajara; in The Westin San Luis Potosi. **Parking:** on-site and valet. **Cards:** AX, DC, MC, VI.

The following restaurants have not been evaluated by AAA but are listed for your information only.

LA CASA DE LAS FLORES — **Phone:** 444/813-4333

fyi

Not evaluated. European influences continue to dominate this upscale restaurant. Featured cuisine includes Potosino dishes along with traditional Continental selections. **Address:** Arista 1205 **Location:** Arista at Ave Emilio Carranza; 1 blk s of Jardin de Tequisquiapan; in Zona Rosa.

LA CORRIENTE — **Phone:** 444/812-9304

fyi

Not evaluated. Located in a historic house, La Corriente offers a wide variety of Mexican dishes with traditional sauces such as chipotle and mole. Service is typically strong and prices are reasonable. **Address:** Ave Carranza No 700 **Location:** Colonia Centro.

LA GRAN VIA — **Phone:** 444/812-2899

fyi

Not evaluated. Translated to read the great street, this well known local favorite offers diners a wide variety of classic Mexican dishes in an informal and relaxed setting. **Address:** Ave V Carranza No 560 **Location:** Colonia Centro.

SAN MIGUEL DE ALLENDE, GUANAJUATO pop. 134,880

WHERE TO STAY

ANTIGUA VILLA SANTA MONICA — Phone: 415/152-0427

Country Inn
$240-$310 All Year

Address: Fray Jose Guadalupe Mojica #22 **Location:** Facing Benito Juarez Park. **Facility:** Very attractive, intimate inn. All rooms unique; all facing interior courtyard. Well-landscaped. Building is over 230 years old. 14 one-bedroom standard units, some with whirlpools. 1 story, exterior corridors. **Parking:** on-site. **Terms:** check-in 3:30 pm, 10 day cancellation notice-fee imposed. **Amenities:** hair dryers. **Pool(s):** heated outdoor. **Guest Services:** valet laundry, wireless Internet. **Business Services:** fax (fee). **Cards:** AX, MC, VI.

/ SOME UNITS

ATOTONILCO EL VIEJO RANCHO HOTEL — Phone: 415/185-2131

Hotel
$120-$225 All Year

Address: Carr Santuario Atotonilco s/n **Location:** 0.6 mi (1 km) off Dolores Hidalgo Hwy to Atotonilco. **Facility:** Smoke free premises. 19 units. 18 one- and 1 two-bedroom standard units, some with whirlpools. 2 stories (no elevator), exterior corridors. **Parking:** on-site. **Terms:** office hours 8 am-10 pm. **Pool(s):** heated outdoor, heated indoor. **Leisure Activities:** steamroom, tennis court, playground, game room. *Fee:* massage. **Business Services:** meeting rooms, PC. **Cards:** AX, MC, VI.

BEST WESTERN HOTEL MONTEVERDE EXPRESS — *Book great rates at AAA.com* — **Phone:** (415)152-1814

Hotel
$68-$130 All Year

Address: Volanteros #2, Col Centro **Location:** Mex 57, exit 111; 55 KM. **Facility:** 29 units. 28 one-bedroom standard units. 1 three-bedroom suite with kitchen (no utensils). 2 stories (no elevator), exterior corridors. *Bath:* shower only. **Parking:** on-site. **Amenities:** high-speed Internet, hair dryers. **Guest Services:** valet laundry, wireless Internet. **Business Services:** meeting rooms. **Cards:** AX, MC, VI.

/ SOME UNITS

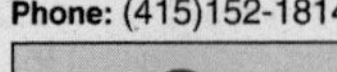

AAA Benefit:

Members save up to 20%, plus 10% bonus points with rewards program.

CASA DE LIZA VILLAS EN EL PARQUE — **Phone:** (415)152-0352

Bed & Breakfast
$140-$379 All Year

Address: Bajada del Chorro #7-Centro **Location:** 3 blks se of main plaza; between Recreo and Calle de Chorro. Located at the edge of the historic district. **Facility:** Lush gardens invite outdoor lounging at this B&B notable for its personalized service and exceptional guest-room decor. Designated smoking area. 7 units. 5 one-bedroom standard units, some with kitchens and/or whirlpools. 2 one-bedroom suites. 2 stories (no elevator), exterior corridors. *Bath:* combo or shower only. **Parking:** on-site. **Terms:** 7 day cancellation notice-fee imposed. **Amenities:** hair dryers. *Some:* safes. **Leisure Activities:** whirlpool. *Fee:* massage. **Guest Services:** valet laundry, wireless Internet. **Business Services:** meeting rooms, PC, fax (fee). **Cards:** AX, MC, VI.

/ SOME UNITS

CASA DE SIERRA NEVADA ORIENT EXPRESS — *Book at AAA.com* — **Phone:** (415)152-7040

Historic Country Inn
$330-$660 All Year

Address: Hospicio 42 **Location:** Just se of main plaza; 1/2 blk off Recreo. **Facility:** Set in a quiet area of San Miguel, this property has luxurious rooms, impeccable service and world-class dining; some rooms are near El Parque. Designated smoking area. 33 units. 27 one-bedroom standard units. 6 one-bedroom suites, some with whirlpools. 2 stories (no elevator), exterior corridors. **Parking:** valet. **Terms:** 2 night minimum stay - weekends, age restrictions may apply, 3 day cancellation notice. **Amenities:** video library, DVD players, safes, honor bars, hair dryers. *Some:* high-speed Internet. **Dining:** Casa de Sierra Nevada en el Parque, Sierra Nevada Restaurant, see separate listings. **Pool(s):** heated outdoor. **Leisure Activities:** exercise room, spa. **Guest Services:** valet laundry, wireless Internet. **Business Services:** meeting rooms, PC, fax (fee). **Cards:** AX, MC, VI.

/ SOME UNITS

CASA PUESTA DEL SOL — **Phone:** 415/152-0220

Bed & Breakfast
$120-$195 All Year

Address: Fuentes #12 **Location:** Jct Pedro Vargas (Queretero Hwy), just e on Santo Domingo, just ne. **Facility:** High in the residential area above the village and tucked into a tiered garden, you'll find a waterfall with fountains to cool the day at this inn. Designated smoking area. 7 units. 6 one-bedroom standard units. 1 two-bedroom suite with kitchen. 2 stories (no elevator), interior/exterior corridors. **Parking:** street. **Terms:** age restrictions may apply, cancellation fee imposed. **Amenities:** *Some:* DVD players. **Leisure Activities:** *Fee:* massage. **Guest Services:** valet laundry, wireless Internet. **Business Services:** PC, fax (fee). **Cards:** MC, VI.

/ SOME UNITS

CASA SCHUCK BOUTIQUE B&B — **Phone:** (415)152-6618

Bed & Breakfast
$178-$262 All Year

Address: Bajada de la Garita #3 **Location:** 4 blks e of main plaza. **Facility:** A lovely courtyard with a fountain, and a rooftop patio with a view to the Parroquia provide a tranquil environment at this B&B. Designated smoking area. 10 one-bedroom standard units. 2 stories (no elevator), exterior corridors. **Parking:** no self-parking. **Terms:** 30 day cancellation notice-fee imposed. **Amenities:** high-speed Internet, safes, hair dryers. *Some:* CD players. **Pool(s):** heated outdoor. **Leisure Activities:** *Fee:* massage. **Guest Services:** TV in common area, valet laundry. **Business Services:** meeting rooms, fax (fee). **Cards:** DC, DS, MC, VI.

FEE

GUADIANA BED AND BREAKFAST ON THE PARK **Phone:** (415)152-5171

Hotel
$75-$99 All Year

Address: Mesquite #11 **Location:** 0.5 mi (0.8 km) s of main plaza; 1/2 blk e of Calle Potranca. Located in a quiet residential area. **Facility:** 9 one-bedroom standard units. 3 stories (no elevator), interior corridors. *Bath:* shower only. **Parking:** street. **Terms:** 15 day cancellation notice. **Guest Services:** valet laundry. **Cards:** MC, VI.

/ SOME UNITS

HACIENDA DE LAS FLORES Book great rates at AAA.com **Phone:** (415)152-1808

Bed & Breakfast
$90-$154 All Year

Address: Hospicio 16 **Location:** 2.5 blks s of main plaza. **Facility:** Colonial-style converted hacienda. Very pretty setting. Attractive, well-maintained guest rooms. Roof garden overlooks bull ring. 16 units. 10 one-bedroom standard units. 6 one-bedroom suites with kitchens. 2 stories, exterior corridors. **Parking:** no self-parking. **Terms:** 11 day cancellation notice, 4 day off season. **Pool(s):** outdoor. **Guest Services:** valet laundry. **Business Services:** meeting rooms, fax (fee). **Cards:** MC, VI.

/ SOME UNITS

HACIENDA EL SANTUARIO HOTEL, SPA & GOLF **Phone:** (415)185-2036

Country Inn
$155-$235 All Year

Address: Dolores Hidalgo Hwy KM 13 **Location:** 7.8 mi (13 km) n on San Miguel de Allende Dolores Hidalgo Hwy (Mex 51), follow signs. **Facility:** Outside of town you will find this property with very attractive guest rooms and grounds that will make for a relaxing stay. 9 units. 8 one-bedroom standard units. 1 one-bedroom suite with whirlpool. 1 story, exterior corridors. **Parking:** on-site. **Terms:** 3 day cancellation notice-fee imposed. **Amenities:** CD players, safes, hair dryers. **Pool(s):** outdoor. **Leisure Activities:** whirlpool, golf-9 holes, tennis court, bicycles, exercise room, spa.. **Guest Services:** valet laundry. **Business Services:** meeting rooms, fax (fee). **Cards:** AX, DC, JC, MC, VI.

FEE D

HOTEL HACIENDA TABOADA **Phone:** (415)152-9250

Hotel
$159-$330 All Year

Address: KM 8 Carr a Dolores Hidalgo Hwy **Location:** 4.8 mi (8 km) on San Miguel de Allende Dolores Hidalgo Hwy (Mex 51), 1.8 mi (3 km) w, follow signs. Located in a quiet area. **Facility:** 70 units. 66 one-bedroom standard units. 4 one-bedroom suites. 3 stories (no elevator), exterior corridors. **Parking:** on-site. **Terms:** cancellation fee imposed. **Pool(s):** heated outdoor. **Leisure Activities:** 2 tennis courts, hiking trails, horseback riding, playground, exercise room, volleyball. *Fee:* massage. **Guest Services:** valet laundry. **Business Services:** meeting rooms. **Cards:** AX, DC, MC, VI.

HOTEL LA SIESTA **Phone:** (415)152-0207

Motel
$60-$83 All Year

Address: Carr a Celaya **Location:** On Mex 49 (Celaya Hwy), just e of Libramiento Hwy. **Facility:** 29 one-bedroom standard units. 1 story, exterior corridors. *Bath:* shower only. **Parking:** on-site. **Terms:** 5 day cancellation notice. **Pool(s):** heated outdoor. **Leisure Activities:** playground. **Guest Services:** valet laundry. **Business Services:** fax (fee). **Cards:** AX, MC, VI.

/ SOME UNITS

HOTEL POSADA DE LA ALDEA **Phone:** 415/152-1022

Historic Hotel
$85-$170 All Year

Address: Calle Ancha de San Antonio #15 **Location:** 0.6 mi (1 km) s on Mex 49 (Celaya Hwy). **Facility:** Within walking distance of the plaza, this hotel on the southwest end of town includes a large parking lot. 65 one-bedroom standard units. 3 stories, interior corridors. *Bath:* shower only. **Parking:** on-site. **Terms:** 5 day cancellation notice. **Pool(s):** heated outdoor. **Leisure Activities:** 2 tennis courts. **Guest Services:** valet laundry, beauty salon. **Business Services:** meeting rooms, fax (fee). **Cards:** AX, MC, VI.

/ SOME UNITS

LA PUERTECITA BOUTIQUE 'OTELS Book great rates at AAA.com **Phone:** (415)152-5011

Country Inn
$200-$500 All Year

Address: Santo Domingo #75 **Location:** Jct Pedro Vargas (Queretero Hwy), 0.4 mi (0.6 km) e. Located in the affluent Atascadero neighborhood. **Facility:** The property's picturesque gardens and waterfalls create a retreat-like ambience; many rooms feature fireplaces. Designated smoking area. 30 units. 22 one-bedroom standard units, some with whirlpools. 8 one-bedroom suites with kitchens, some with whirlpools. 3 stories (no elevator), interior/exterior corridors. **Parking:** on-site. **Terms:** cancellation fee imposed. **Amenities:** safes, hair dryers. **Pool(s):** outdoor, heated outdoor. **Leisure Activities:** whirlpool, library, walking tours, painting and Spanish instruction, exercise room, spa. **Guest Services:** valet laundry, area transportation-town center. **Business Services:** meeting rooms, fax (fee). **Cards:** AX, MC, VI.

FEE / SOME UNITS

VILLA MIRASOL HOTEL **Phone:** (415)152-6685

Hotel
$97-$149 All Year

Address: Pila Seca #35 **Location:** Just 4 blks sw of main plaza. **Facility:** Designated smoking area. 12 one-bedroom standard units. 3 stories (no elevator), exterior corridors. *Bath:* combo or shower only. **Parking:** street. **Terms:** 15 day cancellation notice-fee imposed. **Guest Services:** valet laundry, area transportation (fee), wireless Internet. **Business Services:** fax (fee). **Cards:** AX, MC, VI.

FEE / SOME UNITS

VILLA RIVERA HOTEL Book at AAA.com **Phone:** (415)152-2289

Hotel
$210-$295 All Year

Address: Cuadrante #3 **Location:** 1 blk s of main plaza; center. **Facility:** 12 one-bedroom standard units, some with whirlpools. 3 stories (no elevator), interior/exterior corridors. **Parking:** valet. **Amenities:** high-speed Internet, honor bars, hair dryers. **Pool(s):** outdoor. **Guest Services:** valet laundry. **Business Services:** fax (fee). **Cards:** MC, VI.

/ SOME UNITS

The following lodging was either not evaluated or did not meet AAA rating requirements but is listed for your information only.

HOTEL SPA CASCADA VIEJA **Phone:** 415/155-8050

fyi

Not evaluated. **Address:** KM 12.5 Carr San Miguel-Dolores Hidalgo **Location:** 7.8 mi (12.5 km) nw on highway to Dolores Hidalgo. Facilities, services, and decor characterize a mid-scale property.

WHERE TO DINE

ANTIGUA TRATTORIA ROMANA **Phone:** 415/152-3790

Italian
$10-$18

Popular with the locals and a stone's throw from Instituto Allende, the restaurant prepares a modest selection of pasta entrees in a friendly, laid-back, village-style atmosphere. Inconsistent numbering can make this place hard to find, but it's sited at the apex of a triangular block and where the street makes a sharp turn. At the few tables inside, diners try pizza, salads, pasta dishes and other traditional Italian fare that's big on flavor. Casual dress. **Bar:** Full bar. **Reservations:** accepted. **Hours:** noon-10:30 pm. Closed: Wed. **Address:** CODO #9 **Location:** 3 blks s of main plaza. **Parking:** street. **Cards:** MC, VI.

BUGAMBILIA **Phone:** 415/152-0127

Mexican
$6-$20

In business for more than 60 years, this place gets guests started with flavorful molcajete salsa. Attentive and remarkably friendly servers move through the casual dining room with plates of good food, including freshly prepared dishes such as caldo Xochitl soup and the renowned chili en nogada, with colors representing the Mexican flag. Evening entertainment kicks up the atmosphere in the enchanting courtyard dining room, which has bright pink walls, tin-star lanterns and twinkling lights. Casual dress. Entertainment. **Bar:** Full bar. **Reservations:** accepted. **Hours:** noon-10:30 pm. **Address:** Hidalgo 42 **Location:** Just n of main plaza; center. **Parking:** street. **Cards:** MC, VI.

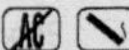

CASA DE SIERRA NEVADA EN EL PARQUE **Phone:** 415/152-7153

Mexican
$6-$20

Mexican specialties are prepared in a colonial Mexican atmosphere. The dining room has an elegant feel, while the patio is tranquil. Weekend entertainment lends to the mood. Art vendors set up within steps of the front entrance on Sunday during breakfast and lunch. The harmonious sounds of a trio bring in people strolling near the park. Casual dress. **Bar:** Full bar. **Reservations:** suggested. **Hours:** 7 am-11 pm. **Address:** Santa Elena 2 **Location:** Just se of main plaza; at Benito Juarez Park. **Parking:** street. **Cards:** AX, MC, VI.

CASA PAYO-ARGENTINIAN GRILL **Phone:** 415/152-7277

Argentine
$10-$25

Steaks are custom-cooked, and the portions are plentiful. With stars overhead and strolling musicians, the attractive courtyard dining area is charming. Casual dress. **Bar:** Full bar. **Hours:** noon-11 pm. **Address:** Zacateros #26 **Location:** Southeast corner of Pila Seca; center. **Parking:** valet. **Cards:** AX, MC, VI.

EL PEGASO **Phone:** 415/152-1351

International
$4-$9

Few of the city's many restaurants offer the charming service for which this place is known—friendly and laid-back but with an eye and instinct for anticipating a diner's every need. The international menu offers something for everyone, including burgers, seviche, tacos de lengua and Thai salad. Among varied desserts are cakes, flan and pies. Local artists' creations, some humorous, line the walls. Casual dress. **Bar:** Full bar. **Hours:** 8:30 am-10 pm. Closed major holidays; also Sun & 5/1-5/14. **Address:** Corregidora #6 **Location:** 1 blk w of main plaza; center. **Parking:** street. **Cards:** MC, VI.

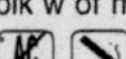

EL TOMATO, COCINA NATURISTA **Phone:** 415/151-6057

Vegetarian
$6-$8

A favorite spot among American tourists, the eatery prepares dishes that are healthful, homemade and then some. Offerings from this diminutive eatery include fresh tuna sandwiches dressed with bits of apple and raisins and served on whole grain breads, tofu burgers, varied salads and courses on the prix fixe menus. Aguas frescas and fresh carrot juice are among beverage choices. Casual dress. **Bar:** Beer & wine. **Reservations:** accepted. **Hours:** 9 am-9 pm. Closed: 1/1, 12/25; also Sun. **Address:** Mesones #62 A & B, Centro **Location:** Just n of main plaza. **Parking:** street.

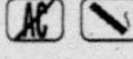

HARRY'S NEW ORLEANS CAFE **Phone:** 415/152-2645

Cajun
$10-$22

Cajun fare served in stylish, contemporary surroundings offering a definite American experience. Casual dress. **Bar:** Full bar. **Reservations:** suggested. **Hours:** 11:30 am-11 pm, Fri & Sat-midnight, Sun 10 am-midnight. **Address:** Hidalgo #12 **Location:** Just n of main plaza; center. **Parking:** street. **Cards:** AX, MC, VI.

HECHO EN MEXICO **Phone:** 415/154-6383

Mexican
$5-$13

The bilingual staff greets guests with friendly smiles. The menu is heavy on sandwiches and salads. Southern touches enhance dishes such as sweet potato casserole, while others, such as cactus salad, center on Mexican elements. Dessert portions are ample enough to share. Simple decor characterizes the inviting enclosed courtyard at this spot next to Instituto Allende. Casual dress. **Bar:** Full bar. **Hours:** noon-10 pm, Fri & Sat-11 pm. Closed: 1/1, 12/24, 12/25. **Address:** Calle Ancha de San Antonio 8 **Location:** 0.6 mi (1 km) s on Mex 49 (Celaya Hwy). **Parking:** street. **Cards:** MC, VI.

LA BELLA ITALIA

Italian
$12-$30

Phone: 415/152-4989

Tucked into the garden courtyard of the Plaza Colonial shopping complex, this Italian bistro boasts a wide ranging menu including seafood pasta, veal chops and sweet desserts. Casual dress. **Bar:** Full bar. **Reservations:** suggested. **Hours:** 1 pm-10 pm, Wed-Sat to 11 pm. Closed: 12/25. **Address:** Canal 21 Col Centro **Location:** 2 blks w from main plaza; in Plaza Colonial. **Parking:** street. **Cards:** MC, VI.

LA CAPILLA

International
$8-$32

Phone: 415/152-0698

In a restored 16th-century building, the restaurant is set against a Gothic-style church. The changing menu incorporates creative, far-from-traditional cuisine from Mexico as well as other countries. Al fresco dining on the upstairs terrace includes views of the mountains and church. Those without reservations could be stuck outside even in uncooperative weather. Casual dress. **Bar:** Full bar. **Reservations:** suggested. **Hours:** 5 pm-11 pm, Sat & Sun from 1 pm. Closed: Mon-Wed. **Address:** Cuna de Allende 10 Centro Historico **Location:** 1 blk s of main plaza; center. **Parking:** street. **Cards:** AX, MC, VI. **Classic**

NIRVANA

International
$7-$18

Phone: 415/150-0067

Upscale decor and friendly, attentive service are found in the casual bistro. Chef Juan Carlos, who trained at the Culinary Institute of America, brings a fresh view to the table with dishes such as watermelon gazpacho, hibiscus quesadillas, venison in dry chili sauce and Camembert with blackberry sauce. The dining room splits between an upscale interior and more casual enclosed courtyard, both displaying original artwork. Original ceramic dishware, whimsical flatware and an artistic menu show attention to detail. Casual dress. **Bar:** Full bar. **Reservations:** accepted. **Hours:** 8 am-11 pm. Closed: 1/1, 12/25; also Tues. **Address:** Mesones #101 **Location:** Just w of main plaza; center. **Parking:** street. **Cards:** MC, VI.

SIERRA NEVADA RESTAURANT

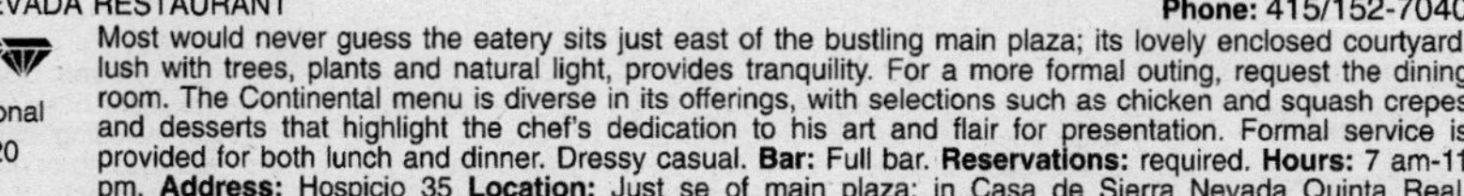

International
$12-$20

Phone: 415/152-7040

Most would never guess the eatery sits just east of the bustling main plaza; its lovely enclosed courtyard, lush with trees, plants and natural light, provides tranquility. For a more formal outing, request the dining room. The Continental menu is diverse in its offerings, with selections such as chicken and squash crepes and desserts that highlight the chef's dedication to his art and flair for presentation. Formal service is provided for both lunch and dinner. Dressy casual. **Bar:** Full bar. **Reservations:** required. **Hours:** 7 am-11 pm. **Address:** Hospicio 35 **Location:** Just se of main plaza; in Casa de Sierra Nevada Quinta Real. **Parking:** street. **Cards:** AX, MC, VI. **Historic**

TIO LUCAS

Regional Steak
$9-$27

Phone: 415/152-4996

Specializing in American cuts, the restaurant offers thick steaks, moist and full of flavor, but the staff truly makes the difference at this small and inviting spot. Personalized attention makes meals memorable in the lovely enclosed courtyard, which has a fountain, greenery and tin-star lanterns. Entertainers perform regularly. Delicious crepes prepared tableside are a fitting dessert choice. Casual dress. **Bar:** Full bar. **Reservations:** accepted. **Hours:** noon-midnight. Closed: 12/24. **Address:** 103 Mesones Centro **Location:** 2 blks w of main plaza. **Parking:** street. **Cards:** AX, MC, VI.

SILAO, GUANAJUATO pop. 134,337

WHERE TO STAY

HOLIDAY INN EXPRESS SILAO-AEROPUERTO BAJIO *Book at AAA.com*

Hotel
$130 10/1-11/30
$120 12/1-9/30

Phone: (472)722-8000

Address: Libramiento Norte #3360 **Location:** On Mex 45 at Silao exit. **Facility:** Meets AAA guest room security requirements. 165 units. 163 one-bedroom standard units. 2 one-bedroom suites. 5 stories, interior corridors. *Bath:* combo or shower only. **Parking:** on-site. **Terms:** cancellation fee imposed. **Amenities:** high-speed Internet, dual phone lines, voice mail, irons, hair dryers. **Pool(s):** heated indoor. **Leisure Activities:** exercise room. **Guest Services:** valet and coin laundry, area transportation, wireless Internet. **Business Services:** meeting rooms, business center. **Cards:** AX, MC, VI.

/ SOME UNITS

TLAQUEPAQUE, JALISCO pop. 474,178

WHERE TO STAY

CASA DE LAS FLORES

Bed & Breakfast
$95-$105 All Year

Phone: (33)3659-3186

Address: Santos Degollado #175 **Location:** 4 blks s of Plaza Hidalgo; center. **Facility:** In a restored historic home, this B&B features colorful local decor and artwork; a well-cared-for garden is relaxing. 7 one-bedroom standard units. 2 stories (no elevator), exterior corridors. *Bath:* shower only. **Parking:** on-site. **Terms:** age restrictions may apply, 21 day cancellation notice-fee imposed. **Guest Services:** coin laundry, wireless Internet. **Business Services:** PC. **Cards:** MC, VI.

/ SOME UNITS

LA VILLA DEL ENSUENO

Hotel
$85-$110 All Year

Phone: (33)3635-8792

Address: Florida 305 **Location:** 0.6 mi (1 km) w of El Parian. **Facility:** Designated smoking area. 20 units. 15 one- and 3 two-bedroom standard units, some with efficiencies and/or whirlpools. 2 one-bedroom suites. 2 stories (no elevator), interior corridors. *Bath:* combo or shower only. **Parking:** on-site. **Terms:** 14 day cancellation notice. **Amenities:** high-speed Internet, safes, hair dryers. **Pool(s):** 2 heated outdoor. **Leisure Activities:** whirlpool. **Guest Services:** valet laundry, wireless Internet. **Business Services:** meeting rooms, business center. **Cards:** AX, MC, VI.

/ SOME UNITS

QUINTA DON JOSE BOUTIQUE HOTEL Phone: 33/3635-7522

Boutique Hotel
$80-$140 All Year

Address: Reforma #139 Centro **Location:** Center. **Facility:** This in-town boutique hotel has a variety of rooms from single to family units; a classic, colorful Mexican decor adorns each unit. 15 units. 10 one-bedroom standard units, some with whirlpools. 4 one- and 1 two-bedroom suites, some with kitchens. 2 stories (no elevator), interior/exterior corridors. *Bath:* combo or shower only. **Parking:** on-site. **Amenities:** irons, hair dryers. **Pool(s):** outdoor. **Guest Services:** valet laundry, wireless Internet. **Business Services:** PC. **Cards:** AX, MC, VI.

WHERE TO DINE

ADOBE RESTAURANTE & BAR **Phone:** 33/3657-2792

Mexican
$7-$20

Combined with a pottery and crafts shop, the colorful, lively restaurant and cantina serves large portions of well-prepared beef and chicken as well as a good selection of spirits. Casual dress. Entertainment. **Bar:** Full bar. **Reservations:** accepted. **Hours:** noon-6:30 pm, Sat-8 pm. Closed major holidays. **Address:** Francisco de Miranda #27 **Location:** Center. **Parking:** on-site (fee). **Cards:** AX, MC, VI.

CASA FUERTE RESTAURANTE **Phone:** 33/3639-6481

Mexican
$10-$19

This lively restaurant presents a fine menu of freshly prepared Mexican fare. Diners can request seating on the streetfront patio, in the lovely open-air center courtyard or in the more sophisticated interior dining room. Live music adds to the ambience. Menu highlights include stuffed peppers, sizzling fajitas and freshly grilled fish and other seafood. Tortillas here are always fresh. Casual dress. Entertainment. **Bar:** Full bar. **Reservations:** suggested. **Hours:** noon-9 pm. **Address:** Independencia 224 **Location:** Centre. **Parking:** no self-parking. **Cards:** MC, VI.

EL NAHUAL **Phone:** 33/3044-2525

International
$10-$28

Creative regional artwork decorates the large dining room, where live entertainment often enhances the dining experience. Mexican influences pepper the chef's international offerings, including starters of fresh soup, local cheese or salad; and entrees of rock Cornish hen, fresh seafood, rack of lamb or beef sided with Mexican sauces. Hot cheese-stuffed bread is served with herb butter. Although it's easy to overindulge, it's best to hold something back for one of the excellent desserts. Casual dress. Entertainment. **Bar:** Full bar. **Reservations:** suggested. **Hours:** 1 pm-midnight. **Address:** Juarez No 17 **Location:** Centre; 1/2 blk from Parian. **Parking:** valet. **Cards:** MC, VI.

EL PATIO **Phone:** 33/3635-1108

Mexican
$8-$15

Patrons should call ahead for reservations so as not to miss an opportunity to dine at this bustling Mexican restaurant. Plants and flowers surround the wonderful patio courtyard that nurtures a relaxed atmosphere. Live entertainment and two-for-one margaritas enhance the laid-back feel. The fresh tortillas that factor into many of the home-style Mexican dishes are prepared as guests look on. A large glass case near the entrance displays the hard-to-resist desserts. Casual dress. Entertainment. **Bar:** Full bar. **Reservations:** suggested. **Hours:** 9 am-9 pm. **Address:** Calle Peatonal Independencia #186 **Location:** Centre. **Parking:** no self-parking. **Cards:** MC, VI.

VIPS **Phone:** 33/3659-6553

Mexican
$5-$9

Owned by Wal-Mart of Mexico and found in most major cities, the budget-friendly chain serves a good variety of Mexican and American dishes, including burgers, sandwiches, salads, spaghetti and enchiladas, as well as a fine selection of desserts. Casual dress. **Hours:** 7 am-11 pm, Fri & Sat-midnight. **Address:** Prol Revolucion #501 **Location:** Center. **Parking:** on-site. **Cards:** MC, VI.

URUAPAN, MICHOACAN pop. 265,699

WHERE TO STAY

HOTEL MANSION DEL CUPATITZIO **Phone:** (452)523-2100

Hotel
$156-$320 All Year

Address: Calz de La Rodilla del Diablo #20 **Location:** 0.3 mi (0.5 km) se of Mex 37 on Calz Fray Juan de San Miguel. **Facility:** 57 one-bedroom standard units. 2 stories (no elevator), exterior corridors. *Bath:* combo or shower only. **Parking:** on-site. **Terms:** 3 day cancellation notice-fee imposed. **Amenities:** hair dryers. *Some:* safes, irons. **Pool(s):** heated outdoor. **Leisure Activities:** exercise room. **Guest Services:** valet laundry, wireless Internet. **Business Services:** meeting rooms. **Cards:** AX, MC, VI.

/ SOME UNITS

ZACATECAS, ZACATECAS pop. 123,899

WHERE TO STAY

HOTEL DEL BOSQUE-TELEFERICO **Phone:** 492/922-0745

Hotel
$118-$275 All Year

Address: Paseo Diaz Ordaz #602, Colonia Centro **Location:** Center. **Facility:** 60 units. 50 one-bedroom standard units, some with kitchens. 8 one-, 1 two- and 1 three-bedroom suites, some with kitchens. 1 story, interior corridors. *Bath:* combo or shower only. **Parking:** on-site. **Amenities:** voice mail, irons, hair dryers. **Leisure Activities:** *Fee:* massage. **Guest Services:** valet laundry, wireless Internet. **Business Services:** meeting rooms, PC (fee). **Cards:** AX, MC, VI.

HOTEL EMPORIO ZACATECAS **Phone:** 492/925-6500

Historic Hotel
$110-$165 All Year

Address: Ave Hidalgo 703 **Location:** On Plaza de Armas; center. Located in historic district; opposite cathedral. **Facility:** Many of the property's rooms overlook a courtyard with a fountain, while some have patios. 113 units. 112 one-bedroom standard units. 1 one-bedroom suite. 6 stories, interior corridors. *Bath:* combo or shower only. **Parking:** on-site (fee). **Amenities:** video library, DVD players, voice mail, safes, irons, hair dryers. **Leisure Activities:** sauna, exercise room. **Guest Services:** valet laundry, wireless Internet. **Business Services:** meeting rooms, business center. **Cards:** AX, MC, VI.

SOME UNITS

HOTEL HACIENDA DEL BOSQUE *Book at AAA.com* **Phone:** (492)924-6666

Hotel
$95-$185 All Year

Address: Heroes de Chapultepec 801 **Location:** 2.4 mi (4 km) ne of center on Guadalajara Rd; jct Mex 54. **Facility:** 79 units. 78 one-bedroom standard units. 1 one-bedroom suite with kitchen and whirlpool. 2 stories (no elevator), interior corridors. **Parking:** on-site. **Terms:** 3 day cancellation notice-fee imposed. **Amenities:** irons, hair dryers. **Pool(s):** heated indoor. **Leisure Activities:** steamroom, playground, exercise room, game room. *Fee:* massage. **Guest Services:** valet laundry, area transportation, wireless Internet. **Business Services:** meeting rooms, business center. **Cards:** AX, MC, VI.

QUINTA REAL ZACATECAS **Phone:** (492)922-9104

Hotel
$200 All Year

Address: Ave Rayon 434 **Location:** 5 blks w of cathedral; beside Elcubo Aqueduct on Ave Gonzalez Ortega. **Facility:** The facade of this beautiful hotel is built around the ruins of an old bull ring. 49 units. 48 one-bedroom standard units, some with whirlpools. 1 one-bedroom suite with whirlpool. 5 stories, interior corridors. **Parking:** valet. **Amenities:** high-speed Internet, voice mail, honor bars, irons, hair dryers. **Dining:** La Plaza Restaurant, see separate listing. **Leisure Activities:** exercise room. **Guest Services:** valet laundry, wireless Internet. **Business Services:** meeting rooms, business center. **Cards:** AX, MC, VI. Affiliated with A Preferred Hotel. ***(See color ad p 8)***

SOME UNITS

SANTA RITA HOTEL *Book at AAA.com* **Phone:** 492/925-1194

Boutique Hotel
$170-$270 All Year

Address: Ave Hidalgo #507A **Location:** Center. **Facility:** Suspended walkways and modern art define the corridors while warm, wood floors and luxurious linens create an inviting oasis within the guest rooms. 35 one-bedroom standard units, some with whirlpools. 7 stories, interior corridors. *Bath:* combo or shower only. **Parking:** valet. **Amenities:** safes, honor bars, hair dryers. *Some:* DVD players. **Leisure Activities:** exercise room. *Fee:* massage. **Guest Services:** valet laundry, wireless Internet. **Business Services:** meeting rooms, PC. **Cards:** AX, MC, VI.

SOME UNITS

WHERE TO DINE

LA PLAZA RESTAURANT **Phone:** 492/922-9104

Continental
$7-$30

The elegant, formal dining room overlooks picturesque bull ring ruins. Featured on the menu are some seafood and Mexican items. Dressy casual. **Bar:** Full bar. **Reservations:** suggested. **Hours:** 7 am-midnight. **Address:** Ave Rayon 434 **Location:** 5 blks w of cathedral; beside Elcubo Aqueduct on Ave Gonzalez Ortega; in Quinta Real Zacatecas. **Parking:** valet. **Cards:** AX, MC, VI.

LOS DORADOS DE VILLA **Phone:** 492/922-5722

Mexican
$5-$7

For traditional Northern Mexican cuisine, there aren't many better places than this tiny spot, which is appointed in folkloric decor. For a true taste of regional cuisine—and as they say, "When in Rome .."—enchiladas Zacatecanas stands out. The staff takes great pride in making menu items a la minute so guests can sit back, relax and rest assured it will be worth the wait. Reservations are a must; those who don't make one risk being disappointed. Casual dress. **Bar:** Beer only. **Reservations:** suggested. **Hours:** 3 pm-1 am. Closed: 1/1, 12/25. **Address:** Plazuela de Garcia #1314 **Location:** Center; n of cathedral; next to Museo Rafael Coronel. **Parking:** street.

SANBORN'S **Phone:** 492/922-1298

Mexican
$8-$18

Restaurants in the casual chain, which includes more than 100 locations throughout Mexico, offer a good selection of American-style sandwiches, salads, soups and both Mexican and American entrees. The selection of desserts is impressive. Casual dress. **Bar:** Full bar. **Hours:** 7:30 am-1 am. **Address:** Ave Hidalgo #212 **Location:** Jct Ave Hidalgo and Calle Allende; in historic center of town. **Parking:** on-site (fee). **Cards:** MC, VI.

VIPS **Phone:** 492/924-2798

Mexican
$5-$9

Owned by Wal-Mart of Mexico and found in most major cities, the budget-friendly chain serves a good variety of Mexican and American dishes, including burgers, sandwiches, salads, spaghetti and enchiladas, as well as a fine selection of desserts. Casual dress. **Hours:** 7 am-midnight. **Address:** Blvd Lopez Portillo #746 **Location:** Jct Ave Universidad and Blvd Lopez Portillo, just e. **Parking:** on-site. **Cards:** MC, VI.

VIPS **Phone:** 492/924-0267

Mexican
$5-$9

Owned by Wal-Mart of Mexico and found in most major cities, the budget-friendly chain serves a good variety of Mexican and American dishes, including burgers, sandwiches, salads, spaghetti and enchiladas, as well as a fine selection of desserts. Casual dress. **Hours:** 7 am-11 pm, Fri & Sat-midnight. **Address:** Ave Gonzalez Ortega #203 **Location:** Jct Ave Rayon and Calle Resbadon, just e; center. **Parking:** on-site. **Cards:** MC, VI.

SOUTHERN MEXICO

JALAPA, VERACRUZ pop. 390,590

WHERE TO DINE

VIPS

Phone: 228/840-7640

Regional Mexican
$7-$24

Owned by Wal-Mart of Mexico and found in most major cities, the budget-friendly chain serves a good variety of Mexican and American dishes, including burgers, sandwiches, salads, spaghetti and enchiladas, as well as a fine selection of desserts. Casual dress. **Bar:** Beer & wine. **Hours:** 7 am-midnight, Fri & Sat-1 am. **Address:** Ave Laza ro Cardenas No 321, Col Encanto de **Location:** In front of Plaza Cristal. **Parking:** on-site. **Cards:** AX, MC, VI.

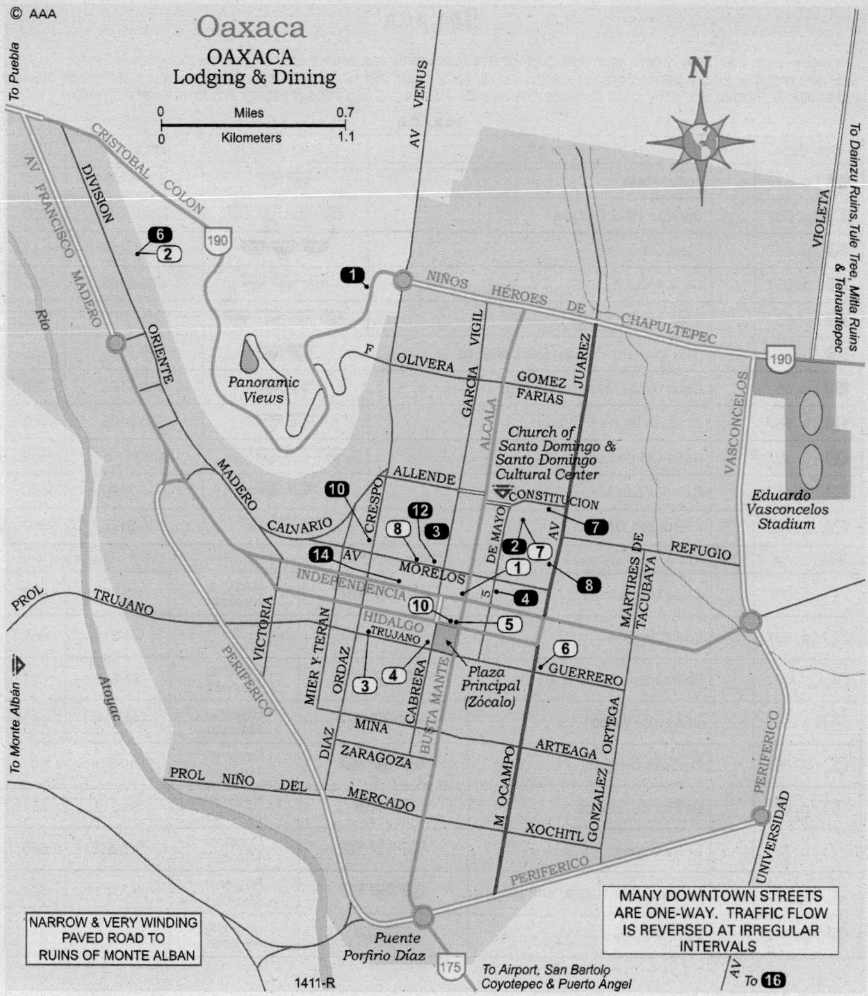

© AAA

Oaxaca

OAXACA
Lodging & Dining

0 Miles 0.7
0 Kilometers 1.1

N

To Puebla

To Dainzu Ruins, Tule Tree, Mitla Ruins & Tehuantepec

To Monte Albán

To Airport, San Bartolo Coyotepec & Puerto Ángel

To 16

CRISTOBAL COLON
AV FRANCISCO MADERO
DIVISION ORIENTE
AV VENUS
NIÑOS HÉROES DE CHAPULTEPEC
VIOLETA
VASCONCELOS
190
Río Atoyac
Panoramic Views
F OLIVERA
GARCIA VIGIL
ALCALA
GOMEZ FARIAS
AV JUAREZ
Church of Santo Domingo & Santo Domingo Cultural Center
ALLENDE
CONSTITUCION
CRESPO
MADERO
CALVARIO
DE MAYO
5
REFUGIO
MARTIRES DE TACUBAYA
Eduardo Vasconcelos Stadium
AV MORELOS
AV INDEPENDENCIA
PROL TRUJANO
VICTORIA
MIER Y TERAN
HIDALGO
TRUJANO
ORDAZ
CABRERA
BUSTA MANTE
Plaza Principal (Zócalo)
GUERRERO
PERIFERICO
MINA
DIAZ
ZARAGOZA
ARTEAGA
ORTEGA
M OCAMPO
GONZALEZ
PROL NIÑO DEL MERCADO
XOCHITL
UNIVERSIDAD
AV
175
Puente Porfirio Díaz

NARROW & VERY WINDING PAVED ROAD TO RUINS OF MONTE ALBAN

MANY DOWNTOWN STREETS ARE ONE-WAY. TRAFFIC FLOW IS REVERSED AT IRREGULAR INTERVALS

1411-R

Oaxaca

This index helps you "spot" where approved lodgings and restaurants are located on the corresponding detailed maps. Lodging daily rate range is for comparison only and show the property's high season. Restaurant rate range is a combination of lunch and/or dinner. Turn to the listing page for more detailed rate information and consult display ads for special promotions.

OAXACA

Map Page	OA	Lodgings	Diamond Rated	High Season	Page
1 / p. 657		Fortin Plaza	◆◆	$99-$135	659
2 / p. 657	AAA	**Camino Real Oaxaca**	◆◆◆◆	$200-$360	659
3 / p. 657		Casa Oaxaca	◆◆◆	$150-$300	659
4 / p. 657		Casa Antiqua	◆◆◆	$85-$165	659
6 / p. 657		Hotel Hacienda Los Laureles	◆◆◆◆	$255-$370	660
7 / p. 657		Best Western Parador Del Dominico	◆◆	$99-$115	659
8 / p. 657		Casa de las Bugambilias B&B	◆◆	$60-$105	659
10 / p. 657		La Casa de los Milagros	◆◆	$85-$105	660
12 / p. 657		Casa Cid de Leon	◆◆◆◆	$200-$230	659
14 / p. 657		Parador San Miguel Oaxaca	◆◆	$74-$220	660
16 / p. 657	AAA	**Fiesta Inn Oaxaca**	◆◆◆	$95-$176	659

Map Page	OA	Restaurants	Diamond Rated	Cuisine	Meal Range	Page
1 / p. 657		Casa Mayordomo	◆◆◆	Regional Mexican	$6-$25	660
2 / p. 657	AAA	**Los Cipreses**	◆◆◆	Regional Mexican	$8-$14	661
3 / p. 657		Restaurante El Naranjo	◆◆◆	Regional Mexican	$8-$28	661
4 / p. 657		El Asador Vasco	◆◆◆	Regional Mexican	$8-$25	660
5 / p. 657		La Casa de la Abuela	◆◆◆	Regional Mexican	$10-$18	661
6 / p. 657		La Flor de Oaxaca	◆◆	Regional Mexican	$6-$18	661
7 / p. 657		El Refectorio	◆◆◆	Regional Mexican	$18-$35	660
8 / p. 657		Catedral Restaurante and Bar	◆◆◆	Regional Mexican	$7-$21	660
10 / p. 657		La Primavera	◆◆	Regional Mexican	$5-$10	661

OAXACA, OAXACA pop. 256,130 (See map and index starting on p. 657)

WHERE TO STAY

BEST WESTERN PARADOR DEL DOMINICO — **Phone:** 951/513-1812 — 7

Hotel
$99-$115 All Year

Address: Pino Suarez No 410 Centro C **Location:** In historic centre. **Facility:** 32 one-bedroom standard units. 3 stories (no elevator), interior corridors. *Bath:* shower only. **Parking:** street. **Amenities:** high-speed Internet, voice mail, safes, honor bars, irons, hair dryers. **Guest Services:** wireless Internet. **Cards:** AX, MC, VI.

/ SOME UNITS

AAA Benefit: Members save up to 20%, plus 10% bonus points with rewards program.

CAMINO REAL OAXACA — *Book great rates at AAA.com* — **Phone:** (951)501-6100 — 2

Classic Historic Country Inn
$200-$360 All Year

Address: 5 de Mayo 300 **Location:** 4 blks n of Zocalo; between Murguia and Abasolo sts; center. **Facility:** The picturesque 16th-century former convent has arched cloisters and a courtyard with fountains; modern rooms have high ceilings and colorful decor. 91 one-bedroom standard units. 2 stories (no elevator), interior/exterior corridors. **Parking:** on-site (fee) and valet. **Amenities:** voice mail, safes, honor bars, hair dryers. **Dining:** El Refectorio, see separate listing, entertainment. **Pool(s):** outdoor. **Guest Services:** valet laundry, wireless Internet. **Business Services:** conference facilities. *Fee:* PC, fax. **Cards:** AX, DC, MC, VI.

FEE / SOME UNITS

CASA ANTIQUA — **Phone:** 951/501-1240 — 4

Hotel
$85-$165 All Year

Address: 5 de Mayo 206 **Location:** In historic downtown. **Facility:** 15 units. 14 one-bedroom standard units. 1 one-bedroom suite with whirlpool. 2 stories, interior corridors. *Bath:* combo or shower only. **Parking:** street. **Terms:** 7 day cancellation notice. **Amenities:** high-speed Internet, safes, hair dryers. **Guest Services:** wireless Internet. **Cards:** AX, CB, DC, DS, MC, VI.

CASA CID DE LEON — **Phone:** 951/514-1893 — 12

Historic Hotel
$200-$230 All Year

Address: Ave Morelos, #602 **Location:** In historic centre. **Facility:** The small, boutique hotel features elegantly-appointed guest rooms adorned with fine furnishings and upgraded decor accents. 4 one-bedroom suites, some with whirlpools. 3 stories (no elevator), interior corridors. *Bath:* combo or shower only. **Parking:** street. **Amenities:** video library, DVD players, CD players, safes, hair dryers. **Guest Services:** wireless Internet. **Cards:** AX, MC, VI.

D / SOME UNITS

CASA DE LAS BUGAMBILIAS B&B — **Phone:** 951/516-1165 — 8

Bed & Breakfast
$60-$105 All Year

Address: Reforma #402 Col Centro **Location:** In historic downtown. **Facility:** Smoke free premises. 9 one-bedroom standard units. 2 stories (no elevator), interior corridors. *Bath:* combo or shower only. **Parking:** street. **Terms:** 20 day cancellation notice. **Amenities:** video library, safes, hair dryers. *Some:* DVD players. **Guest Services:** TV in common area, wireless Internet. **Business Services:** PC. **Cards:** DC, DS, MC, VI.

/ SOME UNITS

CASA OAXACA — **Phone:** 951/514-4173 — 3

Bed & Breakfast
$150-$300 All Year

Address: Garcia Vigil 407 **Location:** 4 blks n of Zocalo; in historic downtown. **Facility:** Rooms surround a lovely courtyard where local artists' work is displayed. The property's environment is very quiet and serene. Designated smoking area. 7 units. 6 one-bedroom standard units. 1 one-bedroom suite. 2 stories, interior corridors. *Bath:* combo or shower only. **Parking:** on-site. **Terms:** 10 day cancellation notice. **Amenities:** safes, irons, hair dryers. **Pool(s):** outdoor. **Leisure Activities:** sauna. *Fee:* massage. **Guest Services:** complimentary laundry, wireless Internet. **Business Services:** PC. **Cards:** AX, MC, VI.

FEE

FIESTA INN OAXACA — *Book great rates at AAA.com* — **Phone:** (951)501-6000 — 16

Hotel
$95-$176 All Year

Address: Ave Universidad, 140 Ex-Hacienda **Location:** At Plaza del Valle. **Facility:** 143 units. 141 one-bedroom standard units. 2 one-bedroom suites. 3 stories, interior corridors. **Parking:** on-site. **Amenities:** irons, hair dryers. **Pool(s):** outdoor. **Leisure Activities:** playground, exercise room. **Guest Services:** valet laundry, area transportation-city centre, wireless Internet. **Business Services:** meeting rooms, business center. **Cards:** AX, DC, MC, VI. *(See color ad on insert)*

/ SOME UNITS

FORTIN PLAZA — **Phone:** (951)515-7777 — 1

Hotel
$99-$135 All Year

Address: Ave Venus 118 **Location:** On north side; in Colonia Estrella on Mex 190. **Facility:** 90 one-bedroom standard units. 6 stories, interior/exterior corridors. *Bath:* combo or shower only. **Parking:** on-site. **Terms:** 5 day cancellation notice. **Amenities:** hair dryers. **Pool(s):** outdoor. **Guest Services:** valet laundry, wireless Internet. **Business Services:** meeting rooms, business center. **Cards:** AX, MC, VI.

/ SOME UNITS

(See map and index starting on p. 657)

HOTEL HACIENDA LOS LAURELES Book at AAA.com **Phone:** (951)501-5300 6

Boutique Hotel
$255-$370 All Year

Address: Hidalgo #21 **Location:** 9 mi (15 km) n of airport. **Facility:** Located north of town, the boutique inn offers tastefully-decorated guest rooms with a distinct Mexican flair. 23 one-bedroom standard units. 2 stories (no elevator), exterior corridors. *Bath:* combo or shower only. **Parking:** on-site. **Terms:** 4 day cancellation notice, in season. **Amenities:** safes, honor bars, irons, hair dryers. **Dining:** Los Cipreses, see separate listing. **Pool(s):** outdoor. **Leisure Activities:** exercise room, spa. **Guest Services:** valet laundry, wireless Internet. **Business Services:** business center. **Cards:** AX, MC, VI.

/ SOME UNITS

LA CASA DE LOS MILAGROS **Phone:** 951/501-2262 10

Bed & Breakfast
$85-$105 All Year

Address: Matamoros #500-C **Location:** In historic downtown. **Facility:** Smoke free premises. 3 one-bedroom standard units. 2 stories (no elevator), interior corridors. *Bath:* shower only. **Parking:** no self-parking. **Terms:** 20 day cancellation notice. **Amenities:** safes, hair dryers. **Guest Services:** TV in common area, wireless Internet. **Business Services:** PC. **Cards:** MC, VI.

D / SOME UNITS

PARADOR SAN MIGUEL OAXACA Book at AAA.com **Phone:** (951)514-9331 14

Hotel
$74-$220 All Year

Address: Ave Independencia #503 **Location:** In historic downtown. **Facility:** 23 one-bedroom standard units, some with whirlpools. 3 stories (no elevator), interior corridors. *Bath:* combo or shower only. **Parking:** no self-parking. **Amenities:** high-speed Internet, safes, hair dryers. **Guest Services:** valet laundry, wireless Internet. **Business Services:** PC. **Cards:** AX, MC, VI.

/ SOME UNITS

The following lodgings were either not evaluated or did not meet AAA rating requirements but are listed for your information only.

CASA CATRINA **Phone:** 951/514-5322

fyi

Not evaluated. **Address:** Garcia 703, Centro. Facilities, services, and decor characterize a mid-scale property.

HOLIDAY INN EXPRESS **Phone:** 951/512-9200

fyi

Not evaluated. **Address:** Diaz Quintas No 115. Facilities, services, and decor characterize a mid-scale property.

HOTEL VICTORIA **Phone:** 951/515-2633

fyi

Not evaluated. **Address:** Lomas del Fortin No 21. Facilities, services, and decor characterize a mid-scale property.

WHERE TO DINE

CASA MAYORDOMO **Phone:** 951/516-6113 1

Regional Mexican
$6-$25

Within walking distance of El Zocalo, this restaurant will please everyone with a wide assortment of mole, chiles stuffed with diced chicken, tomatoes, almonds, raisins and more, as well as burgers for the kids. Casual dress. **Bar:** Full bar. **Reservations:** accepted. **Hours:** 8 am-midnight. **Address:** Calle Alcala #302 **Location:** Calle Alcala at Calle Mariano Matamoros. **Parking:** no self-parking. **Cards:** MC, VI.

CATEDRAL RESTAURANTE AND BAR **Phone:** 951/516-3285 8

Regional Mexican
$7-$21

This centrally located restaurant presents a fine menu of local and regional Mexican fare, including moles, spicy sauces, grilled meats, poultry, seafood and, of course, freshly prepared tortillas. The lovely and sophisticated setting includes candlelit tables and a Mexican fountain in the courtyard area. Semi-formal attire. **Bar:** Full bar. **Hours:** 8 am-midnight. Closed: Tues. **Address:** Garcia Vigil No. 105 **Location:** In historical centre. **Parking:** no self-parking. **Cards:** MC, VI.

EL ASADOR VASCO **Phone:** 951/514-4755 4

Regional Mexican
$8-$25

The restaurant enables guests to dine amid the entertaining surroundings of the Zocalo. On the second floor of a historic building facing the main square, terrace seating is highly sought after on any given night. The menu's International influences provide variety. Service is consistent. Casual dress. **Bar:** Full bar. **Reservations:** accepted. **Hours:** 1 pm-11:30 pm, Sun 2 pm-11 pm. **Address:** Portal de Flores #10A **Location:** On west side of Zocalo. **Parking:** no self-parking. **Cards:** AX, MC, VI.

EL REFECTORIO **Phone:** 951/501-6100 7

Regional Mexican
$18-$35

Diners enjoy live Mexican music and a varied menu of regional Mexican and international fare at this stunning setting in the middle of a converted historic convent. A choice of terrace or indoor seating is offered. Casual dress. **Bar:** Full bar. **Reservations:** suggested. **Hours:** 7 am-10:30 pm. **Address:** 5 Mayo 300 **Location:** 4 blks n of Zocalo; between Murguia and Abasolo sts; center; in Camino Real Oaxaca. **Parking:** valet. **Cards:** AX, DC, MC, VI.

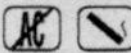

(See map and index starting on p. 657)

LA CASA DE LA ABUELA

Phone: 951/516-3544 (5)

Regional Mexican
$10-$18

Located on the second floor facing the main plaza, the restaurant offers classic Oaxacan dining with variety of mole sauce and crumbly Oaxacan white cheese. Call ahead and reserve and window table. Casual dress. **Bar:** Full bar. **Reservations:** suggested. **Hours:** 1 pm-11 pm. **Address:** Ave Hidalgo 616 Altos **Location:** Overlooking the Zocalo. **Parking:** no self-parking. **Cards:** MC, VI.

LA FLOR DE OAXACA

Phone: 951/516-5522 (6)

Regional Mexican
$6-$18

Tucked away next to and a bit overshadowed by the adjacent church, the restaurant centers on classic local dishes. Among simply prepared favorites are the varied moles for which this state is known. The environment is modest and casual. Casual dress. **Bar:** Full bar. **Hours:** 8 am-10 pm, Sun 9 am-3 pm. **Address:** Armenta y Lopez 311 **Location:** Just e of Zocalo; adjacent to chapel. **Parking:** no self-parking. **Cards:** DC, DS, MC, VI.

LA PRIMAVERA

Phone: 951/516-2595 (10)

Regional Mexican
$5-$10

Adjacent to the Plaza el Zocalo, this authentic Oaxacan restaurant features various moles, stuffed peppers and typical dishes of the area. Casual dress. **Bar:** Beer only. **Hours:** 7 am-midnight. **Address:** Ave Hidalgo con Portal de Fls **Location:** In historic downtown area. **Parking:** no self-parking. **Cards:** MC, VI.

LOS CIPRESES

Phone: 951/501-5300 (2)

Regional Mexican
$8-$14

Diners enjoy a tranquil setting on a covered terrace filled with fresh plants and flowers and glass doors that can be opened on mild evenings. The menu features a wide selection of fresh international cuisine prepared with a Mexican flair. The chef focuses on the use of fresh local and regional ingredients and enhances the flavor of dishes with a fine use of herbs and spices. Casual dress. **Bar:** Full bar. **Reservations:** suggested. **Hours:** 7:30 am-10:30 pm. **Address:** Hidalgo #21 **Location:** 9 mi (15 km) n of airport; in Hotel Hacienda Los Laureles. **Parking:** on-site. **Cards:** AX, MC, VI.

RESTAURANTE EL NARANJO

Phone: 951/514-1878 (3)

Regional Mexican
$8-$28

This is the one restaurant not to miss in this ancient city; if Oaxaca is the soul of Mexican cuisine, then El Naranjo is its cathedral. Everyone talks about this place. All the mole sauces are featured here and the chile relleno is a must. Reasonably priced cooking classes from world renowned Oaxacan chefs are also available. Casual dress. **Bar:** Full bar. **Reservations:** suggested. **Hours:** 1 pm-10 pm. Closed: Sun. **Address:** Valerio Trujano 203, Col Centro **Location:** 1 blk w of El Zocalo main plaza. **Parking:** street. **Cards:** MC, VI.

VIPS

Phone: 951/515-9341

Regional Mexican
$7-$25

Owned by Wal-Mart of Mexico and found in most major cities, the budget-friendly chain serves a good variety of Mexican and American dishes, including burgers, sandwiches, salads, spaghetti and enchiladas, as well as a fine selection of desserts. Casual dress. **Bar:** Beer & wine. **Hours:** 7 am-11 pm, Fri & Sat-2 am. **Address:** Ave B Juarez No 809, Col Centro **Location:** Jct Ave Jacobo Delavuelta. **Parking:** on-site. **Cards:** AX, MC, VI.

PALENQUE, CHIAPAS pop. 85,464

WHERE TO STAY

BEST WESTERN MAYA PALENQUE *Book great rates at AAA.com*

Phone: (916)345-0780

Hotel
$70-$110 All Year

Address: Merle Green y Ave Juarez S/N **Location:** At Glorieta La Cabeza Maya. **Facility:** 50 one-bedroom standard units. 3 stories (no elevator), interior corridors. *Bath:* shower only. **Parking:** on-site. **Amenities:** hair dryers. **Pool(s):** outdoor. **Guest Services:** valet laundry. **Business Services:** meeting rooms, PC. **Cards:** AX, CB, DC, DS, JC, MC, VI.

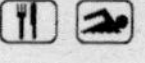

AAA Benefit:
Members save up to 20%, plus 10% bonus points with rewards program.

CHAN-KAH RESORT VILLAGE

Phone: 916/345-1100

Hotel
$120-$240 All Year

Address: KM 3 Carr a las Ruinas **Location:** 1.1 mi (1.8 km) n of main entrance to Palenque ruins. **Facility:** 85 units. 79 one-bedroom standard units. 6 one-bedroom suites. 1 story, exterior corridors. *Bath:* shower only. **Parking:** on-site. **Pool(s):** 4 outdoor. **Business Services:** meeting rooms, PC. **Cards:** MC, VI.

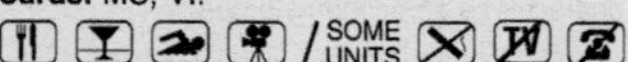

HOWARD JOHNSON HOTEL D'MARCO PALENQUE **Phone:** (916)345-0098

Hotel
$80 All Year

Address: Zona Hotelera KM 1.2 **Location:** 0.3 mi (0.5 km) n of Glorieta La Cabeza Maya. **Facility:** 40 one-bedroom standard units. 2-3 stories (no elevator), interior corridors. *Bath:* shower only. **Parking:** on-site. **Pool(s):** outdoor. **Guest Services:** valet laundry, area transportation (fee). **Business Services:** meeting rooms. **Cards:** MC, VI.

The following lodgings were either not evaluated or did not meet AAA rating requirements but are listed for your information only.

HOTEL MISION PALENQUE PARK PLAZA **Phone:** 916/345-0241

fyi

Not evaluated. **Address:** Rancho San Martin de Porres **Location:** 4 blks e of center, follow signs. Facilities, services, and decor characterize a mid-scale property.

HOTEL NUTUTUN PALENQUE **Phone:** 916/345-0100

fyi

Not evaluated. **Address:** KM 3.5 Carr Palenque-Ocosingo **Location:** 3 mi (5 km) s on Mex 199 to Agua Azul. Facilities, services, and decor characterize an economy property.

HOTEL PLAZA PALENQUE **Phone:** 916/345-0555

fyi

Not evaluated; located in area of political unrest. **Address:** KM 27 Carr Caletaja-Palenque **Location:** 0.6 mi (1 km) n on Mex 199. Facilities, services, and decor characterize a mid-scale property.

SAN CRISTOBAL DE LAS CASAS, CHIAPAS pop. 132,421

WHERE TO STAY

The following lodgings were either not evaluated or did not meet AAA rating requirements but are listed for your information only.

DIEGO DE MAZARIEGOS HOTEL **Phone:** 967/678-0833

fyi

Not evaluated. **Address:** Ma Adelina Flores 2 **Location:** Just n of Parque Espinosa. Facilities, services, and decor characterize a mid-scale property.

HOLIDAY INN **Phone:** 967/678-0045

fyi

Not evaluated. **Address:** Ave 16 de Septiembre y Primero **Location:** In town; just n of Parque Espinosa. Facilities, services, and decor characterize a mid-scale property.

HOTEL BONAMPAK **Phone:** 967/678-1621

fyi

Not evaluated. **Address:** Calzada Mexico 5 **Location:** On Mex 190, north entrance to town at statue. Facilities, services, and decor characterize an economy property.

TAXCO, GUERRERO pop. 100,245

WHERE TO STAY

The following lodgings were either not evaluated or did not meet AAA rating requirements but are listed for your information only.

HACIENDA DEL SOLAR **Phone:** 762/622-0587

fyi

Not evaluated. **Address:** Paraje del Solar S/N Col El Solar **Location:** 2 mi (3.5 km) s off Mex 95, just e. Facilities, services, and decor characterize an economy property.

HOTEL MONTE TAXCO **Phone:** 762/622-1300

fyi

Not evaluated. **Address:** Fracc Lomas de T **Location:** On steep mountain, just n of Mex 95; at entrance of city. Facilities, services, and decor characterize an economy property.

HOTEL VICTORIA **Phone:** 762/622-0004

fyi

Not evaluated. **Address:** Carlos J Nibbi 5 y 7 **Location:** 2 1/2 blks s of Santa Prisca Church; on hill overlooking town. Facilities, services, and decor characterize an economy property.

POSADA DE LA MISION **Phone:** 762/622-0063

fyi

Not evaluated. **Address:** Cerro de la Mision 32 **Location:** On Mex 95; opposite Pemex station. Facilities, services, and decor characterize an economy property.

WHERE TO DINE

The following restaurant has not been evaluated by AAA but is listed for your information only.

LA VENTANA DE TAXCO — **Phone:** 762/622-0587

fyi

Not evaluated. Diners can take in a panoramic view of the city while enjoying International cuisine, including many Italian specialties. Upscale Western decor is reminiscent of the town's rich, silver-mining days. An attentive staff ensures a memorable dinner. **Location:** 2 mi (3.5 km) s off Mex 95, just e; in Hacienda del Solar.

TUXTLA GUTIERREZ, CHIAPAS pop. 434,143

WHERE TO STAY

The following lodgings were either not evaluated or did not meet AAA rating requirements but are listed for your information only.

CAMINO REAL TUXTLA GUTIERREZ — **Phone:** 961/617-7777

fyi

Not evaluated. **Address:** #1195 Blvd Belisario Dominguez **Location:** 0.9 mi (1.5 km) e. Facilities, services, and decor characterize an upscale property.

HOLIDAY INN — **Phone:** 961/617-1000

fyi

Not evaluated. **Address:** Blvd Belisario Dominguez #1821 **Location:** 3 mi (4.5 km) w on Mex 190. Facilities, services, and decor characterize a mid-scale property.

WHERE TO DINE

SANBORN'S — **Phone:** 961/671-8087

Regional Mexican
$8-$28

Restaurants in the casual chain, which includes more than 100 locations throughout Mexico, offer a good selection of American-style sandwiches, salads, soups and both Mexican and American entrees. The selection of desserts is impressive. Casual dress. **Bar:** Full bar. **Hours:** 7:30 am-10 pm, Fri & Sat-1 am. **Address:** Blvd Dominguez No. 1861, Col Bugambilia **Location:** 1.2 mi (2 km) e of Zocalo. **Parking:** on-site (fee). **Cards:** AX, MC, VI.

The following restaurant has not been evaluated by AAA but is listed for your information only.

MONTEBELLO — **Phone:** 961/617-7777

fyi

Not evaluated. Contemporary decor and a high degree of tableside service characterize this comfortably upscale restaurant. Ingredients are blended in complex compositions—ranging from regional Yucatan or Chapeneco dishes to more Continental selections—that are presented artistically. **Address:** #1195 Blvd Belisario Dominguez **Location:** 0.9 mi (1.5 km) e; in Camino Real Tuxtla Gutierrez.

VERACRUZ, VERACRUZ pop. 457,377

WHERE TO STAY

CAMINO REAL — *Book at AAA.com* — **Phone:** (229)923-5500

Hotel
$165-$208 All Year

Address: Blvd Manuel Avila Camacho #3650 **Location:** Oceanfront. In Costa de Oro area; adjacent to Boca del Rio. **Facility:** 156 units. 150 one-bedroom standard units. 6 one-bedroom suites, some with whirlpools. 12 stories, interior corridors. *Bath:* shower only. **Parking:** on-site and valet. **Terms:** 10 day cancellation notice. **Amenities:** high-speed Internet, voice mail, irons, hair dryers. **Pool(s):** outdoor. **Leisure Activities:** whirlpool, exercise room. *Fee:* charter fishing, massage. **Guest Services:** valet laundry, area transportation (fee), wireless Internet. **Business Services:** meeting rooms, business center. **Cards:** AX, MC, VI.

FEE / SOME UNITS

CROWNE PLAZA VERACRUZ TORREMAR — **Phone:** (229)989-2100

Hotel
$175-$230 All Year

Address: Blvd Aldolfo Ruiz Cortines 4300 **Location:** Oceanfront. 5 mi (8 km) sw from Plaza de Armas on Blvd Veracruz Mocambo. Located on the beach. **Facility:** Meets AAA guest room security requirements. 230 units. 210 one-bedroom standard units. 20 one-bedroom suites, some with whirlpools. 9 stories, interior/exterior corridors. **Parking:** on-site. **Terms:** cancellation fee imposed. **Amenities:** CD players, high-speed Internet, voice mail, safes, honor bars, irons, hair dryers. *Some:* dual phone lines. **Pool(s):** 3 outdoor. **Leisure Activities:** whirlpool, playground, exercise room. *Fee:* sailboats, windsurfing, charter fishing, massage. **Guest Services:** valet laundry, area transportation (fee), wireless Internet. **Business Services:** conference facilities, business center. **Cards:** AX, MC, VI.

FEE / SOME UNITS

FIESTA AMERICANA VERACRUZ **Phone:** (229)989-8989

Hotel
$275-$375 All Year

Address: Prol Blvd Avila Camacho **Location:** Oceanfront. 3.8 mi (6 km) sw from Plaza de Armas on Ave Avila Camacho. Located on the beach in a modern commercial area. **Facility:** Located on the beach in an upscale area of town, this is a full-service business and resort hotel. The friendly staff is bilingual. 233 units. 209 one-bedroom standard units. 23 one- and 1 two-bedroom suites, some with whirlpools. 7 stories, interior corridors. **Parking:** on-site and valet. **Amenities:** voice mail, safes, honor bars, irons, hair dryers. *Fee:* video games, high-speed Internet. *Some:* CD players. **Dining:** 2 restaurants. **Pool(s):** outdoor, heated indoor/outdoor. **Leisure Activities:** sauna, bicycles, exercise room. *Fee:* charter fishing, massage. **Guest Services:** valet laundry, wireless Internet. **Business Services:** meeting rooms, business center. **Cards:** AX, DC, MC, VI. *(See color ad on insert)*

/ SOME UNITS FEE VCR

HOTEL EMPORIO **Phone:** (229)932-2222

Hotel
$80-$160 All Year

Address: Paseo del Malecon #244 **Location:** Facing Malecon; in heart of historical downtown district. **Facility:** 203 one-bedroom standard units, some with whirlpools. 10 stories, interior corridors. *Bath:* shower only. **Parking:** on-site. **Terms:** 14 day cancellation notice, in season. **Amenities:** high-speed Internet, safes, hair dryers. **Pool(s):** outdoor, heated indoor. **Leisure Activities:** sauna, exercise room. **Guest Services:** wireless Internet. **Business Services:** meeting rooms, PC (fee). **Cards:** AX, MC, VI.

FEE / SOME UNITS

HOTEL VERACRUZ CALINDA **Phone:** (229)989-3800

Hotel
$93-$150 All Year

Address: Ave Independencia s/n Esq Mig **Location:** Jct Ave Independencia at M Lerdo St. Located adjacent to historic area of downtown. **Facility:** 116 one-bedroom standard units. 6 stories, interior corridors. *Bath:* shower only. **Parking:** on-site and valet. **Amenities:** high-speed Internet, safes, honor bars, hair dryers. **Pool(s):** outdoor. **Guest Services:** valet laundry, wireless Internet. **Business Services:** meeting rooms, business center. **Cards:** AX, MC, VI.

/ SOME UNITS

The following lodging was either not evaluated or did not meet AAA rating requirements but is listed for your information only.

GALERIA PLAZA VERACRUZ **Phone:** 229/989-0504

fyi

Not evaluated. **Address:** Blvd Adolfo Ruiz Cortinez No 3495. Facilities, services, and decor characterize a mid-scale property.

WHERE TO DINE

CAFE DE LA PARROQUIA **Phone:** 229/932-1855

Regional Seafood
$8-$25

In existence for more than 200 years, the well-known cafe and full-service restaurant is adjacent to the main waterfront walkway, el malecon, which always teems with locals. Servers made a big show of preparing the popular cafe con leche, raising the large metal teapot way up and bring it back down as they pour scalding milk into a cup of triple espresso. Diners get a true feel for the city at this great spot for breakfast, lunch or dinner. Casual dress. **Bar:** Full bar. **Hours:** 8 am-midnight. **Address:** Paseo del Malecon #340 **Location:** Facing the Malecon water front walkway; at corner of Ave 16 de Septiembre. **Parking:** street. **Cards:** MC, VI.

MARISCOS VILLA RICA **Phone:** 229/922-3743

Regional Seafood
$12-$38

The rustic spot is among the country's best-known seafood restaurants. Large palapas provide shade and open windows enhance beautiful views of the gulf, sandy beaches and towering palms. The extensive menu centers on snails, octopus, squid, clams and all types of fish caught that morning. Whole sea bass, presented with head and tail for effect, is scored across the thick side. Also delicious are crunchy seafood tostadas and refreshing seviche. Casual dress. **Bar:** Full bar. **Reservations:** accepted. **Hours:** 11 am-10 pm, Thurs-Sat to midnight. **Address:** Lalz Mocambo #527 Col Boca del Rio **Location:** In Mocamba neighborhood; Boca de Rio. **Parking:** on-site. **Cards:** AX, MC, VI.

SANBORN'S **Phone:** 229/931-0088

Regional Mexican
$8-$28

Restaurants in the casual chain, which includes more than 100 locations throughout Mexico, offer a good selection of American-style sandwiches, salads, soups and both Mexican and American entrees. The selection of desserts is impressive. Casual dress. **Bar:** Full bar. **Hours:** 7 am-midnight, Fri & Sat-2 am. **Address:** Ave Independencia No 1069, Col Centro **Location:** 2 blks sw of jct Ave Ignacio Zaragoza. **Parking:** on-site (fee). **Cards:** AX, MC, VI.

SANBORN'S **Phone:** 229/921-9634

Regional Mexican
$8-$28

Restaurants in the casual chain, which includes more than 100 locations throughout Mexico, offer a good selection of American-style sandwiches, salads, soups and both Mexican and American entrees. The selection of desserts is impressive. Casual dress. **Bar:** Full bar. **Hours:** 7 am-10 pm, Fri & Sat-1 am. **Location:** Just s of jct Ave Antonio Lizardo. Blvd Aldolfo Ruiz Cortinez Esq Las Americas. **Parking:** on-site (fee). **Cards:** AX, MC, VI.

VILLAHERMOSA, TABASCO pop. 342,200

WHERE TO STAY

BEST WESTERN HOTEL MAYA TABASCO

Phone: (993)358-1111

Hotel
$95 All Year

Address: Blvd Pte A Ruiz Ruiz Cortinez #907 **Location:** On Ave Ruiz Cortinez, just w of Ave Francisco Mina. **Facility:** 151 one-bedroom standard units. 6 stories, interior corridors. *Bath:* shower only. **Parking:** on-site. **Terms:** cancellation fee imposed. **Amenities:** high-speed Internet, voice mail, safes, hair dryers. **Pool(s):** outdoor. **Guest Services:** valet laundry, area transportation (fee), wireless Internet. **Business Services:** meeting rooms, PC, fax (fee). **Cards:** AX, CB, DC, DS, JC, MC, VI.

FEE D

AAA Benefit:
Members save up to 20%, plus 10% bonus points with rewards program.

CAMINO REAL VILLAHERMOSA

Book at AAA.com

Phone: (993)310-0201

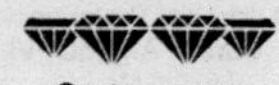

Contemporary Hotel
$150-$280 All Year

Address: Prolongacion Paseo Tabasco 1407 **Location:** Just off Paseo Tabasco, 4 blks nw of jct Ave A Ruiz Cortinez. **Facility:** A modern high-rise structure, this full-service hotel with a restaurant and direct access to the mall caters to business travelers and tourists. 267 units. 241 one-bedroom standard units. 25 one- and 1 two-bedroom suites. 11 stories, interior corridors. **Parking:** on-site and valet. **Amenities:** high-speed Internet, voice mail, safes, irons, hair dryers. **Pool(s):** outdoor. **Leisure Activities:** playground, exercise room. *Fee:* massage. **Guest Services:** valet laundry, area transportation (fee), wireless Internet. **Business Services:** conference facilities, business center. **Cards:** AX, CB, DC, DS, JC, MC, VI.

24 D / SOME UNITS

FIESTA INN

Phone: (993)310-1600

Hotel
$120-$260 All Year

Address: Paseo de la Choca #107 **Location:** Periferico Carlos Pellicer, jct Paseo Tabasco. **Facility:** 145 one-bedroom standard units. 6 stories, interior corridors. **Parking:** on-site. **Amenities:** high-speed Internet, voice mail, irons, hair dryers. **Pool(s):** outdoor. **Leisure Activities:** exercise room. **Guest Services:** valet laundry, wireless Internet. **Business Services:** meeting rooms. **Cards:** AX, DS, MC, VI. *(See color ad on insert)*

D / SOME UNITS

HILTON VILLAHERMOSA AND CONFERENCE CENTER

Book great rates at AAA.com

Phone: (993)313-6800

Contemporary Hotel
$120-$210 All Year

Address: KM 11 Ave AD Cortines Oriente **Location:** At entrance to Villahermosa Airport. **Facility:** Located near the airport, this newer hotel offers modern guest rooms and loads of amenities; the dining room offers a buffet or a la carte dining. Meets AAA guest room security requirements. 220 units. 212 one-bedroom standard units. 8 one-bedroom suites with whirlpools. 4 stories, interior corridors. **Parking:** on-site and valet. **Amenities:** high-speed Internet, dual phone lines, voice mail, safes, irons, hair dryers. **Pool(s):** 2 outdoor. **Leisure Activities:** 2 lighted tennis courts, exercise room, spa. **Guest Services:** valet laundry, area transportation. **Business Services:** conference facilities, business center. **Cards:** AX, CB, DC, DS, JC, MC, VI.

24 CALL S D / SOME UNITS

AAA Benefit:
Members save 5% or more everyday!

HOTEL HYATT REGENCY VILLAHERMOSA

Phone: (993)310-1234

Hotel
$78-$165 All Year

Address: Ave Juarez #106, Col Linda Vista **Location:** 0.8 mi (1.5 km) n on Mex 180; near Tabasco 2000 Commercial Complex. **Facility:** Meets AAA guest room security requirements. 207 one-bedroom standard units. 9 stories, interior corridors. **Parking:** on-site. **Terms:** 3 day cancellation notice-fee imposed. **Amenities:** high-speed Internet (fee), voice mail, safes, honor bars, irons, hair dryers. **Dining:** 2 restaurants, nightclub, entertainment. **Pool(s):** outdoor. **Leisure Activities:** 2 lighted tennis courts, playground. **Guest Services:** valet laundry, wireless Internet. **Business Services:** conference facilities, business center. **Cards:** AX, CB, DC, MC, VI.

D / SOME UNITS

AAA Benefit:
Ask for the AAA rate and save 10%.

The following lodging was either not evaluated or did not meet AAA rating requirements but is listed for your information only.

CALINDA VIVA SPA VILLAHERMOSA

Phone: 993/315-0000

fyi

Not evaluated. **Address:** Adolfo Ruiz Cortinez con Paseo **Location:** 0.8 mi (1.5 km) n on Mex 180; near Tabasco 2000 Commercial Complex. Facilities, services, and decor characterize a mid-scale property.

WHERE TO DINE

LOS TULIPANES — **Phone:** 993/312-9209

Regional Seafood
$10-$25

This long-time local favorite overlooking a busy river features local seafood and soups that integrate local herbs and spices; this is authentic Tabasco cuisine. Try the fish wrapped in banana leaves with momo herbs. Casual dress. **Bar:** Full bar. **Reservations:** accepted. **Hours:** 9 am-10 pm. **Address:** Ave Carlos Pellicer 511 Conjuncto Cicom **Location:** Just off Ave Carlos Pellicer; on riverbank. **Parking:** on-site. **Cards:** AX, MC, VI.

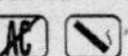

SANBORN'S — **Phone:** 993/357-3377

Regional Mexican
$8-$28

Restaurants in the casual chain, which includes more than 100 locations throughout Mexico, offer a good selection of American-style sandwiches, salads, soups and both Mexican and American entrees. The selection of desserts is impressive. Casual dress. **Bar:** Full bar. **Hours:** 7 am-1 am. **Address:** Ave Roma n Mendoza Herrera Esq Universidad **Location:** Jct aves Ramon Mendoza Herrera and Universidad. **Parking:** on-site (fee). **Cards:** AX, MC, VI.

SANBORN'S — **Phone:** 993/316-9650

Regional Mexican
$8-$28

Restaurants in the casual chain, which includes more than 100 locations throughout Mexico, offer a good selection of American-style sandwiches, salads, soups and both Mexican and American entrees. The selection of desserts is impressive. Casual dress. **Bar:** Full bar. **Hours:** 7 am-1 am. **Address:** Prolongacion Paseo No 1405 **Location:** In Tabasco 2000 Shopping District. **Parking:** on-site (fee). **Cards:** AX, MC, VI.

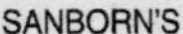

SANBORN'S — **Phone:** 993/316-5710

Regional Mexican
$8-$28

Restaurants in the casual chain, which includes more than 100 locations throughout Mexico, offer a good selection of American-style sandwiches, salads, soups and both Mexican and American entrees. The selection of desserts is impressive. Casual dress. **Bar:** Full bar. **Hours:** 7 am-11 pm, Fri & Sat-1 am. **Address:** Ave Ruiz Cortinez No 1310 **Location:** Downtown. **Parking:** on-site. **Cards:** AX, MC, VI.

VIPS — **Phone:** 993/314-3970

Regional Mexican
$7-$25

Owned by Wal-Mart of Mexico and found in most major cities, the budget-friendly chain serves a good variety of Mexican and American dishes, including burgers, sandwiches, salads, spaghetti and enchiladas, as well as a fine selection of desserts. Casual dress. **Bar:** Beer & wine. **Hours:** 7 am-midnight. **Address:** Ave F I Madero No 402, Col Centro **Location:** Just e of jct Ave Reforma. **Parking:** on-site. **Cards:** AX, MC, VI.

The following restaurant has not been evaluated by AAA but is listed for your information only.

BOUGANVILLAS RESTAURANT — **Phone:** 993/310-1234

fyi

Not evaluated. Elegant continental dining. **Address:** Ave Juarez #106, Col Linda Vista **Location:** 0.8 mi (1.5 km) n on Mex 180; near Tabasco 2000 Commercial Complex; in Hotel Hyatt Regency Villahermosa.

Club Contacts in Mexico

The Mexican Automobile Association (Asociación Mexicana Automovilística, or AMA) has seven club offices throughout Mexico (in Cuernavaca, Mexico City, Puebla, Querétaro, Tampico, Tijuana and Veracruz) that may be able to help visiting AAA/CAA members or provide roadside assistance in the event of a vehicle breakdown. Members also are eligible for discounted repair fees. For information phone 5242-0262 in Mexico City, (55) 5242-0262 elsewhere within Mexico, or 01 (800) 010-7100 (toll-free long distance within Mexico). AMA headquarters is located at Av. Orizaba #7 at Avenida Chapultepec (behind the Metro Insurgentes station), just outside the Zona Rosa in the Roma neighborhood (M: Insurgentes, line 1).

As part of AAA's "Show Your Card & Save" program and a SYC&S alliance between AAA/CAA and AMA, U.S. and Canadian members can enjoy savings from Xel-Ha, Tony Roma restaurants, Romano's Macaroni Grill and Six Flags of Mexico. AMA is continuously expanding the number of *"Ahorra con AMA"* (SYC&S) program partners; for up-to-date information members can visit the SYC&S section of www.AAA.com on their local club's web site.

Speaking of Spanish

ON THE FOLLOWING PAGES are listed some of the Spanish phrases and sentences that are most useful to an English-speaking visitor in Mexico. Although not essential, a basic knowledge of the language will be helpful. Most Mexicans who deal with tourists speak at least some English, and those who don't will be only too glad to help you along with your attempts at Spanish. Fortunately, the language is not that difficult to speak. A little study of the following rules of pronunciation will be sufficient to make yourself understood.

Even if your knowledge of Spanish is rudimentary, using such everyday expressions as por favor (please), gracias (thank you), buenos días (good morning), buenas tardes (good afternoon) and buenas noches (good evening) shows respect. Mexicans are very polite and use these terms all the time; you should also. Good manners mean more than being able to speak the language fluently.

Pronunciation

The pronunciation of the Spanish language presents very few difficulties. The spelling is almost phonetic; nearly every letter has one sound that it retains at all times.

Vowels

A—pronounced as "a" in father.
E—pronounced as "e" in them.
I—pronounced as "e" in me.
O—pronounced as "o" in hold.
U—pronounced as "oo" in food.

Consonants

Consonants do not differ materially from those in English. The few differences are as follows:

b and v—in Mexico are pronounced as in "boy."

c—is pronounced with an "s" sound before e and i. Otherwise it has a "k" sound. Ex. cinco—seen-koh.

g—is soft, like a strong English "h," when it precedes e and i. Ex. gente—hente. In all other cases, it is a hard "g" as in go. Ex. gato—gahtoh. If gu precedes an e or i, the "g" has a hard sound and the "u" is not pronounced. Ex. guerra—geh-rah, guiso—geeh-so. If the "u" has an umlaut it is pronounced güera—gweh-rah, güiro—gwee-roh.

h—always silent, except after c, which makes a "ch" sound as in English.

j—pronounced like the English "h."

ll—pronounced like the English "y." Ex. caballo—kah-BAH-yo.

ñ—combination of "n" and "y," like cognac. Ex. niño—neenyoh.

qu—pronounced like "k." Ex. que—keh.

r—in Mexico the "r" is trilled; the "r" at the beginning of a word and the double "rr" are trilled quite strongly.

x—pronounced as in English, and also pronounced like the English "s" as in Xochimilco (soh-chih-MEEL-coh), and the English "h," as in México

(ME-hee-coh). In Mexico "x" also is used to represent the "sh" sound in native languages, as in Xel-Ha (Shehl-HAH).

z—in Mexico is always pronounced like the English "s."

ch, ll, ñ—these are all letters in the Spanish alphabet and are found after the single letter: "ch" after "c," "ll" after "l," "ñ" after "n."

Diphthongs

Spanish diphthongs are pronounced as very swift omissions of the component vowels.

Ex. "ue" as in weh—fuente.

Ex. "au" as in English ouch—gaucho.

Accent or Stress

1. The stress falls on the next to the last syllable when a word ends in a vowel, "n" or "s."

Ex. hombre—OHM-breh.

Ex. hablan—AH-blahn.

Ex. estos—EHS-tos.

2. The stress falls on the last syllable when the word ends in a consonant other than "n" or "s."

Ex. hablar—ah-BLAR.

3. In some cases an accent mark will be found over a vowel. This does not change the pronunciation of that vowel but indicates that the stress falls on that syllable.

Ex. gramática—grah-MAH-teeh-cah.

Words and Phrases

Note: All nouns in Spanish are either masculine or feminine, and there are two words meaning "the": *el* is used before masculine nouns, *la* before feminine nouns. Masculine words end with an *o*, feminine words end with an *a* (although there are a few exceptions). An adjective agrees in gender with the noun it modifies. The plural of *el* is *los*, of *la* is *las*. After words given on these pages the gender is indicated by (m.) for masculine, (f.) for feminine. For instance, say *el hotel* and *los hoteles; la posada* and *las posadas*. The word *"usted,"* meaning "you," is always abbreviated *Ud.* (*Vd.* in old writings).

Language

Do you understand English? .... ¿Entiende Ud. el inglés?
I do not speak Spanish .... No hablo español.
Yes, sir; no, madam .... Si, señor; no, señora.
Very little .... Muy poco.
I do not understand .... No entiendo.
Do you understand me? .... ¿Me entiende Ud.?
Please speak slowly .... Por favor hable despacio.
I wish to speak with an interpreter .... Quisiera hablar con un intérprete.
What did you say? .... ¿Cómo dice?

Polite Phrases

Good morning .... Buenos días.
Good afternoon .... Buenas tardes.
Good night .... Buenas noches.
Goodbye; see you later .... Adios; hasta la vista.
Thank you .... Gracias.
Yes; very good .... Sí; muy bien.
Please .... Por favor.
Excuse me .... Perdóneme.
I am very sorry .... Lo siento mucho.

To Explain Your Needs

I need; we need .... Necesito; necesitamos.
I would like to telephone .... Quisiera telefonear.
I am hungry; we are hungry .... Tengo hambre; tenemos hambre.
I am thirsty; we are thirsty .... Tengo sed; tenemos sed.
I am cold; we are cold .... Tengo frío; tenemos frío.
I am warm; we are warm .... Tengo calor; tenemos calor.
I am tired; we are tired .... Estoy cansado; estamos cansados.
I am sick; we are sick .... Estoy enfermo; estamos enfermos.
The child is sick; tired .... El niño (la niña) está enfermo (a); cansado (a).
Men's room, ladies' room .... El baño de hombres, de damas.
Fire .... Fuego (m.).
Help .... Auxilio; socorro (m.).

Time

today .... hoy
the morning .... a mañana

tomorrow .... mañana
noon .... el mediodía
yesterday .... ayer
the afternoon .... la tarde
tonight .... esta noche
night .... la noche
last night .... anoche
midnight .... la media noche
What time is it? .... ¿Qué hora es?
It is one o'clock .... Es la una.
It is ten minutes past two .... Son las dos y diez.
It is quarter past three .... Son las tres y cuarto.
It is a quarter of five .... Es un cuarto para las cinco.
It is 25 minutes of six .... Son veinticinco para las seis.
It is half past four .... Son las cuatro y media.

Days of the Week

Sunday .... domingo (m.)
Monday .... lunes (m.)
Tuesday .... martes (m.)
Wednesday .... miércoles (m.)
Thursday .... jueves (m.)
Friday .... viernes (m.)
Saturday .... sábado (m.)

Months of the Year

January .... enero (m.)
February .... febrero (m.)
March .... marzo (m.)
April .... abril (m.)
May .... mayo (m.)
June .... junio (m.)
July .... julio (m.)
August .... agosto (m.)
September .... septiembre (m.)
October .... octubre (m.)
November .... noviembre (m.)
December .... diciembre (m.)

Colors

white .... blanco
black .... negro
gray .... gris
brown .... café
red .... rojo
pink .... rosa
blue; dark blue .... azul; azul oscuro
green; light green .... verde; verde claro
purple .... morado
yellow .... amarillo

Useful Adjectives

Note: These adjectives are in their masculine forms. End them with an "a" if you want the feminine form (except for grande, tarde and fácil, which are used for both genders).

bad .... malo
high .... alto
beautiful .... bello
kind .... bondadoso
cheap .... barato
large .... grande
clean .... limpio
late .... tarde
difficult .... difícil
low .... bajo
dirty .... sucio
polite .... cortés
early .... temprano

sharp ....agudo
easy ....fácil
slow..................lento
expensive ....caro
small..................pequeño
fast..................rápido
ugly ....feo
good..................bueno
unkind..................despiadado, duro
long ....largo
short..................corto
narrow ....angosto
dangerous..................peligroso

Numerals

1. uno	8. ocho	15. quince	30. treinta	90. noventa
2. dos	9. nueve	16. diez y seis	31. treinta y uno	100. cien
3. tres	10. diez	17. diez y siete	40. cuarenta	200. doscientos
4. cuatro	11. once	18. diez y ocho	50. cincuenta	500. quinientos
5. cinco	12. doce	19. diez y nueve	60. sesenta	1,000. mil
6. seis	13. trece	20. veinte	70. setenta	1,000,000. un
7. siete	14. catorce	21. veintiuno	80. ochenta	millón

Points of the Compass

north ....norte (m.) south ....sur (m.) east ....este (m.) west ....oeste (m.)

Note: In addresses, east is oriente, abbreviated Ote.; west is poniente, abbreviated Pte.

At the Border

passport .... pasaporte
tourist card .... tarjeta de turista
age .... edad
marital status .... estado civil
single .... soltero
married .... casado
widowed .... viudo
divorced .... divorciado
profession or occupation .... profesión; ocupación
vaccination card .... certificado de vacuna
car owner's title (registration) .... título de propiedad (registro)
driver's license .... licencia de manejar
year of car .... modelo (o año)
make (Ford, Plymouth, etc.) .... marca
license plate number and state .... número y estado de placa
chassis and motor number .... número de chasis y motor
number of doors .... número de puertas
number of cylinders .... número de cilindros
number of passengers .... número de pasajeros

On the Road

highway .... carretera (f.)
road .... camino (m.)
street .... calle (f.)
avenue .... avenida (f.)
boulevard .... bulevar (m.)
corner .... esquina (f.)
kilometer .... kilómetro (m.)
block .... cuadra (f.)
left side .... lado izquierdo (m.)
right side .... lado derecho (m.)

Please show me the road to .... Enséñeme el camino a.. . .
How far is?.................. ¿Qué tan lejos está.. . ?
Can we get to.. . .before dark? .... ¿Podemos llegar a.. . .antes del anochecer?
Is this road dangerous? .... ¿Es peligroso este camino?
Is that road in good condition?.................. ¿Está en buen estado ese camino?
Is it paved or is it a dirt road? .... ¿Está pavimentado o es de tierra?

Go straight ahead.	Siga adelante.
Turn to the right; left.	Vuelta a la derecha; izquierda.
What city, town, is this?	¿Qué ciudad, pueblo, es éste?
Where does this road lead?	¿A dónde va este camino?

In Case of Car Trouble

I want to ask you a favor.	Quiero pedirle un favor.
My car broke down.	Se me descompuso el carro.
I need a tow truck.	Necesito una grúa.
My lights don't work.	Mis faros no funcionan.
My engine's overheating.	Mi motor se está sobrecalentando.
I have run out of gasoline.	Se me acabó la gasolina.
Is there a gasoline station near here?	¿Hay alguna gasolinería cerca de aquí?
Is there a garage near here?	¿Hay algún taller cerca?
Please send a mechanic.	Por favor mándeme un mecánico.
May I go with you to get a mechanic?	¿Puedo ir con usted a conseguir un mecánico?
Do you have a rope to tow my car?	¿Tiene un cable para remolcar mi carro?
The starter does not work.	El arranque no funciona.
Can you help me push the car to one side of the road?	¿Puede ayudarme a empujar el coche a un lado del camino?
Do you want to be my witness?	¿Quiere ser mi testigo?
Do you want to help me change a tire?	¿Quiere ayudarme a cambiar una llanta?

Arriving in Town

Is English spoken here?	¿Se habla inglés aquí?
Where is the center of town?	¿Dónde está el centro de la ciudad?
May I park here?	¿Puedo estacionarme aquí?
Could you recommend a good restaurant; a good small hotel; a first class hotel?	¿Puede Ud. recomendar un buen restaurante; unbuen hotel pequeño; un hotel de primera clase?
Please direct me to the nearest post office	Por favor diríjame a la oficina de correos mas cercana.
I wish to telephone, to telegraph, to cable	Quiero telefonear, telegrafiar, cablegrafiar.
Please direct me to the railroad station, the bus station	Por favor diríjame a la estación del ferrocarril, a la estación del autobús.
Where is X Street, X Square, the X Hotel?	¿Dónde está la Calle X, la Plaza X, el Hotel X?
How often does the bus go by?	¿Que tan seguido pasa el autobús?
Does the streetcar stop here?	¿Para aquí el tranvía?
I wish to change some money.	Quiero cambiar dinero.
What is the rate of exchange?	¿Cuál es el tipo de cambio?
I want to cash a check.	Quiero cambiar un cheque.
I have lost my traveler's checks.	He perdido mis cheques de viajero.
Where can I find a policeman, a hairdresser, a doctor, a drug store?	¿Dónde puedo hallar un policía, un peinador, un médico, una farmacia?
Where is the police station; the chamber of commerce; the automobile club?	¿Dónde está la comisaría, la cámara de comerciola asociación automovilística?
Where can I find guidebooks, road maps, postcards, American newspapers?	¿Dónde se pueden hallar guías turísticas, mapas de carreteras, tarjetas postales, periódicos norteamericanos?

At the Hotel

hotel	hotel (m.)
inn	posada (f.)
guesthouse	casa de huéspedes (f.)
apartment house	apartamentos (m.)
furnished room	cuarto amueblado (m.)
stairway	escalera (f.)
bedroom	recámara (f.)
bathroom	cuarto de baño (m.)
kitchen	cocina (f.)
towel	toalla (f.)
washcloth	toallita facial (f.)
soap	jabón (m.)

air conditioning	aire acondicionado
room	cuarto (m.)
hot water	agua caliente
office	oficina (f.)
elevator	elevador (m.)
dining room	comedor (m.)
guest	huésped (m.)
manager	gerente
office employee	empleado de oficina
maid	camarera (f.)
key	llave (f.)
porter	mozo (m.) de servicios
bellboy	botones (m.)
ice water	agua con hielo
I want a single room, with bath	Deseo un cuarto para una persona, con baño.
I want a room for two, with twin beds	Deseo un cuarto para dos, con camas gemelas.
I want two connecting rooms	Deseo dos cuartos comunicados.
On the lower floor; upper floor	En el piso bajo; piso alto.
A front room; a back room	Un cuarto al frente; al fondo.
Do you have hot running water?	¿Hay agua corriente y caliente?
What is the price?	¿Cuál es el precio?
What is the minimum rate?	¿Cuál es el precio mínimo?
Do you accept checks in payment?	¿Acepta Ud. cheques en pago?
Is there a garage?	¿Hay garage?
Please call me at six o'clock	Hágame el favor de llamarme a las seis.
Where is the ladies' room, men's room?	¿Dónde está el lavabo de señoras, de señores?
Will you have the baggage brought up? down?	¿Quiere Ud. hacer subir.. . .bajar el equipaje?
We are leaving tomorrow	Partimos mañana.
We are staying several days.. . .Just tonight	Nos quedaremos aquí unos pocos días.. . .solamente esta noche.
Please send these clothes to the laundry	Hágame el favor de mandar esta ropa a la lavandería.
Please clean and press this suit	Hágame el favor de limpiar y planchar este traje.
I want it today; tomorrow.	Lo quiero hoy; mañana.
Where is a barber shop?	¿Dónde hay una peluquería?
I wish my bill, please.	Quiero mi cuenta, por favor.
Please forward my correspondence to this address.	Por favor reexpida mi correspondencia a esta dirección.
Do you want to prepare a lunch for us to carry with us?	¿Quiere Ud. prepararnos un almuerzo para llevárnoslo?

At the Garage

Fill up the gasoline tank; the radiator	Llene el tanque de gasolina; el radiador.
Give me five, ten, fifteen, twenty liters	Deme cinco, diez, quince, veinte litros.
Do you have unleaded gasoline?	¿Tiene gasolina sin plomo?
How much is gasoline per liter?	¿Cuánto vale el litro de gasolina?
Check the oil; change the oil, antifreeze	Vea el aceite; cambie el aceite, anticongelante.
Please lubricate the car; wash the car	Favor de lubricar el automóvil; lavar el automóvil.
Please tighten the brakes; adjust the brakes	Favor de apretar los frenos; ajustar los frenos.
Please tune the engine; change the spark plugs	Favor de afinarme el motor; cambiar las bujías.
My tire has a puncture. Can you repair it?	Mi llanta está picada. ¿Puede repararla?
The tire is flat.	La llanta está desinflada.
Put water in the battery.	Por favor, pónga agua en la batería.
The horn is not working.	La bocina no funciona.
The battery needs charging	La batería necesita carga.
Please replace this headlamp	Por favor, cámbieme este farol.
the fan belt	la banda del ventilador.
the radiator hose	la manguera del radiador.
The gas line is clogged	La tubería de gasolina está tapada.
My engine's overheating	Mi motor se está sobrecalentando.
The exhaust is choked	Está obstruido el tubo de escape.
The steering gear is out of order	La dirección está descompuesta.
The radiator leaks	El radiador gotea.
The clutch slips	El clutch se derrapa.
The gasoline tank is leaking	El tanque de gasolina está goteando.
There is a short circuit	Hay un cortocircuito.

The windshield wiper does not work .... El limpiavidrios del parabrisa no funciona.
The taillight does not work .... La calavera no funciona.
The water pump does not work .... La bomba de agua no funciona.
Please clean the windshield .... Favor de limpiar el parabrisa.
When will the repairs be finished? .... ¿Cuándo terminará la reparación?
How much do I owe you? .... ¿Cuánto le debo?

In Restaurants

breakfast .... desayuno (m).
lunch .... almuerzo (m.)
midday meal .... comida (f.)
dinner; supper .... cena (f.); merienda (f.)
spoon .... cuchara (f.)
cup .... taza (f.)
glass .... vaso (m.)
napkin .... servilleta (f.)
bill .... cuenta (f.)
tip .... propina (f.)
knife .... cuchillo (m.)
fork .... tenedor (m.)

Meat, Eggs, Fish

bacon .... tocino (m.)
beef .... carne (f.) de res (m.)
beefsteak .... bistec (m.)
chicken .... pollo (m.)
duck .... pato (m.)
egg .... huevo (m.)
fried .... frito
soft-boiled .... tibio
hard-boiled .... duro
fish .... pescado (m.)
ham .... jamón (m.)
lamb .... carne (f.) de carnero (m.)
lamb chops .... chuletas (f.) de carnero (m.)
meat .... carne (f.)
omelet .... omelete de huevo (m.)
pork .... carne (f.) de puerco (m.)
roast .... asado (m.)
sausage .... salchicha (f.)
turkey .... guajolote (m.); pavo (m.)
veal .... ternera (f.)

Vegetables

salad .... ensalada (f.)
beans .... frijoles (m.)
beets .... betabeles (f.)
cabbage .... repollo (m.); col (f.)
corn; young corn .... maiz (m.); elote (m.)
lettuce .... lechuga (f.)
onion .... cebolla (f.)
peas .... chícharos (m.)
potatoes .... papas (f.)
rice .... arroz (m.)
string beans .... ejotes (m.)
sweet potatoes .... camotes (m.)
tomatoes .... jitomates (m.)
vegetables .... legumbres (f.); verduras (f.)

Bread

bread .... pan (m.)
crackers .... galletas (f.)
toast .... pan tostado (m.)

Beverages, Liquors

beer .... cerveza (f.)
brandy .... brandy (m.)

coffee ....café (m.)
with cream ....con crema (f.)
without cream ....sin crema
gin ....ginebra (f.)
juice ....jugo (m.)
milk ....leche (f.)
rum ....ron (m.)
tea ....té (m.)
whiskey ....whisky (m.)
table wine ....vino de mesa (m.)

Sweets

dessert ....postre (m.)
sweet rolls ....pan dulce (m.)
cake ....pastel (m.)
candies ....dulces (m.)
cookies ....galletas (f.)
custard ....flan (m.)
ice cream ....helado (m.)
sherbets ....nieves (f.)
pastries ....pasteles (m.)
pie ....pastel (m.)

Fruits, Nuts

apple ....manzana (f.)
avocado ....aguacate (m.)
banana ....plátano (m.)
cantaloupe ....melón (m.)
figs ....higos (m.)
fruit ....fruta (f.)
grapes ....uvas (f.)
guava ....guayaba (f.)
grapefruit ....toronja (f.)
lemon ....limón amarillo (m.)
lime (sweet) ....limón (m.)
nuts ....nueces (f.)
olives ....aceitunas (f.)
orange ....naranja (f.)
peach ....durazno (m.)
peanuts ....cacahuates (m.)
pecans ....nueces (f.)
pineapple ....piña (f.)
strawberries ....fresas (f.)
walnut ....nuez (f.) de castilla
watermelon ....sandía (f.)

Miscellaneous

sugar ....azúcar (m.)
salt ....sal (f.)
pepper ....pimienta (f.)
butter ....mantequilla (f.)
soup; broth ....sopa (f.); caldo (m.)
cheese ....queso (m.)
honey ....miel de abejas (f.)
cigarette; cigar ....cigarrillo (m.); puro (m.)
Please bring me the menu ....Por favor tráigame el menú.
I like my meat rare, medium, well done ....Quiero la carne roja, término medio, bien cocida

Fiestas and Holidays

NOTE: The dates listed here for local celebrations are often variable and may be moved forward or back when the fiesta must be celebrated on a specific day of the week or time of the month or year. Confirm dates in advance with your hotel, at a local tourist information office or at city hall. For background information about widely observed events *see Celebrations, p. 42.*

National Holidays

All banks and most businesses close on these days.

Jan. 1	New Year's Day (Año Nuevo)
Feb. 5	Constitution Day (Día de la Constitución) commemorates the Constitutions of 1857 and 1917.
Mar. 21	Birthday of Benito Juárez, Mexican president and national hero.
May 1	Labor Day (Día del Trabajo), with workers' parades throughout the country.
May 5	Battle of Puebla (Batalla de Puebla), commonly known as Cinco de Mayo, commemorates the Mexican victory over the French at Puebla in 1862.
Sept. 1	The president of Mexico delivers the annual State of the Nation Address (Informe Presidencial).
Sept. 16	Independence Day (Día de la Independencia). The president presides at the ceremony of the *Grito de Dolores* in Mexico City's *Zócalo,* or sometimes at the parish church in Dolores Hidalgo, Gto., where Father Miguel Hidalgo y Costilla issued the *Grito* in 1810. Special celebrations take place in each state capital and start the night of Sept. 15.
Oct. 12	Discovery of the New World by Christopher Columbus, known as Día de la Raza (Day of the Race).
Dec. 25	Christmas Day (Navidad). Plays, religious ceremonies.

Fiestas and Fairs in Mexico

The following fiestas and holiday periods are celebrated in many parts of the country.

Jan. 6	Day of the Three Kings (Día de Los Reyes Magos) features an exchange of gifts as on Christmas in other parts of the world. This also is the day when *Rosca de Los Reyes* (King's Loaf) is served. The round, doughnut-like cake has a plastic doll inside; if you are served the slice containing the doll, tradition says you must host a party on Candlemas Day.
Feb. 2	Candlemas (Día de la Candelaria) is celebrated with processions, dancing, music and food to observe the passing of winter.
Mar. 19	St. Joseph's Day (Día de San José). Especially colorful in Tamuín, S.L.P.
3 days preceding Ash Wednesday	Carnaval is marked with parades, processions, fireworks, music, dancing and a general celebration of fun. Especially spirited in Acapulco, Gro.; Cozumel, Q.R.; Cuernavaca, Mor.; Mazatlán, Sin.; San Cristóbal de Las Casas, Chis.; and Veracruz, Ver.
Palm Sunday to Easter Sunday	Holy Week (Semana Santa). Particularly impressive are the candlelight processions in Taxco, the Passion Play in Iztapalapa (Mexico City), and the Processions of Silence in San Luis Potosí, S.L.P. and San Miguel de Allende, Gto. Other notable observances occur in Pátzcuaro, Mich.; Querétaro, Qro.; Tzintzuntzan, Mich.; and Zinacantán, Chis.
Holy Saturday	Judas Day. Grotesque papier-mâché figures representing Judas are burned the day before Easter Sunday. Especially dramatic in Mexico City and vicinity.
June 24	Saint John the Baptist Day (Día de San Juan Bautista) is celebrated with popular fairs, religious festivities and practical jokes associated with dunking.
Aug. 15-16 and 20-22	Celebration for the Day of the Virgin of Charity and Assumption Day (Día de la Asunción). Flowers and sawdust adorn the streets for processions and special masses. Especially significant in Huamantla, Pue. Fair, Indian dances, *tianguis.*
Oct. 4	St. Francis' Day. Especially interesting in Real de Catorce, S.L.P., and San Francisquito, Son.
Nov. 1-2	Day of the Dead (Día de Los Muertos). A 2-day religious festival celebrated throughout Mexico and marked by visits to cemeteries, flower and culinary offerings, candlelight vigils, elaborately decorated home altars and general merrymaking. It is especially impressive on Isla Janitzio, Mich. Other noteworthy observances take place in Tzintzuntzan, Mich.; Oaxaca, Oax.; and Chiapa de Corzo, Chis.
Nov. 20	Revolution Day (Día de la Revolución). Not a national holiday, but a day marking the anniversary of the Mexican Revolution of 1910 with speeches and official ceremonies.

Dec. 8 — Immaculate Conception. San Juan de los Lagos, Jal., and Pátzcuaro, Mich. are among the many towns with noteworthy celebrations.

Dec. 12 — Feast Day of the Virgin of Guadalupe. Religious festival that pays tribute to the Guadalupe Virgin. This is Mexico's largest religious pilgrimage. Especially dramatic in Mexico City and Monterrey, N.L., but celebrations take place throughout the country.

Dec. 24-25 — Christmas. Celebrations usually begin on Dec. 16 with the *posadas,* re-enactments of Mary and Joseph's search for an inn. At Salamanca, Gto., the fiesta lasts until Feb. 2 and includes numerous Nativity scenes enhanced by moving parts and sound-and-light effects. The entire country celebrates, with particularly notable events taking place in Aguascalientes, Ags.; Oaxaca, Oax.; San Juan del Río, Qro.; San Luis Potosí, S.L.P.; San Miguel de Allende, Gto.; Santiago Tuxtla, Ver.; and Tepotzotlán, Mex.

Dec. 31 — New Year's Eve and Thanksgiving (Fin de Año y Día de Gracias). Especially vibrant in Mexico City, where empty eggshells filled with confetti and food coloring are tossed into the air.

Other Selected Local Festivals and Events

Date	Place	Event
Jan. 17	Taxco, Gro.	St. Anthony's Day. Blessing of pets and other animals in the parish church.
Jan. 18	Taxco, Gro.	Day of Santa Prisca, town patroness, begins with parishioners singing early morning wake-up songs *(mañanitas)* to the Virgin. Celebration and dancing last all day.
Feb. 1-3	San Blas, Nay.	Blessing of the Sea. Dancing and horse races.
Mar. 6	Taxco, Gro.	Day of Our Lord of Xalpa. Indian dances include Los Tlacololeros, Santiagos, Diablos and Pescadores.
Mar. 18-Apr. 4	Tonalá, Jal.	Ceramics Fair. Handicraft exhibits and sales.
Mar. or Apr.	Uruapan, Mich.	Palm Sunday celebration with a huge, weeklong ceramics contest and exhibition, handicraft sales.
Apr. 1-7	Cuernavaca, Mor.	Flower Fair. Exhibits and competitions in floriculture and gardening. Sound-and-light show; popular entertainers.
Apr. 16-May 6	Aguascalientes, Ags.	San Marcos Fair. A major commercial, industrial and agricultural exposition. Handicrafts, local food and beverages, bullfights, exhibits.
Apr. 20-26	Tuxtla Gutiérrez, Chis.	Fiesta of St. Mark the Evangelist. A regional commercial and crafts fair, with *charreadas,* theatrical presentations, marimba contests and sports events.
Apr. (last week)	Villahermosa, Tab.	Tabasco State Fair. People from throughout the state present their music, dances and traditions. Folkloric ballet.
May (last 3 weekends)	Taxco, Gro.	Alarcón Days. Cultural and artistic festival with band serenades, musical performances and presentations of plays by Taxco-born playwright Juan Ruiz de Alarcón.
May (3 weeks)	Morelia, Mich.	Michoacán State Fair (Feria de Morelia). Handicrafts, livestock and agricultural exhibitions, regional dances, bullfights. Fireworks on May 18 mark the anniversary of the city's founding in 1541.
May 3-15	Tepic, Nay.	Fiesta of St. Isador the Farmer. A commercial and cultural fair that includes the blessing of seeds, animals and water.
May 19-22	Chihuahua, Chih.	Fiesta of Santa Rita. A major fair with commercial exhibits, cultural events, food and Indian dances.
May 20-June 10	Monterrey, N.L.	Commercial and agricultural fair.
May 20-30	Tequisquiapan, Qro.	National Wine and Cheese Fair. Tastings and sales, *tianguis,* cultural events.
June 1	Guaymas, Son.	Mexican Navy Day features a naval battle with fireworks.
June (1st Thurs.)	Temascalcingo, Mex.	Corpus Christi Thursday. Blessing of farm animals and equipment; children in Indian costumes.
June 15-July 2	Tlaquepaque, Jal.	National Ceramics Fair and June Fiestas. Craft competitions, exhibits and demonstrations; cultural events.
June 18	Papantla, Ver.	Corpus Christi Day and Vanilla Festival. The famous Flying Pole dancers perform in their place of origin. Regional food and beverages, booths with vanilla products.
July 25	Santiago Tuxtla, Ver.	Day of St. James the Apostle. Líseres (in which participants wear jaguar costumes), Negritos and other local Indian dances.
Mid- to late July (two successive Mondays)	Oaxaca, Oax.	Guelaguetza (Festival of Cooperation). Elaborate, dynamic folkloric festival with dances, regional costumes, music and food.
July 12-Aug. 9	Santa Ana Chiautempan, Tlax.	National Sarape Fair (Feria Nacional del Sarape). This fair takes place simultaneously with the celebration of the town's patron saint on July 26.
Aug. (variable)	Santa Clara del Cobre, Mich.	Copper Fair. Copper handicrafts. Indian dancers, floats.

Aug. 2	Mexico City, D.F.	Cuauhtémoc Day. Dances and ceremonies at Cuauhtémoc Circle honor the last Aztec emperor.
Aug. 18-31	San Luis Potosí, S.L.P.	National Fair of Potosí (Feria Nacional Potosina). Concerts, bullfights, rodeos, sports events, agricultural and livestock exhibitions. The Day of St. Louis the King Aug. 25 honors the city's patron saint with floats and *gigantes* (papier-mâché figures).
Aug. 27-Sept. 1	Zacatecas, Zac.	Festival of La Morisma. Spectacular re-enactment of a 3-day battle between Moors and Spaniards. *Pastorelas;* Indian dances, church services.
Sept. 5-21	Zacatecas, Zac.	National Fair (Feria de Zacatecas). Agricultural and livestock exhibitions, handicrafts, bullfights, rodeos, cultural events.
Sept. 10-17	Dolores Hidalgo, Gto.	Independence Fair and Regional Exposition. *El Grito de Dolores* is reissued by the president on Sept. 15 of most years; there is television coverage of the Mexico City ceremony.
Sept. 15-end of Oct.	Puebla, Pue.	International Fair, a major cultural event focusing on music. The Regional Fair of Hard Cider is an industrial, agricultural and handicrafts exposition.
Sept. 25-Oct. 10	Real de Catorce, S.L.P.	Fiesta of St. Francis and Regional Fair. More than 150,000 pilgrims flock to Real de Catorce for religious and traditional ceremonies honoring St. Francis of Assisi.
Oct. (all)	Guadalajara, Jal.	October Festivals (Fiestas de Octubre). Major fair with many shows, races and other events in the arts and sports.
Oct. (most)	Guanajuato, Gto.	Cervantes International Festival (Festival Internacional Cervantino). One of Mexico's leading cultural events, it draws participants from many countries. *Entremeses,* skits based on the author's work, are featured.
Nov. (last week) or Dec. (1st week)	Taxco, Gro.	National Silver Fair. Show and sale of silver items by craftsmen from around the world.
Dec. 10-12	San Cristóbal de Las Casas, Chis.	Fiesta of the Virgin of Guadalupe. Tzotzil and Tzeltal Indians in procession; marimba music, equestrian parades.
Dec. 23	Oaxaca, Oax.	Night of the Radishes features huge radishes carved into fanciful shapes and thin, fried radish cakes covered with molasses. The cakes are served in a clay dish that must be broken after the cakes are eaten. A parade of floats through the city center takes place the following night.

How to Read a Campground Listing

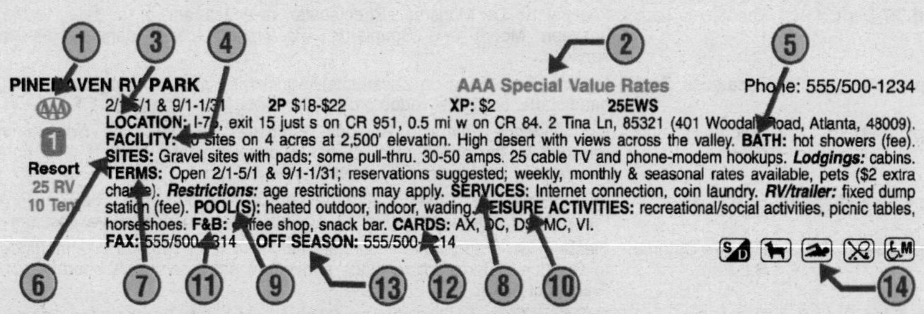

1 or indicates an Official Appointment campground. The OA program permits privately operated campgrounds to display and advertise the or emblem. Red helps you easily locate those OA campgrounds that want AAA/CAA member business.

RATING - AAA professionally trained inspectors evaluate and rate, on a scale of 1 to 3, all privately operated campgrounds based on the overall visual appeal, environmental quality, and completeness, cleanliness and condition of the facilities. The number awarded, not the color, informs you of the overall level of quality you can expect.

1 Surroundings are adequate with modest natural appeal and limited facilities. Sites are visibly rustic and include basic essentials. Showers, toilets and other comforts are not consistently available within direct proximity of each site.

2 Surroundings provide an enhanced natural setting. Sites are visibly appealing, easily identifiable and well defined. There is at least one general service facility onsite such as a visitor's center, store, meeting room or mail center.

3 Surroundings reflect the ultimate camping location featuring prominent natural elements. Extensive recreational facilities and social programs are available. All sites are groomed and enhance the natural beauty of the environment. A variety of services are offered such as a visitor's center, store, meeting room and mail center.

RESORT - A campground classified as a Resort will be denoted as such immediately below the rating. Travel packages, meal plans, entertainment, social and recreational programs, and extensive recreational facilities are typically available.

Campgrounds operated by a public/government agency are included but have not been evaluated or rated by AAA.

SITE COUNT defines the total number and type of short-term sites available.

2 **RATE LINES** shown from left to right: dates or days that the fees are in effect; the daily fee charged per site; how many persons the rate applies to; fee for an extra person (XP) staying at the site; and total sites with electric, water or sewer hookups and any fees charged for the service. Rates do not include taxes.

Rates for campgrounds operated by a public/government agency vary due to governing regulations. We recommend you contact these campgrounds to validate current rates and fees.

RATE OPTIONS:

Special Value Rates - The campground not only guarantees that rates will not exceed the maximum rates printed in the CampBook, but it also offers a minimum discount of 10 percent off printed rates. This is the only rate option that contains a discount.

Guaranteed Rates - The campground guarantees that AAA/CAA members will not be charged more than the maximum rate printed in the CampBook.

Rates Subject To Change - Rates may vary for the life of the CampBook; however, they are guaranteed not to exceed a 15 percent increase on the rates printed.

Exceptions - A campground may temporarily increase rates or modify policies during a special event or for those traveling as part of a group or convention. At these times the ***Special Value*** and ***Guaranteed*** rate options and senior discounts do not apply. Members may take advantage of either the ***Special Value Rate*** or the senior discount, but not both.

3 **LOCATION** includes driving directions, street address and zip or postal code; and mailing address in parenthesis; U.S. directions include the following abbreviations: I (interstate highway), US (federal highway), SR (state road), CR (county road), FR (forest road) and FM (farm to market). For province directions, the following abbreviations are used: Hwy (provincial highway), Rt (route) and CR (county road). Distances are from the nearest town or community unless otherwise noted.

4 **FACILITY** details the physical attributes of the campground, including acreage, elevation and total number of campsites.

5 **BATH** describes types of bathing facilities and any associated fees. Flush toilets and hot showers are available and at no charge unless otherwise noted.

6 **SITES** describes the physical attributes of the average individual campsite, hookup availability and associated fees. ***Lodgings*** shows additional permanent lodgings available to rent. (These may or may not be AAA/CAA approved.)

7 **TERMS** describes reservation policies, conditions and fees imposed. At check-in, some campgrounds require full payment in cash or by credit card for the period reserved. Any subsequent cancellation or refund might then be subject to the advance notice requirement or to the re-rental of the site. ***Restrictions*** details any limits imposed by the campground.

8 **SERVICES** lists services and amenities available at the campground. ***RV/trailer*** describes special services and amenities offered for use by RV and trailers.

9 **POOL(S)** describes types and number of pools.

10 **LEISURE ACTIVITIES** lists the recreational opportunities and activities and any associated fees. Equipment available at a cost is preceded by "rental."

11 **F&B** lists the food or beverage outlets located within the campground.

12 **CARDS:** AX = American Express CB = Carte Blanche DC = Diners Club
DS = Discover JC = Japan Credit Bureau MC = MasterCard VI = Visa

13 The property's main **TELEPHONE NUMBER** appears in the upper right-hand corner. The **RESERVATION** phone number is included for public campgrounds using a central reservations service. The **OFF SEASON** phone number is included for private campgrounds not open year round.

14 **ICONS** help members quickly identify services and amenities available at the campground.

- 10% senior discount for members over 59
- Pool
- Pets Allowed
- Recreational Activities
- No Tents
- Accessible Features *(call property for available services and amenities)*

BAHIA KINO, SONORA

Where to Camp

KINO BAY RV PARK — Rates Subject to Change — Phone: 662/242-0216

2 — 200 RV/Tent

All Year 2P $19-$22 XP: $5 200EWS

LOCATION: 4.8 mi (8 km) nw on beach highway; near pavement end. Mar de Cortez S/N (Apdo Postal 57). **FACILITY:** 200 sites on 4 acres. **SITES:** Level, hardpan and gravel sites with concrete patio; some with corrugated metal sun cover for shade. 30 amps. **TERMS:** monthly rates available. **SERVICES:** propane, Internet connection, coin laundry. ***RV/trailer:*** fixed dump station, supplies, storage. **LEISURE ACTIVITIES:** beach, boat storage, recreational/social activities, bocci, recreation room.
FAX: 662/242-0083

CABO SAN LUCAS, BAJA CALIFORNIA SUR

Where to Camp

VAGABUNDOS DEL MAR RV PARK — Rates Subject to Change — Phone: 624/143-0290

2 — 85 RV

All Year 2P $20-$22 XP: $5 85EWS

LOCATION: On Mex 1; jct Blvd Constituyentes, 0.5 mi (0.9 km) ne at KM 3. Carr Transpeninsular KM 3 (Apdo Postal 197). **FACILITY:** 85 sites on 3 acres. Walled park on the edge of town, beachside of Carr Transpeninsular. **SITES:** Open, gravel sites with cement pads. 30 amps. 85 cable TV hookups. **TERMS:** reservation deposit, 30 day cancellation notice-fee imposed; weekly & monthly rates available. **SERVICES:** Internet connection and wireless, coin laundry, groceries nearby. **POOL(S):** heated outdoor. **LEISURE ACTIVITIES:** recreation room. **F&B:** restaurant, lounge. **CARDS:** MC, VI.
FAX: 624/143-0511

VILLA SERENA RV PARK — Rates Subject to Change — Phone: 624/145-8165

2 — 56 RV/Tent

All Year 2P $21 XP: $2 56EWS

LOCATION: On Mex 1, 4.5 mi (7.5 km) e of town. Carr Transpeninsular KM 7.5 (16175 Monterey Rd, Suite B, MORGAN HILL). **FACILITY:** 56 sites. RV park overlooks home sites and the sea. **SITES:** Open, dirt sites. **TERMS:** weekly & monthly rates available; check-out 10 am. **SERVICES:** wireless Internet, guest laundry, groceries nearby. **POOL(S):** outdoor. **LEISURE ACTIVITIES:** whirlpool, recreation room. **F&B:** restaurant, lounge.
FAX: 624/145-8165

CANCUN, QUINTANA ROO

Where to Camp

CANCUN MECOLOCO TRAILER PARK Rates Subject to Change Phone: 998/843-0324

1
70 RV/Tent

All Year $15-$25 70EWS

LOCATION: On beach road; between Puerto Juarez and Punta Sam. KM 3 Carr Puerto Juarez-Punta Sam. **FACILITY:** 100 sites on 8 acres. Rural location across the road from beach. Adjacent to Mayan ruin excavation. 30 amps. **SERVICES:** groceries, Internet connection. ***RV/trailer:*** fixed dump station. **POOL(S):** outdoor. **LEISURE ACTIVITIES:** sailboats, scuba diving, snorkeling. **CARDS:** MC, VI.

CIUDAD CONSTITUCION, BAJA CALIFORNIA SUR

Where to Camp

MISIONES RV PARK Rates Subject to Change Phone: 613/132-1103

2
40 RV/Tent

All Year 2P $18-$20 XP: $3 40EWS

LOCATION: On Mex 1, 0.6 mi (1 km) n of town. Carr Transpeninsular KM 213 (Colonia Vargas). **FACILITY:** 40 sites on 3 acres. Fully walled park on the edge of town. **SITES:** Gravel sites among flowering plants and trees; some pull-thru. 15-30 amps. ***Lodgings:*** motel units. **SERVICES:** wireless Internet, groceries nearby. **POOL(S):** outdoor. **LEISURE ACTIVITIES:** recreation room. **F&B:** lounge.
FAX: 613/132-1103

CREEL, CHIHUAHUA

Where to Camp

VILLA MEXICANA RV PARK Rates Subject to Change Phone: 635/456-0666

3
73 RV
30 Tent

All Year 2P $10-$20 35EW 38S

LOCATION: 0.6 mi (1 km) se; adjacent to Villa Mexicana Hotel. Calle Lopez Mateos S/N. **FACILITY:** 104 sites. Very nicely done campground. **SITES:** Open, hardpan sites with picnic table and charcoal grill. 30-50 amps. ***Lodgings:*** camping cabins. **TERMS:** weekly & monthly rates available. **SERVICES:** groceries, Internet connection, gift shop, coin laundry, area transportation-train & bus station. ***RV/trailer:*** fixed dump station, storage. **LEISURE ACTIVITIES:** playground, basketball, volleyball, soccer field. **F&B:** restaurant, lounge. **CARDS:** AX, MC, VI.
FAX: 635/426-0065

ENSENADA, BAJA CALIFORNIA

Where to Camp

BAJA SEASONS RV BEACH RESORT Rates Subject to Change Phone: 646/155-4015

2
140 RV

All Year 2P $36-$80 XP: $18 140EWS

LOCATION: On Mex 1-D (toll road), exit Alisitos northbound, U-turn, then 6 mi (10 km) s; 25.2 mi (42 km) n of town. Carr Cuota KM 72. **FACILITY:** 140 sites on 50 acres. Beachfront RV park between Rosarito and Ensenada. **SITES:** Open sites with cement pads. 30 amps. ***Lodgings:*** motel units, villas. **TERMS:** reservation deposit, 14 day cancellation notice; check-in 3 pm. **SERVICES:** groceries, coin laundry. **POOL(S):** outdoor. **LEISURE ACTIVITIES:** whirlpool, playground, recreation room, basketball, volleyball. Fee: miniature golf, 2 lighted tennis courts. **F&B:** restaurant, lounge. **CARDS:** MC, VI.
FAX: 646/155-4019

ESTERO BEACH RV PARK Rates Subject to Change Phone: 646/176-6225

2
38 RV

All Year 2P $30-$45 XP: $5 38EWS

LOCATION: 6.3 mi (10.5 km) s of town on Mex 1, 0.9 mi (1.5 km) w on Ave Jose M Morelos and Lupita Novelo O; at Estero Beach Resort Hotel. (482 W San Ysidro Blvd, PMB 1186, SAN YSIDRO). **FACILITY:** 38 sites on 4 acres. Located at the bay; extensive grounds. **SITES:** Open sites. **TERMS:** reservation deposit, 3 day cancellation notice-fee imposed; monthly rates available; check-in 3 pm. **SERVICES:** coin laundry. ***RV/trailer:*** fixed dump station. **POOL(S):** outdoor. **LEISURE ACTIVITIES:** beach, rental paddleboats, boat ramp, fishing, banana rides, personal watercraft, 3 tennis courts, playground. Fee: bicycles. **F&B:** restaurant, lounge. **CARDS:** MC, VI.
FAX: 646/176-6925

GUADALAJARA, JALISCO

Where to Camp

SAN JOSE DEL TAJO TRAILER PARK Rates Subject to Change Phone: 33/3686-1738

1
125 RV

All Year 2P $18 XP: $2 125EWS

LOCATION: 9.3 mi (15.5 km) s on Mex 15 and 80. Ave Presidente Lopez Mateos (Apdo Postal 31-242). **FACILITY:** 125 sites on 16 acres. Secluded area with quiet residential feel. **SITES:** Some shaded sites; in-line and mixed with permanent houses; trees vary. 30-50 amps. **TERMS:** reservation deposit, 30 day cancellation notice-fee imposed; monthly & seasonal rates available. **SERVICES:** groceries, coin laundry. **POOL(S):** outdoor. **LEISURE ACTIVITIES:** 1 tennis court, recreational/social activities, recreation room, horseshoes, shuffleboard, library. **CARDS:** MC, VI.
FAX: 33/3686-1738

LA PAZ, BAJA CALIFORNIA SUR

Where to Camp

CASA BLANCA RV PARK Rates Subject to Change Phone: 612/124-2477

2
43 RV/Tent

All Year 2P $18 XP: $3 43EWS

LOCATION: On Mex 1 (Abasolo), KM 4.5; west entrance to town. Esq Ave Pez Vela. **FACILITY:** 43 sites on 2 acres. Walled park with modest restrooms and facilities. On the edge of town. **SITES:** Open sites with cement pads. **TERMS:** monthly rates available. **SERVICES:** coin laundry. **POOL(S):** outdoor.
FAX: 612/124-0009

LORETO, BAJA CALIFORNIA SUR

Where to Camp

LORETO SHORES VILLAS & RV PARK Rates Subject to Change Phone: 613/135-1513

2
34 RV

All Year 2P $17-$21 XP: $4 34EWS

LOCATION: 0.6 mi (1 km) s of town center via Francisco Madero. Colonia Zaragoza (Apdo Postal 219). **FACILITY:** 34 sites on 5 acres. At the beach. **SITES:** Open sites; mostly pull-thru. 30 amps. **TERMS:** reservation deposit; weekly rates available. **SERVICES:** coin laundry. ***RV/trailer:*** fixed dump station. **POOL(S):** outdoor. **LEISURE ACTIVITIES:** beach.
FAX: 613/135-0711

TRIPUI RESORT RV PARK Rates Subject to Change Phone: 613/133-0814

1
30 RV

All Year 2P $20 XP: $5 30EWS

LOCATION: 12 mi (20 km) s of town via Mex 1, 0.6 mi (1 km) e at KM 94. (Apdo Postal 73). **FACILITY:** 30 sites on 5 acres. **SITES:** Open, compact sites with palm trees. **TERMS:** reservation deposit, 3 day cancellation notice; weekly & monthly rates available. **SERVICES:** groceries.

LOS BARRILES, BAJA CALIFORNIA SUR

Where to Camp

MARTIN VERDUGO'S BEACH RESORT Rates Subject to Change Phone: 624/141-0054

2
60 RV
25 Tent

All Year 2P $13-$16 XP: $4 60EWS

LOCATION: 0.6 mi (1 km) e of Mex 1. 20 de Noviembre (Apdo Postal 17). **FACILITY:** 85 sites on 5 acres. RV park at the bay, behind motel. **SITES:** Some partially shaded sites in crowded park. 20-30 amps. ***Lodgings:*** motel units. **TERMS:** weekly & monthly rates available. **SERVICES:** wireless Internet, coin laundry, groceries nearby. **POOL(S):** outdoor. **LEISURE ACTIVITIES:** beach, fishing. Fee: boats, charter fishing. **F&B:** lounge. **CARDS:** MC, VI.
FAX: 624/141-0054

MATEHUALA, SAN LUIS POTOSI

Where to Camp

LAS PALMAS TRAILER PARK Rates Subject to Change Phone: 488/882-0001

1
35 RV

All Year $5-$7 35EWS

LOCATION: On Mex 57, by north entrance road to Matehuala; on grounds of Las Palmas Midway Inn and Restaurant. Carr Central KM 617 (Apdo Postal 73). **FACILITY:** 35 sites on 4 acres. Quiet well-maintained grounds. Valet laundry service. **SITES:** Open, spacious sites. **TERMS:** weekly & monthly rates available. **SERVICES:** ***RV/trailer:*** fixed dump station. **POOL(S):** outdoor. **LEISURE ACTIVITIES:** rental bicycles. Fee: miniature golf, bowling. **F&B:** restaurant, lounge. **CARDS:** AX, MC, VI.

MULEGE, BAJA CALIFORNIA SUR

Where to Camp

VILLA MARIA ISABEL RECREATIONAL PARK Rates Subject to Change Phone: 615/153-0246

2

25 Tent
33 RV/Tent

All Year 2P $20 XP: $7 33EW 25S

LOCATION: 1.5 mi (2.5 km) s of town on Mex 1. (Apdo Postal 5). **FACILITY:** 58 sites on 5 acres. At the river. **SITES:** Open, pull-thru sites; tent sites with palapas. 15 amps. **TERMS:** weekly rates available. **SERVICES:** coin laundry. ***RV/trailer:*** fixed dump station. **POOL(S):** outdoor.
FAX: 615/153-0246

PATZCUARO, MICHOACAN

Where to Camp

EL POZO TRAILER PARK Rates Subject to Change Phone: 434/342-0937

1

20 RV/Tent

All Year 2P $15 XP: $4 20EWS

LOCATION: 0.9 mi (1.5 km) ne on Mex 120 (Morelia Hwy). KM 20 Carretera Quiroga Patzcuaro (Apdo Postal 142). **FACILITY:** 20 sites on 3 acres at 2,154m elevation. Basic facilities with gravel roads. **SITES:** Open sites with lots of grass and good separation between sites. 15 amps. **TERMS:** 30 day cancellation notice. **LEISURE ACTIVITIES:** playground.
FAX: 434/342-0937

PUERTO PENASCO, SONORA

Where to Camp

PLAYA BONITA RV PARK Rates Subject to Change Phone: 638/383-2596

2

300 RV/Tent

All Year 2P $22-$27 XP: $2 300EWS

LOCATION: Center; on Playa Bonita Beach west of town. Paseo Balboa Final (PO Box 254, LUKEVILLE). **FACILITY:** 300 sites on 20 acres. **SITES:** Gravel sites, some beach front. 30-50 amps. **TERMS:** reservations accepted; weekly & monthly rates available. **SERVICES:** wireless Internet, coin laundry. **LEISURE ACTIVITIES:** whirlpool, beach, fishing, pavilion, recreation room, barbecue grills. **F&B:** restaurant.

PLAYA DE ORO RV PARK Rates Subject to Change Phone: 638/383-4833

3

320 RV
5 RV/Tent

All Year $21-$27 XP: $3 325EW 320S

LOCATION: Jct Blvd B Juarez, 0.5 mi (0.8 km) e on Blvd Fremont , then 0.5 mi (0.8 km) s on Calle Sinaloa; center. Matamoros y Jalisco S/N (PO Box 583, LUKEVILLE). **FACILITY:** 325 sites on 8 acres. **SITES:** Level, hardpan and gravel sites; some oceanfront. 20-30 amps. 325 cable TV hookups. **TERMS:** weekly & monthly rates available. **SERVICES:** limited groceries, Internet connection and wireless, coin laundry. **LEISURE ACTIVITIES:** beach, boat ramp, fishing, recreation room. **F&B:** restaurant.
OFF SEASON: 602/476-2242

THE REEF RV PARK AT SANDY BEACH Rates Subject to Change Phone: 638/383-0650

1

219 RV/Tent

All Year $17-$40 XP: $2 219EWS

LOCATION: Jct Mex 8 and La Cholla Rd, 2.3 mi (3.7 km) w, 0.6 mi (1 km) s at sign. Camino a La Cholla KM 3.7 (PO Box 742, LUKEVILLE). **FACILITY:** 219 sites on 25 acres. Hardpan roads, security fence and 24 hour guard. **SITES:** Level, hardpan sites; some beachfront. 30-50 amps. **TERMS:** reservation deposit; weekly & monthly rates available. ***Restrictions:*** fireworks prohibited. **SERVICES:** groceries, Internet connection and wireless. ***RV/trailer:*** storage. **LEISURE ACTIVITIES:** beach. **F&B:** restaurant, lounge. **CARDS:** MC, VI.
FAX: 638/383-5790

SAN BARTOLO, BAJA CALIFORNIA SUR

Where to Camp

RANCHO VERDE RV PARK Rates Subject to Change Phone: 612/111-6366

1

30 RV/Tent

All Year 2P $8-$12 XP: $2 30WS

LOCATION: On Mex 1. KM 142 (PO Box 1050, EUREKA). **FACILITY:** 30 sites at 2,000m elevation. RV park in a home-site development in remote mountain area. **SITES:** Well-spaced gravel and dirt sites. **SERVICES:** wireless Internet, area transportation. **LEISURE ACTIVITIES:** hiking trails, recreation room.

SAN CARLOS, SONORA

Where to Camp

HACIENDA TETA KAWI TRAILER PARK — AAA Special Value Rates — Phone: 622/226-0248

1

45 RV/Tent

All Year $20-$24 45EWS

LOCATION: 6.4 mi (10.7 km) nw on Mex 15, 5.6 mi (9.3 km) w on San Carlos turn-off. Across from Bahia de San Carlos S/N KM 5 (Apdo Postal 71, GUAYMAS). **FACILITY:** 45 sites on 3 acres. Across from beach, behind motel. **SITES:** Open sites with concrete patio; some with sheet metal awning. 30 amps. **TERMS:** reservation deposit, 7 day cancellation notice; weekly & monthly rates available. **SERVICES:** wireless Internet. ***RV/trailer:*** storage. **POOL(S):** outdoor. **F&B:** lounge. **CARDS:** AX, DS, MC, VI.
FAX: 622/226-0248

SAN CRISTOBAL DE LAS CASAS, CHIAPAS

Where to Camp

BONAMPAK TRAILER PARK — Rates Subject to Change — Phone: 967/678-1621

1

8 Tent
22 RV/Tent

All Year 1P $9 XP: $9 22EWS

LOCATION: On Mex 190, north entrance to town, at statue; at Hotel Bonampak. Calz Mexico 5 (Apdo Postal 75). **FACILITY:** 30 sites at 2,113m elevation. At entrance to ruins. **LEISURE ACTIVITIES:** playground. **F&B:** lounge. **CARDS:** AX, CB, DC, MC, VI.

SAN MIGUEL DE ALLENDE, GUANAJUATO

Where to Camp

SAN MIGUEL RV PARK — Rates Subject to Change — Phone: 415/152-0659

1

13 RV

All Year $17 XP: $3 13EWS

LOCATION: 0.6 mi (1 km) n of Carr a Celaya. Callejon de San Antonio #16. **FACILITY:** 13 sites. 30 amps. Fee: A/C $2.50. ***Restrictions:*** limited facilities in winter. **SERVICES:** propane, wireless Internet.

TRAILER PARK LA SIESTA — AAA Special Value Rates — Phone: 415/152-0207

1

64 RV/Tent

All Year 2P $17 XP: $10 64EWS

LOCATION: 1.2 mi (2 km) s on Mex 49 (Celaya Hwy). Salida Celaya #82 (Apdo Postal 72). **FACILITY:** 64 sites on 5 acres at 1,800m elevation. Campground located on motel property. Guests have use of motel facilities. **SITES:** Open, grassy, level sites. **TERMS:** reservation deposit, 7 day cancellation notice. **SERVICES:** wireless Internet, coin laundry. **POOL(S):** heated outdoor. **LEISURE ACTIVITIES:** playground. **CARDS:** AX, MC, VI.
FAX: 415/154-4357

TECATE, BAJA CALIFORNIA

Where to Camp

RANCHO OJAI CAMPGROUND AND RV PARK — Rates Subject to Change — Phone: 665/655-3014

3

35 RV
55 Tent

All Year 4P $30 XP: $11 30EWS

LOCATION: On Mex 2, 12 mi (20 km) e of town; near KM 112. Carr Mexicali-Tijuana KM 112 (PO Box 280, TECATE). **FACILITY:** 90 sites on 40 acres. A working ranch in oak-covered mountains. **SITES:** Pull-thru sites with table and barbecue grill. 30-50 amps. ***Lodgings:*** camping cabins. **TERMS:** reservation deposit, 4 day cancellation notice; weekly & monthly rates available. **SERVICES:** groceries, gift shop, coin laundry. **POOL(S):** outdoor. **LEISURE ACTIVITIES:** whirlpool, playground, pavilion, game room, recreation room, basketball, horseshoes, volleyball, pool table. Fee: bicycles. **CARDS:** MC, VI.
FAX: 665/655-3015

ZACATECAS, ZACATECAS

Where to Camp

HOTEL HACIENDA DEL BOSQUE RV PARK — Rates Subject to Change — Phone: 492/924-6666

2

30 RV

All Year 2P $30 30EWS

LOCATION: 2.4 mi (4 km) ne of center on Guadalajara Rd; jct Mex 54. Heroes de Chapultepec 801. **FACILITY:** 30 sites on 2 acres at 5,000m elevation. This is a popular overnight stopping place; access to hotel business center. **SITES:** Flagstone paved sites. 50 amps. **TERMS:** reservation deposit, 15 day cancellation notice; check-in 3 pm. **POOL(S):** heated indoor. **LEISURE ACTIVITIES:** playground, area tours, exercise room. **F&B:** lounge. **CARDS:** AX, MC, VI.
FAX: 492/924-6565

Metric Equivalents

TEMPERATURE

To convert Fahrenheit to Celsius, subtract 32 from the Fahrenheit temperature, multiply by 5 and divide by 9. To convert Celsius to Fahrenheit, multipy by 9, divide by 5 and add 32.

Celsius °		Fahrenheit °
100	BOILING	212
37		100
35		95
32		90
29		85
27		80
24		75
21		70
18		65
16		60
13		55
10		50
7		45
4		40
2		35
0	**FREEZING**	**32**
-4		25
-7		20
-9		15
-12		10
-15		5
-18		0
-21		-5
-24		-10
-27		-15

ACRES

1 acre = 0.4 hectare (ha)   1 hectare = 2.47 acres

MILES AND KILOMETERS

Note: A kilometer is approximately 5/8 or 0.6 of a mile. To convert kilometers to miles multiply by 0.6.

Miles/Kilometers		Kilometers/Miles	
15	24.1	30	18.6
20	32.2	35	21.7
25	40.2	40	24.8
30	48.3	45	27.9
35	56.3	50	31.0
40	64.4	55	34.1
45	72.4	60	37.2
50	80.5	65	40.3
55	88.5	70	43.4
60	96.6	75	46.6
65	104.6	80	49.7
70	112.7	85	52.8
75	120.7	90	55.9
80	128.7	95	59.0
85	136.8	100	62.1
90	144.8	105	65.2
95	152.9	110	68.3
100	160.9	115	71.4

WEIGHT

If You Know:	Multiply By:	To Find:
Ounces	28	Grams
Pounds	0.45	Kilograms
Grams	0.035	Ounces
Kilograms	2.2	Pounds

LINEAR MEASURE

Customary	Metric
1 inch = 2.54 centimeters	1 centimeter = 0.4 inches
1 foot = 30 centimeters	1 meter = 3.3 feet
1 yard = 0.91 meters	1 meter = 1.09 yards
1 mile = 1.6 kilometers	1 kilometer = .62 miles

PRESSURE

Air pressure in automobile tires is expressed in kilopascals. Multiply pound-force per square inch (psi) by 6.89 to find kilopascals (kPa).

24 psi = 165 kPa   28 psi = 193 kPa
26 psi = 179 kPa   30 psi = 207 kPa

LIQUID MEASURE

Customary	Metric
1 fluid ounce = 30 milliliters	1 milliliter = .03 fluid ounces
1 cup = .24 liters	1 liter = 2.1 pints
1 pint = .47 liters	1 liter = 1.06 quarts
1 quart = .95 liters	1 liter = .26 gallons
1 gallon = 3.8 liters	

GALLONS AND LITERS

Gallons/Liters				Liters/Gallons			
5	19.0	12	45.6	10	2.6	40	10.4
6	22.8	14	53.2	15	3.9	50	13.0
7	26.6	16	60.8	20	5.2	60	15.6
8	30.4	18	68.4	25	6.5	70	18.2
9	34.2	20	76.0	30	7.8	80	20.8
10	38.0	25	95.0	35	9.1	90	23.4

Highway Signs

Stop

No Passing

Horizontal Clearance

Maximum Weight (Metric Tons)

No Pedestrians

Parking Limit

One-Hour Parking

No Left Turn

No U Turn

No Parking

Keep to the Right

Inspection

No Trucks

Pedestrians Keep Left

Speed Limit (In K.P.H.)

Right Turn on Red Permitted

No Bicycles

Keep Right

Do Not Enter

Road Signs In Spanish	*Descriptions In English*
Topes, Vibradores	Speed Bumps
Un Solo Carril	One Lane
Pavimento Derrapante	Pavement Slippery
Prohibido Seguir de Frente	Do Not Enter
Vado	Dip

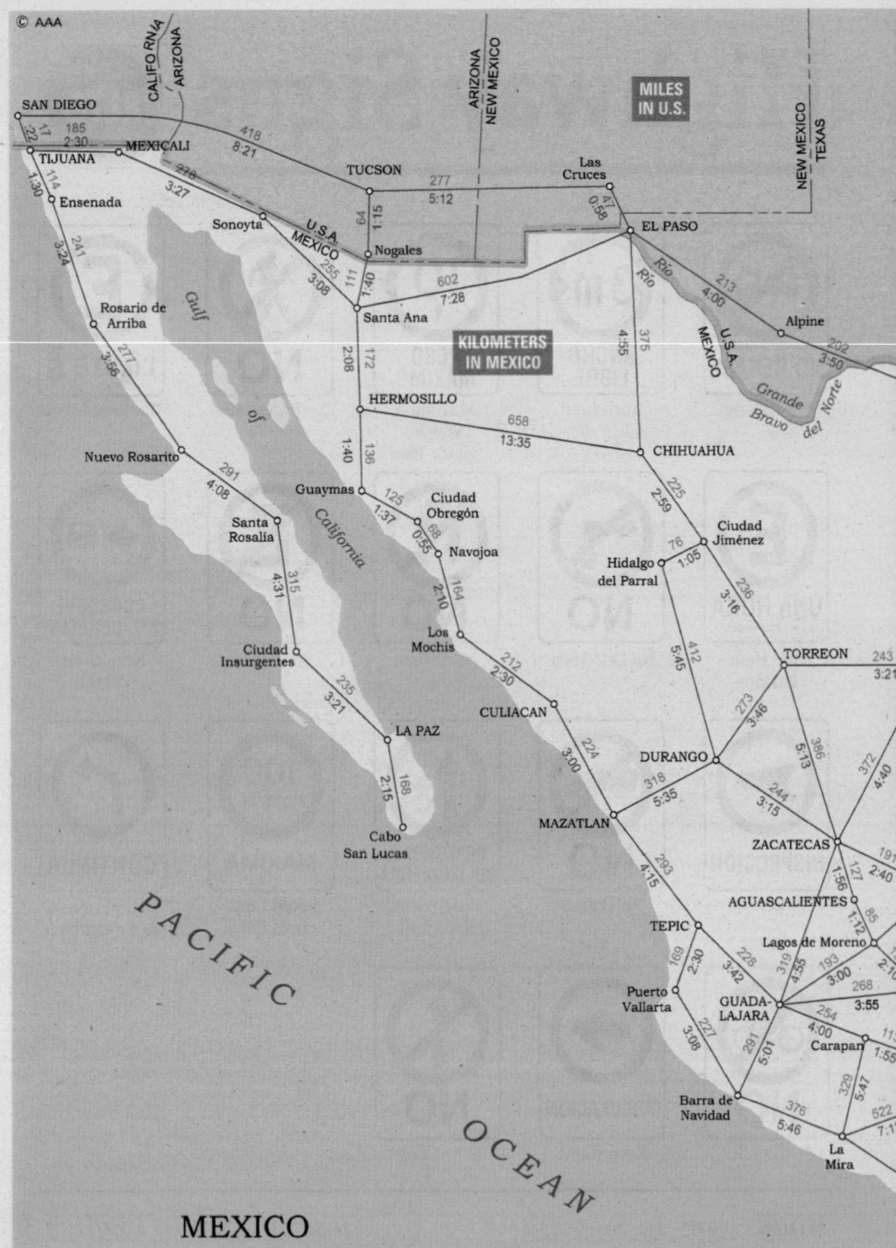
© AAA
MILES IN U.S.
KILOMETERS IN MEXICO
SAN DIEGO
TIJUANA
MEXICALI
Ensenada
Sonoyta
TUCSON
Nogales
Las Cruces
EL PASO
Santa Ana
HERMOSILLO
CHIHUAHUA
Alpine
Rosario de Arriba
Nuevo Rosarito
Guaymas
Ciudad Obregón
Navojoa
Santa Rosalía
Ciudad Jiménez
Hidalgo del Parral
Los Mochis
Ciudad Insurgentes
TORREON
CULIACAN
LA PAZ
DURANGO
MAZATLAN
Cabo San Lucas
ZACATECAS
AGUASCALIENTES
TEPIC
Lagos de Moreno
Puerto Vallarta
GUADALAJARA
Carapan
Barra de Navidad
La Mira
Gulf of California
PACIFIC OCEAN
Río Bravo del Norte
Río Grande
U.S.A.
MEXICO
CALIFORNIA
ARIZONA
NEW MEXICO
TEXAS
MEXICO
DRIVING DISTANCES
100 KILOMETERS IN MEXICO/MILES IN US
2:00 AVERAGE TIME (EXCLUDING STOPS)
3632-R

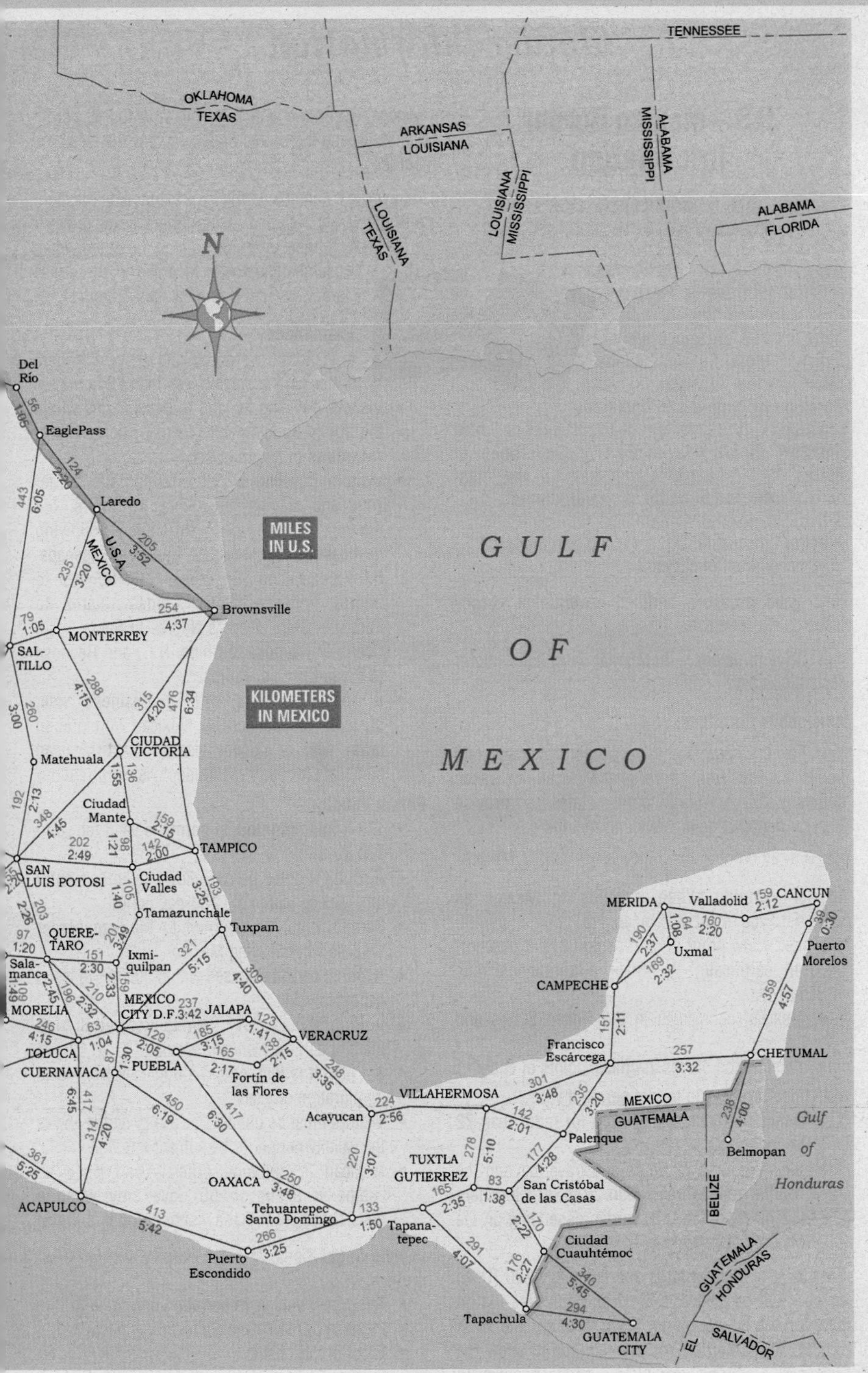

TENNESSEE
OKLAHOMA
TEXAS
ARKANSAS
LOUISIANA
ALABAMA
MISSISSIPPI
LOUISIANA
TEXAS
LOUISIANA
MISSISSIPPI
ALABAMA
FLORIDA
N
MILES IN U.S.
KILOMETERS IN MEXICO
GULF OF MEXICO
U.S.A.
MEXICO
Del Río
EaglePass
Laredo
Brownsville
MONTERREY
SAL-TILLO
CIUDAD VICTORIA
Matehuala
Ciudad Mante
TAMPICO
SAN LUIS POTOSI
Ciudad Valles
Tamazunchale
Tuxpam
QUERE-TARO
Ixmi-quilpan
Salamanca
MORELIA
MEXICO CITY D.F.
JALAPA
VERACRUZ
TOLUCA
CUERNAVACA
PUEBLA
Fortín de las Flores
Acayucan
VILLAHERMOSA
OAXACA
Tehuantepec Santo Domingo
ACAPULCO
Puerto Escondido
Tapanatepec
TUXTLA GUTIERREZ
San Cristóbal de las Casas
Palenque
Ciudad Cuauhtémoc
Tapachula
GUATEMALA CITY
MERIDA
Valladolid
CANCUN
Uxmal
Puerto Morelos
CAMPECHE
Francisco Escárcega
CHETUMAL
MEXICO
GUATEMALA
Belmopan
BELIZE
Gulf of Honduras
GUATEMALA
HONDURAS
EL SALVADOR

Border Information

U.S.–Mexico Border Information

For U.S. and Canadian Residents Traveling to Mexico

Passports for air travel are now required for travel to Mexico. It is expected that at some point in 2009, citizens traveling between the U.S. and Canada, Mexico, the Caribbean, and Bermuda by land or sea (including ferries), will be required to present a valid passport. Please refer to the U.S. Department of State's Web site travel.state.gov for the most current information on these requirements.

Proof of Citizenship: U.S. and Canadian tourists must carry proof of citizenship.

Yes: Valid passport, certified government agency issued birth certificate

No: Driver's license, baptismal certificate, voter registration card

Automobile Insurance:

Yes: Full coverage, including property damage and public liability, from a reliable Mexican insurance company. AAA offices in border states can provide Mexican automobile insurance to members.

No: U.S. automobile insurance is not valid in Mexico.

Tourist Permits: When traveling to Mexico as a tourist, you must obtain an FMT tourist permit. You must show proof of citizenship (a valid passport or birth certificate) to obtain a permit. Permits issued at:

- Mexican consulates in the United States and Canada
- Immigration offices at official points of entry

You must have a valid tourist permit if you:

- Remain anywhere in Mexico for more than 72 hours **or**
- Stay less than 72 hours and travel beyond the "border zone" (area within 20 to 30 kilometers (12 miles) of the U.S. border, depending on the Mexican state)

Cost for a tourist permit is approximately $20 (U.S.) which must be paid at a Mexican bank (see list on back of tourist permit form) or through the bank window at the border. You are required to show the "Fee Paid" stamp on your tourist permit when leaving Mexico. Recommendation: obtain your tourist permit before leaving the United States and pay the fee at the border.

If traveling by air, the permit is distributed on the flight and the fee is included in the airline ticket price. If arriving by cruise ship, the fee is collected when disembarking or is included in the cruise fare if the stay is longer than 72 hours.

Exemptions

- Visitors traveling by land or sea anywhere in Mexico and staying less than 72 hours
- Visitors traveling by land to destinations within the 20- to 30-kilometer (12-mile) border zone, regardless of length of stay
- Visitors traveling by land beyond the border zone and staying more than 72 hours, but limiting their visit to the following destinations/tourist routes: Tijuana to Ensenada, B.C.; Mexicali to San Felipe, B.C.; Sonoyta to Puerto Peñasco, Son.; Ciudad Juárez to Paquime, Chih.; Piedras Negras to Santa Rosa, Coah.; or Reynosa to China, N.L., and Reynosa to Presa Cuchillo, Tamps.
- Business travelers with a business visa; students (as defined by Mexican immigration laws) with a student visa (contact Mexican consulate for business/student visa information)

Permit Validity

- The single-entry tourist permit is valid for up to 180 days
- A multiple-entry permit allows unlimited entry into Mexico within the 180-day period
- Permits must be returned to Mexican border officials when leaving Mexico
- A tourist permit not used within 90 days of issue becomes void
- Visitors should carry their tourist permit with them at all times while in Mexico
- If a permit is lost, obtain a duplicate from local immigration officials
- Visitors must be out of the country by the end of the validity period, or be subject to a fine
- Mexican immigration officials can issue an extension of up to 90 days only when a physician verifies that a visitor is too ill to travel

Vehicle Regulations: At point of entry, visitors must present:

- Temporary vehicle importation permit
- Promise to return vehicle form
- Proof of citizenship

- Valid driver's license
- Tourist permit
- Current vehicle license/registration receipt (original and 2 copies)

Vehicle travel beyond the 20- to 30-kilometer border zone requires:

- Temporary vehicle importation permit
- Promise to return vehicle form

Permits not required in the Baja California peninsula (the states of Baja California and Baja California Sur) unless the vehicle is put on a ferry bound for the mainland.

To obtain these documents from a Mexican consulate or an immigration office at an official point of entry, the vehicle owner must:

- Be 18 years of age or older
- Have a valid U.S. or Canadian driver's license
- Present proof of citizenship
- Provide proof of ownership (current registration) for each vehicle being taken into Mexico

Information on the application for temporary vehicle importation must match the information on the promise to return vehicle form; the same requirements apply to both.

A $25 administrative fee plus tax must be paid at the point of entry (mainland border crossing or ferry crossing from Baja California to the mainland) to receive a temporary importation permit windshield sticker.

Yes: Use major credit card (American Express, MasterCard or VISA), which must be in the registered vehicle owner's name and issued by a U.S. or Canadian bank or lending institution. Vehicle owners without a major credit card may post a bond ($200 to $400 based on vehicle value) with a Mexican bonding firm (Afianzadora) at the point of entry.

No: Cash, checks, money orders or credit cards issued by a Mexican bank are not accepted.

More About Temporary Importation Permits

- Generally issued for 90 days
- Obtain extensions of up to 90 days from Mexican immigration officials
- Only 1 permit will be issued per person, for 1 motorized vehicle at a time
- Carry permit with you – do not leave it in the vehicle
- Return permit, promise to return vehicle form and windshield sticker to Mexican customs officials at the border before or on the expiration date shown on the promise to return vehicle form, or be subject to a fine
- If permit or promise to return vehicle form is lost or stolen, Mexican customs offices can issue replacement documentation provided you obtain a certified document attesting to the loss from your homeland (U.S. or Canada) embassy or consulate
- Permit must be cancelled at customs when you leave Mexico
- If you are found in Mexico beyond the authorized time or without proper documentation, your car will be immediately confiscated

Pets: U.S. visitors may bring a dog, cat, birds and some other pets into Mexico with government approval. A pet health certificate signed not more than 15 days before the animal enters Mexico and a pet vaccination certificate showing that the animal has been treated for rabies, hepatitis, pip and leptospirosis are required at the border for each pet. A pet permit fee will be charged at the time of entry.

For U.S. and Canadian Residents Leaving Mexico

When Leaving the Country:

- Temporary vehicle importation permits, promise to return vehicle forms and windshield stickers must be returned to Mexican immigration and customs officials at the border (or at an interior inspection point)
- Those entering Mexico with a motor vehicle must leave the country with the vehicle
- At stations along the highways, Mexican agricultural officials will inspect those traveling north to the U.S. border
- Officials will inspect all fruits, vegetables, houseplants and other plant matter

Yes: You must have an export certificate to take cultural artifacts or property items (e.g., pre-Columbian monumental and architectural sculpture or murals, clay figurines, original paintings or other works of art excluding handicrafts) out of the country.

No: You may not take valuable religious or archeological relics out of the country.

Returning to the United States: Everyone who seeks entry into the United States – whether foreign visitors, U.S. citizens, or U.S. lawful permanent residents – must be inspected at the point of entry. Random searches may be conducted by U.S. Customs and Border Protection agents.

Returning U.S. citizens must present proof of citizenship. Once customs officials are satisfied that U.S. or Canadian residents have the right to be admitted to the United States, they may examine baggage thoroughly. To expedite the trip through customs, keep sales slips handy and have all purchases in 1 bag, if possible.

U.S. Exemptions:

- You may bring back duty-free articles not exceeding $800 in retail value from a stay abroad of at least 48 hours
- The exemption is allowed once every 30 days
- A family (related persons living in the same household) may combine its exemptions (a family of 6 is entitled to $4,800 worth of goods duty-free on 1 declaration, even if the articles claimed by 1 member exceed that individual's $800 amount)
- Duty must be paid on all items in excess of the exemption amount
- Payment of duty is required upon arrival
- Gifts taken across the U.S./Mexico border are considered to be for personal use and are included in the $800 exemption
- Articles purchased and left for alterations or other reasons do not qualify for the $800 exemption when shipped at a later date
- The $800 exemption may include no more than 2 liters of alcoholic beverages and no more than 200 cigarettes and 100 cigars

Restricted or Prohibited Articles: To prevent the introduction of plant and animal pests and diseases into the United States, the agricultural quarantine bans the importation of certain fruits, vegetables, plants, livestock, poultry and meats. All food products brought into the United States must be declared. The U.S. Department of Agriculture also prohibits the importation of any kind of pet obtained in Mexico. Write to APHIS, Dept. of Agriculture, Room 1147-S, Wash., DC 20250, www.aphis.usda.gov, for a free copy of *Traveler's Tips.* Write to U.S. Customs, P.O. Box 7407, Washington, D.C. 20044 for other helpful leaflets: *Visiting the U.S.: Requirements for Non-Residents, Know Before You Go, Importing a Car,* and *Pets, Wildlife and U.S. Customs.*

Yes: One foreign-made article carrying a protected U.S. trademark (e.g., camera, binoculars, musical instrument, jewelry or watch) may usually be brought into the United States under your personal exemption, provided it's for your private use and not sold within 1 year of importation. Some perfumes are limited to 1 bottle and others are prohibited. If you intend to purchase perfume, inquire about trademark restrictions beforehand.

No: Articles considered detrimental to the general welfare of the United States are prohibited entry: narcotics and dangerous drugs, drug paraphernalia, obscene articles and publications, seditious or treasonable matter, lottery tickets, hazardous items (fireworks, dangerous toys, toxic or poisonous substances) and switchblade knives. Any goods originating in the following countries are prohibited: Balkans, Burma, Cuba, Iran, Iraq, Liberia, Libya, North Korea, Sudan, Syria and Zimbabwe. Please note embargoes are not limited to these countries.

Yes: Live birds, such as parrots, parakeets or birds of prey, widely available on the market in Mexico, can be brought into the United States subject to inspection by the U.S. Department of Agriculture. Birds must be quarantined upon arrival for at least 30 days in a USDA-operated facility at the owner's expense. Quarantine space must be reserved in advance. Contact a USDA office.

No: Endangered wildlife species or products made of any part of these species are prohibited including ivory and products made from elephant or marine mammal ivory or sea turtles.

If you plan to return to the United States with any purchased articles made of fur, any animal skin other than cowhide leather, whalebone or any product manufactured wholly or in part from any type of wildlife, contact: Office of Law Enforcement, U.S. Fish and Wildlife Service, 4401 N. Fairfax Dr., MS-LE-3000, Arlington, VA 22203, (703) 358-1949 for regulations.

Alcoholic Beverages: Both federal and state laws govern the importation of alcoholic beverages. When regulations conflict state laws supersede, so it's important to know the import limits of your state of residence and the state of entry.

U.S. residents 21 years of age or older may bring into the United States 1 liter of alcohol duty-free once every 30 days. However, if you arrive in a state that permits a lesser amount than what you have legally brought into the United States, state law prevails.

Gifts

- Gifts in packages with a total retail value not exceeding $100 may be sent to friends or relatives in the United States free of U.S. customs duty or tax, provided no recipient receives more than 1 gift shipment per day
- Gifts may be sent to more than 1 person in the same package if they are individually wrapped and labeled with each recipient's name
- Perfumes valued at more than $5 retail, tobacco products or alcoholic beverages may not be included in gift packages

- Clearly mark on the package the designation "Unsolicited Gift," the donor's name and the contents' retail value

Duties

- A flat rate duty of 3 percent is applied to the first $1,000 (fair retail value) worth of merchandise in excess of the $800 customs exemption
- Sales receipt functions as proof of value
- Family members residing in 1 household and traveling together may group articles for application of the flat-duty rate
- Flat-duty rate may be taken once every 30 days
- Articles must accompany you to the U.S. border

Canadian Exemptions

- Citizens who have been outside Canada at least 48 hours may bring back duty- and tax-free goods not exceeding $200 (Canadian) in retail value. The exemption can be claimed any number of times a year.
- Citizens who have been outside Canada 7 days or more may bring back duty- and tax-free goods not exceeding $750 in retail value. The $750 exemption can be claimed regardless of any $200 exemption taken on a previous trip and requires a written declaration. The 2 exemptions may not be combined.
- Citizens may claim duty- and tax-free entry for articles (excluding tobacco products or alcoholic beverages) not exceeding $50 in retail value when returning from a trip abroad of at least 24 hours. Items brought into Canada under a personal exemption must be for personal or household use, souvenirs or gifts.

Limitations (on either $200 or $750 exemption): 50 cigars, 200 cigarettes, 200 tobacco sticks and 200 grams (6.4 ounces) of tobacco, and 40 ounces (1.1 liters) of liquor or 53 ounces of wine or 300 ounces (8.5 liters) of beer or ale (equivalent to 24 12-ounce bottles/cans). All exemptions are individual and may not be combined with that of another person to cover an article valued at more than the maximum exemption. You may be asked to prove the length of your visit outside Canada. Keep dated sales receipts for goods or services as they constitute valid proof.

- All declared goods associated with the $200 personal exemption must accompany the purchaser to the Canadian border.
- Declared goods associated with the $750 personal exemption may follow the purchaser by mail.
- Gifts sent to friends or relatives from Mexico do not count against a resident's personal exemption if valued at no more than $60 Canadian and not consisting of alcoholic beverages, tobacco products or advertising matter. Enclose a gift card to avoid misunderstanding. Mexican government customs officials must examine parcels before they ship so consider having a customs broker or forwarding agent handle the details before you leave Mexico.

When you exceed your $200 or $750 exemption, a special GST rate of 7 percent is applied to the next $300 value in goods (except tobacco and/or alcohol) in excess of the maximum exemption, provided the goods are of Mexican origin. Regular duties apply on any additional amount.

While AAA makes every effort to provide accurate and complete information, AAA makes no warranty, express or implied, and assumes no legal liability or responsibility for the accuracy or completeness of any information contained herein.

Points of Interest Index

AIRPORTS

AMUSEMENTS & THEME PARKS

AQUARIUMS

ARCHEOLOGICAL SITES

ART GALLERIES & MUSEUMS

Index Legend

NB....national battlefield
NBP....national battlefield park
NC....national cemetery
NF....national forest
NHM....national historic(al) monument
NHP....national historic(al) park
NHS....national historic(al) site
NL....national lakeshore
NME....national memorial
NMO....national monument
NMP....national military park
NP....national park
NRA....national recreation area
NR....national river
NS....national seashore
NWR....national wildlife refuge
PHP....provincial historic(al) park
PHS....provincial historic(al) site
PP....provincial park
SF....state forest
SHM....state historic(al) monument
SHP....state historic(al) park
SHS....state historic(al) site
SME....state memorial
SP....state park
SRA....state recreation area

GEM: Points of Interest Offering a *Great Experience for Members*®

MUSIC HALLS & OPERA HOUSES

NATURAL PHENOMENA

PAINTINGS

PARKS, CITY; STATE; PROVINCIAL

PARKS, NATIONAL

THEATERS-IMAX & OMNIMAX

TOWERS

TRAILS-SUMMER RECREATION

TUNNELS

VIEWS

VISITOR CENTERS

WALKING TOURS

WATERFALLS

WATER PARKS

WAX MUSEUMS

WILDERNESS AREAS

WILDLIFE SANCTUARIES

WINERIES

ZIPLINES

ZOOLOGICAL PARKS & EXHIBITS

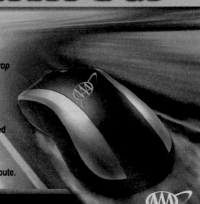

Bed & Breakfast Lodgings Index

Some bed and breakfasts listed below might have historical significance.
Those properties are also referenced in the Historical index.

Country Inns Index

Some of the following country inns can also be considered as bed-and-breakfast operations.

Historical Lodgings & Restaurants Index

Some of the following historical lodgings can also be considered as bed-and-breakfast operations.

Historical Lodgings & Restaurants (cont'd)

THE PACIFIC COAST

ACCOMMODATION

YUCATAN PENINSULA

ACCOMMODATIONS

RESTAURANT

Resorts Index

Many establishments are located in resort areas; however, the following places have extensive on-premises recreational facilities:

BAJA CALIFORNIA

ACCOMMODATIONS

MEXICO CITY AND VICINITY

ACCOMMODATION

NORTHWESTERN MEXICO

ACCOMMODATIONS

THE PACIFIC COAST

ACCOMMODATIONS

YUCATAN PENINSULA

ACCOMMODATIONS

Comprehensive City Index

Here is an alphabetical list of all cities and places appearing in this TourBook® guide. Each city includes the state in which it is located. Page numbers under the POI column indicate where points of interest text begins. Page numbers under the L&R column indicate where lodging and restaurant listings begin.

Comprehensive City Index (cont'd)

AAA

At 60 mph, if you reach down
to change the radio station
you can travel the length
of a football field.

Stay Focused
Keep your mind on the road.